T0135104

Lecture Notes in Computer Science 969
Edited by G. Goos, J. Hartmanis and J. van Leeuwen

Springer

Berlin
Heidelberg
New York
Barcelona
Budapest
Hong Kong
London
Milan
Paris
Tokyo

Jiří Wiedermann Petr Hájek (Eds.)

Mathematical Foundations of Computer Science 1995

20th International Symposium, MFCS '95
Prague, Czech Republic
August 28 - September 1, 1995
Proceedings

Springer

Series Editors

Gerhard Goos, Karlsruhe University, Germany

Juris Hartmanis, Cornell University, NY, USA

Jan van Leeuwen, Utrecht University, The Netherlands

Volume Editors

Jiří Wiedermann
Petr Hájek
Institute of Computer Science, Academy of Sciences of the Czech Republic
Pod vodárenskou věží 2, 182 07 Prague, Czech Republic

Cataloging-in-Publication data applied for

Die Deutsche Bibliothek - CIP-Einheitsaufnahme

Mathematical foundations of computer science 1995 : 20th international symposium ; proceedings / MFCS '95, Prague, Czech Republic, August 28 - September 1, 1995. Jiří Wiedermann ; Petr Hájek (ed.). - Berlin ; Heidelberg ; New York ; Barcelona ; Budapest ; Hong Kong ; London ; Milan ; Paris ; Tokyo : Springer, 1995
(Lecture notes in computer science ; Vol. 969)
ISBN 3-540-60246-1
NE: Wiedermann, Jiří [Hrsg.]; MFCS <20, 1995, Praha>; GT

CR Subject Classification (1991): F.1-4, D.2-3, G.2

ISBN 3-540-60246-1 Springer-Verlag Berlin Heidelberg New York

Typesetting: Camera-ready by author
SPIN 10485448 06/3142 - 5 4 3 2 1 0 Printed on acid-free paper

Foreword

The International Symposium on Mathematical Foundations of Computer Science (MFCS'95) was held August 28 – September 1, 1995, in Prague, the capital of the Czech Republic, in the conference facilities of the Krystal Hotel. It was the 20th anniversary in the series of symposia organized in the Czech Republic, Poland, and the Slovak Republic.

MFCS'95 was organized by the Institute of Computer Science of the Academy of Sciences of the Czech Republic; Charles University, Prague; Prague School of Economics; Center for Theoretical Study of the Institute of Advanced Studies at Charles University and the Academy of Sciences of the Czech Republic, and Czech Society for Computer Science.

The previous meetings took place in Jablona, 1972, Štrbské Pleso, 1973; Jadwisin, 1974; Mariánské Lázně, 1975; Gdańsk, 1976; Tatranská Lomnica, 1977; Zakopane, 1978; Olomouc, 1979; Rydzina, 1980; Štrbské Pleso, 1981; Prague 1984; Bratislava, 1986; Carlsbad, 1988; Porąbka–Kozubnik, 1989; Banská Bystrica, 1990; Kazimierz Dolny, 1991; Prague, 1992; Gdańsk, 1993; and Košice, 1994.

The purpose of all these symposia has been to encourage high-quality research in all branches of theoretical computer science and to bring together specialists active in the field.

To stress the 20th anniversary of the conference the program committee took special care in preparing an interesting scientific program reflecting the recent trends in computer science. The keynote address was be held by Professor Juris Hartmanis with his talk " On the Computational Paradigm and Computational Complexity". It is a great pleasure to announce that Professor Hartmanis was be awarded the Golden Medal of B. Bolzano during this occasion. This medal is awarded by the Academy of Sciences of the Czech Republic to those outstanding foreign scientists who by their work have substantially contributed not only to the development in the field of mathematics and informatics in general, but also to the development of Czech science in particular. In the case of Professor Hartmanis we much appreciate his continuous long term support of the series of the MFCS conferences from its very beginning. He has participated not only as an editor of the LNCS series, but has been also repeatedly an invited lecturer and a member of MFCS program committee. In this way he has positively influenced the development in computer science in our country. We acknowledge his efforts in the field.

The program committee received 104 submissions in response to the Call for Papers for MFCS'95. The program committee for MFCS'95 consisted of:

Giorgio Ausiello (Rome)
Dines Bjørner (Macau)
Manfred Broy (Munich)
Peter Clote (Boston)
Bruno Courcelle (Bordeaux)*
Josep Diaz (Barcelona)
Jerry Feldman (Berkeley)*
Petr Hájek (co-chair, Prague)*
Juhani Karhumäki (Turku)*
Václav Koubek (Prague)*
Mogens Nielsen (Aarhus)*
Wojciech Penczek (Warsaw)*
Igor Prívara (Bratislava)*
Pavel Pudlák (Prague)
Branislav Rovan (Bratislava)*
Grzegorz Rozenberg (Leiden)
Eli Shamir (Jerusalem)
Mike Sipser (Cambridge)
Colin Stirling (Edinburgh)
Peter van Emde Boas (Amsterdam)*
Gerd Wechsung (Jena)*
Ingo Wegener (Dortmund)*
Avi Wigderson (Jerusalem)
Jiří Wiedermann (co-chair, Prague)*
Derek Wood (London)
Jiří Zlatuška (Brno)*

Those members of programming committee denoted by an asterisk in the above list took part at the selection meeting on March 18, 1995, in Prague. Altogether 44 of the contributed papers have been selected for inclusion into the scientific program of MFCS'95. Thus the present volume contains all of the 44 contributed papers, plus 8 invited papers and 2 abstracts of the invited talks.

We wish to thank all those who submitted their papers for consideration, all Program Committee members for their meritorious work in evaluating the submitted papers, as well as the following referees who assisted the Program Committee members in the extensive evaluation process:

L. Aceto, J. Adámek, S. Albers, C. Àlvarez, A. Arnold, J.C.M. Baeten, J. Balcazar, M.A. Bednarczyk, L.S. Bertrand, A. Birkendorf, J. Bloemer, A.M. Borzyszkowski, J. Bradfield, L. Brim, G. Bruns, R. Casas, P. Casteran, I. Černá, V. Černý, Z. Chaochen, A. Corradini, F. Cucker, P. Darondeau, V. Diekert, M. Dietzfelbinger, P. Ďuriš, J. Edmonds, J. Elbro, U.H. Engberg, E. Feuerstein, P. Fischer, P.G. Franciosa, G. Gambosi, R. Gavaldà, V. Geffert, Ch. George, R. Gerth, M. Golin, D. Gruska, T. Harju, I. Havel, H.D. Hecker, J.G. Henriksen, V. Heun, T. Hofmeister, I. Honkala, J. Honkala, J. Hromkovič, M. Hühne, H. Huttel, D. Janin, K. Jansen, B. Juurlink, R. Kaivola, J. Karhumäki, N. Klarlund, C. Klein, J.W. Klop, I. Korec, J. Krajíček, I. Kramosil, M. Krause, K. Kühnle, M. Křetínský, K.J. Lange, H. Lefmann, S. Leonardi, M. Lightner, G. Lischke, M. Loebbing, J. Longley, C. Martinez, A. Mateescu, J. Matoušek, S. Mauw, E. Mayordomo, A. Mazurkiewicz, Ch. Meinel, S. Merz, Y. Metivier, J.J.Ch. Meyer, F. Mignosi, P.D. Mosses, O. Mueller, R. Muller, L. Niepel, D. Olejár, D. Pardubská, G. Paun, M. Penttonen, F. Petrini, D. Plump, A. Poetzsch-Heffter, J. Pokorný, G. Radu, F. Regensburger, E. Robinson, J.M. Robson, J. Rosický, J. Rothe, G. Rozenberg, B. Rumpe, P. Ružička, W. Rytter, A. Salomaa, K. Salomaa,

A. Sandholm, P. Savický, M. Serna, J.R.J. Schirra, D. Sieling, H.U. Simon, A. Simpson, Y. Singer, K. Slind, O. Slotosch, E. Smith, K. Stoelen, J. Šturc, K. Sunesen, O. Sýkora, R. Szelepcsényi, A. Tarlecki, J. Toran, J. van der Woude, P. Vana, D. van Hung, J.J. Vereijken, P.J. Voda, J. Vogel, B. von Stengel, J. Vyskoč, R. Wegner, E. Welzl, R. Werchner, J. Winkowski, G. Winskel, L. Xiaoshan, Q. Xu, S. Žák, W. Zielonka, A. Zvonkin.

We are much indebted to all authors of the invited papers and of the accepted contribution papers who all (with a single exception) prepared their papers according to the instructions using the LNCS LaTeX style.

Many thanks are due also to Roman Neruda and Arnošt Štědrý for the preparation and maintenance of the MFCS'95 database, software support for automatic sending and evaluating of MFCS'95 referee forms, and typesetting of the MFCS'95 Information Bulletin. Tereza Bedaňová did a good job in the secretarial work for the symposium. The occasional assistence of Kateřina Hlaváčková and of Jiří Šíma was also useful.

Special thanks go to Peter van Emde Boas who helped enormously in preparing the presentation schedule for the scientific program at the conference.

We thank the European Association for Theoretical Computer Science (EATCS), IBM Czech Republic, H.E.M. Informatics, FCC Folprecht Praha, SINCO and I.C.C.C. for their support of MFCS'95. The organizational support of the conference provided by Action M Agency is highly appreciated as well.

Last but not least we want to thank Springer-Verlag for proposals that have led to improvements in the logical structure of the volume and for excellent co-operation in its publication.

Prague, June 1995 Petr Hájek, Jiří Wiedermann

Contents

Invited Papers

Contributed Papers

Structural Complexity Theory

Algorithms

Complexity Theory

Graphs in Models of Computations

Lower Bounds

Formal Languages

Unification, Rewriting, Type Theory

Distributed Computation

Concurrency

Semantics

Model Checking

Formal Calculi

Scheduling Parallel Communication: The h-relation Problem

Micah Adler *
Computer Science Division
UC Berkeley
Berkeley, CA 94720

John W. Byers **
Computer Science Division
UC Berkeley
Berkeley, CA 94720

Richard M. Karp ***
International Computer Science Institute
and
Computer Science Division
UC Berkeley
Berkeley, CA 94720

Abstract. This paper is concerned with the efficient scheduling and routing of point-to-point messages in a distributed computing system with n processors. We examine the h-relation problem, a routing problem where each processor has at most h messages to send and at most h messages to receive. Communication is carried out in rounds. Direct communication is possible from any processor to any other, and in each round a processor can send one message and receive one message. The off-line version of the problem arises when every processor knows the source and destination of every message. In this case the messages can be routed in at most h rounds. More interesting, and more typical, is the on-line version, in which each processor has knowledge only of h and of the destinations of those messages which it must send. The on-line version of the problem is the focus of this paper.

The difficulty of the h-relation problem stems from *message conflicts*, in which two or more messages are sent to the same processor in a given round, but at most one can be received. The problem has been well studied in the OCPC optical network model, but not for other contemporary network architectures which resolve message conflicts using other techniques. In this paper, we study the h-relation problem under alternative models of conflict resolution, most notably a FIFO queue discipline motivated by wormhole routing and an arbitrary write discipline motivated by packet-switching networks. In each model the problem can be solved by a randomized algorithm in an expected number of rounds of the form

* Supported by a Schlumberger Foundation Graduate Fellowship.
** Supported by a GAANN Graduate Fellowship.
*** Supported by NSF grant number CCR-9005448

$ch+o(h) + \log^{\Theta(1)} n$, and we focus on obtaining the smallest possible asymptotic constant factor c. We first present a lower bound, proving that a constant factor of 1 is not achievable in general. We then present a randomized algorithm for each discipline and show that they achieve small constant factors.

1 Introduction

We assume that a communication task to be performed by a parallel computer with n processors is specified by an $n \times n$ matrix $K = (k_{ij})$, where k_{ij} gives the number of messages originating at processor i and destined for processor j. If we let h be the maximum sum of any row or column of this matrix; then the matrix specifies an h-relation [Val 90]. The problem of solving this communication task is called the *h-relation problem.* An h-relation can be thought of as a generic model of irregular communication. Routing an h-relation is the fundamental communication step in Valiant's BSP model of parallel computation. The on-line version of the problem is also central to the simulation of a PRAM with many processors on a PRAM with fewer processors, and, in general, to the scheduling of concurrent memory accesses in distributed memory machines.

To define the problem further, we must model the performance characteristics of the communication medium, or network, through which the messages are transmitted. Much of the existing work on the h-relation problem [AM 88], [Val1 90], [GJL+ 93] has been under the Optically Connected Parallel Computer (OCPC) model. In this model of computation, processors communicate by point-to-point messages in synchronous rounds, with the restriction that whenever two or more messages are sent concurrently to the same processor, the messages are destroyed and must be retransmitted. We provide a survey of the theoretical literature on routing h-relations under the OCPC discipline in Section 3.

In this paper, we consider the problem of routing h-relations in other communication media. It is assumed that any processor can communicate directly with any other processor. Communication occurs in synchronous rounds, during which each processor may send and receive one point-to-point message. The models are differentiated by the manner in which they handle *contention*, which occurs when several messages are sent concurrently to the same processor. We consider several disciplines for the handling of contention:

- The *FIFO discipline*, in which incoming messages destined for a given receiver are placed in a first-in first-out queue from which they are extracted by the receiving processor at the rate of one message per round. A sender is temporarily blocked after a transmission, unable to transmit more messages until the original message is extracted from the target processor's queue.
- The *arbitrary write discipline*, in which a receiving processor receives exactly one of its incoming messages at random at each time step; all other incoming messages must be retransmitted. Immediately after each round, every sender is informed as to whether its message has been received.

- The *priority queue discipline* in which incoming messages carry priorities, and are placed in a priority queue. As in the FIFO model, no two messages from the same processor may reside in queues at the same time.

In existing network architectures, message contention is primarily due to limited buffering at internal switches. The arbitrary write discipline is motivated by packet-switched architectures such as the BBN butterfly and the ATM network, where messages traverse the network as a single unit, with their final destination prepended to the message. When packet-switched messages simultaneously arrive at a switch with insufficient buffering, the switch may drop messages it cannot handle. The sender's ability to detect the successful or unsuccessful transmission of a message is often left to higher-level software, rather than the hardware itself. Modeling a packet-switched network is made more challenging by the wide variety of network topologies and internal switches used in practice. However, our arbitrary write discipline captures the essence of the conflict resolution strategy used in packet-switched networks. The contention rule in the arbitrary write discipline is similar to the contention rule of an arbitrary write CRCW PRAM.

The queued models are based on another approach used for routing messages in tightly coupled networks. These use the closely related techniques of wormhole routing and virtual cut-through routing, used for example in the J Machine [ND 90] and the CM-5 [Lei+ 94]. In wormhole routing, messages are divided into very small flow control units (flits) which are then transmitted along a fixed path through the network to the destination. A message can thereby occupy buffer space in several adjacent switches simultaneously. If the first flit of a message arrives at a switch with insufficient buffer space, the entire chain of flits stalls, often stalling the sending processor as well. This style of message-passing motivates the FIFO discipline, which stalls the sending processor until the target processor receives each transmission. Contention in the FIFO model is similar to the capacity constraint of the LogP model [CKP+ 93] and to the asynchronous version of the QRQW PRAM [GMR2 94].

To provide a preliminary comparison of the disciplines, we note that OCPC algorithms can be simulated with no slowdown in the arbitrary write model and FIFO algorithms can be simulated with no slowdown in the priority queue model. The disciplines using queues seem to be incomparable to the disciplines without queues because of the effect of stalling; in the queued disciplines, sending processors must wait until their transmission is successfully sent before proceeding.

We here concentrate our efforts on achieving the best possible leading constant for *direct* algorithms, that is algorithms where each message is routed directly from its source to its destination, without passing through any intermediate processors. Aside from their simplicity, direct algorithms require a smaller total number of successfully transmitted messages than indirect algorithms. Also, when the destinations of the messages are memory modules, messages cannot be forwarded, and direct algorithms are required.

When introducing the OCPC model, Anderson and Miller showed that in the off-line case, an arbitrary h-relation could be routed in time h [AM 88]. Recent efforts have tried to achieve *1-optimal* randomized on-line algorithms [RSTG 95]; i.e., on-line algorithms that route an h-relation in expected time $h + o(h)$. We here provide evidence that no 1-optimal algorithm exists in the FIFO discipline, the arbitrary write discipline, or the OCPC discipline. More specifically, we show that for a natural class of algorithms, there exists an h-relation input for every $h < n^{1/3}$ such that every randomized on-line algorithm for these disciplines requires time at least $1.1h$ to route that input. The class of algorithms can be informally described as those algorithms such that, if $k_{ij} = k_{ir} > 0$, then the first transmission from i to j is as likely to precede as it is to follow the first transmission from i to r.

We can, however, achieve within a small constant factor of optimal for all three disciplines. We present the following.

- In the FIFO discipline, a direct randomized algorithm that runs in time $3.41h + o(h) + O(\log^3 n \log\log n)$ with high probability. The analysis of this algorithm is based on introducing martingales associated with the progress of the algorithm, showing that the martingales have bounded differences with high probability, and then applying Azuma's tail inequality for martingales with bounded differences.
- In the arbitrary write discipline, a direct randomized algorithm that runs in time $1.62h + o(h) + O(\log n \log\log n)$ with high probability.
- In the priority queue discipline, a simple and direct randomized algorithm that runs in time $(2e - 1)h + o(h) + O(\log n)$ with high probability, where e denotes the base of the natural logarithm. The analysis of this algorithm is based on a delay sequence argument.

We also report on simulations in which the following constant factors are observed: $2.08h$ for the FIFO algorithm, $1.57h$ for the arbitrary write algorithm, and $1.85h$ for the priority queue algorithm.

Throughout the paper, we say that an event holds with high probability if, for some $c > 1$, the event holds with probability $\geq 1 - 1/n^c$.

2 Previous Work

In this section, we survey the body of work on routing h-relations, most of which has been done in the Optically Connected Parallel Computer (OCPC). In the OCPC, each of n processors can transmit a message to any of the other processors at each time step. If a processor receives two or more messages at a given time step, the data in those messages is lost and the messages must be retransmitted. Successful transmissions are acknowledged by the receiving processor, and failure to acknowledge implies that the data in the message was lost. This model was introduced by Anderson and Miller [AM 88].

Anderson and Miller were also the first to observe that if all processors have complete information about a given h-relation, there exists a schedule which routes the relation using exactly h communication steps. This observation follows by viewing the relation as a bipartite multigraph of maximum degree h, which is edge-colorable using h colors. Drawing a correspondence between colors and communication steps gives the communication pattern that can be routed in time exactly h, which is also an immediate lower bound.

2.1 Asymptotically Efficient Protocols

A primary theme in the literature on routing h-relations has been to provide routing protocols which are asymptotically efficient, especially for small values of h. Two types of algorithms are considered, *direct* algorithms, in which messages are always transmitted from the sender directly to the final receiver and *indirect* algorithms, in which senders may forward messages through intermediate locations en route to the final destination. The simplicity of direct algorithms makes them appealing from a practical standpoint, but they have theoretical limitations, which will be described momentarily. In all the algorithms we describe, the use of randomness is fundamental; to our knowledge, the best upper bound for deterministically routing an arbitrary h-relation on an OCPC is $O(h \log n)$.

The direct algorithm with the best asymptotic running time for the OCPC is the simple randomized algorithm of Gereb-Graus and Tsantilas [GT 92]. For any fixed $\epsilon > 0$, their algorithm with high probability transmits an arbitrary h-relation in time

$$\frac{e}{1-\epsilon}h + \Theta(\sqrt{h \log n} + \log n \log\log n).$$

This is done with $\log_{1/(1-\epsilon)} h = \frac{\log h}{-\log(1-\epsilon)}$ phases, where the problem remaining at the start of phase i is w.h.p. a $k_i = (1-\epsilon)^i h$-relation, and at the end of phase i is a $k_{i+1} = (1-\epsilon)^{i+1} h$-relation. Each phase transmits some ϵk_i-relation w.h.p. as follows. At each step, every processor uniformly at random picks one of its $r \leq k_i$ packets to send, and attempts to transmit that packet with probability $\frac{r}{k_i}$. With probability $\frac{k_i - r}{k_i}$, the processor does nothing. Using the fact that each processor successfully transmits a packet that has been sent with probability at least $\frac{1-\epsilon}{e}$, they show that the number of steps round i requires is no more than

$$\frac{e}{1-\epsilon}(\epsilon k_i + O(\sqrt{\epsilon k_i \log n} + \log n).$$

The bound on the total amount of time follows.

In [GJLR 92], Goldberg, Jerrum, Leighton and Rao prove a lower bound of $\Omega(\log n)$ for direct algorithms for the h-relation problem on the OCPC. The lower bound motivates study of indirect algorithms as a means to achieve sub-logarithmic time for routing h-relations for small values of h. The bound is a formalization of the following intuition. Consider a 2-relation in which $2n$ senders each transmit a single message to n receivers and where the senders do not know the whereabouts or the sending strategy of their partner. Random direct sending strategies are likely to lead to a pair which conflicts for $\Omega(\log n)$ rounds, thereby acheiving the lower bound. The same authors then present an indirect protocol for routing h-relations on the OCPC which we sketch below that runs in time $O(h + \log\log n)$.

In the first phase of their protocol, the h-relation is thinned by a direct algorithm which routes many of the messages to their final destinations, using a procedure somewhat similar to that of [AM 88]. With high probability, the procedure transmits all but $O(n/h \log\log n)$ messages in time $O(h+\log h \log\log\log n)$. The protocol runs for $O(\log h)$ rounds, round i of which reduces an $\frac{h}{2^{i-1}}$ relation to an $\frac{h}{2^i}$ relation across all but a small fraction of the processors who drop out of the remainder of this phase of the protocol if they are left with too many undelivered messages. During round i, for each of $O(h/2^{i-1} + \log h + \log\log\log n)$ steps, each sender which has survived transmits each of its messages with probability $\frac{2^{i-1}}{h}$. The analysis uses the method of bounded differences to derive the bound on the number of undelivered messages.

Next, in the second phase of the protocol, the undelivered messages are smoothly redistributed across all the processors, so that each processor has at most one undelivered message. The final two phases employ the concept of target groups, $\frac{n}{k}$ disjoint sets of processors of size $k = \log^{c_1} n$. In phase three, all messages are delivered to the target groups of the destination processor, but perhaps not to the destination processor itself. The technique employed is dart-throwing, where those messages which cannot be routed directly to the target group with high probability are copied to many processors, each of which then attempts to transmit the message to the target group. Messages for which more than one copy arrive at the target group select a leader and eliminate duplicates. With high probability, each of the messages has now been delivered at its target group, and furthermore, every processor has at most two messages. In the final phase, running a deterministic procedure such as Valiant's algorithm [Val2 90] (a simple indirect protocol outlined below) within each target group sorts and routes each of the messages to their final destinations in time $O(\log k) = O(\log\log n)$.

Prior to the [GJLR93] result, the algorithm that achieved optimality for the smallest value of h was that of Valiant, an indirect algorithm which routes an h-relation in time $O(h + \log n)$, for any $h = \Omega(\log n)$. The algorithm consists of two steps, the first of which is a thinning step, which insures that within $O(h)$ rounds, the total number of unsent messages is $O(\frac{hn}{\log n})$ w.h.p. The remaining messages are sent by a deterministic subroutine requiring time $O(h+\log n)$. This subroutine proceeds by first performing a parallel prefix with all the processors that informs the processors of the total number of messages, along with the rank of the processor's messages within that total. This allows the processors to redistribute the messages so that every processor has exactly the same number of messages. Once this has been accomplished, the messages can be sorted by various means, such as Cole's parallel merge sort [Col 88], in time $O(h + \log n)$. The keys to be sorted consist of the identifier of the destination processor concatenated with the message itself, and thus all messages destined for the same processor will end up in consecutive processors. Thus, the remaining messages can be deterministically routed to their final destinations in time $O(h)$.

Finally, it is worth remarking that even for indirect algorithms, time bounds of the form $O(h)$ are not possible for small values of h. Goldberg, Jerrum and MacKenzie [GJM 94] prove a lower bound of $\Omega(h + \sqrt{\log\log n})$ for realizing an h-relation on the OCPC.

2.2 1-Optimal Protocols

For much larger values of h, recent research has focused not on asymptotic behavior, but on leading constant factors of asymptotically optimal algorithms. Gerbessiotis and Valiant [GV 94] define a 1-optimal protocol for the OCPC as a protocol which can route a random h-relation in time at most $(1 + o(1))h$ with high probability. To derive 1-optimal algorithms, they employ the total-exchange communication primitive (also known as all-to-all personalized communication), in which every processor has a distinct message to transmit to every other processor. Extremely simple and contention-free strategies solve this communication problem in time n on the OCPC. Using these tools, the same authors present a protocol to route random h-relations using at most $\frac{h}{n}(1 + o(1) + O(\log\log n))$ total-exchange rounds with high probability, and so this algorithm is 1-optimal. Recent work [RSTG 95] has improved this bound to $\frac{h}{n}(1+o(1)+O(\log^* n))$ total-exchange rounds and has provided experimental results which confirm that the algorithm is very fast in practice. A drawback of this approach is that h must be extremely large for the algorithms to achieve 1-optimality, i.e. at least $\omega(n)$.

3 Direct 1-Optimal Algorithms Are Not Possible

In this section, we prove a lower bound for direct, on-line algorithms that are *uniform*, or, informally, algorithms where, at a given sender, a target destination is treated identically to other target destination receiving the same number of messages until the first attempt to send. To be more formal, let an *untried* destination for a processor be a destination to which that processor has not yet attempted to transmit a message. Then, we say that an algorithm is *uniform* if, at every time step, the probability that a processor sends to a given untried destination is the same for all untried destinations receiving the same number of messages. Restricting our attention to the class of uniform algorithms is justified by the fact that all untried destinations receiving the same number of messages look equivalent to a sending processor routing an arbitrary h-relation.

In addition, we assume that each processor is using the same program, and if sender A attempts the first transmission of a message to receiver X at the same time t as at least one other sender, then the probability that the message from A is successfully received at t is $\leq \frac{1}{2}$. If it is not successfully received, it will take at least one more time step for A to successfully send that message. We note that the last assumption holds for the concurrent write, FIFO and OCPC disciplines, but not the priority queue discipline. We prove a lower bound of $1.1h$ for any uniform, direct, on-line algorithm for any model meeting these assumptions, provided that $h \leq n^{1/3}$. Thus, no 1-optimal algorithms exist which meet these criteria.

Theorem 1. *When $h \leq n^{1/3}$, there does not exist a uniform and direct on-line algorithm that routes every h-relation in time less than $1.1h$ with probability greater than $\frac{1}{2}$.*

We assume such an algorithm exists, and work towards a contradiction. Any such algorithm must successfully route h-relations of the form diagrammed below, which we will refer to as *difficult* h-relations. In such an h-relation, Processor 1 has h messages to send to distinct destination processors $j_1, \ldots j_h$. Each of these destinations receives an additional $h-1$ *conflicting* messages from distinct processors. The $h(h-1)$ processors which transmit conflicting messages are referred to as *blocking* processors. Each blocking processor transmits h messages in all, and all non-conflicting messages which they transmit have distinct destinations.

```
1                   1                   1                   1                   1
11111
1    1111
1         1111
1              1111
                    11111
                    1    1111
                    1         1111
                    1              1111
                                        11111
                                        1    1111
                                        1         1111
                                        1              1111
                                                            11111
                                                            1    1111
                                                            1         1111
                                                            1              1111
                                                                                11111
                                                                                1    1111
                                                                                1         1111
                                                                                1              1111
```

Fig. 1. A difficult matrix

We call a time slot *crowded* if all blocking processors attempt the first transmission of a conflicting message during that time slot with probability at least $\frac{1}{2h} - \frac{1}{h^2}$.

Lemma 2. *In any uniform algorithm that routes an h-relation in time $1.1h$ with probability at least $\frac{1}{2}$, there are at least $0.9h$ crowded time slots in the $1.1h$ possible time slots.*

Proof: Since the algorithm is uniform and all processors execute the same code, it suffices to show that the lemma holds for any given blocking processor. To see that this is the case, consider the behavior of an *isolated* processor, i.e. a processor that sends h messages to distinct destinations, none of which conflict with any other messages. Until the time of the first attempted transmission of a conflicting message, the behavior of each blocking processor is identical to that of the isolated processor. For all of n/h isolated processors to succeed with probability $1/2$, each of the isolated processors must succeed with probability $(1/2)^{h/n}$, which is at least $1 - \frac{1}{h^2}$ for h sufficiently large. To complete in time $1.1h$ an isolated processor must choose h time slots to send its messages. If more than $0.2h$ slots are selected with probability $< \frac{1}{2}$, the number of slots utilized is strictly less than $.2h * .5 + .8h * 1 = h$. Thus, to complete in time $1.1h$, there must exist at least $0.9h$ slots that the isolated processor chooses with probability at least $\frac{1}{2}$. Furthermore, each of the $0.9h$ slots has a $\frac{1}{h}$ chance of being the slot chosen for a blocking processor's conflicting message, so the probability that a given conflicting message is scheduled in a crowded time slot is $\geq \frac{1}{2h} - \frac{1}{h^2}$.

Lemma 3. *The probability that processor 1 successfully sends a message on the first attempt, given that the attempt is during a crowded time slot, is no more than* $\frac{1+\exp(-\frac{h-3}{2h})}{2}$.

Proof: There are $h-1$ blocking processors sending conflicting messages coinciding with each message from processor 1. Thus, the probability that processor 1 sends during a time slot where no blocking processor attempts its first transmission is

$$\leq \left(1 - \frac{1}{2h} + \frac{1}{h^2}\right)^{h-1} \leq \exp\left(-\frac{h-3}{2h}\right)$$

During the other time slots, the probability that processor 1 sends successfully is no more than $\frac{1}{2}$. Thus, the total probability that processor 1 sends successfully is

$$\leq \exp\left(-\frac{h-3}{2h}\right) + \frac{1}{2}\left(1 - \exp\left(-\frac{h-3}{2h}\right)\right) = \frac{1}{2}\left(1 + \exp\left(-\frac{h-3}{2h}\right)\right).$$

Proof of Theorem 1 : To complete in time $1.1h$, processor 1 must attempt at least once to send each of its h messages during the first $1.1h$ time slots. But, by Lemma 1, at most $0.2h$ of these slots are not crowded, so processor 1 would have to attempt to send during at least $0.8h$ crowded time slots. Using lemma 2, it is a simple exercise in Chernoff bounds to show that with high probability, at least $0.11h$ of the messages from processor 1 are not transmitted successfully on the first try. Thus, processor 1 needs total time at least $1.11h$, and we have reached a contradiction.

4 Scheduling h-relations under the FIFO Discipline

We now turn our attention to the FIFO discipline. In this discipline, transmission of the h-relation is divided into synchronous rounds, where each processor is allowed to send and receive one message during each round. Messages in transit to a given target processor are viewed as residing in a First-In First-Out queue.

In each round a processor receives the message, if any, at the head of its queue, and that message is deleted from the queue. Network capacity constraints are enforced by ensuring that at most one message is in transit from any given processor at any time. Thus, as long as a message from a sending processor resides in the input queue of some processor, the sending processor is stalled and cannot send further messages, but it can receive messages. As described in the introduction, the FIFO discipline models contemporary machines that use wormhole routing or virtual cut-through routing to transmit messages.

Theorem 4. *There exists a direct randomized algorithm which routes an arbitrary h-relation in the FIFO discipline within time* $3.41h + o(h) + O(log^3 n \log\log n)$ *w.h.p.*

We begin by describing a generic parameterized algorithm for the FIFO discipline with parameters k and μ. The algorithm runs in $m = log_{\frac{1}{\mu}} h$ stages, where with high probability, the following invariant is maintained: at the end of each stage $i, 1 \leq i \leq m$, the undelivered messages form an h_i relation, where $h_i = h\mu^i$. Stage i consists of kh_{i-1} rounds of communication scheduled in a manner described below.

Before stage i begins, each processor schedules the sending times of all of its undelivered messages. These sending times are chosen by sampling without replacement from the uniform distribution over the integers between 1 and kh_{i-1}. Thus the sending time of any given message is uniformly distributed over $[1..khi - 1]$, and no two messages from the same processor have the same sending time. During stage i, each processor sends its messages according to their scheduled sending times. However, if a processor is stalled at the scheduled sending time of one of its messages, then the message is not sent, but is deferred to the next stage. Thus, if a message sent at time t_1 by a processor ρ resides in the input queue of its target processor until time t_2, then all messages scheduled to be sent by ρ in the interval $[t_1 + 1..t_2]$ are deferred to the next stage, and ρ resumes its transmissions at time t_2+1. The algorithm halts at a stage i such that $h_i \leq h^{2/5}$, at which time all remaining messages can be transmitted deterministically in time $o(h)$. The algorithm described in Theorem 4 is an instantiation of the parameterized algorithm with $k = 2.5$ and $\mu = 0.267$. In the following discussion ϵ is a positive constant which may be chosen as small as desired.

Theorem 4 is a consequence of the following lemma, which we will prove momentarily.

Lemma 5. *In stage i, with probability* $1 - 2n \cdot \exp(-\Theta(h_i^{\frac{1}{3}}))$*:*

- *All processors with at least* $0.267h_i$ *unsent messages transmit at least a* $(0.733 - \epsilon)$ *fraction of those messages.*
- *All processors with at least* $0.267h_i$ *unreceived messages receive at least a* $(0.733 - \epsilon)$ *fraction of those messages.*

Proof of Theorem 4 : From Lemma 5, we see that during stage i, which runs in $2.5h_i$ rounds, we have reduced the problem size by a factor of $0.733 - \epsilon$ w.h.p.

We recurse until the resulting problem forms an $h^{2/5}$-relation, which takes time $2.5\cdot\sum_{i=0}^{m}(0.267+\epsilon)^i\,h = \frac{3}{0.733-\epsilon}h$. Then, all messages are sent in any order, and since no message can be delayed by more than $h^{2/5}$ time slots, and no processor needs to send more than $h^{2/5}$ messages, the algorithm finishes in time $o(h)$. Since the failure probability during stage i is at most $2n\cdot exp(-\Theta(h_i^{0.267}))$, the m stages succeed with high probability when for all i, $h_i = \Omega(\log^3 n)$, or equivalently, $h = \Omega(\log^{15/2} n)$. When $h \in [\log^3 n \ldots \log^{15/2} n]$, we can run until $h_i = \Theta(\log^3 n)$, and then complete in time $O(\log^3 n \log\log n)$. Thus, the algorithm completes w.h.p. in time $3.41h + o(h) + O(\log^3 n \log\log n)$. □

In the proof of Lemma 5, we use the following terminology. We say that a schedule chosen for stage i of our protocol is *well-distributed* if no processor receives more than $0.9h_i^{\frac{1}{3}}$ messages in any $h_i^{\frac{1}{3}}$ consecutive rounds. We say that a receiving processor j is *idle* at time t if its input queue is empty during the tth round. Otherwise, we say that the processor is *active* at time t. If the schedule for stage i is well-distributed, no receiving processor is active for more than $h_i^{1/3}$ consecutive rounds in stage i.

The proof also uses the following Martingale Tail Inequality due to Azuma. Recall that a Martingale is a sequence of random variables Y_i, $i = 0, 1, \cdots, n$, such that, for all i, $E[Y_i|Y_0, Y_1, \ldots, Y_{i-1}] = Y_{i-1}$.

Theorem 6 Azuma. *Let $\{Y_i\}$ be a Martingale, and let $a_1, a_2, \ldots, a_n$ be such that, for $i = 1, 2, \cdots, n$, $|Y_i - Y_{i-1}| \le a_i$. Then the probability that $Y_n - Y_0 > \lambda\sqrt{a_1^2 + \cdots a_n^2}$ is less than or equal to $e^{-\frac{\lambda^2}{2}}$.*

The application of this theorem is often called the method of bounded differences.

Proof of Lemma 5: We begin by deriving an upper bound of $\frac{2}{3}$ on the a priori expected time a processor stalls during the transmission of any message. We then apply the method of bounded differences to show that the schedules chosen in stage i (which are well-behaved w.h.p.) cause a processor which schedules x messages to experience a delay of at most $\frac{2x}{3}$ rounds with high probability. A final application of the method of bounded differences reveals that with high probability in stage i, each sender which begins with more than h_i undelivered messages successfully transmits at least $0.733h_i$ of these messages with high probability. A similar statement holds for the receivers and the lemma then follows.

Let x messages to be sent to processor j be partitioned into m sets, where set r contains n_r messages, and $\sum_{r=1}^{m} n_r = x$. The *arrival time* of a message is defined as the number of the round in which it is sent to processor j, or, equivalently, the number of the round in which it arrives at the input queue of processor j. The arrival times of the messages within set r are n_r slots chosen uniformly at random without replacement from the range $[1..S]$. The arrival times of the messages in each set are independent of the arrival times in the other sets. We call the distribution of arrival times associated with any partition an *arrival distribution*. We sometimes use the same notation to refer to both a partition and its arrival distribution.

A message is said to be stalled in a given round if, at the end of the round, it resides in the input queue of processor j. For any message p among the x messages, let $D(p)$, the *delay* of p, be the number of rounds in which message p is stalled.

Lemma 7. *For any message p and any arrival distribution for x messages including p, onto the range $[1\ldots S]$, the expected value of $D(p)$ is less than or equal to $\frac{x}{S-x}$.*

Proof: We first consider the partition consisting of x singleton sets. In this case the arrival times are independent identically distributed random variables, each with the uniform distribution over $[1..S]$. We call this the *uniform and independent arrival distribution.* We say that message p is in the system for $D(p)+1$ rounds. Let $S(j)$ be the time spent in the system of message j. Let $Y(i)$ be the number of messages in the system at time i. By counting the number of message-time pairs, we have that $\sum_{j=1}^{x} S(j) \geq \sum_{i=1}^{S} Y(i)$. For p to be in the system for z rounds, it must be stalled for $z-1$ rounds, and so there must be at least $z-1$ other messages that are either already in the system at the time p arrives, or that have the same arrival time as p. Since the arrival time of p is uniform and independent of the other arrivals,

$$\mathrm{E}[S(p)] \leq 1 + \mathrm{E}[\frac{1}{S}\sum_{i=1}^{S} Y(i)] \leq 1 + \mathrm{E}[\frac{1}{S}\sum_{j=1}^{x} S(j)].$$

By symmetry, $\mathrm{E}[S(p)] \leq 1 + \frac{1}{S}x\mathrm{E}[S(p)]$. This gives us $\mathrm{E}[S(p)] \leq \frac{S}{S-x}$, or that $\mathrm{E}[D(p)] \leq \frac{x}{S-x}$.

To complete the proof we show that of all possible arrival distributions, the expected delay of each message is greatest in the case of the uniform and independent arrival distribution. We compare two partitions: M, which contains a singleton set $\{s\}$, and M_d, which is the same as M, except that s has been merged with some other set U. We show that the expected delay of every message in M is at least as large as the corresponding message in M_d. This shows that the expected delay of any message in any arrival partition is no greater than the expected delay of a message in the uniform and independent partition, since any arrival partition can be made by a series of such transformations, starting with the uniform and independent partition.

To see that the expected delay of any message in M is no greater than that of the corresponding message in M_d, we compare M_d with M_o, where M_o is the same as M with the additional constraint that the message s must be scheduled at the same time as a message in U. Since the arrival distribution M is just a weighted sum of M_o and M_d, showing that each message has smaller expected delay in M_d than in M_o shows that each message has smaller expected delay in M_d than in M.

We first assign a number to each of the x messages in M_o and in M_d, with the constraint that a message in M_o has the same number as its corresponding message in M_d. Also, s is assigned x in M_o, and the message in U that overlaps with s is assigned $x-1$. In M_d, x and $x-1$ are any two elements of U. We henceforth refer to messages by their assigned numbers.

Let $\mathrm{E}_o[i]$ and $\mathrm{E}_d[i]$ be the expected delay of message i when the schedule is defined by arrival distributions M_o and M_d respectively. We shall show that $\forall i$, $\mathrm{E}_o[i] \geq \mathrm{E}_d[i]$. This is proved in two parts.

Claim 1: $\mathrm{E}_o[x] \geq \mathrm{E}_d[x]$ and $\mathrm{E}_o[x-1] \geq \mathrm{E}_d[x-1]$.

Proof: Fix the location of messages $1 \ldots x-2$. Let Z be the expected delay of a single additional message arriving with these fixed messages. Then, $\mathrm{E}_o[x] = \mathrm{E}_o[x-1] = Z + \frac{1}{2}$, since the messages have an expected delay of Z due to the other messages, and $\frac{1}{2}$ due to each other. $\mathrm{E}_d[x] = \mathrm{E}_d[x-1] \leq Z + \frac{1}{2}$, since message x is scheduled after $x-1$ with probability $\frac{1}{2}$.

To analyze the delay of the other messages, we introduce a method of calculating the delay of a given message i, given a fixed schedule. Set a counter to 0. Start at the beginning of the scheduling period. Scan from left to right, one time slot at a time. For every time slot, increment the counter by the number of arrivals, and then decrement it by 1, never letting the counter decrease below 0. The value of this counter when we reach the time slot that i arrives in (before accounting for that time slot), plus $\frac{1}{2}$ times the number of other arrivals during time slot i, is the expected delay of i, with the given schedule.

We can do the same thing by maintaining a *delay list*, where at every time step, each arrival for that time step is placed on the list, after which the smallest numbered message is removed from the list. The number of messages in the delay list when we reach i will be the delay of the first message serviced of those arriving at the same time slot as i. Note that the messages in the delay list are not necessarily the messages that are waiting for service at the time. But, from this we see that if, for a schedule chosen from arrival distribution M_d, we define indicator variables I_{ij}, where $I_{ij} = 1$ if message i is in the delay list when it reaches message j, $\frac{1}{2}$ if message i arrives at the same time as j, and 0 otherwise, then we see that $\mathrm{E}_d[j] = \sum_{i=1}^{x} \mathrm{E}[I_{ij}]$. We can define the same indicator variable J_{ij} for arrival distribution M_o, which gives us $\mathrm{E}_o[j] = \sum_{i=1}^{x} \mathrm{E}[J_{ij}]$, from which we see that lemma 7 follows from the following claim.

Claim 2: $\forall i, 1 \leq i \leq x, \forall j 1 \leq i \leq x-2$, $\mathrm{E}[I_{ij}] \leq \mathrm{E}[J_{ij}]$

Proof: When $i \leq x-1$, then $\mathrm{E}[I_{ij}] = \mathrm{E}[J_{ij}]$ follows from the fact that the location of messages numbered higher than i have no effect on either I_{ij} or J_{ij}, and thus neither does the distribution of those messages. To see that $\mathrm{E}[I_{xj}] \leq \mathrm{E}[J_{xj}]$, fix the location of all messages but $x-1$. This schedule of messages $1 \ldots x-2, x$ is as likely in M_d as it is in M_o. The only effect on I_{xj} or J_{xj} that adding $x-1$ to the other messages can have is changing I_{xj} or J_{xj} from a 0 to a 1. But, if it changes I_{xj} from a 0 to a 1, then J_{xj} will also be changed to a 1, and thus $\mathrm{E}[I_{xj}] \leq \mathrm{E}[J_{xj}]$.

□

Given a bound on the expected delay incurred by a given message, we now let D_j denote the total delay incurred by sending processor j during stage i. Setting $x = h$ and $S = 2.5h$ in Lemma 2, we find that the expected delay of each message transmitted by processor j is at most $2/3$, and thus $\mathrm{E}[D_j] \leq \frac{2h_i}{3}$.

We now show that w.h.p. the actual delay D_j is unlikely to deviate significantly from its expectation. The following lemma assumes that the schedule for stage i is well-distributed; using a Chernoff bound, this can be verified to hold for all processors with high probability, assuming that $h = \Omega(\log^3 n)$.

Lemma 8. *Given that the schedule for stage i is well-distributed, $Pr[|D_j - E[D_j]| > \beta h_i] \leq exp(-\beta^2 h_i^{\frac{1}{3}})$.*

Proof: We define the Martingale A_t, where $A(t) = \mathrm{E}[D_j|S_1 \ldots S_t]$ and S_t represents the scheduled actions of all processors at time t. To apply Azuma's inequality, we must provide a bound on $|A_{t+1} - A_t|$, the increase in expected delay at processor j after seeing a single additional round of the algorithm. Since we are given that the schedule is well-distributed, every receiving processor is guaranteed to be idle some time before time $t+1+h_i^{1/3}$, and therefore $h_i^{1/3}$ serves as a bound on $|A_{t+1} - A_t|$. The lemma follows immediately by an application of Azuma's inequality. □

Lemma 9. *Given that $D_j \leq \frac{2}{3}h_i$, the a priori probability that a given message from processor j is successfully sent during stage i is at least $\frac{11}{15}$.*

Proof: When $D_j \leq \frac{2}{3}h_i$, at most $\frac{4}{11}$ of the scheduled sending slots for processor j are invalidated due to processor j being stalled while sending other messages. Therefore, each message has probability of at least 0.733 of being sent in stage i. □

We can now sketch the proof of Lemma 5 for a sending processor; the proof for a receiving processor is similar. Let j denote an arbitrary processor with $h' \geq (0.267+\epsilon)h_i$ messages left to send at the start of stage i, and let R_j be the random variable that denotes how many of j's messages are actually sent during stage i. From Lemma 8, we see that when $h = \Omega(\log^3 n)$, then for each processor j, $D_j \leq \frac{2}{3}h_i$ with high probability, and so we may restrict attention to the case where this inequality holds. Thus, from the previous lemma, before we choose the schedule for stage i, $\mathrm{E}[R_j] \geq 0.733h'$. We then define the Martingale $B_t = \mathrm{E}[R_j|S_1 \ldots S_t]$, where S_t again represents the actions which all processors take at time t. Since the schedule is well distributed with high probability, we have that $|B_{t+1} - B_t| \leq h^{1/3}$, so Azuma's inequality shows that with high probability, R_j does not deviate substantially from $E[R_j]$. Therefore, processor j transmits at least $(0.733 - \epsilon)\,h'$ of its messages with probability $\exp(\frac{-\epsilon^2}{4}h_i^{1/3})$ and the lemma follows. □

5 Scheduling h-relations under the Arbitrary Write Discipline

In this section we analyze algorithms employing the arbitrary write discipline, which is analogous to the concurrent-write PRAM discipline of the same name.

Each processor is able to send and receive up to one message during each synchronous round. If more than one processor sends a message to the same destination processor in a single round, then that destination processor receives one of the messages chosen at random, while the other messages are lost. The arbitrary write discipline can be contrasted with the somewhat more pessimistic OCPC model, in which all conflicting messages are lost. As in the OCPC discipline, successful receipt of a message can be acknowledged in unit time; those processors which do not receive an acknowledgment can assume their messages were not transmitted successfully.

The algorithm we employ is similar to the direct algorithm for routing h-relations on the OCPC due to Geréb-Graus and Tsantilas [GT 92]. By continuously updating weighted transmission probabilities for messages from sender i to receiver j, we obtain an algorithm which routes h-relations in the arbitrary write model with a small leading constant. We work toward the proof of the following theorem, which gives us a bound on routing h-relations in the arbitrary write model of $1.62h + o(h) + O(\log n \log\log n)$ as compared with the OCPC protocol which runs in time $eh+ o(h) + O(\log n \log\log n)$ achieved by [GT 92] in a less favorable model.

Theorem 10. *There exists a protocol which solves any instance of the h-relation problem under the arbitrary write discipline within time $1.62h + o(h) + O(\log n \log\log n)$ rounds, with high probability.*

The first phase of the protocol is a thinning procedure which runs in a sequence of m stages, where in stage i, the problem is reduced from an h_{i-1}-relation to an h_i-relation with high probability, where $h_i = (1-\beta)^i h$ for $i \leq m$ and $h_0 = h$. The parameter β is a positive real parameter chosen arbitrarily close to zero and the parameter m is chosen as the smallest integer such that $h(1-\beta)^m < h^{2/5}$. After each of the stages, the transmission probabilities at each of the senders are recomputed in a method that will be described momentarily. After m such stages, the second phase of the algorithm routes the remaining messages (of which there are at most $h^{2/5}$) in time $O(h^{4/5})$ using an obvious direct deterministic algorithm which processes any t-relation in time t^2 under the arbitrary write discipline.

Stage k of the first phase of the protocol consists of $t_k = \frac{\alpha\beta(1+\beta)}{1-\beta}(h_k + \log n)$ rounds where α is the reciprocal of the quantity $4(1-e^{-1/2})^2)$, or approximately 1.62. With high probability, the following invariant assertion holds: no processor has more than h_{k-1} messages left to send or receive at the beginning of stage k. If we let d_{ij} denote the number of undelivered messages originating at processor i and destined for processor j at some instant during stage k, we have by the invariant that the row and column sums of the matrix (d_{ij}) are less than or equal to h_{k-1}. At each round of stage k, processor i chooses at most one message to send; the probability that it sends to processor j is $1 - \exp\left(-\frac{d_{ij}}{(1-\alpha)^{k-1}h}\right)$. It is easily verified that these probabilities sum to at most 1. The following sequence of lemmas culminate in the main theorem.

Lemma 11. *The following holds at each round of stage k: if processor 1 sends to processor j, then the probability that its message gets delivered successfully is at least $\frac{1-e^{-\lambda_j}}{\lambda_j}$, where $\lambda_j = (1/h_{k-1}) \sum_{k=2}^{n} d_{kj}$.*

Proof: Let the random variable X be the number of sources other than 1 that send to j. Then the probability that the message from source 1 is selected for transmission, given that source 1 sends to destination j, is $E[\frac{1}{1+X}]$, where E denotes expectation. It is easily seen that the distribution of X is stochastically larger than the Poisson distribution with rate λ_j. This follows from the fact that the random variable X becomes stochastically larger whenever a source i is split into two sources whose demand vectors sum to the original demand vector of source i. If we split each source until each remaining source has exactly one message to send, and then recursively split each of these, then as the number of times the sources are split approaches infinity, the distribution of X_i approaches a Poisson distribution. The lemma then follows from the fact that, when X has the Poisson distribution with mean λ_j, $E[\frac{1}{1+X}] = \frac{1-e^{-\lambda_j}}{\lambda_j}$. □

Lemma 12. *Consider some fixed processor ρ for which at some round during stage k, $\sum_{j=1}^{n} d_{\rho j} = V$ and $\sum_{i=1}^{n} d_{i\rho} = W$. Then during this round:*

- *Processor ρ successfully transmits a message with probability at least $\frac{V}{\alpha^2 h_{k-1}}$.*
- *Processor ρ successfully receives a message with probability at least $1 - e^{-W/h_k}$.*

Proof: The second claim in the lemma is immediate. To prove the first claim, let $F(x)$ be defined as $\frac{1-e^{-x}}{x}$. Then, by Lemma 5, the probability of processor ρ successfully transmitting a message is at least $\sum_{j=1}^{n} \mu_j F(\mu_j) F(\lambda_j)$ where $\mu_j = \frac{d_{\rho j}}{h_{k-1}}$ and λ_j is as defined in the above lemma. Since F is a log-convex function, the product $F(\mu_j)F(\lambda_j)$ is minimized, subject to $\mu_j \geq 0$, $\lambda_j \geq 0$ and $\mu_j + \lambda_j \leq 1$, when $\mu_j = \lambda_j = \frac{1}{2}$. The value of the product at the minimum is $\frac{1}{\alpha^2}$, and the result follows from the fact that $\sum_j \mu_j = \frac{V}{h_{k-1}}$. □

Lemma 13. *Given that the invariant assertion holds at the beginning of stage k, the probability that it fails to hold at the beginning of stage $k+1$ is at most $2n \exp\left(-\frac{(\beta^3 h_k)}{3}\right)$.*

Proof: (Sketch) By Lemma 2 we see that at each round within stage k at which a processor has at least h_k messages left to send, its probability of sending successfully is at least $\frac{1-\beta}{\alpha}$. Now by transmitting with this probability for $t_k = \frac{\alpha\beta(1+\beta)}{1-\beta}(h_k + \log n)$ rounds, by a Chernoff bound, each of the n processors achieves the goal of transmitting at least βh_k of these messages with failure probability only $\exp\left(-\frac{(\beta^3(h_k + \log n))}{3}\right)$ for $h_k = \omega(\log n)$. Likewise, since a processor with at least h_k unreceived messages in stage k receives a message at each round with probability at least $1 - \exp(-\frac{1}{1-\beta}) > \frac{1-\beta}{\alpha}$, the goal of receiving at least βh_k of these messages is also realized with even smaller failure probability in the same time bound, and the lemma follows from a union bound. □

Proof of Theorem:

By Lemma 8, the invariant assertion holds throughout the $O(\log h)$ stages of the first phase of the protocol with high probability. To compute the amount of time that the protocol requires, we first bound the total time measured in rounds used through stage j, where j is the largest integer such that $h_j > \log n$ by

$$\frac{\alpha\beta(1+\beta)}{1-\beta}\sum_{i=0}^{j} h_i < \left(\frac{1+\beta}{1-\beta}\right)\alpha h.$$

The remaining $O(\log\log n)$ stages, $h_{j+1}, \ldots, h_m$, each take $O(\log n)$ rounds, so the first phase of the protocol completes in $\frac{1+\beta}{1-\beta}\alpha h + O(\log n \log\log n)$ rounds. In the second and final phase of the protocol, we route the remaining $h^{2/5}$-relation in time $o(h)$. To accomplish this, note that a single undelivered message will be transmitted unsuccessfully at most $h^{2/5}$ times. Therefore, each processor simply transmits each of its at most $h^{2/5}$ messages until they all arrive successfully, in total time $h^{4/5}$. □

6 Scheduling h-relations under the Priority Queue Discipline

The priority queue discipline is similar to the FIFO discipline in that messages wait in a queue until they are transmitted to their respective destinations, and the sending processor stalls until the message has been sent. The distinction between the two disciplines is that in the priority queue discipline, a sending processor assigns a priority to each sent message, and the message with the highest priority is the first to leave each queue, with any ties being broken arbitrarily. It is easy to see that a protocol for the FIFO discipline can be simulated in the priority queue discipline by assigning each message a priority equal to the time at which it was transmitted. Therefore, the FIFO protocol presented in section 4 can be easily modified to run in this discipline. However, the analysis of the following algorithm is very simple, and the additive term dependent on the number of processors is much smaller.

Under this discipline, we present an algorithm for scheduling an h-relation that yields a running time of $(2e-1)h + o(h) + \log n$. Each of the P processors assigns each message a priority r, chosen independently and uniformly from $[1 \ldots R]$, R sufficiently large to guarantee that all priorities selected are distinct with high probability. Each processor then sends its messages in order of the chosen priorities, from highest to lowest.

Theorem 14. *An h-relation can be routed under the priority queue discipline in time $(2e-1)h + o(h) + \log n$ w.h.p.*

Proof: We begin by providing a simple proof for a bound of $(2e+\epsilon)h$ which uses the delay sequence argument of [Ran 88]. We focus attention on the last message to arrive at its destination, and retrace the sequence of delays which resulted in this message's delayed arrival. In the context of this problem, a delay sequence for a message p_0 with priority r_0 consists of a sequence of messages with increasing priorities all greater than r_0 in which the messages either have the same source as p_0 or the same destination as p_0.

We derive a bound on the probability that there exists a delay sequence of length t for any message. For any fixed message p_0, there are fewer than $2h$ messages with either the same source or the same destination, so each successive message in the delay sequence could be one of at most $2h$. Therefore, there are at most $(2h)^t$ possible delay sequences for each message, and at most hP messages, for a total of at most $hP(2h)^t$ possible delay sequences. Now since each possible delay sequence is actually a delay sequence only when the priorities are strictly increasing, this happens with probability $\frac{1}{t!}$. Using Stirling's approximation, we approximate the probability of any delay sequence actually occurring by

$$\frac{hP(2h)^t}{t!} \leq \frac{hP(2h)^t}{(\frac{t}{e})^t\sqrt{2\pi t}}$$

Thus, when $t > (2e+\epsilon)h = 5.44h$, we see that a delay sequence of length t does not exist w.h.p. By refining the technique used to count the number of delay sequences of a given length to give an improved bound, the leading constant can be improved to $2e-1$, as stated in Theorem 14. □

7 Simulation Results and Conclusion

We have obtained some preliminary simulation results on the algorithms described and analyzed in the previous sections. Our empirical results focus on the 1-relation also known as all-to-all personalized communication, a special case of the h-relation in which each processor pair must exchange a single distinct message. Our analysis of the parameterized algorithm for the FIFO discipline predicted a minimum running time of $3.4h$ by setting $K = 1.9$. Our empirical results show that for this setting of K, the theoretical analysis closely predicts the observed running time. However, as K decreases below 1.9, our analysis does not model the empirical performance of the algorithm, whose running time continues to improve, reaching a minimum of $2.08h$ at $K = 1$. A comparison of theoretically predicted performance vs. empirically observed performance appears in Figure 2.

For the arbitrary write discipline, we discovered that the theoretical bound of $1.62h$ closely predicts the empirically observed running time. Furthermore, we found that the probabilistic weighting scheme was not merely an artifact of the proof; we were not able to achieve running times better than $1.7h$ for any algorithm in the arbitrary write discipline which transmitted all unsent messages with equal probability. Finally, we found that the algorithm used in the priority queue discipline with priorities chosen uniformly at random worked extremely

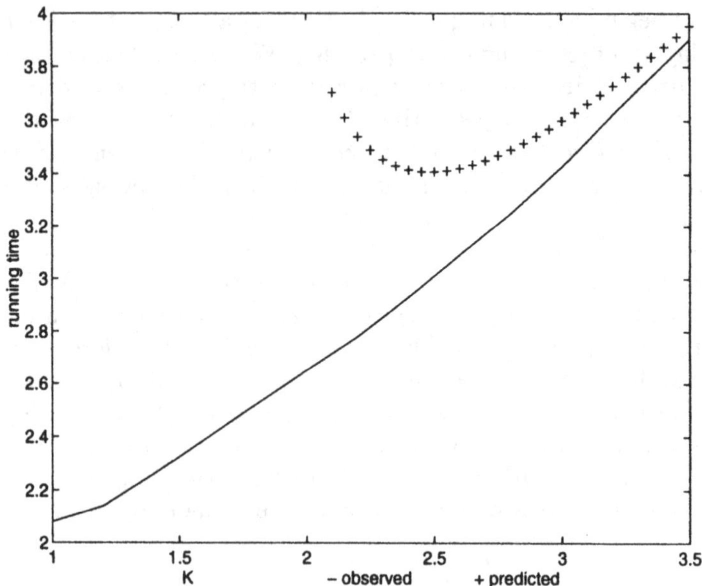

Fig. 2. The dependence of running time on K.

well in practice. Observed running times were approximately $1.85h$, a marked improvement over the running time of the algorithm for the FIFO discipline.

It remains an open problem to reduce the gap between the upper and lower bounds for all the disciplines, most notably the sizable gap remaining for the FIFO discipline. A related problem of interest would be to improve the analysis to reduce the additive polylogarithmic factors associated with the running times of algorithms in the FIFO discipline.

8 Acknowledgments

We would like to thank David Culler for a fruitful discussion of contemporary parallel architectures and network routing techniques.

References

[AM 88] R. A. Anderson and G. L. Miller. "Optical Communication for Pointer-Based Algorithms," *Technical Report CRI 88-14*, Computer Science Department, University of Southern California, Los Angeles, CA, 1988.

[BHK+ 94] J. Bruck, C. Ho, S. Kipnis, D. Weathersby. "Efficient Algorithms for All-to-All Communications in Multi-Port Message-Passing Systems," *Proc. 6th ACM Symp. on Parallel Algorithms and Architectures*, pp. 298-309, June 1994.

[Col 88] R. Cole. "Parallel Merge Sort," *SIAM Journal of Computing 17(4)*, pp. 770-785, 1988.

[CKP+ 93] D. Culler, R. Karp, D. Patterson, A. Sahay, K. E. Schauser, E. Santos, R. Subramonian, and T. von Eicken. "LogP: Towards a Realistic Model of Parallel Computation," *Proc. 4th ACM SIGPLAN Symp. on Principles and Practice of Parallel Programming*, pp. 1-12, January 1993.

[GV 94] A. Gerbessiotis and L. Valiant. "Direct Bulk-Synchronous Parallel Algorithms," *Journal of Parallel and Distributed Computing 22*, pp. 251-267, 1994.

[GT 92] M. Geréb-Graus and T. Tsantilas. "Efficient Optical Communication in Parallel Computers," *Proc. 4th ACM Symp. on Parallel Algorithms and Architectures*, pp. 41-48, June 1992.

[GMR1 94] P. Gibbons, Y. Matias and V. Ramachandran. "The QRQW PRAM: Accounting for contention in parallel algorithms," *Proc. 5th ACM Symp. on Discrete Algorithms*, pp. 638-648, January 1994.

[GMR2 94] P. Gibbons, Y. Matias and V. Ramachandran. "Efficient Low-Contention Parallel Algorithms," *Proc. 6th ACM Symp. on Parallel Algorithms and Architectures*, pp. 236-247, June 1994.

[GJL+ 93] L. A. Goldberg, M. Jerrum, T. Leighton, and S. Rao. "A Doubly Logarithmic Communication Algorithm for the Completely Connected Optical Communication Parallel Computer," *Proc. 5th ACM Symp. on Parallel Algorithms and Architectures*, pp. 300-309, June-July 1993.

[GJM 94] L. A. Goldberg, M. Jerrum and P. MacKenzie. "An $\Omega(\sqrt{\log\log n})$ Lower Bound for Routing on Optical Networks," *Proc. 6th ACM Symp. on Parallel Algorithms and Architectures*, pp. 147-156, June 1994.

[Lei 92] F. T. Leighton. *Introduction to Parallel Algorithms and Architectures: Arrays · Trees · Hypercubes* Morgan Kaufmann Publishers, San Mateo, CA, 1992.

[Lei+ 94] C. E. Leiserson, et al. "The Network Architecture of the Connection Machine CM-5," *Proc. 4th ACM Symp. on Parallel Algorithms and Architectures*, June 1992. Revised March 21, 1994.

[ND 90] M. Noakes and W. J. Dally. "System Design of the J Machine," *Sixth MIT Conference on Advanced Research in VLSI*, pp. 179-194. MIT Press, 1990.

[Ran 88] A. Ranade. *Fluent Parallel Computation*. PhD thesis, Yale University, New Haven, CT, 1988.

[RSTG 95] S. Rao, T. Suel, T. Tsantilas and M. Goudreau. "Efficient Communication Using Total-Exchange," *Proc. 9th IEEE International Parallel Processing Symposium*, pp. 544-555, April 1995.

[Val1 90] L. G. Valiant. "General Purpose Parallel Architectures." In J. van Leeuwen, ed., *Handbook of Theoretical Computer Science, Volume A*, pp. 943-972. Elsevier Science Publishers B.V., Amsterdam, The Netherlands, 1990.

[Val2 90] L. G. Valiant. "A Bridging Model for Parallel Computation," *Communications of the ACM 33*, pp. 103-111, 1990.

[Wol 89] R. W. Wolff, *Stochastic Modeling and the Theory of Queues*, Prentice-Hall, Inc., Englewood Cliffs, New Jersey, 1989.

Decomposable Structures, Boolean Function Representations, and Optimization

Stefan Arnborg

Kungliga Tekniska Högskolan
NADA, S-100 44 Stockholm, Sverige
stefan@nada.kth.se

Abstract. We show the connection between the theory of bounded treewidth graphs, monadic second order definable structures and sets, and boolean decision diagrams. We survey recent results in algorithms for bounded treewidth, symbolic model checking and representation schemes for Boolean functions. Some practical applications are indicated.

1 Introduction

This is a survey of a theory of tree-like graphs and other structures. Many aspects of the corresponding method have been known and practised in operations research, reliability engineering, artificial intelligence, and as special applications of dynamic programming. Problems amenable to solution by the methods are discrete optimization, reliability and dependability problems for complex systems, verification of digital designs and software and reasoning with uncertainty. I want to relate the theory of decomposability or tree-likeness to the BDD and symbolic model checking methods used in circuit and program verification and also to methods designed for reasoning in various applied logics in knowledge systems. In these areas, particularly where unstructured problems are solved, it is difficult to formulate a model and to prepare corresponding inputs to optimization programs. One solution to this problem could be the adoption by practitioners of relatively simple logical notations based on second order logic and high-level definition facilities. Similar developments have already taken place in circuit verification.

Since a complete exposition of this problem area will not fit into the present page allowance, we emphasize those aspects that fit in nicely with the presentation strategy and those that seem the most useful in applications. For a very careful and complete exposition, see the series of papers and surveys on the monadic second order logic of graphs by Bruno Courcelle. A recent bibliography is [16].

1.1 Signatures and structures

Graphs and other combinatorial objects will be represented as *structures*. A *signature* F is a set of sorts and a collection of relation and function constants. A symbol is recognized as either of these. Every relation and function constant has a *profile*, which is a finite sequence of sorts. A relation constant with empty profile is called a propositional constant. A function constant with singleton profile is called an object constant. We will write a signature by listing its sorts, a semicolon, its relation constants, each followed by its profile in parentheses, another semicolon, and its function constants in a similar way. Thus, a one-sorted signature with the unary relation constant P and a binary function constant f is written $(u; P(u); f(u,u) : u)$. A ***structure*** over a signature F is a set of disjoint *domains* D_s, one for each sort s, and, for each relation constant in F of profile $s_1, \ldots, s_n$, an n-ary relation table over $D_{s_1} \times \cdots \times D_{s_n}$, and, for every function constant, a function table compatible with its profile. We consider only finite domains, but also infinite families of structures with unbounded domain.

Objects easily defined using structures are various types of graphs (directed, undirected, multi-), oriented and unoriented matroids, trees (ordered and unordered) etc. Another example:

Example 1. A *propositional formula* is representable as a structure relating formulas and subformulas. Each logical operator used binds a formula together with its operands. There are a number of possible signatures representing propositional formulas. If the objects are formulas and subformulas, then one can have unary relations to represent the operator of a formula, and a number of incidence relations for pointing out the operator-operand relations. For propositional logic one can thus have the signature
$F = (u; P_\neg(u), P_\wedge(u), P_\vee(u), \mathrm{Op}_1(u,u), \mathrm{Op}_2(u,u); \mathrm{Root}() : u)$. As an example, the formula $p \wedge (q \vee \neg p)$ is represented in signature F with domain $\{a, b, c, p, q\}$ as

$$\begin{aligned}
\mathrm{Root} &: a \\
P_\neg &: \{c\} \\
P_\vee &: \{b\} \\
P_\wedge &: \{a\} \\
\mathrm{Op}_1 &: \{(a,p),(b,q),(c,p)\} \\
\mathrm{Op}_2 &: \{(a,b),(b,c)\}.
\end{aligned}$$

Many applications deal with propositional formulas and depend on solving their satisfiability and related problems. Note that not all structures over F correspond to well formed propositional formulas.

We assume known the concept of first-order formula and satisfaction of a formula by a structure, using the intermediate concept of variable assignment[28]. Thus, if a formula is satisfied by structure I under variable assignment V we write $I \models \phi[V]$.

A structure that satisfies a formula ϕ for all variable assignments V is called a *model* for ϕ, written $I \models \phi$. If a set of structures is exactly the set of models of a first order formula ϕ, then the set is said to be a (first-order) *definable* set of structures (and defined by ϕ).

Example 2. The class of simple graphs is the class of structures over $\mathcal{G}_1 = (u; \mathrm{Adj}(u,u);)$ defined by: $\forall x \forall y\ \mathrm{Adj}(x,y) \leftrightarrow \mathrm{Adj}(y,x)$. This formula says that the adjacency relation Adj must be symmetric in a graph. Similarly, the class of directed multi-graphs can be defined in a two-sorted signature,
$\mathcal{G}_2 = (u, v; I_t(u,v), I_h(u,v);)$ with sort 'edge' u and 'vertex' v, using the head and tail incidence relations $I_h(u,v)$ and $I_t(u,v)$ and the conditions: "Every edge is the tail of exactly one vertex and the head of exactly one vertex". This condition can, somewhat tediously, be defined in first-order logic with equality. But the condition could also be built into the signature by regarding tail and head as two functions from edge to vertex.

The *second order logic* is obtained from first order logic by adding variables of a new kind denoting relations or functions of a known profile and quantification over such variables. These variables can be used as the corresponding constants in atoms and terms. The satisfaction relation of first order logic is augmented so that in an assignment, a relation or function table of the right profile is assigned to a second order variable. It turns out that full second order logic is too general for our main purpose here. The *monadic second order logic* is the restricted logic where second order variables can only be unary relation variables, which naturally denote sets from the domain. In monadic second order logic we use set variables for unary relation variables and the set inclusion operator $\subset$ and the membership operator $\in$. Thus, $x \in Y$ is used for what in second order logic would be $Y(x)$. We define a *monadic second order definable set of structures* L to be the set of structures satisfying some monadic second order formula ϕ, $L = \{I \mid I \models \phi\}$.

For a formula with free variables, and for a compatible structure, satisfaction depends on a variable assignment. The *set of satisfying assignments* of a formula φ with respect to a structure I is the set of variable assignments for which I satisfies φ, $\{V \mid I \models \varphi[V]\}$. If we have ordered the m free variables, we can represent the satisfying assignments as m-tuples, with one component for each free variable of φ (it is not difficult to see that satisfaction depends only on the assignment to the free variables). Such a set of m-tuples is called a *monadic second order definable set of tuples* in a structure.

It was shown by Courcelle[13] that it is not possible to 'do counting' in monadic second order logic, *i.e.*, it is not possible to express conditions like: 'set X has more elements than set Y' or 'set X has an odd number of elements'. Following Courcelle we add to monadic second order logic the modular counting relation constants $\mathrm{Mod}_{r,p}$ for $p = 2, 3, \ldots$ and $r = 0, \ldots, p-1$. The meaning of $\mathrm{Mod}_{r,p}(X)$ is: 'the size of X modulo p is r'. This extended logic is called *MS logic*. Similarly, *MS-definable families of structures* and *MS definable sets of tuples* are obtained by just adding modular counting to the corresponding definitions for monadic second order logic.

1.2 Interpretation of structures in structures.

Interpretation is a method for defining a map from structures over one signature F to structures over another signature F'. We present here an extension of Rabins interpretation concept[25]. An interpretation from signature F to signature F' is a set of MS formulas and terms over signature F. First, we have a closed formula γ and a formula α with one free individual variable. The map is only defined for structures satisfying γ and for those structures only objects satisfying α will correspond to objects in the target structure. For every relation constant R_n in F' of profile p with $|p| = n$, we have in the interpretation an MS formula ϕ_{R_n} over F with free individual variables $x_1, \ldots, x_n$, and for every function constant f_m of profile p with $|p| = m+1$ we have a formula φ_{f_m} with the free variables $x_1, \ldots, x_{m+1}$. From a structure G over F we can now produce a structure G' over F' using the following method: The domain of G' is the set of objects in G satisfying α. The relation table for a relation constant R_n is the set of tuples $(a_1, \ldots, a_n)$ such that $G \models \phi_{R_n}[x_1 = a_1, \ldots x_n = a_n]$. The function table for a function constant f_m is a similar table with rows $(a_1, \ldots, a_{m+1})$, where $G \models \phi_{R_n}[x_1 = a_1, \ldots x_{m+1} = a_{m+1}]$. Note that it is not significant how a structure not satisfying γ is mapped, and that we assume that the construction method gives only relation and function tables over the set of objects satisfying α. If we have two classes of structures, C_1 and C_2, and C_2 is contained in the image, by an MS-interpretation map, of C_1, then we say that C_2 is *MS interpretable* in C_1. It is important to note that the interpretability relation is transitive[5].

Example 3. A *co-graph* is either a single vertex graph, or the disjoint union of two co-graphs, or the edge complement of a co-graph[12]. We can represent a co-graph in the signature $(u; \mathrm{Adj}(u, u);)$ and interpret it in a family of labeled binary trees so that a particular graph is represented by a tree showing the construction of the graph. Thus, a leaf of the construction tree represents a vertex of the co-graph. An internal node represents either disjoint union or disjoint union followed by edge complementation. Thus, the family of co-graphs can be interpreted in the family of binary trees with one label: $(u; R(u, u), L(u, u), P_c(u); \mathrm{Root}() : u)$. We express the interpretation in terms of predicates which are easy to define: The condition $\mathrm{Term}(x)$ means that x has neither a left nor a right son, *i.e.*, x is a leaf; $\mathrm{Bintree}()$ means that the whole structure is a binary tree; and $\mathrm{Path}(x, Z, y)$ means that the nodes in Z form an upward path from x to y inclusive. We define two vertices of the interpreted graph to be adjacent if the path to the root from their lowest common ancestor in the construction tree contains an odd number of nodes representing edge complementation:

$$
\begin{aligned}
\gamma &\equiv \mathrm{Bintree}() \\
\alpha(x) &\equiv \mathrm{Term}(x) \\
\mathrm{Adj}(x, y) &\equiv \exists z X Y Z Z_c\ \mathrm{Path}(x, X, z) \wedge \mathrm{Path}(y, Y, z) \wedge \mathrm{Path}(z, Z, \mathrm{Root}()) \wedge \\
&\quad \forall v\ v \in Z_c \leftrightarrow (v \in Z \wedge P_c(v)) \wedge \mathrm{Mod}_{1,2}(Z_c) \wedge \\
&\quad \forall v\ (v \in X \wedge v \in Y) \rightarrow (v = z)
\end{aligned}
$$

The following facts are well known from the classical studies of monadic logic on strings and trees:

- The family of binary trees labeled over a finite alphabet Σ is interpretable in the family of unlabeled binary trees.
- Every family of finitely labeled trees is interpretable in the family of finitely labeled binary trees.

Moreover, every graph family of bounded treewidth, represented in signature $\mathcal{G}_2$, is interpretable in the family of labelled trees[5]. The corresponding proposition for graphs represented in signature $\mathcal{G}_1$ is less intuitive.

The related concept MS definable *transduction* introduced by Courcelle[14] is slightly more powerful than interpretation: the formulas of a transduction can have free variables, and one object in the domain structure can represent several, but only a uniformly bounded number of, objects in the image structure.

1.3 Structure Algebras.

A closely related way of defining structures, advocated by Courcelle, uses techniques of universal algebra. We will now use the terms sort and signature in a different way from before, since the algebraic view focuses on functions and values of terms.

Let S be a finite set of sorts. A set F is a finite $\mathcal{S}$-sorted signature if F is a finite set of operator symbols and every f in F has a profile $s_1 \times \cdots \times s_\beta \rightarrow s$, where β is nonnegative and finite (it may be zero, which corresponds to a constant, *i.e.*, nullary operator), and $s_1, \ldots, s_\beta, s$ are sorts in $\mathcal{S}$.

An *F-algebra* M, where F is a signature, is an association of a (not necessarily finite) domain M_s to each sort s and a total mapping to each operator symbol, so that f with profile $s_1 \times \cdots \times s_\beta \rightarrow s$ is associated with a map $f_M : M_{s_1} \times \cdots \times M_{s_\beta} \rightarrow M_s$. The union of the domains is the *carrier* of F. We write $|M|$ for the carrier of M as customary. A *finite algebra* is an algebra with a finite carrier. A *structure algebra* is an algebra where the domains are structures, usually each with a different signature.

We denote by $T(F)$ the initial F-algebra (term algebra over F), and write $h_M : |T(F)| \rightarrow |M|$ for the unique homomorphism associated with M. A *context* is a mapping defined with a sort-compatible term t with sort s' that contains a variable x of some sort s. The context defines the map from M_s to $M_{s'}$: $m \mapsto \lambda x.t(m)$. We shall write $f[\,]$ for a general context.

The equivalence relation $\approx$ is *finite* if it has a finite number of equivalence classes. The class that includes an element d is denoted $[d]$ when the intended equivalence is clear from the context. A *congruence* on M is an equivalence relation $\approx$ on $|M|$ such that (i) any two elements equivalent under $\approx$ are of the same sort and (ii) the relation $\approx$ is stable under the operations of M, i.e., if $v_i \approx u_i$ for $0 < i \leq \beta$, then $f_M(v_1, \ldots, v_\beta) \approx f_M(u_1, \ldots, u_\beta)$. As a consequence, $\approx$ is stable under the contexts of M.

Let $L \subset |M|$. We denote by $\sim_L$ the congruence on M defined by: $m \sim_L m'$ if and only if, for every context $f[\,]$, $f[m] \in L$ if and only if $f[m'] \in L$. We say that L is *generated* by F if $L \subset h_M(|T(F)|)$, *i.e.*, if every member of L can be written as an expression over F. We say that L is *M-recognizable* if L is a union of classes of a finite congruence on M, all of the same sort.

Proposition 1 (Courcelle). *Let M be an F-algebra and $L \subset M_s$ for some $s \in \mathcal{S}$. The following conditions are equivalent:*

(1) L is M-recognizable.
(2) $\sim_L$ is finite.
(3) $L = h^{-1}(C)$ where h is an F-homomorphism onto a finite algebra M' and $C \subset M'_s$.

Structure algebras are too general to be useful. In an *MS definable structure algebra*, the value $h_M(t)$ of a term t is obtained by an MS interpretation of the term t represented as a tree. Even more useful is the concept if the objects of $h_M(t)$, $t = f_M(t_1, \ldots, t_n)$ are easily obtained from the objects of $h_M(t_i)$, as in the following examples:

Example 4. The classical construction method of a two-terminal series parallel graphs can be described in this framework, in an algebra with the nullary operator creating an edge, and two binary operations for series and parallel composition. The domain consists of structures in $\mathcal{G}_2$ augmented with two object constants pointing to the two terminals. This was generalized to k-terminal graphs by Wimer[33]. Also, the interpretation for co-graphs described above can be interpreted as a structure algebra in signature $\mathcal{G}_1$, whose operations are: an object constant v for a vertex, a unary operation P_c for edge complementation, and a binary operation $\oplus$ for disjoint union.

1.4 Recognizability of MS-definable sets of binary trees

A linear time algorithm for satisfaction of a fixed formula ϕ by a tree follows immediately from:

Theorem 2 [30]. *For every MS definable set K of binary trees, the congruence $\sim_K$ is finite.*

Via transitivity of the interpretability relation, we get a linear time algorithm to decide membership in any MS-definable set of graphs of bounded treewidth, if the graph is given with its interpretation.

An interesting consequence of the finiteness of the congruence relation is that any family interpretable in the family of binary trees must have certain restrictions. Specifically, if a binary relation is interpreted, the number of different objects in a subtree of node n, seen from outside the subtree, is uniformly bounded by the number of congruence classes. If the relation is the Adj relation of a graph represented in signature $\mathcal{G}_1$, the restriction is that the graph family must have uniformly bounded clique-width. If the relation is the incidence relation of a graph represented in signature $\mathcal{G}_2$, the restriction is that the graph family must have uniformly bounded tree-width. This follows, e.g., from an analysis of the restrictions (functional dependence of tail and head vertex of edge) on the incidence relations.

1.5 Powerset algebras and equational sets

For an F-algebra M, the *powerset algebra* $\mathcal{P}(M)$ is an algebra with domains 2^{M_s} and for every operator f of F there is an operator f' of $\mathcal{P}(M)$ such that $f'_{\mathcal{P}(M)}(A_1, \ldots, A_\beta) = \{f_M(a_1, \ldots, a_\beta) \mid a_1 \in A_1, \ldots, a_\beta \in A_\beta)\}$. As a special case of this, nullary operators in M evaluate to singleton sets in $\mathcal{P}(M)$. Moreover, the powerset algebra of M has a union operator $+_s$ for every sort s.

A formal language grammar can be seen as a simple example of an equation system over a the powerset algebra over a structure algebra generating strings. This algebra has a binary concatenation operator and nullary operators for the letters of the alphabet. The non-terminals can be seen as set variables (for sets of strings) and the alternative productions for a non-terminal as a (usually recursive) definition of a set as a union of sets. This view easily extends to structure grammars in general[6]:

Definition 3. An *equational set* over a structure algebra M is the least solution to a system of equations over $\mathcal{P}(M)$. Such a system consists of a number of structure set symbols, each with an associated sort of M, and a number of set equations, one for each set symbol. The left side of the equation is the associated set symbol, the right side is a well-sorted expression over $\mathcal{P}(M)$. As the solution of such a system we shall mean the unique minimal solution, obtained by (infinite)iteration of the equations starting with the empty set for each set variable.

Example 5. Let the parallel and series composition operators of a ttsp graph construction be denoted as operators // and $-$ of a structure algebra, and let e be the nullary operator evaluating to an edge. The set of ttsp graphs is the equational set defined by the system of a single equation:

$$S = e + (S//S) + (S - S)$$

The iteration mentioned in Definition 3 for the set S starts with $S^{(0)} = \emptyset$, $S^{(1)} = \{e\} \cup (S^{(0)}//S^{(0)}) \cup (S^{(0)} - S^{(0)}) = \{e\}$, $S^{(2)} = \{e, e//e, e - e\}, \ldots$. Ultimately, every expression over the algebra will become included in some $S^{(i)}$. Thus, the set S above is the whole set of graphs generated by the structure algebra. The set of ttsp graphs consisting of two parallel edges with a path of length n on both sides, for any n, would be generated by the equation system:

$$S = (e//e) + (e - (S - e))$$

The latter set is not MS definable since it is not possible to do unbounded counting in MS logic, like saying that two paths have equal but unbounded length. However, the 'syntax tree', or rather, the term evaluating to a member of the set, is MS definable as a structure:

Proposition 4 (Courcelle). *Every equational set is the image under MS interpretation of an MS definable set of trees.*

Equational sets over the signatures $\mathcal{G}_1$ and $\mathcal{G}_2$ are important in relation to graph grammars. Essentially, hyperedge replacement systems can generate equational sets over $\mathcal{G}_2$, and node label controlled replacement systems can generate the equational sets over $\mathcal{G}_1$.

2 Algorithms

In this section we review algorithms for solving problems on binary trees defined in MS-logic. These algorithms also work on structures interpreted in binary trees in the following sense: The problems we define here are the computation of characteristics of a set of m-tuples of a tree defined by an MS formula over the signature of binary trees. If instead we ask for a characteristic of the set of m-tuples defined by a formula ϕ over a structure I defined by interpretation from a binary tree T, then it is possible, simply by substitution of the interpretation formulas into the formula ϕ, to obtain an isomorphic set of m-tuples of T defined by an MS formula ϕ'. A similar technique works for decision problems over families of structures obtained as the image by interpretation of an MS definable set of trees. Note that we are not investigating the 'parsing problem' here; that is the problem of finding, given an MS interpretation, the tree with a given image. This problem has been satisfactorily solved (linear time) for graphs represented in signature $\mathcal{G}_2$, by means of tree-decompositions, but in general the problem is not well understood.

2.1 EMS problems and their solution

Let an MS-problem be the problem of deciding membership in a MS-definable class L of structures. The finiteness of $\sim_L$ for every MS-definable class of structures of binary trees implies not only that MS problems are linear time solvable on trees but also on every class of structures interpretable over the class of binary trees, if the structure is represented by its derivation tree and if there is an efficient representation of every structure (we will prove later that an efficient representation can be found). We gave in[5] a large number of MS-problems on graphs from Garey and Johnson[19]. The concept of an MS problem is useful also for other combinatorial objects than graphs. Consider a propositional formula P represented as in Section 1.1 in signature
$F = (u; P_\neg(u), P_\wedge(u), \mathrm{Op}_1(u,u), \mathrm{Op}_2(u,u); \mathrm{Root}() : u)$. An interpretation is a subset of its propositional variables (the ones that are true in the interpretation) and its standard extension to include all subformulas of P that are true in the interpretation. So an interpretation is any set S satisfying:

$$\begin{aligned}\mathrm{Interp}(S) = \forall xyz\ & \mathrm{Op}_1(x,y) \wedge P_\neg(x) \rightarrow (x \in S \leftrightarrow y \notin S) \\ & \mathrm{Op}_1(x,y) \wedge \mathrm{Op}_2(x,z) \wedge P_\wedge(x) \rightarrow \\ & (x \in S \leftrightarrow (y \in S \wedge z \in S))\end{aligned}$$

Validity of a propositional logic formula can now easily be expressed as the property that every interpretation makes the formula true:

$$\text{Valid}() = \forall S\ \text{Interp}(S) \rightarrow \text{Root} \in S$$

In most applications it will be necessary to know not only if a formula $\phi(x_1, \ldots, x_n)$ has a satisfying set of m-tuples, but also if there is such an set consistent with a partial assignment that includes some elements I_i and excludes other, O_i, from tuple i. Such problems are easily solved using standard dynamic programming techniques[5]. EMS-problems are defined in [5] as problems involving MS definable sets in structures. A closely related development was presented by Courcelle and Mosbah[15]. We also use some ideas of Bodlaender[7]. Let a structure I and an MS-formula with m free variables $X_1, \ldots, X_m$ be given. This formula defines a set of m-tuples of subsets of I. The set is of exponential size in general, so we cannot hope to list it efficiently. There may still be a number of things we want to know about the set, without actually listing it: we may consider its size (particularly whether it is non-empty), its largest/smallest members size, the sum of all members sizes, the lexicographically (given some ordering of the domain of I) first element, the first element after a given one. We may want to answer the same questions for a derived set of tuples, like the maximal members the members consistent with a partial assignment, or the set of members in closures under various substructure operations like a quotient structure of a given structure, or related structures corresponding to the graph concepts induced graph, partial graph or minor. These problems are solvable by either systematic transformations of the formulas involved[7, 1] or standard variations of the dynamic programming paradigm[5]. Most of these problem remain solvable if the problem has valuations $w_j^{(i)}$, where i ranges over the variable indices and j ranges over the elements of the corresponding domain. These weights give rise to a weighted problem, where each defined tuple $(A_1, \ldots, A_m)$ has weight $\sum_i \sum_{x_i \in A_i} w_{x_i}^{(i)}$. Analysis of well known computational problems on graphs lead us to the observation in [5] that dozens of well known optimization problems on graphs are largest tuple or weighted largest tuple problems. Counting sets of solutions has its most important applications in probability problems, which can be seen as weighted counting problems. In [5] we describe how network and systems reliability problems can be handled by assigning probabilities to sets and finding the relative weight of sets with a systems property such as disconnecting a communication network. In [1] we describe the use of counting for Bayesian statistical inference in expert systems. The technique is used in several commercial systems, and, with a small variation, for possibilistic logic analyses[18, 26, 27].

The congruence relation for an MS formula with m free variables developed in the proof of Theorem 2 can be seen as a transition function $\delta : S \times S \times B^m \rightarrow S$, where $B = \{0, 1\}$. The set of states that correspond to the satisfying assignments is called the accepting set A. For a node n with subnodes n_1 and n_2 having states s_1 and s_2 with respect to the current variable assignment, the class assigned to n will be $\delta(s_1, s_2, c)$, where c is an m-bit string describing the memberships of node n in the sets assigned to $X_1, \ldots, X_m$, *i.e.*, bit i of c is 0 if $n \notin X_i$, otherwise it is

1. The assignment is satisfying if the root is assigned a class in A. The function δ is often the key to solving EMS problems involving the MS formula ϕ. Some recent extensions of the methodology follow:

Lexicographically first and lexicographic successor. Assume we have an ordering $\{o_1, o_2, \ldots, o_N\}$ of the nodes of a binary tree, and an MS formula ϕ with one free variable X. The lexicographically first set of nodes satisfying ϕ is obtained by first building a maximal initial segment $O_1 = \{o_1, \ldots, o_l\}$ that can be put in the 'out' set O of a partial assignment (with non-empty solution set), then putting o_{l+1} in the 'in' set I, building a maximal segment $O_2 = \{o_{l+2}, \ldots, o_p\}$ such that $O = O_1 \cup O_2$ and $I = \{o_{l+1}\}$ is a partial assignment consistent with ϕ, etc. This procedure forces us to solve N partial assignment problems, each in time $O(N)$. The lexicographically first set of nodes satisfying ϕ can thus be obtained in time quadratic in the size of the binary tree. The lexicographic successor of a set in an MS definable family is similarly computed in quadratic time. It is helpful to consider a set of elements represented as an N-string over $\{0,1\}$. A partial assignment likewise corresponds to an N-string over $\{0,1,*\}$. The total number of lexicographic successors is easily obtained. For example, the number of lexicographic successors of (0011001100) in the set defined by φ is $p(00110011**) + p(001101****) + p(00111*****) + p(01********) + p(1*********) - p(0011001100)$, where $p(s)$ is the number of sets satisfying φ and consistent with the partial assignment s. It is easy to compute $p(s)$ using a combination of the techniques of the previous subsections. This problem is also studied, using different methods, in[15].

Weighted sets and linear size inequalities. Assume again that a set of sets of nodes is defined with an MS-formula ϕ. We want to assign weights on these sets and ask about the induced weights on some nodes given weights or weight bounds on other nodes. The induced weight of a node is of course the sum of weights of sets containing the node. We can generalize our problem to MS definable sets of tuples: Each m-tuple is assigned an m-component weight vector and the induced weight of a node becomes an m-vector. For each node we allow an equality or inequality to be specified for each of the components of its induced weight vector. We can also allow arbitrary linear inequalities and equalities involving the components of induced weight vectors of any number of nodes. We want to find out the possible values of one component of an induced weight vector or any linear combination of such components.

At first sight, this problem appears to call for a linear program containing the full incidence matrix between the tuples of sets defined by ϕ and the nodes of the tree, and a variable for each such tuple. The number of satisfying tuples can be exponential in the size of the tree, so the problem is not feasibly solvable in this way. However, it is possible to introduce variables reflecting the structure of the tree automaton, giving a polynomial size linear program and thus, using Karmarkars linear programming algorithm, a polynomial time algorithm for a family of structures MS-interpretable into the set of binary trees. We introduce a family of indexed variables describing the 'flow' of weight through the binary tree:

x_{nc} weight of tuples with membership vector c of node n
y_{ne} weight of tuples assigning state e to node n
$z_{ne_1e_2c}$ weight of tuples assigning states e_1 and e_2 to sons of n and membership vector c in n

Constraints on weights of nodes can now be added, as linear conditions on the x_{nc}, to the following set of flow equations:

$$
\begin{aligned}
y_{ne} &= \sum_{\delta_n(e_1,e_2,c)=e} z_{ne_1e_2c} &&, n \text{ non-leaf,}\\
x_{nc} &= \sum_{\delta_n(e_1,e_2,c)=e} z_{ne_1e_2c} &&, n \text{ non-leaf,}\\
y_{n_1e} &= \sum_{e_2c} z_{nee_2c} &&, n_1 \text{ right son of } n,\\
y_{n_2e} &= \sum_{e_1c} z_{ne_1ec} &&, n_2 \text{ left son of } n,\\
y_{re} &= 0 &&, e \notin A
\end{aligned}
$$

Example 6. In Nilssons probabilistic logic[22] it is possible to define a set of propositional logic formulas and to give bounds on probabilities of some of these. It is asked what the probability of some other formula can be. This is a problem of the above type where the set of tuple sets is the set of interpretations of the propositional formulas (cf the predicate Interp of Section 2.1).

Extended partitioning, packing and covering problems The following family (approximately) was shown solvable by Borie[8]: Consider a number of members of an MS-definable set of node sets in a binary tree. For every node, a number of incidence conditions are given: the node participates in exactly, at most, or at least m of these sets, where m is a member of a finite set M of integers. We may want to maximize or minimize the number of sets, or their total size. What we have here is a linear optimization problem that can be arranged as in the previous section. However, it is an integer programming problem since we count sets. Normally, an integer programming problem is NP-complete and not known to be solvable in polynomial time. However, in this problem one can get a polynomial time algorithm by careful analysis of the problem. First, note that the number of sets in an optimal solution is less than mN, where m is the largest member of M and N is the number of nodes of the tree. If more than mN sets can be packed, then the maximization problem has no solution (the number of sets is unbounded). If there is no solution with mN or fewer members, then there is no feasible solution at all. Now, look at the system of the previous section, with $m = 1$. The sum of $x_{n,c}$ over c, of y_{ne} over e, and of $z_{ne_1e_2c}$ over e_1, e_2 and c is less than mN, since each of the sums, for each n, is equal to the number of sets. But each of those sums are taken over a constant number of variables, independent of the size of the tree (but it is of course dependent on the formula and its number of free variables). Thus, the number of possibilities for each of the groups of variables is polynomial (a polynomial number of items can be distributed over a constant number of bags in a polynomial number of ways). Going from the leaves upwards we can find the sets of assignments of the variables ($x_{n,c}$, y_{ne} and $z_{ne_1e_2c}$) for each node that can be extended downwards in the tree and is consistent with all equations involving nodes of the subtree. Those solutions for the root with only accepting states are the real solutions. We can examine them and see which one involves the smallest number of sets. Alternatively, we can propagate the smallest (or largest) possible total sets size for each solution and find the largest or smallest total set size satisfying the partitioning/packing/covering conditions.

Example 7. Borie[8] mentions the following examples of graph problems solvable with this method, if the graph is represented in signature $\mathcal{G}_2$ where both vertices and edges are objects:

1. Cycle packing (maximizing the number of disjoint cycles in a graph),
2. generalized matching (maximizing the number of disjoint vertex sets such that each set induces a given fixed graph H),
3. m-multichromatic number (minimizing the number of independent vertex sets such that each vertex is in exactly m sets),
4. chromatic index (minimize the number of matchings into which the edge set can be partitioned),
5. induced tree cover (minimize the number of vertex sets such that each set induces a tree and each vertex is in at least one set).

Some of these problems might be solvable in linear time, because of special combinatorial theorems that do not fit into the general picture. As an example, Zhou, Nakano and Nishizeki[34] show how the chromatic index problem for graphs interpretable in binary trees can be solved efficiently (with small constants) in linear time.

Partial evaluation and BDD structures. The problems above involve a fixed tree into which a structure is interpreted. Instead of computing the tree automaton for MS formula ϕ by a recursion over the formula, it is often advantageous to compute a partial evaluation δ_n of the transition function δ to a node n. Consider also these node transition functions as being represented by matrices, row indexed by left subnode state and column indexed by right subnode state. This has the advantage that state set minimization can be performed 'on the fly' in the recursion over the formula structure. Thus, when $\delta_{n\varphi}$ has been produced for node n and formula φ by combination of the transition tables for the subformulas of φ for the subnodes of n, a construction that goes bottom-up in the interpretation tree, it is possible to fuse states top-down in the tree by joining two states in the left subnode of n if the corresponding rows are equal, and joining states in the right subnode when the corresponding row of δ_n are equal. The resulting data structure is a slight generalization of the popular OBDD structure[9]. Whereas the OBDD is a slight generalization of the minimal DFA accepting the satisfying assignments of a formula, represented as strings over $\{0,1\}$, our structure accepts satisfying assignments represented as trees labeled by $\{0,1\}^m$. The relations between these views were explained in [11, 21]. One can note that if the size of the tree is n and the range of $\delta_{n\varphi}$ is bounded by w (uniformly over n), then the size of the OBDD is (in the worst case) $O(n \log nw)$.

On closer examination we find that it is not necessary to find an explicit interpretation on an MS problem on a structure in order to compute the tree automaton. There is a straightforward way to translate a problem involving second order logic formula ϕ and a given set of domains into a problem of propositional logic. An individual (first-order) variable is translated to a set of one boolean variable for each element of its domain, and a second-order relation variable is translated to one boolean variable for each domain tuple that it could contain (given the profile of the variable). Set operators have an obvious translation to disjunctions and quantification over a relation variable is translated to a quantification over the corresponding set of boolean variables. If there is no universal quantifier in ϕ, the second order logic problem will be translated to a satisfiability problem, and one of the many practical satisfyability checkers can be applied (although it is true that this problem is infeasible in the worst case). Otherwise, we get a quantified boolean formula. We can compute its OBDD or tree representation by guessing either an ordering of its variables, or a tree labelled with its variables. If our guess corresponds to a path or tree into which the problems relational structure can be efficiently interpreted (i.e., with formulas that compile to transition functions over small state sets), then we can also solve related EMS problems. The theory of tree- and path decompositions tell us that if our guess corresponds to a decomposition of small width, then the transition tables will be small. But the opposite is not necessarily true, since there are other possible reasons for the state space to collapse, such as symmetries in the represented functions [10].

The outlined method is applicable to model-checking full second order logic, since a finite propositional formula obtained from the structure will generate finite node state sets. In general, this method will yield exponentially large state sets (in the size of the structure). However, there are problems like validity in intuitionistic and modal logics which are easily expressed in full second order logic (on a structure representing the formula) and where there are indirect proofs of recognizability for bounded treewidth[1]. For such problem families this method will be polynomial.

3 Some properties of MS definable sets of structures.

In this section we will investigate various ways of defining structures using MS definitions and interpretations. We will relate our methods to the area of graph grammars. The problems investigated will be decision problems, *i.e.*, we want to know if every or some member of an infinite family has a certain property. The problems we study were investigated by Wanke[31], in the context of graph grammars.

By a *semilinear set* we mean the union of a finite number of linear sets. A *linear set* is the set of N-vectors $\mathbf{o} + \sum c_i\mathbf{b}_i$ where i ranges over a finite set, the c_i range over the set of natural numbers $0, 1, \ldots$, and $\mathbf{o}$ and $\mathbf{b}_i$ are N-vectors called the *basis* of the set. For an effectively presented semilinear set we have the participating linear sets given with their basis systems. It is clear by application of linear integer programming that both emptiness and finiteness of the intersection of an effectively presented semilinear set and a polytope can be decided.

For a binary tree T, an MS formula ϕ with p congruence classes and a satisfying assignment V of sets of nodes of T to the m free variables of ϕ, we define the *Parikh map* $\Phi_\phi(T, V)$ as a vector in $\mathbf{N}^{p2^m}$ such that a component corresponds to a pair of a class k and membership vector $c \in \{0,1\}^m$ and is the number of nodes in T assigned congruence class k and with membership vector c. Let $\Phi_\phi(T)$ be the union of $\Phi_\phi(T, V)$ over all assignments V giving an accepting state to the root of T. Define $\Psi_{\phi\varphi}$ to be the union of $\Phi_\phi(T)$ over a set $\{T \mid T \models \varphi\}$.

Theorem 5 (Wanke). *For every MS-definable family F of binary trees defined by formula φ, and MS definable family of tuples defined by formula ϕ, $\Psi_{\phi\varphi}$ is a semi-linear set.*

Proof. The following proof is adapted from Parikh[23]. Assume that the formula ϕ has congruence classes S_ϕ, the formula φ has classes $S_\varphi$and m free variables. Let $\Sigma = S_\phi \times S_\varphi \times \{0,1\}^m$ and consider the family $T_{\phi\varphi}$ of trees labeled as defined by the transition functions of ϕ and φ: For a node n of label (s_ϕ, s_φ, c) with subnode states $(s_{\phi 1}, s_{\varphi 1}, c_1)$ and $(s_{\phi 2}, s_{\varphi 2}, c_2)$ we have $s_\phi = \delta_\phi(s_{\phi 1}, s_{\phi 2})$ and $s_\varphi = \delta_\varphi(s_{\varphi 1}, s_{\varphi 2}, c)$. The empty tree is considered labeled with $(s_{\phi 0}, s_{\varphi 0}, 0)$. Clearly, $\Psi_{\phi\varphi}$ is the Parikh map of the subset of these trees whose root is labeled with two accepting states. We will prove that the set of such trees having label set exactly $\Sigma' \subset \Sigma$ has a semilinear set as its Parikh map. The theorem follows from this since a finite union (over the subsets of Σ) of semilinear sets is itself semilinear. So consider $T_{\Sigma'}$, the set of such trees containing exactly label set Σ' and with no unnecessary label repetition along a root-leaf path. An unnecessary label repetition is one where contraction of the path between the repeated labels does not change the label set of the tree. There are finitely many such trees. Also, for every $\sigma \in \Sigma'$, form the finite set C_σ of Σ'-labeled trees with root and one leaf labeled σ, and with no other label repetition along a top-down path. The Parikh map of the accepted trees with label set exactly Σ' is obviously the union over $b \in T_{\Sigma'}$ of a linear set whose offset vector is $\Phi(b)$ and whose basis set is $\{\Phi(t) \mid \sigma \in \Sigma', t \in C_\sigma\}$

Example 8. Wanke gives the following example of an application where this technique is useful: A VLSI cell generator can sometimes be described as the interpretation image of an MS definable tree family. One correctness condition is that signal path lengths between two given vertices must not straddle a signal path length between two other vertices . This condition is a problem of the kind above: If Path(f, P, t) is a MS formula saying that P is a path from f to t, the condition says that there is no graph in the family satisfying

$$\text{Path}(f_1, P_1, t_1) \wedge \text{Path}(f_2, P_2, t_2) \wedge \text{Path}(f_1, P_1', t_1)$$

and with $|P_1| < |P_2| < |P_1'|$. Since $(|P_1|, |P_2|, |P_1'|)$ over the satisfying tuples over the family of graphs is a linear map of a semi-linear set, the condition is decidable with integer linear programming.

4 Conclusion.

Discrete optimization and decision methods based on efficient handling of large state spaces used to be delicate and error-prone. With the emergence of efficient tools based on BDD-related technology and comprehensible logical definition methods[3, 20], applications will multiply. Among interesting application possibilities, besides those already mentioned, are image and geometry codings[29] as used e.g., in geographic information systems, and intelligent systems.

References

1. S. ARNBORG, Graph decompositions and tree automata in reasoning with uncertainty, *Journal of Theoretical and Experimental Artificial Intelligence* **5***(1993) 335-357*
2. S. ARNBORG, Decomposability helps for logics of knowledge and belief. *Graph Transformations in Computer Science, Dagstuhl 1993, LNCS* **776** *37 – 50;*
3. S. ARNBORG, A general purpose MSOL model checker and optimizer based on Boolean function representations. presented at the Fifth International Workshop on Graph Grammars and Their Application to Computer Science, Williamsburg, Nov 1994. `http://www.nada.kth.se/~ stefan`
4. S. ARNBORG, B. COURCELLE A. PROSKUROWSKI AND D. SEESE, An Algebraic Theory of Graph Reduction, *Journ. ACM* **40***(1993) 1134-1164.*
5. S. ARNBORG, J. LAGERGREN AND D. SEESE, Easy Problems for Tree-decomposable graphs *J. of Algorithms* **12***(1991) 308-340.*
6. M. BAUDERON AND B. COURCELLE, Graph expressions and graph rewritings, *Mathematical Systems Theory* **20** (1987), 83-127;
7. H.L. BODLAENDER, Improved self-reduction algorithms for graphs with bounded treewidth. *Discrete Applied Mathematics* **54***(1994) 101-116.*
8. R. B. BORIE, Generation of polynomial time algorithms for some optimization problems on tree-decomposable graphs.
9. R. BRYANT, Graph Based Algorithms for Boolean Function Manipulation *IEEE Trans. Computers* **C-35***(1986) 677-691.*
10. R. BRYANT, Symbolic Boolean Manipulation with Ordered Bolean-Decision Diagrams. *ACM Computing Surveys* **24***(1992) 293-318.*
11. J. R. BURCH, E. M. CLARKE, K. L. McMILLAN, D.L. DILL AND L. J. HWANG, Symbolic Model Checking: 10^{20} states and beyond *Information and Computation* **98** *(1992) 142-170.*

12. D.G. CORNEIL, H. LERCHS AND L. STEWART BURLINGHAM, Complement Reducible Graphs, *Discrete Appl. Math.* **3** *(1981), 163-174.*
13. B. COURCELLE, The monadic second order logic of graphs I: Recognizable sets of finite graphs, *Information and Computation* **85**(1) March 1990, 12-75;
14. B. COURCELLE, Monadic second order definable graph transductions: a survey, *Theoretical Computer Science* **126**(1994), 53-75;
15. B. COURCELLE AND M.MOSBAH, Monadic second order evaluations on tree-decomposable graphs, *Theoretical Computer Science* **109**(1993), 49-82;
16. *Discrete Applied Mathematics* **54***(1994) 281-290.*
17. J.E. DONER, Decidability of the Weak Second-Order theory of two Successors, *Abstract 65T-468, Notices Amer. Math. Soc.* **12** *(1965), 819, ibid. (1966), 513*
18. D. DUBOIS AND H. PRADE Inference in possibilistic hypergraphs. *Proc. 3rd Int. Conf. Information Processing and Management of Uncertainty in Knowledge based Systems (IPMU), Paris, July 1990.*
19. M.R. GAREY AND D.S. JOHNSON, Computers and Intractability, *W.H. Freeman and Company, San Francisco (1979).*
20. J.G. HENRIKSEN, O.J.L. JENSEN, M.E. JØRGENSEN, N. KLARLUND, R. PAIGE, T. RAUHE AND A.B. SANDHOLM, MONA: Monadic Second-Order Logic in Practice. *BRICS Report RS-95-21*
21. K. L. McMILLAN, Hierarchical representations of discrete functions, with applications to model checking *6th International conference on Computer Aided Verification, LNCS* **818** (1994) 41-54,
22. N. NILSSON, Probabilistic logic, *Artificial Intelligence* **28** (1986) 71-87,
23. R. PARIKH, On context-free languages, *JACM* **13**(1966) 570-581,
24. J. PEARL, Probabilistic reasoning in intelligent systems: Networks of plausible inference. *Morgan Kaufmann Publishers, Inc. San Mateo 1988*
25. M.O.RABIN, Decidable theories, *In Handbook of Mathematical Logic, ed. by K.J. Barwise, North-Holland Publishing Company, 1977 595-629.*
26. P. SHENOY, A valuation-based language for expert systems. *Int. Journal of Approximate Reasoning* **3** (1989) 383-411.
27. P. SHENOY, G. SHAFER, Axioms for probability and belief function propagation, in *Uncertainty in Artificial Intelligence* **4** (R.D. Shachter, T.S. Levitt, L.N. Kanal, J.F.Lemmer, Eds.) Elsevier Science Publishers B.V. 1990.
28. J.R. SHOENFIELD, Mathematical Logic, *Reading 1967, Addison-Wesley.*
29. M. STARKEY AND R. BRYANT, Using Ordered Binary-Decision Diagrams for Compressing Images and Image Sequences , *Carnegie Mellon University CMU-CS-95-105*
30. J.W.THATCHER, J.B.WRIGHT, Generalized Finite Automata Theory with an Application to a Decision Problem in Second-Order Logic, *Mathematical Systems Theory* **2** *(1968), 57-81.*
31. E. WANKE On the decidability of certain integer subgraph problems on context-free graph languages, *Information and Computation,* **113** *(1994) 26-49*
32. E. WANKE k-NLC graphs and polynomial algorithms *Discrete Applied Mathematics* **54** *(1994) 251-266.*
33. T.V. WIMER, Linear algorithms on k-terminal graphs, PhD. Thesis, Clemson University (1988).
34. X. ZHOU, S. NAKANO AND T. NISHIZEKI, A Linear Algorithm for edge-coloring partial k-trees, *ESA93, LNCS* **726**, *409-418.*

The Complexity of Interval Routing on Random Graphs *

(Extended Abstract)

Michele Flammini[1,3], Jan van Leeuwen[2] and Alberto Marchetti-Spaccamela[3]

[1] Dip. di Informatica e Sistemistica, University of Rome "La Sapienza", via Salaria 113, I-00198 Rome, Italy

[2] Department of Computer Science, Utrecht University, Padualaan 14, 3584 CH Utrecht, the Netherlands.

[3] Dip. di Matematica Pura e Applicata, University of L'Aquila, via Vetoio loc. Coppito, I-67010 l'Aquila, Italy

Abstract. Several methods exist for routing messages in a network without using complete routing tables (compact routing). In k-interval routing schemes (k-IRS), nodes assign up to k intervals to each incident link. A message is routed over a link if its destination belongs to one of the intervals of the link. We give some results for the necessary value of k in order to achieve shortest path routing. Even though for very structured networks low values of k suffice, we show that for 'general graphs' interval routing cannot significantly reduce the space-requirements for shortest path routing. In particular, for any $\delta > 0$, there exist classes of random graphs $\mathcal{G}_{n,p}$ for all n sufficiently large such that with high probability an optimal k-IRS for a graph $G \in \mathcal{G}_{n,p}$ requires $k = \Omega(n^{1-\delta})$.

1 Introduction

Routing messages is a fundamental operation in distributed systems. But how much information needs to be stored in the processors in order to do it well? As usual we model a network of processors by a connected, undirected graph of n nodes and e edges: the nodes represent the processors, and the edges represent the communication links. We consider routing methods that lead to shortest paths for every source-destination pair.

Shortest routes can be represented trivially by storing a complete routing table at each node v that specifies, for each destination u, a link incident to v which is on a shortest path from v to u. In large networks of processors where processor memory is at a premium, this is space-consuming and thus unattractive. A complete routing table has n entries of $\log d$-bits each, where d is the degree

* This research was supported by the ESPRIT II Basic Research Actions under contract No. 7141 (project ALCOM II: "Algorithms and Complexity II"), by the EC Human Capital and Mobility Program (the MAP project), and by the Italian MURST 40% project "Algoritmi, Modelli di Calcolo e Strutture Informative".

of the node where it is stored. For the entire network this leads to a total of $\sum_{v=1}^{n} n \log d_v = \mathcal{O}\left(n^2 \log \frac{e}{n}\right)$ bits. Fraigniaud and Gavoille [21] recently proved that reasonable shortest-path routing schemes require at least $\Omega(n^2)$ bits.

Practical networking environments have introduced the need for routing methods with smaller tables (*compact routing*), even allowing the possibility of routing messages along paths which are not necessarily shortest. For many practical network topologies the shortest path information can indeed be coded more succinctly at the nodes (see the references or [40, 41]). Tables typically use in the order of $d \log n$ bits per node, hence $\mathcal{O}(e \log n)$ bits total. We will consider a technique called 'interval routing' and show that for general networks it is not likely to be very effective.

Interval routing is based on a suitable naming scheme for the nodes and edges in a network. A node label is any element of the set $\{1, \ldots, n\}$, and an edge label is any 'interval' $[a, b]$ with $a, b \in \{1, \ldots, n\}$. Assuming that the labels 1 through n are arranged clockwise around a circle, an interval $[a, b]$ represents the node labels from a through b in clockwise order. (Thus for $n = 5$, the interval $[4, 2]$ represents the node labels 4, 5, 1, and 2.) A *k-interval labeling scheme* or k-ILS ([39]) consists of (i) a node labeling such that every node gets a unique label, and (ii) at every node, some assignment of up to k intervals to each link leaving that node (an edge labeling). The two ends of an edge may be assigned different sets of up to k edge labels. When no edge label contains the interval $[n, 1]$, the k-ILS is called *linear* [5, 6].

Given a k-ILS, a routing strategy is devised as follows. Let a message m be destined for v, suppose it has reached some node u on its way, and suppose $u \neq v$. Then an edge $e = (u, u')$ incident to u is determined such that v belongs to one of the intervals assigned to e at u, and m is transmitted over e from u to u', to reach the next node on its way to v. If this routing strategy guarantees that messages always arrive at their destination, no matter where they originate and what their destination is, then a k-ILS is termed a *k-interval routing scheme* or k-IRS. If the implied routes are always the shortest, then the k-IRS is called *optimal.*

Interval routing is generally applicable. It can be shown that every network admits a 1-IRS in which at every node an interval is assigned to each edge and the assigned intervals are disjoint ([38, 39]). Many interesting processor interconnection networks have optimum k-interval routing schemes for small k (see e.g. [35, 39, 23, 25, 26, 19, 12]). Interval routing has also found industrial application, e.g. in the design of the C104 router chip of the INMOS T9000 Transputer [30] and in other practical contexts [28, 42, 43, 44, 45]. Several variants have been explored to obtain more flexible compact routing schemes ([7], [11, 14]).

Interval routing seems effective for networks having particular regularities. Observe that every network admits an optimal k-IRS for $k = \frac{1}{2}n$ (note that any assignment of more than $\frac{1}{2}n$ destinations to an edge can be represented by at most $\frac{1}{2}n$ intervals). But it appears to be much harder to decide whether a network admits an optimal k-IRS for some smaller value of k (see [15]). Some results exist that show that 1-IRS [33, 34, 36] and 2-IRS schemes [37] cannot even come close to optimality for some classes of networks. Indeed, when no specific assumption about the topology of a network is made, interval routing does not seem to reduce the space requirement for the routing information in the nodes significantly. Our aim is to demonstrate this through the following results.

(*i*) First we develop a technique for proving lowerbounds on the complexity of optimal k-interval routing schemes for given graphs G. It is used to show that for each n there *exist* graphs on n nodes for which any optimal k-IRS requires a large k.

(*ii*) Next we show for the random graph model $\mathcal{G}_{n,p}$ that for every n sufficiently large there exist p such that with sufficiently high probability any optimal k-IRS scheme for a graph $G \in \mathcal{G}_{n,p}$ has $k \geq \frac{1}{20}n^{1-2\sqrt{6}/\sqrt{\ln n}}$.

This also shows that it is easy to construct many concrete networks that require a 'large k' for optimal k-IRS routing, for the case of uniform edge costs. Large k's are indeed the more common situation if we allow *dynamic* edge costs and require that a graph can be optimally routed by a k-IRS for every cost assignment to the edges. This follows from recent work of Bodlaender *et al.* [8].

In section 2 we develop the technique for proving lowerbounds on the number of intervals needed in an optimal k-IRS. It extends ideas used in Flammini, Gambosi and Salomone [11, 13, 15]. In sections 3 and 4 we develop the main result (*ii*). Some conclusions follow in section 5. For a number of proofs the reader is referred to [16, 17].

2 A Lowerbound Technique for k-Interval Routing Schemes

Let $G = (V, E)$ be a graph with $| V |= n$. How can one bound the value of k needed in an optimal k-IRS for G. We will develop a technique that will be essential for the constructions later. A simple observation learns that one can restrict to deterministic schemes. Also, one can project optimal schemes to optimal schemes for subsets $U \subseteq V$.

Proposition 1. (a) *If G admits an optimal k-IRS, then G admits an optimal k-IRS in which at every node v the assigned edge labels are all disjoint.*
(b) *For every $U \subseteq V$, any optimal k-IRS of G can be reduced to a k-IRS that is optimal for routing to destinations in U only.*

Assume that the set *Opt* of optimal routes is given. For nodes $v \in V$, let $I(v)$ be the set of edges incident to v. For nodes v and edges $e \in I(v)$, let $Opt(v, e)$ be the subset of nodes $u \in V$ optimally reachable from v through its outgoing link e. Any pair (v, e) with $e \in I(v)$ will be called a 'source-pair' (the beginning of a route from v over e). If the routes are defined by a k-IRS, then $Opt(v, e)$ is the union of the intervals assigned to e at v. Conversely, given a node labeling, the sets $Opt(v, e)$ should lead us to the interval labels needed in any optimal IRS for G. Consider the following representation of the optimal routes.

Definition 2. Given a set of destinations $U = \{u_1, ..., u_l\} \subseteq V$ and a set of source-pairs $S = \{(v_j, e_j) \mid e_j \in I(v_j), 1 \leq j \leq m\}$, the *Matrix Representation* of *Opt* w.r.t. U and S is the $l \times m$ Boolean matrix $M(U,S)$ with $M(U,S)[i,j] = 1$ if $u_i \in Opt(v_j, e_j)$ and $M(U,S)[i,j] = 0$ otherwise, for every $1 \leq i \leq l$ and $1 \leq j \leq m$.

Observe that the j-th column of $M(U,S)$ has a '1' precisely in the rows corresponding to destination nodes $u \in U$ which can be reached optimally from v_j over its outgoing link e_j.

An optimal k-IRS for G need not represent *all* optimal routes for every source-destination pair. Thus we cannot just decompose the sets $Opt(v,e)$ into unions of intervals, to find a lowerbound on the number of intervals needed. We have to restrict to a set of routes which any k-IRS for G must represent. Thus we look for sets U and S such that optimal routes to U have unique directions at the nodes in S. We exclude routes 'back to source nodes' because k-IRS schemes do not send messages out if source and destination of a message are equal.

Definition 3. Given a set of destinations U and a set of source-pairs S, *Opt* is called *unique* w.r.t. U and S if and only if it satisfies the following properties:

- for each $u \in U$ and $(v_j, e_j) \in S$ with $u \in Opt(v_j, e_j)$, there exists no $e \in I(v_j)$ with $e \neq e_j$ such that $u \in Opt(v_j, e)$.
- for each $(v_j, e_j) \in S$, $v_j \notin U$.

Informally, if *Opt* is unique w.r.t. U and S, then any optimal IRS scheme for G must reflect the optimal directions as given by *Opt* if we restrict our observation to U and S.

Definition 4. Let M be a $l \times m$ Boolean matrix. The Hamming score $c_M(i,j)$ of rows i and j in M is equal to $\frac{1}{2}d_H(i,j)$, where $d_H(i,j)$ is the Hamming distance between the i-th and j-th row. The Hamming index of M is equal to $Ind(M) = \min\{c_M(i,j) \mid 1 \leq i,j \leq l\}$.

Lemma 5. *Let Opt be unique w.r.t. U and S and let $M = M(U,S)$ be the Matrix Representation of Opt w.r.t. U and S. Then for any optimal k-IRS scheme for G: $k \geq \frac{l}{m} \cdot Ind(M)$, where $|U| = l$ and $|S| = m$.*

Proof. Let $U = \{u_1, \ldots, u_l\}$, let $S = \{(v_j, e_j) \mid e_j \in I(v_j), 1 \leq j \leq m\}$ and let $S' = \{v \mid (v,e) \in S \textit{ for some } e\}$. Using proposition 1 any optimal k-IRS for G must reduce to a k-IRS for G that is optimal if we restrict the set of destinations to U. If we now restrict the set of source-pairs to S as well, uniqueness of *Opt* w.r.t. U and S implies that at every node $v \in S'$ this k-IRS must assign disjoint interval labels to all edges e with $(v,e) \in S$ leaving v.

Considering the j-th column of M for any $1 \leq j \leq m$, the blocks of 1's separated by 0's down the column 'and around' precisely correspond to the intervals assigned to the edge e_j at v_j by the scheme, assuming that $u_1, \ldots, u_l$ are labeled in this order. The number of blocks, and hence the number of intervals needed, is equal to half the number of occurrences of the patterns 01 and 10 down the column and around. (Note that the number of occurrences of 01 is equal to the number of occurrences of 10.) Using Hamming scores and summing for all columns this gives $\sum_{i=1}^{l} c_M(i,(i+1) mod\ l) \geq l \cdot Ind(M)$ blocks total. Hence there is a column in M which has at least $\frac{l}{m} \cdot Ind(M)$ blocks, and the corresponding edge e_j must have at least this number of labels at v_j.

The same argument applies if the nodes $u_1, \ldots, u_l$ are labeled in any other way and the rows of M are permuted accordingly. Hence *any* optimal k-IRS for G must assign at least $\frac{l}{m} Ind(M)$ intervals to some edge.

The Matrix Representation can also be employed to construct k-IRS schemes, by taking $U = V$ and $S = \{(v,e) \mid v \in V, e \in I(v)\}$ and representing *all* routes $\in Opt$. Minimizing the maximum number of 1-blocks per column over all possible permutations of the rows of $M = M(U,S)$ leads to an optimal k-IRS with the smallest k. If $c_M(i,j) \leq d$ for all $1 \leq i,j \leq \mid U \mid = n$, then any node-labeling will lead to an optimal IRS with at most $d.n$ labels total.

Kranakis, Krizanc, and Ravi [29] recently showed that for every n there exist graphs on n nodes for which any optimal *linear* k-IRS requires $k \geq \Omega(n^{1/3})$. Lemma 5 enables one to improve the bound considerably, even for optimal k-IRS that are not necessarily linear.

Proposition 6. *For every n there exist a graph G with n nodes and $O(n \log n)$ edges such that for each optimal k-IRS scheme of G one has $k = \Omega(n/\log n)$.*

Proof. It is sufficient to show that for each integer r there exists a graph G with $n = (3r + 2^r)$ nodes and $(2r + r.2^r)$ edges such that any optimal k-IRS for G has $k \geq \frac{2^{r-1}}{r}$. For integers j let $bin(j)$ denote the binary representation of j. Define $G = (V,E)$ where $V = V_1 \cup V_2 \cup V_3 \cup V_4$ and $E = E_1 \cup E_2 \cup E_3 \cup E_4$ are as follows: $V_1 = \{v_i \mid i = 1,\ldots,r\}$, $V_2 = \{w_{0,i} \mid i = 1,\ldots,r\}$, $V_3 = \{w_{1,i} \mid i = 1,\ldots,r\}$, $V_4 = \{u_j \mid j = 0,\ldots,2^r - 1\}$, $E_1 = \{e_{0,i} = (v_i, w_{0,i}) \mid i = 1,\ldots,r\}$, $E_2 = \{e_{1,i} = (v_i, w_{1,i}) \mid i = 1,\ldots,r\}$, $E_3 = \{(w_{0,i}, u_j) \mid i = 1,\ldots,r, j = 0,\ldots,2^r - 1 \textit{ and the } i-th \textit{ bit of } bin(j) \textit{ is } 0\}$, and $E_4 = \{(w_{1,i}, u_j) \mid i = 1,\ldots,r, j = 0,\ldots,2^r - 1 \textit{ and the } i-th \textit{ bit of } bin(j) \textit{ is } 1\}$.

Consider the optimal routes in G from V_1 to V_4. Taking $U = V_4$ and $S = \{(v_i, e_{1,i}) \mid 1 \leq i \leq r\}$, it easily follows that the set of optimal routes of G is unique w.r.t. U and S. Consider $M = M(U,S)$ and observe that its rows are precisely the 2^r different r-bit strings. Thus $Ind(M) = \frac{1}{2}$. By lemma 5 any optimal k-IRS for G requires $k \geq \frac{2^r}{r} \cdot \frac{1}{2} = \frac{2^{r-1}}{r}$.

The lowerbound technique has been used recently by Gavoille and Guévremont [27] to construct graphs G with n nodes that actually require $k = \Theta(n)$. They also proved that for bounded-degree networks there are graphs of n nodes that require $k = \Omega(\sqrt{n})$. A similar technique was used in [21].

3 Interval Routing in Random Graphs: Preliminaries

We adopt the $\mathcal{G}_{n,p}$ model of random graphs, which consists of all graphs with node set $V = \{1, \ldots, n\}$ and edges chosen independently with probability p (see [9]). We will assume throughout that $\frac{\ln^{1+\epsilon} n}{n} < p < n^{-0.5-\varepsilon}$ for some $\varepsilon > 0$. The (lower)bound on p guarantees that a graph in $\mathcal{G}_{n,p}$ is indeed connected, with high probability ([9], Chapter IV). In this section we prove some useful preliminaries concerning the $\mathcal{G}_{n,p}$ model. Let G be a random graph from $\mathcal{G}_{n,p}$. Let $d(u, v)$ denote the length of the shortest path between u and v.

Definition 7. Given a node $v \in V$, we say that $u \in V$ is *uniquely reachable* from v if and only if all shortest paths from v to u exit v over the same edge (v, w) for some w. For any $h > 0$, let $D(v, h)$ be the set of nodes u with $d(v, u) = h$ and let $U_{v,h} \subseteq D(v, h)$ be the set of nodes u that are uniquely reachable from v and have $d(v, u) = h$.

Observe that a node $u \in V$ is not uniquely reachable from some node v if there exist at least two optimal paths between v and u that exit at v through two different outgoing edges. Let us call such paths *not v-unique* (or *not i-unique* if nodes are indexed and $v = v_i$).

Let $c = \lfloor \frac{\ln n}{\ln(np)} \rfloor = \frac{\ln n}{\ln(np)} - \beta$ (for some $0 \leq \beta < 1$). Consider some set of c source nodes $S' = \{v_1, \ldots, v_c\}$ in G, and let $\mathcal{U} = \bigcap_{i=1}^{c} U_{v_i,c}$ be a set of destinations. $\mathcal{U}$ is the intersection of the sets of nodes at distance c uniquely reachable from each v_i. Intuitively, routing messages from nodes in S' to nodes in $\mathcal{U}$ will require many different intervals at certain nodes, in any optimal k-IRS. We will show that the set $\mathcal{U}$ is sufficiently large with high probability.

Lemma 8. *[9] Let $K > 14$ be a constant. If n is sufficiently large, then with probability $\geq 1 - n^{-K}$, for every node v and every natural number h with $1 \leq h \leq c - 1$:*

$$|\,|D(v,h)| - (np)^h\,| \leq (np)^h/4$$

and

$$\sum_{j=1}^{h} |D(v,j)| \leq 2(np)^h.$$

Lemma 9. *Given a random node u then, if n is sufficiently large, for each vertex v_i, $i = 1, 2 \ldots, c$ and for any natural number h with $1 \leq h \leq c - 1$:*

$$\frac{2(np)^h}{3n} \leq Prob(d(v_i, u) = h) \leq \frac{4(np)^h}{3n}$$

and

$$Prob(d(v_i, u) \leq h) \leq \frac{7(np)^h}{3n}.$$

We need two further lemmas. First observe that

$$(np)^{c-1}p = e^{(\frac{\ln n}{\ln(np)}-\beta-1)\ln(np)}p = \frac{1}{(np)^{\beta}},$$

which implies that for n sufficiently large:

$$(np)^{c-1} \leq \frac{1}{p} \leq \frac{n}{\ln^{1+\varepsilon} n} \leq \frac{n}{4} \quad and \quad (np)^{c-1} \geq \frac{1}{np^2} \geq n^{2\varepsilon},$$

and, since $np \geq \ln^{1+\varepsilon} n$:

$$\frac{c(np)^{c-1}}{n} = \frac{c}{(np)^{1+\beta}} \leq \frac{\ln n}{np\ln(np)} \leq \frac{1}{(1+\varepsilon).\ln^{\varepsilon} n.\ln\ln n} = o(1).$$

By lemma 8, $\sum_{j=1}^{c-1} \mid D(v,j) \mid \leq 2(np)^{c-1} \leq n/2$, hence with probability $\geq (1-n^{-K})$ there are at least $n/2$ nodes at distance $\geq c-1$ from v for n sufficiently large.

Lemma 10. *Given $v_i \in S'$ and $u \in V$, the probability that there exist at least two not i-unique paths of length $c-1$ between v_i and u is $\leq 2(np)^{2c-2}n^{-2}$.*

Lemma 11. *Given $v_i \in S'$ and $u \in V$ then, for n sufficiently large:*

$$Prob(d(v_i,u) = c-1 \, and \, for \, each \, j \neq i \;\; d(v_j,u) > c-1) \geq \frac{(np)^{c-1}}{2n}.$$

We also use the following result due to Chernoff [10]:

Lemma 12. *[10] Let $0 \leq p \leq 1$, let X be a Bernoulli variable with success probability p, let $0 \leq \gamma \leq 1$, and let m be any positive integer. The probability of at most $(1-\gamma)mp$ successes in m independent trials of X is less than $e^{-\gamma^2 mp/2}$. The probability of at least $(1+\gamma)mp$ successes is less than $e^{-\gamma^2 mp/3}$.*

Theorem 13. *For n sufficiently large we have, with probability $1-o(1)$:*

$$\mid \mathcal{U} \mid \geq \frac{1}{4}\left(\frac{e^{-\frac{5}{2(np)^{\beta}}}}{8}\right)^{c} n^{1+\beta^2-\beta}p^{\beta^2}.$$

Proof. For each i write $U_{v_i,c-1} = U_i' \cup U_i''$, where U_i' is the set of nodes $u \in U_{v_i,c-1}$ with $d(v_j,u) > c-1$ for each $j \neq i$, and U_i'' is the set of nodes $u \in U_{v_i,c-1}$ with $d(v_j,u) \leq c-1$ for some $j \neq i$. Observe that, if a node u has distance at least c from v_i and is connected to exactly one node in U_i' and *not* connected to any node in U_i'' for each i, then it has distance c from each v_i and is uniquely reachable from each v_i and, consequently, $u \in \mathcal{U}$. Thus, a lower bound on the number of nodes u with the stated property is also a lower bound on $\mid \mathcal{U} \mid$.

By definition, U_i' is the set of nodes u satisfying the event $A(i,u)$ defined by: "$d(v_i,u) = c-1$ and u is uniquely reachable from v_i and for each $j \neq i$

$d(v_j, u) > c-1$". Thus, given $v_i \in V$ and using lemmas 10 and 11 and the fact that $\frac{(np)^{c-1}}{n} < \frac{c(np)^{c-1}}{n} = o(1)$, we have for suitably large n:

$$Prob(A(i,u)) \geq$$
$$Prob(d(v_i,u) = c-1\, and\, for\, each\, j \neq i,\, d(v_j,u) > c-1) -$$
$$Prob(there\, exist\, at\, least\, two\, not\, i\text{-}unique\, paths\, of\, length\, c-1\, from\, v_i\, to\, u\,) \geq$$

$$\frac{(np)^{c-1}}{2n} - \frac{2(np)^{2c-2}}{n^2} \geq \frac{(np)^{c-1}}{4n}.$$

This implies that $E(|U_i'|) \geq \frac{(np)^{c-1}}{4}$, where $E(|U_i'|)$ denotes the expected value of $|U_i'|$. By applying Chernoff's bound it follows that for suitably large n, the probability that $|U_i'| \leq \frac{(np)^{c-1}}{8}$ is at most $e^{-\frac{(np)^{c-1}}{32}}$. Thus the probability that for each i, $|U_i'| \leq \frac{(np)^{c-1}}{8}$ is at most $ce^{-\frac{(np)^{c-1}}{32}}$ and, hence, the probability that for each i $|U_i'| \geq \frac{(np)^{c-1}}{8}$ is at least $1 - ce^{-\frac{(np)^{c-1}}{32}}$.

An upper bound on $|U_i'|$ and $|U_i''|$ is immediately obtained using lemma 8. In fact, $|U_i'|$ and $|U_i''|$ are both $\leq |D(v_i, c-1)|$ for each i and the probability that for each i, $|U_i'|, |U_i''| \leq \frac{5(np)^{c-1}}{4}$ is at least $1 - cn^{-K}$, with K as in the lemma. In fact, if we let $m_i' = |U_i'|$ and $m_i'' = |U_i''|$, then the given bound is actually a bound on $m_i' + m_i''$.

Let us now bound the number of 'special' nodes $u \in \mathcal{U}$. For any node u such that for each i $d(v_i,u) \geq c$, the probability that u is connected to exactly one node in U_i' and no nodes in U_i'' for each i is equal to:

$$m_1'p(1-p)^{m_1'-1}(1-p)^{m_1''} \cdot \ldots \cdot m_c'p(1-p)^{m_c'-1}(1-p)^{m_c''} \geq$$
$$(\frac{(np)^{c-1}}{8}p(1-p)^{\frac{5(np)^{c-1}}{4}})^c = (\frac{(np)^{c-1}p}{8}(1-p)^{\frac{5}{4}(np)^{c-1}})^c \geq$$
$$(\frac{(np)^{c-1}p}{8}e^{-\frac{5}{2}(np)^{c-1}p})^c = (\frac{e^{-\frac{5}{2(np)^\beta}}}{8(np)^\beta})^c = (\frac{e^{-\frac{5}{2(np)^\beta}}}{8})^c(\frac{1}{(np)^c})^\beta =$$
$$(\frac{e^{-\frac{5}{2(np)^\beta}}}{8})^c(\frac{1}{(np)^{c-1}p})^\beta(\frac{p}{np})^\beta = (\frac{e^{-\frac{5}{2(np)^\beta}}}{8})^c(np)^{\beta^2}\frac{1}{n^\beta} = (\frac{e^{-\frac{5}{2(np)^\beta}}}{8})^c n^{\beta^2-\beta}p^{\beta^2}.$$

For n suitably large, with probability $\geq (1-n^{-K})$ there are at least $n/2$ nodes u at distance $\geq c-1$ from v. Hence an expected number of $(\frac{e^{-\frac{5}{2(np)^\beta}}}{8})^c n^{1+\beta^2-\beta}p^{\beta^2}$ nodes u will have the desired special property. By applying Chernoff's bound, it follows that the probability that $|\mathcal{U}| \geq \frac{(\frac{e^{-\frac{5}{2(np)^\beta}}}{8})^c n^{1+\beta^2-\beta}p^{\beta^2}}{4}$ is at least $1 - e^{-\frac{(\frac{e^{-\frac{5}{2(np)^\beta}}}{8})^c n^{1+\beta^2-\beta}p^{\beta^2}}{16}}$.

Finally, the probability that for each i, $m_i' \geq \frac{(np)^{c-1}}{8}$ and $m_i' + m_i'' \leq \frac{5(np)^{c-1}}{4}$, that there exist at least $\frac{n}{2}$ nodes u such that for each i, $d(v_i,u) \geq c$ and, consequently, that $|\mathcal{U}| \geq \frac{(\frac{e^{-\frac{5}{2(np)^\beta}}}{8})^c n^{1+\beta^2-\beta}p^{\beta^2}}{4}$, is at least $1 - o(1)$.

4 Interval Routing in Random Graphs: A Lower Bound

In this section we prove that for n sufficiently large and for suitable values of p, an optimal k-IRS scheme for a random graph $G \in \mathcal{G}_{n,p}$ requires $k = \Omega(n^{1-\frac{6}{\ln(np)}-\frac{\ln(np)}{\ln n}}) = \Omega(\frac{1}{p}n^{-\frac{6}{\ln np}})$ with high probability. This leads to classes of random graphs for which optimal k-IRS schemes require $k = \Omega(n^{1-\delta})$ with high probability, for any constant $\delta > 0$.

In lemma 15 we will need a version of the 'Coupon Collectors Problem' (see [32]). In this problem there are N cells, and balls are distributed one by one into the cells. Let a trial consist of placing one ball into one cell. The trials are independent and in each trial the probability that a ball lands in a specified cell is N^{-1}. We are interested in T_s, the number of trials needed until for the first time precisely s cells have received at least one ball.

Proposition 14. *If $s \leq \frac{N}{4}$, then $Prob(T_s > 2s) \leq \frac{4}{N}$.*

Let $G \in \mathcal{G}_{n,p}$ be a random graph, with $\frac{\ln^{1+\epsilon} n}{n} < p < n^{-0.5-\epsilon}$. Let S' and $\mathcal{U} = \bigcap_{i=1}^{c} U_{v_i,c}$ be as defined in section 3. Define s by

$$s = \frac{1}{8}(\frac{e^{-\frac{5}{2(np)^{\beta}}}}{8})^c n^{1+\beta^2-\beta} p^{\beta^2},$$

and observe that $s \leq \frac{1}{8}e^{-2c}n^{1+\beta^2-\beta}p^{\beta^2}$.

Lemma 15. *For n sufficiently large, any optimal k-IRS scheme for G must have*

$$k \geq \frac{1}{10}\frac{\ln(np)}{np\ln n}(\frac{e^{-\frac{5}{2(np)^{\beta}}}}{8})^c n^{1+\beta^2-\beta} p^{\beta^2},$$

with probability $1 - o(1)$.

Proof. Each node $u \in \mathcal{U}$ is optimally reachable from each v_i through a unique incident link, thus if we let $U = \mathcal{U}$ and $S = \{(v_i, e) \mid e \in I(v_i)\}$, then the set of optimal paths in G is unique w.r.t. U and S. Let $M = M(U, S)$. We will estimate $\mid U \mid$, $\mid S \mid$ and $Ind(M)$ so as to apply lemma 5. We know that $\mid U \mid = l \geq 2s$ with probability $1 - o(1)$.

To estimate $\mid S \mid$ observe from lemma 8 that with probability $1 - cn^{-K}$ we have for each i, $\mid D(v_i, 1) \mid \leq \frac{5}{4}np$. Thus $\mid S \mid = m \leq \frac{5}{4}cnp \leq \frac{5np\ln n}{4\ln(np)}$ with probability $1 - cn^{-K}$, with K as in the lemma. Bounding $Ind(M)$ poses more difficulties, because one might have $Ind(M) = 0$. We will get around this by selecting a sufficiently large submatrix with all rows different.

By lemma 8 we know that for every i $\mid D(v_i, 1) \mid \geq \frac{3}{4}np$ with probability at least $1 - cn^{-K}$, with K as in the lemma. Assume that this bound on each $\mid D(v_i, 1) \mid$ holds. We can view the columns of M as being divided into c disjoint groups, each group corresponding to the source-pairs $(v_i, e) \in S$ for some fixed v_i. By the common bound on the $\mid D(v_i, 1) \mid$, each group will have $\geq \frac{3}{4}np$ columns.

Considering any row of M as it is divided by the c groups of columns into sectors of at least $\frac{3}{4}np$ bits each, it follows from the uniqueness w.r.t. U and S that each sector of a row has exactly one of its bits set to 1, while the other bits in the sector are equal to 0.

Consider the set R of all possible rows that satisfy the stated condition. It follows that $| R | \geq (\frac{3}{4}np)^c \geq (\frac{1}{e})^c \frac{n}{(np)^\beta}$. By symmetry, each row $\in R$ occurs with equal probability as a row in M. Estimating the number of different rows in M can now be viewed as an instance of the Coupon Collectors Problem in the following way. The cells are the elements of R and a trial that places a ball into a certain cell corresponds to an occurrence of the corresponding row in M. In the notation used earlier we have $N \geq (\frac{1}{e})^c \frac{n}{(np)^\beta}$. Consider a series of trials and note that with probability $1 - o(1)$, M has at least $2s$ rows and thus needs at least $2s$ trials with probability $1 - o(1)$. Note that for n sufficiently large, $\frac{N}{s} \geq 8e^c n^{\beta^2} p^{\beta^2 - \beta} \geq 4$ and hence $s \leq \frac{N}{4}$. By proposition 14, $Prob(T_s > 2s) \leq \frac{4}{N}$ and with high probability M will have at least s mutually different rows.

Let U' be the subset of U consisting of the s mutually different rows which are likely to occur in M. Then the set of optimal paths is unique w.r.t. U' and S as well but now, with $M' = M(U', S)$, we have $Ind(M') \geq 1$ (because different rows will differ in at least two positions). By lemma 5

$$k \geq \frac{s}{m} \geq$$

$$\geq \left(\frac{(\frac{e^{-\frac{5}{2(np)^\beta}}}{8})^c n^{1+\beta^2-\beta} p^{\beta^2}}{8}\right) / \left(\frac{5np\ln n}{4\ln(np)}\right) = \frac{1}{10}\frac{\ln(np)}{np\ln n}\left(\frac{e^{-\frac{5}{2(np)^\beta}}}{8}\right)^c n^{1+\beta^2-\beta} p^{\beta^2}.$$

Finally, the probability that the above bounds on $| D(v_i, 1) |$ for each i and on the number of different rows in $M(U, P)$ hold is at least $(1 - o(1))$.

Using lemma 15 one obtains:

Theorem 16. *For any n, let $p = n^{-\frac{t-1}{t}}$ for an integer $t > 0$ such that $\frac{\ln^{1+\epsilon} n}{n} < p < n^{-0.5-\epsilon}$. Then, for n sufficiently large, an optimal k-IRS scheme for a random graph $G \in \mathcal{G}_{n,p}$ has $k \geq \frac{1}{10} n^{1 - \frac{6}{\ln(np)} - \frac{\ln(np)}{\ln n}}$ with probability* $1 - 0(1)$.

Taking $t = \lceil \sqrt{\ln n} / \sqrt{6} \rceil$ in theorem 16 leads to the following result.

Theorem 17. *For all n sufficiently large, there exist $p > 0$ such that for any random graph $G \in \mathcal{G}_{n,p}$, an optimal k-IRS scheme for G has $k \geq \frac{1}{20} n^{1 - 2\sqrt{6}/\sqrt{\ln n}}$ with probability* $1 - o(1)$.

5 Conclusion

We considered the complexity of optimal routing in processor networks by means of k-interval routing schemes. The technique has gained popularity, because it is applicable to a range of commonly used networks, with reasonably small values of k. These networks are usually quite regular.

We have shown that in general networks small values of k are the exception rather than the rule for optimal k-interval routing schemes. Theorem 17 implies that for any $\delta > 0$, there exist classes of random graphs $\mathcal{G}_{n,p}$ for any n sufficiently large such that with high probability an optimal k-IRS for a graph $G \in \mathcal{G}_{n,p}$ requires $k = \Omega(n^{1-\delta})$. The result is proved by means of a technique that is useful for other lowerbound problems in interval routing as well.

Optimal k-interval routing on random graphs might actually require $k = \Theta(n)$ in many cases, but this remains to be proved. A result of this kind does hold in a slightly stronger version of the problem, namely for dynamic optimal k-interval routing [8].

References

1. Y. Afek, E. Gafni, M. Ricklin. *Upper and lower bounds for routing schemes in dynamic networks.* Proc. 30th Annual IEEE Symp. on Foundations of Computer Science, pp. 370-375, 1989.
2. B. Awerbuch, A. Bar-Noy, N. Linial, D. Peleg. *Compact distributed data structures for adaptive routing.* Proc. 21st Annual ACM Symp. on Theory of Computing, pp. 479-489, 1989.
3. B. Awerbuch, A. Bar-Noy, N. Linial, D. Peleg. *Improved routing strategies with succinct tables.* Journal of Algorithms, 11, pp. 307-341, 1990.
4. B. Awerbuch, D. Peleg. *Routing with polynomial communication-space tradeoff.* SIAM Journal on Discrete Math, 5, pp. 151-162, 1992.
5. E.M. Bakker. *Combinatorial Problems in Information Networks and Distributed Datastructuring,* Ph.D. Thesis, Dept. of Computer Science, Utrecht University, 1991.
6. E.M. Bakker, J. van Leeuwen, R.B. Tan. *Linear interval routing.* Algorithms Review, 2, 2, pp. 45-61, 1991.
7. E.M. Bakker, J. van Leeuwen, R.B. Tan. *Prefix routing schemes in dynamic networks,* Computer Networks and ISDN Systems 26, pp. 403-421, 1993.
8. H.L. Bodlaender, R.B. Tan, D. Thilikos, J. van Leeuwen. *On interval routing schemes and treewidth,* extended abstract, Dept. of Computer Science, Utrecht University, 1995.
9. B. Bollobás. *Random Graphs,* Academic Press, London, 1985.
10. H. Chernoff. *A measure of the asymptotic efficiency for tests of a hypothesis based on the sum of observations,* Ann. Math. Statistics 23, pp. 493-509, 1952.
11. M. Flammini, G. Gambosi, S. Salomone: *Boolean routing,* in: A. Schiper (Ed.), Distributed Algorithms, Proc. 7th Int. Workshop (WDAG '93), Lecture Notes in Computer Science 725, Springer-Verlag, Berlin, pp. 219-233, 1993.
12. M. Flammini, G. Gambosi, and S. Salomone. *Interval labeling schemes for chordal rings* Technical Report Nr. 52, Department of Pure and Applied Mathematics, University of L'Aquila, L'Aquila, 1994.
13. M. Flammini, G. Gambosi, S. Salomone. *On the complexity of devising interval routing schemes.* Submitted for publication, 1994.
14. M. Flammini, G. Gambosi, S. Salomone. *On devising Boolean routing schemes,* Submitted for publication, 1994.

15. M. Flammini, G. Gambosi, S. Salomone. *Interval routing schemes*, in: E. W. Mayr and C. Puech (Eds.), STACS 95 - 12th Annual Symposium on Theoretical Aspects of Computer Science, Lecture Notes in Computer Science 900, Springer-Verlag, Berlin, pp. 279-290, 1995.
16. M. Flammini, J. van Leeuwen, A. Marchetti-Spaccamela. *Lower bounds on interval routing*, Technical Report Nr. 69, Department of Pure and Applied Mathematics, University of L'Aquila, L'Aquila, 1994.
17. M. Flammini, J. van Leeuwen, A. Marchetti-Spaccamela. *The complexity of interval routing on random graphs* (revised version of reference [16]), Technical Report UU-CS-95-16, Department of Computer Science, Utrecht University, Utrecht, 1995.
18. P. Fraigniaud, C. Gavoille. *Interval routing schemes*, Research Rep 94-04, Lab. de l'Informatique du Parallélisme, Ecole Normale Supérieure de Lyon. 1994.
19. P. Fraigniaud, C. Gavoille. *Optimal interval routing*, in: B. Buchberger, J. Volkert (Eds.), Parallel Processing: CONPAR 94 - VAPP VI, Proc. Third Joint Int. Conference, Lecture Notes in Computer Science 854, Springer-Verlag, Berlin, pp. 785-796, 1994.
20. P. Fraigniaud, C. Gavoille. *A characterisation of networks supporting linear interval routing schemes*, in: Proc. 13th Annual ACM Symp. on Principles of Distributed Computing (PODC'94), pp. 216-224, 1994.
21. P. Fraigniaud, C. Gavoille. *Memory requirement for universal routing schemes*, Research Rep. 95-05, Lab. de l'Informatique du Parallélisme, Ecole Normale Supérieure de Lyon. 1995.
22. G.N. Frederickson. *Searching among intervals and compact routing tables*, in: A. Lingas, R. Karlsson, S. Carlsson (Eds.), Automata, Languages and Programming, 20 the Int. Colloquium (ICALP 93), Lecture Notes in Computer Science 700, Springer-Verlag, Berlin, pp. 28-39, 1993.
23. G.N. Frederickson, R. Janardan. *Designing networks with compact routing tables*. Algorithmica, 3, pp. 171-190, 1988.
24. G.N. Frederickson, R. Janardan. *Space-efficient and fault-tolerant message routing in outerplanar networks*, IEEE Trans. on Computers, 37, pp. 1529-1540, 1988.
25. G.N. Frederickson, R. Janardan. *Efficient message routing in planar networks*. SIAM Journal on Computing, 18, pp. 843-857, 1989.
26. G.N. Frederickson, R. Janardan. *Space-efficient message routing in c-decomposable networks*. SIAM Journal on Computing, 19, pp. 164-181, 1990.
27. C. Gavoille, E. Guévremont, *Worst case bounds for shortest path interval routing*, Research Rep 95-02, Lab. de l'Informatique du Parallélisme, Ecole Normale Supérieure de Lyon. 1995.
28. H. Hofestädt, A. Klein, E. Reyzl. *Performance benefits from locally adaptive interval routing in dynamically switched interconnection networks*, in: A. Bode (Ed.), Distributed Memory Computing, Proc. 2nd European Conference, Lecture Notes in Computer Science 487, Springer-Verlag, Berlin, pp. 193-202, 1991.
29. E. Kranakis, D. Krizanc, S.S. Ravi. *On multi-label linear interval routing schemes*, in: J. van Leeuwen (Ed.), Graph-Theoretic Concepts in Computer Science, Proc. 19-th Int. Workshop (WG '93), Lecture Notes in Computer Science 790, Springer-Verlag, Berlin, pp. 338-349, 1994.
30. D. May, P. Thompson. *Transputers and Routers: Components for Concurrent Machines*, Inmos, 1991.
31. D. Peleg, E. Upfal. *A trade-off between space and efficiency for routing tables*. Journal of the ACM, 36, 3, pp. 510-530, 1989.

32. S.C. Port. *Theoretical Probability for Applications*. J. Wiley & Sons, New York, 1994.
33. P. Ružička. *On efficiency of interval routing algorithms*, in: M.P. Chytil, L. Janiga, V. Koubek (Eds.), Mathematical Foundations of Computer Science 1988, Lecture Notes in Computer Science 324, Springer-Verlag, Berlin, pp. 492-500, 1988.
34. P. Ružička. *A note on the efficiency of an interval routing algorithm*, The Computer Journal, 34, pp. 475-476, 1991.
35. M. Santoro, R. Khatib. *Labelling and implicit routing in networks*. The Computer Journal, 28, pp. 5-8, 1985.
36. S.S.H. Tse, F.C.M. Lau. *A lower bound for interval routing in general networks*. Techn. Report, Dept. of Computer Science, The University of Hong Kong, Hong Kong, 1994.
37. S.S.H. Tse, F.C.M. Lau. *On 2-label interval routing*, Techn. Report, Dept. of Computer Science, The University of Hong Kong, Hong Kong, 1995.
38. J. van Leeuwen, R.B. Tan. *Routing with compact routing tables*. In: G. Rozenberg and A. Salomaa (eds.), The book of L, Springer-Verlag, Berlin, pp. 259-273, 1986.
39. J. van Leeuwen, R.B. Tan. *Interval routing*. The Computer Journal, 30, pp. 298-307, 1987.
40. J. van Leeuwen, R.B. Tan. *Compact routing methods: a survey*, Techn. Report RUU-CS-95-05, Dept. of Computer Science, Utrecht University, 1995.
41. J. Vounckx, G. Deconinck, R. Cuyvers, R. Lauwereins, J.A. Peperstraete. *A survey of compact routing techniques*, Internal Report, Electrotechnical Dept (ESAT-ACCA), Kath. Universiteit Leuven, Heverlee, 1993.
42. J. Vounckx, G. Deconinck, R. Cuyvers, R. Lauwereins, J.A. Peperstraete. *Network fault-tolerance with interval routing devices*, in: Proceedings 11th IASTED Int. Symposium on Applied Informatics, Annecy, France, pp. 293-296, 1993. Revised version to appear in Int. J. of Mini and Microcomputers.
43. J. Vounckx, G. Deconinck, R. Lauwereins, J.A. Peperstraete. *Fault-tolerant compact routing based on reduced structural information in wormhole-switching based networks*, in: Colloquium on Structural Information Information and Communication Complexity (SICC 94), Pre-Proceedings, School of Computer Science, Carleton University, Ottawa, 1994.
44. J. Vounckx, G. Deconinck, R. Lauwereins, J.A. Peperstraete. *Deadlock-free fault-tolerant wormhole routing in mesh-based massively parallel systems*, in: Technical Committee on Computer Architecture (TCCA) Newsletter, IEEE Computer Society, Summer-Fall issue, pp. 49 -54, 1994.
45. J. Vounckx, G. Deconinck, R. Cuyvers, R. Lauwereins, *Minimal deadlock-free compact routing in wormhole-switching based injured meshes*, Internal Report, Electrotechnical Dept (ESAT-ACCA), Kath. Universiteit Leuven, Heverlee, 1994, also in: Proc. 2nd Reconfigurable Architectures Workshop, Santa Barbara, Ca. 1995.
46. B. Zerrouk. *Du routage par intervalles*, Technical Report MASI-RR-93-12, Institut Blaise Pascal, Univ. Pierre et Marie Curie, Paris, 1994, also in: Actes du Congrès Biennal de l'AFCET sur les Technologies de l'Information, Versailles, 1993.
47. B. Zerrouk, J.M. Blin, A. Greiner. *Encapsulating networks and routing*, in: Proc. 8th Int. Parallel Processing Symposium (IPPS'94), Cancùn, pp. 547-553, 1994.
48. B. Zerrouk, S. Tricot, B. Rottembourg. *Proper linear interval routing schemes*, Technical Report, Institut Blaise Pascal, Univ. Pierre et Marie Curie, Paris, 1993.
49. B. Zerrouk, S. Tricot, B. Rottembourg. *Improved results on the characterisation of biased interval labeling schemes*, Parallel Processing Letters, 1995 (to appear).

Bridging Across the log(n) Space Frontier

Viliam Geffert

Department of Computer Science
P.J. Šafárik University
Jesenná 5 - 04154 Košice - Slovakia
geffert@kosice.upjs.sk

Abstract. We believe that now is the opportune time to unify the theory of space bounded computations below $\log n$ with higher complexity classes. This needs to review the basic concepts of the space complexity theory and clarify the role of the space constructibility. Despite of the fact that the space below $\log n$ behaves radically different from the higher bounds, many important techniques do work on the both sides of this boundary. In addition, several important problems are closely related across the $\log n$ space bound.

1 Introduction

The classical structural complexity theory concerns the analysis of computational resource requirements for certain classes of problems and the study of relations between various complexity classes. The recent few years brought some light to the theory of space bounded computations. First, we have the surprisingly short proof that the nondeterministic space is closed under complement for $s(n) \geq \log n$ [16, 24]. This implies that the alternating hierarchy of space bounded computations collapses to the first level, i.e.,

$$NSPACE(s(n)) = \Sigma_k\text{-}SPACE(s(n)) = \Pi_k\text{-}SPACE(s(n)),$$

for each $k \geq 1$ and $s(n) \geq \log n$. Second, by much more complicated arguments [6, 12, 18], we know that this hierarchy is infinite for space bounds below $\log n$. Moreover, there is a substantial difference between the uniform and non-uniform models of computation, since the non-uniform hierarchy does collapse even below $\log n$ [7].

This clearly shows that the space below $\log n$ is radically different. The situation is much more complicated below $\log n$ than above, because we do not have enough space, for example, to count the number of reachable configurations, to remember an input head position, or to detect an infinite cycle by counting the executed steps. This inability to count, however, has been utilized in many applications heavily dependent on the assumption $s(n) \in o(\log n)$.

On the other hand, we do have the deterministic space closed under complement independent of whether $s(n) \geq \log n$ [22]. Taking this into consideration, a natural question arises; which of the known results can be extended to all space bounds, using some more sophisticated arguments. It seems that if we consider the sequential computations only, both deterministic and nondeterministic, then many important techniques (but not all), work on the both sides of this boundary. This includes several upward and downward translation techniques, diagonalization, as well as reducibility and completeness. Moreover, there is a tight connection between the computations using extremely little space and those using "large" amount of space. For example, the following statements are equivalent:

(i) Each nondeterministically fully space constructible function in $O(\log\log n)$ is constructible deterministically as well,

(ii) $DLOG = NLOG$,

(iii) the oracle machines using linear space do not have contradictory relativizations for space bounded queries.

The separation is more difficult if we consider the languages with low information content, e.g., the separation (or collapse) of the "simplest" classes $DSPACE(\log\log n) \cap 1^* \stackrel{?}{=} NSPACE(\log\log n) \cap 1^*$ solves at least $DLOG \stackrel{?}{=} NLOG$, the notorious open problem of the *Fundamental Hierarchy* $DLOG \stackrel{?}{=} NLOG \stackrel{?}{=} P \stackrel{?}{=} NP \stackrel{?}{=} PSPACE \stackrel{?}{=} EXPTIME \stackrel{?}{=} \ldots$.

2 The Basic Computational Models

As *a standard model (acceptor)*, we shall consider a nondeterministic Turing machine having a finite state control, a two-way read-only input tape, and a separate semi-infinite two-way read-write work tape.

Definition 1 *(a) A memory state* of a Turing machine is an ordered triple $q = \langle r, u, j \rangle$, where r is a state of the machine's finite control, u is a string of symbols written on the work tape (not including the blank symbols), and j is a position of the work tape head.

(b) A configuration is an ordered pair $k = \langle q, i \rangle$, where q is a memory state and i is a position of the input tape head.

It is easy to see that, for each machine A, there exists a constant $c \geq 6$ such that, for each $s \geq 0$ and each input of length n,

$$\textit{Number of memory states of size at most } s \leq c^{s+1} . \tag{1}$$

Sometimes we use *a deterministic transducer* equipped with an additional write-only output tape. The content of the output is not incorporated into the memory state or configuration.

A further variation will be *an oracle machine*, making queries to an oracle language $\mathcal{A}$, both for the acceptors and transducers. Such query is performed by writing x on a separate second work tape and entering a special query state $r_{\text{in?}}$. The result is passed back via two possible return states r_{yes}, r_{no}, the oracle tape is cleared. The content of the oracle tape now becomes a component of the memory state. A machine B relativized by an oracle $\mathcal{A}$ will be denoted by $B^{S(\mathcal{A})}$, to emphasize the use of space bounded queries.

Before passing further, we shall put our Turing machines in the following normal form.

Lemma 2 *For each Turing machine A, there exists an equivalent machine A' using the same amount of space such that, for each $s \geq 0$, (a) A' has a unique accepting configuration, (b) A' has a unique configuration going to extend the work tape space from s to $s+1$.*

Proof. We shall replace the original machine A by A' that uses two additional symbols $\tilde{b}$,$\tilde{b}_R$ that are not distinguished from the original blanks when being read but the following exception: At the beginning, A' rewrites the first blank by $\tilde{b}_R$. From now on, $\tilde{b}_R$ is placed always as the rightmost nonblank symbol on the work tape. Each time the simulation drives A' to visit $\tilde{b}_R$, A' "resets", i.e., *(i)* A' moves the input head to the left end marker, *(ii)* clears up the work tape by rewriting the used cells by $\tilde{b}$ (including $\tilde{b}_R$), *(iii)* then rewrites the first unused cell by $\tilde{b}_R$. *(iv)* Finally, it restarts from the very beginning, now having marked one more work tape cell. Similarly, the tape is cleared before acceptation. □

We shall now review the basic concepts of space complexity and clarify how they are related to each other, as well as the role of space constructibility. There were two main modes of $s(n)$ space bounded computations studied in the literature, namely, strongly and weakly space bounded machines.

Definition 3 For a function $s: \mathbb{N} \to \mathbb{N}$, call a nondeterministic Turing machine *(a) strongly $s(n)$ space bounded*, if, for each input of length n, no computation path uses more than $s(n)$ cells on the work tape, *(b) weakly $s(n)$ space bounded*, if each accepted input of length n has at least one accepting computation path using at most $s(n)$ work tape cells.

The classes of languages accepted by strongly and weakly $O(s(n))$ space bounded machines will be denoted by *strong-NSPACE(s(n))*, *weak-NSPACE(s(n))*, their deterministic variants by *strong-DSPACE(s(n))* and *weak-DSPACE(s(n))*, respectively. The class of functions computed by the strongly $O(s(n))$ space bounded deterministic transducers will be denoted by *FSPACE(s(n))*.

DLOG, NLOG, FLOG, DLBA, NLBA, and FLBA denote the corresponding logarithmic *strong-xSPACE(log n)* or linear *strong-xSPACE(n)* classes. The shorthand notation *SPACE(s(n))*, with no prefix *"N"* or *"D"*, will be used to indicate that some results hold both for the deterministic and nondeterministic machines.

For example, the fact that $L = \{a^n b^m;\, n \neq m\} \in$ *weak-DSPACE(log log n) – strong-DSPACE(o(log n))* means that *(i)* we have a machine A not using more than $\log\log n$ space to prove that "good" inputs are in L, *(ii)* each machine A' *(including A itself)* must use at least $\log n$ space to prove that $w \notin L$, for some "bad" inputs. This reminds the difference between the best and worst case analyses for the same algorithm. We shall show that the relation of *strong-SPACE(s(n))* to *weak-SPACE(s(n))* replicates, in a much smaller scale, the *Recursive : Recursively Enumerable* relation.

Several "middle" modes in between have been studied (*see* e.g. [5, 26]). The difference disappears for constructible bounds, since then the computations consuming too much space may be aborted. We know that the *exact constructibility* is seldom required, an *approximate constructibility* is sufficient in most applications [27].

The exact constructibility is connected with the third important mode, the so-called demon machine, whose importance has been somehow overlooked. The demon machines were introduced in [20] to study what might be computed if s(n) were fully space constructible.

Definition 4 *A demon $s(n)$ space bounded machine* begins its computation with a special space limit marker placed exactly $s(n)$ positions away from the initial position of the work tape, for every input of length n. The space marker can be detected. The machine rejects if it ever tries to use more than $s(n)$ space.

The corresponding classes of languages will be denoted by *demon-NSPACE(s(n))* and *demon-DSPACE(s(n))*.

Definition 5 *(a)* A function $s: \mathbb{N} \to \mathbb{N}$ is *fully space constructible nondeterministically* if there exists a nondeterministic Turing machine A which is strongly $s(n)$ space bounded and uses exactly $s(n)$ space on at least one computation path for each input of length n.

(b) If A is deterministic, then $s(n)$ is *(deterministically) fully space constructible.*

(c) A function $s: \mathbb{N} \to \mathbb{N}$ is *(nondeterministically) fully space approximable* if there exists a (nondeterministically) fully space constructible $s'(n) \in \Theta(s(n))$.

Clearly, *strong-SPACE(s(n))* $\subseteq$ *weak-SPACE(s(n))* $\subseteq$ *demon-SPACE(s(n))*. It is well-known that *strong-* and *weak-SPACE* complexity classes are equal for fully space constructible functions, but what remained obscured is the fact that this can easily be drawn from some more general statements:

Corollary 6 *(a) For each fully space approximable function $s(n)$, weak-SPACE(s(n)) $\subseteq$ strong-SPACE(s(n)), hence, strong-SPACE(s(n)) = weak-SPACE(s(n)). (b) If, moreover, $s(n)$ is fully space constructible, then demon-SPACE(s(n)) $\subseteq$ strong-SPACE(s(n)), and hence we have strong-SPACE(s(n)) = weak-SPACE(s(n)) = demon-SPACE(s(n)).*

We omit the prefixes strong-, weak-, or demon- if the space bound is fully space constructible since then all these classes are equal. All "normal" functions we usually deal with are fully space constructible (*see* e.g. [15, 26]). Moreover, each fully space constructible function is also approximable. On the other hand, a fully space approximable function need not even be recursive; e.g.,

$$H(n) = n^2 + h_n, \quad \text{where } h_n = 1 \text{ or } 0, \text{ depending on whether the Turing machine } T_n \text{ (in the standard enumeration) halts on every input}, \tag{2}$$

approximated by $H'(n) = n^2$. To illustrate the different space modes and put them in the context with the *constructibility*, we shall now review some important results, beginning with the early result of Savitch [21] relating nondeterminism with space in 1970.

Theorem 7 *Let $x \in \{strong, weak, demon\}$. Then x-NSPACE(s(n)) $\subseteq$ x-DSPACE($s(n)^2$), for each $s(n) \geq \log n$.*

We do not know whether this relationship holds below $\log n$. Some partial extensions for space bounds below $\log n$ are in [10, 19]. Another extensions can be found e.g. in [27]. The situation is different for the closure under complement, since the closure of the *weak-SPACE(s(n))* depends on the space bound $s(n)$.

Theorem 8 *Let $x \in \{strong, demon\}$. Then x-DSPACE(s(n)) = co-x-DSPACE(s(n)), for each $s(n)$.*

The argument is trivial for space bounds above $\log n$. Below $\log n$, however, we do not have enough space to count up to $(n+2) \cdot c^{s(n)+1}$ and accept if the machine A rejects by cycling. Still, Sipser [22] showed by an elegant argument that we cannot get into a cycle running a *Backward Depth-First Search* from a configuration k that is known to be out of any cycle, e.g., if k is a halting configuration. By "backward" we mean examining the tree of all possible predecessors of k. If the machine uses space $s(n)$, then this search can be carried out in $O(s(n))$ space, since the depth-first search does not require an extra space as the previous nodes can be computed from the machine transitions.

Theorem 9 *Let $x \in \{strong, demon\}$. Then x-NSPACE(s(n)) = co-x-NSPACE(s(n)), for each $s(n) \geq \log n$.*

The proof is based on the Immerman-Szelepcsényi method of *Inductive Counting* [16, 24], which generates all configurations reachable from the initial configuration and accepts only if none of these is accepting. Since we visit all reachable configurations, this gives *strong-NSPACE(s(n)) = co-strong-NSPACE(s(n))*. The method can be adapted for the demon machines.

The most frequently cited application using constructibility is *Diagonalization*. In 1965, Stearns, Hartmanis, and Lewis showed in their pioneering work [23] that, with a small increase in space, the deterministic machines can solve new problems that could not be solved before. More precisely, there exists $L \in$ *strong-DSPACE($s_2(n)$) − strong-DSPACE($s_1(n)$)*, if $s_2(n)$ is space constructible, $s_2(n) \geq \log n$, and it grows faster than $s_1(n)$ on at least one infinite sequence of n's, i.e., if $\inf_{n\to\infty} s_1(n)/s_2(n) = 0$.

Using the Backward Depth-First Search, we have the diagonalization below $\log n$. Further, by the Inductive Counting, we have an easy extension for the nondeterministic space bounds, if $s_2(n) \geq \log n$. Without the inductive counting, the proof could be very cumbersome (*see* e.g. [15]). We do not know whether the inductive counting can be used below

$\log n$. However, by [10] (*see* also Thm.30 below), we can use the inductive counting below $\log n$ for bounded languages, e.g., for subsets of 1^*01^*. This is sufficient for us.

The *approximate constructibility* of the larger bound $s_2(n)$ suffices for a strongly bounded machine to diagonalize even *against weakly bounded machines*, hence, the complement of the larger bound $s_2(n)$ is essential, since *weak-SPACE($s_1(n)$)* need not be closed under complement (*see* Thm.12 below).

Theorem 10 *Let $s_1(n) \geq 1$ and let $s_2(n)$ be fully space approximable. Then*
(a) $\inf_{n\to\infty} s_1(n)/s_2(n) = 0$ *implies strong-SPACE($s_2(n)$) − weak-SPACE($s_1(n)$) $\neq \emptyset$,*
(b) $\lim_{n\to\infty} s_1(n)/s_2(n) = 0$ *implies weak-SPACE($s_1(n)$) $\subset$ strong-SPACE($s_2(n)$).*
This holds both for the deterministic and nondeterministic space bounds.

Proof. We shall review (a) for the nondeterministic case. Let $s_2'(n)$ be a fully space constructible function approximating $s_2(n)$, i.e., $s_2'(n) \in \Theta(s_2(n))$. Define

$L_\Delta = \{1^k01^\ell;$ such that *(i)* $\log k \leq s_2'(k+1+\ell)$, and *(ii)* each computation path of T_k on the input 1^k01^ℓ either rejects, loops, or uses space $s > s_2'(k+1+\ell)/\alpha(k)\}$,

where $T_1, T_2, T_3, \ldots$ denotes the enumeration of nondeterministic Turing machines and $\alpha(k)$ equals to the logarithm of the cardinality of the work tape alphabet of T_k.

First, $L_\Delta^c = 1^*01^* - L_\Delta$ is in *strong-NSPACE($s_2'(n)$)*. Construct $s_2'(k+1+\ell)$ and accept if $\log k > s_2'(k+1+\ell)$. Otherwise, having loaded the binary code for T_k on the work tape, accept if T_k has an accepting computation path not using more than $s_2'(k+1+\ell)/\alpha(k)$ space on the input 1^k01^ℓ. Reject if the chosen computation path exceeds this space limit. Note that $s \cdot \alpha(k)$ space is sufficient to simulate the s bounded computation paths of T_k. This gives that $L_\Delta^c \in$ *strong-NSPACE($s_2'(n)$)*. But then, by Thm.30, $L_\Delta \in$ *strong-NSPACE($s_2'(n)$)*, since $L_\Delta^c \subseteq 1^*01^*$. Finally, $L_\Delta \in$ *strong-NSPACE($s_2(n)$)*, using $s_2'(n) \in \Theta(s_2(n))$.

Now, let T_{k_0} be a nondeterministic weakly $O(s_1(n))$ space bounded machine. Since $s_2'(n) \in \Theta(s_2(n))$, we have $\inf_{n\to\infty} s_1(n)/s_2'(n) = 0$, and therefore, for each fixed k_0, there exists $\ell' \geq 0$ such that $s_1(k_0+1+\ell')/s_2'(k_0+1+\ell') < 1/(\alpha(k_0)\cdot\log k_0)$. This gives

$$\begin{array}{rcl} \log k_0 & \leq & s_2'(k_0+1+\ell'), \\ s_1(k_0+1+\ell') & < & s_2'(k_0+1+\ell')/\alpha(k_0), \end{array}$$

using $s_1(n) \geq 1$. Clearly, $1^{k_0}01^{\ell'}$ is in $L(T_{k_0})$ if and only if there exists an accepting path of T_{k_0} on the input $1^{k_0}01^{\ell'}$ that uses space below $s_1(k_0+1+\ell') < s_2'(k_0+1+\ell')/\alpha(k_0)$. On the other hand, $1^{k_0}01^{\ell'}$ is in L_Δ if and only if each computation path of T_{k_0} on the input $1^{k_0}01^{\ell'}$ either rejects, loops, or uses space above $s_2'(k_0+1+\ell')/\alpha(k_0)$. From this we have that T_{k_0} does not recognize L_Δ. □

Corollary 11 *If* $\lim_{n\to\infty} s_1(n)/s_2(n) = 0$ *and* $s_1(n) \geq 1$ *is constructible in demon-$s_2(n)$ space, then demon-SPACE($s_1(n)$) $\subset$ demon-SPACE($s_2(n)$).*

This is the only application so far where the exact constructibility *must* be used, even if $s_2(n)$ grows much faster than $s_1(n)$. For example, consider $H(n)$ defined by (2). It is easy to see that *demon-SPACE($H(n)$)* contains languages that are not recursively enumerable and therefore *demon-SPACE($H(n)$) $\not\subseteq$ demon-SPACE(2^n)*, though $H(n) \in \Theta(n^2)$.

We do not know whether $s_2(n) \geq \log n$ can be discarded if the witness language is a tally set. This is used to prove that *weak-SPACE* is not closed under complement [26].

Theorem 12 *For each two fully space constructible functions with* $\lim_{n\to\infty} s_1(n)/s_2(n) = 0$ *and* $s_1(n) \geq 1$, *there exists a function $s_\Delta(n)$ such that weak-SPACE($s_\Delta(n)$) $\neq$ co-weak-SPACE($s_\Delta(n)$), with $s_1(n) \leq s_\Delta(n) \leq s_2(n)$. This holds both for the nondeterministic and deterministic classes.*

Proof. Let

$L_\upsilon = \{1^n;$ such that *(i)* $n = 2^k(2\ell+1)$, $k \le s_2(n)$, for some $k, \ell \in N$, and *(ii)* each computation path of T_k on the input 1^n either rejects, loops, or uses space $s > s_2(n)/\alpha(k)\,\}$.

$L_\upsilon \subsetneq 1^*$ is a tally variant of $L_\Delta \subsetneq 1^*01^*$ (*see* Thm.10), by the use of a suitable pairing function. It is easy to see that $L_\upsilon \in$ *strong-SPACE*$(s_2(n))$ $-$ *weak-SPACE*$(s_1(n))$.

The assumption $s_2(n) \in \Omega(\log n)$ is hidden in $\lim_{n\to\infty} s_1(n)/s_2(n) = 0$ combined with the full space constructibility of $s_2(n)$. If $s_2(n) \notin \Omega(\log n)$, then, for a sufficiently large n_0, we have $s_2(n_0) = s_2(n_0 + in_0!)$ for each $i \in N$, by [9, Thm.3] (*see* also Sect.4). Hence, $\lim_{n\to\infty} s_1(n)/s_2(n) \ne 0$ for $s_1(n) \ge 1$. Now, define

$$s_\Delta(n) = \begin{cases} s_2(n) & \text{if } 1^n \in L_\upsilon\,, \\ s_1(n) & \text{otherwise}\,. \end{cases}$$

$L_\upsilon \in$ *weak-SPACE*$(s_\Delta(n))$, since $L_\upsilon \in$ *strong-SPACE*$(s_2(n))$ and for each $1^n \in L_\upsilon$ we have $s_\Delta(n) = s_2(n)$. On the other hand, we do not care for $s_\Delta(n)$ if $1^n \notin L_\upsilon$. But we have also $L_\upsilon^c \notin$ *weak-SPACE*$(s_\Delta(n))$ or else $L_\upsilon^c \in$ *strong-SPACE*$(s_1(n))$: Construct $s_1(n)$ and simulate A^c, the hypothetical weakly $s_\Delta(n)$ space bounded recognizer for L_υ^c. Note that A^c must have an accepting path within $s_1(n)$ space for $1^n \in L_\upsilon^c$. Thus, accept if and only if A^c does have such path. This gives $L_\upsilon^c \in$ *strong-SPACE*$(s_1(n))$. But then $L_\upsilon \in$ *strong-SPACE*$(s_1(n))$ (even if $s_1(n)$ is below $\log n$, since $L_\upsilon \subsetneq 1^*$, using Thm.30), which is a contradiction. □

Corollary 13 *There exist (monotone) recursive functions $s_\Delta(n)$ such that (a) $s_\Delta(n)$ are not fully space approximable, (b) strong-SPACE$(s_\Delta(n)) \subset$ weak-SPACE$(s_\Delta(n)) \subset$ demon-SPACE$(s_\Delta(n))$.*

Since both *strong-SPACE*$(s_\Delta(n))$ and *demon-SPACE*$(s_\Delta(n))$ are closed under complement for tally sets, by Thm.30 or 8, they are separated from *weak-SPACE*$(s_\Delta(n))$. Hence, $s_\Delta(n)$ is not approximable, or else *weak-SPACE*$(s_\Delta(n))$ = *strong-SPACE*$(s_\Delta(n))$. Finally, $s_\Delta(n)$ is *monotone* if $s_2(n) \le s_1(n+1)$, e.g., consider $s_1(n) = 2^{n^2}$ and $s_2(n) = 2^{n^2+2n+1}$.

Theorem 14 [26] *(a) For each $s(n)$, weak-DSPACE$(s(n))$ = co-weak-DSPACE$(s(n))$ if and only if weak-DSPACE$(s(n))$ = strong-DSPACE$(s(n))$. (b) For each $s(n) \ge \log n$, weak-NSPACE$(s(n))$ = co-weak-NSPACE$(s(n))$ if and only if weak-NSPACE$(s(n))$ = strong-NSPACE$(s(n))$.*

Proof. The "$\Leftarrow$" part is obvious, since *strong-SPACE*$(s(n))$ is closed under complement. Conversely, *weak-NSPACE*$(s(n))$ = *co-weak-NSPACE*$(s(n))$ implies *weak-NSPACE*$(s(n)) \subseteq$ *strong-NSPACE*$(s(n))$, hence, these classes are equal:

Suppose that $L \in$ *weak-NSPACE*$(s(n))$. By hypothesis, we have two weakly $s(n)$ space bounded machines A, A^c for L, L^c, respectively. We design a strongly bounded machine A' for L: Beginning with $s = \log n$, *(i)* A' accepts if A has an accepting path not using space above s, *(ii)* A' rejects if A^c has such path, *(iii)* A' extends the space from s to $s+1$ and repeats (i) and (ii), only if neither A nor A^c have accepting paths within the space s. This is verified by the inductive counting applied to the both machines.

The argument for (a) uses the backward search instead of the inductive counting. □

Corollary 15 *$L \in$ strong-SPACE$(s(n))$ if and only if $L, L^c \in$ weak-SPACE$(s(n))$, for each $s(n) \ge \log n$.*

The above corollary clearly shows that the relation of *strong-SPACE(s(n))* to *weak-SPACE(s(n))* replicates, in a much smaller scale, the *Recursive : Recursively Enumerable* relation, regardless of whether we consider deterministic or nondeterministic machines. Removing all $s(n)$-space limitations from the Thm.14, we get the classical proof stating that L is recursive if and only if L, L^c are recursively enumerable. This observation is also supported by the behavior at the "topmost" space level:

Let $D_1, D_2, \ldots$ be the enumeration of deterministic Turing machines and $w_1, w_2, \ldots$ be the enumeration of strings in $\{0,1\}^*$ such that $|w_i| \leq |w_j|$ for $i \leq j$. Define

$$\begin{aligned} S_{ij} &= \begin{cases} \text{the space used by } D_i \text{ on input } w_j, \text{ if } D_i \text{ halts on } w_j, \\ 1, \text{ if } D_i \text{ does not halt on } w_j, \end{cases} \\ G(n) &= \max\{S_{ij};\ \text{for } i,j \text{ satisfying } i \leq j \text{ and } |w_j| \leq n\}. \end{aligned}$$

Theorem 16 *(a) strong-DSPACE(G(n)) = strong-NSPACE(G(n)) = REC (recursive sets), (b) weak-DSPACE(G(n)) = weak-NSPACE(G(n)) = RE (recursively enumerable sets), (c) RE ⊂ demon-DSPACE(G(n)).*

To clarify the role of demon machines and their connection with the space constructibility, consider the relation, that extends far beyond the range of all tractable computations:

Theorem 17 *(a) Let $s(n) \leq d^{d^n}$, for some constant d. Then $s(n)$ is fully space constructible if and only if strong-SPACE(s(n)) = weak-SPACE(s(n)) = demon-SPACE(s(n)), and if and only if demon-SPACE(s(n)) ⊆ weak-SPACE(s(n)).*

(b) Let $s(n) \leq d^{d^{d^n}}$. Then demon-SPACE(s(n)) ⊆ weak-SPACE(s(n)) implies that $s(n)$ is fully space approximable and that strong-SPACE(s(n)) = weak-SPACE(s(n)) = demon-SPACE(s(n)).

Proof. (a) We first present the argument for $d=2$. The "⇒" part is obvious, by Coroll.6. Let $\mathrm{str}(x) \in \{0,1\}^*$ denote the binary string representation of the integer $x \in \mathbb{N}$. Define

$L_{\approx} = \{\mathrm{str}\,x \in \{0,1\}^*;\ x = \lfloor \log s(n) \rfloor\}$,

$L_0 = \{\mathrm{str}\,x \in \{0,1\}^*;\ \text{the } x\text{th bit of } s(n) \text{ is } 0\}$.

Clearly, $L_{\approx}, L_0 \in$ *demon-SPACE(s(n))*: Having marked-off $s(n)$ space, compute the binary representation for $\lfloor \log s(n) \rfloor$ and compare with the significant digits of the input $\mathrm{str}\,x$.

By hypothesis, we have $A_{\approx}, A_0$, the *weak-SPACE(s(n)) = weak-SPACE($2^{\lfloor \log s(n) \rfloor}$)* recognizers for $L_{\approx}, L_0$, respectively. The machine A_s constructing $s(n)$ works as follows. For $x = 1,2,3,\ldots$, *(i)* compute $\mathrm{str}\,x$ (no leading zeros), mark-off 2^x space on the work tape, and simulate $A_{\approx}$ on the input $0^{n-|\mathrm{str}\,x|}\mathrm{str}(x)$. If $A_{\approx}$ does not have an accepting path within the space 2^x, repeat for $x+1$. If $x = \lfloor \log s(n) \rfloor$, then $0^{n-|\mathrm{str}\,x|}\mathrm{str}(x)$ is accepted in $2^{\lfloor \log s(n) \rfloor} = 2^x$ space by $A_{\approx}$. This happens for some $\mathrm{str}\,x \in \{0,1\}^*$ of length at most n, since $s(n) \leq 2^{2^n}$.

(ii) Finally, A_s "tunes-in" the exact value of $s(n)$: A_s simulates A_0 in the $2^{\lfloor \log s(n) \rfloor}$ space and computes the xth bit of $s(n)$, for each $x = 0, \ldots, \lfloor \log s(n) \rfloor$.

An $s(n)$ far below $\log n$ does not harm either, even if we consider the constructibility by nondeterministic machines: A_s needs only $O(\log\log s(n))$ space to store the significant part $\mathrm{str}\,x$ but no space is required for the tally segment of the leading zeros $0^{n-|\mathrm{str}\,x|}$. We use the variant of the inductive counting described in Thm.30, which works in space $2^x + \log(|\mathrm{str}\,x|) \in O(2^{\lfloor \log s(n) \rfloor})$ for the input $0^{n-|\mathrm{str}\,x|}\mathrm{str}(x)$.

It is easy to generalize the above argument to any $d>2$; instead of the binary numbers, we use the base d. The more sophisticated argument for (b) is based on the fact that $s(n) \leq d^{d^{d^n}}$ can be approximated by $d^{\tilde{s}(n)}$, with $\tilde{s}(n) = \lfloor \log_d s(n) \rfloor \leq d^{d^n}$. □

The above theorem indicates that, along with n, $\log n$, and $\log\log n$, there may exist another "critical" boundaries.

3 Traveling in Graphs — the "Hardest" Problems

In 1970 [21], Savitch observed that *GAP*, the set of directed graphs having a path connecting the first and last nodes, is *NSPACE(log n)* complete. The directed graph $G = (V, E)$, with $V \subseteq \{1, \ldots, n\}$ and $E \subseteq V \times V$, can be represented by a Boolean $n \times n$ adjacency matrix written on the tape row by row, i.e.,

$$\mathbb{E} = e_{11} \ldots e_{1n} \sharp e_{21} \ldots e_{2n} \sharp \ldots \ \ldots \sharp e_{n1} \ldots e_{nn},$$

with $e_{ij} = 1$ if and only if the edge $i \to j \in E$. Then the language *GAP* can be defined as a set of matrices with the reflexive transitive closure having $e^*_{1n} = 1$ in the upper right corner.

Lemma 18 *(a) The language GAP $\in$ NLOG = NSPACE(log n).*
(b) GAP is complete for NLOG under FLOG = FSPACE(log n) reductions.

Proof. (a) The machine N_{GAP} guesses the path from 1 to n. First, let $i = 1$. Then, for the "current" node i, N_{GAP} finds the ith row of the matrix and replaces nondeterministically i by j, for some j satisfying $e_{ij} = 1$. This is repeated until N_{GAP} reaches $i = n$.

(b) Now, let A be an arbitrary *NLOG* machine. For any input w of length n, we can consider a directed graph $G_{A,w}$ the edges of which represent the single computation steps of A on w and the nodes are labeled by the numbers corresponding to the binary coded configurations of A using at most $O(\log n)$ space.

The finite control state, the content of the work tape, and the head positions can be decoded from the binary strings representing the row or column numbers. Note that the input w is not included in the configurations (*see* Def.1), hence, the node numbers are in range $1, 2, 3, \ldots, 2^{d \cdot \log n}$, for some machine dependent constant d.

We can now construct a log-space transducer F_A that prints on the one-way output tape the matrix $\mathbb{E}_{A,w}$. F_A simply executes two nested loops, for $i, j = 1, \ldots, 2^{d \cdot \log n}$, and prints $e_{ij} = 1$ or 0, depending on whether there is a legal single-step move from the configuration i to j, consulting its input tape for the symbol scanned by A in the configuration i.

Thus, for each *NLOG* acceptor A, we have a deterministic *FLOG* transducer F_A, such that its output $w' = F_A(w) \in GAP$ if and only if $w \in L(A)$, for each $w \in \{0, 1\}^*$. □

Lemma 19 *If GAP $\in$ DLOG, then DLOG = NLOG.*

Proof. For a given *NLOG* machine A, the corresponding deterministic A' simulates the deterministic *GAP* recognizer D_{GAP} on $w' = F_A(w)$ and accepts if and only if $w' \in GAP$.

Since A' does not have enough space to store w', the *FLOG* transducer F_A is used to imitate a virtual input tape with w': A' reruns F_A on w each time the ith cell of w' (for some i) is needed to simulate the next step of D_{GAP}. A' remembers only the work tapes for F_A, D_{GAP}, and the tape positions of all heads for the both machines. Since w' is of length $2^{d \cdot \log n} \times 2^{d \cdot \log n}$ and D_{GAP} is a *DLOG* machine, an $O(\log n)$ space suffices for A'. □

An interesting extension of the above results has been used in [13] to show that the logarithmic space does not have contradictory relativizations: *DLOG* = *NLOG* if and only if, for each oracle $\mathcal{A}$, $DLOG^{S(\mathcal{A})} = NLOG^{S(\mathcal{A})}$. The argument hides a slightly stronger statement than claimed, namely, *DLOG* = *NLOG* if and only if $DLOG^{S(\cdot)} \equiv NLOG^{S(\cdot)}$, that is, the construction of the deterministic machine does not depend on the oracle $\mathcal{A}$.

Definition 20 Let $C_1^{S(\cdot)}$, $C_2^{S(\cdot)}$ be two classes of oracle machines. We say that $C_1^{S(\cdot)}$ *and* $C_2^{S(\cdot)}$ *are equivalent*, written $C_1^{S(\cdot)} \equiv C_2^{S(\cdot)}$, if, for each machine $M_1^{S(\cdot)} \in C_1^{S(\cdot)}$, there exists $M_2^{S(\cdot)} \in C_2^{S(\cdot)}$ such that $L(M_1^{S(\mathcal{A})}) = L(M_2^{S(\mathcal{A})})$, for each oracle $\mathcal{A}$, and vice versa.

Note that to separate $DSPACE(s(n))^{S(\cdot)}$ from $NSPACE(s(n))^{S(\cdot)}$ it is sufficient to present a machine $N \in NSPACE(s(n))^{S(\cdot)}$ such that for each $D \in DSPACE(s(n))^{S(\cdot)}$ we can find an oracle $\mathcal{A}$ satisfying $L(N^{S(\mathcal{A})}) \neq L(D^{S(\mathcal{A})})$. On the other hand, to negate $(\forall \mathcal{A})(DSPACE(s(n))^{S(\mathcal{A})} = NSPACE(s(n))^{S(\mathcal{A})})$, we must show, for some $\mathcal{A}$ and some $N \in NSPACE(s(n))^{S(\cdot)}$, that $L(N^{S(\mathcal{A})}) \neq L(D^{S(\mathcal{A})})$ for each $D \in DSPACE(s(n))^{S(\cdot)}$.

Theorem 21 [13] *GAP is complete for $NLOG^{S(\cdot)} = NSPACE(\log n)^{S(\cdot)}$ under $FLOG^{S(\cdot)} = FSPACE(\log n)^{S(\cdot)}$ reductions.*

Proof. Let $N^{S(\cdot)}$ be an arbitrary $NLOG^{S(\cdot)}$ machine. For each oracle $\mathcal{A}$ and input w, we can again compute a directed graph of configurations $G^{\mathcal{A}}_{N,w}$, of size $2^{d\cdot\log n} \times 2^{d\cdot\log n}$. Now the oracle query tape and its head position are also incorporated into the configuration.

Again, the deterministic $FLOG^{S(\cdot)}$ transducer $F^{S(\cdot)}_N$ printing $\mathbb{E}^{\mathcal{A}}_{N,w}$ writes $e_{ij} = 1$ if and only if there is a legal single-step move from the configuration i to j, but it consults its oracle if $N^{S(\cdot)}$ enters a query state (recall that the content of the query tape can be decoded from i). Thus, $F^{S(\cdot)}_N$ prints $w' = F^{S(\mathcal{A})}_N(w) \in GAP$ if and only if $w \in L(N^{S(\mathcal{A})})$. □

Theorem 22 *The following statements are equivalent: (a) $GAP \in DLOG$, (b) $DLOG = NLOG$, (c) $DLOG^{S(\mathcal{A})} = NLOG^{S(\mathcal{A})}$, for each oracle $\mathcal{A}$, (d) $DLOG^{S(\cdot)} \equiv NLOG^{S(\cdot)}$.*

Proof. The "⇐" part is obvious, if $DLOG^{S(\cdot)} \equiv NLOG^{S(\cdot)}$, then $DLOG^{S(\mathcal{A})} = NLOG^{S(\mathcal{A})}$, for each oracle $\mathcal{A}$. For $\mathcal{A} = \emptyset$ we get $DLOG = NLOG$, hence, $GAP \in DLOG$.

The rest of the proof mirrors Lem.19: For a given $NLOG^{S(\cdot)}$ machine $N^{S(\cdot)}$, the corresponding $D^{S(\cdot)}$ machine again simulates the deterministic GAP recognizer D_{GAP}, now using the deterministic $FLOG^{S(\cdot)}$ transducer $F^{S(\cdot)}_N$ of Thm.21, equipped with an additional query tape. $D^{S(\mathcal{A})}$ accepts w if and only if $w' = F^{S(\mathcal{A})}_N(w) \in GAP$. □

An important application using constructibility is the *Padding Argument* of Savitch [21], used to translate results from some low complexity levels to higher levels. It can be easily extended to the relativized classes; we only equip all machines with the query tape. The new assumption $s_1(n) \leq d \cdot \max\{s_1(1), s_1(2), \ldots, s_1(n-1)\}$ does not force $s_1(n)$ to approximate some "smooth" curve so strictly than does the usual $s_1(n) \leq d \cdot s_1(n-1)$. Still, $s_1(n) \leq d^n$.

Theorem 23 *Let $s_1(n) \geq \log n$ be fully space constructible, such that, for some constant $d \geq 1$, $s_1(n) \leq d \cdot \max\{s_1(1), s_1(2), \ldots, s_1(n-1)\}$. Then x-$DSPACE(s_1(n))^{S(\cdot)} \equiv x$-$NSPACE(s_1(n))^{S(\cdot)}$ implies y-$DSPACE(s_2(n))^{S(\cdot)} \equiv y$-$NSPACE(s_2(n))^{S(\cdot)}$, for each $s_2(n) \geq s_1(n)$ and each of the modes $x, y \in \{strong, weak, demon\}$.*

The assumptions of the above theorem can be improved. For example, we know from [25] that $DSPACE(\log\log n) = NSPACE(\log\log n)$ implies $DSPACE(\log n) = NSPACE(\log n)$. There exists also a partial "downward" translation. For example, Savitch [21] observed that $DLBA = NLBA$ if and only if $DLOG \cap 1^* = NLOG \cap 1^*$. In Sect.4, we shall improve the above results and show that the "downward" translation begins at $s(n) \geq \log n$, which gives $s(\log n) \geq \log\log n$. A very strong result holds for $s_1(n) = \log n$ combined with the constructibility of $s_2(n)$ [13]:

Theorem 24 *$DLOG = NLOG$ if and only if $DSPACE(s(n))^{S(\mathcal{A})} = NSPACE(s(n))^{S(\mathcal{A})}$, for each fully space constructible $s(n) \geq \log n$ and each oracle $\mathcal{A}$.*

The "⇒" part is obvious, by Thm.23. Conversely, $GAP \in NLOG - DLOG$ yields an oracle separating $DSPACE(s(n))^{S(\mathcal{A})}$ from $NSPACE(s(n))^{S(\mathcal{A})}$. For details, *see* [13].

4 Divisibility Checking — the "Easiest" Problems

This section establishes the importance of even the lowest possible level of space bounded computations. From the early works [23, 14] we know that the recognition of a nonregular language in *strong-SPACE(s(n))* implies $s(n) \notin o(\log\log n)$. Later [1], the same was shown for *weak-SPACE(s(n))*. On the other hand, the demon machines can recognize nonregular languages within $o(\log\log n)$ space, e.g.,

$$L_{\log\log\log} = \{a^n;\ n \bmod \lceil \log\log\log n \rceil = 0\},$$

which belongs to *demon-DSPACE(log log log log n)*. This shows that the gap between the constant space and $\log\log n$ is due to the constructibility properties. The gap is known to be tight, since we have fully space constructible functions in $O(\log\log n)$, e.g.,

$$\text{frs}(n) = \lfloor \text{logarithm of the first integer that does not divide } n \rfloor.$$

The first example of a nonregular language in *strong-DSPACE(log log n)* appears in [23]. There exist also tally languages in *strong-DSPACE(log log n)*, e.g., consider [3]

$$L_{2^{\text{P}}} = \{1^n;\ \text{the first integer not dividing } n \text{ is a power of } 2\}.$$

Still, the number of bits we have to transfer is at least $\log n$. Formally, *(a)* if a nonregular language L is accepted by a *one-way* nondeterministic strongly $s(n)$ space bounded machine, then $s(n) \notin o(\log n)$ [14]. *(b)* We have $s(n) \cdot i(n) \notin o(\log n)$ for the product of the space and the number of input head reversals, for each strongly bounded *two-way* machine. It is interesting that this bound is also tight, since the language $L_{2^{\text{P}}}$ can be accepted within $O(\log\log n)$ space and $O(\log n/\log\log n)$ input head reversals simultaneously [4, 5].

Even between $\log\log n$ and $\log n$, there is no unbounded fully space constructible function $s(n)$ that is monotone [8]. By (1), any given *strong-DSPACE(o(log n))* machine A must enter a loop when it traverses the whole input 1^n, for a sufficiently large n.

A loop of length ℓ is a computation path beginning in configuration $<q, i>$ and ending in $<q, i+\ell>$, visiting neither of the margins.

Since the length of the loop ℓ is less than n, $n!$ is an integer multiple of ℓ, and therefore A reaches the same configuration at the other margin if the input 1^n is replaced by $1^{n+n!}$. The computations differ only in the number of the loop iterations. By an easy induction on the number of visits at the end markers, we have that A cannot distinguish 1^n from $1^{n+n!}$. In particular, A marks-off the same amount of space for the both inputs. Hence, A does not construct e.g. $s(n) = \log\log n$. This "$n \to n+n!$" trick was used first in [23].

Clearly, a nondeterministic machine is far from repeating regularly any loop it gets into, it can jump out by making a nondeterministic decision. Still, by [9], we have that even if a nondeterministic machine A travels across 1^n using too little space s, e.g., with $M^6 = (c^{s+1})^6 < n$, an iteration of a single "short" loop dominates over each traversal. Here c denotes the machine dependent constant satisfying (1). Similarly, we can replace "long U-turns" beginning and ending at the same margin (and not visiting the other one) by "short-cuts" not travelling "too far".

Lemma 25 [9, Lem.3] *If there exists a computation path using at most s space from the configuration $k_1 = <q_1, i_1>$ to the configuration $k_2 = <q_2, i_2>$ on the input 1^n, with $M^6 = (c^{s+1})^6 < n$, such that the input head does not visit either of the margins in the meantime, then the shortest path from k_1 to k_2 never moves the input head more than M^2 positions to the right of* $\max\{i_1, i_2\}$, *nor M^2 positions to the left of* $\min\{i_1, i_2\}$.

Theorem 26 [9, Thm.1] *If $M^6 = (c^{s+1})^6 < n$, then each computation path using at most s space from the configuration $k_1 = <q_1, 0>$ to $k_2 = <q_2, n+1>$ on the input 1^n, visiting the margins only in k_1 and k_2, can be replaced by an equivalent path such that*

(a) having traversed s_1 input tape positions,

(b) gets into a memory state q in which a loop of length ℓ is iterated r times, and

(c) then traverses the rest of the input tape of length s_2,

for some s_1, ℓ, r, s_2 satisfying $M^2+1 \leq s_1 \leq M^4$, $M^2+1 \leq s_2 \leq M^4$, and $1 \leq \ell \leq M$. (See Fig.1). The same holds for traversals from right to left.

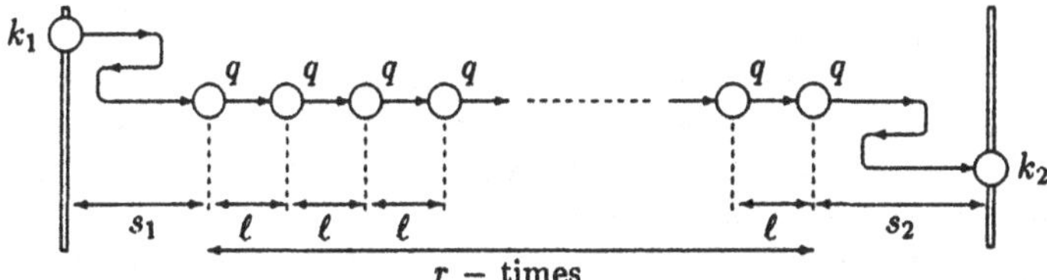

Figure 1: Dominant loop

For such "pseudo-deterministic" computation paths, we can apply the "$n \to n+n!$" method and show that even the nondeterministic machines cannot construct monotone functions below $\log n$ [9, Thm.3]. Theorem 26 has several other applications [2, 9, 10] and later it was generalized to alternating machines [11, 12, 17, 18]. Our next extension will be different, we shall reduce nondeterminism to a "deterministic-but-left-end-marker" machine:

Theorem 27 *Let $x \in \{strong, weak, demon\}$. Then, for each x-$s(n)$ space bounded nondeterministic machine A recognizing a language $L \subseteq 1^*$, there exists $d \geq 1$ and an equivalent $O(s(n))$ space bounded machine A' such that, for each input 1^n, the input head leaves the left margin only if*

(a) A' wants to check if $n \bmod i = j$, for some $i, j \leq d^{s(n)+1}$,

(b) or A' wants to check if $n \leq j$, for some $j \leq d^{s(n)+1}$.

Moreover, if A is deterministic, then A' is also deterministic.

Remark Before passing further, we have to *define formally* what we mean by saying that *A' wants to check* (a) or (b). Most important, A' uses two work tapes:

(i) A binary coded pair $<i, j>$ is written on the second work tape each time A' leaves the left margin of the input, $i = 0$ if the condition (b) is checked. A' leaves the left margin only in the special control state $r_?$ and the head of the first work tape does not move from its initial position until the input head returns back to the left end marker. (Hence, A' does not rely on any other information but $<i, j>$, using the *second* work tape only).

(ii) A' returns back to left margin of the input in one of the two finite control states r_{yes}, r_{no}, depending on whether the checked condition is satisfied. The second work tape is cleared before A' returns back. (Hence, A' performs no additional computations).

Proof. The machine A' simulates A until it leaves the end marker. Then A' first checks if $M^6 = (c^{s+1})^6 \geq n$, where s denotes the current amount of space used by A.

If YES, then $\log n \in O(s)$ and we have enough space to simulate A directly. A' checks $j = M^6, M^6-1, M^6-2, \ldots, 0$ if $j \geq n$ until it finds $j_0 < n$. Then $j_0+1 = n$ and A' completes the simulation not moving from the left end marker any more.

If NO, then $M^6 < n$, and therefore each path *(i)* either returns back to the same end marker not moving farther than M^2 positions away, by Lem.25, *(ii)* or it traverses across the input iterating a single loop, by Thm.26. The space will not be extended from s to $s+1$ in the meantime, by Lem.2. A' first guesses between (i) and (ii). The situation (i) can be simulated by A' within $O(s)$ space, not moving the input head at all.

The situation (ii) is simulated as follows: Let q_1 be the current memory state, say, at the left end marker, i.e., $k_1 = <q_1, 0>$. Guess $s_1, s_2 \in \{M^2+1, \ldots, M^4\}$, $\ell \in \{1, \ldots, M\}$, a loop memory state q, and a target configuration $k_2 = <q_2, n+1>$. Check if

(1) $<q,s_1>$ is reachable from $k_1 = <q_1,0>$,

(2) $<q,s_1+\ell>$ is reachable from $<q,s_1>$, visiting neither of the margins,

(3) $k_2 = <q_2,n+1>$ is reachable from $<q,n+1-s_2>$,

(4) $s_1 + r\cdot\ell + s_2 = n+1$, for some $r \geq 0$.

(*See* Thm.26 and Fig.1 for details). If all tests above are successful, A' goes ahead with q_2 as the "current" memory state at the right end marker.

Conditions (1)–(3) can be verified by A' within $O(s)$ space not using the input head at all, since A does not move farther than $M^4+M+M^2 < M^6$ positions away from the left/right end marker along any of the above paths, by Lem.25, and A' can remember all input head positions relative to the nearest end marker.

Condition (4) is equivalent to $(s_1+s_2-1) \bmod \ell = n \bmod \ell$. Thus A' checks if $n \bmod i = j$, for $i = \ell$ and $j = (s_1+s_2-1) \bmod \ell$.

Carefully implemented, we can satisfy the strong requirements mentioned in the Remark above: Before checking (a) or (b), a copy of i,j, as well as the current and target configurations k_1, k_2 are recorded on the first work tape. Since A' "forgets" by switching to $r_?$, the subprogram beginning in $r_?$ first checks if $i = 0$ to detect which kind of test should be performed on 1^n. r_{yes}, r_{no} can restore the recorded information and proceed further.

The basic difference for the deterministic case is that, instead of guessing s_1, s_2, ℓ, q, and k_2, A' can iterate deterministically over all possible values and find the combination of s_1, s_2, ℓ, q, and k_2 satisfying (1)–(4). Since A is deterministic, these values are unique for each k_1, provided we minimize s_1, s_2, and ℓ. Hence, k_2 is unique for k_1. □

The above idea can be extended to the binary inputs with low information content, we can think of $w \in \{0,1\}^*$ as a sequence of unary strings separated by delimiters, i.e., $w = 1^{h_1}01^{h_2}0\ldots01^{h_m}$, for some $h_1, h_2, \ldots, h_m \geq 0$, with $m \geq 1$.

Definition 28 A language $L \subseteq \{0,1\}^*$ is *$z(n)$–bounded*, if each $w \in L$ of length n contains at most $z(n)$ zeros. L is *bounded*, if it is $z(n)$–bounded for some constant function z. L is *tally*, if it is 0–bounded, i.e., if $L \subseteq 1^*$.

Theorem 29 *Let $x \in \{strong, weak, demon\}$. Then, for each x-$s(n)$ space bounded Turing machine A recognizing $L \subseteq \{0,1\}^*$, there exists an equivalent $O(s(n))$ space bounded machine A' making nondeterministic decisions only if the input head scans a zero or the left end marker.*

Proof. The construction is very similar to Thm.27. A' computes the traversals of A across each segment $\ldots01^{h_e}0\ldots$ with the input head positioned at the left zero of the current segment. A' scans 1^{h_e} only to check if $h_e \leq j$, or $h_e \bmod i = j$, for some $i,j \leq d^{s(n)+1}$. □

Theorem 30 *(a) The space required by the Inductive Counting can be reduced from $O(s(n)+\log n)$ to $O(s(n)+\log z)$, where z denotes the number of zeros in the input word.*

(b) Let $L \subseteq \{0,1\}^*$ be $z(n)$–bounded, with $\log z(n)$ fully constructible in $O(s(n)+\log z(n))$ space. Then $L \in x$-NSPACE$(s(n))$ implies $L^c \in x$-NSPACE$(s(n)+\log z(n))$, for $x \in \{strong, demon\}$. If $z(n) \leq d^{s(n)}$, for some constant d, then $L^c \in x$-NSPACE$(s(n))$.

Proof. We can modify the Inductive Counting procedure so that it generates and counts all reachable configurations that scan zeros on the input tape. Instead of single computation steps, it uses induction on the number of times the input head scans zero. By Thm.29, the traversal of a segment $01^{h_e}0$ becomes a single deterministic macro-step while the input head position is measured by the number of segments lying to the left. (For details, *see* [10]). □

Note that, for bounded languages with constant $z(n)$, we have the closure under complement for each $s(n)$ independent of whether $s(n)$ is above $\log n$ or space constructible, since the constant functions can be constructed in any space.

The machine A' of Thm.27 handles its second tape as if it were an oracle tape, which changes each machine recognizing a tally input into a relativized *LBA* machine, independent of its original space bound $s(n)$. For each $n \in \mathbb{N}$, let *the characteristic oracle* be defined by

$$\mathcal{A}_n = \{<i,j>;\ n \bmod i = j,\ i > j \geq 0\}\ \cup\ \{<0,j>;\ n \leq j,\ j \geq 0\}.$$

Theorem 31 *For each (non)deterministic Turing machine A recognizing $L \subseteq 1^*$, there exists a (non)deterministic linear bounded oracle machine $B^{S(\cdot)}$ such that, for each $n \geq 0$, the configuration $<q,0>$ is reachable by A on 1^n if and only if $B^{S(\mathcal{A}_n)}$ accepts q, presented as the input for $B^{S(\mathcal{A}_n)}$.*

Proof. The machine $B^{S(\cdot)}$ begins its simulation from the initial configuration of A. $B^{S(\cdot)}$ uses the same technique as A' in Thm.27, but, instead of traversing 1^n, it consults its oracle $\mathcal{A}_n$ to determine if $n \bmod i = j$ or $n \leq j$, for some $i,j \leq d^{s+1}$, where s denotes the current space used by A. $B^{S(\cdot)}$ accepts as soon as it reaches the target $<q,0>$ and rejects if A tries to halt or use more space than $|\,q\,|$. Since A cannot reduce its work tape space, $B^{S(\cdot)}$ uses linear space (in the length of q, the input presented to $B^{S(\cdot)}$). □

This shows that *DLOG* and *NLOG* can be separated by exhibiting a tally set in *NSPACE(s(n)) – DSPACE(s(n))*, for arbitrary $s(n)$.

Theorem 32 *If DLOG = NLOG, then x-DSPACE(s(n)) $\cap\, 1^*$ = x-NSPACE(s(n)) $\cap\, 1^*$, for each $s(n)$ and each of the modes $x \in \{strong, weak, demon\}$.*

Proof. Let A be a nondeterministic $s(n)$ space bounded machine for $L \subseteq 1^*$. By Lem.2, we assume that A has the unique accepting and space extending configurations, for each $s \geq 0$.

Now, let $B^{S(\cdot)}$ be the nondeterministic linear bounded oracle machine of Thm.31, i.e., for each $n \geq 0$ and each q, $B^{S(\mathcal{A}_n)}$ accepts q if and only if $<q,0>$ is reachable by A on 1^n. By Thm.22 and 23, *DLOG* = *NLOG* implies that $DLBA^{S(\cdot)} \equiv NLBA^{S(\cdot)}$, i.e., that $B^{S(\cdot)}$ can be replaced by a deterministic linear bounded machine $\tilde{B}^{S(\cdot)}$ such that $L(\tilde{B}^{S(\mathcal{A})}) = L(B^{S(\mathcal{A})})$, for each oracle $\mathcal{A}$. Among others, $\tilde{B}^{S(\mathcal{A}_n)}$ accepts q if and only if $<q,0>$ is reachable by A on 1^n, for each $n \geq 0$.

Now we construct a deterministic $O(s(n))$ space machine $\tilde{A}$ for L: Beginning with $s = 1$,

(i) $\tilde{A}$ accepts, if the unique accepting configuration of size s is reachable by A on 1^n,

(ii) $\tilde{A}$ rejects, if the unique configuration extending space to $s+1$ is not reachable by A.

(iii) Otherwise, $\tilde{A}$ extends the space from s to $s+1$ and repeats (i) and (ii).

By Lem.2, both the space extension and acceptation take place at the left end marker of A, therefore, $\tilde{A}$ can check (i) or (ii) by simulation of $\tilde{B}^{S(\mathcal{A}_n)}$. If $\tilde{B}^{S(\mathcal{A}_n)}$ makes an oracle query to $\mathcal{A}_n$, i.e., if it enters $r_{\text{in?}}$ with some $<i,j>$ on the query tape, $\tilde{A}$ computes the oracle answer by itself: $\tilde{A}$ checks if $n \bmod i = j$, or $n \leq j$, depending on whether $i = 0$. Thus, $\tilde{A}$ can properly resume the simulation from the corresponding return point r_{yes} or r_{no} so we need no oracle any more.

The resulting machine $\tilde{A}$ is non-relativized, deterministic, and $O(s(n))$ space bounded: For each $s = 1,\ldots,s(n)$, $\tilde{A}$ checks (i) or (ii) for some configuration $<q,0>$ of size s, simulating $\tilde{B}^{S(\mathcal{A}_n)}$. But $\tilde{B}^{S(\mathcal{A}_n)}$ is deterministic, its space bound is linear in $|\,q\,|$, i.e., it works in $O(s)$ space. The oracle answers are also computed in $O(s)$ space. □

Corollary 33 *If DLOG = NLOG, then, for each $s(n)$ and each $x \in \{strong, weak, demon\}$, $L \in$ x-NSPACE(s(n)) implies $L \in$ x-DSPACE(s(n)+log z(n)), for each $z(n)$–bounded language $L \subseteq \{0,1\}^*$, with $\log z(n)$ fully constructible in $O(s(n) + \log z(n))$ space. This gives $L \in$ x-DSPACE(s(n)), if $z(n) \leq d^{s(n)}$, for some constant d.*

The above corollary extends the Thm.32 to bounded languages, but now, for each $w = 1^{h_1}01^{h_2}0\ldots01^{h_m} \in \{0,1\}^*$, we use the oracle

$$\begin{aligned} \mathcal{B}_w = \; & \{<e,i,j>;\ h_e \bmod i = j,\ i > j \geq 0,\ m \geq e \geq 1\} \cup \\ & \{<e,0,j>;\ h_e \leq j,\ j \geq 0,\ m \geq e \geq 1\}. \end{aligned}$$

Corollary 34 *If DLOG = NLOG, then all nondeterministically fully space constructible (approximable) functions are also constructible (approximable) deterministically.*

The argument is obvious, $\tilde{A}$ of Thm.32 stops as soon as it finds s such that the space extending configuration of size s is not reachable by A on 1^n. Now all symbols of the binary input $w \in \{0,1\}^*$ are interpreted as ones.

From 1989 [9] we know that *monotone functions* below $\log n$ cannot be constructed even nondeterministically, but it still did not rule out the possibility of separating non-deterministic and deterministic space classes using the space constructibility [20], with $\{0^k1^n;\ k \leq s(n)\}$ as the desired witness language. The above Coroll.34 clearly shows that this task is much harder than we expected, since even a small $s(n) \in O(\log\log n)$ separates at least *DLOG* from *NLOG*.

We shall now complete the *Big Loop*, showing that the converse is also true: If determinism and nondeterminism are equal for fully space constructible functions in any low level range containing $O(\log\log n)$, then the same holds for all levels, since then *DLOG* = *NLOG*. First, we need some facts about the distribution of the prime numbers.

Lemma 35 *Let p_i denote the ith prime. Then $p_i \in \Theta(i \cdot \log i)$ and the first prime that does not divide n is in $O(\log n)$.*

Theorem 36 *If strong-NSPACE(log log n) $\cap\ 1^* \subseteq$ weak-DSPACE(log log n) $\cap\ 1^*$, then DLOG = NLOG.*

Proof. Let N be an arbitrary *NLOG* machine. We now construct a padded machine P_N such that P_N accepts 1^n if and only if

(1) $n = p_1^{\alpha_1} \cdot p_2^{\alpha_2} \cdot \ldots \cdot p_\ell^{\alpha_\ell} \cdot K$, for some $K \geq 1$, where p_i denotes the ith prime. K is not divisible by any of $p_1, p_2, \ldots, p_{\ell+1}$ and $p_{\ell+1}$ is the first prime that does not divide n.

(2) The input $w = b_1 b_2 \ldots b_\ell$ is accepted by N, where

$$b_i = \begin{cases} 1 & \text{if } \alpha_i > 1, \\ 0 & \text{if } \alpha_i = 1, \end{cases} \qquad \text{for each } i = 1, \ldots, \ell.$$

P_N works as follows: First, P_N checks $j = 2,3,4,\ldots$ if j is a prime and if it divides n, until it finds the first prime $p_{\ell+1}$ that does not divide n. By Lem.35, the $O(\log\log n)$ space is sufficient, since $\ell+1 \leq p_{\ell+1} \leq d_0 \cdot \log n$, for some constant d_0.

Then P_N nondeterministically simulates the *NLOG* machine N, pretending that $w = b_1 \ldots b_\ell$ is present on the input tape. If N moves one position to the right (left), P_N increments (decrements, respectively) the current input head position i by one, computes p_i, and checks if n is divisible by p_i^2 to determine whether the current input tape symbol scanned by N is $b_i = 1$ or 0. The right/left end marker is imitated if the input head position reaches $i = \ell+1$ or $i = 0$, respectively.

Since $i \leq p_i \leq p_i^2 \leq p_{\ell+1}^2 \leq (d_0 \cdot \log n)^2$, the $O(\log\log n)$ space suffices to simulate the head movement. The work tape of N is also stored in space $O(\log\log n)$.

By hypothesis, we have a deterministic *weak-DSPACE(log log n)* version D_{P_N} for P_N. We can use it to construct D, a *DLOG* equivalent for N. To recognize $w = b_1 \ldots b_n \in \{0,1\}^*$,

D simulates D_{P_N} imitating the input 1^m, where $m = p_1^{\beta_1} \cdot \ldots \cdot p_n^{\beta_n}$, with $\beta_i = 1+b_i$, for each $i = 1, \ldots, n$. If the input 1^m is accepted by D_{P_N}, then it uses the space at most $d_1 \cdot \log\log m \leq d_1 \cdot \log\log(\prod_{i=1}^n p_i^2) \in O(\log n)$, using $p_i \in O(i \cdot \ln i)$, by Lem.35.

We do not have enough space to store the input head position of D_{P_N}, since $\log m \in \Omega(n)$. However, $L(D_{P_N})$ is a tally set, hence, by Thm.27, we may assume that D_{P_N} leaves the left end marker only to check *(a)* whether $m \bmod x = y$, or *(b)* if $m \leq y$, for some $x, y \leq d_2^{\log\log(m)+1}$. Since $\log\log m \in O(\log n)$, such numbers can be stored in $O(\log n)$ space. Thus, each time D_{P_N} leaves the end marker in the special state $r_?$ with $<x,y>$ stored on the second work tape (*see* Thm.27 for details), D computes the answer by itself:

(a) For $x \neq 0$, D compares y with $\left(\prod_{i=1}^n p_i^{\beta_i}\right) \bmod x$, performing all arithmetic modulo x in $O(\log n)$ space. We use the fact that $(e \cdot f) \bmod g = ((e \bmod g) \cdot (f \bmod g)) \bmod g$.

(b) For $x = 0$, D checks whether $\prod_{i=1}^n p_i^{\beta_i} \leq y$. If the space overflows $O(\log n)$ during the iteration of $H := H \cdot p_i^{\beta_i}$, for some $i \in \{1, \ldots, n\}$, D knows that $\prod_{i=1}^n p_i^{\beta_i} > y$.

In either case, D can resume from the correct return point r_{yes} or r_{no}. □

It is not too hard to see that the above simulation works for any $s(n) \geq \log n$. This gives (almost) optimal $s(\log n) \geq \log\log n$, which improves the related result of Savitch, using $s(n) \geq n$ so that $s(\log n) \geq \log n$. (*See* e.g. [21, 27]). Another variant is obtained by "forgetting" that the padded languages are tally sets.

Theorem 37 *(a) If x-DSPACE(s(log n))* $\cap$ 1^* = *x-NSPACE(s(log n))* $\cap$ 1^*, *then x-DSPACE(s(n)) = x-NSPACE(s(n)), (b) if x-DSPACE(s(log n)) = x-NSPACE(s(log n)), then x-DSPACE(s(n)) = x-NSPACE(s(n)), for each* $s(n) \geq \log n$ *and* $x \in$ *{strong,weak}.*

Corollary 38 *(a) DLBA = NLBA if and only if DLOG* $\cap$ 1^* = *NLOG* $\cap$ 1^*,
(b) DLOG = NLOG if and only if DSPACE(log log n) $\cap$ 1^* = *NSPACE(log log n)* $\cap$ 1^*.

The shifted version (b) is now an easy consequence of Thm.32 and 36. Now we can present the "hardest" constructible function:

Corollary 39 *There exists* $s_\square(n) \in O(\log\log n)$, *a nondeterministically fully space constructible function, such that* $s_\square(n)$ *is constructible deterministically if and only if all nondeterministically fully space constructible functions are constructible deterministically as well.*

The function $s_\square(n)$ is defined as follows:

(1) Let $n = p_1^{\alpha_1} \cdot \ldots \cdot p_\ell^{\alpha_\ell} \cdot K$, with K not divisible by any of $p_1, \ldots, p_{\ell+1}$ and $\alpha_i \geq 1$, for $i = 1, \ldots, \ell$.

(2) Let $w = b_1 \ldots b_\ell$ be defined by $b_i = 1$ or 0, depending on whether $\alpha_i > 1$. Now, let

$$s_\square(n) = \begin{cases} 1 + \lceil \log p_{\ell+1} \rceil & \text{if } w \in GAP, \\ \lceil \log p_{\ell+1} \rceil & \text{otherwise}. \end{cases}$$

References

[1] M. Albers. Space complexity of alternating Turing machines. In *Fundamentals of Computation Theory*, LNCS 199, Springer-Verlag, 1–7, 1985.

[2] H. Alt, V. Geffert, and K. Mehlhorn. A lower bound for the nondeterministic space complexity of context-free recognition. *Inform. Process. Letters*, 42, 25–27, 1992.

[3] H. Alt and K. Mehlhorn. A language over a one symbol alphabet requiring only $O(\log\log n)$ space. *SIGACT News*, 7, 31–33, 1975.

[4] A. Bertoni, C. Mereghetti, and G. Pighizzini. An optimal lower bound for nonregular languages. *Inform. Process. Letters*, 50, 289–92, 1994. (Erratum: 52, 339, 1994).

[5] A. Bertoni, C. Mereghetti, and G. Pighizzini. Strong optimal lower bounds for Turing machines that accept nonregular languages. In *Proc. of MFCS'95*, this volume, 1995.

[6] B. von Braunmühl, R. Gengler, and R. Rettinger. The alternation hierarchy for machines with sublogarithmic space is infinite. In *Proc. of STACS'94*, LNCS 775, Springer-Verlag, 85–96, 1994.

[7] C. Damm and M. Holtzer. Inductive counting below *LOGSPACE*. In *Proc. of MFCS'94*, LNCS 841, Springer-Verlag, 276–85, 1994.

[8] A.R. Freedman and R.E. Ladner. Space bounds for processing contentless inputs. *J. Comput. System Sci.*, 11, 118–28, 1975.

[9] V. Geffert. Nondeterministic computations in sublogarithmic space and space constructibility. *SIAM J. Comput.*, 20, 484–98, 1991.

[10] V. Geffert. Tally versions of the Savitch and Immerman-Szelepcsényi theorems for sublogarithmic space. *SIAM J. Comput.*, 22, 102–13, 1993.

[11] V. Geffert. Sublogarithmic Σ_2-*SPACE* is not closed under complement and other separation results. *RAIRO Theoret. Informatics & Appl.*, 27, 349–66, 1993.

[12] V. Geffert. A hierarchy that does not collapse: Alternations in low level space. *RAIRO Theoret. Informatics & Appl.*, 28, 465–512, 1994.

[13] J. Hartmanis. New developments in structural complexity theory. *Theoret. Comput. Sci.*, 71, 79–93, 1990.

[14] J.E. Hopcroft and J.D. Ullman. Some results on tape-bounded Turing machines. *Journal of the ACM*, 16, 168–77, 1969.

[15] J.E. Hopcroft and J.D. Ullman. *Introduction to automata theory, languages, and computation.* Addison-Wesley, 1979.

[16] N. Immerman. Nondeterministic space is closed under complement. *SIAM J. Comput.*, 17, 935–38, 1988.

[17] M. Liśkiewicz and R. Reischuk. Separating the lower levels of the sublogarithmic space hierarchy. In *Proc. of STACS'93*, LNCS 665, Springer-Verlag, 16–27, 1993.

[18] M. Liśkiewicz and R. Reischuk. The complexity world below logarithmic space. In *Proc. of the Structure in Complexity Theory*, 64–78, 1994.

[19] B. Monien and H. Sudborough. On eliminating nondeterminism from Turing machines which use less than logarithm work tape space. *Theoret. Comput. Sci.*, 21, 237–53, 1982.

[20] D. Ranjan, R. Chang, and J. Hartmanis. Space bounded computations: Review and new separation results. *Theoret. Comput. Sci.*, 80, 289–302, 1991.

[21] W.J. Savitch. Relationships between nondeterministic and deterministic tape complexities. *J. Comput. System Sci.*, 4, 177–92, 1970.

[22] M. Sipser. Halting space bounded computations. *Theoret. Comput. Sci.*, 10, 335–38, 1980.

[23] R.E. Stearns, J. Hartmanis, and P.M. Lewis II. Hierarchies of memory limited computations. In *IEEE Conf. Record on Switching Circuit Theory and Logical Design*, 179–90, 1965.

[24] R. Szelepcsényi. The method of forced enumeration for nondeterministic automata. *Acta Informatica*, 26, 279–84, 1988.

[25] A. Szepietowski. If deterministic and nondeterministic space complexities are equal for $\log\log n$ then they are also equal for $\log n$. *Theoret. Comput. Sci.*, 74, 115–19, 1990.

[26] A. Szepietowski. *Turing machines with sublogarithmic space.* LNCS 843, Springer-Verlag, 1994.

[27] Ch.K. Yap. *Theory of complexity classes.* To be published by Oxford University Press.

Second Order Logic and the Weak Exponential Hierarchies*

Georg Gottlob* Nicola Leone*+ Helmut Veith*

* Christian Doppler Laboratories for Expert Systems,
Information Systems Department, TU Vienna
A-1040 Wien, Paniglgasse 16, Austria
(gottlob|leone|veith)@vexpert.dbai.tuwien.ac.at

+ ISI-CNR,
c/o DEIS-UNICAL
87030 Rende, Italy.

Abstract. Second order logic over finite structures is well-known to capture the levels of the polynomial hierarchy PH. Recently, it has been shown that Θ_k^1 – the first order closure of second order Σ_k^1 – captures the class $\Theta_k^P = L^{\Sigma_k^P}$, a natural intermediate class of the polynomial hierarchy [12].
In this paper we show that with respect to expression complexity, second order logic characterizes the levels of the weak exponential hierarchy EH. Moreover, we extend these results to intermediate classes $E\Theta_k^P$ in EH which correspond to the Θ_k^P classes in PH.
To this end, in extending previous results, we show completeness under projection translations of certain quantified propositional formula languages for Θ_k^P. Those, as well as quantified Boolean formulas are applied to improved complexity upgrade techniques based on the "succinct input" paradigm.
Thus, we obtain a uniform treatment for obtaining expression complexity results for a large number of natural languages. We exhibit examples from database theory and nonmonotonic reasoning. In particular, we investigate the expression complexity of first order logic with Henkin quantifiers and default logic.

1 Introduction

Second order logic is a major framework for both the fields of descriptive complexity theory and database theory, providing a link between computational complexity and logical expressibility over finite models.

* Short abridged version, omitting several proofs. The full paper [13] is available from the authors.

The levels of second order logic are well-known to capture the corresponding levels of the polynomial hierarchy PH [10, 30]. Recently, it has been shown that Θ_k^1 – the first order closure of Σ_k^1 – captures the class $\Theta_k^P = L^{\Sigma_k^P}$, a natural intermediate class in PH. (This is an immediate consequence of Theorem 4.10 in [12].)

In [32], Vardi defined the concepts of data complexity and expression complexity. While the more common notion of data complexity measures the complexity of checking a fixed property over structures of varying size (that is, over different *data*), expression complexity measures the complexity of checking varying expressions of a given language over a fixed structure.

Results about both data and expression complexity of many languages can be found in [32, 6, 8].

In this paper, we provide a general approach for settling the expression complexity for a large class of languages. To this end, we further develop complexity upgrade methods based on succinct data representation, originating in [2, 25, 3] and used previously in [8]. Thus, we are able to characterize the expression complexity of the levels of second order logic, including Θ_k^1.

We shall see that expression complexity tends to be one exponential higher than data complexity. The reason is the fact that a program of size n can encode structures of considerably larger size. Therefore, the expression complexity of second order logic lies in the exponential hierarchy.

Two computational classes, namely, E $= \bigcup_k DTIME[2^{kn}]$ and EXP $= \bigcup_k DTIME[2^{n^k}]$, are commonly referred to as exponential time.

Starting from E and EXP two different exponential hierarchies have been defined: the ***weak exponential hierarchy*** (EH) [15], composed of the levels E, NE, E^{NP}, $\mathrm{NE}^{\mathrm{NP}}$, etc.; and, the ***weak* EXP *hierarchy*** (ExpH) [17], consisting of EXP, NEXP, $\mathrm{EXP}^{\mathrm{NP}}$, $\mathrm{NEXP}^{\mathrm{NP}}$, etc.

In terms of structural complexity, we show that the classes at any level of both exponential hierarchies have natural complete problems via logspace reductions involving logical languages over finite universes and propositional languages. Moreover, we refine the exponential hierarchies by exhibiting natural intermediate classes of EH corresponding to the Θ_k^P levels of PH.

Our starting point, and a main contribution of the paper, will be the proof that the expression complexity of Σ_k^1 formulae is $\mathrm{NE}^{\Sigma_{k-1}^P}$-complete under logspace reductions. Using this result and its paradigmatic methodology (a combination of complexity upgrading techniques and problem vectorization) we show that Θ_k^1 has expression complexity $\mathrm{E}^{\Sigma_{k-1}^P}$. This will be derived as an immediate consequence of the fact that a certain propositional language L_k has complexity Θ_k^P.

We apply our results to determine the expression complexity of first order logic with Henkin quantifiers and of default logic.

Henkin quantifiers, introduced by Henkin in [18], are important in both model theory and theoretical linguistics [19, 31]. The expressibility of Henkin quantifiers over finite models has been recently characterized [5, 12]. We show that first order logic with Henkin quantifiers has expression complexity $\mathrm{LinSpace}^{\mathrm{NP}}$.

Default logic is one of the most used languages in Artifical Intelligence. It was proposed by Reiter [27] as a language incorporating *default* conclusions; that is conclusions are drawn unless counter evidence is available. The expressibility of default logic was investigated in [6, 11]. We show that first order credulous default logic has expression complexity NE^{NP} by an embedding of Skolemized Σ_2^1 into first order default logic.

All results mentioned above are shown to hold as well for the EXP hierarchy. Due to space limitations, we omit the proofs of some statements and focus the presentation on topics related to logic. Detailed proofs, in particular the case of abduction over logic programs are reported in the full version [13].

2 Second Order Logic over Finite Structures

A *signature* is a tuple $\tau = (R_1^{a_1}, \ldots, R_k^{a_k}, c_1, \ldots, c_r)$, where $R_i, 1 \leq i \leq k$, is a relation symbol with arity $a_i \geq 0$, and $c_1, \ldots, c_r$ are constant symbols. Since constants can be simulated by unary predicates which hold on unique elements, we will assume throughout the paper that the signatures dealt with are constant free. Consequently, in writing $x = c$, we mean $C(x)$, where C is the unary predicate for c.

First order logic over a signature τ ($FO(\tau)$) is defined in the standard way apart from the fact that the language always contains the additional binary relation symbols $=, s$ denoting equality, successor, and two constants $0, max$.

A *second order prenex formula* is a formula Ψ of the form $Q_1\text{X}_1 Q_2\text{X}_2 \ldots Q_k\text{X}_k : \phi$, where: (i) $\text{X}_i, 1 \leq i \leq k$ is a tuple of predicate variables taken from an enumerable set $\{P_i^j : i, j \geq 0\}$ of designators (where the symbol P_i^j has arity j), (ii) ϕ is a first order formula with signature $\tau \cup \text{X}_1 \cup \ldots \cup \text{X}_k$, and (iii) $Q_i, 1 \leq i \leq k$ is a quantifier from $\{\forall, \exists\}$.

If the quantifiers $Q_1, \cdots, Q_k$ are alternating and the first quantifier Q_1 is $\exists$, then Ψ is called a Σ_k^1 formula; if the quantifiers $Q_1, \cdots, Q_k$ are alternating and the first quantifier Q_1 is $\forall$, then Ψ is a Π_k^1 formula.

A formula with second order quantifiers where all subformulas with a leading second order quantifier are Σ_k^1 or Π_k^1 is called a Θ_k^1 formula. (For instance, $\exists x, y((\exists P^3 : \forall z E(x, z) \Rightarrow P(x, y, z)) \wedge (\forall Q^1 : E(x, x) \Rightarrow Q(x))$ is a Θ_1^1 formula.) Thus, Θ_k^1 is the natural first order closure of Σ_k^1.

$\Sigma_k^1(\tau)$ (resp. $\Pi_k^1(\tau)$, $\Theta_k^1(\tau)$) is the language of all Σ_k^1 (resp. Π_k^1, Θ_k^1) formulae over τ. *Second order logic* $\Sigma_\omega^1(\tau)$ is the language of all second order formulae over τ.

The notions of finite structure, finite model and satisfaction are standard apart from the fact that we require all structures to have domain size at least 2. For a sentence ϕ, let $\text{Mod}(\phi)$ denote the set of its finite models, and for a signature τ, let $\text{Struct}(\tau)$ denote the set of finite structures over τ. For exact definitions, refer to [13].

In descriptive complexity theory, problems are considered sets of structures. In particular, a problem is usually defined as the set of finite models of its *defining formula*. That is, if ϕ is a sentence of a logic $\mathcal{F}$ over signature τ, then

$\text{Mod}(\phi) \subseteq \text{Struct}(\tau)$ is the problem associated with ϕ. Of course, $\text{Mod}(\phi)$ can itself be considered a set of words over $\{0,1\}^*$. If a logic $\mathcal{L}$ expresses exactly those sets of structures which are recognized by Turing machines of a computational class C, we say that $\mathcal{L}$ *captures* C and write $\mathcal{L} = C$. The following capturing results will be useful.

Theorem 1 [10, 30, 12]. $\Sigma^1_k = \Sigma^P_k,\ \Pi^1_k = \Pi^P_k,\ \Theta^1_k = \Theta^P_k$

Note that the first two equations also hold for second order logic without logical successor predicates whilst the third one presupposes the presence either of a logical successor or of ordered structures.

Let $\Pi \subseteq \text{Struct}(\pi)$ be some problem. We say that Π is *self-embeddable* if membership in Π is stable under domain extensions, i.e. if $\mathcal{G} = (n, R^{\mathcal{G}}_1, \ldots, R^{\mathcal{G}}_r) \in \Pi$ implies $(n+1, R^{\mathcal{G}}_1, \ldots, R^{\mathcal{G}}_r) \in \Pi$. Intuitively, a self-embeddable encoding of a problem provides a very explicit description of the problem instances because only those domain elements where some relation actually holds are relevant for membership. 3-colorability of graphs is self-embeddable because adding isolated vertices does not offend 3-colorability, while Hamiltonicity immediately vanishes. For a problem A and an integer k, let $A^{(k)}$ denote the *vectorized* problem A over k-tuples of domain elements. The notion of vectorized problems is made exact in the following definitions:

Definition 2. Let $\tau = (R^{a_1}_1, \ldots, R^{a_r}_r)$ be a signature, $\phi \in \Sigma^1_\omega(\tau)$, and $k \geq 1$. Then we define:

- $\tau^{(k)} = (R^{a_1 k}_1, \ldots, R^{a_r k}_r)$;
- $\phi^{(k)}$ is the formula obtained from ϕ by replacing, for each variable x occurring in ϕ, every occurrence of x by the k-tuple of variables $x_1, \ldots, x_k$. Then, each occurring $x_1, \cdots, x_k = y_1, \cdots, y_k$ (resulting from the previous step) is replaced by $\bigwedge_{i=1}^k x_i = y_i$.
- Let R be a $k * l$ ary relation over domain n. Then we define $R^{(\frac{1}{k})} = \{((x_{11}, \ldots, x_{1k})_n, \ldots (x_{l1}, \ldots, x_{lk})_n) | (x_{11}, \ldots, x_{1k}, \ldots, x_{l1}, \ldots, x_{lk}) \in R\}$ where $(x_1, x_2, \ldots, x_k)_n$ denotes the integer number j whose n-ary number representation is $x_1 x_2 \ldots x_k$, i.e., $j = \Sigma_{i=0}^{k-1} n^i x_{i+1}$.
  Consequently, $(n, R_1, \ldots, R_r)^{(\frac{1}{k})} = (n^k, R_1^{(\frac{1}{k})}, \ldots, R_r^{(\frac{1}{k})})$.
- Let $\Pi \subseteq \text{Struct}(\tau)$ be a problem over τ. Then the k-ary variant $\Pi^{(k)}$ of Π is defined as $\Pi^{(k)} = \{\mathcal{C} \in \text{Struct}(\tau^{(k)}) \mid \mathcal{C}^{(\frac{1}{k})} \in \Pi\}$ □

From this definition we see that only structures with domain size n^k can be directly translated to vectorized versions of arity k. The situation changes for structures which are instances of self-embeddable problems. Suppose we want to compute $\mathcal{A}^{(k)}$ for some given structure $\mathcal{A}$ of size $|\mathcal{A}| = n$. Then we embed $\mathcal{A}$ into a structure $\mathcal{A}'$ of size $\lceil \sqrt[k]{n} \rceil^k \geq n$. For $\mathcal{A}'$, the vectorization $\mathcal{A}'^{(k)}$ is well-defined and describes the same instance (though over vectors) as $\mathcal{A}$ and $\mathcal{A}'$ do.

The following Lemma follows immediately from the definitions:

Lemma 3. *Let ϕ be a formula, s.t.* $\mathrm{Mod}(\phi)$ *is closed under isomorphisms. Then* $\mathrm{Mod}(\phi^{(k)}) = \mathrm{Mod}(\phi)^{(k)}$. *If* $\mathrm{Mod}(\phi)$ *is self-embeddable then* $\mathcal{G} \models \phi \underset{\text{iff}}{\longleftrightarrow} \mathcal{G}^{(i)} \models \phi^{(i)}$ *for arbitrary* i.

Note that $\mathrm{Mod}(\phi)$ is closed under isomorphisms if ϕ contains no logical predicates except equality.

A *logical reduction* [9, 20, 7, 29] is a reduction between logically defined problems. Let $A \subseteq \mathrm{Struct}(\alpha), B \subseteq \mathrm{Struct}(\beta)$. An *interpretation* of A into B is a set of formulas, which defines structures over β in terms of α. A k-ary reduction of A to B is an interpretation ϕ of A into $B^{(k)}$ where for all structures $\mathcal{A} \in \mathrm{Struct}(\alpha)$ it holds that $\mathcal{A} \in A$ iff $\phi(\mathcal{A}) \in B^{(k)}$.

A *projection reduction*[20, 29] is a logical reduction where the interpretative formulae are quantifierfree and in disjunctive normal form, s.t. each clause contains at most one non-logical predicate and no two clauses are simultaneoulsy satisfied. We shall use the following Lemma:

Lemma 4. [33] *If A is projection reducible to B then A is PLT-reducible to B.*

3 Polynomial and Exponential Hierarchies

3.1 The Hierarchies

We assume that the reader is familiar with the polynomial hierarchy. Recall that $\Theta^P_{k+1} = L^{\Sigma^P_k}$. In this paper, we use the Ladner-Lynch oracle model [23].

E (NE, resp.) is the class of decisional problems recognizable by a deterministic (nondeterministic, resp.) Turing machine in time $O(2^{kn})$, where n is the size of the input and k is a constant. The *weak exponential time hierarchy* (EH) [15] is a hierarchy symmetric to the polynomial one, where E and NE play the roles of P and NP, respectively:

$\mathrm{E}\Delta^P_0 = \mathrm{E}\Sigma^P_0 = \mathrm{E}\Pi^P_0 = \mathrm{E}\Theta^P_0 = \mathrm{E}$ and for all $k \geq 0$, $\mathrm{E}\Delta^P_{k+1} = \mathrm{E}^{\Sigma^P_k}$, $\mathrm{E}\Sigma^P_{k+1} = \mathrm{NE}^{\Sigma^P_k}$, $\mathrm{E}\Pi^P_{k+1} = \text{co-}\mathrm{E}\Sigma^P_{k+1}$, $\mathrm{E}\Theta^P_{k+1} = \mathrm{LinSpace}^{\mathrm{E}\Sigma^P_{k+1}}$.

EH is equal to $\bigcup_{k=0}^{\infty} \mathrm{E}\Sigma^P_k$. Note that our definition of $\mathrm{E}\Theta^P_k$ is new and will be justified by the results to follow. The *weak* exponential hierarchy (ExpH) [17] is defined analogously, using EXP instead of E as the class to start with.

Let *classes_of*(PH) denote the subclasses of PH we defined above. For $C \in$ *classes_of*(PH), let $E(C)$ and $Exp(C)$ denote the classes at the corresponding level of the exponential hierarchies. C, $E(C)$ and $Exp(C)$ are called analogues of each other.

3.2 PH vs. EH

It follows from the definition that the exponential hierarchy solves problems exponentially harder than PH. This section shows that a mapping due to [3] allows to reduce the complexity of problems in EH to PH by an exponential blow-up of the instance size. Given a binary string w, let $|w|$ denote its length.

Given an integer number n, let $bin(n)$ denote the binary representation of n. Conversely, given a binary string w, $int(w)$ denotes the positive integer whose binary representation is w.

Definition 5. [3] Let A be a decisional problem. The *long version* $long(A)$ of A is the problem $long(A) = \{w \in \{0,1\}^* \mid bin(|w|) \in 1A\}$ where $1A = \{1w \in \{0,1\}^* \mid w \in A\}$. □

Theorem 6. *For all classes C in the polynomial hierarchy, it holds that* $long(A) \in C \underset{\text{iff}}{\longleftrightarrow} A \in E(C)$.

Proof. Straightforward Turing Machine simulations. See [13] for the proof. □

3.3 EH vs. ExpH

It is well-known that, even if E has a lower time bound than EXP, problems hard under logspace reductions for E are hard for EXP as well [21]. This result extends to an arbitrary pair of analogue classes of EH and ExpH.

Theorem 7. [13] *Let Ex be a class in* EH *and $EXPx$ its analogue class in* ExpH. *If problem A is complete for Ex under logspace reductions, then it is complete for $EXPx$ under logspace reductions.*

The results of this section show that it will be sufficient to prove completeness results for the classes in EH if possible. It follows from the time hierarchy Theorems by Hartmanis and Stearns [14] that the converse implication does not hold. We assume that the reader is familiar with the concept of bounded oracle queries, see e.g. [34]. In the following we shall need several complexity theoretic identities. For the proofs, consult the full version [13].

Theorem 8. [34, 13]

1. $L^{\Sigma_k^P} = P^{\Sigma_k^P}[O(\log n)]$
2. $\mathrm{E}\Theta_k^P = \mathrm{LinSpace}^{\Sigma_k^P} = E^{\Sigma_k^P}[Pol(n)]$
3. $\mathrm{Exp}\Theta_k^P = \mathrm{PSPACE}^{\Sigma_k^P} = \mathrm{EXP}^{\Sigma_k^P}[Pol(n)]$
4. *The strong exponential hierarchy coincides with* $\mathrm{Exp}\Theta_2^P$.

3.4 The Complexity Upgrade Technique

In this section we describe the complexity upgrade technique, based on a generalization of the results in [25, 3, 8], which will be the basic tool to derive hardness results for second order logics. Due to space restricitions, we announce the results without proofs.

The results and techniques of [25] were extended in [3] to a general concept of succinctness for arbitrary problems. The succinct representation of a binary word w is a Boolean circuit that on input of a number i (in binary), outputs whether $i \leq |w|$, and in that case, the i-th bit of w. The succinct version sA of A is as follows: Given a Boolean circuit C describing an instance w, decide whether $w \in A$.

Theorem 9. [13] *Let C_1 and C_2 be complexity classes, such that, for each problem $A \in C_1$, long$(A) \in C_2$. If B is C_2-hard under PLT-reductions then sB is C_1-hard under L-reductions.*

This Theorem is a generalization of Theorem 5, [3], where hardness for the succinct problem version under polynomial transformability is obtained from hardness of the standard problem under the more restrictive logtime transformability.

4 The Complexity of Second Order Formulae

In this section we determine the expression complexity of function-free second order formulae over finite models. In particular, we show that, wrt expression complexity, Σ_k^1 is complete for both $\mathrm{E}\Sigma_k^P$ and $\mathrm{Exp}\Sigma_k^P$ under logspace reductions, and that Θ_k^1 is complete for both $\mathrm{E}\Theta_k^P$ and $\mathrm{Exp}\Theta_k^P$. In the following, we shall not repeat the results for ExpH since they follow trivially from Theorem 7.

4.1 Succinct k-QBF is $E\Sigma_k^P$-complete

A QBF (Quantified Boolean Formula) is a propositional formula of the form $Q_1X_1Q_2X_2 \cdots Q_kX_k E$, $k \geq 1$, where E is a Boolean expression whose atoms are from pairwise disjoint nonempty sets of variables $X_1, \ldots, X_k$, and the Q_i's are alternating quantifiers from $\{\exists, \forall\}$, for all $i = 1, \ldots, k$. A k-QBF is a QBF where the first quantifier is existential (i.e., $Q_1 = \exists$) and the Boolean expression E is either in CNF or in DNF according to whether k is odd or even. Validity of QBFs is defined in the obvious way by recursion to variable-free Boolean expressions.

In [29], Stewart shows that validity checking of a k-QBF formula is Σ_k^P-complete via successor-free projection translations. In Stewart's encoding, k-QBF are described by two predicates $P(x,y)$ and $N(x,y)$ expressing 'variable x occurs positively (resp. negatively) in clause y'. Moreover, for each quantifier $Q_i, 1 \leq i \leq k$, in the prefix of the QBF formula, there is a unary predicate $M_i(x)$, s.t. $M_i(x)$ holds iff x is bound by Q_i. Let $\tau_k = (N^2, P^2, M_1^1, \ldots, M_k^1)$ be the signature of this representation. For each structure $\mathcal{C} = (n, N^{\mathcal{C}}, P^{\mathcal{C}}, M_1^{\mathcal{C}}, \ldots, M_k^{\mathcal{C}}) \in \mathrm{Struct}(\tau_k)$, let $\mathbf{qbf}(\mathcal{C})$ denote the k-QBF formula expressed by $\mathcal{C}$.

Define k-QBF $= \{\mathcal{G} \in \mathrm{Struct}(\tau_k) | \mathbf{qbf}(\mathcal{G})$is valid$\}$, i.e. k-QBF is the set of structures describing valid k-QBF formulae. The following Theorem from [29] establishes the complexity of k-QBF.

Theorem 10. [29] *For each $k \geq 0$,* k-QBF *is Σ_k^P-complete under successor-free projection translations.*

Since successor-free projection translations are subsumed by polylogtime translations, we conclude that succinct k-QBF is $\mathrm{E}\Sigma_k^P$ hard by Theorem 9.

Recall that a boolean circuit of size n is described by a function $f : n \to \{and, or, neg, in\} \times n \times n$, where $f(i) = (T, j, k)$ iff the i-th gate is a T-gate (e.g., or-gate) and $j, k < i$ are the inputs of the gate, unless i is an in-gate, in which case, say, $j = k = 0$. For not-gates, $j = k$ (cf. [22]). We assume that all the input gates coincide with a starting sequence $0, \ldots, u$ of the naturals and that the n-th gate is regarded as the output gate.

A circuit of size n can be encoded as an ordered structure over signature (F^4), where F encodes the function f and the numbers $1, 2, 3, 4$ denote and, or, neg, and in, respectively. Therefore, the set of boolean circuits is definable as a logical problem over Struct(F^4). (Not all $X \in$ Struct(F^4) are circuits in the sense of the above definition, but only those which satisfy the above syntactic requirements.)

The succinct representation of a structure $\mathcal{G}$ consists of several circuits, each describing one relation of $\mathcal{G}$. Those circuits are written as relations themselves. Thus, in the succinct representation of $\mathcal{G}$, each relation $R^{\mathcal{G}}$ of $\mathcal{G}$ gets replaced by a circuit which computes $R^{\mathcal{G}}$.

Let $\tau = (R_1, \ldots R_r)$ be the signature of a self-embeddable problem. In order to describe an instance $\mathcal{A} \in$ Struct(τ) we shall need r circuits, representing the predicates $R_1^{\mathcal{A}}, \ldots R_r^{\mathcal{A}}$. Therefore, its *succinct signature* $s(\tau)$ is $(F_1^4, \ldots, F_r^4)$.

It is easy to see that for each problem there exists a self-embeddable description obtained by adding a unary relation R to the signature, s.t. the problem is considered only over those domain elements a, where $R(a)$ holds.

Let τ be a signature. Then each circuit $\mathcal{C} \in$ Struct$(s(\tau))$ describes a structure over signature τ. We call this structure gen$(\mathcal{C})$. (If $\mathcal{C}$ is not evaluable as a circuit, let gen$(\mathcal{C})$ by default denote some fixed $T \in$ Struct(τ).) Note that $|\mathrm{gen}(\mathcal{G})| \leq 2^{|\mathcal{G}|}$.

The succinct k-QBF problem s(k-QBF) is defined by
$s(\text{k-QBF}) = \{\mathcal{C} \in \text{Struct}(s(\tau_k)) \,|\, \text{gen}(\mathcal{C}) \in \text{k-QBF}\}$.

Theorem 11. *For each $k \geq 0$, s(k-QBF) is complete for $\mathrm{E}\Sigma_k^P$ under logspace reductions.*

Proof. From Lemma 4 we know that if problem A is reducible to problem B by successor-free projection translations, then $A \leq_m^{PLT} B$. Therefore, the statement follows by Theorem 9 and Theorem 10. □

4.2 Σ_k^1 has Expression Complexity $\mathrm{E}\Sigma_k^P$

Using last section's generic problems for the classes of EH, we are now ready to turn to expression complexity of second order logic and prove that satisfaction of Σ_k^1 is complete for the complexity classes $\mathrm{E}\Sigma_k^P$ and $\mathrm{Exp}\Sigma_k^P$. We first show hardness of the problems in the complexity classes.

We start with constructing first order sentences over the fixed structure $\mathcal{B} = (\{0,1\})$ which simulate given circuits.

Note that $\mathcal{B}$ is the weakest possible structure in our framework. In the following, we shall write 1 to denote the constant *max*.

Lemma 12. *Let $C = (n, F^4)$ be a circuit with k input gates. Then there exists a first order formula $circ(C)(y_1, \ldots, y_k)$ of size $O(n)$, s.t. for all $\mathbf{y} \in \{0,1\}^k$ it holds that $\mathcal{B} \models circ(C)(\mathbf{y})$ iff the output gate of C contains 1 on input of $\mathbf{y}$. Moreover, $circ(C)$ is computable from C in logspace.*

Proof. Let $circ(C)(\mathbf{y}) = \exists x_1 \ldots x_n \; x_n = 1 \wedge \bigwedge_{i=1}^{n} \Phi_i \wedge (x_i = 1 \vee x_i = 0)$, where

$$\Phi_i = \begin{cases} x_i = 1 \equiv (x_j = 1 \wedge x_k = 1) & \text{if } C \models F(i,1,j,k) \\ x_i = 1 \equiv (x_j = 1 \vee x_k = 1) & \text{if } C \models F(i,2,j,k) \\ x_i = 1 \equiv x_j = 0 & \text{if } C \models F(i,3,j,j) \\ x_i = y_i & \text{if } C \models F(i,4,0,0) \end{cases}$$

It is easy to see that the formula gains the wished effect by simulating the circuit: Each variable corresponds to a circuit gate and is defined from other variables just like the gates in C. Evidently, $circ(C)$ is logspace–computable. □

Note that, for readability reasons we have stated the above Lemma for a simple circuit $C = (n, F^4)$; however, it is immediately seen that the same construction applies for circuits $C = (n, F^4, \cdots)$.

The following Lemma is crucial to the proof. It shows that, given a circuit C of size n, it is essentially equivalent to use either the vectorized version $\text{gen}(C)^{(n)}$ of the structure which C represents, or to use the formula $circ(C)$. This settles the compatibility between vectorized variants and the circ formulae.

Lemma 13. [13] *Let $\tau = (P^k)$ be a signature, and $C \in \text{Struct}(s(\tau))$, $|C| = n$, be a circuit for τ with l input gates. Then, for all $\mathbf{x} \in \{0,1\}^l$, it holds that*

$$\mathcal{B} \models circ(C)(\mathbf{x}) \underset{\text{iff}}{\longleftrightarrow} \text{gen}(C)^{(n)} \models P(\mathbf{x})$$

Now we are ready to prove hardness of the expression complexity of Σ_k^1: We have shown how to simulate circuits by formulae and how to adapt the other formulae to the simulation formulae. It remains putting everything together:

Theorem 14. *Σ_k^1 is $\text{E}\Sigma_{k-1}^P$ hard with respect to expression complexity and logspace reductions.*

Proof. Recall that given an instance $C \in \text{Struct}(s(\tau_k))$ over domain n, we have to find a reduction f by a logspace algorithm to a Σ_k^1 formula $f(C) = \Psi$, s.t.

$$\text{gen}(C) \in \text{k-QBF} \underset{\text{iff}}{\longleftrightarrow} \mathcal{B} \models \Psi$$

By Stockmeyer's generalization [30] of Fagin's Theorem [10] we conclude from Theorem 10 that there exist Σ_k^1 second order sentences ϕ_k, s.t. $\text{Mod}(\phi_k) =$ k-QBF. Note that apart from the second order predicate variables, the only predicates occurring in ϕ_k are $N, P, M_1, \ldots, M_k$. We express this by writing $\phi_k[N, P, M_1, \ldots, M_k]$. The crucial idea is that starting from signature τ_k we can use Lemma 3 to go over to the bit vector problem over signature $\tau_k^{(n)}$:

$$\mathcal{G} \in \text{k-QBF} \underset{\text{iff}}{\longleftrightarrow} \mathcal{G} \models \phi_k \underset{\text{iff}}{\longleftrightarrow} \mathcal{G}^{(n)} \models \phi_k^{(n)}$$

In particular, this holds for $\mathcal{G} = \text{gen}(\mathcal{C})$. In this case, the information about the relations $N^{\mathcal{G}}, P^{\mathcal{G}}, M_1^{\mathcal{G}}, \ldots, M_k^{\mathcal{G}}$ is provided by the circuit $\mathcal{C}$. Lemmas 12 and 13 say that the circuit computation is expressed by formulae $circ_1(\mathcal{C}), \ldots, circ_{k+2}(\mathcal{C})$ over $\mathcal{B}$.

Therefore, $\mathcal{G}^{(n)} \models \phi_k^{(n)} \underset{\text{iff}}{\longleftrightarrow} \mathcal{B} \models \underbrace{\phi_k^{(n)}[circ_1(\mathcal{C}), \ldots, circ_{k+2}(\mathcal{C})]}_{\text{hard}_k}$.

hard_k is logspace computable, because ϕ_k is constant, and both the *circ* formulas and the vectorization are logspace computable. In later proofs, we shall refer to hard_k as a prototypical formula with high expression complexity. □

To show completeness is comparatively easy; we defer the proof to [13], the full version of this paper.

Theorem 15. [13] *Over finite structures, Σ_k^1 is $\text{E}\Sigma_k^P$ complete with respect to expression complexity and logspace reductions.*

Corollary 16. *Σ_k^1 is $\text{Exp}\Sigma_k^P$ complete with respect to expression complexity and logspace reductions.*

Proof. Immediate from Theorem 15 and Corollary 7. □

Corollary 17. *Over finite structures, Π_k^1 is $\text{E}\Pi_k^P$-complete with respect to expression complexity and logspace reductions.*

Proof. Immediately from the fact that a Π_k^1 formula is satisfied by a certain structure iff its negation, in logspace rewritten as a Σ_k^1 formula, is not satisfied by that structure. □

Let us investigate an example of expression complexity within second order logic:

Example 1. Consider the language of Σ_1^1, restricted to its Skolem Normal Form $\exists P : \forall \mathbf{x} \exists \mathbf{y} : \phi$ where ϕ is quantifierfree. The Skolemization procedure can be easily done in logspace, consult [22] for the procedure. Therefore, each Σ_1^1 sentence is equivalent to a logspace-computable sentence in Skolemized Σ_1^1 (and of course vice versa). In particular, hard_k from Theorem 14 can be converted into Skolem Normal Form, thus providing a hard formula for Skolemized Σ_1^1. Hence, we conclude that the expression complexity of Σ_1^1 remains NE hard even for Skolemized Σ_1^1. This result easily generalizes to the classes Σ_k^1 and Π_k^1.

4.3 Θ_k^1 has Expression Complexity $E\Theta_k^P$

In this section, we combine the techniques developed above to characterize the expression complexity of second order formulas with second order quantifier nesting depth k (i.e. Θ_k^1 formulas). In order to proceed like in Theorem 14 above, we use a problem complete under projection translations for the class Θ_k^P, since it follows from results in [12] that Θ_k^1 captures Θ_k^P. (Note that a problem which is Θ_k^P complete under PLT reductions would be sufficient.) How to find such a problem? Take $\Theta_1^P = L^{\mathrm{NP}}$. The following problem MAX-CLIQUE has been shown complete for Θ_1^P under L-reductions by [34]:

MAX-CLIQUE:
Instance: A graph E
Query: Does the maximum clique of E have an *even* number of vertices?

Consider in contrast the problem CLIQUE which is well-known to be NP-complete under L-reductions:

CLIQUE:
Instance: A graph E and a constant $k \leq |E|$
Query: Does E contain a clique of size $\geq k$?

It is easy to see that the following boolean combination of queries to an NP-CLIQUE oracle evaluates to true iff E ∈MAX-CLIQUE:

$\bigvee_{i=0}^{n}$ $[(E, 2i) \in \mathrm{CLIQUE} \wedge (E, 2i+1) \notin \mathrm{CLIQUE}]$, where n is the domain size.

Taking into account that the oracle calls can be substituted by calls to satisfiability oracles, we define the language L_k as an extension of k-QBF. L_k consists of propositional formulas $\bigwedge_{i=1}^{n} S_i \vee \neg T_i$ where S_i and T_i are k-QBF formulas.

Since we want to go for completeness under projection reductions, we need an encoding of L_k formulas by finite structures. For this purpose we define a signature $2\tau_k$ which as its name suggests is a natural generalization of the signature τ_k which we used for describing k-QBF formulas.

Recall that $\tau_k = (M_1, \ldots, M_k, P, N)$. From the definition of L_k it follows that an L_k formula can be seen as a $2 \times n$ array of k-QBF formulas. Therefore, we choose the signature $2\tau_k$ to be $(M_1, \ldots, M_k, P, N, M_1^{\neg}, \ldots M_k^{\neg}, P^{\neg}, N^{\neg})$

where the $M_i, M_i^{\neg}$ have arity 2 and $N, P, N^{\neg}, P^{\neg}$ have arity 3. Here the additional predicate argument serves for indexing the clauses. The two copies of τ_k correspond to the S_i and T_i k-QBF formulas above. Actually, an instance of Struct$(2\tau_k)$ over domain n describes $2n$ instances of Struct(τ_k) over domain n.

In order to apply the upgrading technique, we have to find a logical characterization of L_k. Recall the original problem k-QBF over signature τ_k. Its generic generalized quantifier $\boxed{k}$ is defined as follows: (for a general concept, see [20, 29])

Definition 18. For any formula $\psi(x_1, \ldots, x_r) \in FO(\delta)$ and structure $C \in$ Struct(δ), let ψ^C denote $\{(i_1, \ldots, i_r) \in |C|^r \mid C \models \psi(i_1, \ldots, i_r)\}$. Let $C \in$ Struct(δ), and let $\rho_1(x), \ldots, \rho_k(x), \rho_{k+1}(x,y), \rho_{k+2}(x,y) \in FO(\delta)$.

Then we define

$$C \models \boxed{k}(\lambda x \rho_1(x); \ldots; \lambda x \rho_k(x); \lambda x, y \rho_{k+1}(x,y); \lambda x, y \rho_{k+2}(x,y))$$

$$\underset{\text{iff}}{\longleftrightarrow}$$

$$(|C|, \rho_1^C, \ldots, \rho_{k+2}^C) \models \phi_k$$

where ϕ_k is the formula defining k-QBF via k-QBF= Mod(ϕ_k). □

Using this terminology, it is easy to see that we can characterize the language L_k in the following manner:

$$L_k = \text{Mod}\left(\forall y : \begin{array}{l}(\boxed{k}\lambda x M_1(x,y); \ldots \lambda x M_k(x,y); \lambda xzyP(x,z,y); \lambda xzyN(x,z,y)) \Rightarrow \\ (\boxed{k}\lambda x M_1^{\neg}(x,y); \ldots \lambda x M_k^{\neg}(x,y); \lambda xzyP^{\neg}(x,z,y); \lambda xzyN^{\neg}(x,z,y))\end{array}\right)$$

Note that $\neg A \vee B$ got rewritten as $A \Rightarrow B$. The result goes as follows:

Theorem 19. [13] *L_k is complete for Θ_k^P under projection reductions.*

Proof. (Idea) It follows from [12] that all problems in Θ_k^P are expressible in *Stewart Normal Form*, i.e. as a Θ_k^1 formula of the form $\forall \mathbf{y}(A(\mathbf{y}) \Rightarrow B(\mathbf{y}))$ where $A(\mathbf{y})$ and $B(\mathbf{y})$ are Σ_k^1 formulae with free variables $\mathbf{y}$. Self-embeddability and completeness under projection reductions for k-QBF can be seen to carry over to the quantifier $\boxed{k}$. The result follows. □

It is clear that each $\boxed{k}$ quantifier can be replaced by its defining formula ϕ_k. On the other hand, each Σ_k^1 subformula can be replaced by a quantifier $\boxed{k}$ because the underlying problem k-QBF is complete under projection reductions. Recall that Θ_k^1 denotes the logic of first order combinations of Σ_k^1 formulas. Then we can rewrite our result as follows:

Corollary 20. [13] *Θ_k^1 has data complexity Θ_k^P, captures Θ_k^P and has expression complexity* $\text{LinSpace}^{\Sigma_k^P}$.

5 Applications

5.1 Henkin Quantifiers

Henkin quantifiers are a natural generalization of first order formulas. Consider an expression $\begin{pmatrix}\forall u \exists v \\ \forall x \exists y\end{pmatrix} \phi(u,v,x,y)$

where ϕ is a first order formula with free variables u, v, x, y. The semantics of the above sentence is defined by the following second order sentence:

$\exists F_1, F_2 :$

$$(\forall x \exists ! y F_1(x,y)) \wedge (\forall x \exists ! y F_2(x,y)) \wedge (\forall u,v,x,y : F_1(u,v) \wedge F_2(x,y) \Rightarrow \phi(u,v,x,y))$$

In other words, there exist distinct Skolem functions for $v = f_1(u), y = f_2(x)$ which depend only on u, x respectively.

Lemma 21. *There exists a logspace transducer which translates Σ_1^1 formulas into equivalent Henkin formulas of the form* $\begin{pmatrix}\forall x_1, \ldots x_n \exists y_1, \ldots y_n \\ \forall u_1, \ldots u_n \exists v_1, \ldots v_n\end{pmatrix} \Psi$ *where Ψ is first order.*

Proof. A careful examination of Walkoe's proof [35] yields the result. Consult [13] for a recast. □

Like with second order logic we can investigate two Henkin languages corresponding to the classes Σ_1^1, Θ_1^1: First order logic with prenex Henkin quantifiers and its first order closure (termed ***first order logic with Henkin quantifiers***).

Theorem 22. *First order logic with prenex Henkin quantifiers has expression complexity* NE *wrt logspace reductions. First order logic with Henkin quantifiers has expression complexity* $\text{LinSpace}^{\text{NP}}$

Proof. Immediate from Lemma 21. □

5.2 Default Logic

Propositional Default Logic

In [11], the complexity of propositional default logic was investigated. In particular the problem of deciding if there exists an extension of a given set of formulas was shown to be Σ_2^P complete for both systems.

Let us first consider propositional default logic. A default theory is a pair $< W, D >$ where W is a finite set of propositional sentences and D is a set of defaults. A default is an expression of the form

$$\frac{\alpha : M\gamma}{\omega}$$

where α, γ, ω are propositional formulas. α is called the ***prerequisite***, γ is called the ***justification*** and ω the ***consequence*** of the default. (In the literature, there are usually several justifications, but for the purpose of our exposition this language is sufficient.) The intended interpretation of a default is: *If α holds, and there is no counterevidence for γ, then ω can be inferred by default.*

An *extension* of $< W, D >$ is a set of propositional formulas which is based on a series of default conclusions starting from W, and which is closed under both propositional inference and default application. In formal terms: E is an extension of $< W, D > \underset{\text{iff}}{\longleftrightarrow} E = \bigcup_{i \geq 0} E_i$, where $E_0 = W$ and $E_{i+1} = \{\gamma | \frac{\alpha : M\beta}{\gamma} \in D, \alpha \in E_i, \neg\beta \notin E\} \cup Cons(E_i)$. Here, $Cons(E_i)$ denotes the propositional deductive closure.

Obviously, a default theory in general does not have a unique extension. This gives rise to ***credulous*** and ***skeptical*** semantics. We say that $< W, D >$ entails ϕ skeptically (resp. credulously) if ϕ is contained in all (some) extensions of $< W, D >$. Note that extensions are infinite sets. Formally, we write $< W, D > \vdash^{sk} \phi$ ($< W, D > \vdash^{cr} \phi$). We call the corresponding decision problems DEF-sk and DEF-cr.

Theorem 23. [11] DEF-cr *is Σ_2^P-complete and* DEF-sk *is Π_2^P-complete.*

Full Default Logic

In [6], default logic was adopted as a database query language. It was shown there that credulous default logic over quantifierfree first order logic captures Σ_2^P. In other words, default logic is another way of looking at the Σ_2^1 fragment of second order logic.

We show how to extend the propositional definitions to the first order case. In the following, the term *formula* will subsume both ordinary first order and default formulas.

Let $\mathcal{A} \in \mathrm{Struct}(\tau)$ be a structure. Then the completion $\mathtt{COMP}(\mathcal{A})$ of $\mathcal{A}$ is defined as $\{R(\mathbf{x}) | \mathcal{A} \models R(\mathbf{x}), R \in \tau, \mathbf{x} \in |\mathcal{A}|^{ar(R)}\} \cup \{\neg R(\mathbf{x}) | \mathcal{A} \not\models R(\mathbf{x}), R \in \tau, \mathbf{x} \in |\mathcal{A}|^{ar(R)}\}$, i.e. the Herbrand model corresponding to $\mathcal{A}$.

Let $\phi(\mathbf{x})$ be a formula with free variables $\mathbf{x}$. Then $\mathtt{INST}_{\mathcal{A}}(\phi(\mathbf{x}))$ is the set of formulas obtained by replacing domain elements from $\mathcal{A}$ for $\mathbf{x}$. For a set S of formulas, let $\mathtt{INST}_{\mathcal{A}}(S) = \bigcup_{\phi \in S} \mathtt{INST}_{\mathcal{A}}(\phi)$. Thus, for each set of formulas S and structure $\mathcal{A}$, $\mathtt{INST}_{\mathcal{A}}(S)$ is a set of closed formulas equivalent to S over $\mathcal{A}$.

Let us turn to full first order formulas. Over a fixed domain, first order formulas can be seen as large quantifier-free formulas with the quantifiers replaced by conjunctions and disjunctions. This gives rise to the following definition:

Let ϕ be a default formula over signature τ, $\mathcal{A} \in \mathrm{Struct}(\tau)$. Then $\mathbf{prop}_{\mathcal{A}}(\phi)$ denotes the formula obtained from ϕ by recursively replacing each subformula $\forall x \psi(x)$ by $\bigwedge_{c \in |\mathcal{A}|} \psi(c)$ and $\exists x \psi(x)$ by $\bigvee_{c \in |\mathcal{A}|} \psi(c)$. Then we define $\mathbf{ground}_{\mathcal{A}}(\phi) = \mathtt{INST}_{\mathcal{A}}(\mathbf{prop}_{\mathcal{A}}(\phi))$.

As with $\mathtt{INST}$, this definition generalizes to sets of formulas. Now it is easy to define the semantics for first order default logic: Given a model $\mathcal{A}$, and a first order default theory $< W, D >$, we consider the extensions of the propositional default theory $\mathbf{ground}_{\mathcal{A}}(< W, D >) =< \mathtt{COMP}(\mathcal{A}) \cup \mathbf{ground}_{\mathcal{A}}(W), \mathbf{ground}_{\mathcal{A}}(D) >$. Hence, we can define entailment for both skeptical and credulous reasoning: $\mathcal{A} \vdash_{<W,D>} \phi \underset{\text{iff}}{\longleftrightarrow} \mathbf{ground}_{\mathcal{A}}(< W, D >) \vdash \mathbf{ground}_{\mathcal{A}}(\phi)$. It is easy to show that first order default logic with credulous semantics captures Σ_2^P. From [6] we know that the quantifierfree fragment captures Σ_2^P, therefore we only have to prove the membership part by showing that first order default logic credulous entailment can be polynomially reduced to DEF-cr. This follows immediately from the fact that the computation of $\mathbf{ground}_{\mathcal{A}}$ is polynomial in $|\mathcal{A}|$ and from the definition of entailment above. Thus we obtain:

Theorem 24. *First order default logic with credulous semantics captures* Σ_2^P.

In a similar way we can obtain results about expression complexity. For a default d, let $|d|$ denote the cummulated length of its constituting first order formulas.

First we can conclude $\mathrm{NE}^{\mathrm{NP}}$ hardness: From Example 1 we know that the restriction of Σ_2^1 to the Skolemized form $\exists \mathbf{S} \forall \mathbf{T} \exists \mathbf{x} \forall \mathbf{y} \phi$, where ϕ is quantifierfree, is $\mathrm{NE}^{\mathrm{NP}}$ hard wrt expression complexity. The capturing proof for quantifierfree default logic from [6] features a logspace mapping f which associates with each skolemized Σ_2^1 formula ϕ a default theory $f(\phi)$, s.t. $\mathcal{A} \models \phi$ iff $\mathcal{A} \vdash_{f(\phi)} V$, for a fixed literal V. Therefore, we can further proceed like in example 1: Given a circuit C, take the hard formula hard$_2 = \phi_2^{(|C|)}[circ_1(C), circ_2(C), circ_3(C), circ_4(C)]$ from Theorem 14, Skolemize it and apply f. The resulting quantifierfree default theory is equivalent to the original formula and computable from C in logspace.

As for membership, note that the computation of $\mathbf{ground}_{\mathcal{A}}(\phi)$ for fixed $\mathcal{A}$ is exponential in $|\phi|$. Therefore, each instance of the expression complexity problem can be deterministically reduced to an exponential size instance of DEF-cr, hence its complexity is bounded above by $\mathrm{NE}^{\mathrm{NP}}$. Thus we have proved the following Theorem:

Theorem 25. *First order default logic under credulous semantics is* $\mathrm{NE}^{\mathrm{NP}}$ *complete with respect to expression complexity. Hardness even holds for the quantifierfree case.*

5.3 Abduction

In the full paper [13] we apply our methods to derive the expression complexity of abduction from logic programs under cautious inference with stable model semantics. In particular, we analyze the expression complexity of the main problems in abductive reasoning which are: Given an instance of an abduction problem (i) does the problem have a solution (i.e., an explanation); (ii) does a given hypothesis belong to some explanation; and (iii) does a given hypothesis belong to all explanations. We obtain completeness results for the classes $\mathrm{E}\Sigma_2^P, \mathrm{E}\Sigma_3^P, \mathrm{E}\Theta_3^P$.

References

1. J.L.Balcázar, J.Diaz, J.Gabarro: Structural Complexity I. Springer Verlag, 1988.
2. A.Lozano, J.L.Balcázar. The Complexity of Graph Problems for Succinctly Represented Graphs. In: G.Goos,J.Hartmanis, eds., *Graph-Theoretic Concepts in Computer Science*, LNCS 411:277–286, Springer-Verlag, 1989.
3. J.L. Balcázar and A. Lozano and J. Torán. The Complexity of Algorithmic Problems on Succinct Instances. In R. Baeta-Yates and U. Manber, editors, *Computer Science*, pp. 351–377, Plenum Press, New York, 1992.
4. D.A. Barrington, N.Immerman, and H.Straubing. On Uniformity within NC^1. Journal of Computer and System Sciences, 41, 274-306, 1990.
5. A. Blass, Y. Gurevich. Henkin Quantifiers and Complete Problems. Annals of Pure and Applied Logic, 32(1986), 1-16.
6. M.Cadoli, T.Eiter, G.Gottlob. Using Default Logic as a Query Language. Proceedings (KR-94), pp.99–108.
7. E.Dahlhaus. Reductions to NP-complete Problems by Interpretations. Lecture Notes in Computer Science 171 (1984), 357-365.
8. T. Eiter and G. Gottlob and H. Mannila. Adding Disjunction to Datalog. *Proceedings ACM PODS-94* , May 1994, pp. 267–278.
9. H.Enderton. *A Mathematical Introduction to Logic*. Academic Press, 1972.
10. R. Fagin. Generalized First-Order Spectra and Polynomial-Time Recognizable Sets. In R. M. Karp editor *Complexity of Computation*, pp. 43–74, 1974.

11. G.Gottlob. Complexity Results for Nonmonotonic Logics. J.Logic Computation, Vol.2 No.3, pp.397-425, 1992.
12. G.Gottlob. Relativized Logspace and Generalized Quantifiers over Finite Structures. Available as Technical Report CD-TR/95/76. Extended Abstract to appear in *Proceedings of the 10th IEEE Symposium on Logic in Computer Science 1995.*
13. G.Gottlob, N.Leone, H.Veith. Second Order Logic and the Weak Exponential Hierarchies. Technical Report TR 95-80 Christian Doppler Lab for Expert Systems, Information Systems Department, TU Vienna.
14. J.Hartmanis, R.E.Stearns. On the computational complexity of algorithms. Trans.Amer.Math.Soc.117 (1965), pp.285-306.
15. J. Hartmanis, N. Immerman, and V. Sewelson. Sparse Sets in NP-P: $EXPTIME$ versus $NEXPTIME$. *Information and Control*, 65:159–181, 1985.
16. J. Hartmanis and Y. Yesha. Computation Times of NP Sets of Different Densities. *Theoretical Computer Science*, 34:17–32, 1984.
17. Lane A. Hemachandra. The Strong Exponential Hierarchy Collapses *Journal of Computer and System Sciences*, 39:299–322, 1989.
18. L.Henkin. Some remarks on infinitely long formulas. Proceedings of the Symposium on the Foundations of Mathematics, Warsaw, 1959, pp.167-183.
19. J.Hintikka. Quantifiers in Logic and Quantifiers in Natural Languages. In S.Körner, editor, *Philosophy of Logic*, Basil Blackwell, Oxford.
20. N. Immerman. Languages that Capture Complexity Classes. *SIAM J. Computation*, 16(4):760-778, 1987.
21. D.S.Johnson. A Catalog of Complexity Classes. In van Leeuwen, ed., *Handbook of Theoretical Computer Science*, pp.67–162, Elsevier 1990.
22. P.G. Kolaitis and C.H. Papadimitriou. Why Not Negation by Fixpoint? *Journal of Computer and System Sciences*, 43, 125-144(1991).
23. R.E.Ladner, N.E.Lynch. Relativizations about Questions of logspace Computability. J.Comp.Sys.Sci. 10(1976), pp.19-32.
24. C. H. Papadimitriou. *Computational Complexity.* Addison-Wesley, 1994.
25. C.H. Papadimitriou and M. Yannakakis, A Note on Succinct Representations of Graphs, *Information and Computation*, 71:181–185, 1985.
26. C.S.Peirce. Abduction and Induction. In J.Buchler, editor, *Philosophical Writings of Peirce*, chapter 11. Dover, New York, 1955.
27. R.Reiter. A Logic for Default Reasoning. Artifical Intelligence, 13:81-132, 1980.
28. A. Selman. *Proc., 1st. Structure in Complexity Theory Conference*, LNCS 223, Springer-Verlag, New York/Berlin, June 1986.
29. I.A. Stewart. Complete Problems Involving Boolean Labelled Structures and Projection Transactions. *J.Logic Computation*, 1(6):861–882, 1991.
30. L. J. Stockmeyer. The Polynomial-Time Hierarchy. *Theoretical Computer Science*, 3:1–22,1977.
31. J.Väänänen. Remarks on generalized quantifiers and second order logics. Prace Naukowe Inst. Mat. Politech. Wroclawski ser. kon. (1977), 117-123.
32. M. Vardi. Complexity of Relational Query Languages. In *Proceedings 14th STOC*, pp. 137–146, 1982.
33. H.Veith. Logical Reducibilities in Finite Model Theory. Master's Thesis, Technical University of Vienna, Vienna, 1994.
34. K.Wagner. Bounded Query Classes. SIAM J.Comput., 19(5):833-846, 1990.
35. W.Walkoe. Finite partially ordered quantification. JSL 35(1970), 535-550.

On the Computing Paradigm and Computational Complexity

Juris Hartmanis*
Department of Computer Science
Cornell University
Ithaca NY 14853
USA

Abstract. Computational complexity theory is the study of the quantitative laws that govern computing. Since the computing paradigm is universal and pervasive, the quantitative laws of computational complexity apply to all information processing from numerical computations and simulation to logical reasoning and formal theorem proving, as well as processes of rational reasoning.

In this view, the search for what is and is not feasibly computable takes on an even deeper significance than just a central problem in theoretical computer science. The search for the limits of what is feasibly computable is the search for the limits of scientific theories and, possibly, rational reasoning.

1 Introduction

We all are witnessing the explosive and unprecedented growth of computer and communications technology which is profoundly changing our societies. At the same time, in parallel to and intertwined with technological developments, are exciting and far reaching intellectual developments which have yielded new concepts and results about computing, the nature of mathematical proofs and possibly intellectual processes.

The computing paradigm (as we know it today) is universal and encompasses the full power of formal mathematical reasoning — humankind's most powerful scientific tool. But the same computing paradigm also revealed very clearly the limitations of formal mathematical systems; as already shown by Goedel, we will never establish the completeness and consistency of these formal systems.

Following Goedel's work, recursive function theory clarified what is and is not effectively computable — computable in principle without any feasibility considerations. The central task of computational complexity theory is to determine what is and is not feasibly computable — what are the limits of what is (will be) practically computable.

Since computing is universal, we believe that the quantitative laws about computing apply broadly to all rational (formal?) reasoning processes. Therefore,

* Supported in part by National Science Foundation Grant CCR-91-23730

the search for the limits of the feasibly computable may yield insights about the limits of scientific theories and, ultimately, limits of what is knowable.

I believe that the understanding of what quantitative laws govern information processing in physical and biological systems will parallel the developments in physics. Just as physical laws were known to govern the physical world, and later were seen to also govern the biological world — so I am convinced, we will see that the computing paradigm and the quantitative laws that govern computing apply to all information processing in hardware as well as biological systems.

To understand what is and is not feasibly computable we face two different aspects of this problem, one technological and one theoretical. First of all, we have to estimate what kind of computing technologies will be available and how much computing power will they provide. Second, we have to determine what computations can be performed with the projected computing technologies and computing power.

Both of these are central problems in computer science and engineering. Computer science is actively involved in improving the performance of our computing devices and exploring new computing technologies and the limits of these technologies. The task of theoretical computer science is to clarify what problems can be solved with what computing resources.

The problems facing theoretical computer science seem formidable. A lot of progress has been made, but we have to admit that the key open problems have not yet been seriously threatened. We have a long way to go before we can hope for real understanding of the complexity of computations and grasp the limits of feasible computations.

As a matter of fact, this is a very exciting time in the search for what is feasibly computable. There are many new theoretical insights about computational complexity and particularly interesting results about interactive proofs which shed new light on the nature of mathematical proofs, nonapproximability of hard problems and even on the meaning of relativization results in complexity theory. There are new insights about the computational power of "quantum computing technology" and very impressive demonstration about "molecular computing" followed by more recent theoretical results about it. It will be very interesting to see how these new computing technologies develop and if they can compete or even best the current, more mature technologies.

Finally, these developments raise again deeper questions about the relations between computing and physical processes. In particular, what physical processes, if any, can go beyond the Turing computability (say, in generation of unbounded random sequences) and which processes can go beyond feasible Turing computation. Stated differently, what limits, if any, do quantitative laws about complexity impose on the physical world and vice versa.

2 Separation Problems in Computational Complexity

The research in computational complexity has yielded many interesting results with some surprising insights. Still, the key separation problems remain open and at this time we may not yet have the needed mathematical techniques to resolve them.

The state of affairs in complexity theory can be epitomized by Figure 1. representing the structure of the main complexity classes. Please note that this is a highly simplified picture which leaves out many important complexity classes. Most probabilistic (randomized) complexity classes are not shown, nor is the fine structure below P.

The encouraging aspect of this situation is, that it is clear that these and other complexity classes are important and robust mathematical objects. Many of these classes can be defined by their natural complete problems or by the computational resource bounds and they stay invariant under reasonable modifications of our computing mode. Furthermore, many of these classes appear naturally in other settings or disciplines not directly related to computing. For example, they can appear as classes definable in various logical systems or classes defined as closures under various mathematical operations.

The discouraging part of the situation is that in spite of a serious twenty-five-year effort, we have not been able to show that these classes are different nor by how much they differ. In our picture, we have not been able to separate any of the classes between P and $PSPACE$.

It is quite surprising that in the whole awesome mathematical arsenal of results and proof techniques there does not seem to be any technique to attack these separation problems. At the same time, these separation problems are among the most important problems in theoretical computer science and possibly in all of mathematics (but they are not yet so recognized by most mathematicians).

I personally believe that the separation problems can and will be solved, but it is also clear that among lower bound problems or separations problems are many problems not provable in our formal mathematical systems — they are independent of the formal systems. The logical structure of the separation problems forces independence results to exist and this may be a (partial) reason why they appear to be so hard.

To exhibit the independence results we just have to observe that the sets of machines naming the languages in the difference sets, such as $NP - P$, $PSPACE - NP$ or even $TIME[n^3] - TIME[n^2]$, are complete sets for Π_2 of the Kleene Hierarchy [13]. More explicitly let $N_1, N_2, N_3, \ldots$ be the standard enumeration of NP-machines and let $L(N_i)$ denote the language accepted by N_i. Then, if $P \neq NP$, we can easily show that

$$\Delta = \{N_i \mid L(N_i) \in NP - P\}$$

is a Π_2 -complete set in the Kleene Hierarchy. From this follows:

Theorem: Let F by a sound and axiomatizable formal system. If $P \neq NP$ then there exists a language $A \in NP - P$, such that for no N_i, with $L(N_i) = A$, is there a proof in F that $L(N_i) \notin P$.

Proof: If for every $A \in NP - P$ there is a proof in F for some N_i, $L(N_i) = A$, that $L(N_i) \notin P$, then there is an r.e. set (and therefore a recursive set)

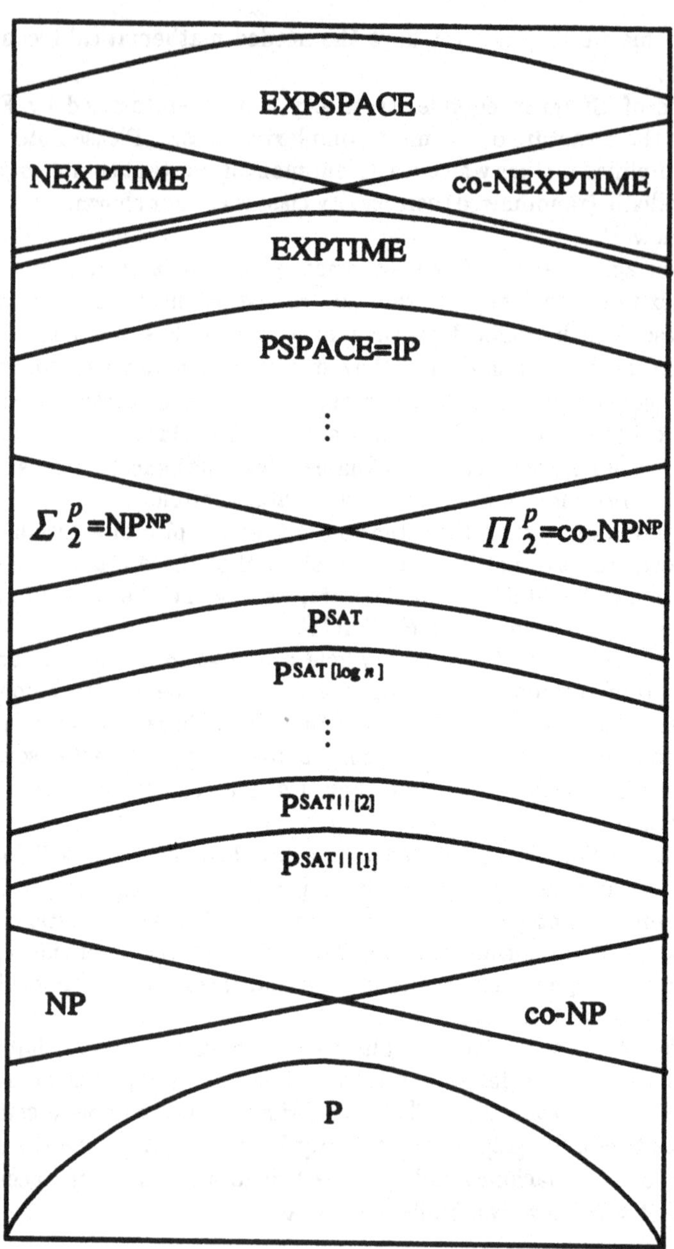
EXPSPACE
NEXPTIME
co-NEXPTIME
EXPTIME
PSPACE=IP
Σ_2^p=NP^{NP}
Π_2^p=co-NP^{NP}
P^{SAT}
P$^{SAT[\log n]}$
P$^{SAT||[2]}$
P$^{SAT||[1]}$
NP
co-NP
P

Fig. 1.

$\{N_{ij} \mid j \geq 1\}$ such that

$$\{L(N_{ij}) \mid j \geq 1\} = NP - P.$$

But then we could write

$$\Delta = \{N_k | (\exists_j)\ (\forall_x)\ [N_k(x) = N_{ij}(x)]\}$$

as a $\sum_2$ set. This is a contradiction to Δ being Π_2-complete. Thus, the desired language A in $NP - P$ exists and there is no proof for any $N_i, L(N_i) = A$, that $L(N_i) \notin P$. □

It should be observed that the above result is not simply based on the fact that we can not decide what a Turing machines does; it is not based on a specific (opaque) machine accepting the set A. The result states that for no representation of A can it be shown that A is not in P.

This result shows that there is no total victory over the NP problem. Even if we could prove in F that $P \neq NP$, there will remain an infinite number of languages in $NP - P$ for which there is no proof in F(for any of their representations) that they are not in P.

As a matter of fact, this is also the situation for time or space bounded classes. For example, we know that

$$TIME[n^3] \neq TIME[n^2]$$

and still there are, by a proof of the same type, infinitely many languages in $TIME\ [n^3] - TIME\ [n^2]$ for which there are no proofs in F that they are not in $TIME\ [n^2]$, for any representation of these languages.

On the other hand, there are more encouraging news. For a long time it was a widely held opinion that problems which have contradictory randomization, which most separation problems have, are beyond the power of current mathematical techniques. Since there exist recursive oracles A and B, such that

$$P^A = NP^A \ \ and \ \ P^B \neq NP^B,$$

we know that certain proof techniques will not solve this problem and it was believed that the needed techniques were not yet discovered [14].

The results about interactive proofs show that this is not the case and, furthermore, that the Random Oracle Hypothesis (ROH) points in the wrong direction in this case [5].

First of all, let me say that I consider the stream of research results about and emanating from the interactive proof concept as one of the most impressive developments in complexity theory during the last decade. I believe that this work represents a beautiful example how the computing paradigm, in two different settings [2, 12], led to new computing models whose exploration led to surprising new insights about the unexpected computational power of randomization and interaction. This research led also to new understanding of the nature of probabilistic checking of long mathematical proofs to gain confidence that there exists a proof without seeing the whole proof. Furthermore, it lead to a whole new set of nonapproximability results about NP problems, which had been open for a long time. Finally, these results shed also some new light on the meaning of oracle results in the search for solutions to the separation problems.

Recall that Shamir [19] showed that

$$IP = PSPACE.$$

Thus resolving a very interesting problem which had contradictory relativizations, since these are recursive oracles A and B such that

$$IP^A = PSPACE^A \text{ and } IP^B \neq PSPACE^B.$$

Furthermore, it can be shown that [5, 11] for almost all oracles (i.e. for random oracles with probability 1)

$$IP^A \neq PSPACE^A,$$

or even more dramatically that

$$co - NP^A \not\subseteq IP^A.$$

This demonstrates that the Random Oracle Hypothesis, attributed to Bennett and Gill [4], is false. This hypothesis essentially states that the relationships between complexity classes which hold for almost all relativized words must also hold in the unrelativized case. There have been previous counterexamples to the ROH [15] but this is the most compelling one. Furthermore, it can be seen [5] that the ROH is very sensitive to small changes in the definition. For the class $IPP, IPP = IP$, defined with slightly different probability condition than IP, for almost all oracles A

$$IPP^A = PSPACE^A.$$

Such sensitivity to small changes in the model makes ROH an unlikely touchstone to indicate the direction the results are likely to go. Nevertheless, in many cases ROH points in the same direction as our current intuition. For example, for almost all oracles A,

$$P^A \neq NP^A \neq co - NP^A$$

$$SPACE^A[logn] \neq P^A$$

$$PSPACE^A \neq EXPTIME^A$$

$$PH^A \subsetneq PSPACE^A$$

$$| PH^A |= \infty.$$

And contrary to some beliefs

$$P^A = RP^A = BPP^A.$$

Also somewhat to my embarrassment, the Berman-Hartmanis conjecture that all NP-complete sets are P-isomorphic, fails for almost all oracles, but not all [3, 10, 16].

The $IP = PSPACE$ result demonstrates that problems with contradictory relativizations can indeed be solved and should encourage us to attack the separation problems with new vigor.

The only negative note here is that in this case the two classes, IP and $PSPACE$, were shown to be equal and that we still do not have any result showing two natural complexity classes with contradictory relativizations to be distinct.

3 The Computing Paradigm and Nature

To assess the limits of the computing paradigm and in particular the limits of the feasibly computable, we must have the right models of computing and explore what computations can be performed by various physical and biological processes.

At this time, I believe that the Church-Turing thesis properly captures what is and is not effectively computable (even if there are skeptics on this issue [20]). Still, there remain open questions if there are processes in nature which are beyond effective computability. Particularly intriguing is the question about random sequences. We know that Turing machines can not compute Kolomogorov random strings longer than the machine description. Thus there is a very definite limitation on effective computability when it comes to randomness. On the other hand, the standard interpretation of quantum mechanics is probabilistic and thus it seems that nature may not be bound by the same limitations as effective computing. At closer inspection, the situation does not seem that clear. The often suggested source of natural randomness, the process of radioactive decay, does not violate the "computing" restriction. The radioactive decay uses up a finite resource and after it has decayed, the randomness has been used up. This in essence corresponds to encoding long random strings in a Turing machine and then printing it out.

A convincing demonstration that nature can violate the "computing" restrictions requires a finite physical system that can produce arbitrary long random strings. Clearly this can not be achieved without putting energy in the finite physical system to be able to output (signal) the long random string. The trick is how to get the energy into the finite physical system without adding randomness. It would be very interesting to see if there is a nice, crisp, finite physical model that can generate arbitrary long random strings (with energy added to it without adding randomness). So far I have not seen a convincing argument how to do this.

A related theoretical problem is raised by the alleged unpredictability of chaotic systems. Much has been said and written about chaotic systems, but we do not seem to have a proof that they indeed are not predictable. In a sense, this is a classic computational complexity problem. Consider a dynamic system, for example,

$$x = \lambda x(1 - x),$$

and prove how hard it is to decide some property of x after n iterations. If the complexity of the decision requires roughly the same number of operations as the iterations, then this system can be justly called unpredictable.

So far we have no proof that there are no mathematical shortcuts which allow to make computationally easy predictions about the very complex behavior of a chaotic system. I consider this as a key complexity problem about dynamic systems and hope that it is resolved reasonably soon.

In order to estimate what computing power will be available in the future we face the very interesting question about what natural phenomena can be exploited for computing devices and how powerful could these devices be eventually.

It seems that we can reasonably well estimate the growth potential for the current "mature" computer technologies. Even for several related new technologies (based on various quantum theoretic effects) the ultimate limits can be estimated. In all these cases, though the projected computing power has the potential to grow by orders of magnitude, the problems requiring exponential time on Turing machines remain out of reach for the projected machines already for fair size problems.

The intriguing question is if there are natural phenomena that could be exploited to break the exponential barrier. Quite recently two new potential computing techniques have caused considerable excitement: quantum computing and melocular computing. Both are bold and interesting scientific explorations.

Feynman [8, 9] discussed the possibly intrinsic difficulty of computational simulation of quantum mechanics and suggested using quantum mechanical principles to build computers to overcome these computational difficulties. Deutsch [6, 7] has outlined a model of quantum computation. The latest excitement about quantum computing was ignited by Shor's result [18] that factoring and finding discrete logarithms can be done on a quantum computer in polynomial time, i.e. they are in the complexity class BQP (problems solvable with bounded probability on a quantum computer in polynomial time). At the present, no polynomial time Turing machine algorithms are known for these problems.

These results raise interesting theoretical questions about the relations of BQP to the classical complexity classes—and thus the power of the quantum computing model. It is know [18] that

$$BQP \subseteq P^{\sharp P} \subseteq PSPACE$$

leaving open the fascinating questions about relations between BQP and BPP and NP.

The questions about the feasibility of quantum computers are very complex and at this time it is not at all clear that even simple demonstration models can be realized. At the same time, even the possibility of just building special purpose quantum computers for fast factoring of large integers should already send shockwaves through the cryptographic community.

The interest in molecular computing was ignited by Adleman's recent paper "Molecular Computation of Solutions of Combinatorial Problems" [1, 17]. Adleman's paper appeared on November 11, 1994, and has received a lot of national publicity since then, including a *New York Times* article on December 13, 1995, about Adleman's scientific career.

The paper describes how the Hamiltonian path problem for a seven node graph was encoded in DNA sequences and the Hamiltonian path was extracted as a single DNA string using standard lab techniques after seven days of lab work. This is indeed a very impressive achievement and may stimulate thorough exploration of the potential of molecular computing. As pointed out in this article, the numbers of "operations" performed in biological computing can be very high and the energy requirements are surprisingly small. At the same time, as we will observe later, even these computations can not escape the exponential curse; if the computations are indeed exponential, then their weight is prohibitive.

The following nondeterministic algorithm was used to solve the directed Hamiltonian path problem:

Step 1: Generate random paths through the graph.
Step 2: Keep only paths that begin with *in-node* and end with *out-node*.
Step 3: If the graph has n vertices, then keep only those paths that enter exactly n vertices.
Step 4: Keep only those paths that enter all of the vertices of the graph at least once.
Step 5: If any paths remain, say "Yes;" otherwise, say "No."

If this algorithm is used then in step 1 one has to expect to generate almost all possible paths through the graph to find a path satisfying the remaining conditions. Though the paths are encoded molecularly (with DNA strands) they have weight and the question arises: How heavy will these computations get? In short, we have to consider a new computational complexity measure: the weight of the computation to assess its feasibility.

Consider a graph with 200 nodes and assume that to extract a Hamiltonian path we need to generate an exponential number of paths of length n. A lower bound for the encoding of the edges and the paths in the graph in DNA sequences is $log_4 200$ bases per edge and a low estimate of the weight per base is $10^{-25}kg$. Thus the biologically encoded set of paths will weigh more than

$$2^{200} \cdot log_4 200 \cdot 10^{-25}kg \geq (2^4)^{50} \cdot 3 \cdot 10^{-25}kg \geq 3 \cdot 10^{25}kg$$

which is more than the weight of the Earth.

Adleman's molecular solution of the Hamiltonian path problem is indeed a magnificent achievement and may initiate an intensive exploration of molecular computing and computing in biological systems. At the same time, the exponential function grows too fast and the atoms are a bit too heavy to hope that molecular computing can break the exponential barrier, this time the weight barrier.

4 Conclusion

We have argued that the quantitative laws that govern computing apply generally to rational reasoning and thus further emphasize the importance of clarifying what is and is not feasibly computable.

At the present, though some existing new computing technologies are being explored, we can only count on the steady and more easily predictable improvement of computing power via the "mature" computing technologies.

The understanding of what can be computed with the projected computing power leads back to the need to resolve the classic separation problems, which have so far resisted all direct attacks. At the same time, many new insights have been gained about the complexity of computations and the nature of mathematical proofs.

5 References

1. Adleman, Leonard M.: Molecular Computation of Solutions of Combinatorial Problems. *Science* **266** (Nov. 1994) 1021-1024
2. Babai, L.: Trading group theory for randomness. ACM Symposium on Theory of Computing, (1985) 421-429
3. Berman, L. and Hartmanis, J.: On isomorphism and density of NP and other complete sets. *SIAM Journal on Computing* **6** (1977) 305-322
4. Bennett, C. and J. Gill: Relative to a Random Oracle $A, P^A \neq NP^A \neq co-NP^A$ with probability 1. *SIAM J. Comput.* **10** No. 1 (1981) 96-113
5. Chang, Richard, Benny Chor, Oded Goldreich, Juris Hartmanis, Johan Hastad, Desh Ranjan and Pankaj Rohatgi: The Random Oracle Hypothesis is False. *J. Computer and System Sciences* **49** (August 1994) 24-39
6. Deutsch, D.: Quantum theory, the Church-Turing principle and the universal quantum computer. *Proc. Roy. Soc. Lond.* **A400** (1985) 96-117
7. Deutsch, D. and Jozsa, R.: Rapid solution of problems by quantum computation. *Proc. Roy. Soc. Lond.* **A39** (1992) 553-558
8. Feynman, R.: Simulating physics with computers. *International Journal of Theoretical Physics* **21** No. 6/7 (1982) 467-488
9. Feynman, R.: Quantum mechanical computers. *Foundations of Physics* **16** (1986) 507-531 (Originally appeared in *Optics News*, Feb. 1985)
10. Fenner, S. and Fortnow, and Kurtz, S.: The isomorphism conjecture holds relative to an oracle. *SIAM J. Comp.* to appear.
11. Fortnow, L. and Sipser, M.: Are there interactive protocols for co-NP languages? *Inform. Proc. Lett.* **28** (1988) 249-251

12. Goldwasser, S. Micali, S. and Rackoff, C.: The knowledge complexity of interactive proof systems. *SIAM J. Comput.* **18** No. 1 (1989) 186-208
13. Hartmanis, J.: Structural Complexity Column: "On the Importance of Being Π_2 Hard. *Bulletin of the European Association of Theoretical Computer Science (EATCS)* **37** (Feb. 1989) 117-127
14. Hopcroft, J. E.: Turing machines. *Sci. Amer.*, (May 1984) 86-98
15. Kurtz, S. A.: On the random oracle hypothesis. ACM Symposium on Theory of Computing, 1982. 224-230
16. Kurtz, S.A. with Mahaney, S.R. and Royer, J.S.: The isomorphism conjecture fails relative to a random oracle. ACM Symposium on Theory of Computing, 1989. 157-166
17. Lipton, Richard J.: DNA Solutions to Hard Computational Problems. *Science* **262** (April, 1995) 542-545
18. Schor, Peter W.: Algorithms for Quantum Computation: Discrete Logarithms and Factoring. "Proceedings 35th Annual Symposium on Foundations of Computer Science." (Nov. 1994)
19. Shamir, A.: $IP = PSPACE$. Journal of the ACM **39** (1992) 869-877
20. Siegelman, Hava T.: Computation Beyond the Turing Limit *Science* **262** (April, 1995) 545-548

Ranked Structures in Nonmonotonic Reasoning and Belief Revision: Abstract

Daniel Lehmann[1]

Institute of Computer Science, Hebrew University, Jerusalem 91904, Israel

Recent results have shown the intimate connections existing between belief revision, nonmonotonic reasoning and some ordered structures. Belief Revision studies how one should revise its beliefs in the presence of new information that may contradict those beliefs. In [1], a set of postulates, the AGM postulates, for belief revision was proposed. An equivalent description in terms of a binary relation, epistemic entrenchment, on formulas was discovered in [2]. Nonmonotonic Reasoning is deduction in the presence of default information. A system of nonmonotonic reasoning may be described by a binary relation on formulas, the corresponding nonmonotonic consequence relation. In [5], the family of rational relations was proposed to describe disciplined nonmonotonic reasoning. Rational relations are representable by modular order relations on the set of propositional models. In [3], it was shown that the revisions that satisfy the AGM postulates are exactly those for which the revision of every fixed theory defines a consistency-preserving rational relation. Modular order relations on propositional models also provide interesting models for belief revision. Revision procedures that may be defined this way cannot be studied in the original AGM framework, but, in [4], they have been characterized by postulates in an extended framework in which iterated revisions are explicit in the formalism.

References

1. Alchourrón, C.A., Gärdenfors, P., Makinson, D.: On the logic of theory change: partial meet contraction and revision functions. J. of Symbolic Logic **50** (1985) 510–530
2. Gärdenfors, P., Makinson, D.: Revisions of knowledge systems using epistemic entrenchment. Proceedings of the Second Conference on Theoretical Aspects of Reasoning About Knowledge (Vardi, ed.) Morgan Kaufmann (1988) 83–95
3. Gärdenfors, P., Makinson, D.: Nonmonotonic inference based on expectations. J. of Artificial Intelligence **65** (1994) 197–245
4. Lehmann, D.: Belief revision, revised. Proc. of 14th I.J.C.A.I., Montreal, Canada, (1995)
5. Lehmann, D., Magidor, M.: What does a conditional knowledge base entail? J. of Artificial Intelligence **55** (1992) 1–60

* This work was partially supported by the Jean and Helene Alfassa fund for research in Artificial Intelligence and by grant 136/94-1 of the Israel Science Foundation on "New Perspectives on Nonmonotonic Reasoning".

Symbolic Dynamics and Finite Automata

Dominique Perrin

Université de Marne la Vallée
93166 Noisy le Grand
France

Abstract. In this survey, we present some connections between notions and results in automata theory and other ones in symbolic dynamics.

1 Introduction

Symbolic dynamics is a field born with the work in topology of Marston Morse at the beginning of the years 20 [25]. It is, according to Morse, an *"algebra and geometry of recurrence"*. The idea is to study the sequences of symbols obtained by scanning the successive regions of a surface met while following a trajectory starting from a given point. A further paper by Morse and Hedlund ([24]) gives the basic results of this theory. Later, the theory was developed by many authors as a branch of ergodic theory (see for example the collected works in [32] or [7]). One of the main directions of research has been the problem of the *isomorphism of subshifts of finite type* (see below the definition of these objects). It is not yet completely solved although the last results of Kim and Roush [21] indicate a counterexample to a long-standing conjecture formulated by F. Williams [34].

There are many links between symbolic dynamics and the theory of automata, as pointed out by R. Adler and B. Weiss ([33]). The interplay is interesting to explore since it brings new problems and methods. In this paper, I will present some of these interconnections and report some of the new results that have been obtained in this direction together with some interesting open problems.

The material presented here does not cover all existing connections of this kind. There are in particular interesting links between symbolic dynamics and representation of numbers that are not presented here (see [17]). There are also important connections with cellular automata (see e.g. [11]).

2 What is symbolic dynamics about?

We present in this Section a short introduction to the concepts of symbolic dynamics. For a more detailed exposition, we refer to [32].

We consider the set $A^{\mathbb{Z}}$ of two-sided infinite words as a topological space with respect to the usual product topology. The *shift* transformation σ acts on $A^{\mathbb{Z}}$ bijectively. It associates to $x \in A^{\mathbb{Z}}$ the element $y = \sigma(x) \in A^{\mathbb{Z}}$ defined for $n \in \mathbb{Z}$ by

$$y_n = x_{n+1}$$

A *symbolic dynamical system* or *subshift* is a subset S of $A^{\mathbb{Z}}$ which is both

1. closed and,
2. shift-invariant i.e. such that $\sigma(S) = S$.

The system is denoted S or (S, σ) to emphasize the role of the shift σ. For example, $(A^{\mathbb{Z}}, \sigma)$ itself is a symbolic dynamical system, often called the *full shift* in contrast with other ones called *subshifts* to refer to the embedding in $A^{\mathbb{Z}}$.

It is not difficult to verify that a subshift is given unambiguously by a set of ordinary finite words $F = F_S \subset A^*$ subject to the conditions to be

1. factorial: $uvw \in F \Rightarrow v \in F$.
2. extensible: $\forall v \in F, \exists u, w \in F : uvw \in F$

The subshift S is said to be *irreducible* if for any $x, y \in F$ there is a word u such that $xuy \in F$. It is said to be *primitive* if there is an integer $n > 0$ such that all such words u can be chosen of length n.

A *morphism* between two subshifts (S, σ) and (T, τ) is a map $f : S \to T$ which is continuous and commutes with the shift, i.e. such that $f\sigma = \tau f$. When f is a morphism from S onto T, it is said that T is a *factor* of S.

An *isomorphism* or a *conjugacy* is a bijective morphism. If f is an isomorphism from S onto T, then S and T are said to be *conjugate*.

Let $k \geq 1$ and let $f : A^k \to B$ be a function. We still denote by f the mapping from $A^{\mathbb{Z}}$ into $B^{\mathbb{Z}}$ associating to a word $x \in A^{\mathbb{Z}}$ the word $y = f(x)$ defined for $n \in \mathbb{Z}$ by

$$y_n = f(x_n x_{n+1} \cdots x_{n+k-1})$$

Such a function f is said to be *k-local.* It is well-known that a function $f : S \subset A^{\mathbb{Z}} \to Y \subset B^{\mathbb{Z}}$ is a morphism if it is, up to some composition with the shift, k-local for some $k \geq 0$.

A morphism between subshifts can be realized by a local automaton with set of states the set A^{k-1} of words of length $k-1$ and an edge between au and ub labelled $(b, f(aub))$. The morphism is said to be *right-resolving* if the automaton is deterministic.

A *sofic system* is a subshift S which is the set of labels of infinite paths in a finite graph labelled by the symbols of A. A sofic system is thus essentially the same as a subshift recognizable by a finite automaton.

A *system of finite type* is a subshift which is made of all infinite words avoiding a given finite set of words. One can prove that this notion, (as that of a sofic system) is invariant under conjugacy in the sense that any conjugate of a system of finite type is again of finite type.

Any system of finite type can be obtained, up to conjugacy, as follows: let G be a finite graph with E as its set of edges. Let S_G be the subshift of $E^{\mathbb{Z}}$ formed of all biinfinite paths in G. It is clear that S_G is a subshift of finite type and that any subshift of finite type defined by a set of forbidden blocks of length 2 is of that form. Clearly, any system of finite type is also a sofic system. Conversely, it follows from the definition of a sofic system that any sofic system is a factor of some system of finite type.

3 The Shannon cover

The close connection between a subshift S and the set F_S of its finite blocks leads to a possibility of studying the same objects from both points of view of symbolic dynamics and of finite automata as first shown by F. Blanchard and G. Hansel [10].

As a first example of a result with equivalent formulations in terms of symbolic dynamics and in terms of finite automata, the existence of a unique minimal automaton takes the following form for sofic systems.

A *right-resolving cover* of a sofic system S is a right-resolving morphism $f : T \to S$ from a system of finite type $T = T_G$ onto S. It is *minimal* if the graph G has the minimal possible number of vertices.

It has been shown by Fischer [16] that an irreducible sofic system has a unique minimal right-resolving cover. It is often called the *Shannon cover*. It is actually essentially equivalent to the minimal deterministic automaton of the set F_S as shown by Danièle Beauquier (see [6],[4]).

4 Codes and finite-to-one maps

A morphism $\varphi : S \to Y$ is said to be *finite-to-one* if, for all $y \in Y$, the set $\varphi^{-1}(y)$ is finite. There is a close connection between this notion and that of codes and *unambiguous automata.*

Indeed, let $\mathcal{A} = (Q, 1, 1)$ be a strongly connected automaton with a unique initial and final state $1 \in Q$. Let X be the set of labels of simple paths from 1 to 1. The map going from paths in the automaton to their labels is finite-to-one iff the automaton is unambiguous. Moreover, the automaton is unambiguous iff the set X is recognized unambiguously and is a code.

This connection allows to translate results from codes to finite-to-one maps and conversely. For instance, a result due to Ehrenfeucht and Rosenberg says that any rational code is included in a finite maximal one (see [8] p. 62). An analogous proof can be used to obtain the following result [2]:

Theorem 1. *If S, T are irreducible subshifts of finite type, and $\varphi : S \to T$ is a finite-to-one morphism, then there is a subshift of finite type U containing S and a finite-to-one morphism from U onto T extending φ.*

The theorem of Ehrenfeucht and Rozenberg corresponds to the case where T is the full shift. The more general case where a code X is constraint to be included in a fixed factorial set F has been studied by A. Restivo who has shown that the results known previously extend to this case [28].

The paper [2] contains other results of the same kind. One of them deals with *right-closing* morphisms, a notion intermediary between finite-to-one and right-resolving which is defined precisely as follows.

A function $\varphi : S \to T$ is right-closing if whenever $x, y \in S$ have a common left-infinite tail and $\varphi(x) = \varphi(y)$ then $x = y$. Right-closing morphisms correspond to automata with ***bounded delay*** in the same way as right-resolving morphisms correspond to deterministic automata. The result on right-closing morphisms proved in [2] corresponds to one on codes with bounded deciphering delay proved by V. Bruyère, L. Wong and L. Zhang in [14]: any rational code with finite deciphering delay may be embedded into a rational maximal one.

Finally, the paper [2] contains an analogous result on extending morphisms belonging this time to the class of ***biclosing*** morphisms i.e. morphisms that are both left and right closing. This is related to a result proved recently by L. Zhang: any rational biprefix code can be embedded into a rational maximal one [35].

5 Shift equivalence

Let $S = S_G, T = T_H$ be two subshifts of finite type given by the adjacency matrices M, N of the graphs G, H. In [34], R. F. Williams has introduced two equivalence relations on matrices allowing to formulate in algebraic terms the relation of conjugacy on the subshifts.

Two square matrices M, N with nonnegative coefficients are said to be *elementary shift equivalent* if there exist two nonnegative integral matrices U, V such that

$$M = UV, \qquad N = VU \tag{1}$$

Note that M and N may be of different dimensions.

Then M and N are called ***strong shift equivalent*** if there is a chain of elementary shift equivalences between M and N. We then have the following result

Theorem 2. (Williams [34]) *Two subshifts of finite type S and T given by the matrices M, N as above are conjugate iff the matrices M, N are strong shift equivalent.*

Before introducing the second equivalence relation, we make two observations about strong shift equivalence.

First, the relation of strong shift equivalence is not easy to compute because in a chain $(M_1, M_2, \ldots, M_n)$ of elementary equivalences, the dimensions of the matrices M_i is not a priori bounded. It is actually not known whether it is recursively computable or not.

Second, it is worth noting that there is a combinatorial version of the elementary equivalence in terms of *state splitting*. The operation of (output) splitting is the following. It operates on a graph G transforming it in a graph G'. Let v be a vertex of G. Let I be the set of edges of G entering v and S the set of edges going out of v. Let $S = S' + S''$ be a partition of the set S. We transform the vertex v into two vertices v', v'' with both the set I of input edges and with S' (resp. S'') as set of outgoing edges for v' (resp. v''). The operation of output split is dual and obtained by partitioning the set I of in-going edges instead of S.

Then it can be proved that a strong shift equivalence can be obtained by a sequence of input and output splitting and conversely [34].

We now come to the second equivalence relation on square matrices. Two square matrices M and N are called *shift equivalent* if there exist two nonnegative integral matrices U, V and an integer k such that

$$\begin{array}{ccc} MU = UN & , & NV = VM \\ M^k = UV & , & N^k = VU \end{array} \tag{2}$$

It is clear that $k = 1$ corresponds to an elementary shift equivalence and thus that strong shift equivalence implies shift equivalence.

The converse was posed by Williams as a problem: does shift equivalence imply strong shift equivalence? It was shown by Kim and Roush in [21] that the answer is negative in general. However the subshifts of their counterexample are reducible and the conjecture is still pending for irreducible subshifts of finite type.

It is interesting to note that shift equivalence has been proved decidable by Kim and Roush [20]. Also, the problem of comparing, inside a given semigroup, the various relations generalising the group conjugacy has been studied by several authors (see [15]). It is however a different problem here since the relation is defined among square matrices of different dimensions and not inside a semigroup.

6 Entropy

The *entropy* of a subshift S is the limit

$$h(S) = \lim_{n\to\infty} \frac{1}{n} \log s_n$$

where s_n is the number of blocks of length n appearing in the elements of S.

Let X be a rational code and let S be the associated sofic system formed of all biinfinite sequences of elements of X. The entropy of S is equal to $\log(1/r)$ where $r = r_X$ is the unique positive real number r such that

$$\sum_{x\in X} r^{|x|} = 1.$$

In other terms, if $\alpha_n = \mathrm{Card}(X \cap A^n)$ and $f_X(z) = \sum_{n\geq 0} \alpha_n z^n$, then r_X is the unique positive root of $f_X(z) = 1$. If the alphabet A has k elements, then $r_X \leq 1/k$ or equivalently

$$f_X(1/k) \leq 1 \tag{3}$$

which is Kraft's inequality. Conversely, for any series f with positive coefficients satisfying (3), it is well-known that there exists a prefix code X on a k-symbol alphabet such that $f = f_X$.

Recall that a series $f = \sum_{k\geq 0} f_k z^k$ is said to be an $\mathbb{N}$-rational series if there exists a nonnegative integral $n \times n$ matrix M, and two vectors $i \in \mathbb{N}^{1\times n}, t \in \mathbb{N}^{n\times 1}$ such that identically $f_k = iM^k t$.

If X is a rational code, then f_X satisfies (3) and is additionally an $\mathbb{N}$-rational series. What can be said conversely? It is tempting to conjecture that for any $\mathbb{N}$-rational series $f = \sum_{n\geq 0} \alpha_n z^n$, such that $f(1/k) \leq 1$, there exists a rational prefix code X over a k-letter alphabet such that $f = f_X$.

A particular case of this is proved in [26].

If X is a finite code, then f_X is a polynomial and r_X has the property that it has no other positive real conjugate. The following result has been proved conversely by Handelman:

Theorem 3. (Handelman [19]) *An algebraic integer r satisfies $r = r_X$ for some finite code X iff it has no other real positive algebraic conjugate.*

This result has been extended to study the star height of one-variable rational series by F. Bassino. It was known that the star height of a one variable $\mathbb{N}$-rational series is at most two (see [30]). She has obtained, in the primitive case, a characterisation of the series of star height one [3].

7 The road colouring problem

A classical notion in automata theory is that of a *synchronizing word.* We recall that, given a deterministic and complete automaton $\mathcal{A}$ on a state set Q, a word w is said to be synchronizing if the state reached from any state $q \in Q$ after reading w is independent of q. The automaton itself is called synchronizing if there exists a synchronizing word.

A maximal prefix code X is called synchronizing if it is the set of first returns to the initial state in a synchronizing automaton.

It is clear that a necessary (but not sufficient) condition for an automaton to be synchronizing is that the underlying graph is primitive (i.e. strongly connected and the gcd of the cycle lengths is 1). The same holds for a prefix code (which is called aperiodic if it is maximal and the gcd of the word lengths is 1).

The following problem was raised in [1]. Let G be a finite directed graph with the following properties:

1. All the vertices of G have the same out-degree.
2. G is primitive.

The problem is to find, for any graph G satisfying these hypotheses, a labelling turning G into a synchronizing deterministic automaton. The problem is called the *road-colouring problem* because of the following interpretation: a labelling (or colouring) making the automaton synchronizing allows a traveller lost on the graph G to follow a path which is a succession of Coors leading back home wherever he actually started from.

In terms of symbolic dynamics, such a labelling defines a right-resolving map $f : S_G \to A^{\mathbb{Z}}$ from the system of finite type S_G onto a full shift which is 1-to-1 almost everywhere. In this context, a synchronizing word is called a *resolving block.*

It is proved in [1] that there exists a conjugate T of S_G such that such a map $f : T \to A^{\mathbb{Z}}$ exists. The proof consists in considering the subshift $S_{G^{(n)}}$, for large enough n, where $G^{(n)}$ is the graph having as edges the paths of length n in G. Actually, it is shown in [27] that this result can also be obtained applying a construction from [31].

The following result is proved in [27], providing a partial answer to the problem. For a prefix code X, we denote by T_X the usual (unlabelled) tree whose leaves correspond to the elements of X. Several prefix codes may thus correspond to the same tree according to the choice of a labelling of the sons of each node.

Theorem 4. *Given a finite aperiodic prefix code X, there is a synchronizing prefix code Y such that $T_X = T_Y$.*

The proof uses heavily the theorem of C. Reutenauer [29] on the non-commutative polynomial of a code.

In terms of symbolic dynamics, Theorem 4 solves positively the road colouring problem for those graphs G satisfying the following additional assumption:

(3) All vertices except one have in-degree 1.

The road-colouring problem itself remains still open.

8 The zeta function of a subshift

Let (S, σ) be a subshift and let

$$S_n = \{x \in S \mid \sigma^n(x) = x\}$$

be the set of points of period dividing n.

The *zeta function* of a subshift S is the series

$$\zeta_S(z) = \exp \sum \frac{s_n}{n} z^n$$

with $s_n = \mathrm{Card}(S_n)$. It is an invariant under conjugacy. since the same holds for each of the coefficients s_n for $n \geq 1$.

It was proved by R. Bowen and O. Lanford in [12] that the zeta function of a system of finite type S is a rational series. They proved actually that

$$\zeta_S(z) = \det(I - Mz)^{-1}$$

where M is the adjacency matrix of the graph defining S.

It was proved later by A. Manning [23] that the zeta function of a sofic system is also rational.

This has motivated further investigations in several directions. On one hand, J. Berstel and C. Reutenauer have extended the result of Manning to the case of a generalisation of the zeta function to some formal series [9].

On the other hand M. P. Béal has introduced a new operation on finite automata, the *external power* allowing to obtain the zeta function of a sofic system as a combination of the values obtained on the different external powers (see [4]). This gives a different proof of the rationality of the zeta function. This proof has been later extended to a result on sets of cyclic words [5].

9 Circular codes and subshifts of finite type

Recall that $X \subset A^+$ is called a *circular code* if any circular word over A has at most one decomposition as a product of words from X.

There is a close connection between the notion of a subshift of finite type and that of a circular code. Indeed, if $X \subset A^*$ is a finite circular code, then the set of biinfinite words having a factorisation in words of X is a subshift of finite type denoted S.

Let, as in Section 6, $\alpha_n = \mathrm{Card}(X \cap A^n)$ and $f_X(z) = \sum_{n \geq 0} \alpha_n z^n$. The zeta function of S has the simple form

$$\zeta_S = (1 - f_X)^{-1}$$

and the number s_n of points of S of period dividing n can be computed from this formula. The number of points having period exactly n is denoted by $u_n(S)$ or simply u_n. Obviously s_n and u_n are related by $s_n = \sum_{d|n} u_d$. The following inequalities are then satisfied for all $n \geq 1$.

$$u_n \leq l_n(k) \tag{4}$$

where $l_n(k)$ is the number of points of period exactly n in the full shift over k symbols.

The length distribution $(\alpha_n)_{n \geq 1}$ of a circular codes satisfies inequalities stronger than (3) which are obtained after expressing in 4 the integers u_n in terms of the α_n.

The first inequalities are, in explicit form:

$$\alpha_1 \leq k$$
$$\alpha_2 + \frac{1}{2}(\alpha_1^2 - \alpha_1) \leq \frac{1}{2}(k^2 - k)$$
$$\cdots \leq \cdots$$

It was shown by Schützenberger (see [8] p. 343) that conversely

Theorem 5. *A sequence α_n of integers is the length distribution of a circular code over a k-letter alphabet iff it satisfies the above inequalities.*

This is linked in a very interesting way with a theorem of Krieger which gives a necessary and sufficient condition for the existence of a strict embedding of a subshift of finite type into another one.

Theorem 6. (Krieger [22]) *Let S and T be two subshifts of finite type. Then there exists an isomorphism f from S into T with $f(S) \neq T$ iff*

1. *$h_S < h_T$.*
2. *for each $n \geq 1$, $u_n(S) \leq u_n(T)$*

Given a finite sequence $\alpha = (\alpha_i)_{1\leq i\leq n}$, let G be the *renewal graph* made of n simple cycles of lengths $\alpha_1, \ldots, \alpha_n$ with exactly one common point. Any circular code on the alphabet A with length distribution α defines an isomorphism from S_G into $A^{\mathbb{Z}}$. Thus Theorem 5 gives a proof of Theorem 6 in the particular case where S is a the subshift defined by a renewal graph and T is a full shift. This raises the following questions:

1. Is it true that for any $\mathbb{N}$-rational series $f = \sum_{n\geq 0} \alpha_n z^n$ whose coefficients satisfy (4) there is a rational circular code over a k-letter alphabet such that $f = f_X$?
2. Can Theorem 5 be extended to the case where the alphabet A is replaced by a circular code Y?

10 $\mathbb{N}$-rational series and positive matrices

Much of the study of subshifts of finite type is linked to that of *positive matrices.* Indeed, a subshift of finite type is given by a finite graph which in turn is given by its adjacency matrix. The subshift of finite type itself corresponds to a class of equivalent matrices. The study of this equivalence has motivated a lot of research (see [13] for a survey).

One aspect of this research is the study of the cone of positive matrices inside the algebra of all integer matrices. The basic properties of positive matrices were obtained long ago by Perron and Frobenius. The theorem says essentially that a nonnegative real matrix has an eigenvalue of maximal modulus which is a positive real number. If it is irreducible, it has a corresponding eigenvector with positive coefficients. And if is primitive, there is only one eigenvalue of maximal modulus.

In a more recent work, Handelman [18] has proved a kind of converse of the Perron Frobenius theorem. A matrix is said to be *eventually positive* if some power has only strictly positive coefficients. A *dominant eigenvalue* is an eigenvalue α such that $\alpha > |\beta|$ for any other eigenvalue.

Theorem 7. (Handelman [18]) *A matrix with integer coefficients is conjugate to an eventually positive matrix iff it has a dominant eigenvalue.*

This result is very close to one due to M. Soittola (see [30]) characterising $\mathbb{N}$-rational series in one variable among $\mathbb{Z}$-rational series. We quote it for series having a *minimal pole* i.e. a unique pole with minimal modulus.

Theorem 8. (Soittola) *A $\mathbb{Z}$-rational series with nonnegative integer coefficients*

$$f = \sum_{n\geq 0} \alpha_n z^n$$

having a minimal pole is $\mathbb{N}$-rational.

In [27] we show how both theorems can be deduced from a construction leading to a basis in which the matrices have the appropriate properties.

References

1. Roy Adler, I. Goodwin, and Benjamin Weiss. Equivalence of topological Markov shifts. *Israel J. Math.*, 27:49–63, 1977.
2. John Ashley, Brian Marcus, Dominique Perrin, and Selim Tuncel. Surjective extensions of sliding block codes. *SIAM J. Discrete Math.*, 6:582–611, 1993.
3. Frédérique Bassino. Hauteur d'étoile d'une série IN-rationnelle. Technical report, Institut Gaspard Monge, 1995.
4. Marie-Pierre Béal. *Codage Symbolique*. Masson, 1993.
5. Marie-Pierre Béal and Olivier Carton. Cyclic languages and languages of stabilizers. Technical report, Institut Gaspard Monge, 1995.
6. Danièle Beauquier. Minimal automaton for a factorial, transitive rational language. *Theoret. Comput. Sci.*, 67:65–73, 1989.
7. Tim Bedford, Michael Keane, and Caroline Series, editors. *Ergodic Theory, Symbolic Dynamics and Hyperbolic Spaces*. Oxford University Press, 1991.
8. Jean Berstel and Dominique Perrin. *Theory of codes*. Academic Press, 1985.
9. Jean Berstel and Christophe Reutenauer. Zeta functions of formal languages. *Trans. Amer. Math. Soc.*, 321:533–546, 1990.
10. François Blanchard and Georges Hansel. Languages and subshifts. In M. Nivat and D. Perrin, editors, *Automata on Infinite Words*, volume 192 of *Lecture notes in Computer Science*, pages 138–146. Springer Verlag, 1985.
11. François Blanchard and Alejandro Maass. On dynamical properties of generalized cellular automata. In Ricardo Baeeza-Yates and Eric Goles, editors, *LATIN 95: Theoretical Informatics*, volume 911 of *Lecture Notes in Comput. Sci.*, pages 84–98, 1995.
12. Rufus Bowen and O. Lanford. Zeta functions of restrictions of the shift transformation. *Proc. Symp. Pure Math.*, 14:43–50, ?
13. Mike Boyle. Symbolic dynamics and matrices. In S Friedland, V. Brualdi, and V. Klee, editors, *Combinatorial and Graph-Theoretic Problems in Linear Algebra*, volume 50 of *IMA Volumes in Mathematics and its Applications*. 1993.
14. Véronique Bruyère, L. Wong, and Liang Zhang. On completion of codes with finite deciphering delay. *European J. Combin.*, 11:513–521, 1990.
15. Christian Choffrut. Conjugacy in free inverse monoids. *Int. J. Alg. Comput.*, 3:169–188, 1993.
16. R. Fischer. Sofic systems and graphs. *Monatshefte Math.*, 80:179–186, 1975.
17. Christiane Frougny and Boris Solomyak. Finite beta-expansions. *Ergod. Th. & Dynam. Syst.*, 12:45–82, 1992.
18. David Handelman. Positive matrices and dimension groups affiliated to C^*-algebras and topological Markov chains. *J. Operator Theory*, 6:55–74, 1981.
19. David Handelman. Spectral radii of primitive integral companion matrices and log-concave poynomials. In Peter Walters, editor, *Symbolic Dynamics and its Applications*, volume 135 of *Contemporary Mathematics*, pages 231–238. Amer. Math. Soc., 1992.
20. K. H. Kim and F. W. Roush. Decidability of shift equivalence. In *Symbolic Dynamics*, volume 1342 of *Lecture Notes in Mathematics*, pages 374–424. Springer, 1988.
21. K. H. Kim and F. W. Roush. William's conjecture is false for reducible matrices. *J. Amer. Math. Soc.*, 5:213–215, 1992.
22. Wolfgang Krieger. On the subsystems of topological Markov chains. *Ergod. Th. & Dynam. Syst.*, 2:195–202, 1982.

23. Anthony Manning. Axiom a diffeomorphisms have rational zeta function. *Bull. London Math. Soc.*, 3:215–220, 1971.
24. M. Morse and G. Hedlund. Symbolic dynamics. *Amer. J. of Math.*, 3:286–303, 1936.
25. Marston Morse. Recurrent geodesics on a surface of negative curvature. *Trans. Amer. Math. Soc.*, 22:84–110, 1921.
26. Dominique Perrin. Arbres et séries rationnelles. *C. R. Acad. Sci. Paris*, 309:713–716, 1989.
27. Dominique Perrin and Marcel-Paul Schützenberger. Synchronizing prefix codes and automata and the road coloring problem. In Peter Walters, editor, *Symbolic Dynamics and its Applications*, volume 135 of *Contemporary Mathematics*, pages 295–318. Amer. Math. Soc., 1992.
28. Antonio Restivo. Codes and local constraints. *Theoret. Comput. Sci.*, 72:55–64, 1990.
29. Christophe Reutenauer. Non commutative factorization of variable length codes. *J. Pure and Applied Algebra*, 36:157–186, 1985.
30. A. Salomaa and Matti Soittola. *Automatic-Theoretic Aspects of Formal Power Series*. New York, Springer-Verlag, 1978.
31. Marcel-Paul Schützenberger. On synchronizing prefix codes. *Inform and Control*, 11:396–401, 1967.
32. Peter Walters, editor. *Symbolic Dynamics and its Applications*, volume 135 of *Contemporary Mathematics*. Amer. Math. Soc., 1992.
33. Benjamin Weiss. Subshifts of finite type and sofic systems. *Monats. Math.*, 77:462–474, 1973.
34. Frank Williams. Classification of subshifts of finite type. *Ann. of Math.*, 98:120–153, 1973. (Errata ibid. **99**:380-381,1974).
35. Liang Zhang and Zhonghui Shen. Completion of recognizable bifix codes. *Theoret. Comput. Sci.*, 145:345–355, 1995.

Lower Bounds for Propositional Proofs and Independence Results in Bounded Arithmetic (Abstract)

Alexander A. Razborov

Steklov Mathematical Institute, Moscow, RUSSIA

Previously known results about the complexity of propositional proofs relied on difficult combinatorial machinery and ideas borrowed from Boolean complexity. A natural limit for this approach, however, is put by our inability to apply this machinery even to sufficiently strong Boolean models. The corresponding problems in the complexity of proofs appear to be even harder. On the contrary, in the field of Bounded Arithmetic it became customary to show conditional independence results via powerful witnessing technique which allows us to reduce the statement of interest to some well-studied hypothesis in pure Complexity Theory.

In this talk we survey a very recent research (work in progress) intending to develop an analogue of this witnessing technique for propositional proofs (which are about the same as proofs of Δ_1^b-formulae in Bounded Arithmetic) and thus reduce the questions about their complexity to purely complexity asssumptions. We present both the general framework (interpolation theorems, complexity of disjoint NP-pairs) and concrete results already obtained in this way.

Physics and the New Computation

Paul Vitányi*

CWI and University of Amsterdam

Abstract. New computation devices increasingly depend on particular physical properties rather than on logical organization alone as used to be the case in conventional technologies. This has impact on the synthesis and analysis of algorithms and the computation models on which they are to run. Therefore, scientists working in these areas will have to understand and apply physical law in their considerations. We discuss three cases in some detail: interconnect length and communication in massive multicomputers which depend on the geometry of space and speed of light; energy dissipation and reversible (adiabatic) computation which depend on thermodynamics; and quantum coherent parallel computing which depends on quantum mechanics.

1 Introduction

In a sequential computation such as performed by a Turing machine or a von Neumann architecture computer, one can safely ignore many physical aspects of the underlying computer system and analyse the computational complexity of a program in a purely logical fashion. In the realm of nonsequential computation one cannot ignore the reality of the physical world we live in to such an extent. The appropriateness of the analysis may stand or fall with the account taken of physical reality. Moreover, nonclassical or nonstandard physical realizations of computers may have totally unexpected properties.

A popular model to analyse parallel algorithms is the parallel random access machine (PRAM) were many processors can read and write a single shared memory in unit time per operation. Typically, for n inputs we have $p(n)$ processors and clever algorithms are designed which, say, add n numbers of n^{ϵ} bits in $O(\log n)$ parallel time (the longest chain of operations executed by any single processor in the lot). However, something is wrong here. Since $p(n)$ processors are necessary and sufficient for the algorithm, we cannot dispense with any one of them, and hence the results of the calculations of each pair of processors must interact somewhere. This means that we have to signal between each pair of processors, and, taking the outermost ones, the distance between them is

* Partially supported by the European Union through NeuroCOLT ESPRIT Working Group Nr. 8556, and by NWO through NFI Project ALADDIN under Contract number NF 62-376 and NSERC under International Scientific Exchange Award ISE0125663. Address: CWI, Kruislaan 413, 1098 SJ Amsterdam, The Netherlands. Email: paulv@cwi.nl

$\Omega(p(n)^{1/3})$ because of the geometry of space. Hence the time required for interaction is $\Omega(p(n)^{1/3})$ by the bounded speed of light. That is, what we called 'parallel time' is in fact a series of 'consecutive steps' were the length of each step depends on physical considerations. A similar problem of relation between the theoretical model and physical realization occurs with NC networks (polynomial number of processors and polylogarithmic depth).

In fact, optimality of PRAM algorithms may be misleading, because in any physically realizable machine architecture it may be the case that a much simpler and unsophisticated algorithm outperforms the optimal PRAM algorithm. Do networks help with this problem? We can simulate PRAMs fast by networks of processors communicating by message passing at the cost of a multiplicative slowdown square logarithmic in the number of processors n for simulation on a $\log n$-dimensional hypercube, [Upfal and Wigderson, 1987]. This doesn't solve the problem mentioned above, since the hypercube nodes need to be order $n^{1/3}$ apart for the majority of pairs (see below). Together it turns out that rather than saving time, the simulation costs at least a logarithmic in n factor more time than the original. Rolf Landauer, [Landauer, 1991] has emphasized "information is physical". So is communication.

At the outset of high density electronic chip technology (VLSI = Very Large Scale Integration), a flurry of activity in analyzing computational complexity focussed on the AT^2 measure, where A is the total (two dimensional) chip area and T is the time (maximal number of transitions or steps of any component on the chip). Typically, up to a polylogarithmic factor the results say $AT^2 = \Omega(n^2)$ for many problems (for example input n bits and determine whether or not they sum to $n/2$). It seems difficult to reach significantly higher lower bounds. Superficially, it seems that this measure is nice since it gives a lower bound tradeoff for time versus area. However, it does not say much about *physical* chips. For n input bits, assume that at the start of the computation we have them on chip. Since each bit physically takes $\Omega(1)$ area we have that $A = \Omega(n)$ outright (for example for the Kolmogorov random inputs which are the overwhelming majority). That means that most input bits are $\Omega(n^{1/2})$ distant from most other input bits by the geometry of space argument. In any computation where none of the input bits can be ignored, each pair of bits needs to interact somewhere, and hence information must be exchanged across $\Omega(n^{1/2})$ distance. This means, by the bounded speed of light, that $T = \Omega(n^{1/2})$. Together this trivially shows $AT^2 = \Omega(n^2)$.

Even if we assume that $A = n/f(n)$ ($f(n)$ unbounded) then the chip can contain at most $n/f(n)$ input bits and the computation needs to proceed through entering about n input bits. Since the circumference of the chip is $\Omega(\sqrt{n/f(n)})$ this takes at least $\Omega(\sqrt{n \cdot f(n)})$ time, resulting in $AT^2 = \Omega(n^2)$ again. If we account for the bounded 'pinability', bounded number of pins through which the input can be entered, we find $AT^2 = \Omega(n^3/f(n))$. All these estimates are gross underestimates because they ignore actual computing time on chip.

The AT^2 measure was widely studied [Thompson, 1979, Ullman, 1984] perhaps due to the fact that the argument used is to bisect the postulated but unknown embedded communication network (divide them into two parts whith approximately equal number of nodes by a cut of the layout), and express both A and T in terms of the unknown *minimum bisection width* of the network (minimum number of edges and nodes on the cut). Fortuitiously, using AT^2, the unknown minimum bisection width gets divided out. According to [Mead & Conway, 1980], a measure like AT has physical significance because it is related to the maximal energy consumption and energy disipation of a chip. If the gates constitute a constant fraction of A, and if all gates switch at each clock cycle, conventional technologies dissipate $\Omega(AT)$ energy in the form of heat. Because of overheating and meltdown this is a main factor which determines viability. Related measures were defined and first investigated in [Kissin, 1982–1991].

Physics has a treasure trove of nonconventional technologies which may yield computation opportunities. We cite three novel items. The first one is quantum cryptography, [Bennett, *et al.*, 1992]. Viewed first as science fiction, after a working prototype had been demonstrated this idea has now been taken on by commercial developers. British Telecom recently announced a working setup using optical fiber communication in excess of 10 kilometer. A second new development is quantum coherent computation. Because new developments in quantum coherent computation (if physically realizable) allow breaking most commonly used cryptosystems, see Section 4, quantum cryptography may be the only safe principle for public cryptography currently known, [Brassard, 1994]. In contrast with other systems, whose safety rests (or rested) on unproven cryptographic assumptions, the safety of quantum cryptography rests on the validity of quantum mechanics.

A third new principle is computation using DNA. Recently a small instance of the 'Hamiltonian path problem' was encoded in molecules of DNA and solved inside of a test tube using standard methods of molecular biology, [Adleman, 1994]. This has raised excitement about the following questions: Can practical molecular computers actually be built? Might they be as much as a billion times faster that current super computers? According to [Adleman, 1994], "To some, a computer is a physical device in the real world. But being a computer is something that we externally impose on an object. There might be a lot of computers out there, and I suspect there are".

Acknowledgements Section 3 is based on joint work with Ming Li. Discussions and help from André Berthiaume, Harry Buhrman, Tao Jiang, and John Tromp are gratefully acknowledged.

2 Geometry of Space

Models of parallel computation that allow processors to randomly access a large shared memory, such as PRAMs, or rapidly access a member of a large number of other processors, will necessarily have large latency. If we use n processing elements of, say, unit size each, then the tightest they can be packed is in a 3-dimensional sphere of volume n. Assuming that the units have no "funny" shapes, e.g., are spherical themselves, no unit in the enveloping sphere can be closer to all other units than a distance of radius R,

$$R = \left(\frac{3 \cdot n}{4\pi} \right)^{1/3} \tag{1}$$

Because of the bounded speed of light, it is impossible to transport signals over n^α ($\alpha > 0$) distance in $o(n)$ time. In fact, the assumption of the bounded speed of light says that the lower time bound on *any* computation using n processing elements is $\Omega(n^{1/3})$ outright.

We study the following problem. Let $G = (V, E)$ be a finite undirected graph, without loops or multiple edges, *embedded* in 3-dimensional Euclidean space. Let each embedded node have unit *volume*. For convenience of the argument, each node is embedded as a sphere, and is *represented* by the single point in the center. The *distance* between a pair of nodes is the Euclidean distance between the points representing them. The *length* of the embedding of an edge between two nodes is the distance between the nodes. How large does the *average* edge length need to be?

We illustrate the approach with a popular architecture, say the *binary d-cube*. Recall, that this is the network with $n = 2^d$ nodes, each of which is identified by a d-bit name. There is a two-way communication link between two nodes if their identifiers differ by a single bit. The network is represented by an undirected graph $C = (V, E)$, with V the set of nodes and $E \subseteq V \times V$ the set of edges, each edge corresponding with a communication link. There are $d2^{d-1}$ edges in C. Let C be embedded in 3-dimensional Euclidean space, each node as a sphere with unit volume. The distance between two nodes is the Euclidean distance between their centers. Let x be any node of C. There are at most $2^d/8$ nodes within Euclidean distance $R/2$ of x, with R as in Equation 1. Then, there are $\geq 7 \cdot 2^d/8$ nodes at Euclidean distance $\geq R/2$ from x. Construct a spanning tree T_x in C of depth d with node x as the root. Since the binary d-cube has diameter d, such a shallow tree exists. There are n nodes in T_x, and $n-1$ paths from root x to another node in T_x. Let P be such a path, and let $|P|$ be the *number of edges* in P. Then $|P| \leq d$. Let $length(P)$ denote the Euclidean length of the embedding of P. Since 7/8th of all nodes are at Euclidean distance at least $R/2$ of root x, the average of $length(P)$ satisfies

$$(n-1)^{-1} \sum_{P \in T_x} length(P) \geq \frac{7R}{16}$$

The average Euclidean length of an embedded edge *in a path* P is bounded below as follows:

$$(n-1)^{-1} \sum_{P \in T_x} \left(|P|^{-1} \sum_{e \in P} length(e) \right) \geq \frac{7R}{16d}. \tag{2}$$

This does *not yet* give a lower bound on the average Euclidean length of an edge, the average taken *over all edges* in T_x. To see this, note that if the edges incident with x have Euclidean length $7R/16$, then the average edge length *in each path* from the root x to a node in T_x is $\geq 7R/16d$, even if all edges not incident with x have length 0. However, the average edge length *in the tree* is dominated by the many short edges near the leaves, rather than the few long edges near the root. In contrast, in the case of the binary d-cube, because of its symmetry, if we squeeze a subset of nodes together to decrease local edge length, then other nodes are pushed farther apart increasing edge length again. We can make this intuition precise, [Vitányi, 1986, Vitányi, 1988].

Lemma 1. *The average Euclidean length of the edges in the 3-space embedding of C is at least* $7R/(16d)$.

The symmetry property yielding such huge edge length is 'edge-symmetry.' To formulate the generalization of Lemma 1 for arbitrary graphs, we need some mathematical machinery. Let $G = (V, E)$ be a simple undirected graph, and let Γ be the automorphism group of G. Two edges $e_1 = (u_1, v_1)$ and $e_2 = (u_2, v_2)$ of G are *similar* if there is an automorphism γ of G such that $\gamma(\{u_1, v_1\}) = \{u_2, v_2\}$. We consider only connected graphs. The relation 'similar' is an equivalence relation, and partitions E into nonempty equivalence classes, called *orbits*, $E_1, ..., E_m$. We say that Γ *acts transitively* on each E_i, $i = 1, ..., m$. A graph is *edge-symmetric* if every pair of edges are similar ($m = 1$).

Additionally, we need the following notions. If x and y are nodes, then $d(x, y)$ denotes the number of edges in a *shortest path* between them. Let D denote the *diameter* of G defined by D is the maximum over all node pairs x, y of $d(x, y)$. For $i = 1, ..., m$, define $d_i(x, y)$ as follows. For edges $\{x, y\} \in E$, if $\{x, y\} \in E_i$ then $d_i(x, y) = 1$, else $d_i(x, y) = 0$. Let Π be the set of shortest paths between x and y along edges in E. If x and y are not incident on the same edge ($\{x, y\} \notin E$), then $d_i(x, y) = |\Pi|^{-1} \sum_{P \in \Pi} \sum_{e \in P} d_i(e)$. Clearly,

$$d_1(x, y) + \cdots + d_m(x, y) = d(x, y) \leq D$$

Denote $|V|$ by n. The ith *orbit frequency* is

$$\delta_i = n^{-2} \sum_{x, y \in V} \frac{d_i(x, y)}{d(x, y)},$$

$i = 1, ..., m$. Finally, define the *orbit skew coefficient* of G as $M = \min\{|E_i|/|E| : 1 \leq i \leq m\}$. Consider a d-dimensional Euclidean space embedding of G, with embedded nodes, distance between nodes, and edge length as above. Let R be the *radius* of a d-space sphere with volume n, corresponding to Equation 1 for d = 3. We are now ready to state the main result.

Theorem 2. *Let graph G be embedded in d-space with the parameters above, and let* $C = (2^{\mathrm{d}} - 1)/2^{\mathrm{d}+1}$.

(i) Let $l_i = |E_i|^{-1} \sum_{e \in E_i} l(e)$ *be the average length of the edges in orbit* E_i, $i = 1, ..., m$. *Then,* $\sum_{1 \leq i \leq m} l_i \geq \sum_{1 \leq i \leq m} \delta_i l_i \geq CRD^{-1}$.

(ii) Let $l = |E|^{-1} \sum_{e \in E} l(e)$ *be the average length of an edge in E. Then,* $l \geq CRMD^{-1}$.

For the proof we refer to [Vitányi, 1988], where the theorem is applied to binary d-Cube, Cube-Connected Cycles, edge-symmetric graphs (including complete graph, star graph, δ-dimensional meshes with wrap-around), and complete binary tree. The lower bound is optimal in the sense of being within a constant multiplicative factor of an upper bound for several example graphs of various diameters, [Vitányi, 1988]. An extension of the argument shows the same for related networks like the Bruijn networks, shuffle-exchange graphs, and so on, [Koppelman, 1995].

2.1 Irregular Networks

Since low-diameter symmetric network topologies lead to high average interconnect length, it is natural to ask what happens with irregular topologies. In fact, it is sometimes proposed that since symmetric networks of low diameter lead to high interconnect length, one should use random networks where the presence or absence of a connection is determined by a coin flip. We report on some work in [Vitányi, 1994] that such networks will also have impossibly high average interconnect length.

Kolmogorov complexity The Kolmogorov complexity, [Kolmogorov, 1965], of x is the length of the ***shortest*** effective description of x. That is, the *Kolmogorov complexity* $C(x)$ of a finite string x is simply the length of the shortest program, say in FORTRAN[2] encoded in binary, which prints x without any input. A similar definition holds conditionally, in the sense that $C(x|y)$ is the length of the shortest binary program which computes x given y as input. It can be shown that the Kolmogorov complexity is absolute in the sense of being independent of the programming language, up to a fixed additional constant term which depends on the programming language but not on x. We now fix one canonical programming language once and for all as reference programming language, and thereby we fix $C()$ uniquely.

For the theory and applications, see [Li & Vitányi, 1993]. Let $x, y, z \in \mathcal{N}$, where $\mathcal{N}$ denotes the natural numbers and we identify $\mathcal{N}$ and $\{0,1\}^*$ according to the correspondence $(0,\epsilon), (1,0), (2,1), (3,00), (4,01), \ldots$. Hence, the length $|x|$ of x is the number of bits in the binary string x. Let $T_1, T_2, \ldots$ be a standard enumeration of all Turing machines. Let $\langle \cdot, \cdot \rangle$ be a standard invertible effective bijection from $\mathcal{N} \times \mathcal{N}$ to $\mathcal{N}$. This can iterated to $\langle \langle \cdot, \cdot \rangle, \cdot \rangle$.

Definition 3. Let U be an appropriate universal Turing machine such that $U(\langle \langle i, p \rangle, y \rangle) = T_i(\langle p, y \rangle)$ for all i and $\langle p, y \rangle$. The *Kolmogorov complexity* of x given y (for free) is

$$C(x|y) = \min\{|p| : U(\langle p, y \rangle) = x, p \in \{0,1\}^*, i \in \mathcal{N}\}.$$

[2] Or in Turing machine codes.

One way to express irregularity or *randomness* of an individual network topology is by a modern notion of randomness like Kolmogorov complexity. A simple counting argument shows that for each y in the condition and each length n there exists at least one x of length n which is *incompressible* in the sense of $C(x|y) \geq n$, 50% of all x's of length n is incompressible but for 1 bit ($C(x|y) \geq n-1$), 75% of all x's is incompressible but for 2 bits ($C(x|y) \geq n-2$) and in general a fraction of $1-2^{-c}$ of all strings cannot be compressed by more than c bits. (This is because there are 2^n strings of length n and only $2^{n-c}-1$ binary programs of length at most $n-c$, [Li & Vitányi, 1993]. A more sophisticated argument shows that there are a large number of strings of length n with complexity at least n.)

Random Graphs Each graph $G=(V,E)$ on n nodes $V=\{0,\ldots,n-1\}$ can be coded (up to isomorphism) by a binary string of length $n(n-1)/2$. We enumerate the $n(n-1)/2$ possible edges in a graph on n nodes in standard order and set the ith bit in the string to 1 if the edge is present and to 0 otherwise. Conversely, each binary string of length $n(n-1)/2$ encodes a graph on n nodes. Hence we can identify each such graph with its corresponding binary string.

We shall call a graph G on n nodes *random* if it satisfies

$$C(G|n) \geq n(n-1)/2 - cn, \tag{3}$$

where c is an appropriate constant ($c = 0.09$ suffices for n large enough). Elementary counting shows that *a fraction* of at least

$$1 - 1/2^{cn}$$

of all graphs on n nodes has that high complexity.

Lemma 4. *The degree d of each node of a random graph satisfies $|d-(n-1)/2| < n/4$.* [3]

Proof. Assume that the deviation of the degree d of a node v in G from $(n-1)/2$ is at least k. From the lower bound on $C(G|n)$ corresponding to the assumption that G is random, we can estimate an upper bound on k, as follows.

Describe G given n as follows. We can indicate which edges are incident on node v by giving the index of the connection pattern in the ensemble of

$$m = \sum_{|d-(n-1)/2| \geq k} \binom{n}{d} \leq 2^n e^{-k^2/(n-1)} \tag{4}$$

[3] One can replace cn in Equation 3 by $o(n)$. Then in Lemma 4 we can replace $n/4$ by $o(n)$. The random graphs under this definition contain only nodes with vertex degree about $n/2$. With $n/\log n$ substituted for $o(n)$, they constitute a slightly smaller fraction $1-1/2^{n/\log n}$ of all graphs on n nodes, but still a fraction which goes to 1 fast with n. With Harry Buhrman we have proved in a forthcoming paper that there are $2^n/d$ graphs G satisfying $C(G|n) \geq n(n-1)/2$, where d is a constant. For such complex G we have $|d-(n-1)/2| = O(\sqrt{n})$. The fraction of such G among all graphs on n nodes is at least $1/d$.

possibilities. The last inequality follows from a general estimate of the tail probability of the binomial distribution, Chernoff's bounds, [Li & Vitányi, 1993], pp. 127-130. To describe G it then suffices to modify the old code of G by prefixing it with

- the identity of the node concerned in $\lceil \log n \rceil$ bits,
- the value of d in $\lceil \log n \rceil$ bits, possibly adding nonsignificant 0's to pad up to this amount,
- the index of the interconnection pattern in $\log m + 2 \log \log m$ bits in self-delimiting form (this form requirement allows the concatenated binary sub-descriptions to be parsed and unpacked into the individual items: it encodes a separation delimiter in $< 2 \log \log m$ bits, [Li & Vitányi, 1993]),

followed by the old code for G with the bits in the code denoting the presence or absence of the possible edges which are incident on the node v deleted.

Clearly, given n we can reconstruct the graph G from the new description. The total description we have achieved is an effective program of

$$\log m + 2 \log \log m + O(\log n) + n(n-1)/2 - (n-1)$$

bits. This must be at least the length of the shortest effective binary program, which is $C(G|n)$ satisfying Equation 3. Therefore,

$$\log m + 2 \log \log m \geq n - 1 - O(\log n) - cn.$$

Since we have estimated in Equation 4 that

$$\log m \leq n - (k^2/(n-1)) \log e,$$

it follows that, with $c = 0.09$,

$$k < n/4.$$

The lemma shows that each node is connected by an edge with about 25% of all nodes in G. Hence G contains a subgraph on about 25 % of its nodes of diameter 1. This is all we need. [4]

Theorem 5. *A fraction of at least* $1 - 1/2^{cn}$ *(*$c = 0.09$*) of all graphs on* n *nodes (the incompressible, random, graphs) have total interconnect length of* $\Omega(n^{7/3})$ *in each 3-dimensional Euclidean space embedding (or* $\Omega(n^{5/2})$ *in each 2-dimensional Euclidean space embedding).*

Proof. By lemma 4 we know that in a random graph G each node x is at distance 1 of $(n-1)/2 \pm n/4$ other nodes y, and 7/8th of these nodes y (in 3 dimensions) is at distance $\Omega(n^{1/3})$ of x by Equation 1. The argument for 2 dimensions is analogous. By Lemma 4 we know that a random graph G on n nodes has $\Omega(n^2)$ edges since each node has at least $n/4$ incident edges.

[4] Using another standard incompressibility argument, as suggested by Harry Buhrman, one can show that all graphs which are random in the sense above have diameter precisely 2.

Since both the very regular symmetric low diameter graphs and the random graphs have high average interconnect length which sharply rises with n, the only graphs which will scale feasibly up are symmetric fairly high diameter topologies like the mesh—which therefore will most likely be the interconnection pattern of the future massive multiprocessor systems.

2.2 Interpretation of the Results

An effect that becomes increasingly important at the present time is that most space in the device executing the computation is taken up by the wires. Under very conservative estimates that the unit length of a wire has a volume which is a constant fraction of that of a component it connects, we have shown in [Vitányi, 1988] that in 3-dimensional layouts for binary d-cubes, the volume of the $n = 2^d$ components (nodes) performing the actual computation operations is an asymptotic fastly vanishing fraction of the volume of the wires needed for communication:

$$\frac{\text{volume computing components}}{\text{volume communication wires}} = o(n^{-1/3})$$

If we charge a constant fraction of the unit volume for a unit wire length, and add the volume of the wires to the volume of the nodes, then the volume necessary to embed the binary d-cube is $\Omega(n^{4/3})$. However, this lower bound ignores the fact that the added volume of the wires pushes the nodes further apart, thus necessitating longer wires again. How far does this go? A rigorous analysis is complicated, and not important here. The following intuitive argument indicates what we can expect well enough. Denote the volume taken by the nodes as V_n, and the volume taken by the wires as V_w. The total volume taken by the embedding of the cube is $V_t = V_n + V_w$. The total wire length required to lay out a binary d-cube as a function of the volume taken by the embedding is, substituting radius R obtained from $V_t = 4\pi R^3/3$ in the formula for the total wire length obtained in [Vitányi, 1988],

$$L(V_t) \geq \frac{7n}{32}\left(\frac{3V_t}{4\pi}\right)^{1/3}$$

Since $\lim_{n\to\infty} V_n/V_w \to 0$, assuming unit wire length of unit volume, we set the total interconnect length $L(V_t)$ at $L(V_t) \approx V_t$. This results in a better estimate of $\Omega(n^{3/2})$ for the volume needed to embed the binary d-cube. When we want to investigate an upper bound to embed the binary d-cube under the current assumption, we have a problem with the unbounded degree of unit volume nodes. There is no room for the wires to come together at a node. For comparison, therefore, consider the fixed degree version of the binary d-cube, the CCC (see above), with $n = d2^d$ trivalent nodes and $3n/2$ edges. The same argument yields $\Omega(n^{3/2}\log^{-3/2} n)$ for the volume required to embed CCC with unit volume per unit length wire. It is known, that every small degree n-vertex graph, e.g., CCC, can be laid out in a 3-dimensional grid with volume $O(n^{3/2})$ using a unit volume per unit wire length assumption, [Mead & Conway, 1980, Ullman, 1984]. This neatly matches the lower bound.

Just like for the complete graph, the situation for the random graph which we consider here, is far worse. For a random graph we have, under the assumption that the wires have unit volume per unit length, that the total wire length in 3 dimensional embeddings is $\Omega(n^{7/3})$ by Theorem 5, and that

$$\frac{\text{volume communication wires}}{\text{volume computing components}} = \Omega(n^{4/3})$$

The proof of Theorem 5 actually shows that the total interconnect length of an embedded random graph is $L(V_t) = \Omega(n^2 V_t^{1/3})$, where the radius of an as tight as possibly packed 3-dimensional sphere of the total volume V_t of nodes and wires together is $\Omega(V_t^{1/3})$. Considering that the larger volume will cause the average interconnect length to increase, as above for the binary d-cube, setting the total interconnect length $L(V_t) \approx V_t$ since the volume of the computing nodes add a negligible term, we find for a random graph that on n nodes that the total volume satisfies

$$V_t = \Omega(n^3).$$

Here we have not yet taken into account that longer wires need larger drivers and have a larger diameter, that the larger volume will again cause the average interconnect length to increase, and so on, which explosion may make embedding altogether impossible with finite length interconnects as exhibited in related contexts in [Vitányi, 1985].

3 Adiabatic Computation and Thermodynamics

All computations can be performed logically reversibly, [Bennett, 1973], at the cost of eventually filling up the memory with unwanted garbage information. This means that reversible computers with bounded memories require in the long run irreversible bit operations, for example, to erase records irreversibly to create free memory space. The minimal possible number of irreversibly erased bits to do so is believed to determine the ultimate limit of heat dissipation of the computation by Landauer's principle, [Landauer, 1961, Bennett, 1973, Bennett, 1982, Proc. PhysComp, 1981, 1992, 1994]. In reference [Bennett *et al.*, 1993] we and others developed a mathematical theory for the unavoidable number of irreversible bit operations in an otherwise reversible computation.

Methods to implement (almost) reversible and dissipationless computation using conventional technologies appear in [Proc. PhysComp, 1981, 1992, 1994], often designated by the catch phrase 'adiabatic switching'. Many currently proposed physical schemes implementing adiabatic computation reduce irreversibility by using longer switching times. This is done typically by switching over equal voltage gates after voltage has been equalized slowly. This type of switching does not dissipate energy, [Proc. PhysComp, 1981, 1992, 1994], the only energy dissipation is incurred by pulling voltage up and down: the slower it goes the less energy is dissipated. If the computation goes infinitely slow, zero energy is dissipated. Clearly, this counteracts the purpose of low energy dissipation which is faster computation.

In [Li & Vitányi, 1994] it is demonstrated that even if adiabatic computation technology advances to switching with no time loss, a similar phenomenon arises when we try to approach the ultimate limits of minimal irreversibility of an otherwise reversible computation, and hence minimal energy dissipation. This time the effect is due to the logical method of reducing the number of irreversible bit erasures in the computation irrespective of individual switching times. By computing longer and longer (in the sense of using more computation steps), the amount of dissipated energy gets closer to ultimate limits. Moreover, one can trade-off time (number of steps) for energy: there is a new time-irreversibility (time-energy) trade-off hierarchy. The bounds we derive are also relevant for quantum computations which are reversible except for the irreversible observation steps, [Deutsch, 1985–1992, Benioff, 1980–1986, Benioff, 1995].

3.1 Background

The ultimate limits of miniaturization of computing devices, and therefore the speed of computation, are governed by unavoidable heating up attending rising energy dissipation caused by increasing density of switching elements in the device. On a basically two dimensional device, linear speed up by shortening interconnects is essentially attended by squaring the dissipated energy per area unit per second because we square the number of switching elements per area unit, [Mead & Conway, 1980].

Therefore, the question of how to reduce the energy dissipation of computation determines future advances in computing power. Around 1940 a computing device dissipated about 10^{-2} Joule per bit operation at room temperature. Since that time the dissipated energy per bit operation has roughly decreased by one order of magnitude (tenfold) every five years. Currently, a bit operation dissipates[5] about 10^{-17} Joule. Extrapolations of current trends show that the energy dissipation per binary logic operation needs to be reduced below kT (thermal noise) within 20 years. Here k is Boltzmann's constant and T the absolute temperature in degrees Kelvin, so that $kT \approx 3 \times 10^{-21}$ Joule at room temperature. Even at kT level, a future laptop containing 10^{18} gates in a cubic centimeter operating at a gigahertz dissipates 3 million watts/second. For thermodynamic reasons, cooling the operating temperature of such a computing device to almost absolute zero (to get kT down) must dissipate at least as much energy in the cooling as it saves for the computing.

Considerations of thermodynamics of computing started in the early fifties. J. von Neumann [Burks, 1966] reputedly thought that a computer operating at temperature T must dissipate at least $kT \ln 2$ Joule per elementary bit operation (about 3×10^{-21} J at room temperature).

---

[5] After R.W. Keyes, IBM Research.

Around 1960, R. Landauer [Landauer, 1961] more thoroughly analyzed this question and concluded that it is only 'logically irreversible' operations that dissipate energy. An operation is *logically reversible* if its inputs can always be deduced from the outputs. Erasure of information in a way such that it cannot be retrieved is not reversible. Erasing each bit costs $kT \ln 2$ energy, when computer operates at temperature T.

One should sharply distinguish between the issue of logical reversibility and the issue of energy dissipation freeness. The fact that some computers operates in a logically reversible manner says nothing about whether they dissipate heat. It only says is that the laws of physics do not preclude that one can invent a technology in which to implement a logically similar computer to operate physically in a dissipationless manner. Computers built from reversible circuits, or the reversible Turing machine, [Bennett, 1973, Bennett, 1982, Fredkin & Toffoli, 1982], implemented with current technology will presumably dissipate energy but may conceivably be implemented by future technology in an adiabatic fashion. For non-reversible computers adiabatic implementation is widely considered impossible.

Thought experiments can exhibit a computer that is both logically and physically perfectly reversible and hence perfectly dissipationless. An example is the billiard ball computer, [Fredkin & Toffoli, 1982], and similarly the possibility of a coherent quantum computer, [Feynman, 1982—1987, Deutsch, 1985–1992]. Our purpose is to determine the theoretical ultimate limits to which the irreversible actions in an otherwise reversible computation can be reduced.

3.2 Irreversibility Cost of Computation

The ultimate limits of energy dissipation by computation will be expressed in number of irreversibly erased bits. Hence we consider compactification of records. In analogy of garbage collection by a garbage truck, the cost is less if we compact the garbage before we throw it away. The ultimate compactification which can be effectively exploited is expressed in terms of Kolmogorov complexity.

Let $\mathbf{R} = R_1, R_2, \ldots$ be a standard enumeration of reversible Turing machines, [Bennett, 1973]. We define $E(\cdot,\cdot)$ as in [Bennett *et al.*, 1993] (where it is denoted as $E_3(\cdot,\cdot)$).

Definition 6. The *irreversibility cost* $E_R(x, y)$ of computing y from x by a reversible Turing machine R is is

$$E_R(x, y) = \min\{|p| + |q| : R(\langle x, p\rangle) = \langle y, q\rangle\}.$$

We denote the class of all such cost functions by $\mathcal{E}$.

We call an element E_Q of $\mathcal{E}$ a *universal irreversibility cost function*, if $Q \in \mathbf{R}$, and for all R in $\mathbf{R}$

$$E_Q(x, y) \leq E_R(x, y) + c_R,$$

for all x and y, where c_R is a constant which depends on R but not on x or y. Standard arguments from the theory of Turing machines show the following.

Lemma 7. *There is a universal irreversibility cost function in $\mathcal{E}$. Denote it by E_{UR}.*

Proof. In [Bennett, 1973] a universal reversible Turing machine UR is constructed which satisfies the optimality requirement.

Two such universal (or optimal) machines UR and UR' will assign the same irreversibility cost to a computation apart from an additive constant term c which is *independent* of x and y (but does depend on UR and UR'). We select a reference universal function UR and define the *irreversibility cost* $E(x,y)$ of computing y from x as

$$E(x,y) \equiv E_{UR}(x,y).$$

Because of the expression for $E(x,y)$ in Theorem 8 below it is called the *sum cost* measure in [Bennett *et al.*, 1993].

In physical terms this cost is in units of $kT \ln 2$, where k is Boltzmann's constant, T is the absolute temperature in degrees Kelvin, and ln is the natural logarithm.

Because the computation is reversible, this definition is *symmetric*: we have $E(x,y) = E(y,x)$.

In our definitions we have pushed all bits to be irreversibly provided to the start of the computation and all bits to be erased to the end of the computation. It is easy to see that this is no restriction. If we have a computation where irreversible acts happen throughout the computation, then we can always mark the bits to be erased, waiting with actual erasure until the end of the computation. Similarly, the bits to be provided can be provided (marked) at the start of the computation while the actual reading of them (simultaneously unmarking them) takes place throughout the computation).

Now let us consider a general computation which outputs string y from input string x. We want to know the minimum irreversibility cost for such computation. This leads to the following theorem, for two different proofs see [Bennett *et al.*, 1993, Li & Vitányi, 1994].

Theorem 8 Fundamental theorem. *Up to an additive logarithmic term*

$$E(x,y) = C(x|y) + C(y|x).$$

Erasing a record x is actually a computation from x to the empty string ϵ. Hence its irreversibility cost is $E(x,\epsilon)$.

Corollary 9. *Up to a logarithmic additive term, the irreversibility cost of erasure is $E(x,\epsilon) = C(x)$.*

3.3 Trading Time for Energy

Because now the time bounds are important we consider the universal Turing machine U to be the machine with two work tapes which can simulate t steps of a multitape Turing machine T in $O(t \log t)$ steps (the Hennie-Stearns simulation). If some multitape Turing machine T computes x in time t from a program p, then U computes x in time $O(t \log t)$ from p plus a description of T.

Definition 10. Let $C^t(x|y)$ be the *minimal length* of binary program (not necessarily reversibly) for the two work tape universal Turing machine U computing x given y (for free) *in time* t. Formally,

$$C^t(x|y) = \min_{p \in \mathcal{N}} \{|p| : U(\langle p, y \rangle) = x \text{ in } \leq t(|x|) \text{ steps}\}.$$

$C^t(x|y)$ is called the *t-time-limited conditional Kolmogorov complexity* of x given y. The unconditional version is defined as $C^t(x) := C^t(x, \epsilon)$. A program p such that $U(p) = x$ in $\leq t(|x|)$ steps and $|p| = C^t(x)$ is denoted as x_t^*.

Note that with $C_T^t(x|y)$ the conditional t-time-limited Kolmogorov complexity with respect to Turing machine T, for all x, y, $C^{t'}(x|y) \leq C_T^t(x|y) + c_T$, where $t' = O(t \log t)$ and c_T is a constant depending on T but not on x and y.

This $C^t(\cdot)$ is the standard definition of time-limited Kolmogorov complexity, [Li & Vitányi, 1993]. However, in the remainder of the paper we always need to use reversible computations. Fortunately, in [Bennett, 1989] it is shown that for any $\epsilon > 0$, ordinary multitape Turing machines using T time and S space can be simulated by reversible ones using time $O(T)$ and space $O(ST^\epsilon)$.

To do effective erasure of compacted information, we must at the start of the computation provide a time bound t. Typically, t is a recursive function and the complexity of its description is small, say $O(1)$. However, in Theorem 11 we allow for very large running times in order to obtain smaller $C^t(\cdot)$ values.

Theorem 11 Irreversibility cost of effective erasure. *If $t(|x|) \geq |x|$ is a time bound which is provided at the start of the computation, then erasing an n bit record x by an otherwise reversible computation can be done in time (number of steps) $O(2^{|x|} t(|x|))$ at irreversibility cost (hence also thermodynamic cost) $C^t(x) + 2C^t(t|x) + 4 \log C^t(t|x)$ bits. (Typically we consider t as some standard explicit time bound and the last two terms adding up to $O(1)$.)*

Proof. Initially we have in memory input x and a program p of length $C^t(t, x)$ to compute reversibly t from x. To separate binary x and binary p we need to encode a delimiter in at most $2 \log C^t(t|x)$ bits.

1. Use x and p to reversibly compute t. Copy t and reverse the computation. Now we have x, p and t.
2. Use t to reversibly dovetail the running of all programs of length less than x to find the shortest one halting in time t with output x. This is x_t^*. The computation has produced garbage bits $g(x, x_t^*)$. Copy x_t^*, and reverse the computation to obtain x erasing all garbage bits $g(x, x_t^*)$. Now we have x, p, x_t^*, t in memory.
3. Reversibly compute t from x by p, cancel one copy of t, and reverse the computation. Now we have x, p, x_t^* in memory.
4. Reversibly cancel x using x_t^* by the standard method, and then erase x_t^* and p irreversibly.

Corollary 12. *$E(x, \epsilon) \geq \lim_{t \to \infty} C^t(x) = C(x)$, and by Theorem 8 up to an additional logarithmic term, $E(x, \epsilon) = C(x)$.*

Essentially, by spending more time we can reduce the thermodynamic cost of erasure of x_t^* to its absolute minimum. In the limit we spend the optimal value $C(x)$ by erasing x^*, since $\lim_{t\to\infty} x_t^* = x^*$. This suggests the existence of a trade-off hierarchy between time and energy. The longer one reversibly computes to perform final irreversible erasures, the less bits are erased and energy is dissipated. This intuitive assertion will be formally stated and rigourously proved below.

Definition 13. Let UR be the reversible version of the two worktape universal Turing machine, simulating the latter in linear time by Bennett's result mentioned above. Let $E^t(x,y)$ be the *minimum irreversibility cost* of an otherwise reversible computation from x to y *in time* t. Formally,

$$E^t(x,y) = \min_{p,q\in\mathcal{N}} \{|p| + |q| : UR(\langle x,p\rangle) = \langle y,q\rangle \text{ in} \le t(|x|) \text{ steps}\}.$$

Because of the similarity with Corollary 12 ($E(x,\epsilon)$ is about $C(x)$) one is erroneously led to believe that $E^t(x,\epsilon) = C^t(x)$ up to a log additive term. However, the time-bounds introduce many differences. To reversibly compute x_t^* we may require (because of the halting problem) at least $O(2^{|x|}t(|x|))$ steps after having decoded t, as indeed is the case in the proof of Theorem 11. In contrast, $E^t(x,\epsilon)$ is about the number of bits erased in an otherwise reversible computation which uses at most t steps. Therefore, as far as we know possibly $C^t(x) \ge E^{t'}(x,\epsilon)$ implies $t' = \Omega(2^{|x|}t(|x|))$. More concretely, it is easy to see that for each x and $t(|x|) \ge |x|$,

$$E^t(x,\epsilon) \ge C^t(x) \ge E^{t'}(x,\epsilon)/2, \tag{5}$$

with $t'(|x|) = O(t(|x|)$. Theorem 11 can be restated in terms of $E^t(\cdot)$ as

$$E^{t'}(x,\epsilon) \le C^t(x) + 2C^t(t|x) + 4\log C^t(t|x),$$

with $t'(|x|) = O(2^{|x|}t(|x|))$. Comparing this to the righthand inequality of Equation 5 we have improved the upper bound on erasure cost at the expense of increasing erasure time. However, these bounds only suggest but do not actually prove that we can exchange irreversibility for time. The following result definitely establishes the existence of a trade-off, [Li & Vitányi, 1994].

Theorem 14 Irreversibility-time trade-off hierarchy. *For each large enough n there is a string x of length n and a sequence of $m = \frac{1}{2}\sqrt{n}$ time functions $t_1(n) < t_2(n) < \ldots < t_m(n)$, such that*

$$E^{t_1}(x,\epsilon) > E^{t_2}(x,\epsilon) > \ldots > E^{t_m}(x,\epsilon).$$

In the cost measures like $E^t(\cdot,\cdot)$ we have counted both the irreversibly provided and the irreversibly erased bits. But Landauer's principle only charges energy dissipation costs for irreversibly erased bits. It is conceivable that the above results would not hold if one considers as the cost of erasure of a record only the irreversibly erased bits. However, we have show that Theorem 14 also holds for Landauer's dissipation measure, [Li & Vitányi, 1994], in exactly the same form and by almost the same proof.

4 Quantum Coherent Parallel Computation

Classical methods of parallel computation are plagued by wiring problems (Section 2) and heat dissipation problems (Section 3). To counteract such problems attending further miniaturization of parallel computing devices current research considers quantum mechanics based technologies. Classical use of such technologies deals with reducing feature width on chip to below the nanometer level, [Kiehl, 1994], or interacting quantum dots subnanotechnology layouts for cellular automata, [Lent *et al.*, 1994].

This section deals with the prospect of a very *nonclassical* emergent possible computer technology (quantum coherent computing or QCC) which has recently acquired great anticipated economic value. This happened by one of the most fortuitious demonstrations in computing that QCC can break the universally used public key cryptosystems by being able to factor and do the discrete logarithm in polynomial time, [Shor, 1994] with preliminary work in [Deutsch, 1985–1992, Bernstein and Vazirani, 1993, Simon, 1994]. This result opened the vista of a veritable breakthrough in computing. There are apparently formidable obstacles to surmount before a workable technology can be obtained, [Unruh, 1995].

The QCC approach as first advocated in [Benioff, 1980–1986] is currently aimed to exploit the accepted theory that quantum evolution of an appropriate system consists in a superposition of many (potentially infinitely many) simultaneous computation paths. It is theoretically possible that through the specific quantum mechanical rules of interference of the different paths one can boost the probability associated with desirable evolutions and suppress undesirable ones for certain algorithms. Upon observation of the system state one of the states in superposition is realized. By quantum specific algorithmic techniques the desired outcome can theoretically by observed with arbitrary high probability, or the desired outcome can be computed from the observed data with arbitrary high probability.

The QCC approach will partially alleviate the wiring problem (Section 2) because an exploding number of different computation paths will be simultaneously followed (with appropriate probability amplitudes, to be sure) by the same single physical apparatus requiring but a tiny amount of physical space. This is the substance of R. Feynman's dictum "there is room at the bottom" in the context of his proposal of QCC, [Feynman, 1982—1987]. Of course, since the different computation paths of a quantum computation cannot communicate as is often a main feature in a parallel distributed computation, it is only a very special type of room which is available at the bottom. Moreover, since the quantum evolution in a computation if unobstructed by observation and decoherence is reversible, the pure form of QCC, apart from the irreversible observation phase, is energy dissipation free. QCC seems to a very large extent to achieve the optimal adiabatic computation aimed for in Section 3. Although there seems to be agreement that energy gets dissipated in the irreversible observation phase, to the author's knowledge it is not yet clear how much. This seems to require a quantum Kolmogorov complexity based on 'qubits' (quantum bits) as defined in context of quantum information theory by [Schuhmacher, 1994], analogous to the classical bits of information theory of [Shannon, 1948]. Through a sequence of proposals [Benioff, 1980–1986], [Feynman, 1982—1987], [Deutsch, 1985–1992], there has emerged a Turing machine model of quantum coherent computing.

4.1 Background: Probabilistic Turing Machines

The simplest way to describe it seems by way of probabilistic machines. Suppose we consider the well known probabilistic Turing machine which is just like an ordinary Turing machine, except that at each step the machine can make a probabilistic move which consists in flipping a (say fair) coin and depending on the outcome changing its state to either one of two alternatives. This means that at each such probabilistic move the computation of the machine splits into two distinct further computations each with probability $1/2$. Ignoring the deterministic computation steps, a computation involving m coinflips can be viewed as a binary computation tree of depth m with 2^m leaves, where each node at level $t \leq m$ corresponds to a state of the system which after t coinflips occurs with probability $1/2^t$. For convenience, we can label the edges connecting a state x directly with a state y with the probability that a state x changes into state y in a single coin flip (in this example all edges are labeled '1/2').

As an example, given an arbitrary Boolean formula containing n variables, a probabilistic machine can flip its coin n times to check each of the 2^n possible truth assignments to determine wether there exists an assignment to the variables which makes the formula true. If there are m distinct such assignments then the probabilistic machine finds that the formula is satisfyable with probability at least $m/2^n$—since there are m distinct computation paths leading to a satisfyable assignment.

Now suppose the probabilistic machine is hidden in a black box and the computation proceeds without us knowing the outcomes of the coin flips. Suppose that after t coin flips in the computation we open part of the black box and observe the bit at the position of the Turing machine tape which denotes the truth assignment for variable x_5 ($5 \leq t$) which already received its truth assignment. Before we opened the black box all 2^t initial truth assignments to variables $x_1, \ldots, x_t$ were equally possible, each had probability $1/2^t$. After we observed the state of variable x_5, say 0, the probability space of possibilities has collapsed to the truth assignments which consist of all binary vectors with a 0 in the 5th position each of which has probability renormalized at $1/2^{t-1}$.

4.2 Quantum Turing Machines

A quantum Turing machine is related to the probabilistic Turing machine. Consider the same computation tree. However, instead of a probability $p_i \geq 0$ associated with each node i, such that $\sum p_i = 1$, the summation taking place over the states a computation can possible be in at a particular time instant, there is an amplitude α_i associated with each state $|i\rangle$ of an observable of the system (the notation $|\cdot\rangle$ has good reasons in quantum mechanics notation related to the particular matrix mathematics involved). The amplitudes are complex numbers satisfying $\sum ||\alpha_i||^2 = 1$, where if $\alpha_i = a + b\sqrt{-1}$ then $||\alpha_i|| = \sqrt{a^2+b^2}$ and the summation is taken over all distinct states of the observable at a particular instant. The transitions are governed by a matrix U which represents the program executed. This program has to satisfy the following constraints. If the set of possible ID's (complete instantaneous description) of the Turing machine is X, where X is say $\{0,1\}^n$ to simplify the discussion, then U maps the column vector $\underline{\alpha} = (\alpha_x)_{x \in X}$ to $U\underline{\alpha}$. Here $\underline{\alpha}$ is a vector of amplitudes of the quantum superposition of the distinct possible states in X before a step, and $U\underline{\alpha}$ the same after the step concerned. The special property which U needs to satisfy in quantum mechanics is that it is *unitary*, that is, $U \times U^\dagger = I$ where I is the identity matrix and $U^\dagger$ is the conjugate transpose of U ('conjugate' means that all $\sqrt{-1}$'s are replaced by $-\sqrt{-1}$'s and 'transpose' means that the rows and columns are interchanged). In other words, U is unitary iff $U^\dagger = U^{-1}$.

The unitary constraint on the evolution of the computation enforces two facts.

1. If $U^0\underline{\alpha} = \underline{\alpha}$ and $U^t = U \cdot U^{t-1}$ then $\sum_{x \in X} ||(U^t\underline{\alpha})_x||^2 = 1$ for all t (discretizing time for convenience).
2. A quantum computation is reversible (replacing U by $U^\dagger = U^{-1}$).

The common example here is a simple computation on a one-bit computer. The quantum superposition of states of the computer is denoted by

$$|\Psi\rangle = \alpha\ |0\rangle + \beta\ |1\rangle,$$

where $||\alpha||^2 + ||\beta||^2 = 1$. The different possible states are $|0\rangle = \binom{1}{0}$ and $|1\rangle = \binom{0}{1}$. Our unitary operator will be

$$U = \frac{\sqrt{2}}{2}\begin{pmatrix} 1 & 1 \\ -1 & 1 \end{pmatrix}.$$

It is easy to verify using common matrix calculation that

$$\begin{aligned} U\ |0\rangle &= \sqrt{2}/2\ |0\rangle - \sqrt{2}/2\ |1\rangle \\ U\ |1\rangle &= \sqrt{2}/2\ |0\rangle + \sqrt{2}/2\ |1\rangle \\ U^2\ |0\rangle &= 0\ |0\rangle - 1\ |1\rangle = -\ |1\rangle \\ U^2\ |1\rangle &= 1\ |0\rangle + 0\ |1\rangle = \ |0\rangle \end{aligned}$$

If we observe the computer in state $U\ |0\rangle$, then the probability of observing state $|0\rangle$ is $(\sqrt{2}/2)^2 = 1/2$ and the probability to observe $|1\rangle$ is $(-\sqrt{2}/2)^2 = 1/2$. However, if we observe the computer in state $U^2\ |0\rangle$, then the probability of observing state $|0\rangle$ is 0 and the probability to observe $|1\rangle$ is 1. Similarly, if we observe the computer in state $U\ |1\rangle$, then the probability of observing state $|0\rangle$ is $(\sqrt{2}/2)^2 = 1/2$ and the probability to observe $|1\rangle$ is $(\sqrt{2}/2)^2 = 1/2$. But now, if we observe the computer in state $U^2\ |1\rangle$, then the probability of observing state $|0\rangle$ is 1 and the probability to observe $|1\rangle$ is 0. Therefore, the operator

U inverts a bit when it is applied twice in a row, and hence has acquired the charming name *square root of 'not'*. It is a simple exercise to write U in terms of an if–then–else program:

$$\begin{aligned} \textbf{if } |\Psi\rangle = |0\rangle \textbf{ then } |\Psi\rangle &:= \sqrt{2}/2\ |0\rangle - \sqrt{2}/2\ |1\rangle \\ \textbf{else } |\Psi\rangle &:= \sqrt{2}/2\ |0\rangle + \sqrt{2}/2\ |1\rangle \end{aligned}$$

Without mentioning it, and perhaps without the reader even noticing, we have applied as a matter of course an absolutely crucial difference between quantum computation and probabilistic computation.

4.3 Observables

According to quantum mechanics a physical system gives rise to a complex linear vector space $\mathcal{H}$, such that each vector of unit length represents a state of the system $|\Psi\rangle \in \mathcal{H}$.

A *quantum measurement* gives rise to a Hermitian operator $\hat{A}$ (the *observable*) and a decomposition of $\mathcal{H}$ into orthogonal subspaces (different *states* of the observable)

$$\mathcal{H} = A_1 \oplus A_2 \oplus \cdots \oplus A_n,$$

with $\hat{A} = \sum_{i=1}^{n} \alpha_i P_i$ where P_i is the projector of state $|\Psi\rangle$ on A_i (say, $|a_i\rangle$). If we measure observable $\hat{A}$ in system state $|\Psi\rangle$, with $|\Psi\rangle = \sum_{i=1}^{n} c_i\ |a_i\rangle$, then the following happens with probability $||c_k||^2$:

1. The outcome of the measurement α_k is registered.
2. The superposition $|\Psi\rangle$ collapses to superposition $|a_k\rangle \in A_k$.
3. The probability of observing $|a_k\rangle$ is renormalized to 1.

4.4 Interference

In computing the above amplitudes, subsequent to two applications of U, according to matrix calculus we found that

$$\begin{aligned} U^2\ |1\rangle &= \sqrt{2}/2\,(\sqrt{2}/2(\ |0\rangle -\ |1\rangle) + \sqrt{2}/2(\ |0\rangle +\ |1\rangle)) \\ &= \tfrac{1}{2}(\ |0\rangle -\ |1\rangle +\ |0\rangle +\ |1\rangle)\ =\ |0\rangle. \end{aligned}$$

In a probabilistic calculation, flipping a coin two times in a row, we would have found that the probability of each computation path in the complete binary computation tree of depth 2 was $1/4$, and the states at the four leaves of the tree were $|0\rangle$, $|1\rangle$, $|0\rangle$, $|1\rangle$, resulting in a total probability of observing $|0\rangle$ being $1/2$ and the total probability of observing $|1\rangle$ being $1/2$ as well.

The principle involved is called *interference*, like with light. If we put a screen with a single small enough hole in between a light source and a target, then we observe a gradually dimming illumination of the target screen, the brightest spot being colinear with the light source and the hole. If we put a screen with two small holes in between, then we observe a diffraction pattern of bright and dark stripes due to interference. Namely, the light hits all of the screen via two different routes (through the two different holes). If the two routes differ by an even number of half wave lengths, then the wave amplitudes at the target are added, resulting in twice the amplitude and a bright spot, and if they differ by an odd number of half wave lengths then the wave amplitudes are in opposite phase and are subtracted resulting in zero and a dark spot. Similarly, with quantum computation, if the quantum state is

$$|\Psi\rangle = \alpha\ |x\rangle + \beta\ |y\rangle,$$

then for $x = y$ we have a probability of observing $|x\rangle$ of $||\alpha + \beta||^2$, rather than $||\alpha||^2 + ||\beta||^2$ which it would have been in a probabilistic fashion. For example, if $\alpha = \sqrt{2}/2$ and $\beta = -\sqrt{2}/2$ then the probability of observing $|x\rangle$ is 0 rather than 1/2, and with the sign of β inverted we observe $|x\rangle$ with probability 1.

4.5 Quantum Parallelism and Realizations

The currently successful trick used in [Shor, 1994, Simon, 1994] is to use a sequence S_n of n unitary operations S (similar to U above) on a register of n bits originally in the all-0 state $|\Psi\rangle = |00\ldots0\rangle$. The result is a superposition of

$$S_n\ |\Psi\rangle = \sum_{x\in\{0,1\}^n} 1/\sqrt{2^n}\ \ |x\rangle$$

of all the 2^n possible states of the register, each with amplitude $1/\sqrt{2^n}$ (and hence probability of being observed of $1/2^n$.) Now the computation proceeds in parallel along the exponentially many computation paths in quantum coherent superposition. A sequence of tricky further unitary operations and observations serves to exploit interference (and so-called entanglement) phenomena to effect a high probability of eventually observing a desired outcome.

Physical realizations of QCC will have to struggle with the fact that the coherent states of the superposition will tend to deteriorate by interaction with each other and the universe, a phenomenon called *decoherence*. In [Unruh, 1995] it is calculated that that QCC calculations using physical realizations based on spin lattices will have to be finished in an extremely short time. For example, factoring a 1000 bit number in square quantum factoring time we have to perform 10^6 steps in less than the thermal time scale $\hbar/kT$ which at 1 K is of order 10^{-9} seconds. Such a QCC computation would need to proceed at optical frequencies. See also [Chuang, *et al.*, 1995].

Another problem is *error correction*: measurements to detect errors will destroy the computation. A novel partial method for error correction has been suggested in [Berthiaume *et al.*, 1994]. A comprehensive discussion on these problems in practically applying QCC is contained in [Landauer, 1995].

References

[Adleman, 1994] L. Adleman, Molecular computation of solutions to combinatorial problems, *Science*, Vol 266, Nov 1994, 1021-1024; A Vat of DNA May Become Fast Computer Of the Future, Gina Kolata in: *The New York Times*, April 11, 1995, Science Times, pp. C1, C10.

[Barenco *et. al*] A. Barenco, C.H. Bennett, R. Cleve, D.P. DiVicenzo, N. Margolus, P. Shor, T. Sleator, J. Smolin, and H. Weinfurter, Elementary gates for quantum computation, submitted to *Physical Review A*, March 1995.

[Benioff, 1980–1986] P. Benioff, J. Stat. Phys., 22(1980), 563-591, also *J. Math. Phys.*, 22(1981), 495-507, *Int. J. Theoret. Phys.*, 21(1982), 177-201, *Phys. Rev. Letters*, 48(1982), 1581-1585, *J. Stat. Phys.*, 29(1982), 515-546, *Phys. Rev. Letters*, 53(1984), 1203, *Ann. New York Acad. Sci.*, 480(1986), 475-486.

[Benioff, 1995] P. Benioff, Review of quantum computation, In: *Trends in Statistical Physics*, Council of Scientific Information, Trivandrum, India, To be published.

[Bennett, 1973] C.H. Bennett. Logical reversibility of computation. *IBM J. Res. Develop.*, 17:525–532, 1973.

[Bennett, 1982] C.H. Bennett. The thermodynamics of computation—a review. *Int. J. Theoret. Phys.*, 21(1982), 905-940.

[Bennett, 1989] C.H. Bennett. Time-space trade-offs for reversible computation. *SIAM J. Comput.*, 18(1989), 766-776.

[Bennett, *et al.*, 1992] C.H. Bennett, F. Bessette, G. Brassard, L. Salvail and J. Smolin, Experimental quantum cryptography, *J. Cryptology*, 5:1(1992), 3-28; C.H. Bennett, G. Brassard and A. Ekert, Quantum cryptography, *Scientific American*, Oct. 1992, 50-57.

[Bennett *et al.*, 1993] C.H. Bennett, P. Gács, M. Li, P.M.B. Vitányi and W.H Zurek, Thermodynamics of computation and information distance *Proc. 25th ACM Symp. Theory of Computation.* ACM Press, 1993, 21-30.

[Bernstein and Vazirani, 1993] Bernstein, E. and U. Vazirani, "Quantum complexity theory", *Proc. 25th ACM Symposium on Theory of Computing*, 1993, pp. 11 – 20.

[Berthiaume *et al.*, 1994] A. Berthiaume, D. Deutsch and R. Jozsa, The stabilisation of quantum computations, *Proc. 3rd IEEE Workshop on Physics and Computation (PhysComp '94)*, IEEE Computer Society Press, 1994.

[Brassard, 1994] G. Brassard, Cryptology Column—Quantum computing: The end of classical cryptography? *SIGACT News*, 25:4(Dec 1994), 15-21.

[Chuang, *et al.*, 1995] I.L. Chuang, R. Laflamme, P. Shor, and W.H. Zurek, Quantum computers, factoring and decoherence, Report LA-UR-95-241, Los Alamos National Labs, 1995 (quant-ph/9503007).

[Deutsch, 1985–1992] D. Deutsch, Quantum theory, the Church-Turing principle and the universal quantum computer. *Proc. Royal Society London.* Vol. A400(1985), 97-117; see also *Proc. Royal Society London*, A425(1989), 73-90; with R. Josza, *Proc. Royal Society London*, A439(1992), 553-558.

[Feynman, 1982—1987] R.P. Feynman, Simulating physics with computers, *Int. J. Theoret. Physics*, 21(1982), 467-488; Quantum mechanical computers. *Foundations of Physics*, 16(1986), 507-531. (Originally published in *Optics News*, February 1985); Tiny Computers Obeying Quantum Mechanical Laws. In: *New Directions in Physics: The Los Alamos 40th Anniversary Volume*,, N. Metropolis and D. M. Kerr and G. Rota, Eds.,Academic Press,, Boston, 1987, 7-25.

[Fredkin & Toffoli, 1982] E. Fredkin and T. Toffoli. Conservative logic. *Int. J. Theoret. Phys.*, 21(1982),219-253.

[Kiehl, 1994] R.A. Kiehl, Research toward Nanoelectronic computing technologies in Japan, In: Proc. 3rd Workshop on Physics and Computation (PhysComp'94), IEEE Computer Society Press, 1994, 1-4.

[Kissin, 1982–1991] G. Kissin, Measuring Energy Consumption in VLSI Circuits: a Foundation, Proc. 14th ACM Symp. Theor. Comp., 1982, 99-104; Lower and Upper Bounds on the Switching Energy Consumed by VLSI Circuits, *J. Assoc. Comp. Mach.*,, 38(1991), pp. 222-254.

[Kolmogorov, 1965] A.N. Kolmogorov, Three approaches to the definition of the concept 'quantity of information', *Problems in Information Transmission,* **1:1**(1965), 1-7.

[Koppelman, 1995] D.M. Koppelman, A lower bound on the average physical length of edges in the physical realization of graphs, Manuscript Dept ECE, Lousiana State Univ. Baton Rouge, 1995.

[Landauer, 1961] R. Landauer. Irreversibility and heat generation in the computing process. *IBM J. Res. Develop.*, 5:183–191, 1961.

[Landauer, 1991] R. Landauer, Information is physical, *Physics Today,* 44:May(1991), 23-29.

[Landauer, 1994] R. Landauer, Zig-zag path to understanding. In: Proc. 3nd Workshop on Physics and Computation (PhysComp'94), IEEE Computer Society Press, 1994, 54-59.

[Landauer, 1995] R. Landauer, Is quantum mechanics useful? *Proc. Roy. Soc. Lond.*, to be published.

[Lent *et al.*, 1994] C.S. Lent, P.D. Tougaw, W. Porod, Quantum cellular automata: The physics of computing with arrays of quantum dot molecules. In: Proc. 3nd Workshop on Physics and Computation (PhysComp'94), IEEE Computer Society Press, 1994, 5-13; also J. Appl. Phys., 74(1993), 3558, 4077, 6227, 75(1994), 1818.

[Li & Vitányi, 1993] M. Li and P.M.B. Vitányi. *An Introduction to Kolmogorov Complexity and Its Applications.* Springer-Verlag, New York, 1993.

[Li & Vitányi, 1994] M. Li and P.M.B. Vitányi. *Irreversibility and Adiabatic Computation: Trading time for energy,* submitted.

[Mead & Conway, 1980] C. Mead and L. Conway. *Introduction to VLSI Systems.* Addison-Wesley, 1980.

[Proc. PhysComp, 1981, 1992, 1994] Proc. 1981 Physics and Computation Workshop. *Int. J. Theoret. Phys.*, 21(1982). *Proc. 1992 Physics and Computation Workshop.* IEEE Computer Society Press, 1992. *Proc. 1994 Physics and Computation Workshop.* IEEE Computer Society Press, 1994.

[Schuhmacher, 1994] , B.W. Schumacher, On Quantum coding, *Phys. Rev. A*, in press to appear in 1995; (with R. Josza), A new proof of the quantum noiseless coding theorem, *J. Modern Optics*, 41(1994), 2343-2349.

[Shannon, 1948] C.E. Shannon, A mathematical theory of communication, *Bell System Tech. J.*, **27**(1948), 379-423, 623-656.

[Shor, 1994] Shor, P., Algorithms for quantum computation: Discrete log and factoring, *Proc. 35th IEEE Symposium on Foundations of Computer Science*, 1994, 124-134.

[Simon, 1994] Simon, D., On the power of quantum computation, *Proc. 35th IEEE Symposium on Foundations of Computer Science*, 1994.

[Thompson, 1979] C. Thompson, Area-time complexity for VLSI, Proc. 11th ACM Symp. Theor. Comp., 1979, 81-88.

[Ullman, 1984] J. Ullman, *Computational Aspects of VLSI*, Computer Science Press, Rockville, MD, 1984.

[Unruh, 1995] Unruh, W. G., Maintaining coherence in quantum computers, *Physical Review A*, 51(1995), 992-.

[Upfal and Wigderson, 1987] E. Upfal and A. Wigderson, How to share memory on a distributed system, *J. Assoc. Comp. Mach.*, 34(1987), 116-127.

[Vitányi, 1985] Area penalty for sublinear signal propagation delay on chip, *Proceedings 26th IEEE Symposium on Foundations of Computer Science*, 1985, 197-207.

[Vitányi, 1986] P.M.B. Vitányi, Non-sequential computation and Laws of Nature, In: VLSI Algorithms and Architectures (Proceedings Aegean Workshop on Computing, 2nd International Workshop on Parallel Processing and VLSI), *Lecture Notes In Computer Science 227*, Springer Verlag, 1986, 108-120.

[Vitányi, 1988] P.M.B. Vitányi, Locality, communication and interconnect length in multicomputers, *SIAM J. Computing*, 17 (1988), 659-672.

[Vitányi, 1994] P.M.B. Vitányi, Multiprocessor architectures and physical law. In: Proc. 3rd Workshop on Physics and Computation (PhysComp'94), IEEE Computer Society Press, 1994, 24-29.

[Burks, 1966] J. von Neumann. *Theory of Self-Reproducing Automata.* A.W. Burks, Ed., Univ. Illinois Press, Urbana, 1966.

Measure on P: Robustness of the Notion*

Eric Allender[1] and Martin Strauss[2]

[1] Department of Computer Science, Rutgers University, New Brunswick, NJ 08903, allender@cs.rutgers.edu

[2] Department of Mathematics, Rutgers University, New Brunswick, NJ 08903, mstrauss@math.rutgers.edu

Abstract. In [AS], we defined a notion of measure on the complexity class P (in the spirit of the work of Lutz [L92] that provides a notion of measure on complexity classes at least as large as E, and the work of Mayordomo [M] that provides a measure on PSPACE). In this paper, we show that several other ways of defining measure in terms of covers and martingales yield precisely the same notion as in [AS]. (Similar "robustness" results have been obtained previously for the notions of measure defined by [L92] and [M], but – for reasons that will become apparent below – different proofs are required in our setting.)
To our surprise, and in contrast to the measures of Lutz [L92] and Mayordomo [M], one obtains strictly *more* measurable sets if one considers "nonconservative" martingales that succeed merely in the lim sup rather than having a limit of infinity. For example, it is shown in [AS] that the class of sparse sets does *not* have measure zero in P, whereas here we show that using the "nonconservative" measure, the class of sparse sets (and in fact the class of sets with density $\epsilon < 1/2$) *does* have measure zero. We also show that our "nonconservative" measure on PSPACE is incomparable with that of [M].

1 Introduction

Our purpose in this paper is to prove additional basic properties of the notions of measure on P and PSPACE that were defined in our earlier paper [AS], and to clarify the relationship between our measure on PSPACE and the measure that was presented by Mayordomo in [M]. (Both the notion of measure presented in [AS] and the notion presented in [M] coincide with that of [L92] whenever Lutz's measure is defined. There is by now a large body of interesting work demonstrating the utility and importance of resource-bounded measure; we refer the reader to [AS, L93] for pointers to this material.)

Our definition of a measure on P in [AS] shares the following aspects of the definition of [L92]:

A null cover of a set S of languages is a function $d : \mathbb{N} \times \Sigma^* \to \mathbb{R}$ (where $d(k, w)$ is denoted by $d_k(w)$) such that

* Research supported by NSF grant CCR-9204874.

- $d_k(\lambda) \leq 1/2^k$
- $d_k(w) = \mathrm{avg}\{d_k(w0), d_k(w1)\}$
- For every sequence $\omega \in S$ there is some prefix w of ω such that $d_k(w) \geq 1$.

A function of this sort is called a "density system." Note that any such d_k corresponds to covering S by a sequence of intervals whose sizes sum to $1/2^k$. Measures on specific complexity classes are obtained by putting limits on the complexity of the function d. (Details may be found in Section 2.)

In later work [L93], Lutz defines his measure equivalently using the notion of a "martingale". This is a "betting strategy" that starts with some fixed amount of money and, for each input sequence w, "bets" a fraction of the money it currently has on what the next bit of the sequence will be. It is known that a set S has measure zero if and only if there is a martingale that "succeeds" (i.e., is unbounded) on all sequences in S. (In the setting of resource-unbounded measure, see [Schn]; for the resource-bounded case, see [JL, M].)

In Lutz's setting, and in Mayordomo's setting (as in Lebesgue measure), the class of measure-zero sets one obtains is the same, regardless of which of the following choices one picks in making the definitions:

1. The martingale succeeds on sequence ω if (1) it is unbounded on ω (i.e., the lim sup is infinite), or (2) it succeeds only if it has a limit of infinity on ω.
2. The martingale either (1) must be "conservative" in the sense that the amounts of money after $w0$ and $w1$ exactly average to the amount of money after w, or (2) it can "throw money away" by having the average after $w0$ and $w1$ be less than the amount after w.

(Depending on what one is trying to prove, it can be more convenient to choose more stringent or more lenient conditions.)

In this paper, we show that the class of measure zero sets one obtains using the definition of [AS] is the same as that one obtains by formulating the definition in terms of conservative martingales (both in the lim sup sense and in the limit sense) and it is also equivalent to being covered in the limit sense by a martingale that is not assumed to be conservative.

However, to our surprise (and in contrast to the case for Lebesgue measure and for Lutz's or Mayordomo's notions of measure), one obtains strictly more measurable sets in our setting, if one considers covering sets in the lim sup sense by non-conservative martingales. Furthermore, some of the classes one is able to cover in this sense are fairly interesting and natural. For instance, using the definition presented in [AS], we showed that the class of sparse sets does not have measure zero in P. However, using the more generous notion of measure (non-conservative martingales) we show here that the class of all sets that are not exponentially dense has measure zero in P.

Our previous paper [AS] provided a notion of measure not only for P (and other time-bounded classes), but also for PSPACE (and other space-bounded classes). The measure on PSPACE presented in [AS] provides strictly fewer measurable sets than the measure of [M]. However, if one defines a measure on PSPACE using the non-conservative, lim sup notion, we show here that one obtains a notion that is incomparable with that of [M].

Thus we now have two notions of measure on P: a conservative measure and a non-conservative one. One might now worry that any of a number of other slight modifications to the technical aspects of our definitions could lead to other distinct notions of measure. One goal of the current paper is to demonstrate that this is not the case. In fact, as the following paragraph tries to explain, we find it surprising that the class of sets that are covered by martingales is so robust to the details of how the martingales are computed.

The reason this strikes us as surprising is that one of the technical difficulties that had to be overcome in defining the measure in [AS] was that an appropriate representation for numerical outputs had to be found that could be represented in a small number of bits, but still would allow efficient arithmetic operations. (In [AS], we represented numbers as the difference of two sums of powers of two. Thus we can write $2^n + 2^{-r} - 2^m$ in $\log nrm$ bits.) However, we have been able to show that, at least in the martingale formulation, one can use the more natural binary notation, and obtain the same class of measure zero sets.

Note that the work performed in formulating the delicate definition in [AS] was *not* done in vain. In order that the notion of measure be a "reasonable" notion of big and small, certain axioms have to be satisfied, and this is most easily done in the delicate formulation of [AS], which involves output as differences of formal sums of powers of two, and martingales whose values are approximated rather than computed exactly.

In nearly all cases, the arguments here also apply to the measures of [L92] and [M]. Thus this paper gives a unified treatment of the robustness theorems.

2 Definitions

First we review the measure defined in [AS]. The definitions given there were designed to facilitate proving basic properties of the measure, and so the definitions were in some cases more restrictive and in other cases more general than what is "natural." In this paper we show that in almost all regards (with one important exception), the alternate formulations are all equivalent.

We state the results here for measure on P but note that the results hold for measure on any class DTIME($\mathcal{C}$) (or DSPACE($\mathcal{C}$)) with $\mathcal{C}$ closed under squaring. We equate a language L with its characteristic sequence χ_L. Given a string w (or a sequence ω) we use $w[i..j]$ ($\omega[i..j]$) to denote the string occupying positions i through j of $w(\omega)$. We write $w \sqsubseteq z$ to denote that w is a prefix of z.

Now we present a key notion that is essential to defining the measure in [AS]. Given a natural number n and a Turing machine M having random access to its input, define a *dependency set* $G_{M,n} \subseteq \{0, \ldots, n\}$ to be a set such that for each $i \in G_{M,n} \cup \{n\}$, and each word w of length n, M can compute $M(w[0..i])$ querying only input bits in $G_{M,n} \cap \{0, 1, 2, \ldots i\}$. Note that for all M and n, there is a unique minimal dependency set for M and n, which can easily be computed by expanding the tree of queries that one obtains by assuming both possible values for each queried bit.

A $\Gamma(\mathrm{P})$ machine ($\Gamma(\mathrm{PSPACE})$ machine) M is such that M runs in time (space) $\log^{O(1)} n$ and has dependency sets $G_{M,|w|} \subseteq \{0,\ldots,n\}$ with size bounded by $\log^{O(1)} n$. The machine M is given the length of its input. The output of M is a rational number represented as the difference of formal sums of powers of 2. By convention, numerical arguments are passed to M in both unary and binary (so M has time polylog in the *value* of such arguments, which is enough time to read the binary form of the argument). If M computes a function with numerical arguments then the dependency sets have subscripts to match: If M computes $d_r(w)$ then M has dependency sets $G_{M,|w|,r}$ that must be polylog in $|w|+r$. We will sometimes write $G_{d,|w|,r}$ for $G_{M,|w|,r}$ when M computes d.

A set is said to be $\Gamma(\mathcal{C})$-null if it is covered by a density system d, with $d_k(\lambda) \leq 2^{-k}$, and d is approximated by a $\Gamma(\mathcal{C})$ machine M in the sense that $|d_k(w) - M_{k,r}(w)| \leq 2^{-r}$. If in fact $d_k(w)$ is *equal* to $M_k(w)$ (instead of merely being approximated) then we say that d is *exactly computed.* The approximation to d computed by M is denoted by $\hat{d}$. *A priori* we require only $d_k(w) \geq \frac{d_k(w0)+d_k(w1)}{2}$, not equality.

2.1 Niceness Properties

A *cover* will refer to either a density system or a martingale. Unless specified otherwise, a result for a "cover" is claimed to hold for either martingales or density systems. Note one can build a density system from a martingale by defining $d_k(w)$ to be $2^{-k}d(w)$, and this preserves all the properties discussed below that hold for both notions of cover.

We have already defined what it means for a cover to be exactly computed. Below, we define the other "niceness" properties that will be considered.

Definitions: Consider a cover d with dependency set G_d.

- A martingale d covering set A is a *limit* martingale if d has a limit of infinity (and not just a lim sup) along languages in A.
- A density system d is *regular* if $d_k(z) \geq 1$ and $z \sqsubseteq w$ imply $d_k(w) \geq 1$ for all k.
- d is *conservative* if $d(w) = \frac{d(w0)+d(w1)}{2}$. (A function satisfying

  $$d(w) \geq \frac{d(w0)+d(w1)}{2}$$

  but not necessarily with equality is sometimes called a supermartingale.)
- d is *monotone* if $G_{d,m} \subseteq G_{d,n}$ for $m \leq n$.
- d is *slothful* if (1) d is exactly computed, and (2) given input (n,k), we can compute in time polylog in $n+k$ a list of indices from $\{0,\ldots,n\}$ such that, if i is *not* in this list, then for any string w of length n, $d_k(w[0..i-1]) = d_k(w[0..i])$. (If d is a martingale disregard k.) The condition of sloth is merely a technical notion that is useful in our proofs.

In subsequent sections we will prove that without loss of generality one may assume that the density systems come from martingales, i.e., $d_k = 2^{-k}d$ for a martingale d, and that d and d_k are exactly computable. We will also show, curiously, that if one assumes *any* of the other niceness conditions above, then *all* the others follow.

Due to space limitations, the proofs have been omitted from this extended abstract. A version of the complete paper is available through the Electronic Colloquium on Computational Complexity (`http://www.eccc.uni-trier.de/eccc`).

3 Equivalence

First we discuss several simplifications that are possible without assuming the niceness conditions. Later we discuss the equivalence of the niceness conditions.

3.1 General Equivalence

Lemma 1. *Let $G_{\hat{d},|w|,r}$ be dependency sets for a computation $\hat{d}_r(w)$. Without loss of generality we may assume $G_{\hat{d},|w|,r} \subseteq G_{\hat{d},|w|,s}$ for $r \leq s$.* □

While the observation of Lemma 1 is immediate, it is important for the constructions in this paper, as well as for Theorem 4 in [AS]. ([AS] was somewhat unclear on this point.) The reader should not confuse monotonicity in r (which is always possible and henceforth always assumed) with the niceness property "monotonicity" (i.e., monotonicity in $|w|$).

Next we give an exact computation lemma for martingales and density systems in our setting. The reader should also see Theorem 10 for an exponentially better exact-computation lemma for martingales in both our setting and Lutz's setting.

Theorem 2. *Given any cover d, one can construct an exactly-computed cover d' covering the same sets. This construction preserves coverage in the limit and monotonicity.* □

Next we show that for nonconservative covers the density system and martingale formulations coincide.

Theorem 3. *A set covered by a density system is covered by a nonconservative martingale.* □

This construction destroys conservation, so one cannot use it to convert a conservative density system into a conservative martingale. The entire next subsection is devoted to this conversion.

Fig. 1. Order of constructions

$$\begin{array}{ccccc} \text{conservative} & \leftrightarrow & \text{slothful} & \leftarrow & \text{monotone} \\ & & \downarrow & & \uparrow \\ & & \text{regular} & \rightarrow & \text{limit} \end{array}$$

3.2 Equivalence of Niceness conditions

In this subsection we show the niceness conditions are equivalent. Requiring any one of the niceness conditions places a severe restriction on the measure, as is discussed in the next section.

We prove the equivalence according to Fig. 1. The reader is cautioned that some of the constructions destroy some properties. Fig. 1 is used as follows:

- Given a martingale or density system covering a set A and satisfying any of the five properties above, one can construct a limit martingale and a monotone density system covering A.
- Given a limit martingale one can make the martingale in turn monotone, slothful and conservative, and these properties accumulate.
- Given a monotone density system one can make the density system in turn slothful, regular and conservative, and these properties accumulate.

We recall that regularity is predicated of density systems and limit coverage is predicated of martingales.

In summary:

Theorem 4. *All sets with covers have exactly computed covers. A set is covered by a density system iff it is covered by a martingale. If a set is covered by a conservative, monotone, regular,* or *limit cover, then it is covered by an exactly-computed, conservative, monotone, regular density system and covered in the limit by an exactly-computed, conservative, monotone martingale.* □

The double arrow of Fig. 1 gives us an exact computation lemma for conservative covers: Given a conservative cover make a slothful cover, then make a conservative, slothful (and hence exactly computed) cover. Also, Theorem 4 shows that the conservative density sytem and martingale formulations coincide.

(Although we have had to omit the proof of Theorem 4 here, it is appropriate to mention that some parts of the proof draw on similar material from [JLM, M].)

3.3 Space

The notion of measure of [AS] can be defined for space as well as time. We conclude this section by comparing that measure, denoted $\mu_{\Gamma(\text{PSPACE})}$, with the measure of [M], here denoted $\mu_{\Phi(\text{PSPACE})}$.

Theorem 5. *If a set has a $\mu_{\Gamma(\text{PSPACE})}$ cover, than it also has a $\mu_{\Phi(\text{PSPACE})}$ cover.* □

In [AS] it is shown that SPARSE does not have $\mu_{\Gamma(\mathbf{PSPACE})}$ measure zero. It is easy to see that SPARSE does have $\mu_{\Phi(\mathbf{PSPACE})}$ measure zero, so the measure of [M] is strictly richer.

4 Inequivalence

Henceforth we will denote the conservative measure by $\mu_{\Gamma(C)}$ and the nonconservative measure by $\mu_{\Gamma'(C)}$. In this section we show that the two measures differ almost exponentially in the largest f such that $\{L : L \text{ has density at most } f\}$ has measure zero. In the previous section we showed $\mu_{\Gamma(\mathbf{PSPACE})}$ is strictly weaker than $\mu_{\Phi(\mathbf{PSPACE})}$; here we show that $\mu_{\Gamma'(\mathbf{PSPACE})}$ is incomparable with $\mu_{\Phi(\mathbf{PSPACE})}$.

4.1 Conservative versus Nonconservative measure

In [AS] it was shown that SPARSE, the set of languages with at most polynomially many words of a given length, does not have an exactly-computable conservative cover. The theorems of the last section show that SPARSE has no conservative cover at all. In this section we show that SPARSE does have a nonconservative cover (which is not monotone, not regular if a density system, and not limit if a martingale). We also show that there are sets A and B such that $\mu_{\Gamma'(\mathbf{PSPACE})}(A) = 0$ but $\mu_{\Phi(\mathbf{PSPACE})}(A) \neq 0$ and $\mu_{\Gamma'(\mathbf{PSPACE})}(B) \neq 0$ but $\mu_{\Phi(\mathbf{PSPACE})}(B) = 0$, so the nonconservative versions of our measure on PSPACE is incomparable with that of [M].

Theorem 6. *The set of languages with density less than $\epsilon < 1/2$ is $\mu_{\Gamma'(\mathbf{P})}$-null.* □

In [AS] it is noted that the set of languages with density n^k (fixed k) is Γ(P)-null, whereas all of SPARSE is not. Thus [AS] presents a threshold density for Γ(P)-measure. Theorem 6 shows that Γ'(P)-measure is significantly stronger in this regard.

4.2 Space

Now we compare our PSPACE measure to that of [M].

Definition 7. Let ODD denote the set of languages L such that for each n, L has an odd number of words of length n.

Note that ODD has Lebesgue measure zero.

Definition 8. Let DOUBLE be the set of sequences ω such that for almost all n there exists $x \leq 2^n$ with

$$\begin{aligned}\omega[3^n + xn^2..3^n + (x+1)n^2 - 1] \\ = \omega[2 \cdot 3^n + xn^2..2 \cdot 3^n + (x+1)n^2]\ .\end{aligned}$$

That is, in the sequence ω, the same sequence of n^2 bits appears at positions $3^n + xn^2$ and at $2 \cdot 3^n + xn^2$. Note that for large n we have $\sum_{j=0}^{n} 2^j j^2 < 3^n$.

Theorem 9. *The set* ODD *has* $\mu_{\Phi(\mathrm{PSPACE})}$*-measure zero, but the set* ODD $\cap$ PSPACE *does not have* $\mu_{\Gamma'(\mathrm{PSPACE})}$*-measure zero.*

The set DOUBLE *has* $\mu_{\Gamma'(\mathrm{PSPACE})}$*-measure zero, but the set* DOUBLE $\cap$ PSPACE *does not have* $\mu_{\Phi(\mathrm{PSPACE})}$*-measure zero.* □

To cover ODD a martingale needs to look at all its input, whereas to cover DOUBLE a martingale needs to be able to look at input in a dynamically-determined order. In this regard these examples are complementary, and we see that the two measures are very different.

We've shown our notion of measure on PSPACE is incomparable to that of [M]. One might ask about a join, a measure on PSPACE strictly richer than both, and one might hope that a join can be constructed without defining a new model of computation (say by adding a Γ'(PSPACE) martingale to a Φ(PSPACE) martingale.) It seems, however, that "clean-hands" approaches fail, and a new model of computation *would* be needed. Such a model would likely be quite complicated, however, in regards to giving the machine the length of its input: $\mu_{\Gamma'(\mathrm{PSPACE})}$ machines get the exact length of their input and make good use of this information, whereas $\mu_{\Phi(\mathrm{PSPACE})}$ machines *must not* be given their exact input length. (This is so that $M(z)$ and $M(w)$ are initially the same computation for $z \sqsubseteq w$ and approximately the same length, which guarantees that a PSPACE machine can diagonalize against M. See [M].)

5 Quasipolynomial Precision

A cover d is required to have a computation $\hat{d}_r$ such that for all w we have $|d(w) - \hat{d}_r(w)| \leq 2^{-r}$, and in Theorem 2, we showed that a set A has such a cover iff A has an exactly computable cover. In this section, we first show how to weaken the hypothesis to $|d(w) - \hat{d}_r(w)| \leq \frac{1}{r^2}$ (one could substitute any reasonable function $f(r)$ such that $\sum_{r=1}^{\infty} f(r)$ is finite). Next, we observe that $d_k(w) \leq 2^{\mathrm{polylog}(k + |w|)} d_k(\lambda)$, since $d_k(w[0..j]) \leq 2d_k(w[0..i])$, where i and j are consecutive elements of $G_{d,|w|,k}$. From this it follows that two-sided quasipolynomial precision suffices for our machines, i.e., our machines need only output a polylog number of significant bits to either side of the radix point. We draw two important corollaries:

- The usual way that sublinear-time machines compute functions is to output the ith bit as a function of i. The most natural way is to output the value in binary. In [AS] functions output "differences of formal sums of powers of two." Now, since two-sided quasipolyonmial precision suffices, we see that all three conventions are equivalent.
- If a set A has a cover d with approximation $\hat{d}$, such that $|d - \hat{d}_r| \leq \frac{1}{r^2}$ and $\hat{d}$ is computable if output is expressed as a "differences of formal sums of

powers of p" for $p \neq 2$, then A also has a base-two cover. (Essentially, this is because two-sided quasipolynomial precision is a concept independent of base.)

The results of this section hold for both Γ(P)- and Γ'(P)- martingales.

The following is similar to Theorem 2, but exponentially better, in the sense that the assumption about the goodness of approximation has been relaxed:

Theorem 10. *Let A be a set for which there exists a martingale d and a computable function $\hat{d}_r(w)$ such that for all w we have $|d(w) - \hat{d}_r(w)| \leq \frac{1}{r^2+1}$. Then A has an exactly computed martingale d'.* □

As in Sect. 3, we have to treat conservative martingales specially:

Theorem 11. *Under the hypotheses of Theorem 10, if d is conservative then d' of the conclusion can be made conservative.* □

Next we observe that these martingales can't grow too quickly:

Theorem 12. *Let d be a computable martingale. Then $d(w) \leq 2^{\mathrm{polylog}(|w|)}$.* □

Combining the last two theorems, we get

Theorem 13. *If A is covered by a (conservative) martingale d, then A is covered by a (conservative) martingale with at most polylog-many nonzero bits on either side of the radix point.* □

Corollary 14. *If A is covered by a martingale $d(w)$, and a there is a function $\hat{d}_r(w)$ such that $|d(w) - \hat{d}_r(w)| \leq 1/r^2$ and the ith bit of $\hat{d}_r(w)$ can be computed on input i, then A has an exactly-computed null cover whose value is output in binary.* □

Corollary 15. *Fix a base p. If A has a martingale d with a computation $\hat{d}_r$ such that $|d - \hat{d}_r| \leq 1/r^2$ and the ith base-p digit of $\hat{d}_r$ can be computed on input i, then A has a base-two cover.* □

The situation is similar for density systems, but the density system notation makes the situation *appear* worse. Since martingales are normalized in the sense that $d(\lambda) = 1$, when we claim that $|d(w) - \hat{d}_r(w)| \leq f(r)$ we are really giving a *relative* error. To get comparable results for density systems, it seems we need a computation $\hat{d}_{k,r}(w)$ with $|d_k(w) - \hat{d}_{k,r}(w)| \leq 2^{-k}/r^2$ (exponential in k but a power in r). But relaxing the precision of a computation of a density system from $1/2^r$ to $1/2^k r^2$ is no big feat, since given a computation satisfying the latter, it's easy to get a computation satsifying the former: $\hat{d}_{k+r,r}$ satisfies $|d_k(w) - \hat{d}_{k,r}(w)| \leq 2^{-r}$. Next, while a martingale can easily output 1 in binary, a density function d_k cannot output 2^{-k} in binary in polylog time, which would be analogous. Therefore density systems must settle for scientific notation. We omit the density-system analogs of the above corollaries.

6 Conclusions

The study of resource-bounded measure is still new, and it is useful to note that the definitions presented in [L92] have evolved slightly over time. Still, a large and growing body of results have shown that resource-bounded measure is a useful tool providing surprising connections to other questions in computer science [RSC].

The extension of this notion to small classes such as P is a much newer notion, and although the results of [AS] have shown that interesting results can be obtained using one definition of a measure on P, we should not be surprised if this notion evolves as further experience is gained.

This paper represents the next step of such an evolution. Although we were able to show here that the measure of [AS] is robust under many changes to the details of the definition, we have learned the surprising fact that one can obtain strictly more measurable sets by considering betting strategies that throw away information periodically.

References

[AS] E. Allender and M. Strauss, Measure on small complexity classes, with applications for BPP, *Proc. 35th FOCS conference,* 1994 pp. 807–818.

[JL] D. Juedes and J. Lutz, The complexity and distribution of hard problems, *Proc. 34th FOCS Conference*, pp. 177–185, 1993.

[JLM] D. Juedes, J. Lutz and E. Mayordomo, private communication, 1993-94.

[L92] J. Lutz, Almost Everywhere High Nonuniform Complexity, *Journal of Computer and System Sciences* 44 (1992), pp. 220-258.

[L93] J. Lutz, The quantitative structure of exponential time, *Proc. 8th Structure in Complexity Theory Conference*, pp. 158–175, 1993.

[M] E. Mayordomo, *Contributions to the Study of Resource-Bounded Measure,* PhD Thesis, Universitat Politècnica de Catalunya, Barcelona, 1994. See also [M2], in which a preliminary version of the PSPACE measure appears.

[M2] E. Mayordomo, Measuring in PSPACE, to appear in *Proc. International Meeting of Young Computer Scientists '92*, Topics in Computer Science series, Gordon and Breach.

[RS] K. Regan and D. Sivakumar. Improved resource-bounded Borel-Cantelli and stochasticity theorems. Technical Report UB-CS-TR 95-08, Computer Science Dept., University at Buffalo, February 1995.

[RSC] K. Regan, D. Sivakumar, and J.-Y. Cai. Pseudorandom generators, measure theory, and natural proofs. Technical Report UB-CS-TR 95-02, Computer Science Dept., University at Buffalo, January 1995.

[Schn] C. P. Schnorr, *Zufälligkeit und Wahrscheinlichkeit*, Lecture Notes in Mathematics 218 (1971).

Comparing Counting Classes for Logspace, One-way Logspace, and First-order

Hans-Jörg Burtschick

TU - Berlin, Sekr.: FR 6-2, Franklinstr. 28/29, D-10587 Berlin

Abstract. We consider one-way logspace counting classes which are defined via Turing machines that scan their input only in one direction. The one-way logspace counting classes #1L and span-1L are strict subclasses of the corresponding (two-way) logspace classes #L and span-L, resp. We separate the one-way classes 1UL and 1NL which correspond to the classes UL and NL. It follows that F1L $\subset$ #1L $\subset$ span-1L $\subset$ #P.
We generalize first-order counting classes to use $<$, $SUCC$, and $+$ as linear orderings. It turns out that with respect to certain natural encodings for $op \in \{<, SUCC, +\}$ the classes $\#\Sigma_0[op]$ and $\#\Sigma_1[op]$ are subclasses of #1L and span-1L. It holds that $\#\Pi_2[<] = \#\Pi_1[\text{SUCC}] = \#\Pi_1[+]$, and that this class characterizes #P.
From that, we obtain a characterization of #P via universally branching alternating logtime Turing machines.

1 Introduction

An important open question in complexity theory is whether the two classes NL and NP are equal. Although in the case of computing partial multivalued functions nondeterministically the corresponding classes can be separated [Bur89], a solution for the class of decision problems is not in sight.

Counting classes, such as #P [Val79] or the corresponding logspace counting class #L, contain the functions that count the accepting paths of polynomial time bounded (or logarithmic space bounded resp.) nondeterministic Turing machines. Thus they may be seen as intermediate between NP and NPMV. That is, the complexity of 'counting the number of solutions' may be seen as between that of 'computing the solution' and that of 'checking the existence of a solution'. But, as for NL and NP, the question whether #L equals #P is open.

Considering this, the existence of strict subclasses of #P, proven by Saluja, Subrahmanyam, and Thakur [SST92], is surprising. Their results use notions from finite model theory to obtain logical characterizations of complexity classes. This line of research was initiated by [Fag74]. In [SST92] the descriptional complexity of counting functions is considered. The number of alternations of first-order quantifiers in formulas is used as a measure of the complexity. For example, formulas of the form $\forall \mathbf{x} \exists \mathbf{y}\, \varphi(\mathbf{x}, \mathbf{y})$ are called Π_2-formulas. The class $\#\Pi_2$ contains the counting functions that are definable by Π_2-formulas (see Section 2 for precise definitions). One of their main results is: $\#\Sigma_0 \subset \#\Sigma_1 \subset \#\Pi_1 \subset \#\Sigma_2 \subset \#\Pi_2\ (= \#\text{P})$.

There are functions in $\#\Sigma_2 \setminus \#\Pi_1$ that are computable by deterministic logspace bounded Turing machines. On the other hand, $\#\Pi_1$ contains a function that is complete for #P via logspace reductions that preserve the number of solutions. Thus at first sight, these results seem not to fit into the structure of more traditional Turing machine based counting classes.

The aim of this paper is to compare logically characterized counting classes to counting classes based on Turing machines.

In section 3 we consider one-way logspace counting classes. A one-way Turing machine scans its input only once (from left to right, say). Studying this type of Turing machines has a long tradition in theoretical computer science [HU69] [HIM78]. It is obvious that one can define the counting classes #1L and span-1L via one-way logspace Turing machines, similar to the well-known classes #L and span-L. We get the following results: We separate 1NL and 1UL. In [AJ93] it is shown that $1UL = 1NL \Leftrightarrow \#1L = \text{span-}1L \Leftrightarrow \#1L \subseteq \text{opt-}1L$, thus it follows that $\#1L \subset \text{span-}1L$. From $1NL \neq 1UL$ we conclude also that $F1L \subset \#L$. Furthermore, all the one-way logspace counting classes are strictly included in the corresponding (two-way) logspace counting classes.

In Section 4 we relate these counting classes to logically characterized classes. First, we generalize the notion of first-order counting function as defined in [SST92] with respect to the ordering. First-order counting functions map ordered finite structures to nonnegative integers. It is crucial here that the structure is ordered. If isomorphic copies of the same solution are indistinguishable, the counting function will not only count the distinct solutions, but also all isomorphic copies of the each solution! There are interesting results in the case of counting functions on unordered structures (see [CG94]). But for the comparison of first-order and Turing machine based counting classes it is useful to consider ordered structures. In [SST92] a linear ordering is used. If we look at Turing machines (and thus at strings) it seems artificial, not to consider the succ relation or the plus relation as orderings as well. For $k \in \mathbb{N}$ and $op \in \{<, SUCC, +\}$ we therefore define the classes $\#\Sigma_k[op]$ and $\#\Pi_k[op]$ of counting functions definable by first-order Π_k and Σ_k formulas using op as linear ordering. The classes $\#\Sigma_k[<]$ and $\#\Pi_k[<]$ coincide with $\#\Sigma_k$ and $\#\Pi_k$.

In [SST92] it is shown that $\#\Pi_1[<] \subset \#\Sigma_2[<] \subset \#\Pi_2[<] = \#P$ which is surprising, since $\#3SAT$ (a #P complete function) is contained in $\#\Pi_1[<]$. But these results depend heavily on the use of the linear order instead of the $SUCC$ relation or the + relation. It turns out that $\#\Pi_2[<] = \#\Pi_1[\text{SUCC}] = \#\Pi_1[+]$. (It follows, that $\#\Pi_1[+] = \#\Pi_2[+]$. This may also be seen as an answer to the question posed in [Lyn90], whether $\Sigma_1^1\Pi_1^0[+]$ is strictly included in $\Sigma_1^1\Pi_2^0[+]$.)

In order to compare first-order and Turing machine based counting functions we have to take into account that they differ in their domain. In [SST92] the authors redefine #P such that the polynomial time bounded Turing machines have ordered finite structures as input. We want to keep the definition of #P to be based on strings. Thus we have to encode finite ordered structures in strings and vice versa. We define a natural encoding of finite ordered structures into strings. Under that encoding, the class $\#\Sigma_0[op]$ is a subclass of #1L and $\#\Sigma_1[op]$ is a subclass of span-1L. Since this encoding is one-one but not onto, the inclusions are strict by definition. But from results in [SST92] it follows that #1L and $\#\Sigma_0[<]$, and also span-1L and $\#\Sigma_1[<]$, are separated even in the range of the encoding.

Based on Fagins Theorem [Fag74] one can show that (under a natural encoding of strings into finite ordered structures) #P is a subclass of $\#\Pi_1$[SUCC]. Therefore, the classes $\#\Pi_1$[SUCC] and $\#\Pi_1$[+] may be seen as logical characterizations of #P.

In [BIS90] it is shown, that the class of first-order definable sets equals the logarithmic time hierarchy LH. So this leads obviously to the question whether it is possible to define certain classes of logtime counting functions and to show that these classes are intermediate between the first-order counting classes and the one-way logspace counting classes. It turns out that this is, in some sense, possible (see [Bur95] for a detailed discussion and for results). In this paper we define a class of certain Π_1 logtime counting functions. We show that every Π_1 definable counting function is (with respect to a certain encoding) a Π_1 logtime counting function.

From this, we obtain a characterization of #P via universally branching logtime Turing machines.

2 Preliminaries

We will use standard notation as e.g. in [BDG89]. We write $\mathbb{N}$ for the set of nonnegative integers. If A is a finite set then $||A||$ denotes its cardinality. For any set A let χ_A be the characteristic function of A, that is, $\chi_A(x) = 1$ if $x \in A$ and $\chi_A(x) = 0$ otherwise. For a string $w \in \Sigma^*$ we write $|w|$ for the length of w. If $i \leq |w|$ we denote the ith bit of w by $w(i)$. We write $bin(n)$ to denote the binary representation of $n \in \mathbb{N}$ and let $bin(k, n)$ denote the binary representation of n with leading zeroes such that $|bin(k, n)| = k$, if $k \geq |bin(n)|$.

We use the standard definitions for the complexity classes L, FL, UL, NL, P, and NP. Let #P (#L) be the class of functions $f : \Sigma^* \to \mathbb{N}$ such that there exists a polynomial time bounded (logarithmic space bounded) NTM M which for all $x \in \Sigma^*$ on input x has exactly $f(x)$ accepting paths. A NTM computes a binary relation R, if $(x, y) \in R$ iff on input x there exists a computation path such that M outputs y and accepts. A relation R is logspace computable if there exists a logspace NTM that computes R. NLMV is the class of logspace computable relations. Let span-L be the class of functions f, such that there exists a logspace computable relation R and for all x it holds that $f(x) = ||\{y : (x, y) \in R\}||$.

A one-way logspace TM (NTM, ATM) is a Turing machine with a logarithmic space bound, a one-way read-only input tape, and a one-way write-only output tape. We follow the definition (as, e.g., in [HIM78]) that $c \cdot \lceil \log(n) \rceil$ tape cells are marked on the work tapes before the beginning of a computation on an input of size n (c is a constant). We define F1L, 1NL, 1UL, #1L, 1NLMV, and span-1L similar to the classes FL, NL, UL, #L, NLMV, and span-L except that we use one-way logspace Turing machines instead of ordinary (two-way) Turing machines.

A signature $\sigma = (R_1, \ldots, R_k, c_1, \ldots, c_l)$ consists of relation symbols R_i with arities a_i and of constant symbols c_i for $1 \leq i \leq k$. A finite σ-structure $\mathcal{A} = (U^{\mathcal{A}}, R_1^{\mathcal{A}}, \ldots, R_k^{\mathcal{A}}, c_1^{\mathcal{A}}, \ldots, c_l^{\mathcal{A}})$ consists of a finite set $U^{\mathcal{A}}$ called the universe of $\mathcal{A}$, relations over $U^{\mathcal{A}}$ corresponding to the relation symbols, and constants from the universe corresponding to the constant symbols in σ. Let τ be a signature such that $\tau \cap \sigma = \emptyset$. A τ-expansion $\mathcal{T}$ of $\mathcal{A}$ consists of relations and constants over $U^{\mathcal{A}}$ corresponding to the relation symbols and constant symbols in τ. Let $\prec^{\mathcal{A}}$ be a linear ordering on

$U^{\mathcal{A}}$. We call $(\mathcal{A}, \prec^{\mathcal{A}})$ an ordered σ-structure. A formula of the form $\exists \mathbf{x_1} \forall \mathbf{x_2} \ldots Q\mathbf{x_k}$ $\varphi(\mathbf{x_1}, \mathbf{x_2}, \ldots, \mathbf{x_k})$ $(\forall \mathbf{x_1} \exists \mathbf{x_2} \ldots Q\mathbf{x_k}\ \varphi(\mathbf{x_1}, \mathbf{x_2}, \ldots, \mathbf{x_k}))$ such that $\varphi(\mathbf{x_1}, \mathbf{x_2}, \ldots, \mathbf{x_k})$ is quantifier-free is called a Σ_k-formula (Π_k-formula), if $k \geq 1$. A formula without quantifiers and variables is called a Π_0-formula or Σ_0-formula.

In [SST92] for $k \in \mathbb{N}$ the class $\#\Sigma_k$ ($\#\Pi_k$) is defined to be the class of functions f such that there exists a Σ_k-formula (Π_k-formula) ϕ over $(\sigma, \tau, <)$ such that $f(\mathcal{A}, \prec^{\mathcal{A}})$ $= ||\{\mathcal{T} : (\mathcal{A}, \mathcal{T}, \prec^{\mathcal{A}}) \models \phi\}||$ for all ordered σ-structures $(\mathcal{A}, \prec^{\mathcal{A}})$.

In [SST92] it is proven that $\#DEG\_1\_NGB \in \#\Sigma_2 \setminus \#\Pi_1$ and $DIST2 \in \#\Sigma_1 \setminus \#\Sigma_0$, where $\#DEG\_1\_NGB$ counts the nodes of a graph that have a neighbour of degree 1, and $\#DIST2$ counts the pairs of nodes for which the shortest path in the graph is of length two.

3 Logspace and one-way logspace counting classes

Our definitions of logspace counting classes are based on *one-way protocol machines* defined by K.-J. Lange [Lan86]. We call these Turing machines 2-1-, and 1-1-Turing machines to avoid confusion in the definition of one-way logspace counting classes.

Definition 1. A 2-1-TM (2-1-ATM) is a Turing machine (alternating Turing machine) with two input tapes. The first is a two-way and the second is a one-way input tape. A 2-1-Turing machine M accepts a binary Relation R, iff M accepts all $(x, y) \in R$, such that x is on the first input tape and y is on the second input tape. We call x the first input and y the second input.

Analogously, a logspace 1-1-TM (1-1-ATM) is a one-way logspace Turing machine with two one-way input tapes.

For $k > 0$ we call a 2-1-ATM (1-1-ATM) that makes at most $k-1$ alternations a 2-1-Σ_k-TM (1-1-Σ_k-TM) if it starts in an existential configuration and a 2-1-Π_k-TM (1-1-Π_k-TM) if it starts in an universal configuration.

A deterministic 2-1-TM (1-1-TM) is called a 2-1-Σ_0-TM or 2-1-Π_0-TM (1-1-Σ_0-TM or 1-1-Π_0-TM resp.)

Definition 2. For each $k \in \mathbb{N}$ let 2-1-Σ_kL (2-1-Π_kL, 1-1-Σ_kL, 1-1-Π_kL) be the class of polynomially length-bounded binary relations that are accepted by logspace 2-1-Σ_k-Turing machines (2-1-Π_k-Turing machines, 1-1-Σ_k-Turing machines, 1-1-Π_k-Turing machines resp.).

Definition 3. For each $k \in \mathbb{N}$ let $\#\Sigma_k$L ($\#\Pi_k$L) be the class of functions f such that there exists a relation $R \in$ 2-1-Σ_kL ($R \in$ 2-1-Π_kL resp.) and that $f(x) = ||\{y : (x, y) \in R\}||$ holds for every string x. The classes $\#\Sigma_k$1L and $\#\Pi_k$1L are defined analogously.

The above defined counting classes characterize the known logspace counting classes. First, we show that every binary relation R is logspace computable, iff it is acceptable by a logspace 2-1-Σ_1-TM.

Lemma 4. *1.* NLMV = *2-1-$\Sigma_1 L$* *2.* 1NLMV = *1-1-$\Sigma_1 L$*

Proof. (sketch) (1.) (NLMV $\subseteq$ 2-1-Σ_1L): Let $R \in$ NLMV and M_R be the logspace NTM that computes R. A logspace 2-1-Σ_1-TM M simulates M_R and checks bit by bit whether the output of M_R and the second input of M is equal.
(2-1-Σ_1L $\subseteq$ NLMV): Let $R \in$ 2-1-Σ_1L and M_R be the 2-1-Σ_1-TM that accepts R. A logspace NTM simulates M_R and guesses each bit of the second input of M_R and writes it on the output tape. M accepts iff M_R accepts.
(2.) The proof is similar to (1.) since the simulations do not depend on the head-moves. □

Remark. Let $F = (a_1 \vee a_{n+1}) \wedge (a_2 \vee a_{n+2}) \wedge \ldots \wedge (a_n \vee a_{2n})$ be a propositional formula and $b \in \{0,1\}^{2n}$ a truth assignment such that $a_i = b(i)$, for $1 \leq i \leq 2n$. Given F as first input and b as second input a logspace 2-1-NTM cannot check whether b satisfies F [Bur89]. Thus NLMV $\subset$ NPMV.

Theorem 5.
1. $\#\Sigma_0 1L = \#1L$
2. $\#\Sigma_1 1L = span\text{-}1L$
3. $\#\Sigma_0 L = \#L$
4. $\#\Sigma_1 L = span\text{-}L$

Proof. (sketch)
(1.) ($\#\Sigma_0$1L $\subseteq$ #1L): Let $R \in$ 1-1-Σ_0L and let M_R be a logspace bounded 1-1-DTM that accepts R. A logspace bounded NTM M simulates M_R and guesses each bit that M_R reads from the second input tape. Since M_R is deterministic, every $(x, y) \in R$ yields at most one accepting path of M.
(#1L $\subseteq$ $\#\Sigma_0$1L): Let M be a logspace NTM. The relation R is in 1-1-Σ_0L: $R = \{(x, y) : y$ denotes an accepting computation of M on input $x\}$.
(3.) The proof is similar to (1.) since the simulations above do not depend on the head-moves on the first tape.
(2. & 4.) $\#\Sigma_1$1L = span-1L and $\#\Sigma_1$L = span-L follow directly from Lemma 4. □

In the following we prove that the one-way logspace counting classes form a strict hierarchy within #P. That is, we show F1L $\subset$ #1L $\subset$ span-1L $\subset$ $\#\Pi_1$1L = #P. In [AJ93] it is shown that 1UL = 1NL $\Leftrightarrow$ #1L = span-1L $\Leftrightarrow$ opt-1L $\subseteq$ #1L. First, we prove that 1UL $\neq$ 1NL. From that it follows that #1L $\neq$ span-1L. (Although this is not in the scope of the paper, we state that therefore opt-1L $\not\subseteq$ #1L.) From 1UL $\neq$ 1NL we also conclude F1L $\neq$ #1L.

For proving the following separations we use the sets $L_= = \{w@w : w \in \{a,b\}^*\}$ and $L_{\neq} = \{w@w' : w, w' \in \{a,b\}^* \wedge |w| = |w'| \wedge \exists i : w(i) \neq w'(i)\}$.

Theorem 6. $L_{\neq} \in$ *1NL* $\setminus$ *1UL*.

Proof. ($L_{\neq} \in$ 1NL) : In order to decide $L_{\neq}$ a one-way logspace NTM $M_{\neq}$ scans the input $w@w'$ from left to right and chooses nondeterministically a position i and stores it in binary. The NTM checks whether $w(i) \neq w'(i)$.
($L_{\neq} \notin$ 1UL) : Assume $L_{\neq}$ to be in 1UL. Let M be the one-way logspace NTM that accepts $L_{\neq}$ and on each input has at most one accepting path. We say that a configuration c is the first configuration in a computation path at position $n+1$, if c contains the input-head position $n+1$ and all previous configurations in that computation path contain smaller input-head positions. Let C_{n+1} be the set of configurations c of M such that for inputs of length $2n+1$ there exists a computation path with

c as first configuration at position $n+1$. Let $(w_i)_{1\le i\le 2^n}$ be an enumeration of all strings $w \in \{a,b\}^n$ and let $(c_i)_{1\le i\le q_M(2n+1)}$ be an enumeration of all configurations $c \in C_{n+1}$. Since M is logspace-bounded, it follows that q_M is a polynomial.

We now define a $2^n \times 2^n$ matrix A_{2^n}. For all $1 \le i,j \le 2^n$ let $a_{i,j}$ be an element of A_{2^n} such that $a_{i,j} = 0$ if $i = j$, and $a_{i,j} = k$ if c_k is the first configuration at position $n+1$ in the accepting path of M on input $w_i@w_j$.
The matrix A_{2^n} satisfies the following two properties. The first follows from the definition:

(i) For all $1 \le i,j \le 2^n$, $a_{i,j} = 0$ iff $i = j$.

The second property follows from the fact that the input head of M never moves to the left. If for two different inputs $w_i@w_j$ and $w_{i'}@w_{j'}$ the first configuration at position $n+1$ on the accepting path is the same, then M will also accept the inputs $w_i@w_{j'}$ and $w_{i'}@w_j$. Furthermore all accepting paths contain the same first configuration at position $n+1$.

(ii) For all $1 \le i,i',j,j' \le 2^n$ such that $i \ne j$ and $i' \ne j'$, it holds that:

$$a_{i,j} = a_{i',j'} \quad \Rightarrow \quad a_{i,j} = a_{i',j'} = a_{i,j'} = a_{i',j}$$

In the following we show that there is a lower bound for the number of distinct elements in A_{2^n} that is linear in the number of rows (and columns). This will yield a contradiction to the assumption, that the number of distinct elements in A_{2^n} is bounded by a polynomial in n.

Let B_m be an $m \times m$ integer matrix and let $upper(B_m) = \{b_{i,j} : i < j\}$ be the set of all elements of B_m which occur above the 'diagonal' elements $b_{i,i}$.
Claim. *Let $m \in \mathbb{N}$, $m \ge 3$, and B_m be a $m \times m$ integer matrix that satisfies the properties (i) and (ii). Then $||upper(B_m)|| \ge m-1$.*

We omit the proof here and refer the reader to [Bur95].

It follows that $||upper(A_{2^n})|| \ge 2^n - 1$. But this yields a contradiction, since $||upper(A_{2^n})|| \le q_M(2n+1)$. □

Remark. In order to prove $L_{\ne} \in$ 1NL we do not use the fact that the workspace is marked in advance. Furthermore this proof also works if we do not use a special symbol to separate the strings w and w'.

From the following Theorem we can conclude that the one-way logspace classes form a strict hierarchy within #P.

Theorem 7. 1. $F1L \subset \#\Sigma_0 1L$ 2. $\#\Sigma_0 1L \subset \#\Sigma_1 1L$

Proof. (sketch)
(1.) Using standard techniques it is easy to see that $\mathrm{F1L} \subseteq \#\Sigma_0 1\mathrm{L}$.
Consider the one-way logspace NTM $M_{\ne}$ that is described in the proof of Theorem 6. Let $f_{\ne}$ be the counting function induced by $M_{\ne}$. Assume $f_{\ne} \in$ F1L, it follows that $L_{\ne} \in$ 1L and thus $L_{\ne} \in$ 1UL. This contradicts Theorem 6.
(2.) In [AJ93] it is shown that 1UL = 1NL $\Leftrightarrow$ #1L = span-1L. From this we get the result, since 1UL $\ne$ 1NL. □

It is shown in [HU69], that $L_= \notin$ 1NL and it is easy to see, that $L_= \in L$ thus $\chi_{L_=} \in \mathrm{FL} \setminus \#\Sigma_1 1\mathrm{L}$. It follows that the one-way logspace counting classes are strict subclasses of the corresponding two-way logspace counting classes.

Observation 8 1. $F1L \subset FL$ 2. $\#\Sigma_0 1L \subset \#\Sigma_0 L$ 3. $\#\Sigma_1 1L \subset \#\Sigma_1 L$

One can prove $\#\Sigma_k 1\mathrm{L} \subseteq \#\Pi_k 1\mathrm{L} \subseteq \#\mathrm{P}$ and $\#\Sigma_k \mathrm{L} \subseteq \#\Pi_k \mathrm{L} \subseteq \#\mathrm{P}$ for all $k \in \mathbb{N}$. But from Theorem 17 and Lemma 15 in Section 4 it will follow that $\#\Pi_1 1\mathrm{L} = \#\Pi_1 \mathrm{L} = \#\mathrm{P}$. Therefore these hierarchies of logspace counting classes collapse to $\#\Pi_1 1\mathrm{L}$.

4 Relating Turing machine based counting classes to logically characterized counting classes

As described in the introduction we consider ordered structures as domain of first-order counting functions. But in order to define these functions, we use not only a linear ordering but also the successor relation or the plus relation.

Definition 9. Let op be one of the following predicates $<$, $SUCC$, $+$. Let σ and τ be signatures that do not contain op and $\prec$. Let $(\mathcal{A}, \prec^{\mathcal{A}})$ be an ordered σ-structure and let $op^{\prec^{\mathcal{A}}}$ be $\prec^{\mathcal{A}}$ or the successor relation or the plus relation that induces $\prec^{\mathcal{A}}$.

For $k \in \mathbb{N}$ we define the class $\#\Sigma_k[op]$ ($\#\Pi_k[op]$) to be the class of functions f such that there exists a Σ_k-formula (Π_k-formula) ϕ over (σ, τ, op) and $f(\mathcal{A}, \prec^{\mathcal{A}}) = ||\{\mathcal{T} : (\mathcal{A}, \mathcal{T}, op^{\prec^{\mathcal{A}}}) \models \phi\}||$ for all ordered σ-structures $(\mathcal{A}, \prec^{\mathcal{A}})$.

Our definition of first-order counting classes is a generalization of the definition given in [SST92]: $\#\Sigma_k = \#\Sigma_k[<]$ and $\#\Pi_k = \#\Pi_k[<]$ for $k \in \mathbb{N}$.

It turns out, that the descriptional complexity may depend on the chosen ordering.

Theorem 10. $\#\Pi_2[<] = \#\Pi_1[SUCC] = \#\Pi_1[+]$

Due to the lack of space, we omit the proof, and refer the reader to [Bur95].

In the following we show that the logically characterized counting classes are subclasses of the corresponding one-way logspace classes.

First, we describe an encoding e_1 of ordered σ-structures into binary strings. Let $(\mathcal{A}, \prec^{\mathcal{A}})$ be a ordered σ-structure and $n = ||U^{\mathcal{A}}||$. $e_1(\mathcal{A}, \prec^{\mathcal{A}})$ starts with 1^n0. We use the enumeration induced by $\prec^{\mathcal{A}}$ to encode the constants and the relations in binary strings. Let R be, for example, a k-ary Relation, then the bit at position $\sum_{i=1}^{k} x_i \cdot n^{i-1}$ in the encoding of R is 1, iff $(x_1, x_2, \ldots, x_k) \in R$. We encode a τ-expansion $\mathcal{T}$ of $\mathcal{A}$ using $\prec^{\mathcal{A}}$ as described above, but without the encoding of n. For all functions $f \in \#\mathcal{FO}[op]$ let $e_1(f)$ be the function such that for all $x \in \{0,1\}^*$, $e_1(f)(x) = f(\mathcal{A}, \prec^{\mathcal{A}})$ if $x = e_1(\mathcal{A}, \prec^{\mathcal{A}})$, and $f(x) = 0$ otherwise. Since our encoding is one-one, the function $e_1(f)$ is well-defined. For any class of first-order counting functions $\mathcal{C} \subseteq \#\mathcal{FO}[op]$ let $e_1(\mathcal{C})$ be the class of functions $e_1(f) : \{0,1\}^* \to \mathbb{N}$ for $f \in \mathcal{C}$.

Theorem 11. *Let op be one of the relations $<$, $SUCC$, or $+$. It holds that*

$$e_1(\#\Sigma_0[op]) \subseteq \#\Sigma_0 1L\,, \quad e_1(\#\Sigma_1[op]) \subseteq \#\Sigma_1 1L\,, \quad e_1(\#\Pi_1[op]) \subseteq \#\Pi_1 1L$$

Proof. Let σ and τ be signatures, $e_1(f)$ a function in $e_1(\#\Sigma_0[op])$ ($e_1(\#\Sigma_1[op])$, or $e_1(\#\Pi_1[op])$ resp.) and let ϕ be the Σ_0-formula (Σ_1-, or Π_1-formula) over (σ, τ, op) such that $f(\mathcal{A}, \prec^{\mathcal{A}}) = ||\{\mathcal{T} : (\mathcal{A}, \mathcal{T}, op^{\prec^{\mathcal{A}}}) \models \phi\}||$ for all ordered σ-structures $(\mathcal{A}, \prec^{\mathcal{A}})$.

We define the binary relation R_ϕ such that $(e_1(\mathcal{A}, \prec^{\mathcal{A}}), e_1(\mathcal{T}, \prec^{\mathcal{A}})) \in R_\phi$ iff $(\mathcal{A}, \mathcal{T}, op^{\prec^{\mathcal{A}}}) \models \phi$. Since our encoding is one-one, for all $x \in \{0,1\}^*$ we have $e_1(f)(x) = ||\{y : (x, y) \in R_\phi\}||$. Thus, it is sufficient to show that $R_\phi \in$ 1-1-Σ_0L ($R_\phi \in$ 1-1-Σ_1L, $R_\phi \in$ 1-1-Π_1L, resp.).

(1. $R_\phi \in$ 1-1-Σ_0L) We describe a logspace-bounded 1-1-Σ_0-TM M_ϕ, that accepts R_ϕ. First M_ϕ reads the cardinality of the universe and then copies all the constants to its work tape. Note that ϕ is a Σ_0-formula and since it is closed, ϕ contains no variables. In order to evaluate the formula M_ϕ has to read a constant number of bits. One sweep over the input is thus sufficient. Parallel to that M_ϕ checks deterministically the correctness of the representation.

(2. $R_\phi \in$ 1-1-Σ_1L) The algorithm is similar to (1.) but ϕ has existentially quantified variables. After reading the cardinality of the universe and the constants M_ϕ guesses the assignments of the variables and evaluates ϕ as above.

(3. $R_\phi \in$ 1-1-Π_1L)M_ϕ works similar to (2.), but instead of existentially guessing the variable assignment M_ϕ uses universal branches. □

It is easy to see that $e_1(\#DEG_1_NGB) \in \#\Sigma_1$1L and that $e_1(\#DIST2) \in \#\Sigma_0$1L. From [SST92] it follows, that $e_1(\#DEG\_1\_NGB) \notin e_1(\#\Sigma_1[<])$ and $e_1(\#DIST_2) \notin e_1(\#\Sigma_0[<])$. Thus, the classes $\#\Sigma_1$1L and $\#\Sigma_1[<]$, and $\#\Sigma_0$1L and $\#\Sigma_1[<]$ are separated within the range of the encoding.

Observation 12
$$e_1(\#DEG\_1\_NGB) \in \#\Sigma_1 1L \setminus e_1(\#\Sigma_1[<])$$
$$e_1(\#DIST2) \in \#\Sigma_0 1L \setminus e_1(\#\Sigma_0[<])$$

We show that #P is (with respect to an encoding) is a subclass of $\#\Pi_1$[SUCC]. In [SST92] it is shown that $\#\Pi_2[<] = \#$P but #P is redefined as the class of polynomial time counting functions having ordered σ-structures as domain. We keep the definition of #P unchanged and use a standard encoding of strings using monadic relations, which we denote by e_2. The elements of the universe are the input positions and it is quite obvious to use the $<$ relation as linear ordering. We define $e_2(f)$ such that for all ordered σ-structures $(\mathcal{A}, \prec^{\mathcal{A}})$, $e_2(f)(\mathcal{A}, \prec) = f(x)$ if $(\mathcal{A}, \prec) = e_2(x)$, and $e_2(f)(\mathcal{A}, \prec) = 0$ otherwise. (Note that if the cardinality of the input alphabet is not a power of two, then the encoding is not onto.) Let $e_2(\#$P$)$ be the class of functions $e_2(f)$ for $f \in \#$P.

Theorem 13 follows from Theorem 10 and the result of [SST92]. But it may also be proven more directly by following the proofs of [Fag74] and [Pap94] that existential second-order characterizes NP. We follow the construction presented in [Pap94].

Theorem 13
$$e_2(\#P) \subseteq \#\Pi_1[SUCC]$$

Proof. (sketch) One can show that for all polynomially time-bounded Turing machines M there exists a Π_1-formula ϕ over $(\sigma, \tau, SUCC)$ such that M accepts an input x iff there is a assignment to the second-order variables $\mathcal{T}$ such that $(e_2(x), \mathcal{T}, SUCC) \models \phi$. We have to add a subformula that checks whether the finite structure is a correct encoding of a string with respect to the input alphabet of the Turing machine. Additionally one has to check whether there exists for each accepting computation path a unique assignment $\mathcal{T}$ that satisfies ϕ. □

Motivated by [BIS90] it is an obvious question whether it is possible to get a closer connection between first-order counting classes and Turing machine counting classes via logtime counting functions. We present a definition of Π_1-logtime counting functions. To define this logtime counting class we use alternating random-access Turing machines, as used for example in [Bus87]. But, to accept binary relations we define random-access Turing machines with two index tapes. We denote these Turing machines by i-i-Π_1-TM to indicate that the input is accessed via two index tapes.

Definition 14. A i-i-Π_1-Turing machine is a alternating random-access Turing machine without existential states and with a first index tape and a second index tape. The input that is accessible via the first index tape, we call first input and the input accessible via the second index tape, we call the second input. A i-i-Π_1-TM accepts a binary relation R iff it accepts $(x, y) \in R$ with x as first input and y as second input.

Let $i\text{-}i_{pol}\text{-}\Pi_1$LOGTIME be the class of polynomially length-bounded relations accepted by logarithmic time bounded i-i-Π_1-TM. Let $\#_{pol}\Pi_1$LOGTIME be the class of functions f such that there exists a binary relation $R \in i\text{-}i_{pol}\text{-}\Pi_1$LOGTIME and that $f(x) = ||\{y : (x, y) \in R\}||$ holds for all strings x.

We first state that this logtime counting class is a subclass of the corresponding one-way logspace counting class, omitting the proof. A detailed proof can be found in [Bur95].

Lemma 15. $\#_{pol}\Pi_1 LOGTIME \subseteq \#\Pi_1 1L$

We now prove an analog of Theorem 11 for the class $\#_{pol}\Pi_1$LOGTIME. But we cannot use the encoding e_1. In order to evaluate $(x_1, \ldots, x_k) \in R$ for a k-ary relation R on an universe of cardinality n, the Turing machine has to determine the input position by computing the polynomial $\sum_{i=1}^{k} x_i \cdot n^{i-1}$. To avoid the multiplication we have to change the definition of e_1. Let $l \in \mathbb{N}$ be the smallest integer such that $n \leq 2^l$ and let $m = 2^l$. A k-ary relation is represented as follows: The bit at position $\sum_{i=1}^{k} x_i \cdot m^{i-1}$ is 1 iff $(x_1, \ldots, x_k) \in R$ and $x_i \leq n$ for all $1 \leq i \leq k$. We denote this encoding by e_3. Using this encoding it is sufficient to concatenate $bin(x_1) \ldots bin(x_k)$ to determine the input position.

Theorem 16. $e_3(\#\Pi_1[SUCC]) \subseteq \#_{pol}\Pi_1 LOGTIME$

Proof. (sketch) The evaluation of the formula is similar as in the proof of Theorem 11. The i-i-Π_1-TM uses binary search to determine the cardinality of the universe. To check the correctness of the encoding, the i-i-Π_1-TM checks the input length and universally checks all input positions. □

It is possible to characterize #P via logtime counting functions. This does not follow directly from the Theorems 13 and 16, since $e_3(e_2(\#\mathrm{P})) \neq \#\mathrm{P}$.

Theorem 17. $\#P = \#_{pol}\Pi_1 LOGTIME$

Proof. (sketch) We show that $\#P \subseteq \#_{pol}\Pi_1$LOGTIME:

Let f be a function in #P. Let ϕ be the Π_1-formula over $(\sigma, \tau, SUCC)$ such that $f(x) = ||\{\mathcal{T} : (e_2(x), \mathcal{T}, SUCC) \models \phi\}$ for all $x \in \Sigma^*$. We define a relation R such that $R = \{(x, e_3(\mathcal{T})) : (e_2(x), \mathcal{T}, SUCC) \models \phi\}$, and describe a logtime i-i-Π_1-TMM_R that accepts R. It follows that $R \in$ *i*-i_{pol}-Π_1LOGTIME and thus $f \in \#_{pol}\Pi_1$LOGTIME.

From the proof of Theorem 16 it follows that there exists a i-i-Π_1-TM M_ϕ that accepts the input $(e_3(e_2(x)), e_3(\mathcal{T}))$ iff $(e_2(x), \mathcal{T}, SUCC) \models \phi$. M_R simulates M_ϕ and computes each bit that M_ϕ queries to $e_3(e_2(x))$ from its first input x. □

Acknowledgments. I would like to thank Thomas Schwentick, Dirk Siefkes, Heribert Vollmer, Klaus Wagner, and especially Arfst Nickelsen for helpful comments and fruitful discussion.

References

[AJ93] C. Àlvarez and B. Jenner. A Very Hard Log Space Counting Class. *Theoretical Computer Science*, 107:3–30, 1993.

[BDG89] J. L. Balcázar, J. Diaz, and J. Gabarró. *Structural complexity I.* EATCS Monographs on Theoretical Computer Science. Springer, 1989.

[BIS90] David A. Mix Barrington, Neil Immerman, and H. Straubing. On Uniformity within NC^1. *Journal of Computer and System Sciences*, 41:274–306, 1990.

[Bur89] H.-J. Burtschick. Vergleich von logarithmischer Platzbschränkung und polynomieller Zeitbeschränkung für Konstruktionsprobleme und Belegmengen. Diplomarbeit, 1989.

[Bur95] H.-J. Burtschick. Comparing counting classes for logspace, one-way logspace, logtime, and first-order. Forschungsberichte des Fachbereichs Informatik 94-39, TU Berlin, 1995.

[Bus87] S. R. Buss. The Boolean formula value problem is in ALOGTIME. In *Proc. 19th. Ann. ACM Symp. on Theory of Computing*, pages 123 - 131, 1987.

[CG94] Kevin J. Compton and Erich Grädel. Logical Definability of Counting Functions. In *9th Ann. Conf. Structure in Complexity Theory*, pages 255–266, 1994.

[Fag74] R. Fagin. Generalized first-order spectra and polynomial time recognizable sets. In R. Karp, editor, *Complexity of Computations*, pages 43–73, 1974.

[HIM78] J. Hartmanis, N. Immerman, and S. Mahaney. One-way log-tape reductions. In *Proc. 19th IEEE Symp. Foundations of Computer Science*, pages 65 - 71. IEEE Computer Society Press, 1978.

[HU69] J. E. Hopcroft and J. D. Ullman. Some Results on Tape-Bounded Turing Machines. *Journal of the ACM*, 16(1):168–177, 1969.

[Lan86] Klaus Jörn Lange. Two characterizations of the logarithmic alternation hierarchy. In *Proc. of the 12th Symp. on Mathematical Foundations of Computer Science*, volume 233 of *LNCS*, pages 518–526. Springer Verlag, August 1986.

[Lyn90] J. F. Lynch. The Quantifier Structure of Sentences that Characterize Nondeterministic Time Complexity. In *5th Ann. Conf. Structure in Complexity Theory*, pages 210–222, 1990.

[Pap94] Christos H. Papadimitriou. *Computational Complexity.* Addison-Wesley, 1994.

[SST92] S. Saluja, K. V. Subrahmanyam, and M. N. Thakur. Descriptive complexity of #P functions. In *7th Ann. Conf. Structure in Complexity Theory*, 1992.

[Val79] Leslie G. Valiant. The complexity of enumeration and reliabilty problems. *SIAM Journal of Computing*, 8(3):411–421, August 1979.

Automata That Take Advice

Carsten Damm[1] and Markus Holzer[2,3]

[1] FB IV-Informatik, Universität Trier, D-54286 Trier, Germany
[2] Wilhelm-Schickard-Institut für Informatik, Universität Tübingen
Sand 13, D-72076 Tübingen, Germany

Abstract. Karp and Lipton introduced advice-taking Turing machines to capture nonuniform complexity classes. We study this concept for automata-like models and compare it to other nonuniform models studied in connection with formal languages in the literature. Based on this we obtain complete separations of the classes of the Chomsky hierarchy relative to advices.

1 Introduction

Language classes investigated in automata and formal language theory traditionally are uniform in nature: A single finite device (finite automata, pushdown automata, grammar, etc.) is responsible to accept or to generate all words of a given language. On the other hand in complexity theory—a field which has many interconnections with formal language theory—one often studies *nonuniform* computational models. These are devices which, depending on the length of the input, may choose from an infinite library of algorithms, e.g., sequences of polynomial size circuits (Pippenger [11]) or finite automata with growing set of states (Ibarra and Ravikumar [7]). The complexity classes arising from these models share many of the properties of uniform complexity classes but in some cases they seem to behave differently (see, e.g., Aleliunas *et al.* [1], Damm and Holzer [3], and Widgerson [13]). Further, lower bound statements for nonuniform complexity are stronger than those for uniform complexity and are therefore in general harder to obtain. In order to better understand the nature of nonuniformity as a resource, it is therefore natural to ask about the impact of introducing nonuniformity into classes studied in this old field of automata and formal language theory.

One universal formalization of the idea of nonuniformity has been proposed and studied in depth by Karp and Lipton in their seminal paper [8]. Given a class $\mathcal{B}$ of languages over some finite alphabet Σ and a set $\mathcal{F}$ of sequences (*advices*) $\alpha = (\alpha_n)$ of strings from Σ^*. Then $\mathcal{B}/\mathcal{F}$ is defined as the class of sets of the form $L : \alpha = \{\, w \mid \alpha_{|w|} w \in L \}$, with $L \in \mathcal{B}$ and $\alpha \in \mathcal{F}$. Mostly one considers the class of polynomial length advices. But also other classes have been considered.

[3] Part of the work done while the author worked at Institut für Informatik, Technische Universität München, Arcisstr. 21, D-80290 München, Germany.

Although several models of nonuniformity were studied in connection with formal languages, to our knowledge the Karp-Lipton approach—despite of it's unifying power—has not been investigated in this field. We try to fill this gap in studying the classes of the Chomsky hierarchy relative to advices. It turns out that for regular languages constant length advices are as powerful as polynomial length advices. For higher classes of the hierarchy this is not the case. Therefore we consider constant length and polynomial length advices separately. Our main results are complete separations of the classes of the Chomsky hierarchy relative to both constant and polynomial length advices. As a means to prove the separations we relate this approach to other nonuniform measures for formal language classes.

We close this section with the following notational conventions:

Let *poly*, (*const*, respectively) denote the set of advices α with $|\alpha_n| \leq n^{O(1)}$ ($|\alpha_n| \leq O(1)$, respectively).

The classes of regular, context-free, context-sensitive, and recursively enumerable languages, respectively, are denoted by **REG**, **CFL**, **CS**, and **RE**, respectively. From the general definition of advices above notations like **REG**/*poly*, **CFL**/*const*, etc., become clear.

We will several times use binary encodings of integers out of a given set. For an integer l with $0 \leq l < k$ let $\text{bin}(l)$ denote the binary encoding of l of length $m = \lfloor \log k \rfloor$ with leading zeroes.

2 Finite automata that take advice

We first consider finite automata with access to advices. It turns out that due to the limited memory only a constant amount of nonuniformity can be used.

Proposition 1. $\mathbf{REG}/\mathit{poly} = \mathbf{REG}/\mathit{const}$.

Proof. Let $L : \alpha \in \mathbf{REG}/\mathit{poly}$ for some sequence $\alpha = (\alpha_n) \in \mathit{poly}$. Then there is a deterministic finite automaton $\mathcal{A}$ with one-way input tape that recognizes L. Hence $\alpha_{|w|}w$ is accepted by $\mathcal{A}$ if and only if the following holds: After reading $\alpha_{|w|}$ on the input tape $\mathcal{A}$ is in some state q and $\mathcal{A}$ started in q accepts w.

Let β_n be the binary encoding of the state $\mathcal{A}$ is in after reading α_n on the input tape. Consider a new automaton $\mathcal{A}'$ that works as follows: With $\beta_{|w|}w$ on the input tape it first uses a tree-like state transition function to find out the state q described by $\beta_{|w|}$. After this it uses the original state transition function of $\mathcal{A}$. Clearly $\mathcal{A}'$ accepts $\beta_{|w|}w$ if and only if $w \in L$. Hence for $\beta = (\beta_n) \in \mathit{const}$ holds $L : \beta \in \mathbf{REG}/\mathit{const}$. □

For a nonnegative integer k let $\mathbf{k}$ be the set of all sequences of binary strings of length at most k. We define: A language $L \subseteq \Sigma^*$ belongs to $\mathbf{REG}/\mathbf{k}$ if there is a sequence $\alpha = (\alpha_n) \in \mathbf{k}$ and $\{\, \alpha_{|w|}w \mid w \in L \,\}$ is a regular language.

For instance $\mathbf{REG} = \mathbf{REG}/\mathbf{0}$. Since $\mathbf{REG}/\mathbf{1}$ contains nonrecursive sets (e.g., all tally languages) we have $\mathbf{REG}/\mathbf{0} \subset \mathbf{REG}/\mathbf{1}$. To separate $\mathbf{REG}/(\mathbf{k}-\mathbf{1})$ from $\mathbf{REG}/\mathbf{k}$ in general we need a structural description of languages in $\mathbf{REG}/\mathbf{k}$. We prove that these languages are *piecewise regular*.

Proposition 2 (Piecewise characterization Theorem). *Let $L \subseteq \Sigma^*$. The following statements are equivalent:*

1. $L \in \mathbf{REG/k}$
2. *There is a mapping $c : \mathbb{N} \rightarrow \{0, \dots, 2^k - 1\}$ and there are regular languages $A_0, \dots, A_{2^k-1} \in \Sigma^*$ such that $L \cap \Sigma^n = A_{c(n)} \cap \Sigma^n$ for all $n \in \mathbb{N}$.*

Proof. $1 \Rightarrow 2$: By reformulation of the definition $L \subseteq \Sigma^*$ belongs to $\mathbf{REG/k}$ if and only if there is a regular language A, a mapping $c : \mathbb{N} \rightarrow \{0, \dots, 2^k - 1\}$ and words $w_0, \dots, w_{2^k-1} \in \{0,1\}^k$ such that $L \cap \Sigma^n = w_{c(n)}^{-1} A \cap \Sigma^n$ for all $n \in \mathbb{N}$, where $w^{-1}A = \{\, u \in \Sigma^* \mid wu \in A \,\}$ for any w. Since for any string w language $w^{-1}A$ is regular if A is, the claim follows.
$2 \Rightarrow 1$: For languages $A_0, \dots, A_{2^k-1}$ let A be the *join of* $A_0, \dots, A_{2^k-1}$, i.e., $A = \bigcup_{i=0}^{2^k-1} \mathrm{bin}(i) A_i$. It is not hard to prove that the join of regular languages is regular itself. Now consider the advice $\alpha \in \mathbf{k}$ defined by $\alpha_n = \mathrm{bin}(i)$ if $c(n) = i$. Obviously $L = A : \alpha$, hence $L \in \mathbf{REG/k}$. □

For the separation of the above hierarchy we need some notions and results from Kolmogorov complexity theory (see Li and Vitányi [9]).

Definition 3. A *partial recursive prefix function* $\phi : \{0,1\}^* \rightarrow \mathbb{N}$ is a partial recursive function with a prefix-free domain, i.e., if ϕ is defined on both x and y then x is not a proper prefix of y.

Let $x \in \{0,1\}^*$. Any partial recursive prefix function $\phi : \{0,1\}^* \rightarrow \mathbb{N}$ together with a string $p \in \{0,1\}^*$ such that $\phi(p) = x$ is a *description* of x. The prefix complexity C_ϕ of x with respect to ϕ is defined by

$$\min\{\, |p| \mid \phi(p) = x \,\}$$

and $C_\phi(x) = \infty$ if there is no such p.

It is known that there is a partial recursive prefix function f such that for any partial recursive prefix function g there is a constant c_{fg} such that for all $x \in \{0,1\}^*$ holds $C_f(x) \leq C_g(x) + c_{fg}$. We fix one such additively optimal partial recursive prefix function ψ_0 and define the prefix complexity of x to be $K(x) = C_{\psi_0}(x)$. Further for an infinite binary sequence ω and $n \in \mathbb{N}$ let $\omega_{0:n}$ denote the prefix of ω of length n.

Proposition 4. *There exists an infinite binary sequence ω that is* random, *i.e., there is a constant c such that $K(\omega_{0:n}) \geq n - c$ for all n.*

Theorem 5. $\mathbf{REG/(k-1)} \subset \mathbf{REG/k}$ *for all $k \geq 1$.*

Proof. We first consider the step $\mathbf{REG/1} \subset \mathbf{REG/2}$. Let

$$L = \{\, \mathrm{bin}(l) 0^{n-1} i \mid \omega_{2n+l} = i \text{ for } 0 \leq l < 2,\ n \geq 0 \,\},$$

where $\omega = \omega_0 \omega_1 \dots$ is a random infinite binary sequence. Consider the languages $L_{00} = \{0,1\}0^*0$, $L_{01} = 00^*0 \cup 10^*1$, $L_{10} = 00^*1 \cup 10^*0$, and $L_{11} = \{0,1\}0^*1$.

Defining $c : \mathbb{N} \rightarrow \{00, 01, 10, 11\}$ accordingly we can form L as a piecewise regular language from these 2^2 languages, thus $L \in \mathbf{REG/2}$.

Assume $L \in \mathbf{REG/1}$ and let $\mathcal{A}$ be the *deterministic* finite automaton that accepts $\{\alpha_{|w|}w \mid w \in L\}$, where $\alpha = (\alpha_n)$ is an 1-bit advice. We describe a program P that computes the first $2n$ bits of ω, given n and $\alpha_2, \ldots, \alpha_{n+1}$.

```
read n;
for i = 2 to n+1 do read α_i od;
for i = 2 to n+1 do
        if A accepts α_i 0^{i-1} 0 then ω_{2(i-2)} = 0 else ω_{2(i-2)} = 1;
        if A accepts α_i 1 0^{i-2} 0 then ω_{2(i-2)+1} = 0 else ω_{2(i-2)+1} = 1;
            od;
```

A universal machine $\mathcal{U}$ given the input $P\#n\#\alpha_2, \ldots, \alpha_{n+1}$ can first check if the input is of the required form and if so, execute P on $(n, \alpha_2, \ldots, \alpha_{n+1})$ using $\mathcal{A}$ as a subroutine and else it starts cycling forever. Clearly $\mathcal{U}$ does not halt on any proper prefix of an admissible input and on admissible inputs computes the first $2n$ bits of ω. Hence $\mathcal{U}$ corresponds to a partial recursive prefix function, and the input $P\#n\#\alpha_2, \ldots, \alpha_{n+1}$ is a description of $\omega_{0:(2n-1)}$ in the sense of Definition 3. This description has length $O(1)+O(\log n)+n$. This contradicts the randomness of ω which requires at least $2n-c$ bit for some c to describe $\omega_{0:(2n-1)}$.

To generalize this idea to higher levels of the hierarchy we define

$$L = \{\operatorname{bin}(l)0^{n-m}i \mid \omega_{k\cdot n+l} = i \text{ for } 0 \leq l < k,\, n \geq 0\},$$

where $m = \lfloor \log k \rfloor$. With similar arguments as above one can show that L is a member of $\mathbf{REG/k}$ but does not belong to $\mathbf{REG/(k-1)}$. □

3 The Chomsky hierarchy relative to constant length advices

We show that pumping lemmata can be used to separate the low levels of Chomsky's hierarchy relative to constant length advices. In order to do this we need a technical lemma which can be proved by van der Waerden's Theorem (see, e.g., Graham *et al.* [5]): If the natural numbers are colored with finitely many colors then there exists a monochromatic arithmetic progression of arbitrary length.

Lemma 6. *Let $N_{\geq q} := \{n \mid n \geq q\}$ for some $q \in \mathbb{N}$ and $S_{a,b}$ a linear set of the form $\{a \cdot n + b \mid n \in \mathbb{N}\}$ for some $a, b \in \mathbb{N}$.*

Let c be a r-coloring of the natural numbers, i.e., $c : \mathbb{N} \rightarrow \{0, 1, \ldots, r\text{-}1\}$, and let l be some constant. Then there exists a monochromatic arithmetic progression in $N_{\geq q} \cap S_{a,b}$ of length l.

Proposition 7. $\{a^n b^n \mid n \in \mathbb{N}\} \notin \mathbf{REG}/const.$

Proof. Assume that $\{ a^n b^n \mid n \in \mathbb{N} \} \in \mathbf{REG/k}$ for some $k \in \mathbb{N}$. Then by the piecewise characterization theorem there is a mapping $c : \mathbb{N} \to \{0, \ldots, 2^k - 1\}$ and there are languages $A_0, \ldots, A_{2^k-1} \in \mathbf{REG}$ such that for all $n \in \mathbb{N}$ holds $L \cap \Sigma^n = A_{c(n)} \cap \Sigma^n$.

Let $q := \max\{ q_i \mid 0 \le i \le 2^k - 1 \}$ where q_i is the constant of the pumping lemma for the language A_i. Mapping c realizes a 2^k-coloring of the natural numbers. Applying Lemma 6 for $l = q + 1$ and the set $S_{2,0}$, there exists a monochromatic arithmetic progression of the form

$$P_1 = \{2n, 2n + d, \ldots, 2n + (l-1) \cdot d\} \subseteq \mathbb{N}_{\ge 2q} \cap S_{2,0}.$$

Without loss of generality we can assume that P_1 is colored by c with 0, hence $a^n b^n \in A_0$.

Because $n \ge q$ we can decompose the word $a^n b^n \in A_0$ by the pumping lemma for regular languages such that there exists u, v, w with

1. $|uv| \le q$,
2. $|v| \neq 0$, and
3. $uv^i w \in A_0$ for all $i \in \mathbb{N}$.

Obviously, the lengths of the words $uv^i w$ form an arithmetic progression

$$P_2 = \{2n, 2n + |v|, 2n + 2 \cdot |v|, \ldots\} \subseteq \mathbb{N}_{\ge 2q}.$$

Observe, $2n + |v| \cdot d$ belongs to both P_1 and P_2. This implies that $uv^{d+1}w$ belongs to A_0 and in addition to L. Since the decomposition was chosen in the above way, the numbers of a's and b's in the word $uv^{d+1}w$ are not equal. Therefore, $uv^{d+1}w \notin L$. This contradicts the assumption, and thus $\{ a^n b^n \mid n \in \mathbb{N} \}$ does not belong to $\mathbf{REG}/const$. □

To separate the Chomsky hierarchy relative to constant length advices in addition we need a theorem due to Mundhenk and Schuler [10] that shows that for space constructible functions there exists a nonuniform space hierarchy. For $h : \mathbb{N} \to \mathbb{N}$ let $\mathcal{A}/h$ denote the class $\mathcal{A}/\mathcal{F}$, where $\mathcal{F}$ is the set $\{g : \mathbb{N} \to \Sigma^* \mid |g(n)| = O(h(n)) \}$.

Theorem 8. *[10] Let f, g, and h be space constructible functions, where n, $g(n)$, $h(n) = o(f(n))$ and $h(n) = o(2^n)$. Then there exists a language in the class $DSpace(f(n))$ which is not in $DSpace(g(n))/h(n)$, i.e., $DSpace(f(n)) \setminus DSpace(g(n))/h(n) \neq \emptyset$.*

Theorem 9. $\mathbf{REG}/const \subset \mathbf{CFL}/const \subset \mathbf{CS}/const \subset \mathbf{RE}/const$.

Proof. $\mathbf{REG}/const \subset \mathbf{CFL}/const$: Immediately from Proposition 7.

$\mathbf{CFL}/const \subset \mathbf{CS}/const$: The essential fact underlying Proposition 7 is that the image of $\{ a^n b^n \mid n \in \mathbb{N} \}$ under Parikh mapping is semilinear. Thus an almost identical argument can be applied to the context-sensitive language $\{ a^n b^n c^n \mid n \in \mathbb{N} \}$.

$\mathbf{CS}/const \subset \mathbf{RE}/const$: By Savitch's Theorem $\mathbf{CS}/const \subseteq DSpace(n^2)/const$. Applying Theorem 8 for $g(n) = n^2$, $h(n) = 1$, and, e.g., $f(n) = 2^n$ we obtain $\mathbf{CS}/const \subseteq DSpace(n^2)/const \subset DSpace(2^n)/const \subseteq \mathbf{RE}/const$. □

4 Nonuniform measures

Most approaches to define nonuniform complexity measures in connection with formal languages are based on quantifying the ability of automata-like devices to approximate languages by finite subsets. Such approaches are made, e.g., by Balcázar *et al.* [2], Huynh [6], and Shallit and Breitbart [12]. The latter reference also contains a historical overview about the different measures.

We use a similar approach, but, for technical reasons we approximate languages be generating devices (grammars) rather than accepting ones.

Definition 10. Given a language $L \subseteq \Sigma^*$, we define the *regular cost* of L as the function $reg_L : \mathbb{N} \to \mathbb{N}$ given by

$$reg_L(n) := \min\{\,|G| \mid G \text{ is a regular grammar such that } L(G) \cap \Sigma^n = L \cap \Sigma^n\,\}$$

where $|G|$ denotes the size of G and is defined as the cardinality of the production-set of G.

We define the class of languages with constant and polynomial regular costs as:

$$\begin{aligned} Const_{reg} &= \{\, L \mid reg_L(n) = O(1)\,\} \\ Poly_{reg} &= \{\, L \mid \exists k : reg_L(n) = O(n^k)\,\}. \end{aligned}$$

In the same manner one can define *context-free cost* cf_L, *context-sensitive cost* cs_L, and *recursive enumerable cost* re_L of a language L. The class of languages with constant context-free (context-sensitive, recursive enumerable, respectively) costs is denoted by $Const_{cf}$ ($Const_{cs}$, $Const_{re}$, respectively), and the class of languages with polynomial context-free (context-sensitive, recursive enumerable, respectively) costs by $Poly_{cf}$ ($Poly_{cs}$, $Poly_{re}$, respectively).

Using the piecewise characterization theorem and the fact that for constantly bounded costs there exists only a *finite* number of devices of a given kind, one can easily prove:

Theorem 11. *1.* $\mathbf{REG}/const = Const_{reg}$,
2. $\mathbf{CFL}/const = Const_{cf}$,
3. $\mathbf{CS}/const = Const_{cs}$, *and*
4. $\mathbf{RE}/const = Const_{re}$. □

Remark. Ibarra and Ravikumar [7] introduced a measure similar to initial index and to our regular cost as follows: A language $L \subseteq \Sigma^*$ belongs to the class $NSpace(s(n))$[nonuniform] if there exists a constant c and a collection $\{A_n\}$, $n = 1, 2, \ldots$, of two-way deterministic finite automata such that the number of states in A_n is at most $c^{s(n)}$, and $L(A_n) \cap \Sigma^n = L \cap \Sigma^n$ for all $n \in \mathbb{N}$. It is easy to see that $\mathbf{REG}/const$ and $NSpace(1)$[nonuniform] coincide.

In comparison to Theorem 11 the situation changes for polynomial length bounded advices. For context-sensitive and recursive enumerable sets we obtain characterizations in terms of polynomially context-sensitive and recursive enumerable costs. The main idea to prove the following theorem is to use the ability of a Turing machine to read the advice on the input tape several times (the input-head works two-way) and to simulate a derivation of a context-sensitive or unrestricted grammar in a given amount of space. Due to the lack of space we omit the proof.

Theorem 12. **CS**/*poly* $= Poly_{cs}$ *and* **RE**/*poly* $= Poly_{re}$. □

Turning to regular and context-free languages and costs, we can show that a similar characterization as in the context-sensitive or recursive enumerable case does not hold.

Theorem 13. **REG**/*const* $\subset Poly_{reg} \subset$ **CFL**/*poly* $\subseteq Poly_{cf} \subset$ **CS**/*poly*.

Proof. **REG**/*const* $\subset Poly_{reg}$: **REG**/*const* coincides with $Const_{reg}$ by Theorem 11, and $\{ a^n b^n \mid n \in \mathbb{N} \}$ has linear regular cost, but does not belong to **REG**/*const* by Proposition 7.

$Poly_{reg} \subset$ **CFL**/*poly*: Let $L \in Poly_{reg}$. Then for every n there exists a regular grammar G_n (of polynomial size) with $L(G_n) \cap \Sigma^n = L \cap \Sigma^n$. For technical reasons we construct a regular grammar G_n^R with $L(G_n^R) = L(G_n)^R$. Here L^R denotes the *mirror image* of L.
The advice α_n for the pushdown automaton is build up by repeating n times a suitable coding of G_n^R. Obviously, α_n is polynomially length bounded. The pushdown automaton that accepts L works on input $\alpha_{|w|}w$ as follows: While reading the advice, the automaton guesses a terminating derivation of length n step by step. After each step the automaton pushes the derived terminal-symbol and verifies with the encoded grammar G_n^R (and with the help of the pushdown) whether this derivation-step is correct. If this is not the case, the automaton rejects. After the advice is read, the automaton checks whether the derived word, which is stored in the pushdown, coincides with w. If this is the case the automaton accepts, otherwise it rejects. This proofs that $L \in$ **CFL**/*poly*.
The proper inclusion follows from the fact, that the context-free language $\{ ww^R \mid w \in \{a, b\}^* \}$ has exponential regular cost (Balcázar *et al.* [2]).

CFL/*poly* $\subseteq Poly_{cf}$: Obviously.

$Poly_{cf} \subset$ **CS**/*poly*: **CS**/*poly* coincides with $Poly_{cs}$ by Theorem 12, and the context-sensitive language $\{ ww \mid w \in \{a, b\}^* \}$ has exponential context-free cost (see Balcázar *et al.* [2] and Goodrich *et al.* [4]). □

The exact relation between context-free languages relative to polynomial length advices and measures is still open, but we conjecture that the inclusion **CFL**/*poly* $\subseteq Poly_{cf}$ is proper. This conjecture is based on the following two facts: First, $Poly_{cf}$ coincides with the class of languages accepted by one-way nondeterministic pushdown automata with an auxiliary log-space bounded work tape working in polynomial time, and with the help of a polynomially length bounded advice (Huynh [6]). Second, let the advice $\alpha = (\alpha_n)$ be given in the following alternative way: For $w = w_1 \ldots w_n \in \Sigma^n$ consider the input (see, e.g., Balcázar *el al.* [2]):

$$\alpha_n w_1 \alpha_n w_2 \alpha_n \ldots \alpha_n w_n \alpha_n.$$

For finite automata this seems to be a more gentle way to provide the advice. But it can be shown that this makes no difference to the classes **REG**/*poly*, **CS**/*poly* and **RE**/*poly*. Moreover with this alternative definition the class of context-free languages with polynomial length advices coincides with $Poly_{cf}$.

5 The Chomsky hierarchy relative to polynomial length advices

Theorem 14. *1.* **CFL**/*const* ⊂ **CFL**/*poly,*
2. **CS**/*const* ⊂ **CS**/*poly, and*
3. **RE**/*const* ⊂ **RE**/*poly.*

Proof. 1. Obviously, if $L \subseteq \Sigma^*$ is a *sparse* language, i.e., there exists a polynomial p such that $|L \cap \Sigma^n| \leq p(n)$, then L belongs to $Poly_{reg}$. Thus language $\{ a^n b^n c^n \mid n \in \mathbb{N} \}$ belongs to $Poly_{reg}$ and therefore also to **CFL**/*poly*, but is not contained in **CFL**/*const* by Theorem 9.
2. and 3. follow from Lemma 15 below and the well-known fact that **CS** is the class of languages recognized by nondeterministic linear space bounded Turing machines. □

A nonnegative integer function $h(n)$ is said to be *constructible* if there is a deterministic Turing machine $\mathcal{M}$, that on input 1^n outputs the string $1^{h(n)}$. The function $h(n)$ is said to be *constructible in DSpace*(n) if additionally $\mathcal{M}$ is linear space bounded.

Lemma 15. *Let* $f(n) = o(g(n))$, *where* $f(n)$ *and* $g(n) \leq 2^n$ *are integer functions. Further let* $m(n) = \lfloor \log g(n) \rfloor$.

If $m(n)$ *is constructible then* **RE**/$f(n)$ ⊂ **RE**/$g(n)$ *and if* $m(n)$ *moreover is constructible in DSpace*(n) *then* **CS**/$f(n)$ ⊂ **CS**/$g(n)$.

Proof. Let $G(n) = g(0) + g(1) + \cdots + g(n)$ and $F(n) = f(0) + \cdots + f(n)$, with $g(0) = 0$ and $f(0) = 0$.

Let ω be a random infinite binary sequence. The separating language L is

$$L = \{ \mathrm{bin}(l) 0^{n-m(n)} i \mid \omega_{G(n)+l} = i \text{ for } 0 \leq l < g(n+1),\ n \geq 0 \}.$$

Let $m(n)$ be constructible, hence $L \in$ **RE**/$g(n)$. In case $L \in$ **RE**/$f(n)$ we could give a description of $\omega_{0:G(n)}$ of length $O(1) + O(\log n) + F(n)$ using a program similar to that in the proof of Theorem 5. But this contradicts the randomness of ω since $\lim_{n\to\infty}[(F(n) + O(\log n))/G(n)] = 0$.

The same argument works for the second inclusion if $m(n)$ is required to be constructible in *DSpace*(n). □

Using Proposition 1, Theorem 8 and 13 we can finally prove:

Theorem 16. $\mathbf{REG}/poly \subset \mathbf{CFL}/poly \subset \mathbf{CS}/poly \subset \mathbf{RE}/poly$. □

6 Conclusions

We investigated nonuniform counterparts of the Chomsky hierarchy based on the Karp-Lipton model and on cost measures. This two models nicely fit together in the case of constant and polynomial length bounded advices and costs, respectively, except for regular and context-free languages relative to polynomial length advices. The relations between the classes considered are shown in Figure 1.

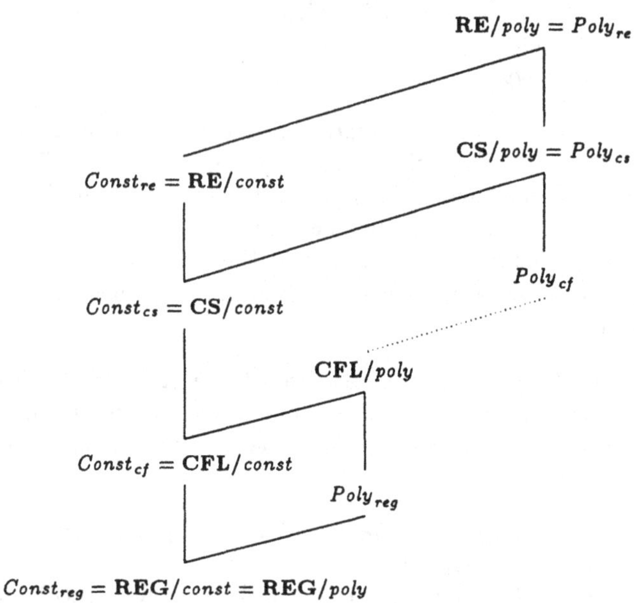

Fig. 1. Inclusion diagram. Dotted lines stand for inclusions, and solid lines for proper inclusions.

For the Karp-Lipton model we have used one of the simplest pairing functions $(\alpha_{|w|}, w) \mapsto \alpha_{|w|}w$. Such a restricted mechanism seems to be inadequate for low levels of the Chomsky hierarchy due to the limited power of computational resource. To avoid this one could allow, e.g., pairing functions computable by regular transducers with two input-tapes. For example, regular languages relative to polynomial length advices with alternative definition gives the class $Poly_{reg}$.

Different cost measures have been considered in the literature. Motivated by our results we feel it worth to study the relations between these measures from the complexity theoretical point of view. The rich collection of tools for formal languages (e.g., pumping lemmata, powerset construction,...) seem to provide a wide area to obtain lower bounds for such nonuniform measures.

7 Acknowledgments

We thank Martin Mundhenk for several fruitful discussions on the subject. The main idea to the proof of Theorem 5 is due to him. Thanks also to Uwe Schöning for drawing our attention to the work of Balcázar *et al.* [2] and to Klaus-Jörn Lange for helpful comments on an earlier version of this work. Finally we would like to thank an unknown referee for useful recommendations.

References

1. R. Aleliunas, R. M. Karp, R. J. Lipton, L. Lovasz, and C. Rackoff. Random walks, universal traversal sequences, and the complexity of MAZE problems. In *Proceedings of the 20th IEEE Annual Symposium on Foundations of Computer Science*, pages 218–223, 1979.
2. J. L. Balcázar, J. Díaz, and J. Gabarró. Uniform characterizations of non-uniform complexity measures. *Information and Control*, 67:53–69, 1985.
3. C. Damm and M. Holzer. Inductive counting below LOGSPACE. In *Proceedings of the 19th Conference on Mathematical Foundations of Computer Science*, number 841 in LNCS, pages 276–285. Springer, August 1994.
4. G. Goodrich, R. Ladner, and M. Fischer. Straight line programs to compute finite languages. In *Conference on Theoretical Computer Science*, Waterloo, 1977.
5. R. L. Graham, B. L. Rothschild, and J. H. Spencer. *Ramsey theory*. Wiley, 1990.
6. D. T. Huynh. Complexity of closeness, sparseness and segment equivalence for context-free and regular languages. In *Informatik, Festschrift zum 60. Geburtstag von Günter Hotz*, pages 235–251. B. G. Teubner, 1992.
7. O. H. Ibarra and B. Ravikumar. Sublogarithmic-space Turing machines, nonuniform space complexity, and closure properties. *Mathematical Systems Theory*, 21:1–17, 1988.
8. R. M. Karp and R. J. Lipton. Turing machines that take advice. *L'Enseignement Mathématique*, 28:191–209, 1982.
9. M. Li and P. Vitányi. *An Introduction to Kolmogorov Complexity and its Applications*. Springer, New York, Berlin, Heidelberg, 1993.
10. M. Mundhenk and R. Schuler. Random languages for nonuniform complexity classes. *Journal of Complexity*, 7:296–310, 1991.
11. N. Pippenger. On simultaneous resource bounds. In *Proceedings of the 20th IEEE Annual Symposium on Foundations of Computer Science*, pages 307–311, 1979.
12. J. Shallit and Y. Breitbart. Automaticity: properties of a measure of descriptional complexity. In *Annual Symposium on Theoretical Aspects of Computing*, number 775 in Lecture Notes in Computer Science, pages 619–630. Springer, 1994.
13. A. Wigderson. NL/poly $\subseteq$ $\oplus$L/poly. In *Proceedings of the 9th Annual Structure in Complexity Theory Conference*, pages 59–62, Juni 1994.

Nonuniform Lower Bounds for Exponential Time Classes

Steven Homer[1] * and Sarah Mocas[2] **

[1] Computer Science Department, Boston University, Boston, MA 02215
[2] Computer Science Department, Portland State University, Portland, Oregon 97207

Abstract. Lower bounds for the first levels of the exponential time hierarchy with respect to circuit and advice classes are studied. Using time bounded Kolmogorov complexity, languages are constructed which witness that various exponential time classes are not included in (fixed) polynomial advice classes. We show as well that these languages are not included in small circuit families where the circuits are of a fixed, polynomial size. The results yield optimal bounds (up to relativization) on efficient nonuniform computation.

1 Introduction

It is well known that a problem can be solved by a family of small (that is polynomial-size) circuits if and only if it is polynomial time Turing reducible to a sparse set. Both of these properties are equivalent to a problem being in the advice class $P/poly$. Formally, a set A is in $P/poly$ if there is a polynomial length bounded *advice function* $f : N \rightarrow \Sigma^*$ and a $B \in P$ such that $x \in A$ if and only if $\langle x, f(|x|)\rangle \in B$. The *advice string*, $f(|x|)$, depends only on the length of x.

Problems in $P/poly$ are often equated with problems which are non-uniformly efficiently computable. Thus it is of interest to exhibit problems which are not so computable, that is finding and determining the complexity of problems which do not have polynomial size circuits. There is an extensive literature relating uniform complexity measures to the central nonuniform classes. Kannan exhibited sets in $NEXP^{NP}$ which are not in $P/poly$ [Kan82]. By results of Wilson [Wil85] we know that any substantial improvement of Kannan's result cannot relativize as there are oracles relative to which $EXP^{NP} \subseteq P/poly$. Of course there is strong evidence, in the form of the well-known theorems of Karp, Lipton, Sipser and others [KL80], that NP (and so larger classes as well) is not contained in P/poly as such containment implies the collapse of the polynomial time hierarchy. Analogous collapsing results for the exponential time hierarchy have been shown in Buhrman and Homer [BH92]. For example, if $EXP^{NP} \subseteq EXP/poly$ then $EXP = EXP^{NP}$.

* Research partially supported by the National Science Foundation under grants CCR-9103055 and CCR-9400229.

** Research partially supported by the National Science Foundation under grant CCR-9410713.

In this paper we are interested in absolute and constructive results rather than hypotheses implying collapses, and consider advice classes slightly smaller than *P/poly* and circuit classes of a fixed polynomial-size. We establish several lower bounds for problems in the exponential time hierarchy with respect to these classes. This is not a new tack to explore. Bin Fu [Fu93] considered lower bounds for polynomial time reductions to sparse sets, where limits are placed on the number of queries to the sparse set. The main result of his paper was that there are sets in EXP which are not polynomial time Turing reducible to a sparse set when the reduction is restricted to querying the sparse set no more than n^α times, for α any constant less than 1. The results presented here are incomparable to Fu's. The lower bounds we present are stronger but they apply only to the size of small circuits or to the length of advice in advice classes, not to the number of queries to sparse sets.

In this work we look directly at families of small circuits and at non-uniform classes. While for polynomial-length advice these classes are equivalent to reductions to sparse sets, the equivalence does not hold when we start bounding the advice further. In particular, it does not hold when we bound the length of the advice below some fixed polynomial. We establish lower bounds for EXP and EXP^{NP} with respect to non-uniform classes where the length of the advice is polynomially bounded. For example, $EXP^{NP} \not\subseteq NP/n^c$ for any fixed integer c. From this we obtain several corollaries as well as an analogous bound for E and E^{NP}.

In Section 2 we use time bounded Kolmogorov complexity to prove nonuniform lower bounds for the classes EXP and E. The main results of this section can also be seen to directly follow from the stronger measure-theoretic techniques of Lutz [L92] and Lutz and Mayordomo [LM93]. Our proofs use simpler techniques by directly applying Kolmogorov complexity to construct languages exhibiting the desired properties. With respect to the complexity of the lower bounds, the results are optimal up to relativization. That is, strengthening the results to hold for full polynomial advice would require methods that do not relativize as, if they did, they would contradict Wilson's oracle results [Wil85] mentioned above. Similar bounds are implied for circuit classes smaller than polynomial size. For example, the theorems imply that E does not have circuits of size cn for any fixed c and that EXP does not have circuits of size n^c for any fixed c. This second statement was previously shown by Kannan [Kan82].

With a bit of care, the proof techniques in Section 2 relativize and yield additional information. These results are discussed in Section 3. In particular we are able to prove that there are problems slightly higher in the exponential hierarchy, at the EXP^{NP} level, which are not computable by larger advice classes such as P^{NP}/n^c or E^{NP}/n^c. We also obtain a theorem concerning the impossibility of having small circuit generators for some uniform classes in the EXP hierarchy. Finally, we consider classes defined by nonadaptive oracle queries and establish similar lower bounds for uniform classes with respect to advice classes which are also nonadaptively defined.

1.1 Basic Definitions and Notation

All languages considered are subsets of $\Sigma^* = \{0,1\}^*$. The *complement* of a language A is $\Sigma^* - A$ and is denoted by $\bar{A}$. Strings are elements of Σ^* and are denoted by small letters $w, x, y, \ldots$ or by $\alpha, \beta, \gamma, \ldots$. We will use $|x|$ to designate the length of x. Let N be the set of natural numbers. For a set A and $n \in N$ define

$$A^n = \{x \in A \mid |x| = n\}.$$

Fix a pairing function $\langle \cdot, \cdot \rangle$. We may assume that this pairing function is polynomial-time computable and invertible, and that for any string x, y, $|\langle x, y\rangle| \leq 2(|x|+|y|)$. When needed we assume a similarly efficient coding of n-tuples.

A set S is *sparse* if $||\{x \in S \mid |x| \leq n\}|| \leq p(n)$ for some polynomial p.

We follow what is now fairly standard notation in naming the exponential time classes.

$E = DTIME(2^{linear})$, $EXP = DTIME(2^{poly})$,
$NE = NTIME(2^{linear})$, $NEXP = NTIME(2^{poly})$,
$EXPSPACE = DSPACE(2^{poly})$.

Most of our results contrast exponential time classes with advice classes and circuit families which we define next.

Definition 1 *An* advice *function is a function $f : \mathrm{N} \rightarrow \Sigma^*$. Let C be a complexity class, and F a family of advice functions. The class C/F is the collection of all sets A such that for some $B \in C$ and function $f \in F$,*

$$x \in A \text{ if and only if } \langle x,\ f(|x|)\rangle \in B.$$

Common classes F of advice functions are

$log = \{f \mid |f(n)| \leq c \cdot \log_2 n$ for some constant $c\}$,
$lin = \{f \mid |f(n)| \leq c \cdot n$ for some constant $c\}$,
$poly = \{f \mid |f(n)| \leq k \cdot n^c$ for some constants $c, k\}$.
$n^c = \{f \mid |f(n)| \leq k \cdot n^c$, for some constant $k\}$.

Familiarity with the standard definitions of Boolean circuit complexity is assumed here (see [BDG88], for example). A class C is said to have f-size circuits if for every set $A \in C$ there is a sequence $\{D_n\}$ of circuits which recognize A and such that for all n, D_n has size $\leq f(n)$.

2 Separating EXP from Advice Classes

In this section we will use bounded Kolmogorov complexity to obtain bounds on the nonuniform complexity of EXP (Theorem 2) and E (Theorem 3). A precursor of this proof technique can be found in Gavaldà and Watanabe [GW91].

The stronger and more complex measure theoretic methods of Lutz [L92] and Lutz and Mayordomo [LM93] can be seen to yield stronger results than our

Theorems 2 and 3. In particular Theorem 3 can be seen to follow from the weak stochasticity theorem for E found in [LM93]. And a similar theorem for EXP can be found in Lutz [L92a]. The proofs here are more elementary and direct. The proof of Theorem 2 is included here as it is needed to obtain the results in Section 3 concerning higher levels of the exponential hierarchy.

The following is a standard definition for time-bounded Kolmogorov complexity [BDG90]. The original notion is due to Hartmanis [Hart83]. Fix any reasonable universal transducer U, and let $U(x)$ denote the output of U on input x.

Definition 2 *Time Bounded Kolmogorov Complexity.*

$K[f,\ g] = \{u \mid \exists w(|w| \leq f(|u|)), U(w) = u$ *and this result is obtained in at most* $g(|u|)$ *steps of* $U\}$.

Strings in $K[f,\ g]$ are said to have low (f,g)-time bounded Kolmogorov complexity. Intuitively $K[f,\ g]$ is the set of strings u which can be computed from some string w that represents a compression of u by a factor of $f(|u|)$ and for which the computation takes time $g(|u|)$. The use of a fixed universal transducer U is justified by the following central lemma which is also due to Hartmanis. Let K_i be the time bounded Kolmogorov complexity measure based on the ith Turing machine in some standard enumeration of Turing transducers.

Lemma 1. *[Hart83] Let i be any index and $g(n), t(n)$ be time constructible functions. Then there exists a $c > 0$ such that $K_i[g(n), t(n)] \subseteq K[g(n)+c, c\, t(n) log\ t(n)+ c]$.*

We can now state the main theorem of this section. The proof is a series of lemmas each of which is reasonably simple, however the Kolmogorov complexity arguments are delicate and care has to be taken in each case to get the sharp results we desire. For this reason, a brief outline of the proof follows the statement of the theorem and precedes its proof.

Theorem 2. *$EXP \not\subseteq DTIME(2^{O(n^{c_1})})/n^{c_2}$ for any fixed integers c_1 and c_2.*

The intuition behind this proof is straightforward. We will need to divide strings x into substrings each of length n. Formally, if $x = x_1x_2\ldots x_k$, where $|x_i| = n$ for all i, $1 \leq i \leq k$, we say that each x_i is a *n-block* of x. Now assume that $EXP \subseteq DTIME(2^{O(n^{c_1})})/n^{c_2}$, for some fixed c_1 and c_2. We construct a set A in EXP by, for each n, finding a string τ_n whose length is polynomial in n, and which has high time bounded Kolmogorov complexity. (That is $\tau_n \notin K[f,g]$, for suitably chosen f,g.) We break τ_n up into its n-blocks and let these n-blocks make up A^n, the strings in A of length n. Using the above assumption, we give an algorithm which, for sufficiently large n, finds a string ξ of sufficiently small length less than τ_n from which τ_n can be efficiently generated. This contradicts the high time-bounded Kolmogorov complexity of τ and therefore our initial assumption.

Proof. Assume $EXP \subseteq DTIME(2^{O(n^{c_1})})/n^{c_2}$ for some fixed integers c_1 and c_2. For each n we construct the set A^n of strings of length n as follows.

Let $m = n^{3+c_1c_2}$. Choose the (lexicographically) least string $\tau \in \Sigma^m$ such that $\tau \notin K[m-1,\ 2^{2m}]$. Set $A^n = \{w_i \mid w_i \text{ is a } n\text{-block of } \tau\}$.
Let $A = \bigcup_{n=1}^{\infty} A^n$.

Claim 2.1 $A \in DTIME(2^{3n^{3+c_1c_2}})$ *(and hence A is in EXP).*

Proof of Claim. To determine if $x \in A$, where $|x| = n$, we find the first string τ of length $m(= n^{3+c_1c_2})$ which is not in $K[m-1,\ 2^{2m}]$. This can be done by simulating the universal transducer $U(z)$ for 2^{2m} steps on all of the (2^m-1)-many $z \in \Sigma^{\leq m-1}$ and then lexicographically listing all strings of length m output by this transducer. τ is the first string in Σ^m that is not in the list. The n-blocks of τ then give the elements of A^n. In this way $x \in A^n$ can be decided in time $2^{m-1}2^{2m} + O(2^{2m}) < 2^{3m} = 2^{3n^{3+c_1c_2}}$, for sufficiently large n. □

Now by the assumption $A \in DTIME(2^{O(n^{c_1})})/n^{c_2}$, so by definition there exists an advice function $f \in n^{c_2}$, and a $B \in DTIME(2^{dn^{c_1}})$, for some fixed integer d, such that

$$x \in A \leftrightarrow \langle x,\ f(|x|)\rangle \in B.$$

Now let M be a Turing machine which runs in $DTIME(2^{O(n^{c_1})})$ and computes B. Fix n and let τ be the advice string not in $K[m-1, 2^{2m}]$ chosen for n. The definition of n^{c_2} advice says there is a constant e such that $|f(n)| \leq e \cdot n^{c_2}$. Without loss of generality we can assume equality here and let $f(n) = \alpha_1\alpha_2\cdots\alpha_{en^{c_2}}$, where $\alpha_i \in \{0,1\}$, be the advice for inputs of length n. The proof of the next claim is mainly technical and quite long and is omitted here.

Claim 2.2 *For all sufficiently large n, given the advice string $\alpha_1\alpha_2\cdots\alpha_{en^{c_2}}$ we can generate the n-blocks of τ (that is A^n) in time $2^{n^{c_1c_2+1}}$*

Now by way of contradiction we will show that for n sufficiently large (and m defined as above), $\tau \in K[m-1,\ 2^{2m}]$. What we need are an encoding of the advice $\alpha_1\alpha_2\cdots\alpha_{en^{c_2}}$, from which we can generate all of the n-blocks of τ, and an encoding of the order in which the n-blocks appear in τ.

Let $LEX(A^n)$ be an enumeration of all of the n-blocks that form strings in A^n in lexicographic order. Let $z_1,\ z_2,\ \ldots,\ z_{n^{2+c_1c_2}}$ be such that z_i is the position in $LEX(A^n)$ of the ith n-block of τ. Clearly $|z_i| \leq \log(n^{2+c_1c_2})$ and there are at most $n^{2+c_1c_2}$ different n-blocks since $m = |\tau| = n^{3+c_1c_2}$. (A simple combinatorial argument (see [Fu93]) shows that in fact there are exactly $n^{2+c_1c_2}$ n-blocks as they all must be different, though this fact is not necessary for this proof.)

Set $\gamma = \langle z_1,\ z_2,\ \ldots,\ z_{n^{2+c_1c_2}}\rangle$. $z_1,\ z_2,\ \ldots,\ z_{n^{2+c_1c_2}}$ can be retrived from γ in $2 * |\gamma|$ steps, and the length of γ is bounded by $2(n^{2+c_1c_2}\log(n^{2+c_1c_2}))$.

Now define $\xi = \langle \alpha_1\alpha_2\cdots\alpha_{en^{c_2}}, \gamma\rangle$. So $|\xi| \leq 2en^{c_2} + 2(n^{2+c_1c_2}\log(n^{2+c_1c_2}))$ which is less than m, for all sufficiently large n. This means that, for sufficiently large n, there is a string with length less than m that generates τ. It remains to show that τ can be generated in 2^{2m} steps.

Given ξ we can compute τ in time 2^{2m} as follows. From ξ we can find both $\alpha_1\alpha_2\cdots\alpha_{en^{c_2}}$ and $z_1, z_2, \ldots, z_{n^{2+c_1c_2}}$ in linear time (in ξ). Given the advice $\alpha_1\alpha_2\cdots\alpha_{en^{c_2}}$ we can generate all n-blocks in A^n in lexicographical order in $2^{n^{c_1c_2+1}}$ steps as above and so construct $LEX(A^n)$. From $LEX(A^n)$ and $z_1, z_2, \ldots, z_{n^{2+c_1c_2}}$ the string τ can be reconstructed in $O(n^{c_1c_2+3})$ steps by reordering the strings in A^n using the positions coded by γ, and for large values of n, $2^{n^{c_1c_2+3}} < 2^{2m}$.

Therefore, for large enough n, τ is generated by a string of length $< m$ within 2^{2m} steps. So $\tau \in K[m-1, 2^{2m}]$ contradicting the construction of A^n. □

In Karp and Lipton [KL80] it was shown that $EXP \not\subseteq P/log$ as this would imply $P = NP$ which in turn implies that $P = PH = EXP$.

Observing that the set A which is constructed in the proof of Theorem 2 is sparse we have the following corollary.

Corollary 2.1 *y*

1. *$EXP \not\subseteq E/n^c$, for any fixed c.*
2. *$NEXP \not\subseteq E/lin$.*
3. *For any fixed c_1 and c_2, there exists a sparse set $S \in EXP$ such that $S \notin DTIME(2^{O(n^{c_1})})/n^{c_2}$.*

In [PY93] the class $LOGSNP$ is defined and several natural problems are shown to be complete for this class. Also it is shown that $LOGSNP \subseteq (NP[\log^2 n] \bigcap DSPACE(\log^2 n))$. The class $NP[\log^2 n]$ is the subclass of NP problems in which only $\log^2 n$ steps are nondeterministic. Kintala and Fischer [KF80] and Díaz and Torán [DT90] previously studied classes that use polylogarithmic amounts of nondeterminism.

Corollary 2.2 *$EXP \not\subseteq LOGSNP/n^{c_1}$.*

Proof. Clearly $NP[\log^2 n] \subseteq DTIME(2^{\log^2 n}p(n))$, where p is a polynomial, since there are at most $2^{\log^2 n}$ possible paths in the entire computation tree of any problem in $NP[\log^2 n]$ and the length of each of these paths is at most polynomial in the length of n. Since, for large enough n, $2^{\log^2 n}p(n) \leq 2^{n^{c_2}}$, for some fixed constant c_2, then $LOGSNP/n^{c_1} \subseteq NP[\log^2 n]/n^{c_1} \subseteq DTIME(2^{n^{c_2}})/n^{c_1}$. This implies, by Theorem 2, that $EXP \not\subseteq LOGSNP/n^{c_1}$. □

With care, the proof of Theorem 2 can be modified to construct a set in E which is not in linear exponential time with fixed linear advice. More precisely,

Theorem 3. *$E \not\subseteq DTIME(2^{c_1 n})/c_2 n$ for fixed integers c_1 and c_2.*

The proof is omitted here. The weak stochasticity theorem of Lutz and Mayordomo [LM93] yields a stronger fact. Namely that there are (measure one) many sets in E which differ in (asymptotically) 1/2 of all elements of any length from any set in $DTIME(2^{c_1 n})/c_2 n$.

The following lemma is obtained by simply looking at the standard proof that problems with polynomial size circuits are in $P/poly$ as found for example in [BDG88]. Recall that n^c advice functions need only be $O(n^c)$ length bounded.

Lemma 4. *Let A be a problem which has $O(n^c)$-size circuits for some c, then $A \in P/n^{2c}$.*

Using the lemma, together with Theorem 2, we obtain the following corollary which is directly implied by an earlier result by Kannan. [Kan82].

Corollary 2.3 *EXP does not have $O(n^c)$-size circuits, for any fixed c.*

From Theorem 3 and a similar lemma we obtain,

Corollary 2.4 *E does not have circuits of size cn, for any fixed c.*

3 Separating EXP^{NP} and EXP_{tt}^{NP} from Advice Classes

Using relativized resource-bounded Kolmogorov complexity, we now present two relativized versions of Theorem 2 and use them to prove lower bounds for larger classes in the exponential hierarchy and for oracle classes where the oracle is only accessed nonadaptively. By the original work of Kannan [Kan82] and the relativization of Wilson [Wil85], we know that EXP^{NP} is the largest class in the EXP-hierarchy which may have polynomial size circuits. The first results in this section enable us to bound the nonuniform complexity of this level of the hierarchy.

We can assume that a universal machine used to measure Kolmogorov complexity can query an oracle. Let $K^D[f, g]$ denote the set of strings u such that there exists a word w, $|w| \leq f(|u|)$, so that U with oracle D on input w outputs u in at most $g(|u|)$ steps. In the following $DTIME(f(n), D)$ denotes the class of problems computable in deterministic time f where the machines are allowed access to a set D as an oracle.

It is straightforward to check that the proof of Theorem 2 relativizes to yield the following theorem whose proof we omit in this abstract.

Theorem 5. *For any set D, $EXP^D \not\subseteq DTIME(2^{O(n^{c_1})}, D)/n^{c_2}$ for any fixed integers c_1 and c_2.*

Corollary 3.1
1. *$EXP^{NP} \not\subseteq NP/n^c$, for any fixed integer c.*
2. *$EXP^{NP} \not\subseteq E^{NP}/n^c$, for any fixed integer c.*

A circuit generator is an extension of a circuit family by allowing the circuits to compute (partial) functions. Saying that a language has polynomial size circuit generators is slightly weaker than its having polynomial size circuits. (For the definitions and main results see Schöning [Sch85].) It is known that a set has polynomial size circuit generators if and only if it is in $NP/poly$. From Corollary 3.1 we have,

Corollary 3.2 *For any fixed c, EXP^{NP} does not have circuit generators of size n^c.*

Similarly, Theorem 3 relativizes and yields,

Theorem 6. $E^{NP} \not\subseteq DTIME(2^{cn}, NP)/dn$, *for any fixed constants c and d.*

Evidence for a stronger separation is provided by Buhrman and Homer in [BH92]. They show that if $EXP^{NP} \subseteq EXP/poly$ then $EXP^{NP} = EXP$ and that if $EXP^{NP} \subseteq P/poly$ then $EXP = \Sigma_2^P \bigcup \Pi_2^P$. So again our results here are nearly optimal.

Finally we consider the case that the queries to the oracle are made nonadaptively. Oracle classes defined by nonadaptive or truth-table queries to the oracle in their definition are natural and useful weakenings of the corresponding adaptive classes. Such classes in the polynomial hierarchy have been extensively studied and seen to play an important role. The corresponding classes in the exponential hierarchy have been investigated less, mainly by Hemachandra [Hem87] and more recently by Mocas [M93].

The proof of Theorem 5 can be modified to show that the same result holds with reguard to nonadaptive (i.e. truth-table) computations. Such computations are required to make all of their oracle queries at the start of the computation so that which queries are made to the oracle does not depend on answers to previous oracle queries. The proof requires a slight reformulation of time bounded Kolmogorov complexity. We still make use of a universal oracle Turing transducer, U, in our definition, but we restrict attention to computations of U which are nonadaptive. That is, a string u is in $K_{tt}^D[f, g]$ only if it is in $K^D[f, g]$ and the computation of U witnessing this is nonadaptive. Using this notion the proof of Theorem 3.1 can be modified to work nonadaptively.

In the next theorem $DTIME_{tt}(2^{0(n^{c_1})}, D)$ is the set of languages in $DTIME(2^{0(n^{c_1})}, D)$ that are accepted by oracle Turing machines which make only nonadaptive queries. EXP_{tt}^D is defined similarly. A short sketch of the construction for this theorem is given.

Theorem 7. *For any set D,* $EXP_{tt}^D \not\subseteq DTIME_{tt}(2^{0(n^{c_1})}, D)/n^{c_2}$, *for fixed integers c_1 and c_2.*

Proof(sketch). First we need to modify the oracle Turing machine U with which we define the Kolmogorov complexity so that only nonadaptive computations are considered. This can be done by, on any input, having U output nothing and halt unless it carries out its queries nonadaptively by listing all of its queries on a tape before actually making the oracle queries. (So the strings queried cannot depend on the outcome of previous queries.) Call the corresponding Kolmogorov complexity measure K_{tt}^D.

Now assume for some fixed oracle set D, $EXP_{tt}^{D} \subseteq DTIME_{tt}(2^{0(n^{c_1})}, D)/n^{c_2}$, for fixed integers c_1 and c_2. Construct the set A as follows:

Let $m = n^{3+c_1c_2}$. Choose the (lexicographically) least string $\tau \in \Sigma^m$ such that $\tau \notin K_{tt}^{D}[m-1, 2^{2m}]$. Set $A^n = \{w_i \mid w_i \text{ is a } n\text{-block of } \tau\}$.

Let $A = \bigcup_{n=1}^{\infty} A^n$.

In a manner analogous to the proof of Theorem 2, a series of claims can now be proved showing that the above construction succeeds.

The next two corollaries follow immediately.

Corollary 3.3 *$EXP_{tt}^{NP} \not\subseteq P_{tt}^{NP}/n^c$ for any fixed integer c.*

Corollary 3.4 *$E_{tt}^{NP} \not\subseteq DTIME_{tt}(2^{cn}, NP)/dn$, for fixed constants c and d.*

Of course the major open problems concern $P/poly$ and ask whether $EXP \subseteq P/poly$ and $NEXP \subseteq P/poly$ (or even $NEXP \subseteq NP/poly$). These results will require techniques which do not relativize. Such techniques are now available and the lack of "structural" results which have followed from these techniques has so far been disappointing. (One exception being [BFNW91].) A major challenge is to use these new methods to tell us about properties of complexity classes and hard sets for those classes. Problems such as those discussed here might be reasonable ones on which to try to apply these new methods.

We thanks Jack Lutz for referring us to his previous work and pointing out the relationships to the results in Section 2.

References

[BDG88] J. Balcázar, J. Díaz, and J. Gabarró. *Structural Complexity*, volume I. Springer-Verlag, New York, 1988.

[BDG90] J. Balcázar, J. Díaz, and J. Gabarró. *Structural Complexity*, volume II. Springer-Verlag, New York, 1990.

[BFNW91] L. Babai, L. Fortnow, N. Nisan, and A. Wigderson. BPP has subexponential time simulations unless EXPTIME has publishable proofs. In *Proc. 6th IEEE Structure in Complexity Theory*, pages 213–219, 1991.

[BH92] H. Buhrman and S. Homer. Superpolynomial circuits, almost sparse oracles and the exponential hierarchy. In *Proc. of the Conf. on Foundations of Software Technology and Theoretical Computer Science*, 1992.

[DT90] J. Díaz and J. Torán. Classes of bounded nondeterminism. *Math. Systems Theory*, 23:21–32, 1990.

[Fu93] B. Fu. With quasi-linear queries, EXP is not polynomial time Turing reducible to sparse sets. In *Proc. IEEE Structure in Complexity Theory*, pages 185–191, 1993.

[GW91] R. Gavaldà and O. Watanabe. On the computational complexity of small descriptions. In *Proc. 6th IEEE Structure in Complexity Theory*, pages 89-101, 1991.

[Hem87] L. Hemachandra. Counting in structural complexity theory. Ph.D. Thesis, Cornell University, 1987.

[Hart83] J. Hartmanis. Generalized Kolmogorov complexity and the structure of feasible computations. In *Proc.24th Annual FOCS Conference*, pages 439–445, 1983.

[Kan82] R. Kannan. Circuit-size lower bounds and non-reducibility to sparse sets. *Information and Control*, 55:40–46, 1982.

[KF80] C. M. R. Kintala and P. C. Fischer. Refining nondeterminism in relativized polynomial-time bounded computations. *SIAM Journal on Computing*, 9:46–53, 1980.

[KL80] R. Karp and R. Lipton. Some connections between nonuniform and uniform complexity classes. In *Proc. 12th ACM Symposium on Theory of Computing*, pages 302–309, 1980.

[L92] J. H. Lutz. Almost everywhere high nonuniform complexity. *Journal of Computer and System Sciences*, pages 220-258, 1992.

[L92a] J. H. Lutz. One-way functions and balanced NP. Unpublished manuscript.

[LM93] J. H. Lutz and E. Mayordomo. Measure, stochasticity, and the density of hard languages. *SIAM Journal on Computing*, to appear.

[M93] S. E. Mocas. Separating exponential time classes from polynomial time classes. Ph.D. Thesis, Northeastern University, 1993.

[PY93] C. H. Papadimitriou and M. Yannakakis. On limited nondeterminism and the complexity of the v-c dimension. In *Proc. 8th IEEE Structure in Complexity Theory*, pages 12–18, 1993.

[Sch85] U. Schöning. *Complexity and Structure*, volume 211 of *Lecture Notes in Computer Science*. Springer-Verlag, New York, 1985.

[Wil85] C. B. Wilson. Relativized circuit complexity. *Journal Computer Systems Sci.*, 31:169–181, 1985.

On a Quantitative Notion of Uniformity*

(Extended Abstract)

Susanne Kaufmann**, Martin Kummer

Institut für Logik, Komplexität und Deduktionssysteme, Universität Karlsruhe, D-76128 Karlsruhe, Germany. {srogina; kummer}@ira.uka.de

1 Introduction

Recent work on "Bounded Query Classes" in complexity theory and computability theory (see [5] for a survey) has sparked renewed interest in quantitative aspects of computability theory. A central result in this field is the Nonspeedup Theorem [1, Theorem 9], which states that if any 2^n parallel queries to a set A can be computed with n sequential queries to some oracle, then A must be recursive. More formally, for $A \subseteq \omega$ (ω is the set of all natural numbers) and fixed $n \geq 1$, let $C_n^A(x_1, \ldots, x_n) = (\chi_A(x_1), \ldots, \chi_A(x_n))$ denote the n-fold characteristic function of A. If there is an oracle $B \subseteq \omega$ such that $C_{2^n}^A$ can be computed with n sequential queries to B, then A is recursive. (The bound on the number of queries is tight, i.e., n cannot be replaced by $n+1$.) In [11] the analogous result for the n-place cardinality function $\#_n^A(x_1, \ldots, x_n) = |\{i : x_i \in A\}|$ is obtained (Cardinality Theorem).

There is also a classical result of Trakhtenbrot [18] with a similar flavor, concerning approximative computation of n distinct parallel queries to A: A set A is called (m,n)-recursive for $1 \leq m \leq n$, if there is a recursive function $f : \omega^n \to \{0,1\}^n$ (an "(m,n)-operator") such that for all pairwise distinct $x_1, \ldots, x_n$, $f(x_1, \ldots, x_n)$ and $C_n^A(x_1, \ldots, x_n)$ agree in at least m components. Trakhtenbrot's Theorem states that every (m,n)-recursive set is recursive if $m > \frac{n}{2}$. (Again, this is tight, i.e., the theorem does not hold for $m = \lfloor \frac{n}{2} \rfloor$.)

A typical point of these results is the nonuniform nature of their proofs: A set A is shown to be decidable, but no effective method for deciding A is provided. Beigel et al. [1] and Kinber [9, 10] proved that this nonuniformity is inevitable. More precisely, Kinber [10] proved that, given an index for f, there is no algorithm that computes the characteristic function (up to finitely many errors) of some set A which is (m,n)-recursive via f (if such A exists), even if $m = n-1$. Thus, the following questions naturally arise: Do there exist *two* algorithms such that for every index at least one of them is successful? In general, what is the least number k depending on m,n such that there are k algorithms and for every index at least one of them is successful? This number can also be considered in two other ways. In a probabilistic interpretation, it tells us that A can be computed from an index of an (m,n)-operator with probability $1/k$. From the point of view of descriptional complexity, it tells us that $\lceil \log_2 k \rceil$ bits

* The complete version of this paper will appear in Fundamenta Informaticae.

** Supported by the Deutsche Forschungsgemeinschaft (DFG) grant Me 672/4-2.

of additional information (to specify one of the k possibilities) are needed to compute A from an index of an (m, n)-operator.

For a unified treatment of these questions we move to the domain of infinite binary trees: It is known that each of the above theorems is equivalent to the statement that a certain natural class of recursive or r.e. trees has only recursive branches. These trees are also interesting in their own right.

Owings [15] pointed out that the Nonspeedup Theorem is equivalent to the statement that every branch of an r.e. tree of bounded width is recursive. In this version the question of uniformity amounts to asking whether there is an algorithm that computes a branch from an index of the tree. While there is no uniformity in this strong sense, we get nontrivial positive results by weakening the concept of uniformity as indicated above:

For some fixed number k we want an algorithm which, given an index of a tree, outputs a list of k programs such that at least one of them computes a branch of the tree up to finitely many errors. Now the goal is to determine the least k for which this works.

We show that, for r.e. trees of width at most n, the least possible k is $2n-1$. For trees arising from Trakhtenbrot's Theorem with parameters m, n we determine $k = n - m + 1$ as the optimal value. In addition, several other, related classes of trees will be investigated. The proofs of the upper bounds require refinements of the proofs of the original theorems. The lower bounds are shown by suitable diagonalizations using the recursion theorem. Due to space limitations all proofs have been omitted, except, for illustration, a proof sketch of the upper bound of Theorem 13.

The results of Sections 4, 5 originally appeared in [8] where additional material can be found. Very recently our results have been applied in inductive inference [4].

Notation and Definitions

The notation is standard (see e.g., the textbooks [14, 16, 17]). $\omega = \{0, 1, 2, \ldots\}$. φ_i is the i-th partial recursive function in the standard enumeration, $W_i \subseteq \omega$ is the i-th r.e. set in the standard enumeration ($W_i = dom(\varphi_i)$). For a given r.e. set A, let $\{A_s\}_{s\in\omega}$ denote a recursive enumeration of A such that $\{A_s\}_{s\in\omega}$ is a strong array, $A_s \subseteq A_{s+1}$, and $\bigcup_{s\in\omega} A_s = A$, cf. [17, II.2.7]. P_1 is the set of all partial recursive one-place functions. R_1 is the set of all total recursive one-place functions. For functions f and g let $f =^* g$ denote that f and g agree almost everywhere, i.e., $(\exists x_0)(\forall x \geq x_0)[f(x) = g(x)]$. $f \upharpoonright y$ denotes the restriction of f to arguments $x \leq y$. χ_A is the characteristic function of A. We identify A with χ_A, e.g., we write $A(x)$ instead of $\chi_A(x)$.

$\{0, 1\}^*$ is the set of finite strings of 0s and 1s. λ is the empty string. $|t|$ denotes the length of string t. For instance, $|\lambda| = 0$. For strings t_1 and t_2 we write $t_1 \preceq t_2$ if t_1 is an initial segment of t_2. Let $t(x) = b$ if $x < |t|$ and b is the $(x+1)$-th symbol of t. For $t_1, t_2 \in \{0, 1\}^n$, $t_1 =^e t_2$ means that t_1 and t_2 disagree in at most e components. The concatenation of t_1 and t_2 is denoted by t_1t_2.

A *tree* T is a subset of $\{0, 1\}^*$ which is closed under initial segments. Note that all of our trees are binary. $t \in T$ is called a *node* of T. Let $cod : \{0, 1\}^* \to \omega$

be a recursive bijection. We often identify a tree T with the set $\{cod(t) : t \in T\}$. Then we say that T is r.e. if $W_i = \{cod(t) : t \in T\}$ for some i. Such an i is called a Σ_1-*index* of T. We say that a tree T is recursive if χ_T is a recursive function, in which case i is called a Δ_0-*index* of T if $\varphi_i = \chi_T$.

$f \in \{0,1\}^\omega$ is a *branch* of T if every finite initial segment of f is a node of T. We also say that $A \subseteq \omega$ is a branch of T if χ_A is a branch of T. $[T]$ is the set of all branches of T. The degrees of branches of recursive trees were investigated intensively; see [7] as the basic reference.

The *width* $w(T)$ of a tree T is the maximum number of nodes on any level, i.e., $w(T) = \max\{|T \cap \{0,1\}^n| : n \geq 0\}$.

$B_n = \{0,1\}^{\leq n}$ is the full binary tree of depth n. A mapping $g : B_n \rightarrow T$ is an embedding of B_n into T if $(\forall t)[|t| < n \rightarrow [g(t0) \succeq g(t)0 \wedge g(t1) \succeq g(t)1]]$. $rk(T)$, the *rank* of T, is the maximal n such that B_n is embeddable into T.

For $A, B \subseteq \omega$ let $A \triangle B$ denote the symmetric difference of A and B, i.e., $A \triangle B = (A \setminus B) \cup (B \setminus A)$. For $M \subseteq 2^\omega$ let $(\triangle M) = \max\{|A \triangle B| : A, B \in M\}$. For a tree T we write $(\triangle T)$ instead of $(\triangle [T])$.

2 A Weak Notion of Uniformity

In this section we develop our notion of uniformity, provide a formal definition, and summarize our results. As a starting point consider the following search problem for a class $\mathcal{A}$ of recursive (or r.e.) trees.

Search Problem for $\mathcal{A}$
Input: A Δ_0-index (or Σ_1-index) of a tree $T \in \mathcal{A}$ with $[T] \neq \emptyset$.
Output: An index i of some branch A of T (i.e., $\varphi_i = A$).

This makes sense only if T has at least one *recursive* branch. For the classes $\mathcal{A}$ which we investigate in this paper, we have $[T] \subseteq R_1$, i.e., every branch is recursive. However, it turns out that the search problem for $\mathcal{A}$ is still *algorithmically unsolvable*, even if we allow the function φ_i to make finitely many errors (i.e., $\varphi_i =^* A$ instead of $\varphi_i = A$). Therefore we are led to the following weak version of the search problem.

Weak k-Search Problem for $\mathcal{A}$
Input: An index of a tree $T \in \mathcal{A}$ with $[T] \neq \emptyset$.
Output: A list of k indices $i_1, \ldots, i_k$ such that there is some $1 \leq j \leq k$ and some branch A of T with $\varphi_{i_j} =^* A$.

In this version one has to produce k possibilities such that at least one of them is correct up to finitely many errors. A partial recursive solution g of the Weak k-Search Problem for $\mathcal{A}$ is called a k-*selector* for $\mathcal{A}$. Our goal is to determine the least k such that there is a k-selector for $\mathcal{A}$. The following definition states all this formally.

Definition 1. Let $\mathcal{A}$ be a class of recursive [r.e.] trees. A function $g \in P_1$ is a *k-selector for $\mathcal{A}$* if, whenever i is a Δ_0-index [Σ_1-index] of $T \in \mathcal{A}$ with $[T] \neq \emptyset$, there exist $i_1, \ldots, i_k$ such that $g(i) = \langle i_1, \ldots, i_k \rangle$ and there is some $1 \leq j \leq k$, and some $A \in [T]$, with $\varphi_{i_j} =^* A$. The least k such that there is a k-selector for $\mathcal{A}$ is denoted by $sel(\mathcal{A})$. If no such k exists we write $sel(\mathcal{A}) = \infty$.

Remarks: (1) We may assume that g is total recursive: By the *s-m-n* theorem there is a total recursive function h such that $\varphi_{h(i,j)} = \varphi_{i_j}$ if $g(i) = \langle i_1, \ldots, i_k \rangle \wedge 1 \leq j \leq k$, otherwise $\varphi_{h(i,j)}$ is undefined everywhere. Therefore we may replace g by the total recursive function $g'(i) = \langle h(i,1), \ldots, h(i,k) \rangle$.

(2) Also note that we get the same notion even if we only require $g(i)$ to be an r.e. index of a finite set of size at most k which contains a correct index of a branch. We just define h such that $\varphi_{h(i,j)} = \varphi_z$ if z is the j-th element enumerated into $W_{g(i)}$; then we define g' as above. □

We now introduce the classes of trees which are central to our investigation:

Definition 2. $\mathcal{D}_n := \{T : T \text{ is a recursive tree and } (\Delta T) \leq n\}$.
$\mathcal{B}_n := \{T : T \text{ is an r.e. tree with } w(T) \leq n\}$.
$\mathcal{B}_n^r := \{T : T \text{ is a recursive tree with } w(T) \leq n\}$.
$\mathcal{E}_n := \{T : T \text{ is an r.e. tree with } rk(T) \leq n\}$.
$\mathcal{E}_n^r := \{T : T \text{ is a recursive tree with } rk(T) \leq n\}$.

Trakhtenbrot [18], Owings[15], and Kummer [11, Lemma 1] proved that $[T] \subseteq R_1$ for $T \in \mathcal{D}_n, \mathcal{B}_n, \mathcal{E}_n$, respectively. It is easy to see that $\mathcal{B}_n$ is a subclass of $\mathcal{E}_n$. $\mathcal{D}_n$ is incomparable to the other classes.

The weak search problems for $\mathcal{D}_n$, $\mathcal{B}_n$, and $\mathcal{E}_n$ turn out to be markedly different. For instance, while the weak search problems for $\mathcal{D}_n$ and $\mathcal{B}_n$ are effectively solvable, this is not the case for $\mathcal{E}_n$. Our quantitative results are summarized in the following table:

$\mathcal{A}$	$\mathcal{D}_n$	$\mathcal{B}_n$	$\mathcal{B}_n^r$	$\mathcal{E}_n$	$\mathcal{E}_n^r$
$sel(\mathcal{A})$	$\lceil \frac{n+1}{2} \rceil$	$2n-1$	n	∞	$n+1$

It follows at once that $sel(\mathcal{A}) = \infty$ if $\mathcal{A}$ is the class of all recursive trees with (ΔT) finite ($\bigcup_n \mathcal{D}_n$), the class of all recursive trees of finite width ($\bigcup_n \mathcal{B}_n^r$), or the class of all recursive trees of finite rank ($\bigcup_n \mathcal{E}_n^r$). The results concerning $\mathcal{D}_n$, $\mathcal{B}_n$, $\mathcal{E}_n$ are connected with the uniformity of Trakhtenbrot's Theorem, the Nonspeedup Theorem, and the Cardinality Theorem, respectively. We treat these classes and explain the connections in sections 3, 4, 5 below.

Remarks: (1) The fact that $sel(\mathcal{D}_0) = 1$ is well known: If a recursive tree has exactly one branch then this branch is (uniformly) recursive [17, VI.5.12].
(2) We do not consider the r.e. analogue of $\mathcal{D}_n$, because, even if an r.e. tree has a unique branch, this branch need not be recursive. Owings [15, p. 766] gave the following example: Let $T := \{t \in \{0,1\}^* : (\exists s)[t \preceq (K_s(0), \ldots, K_s(s))]\}$ where $\{K_s\}_{s \in \omega}$ is a recursive enumeration of the halting problem K. Then $[T] = \{K\}$.
(3) Note that $|[T]| \leq n$ for every $T \in \mathcal{B}_n^r$. On the other hand, it is easy to see that, for every recursive tree T with at most n branches, one can uniformly compute a

recursive tree $T' \in \mathcal{B}_n^r$ with $[T] = [T']$. Thus our results on the uniformity of $\mathcal{B}_n^r$ transfer to the class of all recursive trees with at most n branches. In particular, $sel(\mathcal{A}) = \infty$ for the class $\mathcal{A}$ of all recursive trees with finitely many branches.
(4) The result that every branch of a tree of bounded width is recursive appears implicitly already in [13, p. 525 f.] where it is credited to A. R. Meyer. It is the key to the proof that an infinite sequence $\sigma \in \{0,1\}^\omega$ is recursive if the length-conditional Kolmogorov complexity of all its initial segments is bounded by a constant. □

3 Uniformity of Trakhtenbrot's Theorem

In this section we investigate the uniformity of Trakhtenbrot's Theorem in relation to the class $\mathcal{D}_n$. Let us first introduce some further notation. For any recursive function $f : \omega^n \to \{0,1\}^n$ we call $A \subseteq \omega$ (m,n)-recursive *via* f iff for all pairwise distinct $x_1, \dots, x_n$ we have $C_n^A(x_1, \dots, x_n) =^{n-m} f(x_1, \dots, x_n)$. Let $TT_{m,n}(f)$ denote the class of all sets that are (m,n)-recursive via f.

3.1 Previous Results

We can state Trakhtenbrot's Theorem as follows:

Theorem 3. (Trakhtenbrot [18]) *Let $\frac{n}{2} < m \leq n$ and let $f : \omega^n \to \{0,1\}^n$ be a recursive function. Then every set in $TT_{m,n}(f)$ is recursive.*

A more easily accessible reference for the proof of Theorem 3 is [6, Section 1]. A proof also falls out of Theorem 7 and Lemma 6 below. Theorem 3 also follows directly from Lemma 6 and the fact that every recursive tree with only countably many branches (but at least one) has a recursive branch [14, V.5.27] (see also the Tree Lemma of Owings in [15]).
The question of uniformity for Theorem 3 leads to the following weak search problem (for fixed k, m, n with $\frac{n}{2} < m \leq n$).

Weak k-Uniformity Problem for Trakhtenbrot's Theorem with Parameters m, n
Input: An index of $f : \omega^n \to \{0,1\}^n$ with $TT_{m,n}(f) \neq \emptyset$.
Output: A list of k indices $i_1, \dots, i_k$ such that $\varphi_{i_j} =^* A$ for some $1 \leq j \leq k$ and some $A \in TT_{m,n}(f)$.

This problem is uniformly equivalent to a weak search problem for a suitable class of recursive trees which we now define (cf. [6, p. 683], [18]). It consists of all finite initial segments that are consistent with the (m,n)-operator f.

Definition 4. For any recursive function $f : \omega^n \to \{0,1\}^n$ and $m \leq n$ let $T_{m,n}(f) := \{t \in \{0,1\}^* : (\forall x_1 < \dots < x_n < |t|)[(t(x_1), \dots, t(x_n)) =^{n-m} f(x_1, \dots, x_n)]\}$. $T_{m,n}(f)$ is called an *(m,n)-recursive tree* (via f). Let $\mathcal{A}_{m,n}$ denote the class of all (m,n)-recursive trees.

Note that the branches of $T_{m,n}(f)$ are exactly the sets which are (m,n)-recursive via f, i.e., $[T_{m,n}(f)] = TT_{m,n}(f)$. From m,n and an index of $f : \omega^n \to \{0,1\}^n$ we can uniformly compute a Δ_0-index of $T_{m,n}(f)$. Conversely, from m,n and a Δ_0-index of $T_{m,n}(f)$ we can compute an index of $g : \omega^n \to \{0,1\}^n$ such that $T_{m,n}(g) = T_{m,n}(f)$. (Define g by induction on k for all n-tuples $x_1 < \cdots < x_n$ with $x_n = k$.) Therefore, the Weak k-Uniformity Problem for Trakhtenbrot's Theorem with Parameters m,n is uniformly equivalent to the Weak k-Search Problem for $\mathcal{A}_{m,n}$.
Kinber proved the first lower bound on $sel(\mathcal{A}_{m,n})$. His result can be restated as follows:

Theorem 5. (Kinber [9, 10]) *$sel(\mathcal{A}_{m,n}) > 1$ for $\frac{n}{2} < m < n$.*

The connection between $\mathcal{A}_{m,n}$ and $\mathcal{D}_n$ is given by the following observation of Trakhtenbrot, which is essential for his proof of Theorem 3.

Lemma 6. (Trakhtenbrot [18]) *$\mathcal{A}_{m,n} \subseteq \mathcal{D}_{2(n-m)}$ for $\frac{n}{2} < m \leq n$.*

Remarks: (1) By an argument in [6, p. 683], we also have $\mathcal{A}_{m,n} \subseteq \mathcal{E}^r_{n-1}$, for $\frac{n}{2} < m \leq n$.
(2) Fix m,n,k with $\frac{n}{2} < m < n$ and $k \geq 1$. It follows from Kinber's result that there is no k-selector g for $\mathcal{A}_{m,n}$ which, given an infinite tree $T \in \mathcal{A}_{m,n}$, produces at least one index i_j such that $\varphi_{i_j} \in [T]$: Otherwise, there would be a 1-selector for $\mathcal{A}_{m,n}$ which first computes $g(i) = \langle i_1, \ldots, i_k\rangle$ and then outputs an index of the following function f_i:

$f_i(x)$: Search for $1 \leq j \leq k$ with $\varphi_{i_j}(z)\downarrow$ for all $z \leq x+1$ and $\varphi_{i_j} \restriction (x+1) \in T$. Then let $f_i(x) := \varphi_{i_j}(x)$.

Note that for sufficiently large x we have $\varphi_{i_j} \restriction (x+1) \in T$ only if φ_{i_j} is a branch of T. By Lemma 6, all branches of T which are equal to φ_{i_j} for some $1 \leq j \leq k$ agree from some point on. Hence f_i makes only finitely many errors and gives us a 1-selector. By a similar argument, there can be no k-selector g and a fixed error bound $e \in \omega$ such that one of the φ_{i_j} computes a branch up to e errors.

This shows that it would have been too restrictive not to allow a finite (and unbounded) number of errors in the definition of a k-selector. □

3.2 Main Results

The next result gives the exact value of $sel(\mathcal{A}_{m,n})$:

Theorem 7. *$sel(\mathcal{A}_{m,n}) = n - m + 1$ for $\frac{n}{2} < m \leq n$.*

We shall organize the proof of this theorem in such a way that we get in addition the exact value of $sel(\mathcal{D}_n)$:

Theorem 8. *$sel(\mathcal{D}_n) = \lceil \frac{n+1}{2} \rceil$ for $n \geq 0$.*

With Lemma 6 the plan for the proofs of Theorems 7, 8 is clear:

We first show the upper bound $sel(\mathcal{D}_n) \leq \lceil \frac{n+1}{2} \rceil$. Then, using Lemma 6, we get the upper bound of Theorem 7: $sel(\mathcal{A}_{m,n}) \leq sel(\mathcal{D}_{2(n-m)}) \leq n-m+1$.

Second, we show the lower bound $sel(\mathcal{A}_{m,n}) \geq n-m+1$. Then, by Lemma 6, we get the lower bound of Theorem 8: $k+1 \leq sel(\mathcal{A}_{k+1,2k+1}) \leq sel(\mathcal{D}_{2k}) \leq sel(\mathcal{D}_{2k+1})$.

3.3 Total Selectors

We would now like to point out a direct proof for $sel(\mathcal{A}_{m,n}) \leq n-m+1$ which yields a stronger result and provides new insights into the structure of trees that arise from Trakhtenbrot's Theorem.

To this end let $sel_t(\mathcal{A})$ be the least number k for which there is a k-selector for $\mathcal{A}$ such that at least one of the indices which it produces on input $T \in \mathcal{A}$ computes a branch of T almost everywhere *and computes a total function.* Clearly, $sel_t(\mathcal{A}) \geq sel(\mathcal{A})$. The next result shows that the bound in Theorem 7 also holds for total selectors. An analogous result holds for the tree classes $\mathcal{B}_n, \mathcal{B}_n^r, \mathcal{E}_n, \mathcal{E}_n^r$ which we consider in the next sections.

Theorem 9. *$sel_t(\mathcal{A}_{m,n}) = n-m+1$ for $\frac{n}{2} < m \leq n$.*

The lower bound follows from Theorem 7. For the upper bound we need the following combinatorial notion.

Definition 10. A tree T has *dimension* d_0 ($dim(T) = d_0$) if d_0 is the maximal number d such that there exist $x_1 < \cdots < x_d$ with $(\forall v \in \{0,1\}^d)(\exists A \in [T])[v = C_d^A(x_1, \ldots, x_d)]$. If d_0 does not exist then $dim(T) := \infty$.

Remark: In more technical terms $dim(T)$ is the *Vapnik-Chervonenkis dimension* of the concept class $[T] \subseteq 2^\omega$. See [3] for more information on this notion; in [2, Section 2], [12, Theorem 6, Proposition 7] further recursion theoretic applications are given. □

Note that for every $T \in \mathcal{A}_{m,n}$ we have $dim(T) \leq n-m$: If $dim(T) > n-m$ then choose $x_1 < \cdots < x_{n-m+1}$ witnessing this fact. Suppose that T is an (m,n)-recursive tree via f. Let $(b_1, \ldots, b_n) = f(x_1, \ldots, x_{n-m+1}, x_{n-m+1}+1, x_{n-m+1}+m-1)$. Now we can choose a branch A of T such that $1 - A(x_i) = b_i$ for $1 \leq i \leq n-m+1$. But this means that A is not (m,n)-recursive via f, a contradiction.

The next lemma shows how the knowledge of the dimension of T can help to compute a branch of T.

Lemma 11. *Let T be an infinite recursive tree with $dim(T) = d$ and (ΔT) finite. Then, uniformly in a Δ_0-index of T, there is $f \leq_* K$ such that $f =^* A$ for some $A \in [T]$, and in addition f is* total.

The totality of the selector function is not guaranteed by the proof of the upper bound of Theorem 8, in which the correct f'_a may be undefined at two places. We close this section by showing that non-totality is essential for the upper bound $sel(\mathcal{D}_n) \leq \lceil \frac{n+1}{2} \rceil$: By the next result, $sel_t(\mathcal{D}_n)$ is twice as large as $sel(\mathcal{D}_n)$.

Theorem 12. *$sel_t(\mathcal{D}_n) = n + 1$ for $n \geq 0$.*

4 Uniformity of the Nonspeedup Theorem - Trees of Bounded Width

In this section we present optimal bounds for trees of bounded width. The main results are:

Theorem 13. *$sel(\mathcal{B}_n) = 2n - 1$ for $n \geq 1$.*

Theorem 14. *$sel(\mathcal{B}^r_n) = n$ for $n \geq 1$.*

Proof sketch of the upper bound $sel(\mathcal{B}_n) \leq 2n - 1$:
We proceed in two steps. First, we will show that $sel(\mathcal{B}_n) \leq \frac{n(n+1)}{2}$; this will just be a uniform version of a proof of Owings in [15, p. 764]. Second, we will take a closer look at the selector that we have found and define a refined version which, somewhat surprisingly, reduces the quadratic bound to a linear bound and gives us $sel(\mathcal{B}_n) \leq 2n - 1$.

(1) $sel(\mathcal{B}_n) \leq \frac{n(n+1)}{2}$:
For a tree $T \in \mathcal{B}_n$ let $L(T, k) := T \cap \{0,1\}^k$ (the k-th level of T), $a_0 := \|[T]\|$, and define the *supremal width* as $b_0 := \max\{l : (\exists^\infty k)[|L(T,k)| = l]\}$. We assume that $a_0 > 0$. Clearly, $a_0 \leq b_0 \leq n$. We prove that there is a uniform procedure f_{a_0,b_0} which, given a_0, b_0, and a Σ_1-index of T, computes a branch of T up to finitely many errors. Since there are $\frac{n(n+1)}{2}$ possible pairs (a_0, b_0) this gives us an $\frac{n(n+1)}{2}$-selector for $\mathcal{B}_n$.

(2) $sel(\mathcal{B}_n) \leq 2n - 1$: The idea is to "amalgamate" several $f_{a,b}$-functions into one function. If $(a, b) \neq (a_0, b_0)$ but $dom(f_{a,b})$ is finite then $f_{a,b}$ does not hurt in the amalgamation. Therefore we have to consider when $dom(f_{a,b})$ is finite.

Claim: If $(a_0, b_0) \in \{(a, b), (a + 2c, b + c)\}$ for some $a, b, c > 0$ then exactly one of $dom(f_{a,b})$ and $dom(f_{a+2c,b+c})$ is infinite.

By the Claim, we are led to define $2n-1$ functions $g_{a,b}$, for $a = 1, 2$ and $a \leq b \leq n$, as follows:

$g_{a,b}(x)$: Dovetail the computations of $f_{a,b}(x), f_{a+2,b+1}(x), \ldots, f_{a+2c,b+c}(x)$, where c is maximal with $a + 2c \leq b + c$. As soon as a converging computation with output y appears, let $g_{a,b}(x) := y$.

5 Uniformity of the Cardinality Theorem - Trees of Bounded Rank

In this section we prove optimal bounds for trees of bounded rank and discuss the connection with the uniformity of the Cardinality Theorem.

Theorem 15. *$sel(\mathcal{E}_1) = \infty$.*

Theorem 16. *$sel(\mathcal{E}_n^r) = n + 1$ for $n \geq 0$.*

The trees that arise in the Cardinality Theorem (CT) are a proper subclass of the r.e. trees of bounded rank. CT can be stated as follows [11]:

Let $A \subseteq \omega$ and $n \geq 1$. If there is a recursive function $g : \omega^n \to \omega$ such that for every $x_1 < \cdots < x_n$, (1) $W_{g(x_1,\ldots,x_n)} \subset \{0, 1, \ldots, n\}$ (note that it is a proper inclusion), (2) $\#_n^A(x_1, \ldots, x_n) \in W_{g(x_1,\ldots,x_n)}$, then A is recursive.

For a given g as above we can define a uniformly r.e. tree T_g such that the branches of T_g are just the sets A which satisfy conditions (1), (2):

$T_g = \{t \in \{0,1\}^* : (\forall x_1 < \cdots < x_n)[x_n < |t| \to \sum_{i=1}^n t(x_i) \in W_{g(x_1,\ldots,x_n)}]\}$.

We say that T_g arises from CT with parameter n. Let $\mathcal{C}_n$ denote the class of all trees that arise from CT with parameter n. CT is proved by showing that the trees in $\mathcal{C}_n$ have bounded rank. However, there are trees of bounded rank which do not belong to any $\mathcal{C}_n$.

The class $\mathcal{C}_2$ is studied in greater detail in [8, 15]. It is shown in [8] that $\mathcal{E}_1 \not\subseteq \mathcal{C}_2 \subset \mathcal{E}_2$, and that, in contrast to Theorem 15, $sel(\mathcal{C}_2)$ is finite (in fact, $sel(\mathcal{C}_2) \leq 6$). It is not known whether $sel(\mathcal{C}_n)$ is finite for all n.

From Theorem 16 we can derive a positive result for the uniformity of a weak version of CT (proved in [15]), in which $W_{g(x_1,\ldots,x_n)}$ is replaced by $D_{g(x_1,\ldots,x_n)}$ (D_i is the i-th finite set in a canonical enumeration of all finite sets):

Let $\mathcal{C}_n^r$ denote the class of all recursive trees arising from this version of CT with parameter n. It is shown in [11] that the rank of every tree in $\mathcal{C}_n$ is bounded by $4^n - 2$. In particular, $\mathcal{C}_n^r \subseteq \mathcal{E}_{4^n-2}^r$. Thus, by Theorem 16, we get $sel(\mathcal{C}_n^r) \leq 4^n - 1$.

6 Conclusion

We have introduced a new notion of uniformity to investigate the problem of how to compute a branch of a tree. We have obtained precise quantitative descriptions of the borderline between uniformity and nonuniformity for several interesting classes of trees.

Furthermore, we were able to apply these findings to central results of quantitative computability theory such as Trakhtenbrot's Theorem and the Non-speedup Theorem.

In this paper we have studied our quantitative notion of uniformity in a domain which in itself had a quantitative structure, namely classes of trees parameterized by natural numbers. It would be interesting to study this notion in other areas as well.

Acknowledgements: We would like to thank Bill Gasarch, Georgia Martin, and Frank Stephan for helpful comments. We are particularly indebted to Georgia Martin for proofreading and an extensive revision of our prose.

References

1. R. Beigel, W. I. Gasarch, J. Gill, J. C. Owings, Jr. Terse, superterse, and verbose sets. *Information and Computation*, 103:68–85, 1993.
2. R. Beigel, M. Kummer, F. Stephan. Quantifying the amount of verboseness. To appear in: Information and Computation. (A preliminary version appeared in: Lecture Notes in Computer Science, Vol. 620, pp. 21–32, 1992.)
3. A. Blumer, A. Ehrenfeucht, D. Haussler, M. K. Warmuth. Learnability and the Vapnik-Chervonenkis dimension. *Journal of the ACM*, 36:929–966, 1989.
4. J. Case, S. Kaufmann, E. Kinber, M. Kummer. Learning recursive functions from approximations. In: *Proceedings of EuroCOLT'95*. LNCS 904, 140–153, Springer-Verlag, 1995.
5. W. I. Gasarch. Bounded queries in recursion theory: a survey. In *Proceedings of the Sixth Annual Structure in Complexity Theory Conference*. IEEE Computer Society Press, 62–78, 1991.
6. V. Harizanov, M. Kummer, J. C. Owings, Jr. Frequency computation and the cardinality theorem. *J. Symb. Log.*, 57:677–681, 1992.
7. C. G. Jockusch, R. I. Soare. Π_1^0 classes and degrees of theories. *Trans. Amer. Math. Soc.*, 173, 33–56, 1972.
8. S. Kaufmann. *Uniformität bei rekursiv aufzählbaren Bäumen*. Diplomarbeit, Fakultät für Informatik, Universität Karlsruhe, 1991.
9. E. B. Kinber. On frequency calculations of general recursive predicates. *Sov. Math. Dokl.*, 13:873–876, 1972.
10. E. B. Kinber. *Frequency-computable functions and frequency-enumerable sets*. Candidate Dissertation, Riga, 1975. (in Russian)
11. M. Kummer. A proof of Beigel's cardinality conjecture. *J. Symb. Log.*, 57:682–687, 1992.
12. M. Kummer, F. Stephan. Recursion theoretic properties of frequency computation and bounded queries. To appear in: Information and Computation. (A preliminary version appeared in: Lecture Notes in Computer Science, Vol. 713, pp. 243–254, 1993.)
13. D. W. Loveland. A variant of the Kolmogorov concept of complexity. In: *Information and Control*, 15:510–526, 1993.
14. P. Odifreddi. *Classical Recursion Theory*. North-Holland, Amsterdam, 1989.
15. J. C. Owings. A cardinality version of Beigel's nonspeedup theorem. *J. Symb. Log.*, 54:761–767, 1989.
16. J. S. Royer, J. Case. *Subrecursive Programming Systems: Complexity and Succinctness*. Birkhäuser-Verlag, Boston, 1994.
17. R. I. Soare. *Recursively Enumerable Sets and Degrees*. Springer-Verlag, Berlin, 1987.
18. B. A. Trakhtenbrot. On frequency computation of functions. *Algebra i Logika*, 2:25–32, 1963. (in Russian)

Separations by Random Oracles and "Almost" Classes for Generalized Reducibilities

(Extended Abstract)

Wolfgang Merkle and Yongge Wang *

Mathematisches Institut der Universität Heidelberg
Heidelberg, Germany **

Abstract. Given two binary relations $\leq_r$ and $\leq_s$ on 2^ω which are closed under finite variation (of their set arguments) and a set X chosen randomly by independent tosses of a fair coin, one might ask for the probability that the lower cones $\{A \subseteq \omega : A \leq_r X\}$ and $\{A \subseteq \omega : A \leq_s X\}$ w.r.t. $\leq_r$ and $\leq_s$ are different. By closure under finite variation, the Kolmogorov 0-1 Law yields immediately that this probability is either 0 or 1; in the case it is 1, the relations are said to be separable by random oracles. Again by closure under finite variation, the probability that a randomly chosen set X is in the upper cone of a fixed set A w.r.t. $\leq_r$ is either 0 or 1. $Almost_r$ is the class of sets for which the upper cone w.r.t. $\leq_r$ has measure 1.
In the following, results about separations by random oracles and about Almost classes are obtained in the context of generalized reducibilities, that is, for binary relations on 2^ω which can be defined by a countable set of total continuous functionals on 2^ω in the same way as the usual resource bounded reducibilities are defined by an enumeration of appropriate oracle Turing machines. The concept generalized reducibility comprises all natural resource bounded reducibilities, but is more general; in particular, it does not involve any kind of specific machine model or even effectivity. From the results for generalized reducibilities, one obtains corollaries about specific resource bounded reducibilities, including several results which have been shown previously in the setting of time or space bounded Turing machine computations.

1 Introduction

1.1 Introduction and Overview

Given two binary relations $\leq_r$ and $\leq_s$ on 2^ω which are closed under finite variation (of their set arguments) and a set X chosen randomly by independent

* Both authors were partially supported by the EU network *Complexity, Logic and Recursion Theory (COLORET)*, EU Contract No. ERBCHRXCT930415.

** Universität Heidelberg, Mathematisches Institut, Im Neuenheimer Feld 294, 69120 Heidelberg, Germany; e-mail adresses:{merkle | wang}.math.uni-heidelberg.de

tosses of a fair coin, one might ask for the probability that the lower cones $\{A \subseteq \omega : A \leq_r X\}$ and $\{A \subseteq \omega : A \leq_s X\}$ w.r.t. $\leq_r$ and $\leq_s$ are different. By closure under finite variation, the Kolmogorov 0-1 Law yields immediately that this probability is either 0 or 1; in the case it is 1, the relations are said to be separable by random oracles. Again by closure under finite variation, the probability that a randomly chosen set X is in the upper cone of a fixed set A w.r.t. $\leq_r$ is either 0 or 1. $Almost_r$ is the class of sets for which the upper cone w.r.t. $\leq_r$ has measure 1.

It is known that separations by random oracles are possible for the relations $\leq_T^{log}$ vs $\leq_T^p$ and for $\leq^{PSPACE}$ vs $\leq_T^E$ ([BG81]). The same holds for $\leq_{k-tt}^p$ vs $\leq_{(k+1)-tt}^p$ for all $k \geq 0$ ([BT91]), and in [BLM94] it was implicitly shown that this result remains true if one replaces the former reducibility $\leq_{k-tt}^p$ by $\leq_{k-tt}$. Results about Almost classes include $Almost_m^p = Almost_{btt}^p = Almost_{(\log n)-T}^p = P$ ([Am86a], [Am86b], [BT91]) and $Almost_{tt}^p = Almost_T^p = BPP$ ([BG81]).

In the following, results about separations by random oracles and about Almost classes are obtained in the context of generalized reducibilities, that is, for binary relations on 2^ω which can be defined by a countable set of total continuous functionals on 2^ω in the same way as the usual resource bounded reducibilities are defined by an enumeration of appropriate oracle Turing machines. The concept generalized reducibility comprises all natural resource bounded reducibilities, but is more general; in particular, it does not involve any kind of specific machine model or even effectivity.

From the results on generalized reducibilities, one then obtains corollaries about specific resource bounded reducibilities. The corollaries include *all* the results mentioned above. One obtains further, that for most of the generalized reducibilities that can be found in the literature, reducibilities of $k-tt$-type can be separated by random oracles from any reducibility of btt-type which is *not* of $k-tt$-type itself. In addition, for a wide class of reducibilities random separations are possible for reducibilities of btt-type vs reducibilities of truth-table or Turing-type, and the same holds for truth-table vs Turing type. Note that the latter result cannot hold for all pairs of resource bounded reducibilities of truth-table, resp. of Turing type, as for example in the case of reductions restricted to elementary time the corresponding reducibility notions are the same. Concerning Almost classes, it is shown that for *all* generalized reducibilities of btt-type which are closed under finite variation, the class $Almost_r$ is equal to $\mathcal{L}_r := \{A \subseteq \omega : A \leq_r B \text{ for all } B \subseteq \omega\}$, and that $Almost_{(lin)-T}^E = E$ and $Almost_{(poly)-T}^{E_2} = E_2$.

1.2 Notation

For notation not explained here or below in the text, see [BDG] and [Od89]. The set $\omega = \{0,1,\ldots\}$ of natural numbers will be identified with the set $\{0,1\}^* = \{\lambda, 0, 1, 00, \ldots\}$ of finite binary strings via the uniquely determined order isomorphism which takes the standard ordering $\leq$ on ω to the length-lexicographical ordering on $\{0,1\}^*$. Subsets of ω are identified with their characteristic functions and 2^ω denotes the powerset of ω. The set of all functions from ω to ω is denoted by ω^ω. Note that unless explicitely attributed as being partial, all functions and functionals are meant to be total.

Lower-case greek letters $\alpha, \beta, \gamma, \ldots$ denote partial characteristic functions, that is (total) functions from some set $I \subseteq \omega$ to $\{0,1\}$; the domain of a partial characteristic function α is denoted by $dom(\alpha)$; thereby for example $dom(\alpha) = \omega$ iff α is a set. If identified with their graphs, partial characteristic functions become partially ordered by set theoretical inclusion, that is $\alpha \subseteq \beta$ iff $dom(\alpha) \subseteq dom(\beta)$ and $\alpha(x) = \beta(x)$ for all $x \in dom(\alpha)$. Likewise, for partial characteristic functions α and β which are compatible, that is, which agree on the intersection of their domains, $\alpha \cup \beta$ is the partial characteristic function with domain $dom(\alpha) \cup dom(\beta)$ which agrees with α and β on their respective domains. For sets $A, I \subseteq \omega$, $A \mid I$ denotes the uniquely determined partial characteristic function α, such that $dom(\alpha) = I$ and $\alpha \subseteq A$. The α-patch $\langle A, \alpha \rangle \subseteq \omega$ of a set A w.r.t. a partial characteristic function α is the unique set which agrees with the partial characteristic function α on arguments in $dom(\alpha)$ and agrees with the set $A \subseteq \omega$ otherwise.

Upper-case greek letters $\Gamma, \Delta, \ldots$ denote functionals, that is functions from 2^ω to 2^ω. Given a functional Γ and a partial characteristic function α, Γ_α denotes the functional defined by $\Gamma_\alpha(A) := \Gamma(\langle A, \alpha \rangle)$.

A set $A \subseteq \omega$ is a finite variation of a set $B \subseteq \omega$, written $A =^* B$, iff A and B differ at most at finitely many places. An n-ary relation $\mathcal{P}$ on 2^ω is closed under finite variations (c.f.v.) iff for all $A_1, A_1', \ldots A_n, A_n' \in 2^\omega$ where $A_i =^* A_i'$ for all $i \in \{1, \ldots, n\}$, $\mathcal{P}(A_1, \ldots, A_n)$ iff $\mathcal{P}(A_1', \ldots, A_n')$. A binary relation $\leq_r$ on 2^ω is upwards c.f.v. iff for all $A \subseteq \omega$ and all $B_0, B_1 \subseteq \omega$ where $B_0 =^* B_1$, $A \leq_r B_0$ iff $A \leq_r B_1$. Note that a reflexive and transitive relation $\leq_r$ is c.f.v. iff it is upwards c.f.v.

The measure on 2^ω obtained by independent tosses of a fair coin, that is the product measure of the uniform distribution on $\{0,1\}$, is denoted by μ. Conditional measures are written as $\mu(. \mid .)$. In case the abbreviation is not ambiguous, $\mu(\{A \subseteq \omega : \mathcal{P}(A)\})$ is shortened to $\mu(\mathcal{P}(A))$, and likewise for conditional measures. The lower cone $\leq_r (B)$ of a set $B \subseteq \omega$ w.r.t. a binary relation $\leq_r$ on 2^ω is the class $\{A \subseteq \omega : A \leq_r B\}$.

2 Separations

2.1 Generalized Use and Reductions

In the following, the term functional denotes a (total) function from 2^ω to 2^ω. Equivalently, via the equation $\Gamma(A, x) := (\Gamma(A))(x)$, a functional Γ can be viewed as a function from $2^\omega \otimes \omega$ to the set $\{0,1\}$.

Definition 1. A functional Γ is *continuous* iff for all sets $A \in 2^\omega$ and all $x \in \omega$, there is some finite set $I(A, x) \subseteq \omega$, such that for all sets $B \in 2^\omega$ $A \mid I(A, x) = B \mid I(A, x)$ implies $\Gamma(A, x) = \Gamma(B, x)$.

The point of Definition 1 is that for a continuous functional the value $\Gamma(A,x)$ is determined by x and a finite part of the set argument A. Note that a functional is continuous in the sense of Definition 1 iff it is a continuous mapping in the usual topological sense w.r.t. the standard topology on 2^ω.

Proposition 2. *Let Γ be a continuous functional and let $x \in \omega$. Then there is a finite set $I(x) \subseteq \omega$ which satisfies*

$$A \mid I(x) = B \mid I(x) \Rightarrow \Gamma(A,x) = \Gamma(B,x) \quad \text{for all } A, B \in 2^\omega \ , \qquad (1)$$

such that $I(x)$ is minimal w.r.t. set theoretical inclusion among all subsets of ω satisfying (1). (The (uniquely determined) set $I(x)$ is called generalized use of Γ at place x and is denoted by $u(\Gamma, x)$.)

Proof. Let Γ be a continuous functional and let $x \in \omega$. First note that the existence of a finite set $I(x)$ that satisfies (1) amounts to the fact that $\Gamma(A,x)$ can be characterized by a truth table condition on A; that this is the case follows due to compactness of 2^ω by the same argument as in the "effective case" of a (total) recursive functional Γ (see for example [Od89], p.269).

Thus in order to prove Proposition 2, it is sufficient to show that the sets $I(x)$ satisfying (1) are closed under meet. Now let I_0, I_1 be two such sets and let the sets $A, B \in 2^\omega$ agree on $I_0 \cap I_1$. Then there is some set $C \in 2^\omega$ which agrees with A on I_0 and with B on I_1. By totatility of Γ, $\Gamma(.,x)$ is defined on the sets A, B, and C, and $\Gamma(C,x)$ is equal to $\Gamma(A,x)$, by assumption on I_0, and is equal to $\Gamma(B,x)$, by assumption on I_1, that is, $\Gamma(A,x) = \Gamma(B,x)$. □

Definition 3. Let $\leq_r$ be a binary relation on 2^ω.

1. A functional Γ is a reduction iff it is continuous. A reduction Γ is a reduction w.r.t. $\leq_r$ or a $\leq_r$ - reduction, for short, iff $\Gamma(B) \leq_r B$ holds for all sets $B \subseteq \omega$. For $A, B \subseteq \omega$, a fact $A \leq_r B$ is witnessed by the functional Γ, $A \leq_r B$ via Γ for short, iff Γ is a $\leq_r$ - reduction and $A = \Gamma(B)$.
2. A set $\mathcal{R}$ of functionals is a reduction cover for $\leq_r$ iff $\mathcal{R}$ is a countable set of $\leq_r$ - reductions, such that when $A \leq_r B$ holds for sets $A, B \subseteq \omega$, then this fact is witnessed by some $\Gamma \in \mathcal{R}$.
3. The relation $\leq_r$ is a generalized reducibility (on 2^ω) iff there is some reduction cover for $\leq_r$.

The usual time or space bounded reducibilities such as $\leq_T^p$ or $\leq_m^{log}$ are generalized reducibilities which have a reduction cover of the special form $\{\Phi_e : e \in E\}$ where $E \subseteq \omega$ is recursive. (Recall that Φ_e is the partial functional computed by the e-th oracle Turing machine and note that the definition of reduction cover implies that Φ_e is total for all $e \in E$). Such reducibilities were called bounded reducibilities in [BLW94]. An example of a generalized reducibility which is not a bounded reducibility is given by truth-table reducibility $\leq_{tt}$: by compactness of 2^ω (see the proof of Proposition 2) the set of all (total) recursive functionals provides a reduction cover for $\leq_{tt}$, but it can be shown that there is no reduction cover for $\leq_{tt}$ which has the form $\{\Phi_e : e \in E\}$ for recursive E.

Definition 4. Let $\leq_r$ be a binary relation on 2^ω.

1. Let f be a function from ω to ω. A reduction Γ is f(x) use bounded iff $| u(\Gamma, x) | \leq f(x)$ holds for all $x \in \omega$. For $k \in \omega$, Γ is k use bounded iff Γ is $\lambda x.k$ use bounded.
2. Let $\mathcal{F}$ be a class of functions from ω to ω. The relation $\leq_r$ is of $\mathcal{F}$-tt-type iff there is some reduction cover E of $\leq_r$, such that every Δ in E is $f(x)$ use bounded for some $f \in \mathcal{F}$.
3. For $k \in \omega$, the relation $\leq_r$ is of k-tt-type iff it is of $\{\lambda x.k\}$-tt-type. The relation $\leq_r$ is of *btt*-type iff it is of $\{\lambda x.k : k \in \omega\}$-tt-type.

2.2 Probability Amplification and the Kolmogorov 0-1 Law

The follwing lemma contains two useful properties of the measure μ: the first will be refered to as probability amplification (by finite patching), the second is a special case of the Kolmogorov 0-1 law.

Lemma 5. *Let the set $\mathcal{S} \subseteq 2^\omega$ be measurable.*

1. *If $\mu(A \in \mathcal{S}) > 0$, then for any rational $\delta < 1$ there is some partial characteristic function α with finite domain, such that $\mu(A \in \mathcal{S} \mid \alpha \subseteq A) \geq \delta$.*
2. *If $\mathcal{S}$ is c.f.v., then either $\mu(A \in \mathcal{S}) = 0$ or $\mu(A \in \mathcal{S}) = 1$.*

In applications of the first claim, the equation $\mu(\Gamma(A) = \Delta(A) \mid \alpha \subseteq A) = \mu(\Gamma_\alpha(A) = \Delta_\alpha(A))$ will be used. Note that for reductions Γ and Δ classes $\mathcal{S}$ of the form $\{A \subseteq \omega : \Gamma(A, x) \neq \Delta(A, x)\}$ or $\{A \subseteq \omega : \Gamma(A) \neq \Delta(A)\}$ are always measurable, and the same holds for classes such as $\{A \subseteq \omega : \leq_s(A) \neq \leq_r(A)\}$, where $\leq_s$ and $\leq_r$ are generalized reducibilities.

Sketch of Proof. Note that the first property implies the second, because if $\mathcal{S}$ is measurable and c.f.v., then $\mu(A \in \mathcal{S} \mid \alpha \subseteq A)$ exists and must be the same for all partial characteristic functions α with identical finite domain, and consequently one cannot only amplify the conditional measure of $\mathcal{S}$, but also the measure itself. The first property follows from the fact, that by definition for any measurable set $\mathcal{S}$ and any real $\varepsilon > 0$ there are partial characteristic functions α_i, $i \in \omega$, and corresponding sets $\mathcal{O}_i = \{B \subseteq \omega : \alpha_i \subseteq B\} \subseteq 2^\omega$ such that firstly, $\mathcal{S}$ is contained in the union $\mathcal{O}$ of the sets $\mathcal{O}_i$, and secondly, the measure of $\mathcal{S}$ and $\mathcal{O}$ differs at most by ε. Now, for given $\delta < 1$, one can choose ε so small, that $\mu(\mathcal{S}) \geq \mu(\mathcal{O}) \cdot \delta$. But then there must be some α_i, such that $\mu(A \in \mathcal{S} \mid \alpha_i \subseteq A) \geq \delta$; otherwise the sum of the terms $\mu(\alpha_i \subseteq A) \cdot \mu(A \in \mathcal{S} \mid \alpha_i \subseteq A)$ over all i, which is equal to $\mu(\mathcal{S})$ by $\mathcal{S}$ being contained in the union of the sets $\mathcal{O}_i$, would be strictly less than $\mu(\mathcal{O}) \cdot \delta$, contrary to the choice of $\mathcal{O}$. □

2.3 Separations by Random Oracles

By the following lemma, in order to prove that a generalized reducibility $\leq_a$ can be separated by random oracles from a generalized reducibility $\leq_b$, it is sufficent to show that there is a $\leq_b$ - reduction Γ and a reduction cover $\mathcal{R}$ for $\leq_a$, such that for any $\Delta \in \mathcal{R}$ the reductions Δ and Γ differ with probability one. In this situation, the functional Γ will be informally refered to as a diagonalizing reduction. (Diagonalizing reductions correspond to the "test languages" used in [BG81].)

Lemma 6. *Let $\leq_a$ and $\leq_b$ be generalized reducibilities. Let there be a reduction cover $\mathcal{R}$ for $\leq_a$ and let Γ be a $\leq_b$ - reduction, such that $\mu(\Gamma(A) \neq \Delta(A)) = 1$ holds for all $\Delta \in \mathcal{R}$. Then $\leq_a$ and $\leq_b$ can be separated by random oracles, or more precisely, $\mu(\leq_b(A) \not\subseteq \leq_a(A)) = 1$.*

Proof. Let the assumptions of Lemma 6 be satisfied. Then $\{A \subseteq \omega : \Gamma(A) = \Delta(A)\}$ has measure 0 for all $\Delta \in \mathcal{R}$, and therefore the set

$$\begin{aligned}\{A \subseteq \omega : \leq_b(A) \subseteq \leq_a(A)\} &\subseteq \{A \subseteq \omega : \Gamma(A) \in \leq_a(A)\} \\ &= \bigcup_{\Delta \in \mathcal{R}} \{A \subseteq \omega : \Gamma(A) = \Delta(A)\}\end{aligned}$$

has measure 0, by being contained in countable union of measure 0 sets, which then implies the claim. □

The next lemma contains a sufficient condition for two reductions Γ and Δ to differ with probability one. The content and the intended applications of the lemma are basically the same as of lemma 1 in [BG81]; however, by applying Lemma 5, the formulation of the assumptions and the proof become considerably simpler.

Lemma 7. *Let Δ and Γ be reductions. Let there be some rational $\varepsilon > 0$, such that for all partial characteristic functions α with finite domain holds*

$$\mu(\Delta_\alpha(A) \neq \Gamma_\alpha(A)) \;\geq\; \varepsilon \tag{2}$$

Then holds $\mu(\Gamma(A) \neq \Delta(A)) = 1$.

Proof. Assume by contradiction, that the assumptions of the lemma are satisfied, but $\mu(\Gamma(A) = \Delta(A)) > 0$. Then, by probability amplification according to Lemma 5, there is some partial characteristic functions α with finite domain, such that $\mu(\Delta_\alpha(A) = \Gamma_\alpha(A)) > 1 - \varepsilon$, contrary to assumption. □

In connection with Lemma 7, the concept of a honest reduction defined next will be useful.

Definition 8. Let Γ be a reduction and let $I \subseteq \omega$.

1. Γ is honest on I iff there is some function $f : \omega \to \omega$, such that $y \in u(\Gamma, x)$ implies $x \leq f(y)$ for all $x \in I$ and all $y \in \omega$. Γ is honest iff Γ is honest on ω.
2. Γ has disjoint use on I, iff $u(\Gamma, x) \cap u(\Gamma, y) = \emptyset$ holds for all $x, y \in I$ where $x \neq y$.

The concept of an honest reduction has been used by Bennett and Gill (see their Condition 4 in [BG81], p.98 and further references given there). The honest reductions introduced in Definition 8 might more precisely be called ω^ω-honest, in accordance with standard terminology, whereby a reduction is $\mathcal{F}$-honest for some $\mathcal{F} \subseteq \omega^\omega$, iff there is some $f \in \mathcal{F}$, such that $y \in u(\Gamma, x)$ implies $x \leq f(y)$ for all $x, y \in \omega$. (Note that there is a dated use of the term *honest*, whereby *honesty* refers to a concept which now is usually called time-constructibility.)

Obviously, an honest reduction Γ maps finite variations to finite variations, that is, $A =^* B$ implies $\Gamma(A) =^* \Gamma(B)$ for all $A, B \in 2^\omega$. Further, if Γ is honest on some infinite set $I \subseteq \omega$, then I contains an infinite set J, such that Γ has disjoint use on J.

2.4 Separations by Random Oracles Involving Constant Use Bounds

Lemma 9 will be used in proofs of separations by random oracles for reducibilities of *btt*-type, that is, when reductions with a constant use bound are involved.

Lemma 9. *Let Γ be a reduction, let $k_0 \in \omega$ and let $I \subseteq \omega$ be some infinite set, such that Γ is honest on I and $\mid u(\Gamma, x) \mid = k_0$ holds for all $x \in I$.*

1. *If Δ is a reduction, such that $\mid u(\Delta, x) \mid < k_0$ holds for all $x \in I$, then holds $\mu(\Gamma(A) \neq \Delta(A)) = 1$.*
2. *If $\leq_a$ is a generalized reducibility of k-tt-type where $k < k_0$, $k \in \omega$, then holds $\mu(\Gamma(A) \notin \leq_a(A)) = 1$.*

Proof. Part 2 is immediate from Part 1 by Lemma 6. In order to prove Part 1, by Lemma 7 it is sufficient to show, that there is some fixed rational $\varepsilon > 0$, such that $\mu(\Gamma_\alpha(A) \neq \Delta_\alpha(A)) \geq \varepsilon$ holds for every partial characteristic function α with finite domain. Now given such α, by Γ being honest on I, choose $x \in I$, such that $u(\Gamma, x) \cap dom(\alpha) = \emptyset$; then $\Gamma(., x)$ and $\Gamma_\alpha(., x)$ are the same and in particular $u(\Gamma, x) = u(\Gamma_\alpha, x)$. Thus by assumption on Δ, and by $u(\Delta_\alpha, x) \subseteq u(\Delta, x)$, $D{:=}u(\Delta_\alpha, x) \cap u(\Gamma_\alpha, x)$ is strictly contained in $u(\Gamma_\alpha, x)$. Therefore, by definition of generalized use, there are partial characteristic functions β_0 and β_1 with domain $u(\Gamma_\alpha, x)$, such that firstly, β_0 and β_1 agree on D, and secondly, for every set $C \subseteq \omega$, $\Gamma_\alpha(C_{\beta_0}, x) \neq \Gamma_\alpha(C_{\beta_1}, x)$. Therefore, either for $i = 0$ or for $i = 1$, $\Delta_\alpha(C_{\beta_0}, x) = \Delta_\alpha(C_{\beta_1}, x) \neq \Gamma_\alpha(C_{\beta_i}, x)$. Consequently, one obtains $\mu(\Gamma_\alpha(A) \neq \Delta_\alpha(A)) \geq 1/2^{|u(\Gamma_\alpha, x)|}$, that is, one can choose $\varepsilon{:=}1/2^{k_0}$, because by the choice of x, the cardinality of $u(\Gamma_\alpha, x)$ is equal to k_0. □

Corollary 10 contains some easy consequences of Lemma 9. Thereby $\leq_{k-tt}$ and $\leq_{btt}$ are the restrictions of Turing reducibility to reductions of k-question truth-table, resp. bounded truth-table type. The superscript *const* stands for the restriction to constant space bounds, where as usual the space used on the oracle tape shall not be charged against the space bound. Note that the main result in [BLM94] implies that for every algorithmically random language A, $\leq^p_{(k+1)-tt}(A)$ is not contained in $\leq_{k-tt}(A)$ for any fixed $k \geq 0$. From this, Claim 2 is immediate, because the class of algorithmically random languages has measure 1 (see for example [BLW94]).

Corollary 10. *Let $k \geq 0$ be a natural number.*

1. *[Book and Tang]* $\mu(\leq^p_{(k+1)-tt}(A) \not\subseteq \leq^p_{k-tt}(A)) = 1$.
2. *[Book, Lutz, and Martin]* $\mu(\leq^p_{(k+1)-tt}(A) \not\subseteq \leq_{k-tt}(A)) = 1$.
3. $\mu(\leq^p_{btt}(A) \not\subseteq \leq^p_{k-tt}(A)) = 1$. $\quad \mu(\leq^{const}_{btt}(A) \not\subseteq \leq_{k-tt}(A)) = 1$.

Proof. All claims are immediate by Lemma 9, where k_0 is set to $k+1$.

The next proposition can be viewed as the general form of results such as listed in Corollary 10. (Note that a reducibility of k-tt-type is also of *btt*-type.)

Proposition 11. *Let $\leq_a$ be a generalized reducibility of k-tt-type for some $k \in \omega$. Let the generalized reducibility $\leq_b$ be upwards c.f.v., such that $\leq_b$ is of btt-type, but not of k-tt-type. Then $\leq_a$ and $\leq_b$ can be separated by random oracles; more precisely $\mu(\leq_b(A) \not\subseteq \leq_a(A)) = 1$*

Proof. Fix some reduction cover $\mathcal{R}$ for $\leq_b$ which witnesses that $\leq_b$ is of *btt*-type, and by $\leq_b$ being upwards c.f.v., assume that $\Gamma \in \mathcal{R}$ implies $\Gamma_\alpha \in \mathcal{R}$ for all partial characteristic functions α with finite domain. For each reduction $\Gamma \in \mathcal{R}$, let $k(\Gamma)$ be the unique natural number, such that Γ is $k(\Gamma)$, but not $k(\Gamma) - 1$ use bounded. Now, if some reduction in $\mathcal{R}$ satisfies the assumptions of Lemma 9, this obviously finishes the proof; otherwise, one can show for all $\Gamma \in \mathcal{R}$ by induction on $k(\Gamma)$, that for each $A \subseteq \omega$, there is some k use bounded reduction $\Gamma' \in \mathcal{R}$, such that $\Gamma'(A) = \Gamma(A)$. But this contradicts the assumptions on $\leq_b$, because then the subclass of all reductions in $\mathcal{R}$ which are k-use bounded would witness that $\leq_b$ is of k-tt-type.

For the proof by induction, assume that there is no reduction in $\mathcal{R}$ which satisfies the assumptions of Lemma 9. The induction hypothesis is trivially true for all reductions in $\mathcal{R}$ which are k use bounded. So let $\Gamma \in \mathcal{R}$, where $k(\Gamma) > k$, and let $K(\Gamma) := \{x \in \omega : |u(\Gamma, x)| = k(\Gamma)\}$; that is, $K(\Gamma)$ contains all numbers x, such that $u(\Gamma, x)$ has (the largest possible) cardinality $k(\Gamma)$. First assume that there is some finite set D, such that D intersects $u(\Gamma, x)$ for all $x \in K(\Gamma)$. Then given an arbitrary set $A \subseteq \omega$, for $\alpha := A \mid D$, one obtains $\Gamma(A) = \Gamma_\alpha(A)$. By assumption on D, the reduction Γ_α is $k(\Gamma) - 1$ use bounded, and consequently by the induction hypothesis there is some k use bounded reduction Γ' in $\mathcal{R}$, such that $\Gamma(A) = \Gamma_\alpha(A) = \Gamma'(A)$. In case there is no such finite set D, it follows easily that there is some infinite subset I of $K(\Gamma)$, such that Γ is honest on I, that is, contrary to assumption, Γ satisfies the assumptions of Lemma 9, where k_0 is set to $k(\Gamma) > k$. □

The next proposition shows that generalized reducibilities of *btt*-type can be separated by random oracles from a wide class of generalized reducibilities which are not of *btt*-type.

Proposition 12. *Let $\leq_a$ and $\leq_b$ be generalized reducibilities. Let $\leq_a$ be of btt-type and let there be a $\leq_b$-reduction Γ, such that Γ is honest and there are arbitrarily large $k \in \omega$, such that the set $\{x \in \omega : \mid u(\Gamma, x) \mid = k\}$ is infinite. Then holds $\mu(\leq_b(A) \not\subseteq \leq_a(A)) = 1$*

Proof. The proof follows easily from the Lemmata 6 and 9. Due to $\leq_a$ being of *btt*-type there is some reduction cover $\mathcal{R}$ for $\leq_a$, such that each $\Delta \in \mathcal{R}$ is l use bounded for some $l \in \omega$, where l might depend on Δ. Given such Δ and l, apply Lemma 9 with $I := \{x \in \omega : \mid u(\Gamma, x) \mid = k\}$, where $k > l$ is chosen such that I is infinite. □

Corollary 13 follows easily from Proposition 12. The superscript *lin* stands for restriction to linear time bounds.

Corollary 13. $\mu(\leq_{tt}^{p}(A) \not\subseteq \leq_{btt}^{p}(A)) = 1. \quad \mu(\leq_{tt}^{lin}(A) \not\subseteq \leq_{btt}(A)) = 1.$

Note that, given a generalized reducibility $\leq_r$ of *btt*-type, one can construct a generalized reducibility $\leq_s$ which is not of *btt*-type, but which cannot be separated by random oracles from $\leq_r$. In order to define a reduction cover for $\leq_s$, one takes a reduction cover for $\leq_r$ and adds a diagonalizing reduction Γ which is equal to some fixed $\leq_r$ - reduction, except for infinitely many "diagonalization points" x_i, at which Γ is defined such that for all $i \in \omega$ holds $\mid u(\Gamma, x_i) \mid \geq i$ and such that Γ differs at place x_i with "small enough" probability from the i-th $\leq_r$ - reduction.

2.5 Separations by Random Oracles Involving Non-Constant Use Bounds

In the proofs of separations by random oracles given by Bennett and Gill, they use reductions Γ of a special form, which can informally be described as follows: in order to compute $\Gamma(B, x)$, first $\mid D \mid$ non-adaptive queries are made to strings in some finite set D, which might depend on x, followed by a single adaptive query $q(B, x) \in \omega \setminus D$. Thereby $\Gamma(B, x)$ is set equal to $B(q(B, x))$, and the adaptive queries depend on the non-adaptive queries in such a way, that $q(B_0, x) \neq q(B_1, x)$ holds in case the sets B_0 and B_1 differ for some argument in D. Note that consequently, while for each single set B and for each place x exactly $\mid D \mid +1$ queries are made, the size of the generalized use of Γ at x is equal to $\mid D \mid + 2^{\mid D \mid}$. The following definition tries to capture the essential features of such reductions in terms of generalized use.

Definition 14. Let Γ be a reduction and let $x \in \omega$. Γ is (single adaptive query) use boosting at x, iff there is some finite set $D \subseteq \omega$, such that for all partial characteristic functions α, β with domain D hold

1. $\mid u(\Gamma_\alpha, x) \mid = 1$
2. $\alpha \neq \beta$ implies $u(\Gamma_\alpha, x) \cap u(\Gamma_\beta, x) = \emptyset$

The reduction Γ is (single adaptive query) use boosting iff Γ is use boosting at every $x \in \omega$.

Proposition 15. *Let $\leq_a$ and $\leq_b$ be generalized reducibilities. Let there be a reduction cover $\mathcal{R}$ for $\leq_a$ and let Γ be a $\leq_b$-reduction, which is honest and use boosting, such that*

$$\liminf_{x\to\infty} \frac{|u(\Delta,x)|}{|u(\Gamma,x)|} < 1 . \tag{3}$$

holds for all $\Delta \in \mathcal{R}$. Then holds $\mu(\leq_b(A) \not\subseteq \leq_a(A)) = 1$.

Proof. For $x \in \omega$, let $D(x)$ be such that Γ and $D{:=}D(x)$ satisfy the definition of *use boosting at* x. Let $n(x){:=}\mid D(x)\mid$. Note that $\mid u(\Gamma,x)\mid = 2^{n(x)} + n(x)$ for all $x \in \omega$. Let $r(x){:=}\mid u(\Delta,x)\mid / \mid u(\Gamma,x)\mid$ and choose some real δ_0, such that $liminf_{x\to\infty} r(x) < \delta_0 < 1$. Let $I{:=}\{x \in \omega : r(x) \leq \delta_0\}$. In case $\mid u(\Gamma,x)\mid$ is bounded by some constant for all $x \in I$, then the proposition is immediate from Lemma 9. So assume $\mid u(\Gamma,x)\mid$ is not bounded on I. Then elementary calculus shows that there is some $\delta < 1$ and some infinite subset J of I, such that $\mid u(\Delta,x)\mid / 2^{n(x)} \leq \delta$ holds for all $x \in J$. Now in order to apply Lemma 7, given a partial characteristic function α with finite domain, by honesty of Γ choose $x \in J$, such that $u(\Gamma,x) \cap dom(\alpha) = \emptyset$. Then, by definition of J and by $u(\Delta_\alpha,x) \subseteq u(\Delta,x)$, a fraction of at least $1-\delta$ of the $2^{n(x)}$ "adaptive queries" of Γ is *not* contained in $u(\Delta_\alpha,x)$. But this yields immediately that Γ_α and Δ_α differ at place x with probability greater or equal to $(1-\delta)\cdot(1/2)$, because each of the adaptive queries is "selected" with equal probability, and in case the selected adaptive query is not in $u(\Delta_\alpha,x)$, then with probability $1/2$ the two reductions will differ at x. □

Corollary 16. *1. [Bennett and Gill]* $\mu(\leq_T^p(A) \not\subseteq \leq_T^{log}(A)) = 1$.
$\mu(\leq_T^E(A) \not\subseteq \leq_T^{PSPACE}(A)) = 1$.
2. $\mu(\leq_T^p(A) \not\subseteq \leq_{tt}^p(A)) = 1$.
3. $\mu(\leq_{(\log n)-T}^p(A) \not\subseteq \leq_{btt}^p(A)) = 1$.

The reducibilities $\leq_T^{log}$ and $\leq_T^{PSPACE}$ occuring in the second claim are Turing reducibility restricted to logarithmic, resp. polynomial space, E stands for time bounds of type $2^{c|x|}$, $c \in \omega$.

Proof. The last two claims are immediate from Proposition 15, by choosing a use boosting $\leq_T^p$ - reduction, resp. $\leq_{(\log n)-T}^p$ - reduction, with $\mid x \mid$, resp. with $\log \mid x \mid$, non-adaptive queries for each $x \in \omega$.

The first claim follows from the crucial observation due to Bennett and Gill, that the number of potential queries of an oracle Turing machine T, and therefore the size of the generalized use of the reduction computed by T, is bounded by the number of configurations of T: if one assumes as usual a machine model where the query tape is erased after a query has been made, then the configuration after query number k determines the next query. By this argument, it is easy to see that reductions computed by oracle Turing machines which use logarithmic, resp. polynomial space, are polynomially, resp. $2^{c\cdot|x|}$ use bounded. Now Proposition 15 implies the second claim, because there are honest and use boosting $\leq_T^p$ - , resp. $\leq_T^E$ - reductions, with $2^{c\cdot|x|}$, resp. $2^{2^{c\cdot|x|}}$, adaptive queries at each place x. □

3 Almost classses

Note that the techniques used in this section are standard and have mostly, at least implicitly, been used before.

Definition 17. For a generalized reducibility $\leq_r$, let

$$\mathcal{L}_r := \{A \subseteq \omega : A \leq_r B \text{ for all } B \subseteq \omega\}$$
$$Almost_r := \{A \subseteq \omega : \mu(\{B \subseteq \omega : A \leq_r B\}) = 1\}$$

Obviously, $\mathcal{L}_r \subseteq Almost_r$ holds by definition for all generalized reducibilities. Under additional assumptions on $\leq_r$, one can derive that $\mathcal{L}_r$ and $Almost_r$ coincide (see Proposition 20). But this might not hold for all generalized reducibilities, for example $Almost_T^p = BPP$ is not known to be equal to $\mathcal{L}_T^p = P$.

Definition 18. Let $\leq_r$ be a generalized reducibility and let $A \subseteq \omega$. A is in the oracle-based bounded-error probabilistic class w.r.t $\leq_r$, $\underline{A \in BP_o(\leq_r)}$ for short, iff there is some $\leq_r$ - reduction Γ and some rational $\varepsilon > 0$, such that for all $x \in \omega$ holds $\mu(\{B \subseteq \omega : A(x) = \Gamma(B, x)\}) \geq 1/2 + \varepsilon$.

The main difference between the operator BP_o and the usual BP operator is that for BP_o, the random bits are given via some oracle, that is, by a set argument, and not by some advice string of polynomial length which is part of the number input, and that consequently in the case of BP_o the number of available random bits is not bounded in advance by some polynomial p, but by the reduction Γ itself. Using the BP_o operator, one obtains easily an upper bound for the class $Almost_r$.

Proposition 19. *Let the generalized reducibility $\leq_r$ be upwards c.f.v. Then holds*

$$\mathcal{L}_r \subseteq Almost_r \subseteq BP_o(\leq_r) \quad . \tag{4}$$

The proof of Proposition 19 will be contained in the full version of the paper, together with more precise characterizations of the class $Almost_r$ for various types of reducibilities. In particular, it will be shown that $Almost_r$ is equal to $BP_o(\leq_r)$ for all generalized reducibilities which are upwards c.f.v. and which in addition allow a special form of probability amplification similar to the one used in connection with the usual BPP machines (see [BDG]). This result, together with a general lemma about the equivalence of gathering random bits from random oracles and from random advice strings, will then be used to show that $Almost_r$ is equal to $\mathcal{L}_r$ for various specific bounded reducibilities $\leq_r$, and that for $\leq_{tt}^p$ and $\leq_T^p$ the corresponding Almost classes are equal to BPP.

The next proposition, which can be proved without using the lemmata omitted in this version of the paper, shows that the known result $Almost_m^p = Almost_{btt}^p = P$ (see [Am86a], [Am86b], [BT91]) can be extended to a much wider class of generalized reducibilities.

Proposition 20. *Let $\leq_r$ be a generalized reducibility of btt-type, which is upwards c.f.v. Then holds $\mathcal{L}_r = Almost_r$.*

Proof. The set $\mathcal{L}_r$ is always a subset of $Almost_r$, so it remains to show the reverse containment. Let $\mathcal{R}$ be a reduction cover for $\leq_r$, such that each reduction $\Gamma \in \mathcal{R}$ is k use bounded for some $k \in \omega$. Because $\leq_r$ is upwards c.f.v., one can assume that $\Gamma \in \mathcal{R}$ implies $\Gamma_\alpha \in \mathcal{R}$ for every partial characteristic function α with finite domain. Now it is sufficient to show that, given a set $A \notin \mathcal{L}_r$, for all $\Gamma \in \mathcal{R}$ holds $\mu(\Gamma^{-1}(A)) = 0$, whereby $\Gamma^{-1}(A){:=}\{B \subseteq \omega : A \leq_r B\}$, because then $\{B \subseteq \omega : A \leq_r B\} = \bigcup_{\Gamma \in \mathcal{R}} \Gamma^{-1}(A)$ must have measure 0. This is shown for all $\Gamma \in \mathcal{R}$ by induction over $k(\Gamma)$, where $k(\Gamma) \in \omega$ is minimal such that Γ is $k(\Gamma)$ use bounded. In case $k(\Gamma)$ is 0, the reduction Γ is constant on 2^ω and thus $A \neq \Gamma(B)$ for all sets $B \subseteq \omega$, because otherwise A would be in $\mathcal{L}_r$, contrary to assumption. Now let $k(\Gamma) = k + 1$ for some $k \geq 0$ and let $K(\Gamma){:=}\{x \in \omega : |u(\Gamma, x)| = k(\Gamma)\}$ as in the proof of Proposition 11. In case there is some finite set D such that D intersects $u(\Gamma, x)$ for all $x \in K(\Gamma)$, then holds $k(\Gamma_\alpha) < k(\Gamma)$ for all partial characteristic functions α with domain D, and as $\Gamma^{-1}(A)$ is contained in $\bigcup_{\alpha:D\to\{0,1\}} {\Gamma_\alpha}^{-1}(A)$, $\mu(\Gamma^{-1}(A)) = 0$ follows from the induction hypothesis. In case no such set D exists, there must be some infinite set $I \subseteq K(\Gamma)$, such that Γ has disjoint use on I, that is the class of events $\mathcal{E}(x){:=}\{B \subseteq \omega : A(x) = \Gamma(B, x)\}$ for $x \in I$ is stochastically independent. Therefore, as each $\mathcal{E}(x)$ has measure less than $\delta{:=}1 - 1/2^{k(\Gamma)}$ by choice of I, any finite intersection of n such events has measure less than δ^n, which implies $\mu(\Gamma^{-1}(A)) = 0$ as $\Gamma^{-1}(A)$ is contained in all $\mathcal{E}(x)$. □

References

[Am86a] K.Ambos-Spies. Randomness, relativizations, and polynomial reducibilities. *Proc. First Structure in Complexity Theory Conference*, Lecture Notes in Computer Science Vol. 223, Springer Verlag, Heidelberg New York, 1986, 23-34.

[Am86b] K.Ambos-Spies. Randomness, relativizations, and polynomial reducibilities. *Unpublished research paper*, 1986.

[BDG] J.L.Balcázar, J.Díaz, J.Gabarró. *Structural Complexity I and II.* Springer Verlag, Heidelberg New York, 1988 and 1990.

[BG81] C.H. Bennett, J. Gill. Relative to a random oracle A, $P^A \neq NP^A \neq co-NP^A$ with probability 1. *SIAM Journal on Computing* 10 (1981), 96-113.

[BLM94] R.V. Book, J.H. Lutz, D.M. Martin Jr. The global power of additional queries to random oracles. *Symposium on Theoretical Aspects of Computer Science 1994*, Lecture Notes in Computer Science 775, Springer Verlag, Heidelberg New York, 1994, 403-414.

[BLW94] R.V. Book, J.H. Lutz, K.W. Wagner. An observation on probability versus randomness with applications to complexity classes. *Mathematical Systems Theory* 27 (1994), 201-209.

[BT91] R.V. Book, S. Tang. Polynomial-time reducibilities and almost all oracle sets. *Theoretical Computer Science* 81 (1991), 35-47.

[Od89] P.Odifreddi. *Classical Recursion Theory.* North Holland, Amsterdam, 1989.

On the Complexity of Finite Memory Policies for Markov Decision Processes

Danièle Beauquier[1]
Université Paris-12 and L.I.T.P., Institut Blaise Pascal, Paris, France

Dima Burago[2 ♮]
Laboratory for Theory of Algorithms, SPIIRAN[†]*, St-Petersburg, Russia and LRI, Université Paris-Sud, France*

Anatol Slissenko[3 ♭]
Université Paris-12 and L.I.T.P., Institut Blaise Pascal, Paris, France and Laboratory for Theory of Algorithms, SPIIRAN[†]*, St-Petersburg, Russia*

Abstract. We consider some complexity questions concerning a model of uncertainty known as Markov decision processes. Our results concern the problem of constructing optimal policies under a criterion of optimality defined in terms of constraints on the behavior of the process. The constraints are described by regular languages, and the motivation goes from robot motion planning. It is known that, in the case of perfect information, optimal policies under the traditional cost criteria can be found among Markov policies and in polytime. We show, firstly, that for the behavior criterion optimal policies are not Markovian for finite as well as infinite horizon. On the other hand, optimal policies in this case lie in the class of finite memory policies defined in the paper, and can be found in polytime. We remark that in the case of partial information, finite memory policies cannot be optimal in the general situation. Nevertheless, the class of finite memory policies seems to be of interest for probabilistic policies: though probabilistic policies are not better than deterministic ones in the general class of history remembering policies, the former ones can be better in the class of finite memory policies.

[1] *Address: Université Paris-12, Equipe d'Informatique Fondamentale, 61, Ave. du Général de Gaulle, 94010 Créteil, France.*
E-mail: dab@litp.ibp.fr Fax: 33-1-42 07 17 18

[2] *Address: Dept. of Mathematics, University of Pennsylvania, Philadelphia, PA 19104, USA. E-mail: dburago@math.upenn.edu*

♮ *The research of this author was supported by DRET and Armines contract 92-0171.00.1013.*

† *St-Petersburg Inst. for Informatics and Automation of the Acad. Sci. of Russia*

[3] *Address: Université Paris-12, Equipe d'Informatique Fondamentale, 61, Ave. du Général de Gaulle, 94010 Créteil, France. E-mail: sliss@litp.ibp.fr*

♭ *The research of this author was partially supported by DRET contract 91/1061.*

1 Introduction

We consider some algorithmic and combinatorial questions concerning optimal policies for finite stationary Markov decision processes mainly for the case of perfect imformation but under a cost criterion different from traditional ones (e. g. see [6], [1]). The model is constituted by a finite set of states (e. g. points of control of a robot in an environment) which are in a general case colored, and the color is the only information available when arriving at a state. If the coloring is bijective the process is said to be perfectly observable, and if not, we speak about imperfect information or partial observability. But in any case the process is probabilistic, i. e. at any moment of discrete time we may make some action but the result of our action is predictable only with some probability. These probabilistic deviations are described by a function $\mu(\lambda, xy)$ that gives the probability to reach y from x if the action λ has been chosen. Clearly, the process can be represented as a colored graph with states being vertices. A policy is a function from the strings of colors to actions. In the traditional setting every action λ at a vertex x imposes a reward $r(x, \lambda)$ which is interpreted as gain or loss depending on its sign. Usual criterion is the expectation of the sum of rewards, and deals with its maximization. Two cases are distinguished when analyzing the problem of constructing an optimal policy, when the time is bounded (finite horizon) or when the time is unbounded (infinite horizon).

It is known (see [4]) that for the case of perfect information a policy optimal with respect to the traditional criteria can be found among Markovian ones (among non stationary ones for finite horizon, and among stationary ones for infinite horizon), and this can be done in polytime. For the case of imperfect information the problem is known to be PSPACE-hard [5]. When the unobservability is bounded, it rests to be NP-hard, but in some cases polytime approximation is possible, see [2] where one can find also connections of the problem under discussion and the Max Word Problem.

We consider here another criterion of quality of policies motivated by robot motion planning and described in terms of constraints on the admissible behavior of the system. For example, we may demand that the system firstly goes to the state x then to y and then to z, and exactly in this order. Formally, constraints on the behavior are given by a language of admissible sequences (paths) of states (or colors). The basic criterion considered here is the probability to follow admissible paths starting from a source vertex.

We formulate main notions in the next section 2, and then recall related results concerning the traditional criterion of expectation of the total reward.

In section 3 the criterion in terms of behavior is considered. We restrict ourselves to behaviors described by regular (finite automaton) languages, for standard larger classes of languages the problem becomes computationally hard. For the same reason only the case of perfect information is analyzed. Here we show that optimal policies are not Markovian in the general situation, but they can be found among finite memory ones. This class of policies seems to be of interest in more general settings. We prove that optimal finite memory policies can be found in polytime.

Section 4 points out some limits on the power of finite memory policies. We prove that in the case of partial information, when an optimal policy exists (for infinite horizon), maybe no finite memory policy is optimal (opposite to the case of perfect information).
In the last section 5 randomized policies are approached. We remark that for finite horizon history remembering deterministic policies are not worse than randomized ones. But among finite memory policies probabilistic policies can do better.

2 Main Notions

Uncertainty Model. Let V be a finite set. Its elements are interpreted as *states* of a system to control. The set V is supplied with the following additional structure.

• $clr : V \to C$ is the *coloring* function where C is a finite set. It defines a partition of the states into classes $clr^{-1}(c), \;\; c \in C$ which characterizes uncertainty of "positioning" the process. When clr is a bijective function we assume that $V = C$ and $clr = id$, and we are in a *perfect information* situation opposite to the general situation of *partial (imperfect) information.*

• $\mu : D \times V \times V \to [0,1]$ is the transition probability function, such that $\sum_{v \in V} \mu(\lambda, u, v) = 1$ for all $\lambda \in D$ and $u \in V$. (The writings $\mu(\lambda, xy)$ and $\mu(\lambda, x, y)$ are equivalent.)
The finite set D may be interpreted as a set of *actions* (or *moves* or *decisions*), and $\mu(\lambda, uv)$ is the probability to arrive at v from u if the action λ has been made.
To avoid trivialities, we assume $|D|$ is polynomially bounded with respect to $|V|$. When treated as a part of input of algorithms, μ is assumed to have rational values and to be represented as a usual table of its values.
Thus, the main object to consider as input for the problems to analyze is of the form (V, D, C, clr, μ), or (V, D, C, clr, μ, s) when a starting state s is fixed. We will call such an object a *CU-graph* (*CU* from *Control* under *Uncertainty*). Interpreting this structure as a graph with the set of vertices V and edges uv defined by the condition $\exists \lambda \in D \;\; \mu(\lambda, u, v) > 0$ is convenient, especially for describing examples, and will be used below, though formally edges are redundant. For interpretations from motion planning λ maybe treated as a label of an edge and μ as a function describing probabilistic deviations from a chosen direction represented by λ.

Policies. Given a CU-graph G, a (*deterministic*) *policy* is a function $\sigma : C^+ \to D$, where A^+ denotes the set of all non empty strings over alphabet A. One can interprete a policy σ in the following way. If, while applying σ, we have covered a sequence of states (path) $v_1 \ldots v_k$, the only available information is the string of colors $W = clr(v_1) \ldots clr(v_k)$. And our next action to change the state is $\sigma(W)$. Having made this action in state v_k we arrive at a state v with probability $\mu(\sigma(W), v_k v)$.
Denote by $\mathcal{P}_x^k$ the set of all paths in the CU-graph G starting from x and having k vertices, and let $\mathcal{P}_x = \bigcup_{k \geq 1} \mathcal{P}_x^k$.
Assume that a starting state $s \in V$ is fixed.

A policy σ defines probabilistic distributions p^σ on $\mathcal{P}_s^k$ as follows:

$p^\sigma(v_1 \ldots v_{k-1}v_k) = \prod_{i=1}^{k-1} \mu(\sigma(clr(v_1)\ldots clr(v_i)), v_iv_{i+1})$.

Informally speaking, $p^\sigma(P)$ is the probability to follow a given path P of the length k when executing σ.

Criteria of Quality of Policies. Below we consider policies that start from a vertex s. Many criteria are particular cases of the following general criterion $R_k^F(\sigma)$, where F is a function (maybe dependant on σ), $F: \ \mathcal{P}_s \to R$:

$R_k^F(\sigma) = \sum_{P \in \mathcal{P}_s^k} F(P) \cdot p_k^\sigma(P)$.

For every criterion R_k^F we consider also its limit version $R_\infty^F(\sigma) = \limsup_{k\to\infty} R_k^F(\sigma)$. Informally speaking, the limit version of a criterion means that we do not care about the number of steps done to fulfil the task. The criterion R_k^F is called a *finite horizon criterion* and R_∞^F is the *infinite horizon* version. When we do not specify the nature of the horizon, we will write simply R^F.

One of the usual criteria for the Markov decision model is the total expected reward [6]. In this situation, a cost function r is given in the following way: $r_k(v, \lambda)$ is the immediate reward received at step k, if the system is in state v and action λ is chosen. Therefore, $F(P)$ is the total reward received, applying σ and following path P:

$F(v_1 \ldots v_k) = \sum_{t=1}^{k-1} r_t(v_t, \sigma(clr(v_1)\ldots clr(v_t)))$.

Denote this criterion by R^r. The main criterion considered in the paper is different and instead of evaluating some reward, it evaluates the probabilty to respect some specified behavior.

Probability of realizing an allowed behavior. Let L be a set of sequences of states interpreted as a set of allowed realizations. The criterion $R^L(\sigma)$ is defined by $R^L(\sigma) = R^{\chi_L}(\sigma)$ where χ_L is the characteristic function of the set L.

This criterion cannot be modelized by a R^r criterion using some local reward function r. Nevertheless this criterion R^L is a generalization of:

Probability to reach a target in not more than k steps. Let $T \subseteq V$ be a target set to reach. This criterion, denoted by $R_k^{s,T}(\sigma)$, corresponds to the following function:

$F(v_1 \ldots v_k) = \textbf{if } \exists i \le k \ (v_i \in T) \textbf{ then } 1 \textbf{ else } 0.$

Clearly, the $R_k^{s,T}$ criterion is a particular case of $R_k^L(\sigma)$ criterion where L is the set of paths starting in s and arriving in T.

Opposite to the general criterion R^L, the $R^{s,T}$ criterion can be considered as a total expected reward criterion. Actually, given a CU-graph (V, D, C, clr, μ, s), and a target set T, considering the $R^{s,T}$ criterion, w.l.o.g. we can add a trap state t_0 and suppose that

- for every action λ and every state $t \in T$, $\mu(\lambda, tt_0) = 1$ and $r(t, \lambda) = 1$, (here the cost function r does not depend on time).

- for every action λ and every state $t \notin T$, $r(t, \lambda) = 0$.

Clearly, applying σ for horizon $k \in N \cup \{\infty\}$ the total expected reward $R_k^r(\sigma)$ is equal to $R_k^{s,T}(\sigma)$.

So the $R^{s,T}$ criterion is both a particular case of R^L criterion and R^r one.

Notice that criteria $R_k^{s,T}$, R_k^L , and R_k^r in the case of positive rewards, are non

decreasing on k and hence, we can replace lim sup by lim in the definition of its limit version.
A policy σ is *optimal* with respect to a criterion $\boldsymbol{R}^F$, or $\boldsymbol{R}^F$-*optimal* for $k \in \boldsymbol{N} \cup \{\infty\}$ if for every policy σ' we have $\boldsymbol{R}_k^F(\sigma') \leq \boldsymbol{R}_k^F(\sigma)$.

R^r-criterion. Perfect information. A policy is an arbitrary function with potentially unlimited memory and can hardly be considered as a feasible object. But in some particular cases of interest optimal policies exist in classes of rather simple functions [6].
A policy σ is called an $\boldsymbol{M}$-*policy* (or *stationary Markov*) if it depends on the last color of the argument only, i. e. if there exists a function $\sigma' : C \rightarrow D$ such that $\sigma(W) = \sigma'(last.W)$ for all $W \in C^+$, where $last.W$ denotes the last character of the string W.
A policy σ is called a $\boldsymbol{T}$-*policy* (or *non stationary Markov*) if it depends on time and on the last color of its input only, i. e. there exists a function $\sigma' : C \times \boldsymbol{N} \rightarrow D$ such that $\sigma(W) = \sigma'(last.W, \mid W \mid)$ for all $W \in C^+$, where $\mid W \mid$ denotes the length of W.
It is not difficult to prove [1] that in the case of perfect information, an $\boldsymbol{R}_k^r$-optimal $\boldsymbol{T}$-policy can be constructed in polytime (by standard backward dynamic programming). Moreover, the same is true for $\boldsymbol{R}_\infty^r$-optimal $\boldsymbol{M}$-policy in the case of perfect information and positive reward. The proof is much more intricated [4].

R^r-criterion. Partial information. In the case of partial information, problems are computationally more difficult. For finite horizon:
Theorem 1 ([5]) *Given a CU-graph $G = (V, D, C, clr, \mu, s)$ and a reward function r, computing a $\boldsymbol{R}_k^r$-optimal policy is PSPACE- hard, and PSPACE-complete if k is restricted to be smaller than $\mid V \mid$.*
For infinite horizon, even with a positive reward function, in some cases, there is no optimal policy (e. g. see [2]) though there is a maximal total reward. And it seems to be an open problem whether the existence of an optimal policy is decidable.

3 R^L-criterion

We consider the problem of maximizing the probability of realizing an allowed behavior. Such a behavior is defined by regular (finite automaton) constraints on sequences of visited states. Some motivations are illustrated by the following examples of regular constraints:

- the goal is to evolve in such a way that states u, v and w are reached only once, and in this order;

- every time we reach state u we have to reach another given state v before coming back to u.

This setting is attractive for us as a step towards studying policies whose goals are formulated in terms of their behavior.
So, we deal with the $\boldsymbol{R}^L$-criterion for regular (finite automata) languages L of sequences of states. Firstly, we recall the definition of a regular language.

Regular languages [3]. A *finite (complete and deterministic) automaton $\mathcal{A}$* over the alphabet V is a quintuple (Q, V, δ, q_0, F), where

- Q is a finite set of *states*,
- δ is a function: $Q \times V \to V$ called the *transition function*,
- $q_0 \in Q$ is the *initial state*,
- $F \subset Q$ is a set of *final states*. The function δ can be extended to $Q \times V^*$ as follows:

$\delta(q, \Lambda) = q$, $\delta(q, wu) = \delta(\delta(q, w), u)$ for $q \in Q$, $w \in V^*$, $u \in V$.
For short, $\delta(q, w)$ is denoted $q.w$. A string $w \in V^*$ is *accepted by* $\mathcal{A}$ if $\delta(q_0, w)$ belongs to F. The set of strings accepted by $\mathcal{A}$ is denoted by $L(\mathcal{A})$. A language $L \subset V^*$ is a *regular language* if there exists a finite (deterministic and complete) automaton $\mathcal{A}$ such that $L = L(\mathcal{A})$.
If the set of final states is not precised, the automaton is called a *finite transition system*.

R^L-optimal policies are not Markovian. According to the previous section, as far as we consider the $\boldsymbol{R}^r$ criterion, the class of $\boldsymbol{M}$-policies or $\boldsymbol{T}$-policies is sufficient, for infinite and finite horizon respectively. It is no longer the case for the $\boldsymbol{R}^L$ criterion, and this can be proved by a rather simple example.

Proposition 1 *There exists a CU-graph and a regular language L for which no $\boldsymbol{T}$-policy is $\boldsymbol{R}_k^L$-optimal ($k \geq 4$), and no $\boldsymbol{M}$-policy is $\boldsymbol{R}_\infty^L$-optimal.*

Finite memory policies. A natural generalization of $\boldsymbol{M}$-policy is *finite memory* policy. We prove below that the class of finite memory policies contains optimal policies for the $\boldsymbol{R}_\infty^L$ criterion, when L is a regular language. Moreover, for the finite horizon, a generalization of $\boldsymbol{T}$-policy in the same way, leads to optimal solutions.
A (deterministic) policy σ is called a *finite memory policy* or *$\boldsymbol{F}$-policy* if there exists a finite transition system $\mathcal{T} = (States,\ C,\ \delta, p_0)$, and a function σ' : $States \to D$ such that $\forall w : \sigma(w) = \sigma'(p_0.(w)$. The *size of the memory* is the size of the transition system $\mathcal{T}$.
A (deterministic) policy σ is called *dependent only on time and finite memory* or *$\boldsymbol{FT}$-policy* if there exists a finite transition system $\mathcal{T} = (States,\ C,\ \delta, p_0)$, and a function σ' : $States \times \boldsymbol{N} \to D$ such that $\forall w : \sigma(w) = \sigma'(p_0.w, \mid w \mid)$.
Notice that $\boldsymbol{T}$- and $\boldsymbol{FT}$-policies are not finite memory ones.

R^L-optimal policies. Supposing that the information is perfect we prove here that $\boldsymbol{R}^L$-optimal policies can be found in the class of $\boldsymbol{F}$- policies for infinite horizon, and in the class of $\boldsymbol{FT}$-policies for finite horizon, at least when L is a regular language.

Encoding an R^L-criterion into an $R^{s,T}$ one. Let $G = (V, D, \mu, s)$ be a CU-graph with bijective coloring, and L a regular language recognized by the finite automaton $\mathcal{A} = (Q, V, \delta, q_0, F)$. W. l. o. g. we can suppose that D contains a *null* action ω, that is an action ω such that for all state v, $\mu(\omega, v, v) = 1$. We need the following definitions to describe the mentioned reductions. A path in G is called *normal* if it belongs to sV^*. A policy on G is a *normal policy* if its value is ω for not normal paths. Clearly if σ is an $\boldsymbol{R}^L$-optimal policy, then the unique normal policy σ_1 defined as σ on normal paths is also an $\boldsymbol{R}^L$-optimal policy. Moreover if σ is a $\boldsymbol{T}$-policy (resp. a $\boldsymbol{M}$-policy) then σ_1 is a $\boldsymbol{T}$-policy (resp. a $\boldsymbol{M}$-policy).

We define the image $\Phi(G)$ of G as the CU-graph $\Phi(G) = (V', D', \mu', s', T')$ with $V' = V \times Q$, $D' = D$, $\mu'(\lambda, (u, q), (v, q.v)) = \mu(\lambda, u, v)$, $s' = (s, q_0.s)$, $T' = V \times T$. Extending the mapping Φ onto paths and policies one can use this construction to reduce the problem to known results on R^r-criterion with positive reward (mentioned at the end of section 2), and thus prove

Theorem 2 *For every CU-graph with perfect information and every regular language L a policy $\boldsymbol{R}^L$-optimal for a given $k \in \boldsymbol{N}$ does exist among $\boldsymbol{FT}$-policies, and such a $\boldsymbol{FT}$-policy can be constructed in time polynomial in k, in the size of the CU-graph and in the size of the automaton defining L.*

Theorem 3 *For every CU-graph with perfect information and every regular language L $\boldsymbol{R}^L_\infty$-optimal policy does exist among $\boldsymbol{F}$-policies, and such a $\boldsymbol{F}$-policy and can be constructed in time polynomial in the size of the CU-graph and in the size of the automaton defining L.*

4 Limits of finite memory policies

Opposite to the perfect information situation, in the case of partial information, even when there exists a $\boldsymbol{R}^r_\infty$-optimal policy, there may be no finite memory policy which is optimal.

The proof is based on considering the following CU-graph G:

• the set of vertices is $V = \{s_0,\ s_1,\ s_2,\ s_3,\ s'_1,\ s'_2,\ s'_3,\ t,\ trap\}$,

• the set of actions $D = \{d,\ \bar{d}\}$

• transition probability function μ:

$\mu(d, s_0, s_1) = \mu(d, s_0, s'_1) = \mu(\bar{d}, s_0, s_1) = \mu(\bar{d}, s_0, s'_1) = 1/2$,

For $x_i \in \{s_2, s_3, s'_1, s'_3\}$:

$\mu(\lambda,\ x_i,\ x_{i+1}) = \frac{1-\alpha}{2}$, $\mu(\lambda,\ x_i,\ x_i) = \alpha/2$, $\mu(\lambda,\ x_i,\ t) = 1/2$, $\lambda \in \{d, \bar{d}\}$ (the sum of indices is mod 3),

$\mu(d, s_1, s_1) = \alpha/2$, $\mu(d, s_1, s_2) = \frac{1-\alpha}{2}$ $\mu(d, s_1, t) = \beta$, $\mu(d, s_1, trap) = 1/2 - \beta$,
$\mu(\bar{d}, s_1, s_1) = \alpha/2$, $\mu(\bar{d}, s_1, s_2) = \frac{1-\alpha}{2}$ $\mu(d, s_1, t) = 1/2 - \beta$, $\mu(d, s_1, trap) = \beta$,
$\mu(d, s'_2, s'_2) = \alpha/2$, $\mu(d, s'_2, s'_3) = \frac{1-\alpha}{2}$, $\mu(d, s'_2, t) = 1/2 - \beta$, $\mu(d, s'_2, trap) = \beta$,
$\mu(\bar{d}, s'_2, s'_2) = \alpha/2$, $\mu(\bar{d}, s'_2, s'_3) = \frac{1-\alpha}{2}$ $\mu(d, s'_2, t) = \beta$, $\mu(d, s_1, trap) = 1/2 - \beta$,

• vertices $s_1, s_2, s_3, s'_1, s'_2, s'_3$ have the same color, we will call this color c.

After one step, the state of the system has a color c, and while state t or state $trap$ is not reached, the system remains in a state with color c. So, at step $n+1$, a policy σ acts on the word $clr(s_0)c^n$, and can be considered as a $\boldsymbol{T}$-policy.

Let $p_n(s_i)$ (resp. $p_n(s'_i)$) be the probability to be in state s_i (resp. s'_i) after n steps of applying some policy σ, and knowing that the system is in a state with color c. Whatever be σ, we have: $p_n(s_i) = p_n(s'_i) = p_{i,n}$ for $i = 1,\ 2,\ 3$ with

$$\begin{pmatrix} p_{1,n} \\ p_{2,n} \\ p_{3,n} \end{pmatrix} = \frac{1}{2} M^n \begin{pmatrix} 1 \\ 0 \\ 0 \end{pmatrix}, \text{ where } M = \begin{pmatrix} \alpha & 0 & 1-\alpha \\ 1-\alpha & \alpha & 0 \\ 0 & 1-\alpha & \alpha \end{pmatrix}. \quad (1)$$

So, at step n, $n \geq 1$, if the system is in a state with color c, the probability to reach t at the next step depends only on the action made at this moment, because the probability distribution at this moment is independant of σ, and this probability to reach t at the next step is:

$p_n(s_1)\beta + p_n(s'_2)(1/2 - \beta) + 1/2(p_n(s_2) + p_n(s_3) + p_n(s'_1) + p_n(s'_3))$ if action d is made,

$p_n(s_1)(1/2-\beta)+p_n(s'_2)\beta+1/2(p_n(s_2)+p_n(s_3)+p_n(s'_1)+p_n(s'_3))$ if action $\bar{d}$ is made.
So at step n the best action is d if
$p_n(s_1)\beta+p_n(s'_2)(1/2-\beta)>p_n(s_1)(1/2-\beta)+p_n(s'_2)\beta$
which for $\beta<1/4$ is equivalent to

$$p_n(s_1)>p_n(s'_2). \qquad (2)$$

Using M for computing the probabilities $p_n(s_i)$ one can show that (2) is equivalent to :

$$\cos(n\theta+\frac{\pi}{6})>0. \qquad (3)$$

where θ is the argument of $\lambda=\alpha+(1-\alpha)\zeta$, with $\zeta=e^{\frac{2\pi i}{3}}$, where λ is one of the eigenvalues of M, the others are 1 and $\bar{\lambda}$.
The definition of λ leads to the equality:

$$\cos\theta=\frac{1-3\alpha}{2\sqrt{1-3\alpha+3\alpha^2}}. \qquad (4)$$

One can choose a rational α which satisfies (4) and is small enough to obey other constraints mentioned above, and such that θ is not a rational multiple of π.
Denote by D_n the boolean value of (3). Then the sequence $\{D_k\}_{k\in\boldsymbol{N}}$ is not ultimately periodic. Indeed, suppose that the sequence $\{D_k\}_{k\in\boldsymbol{N}}$ is ultimately periodic with period T, and the periodicity begins at k_0. Suppose also, without loss of generality, that $\cos(k_0\theta+\frac{\pi}{6})\in[0,1]$. Then, denoting $\eta_0=k_0\theta+\frac{\pi}{6}$ and $\eta=T\theta$ we have $\cos(\eta_0+i\eta)\in[0,1]$ for all $i\in\boldsymbol{N}$. But η is not commensurable with π, and hence $\{i\eta \pmod{2\pi}\}_{i\in\boldsymbol{N}}$ is dense in $[0,2\pi]$. Thus, the sequence $\{\cos(\eta_0+i\eta)\}_i$ is dense in $[-1,1]$, a contradiction.
Clear, there is a unique (except for the first step where, d or $\bar{d}$ can be chosen arbitrarily) $\boldsymbol{R}^{s,t}_\infty$-optimal policy τ defined by : $\tau(clr(s_0)c^n)$ is equal to d if D_n is true and to $\bar{d}$ otherwise.
We know that the boolean value D_n of (3) is not ultimately periodic. But a $\boldsymbol{T}$-policy which has a finite memory is exactly an ultimately periodic function. Therefore, for every finite memory policy σ there exists infinitely many n such that $\sigma(clr(s_0)c^n)\neq\tau(clr(s_0)c^n)$. So,
Theorem 4 *For the CU-graph G defined above, there exists a $\boldsymbol{R}^{s,t}_\infty$-optimal policy τ, and for every finite memory policy σ we have:*

$$\boldsymbol{R}^{s,t}_\infty(\sigma)<\boldsymbol{R}^{s,t}_\infty(\tau).$$

Since $\boldsymbol{R}^{s,t}$-criterion is a particular case of both $\boldsymbol{R}^r$ and $\boldsymbol{R}^L$ ones we can state that in the case of partial observability and infinite horizon there may be situations when no finite memory policy is optimal even if an optimal policy exists.

5 Randomized policies

We consider a more rich class of policies, namely, randomized policies. As many algorithmic problems related to constructing optimal deterministic policies are computationally hard, one can hope that similar problems for randomized policies will be simpler.
A *randomized policy* is a random function of the same type as deterministic

policy. Such a function τ can be represented by the function Λ^τ that gives a distribution of probabilities to choose this or that action: $\Lambda^\tau : C^+ \times D \rightarrow [0,1]$, such that $\sum_{\lambda \in D} \Lambda^\tau(W, \lambda) = 1$ for all $W \in C^+$.
The distributions $\boldsymbol{p}^\tau(v_1 \dots v_{k-1}v_k, \lambda_1 \dots \lambda_{k-1})$ generated by a randomized policy τ are defined similarly to the deterministic case.

In the case of perfect information it is known that randomized policies are not better than deterministic ones for the $\boldsymbol{R}^r$-criterion [4]. This result can be extended to the partial information case.

Theorem 5 *For every randomized policy τ and for every k there exists a deterministic policy σ such that $\boldsymbol{R}_k^r(\tau) \leq \boldsymbol{R}_k^r(\sigma)$.*

The proof is rather straightforward but technical, and is based on considerations of convexity of $\boldsymbol{R}^r$ with respect to some kind of addition of policies.
In a similar way as for deterministic policies, we define the notion of *finite memory randomized policy.*
A randomized policy τ defined by the function $\Lambda^\tau : C^+ \times D \rightarrow [0,1]$, is a *finite memory policy* if there exists a finite transition system $\mathcal{T} = (States,\ C,\ \delta,\ p_0)$ and a function $\Lambda^{\tau'} : States \times D \rightarrow [0,1]$, such that for all $W \in C^+$

$$\Lambda^\tau(W, \lambda) = \Lambda^{\tau'}(p_0.W, \lambda)$$

and, for all $q \in States$

$$\textstyle\sum_{\lambda \in D} \Lambda^{\tau'}(q, \lambda) = 1.$$

The *size of the memory* is the size of the transition system.

Randomized vs. deterministic finite memory policies. We give here an example when finite memory randomized policies are better than the deterministic ones. Constructing examples of this type it is reasonable to take into account the complexity of CU-graphs and of policies, in particular, the complexity of random number generators with respect to the simple uniform 0-1 Bernoulli source. Our example deals with grids, for less 'geometric' graphs one can find simpler examples.

Proposition 2 *Given an integer M, there exists a CU-graph G_M for which the following property holds: there exists a randomized policy τ with finite memory bounded by M such that for every deterministic policy σ with finite memory bounded by M, we have $\boldsymbol{R}_\infty^{s,T}(\tau) > \boldsymbol{R}_\infty^{s,T}(\sigma)$.*

Proof : Consider the square grid G of size $n \times n$, $n > M$ being odd. The set of actions is $D = \{N,\ E,\ S,\ W\}$, the actions corresponding to cardinal points. One side of the square is fixed as the target. We use two colors, *black* and *white*. All the vertices are *white* except the target vertices which are *black*. We take four copies of the same grid but with four different target sides (with respect to cardinal points) with centres $o_1,\ o_2,\ o_3,\ o_4$. We add a *white* source vertex s. Define the function μ as follows. For s, we put $\mu(d, s, o_i) = 1/4$ whatever be the action d, $i = 1, \dots, 4$. So starting from s, after one step, we reach one of the four centres with the same probability. For every vertex u in the grids and every direction $d \in D$, taking action d in state u, we go to its d-neighbour with probability 1 if this d-neighbour exists otherwise we remain in state u with the same probability 1.
Let σ be a finite memory deterministic policy with memory size bounded by M.

Consider its behavior when it starts from the centre of one grid. While the policy sees white states its behavior is defined by a deterministic automaton without input. But the state transition diagram of such an automaton is a (directed) cycle, say Z, with a directed simple path, say Y, of vertices coming in it. Thus, once having done Y, the policy starts some periodic behavior.

The sequence Y determines some displacement inside the interior of the square. After having done this displacement the policy follows the periodic pattern defined by Z. If this pattern is strictly inside the square the displacement is determined by the vector going from the initial to the end vertex of the pattern. We will call it the *displacement vector*. But when the policy reaches a white boundary, further displacements are along the projection of the vector on the boundary. On the whole the policy can reach vertices situated on at most two adjacent boundaries but without end extremities different from their joint vertex.

Now launch in G a deterministic policy σ with memory bounded by M. Suppose, without loss of generality, that its displacement vector belongs to North-West quadrant. With probability $1/2$ it arrives in a grid where the target is either the North or West boundary. Thus σ reaches the target with probability not more than $1/2$.

On the other hand, the randomized policy τ which defines the usual uniform random walk in the square reaches the target with probability 1. And τ has a very small constant memory even if it uses for random generation of directions the uniform zero-one Bernoulli source. □

References

1. D. P. Bertsekas. *Dynamic Programming and Stochastic Control.* Academic Press, New York, 1976.
2. D. Burago, M. de Rougemont, and A. Slissenko. On the complexity of partially observed Markov decision processes. 19p., accepted to *Theor. Comput. Sci.*, 1995.
3. C. J. Eilenberg. *Automata, Languages and Machines.* Academic Press, New York, 1974. Vol. A.
4. L.C.M. Kallenberg. Linear programming and finite Markovian control problems. Technical Report 148, Mathematics Centrum Tract, Amsterdam, 1983.
5. C. H. Papadimitriou and J. N. Tsitsiklis. The complexity of Markov decision procedures. *Mathematics of Operations Research,* 12(3):441–450, 1987.
6. M.L. Puterman. Markov decision processes. In D.P. Heyman and M.J. Sobel, editors, *Handbooks in Operations Research and Management Science. Stochastic Models.*, pages 331–434. North Holland, 1990. Vol. 2.

Derandomization for Sparse Approximations and Independent Sets

Thomas Hofmeister and Hanno Lefmann

Lehrstuhl Informatik II, Universität Dortmund, D-44221 Dortmund, Germany
hofmeist,lefmann@ls2.informatik.uni-dortmund.de

Abstract. It is known (see Althöfer [A]) that for every $n \times m$-matrix A with entries taken from the interval $[0,1]$ and for every probability vector $\underline{p}$, there is a sparse probability vector $\underline{q}$ with only $O(\ln n/\varepsilon^2)$ nonzero entries such that every component of the vector $A \cdot \underline{q}$ differs from every component of $A \cdot \underline{p}$ in absolute value by at most ε.
In [A], the existence of such a vector is proved by a probabilistic argument. It is stated as an open problem whether there is an efficient, i.e. polynomial-time, deterministic algorithm which actually constructs such a vector $\underline{q}$.
In this paper, we provide such an algorithm which takes time polynomial in n,m, and $1/\varepsilon$. The algorithm is based on the method of "pessimistic estimators", introduced by Raghavan [R].
Moreover, we apply a similar derandomization strategy to the Independent Set Problem for graphs with not too many triangles. Improving recent results of Halldórsson and Radhakrishnan [HR], we give an efficient algorithm which computes an independent set of size $\Omega(\frac{n}{\Delta} \ln \Delta)$ for a graph G on n vertices with maximum degree Δ, if G contains only a little less than the maximum possible number of triangles (say $n\Delta^{2-\epsilon}$ many for a positive constant ε). This algorithm is based on earlier results concerning the independence number of triangle-free graphs due to Ajtai, Komlós, Szemerédi [AKS1] and Shearer [S1].

1 Introduction

In [A], Althöfer proved the following

Theorem 1. *Let $A = (a_{i,j})$ be an $n \times m-$matrix over the real numbers with $0 \leq a_{i,j} \leq 1$ for $1 \leq i \leq n$ and $1 \leq j \leq m$. Let $\underline{p} = (p_1, \ldots, p_m)$ be a probability vector (i.e. $p_i \geq 0$ for $1 \leq i \leq m$ and $\sum_{i=1}^{m} p_i = 1$).*
Then for every real $\varepsilon > 0$ there exists a probability vector $\underline{q} = (q_1, \ldots, q_m)$ with at most $\lceil \ln(2n)/(2\varepsilon^2) \rceil$ nonzero entries such that $A \cdot \underline{q}$ is "ε-close" to $A \cdot \underline{p}$, i.e.,

$$|\sum_{j=1}^{m} a_{i,j} p_j - \sum_{j=1}^{m} a_{i,j} q_j| \leq \varepsilon \quad \textit{for } i = 1, \ldots, n.$$

It should be noted that this theorem is useful provided $\ln n/\varepsilon^2 = o(m)$. This approximation result was crucial in some applications to matrix games, linear

programming, computer chess and uniform sampling spaces, cf. [A]. A variant of von Neumann's Min Max Theorem, which is also related to Theorem 1, has been investigated by Lipton and Young [LY] and Althöfer. Moreover, in [LY], applications of this result to Complexity Theory are given.
For the proof of Theorem 1, probabilistic arguments were used. These yield only the existence of a vector $\underline{q}$ with the desired properties. In [A] it was stated as an open problem whether there exists a fast, i.e. polynomial-time, deterministic algorithm to construct such a vector $\underline{q}$. Here, we give such an algorithm:

Theorem 2. *Let A be an $n \times m$-matrix with real entries from the interval $[0,1]$ and let $\underline{p}$ be a probability vector of length m. Let $0 < \varepsilon \leq 1$.
There exists a deterministic algorithm with running time $O\left(n \cdot m \cdot \ln n/\varepsilon^2\right)$, which constructs a probability vector $\underline{q}$ with at most $2.93 \cdot \ln(4n)/\varepsilon^2$ nonzero entries such that $A \cdot \underline{q}$ is ε-close to $A \cdot \underline{p}$.*

The sequential algorithm from Theorem 2 can easily be parallelized yielding an NC-algorithm for the approximation problem.
Concerning the applications to matrix games, linear programming and others given in [A], Theorem 1 was the central tool. Thus, Theorem 2 provides the corresponding efficient deterministic algorithms for these applications.
In related work, Young [Y] gives an algorithm for finding sparse strategies for two-player zero-sum games given by a matrix A. Given $\varepsilon > 0$, his algorithm finds a sparse distribution $\underline{q}$ such that $\max_i \sum_j A_{i,j} \cdot q_j \leq (\min_{\underline{p}} \max_i \sum_j A_{i,j} \cdot p_j) + \varepsilon$. Thus, his strategy does not require an initial distribution $\underline{p}$ to be known, but controls deviations in one direction, only for the largest entry. Contrary to this, our algorithm works for arbitrarily given distributions $\underline{p}$ and controls deviations from $A \cdot \underline{p}$ in both directions, for *all* coordinates.
In the second part of this paper, we are concerned with another application for the derandomization technique. Namely, we apply it in the context of approximation algorithms for independent sets in graphs and obtain the following result:

Theorem *Let $G = (V, E)$ be a graph with $|V| = n$ and average degree $d \neq 0$. Let G contain $s \geq 1$ triangles. There is a deterministic algorithm with running time $O(|E| \cdot d + n)$ which finds an independent set in G of size at least $c \cdot \frac{n}{d} \cdot \ln(\beta \cdot d)$, where $\beta = \min\{1, \sqrt{\frac{n}{s}}\}$ and c is some fixed positive constant.*

This improves on recent results in [HR], where a Greedy strategy together with the removal of a maximal collection of pairwise disjoint triangles was used.

2 Sparse Approximations

2.1 A Sketch of the Probabilistic Proof

In order to keep this note self-contained and to indicate how our deterministic algorithm mimics the probabilistic argument to guarantee an appropriate sparse vector, we sketch in this section the probabilistic proof of Theorem 1 from [A].

Let $\varepsilon > 0$ be given, and let $0 \leq a_{i,j} \leq 1$ be the entries of the $n \times m$-matrix A and let $\underline{p} = (p_1, \ldots, p_m)$ be a probability vector. Set $\underline{res} = (res_1, \ldots, res_n) = A \cdot \underline{p}$. Then each entry res_z, $z = 1, \ldots, n$, is contained in the interval $[0, 1]$.
The probability vector $\underline{p}$ is used to define a random experiment which consists of r independent identically distributed random variables X_i with range $\{1, \ldots, m\}$. For $i = 1, \ldots, r$, let X_i be defined by choosing $X_i = j$ with probability p_j for $j = 1, \ldots, m$. The meaning behind this is that we choose one of the rows of $\underline{p}$ with the corresponding probability. Then we count for each row j how often it has been chosen during our random experiment, i.e. $count_j := \#\{i \mid X_i = j\}$. The vector $\underline{count}$ is regarded as the outcome of our experiment.
It is easy to see that the expected value of the k−th component $(A \cdot \underline{count})_k$ is equal to $r \cdot res_k$. Large deviations of $(A \cdot \underline{count})_k / r$ from res_k become the more unlikely the larger one chooses r, i.e. the number of random variables, in this experiment. Using Hoeffding's inequality, one can compute a number r to guarantee that there is at least one *good* outcome of the experiment, i.e. one, where the vector $\underline{count}$ has the property that $A \cdot \underline{count}/r$ is ε-close to $A \cdot \underline{p}$. It turns out that r can be chosen such that $r = O(\ln n / \varepsilon^2)$.

2.2 The Deterministic Construction

In this section we will give the proof of Theorem 2. Our construction is closely related to the probabilistic approach. We mimic the random experiment in such a way that in each round we compute *deterministically* how to choose X_i. This strategy is based on the method of "pessimistic estimators" introduced by Raghavan [R], cf. also Alon, Spencer and Erdös [ASE].
For the purpose of a more closed presentation, we generalize the above experiment. Namely, we allow the probability distributions for the X_i to be different for each i. This means that we associate with each X_i its own probability vector $\underline{b_i} = (b_{i,1}, \ldots, b_{i,m})$ for $1 \leq i \leq r$. Thus the probability that $X_i = j$ equals $b_{i,j}$ for $1 \leq i \leq r$ and $1 \leq j \leq m$. In this setting, the experiment used in the probabilistic proof can be described by $\underline{b_i} = \underline{p}$ for $i = 1, \ldots, r$.
We call a probability distribution $\underline{b_i}$ *sharp* if there exists a j such that $b_{i,j} = 1$. Let us denote by $\underline{e_k}$ the sharp distribution which has $e_{k,k} = 1$.
The general idea behind our algorithm is as follows: We will give an upper bound $F(\underline{b_1}, \ldots, \underline{b_r})$ for the probability that the outcome of the random experiment with the probability distributions $\underline{b_1}, \ldots, \underline{b_r}$ is *bad*. This upper bound has two nice properties, i.e.:

- It is easy to compute.
- We can easily find an integer k such that $F(\underline{e_k}, \underline{b_2}, \ldots, \underline{b_r}) \leq F(\underline{b_1}, \underline{b_2}, \ldots, \underline{b_r})$

As the probability distributions $\underline{b_i}$ are assumed to be arbitrary, this means that step by step, we can redefine our experiment, making the distributions sharp one after the other. We end up with an experiment which has only one outcome, hence it is deterministic. The failure bound gives a value which is at most the value of the bound we started with. If this latter bound is smaller than 1, then

the actual probability that the outcome is bad must be smaller than 1, i.e. it is 0. Hence, the deterministic experiment yields a *good* outcome.
Now to the details. We define n new random variables ψ_z, $z = 1, \ldots, n$, which depend on the X_i by $\psi_z = \sum_{i=1}^{r} a_{z,X_i}$. Note that ψ_z corresponds to the value of the z−th component in the vector $A \cdot \underline{count}$. For $z = 1, \ldots, n$, the expected value $E[\psi_z]$ of the random variable ψ_z is given by $E[\psi_z] = \sum_{i=1}^{r} E[a_{z,X_i}] = \sum_{i=1}^{r} \sum_{w=1}^{m} b_{i,w} \cdot a_{z,w}$. Observe that $E[\psi_z] = r \cdot res_z$ if $\underline{b_i} = \underline{p}$ for $i = 1, \ldots, n$. We want to achieve that each ψ_z is contained in a certain interval $[Low_z, Upp_z]$ for $z = 1, \ldots, n$, where Low_z and Upp_z will be specified later. Let P_z and Q_z (we suppress the underlying probability distributions $\underline{b_1}, \ldots, \underline{b_r}$ in the notation) be defined by $P_z := Prob\ (\psi_z > Upp_z)$ and $Q_z := Prob\ (\psi_z < Low_z)$.
Recall Markov's inequality, i.e. for every nonnegative random variable X and every real number $a > 0$ it is valid that $Prob\ (X > a) < \frac{E[X]}{a}$. We infer for every $t > 0$ and every $B > 1$ that

$$\begin{aligned} Prob\ (X > a) &= Prob\ (B^{t \cdot X} > B^{t \cdot a}) < B^{-t \cdot a} \cdot E[B^{t \cdot X}] \\ \text{as well as}\quad Prob\ (X < a) &< B^{t \cdot a} \cdot E[B^{-t \cdot X}]\,. \end{aligned} \tag{1}$$

Hence, for every real $t > 0$, we have $P_z < B^{-t \cdot Upp_z} \cdot E[B^{t \cdot \psi_z}]$ as well as $Q_z < B^{t \cdot Low_z} \cdot E[B^{-t \cdot \psi_z}]$.
For the intuition, let us remark that later on, we will choose t as some number between 0 and 1. By definition of ψ_z, we have

$$P_z < B^{-t \cdot Upp_z} \cdot E[\prod_{i=1}^{r} B^{t a_{z,X_i}}] = B^{-t \cdot Upp_z} \cdot \prod_{i=1}^{r} E[B^{t a_{z,X_i}}]\,,$$

as the random variables X_i are mutually independent. For each term $E[B^{t a_{z,X_i}}]$, we have $E[B^{t a_{z,X_i}}] = b_{i,1} \cdot B^{t a_{z,1}} + \cdots + b_{i,m} \cdot B^{t a_{z,m}}$. This yields

$$P_z < B^{-t \cdot Upp_z} \cdot \prod_{i=1}^{r} \sum_{j=1}^{m} b_{i,j} \cdot B^{t \cdot a_{z,j}}\,. \tag{2}$$

The expression for Q_z is similar - just replace t by $-t$ and Upp_z by Low_z.
By Taylor's formula, with $c_1 = \ln B$ and $c_2 = \frac{(\ln B)^2}{2} + \frac{(\ln B)^3}{6} \cdot B$, we can estimate $B^{t a_{z,i}} \leq 1 + a_{z,i} \cdot (c_1 t + c_2 t^2)$ as well as $B^{-t a_{z,i}} \leq 1 + a_{z,i} \cdot (-c_1 t + c_2 t^2)$ which we can plug into the upper bounds for P_z and Q_z. In doing so, we abbreviate the product terms in the upper bounds for P_z and Q_z by $PT_z(\underline{b_i}) := \sum_{j=1}^{m} b_{i,j} \cdot (1 + a_{z,j} \cdot (c_1 t + c_2 t^2))$ and by $QT_z(\underline{b_i}) := \sum_{j=1}^{m} b_{i,j} \cdot (1 + a_{z,j} \cdot (-c_1 t + c_2 t^2))$.
For the *failure probability* W that there exists at least one integer z such that ψ_z is *not* contained in the interval $[Low_z, Upp_z]$, we have $W \leq \sum_{z=1}^{n} (P_z + Q_z)$, and hence we infer

$$W \leq F(\underline{b_1}, \ldots, \underline{b_r}) := \sum_{z=1}^{n} B^{\lceil -t \cdot Upp_z \rceil} \cdot \prod_{i=1}^{r} PT_z(\underline{b_i}) + \sum_{z=1}^{n} B^{\lceil t \cdot Low_z \rceil} \cdot \prod_{i=1}^{r} QT_z(\underline{b_i})\,.$$

We used here the ceiling function in the exponents of B to make an evaluation of F easier. The algorithm proceeds as follows: For $k = 1, \ldots, m$, the bound $F(\underline{e_k}, \underline{b_2}, \ldots, \underline{b_r})$ is computed and $\underline{b_1}$ is replaced by the first $\underline{e_k}$ such that $F(\underline{e_k}, \underline{b_2}, \ldots, \underline{b_r}) \leq F(\underline{b_1}, \underline{b_2}, \ldots, \underline{b_r})$. We will see that the choice of such a k is always possible. The replacement procedure can of course be applied in r rounds to every $\underline{b_i}$, leaving us with r sharp distributions. This gives the deterministic procedure provided we can find distributions $\underline{b_1}, \ldots, \underline{b_r}$ and values for t and r such that the choice $Low_z = r \cdot res_z - r \cdot \varepsilon$ and $Upp_z = r \cdot res_z + r \cdot \varepsilon$ yields a failure bound F which is smaller than 1. This will be dealt with in the next subsection. First, we show that the choice of an appropriate k is always possible. As $PT_z(\underline{e_j}) = 1 + a_{z,j} \cdot (c_1 t + c_2 t^2)$, we infer that $PT_z(\underline{b_i}) = \sum_{j=1}^{m} b_{i,j} \cdot PT_z(\underline{e_j})$. Using the corresponding identities for QT_z, we obtain $F(\underline{b_1}, \ldots, \underline{b_r}) = \sum_{j=1}^{m} b_{1,j} \cdot F(\underline{e_j}, \underline{b_2}, \ldots, \underline{b_r})$. Since $\underline{b_1}$ is a probability distribution, there is an integer k such that $F(\underline{e_k}, \underline{b_2}, \ldots, \underline{b_r}) \leq F(\underline{b_1}, \underline{b_2}, \ldots, \underline{b_r})$.

2.3 Bounding the Probability in the Beginning

For our strategy to work, it has to be guaranteed that the failure bound F can be made smaller than 1 by choosing r and t appropriately.
To do so, it is near at hand to start with the set of distributions which was used in the existence proof, i.e. $\underline{b_1} = \cdots = \underline{b_r} = \underline{p}$. For this choice of distributions,

$$PT_z(\underline{p}) = \sum_{j=1}^{m} p_j \cdot (1 + a_{z,j} \cdot (c_1 t + c_2 t^2)) \;=\; 1 + (c_2 t^2 + c_1 t) \cdot res_z \,.$$

Again, for $QT_z(\underline{p})$ the same bound holds with t replaced by $-t$. Plugging these into the failure bound $F(\underline{p}, \ldots, \underline{p})$, we obtain

$$F = \sum_{z=1}^{n} B^{\lceil -t \cdot Upp_z \rceil} \cdot (1 + res_z \cdot (c_2 t^2 + c_1 t))^r + \sum_{z=1}^{n} B^{\lceil t \cdot Low_z \rceil} \cdot (1 + res_z \cdot (c_2 t^2 - c_1 t))^r \,.$$

Using the inequality $1 + x \leq e^x = B^{x/\ln B}$ and the property that $1 + res_z \cdot (c_2 \cdot t^2 - c_1 \cdot t) > 0$, we infer that

$$F \leq \sum_{z=1}^{n} B^{\lceil -t \cdot Upp_z \rceil + res_z \cdot (c_2 \cdot t^2 + c_1 \cdot t) \cdot r / \ln B} + \sum_{z=1}^{n} B^{\lceil t \cdot Low_z \rceil + res_z \cdot (c_2 \cdot t^2 - c_1 \cdot t) \cdot r / \ln B} .$$

With $Upp_z = r \cdot (res_z + \varepsilon)$, and $Low_z = r \cdot (res_z - \varepsilon)$, and $c_1 = \ln B$ we obtain

$$F \leq 2 \cdot B \cdot \sum_{z=1}^{n} B^{-t \cdot r \cdot \varepsilon + res_z \cdot c_2 \cdot t^2 \cdot r / \ln B} \leq 2 \cdot B \cdot n \cdot B^{r \cdot (-t \cdot \varepsilon + c_2 \cdot t^2 / \ln B)} \,.$$

The last expression is smaller than 1 (and hence our failure bound in the beginning), if we choose $t = \varepsilon \cdot \ln B / (2 c_2)$ and

$$r \;>\; \frac{\ln(2Bn)}{\varepsilon^2} \cdot \frac{4 \cdot c_2}{(\ln B)^2} \;=\; \frac{\ln(2Bn)}{\varepsilon^2} \cdot 4 \cdot \left(\frac{1}{2} + \frac{B \cdot \ln B}{6} \right) . \tag{3}$$

In particular, for $B = 2$, expression (3) is less than $2.93 \cdot \ln(4n)/\varepsilon^2$.
This means that we have found a deterministic procedure which allows us to determine values for $X_1, \ldots, X_r$ such that the vector $\underline{\psi} = A \cdot \underline{count}$ is $r \cdot \varepsilon$-close to $r \cdot \underline{res}$. This is guaranteed by our choices of Upp_z and Low_z. Thus, defining $\underline{q} := \underline{count}/r$ gives a probability vector $\underline{q}$ such that $A \cdot \underline{q}$ is ε-close to $\underline{res} = A \cdot \underline{p}$. Looking at the way we carried out our experiment, we find that in this vector, only $r = O(\ln n/\varepsilon^2)$ entries are nonzero. Nonzero entries are multiples of $1/r$.

2.4 Computational Aspects

We assume a model of computation where operations with real numbers are possible. The reason for this assumption is that the calculations can easily be done using finite precision arithmetic only. The algorithm would not be affected since our estimates are rather robust.
For estimating the running time of our algorithm we therefore assume a uniform cost model, where each basic operation (addition, multiplication, exponentiation and their inverses) takes one time-unit. First we fix the values of t and r in constant time. Moreover, we compute the vector $\underline{res} = A \cdot \underline{p}$ in time $O(m \cdot n)$. During our algorithm we maintain $r \times n$ matrices PM and QM which contain as entries the values of $PT_z(\underline{b_i})$ and $QT_z(\underline{b_i})$, $1 \leq z \leq n$ and $1 \leq i \leq r$. In the beginning we have $\underline{b_1} = \ldots = \underline{b_r} = \underline{p}$. Using the entries of the vector $\underline{res}$, we can compute the value of each $PT_z(\underline{p})$ or $QT_z(\underline{p})$ in constant time and thus PM and QM can be computed in time $O(n \cdot r)$. Moreover, we compute all products $(PT_z(\underline{p}))^r$ and $(QT_z(\underline{p}))^r$, $1 \leq z \leq n$, and store them in lists PL and QL. This can be done in time $O(n \cdot r)$. Thus for this preprocessing we have a running time of $O(n \cdot (r + m))$.
During our algorithm we update the entries of the matrices PM and QM and of the lists PL and QL after each round, once for fixed i some probability vector $\underline{b_i}$ is replaced by some $\underline{e_k}$. Computing the corresponding values $PT_z(\underline{e_k})$ and $QT_z(\underline{e_k})$, $1 \leq z \leq n$, takes time $O(n)$, as $\underline{e_k}$ is a sharp distribution. Using the entries of the lists PL and QL, we can calculate $F(\underline{b_1}, \underline{b_2}, \ldots, \underline{b_r})$ in time $O(n)$. Computing then, say, $F(\underline{e_j}, \underline{b_2}, \ldots, \underline{b_r})$ for $j = 1, 2, \ldots, m$, the decision about the particular choice for the sharp distribution $\underline{e_j}$ takes time $O(n \cdot m)$ again by using the lists PL and QL (dividing the z–th entry of PL by $PT_z(\underline{b_1})$ and then multiplying by $PT_z(\underline{e_j})$ and similarly for QL). As our algorithm consists of r rounds we obtain an overall running time of $O(r \cdot n \cdot m) = O\left(n \cdot m \cdot \ln n/\varepsilon^2\right)$.
We remark that for each round of our algorithm there is obviously an NC-algorithm for doing the corresponding computations. As the number of rounds is bounded by $O(\ln n/\varepsilon^2)$, this yields an NC-algorithm for the approximation problem, provided that $1/\varepsilon$ is polylogarithmic in $n \cdot m$.

3 Independent Sets

In this section we use derandomization to establish an algorithm which computes large independent sets in graphs with not too many triangles.

For an undirected graph $G = (V, E)$, a vertex subset $V' \subseteq V$ is called *independent* if the subgraph of G induced by V' contains no edges. Let $\alpha(G)$ be the independence number of G, i.e., the maximum size of an independent set in G. Computing $\alpha(G)$ is an NP-hard problem, even for graphs with bounded maximum degree Δ (i.e., maximum number of edges incident to a vertex).
Define the performance ratio ρ_A of an algorithm A by $\rho_A := \sup_G \frac{\alpha(G)}{A(G)}$, where $A(G)$ is the size of an independent set obtained by algorithm A.
The Greedy algorithm picks a vertex of smallest degree, deletes this vertex and its neighbours, and iterates this procedure on the remaining graph. In [HR] it is shown that $\rho_{Greedy} \leq (\Delta + 2)/3$. For triangle-free graphs, a better algorithm is known. Ajtai, Komlós and Szemerédi [AKS1] [AKS2] proved that if G is a triangle-free graph on n vertices with average degree d, then $\alpha(G) \geq \Omega\left(\frac{n}{d} \cdot \ln d\right)$. A random graph argument shows that this is best possible up to a constant factor. Based on this, Shearer gave in [S1], cf. [S2], an algorithm which finds an independent set in G of size $\Omega\left(\frac{n}{d} \cdot \ln d\right)$. Thus, his algorithm has a performance ratio of $O\left(\frac{d}{\ln d}\right)$ on triangle-free graphs which is better than the value which can be guaranteed by the Greedy algorithm. Shearer's algorithm finds a vertex v with degree $d(v)$ such that the average degree $\overline{d(v)}$ of its neighbours satisfies $(d(v)+1) \cdot f(d) \leq 1 + (d \cdot d(v) + d(v) - 2 \cdot d(v) \cdot \overline{d(v)}) \cdot f'(d)$, where $f(d) = \frac{d \cdot \ln d - d + 1}{(d-1)^2}$. Then, v is added to the independent set and removed from the graph, together with its neighbours. The procedure is iterated on the remaining graph. The running time of this algorithm is $O\left(|E| + min\{\Delta^2 \cdot n, n \cdot \ln n\}\right)$.
For graphs which contain triangles, [HR] proposed the following: Find a maximal collection of disjoint triangles in the graph, remove the underlying vertices, and then apply Shearer's algorithm to the remaining graph. However, this simple strategy might result in a very small graph, in which case only trivial conclusions on the independence number can be drawn. For graphs with average degree d we give an algorithm with a performance ratio of $O\left(\frac{d}{\ln d}\right)$ which avoids these difficulties, i.e. the input graphs can still have a lot of triangles.
First we show the following result, which might be of interest on its own.

Lemma 3. *Let $G = (V, E)$ be a graph with $|V| = n$, $|E| = m$, and which contains s triangles. Let its average degree be $d := \frac{2\,|E|}{n}$. There is an algorithm with running time $O(|E| \cdot d + n)$ which on input G, and p, $(0 < p \leq 1)$ finds an induced subgraph $G^* = (V^*, E^*)$ which contains s^* triangles such that:*

$$|V^*| \geq |V| \cdot \frac{p}{6} \quad and \quad |E^*| \leq |E| \cdot 3p^2 \quad and \quad s^* \leq s \cdot 3p^3 .$$

Proof. Let $V = \{v_1, \ldots, v_n\}$ and let T denote the set of triangles in G. The algorithm first checks whether $p \leq 6/n$. If so, it outputs an arbitrary vertex which is a subgraph fulfilling the properties. Hence, we can assume in the rest of the proof that $p > 6/n$.
The existence of the desired subgraph G^* can be shown by picking vertices of V at random, independently of each other with probability p. As we did earlier in this paper, we start by generalizing the probabilistic experiment. Every vertex

v_i is now chosen with probability p_i. Let $X^{(E)}_{p_1,\ldots,p_n}$, $X^{(T)}_{p_1,\ldots,p_n}$ and $X^{(V)}_{p_1,\ldots,p_n}$ be random variables which count in the induced random subgraph the number of edges, triangles and vertices, respectively. First, we want to get a subgraph with at least $Low_V := |V|\, p/3$ vertices, with at most $Upp_E := |E| \cdot 3p^2$ edges and at most $Upp_T := s \cdot 3p^3$ triangles.
In order to apply our deterministic procedure, we estimate the probability P for the "bad event" by $P \leq Prob\ (X^{(E)} > Upp_E) + Prob\ (X^{(T)} > Upp_T) + Prob\ (X^{(V)} < Low_V)$. Applying Markov's inequality to the first two terms and the analogue of inequality (2) in Section 2.2 to the third term, with $B = e$, and $t = \ln 3$, i.e., $B^t = 3$, we obtain

$$P \leq \frac{E[X^{(E)}]}{Upp_E} + \frac{E[X^{(T)}]}{Upp_T} + 3^{Low_V} \cdot \left(1 - \frac{2}{3}p_1\right) \cdots \left(1 - \frac{2}{3}p_n\right) .$$

This suggests to define the failure bound $F(p_1, \ldots, p_n)$ to be the right hand side of the above inequality. Since

$$E[X^{(E)}_{p_1,\ldots,p_n}] = \sum_{\{i,j\} \in E(G)} p_i \cdot p_j \quad \text{as well as} \quad E[X^{(T)}_{p_1,\ldots,p_n}] = \sum_{\{i,j,k\} \in T} p_i \cdot p_j \cdot p_k ,$$

the failure bound is linear in every p_i. Therefore, the following identity holds: $F(p_1, p_2, \ldots, p_n) = p_1 \cdot F(1, p_2, \ldots, p_n) + (1 - p_1) \cdot F(0, p_2, \ldots, p_n)$. This means that our deterministic procedure can be applied to the failure bound since one of the two choices "replace p_1 by 0" or "replace p_1 by 1" does not increase the value of the failure bound, i.e., $\min\{F(0, p_2, \ldots, p_n), F(1, p_2, \ldots, p_n)\} \leq F(p_1, \ldots, p_n)$. We choose v_1 to be in V^* if and only if $F(1, p_2, \ldots, p_n) \leq F(0, p_2, \ldots, p_n)$. Iterating this for all vertices yields the desired set V^*. Starting the algorithm with $p_i = p$ for all i, we start with the failure bound

$$F(p, \ldots, p) = \frac{p^2|E|}{3p^2|E|} + \frac{p^3 s}{3p^3 s} + 3^{Low_V}\left(1 - \frac{2}{3}p\right)^n < \frac{2}{3} + \left(\frac{3}{e^2}\right)^{pn/3} ,$$

which is less than 1 since $pn > 6$. Thus, the subgraph finding procedure works well.
Now to the analysis of its running time; it will be seen why we chose $Low_V = pn/3$ instead of $pn/6$. First, we remove all vertices of G with degree larger than $2d$ and obtain a graph G' with at least $n/2$ vertices and at most $O(|E| \cdot d)$ triangles. To G', we apply the above subgraph finding procedure. It is easily seen that the failure bound $F(p, \ldots, p)$ can be computed in time $O(n)$. If at a stage of the subgraph finding algorithm we have to decide whether we take a vertex v_i or not, we have to determine the values $F(p_1, \ldots, p_i := 0, \ldots, p_n)$ and $F(p_1, \ldots p_i := 1, \ldots, p_n)$. This takes time proportional to the number of edges and triangles incident to v_i since only their corresponding terms in the failure bound might change. Hence the overall running time is bounded by $O(|E| \cdot d + n)$. □

As an application of Lemma 3 we have the following result.

Theorem 4. *Let $G = (V, E)$ be a graph with $|V| = n$ and average degree $d \neq 0$. Let G contain $s \geq 1$ triangles. There is a deterministic algorithm with running time $O(|E| \cdot d + n)$ which finds an independent set in G of size at least $c \cdot \frac{n}{d} \cdot \ln(\beta \cdot d)$, where $\beta = \min\{1, \sqrt{\frac{n}{s}}\}$, and c is some fixed positive constant.*

Proof. We apply Lemma 3 with $p := \min\{\sqrt{\frac{n}{72s}}, 1\}$ and obtain a subgraph G^*. By the choice of p, we have $s3p^3 \leq np/24$, i.e., G^* has at least $pn/6$ vertices, at most $pn/24$ triangles, and average degree bounded by $\frac{2 \cdot 3p^2|E|}{np/6} = 18pd$. Then, we remove all vertices of G^* with degree larger than $36pd$ and call the resulting graph with at least $np/12$ vertices G^{**}. In G^{**}, we remove from every triangle one vertex and obtain a triangle-free subgraph G^{***} on at least $np/12 - np/24 = np/24$ many vertices. All vertices have a degree bounded by $36pd$. Scanning all triangles and removing the vertices can be done in time $O(|E| \cdot d + n)$. To G^{***}, we apply Shearer's algorithm which yields an independent set of size at least $c' \cdot \frac{np/24}{36pd} \cdot \ln(36pd)$. This yields the bound stated in the theorem for some appropriately chosen constant c since $36p \geq \beta$. The running time of Shearer's algorithm applied to G^{***} is $O(|E| + d^2 n) = O(|E| + |E|d)$. □

If we measure the size of the independent sets in terms of the maximum degree Δ, then since $\frac{\ln \Delta}{\Delta} \leq \frac{\ln d}{d}$, our algorithm yields independent sets of size $\Omega(n/\Delta \cdot \ln \Delta)$ even if the number of triangles is very close to the maximum possible number, say $s \leq n\Delta^{2-\epsilon}$. This improves the Greedy algorithm in those cases considerably.

4 Open Problems

It is known that every Boolean function f on n variables can be represented as the product of a $2^n \times 2^n$-Hadamard matrix and some vector v_f. The vector v_f is called the spectrum of f, the 2^n entries of v_f are called the spectral coefficients. Bruck and Smolensky used in [BS] a result very similar to Theorem 1, namely they showed the following. If the sum of the absolute values of the spectral coefficients (the so-called L_1-norm) is bounded by a polynomial, then f can be approximated closely by a linear combination of polynomially many parity functions. This can also be seen as replacing the vector v_f by some sparse vector w_f which only consists of polynomially many – instead of exponentially many – nonzero entries. The result was obtained by a probabilistic argument.
Our algorithm for computing sparse vectors can be used in this environment, but, since the spectrum has exponential size, it would have running time exponential in n. Of course one cannot hope for a general algorithm working in time polynomial in n if the input size is already 2^n, but it might be interesting to investigate whether our algorithm can be applied in situations where the spectrum can be described in a more compact fashion. This interest stems from the fact that there are depth-2 threshold circuits for computing functions with a polynomial L_1-norm [BS]. One such example is the addition function. Meanwhile, for this particular function, a method has beeen found (see e.g. [AB]), to construct the appropriate approximations in time polynomial in n. It might be

interesting to investigate whether there is a nontrivial class of Boolean functions g_n where our algorithm can be adapted in such a way that it provides us with sparse approximations in time only $O(n^k)$ for some fixed integer k.
Halldórsson and Radhakrishnan suggested in [HR] for graphs containing no complete subgraphs K_l on $l \geq 4$ vertices an iterative subgraph removal technique by removing $K_{l-1}, \ldots, K_3$. Besides the problem that their technique might result in an empty graph, the performance guarantee for $l = 4$ was claimed in [HR] to be at most $\frac{\Delta}{3.67} + c$. In [AEKS] it is proved that every graph G on n vertices with average degree d which contains no complete graph $K_l, l \geq 4$, has independence number $\alpha(G) \geq c \cdot \frac{n}{d} \cdot \log(\frac{\log d}{l})$. With the technique above and some additional ideas, their probabilistic argument can be turned into an efficient algorithm with performance ratio $O(\frac{d}{\log \log d})$. However, more interesting might be the question whether the estimate on the independence number can be improved to $\alpha(G) \geq c_l \cdot \frac{n}{d} \cdot \log d$ for K_l-free graphs G, and, in particular, how to achieve this by an efficient algorithm.

References

[AEKS] M. Ajtai, P. Erdös, J. Komlós and E. Szemerédi, *On Turán's Theorem for Sparse Graphs,* Combinatorica 1, 313-317 (1981).

[AKS1] M. Ajtai, J. Komlós and E. Szemerédi, *A Note on Ramsey Numbers,* J. of Combinatorial Theory, Ser. A 29, 354-360 (1980).

[AKS2] M. Ajtai, J. Komlós and E. Szemerédi, *A Dense Infinite Sidon Sequence,* European J. of Combinatorics 2, 2-11 (1981).

[A] I. Althöfer, *On Sparse Approximations to Randomized Strategies and Convex Combinations,* Linear Algebra and its Applications 199, 339-355 (1994).

[AB] N. Alon and J. Bruck, *Explicit Constructions of Depth-2 Majority Circuits for Comparison and Addition,* SIAM J. on Discrete Mathematics 7, 1994, 1-8.

[ASE] N. Alon, J. Spencer and P. Erdös, *The Probabilistic Method,* Wiley & Sons, New York (1992).

[BS] J. Bruck and R. Smolensky, *Polynomial Threshold Functions, AC^0 Functions and Spectral Norms,* SIAM J. on Computing 21, 33-42 (1992).

[HR] M. Halldórsson and J. Radhakrishnan, *Greed is Good: Approximating Independent Sets in Sparse and Bounded-degree Graphs,* Proc. 26th ACM Symp. on Theory of Computing (STOC), 439-448 (1994).

[LY] R. J. Lipton and N. E. Young, *Simple Strategies for Large Zero-Sum Games with Applications to Complexity Theory,* Proc. 26th ACM Symp. on Theory of Computing (STOC), 734-740 (1994).

[R] P. Raghavan, *Probabilistic Construction of Deterministic Algorithms: Approximating Packing Integer Programs,* J. of Computer and System Sciences 37, 130-143 (1988).

[S1] J. Shearer, *A Note on the Independence Number of Triangle-free Graphs,* Discrete Mathematics 46, 83-87 (1983).

[S2] J. Shearer, *A Note on the Independence Number of Triangle-free Graphs, II,* J. of Combinatorial Theory 53, 300-307 (1991).

[Y] N. E. Young, *Greedy Algorithms by Derandomizing Unknown Distributions,* preprint (1994). See also: *Randomized Rounding without Solving the Linear Program,* Proc. 6th ACM-SIAM Symp. on Discrete Algorithms (SODA), to appear (1995).

Asymptotically efficient in-place merging

Jyrki Katajainen[1], Tomi Pasanen[2*], and George Titan[1]

[1] Department of Computer Science, University of Copenhagen, Universitetsparken 1, DK-2100 Copenhagen East, Denmark
[2] Department of Computer Science, University of Turku, Lemminkäisenkatu 14 A, FIN-20520 Turku, Finland

Abstract. Two new linear-time algorithms for *in-place* merging are presented. Both algorithms perform at most $(1+t)m + n/2^t + o(m)$ element comparisons, where m and n are the sizes of the input sequences, $m \le n$, and $t = \lfloor \log_2(n/m) \rfloor$. The first algorithm is for *unstable* merging and it carries out no more than $4(m+n)+o(n)$ element moves. The second algorithm is for *stable* merging and it accomplishes at most $15m + 13n + o(n)$ moves.

1 Introduction

Given two sorted sequences with m and n elements, the classical *merging problem* is to rearrange these to form one sorted sequence of $m+n$ elements. In this merging the primitive operations allowed for the elements are comparisons and moves.

In this paper we study the computational complexity of the *in-place merging problem*, in which the input sequences are given as subarrays of some array $\mathcal{E}$, $\mathcal{E}[1..m]$ and $\mathcal{E}[m+1..m+n]$, and the output is produced into the same array $\mathcal{E}[1..m+n]$. We can assume that the size of the first sequence is less than or equal to that of the second sequence, i.e., $m \le n$. In addition to array $\mathcal{E}$, one more storage location is available for storing elements. This is needed, e.g., when exchanging the places of two elements in $\mathcal{E}$. We assume also that only $O(1)$ storage locations are available for storing array indices, counters, etc. The normal arithmetic operations are used in the manipulation of these.

Assuming that the input sequences are of the same size, $m+n-1$ is the best possible bound for the number of comparisons. However, if one of the sequences is much shorter than the other, the merging problem can be solved with at most $(1+t)m + \lfloor n/2^t \rfloor - 1$ comparisons and $t \cdot m + \lfloor n/2^t \rfloor$ comparisons are known to be necessary to carry out the task, where $t = \lfloor \log_2(n/m) \rfloor$ [5]. The main goal in this paper is to develop in-place merging algorithms, for which the number of comparisons performed is close to the above information-theoretic lower bound.

As to the number of moves, $2m+n$ is the only non-trivial lower bound known by us. This bound can be proved by considering a particular merging instance, where the elements are to be moved according to the following permutation:

$$\begin{pmatrix} 1 & 2 & \cdots & m-1 & m & m+1 & m+2 & \cdots & 2m & 2m+1 & \cdots & m+n \\ m+1 & m+2 & \cdots & 2m-1 & m+n & 1 & 2 & \cdots & m & 2m & \cdots & m+n-1 \end{pmatrix}.$$

* Financially supported by the Graduate School of Turku Centre for Computer Science.

This permutation has m cycles. By [1, Lemma 2.1], at least $2m + n$ moves have to be done when permuting the elements in-place.

A merging algorithm is said to be *stable*, if it retains the original order of elements with equal keys. Many algorithms for in-place merging has been proposed [2, 3, 8, 9, 11]. All these algorithms can be made stable [4, 12, 14, 15], but the resulting algorithms are complicated. According to the analysis of Pasanen [12], the algorithms developed by Huang and Langston [3, 4] have the lowest complexity with respect to the number of moves, if a linear number of comparisons is approved. The only algorithm performing asymptotically the optimal number of comparisons is that by Mannila and Ukkonen [9] as well as its stable variant introduced by Symvonis [15].

For most in-place merging algorithms presented in the literature, the constant factors in their complexity (that is, the number of comparisons and moves performed) are not analysed properly. The only attempts into this direction, we are aware of, appear in [4, 12].

Huang and Langston [3, 4] proved that their unstable algorithm guarantees "a worst-case grand total of something less than" $3.5(m+n)+o(n)$ and that their stable algorithm assures "a worst-case key-comparison and record-exchange grand total bounded above by" $7(m+n)+o(n)$. A more careful analysis shows that the unstable algorithm given in [3] performs at most $1.125(m + n) + o(n)$ element comparisons and $2(m + n) + o(n)$ element exchanges. Note, however, that each element exchange requires 3 moves. Therefore, the number of moves is bounded by $6(m + n) + o(n)$. Katajainen et al. [6] observed that the number of moves can be reduced to $5(m + n) + o(n)$. For the stable algorithm given in [4], the number of comparisons is the same as that required by the unstable algorithm, but the number of exchanges is increased to $5.5(m + n) + o(n)$, which means $16.5(m + n) + o(n)$ moves.

Using the algorithm of Mannila and Ukkonen [9] (cf. Section 3) as our starting point, we show that in-place merging is possible with $(1 + t)m + n/2^t + o(m)$ comparisons and $4(m + n) + o(n)$ moves (Section 4); and that stable in-place merging can also be accomplished with $(1+t)m+n/2^t+o(m)$ comparisons, if the number of moves is increased to $15m + 13n + o(n)$ (Section 5). These results are based on the following observations: (1) the block factor $\sqrt{m}$ used in the original algorithm is not optimal, but a larger factor gives a better performance; (2) the hole technique (cf. Section 2), already in heavy use in [6], can be used to reduce the number of moves.

2 Preliminaries

Throughout this paper we use the following notation. A *block* X is any collection of consecutive elements in the input array $\mathcal{E}$. Any subarray of $\mathcal{E}$ occupying some consecutive elements is called a *zone*. Moreover, $|X|$ denotes the number of elements in X. For two adjacent blocks X and Y, XY is the block consisting of all X-elements followed by all Y-elements. For blocks U, V, X, and Y, if $W = UV$ and $W = XY$, then we write $V = U^{-1}W$ and $X = WY^{-1}$.

2.1 Block interchanging

In *block interchanging* we are given two adjacent blocks, X and Y, not necessarily of the same size, and we want to interchange the order of X-elements and Y-elements.

That is, the task is to produce block YX within the zone originally occupied by XY. Dudziński and Dydek [1] showed how this can be carried out with $|X| + |Y| + \gcd(|X|, |Y|)$ element moves, where $\gcd(a, b)$ denotes the greatest common divisor of positive integers a and b. If the size of X equals to that of Y, it is easy to accomplish the interchanging optimally by exchanging the ith element of X and Y, for all i. In this special case, called *block swapping*, X and Y need not even be adjacent.

The basic requirement in block interchanging (or swapping) is that the order of both X- and Y-elements is retained. However, sometimes the order of elements in one of the blocks is important, whereas the order of elements in the other block is immaterial. In our algorithms this is often the case. If the order of, say, X-elements is immaterial, then the block interchanging can be accomplished as follows. Let us assume that the elements of X (Y) lie on zone A (B). First, the first X-element is taken out from A to create a *hole* in A. Second, the first Y-element is moved into this hole. Third, the second X-element is moved into the hole in B thus creating a new hole in A. This is repeated until Y-elements are exhausted, after which the first X-element can be moved into the hole in B. It is relatively easy to see that the block interchanging for X and Y requires $2|X| + 1$ (resp. $2|Y| + 1$) moves, if the order of X-elements (resp. Y-elements) is to be retained.

2.2 Merging

The merging problem for two adjacent sequences X and Y is easy to solve, if a work-space of size $\min\{|X|, |Y|\}$ is available (see [8, Lemma 3] or [7, Exercise 5.2.4-10]). Actually, the basic idea in most algorithms for in-place merging—as well as in our algorithms—is to reduce the general merging problem to subproblems, where the size of the available work-space is at least the length of the smaller sequence. The work-space is called an *internal buffer* and the technique *internal buffering*.

In our algorithms the following task has to be carried out repeatedly. Given two sorted blocks X, Y, and any block Z on the zones A, B and C, respectively. Pick up the $\min\{|X| + |Y|, |Z|\}$ smallest elements from A and B in sorted order, and replace these with Z-elements originally in C. Here the hole technique can again be applied. First, the first Z-element is removed to create a hole. Second, the smallest remaining X- or Y-element is moved into the hole in C and the Z-element next to this hole into the place of just moved X- or Y-element. This is repeated until zone C is full or both X- and Y-elements are exhausted. Finally, the first Z-element is put into the hole in A or B. The number of moves required by this procedure is clearly $2\min\{|X| + |Y|, |Z|\} + 1$.

3 Basic algorithm

3.1 Binary merge

Let $\mathcal{E}$ be an array of size $m + n$. Assume that the sorted sequences X and Y to be merged lie in consecutive zones of $\mathcal{E}$ and are of size m and n, respectively. Without loss of generality, we assume that $m \leq n$. If this is not the case, the problem can be solved symmetrically by seeing the last entry of $\mathcal{E}$ as the beginning of the input.

Assume that $X = \langle x_1, x_2, \ldots, x_m \rangle$. Let us now mark every 2^tth element in sequence Y, where $t = \lfloor \log_2(n/m) \rfloor$. Observe that this marking is implicit not explicit. In the binary-merge routine of Hwang and Lin [5], the X-elements and the marked Y-elements are first merged by the standard merging algorithm. (In the case of equal elements, X-elements are considered to be smaller.) This will induce a partitioning of Y into blocks Y_i, $i \in \{0, 1, 2, \ldots, m\}$, where every Y-element in Y_i is smaller than x_{i+1} (assume that $x_{m+1} = \infty$). The size of block Y_i is a multiple of 2^t; it can also be zero. To determine the final location of x_i, it is enough to consider the $2^t - 1$ first elements in the first non-empty block Y_j, for which $j \geq i$. Binary search is used to find out how many of those Y-elements are smaller than x_i. When this information is available the sorted output is easy to produce.

From the description above, it should be clear that the total number of element comparisons performed is at most $m + n/2^t + mt$, which is $O(m \log_2(n/m + 1))$.

3.2 Case $m \ll n$

Let us consider how the binary-merge algorithm is implemented with a work-space of size $O(1)$, if the shorter sequence X is much smaller than the longer sequence Y. More precisely, we assume that $m \leq \sqrt{n}$.

We let X' (Y') denote the X-elements (Y-elements) that have not been merged yet. Initially, $X' = X$ and $Y' = Y$. We call the first element x_c (y_c) of X' (Y') the *current X-element* (*Y-element*). Now x_c is compared with the marked Y-element y_* closest to y_c on the right. If $x_c > y_*$, the Y-block—call it Y_1—containing all Y'-elements between y_c and y_* (both included) is interchanged with X', and the first element in block $Y_1^{-1}Y'$ is assigned to be the new current Y-element. If $x_c < y_*$, the Y-block—call it Y_2—containing all Y'-elements smaller than x_c is determined by binary search, X' and Y_2 are interchanged, the first element of $\langle x_c \rangle^{-1}X'$ is assigned to be the new current X-element, and the first element of $Y_2^{-1}Y'$ is assigned to be the new current Y-element. This is repeated until X' or Y' is exhausted.

The number of comparisons performed by the above procedure is at most $m + n/2^t + mt$. Because at each step $\gcd(|X'|, |Y_1|) \leq m$ and $\gcd(|X'|, |Y_2|) \leq m$, the total number of moves performed is bounded by $n + 2m^2$, which is less than or equal to $3n$. One should observe that this procedure merges the blocks stably. Therefore, we shall hereafter assume that $m > \sqrt{n}$.

3.3 In-place merging

Mannila and Ukkonen [9] showed how the binary-merge algorithm can be made in-place. Next we give a detailed description of their algorithm. Observe, however, that some implementation details in our description are different from those given in [9]. This is done in order to get asymptotically a faster algorithm. The basic techniques used in [9] are internal buffering and splitting the smaller input sequence into blocks of size s (to be determined later).

The buffer containing the $2s$ largest elements in the input is created as follows. Observe that a buffer of size $2s$ was already used by Salowe and Steiger [14] in their algorithm for in-place merging. First, the $2s$ largest elements are determinated by scanning the two input sequences X and Y backwards with two cursors. Let $X_{\max}$

($Y_{\max}$) denote the block of X-elements (Y-elements) among the $2s$ largest elements. Further, let X' (Y') be the block $XX_{\max}^{-1}$ ($YY_{\max}^{-1}$). Second, the block X_0 consisting of the $|Y_{\max}|$-largest X-elements in X' and $Y_{\max}$ are swapped. So the buffer elements have been gathered.

Let $X'' = X'X_0^{-1}$ and $r = |X''| \bmod s$. As an initialization, the r first elements of X'' (forming block X_1) are swapped with the r last elements among the s first elements in the buffer. We say that the buffer elements in the beginning of the input array form the *output area*. Initially, the first element of X_1 (Y') is the *current X-element* (*Y-element*). Block X_1 together with the buffer elements in front of it is called the *current X-block*. In general, we can have buffer elements in three places: in the output area, in the current X-block, and in front of Y'.

Now we are ready for merging. The basic idea is simple: Move the elements from the current X-block and Y' in the right order into the output area and increase the size of the output area when necessary. The latter is done by swapping the leftmost X-block with a block containing buffer elements only. As in Subsection 3.2, by using the current X-element x_c we determinate the prefix of Y' that contains all the Y'-elements smaller than x_c. That is, we move m times a Y-block followed by an X-element into the output area. Now there are various special cases that should be handled with care.

Case 1. The output area becomes full. In this case there has to be at least s buffer elements in front of Y'. Now the leftmost X-block (this can be the current X-block) is swapped with the block of s first buffer elements in front of Y'. Here the hole technique is used as described in Subsection 2.1.

Case 2. The current X-block becomes empty. In this case there are s buffer elements in the current X-block. This block is swapped with the leftmost X-block as described in Subsection 2.1. Finally, we scan through the X-blocks to determine, which of them should be the new current X-block. In this scanning the primary key of each block is the key of its first element and the secondary key of each block is the key of its last element. The X-block with the smallest key value is to be processed next. It can also happen that there are no X-blocks left. To handle this, the blocks Y' and X_0 are merged as explained in Subsection 2.2 by using the buffer elements in front of Y' as a work-space.

Case 3. The Y-elements are exhausted. Now the X-elements in the remaining X-blocks are moved forward in the right order. When the output area is full the X-blocks are rotated as in Case 2.

The merging is completed by sorting the buffer elements at the end of the array. For this purpose, heapsort is used.

The correctness of this algorithm should be obvious. At all times the current elements point to the smallest elements in the remaining parts of X and Y. Moreover, the buffer contains the $2s$ largest elements, so these also end up at the right place. We postpone analysing the performance of the algorithm in the next section.

4 Unstable merging

In the original algorithm by Mannila and Ukkonen [9] the block factor $\lceil\sqrt{m}\rceil$ was used. Our basic observation is that a larger block factor gives asymptotically a faster algorithm. In unstable merging, we use $s = \lceil m^{5/8} \rceil$.

The creation of the buffer ($2s$ elements) and all the block swaps in the initialization phase take clearly $O(s)$ time, i.e., $o(m)$ time due to our choice of s. The number of X-blocks is at most $m/\lceil m^{5/8} \rceil \in O(m^{3/8})$. Therefore, the selection of the next current X-block in Cases 2 and 3 requires $O(m^{6/8})$ comparisons in total, which is again $o(m)$. Otherwise the number of comparisons is the same as in the algorithm of Hwang and Lin (cf. Subsection 3.1).

As to the number of moves, each location of the output area takes part in two exchanges. First, an X-element is replaced with a buffer element. Second, the buffer element is replaced by the X-element or Y-element that should be output at the present location. Since we are using the hole technique both in block swapping and in filling the output area, the total number of moves performed is at most $4(m+n) + 2(m+n)/\lceil m^{5/8} \rceil$ (cf. Subsections 2.1 and 2.2). Recall that we assumed that $m > \sqrt{n}$. Hence, the number of moves is bounded by $4(m+n) + o(n)$. Lastly, the buffer sorting takes $O(m^{5/8} \log_2 m)$ time, which is $o(m)$.

The above discussion is summarized in the following

Theorem 1. *Two sorted sequences of size m and n, $m \leq n$, can be merged in-place in $O(m+n)$ time, so that in the worst case the number of comparisons performed is $(1+t)m + n/2^t + o(m)$, $t = \lfloor \log_2(n/m) \rfloor$, and the number of moves $4(m+n) + o(n)$.*

5 Stable merging

In the algorithm presented in Subsection 3.3, the stability can be lost in two places. First, the order of buffer elements is mixed up. Since the buffer might contain equal elements, the original order of these cannot be recovered. Second, the order of X-blocks is mixed up. Since all elements in some blocks can be equal, the order of these homogeneous blocks cannot be recovered. Symvonis [15] presented how these problems can be solved in the algorithm by Mannila and Ukkonen [9]. The basic techniques used by us are similar to those used by Symvonis. However, our goal is again the asymptotical efficiency of the algorithm.

Our purpose in this section is to prove

Theorem 2. *Two sorted sequences of size m and n, $m \leq n$, can be stably merged in-place in $O(m+n)$ time, so that in the worst case the number of comparisons performed is $(1+t)m + n/2^t + o(m)$, $t = \lfloor \log_2(n/m) \rfloor$, and the number of moves $15m + 13n + o(n)$.*

5.1 Creation of the buffer

To avoid the problem with equal buffer elements, we pick up from the X-sequence only distinct elements. This idea was already used in the stable merging algorithm by Huang and Langston [4]. Let $s = \lceil m^{3/8} \rceil + 2\lceil m^{5/8} \rceil$. At most s distinct buffer elements are found by scanning the X-sequence from right to left. Our aim is to gather the buffer elements in front of the remaining X-elements.

Assume that we have already i elements in the buffer B. Let X' denote the block of X-elements not yet processed and let X'' denote the block of those X-elements processed already. These blocks are maintained in order $X'BX''$. Assume that x is the last element in X'. To find the $(i+1)$st buffer element, we use binary search for determining the first element v in X' that is equal to x. Let X_e denote the block of X-elements all equal to x. Now the blocks X_e and B are interchanged resulting the block $B'X_e$ within the zone occupied by X_eB. That is, the order of B-elements may be mixed up. At last, we assign $X' = X'X_e^{-1}$, $X'' = \langle v\rangle^{-1}X_eX''$, and $B = B'\langle v\rangle$. We repeat the above process until the buffer is full or until all the X-elements are exhausted. When the buffer is full, the blocks X' and B are interchanged to get the buffer in front of all other X-elements.

Next we sort the buffer by heapsort. The $\lceil m^{3/8}\rceil$ smallest buffer elements are kept in the beginning of the input array. Their usage is explained in the next subsections. The remaining $2\lceil m^{5/8}\rceil$ buffer elements are used as in Subsection 3.3.

The number of comparisons needed for creating the buffer is $O(m^{5/8}\log_2 m)$. Let h_i denote the size of block X_e at the ith step and h_{s+1} the size of the last X'-block. Since the order of the buffer elements need not be maintained, the number of moves when moving the buffer forward is $\sum_{i=1}^{s+1}(2h_i+1)$. In sorting, $O(m^{5/8}\log_2 m)$ moves are done. Thus, the total number of moves performed is $2m + o(m)$.

5.2 Buffer is very small

Let us first consider the case that the X-sequence contains only at most $2\lceil m^{3/8}\rceil$ distinct elements. That is, the size of the buffer B just created is at most $2\lceil m^{3/8}\rceil$. Let $\ell = |B|$. The configuration of the input array is now $BX''Y$.

Let x_{first} (y_{last}) denote the first (last) element in X'' (Y). Now we use x_{first} to determine the block Y_{small} of all the Y-elements smaller than x_{first}. Let $Y' = Y_{\text{small}}^{-1}Y$. Similarly, we use y_{last} to determine the block X_{large} of all the X-elements larger than y_{last}. Let $X' = X''X_{\text{large}}^{-1}$. Next the configuration of the input array is transformed from $BX'X_{\text{large}}Y_{\text{small}}Y'$ to $BY_{\text{small}}X'Y'X_{\text{large}}$ by suitable block interchanges. The boundaries of X_{large} and Y_{small} are found by binary search. Therefore, only $O(\log_2 n) \in O(\log_2 m)$ comparisons are needed here. For the sake of brevity, we denote $m' = |X'|$ and $n' = |Y'|$. It is easy to see that in the block interchanges at most $3|X_{\text{large}}| + 3|Y_{\text{small}}| + m' + n'$ moves are performed. To complete the merge operation for $X''Y$, the blocks Y_{small} and X_{large} need not be considered any more.

Let $q = \lceil (m'+n')/\ell\rceil$, $p = m' \bmod q$, and $r = n' \bmod q$. The blocks X' and Y' are divided into blocks of size q, except perhaps the first X'-block, which is of size p, and the last Y'-block, which is of size r. Now these blocks are sorted by using the imitation technique introduced by Symvonis [15]. The key of each X'-block (Y'-block) is the key of its *first* (*last*) element. Observe that the key of the first (last) X'-block (Y'-block) is smallest (largest) among all keys. Therefore, the non-full blocks need not be moved during the sorting.

Recall that the buffer is sorted. When sorting the blocks we let one element in the buffer to correspond to each block. Every time two blocks are swapped also their corresponding buffer elements are swapped. The buffer elements are used for two purposes. First, we remember the largest key of a buffer element corresponding to an X'-block. This key value helps us to distinguish X'-blocks from Y'-blocks. Second, the buffer elements are used to recall the original order of homogeneous blocks. This will guarantee the stability of the merging.

The block sorting is carried out by using selection sort. This requires $O(\ell^2) \in o(m)$ element comparisons and ℓ block swaps, i.e., $3(m'+n')+O(1)$ element moves.

After sorting, there are still some elements that should be moved into their final locations. More precisely, some elements in any X'-block that is followed by Y'-blocks are to be moved forwards and some elements in any Y'-block preceded by X'-blocks are to be moved backwards. Let ℓ_1 (ℓ_2) denote the number of such X'-elements (Y'-elements). These elements are moved into their final locations by repeated block interchanges. The boundaries of the blocks that need be interchanged are determined by binary search. In total, at most ℓ block interchanges are to be performed. Therefore, the total number of comparisons done here is $O(\ell \log_2 n)$, which is $o(m)$ due to our assumptions that $\ell \leq 2\lceil m^{3/8} \rceil$ and $m > \sqrt{n}$. The analysis given in Subsection 2.1 easily implies that the total number of moves performed is bounded by $n' + 2\lceil \frac{m'+n'}{\ell} \rceil \ell_1$, when moving X'-elements, and by $m' + 2\lceil \frac{m'+n'}{\ell} \rceil \ell_2$, when moving Y'-elements. Because $\ell_1 + \ell_2 \leq \ell$, the number of moves is at most $3(m'+n')+O(1)$.

Lastly, the buffer elements in the beginning of the input array are to be embedded into the sorted block just created. The buffer is first sorted by using heapsort. Since the size of the buffer is at most $2\lceil m^{3/8} \rceil$, the merging of the buffer with the other block can be carried out efficiently by repeated block interchanges. As earlier, this requires $o(m)$ comparisons and $m+n+o(m)$ moves.

To sum up, this special case can be handled with $o(m)$ comparisons and $8(m+n)+o(m)$ moves.

5.3 Buffer is small

Let us now assume that ℓ, the buffer size is between $2\lceil m^{3/8} \rceil$ and $\lceil m^{3/8} \rceil + 2\lceil m^{5/8} \rceil$. Basically this special case is handled as that in the previous subsection. There are, however, two substantial distinctions. First, the block sorting is carried out by using heapsort, implemented with a $\lceil \ell^{1/2} \rceil$-heap not with a 2-heap as done normally. Second, the final buffer embedding is seen as a merge operation, which is solved by using the algorithm of Subsection 3.3.

Let $d = \lceil \ell^{1/2} \rceil$. The heapsort algorithm implemented with a d-heap is analysed, e.g., in [10] or [13, Section 3.1]. The standard algorithm for creating a d-heap of ℓ elements requires at most 2ℓ comparisons and $\ell^{1/2} + O(1)$ block swaps. Due to the choice of ℓ and m, this totals $o(m)$ comparisons and $o(n)$ moves. With the present choice of d, the d-heap structure has only 3 levels. Therefore, in actual sorting a leaf is swapped to the root and swapped further at most two levels downwards. The number of comparisons required for determining, which swaps should be done, is $2\ell^{3/2} + O(\ell)$ [13]. Since $\ell \in O(m^{5/8})$, the number of comparisons is $o(m)$.

The basic problem when maintaining the heap property is that we have a cycle of at most four equal-sized blocks Y_0, Y_1, Y_2, Y_3 and the task is to move the elements of Y_i into $Y_{(i+1) \bmod 4}$. It is easy to see that this task can be carried out with $5|Y_i|$ element moves. In our heap application the size of the blocks is $\lceil (m'+n')/\ell \rceil$ and ℓ cyclic rotations are performed in total. Hence, the number of element moves performed during this sorting is $5(m'+n')+O(1)$.

Let us next consider how the buffer elements are moved into their final locations. Basically this is nothing but an instance of the merging problem, which we solve by using the algorithm of Subsection 3.3 with a buffer of size $2\lceil m^{3/8}\rceil$. Observe that since the first sequence consists of distinct elements stability is not a problem here. Now the $2\lceil m^{3/8}\rceil$ last elements of the first sequence (the earlier buffer) can be used as a new buffer. When the first sequence is exhausted, the buffer can be embedded into the remaining Y-block by performing repeated block interchanges. This merging increases the number of comparisons by $o(m)$ and the number of moves by $4(m+n)+o(n)$.

By recalling the other costs involved in this special case from the previous subsection, the number of comparisons is seen to be bounded by $(1+t)m+n/2^t+o(m)$ and the number of moves by $13(m+n)+o(n)$.

5.4 Buffer has its normal size

Finally, consider the case that the X-sequence contains at least $\lceil m^{3/8}\rceil + 2\lceil m^{5/8}\rceil$ distinct elements. The $\lceil m^{3/8}\rceil$ first buffer elements are used to imitate the order of X-blocks as in Subsection 5.2. The second part of the buffer is used as in Subsection 3.3. Since the imitation technique will cost only $o(m)$ extra comparisons and moves, the resource requirements in this merging are those stated in Theorem 1.

After merging, the configuration of the input array is $B'ZB''$, where Z denotes the block just merged; B' and B'' are the blocks containing the buffer elements. The elements in B' are merged into Z by repeated block interchanges. Let Z'' denote that part of Z not touch in this process. The final output is obtained by merging Z'' and B'' as described in Subsection 5.3.

All the above requires at most $(1+t)m+n/2^t+o(m)$ comparisons and $8(m+n)+o(n)$ moves.

6 Concluding remarks

In this paper we showed that in-place merging can be accomplished with almost optimal number of comparisons, even if the resulting algorithm is required to be stable. Our development was based on the fundamental ideas introduced by Hwang and Lin [5] and Mannila and Ukkonen [9]. However, the techniques used can be applied to improve the asymptotical performance of other in-place merging algorithms, too. For example, the asymptotical performance of the algorithm by Huang and Langston [3] can be improved such that the total number of element comparisons is $m+n+o(n)$ and that of element moves $4(m+n)+o(n)$.

As to unstable in-place merging, $4(m+n)+o(n)$ seems to be a magical bound for the number of moves carried out by any of the known algorithms. The basic reason for this is that most algorithms operate in two phases: In the first phase every element is moved close to its final location and in the second phase the merge operation is completed. Since a work-space of size $O(1)$ is only available, each time the location of an element is changed one additional element move must be carried out. Therefore, it seems to be difficult to reduce the number of moves performed in either of the two phases below $2(m+n)$. A natural idea is to try to combine the phases, so that most elements are moved directly into their final locations. However, we have not been able to device such an algorithm.

As to stable in-place merging, one may ask whether the number of moves can be reduced below our bounds. Intuitively, the work carried out here should not be much more than twice of that performed by an unstable algorithm. The most difficult special case for stable in-place merging was recognized in Subsection 5.3. However, by using a $\lceil\sqrt{m}\rceil$-partitioning the number of moves could be reduced to $13m + 11n + o(n)$, if we were willing to increase the number of comparisons with a small additive term. We postpone presenting the technical details of this modification in the full version of the present paper and leave any improvement as an open problem.

Acknowledgement

We would like to thank Jukka Teuhola for his comments on an earlier version of this paper.

References

1. Dudziński K., Dydek A., "On stable minimum storage merging algorithm", *Information Processing Letters* **12** (1981) 5–8
2. Dvořák S., Ďurian B., "Towards an efficient merging", *Proc. of the 12th Symposium on Mathematical Foundations of Computer Science* (1986) 290–298
3. Huang B-C., Langston M. A., "Practical in-place merging", *Communications of the ACM* **31** (1988) 348–352
4. Huang B-C., Langston M. A., "Fast stable merging and sorting in constant extra space", *Proc. of the 1st International Conference on Computing and Information* (1989) 71–79
5. Hwang F. K., Lin S., "A simple algorithm for merging two disjoint linearly ordered sets", *SIAM Journal on Computing* **1** (1972) 31–39
6. Katajainen J., Pasanen T., Teuhola J., "Practical in-place mergesort", TR 94/1, Department of Computer Science, University of Copenhagen, Denmark (1994)
7. Knuth D. E., *The Art of Computer Programming* Vol. 3: *Sorting and Searching*, 2nd Printing, Addison-Wesley (1975)
8. Kronrod M. A., "Optimal ordering algorithm without operational field", *Soviet Math. Dokl.* **10** (1969) 744–746
9. Mannila H., Ukkonen E., "A simple linear-time algorithm for in situ merging", *Information Processing Letters* **18** (1984) 203–208
10. Munro J. I, Raman V., "Sorting with minimum data movement", *Journal of Algorithms* **13** (1992) 374–393
11. Pardo L. T., "Stable sorting and merging with optimal space and time bounds", *SIAM Journal on Computing* **6** (1977) 351–372
12. Pasanen T., "Lajittelu minimitilassa", M.Sc. Thesis T-93-3, Department of Computer Science, University of Turku, Finland (1993)
13. Raman V., "Sorting in-place with minimum data movement", Ph.D. Thesis CS-91-12, Computer Science Department, University of Waterloo, Ontario (1991)
14. Salowe J. S., Steiger W. L., "Simplified stable merging tasks", *Journal of Algorithms* **8** (1987) 557–571
15. Symvonis A., "Optimal Stable Merging", *Proc. of the 6th International Conference on Computing and Information* (1994) 124–143

The Complexity of the Falsifiability Problem for Pure Implicational Formulas

Peter Heusch[1]

Abstract. Since it is unlikely that any NP-complete problem will ever be efficiently solvable, one is interested in identifying those special cases that can be solved in polynomial time. We deal with the special case of Boolean formulas where the logical implication $\rightarrow$ is the only operator and any variable (except one) occurs at most twice. For these formulas we show that an infinite hierarchy $S_1 \subseteq S_2 \cdots$ exists such that we can test any formula from S_i for falsifiability in time $O(n^i)$, where n is the number of variables in the formula. We describe an algorithm that finds a falsifying assignment, if one exists. Furthermore we show that the falsifiability problem for $\bigcup_{i=1}^{\infty} S_i$ is NP-complete by reducing the SAT-Problem. In contrast to the hierarchy described by Gallo and Scutella for Boolean formulas in CNF, where the test for membership in the k-th level of the hierarchy needs time $O(n^k)$, our hierarchy permits a linear time membership test. Finally we show that S_1 is neither a sub- nor a superset of some commonly known classes of Boolean formulas, for which the SAT-Problem has linear time complexity (Horn formulas, 2-SAT, nested satisfiability).

Subject classification: algorithms and data structures, logic in computer science.

1 Introduction

The satisfiability problem (SAT) for Boolean formulas in conjunctive normal form (CNF) was the first problem that was shown to be NP–complete, [1]. For this reason, its complexity has been the subject of quite a number of studies. However, CNF–SAT shows a sort of threshold behaviour, yielding the effect that for many input restrictions for which the problem is solvable in polynomial time the problem becomes NP–complete even if the set of inputs is only slightly extended.

One example of such a class is the class of CNF–formulas where every variable may occur at most twice, for inputs from this class the SAT–problem is solvable in linear time, if however three occurrences of a variable are allowed in the input formulas, the satisfiability problem is NP–complete. There are also classes C_i of formulas where for any $F \in C_i$ the satisfiability problem is solvable in time $O(|F|^i)$, $|F|$ denoting the number of variables in the formula, for example the classes C_i where every formula in C_i is satisfiable by setting at most i variables to true, but this classification is quite unsatisfactory in the sense that the test whether a given F belongs to some class C_k may need up to $O(|F|^k)$ steps. Important classes showing this behaviour are the classes Γ_i defined by Gallo and Scutella, [2].

We will present a new hierarchy $S_1 \subseteq S_2 \subseteq \cdots$ with the property that for every $F \in S_i$ the falsifiability can be solved in time $O(|F|^i)$, while the test whether $F \in S_i$ can be solved in linear time. Furthermore, we will prove that every SAT–problem

[1] Universität zu Köln, Pohligstr.1, D-50969 Köln, email: heusch@informatik.uni-koeln.de, Fax: (02 21) 4 70 - 53 87

is polynomially reducible to some problem in $\bigcup_i S_i$, hence the falsifiability problem for $\bigcup_i S_i$ is NP–complete.

The remaining part of this paper is organized in the following way: the rest of this chapter contains the definitions needed, in chapter 2 we prepare our main result while chapter 3 contains the main result. In the last chapter we give a relationship between the class of formulas solvable in linear time by our algorithm and other classes for which satisfiability is solvable in linear time.

A Boolean formula $F = C_1 \wedge C_2 \wedge \ldots \wedge C_r$ in conjunctive normal form (CNF) over n Variables $v_1, \ldots, v_n$ is a conjunction of clauses $C_1, \ldots, C_r$, where each clause C_l is a disjunction of literals $x_{i_1}, \ldots, x_{i_k}$, a literal is either stands for a variable (positive literals) or its complement (negative literals). A Boolean formula is in pure implicational form (PIF), iff it contains only positive literals and the only connective being used is the logical implication. For any implication $A \rightarrow B$ we call A the implicant and B the consequence of the implication. Since the implication is a nonassociative connective, we define $A \rightarrow B \rightarrow C$ to be read as $A \rightarrow (B \rightarrow C)$. An assignment $t : \{v_1, \ldots, v_n\} \mapsto \{true, false\}$ satisfies a Boolean formula F, iff F evaluates to $true$ when every variable v is replaced by $t(v)$ and the usual evaluation rules for Boolean operators are applied, t falsifies F iff F evaluates to $false$. A partial assignment is a function $t : \{v_1, \ldots, v_n\} \mapsto \{true, false, undef\}$, a (partial) assignment t' extends a partial assignment t, iff

$$t(v) \neq undef \Rightarrow t'(v) = t(v).$$

An assignment t' is called 1–extension of a partial assignment t, if t' extends t and $t(v) = undef$ implies $t'(v) = true$.

For any Boolean formula $F = F_1 \rightarrow F_2$ and for any subformula F' of F we define

$$\mathcal{D}_l(F', F) = \begin{cases} 0 & \text{if } F = F', \\ 1 + \mathcal{D}_l(F', F_1) & \text{if } F' \text{ lies in the implicant of } F, \\ \mathcal{D}_l(F', F_2) & \text{if } F' \text{ lies in the consequence of } F. \end{cases}$$

If F is represented by a tree then $D_l(F', F)$ denotes the number of left edges we have to pass on the path from the root of F to the root of F'. The set

$$\mathcal{B}(F) = \{F' | F' \text{ is subformula of } F, D_l(F', F) = 0\}$$

is called the backbone of F, those subformulas F' of F that have $D_l(F', F) = 1$ are called the backbone implicants of F. The backbone of F contains exactly one subformula that is a variable, this variable is the rightmost variable $V_r(F)$. The set of Boolean formulas in PIF where every variable except the rightmost variable occurs at most twice is called 2–PIF. A backbone implicant F' of F is called a critical subformula, w.r.t a partial assignment t, iff $t(V_r(F')) = false$. We will see that the number of critical subformulas plays an important role in the analysis of the falsifying algorithm. If a subformula F' of F is critical and F'' is a backbone implicant of F', we call F'' compensating (w.r.t a partial assignment t), if t falsifies F''. This is due to the fact that a formula F in PIF can be satisfied by setting $V_r(F)$ to $true$ or by falsifying at least one of the backbone implicants, hence to falsify F, $V_r(F)$ must be set to $false$ and all backbone implicants have to be satisfied.

2 A hierarchy for pure implicational formulas

We will now define the formula subsets that subdivide 2–PIF and prove some results about them as well as about 2–PIF itself. We define S_i to contain all those formulas F in 2–PIF, such that $V_r(F)$ occurs at most i times in F. The definition of these sets immediately implies the following lemma:

Lemma 1 *For any Boolean formula F in 2–PIF, the membership problem whether F belongs to S_i can be determined in linear time.*

Proof Obvious.□

Another interesting point that a hierarchy must fulfill to be interesting is that it must also be a real hierarchy, i.e. that it must not collapse beyond a certain class, as in the case of CNF–SAT, where an increase of the number k of literals allowed in one clause does not change the complexity of the problem if $k \geq 3$. The following theorem based on a theorem by Kleine B"uning et al. given in [3], however, gives a strong hint that this is indeed the case with the hierarchy induced by the S_i:

Theorem 1 *The falsifiability problem for formulas in 2–PIF is NP–complete.*

Proof We reduce the wellknown NP–complete SAT–problem for Boolean formulas in CNF where every variable occurs at most 3 times to the falsifiability problem for Boolean formulas in PIF. Let F be such a formula in CNF. W.l.o.g. we may assume that every variable with 3 occurrences occurs exact once positive and twice negative in F. Let a be such a variable and let C_1, C_2 be the clauses such that $C_1 = \neg a \vee C_1'$ and $C_2 = \neg a \vee C_2'$. We then introduce new variables a', a'' and replace C_1, C_2 by $\neg a \vee (a' \wedge a'')$, $\neg a' \vee C_1'$ and $\neg a'' \vee C_2'$. By repeating this process for every variable occurring three times in F we get a new formula F' s.t. every variable is contained at most twice in F'.

The next step is to eliminate the logical operations $\wedge$, $\vee$ and $\neg$. Without changing the number of variables this can be achieved by substitution of $a \rightarrow false$ for $\neg a$, $(a \rightarrow false) \rightarrow b$ for $a \vee b$ and $(a \rightarrow (b \rightarrow false)) \rightarrow false$ for $a \wedge b$. At this point we may apply some simplification rules, e.g. substituting a for $a \rightarrow false \rightarrow false$. To eliminate the logical constant $false$, we replace every occurrence of $false$ by a new variable z, which will forced to be set to $false$ later on.

Let F'' be the result of these transformations. Clearly, F'' contains every variable at most twice and is satisfiable by every assignment that satisfies the original formula F and sets z to $false$, thereby setting those "variables" to $false$, where z was replaced for the constant value $false$. This immediately results in the formula $F'' \rightarrow z$ being falsifiable iff F was satisfiable, hence the falsifiability problem for Boolean formulas in 2–PIF is NP–complete.□

3 Main Theorem

Theorem 1 showed that every NP–complete problem must be contained in one of the set S_i. In the next step we show that our hierarchy is indeed a polynomial hierarchy, i.e. that the falsifiability problem is polynomially solvable for every fixed S_i.

We will formulate this by proving the runtime bound and the correctness for the following algorithm PIF_solve, initially called with the parameters F and $\emptyset$.

```
procedure PIF_solve(F:PIF,Z:set);

begin
  let F = F_1 → ... F_j → ... → F_k → z
  Z = Z ∪ {z}
  if Z ∩ ⋃_i V_r(F_i) = ∅ then begin
    print solution Z and exit
  end
  find the smallest j such that V_r(F_j) ∈ Z
  let F_j = G_1 → ... G_h → z'
  for l=1 to h do begin
    PIF_solve(F_1 → ... F_{j-1} → F_{j+1} → ... → G_l, Z)
  end
end
```

This can also be seen as a graph manipulation process: if the formula is interpreted as a tree where the inner nodes correspond to operators and the outer nodes correspond to variables, then we can falsify the formula from figure 1 iff for at least one i the formula given in figure 2 is falsifiable.

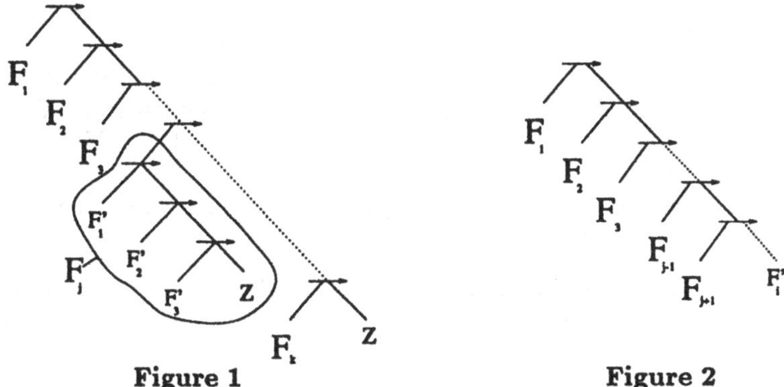

Figure 1 **Figure 2**

As we mentioned, the number of critical subformulas plays an important role for the runtime of the algorithm. The following lemma gives an upper bound for this number:

Lemma 2 *Let F be a formula in 2–PIF containing i occurrences of $V_r(F)$. Then the number of critical formulas in any recursive call of PIF_solve is bounded above by $i-1$.*

Proof The proposition is surely true when PIF_solve starts, since there may be at most $i-1$ backbone implicants whose rightmost variable is $z_0 := V_r(F)$. If, however, we see the process of finding critical and compensating subformulas as a variable renaming process—instead of storing those variables in Z that we have decided to be assigned the value *false*, we could simply rename them to z_0—then we see that the number of occurrences of z_0 can never go beyond i, since whenever two occurrences of z_0 are put into F by selecting a compensating subformula, we delete two other occurrences of z_0 in the formula.□

It remains to prove the correctness of PIF_solve. This is expressed in the following lemma:

Lemma 3 *Let F be a formula in 2–PIF. Then F is falsifiable iff one of the following conditions holds:*

1. *F doesn't contain any critical subformulas.*
2. *An assignment exists such that for every critical subformula F' of F there is a compensating subformula F''.*

Proof If F does not contain any critical subformulas, then it can easily be falsified by assigning $false$ to $V_r(F)$ and assigning $true$ to all other variables, this satisfies all backbone implicants, hence F is falsified. Assume now that F contains critical subformulas. If we can extend the partial assignment implied by Z in such a way that for every critical subformula formula a compensating subformula exists, we get an assignment where for every critical subformula at least one of its backbone implicants is assigned the value $false$, i.e. the critical subformula is satisfied even if its rightmost variable was assigned the value $false$. If we cannot extend the partial assignment given by Z in such a way, then for every assignment at least one critical subformula F' exists such that no backbone implicant of F' is compensating, hence every assignment to the variables of F will falsify F' and therefore satisfy F.□

We note that for any formula $F = F_1 \rightarrow F_{j-1} \rightarrow F_j \rightarrow F_{j+1} \cdots \rightarrow F_r \rightarrow z$ in 2–PIF the test whether a certain subformula F' is compensating for a critical subformula F_j is the same as the test whether after removal of F_j from F there exists an assignment that falsifies F and F' at the same time, this can also be achieved by testing $F = F_1 \rightarrow F_{j-1} \rightarrow F_{j+1} \cdots \rightarrow F_r \rightarrow F'$ for falsifiability under the condition that $z = false$.

Now we state our main result, whose correctness, after the preceeding lemmas is almost obvious:

Theorem 2 *Let F be a formula from 2–PIF with n variables and $i \geq 2$ occurrences of $V_r(F)$, then PIF_solve finds a falsifying assignment for F iff one exists, furthermore the runtime of PIF_solve is bounded by $O(in^{i-1})$.*

Proof Since there are no more than $i-1$ critical formulas in F at the same time, there are at most $\sum_{k=0}^{i-1} \binom{n}{k} = O(n^{i-1})$ ways to distribute them amongst all subformulas. To get a runtime bound, we note that at most $2i$ occurrences of variables in Z are contained in F, hence the test whether $Z \cap \bigcup_i V_r(F_i) = \emptyset$ and the selection of j such that $V_r(F_j) \in Z$ can be carried out in time $O(i)$, all other steps take constant time, hence we get a runtime of $O(in^{i-1})$. The correctness follows from the fact that if no critical subformula is found, then PIF_solve prints a solution, else it enumerates all possible ways to find a compensating subformula for F_j.□

4 Relationships to other input classes

Since CNF–SAT is NP–complete, a number of input restrictions have been developed that permit to test a formula for satisfiability in polynomial time. The most common of these restrictions are restrictions for formulas in CNF, they are defined as follows:

- 2–SAT: Clauses may contain at most 2 literals.
- Horn formulas: Clauses may contain at most 1 positive literal.

- Nested SAT: An ordering of the clauses must exist with the property that if a clause C preceeds another clause C' then no variable from C except the first and the last (w.r.t to an ordering of the variables) may be contained in C'.
- READ–2: No variable may occur more than twice in a formula.

It is well known that for inputs from these classes the satisfiability problem is solvable in time proportional to the length of the formula, see [4, 3]. The following remark formalizes the relationship between S_2 and these classes:

Remark 1 *For any one of the classes 2–SAT, HORN, nested SAT and READ–2 there is a boolean function function whose complement can be expressed in S_2 but that cannot be expressed in 2–SAT, HORN, nested SAT and READ–2, respectively.*

References

1. S. Cook. The Complexity of Theorem Proving Procedures. *Proc. 3rd Ann. ACM Symp. on Theory of Computing*, pages 151–158, 1971.
2. G. Gallo and M.G. Scutella. Polynomially Solvable Satisfiability Problems. *Information Processing Letters*, 29(5):221–227, 1988.
3. H. Kleine Büning and T. Lettman. *Aussagenlogik: Deduktion und Algorithmen*. B. G. Teubner, Stuttgart, 1994.
4. D. E. Knuth. Nested satisfiability. *Acta Informatica*, 28:1–6, 1990.

Strong Lower Bounds on the Approximability of some NPO PB-Complete Maximization Problems

Viggo Kann*

Department of Numerical Analysis and Computing Science,
Royal Institute of Technology, S-100 44 Stockholm, Sweden

Abstract. The approximability of several NP maximization problems is investigated and strong lower bounds for the studied problems are proved. For some of the problems the bounds are the best that can be achieved, unless P = NP.
For example we investigate the approximability of MAX PB 0 − 1 PROGRAMMING, the problem of finding a binary vector x that satisfies a set of linear relations such that the objective value $\sum c_i x_i$ is maximized, where c_i are binary numbers. We show that, unless P = NP, MAX PB 0 − 1 PROGRAMMING is not approximable within the factor $n^{1-\varepsilon}$ for any $\varepsilon > 0$, where n is the number of inequalities, and is not approximable within $m^{1/2-\varepsilon}$ for any $\varepsilon > 0$, where m is the number of variables.
Similar hardness results are shown for other problems on binary linear systems, some problems on the satisfiability of boolean formulas and the longest induced circuit problem.

1 Introduction

Approximation of NP-complete optimization problems is a very interesting and active area of research. Since all NP-complete problems are reducible to each other one could suspect that they should have similar approximation properties, but this is not at all the case.

The range of approximability of NP-complete problems stretches from problems that are approximable within every constant in polynomial time, e.g. the knapsack problem [8], to problems that are not approximable within n^{ε} for some $\varepsilon > 0$, where n is the size of the input instance, unless P = NP. A problem that is known to be this hard to approximate is the minimum independent dominating set problem (minimum maximal independence number) [7].

Even optimization problems whose objective function is bounded by a polynomial in the size of the input may be hard to approximate. Krentel defined a class of optimization problems called OPTP[log n], that consists of all NP optimization problems that are polynomially bounded [12]. This class, which we will call NPO PB, can be divided into two classes, MAX PB and MIN PB, containing maximization and minimization problems respectively [11]. Berman and

* E-mail: `viggo@nada.kth.se`, supported by grants from TFR.

Schnitger started to investigate the approximability of MAX PB problems and proved that there are MAX PB-complete problems, i.e. MAX PB problems to which every MAX PB problem can be reduced using an approximation preserving reduction [4]. Several problems are now known to be MAX PB-complete [9]. Later, some minimization problems were shown to be MIN PB-complete [10], and recently Crescenzi, Kann, Silvestri and Trevisan proved that any MIN PB-complete problem is NPO PB-complete and that any MAX PB-complete problem is NPO PB-complete [6]. The classes of MIN PB-complete, MAX PB-complete and NPO PB-complete problems thus coincide.

For every NPO PB-complete problem there is a constant $\alpha > 0$ such that the problem is not approximable within n^α, where n is the size of the input instance, unless P = NP. For some problems, for example minimum independent dominating set, this constant can be chosen arbitrarily close to 1, which means that these problems are incredible hard to approximate.

The problems known to be this hard to approximate are mainly minimization problems. Only a few maximization problems are known to have such an extreme nonapproximability bound, and they are all problems on graphs where one looks for a maximum induced connected subgraph [13]. The problem MIN DISTINGUISHED ONES, where one look for a satisfying boolean variable assignment containing as few true variables as possible from some distinguished set of variables, is NPO PB-complete and not approximable within $n^{1-\epsilon}$, where n is the number of distinguished variables [10]. The corresponding maximization problem is also NPO PB-complete, but no strong lower bound on the approximability is known. One could ask whether minimization problems in some sense can be harder to approximate than maximization problems.

In this paper we will, however, show that this is not true. We will show that several maximization problems, for example MAX DISTINGUISHED ONES, have nonapproximability bounds similar to $n^{1-\epsilon}$. We will do this by constructing approximation preserving reductions from either MIN INDEPENDENT DOMINATING SET or LONGEST INDUCED PATH and use the fact that these two problems have strong lower bounds on the approximability. We conclude that a convenient way to establish both NPO PB-completess results and strong lower bounds is to reduce from MIN INDEPENDENT DOMINATING SET or LONGEST INDUCED PATH. Note that our results do not make use of the quite complicated machinery of interactive proofs and the PCP model that recently have been used for showing approximation hardness of several optimization problems, see for example [3].

In the appendix all problems treated in the text are defined.

1.1 Preliminaries

Definition 1. An NP *optimization problem* A is a fourtuple $(I, sol, m, goal)$ such that

1. I is the set of the *instances* of A and it is recognizable in polynomial time.
2. Given an instance x of I, $sol(x)$ denotes the set of *feasible solutions* of x. These solutions are short, that is, a polynomial p exists such that, for any

$y \in sol(x)$, $|y| \leq p(|x|)$. Moreover, it is decidable in polynomial time whether, for any x and for any y such that $|y| \leq p(|x|)$, $y \in sol(x)$.
3. Given an instance x and a feasible solution y of x, $m(x,y)$ denotes the positive integer *measure* of y (often also called the value of y). The function m is computable in polynomial time and is also called the *objective* function.
4. $goal \in \{\max, \min\}$.

The *class* NPO is the set of all NP optimization problems. The goal of an NPO problem with respect to an instance x is to find an *optimum solution*, i.e. a feasible solution y such that $m(x,y) = goal\{m(x,y') : y' \in sol(x)\}$. In the following *opt* will denote the function mapping an instance x to the measure of an optimum solution.

An NPO problem is said to be *polynomially bounded* if a polynomial q exists such that, for any instance x and for any solution y of x, $m(x,y) \leq q(|x|)$. The *class* NPO PB is the set of all polynomially bounded NPO problems. NPO PB = MAX PB $\cup$ MIN PB where MAX PB is the set of all maximization problems in NPO PB and MIN PB is the set of all minimization problems in NPO PB.

Given an instance x of an NPO problem and a feasible solution y of x, we define the *performance ratio of y with respect to x* as $R(x,y) = m(x,y)/opt(x)$ for minimization problems and $opt(x)/m(x,y)$ for maximization problems.

Definition 2. Let A be an NPO problem and let T be an algorithm that, for any instance x of A, returns a feasible solution $T(x)$. Given an arbitrary function $r : N \rightarrow (1,\infty)$, we say that T is an *$r(n)$-approximate algorithm for A* if, for any instance x, the performance ratio of the feasible solution $T(x)$ with respect to x verifies the inequality $R(x,T(x)) \leq r(|x|)$.

Several polynomial time approximation preserving reductions have been defined in the literature. The PTAS-reduction [6], which preserves the performance ratio very well, is suitable for defining complete problems in approximation classes. A problem $A \in$ NPO is NPO-*complete* if, for any $B \in$ NPO, there is a PTAS-reduction from B to A. Similarly, a problem $A \in$ NPO PB is NPO PB-*complete* if, for any $B \in$ NPO PB, there is a PTAS-reduction from B to A. In the same way MAX PB-complete and MIN PB-complete problems can be defined.

Proposition 3 [6]. *Any* MIN PB-*complete problem is* NPO PB-*complete and any* MAX PB-*complete problem is* NPO PB-*complete.*

The approximability for problems that are not approximable within a constant is usually described as a function of the size of the problem instance, or more precisely, as a function of some size parameter, like the number of nodes or edges in an input graph. The PTAS-reduction does not preserve size parameters, so this reduction cannot be used when investigating the approximability (or nonapproximability) of problems that are very hard to approximate, like NPO PB-complete problems. For such problems it is not relevant whether the reduction increases the performance ratio by a constant factor. We will use the

S-reduction, defined in [10], which is a reduction that guarantees that the performance ratio is preserved within *some* constant factor, but has full control over the increase of the size if the problem instance.

Definition 4. ([10]) Let A and B be two NPO problems. A is said to be *S-reducible* to B with size amplification a if there exist three functions f, g, a, and a positive constant c such that:

1. for any $x \in I_A$, $f(x,r) \in I_B$ is computable in time polynomial in $|x|$,
2. for any $x \in I_A$, for any $y \in sol_B(f(x))$, $g(x,y) \in sol_A(x)$ is computable in time polynomial in $|x|$ and $|y|$,
3. $a : R^+ \to R^+$ is monotonously increasing, positive and computable,
4. for any $x \in I_A$, for any $y \in sol_B(f(x))$, $R_A(x, g(x,y)) \leq R_B(f(x), y)$,
5. for any $x \in I_A$, $|f(x)| \leq a(|x|)$.

Proposition 5 [10]. *Given two* NPO *problems F and G, if there is an S-reduction from F to G with size amplification $a(n)$ and G is approximable within some monotonously increasing positive function $u(n)$ of the size of the input instance, then F is approximable within $c \cdot u(a(n))$. Conversely, if F is not approximable within $c \cdot u(a(n))$, then G is not approximable within $u(n)$.*

For constant and polylogarithmic approximable problems the S-reduction preserves approximability within a constant for any polynomial size amplification, since $c \log^k(n^p) = p^k c \log^k n = O(\log^k n)$. For n^c approximable problems it only does this for size amplification $O(n)$, since $c \cdot (O(n))^c = O(n^c)$.

2 Lower Bounds

In this section we will prove lover bounds on the approximability of the following NPO PB-complete problems: Max PB $0-1$ Programming [4], Max Number of Satisfiable Formulas [14], Max Distinguished Ones [14], Max Ones [14], Max C Bin Sat$^{\mathcal{R}_1;\mathcal{R}_2}$ (maximum constrained binary satisfiable linear subsystem) [1], Max Bin Irrelevant Sat$^{\mathcal{R}}$ (maximum irrelevant binary variables in linear system) [2], and Longest Induced Circuit.

In the references above the problems are defined and are also shown to be Max PB-complete. The problems are therefore NPO PB-complete by Proposition 3. Formal definitions of the problems can be found in the appendix.

We first show that Max PB $0-1$ Programming is hard to approximate. This result was obtained as a side-effect in the proof of Theorem 5 in [6]. We will then modify this proof to prove hardness results for the other problems.

Theorem 6. Max PB $0-1$ Programming *is not approximable within $n^{1-\varepsilon}$ for any $\varepsilon > 0$, where n is the number of inequalities, and is not approximable within $m^{1/2-\varepsilon}$ for any $\varepsilon > 0$, where m is the number of variables.*

Proof. Halldórsson has proved that, unless P = NP, MIN INDEPENDENT DOMINATING SET is not approximable within $n^{1-\varepsilon}$ for any $\varepsilon > 0$, where n is the sum of the number of nodes and edges in the graph [7]. We will use this fact to show that MAX PB $0-1$ PROGRAMMING is hard to approximate.

We will construct a reduction from MIN INDEPENDENT DOMINATING SET to MAX PB $0-1$ PROGRAMMING using the following idea. The objective function, i.e. the number of nodes in the independent dominating set is encoded by introducing an order of the nodes in the solution. The order is encoded by a squared number of $0-1$ variables in the programming problem, see Fig. 1. A solution of size 1 shall correspond to the $0-1$ programming objective value n, and a solution of size p shall correspond to an objective value of $\lfloor n/p \rfloor$.

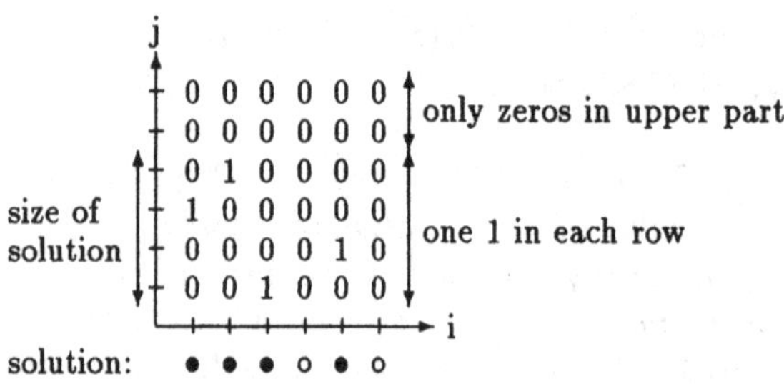

Fig. 1. The idea of the reduction from MIN INDEPENDENT DOMINATING SET to MAX PB $0-1$ PROGRAMMING. The variable $x_i^j = 1$ if and only if v_i is the jth node in the solution. There is at most one 1 in each column and in each row.

Given an instance of MIN INDEPENDENT DOMINATING SET, i.e. a graph with nodes $V = \{v_1, \ldots, v_m\}$ and edges E, construct m^2 variables x_i^j, $1 \leq i, j \leq m$, n variables y_p, $1 \leq p \leq n$, and the following inequalities:

$$\forall i \in [1..m] \quad \sum_{j=1}^{m} x_i^j \leq 1, \quad \text{(at most one 1 in each column)} \tag{1}$$

$$\forall j \in [1..m] \quad \sum_{i=1}^{m} x_i^j \leq 1, \quad \text{(at most one 1 in each row)} \tag{2}$$

$$\forall j \in [1..m-1] \quad \sum_{i=1}^{m} x_i^j - \sum_{i=1}^{m} x_i^{j+1} \geq 0, \quad \text{(only zeros in upper part)} \tag{3}$$

$$\forall (v_i, v_j) \in E \quad \sum_{k=1}^{m} x_i^k + \sum_{k=1}^{m} x_j^k \leq 1, \quad \text{(independence)} \tag{4}$$

$$\forall i \in [1..m] \quad \sum_{k=1}^{m} x_i^k + \sum_{\substack{j:(v_i,v_j)\in E \\ k\in[1..m]}} x_j^k \geq 1, \quad \text{(domination)} \tag{5}$$

$$\forall i \in [1..n] \quad y_i \leq \textstyle\sum_{k=1}^{m} x_k^{\lfloor n/i \rfloor}, \quad \text{(objective variables)} \tag{6}$$

$$y_i \geq \textstyle\sum_{k=1}^{m} x_k^{\lfloor n/i \rfloor}. \tag{7}$$

The objective function is defined as $\sum_{p=1}^{n} y_p$.

One can now verify that an independent dominating set of size s will exactly correspond to a solution of the $0-1$ programming problem with objective value $\lfloor n/s \rfloor$ and vice versa.

Suppose that the minimum independent dominating set has size M, then the performance ratio s/M for the independent dominating set problem will correspond to the performance ratio $\lfloor n/M \rfloor / \lfloor n/s \rfloor = s/M\,(1 \pm m/n)$ for the $0-1$ programming problem, where m/n is the relative error due to the floor operation. By choosing n large enough the relative error can be made arbitrarily small, but for proving the theorem it is enough to choose $n = m$ to obtain a reduction that preserves the approximability within a factor of 2.

The reduction is obviously an S-reduction with amplification $O(m+|E|)$ with respect to the number of inequalities and amplification $O(m^2)$ with respect to the number of variables. The theorem now follows from Proposition 5 together with the fact that MIN INDEPENDENT DOMINATING SET is not approximable within $n^{1-\varepsilon}$ for any $\varepsilon > 0$, where n is the sum of the number of nodes and edges in the graph [7]. □

Theorem 7. MAX NUMBER OF SATISFIABLE FORMULAS *is not approximable within $n^{1-\varepsilon}$ for any $\varepsilon > 0$, where n is the number of formulas, unless* P = NP.

Proof. We modify the construction of the proof of Theorem 6 in the following way. Given a graph with nodes $V = \{v_1, \ldots, v_m\}$ and edges E, construct m^2 variables x_i^j, $1 \le i,j \le m$, m variables y_p, $1 \le p \le m$, and the m boolean formulas $\Phi_p = y_p \wedge \varphi$, $1 \le p \le m$ where φ is the conjunction of the following formulas:

$$\forall i \in [1..m], 1 \le j < k \le m \qquad \overline{x_i^j} \vee \overline{x_i^k}, \tag{8}$$

$$\forall i \in [1..m], 1 \le j < k \le m \qquad \overline{x_j^i} \vee \overline{x_k^i}, \tag{9}$$

$$\forall j \in [1..m-1] \left(\bigvee_{k=1}^{m} x_k^{j+1}\right) \Rightarrow \left(\bigvee_{k=1}^{m} x_k^{j}\right), \tag{10}$$

$$\forall (v_i, v_j) \in E, \forall k,l \in [1..m] \qquad \overline{x_i^k} \vee \overline{x_j^l}, \tag{11}$$

$$\forall i \in [1..m] \qquad \bigvee_{k=1}^{m} x_i^k \vee \bigvee_{\substack{j:(v_i,v_j)\in E \\ k\in[1..m]}} x_j^k, \tag{12}$$

$$\forall p \in [1..m] \qquad y_p \equiv \bigvee_{k=1}^{m} x_k^{\lfloor m/i \rfloor}. \tag{13}$$

It is clear that the boolean formulas (8–13) restrict the variables in exactly the same way as the inequalities (1–7) and that the number of satisfied formulas $y_p \wedge \varphi, 1 \le p \le m$ is the same as the sum $\sum_{p=1}^{m} y_p$ in MAX PB $0-1$ PROGRAMMING. Therefore MAX NUMBER OF SATISFIABLE FORMULAS is not approximable within $n^{1-\varepsilon}$ for any $\varepsilon > 0$, where n is the number of formulas, unless P = NP. □

Theorem 8. MAX DISTINGUISHED ONES *is not approximable within* $n^{1-\varepsilon}$ *for any* $\varepsilon > 0$*, where* n *is the number of distinguished variables, and* MAX ONES *is not approximable within* $n^{1/3-\varepsilon}$ *for any* $\varepsilon > 0$*, where* n *is the number of variables, unless* $\mathrm{P} = \mathrm{NP}$.

Proof. First we prove the result for MAX DISTINGUISHED ONES. This time we modify the construction of the proof of Theorem 7. We first construct a formula with clauses of unbounded size and then rewrite the clauses as 3-SAT clauses.

Let $y_p, 1 \le p \le m$ be the distinguished variables. Apart from the $m^2 + m$ variables x_i^j and y_p we will need m variables t_p, $1 \le p \le m$, and m variables z_p, $1 \le p \le m$. We define these variables by

$$\forall p \in [1..m] \quad t_p \equiv \bigvee_{k=1}^{m} x_k^p, \; z_p \equiv \bigvee_{k=1}^{m} x_p^k. \tag{14}$$

We then can reformulate the formulas (10), (12), and (13) as, respectively,

$$\forall j \in [1..m-1] \quad \overline{t_{j+1}} \vee t_j, \tag{15}$$

$$\forall i \in [1..m] \; z_i \vee \bigvee_{j:(v_i,v_j)\in E} z_j, \tag{16}$$

$$\forall i \in [1..m] \quad y_i \equiv t_{\lfloor m/i \rfloor}. \tag{17}$$

We can now rewrite the equivalences in (14) and (17) as clauses using the rewriting rule $u \equiv v \longrightarrow (u \vee \overline{v}) \wedge (\overline{u} \vee v)$. All clauses now consist of 2 literals except (14) and (16). We use the standard method of rewriting these as clauses of 3 literals. In this process we introduce $O(m^2 + |E|)$ new variables.

The conjunction of all these clauses is equivalent to the formula φ in the proof of Theorem 7, and the number of true distinguished variables in a variable assignment will exactly correspond to the number of satisfied formulas in the other proof. Since the number of distinguished variables is m, MAX DISTINGUISHED ONES is not approximable within $m^{1-\varepsilon}$ for any $\varepsilon > 0$, unless $\mathrm{P} = \mathrm{NP}$.

In order to formulate the problem as a MAX ONES problem instance we use an idea in [14] and create copies of the distinguished variables to make each such variable more valuable than all the nondistinguished variables together. □

Theorem 9. MAX C BIN SAT$^{\mathcal{R}_1;\mathcal{R}_2}$ *is not approximable within* $n^{1-\varepsilon}$ *where* n *is the number of optional relations, and not within* $n^{1/2-\varepsilon}$ *where* n *is the number of variables, for any* $\varepsilon > 0$*, and for any* $\mathcal{R}_1, \mathcal{R}_2 \in \{=, \geq, >, \neq\}$*, unless* $\mathrm{P} = \mathrm{NP}$. MAX BIN IRRELEVANT SAT$^{\mathcal{R}}$ *is not approximable within* $n^{1/3-\varepsilon}$ *for any* $\varepsilon > 0$*, and for any* $\mathcal{R} \in \{=, \geq, >, \neq\}$*, where* n *is the sum of the number of variables and the number of relations, unless* $\mathrm{P} = \mathrm{NP}$.

The proof is by S-reduction from the MAX PB $0-1$ PROGRAMMING instances constructed in the proof of Theorem 6, and will appear in the full version.

Theorem 10. LONGEST INDUCED CIRCUIT *is not approximable within* $n^{1-\varepsilon}$ *for any* $\varepsilon > 0$*, where* n *is the number of nodes, unless* $\mathrm{P} = \mathrm{NP}$.

Proof. We reduce from the problem LONGEST INDUCED PATH that is known to be NPO PB-complete [4] and not approximable within $n^{1-\varepsilon}$ for any $\varepsilon > 0$, where n is the number of nodes, unless P = NP [13].

Given an input graph to LONGEST INDUCED PATH, $G = (V, E)$. We extend this graph by adding one new node w_i for each node $v_i \in V$ and add edges (w_i, v_i) for $1 \le i \le |V|$. We also add one special node w_0 that is connected to all new nodes, i.e. we have edges (w_0, w_i) for $1 \le i \le |V|$.

Every induced path in G (say, starting in node v_s and ending in node v_e) can now be extended to an induced circuit in the new graph by adding the nodes w_s, w_e and w_0. The circuit will have length 4+(length of induced path).

On the other hand, every induced circuit in the new graph that contains the node w_0 will give us an induced path in G containing 4 edges less than the circuit. An induced circuit that does not contain the special node cannot contain any w node, so by removing any node in the circuit we will get an induced path in G containing 2 edges less than the circuit. □

3 Summary and Discussion

The following table summarizes the nonapproximability results in the paper. For each result we give the name of the problem, the nonapproximability exponent b and the size parameter n, saying that the problem is not approximable within $n^{b-\varepsilon}$ for any $\varepsilon > 0$, unless P = NP.

problem	b	size parameter n
MAX PB $0-1$ PROGRAMMING	1	inequalities
	1/2	variables
MAX NUMBER OF SATISFIABLE FORMULAS	1	formulas
MAX DISTINGUISHED ONES	1	distinguished variables
	1/2	variables
MAX ONES	1/3	variables
MAX C BIN SAT$^{\mathcal{R}_1;\mathcal{R}_2}$	1	optional relations
	1/2	variables
MAX BIN IRRELEVANT SAT$^{\mathcal{R}}$	1/3	variables+relations
LONGEST INDUCED CIRCUIT	1	nodes

In all the treated maximization problems except LONGEST INDUCED CIRCUIT it is NP-complete to decide whether there exists a solution. Since an approximation algorithm must be able to in polynomial time return some solution, we have chosen to include a trivial solution in the input instance.

Another way would be to extend the space of solutions with a special solution with objective value 1. This would make it possible to easily show approximation hardness of some of the problems. For example, we can reduce 3-SAT to MAX NUMBER OF SATISFIABLE FORMULAS by constructing n copies of the formula. If the formula is satisfiable the objective value is n, otherwise it is 1. An algorithm approximating the number of satisfied formulas within $n^{1-\varepsilon}$ would therefore solve the NP-hard 3-SAT problem. We thank Magnús Halldórsson for this remark.

Thus the exact formulation of the problems with respect to trivial solutions is of importance. Since the problem should be to find a *good* solution and not to find *any* solution, we think that our definition is the natural definition when studying the approximability of these optimization problems.

References

1. E. Amaldi and V. Kann. The complexity and approximability of finding maximum feasible subsystems of linear relations. Theoretical Comput. Sci., to appear, 1995.
2. E. Amaldi and V. Kann. On the approximability of removing the smallest number of relations from linear systems to achieve feasability. Technical Report ORWP-6-94, Dep. of Mathematics, Swiss Federal Institute of Technology, Lausanne, 1994.
3. M. Bellare and M. Sudan. Improved non-approximability results. In *Proc. Twenty sixth Ann. ACM Symp. on Theory of Comp.*, pages 184–193. ACM, 1994.
4. P. Berman and G. Schnitger. On the complexity of approximating the independent set problem. *Inform. and Comput.*, 96:77–94, 1992.
5. P. Crescenzi and V. Kann. A compendium of NP optimization problems. Technical Report SI/RR-95/02, Dipartimento di Scienze dell'Informazione, Università di Roma "La Sapienza", 1995. The list is updated continuously. The latest version is available by anonymous ftp from `nada.kth.se` as `Theory/Viggo-Kann/compendium.ps.Z`.
6. P. Crescenzi, V. Kann, R. Silvestri, and L. Trevisan. Structure in approximation classes. In *Proc. of First Ann. Int. Computing and Comb. Conf.*, to appear, 1995.
7. M. M. Halldórsson. Approximating the minimum maximal independence number. *Inform. Process. Lett.*, 46:169–172, 1993.
8. O. H. Ibarra and C. E. Kim. Fast approximation for the knapsack and sum of subset problems. *J. ACM*, 22(4):463–468, 1975.
9. V. Kann. *On the Approximability of NP-complete Optimization Problems*. PhD thesis, Dep. of Numerical Analysis and Computing Science, KTH, 1992.
10. V. Kann. Polynomially bounded minimization problems that are hard to approximate. *Nordic J. Computing*, 1:317–331, 1994.
11. P. G. Kolaitis and M. N. Thakur. Logical definability of NP optimization problems. *Inform. and Comput.*, 115:321–353, 1994.
12. M. W. Krentel. The complexity of optimization problems. *J. Comput. System Sci.*, 36:490–509, 1988.
13. C. Lund and M. Yannakakis. The approximation of maximum subgraph problems. In *Proc. of 20th International Colloquium on Automata, Languages and Programming*, pages 40–51. Springer-Verlag, 1993. Lecture Notes in Comput. Sci. 700.
14. A. Panconesi and D. Ranjan. Quantifiers and approximation. *Theoretical Comput. Sci.*, 107:145–163, 1993.

Appendix: A List of NPO Problems

Here follows a list of definitions of problems mentioned in the text. A much larger list of NPO problems can be found in [5].

Since it is NP-hard to decide the existence of solutions of all maximization problems below, except LONGEST INDUCED CIRCUIT, we will demand that a trivial solution is included in each problem instance.

MIN INDEPENDENT DOMINATING SET

Instance: Graph $G = (V, E)$.
Solution: An independent dominating set for G, i.e., a subset $V' \subseteq V$ such that for all $u \in V - V'$ there is a $v \in V'$ for which $(u, v) \in E$, and such that no two nodes in V' are joined by an edge in E.
Measure: Cardinality of the independent dominating set, i.e., $|V'|$.

MAX PB $0-1$ PROGRAMMING

Instance: Integer $m \times n$-matrix $A \in Z^{m \cdot n}$, integer m-vector $b \in Z^m$, nonnegative binary n-vector $c \in \{0,1\}^n$.
Solution: A binary n-vector $x \in \{0,1\}^n$ such that $Ax \geq b$.
Measure: The scalar product of c and x, i.e., $\sum_{i=1}^{n} c_i x_i$.

MAX NUMBER OF SATISFIABLE FORMULAS

Instance: Set U of variables, collection C of 3CNF formulas.
Solution: A subset $C' \subseteq C$ of the formulas such that there is a truth assignment for U that satisfies every formula in C'.
Measure: Number of satisfied formulas, i.e., $|C'|$.

MAX DISTINGUISHED ONES

Instance: Disjoint sets X, Z of variables, collection C of disjunctive clauses of at most 3 literals, where a literal is a variable or a negated variable in $X \cup Z$.
Solution: Truth assignment for X and Z that satisfies every clause in C.
Measure: The number of Z variables that are set to true in the assignment.

MAX ONES

Instance: Set X of variables, collection C of disjunctive clauses of at most 3 literals, where a literal is a variable or a negated variable.
Solution: Truth assignment that satisfies every clause in C.
Measure: The number of variables that are set to true in the assignment.

MAX C BIN SAT$^{\mathcal{R}_1;\mathcal{R}_2}$

Instance: $\mathcal{R}_1, \mathcal{R}_2 \in \{=, \geq, >, \neq\}$ defining the types of relations. Systems $A_1 x_1 \mathcal{R}_1 b_1$ and $A_2 x_2 \mathcal{R}_2 b_2$ of linear relations, where A_1 and A_2 are integer matrices, and b_1 and b_2 are integer vectors.
Solution: Two vectors x_1 and x_2 of binary numbers such that all relations $A_1 x_1 \mathcal{R}_1 b_1$ are satisfied.
Measure: The number of relations in $A_2 x_2 \mathcal{R}_2 b_2$ that are satisfied by x_2.

MAX BIN IRRELEVANT SAT$^{\mathcal{R}}$

Instance: $\mathcal{R} \in \{=, \geq, >, \neq\}$ defining the type of relations. System $Ax\mathcal{R}b$ of linear relations, where A is an integer matrix, and b is an integer vector.
Solution: A vector x of binary numbers such that all relations $Ax\mathcal{R}b$ are satisfied.
Measure: The number of zero elements in x, i.e., $|\{i : x_i = 0\}|$.

LONGEST INDUCED CIRCUIT

Instance: Graph $G = \langle V, E \rangle$.
Solution: A subset $V' \subseteq V$ such that the subgraph induced by V' is a circuit.
Measure: Length of the circuit, i.e., $|V'|$.

Some Typical Properties of Large AND/OR Boolean Formulas

Hanno Lefmann and Petr Savický*

Lehrstuhl Informatik II, Universität Dortmund, D-44221 Dortmund, Germany
lefmann@ls2.informatik.uni-dortmund.de
and
Institute of Computer Science, Academy of Sciences of Czech Republic, Prague, Czech Republic, savicky@uivt.cas.cz

Abstract. In this paper typical properties of large random Boolean AND/OR formulas are investigated. Such formulas with n variables are viewed as rooted binary trees chosen from the uniform distribution of all rooted binary trees with m leaves, where n is fixed and m tends to infinity. The leaves are labeled by literals and the inner nodes by the connectives AND/OR, both uniformly at random. In extending the investigation to infinite trees, we obtain a close relation between the formula size complexity of an arbitrary Boolean function f and the probability of its occurrence under this distribution, i.e., the negative logarithm of this probability differs from the formula size complexity of f only by a polynomial factor.

1 Introduction

In this paper, we study Boolean functions determined by large random AND/OR Boolean formulas with a given number n of variables. Such formulas are rooted binary trees chosen from the uniform distribution on trees with m leaves, where m tends to infinity, labeled by connectives and variables. Each of the $m-1$ inner nodes has degree two and is labeled by AND or OR with probability 1/2 and independently of the labeling of all the other nodes. Each leaf is labeled by a literal, a variable or its negation, from the uniform distribution on the $2n$ literals and independently of the labeling of all the other nodes.
It appears that, with high probability, the function computed by the large random formula is in fact determined only by a small part of it. Using this, for an arbitrary Boolean function f, we establish a close relation between its formula size complexity $L(f)$, which is the minimal size of an AND/OR formula expressing f, and the limit probability $P(f)$ of the occurrence of f under the distribution described above, when m approaches infinity.

Theorem 1. *There exist positive constants $c_1, c_2 > 0$, such that for every Boolean function f of n variables satisfying $L(f) \geq \Omega(n^3)$, the following holds:*

$$e^{-c_1 L(f) \log n} \leq P(f) \leq e^{-c_2 L(f)/n^3} .$$

* This research was supported by GA CR, Grant No. 201/95/0976, and by Heinrich-Hertz-Stiftung while visiting Universität Dortmund, FB Informatik, LS II.

The study of the uniform distribution on AND/OR formulas of size approaching infinity was suggested by Woods [11]. Using a variant of the model described above, he considered formulas with AND/OR gates of unbounded fan-in instead of fan-in 2. Woods proved the existence of the limit probabilities and that these are positive. Moreover, he asked [11], whether these probabilities are related to the formula size complexity of the Boolean functions. Theorem 1 gives an affirmative answer to his question formulated in terms of formulas with fan-in 2 gates.

A related model for studying the relation between the probability of Boolean functions and their complexity was suggested by Friedman [2]. In this model, there is a sequence of probability distributions on formulas of increasing size. Friedman investigated the moments of distributions involved in the random k-SAT problem, which includes iterated conjunction of small random disjunctions. A similar model based on a sequence of distributions on Boolean formulas of increasing size is described in [9]. Functions of different complexity appear with nonzero probability in different steps of the process. The supremum over all steps of the process of the probability of the occurrence of a given function f may be approximated in terms of the formula size complexity of f by $2^{-L(f)^{\Theta(1)}}$.

The model described in the present paper is also based on a sequence of distributions on formulas of increasing size, but here, the relation between probability and complexity appears in the limit distribution. This is not the case in the model from [9], since there, the limit is the uniform distribution on all Boolean functions.

The distribution on functions represented by large AND/OR Boolean formulas was studied also in [4]. The main question there concerns the distribution of the weight of the function represented by the random formula, i.e. the number of ones in its table. For example, the following is proved there. If both the size m of the formula and the number n of variables tend to infinity, then, for constants a, b with $0 \leq a < b \leq 1$, the probability of the event that the weight of the random function is in the interval $[a2^n, b2^n)$ converges to a positive limit.

The limit distribution on formulas described in this paper has the property that disjoint subformulas of the random formula viewed as random variables are independent. Boolean formulas of this kind were already studied by Boppana, Razborov, Valiant and others, and used to prove results on the formula size complexity of the majority function and of the representation of Ramsey graphs, see [1], [7], [8] and [10]. In all these results, the independence of subformulas is the basic tool. In a more general setting, there is a connection to the study of nonlinear dynamical systems defined on finite functions (see [5], [6]).

2 Approximation by an Infinite Tree

First, we will investigate the tree structure of AND/OR formulas. The *size* of a tree is the number of its nodes. A binary tree consisting of two nonempty subtrees connected to the root will be called *1-separable* or only separable, if its two subtrees have different size. In such a tree, the unique maximum subtree will be called *tail*. If the tail is also separable, we say that the original tree is *2-separable*, and so on. Hence, a k-separable tree allows k steps of such a decomposition. The tail obtained in the i-th step will be called *i-th tail*, where the 0-th tail is the whole tree. Moreover, the whole tree with the k-th tail replaced by a new *special leaf* distinguishable from all the other leaves, will be called the *k-head* or, if k follows from the context, simply head. The special leaf is included in order to mark the position, where the tail was connected to. We shall also consider the decomposition of the k-head into k segments, where the *i-th segment* is the $(i-1)$-st tail with the i-th tail replaced by the special leaf denoting the original position of the i-th tail. We do not count the special leaves to the sizes of the segments. Hence, the size of a k-separable tree is the sum of the sizes of its k segments plus the size of the k-th tail.

In the following, we will prove that, if m tends to infinity, then, with probability approaching 1, a random binary tree of size $2m-1$ is 1-separable and the corresponding tail has size at least $(2m-1-t(m))$, where $t(m) \ll m$ is any function tending to infinity with m.

Let $g(x)=\sum_{i=1}^{\infty} a_i x^i$ be the generating function for the nonempty rooted binary trees. That is, a_i counts the number of rooted binary trees of size i. Since $a_1=1$ and $a_i=\sum_{j=1}^{i-2} a_j a_{i-j-1}$ for all $i \geq 2$, we obtain the identity $g(x)=x(1+g(x)^2)$. From this and the fact that $g(0)=0$, we infer that $g(x)=\frac{1}{2x}\cdot\left(1-\sqrt{1-4x^2}\right)$. Using Taylor expansion, we obtain for $0 \leq x \leq 1/2$ that

$$g(x)=\frac{1}{2x}\cdot\left(1-\sum_{i=0}^{\infty}\binom{1/2}{i}\cdot(-4x^2)^i\right)=\sum_{n=1}^{\infty} C(2n-1)\cdot x^{2n-1}, \qquad (1)$$

where $C(2n-1)$ are the Catalan numbers, $C(2n-1)=\frac{1}{n}\cdot\binom{2n-2}{n-1}$, counting the number of rooted binary trees of size $2n-1$ for every $n \geq 1$.

In a k-separable tree, each segment consists of its root and two sons. One of them is the special leaf, the other is a nonempty binary tree. As there are two possible positions for the special leaf, the number of segments of size $2r$ is $2\cdot C(2r-1)$.

Lemma 2. *Let H be a fixed k-head with i-th segment of size $2r_i$ for $i=1,2,\ldots,k$. Let m tend to infinity and let $\sum_{i=1}^{k} r_i = o(m)$. Then, the probability that a random tree of size $2m-1$ is k-separable and that its k-head is H equals*

$$\left(1+O\left(\frac{1}{m}\sum_{i=1}^{k} r_i\right)\right)\cdot\prod_{i=1}^{k} 2^{-2r_i}. \qquad (2)$$

Proof. The required probability P is equal to the quotient of the number of k-separable trees with head H and the number of all trees of size $2m-1$. Every k-separable tree with head H has a tail of size $2(m-\sum_{i=1}^{k} r_i)-1$. Hence, P is equal to the ratio of $C(2(m-\sum_{i=1}^{k} r_i)-1)$ over $C(2m-1)$. The lemma is then obtained using Stirling's formula. The details are left to the full version. □

By the following result, for k not too large, the tree is k-separable with probability approaching 1 for m approaching infinity.

Lemma 3. *Let $kr = o(m)$ and $k = o(r^{1/2})$. Then, for m large the probability P that the tree is k-separable and each of the k corresponding segments has size at most $2r$, equals $P = 1 - O\left(k/r^{1/2}\right) + O\left(kr/m\right)$.*

Proof. We compute the sum of the probabilities of the occurrence of each k-head H with segments of size at most $2r$. By Lemma 2 used for $k = 1$, for $m \to \infty$ the limit of the probability of the occurrence of an individual segment of size $2j$ is 2^{-2j}. There are $2C(2j-1)$ segments of size $2j$. By (1) for $x = 1/2$, we get

$$\sum_{j=1}^{\infty} \frac{2C(2j-1)}{2^{2j}} = 1 . \tag{3}$$

Using Stirling's formula we have $2 \cdot C(2j-1) \cdot 2^{-2j} = O\left(j^{-3/2}\right)$ and hence

$$\sum_{j=r+1}^{\infty} \frac{2C(2j-1)}{2^{2j}} = O\left(\int_r^{\infty} \frac{1}{x^{3/2}} \mathrm{d}x\right) = O\left(\frac{1}{r^{1/2}}\right) . \tag{4}$$

By Lemma 2 and (4), the desired probability P is given by

$$P = \left(1 + O\left(\frac{kr}{m}\right)\right)\left(\sum_{j=1}^{r} \frac{2C(2j-1)}{2^{2j}}\right)^{k} = \left(1 + O\left(\frac{kr}{m}\right)\right)\left(1 - O\left(\frac{1}{r^{1/2}}\right)\right)^{k} .$$

As $kr = o(m)$ and $k = o(r^{1/2})$, we infer $P = 1 - O\left(\frac{k}{r^{1/2}}\right) + O\left(\frac{kr}{m}\right)$. □

By Lemma 2, for $m \to \infty$ the probability of the occurrence of each individual segment of size $2r$ converges to 2^{-2r}. By (3), these limits determine a well-defined distribution on segments. For the random segments from this distribution consider the usual random labeling of the inner nodes and the leaves, except of the special leaf, by connectives AND/OR and literals containing the Boolean variables $x_1, x_2, \ldots, x_n$. From now on, let n be the number of these variables, where n is fixed. The resulting distribution on labeled segments will be denoted by D_1. Moreover, let D_k be the distribution on labeled k-heads formed by choosing k segments independently from D_1 and connecting them via the special leaves in the straightforward manner.

For a labeled head occurring either in the distribution D_k or as the k-head of a k-separable tree, we define the function computed by the head as follows. Assume that the special leaf is labeled by a new variable x_{n+1}. Thus, the head is labeled by $n+1$ variables. The function computed by the labeled head is the partial Boolean function of n original variables, defined for those inputs, for which the value of the formula of $n+1$ variables does not depend on x_{n+1}. If the head of a k-separable tree computes a total function, we say that the head is *closed*.

It is easy to see that the probability $P_k(f)$ of the occurrence of each total Boolean function f in the distributions D_k is nondecreasing with k. Moreover, the probabilities $P_k(f)$ have some positive limits $P(f) = \lim_{k\to\infty} P_k(f)$.

Let D be the distribution on labeled infinite trees, which are formed by connecting an infinite sequence of labeled segments chosen independently from D_1. A

tree chosen from D contains exactly one infinite path. We say that a tree chosen from D *computes a function* f, if for some integer k, the first k labeled segments in the tree form a closed k-head computing f. This happens with probability one and the probability that a tree from D computes f is equal to $P(f)$.
The *size* of a Boolean formula is the number of occurrences of variables contained in the formula, i.e. a formula of size m is based on a tree of size $2m-1$.

Theorem 4. *Let f be a total Boolean function on n variables. Then, the probability that a random AND/OR formula chosen from the uniform distribution on formulas of size m computes f, converges to $P(f)$ with m tending to infinity.*

Proof. It suffices to show that for every total Boolean function f the difference between the probability of computing f by a random formula chosen from the uniform distribution on formulas of size m and $P_k(f)$ converges to zero, if k and m both tend to infinity in a controlled way. Fix some ε, $0<\varepsilon<1/3$, and set $k=\lceil m^{1/3-\varepsilon}\rceil$ and $r=\lceil m^{2/3}\rceil$. Let $\Pr_1(A)$ be the probability of some event A in the uniform distribution on formulas of size m, while $\Pr_2(A)$ will be the probability of A in the distribution D_k. The set of all k-heads containing only segments of size at most $2r$ is denoted by $\mathcal{H}(k,r)$. For any k-head $H\in\mathcal{H}(k,r)$, by $\Pr_1(H)$ ($\Pr_2(H)$) we mean the probability of the event "the tree is k-separable and its k-head is equal to H". By $\mathcal{H}(k,r)$ we mean the disjunction of the events corresponding to all $H\in\mathcal{H}(k,r)$.
To compare the probabilities $\Pr_1(f)$ and $\Pr_2(f)$ of the event that the random formula in the corresponding distribution computes f, we first consider the conditional probabilities $\Pr_1(f\mid H)$ and $\Pr_2(f\mid H)$. The assignments of connectives and literals, which guarantees f in the second of these two events, are exactly the same as the assignments of the k-head H in the first event that make H closed and give f. Hence, $\Pr_2(f\mid H)=\Pr_1(f\wedge(H \text{ is closed})\mid H)$, and

$$\begin{aligned}0&\le \Pr_1(f\mid H)-\Pr_2(f\mid H)=\Pr_1(f\wedge(H\text{ is not closed})\mid H)\\&\le \Pr_1(H\text{ is not closed}\mid H)\,.\end{aligned}$$

Consider a fixed input x. Each of the k nodes on the path from the root to the k-th tail computes either the AND or OR of two subformulas. One of them contains the tail and the other belongs completely to the head. The assignment of connectives and literals is symmetric with respect to the values 0 and 1. Hence, the subformula, which belongs to the head, computes 0 and 1 on input x, each with probability 1/2. With probability 1/2, the value of the subformula, which contains the tail, has no influence on the value computed in the node. Since this happens for all k nodes in the path independently, the probability that the tail is needed to compute the value of the function in the root, is at most $(1/2)^k$. As there are 2^n different inputs, the probability that for at least one of them, the value of the function is not determined by the head is at most 2^{n-k}. Combining the arguments, we obtain for fixed n that

$$|\Pr_1(f\mid H)-\Pr_2(f\mid H)|\le 2^{n-k}=O(2^{-m^{1/3-\varepsilon}})\,. \tag{5}$$

As $kr/m = O(m^{-\varepsilon})$, we have by Lemma 2, that $\Pr_1(H) = \Pr_2(H)\cdot(1+O(m^{-\varepsilon}))$ for every k-head $H \in \mathcal{H}(k,r)$. Moreover, $\Pr_1(\neg\mathcal{H}(k,r)) = O(m^{-\varepsilon})$ by Lemma 3. The leftmost expression in (4) is equal to the probability that the random segment chosen from D_1 has size at least $2r+2$. Hence, as in the proof of Lemma 3, we obtain $\Pr_2(\neg\mathcal{H}(k,r)) = O(k/r^{1/2}) = O(m^{-\varepsilon})$. Using (5), we summarize

$$\begin{aligned}
&\Pr_1(f) - \Pr_2(f) \\
&= \sum_{H\in\mathcal{H}(k,r)} [\Pr_1(f \mid H)\cdot \Pr_1(H) - \Pr_2(f \mid H)\cdot \Pr_2(H)] + O(m^{-\varepsilon}) \\
&= \sum_{H\in\mathcal{H}(k,r)} \Pr_2(H)\cdot[\Pr_1(f \mid H) - \Pr_2(f \mid H) + \Pr_1(f \mid H)O(m^{-\varepsilon})] + O(m^{-\varepsilon}) \\
&= O(m^{-\varepsilon}) ,
\end{aligned}$$

since $\sum_{H\in\mathcal{H}(k,r)} \Pr_2(H) \leq 1$. □

3 Bounding the Limit Probabilities

For any Boolean function f, the *formula size complexity* $L(f)$ is the minimum size of a formula representing f. Our construction of the distribution D yields the following lower bound on the probability $P(f)$ of the occurrence of f.

Theorem 5. *Let f be a Boolean function of n variables. Then*

$$P(f) \geq \frac{1}{4}\cdot\left(\frac{1}{8n}\right)^{L(f)+1} \tag{6}$$

Proof. Let ϕ be any formula of size $L(f)$ representing f. We obtain (6) by calculating the total probability of the closed 2-heads in the two forms $\phi \vee ((x_i \wedge \neg x_i) \wedge y)$ and $\phi \wedge ((x_i \vee \neg x_i) \vee y)$, where $1 \leq i \leq n$ and y denotes the position of the special leaf, and their variants due to the commutativity of AND/OR. □

Pick a random Boolean formula according to the distribution D. As in the proof of Theorem 4, for a fixed input, the first k segments of the tree are sufficient to determine the value of the whole infinite formula with probability $1-2^{-k}$. Thus, with probability at least $1-2^{n-k}$, the first k segments determine the value of the whole formula for all inputs. This is close to 1 if $k \gg n$. Moreover, (4) together with the definition of D_1 implies that the probability for the size of a segment being bigger than $2r$ is at most $O(1/r^{1/2})$. Hence, with high probability, only small parts of the formula are really needed to compute the function. This may be used to prove an upper bound on the probability $P(f)$ of a function f. This upper bound is small, if the formula size $L(f)$ is large, however, it would be only one over a polynomial in $L(f)$. In the following, an upper bound of the magnitude one over an exponential of $L(f)$ will be given. To prove it, we show that in a random formula from distribution D many cancelations may be performed. The resulting equivalent formula is finite with probability 1 and, moreover, it is large with exponentially small probability.

The cancelations are controlled by assigning a set of restrictions to each inner node of the tree. If the set of restrictions assigned to a node is contradictory, the node will be deleted. The restrictions are simply requirements on the values of single variables and they are computed as follows. The root is assigned the empty set. Assume that an inner node v of the formula is assigned a set ρ of restrictions. If both successors of v are inner nodes, the set ρ is assigned to both of them without any change. If only one of the successors is an inner node, say the left one, let x_i be the variable used in the literal in the right successor. Then, the left successor is assigned the set $\rho \cup \{x_i = a\}$ of restrictions, where a is the value of x_i which does not force the AND or OR in the node v to a constant. In the remainder of this section, we always assume that the nodes of a formula from D are assigned to the cancelation controlling restrictions computed by these rules. If some inner node v is assigned a set ρ of restrictions and, for some input, the input variables do not satisfy some of the restrictions, then the value computed in the node v has no influence to the value computed by the whole formula. If ρ contains both $x_i = 0$ and $x_i = 1$ for some i, then the node v has no influence for any input and, hence, it may be deleted. The deletion is performed by replacing the node by any constant and when all such replacements are finished, the formula is transformed to a formula without constants using standard simplification rules. Let ϕ be a random Boolean formula labeled by the sets of restrictions as described. Denote by $||\phi||$ the number of inner nodes in ϕ assigned to a consistent set of restrictions. After the transformation described above, the number of inner nodes in the new equivalent formula is at most $||\phi||$ and hence its formula size is at most $||\phi|| + 1$. To give a small upper bound on the probability that $||\phi||$ is large, where ϕ is chosen from the distribution D, we estimate the expected value $\mathrm{E}\left[(1+\varepsilon)^{||\phi||}\right]$, where $\varepsilon > 0$ is appropriate. To this end, we represent the distribution D as a simple growing process on trees and first consider the expectation of a similar quantity in some finite parts of ϕ.

Consider the following two types of nodes, *c-nodes* and *n-nodes* (connecting and normal, respectively). We start with one c-node. In each step, each node is either expanded into two successors or stopped. A c-node is always expanded into one c-node and one n-node. With probability 1/2, the new c-node is either the left successor or the right successor. An n-node is either expanded or stopped, each with probability 1/2. If expanded, both successors are again n-nodes. The resulting tree consists of an infinite sequence of independently chosen (possibly infinite) segments connected via c-nodes. Moreover, the probability for the event that a given individual segment of size $2r$ occurs is $(1/2)^{2r}$. Thus, the tree structure of a single segment is generated according to the distribution D_1. In particular, each segment is finite with probability 1. By assigning the random labeling by connectives and literals to all segments as before, we obtain a formula from D. We refer to this process as to the *basic growing process*.

The tree is generated level by level. If all the nodes in level $j+1$ are created, it is known for every node in level j, whether it is an inner node or a leaf. At this time, the random labeling of these nodes by connectives and literals is chosen. Since all nodes in level j have their labels, the sets of restrictions for all nodes in level

j may be computed. Let v be an inner node in level j. Note that the distribution of the subtree below v including the labeling and the sets of restrictions depends on the rest of the tree only via the labeling of v. Hence, we can consider v as a starting node of a separate process. The initialization of the process is given by the type of node v (n-node or c-node) and by the set ρ of restrictions in v. If v is an n-node, the process starts by expanding v deterministicaly, as v is an inner node. We refer to this process as to the *generalized growing process*. The basic growing process generating formulas from D is the special case, when the starting node is a c-node and ρ is the empty set.
For a random formula ϕ generated by the generalized growing process and any nonnegative integer d, let $||\phi||_d$ be the number of inner nodes of depth at most d in ϕ, which are assigned a consistent set of restrictions. If ϕ is generated by the growing process started with a set of restrictions ρ, then, by symmetry, the distribution of $||\phi||_d$ is the same for all other consistent starting sets of restrictions of the same size. Hence, only the size of ρ has to be taken into account. In the following, let $\varepsilon > 0$ be a real number, which will be specified later. Let $\alpha(d,k) = \mathrm{E}\left[(1+\varepsilon)^{||\phi||_d}\right]$ respective $\beta(d,k) = \mathrm{E}\left[(1+\varepsilon)^{||\phi||_d}\right]$, where ϕ is generated by the generalized growing process starting at an n-node respective c-node with a consistent set ρ of restrictions of size k.

Lemma 6. *For every real $\varepsilon > 0$ and for all integers $d \geq 0$ and $k = 0, 1, \ldots, n$,*

$$\alpha(0,k) = 1 + \varepsilon$$

$$\alpha(d+1,k) = (1+\varepsilon)\left(\frac{1}{4}\alpha(d,k)^2 + \frac{k}{4n}\alpha(d,k) + \right.$$

$$\left. + \frac{1}{2}\left(1 - \frac{k}{n}\right)\alpha(d,k+1) + \frac{k}{4n} + \frac{1}{4}\right).$$

Proof. The starting node v is an n-node with a consistent k-element set ρ of restrictions. Hence, $||\phi||_0 = 1$ and $\alpha(0,k) = 1 + \varepsilon$. For the second identity, we use the fact that for every d, $||\phi||_{d+1} = 1 + ||\phi_1||_d + ||\phi_2||_d$. The random variables $||\phi_1||_d$ and $||\phi_2||_d$ are dependent, but they are conditionally independent if the labeling of the succesors v_1, v_2 of v is known. Using this, the expected value of $(1+\varepsilon)^{||\phi||_{d+1}}$ is computed by expansion to the conditional expectations according to all possibilities of the labeling of v_1, v_2, i.e., for each node v_1, v_2 independently, we distinguish the cases, whether the node is expanded or stopped and, if stopped, whether the new restriction is independent of the condition in v, contradictory to it or contained in it. The details are skipped. □

Similarly, one can show the following:

Lemma 7. *For every real $\varepsilon > 0$, and for all integers $d \geq 0$ and $k = 0, 1, \ldots, n$,*

$$\beta(0,k) = 1 + \varepsilon$$

$$\beta(d+1,k) = (1+\varepsilon)\left(\frac{1}{2}\alpha(d,k)\beta(d,k) + \frac{k}{4n}\beta(d,k) + \right.$$

$$\left. + \frac{1}{2}\left(1 - \frac{k}{n}\right)\beta(d,k+1) + \frac{k}{4n}\right).$$

Theorem 8. *There exists a constant $c > 1$ such that for every Boolean function f on n variables,*

$$P(f) \leq (1 + O(1/n)) \cdot c^{-L(f)/n^3}.$$

Proof. First we give upper bounds on $\alpha(d,k)$ and $\beta(d,k)$, if ε is 1 over some polynomial in n. With foresight, set $u_k = 5(n-k+1)$ and $v_k = 5(n-k+2)^2$ for every $k = 0,\ldots,n$. We will find a range of ε, such that for $k = 0,1,\ldots,n$ and every nonnegative integer d the following inequalities hold

$$\alpha(d,k) \leq 1 + u_k\varepsilon \tag{7}$$

$$\beta(d,k) \leq 1 + v_k\varepsilon\ . \tag{8}$$

Both these inequalities are satisfied for $d = 0$, any $k = 0,1,\ldots,n$ and any $\varepsilon > 0$. By induction on d, one can show that these two inequalities hold for all $d \geq 0$, provided ε is small enough. For the induction step, we use Lemmas 6 and 7 together with (7) and (8) to prove

$$\begin{aligned}
&1 + u_k\varepsilon - \alpha(d+1,k) \\
&\geq \left[\left(\frac{1}{2} - \frac{k}{4n}\right)u_k - \frac{1}{2}\left(1 - \frac{k}{n}\right)u_{k+1} - 1\right]\varepsilon + O(n^2\varepsilon^2) \\
&\geq \left(\frac{1}{2} - \frac{k}{4n}\right)(u_k - u_{k+1} - 4)\varepsilon + O(n^2\varepsilon^2) \geq \frac{1}{4}\varepsilon + O(n^2\varepsilon^2)
\end{aligned}$$

and

$$\begin{aligned}
&1 + v_k\varepsilon - \beta(d+1,k) \\
&\geq \left[\left(\frac{1}{2} - \frac{k}{4n}\right)v_k - \frac{1}{2}\left(1 - \frac{k}{n}\right)v_{k+1} - \frac{1}{2}u_k - 1\right]\varepsilon + O(n^3\varepsilon^2) \\
&\geq \left(\frac{1}{2} - \frac{k}{4n}\right)(v_k - v_{k+1} - 2u_k - 4)\varepsilon + O(n^3\varepsilon^2) \geq \frac{1}{4}\varepsilon + O(n^3\varepsilon^2)\ .
\end{aligned}$$

We conclude that there is a positive constant δ such that for every ε, $0 < \varepsilon \leq \delta/n^3$, we have $\alpha(d+1,k) \leq 1 + u_k\varepsilon$ and $\beta(d+1,k) \leq 1 + v_k\varepsilon$. By induction, we obtain (7) and (8) for all $d \geq 0$. For the remainder of the proof set $\varepsilon = \delta/n^3$. Let ϕ be a formula from D. By definition of $\beta(d,k)$, it follows that $\mathrm{E}\left[(1+\varepsilon)^{\|\phi\|_d}\right] = \beta(d,0)$. Since $\|\phi\|_d \geq \|\phi\|_{d-1}$, the limit $\lim_{d\to\infty} \mathrm{E}\left[(1+\varepsilon)^{\|\phi\|_d}\right]$ exists and, by (8), is bounded from above by $1 + 5(n+2)^2\varepsilon$.

Lemma 9. (see [3]) *If* $\sum_{d=0}^{\infty} \mathrm{E}[|Y_d|]$ *is convergent for a sequence of random variables* Y_d, *then* $\mathrm{E}\left[\sum_{d=0}^{\infty} Y_d\right] = \sum_{d=0}^{\infty} \mathrm{E}[Y_d]$.

Let $Y_0 = (1+\varepsilon)^{\|\phi\|_0}$ and $Y_d = (1+\varepsilon)^{\|\phi\|_d} - (1+\varepsilon)^{\|\phi\|_{d-1}}$ for every $d \geq 1$. Since $\|\phi\|_d \geq \|\phi\|_{d-1}$, we have $Y_d \geq 0$, and hence

$$\sum_{d=0}^{\infty} \mathrm{E}[|Y_d|] = \sum_{d=0}^{\infty} \mathrm{E}[Y_d] = \lim_{d\to\infty} \mathrm{E}\left[(1+\varepsilon)^{\|\phi\|_d}\right] \leq 1 + 5(n+2)^2\varepsilon = 1 + O(1/n)\ .$$

By Lemma 9 it follows that $\mathrm{E}\left[(1+\varepsilon)^{\|\phi\|}\right] \leq 1+O(1/n)$. If ϕ computes f, then $L(f) \leq \|\phi\|+1$, and hence, by Markov's inequality,

$$\Pr\left(\phi \text{ computes } f\right) \leq \Pr\left((1+\varepsilon)^{\|\phi\|} \geq (1+\varepsilon)^{L(f)-1}\right) \leq \frac{\mathrm{E}\left[(1+\varepsilon)^{\|\phi\|}\right]}{(1+\varepsilon)^{L(f)-1}} \leq$$

$$\leq (1+O(1/n)) \cdot \left(1+\frac{\delta}{n^3}\right)^{-L(f)} \leq (1+O(1/n)) \cdot c^{-L(f)/n^3}$$

for every absolute constant c with $1 < c < \mathrm{e}^{\delta}$ and n large enough. □

Now Theorem 1 is an immediate consequence of Theorems 5 and 8.

Acknowledgement The authors would like to thank to Jan Krajíček for simplifying the limiting argument in the proof of Theorem 8.

References

1. R. B. Boppana: Amplification of Probabilistic Boolean Formulas, *Proc. 26th Ann. IEEE Symp. on Foundations of Computer Science,* 1985, 20–29.
2. J. Friedman: Probabilistic Spaces of Boolean Functions of a Given Complexity: Generalities and Random k-SAT Coefficients, CS-TR-387-92, Princeton University, 1992.
3. A. N. Kolmogorov: *Foundations of the Theory of Probability,* Chelsea Publishing Company, New York, 1950.
4. J. B. Paris, A. Vencovská, G. M. Wilmers: A Natural Prior Probability Distribution Derived from the Propositional Calculus, *Annals of Pure and Applied Logic* 70, 1994, 243-285.
5. Y. Rabani, Y. Rabinovich and A. Sinclair: A Computational View of Population Genetics, preprint.
6. Y. Rabinovich, A. Sinclair and A. Wigderson: Quadratic Dynamical Systems, *Proc. 33rd Ann. IEEE Symp. on Foundations of Computer Science,* 1992, 304-313.
7. A. A. Razborov: Bounded-depth Formulae over $\{\wedge, \oplus\}$ and some Combinatorial Problems. In *Complexity of Algorithms and Applied Mathematical Logic* (in Russian), Ser. *Voprosy Kibernetiky* (Problems in Cybernetics), ed.: S. I. Adian, Moscow, 1988, 149-166.
8. P. Savický: Improved Boolean Formulas for the Ramsey Graphs, to appear in *Random Structures and Algorithms.*
9. P. Savický: Complexity and Probability of some Boolean Formulas, TR 538, FB Informatik, Universität Dortmund, 1994.
10. L. G. Valiant: Short Monotone Formulae for the Majority Function, *J. Algorithms 5,* 1984, 363–366.
11. A. Woods, personal communication.

The Hedge: An Efficient Storage Device for Turing Machines with One Head

(Extended Abstract)

Martin Hühne*

Fachbereich Informatik, Lehrstuhl II, Universität Dortmund, D-44221 Dortmund

huehne@ls2.informatik.uni-dortmund.de

Abstract Which kind of storage device should be used for a time-efficient simulation of multitape Turing machines on deterministic Turing machines with only one access head? In the literature, simulations on Turing machines accessing a tape, a multidimensional array, or a tree have been studied.

We advocate a new storage device for Turing machines, the "hedge."

On a Turing machine accessing one hedge, multitape Turing machines can be simulated faster than on each of the traditional storage devices. E.g., we show how to simulate $t(n)$ steps of a multitape Turing machine by $O(t(n) \log t(n)/ \log \log t(n))$ steps of a Turing machine accessing one hedge.

1 Introduction

Simulations of Turing machines (TMs) with different storage devices among each other have been studied extensively. Here, we consider the efficiency of deterministic Turing machines with *one* access head. The topology of the storage device of the TM is described by a directed, edge-labelled graph of bounded degree. The vertices of the graph are identified with the cells of the storage device. The edges of the graph define the legal movements of the access head.

What is a "good" storage device for Turing machines with one access head? More specific, which storage device should be used for an efficient simulation of multitape TMs? Common storage devices are the linear tape, the multidimensional array, and the tree [CA69, PF79]. Of course, the linear tape is not an efficient storage device, since $\Theta(t(n)^2)$ steps are required to simulate $t(n)$ steps of a multitape TM on one linear tape [HS65, Hen65, Maa85]. On a TM with one d-dimensional storage device, $d \geq 2$, the multitape TM can be simulated in time $\Theta(t(n)^{1+1/d}/ \log t(n))$ [DH94]. For the simulation of a multitape TM, the tree is the most efficient of the common storage devices. On a TM with one storage device in the shape of a tree, $t(n)$ steps of a multitape TM can be simulated in time $O(t(n) \log t(n))$ [folklore]. The same time bound holds for the simulation of a TM accessing several trees on a TM accessing one tree [PR81]. It is not known whether simulations on TMs accessing an X-tree are more efficient than simulations on TMs accessing a tree. An X-tree is a tree with additional edges joining cells on the same level from the left to the right [HL88]. Faster simulations are only known on machines with more than one access head. E.g., on a TM accessing both a tree and a linear tape, the multitape TM can be simulated in linear

* The author gratefully acknowledges the support of Deutsche Forschungsgemeinschaft under Grant Di 412/2-2.

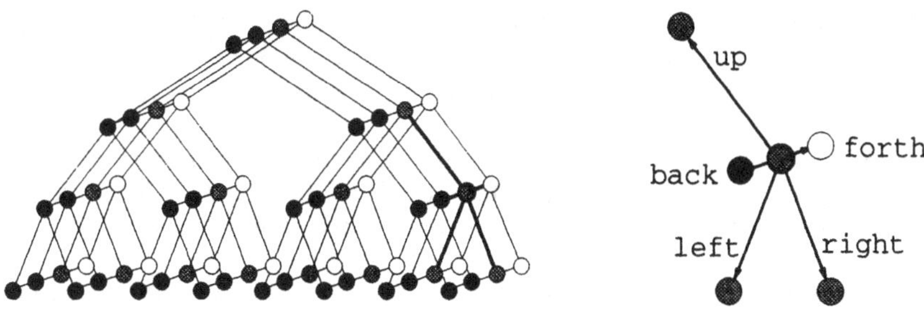

Figure 1. The topology of the storage device "hedge." The first four levels of four bushes of the hedge are shown. Cells with the same colour belong to the same bush. On the right, one cell, its adjacent cells, and the corresponding directions are shown on a larger scale.

time [HPV75, PR81]. The multitree TM can be simulated on this model in time $O(t(n)\ \log t(n)/\log\log t(n))$ [Lou84]. A TM accessing several d-dimensional arrays can be simulated by a multitree TM in time $O(t(n)\,5^{d\log^* t(n)})$, i.e., in almost linear time [Rei82].

Our simulations are based on an efficient implementation of string copying on machines with only one head. Such a copying technique was first presented for TMs with a multidimensional array [DH94]. The basic idea is that information can be transferred faster than in the naive way from one region to the other, if, on the storage device, there are several (short) disjoint paths between these regions. This is impossible on the tree and on the linear tape.

In this paper we present a new, efficient storage device for one-head TMs: the *hedge*. A hedge consists of a sequence of trees where corresponding vertices in adjacent trees are connected by additional edges (cf. Fig. 1 and Sec. 2). The hedge has a regular structure; graphtheoretically, it can be described as the Cartesian product of the tree and the one-dimensional array. The hedge combines the qualities of the tree and the multidimensional array. As on the tree, the number of cells reachable within a fixed distance is exponential. This can be used to look up information in time which is logarithmic in the size of the data base that is searched through. As on the multidimensional array, the cells are connected by several paths. Thus, information looked up in the data base can be copied fast.

We show upper bounds for simulations on Turing machines accessing one hedge. Our main results are as follows.

Theorem 1 *Each $t(n)$ time bounded Turing machine which uses several d-dimensional arrays as work tapes can be simulated by an*

$$O\left(\frac{t(n)\ \log t(n)}{\sqrt[d]{\log\log t(n)}}\right)$$

time bounded Turing machine which uses one hedge as work tape.[2]

[2] Throughout this paper, let $\log t = \max(1, \log_2 t)$.

For $d = 1$, as an immediate corollary this yields an $O(t(n) \log t(n) / \log \log t(n))$ time bounded simulation of several linear tapes on one hedge.

We show how to simulate multitree and multihedge TMs on one hedge.

Theorem 2 *Each $t(n)$ time bounded TM which uses several trees and several hedges as work tapes can be simulated by an $O(t(n) \log t(n) / \log \log \log t(n))$ time bounded Turing machine which uses one hedge as work tape.*

These are the first results where sublogarithmic delay for the deterministic simulation of a machine with several heads on a machine with one head is achieved.

The rest of the paper is organized as follows. The storage device hedge is introduced in Section 2. In Section 3, a fast copy algorithm is implemented on TMs which access one hedge as work tape. This copy algorithm is used in Sections 4 and 5 to prove Theorems 1 and 2, respectively.

2 Storage Devices for Turing Machines

A storage device consists of an infinite set of storage cells each with a finite capability to store information, and of one read/write head to access these cells. At each point of time the head visits one of the cells. Only the contents of this cell can be read or modified by the machine. To access the other cells, the head can be moved according to the topology of the storage device. We consider Turing machines where the topology of the storage device is fixed for all computations of the machine. (For a model where the machine may modify the topology of its storage during the computation, see [Sch80].)

The topology of the storage device is described by a graph ([PR81], [Rei90], see also [CA69]). Let $G = (V, E)$ be an infinite directed edge-labelled multigraph of bounded degree. The labelling $\varphi : E \to D$ of the edges by a finite set D of *directions* is injective when it is restricted to edges with fixed tail. I.e., for each $c \in V$ and each $dir \in D$ there is at most one $c' \in V$ where $\varphi(c, c') = dir$. One cell $c_0 \in V$ is distinguished as the *origin* of G.

In this setting, the storage device *linear tape* is described by the set of cells $V = \mathbb{Z}$ and the set of edges $E = \{ (c, c+1),\ (c, c-1) \mid c \in \mathbb{Z}\}$. The edges $(c, c-1)$ are labelled by the direction $\mathtt{back} \in D$, the edges $(c, c+1)$ are labelled by the direction $\mathtt{forth} \in D$. The storage device *infinite binary rooted tree* has cells $V = \{0,1\}^*$, edges $E = \{(c, ca),\ (ca, c) \mid c \in \{0,1\}^*, a \in \{0,1\}\}$, directions $D = \{\mathtt{left}, \mathtt{right}, \mathtt{up}\}$, and the labelling $\varphi(c, c0) = \mathtt{left}$, $\varphi(c, c1) = \mathtt{right}$, $\varphi(ca, c) = \mathtt{up}$. The origin of the tree is the root ε.

The *hedge* is a storage device with vertices (p, q), $p \in \{0,1\}^*, q \in \mathbb{Z}$. The hedge can be traversed by the access head using the movements $\mathtt{up}$, $\mathtt{left}$, $\mathtt{right}$, $\mathtt{back}$, and $\mathtt{forth}$. For $q \in \mathbb{Z}$ fixed, the cells (p, q), $p \in \{0,1\}^*$, form a complete infinite binary rooted tree, referred to as *bush* q of the hedge. For $\ell \in \mathbb{N}$, the cells (p, q), $p \in \{0,1\}^\ell$, $q \in \mathbb{Z}$, are on *level* ℓ of the hedge. The movements $\mathtt{left}$ and $\mathtt{right}$ move the access head from cell (p, q) to cell $(p0, q)$ and $(p1, q)$, respectively, movement $\mathtt{up}$ moves the head from cell (pa, q), $a \in \{0,1\}$, to (p, q).

The movements **back** and **forth** move the head from a cell in bush q to the corresponding cell in the adjacent bush $q-1$ and $q+1$, respectively. The cell $(\varepsilon, 0)$ is the origin of the hedge. Level zero is called the root of the hedge. More formally, for the hedge we have

- cells $V = \{0,1\}^* \times \mathbb{Z}$,
- edges $E = \{((p,q),(pa,q)),\ ((pa,q),(p,q)),\ ((p,q),(p,q-1)),\ ((p,q),(p,q+1)) \mid p \in \{0,1\}^*, a \in \{0,1\}, q \in \mathbb{Z}\}$,
- directions $D = \{\mathtt{left}, \mathtt{right}, \mathtt{up}, \mathtt{back}, \mathtt{forth}\}$, and the
- labelling $\varphi((p,q),(p0,q)) = \mathtt{left},\quad \varphi((p,q),(p,q-1)) = \mathtt{back}$,
  $\varphi((p,q),(p1,q)) = \mathtt{right},\ \varphi((p,q),(p,q+1)) = \mathtt{forth}$,
  $\varphi((pa,q),(p,q)) = \mathtt{up}$.

In the following, we will also consider the storage device *d-dimensional array*, $d \geq 1$, which is the Cartesian product of d linear tapes. Thus, the corresponding set of cells is $\mathbb{Z}^d$ and the set of directions is $\{\mathtt{back}_i, \mathtt{forth}_i \mid i = 1, \ldots, d\}$.

Now, let G be a storage device. Then, a G Turing machine is a deterministic TM which accesses a storage device G as its "work tape" and a linear tape as one-way input tape. At the beginning of the computation, the head on the input tape visits the leftmost cell and the head on the work tape G visits the origin. The cells on the input tape store the input; each cell on the work tape stores a blank symbol. In the computation, let $c \in V$ be the cell currently visited on the work tape. In one step, after reading the contents of cell c and of the cell currently visited on the input tape, the machine may write to cell c, may move the head on the work tape to a cell c', $(c, c') \in E$ (*movement into direction* $\varphi(c, c') \in D$), and may move the head on the input tape one cell to the right. Multi-G TMs and TMs accessing several different storage devices can be defined in the obvious way. The *distance* between two cells c and c' on the work tape, $c, c' \in V$, is the number of steps required to move the head from c to c'. The *time complexity* of the machine is denoted by $t(n)$, where n is the length of the input. Often, TMs without separate input tape are considered. As to our results, we remark that the separate input tape is not essential for our simulations. The simulations can be adapted to machines where the input is written on the work tape G in a suitable compact fashion, e.g., on the first $\lfloor \log n \rfloor + 1$ levels in bush zero of a hedge.

3 Copying Strings on One Hedge

Consider the following copying task: Let $c_{start} = (p_{start}, q_{start})$ and $c_{end} = (p_{end}, q_{end})$ be two cells on the hedge which are connected by a path of Δ marked cells such that the head of the machine can be moved from c_{start} to c_{end} and back to c_{start} within $O(\Delta)$ steps. Let ℓ be a natural number. The task is to copy the contents of the ℓ cells $(p_{start}, q_{start}+1), \ldots, (p_{start}, q_{start}+\ell)$ to the cells $(p_{end}, q_{end}+1), \ldots, (p_{end}, q_{end}+\ell)$ which are Δ cells away.

Using one head, the TM may copy the contents of the cells along the path bit by bit in time $O(\ell\Delta)$. In [DH94] a fast copying technique for machines accessing one multidimensional array was presented where $\omega(1)$ bits are transferred

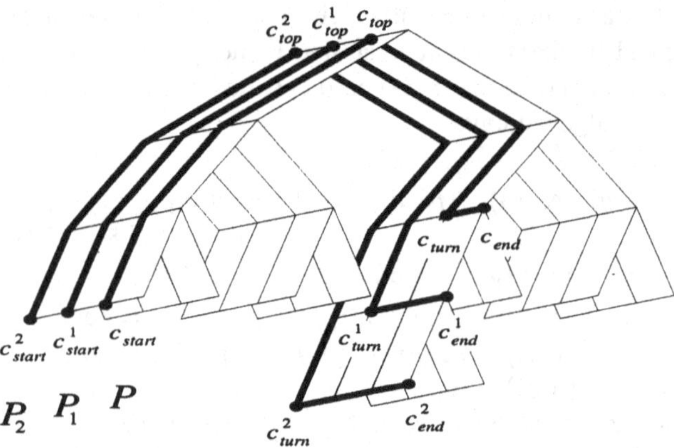

Figure 2. Arrangement of the paths. Here, three paths $P_0 = P$, P_1, and P_2 are constructed. The initial path P leads from c_{start} to c_{end}.

at each traversal. For this, Δ^ε disjoint paths leading from c_{start} to c_{end} are prepared. Then, by choosing one of these paths for the traversal, the machine copies $\Theta(\log \Delta^\varepsilon)$ bits in time $O(\Delta)$, i.e., the ℓ cells are copied in time $O(\ell\Delta/\log\Delta)$. This algorithm cannot be implemented on TMs accessing a linear tape or a tree. In this section, we show that fast copying can be implemented on a machine accessing one hedge. However, since keeping track of head movements on a hedge is not as easy as on the array, to prepare disjoint paths on the hedge is more difficult and requires a longer preprocessing phase. Thus, the new copying technique is only efficient when many different strings are to be copied along the same path.

In what follows, we assume that the path leading from c_{start} to c_{end} has the following structure: Starting in c_{start}, it first leads up to a cell $c_{top} = (p_{top}, q_{top})$, then `left` and `right` to $c_{turn} = (p_{turn}, q_{turn})$, and, eventually, `back` (if $q_{start} > q_{end}$) or `forth` (if $q_{start} < q_{end}$) to c_{end}. I.e., $q_{start} = q_{top} = q_{turn}$ and $p_{turn} = p_{end}$. This will be sufficient for our applications (Thms. 1 and 2).

Lemma 3 *On a TM which uses one hedge, the copying task can be performed in preprocessing time $O(\Delta^{3/2})$ and copying time $O(\Delta + \ell\Delta/\log\Delta)$. The preprocessing phase is independent of the string to be copied, i.e., to copy different strings along the same path it is sufficient to execute the preprocessing phase only once.*

Remark. In the same way, information can be copied from c_{end} to c_{start}.

Proof:

Preprocessing. Let P be the path leading from c_{start} to c_{end}. Using distinguished markers, the machine constructs $\lceil\sqrt{\Delta}\rceil$ paths $P_0, \ldots, P_{\lceil\sqrt{\Delta}\rceil-1}$ as follows. If $q_{start} \le q_{end}$, then path P_i leads from cell $c^i_{start} = (p_{start}, q_{start} - i)$ to $c^i_{end} = (p_{end}0^i, q_{end})$ and has length $\Delta + 2i$. Cells on the path are $c^i_{top} = (p_{top}, q_{top} - i)$ and $c^i_{turn} = (p_{turn}0^i, q_{turn} - i)$. If $q_{start} > q_{end}$, then path P_i leads from $c^i_{start} = (p_{start}, q_{start} + i)$ to $c^i_{end} = (p_{end}0^i, q_{end})$ with $c^i_{top} = (p_{top}, q_{top} + i)$

and $c_{turn}^i = (p_{turn}0^i, q_{turn}+1)$. Thus, the paths P and P_0 coincide, and P_{i+1} can be marked in time $O(\Delta)$ by traversing P_i and copying the markers on P_i to the adjacent cell on P_{i+1}. The construction of the $\sqrt{\Delta}$ paths takes time $O(\Delta^{3/2})$.

Let Σ be the alphabet of the hedge. In the preprocessing phase, the machine also computes the number $b = \lfloor \frac{1}{2} \log_{|\Sigma|} \Delta \rfloor$.

Copying. In time $O(\ell \log b)$, the machine divides the set of cells $(p_{start}, q_{start}+1), \ldots, (p_{start}, q_{start}+\ell)$ into $\lceil \ell/b \rceil$ blocks of at most b cells. The blocks are copied one after another. To copy one block, its contents are viewed as the base $|\Sigma|$ representation of a natural number i, $0 \le i < |\Sigma|^b \le \sqrt{\Delta}$. Within $O(i \log i) = O(\Delta)$ steps the machine selects the start cell c_{start}^i of path P_i. It traverses this path. After $\Delta + 2i$ steps, the machine reaches the end cell c_{end}^i. There, it recovers the base $|\Sigma|$ representation of i, i.e., the contents of the block, from the index of the path in $O(i \log i)$ steps.

If new paths are constructed after the copying of each $\sqrt{\Delta}$ blocks, then the distance between the block and the corresponding start and end cell is $b\sqrt{\Delta}$. The contents of the block can be copied to the start cell and from the end cell to the block in time $O(b^2\sqrt{\Delta}) = O(\Delta)$ by copying bit by bit.

Hence, the ℓ cells are copied in time $O(\ell \log b + \lceil \ell/b \rceil \Delta + \lfloor \lceil \ell/b \rceil / \sqrt{\Delta} \rfloor \Delta^{3/2}) = O(\Delta + \ell\Delta/\log\Delta)$. ■

4 Simulation of Multitape and Multidimensional Turing Machines on One Hedge

In this section we show how to simulate a Turing machine which accesses several d-dimensional arrays on a TM which accesses one hedge (Theorem 1).

Let M be a $t(n)$ time bounded Turing machine which accesses k d-dimensional arrays $A_1, \ldots, A_k$ as its work tapes.

The simulating machine M' accesses one hedge. The machine divides its work tape into $3k$ tracks. For each array A_i of M, $i = 1, \ldots, k$, on the hedge there is a data track, a copy track, and a simulation track. On each copy track at each point of time there are distinct preprocessed paths for up to $2 \cdot 3^d$ different destinations.

The cells of the simulated machine will be stored on the data track of the first $O(\log t(n))$ levels of the hedge. For each array, the simulating machine copies $\Theta(\log\log t(n))$ cells in the surroundings of the M-head to the first level of the hedge, simulates $\Omega(\sqrt[d]{\log\log t(n)})$ steps, and copies the new contents of the cells back to the data tracks. Using fast copying and bounding the number of preprocessing phases, the TM M' simulates these $\Omega(\sqrt[d]{\log\log t(n)})$ steps in time $O(\log t(n))$. This will yield the claimed time bound.

We describe the simulation in more detail.

The simulation proceeds in rounds $r = 1, 2, 3, 4, \ldots$ At the beginning of a new round r, the embedding of the cells of the arrays into the data tracks of the hedge is fixed for this round. We start with a description of this embedding (cf. also Fig. 3).

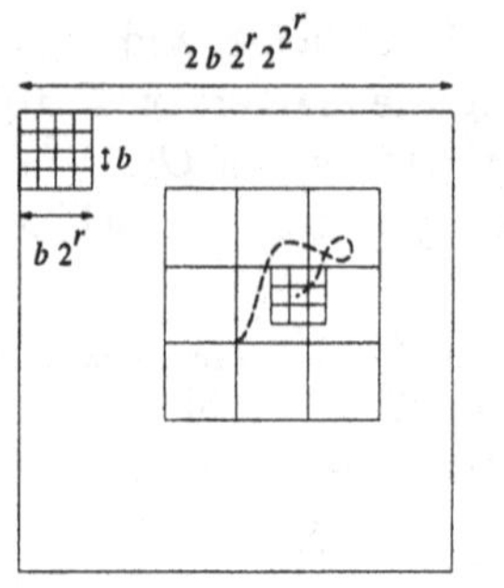

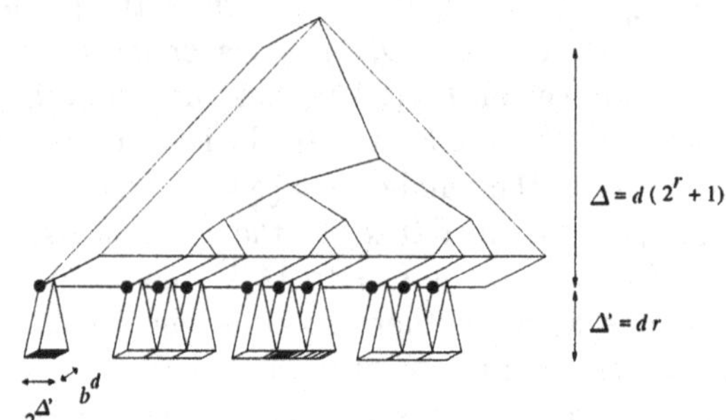

Figure 3. The two-dimensional array on the left is partitioned into blocks and superblocks. The position of the head (broken line) defines the 3^2 active blocks. On the hedge on the right, the meeting places on level Δ are marked (•). Each superblock stores the cells of $2^{\Delta'}$ blocks. The order in which the superblocks are arranged on the hedge is described below. For 3^2 superblocks paths are prepared.

Let $b = \lceil \sqrt[d]{r}\,\rceil$. In round r, up to $b^d\, 2^{d(r+2^r+1)}$ cells of each array can be represented on the data tracks. Each array A_i, $i = 1, \ldots, k$, is divided into $2^{d(r+2^r+1)}$ disjoint *blocks* $B_i^{\beta_1,\ldots,\beta_d}$, $-2^{r+2^r} \le \beta_1, \ldots, \beta_d < 2^{r+2^r}$, of side length b. The block $B_i^{\beta_1,\ldots,\beta_d}$ consists of those cells $(c_1, \ldots, c_d) \in \mathbb{Z}^d$ of the array where, for each $j = 1, \ldots, d$,

$$\beta_j\, b \;\le\; c_j \;<\; (\beta_j + 1)\, b.$$

Moreover, each array is divided into $2^{d(2^r+1)}$ disjoint *superblocks* $S_i^{\sigma_1,\ldots,\sigma_d}$, $-2^{2^r} \le \sigma_1, \ldots, \sigma_d < 2^{2^r}$, of side length $b\,2^r$. The superblock $S_i^{\sigma_1,\ldots,\sigma_d}$ consists of all those cells of the array where, for each $j = 1, \ldots, d$,

$$\sigma_j\, b\, 2^r \;\le\; c_j \;<\; (\sigma_j + 1)\, b\, 2^r.$$

Thus, each superblock consists of the cells of 2^{dr} blocks.

On the hedge, a (super-)block is represented as soon as it is visited by the head of M (or becomes "active," see below). Let $B_i^{\beta_1,\ldots,\beta_d}$ be a block, let $a_{1,j} \cdots a_{r+2^r+1,j} \in \{0,1\}^{r+2^r+1}$ be the binary representation of $\beta_j + 2^{r+2^r}$, $j = 1, \ldots, d$, and let $\mathrm{adr}(\beta_1, \ldots, \beta_d) = a_{1,1}a_{1,2} \cdots a_{1,d} \;\cdots\; a_{r+2^r+1,1} \cdots a_{r+2^r+1,d}$. Using the data track on level $d(r + 2^r + 1)$ that corresponds to array A_i, the machine M' stores the contents of block $B_i^{\beta_1,\ldots,\beta_d}$ in the b^d cells $(\mathrm{adr}(\beta_1, \ldots, \beta_d), 1)$, $\ldots, (\mathrm{adr}(\beta_1, \ldots, \beta_d), b^d)$.

Let $S_i^{\sigma_1,\ldots,\sigma_d}$ be a superblock and let $a_{1,j} \cdots a_{2^r+1,j} \in \{0,1\}^{2^r+1}$ be the binary representation of $\sigma_j + 2^{2^r}$, $j = 1, \ldots, d$. The cell $(a_{1,1}a_{1,2} \cdots a_{1,d} \;\cdots\; a_{2^r+1,1} \cdots a_{2^r+1,d}, 0)$ of the hedge is called the *meeting place* of the superblock $S_i^{\sigma_1,\ldots,\sigma_d}$. Note that on the hedge the distance between the meeting place and any cell used to store the contents of this superblock is at most $dr + b^d = O(r)$.

Two blocks $B_i^{\beta_1,\ldots,\beta_d}$ and $B_i^{\beta'_1,\ldots,\beta'_d}$ are called *adjacent* if $|\beta_j - \beta'_j| \le 1$ for $j = 1, \ldots, d$. The adjacency of superblocks is defined correspondingly.

A block is called *active* if the head visits a cell in one of the adjacent blocks. At each point of time, there are $k\,3^d$ active blocks. The next b steps of M only depend on the contents of these blocks. At the root, the simulation tracks on $3^d b^d$ bushes are used to store a copy of the active blocks. By turns, M' simulates b steps of M, and exchanges blocks between the data and the simulation tracks. First, the $k\,3^d$ active blocks are copied from the data tracks on level $d(r+2^r+1)$ to the simulation tracks at the root. For the copying of each of these blocks, both the bit by bit copy algorithm and the new algorithm are used. From level $d(r+2^r+1)$ to the meeting place of the superblock on level $d(2^r+1)$, the data are copied bit by bit. From the meeting place to the root, fast copying is used. On each copy track and at each point of time, there are preprocessed paths for 3^d meeting places to be used for fast copying. After the simulation of $b\,2^r$ steps of M it may happen that there are no preprocessed paths for the meeting place of the current superblock. In this case, all the preprocessed paths on this copy track are removed and new preprocessed paths are created for this superblock and the adjacent superblocks. Now, copies of the active blocks are stored on the simulation tracks at the root. There, at least b steps of M can be simulated step by step. After the simulation of b steps, the blocks are copied back to the corresponding data track. Then, the blocks which are active at that point of time are identified and copied to the simulation tracks to simulate the next b steps of M. The simulation proceeds in this way, until either this round ends or M stops. Round r ends, if M visits a cell which cannot be represented in this round. Note that this cell has distance $\Omega(b\,2^{r+2^r})$ from the origin of the array.

If M visits a cell which cannot be represented in round r, this round is ceased and the embedding of the blocks for round $r+1$ is prepared. For this, the contents of all the cells already visited are copied from level $2^{d(r+2^r+1)}$ to level $2^{d(r+2^{r+1}+2)}$. On each array A_j, $j = 1, \dots, k$, the simulating machine M' moves the head of M on an Eulerian tour such that each cell visited up to now is visited again. To copy the blocks between the data and the simulation track, the same technique as before is used. However, rather than copying the blocks back to level $2^{d(r+2^r+1)}$, they are copied to level $2^{d(r+2^{r+1}+2)}$. Up to a factor which only depends on d, the length of the tour is bounded by the number of steps already simulated. Thus, the preparation of the new embedding increases the running time of the simulation only by a constant factor.

Let $\Delta = d(2^r+1)$ and $\Delta' = dr$. To estimate the time complexity of this simulation, first we bound the delay in round r. The step by step simulation on the simulation tracks is performed with delay $3^d b^d \log(3^d b^d) = O(r \log r)$. Each b M-steps, $k\,3^d$ blocks of size b^d have to be copied from the root to a meeting place on level Δ (fast copying) and from the meeting place to level $\Delta + \Delta'$ (bit by bit copying). Without preprocessing, the copying of each block takes time $O(b^d \Delta / \log \Delta + b^d \Delta') = O(2^r)$. The same amount of time suffices to copy blocks from the data track to the root. The next active blocks are identified in time $O(\Delta + \Delta'^2) = O(2^r)$. Time $O(\Delta^2 + \Delta^{3/2}) = O(2^{2r})$ is sufficient to identify 3^d new superblocks and to preprocess paths for copying. This is performed each $\Omega(b\,2^r)$ M-steps. Thus, in round r each step is simulated with amortized delay

$$O\left(r \log r + \frac{2^r}{b} + \frac{2^{2r}}{b\,2^r}\right) = O\left(\frac{2^r}{\sqrt[d]{r}}\right).$$

If round $r+1$ is reached, then M' has simulated $t(n) \geq b\,2^{r+2^r}$ steps of M. Thus, $r < 1 + \log\log t(n)$ and M' simulates each step with total delay

$$\sum_{i=1}^{r} O\left(\frac{2^r}{\sqrt[d]{r}}\right) = O\left(\frac{\log t(n)}{\sqrt[d]{\log\log t(n)}}\right). \qquad \blacksquare$$

5 Simulation of Multitree and Multihedge Turing Machines on One Hedge

For the simulation of multitree and multihedge TMs it is favourable to assume that the cells used by the machines are not too far away from the origin. Say, a TM is $r(n)$ *range bounded* if for all inputs of length n on all its work tapes it only visits cells with distance at most $r(n)$ from the origin. Paul and Reischuk have shown that, without loss of generality, $O(t(n))$ time bounded multitree TMs are $O(\log t(n))$ range bounded [PR81].

A similar compactness result holds for multihedge TMs:

Lemma 4 *Each $t(n)$ time bounded multihedge Turing machine can be simulated by a multihedge Turing machine which is $O(\log t(n))$ range bounded and $O(t(n))$ time bounded.*

Proof: Omitted. $\blacksquare$

Now, we prove Theorem 2.

Let M be an $O(t(n))$ time bounded TM that accesses k hedges $H_1, \ldots, H_k$. If M also accesses some trees, these are simulated as if they were hedges. By Lemma 4, we may assume that M is $O(\log t(n))$ range bounded.

The simulating machine M' has one hedge H' which is divided into $3k$ tracks. For each hedge of M there is a data, a copy, and a simulation track. The hedges are stored on the corresponding data track without any change, i.e., machine M' represents cell (p,q) of hedge H_i, $1 \leq i \leq k$, on data track i of cell (p,q). On each copy track there are paths between a meeting place and the root as well as a path between the current position of the simulated head and the meeting place.

Let t be the number of steps already simulated. For each M-hedge, the simulating machine checks whether the distance between the meeting place and the current position of the head exceeds $(\log t)^{3/4}$. If the distance is larger than $(\log t)^{3/4}$, the old paths on this copy track are removed and a preprocessing phase to construct paths between the root and the current position of the head is executed. Now, M' marks the cells in $b = \lfloor(\log\log\log t)/2\rfloor$ bushes and b levels which are reachable from the current head position within $b/2$ steps. These are $O(b\,2^b) = O(\log\log t)$ cells. The contents of these cells are copied to the simulation track on levels 0 to b. To copy the cells to the meeting place, bit by bit copying is used. This takes time $O((\log t)^{3/4} \log\log t) = O(\log t)$. To copy the cells from the meeting place to the root, fast copying is used. This also takes time $O(\log t)$.

If all k blocks are copied to the simulation track, the next $b/2$ steps of M are simulated step by step on the simulation track. Each of these steps is simulated in time $O(b)$. After the simulation of $b/2$ steps, the new contents are copied back to the data tracks in time $O(\log t)$. In this way, $\Omega(\log\log\log t)$ steps of M are simulated in time $O(\log t)$, i.e., without preprocessing phases, the amortized delay of the simulation is $O(\log t(n)/\log\log\log t(n))$.

Between two preprocessing phases on the same copy track the machine M' simulates at least $(\log t)^{3/4}$ steps of M. The preprocessing phase is executed in time $O((\log t)^{3/2})$. Thus, the amortized delay caused by preprocessing is $O((\log t)^{3/4}) = O(\log t(n)/\log\log\log t(n))$.

Hence, M is simulated by one hedge in time $O(t(n)\ \log t(n)/\log\log\log t(n))$. ∎

Acknowledgement

I am indebted to Martin Dietzfelbinger for helpful discussions during the preparation of this paper. The comments of the referees helped to improve the presentation.

References

[CA69] S.A. Cook and S.O. Aanderaa. On the minimum computation time of functions. *Transactions of the AMS*, 142:294–314, 1969.

[DH94] M. Dietzfelbinger and M. Hühne. Matching upper and lower bounds for simulations of several tapes on one multidimensional tape. In *14th Conf. on Found. of Software Technology and Theoretical Computer Science*, 24–35, 1994.

[Hen65] F.C. Hennie. One-tape, off-line Turing machine computations. *Information and Control*, 8:553–578, 1965.

[HL88] A.S. Hodel and M.C. Loui. Optimal dynamic embedding of X-trees into arrays. *Theoretical Computer Science*, 59:259–276, 1988.

[HPV75] J. Hopcroft, W.J. Paul, and L. Valiant. On time versus space and related problems. In *Proc. 16th Symp. on Found. of Computer Science*, 57–64, 1975.

[HS65] J. Hartmanis and R.E. Stearns. On the computational complexity of algorithms. *Transactions of the AMS*, 117:285–306, 1965.

[Lou84] M.C. Loui. Minimizing access pointers into trees and arrays. *Journal of Computer and System Sciences*, 28:359–378, 1984.

[Maa85] W. Maass. Combinatorial lower bound arguments for deterministic and nondeterministic Turing machines. *Transactions of the AMS*, 292:675–693, 1985.

[PF79] N. Pippenger and M.J. Fischer. Relations among complexity measures. *Journal of the ACM*, 26:361–381, 1979.

[PR81] W.J. Paul and K.R. Reischuk. On time versus space II. *Journal of Computer and System Sciences*, 22:312–327, 1981.

[Rei82] K.R. Reischuk. A fast implementation of a multidimensional storage into a tree storage. *Theoretical Computer Science*, 19:253–266, 1982.

[Rei90] K.R. Reischuk. *Einführung in die Komplexitätstheorie*. B.G. Teubner, Stuttgart, 1990.

[Sch80] A. Schönhage. Storage modification machines. *SIAM J. on Computing*, 9:490–508, 1980.

Graph Inference from a Walk for Trees of Bounded Degree 3 is NP-Complete*

Osamu Maruyama[1],** and Satoru Miyano[2]

[1] Department of Information Systems, Kyushu University 39, Kasuga 816, Japan
[2] Research Institute of Fundamental Information Science, Kyushu University 33, Fukuoka, 812, Japan

Abstract. The graph inference from a walk for a class C of undirected edge-colored graphs is, given a string x of colors, finding the smallest graph G in C that allows a traverse of all edges in G whose sequence of edge-colors is x, called a walk for x. We prove that the graph inference from a walk for trees of bounded degree k is NP-complete for any $k \geq 3$, while the problem for trees without any degree bound constraint is known to be solvable in $O(n)$ time, where n is the length of the string. Furthermore, the problem for a special class of trees of bounded degree 3, called (1,1)-caterpillars, is shown to be NP-complete. This contrast with the case that the problem for linear chains is known to be solvable in $O(n \log n)$ time since a (1,1)-caterpillar is obtained by attaching at most one hair of length one to each node of a linear chain. We also show the MAXSNP-hardness of these problems.

1 Introduction

A partial walk in an undirected edge-colored graph G is a path in G. If a partial walk in G contains all edges of G, it is called a *walk* in G. The trace of a partial walk w is the string of colors of the edges traversed in w. Let C be a class of graphs. The *graph inference from a walk for C* is defined as follows: Given a string x, find a graph G in C with the minimum number of edges such that G can realize a walk with trace x.

We can say that the trace of a walk in a graph provides a partial structural information of the graph. Thus the problem can be regarded as that of reconstructing an edge-colored graph only from the trace of a walk in the graph. Several kinds of such problems of reconstructing edge-colored graphs from their partial information have received attentions. Rudich [11] considered the problem of inferring a Markov chain from its output and showed that the smallest Markov chain for a given output can be produced in the limit. Angluin [1] and Gold [5] also considered the problem of identifying a finite automaton of the minimum size which is consistent with given

* This work is partly supported by Grant-in-Aid for Scientific Research on Priority Areas "Genome Informatics" from the Ministry of Education, Science and Culture, Japan.

** Corresponding author. Research Institute of Fundamental Information Science, Kyushu University 33, Fukuoka 812, Japan. Email: maruyama@rifis.kyushu-u.ac.jp. This author is a Research Fellow of the Japan Society for the Promotion of Science (JSPS). The author's research is partly supported by Grants-in-Aid for JSPS research fellows from the Ministry of Education, Science and Culture, Japan.

input/output behaviors. They showed that the problem is, in general, NP-complete. Recently, Maruyama and Miyano [7] discussed the graph inference from partial walks, which is a variant of the graph inference from a walk, and proved that the problem is NP-complete even if the graphs are either trees or linear chains.

The problem of graph inference from a walk was first deeply discussed by Aslam and Rivest [3]. They devised polynomial time algorithms for the graph inference from a walk for graphs of bounded degree 2, i.e., linear chains and cycles. Then Raghavan [10] developed a faster algorithm running in $O(n \log n)$ time. While only bounded degree graphs are considered in [3, 10], Maruyama and Miyano [7] focused on the case of unbounded degree graphs, and proved that the graph inference from a walk for trees without any degree bound constraint is solvable in $O(n)$ time. As a hardness result, Raghavan [10] considered the degree bound constraint on graphs and showed that, given a string x, the problem of finding a graph of bounded degree k with the minimum number of nodes that realizes a walk with trace x is NP-complete for all $k \geq 3$.

These results naturally raise a question whether the graph inference from a walk is tractable for trees with bounded degree 3. This paper settles this question. We prove that the graph inference from a walk for trees of bounded degree 3 is NP-complete even if the number of colors is restricted to 4. Generally, for any $k \geq 3$, we can show that the problem for trees of bounded degree k is NP-complete when the number of colors is $k+1$. The number $k+1$ of colors is optimal since the problem for trees of bounded degree k with at most k colors can be shown solvable in $O(n)$ time by applying the linear-time algorithm in [7].

Recall that the linear chain inference from a walk is solvable in polynomial time [3, 10]. We then consider a special class of graphs called (1,1)-caterpillars. A (1,1)-caterpillar is a graph obtained from a linear chain by attaching at most one edge, called a hair, to each node of the linear chain. Our next result is that the graph inference from a walk for (1,1)-caterpillars is, unfortunately, NP-complete. Namely, attaching at most one edge to each node of a linear chain makes the graph inference problem intractable. This result claims that the graph inference from a walk is computationally hard even for the simplest graphs of bounded degree 3.

In the last section, we discuss the approximability and the MAXSNP-hardness of these problems.

2 Preliminaries

Let Σ be a finite alphabet. The set of all strings over Σ is denoted by Σ^*. The reversal of a string x is written as x^R, and the length of x is denoted by $|x|$. To represent the cardinality of a set S, we use the same notation $|S|$. The concatenation of strings x and y is written as $x \cdot y$, or simply xy. For strings $x_1, \ldots, x_n$, $\prod_{i=1}^n x_i$ denotes $x_1 x_2 \cdots x_n$. Especially, if $x = x_1 = \cdots = x_n$, we denote $\prod_{i=1}^n x_i$ by $(x)^n$, or simply x^n. For convenience, x^0 is defined as the empty string ε.

A *color* is a symbol in Σ. We consider undirected edge-colored graphs $G = (V, E, c)$, where $c : E \rightarrow \Sigma$ is called the *edge-coloring of* G. Hereafter a graph means an undirected edge-colored graph without any notice. For graphs G and G', if G and G' are isomorphic including edge labels, we identify G with G' without any

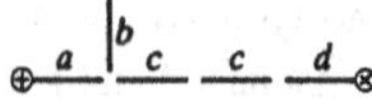

Fig. 1.

notice. A *linear chain* is a graph $l = (V, E, c)$ with $V = \{v_i | i = 1, \ldots, m\}$ and $E = \{\{v_i, v_{i+1}\} | i = 1, \ldots, m-1\}$, and the *label* of l is $\prod_{i=1}^{m-1} c(\{v_i, v_{i+1}\})$.

A *partial walk* w in a graph G is a path in G and $w[i]$ denotes the ith node of G passed by w, where the start node of the partial walk is $w[0]$. If a partial walk in G contains all edges of G, it is called a *walk* in G. We say that a partial walk w is *closed* if the start node of w coincides with the end node. Let $e_1, \ldots, e_n$ be the sequence of edges of a partial walk w in a graph $G = (V, E, c)$. The *trace* of w is $\prod_{i=1}^{n} c(e_i)$. Let x be a string in Σ^*. If w is a partial walk with trace x, w is called a *partial walk for* x. For a graph G, we say that G *realizes* a partial walk for x if there is a partial walk for x in G. Let $x = \prod_{i=1}^{n} s_i$ with s_i in Σ. For a partial walk w for x, the *subwalk* of w for substring $\prod_{i=j}^{k} s_i$ with $1 \leq j \leq k \leq n$ is the partial walk with the node sequence of $w[j-1], w[j], \cdots, w[k]$.

3 Inferring a tree of bounded degree 3 from a walk

Let C be a class of graphs. The *graph inference from a walk for* C, denoted by GIW(C), is defined as follows:

Instance: A string x over a finite alphabet Σ, and a positive integer K.
Problem: Is there a graph $G \in C$ with at most K edges such that G realizes a walk for x?

The class of trees of bounded degree k is denoted by k-Deg-Tree. At first, we consider GIW(3-Deg-Tree), the graph inference from a walk for trees of bounded degree 3.

Example. Let $K = 5$. For a string $x = abbccd$, the graph in Fig. 1 is a tree of bounded degree 3 with K edges which realizes a walk for x with the start node $\oplus$ and the end node $\otimes$. On the other hand, for $y = abbccddccaad$, there is no tree of bounded degree 3 with at most K edges which realizes a walk for y.

Theorem 1. *The graph inference from a walk for trees of bounded degree 3 is NP-complete.*

The following fact is useful when we construct a tree realizing a closed walk.

Fact 2. *Suppose that a tree t realizes a closed walk w for a string x. If a symbol a occurs in x exactly twice, then t includes exactly one edge labeled a and the edge is traversed exactly twice by w in distinct directions.*

Proof of Theorem 1 The proof requires a rather long argument. We just describe the sketch of the reduction. Obviously, GIW(3-Deg-Tree) is in NP. To show that the problem is NP-hard, we give a reduction from the vertex cover problem (VC) [4],

Fig. 2. T_W

which is to decide if, given a graph $G = (V, E)$ and a positive integer K, there is a vertex cover of size at most K for G, that is, a subset $U \subseteq V$ with $|U| \leq K$ such that for each edge $\{u, v\} \in E$ at least one of u and v belongs to U. For an integer k, let k-DEGREE VERTEX COVER be the VC restricted to graphs of bounded degree k without any self-loop. It is known that 3-DEGREE VERTEX COVER remains NP-complete [4]. Let $K \leq |V|$ be a positive integer and $G = (V, E)$ be a graph of bounded degree 3 without any self-loop, where $V = \{v_1, \ldots, v_n\}$ and $E = \{e_1, \ldots, e_m\}$. We will define an alphabet Σ and construct a string x over Σ and a positive integer K' such that there is a tree of bounded degree 3 with at most K' edges which realizes a walk for x if and only if G has a vertex cover of size K or less. Hereafter a tree means a tree of bounded degree 3. The alphabet Σ is defined as follows:

$$\Sigma = \{a_1, a_2\} \cup \{g_1, g_2, g_3\} \cup \{h_1, h_2\} \cup \{r_1, r_2\} \cup \{s_1, s_2\} \cup V \cup \{0, 1, \#\}$$
$$\cup \{\alpha_i, \overline{\alpha}_i \mid i = 1, 2, 3\} \cup \{\beta_{i,j} \mid i = 1, \ldots, n \text{ and } j = 1, 2, 3\}.$$

In order to define the string x, we introduce the four kinds of strings as follows:

(1) W and W': The string W occurs in x many times and W' once. Let $\mu = 53n + m + 2$, where $n = |V|$ and $m = |E|$. Then we define

$$W = \prod_{i=1}^{\mu} b_i \text{ and } W' = \prod_{i=1}^{\mu} (\#\#b_i),$$

where $b_i = 0$ if i is even and $b_i = 1$ if i is odd. It is trivial that only the linear chain with label W realizes a walk for W, and the tree T_W in Fig. 2 is the smallest tree without any degree bound that realizes a walk for W'. Notice that these graphs have μ and 2μ edges, respectively. It will be seen that any tree realizing a walk for x with at most K' edges has exactly one subgraph isomorphic to T_W and all partial walks for W and W' are realized in this unique T_W.

(2) $X_{i,j}$ with $i \in \{1, \ldots, n\}$ and $j \in \{1, 2, 3\}$: First let

$$x_{i,j} = 0 g_1 h_1 h_2 h_2 h_1 g_2 g_2 h_1 \overline{\alpha}_j \overline{\alpha}_j h_2 g_3 g_3 h_2 \alpha_j \alpha_j h_1 g_1 \beta_{i,j} \beta_{i,j} 0,$$

for $i \in \{1, \ldots, n\}$ and $j \in \{1, 2, 3\}$. We define $X_{i,j}$ by using $x_{i,j}$ as

$$X_{i,j} = (a_1\#\#a_1)^i 1 (r_1 r_2 r_2 r_1)^{\lfloor (3-j)/2 \rfloor} (a_2\#\#a_2)^j$$
$$x_{i,j}\ (s_1 s_1)^{\lfloor j/3 \rfloor} (a_2 a_2)^j 1 (s_2 s_2)^{\lfloor i/n \rfloor} (a_1 a_1)^i.$$

Note that $\lfloor (3-j)/2 \rfloor$ is equal to 1 if $j = 1$ and 0 otherwise. Consider the tree $t_{i,j}$ in Fig. 3. Then it is clear from Fact 2 that if a walk w for $X_{i,j}$ is closed then the subwalk of w for the substring $x_{i,j}$ of $X_{i,j}$ must be a closed walk in the tree $t_{i,j}$. A node of a tree is said to be *free* if its degree is less than 3. A prefix of x is a

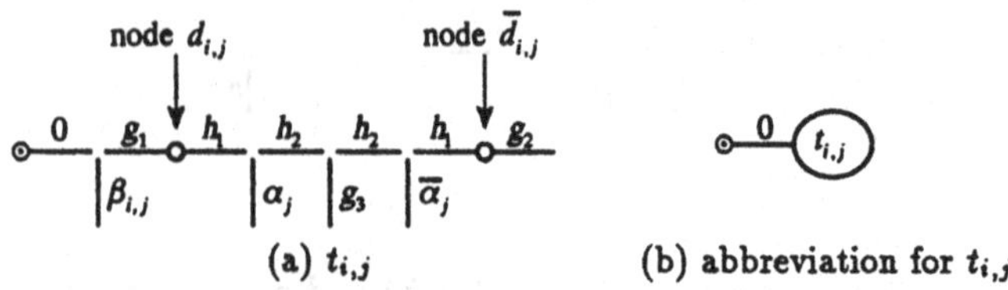

(a) $t_{i,j}$ (b) abbreviation for $t_{i,j}$

Fig. 3. The tree $t_{i,j}$ has two free internal nodes, which are denoted by $d_{i,j}$ and $\bar{d}_{i,j}$. The node $\odot$ is the start and end node of the closed walk for $x_{i,j}$.

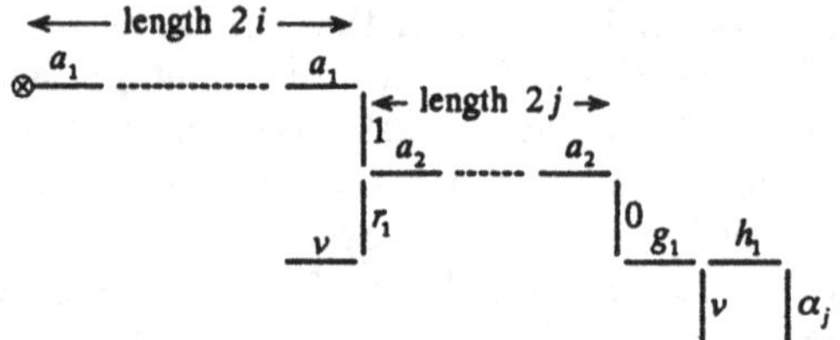

Fig. 4. $i \in \{1, \ldots, n\}$.

concatenation of the strings $X_{i,j}$'s, W's and W', which is called *TEMPLATE*. It will be seen that a tree realizing a walk for *TEMPLATE* with at most K' edges is unique up to isomorphism.

(3) $\langle v, j \rangle$ with $v \in V$ and $j \in \{1,2,3\}$: The string vv appears in $\langle v, j \rangle$ twice. We define

$$\langle v, j \rangle = (a_1a_1)^n 1 r_1 (vv) r_1 (a_2a_2)^j 0 g_1 (vv) h_1 \alpha_j \alpha_j h_1 g_1 0 (a_2a_2)^j 1 (a_1a_1)^n.$$

The tree in Fig. 4 realizes a closed walk for $\langle v, j \rangle$ starting and ending at node $\otimes$.

(4) $\langle e \rangle$ with $e \in E$: Let $e = \{u, v\} \in E$. The strings uu and vv appear in $\langle e \rangle$ once, respectively. We define

$$\langle e \rangle = (a_1a_1)^K 1 (a_2a_2)^3 0 g_1 h_1 h_2 h_2 h_1 (uu) h_1 h_2 h_2 h_1 (vv) h_1 h_2 h_2 h_1 g_1 0 (a_2a_2)^3 1 (a_1a_1)^K.$$

Notice that $(a_1a_1)^n$ is not a prefix of $\langle e \rangle$, but $(a_1a_1)^K$ is a prefix. The tree in Fig. 5 realizes a closed walk for $\langle e \rangle$ starting and ending at node $\otimes$.

Let

$$TEMPLATE = W^R W' W^R \prod_{i=1}^{n} (\prod_{j=1}^{3} (X_{i,j} W W^R)),$$

$$VERTEX = \prod_{j=1}^{3} (\prod_{i=1}^{n} (\langle v_i, j \rangle W W^R)),$$

$$EDGE = \prod_{i=1}^{m} (\langle e_i \rangle W W^R).$$

We then define $x = TEMPLATE \cdot VERTEX \cdot EDGE$. Finally, let $K' = 53n + m + 1 + 2\mu$, which is equal to $3\mu - 1$ since $\mu = 53n + m + 2$.

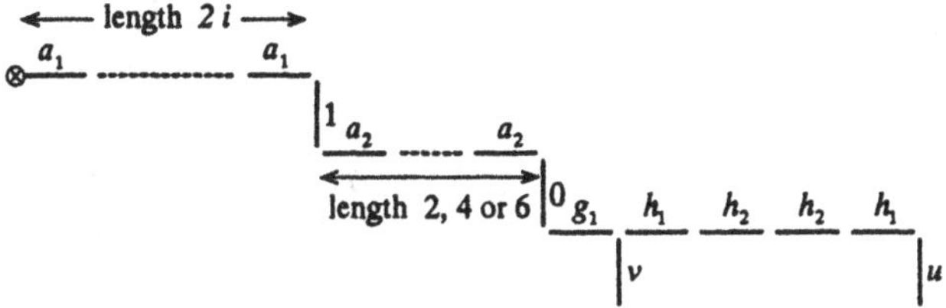

Fig. 5. $i \in \{1, \ldots, K\}$.

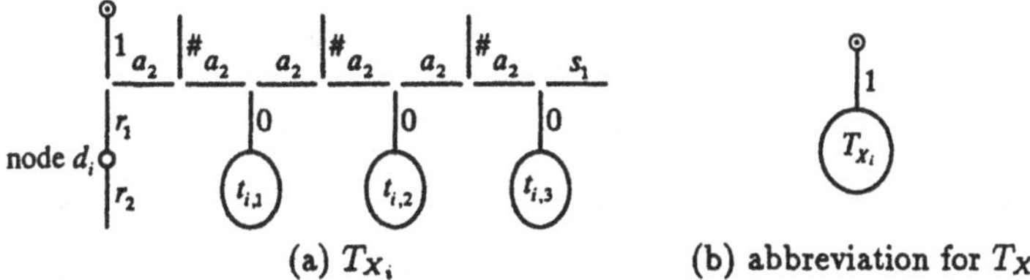

Fig. 6. T_{X_i} has one internal free node d_i in addition to the nodes $d_{i,j}, \overline{d}_{i,j}$ in $t_{i,j}$ for $j = 1, 2, 3$.

This transformation can be done in polynomial time. We claim that there is a vertex cover of G with size at most K if and only if there is a tree of bounded degree 3 with at most K' edges which realizes a walk for x. The verification of this claim will exhaust a heavy discussion and omit the details. The following is a key claim in the verification:

Claim 3. *Any tree of bounded degree 3 with at most K' edges that realizes a walk for the string TEMPLATE is isomorphic to the tree T_{TEM} in Fig. 7.*

□

The alphabet Σ in the proof of Theorem 1 is not bounded by a fixed constant. The following result completely settles the case that the alphabet size is constant:

Theorem 4. *For any integer $k \geq 3$, the graph inference from a walk for trees of bounded degree k is NP-complete even if the alphabet size is restricted to $k + 1$.*

On the other hand, if the number of symbols in a string x is at most k, the linear-time algorithm in [7] produces the smallest tree of bounded degree k that realizes a walk for x. This is because for any string x of k colors, the smallest tree realizing a walk for x has no node with degree exceeding k.

Theorem 4 can be shown by refining the argument of the proof of Theorem 1. In the proof of Theorem 4, Fact 2 is not helpful to determine the tree realizing a closed walk for a long string y since y is over a few symbols. Then we employ Fact 5, which is more precise than Fact 2.

Fact 5. *Suppose that t is an arbitrary tree without any degree bound constraint realizing a closed walk for a string x and t' is the smallest tree without any degree bound*

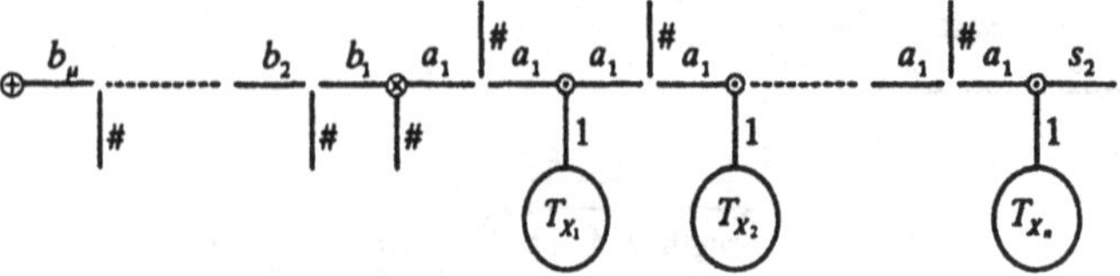

Fig. 7. T_{TEM}

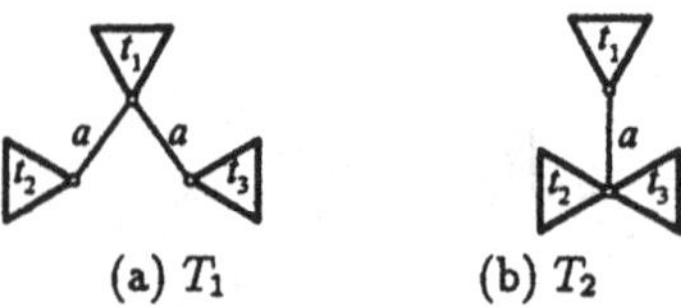

(a) T_1 (b) T_2

Fig. 8. t_1, t_2 and t_3 in (a) and (b) are arbitrary trees and a is an arbitrary color.

constraint realizing a walk for x. Let w and w' be those walks realized in t and t', respectively.

1. *For an edge e of t' traversed in w' exactly twice, let $e = \{w'[i], w'[i+1]\} = \{w'[j], w'[j+1]\}$ with $0 \le i < j \le |x|-1$. Then, $\{w[i], w[i+1]\} = \{w[j], w[j+1]\}$.*
2. *For an edge e of t' traversed in w' exactly four times, let $e = \{w'[i_1], w'[i_1+1]\} = \{w'[i_2], w'[i_2+1]\} = \{w'[i_3], w'[i_3+1]\} = \{w'[i_4], w'[i_4+1]\}$ with $0 \le i_1 < i_2 < i_3 < i_4 \le |x|-1$. Then, one of the following three cases holds:*

Case 1: $\{w[i_1], w[i_1+1]\} = \{w[i_2], w[i_2+1]\}$ $(= e_0)$,
$\{w[i_3], w[i_3+1]\} = \{w[i_4], w[i_4+1]\}$ $(= e_1)$ *and* $e_0 \ne e_1$.
Case 2: $\{w[i_1], w[i_1+1]\} = \{w[i_4], w[i_4+1]\}$ $(= e_0)$,
$\{w[i_2], w[i_2+1]\} = \{w[i_3], w[i_3+1]\}$ $(= e_1)$ *and* $e_0 \ne e_1$.
Case 3: $\{w[i_1], w[i_1+1]\} = \{w[i_2], w[i_2+1]\} =$
$\{w[i_3], w[i_3+1]\} = \{w[i_4], w[i_4+1]\}$.

Fact 5 can be proven by Lemma 7 (4) and the fact that the shortest path between two nodes in a tree is unique.

Definition 6. 1. Let $\rightarrow$ be a binary relation on a set S and $\xrightarrow{*}$ be the transitive and reflexive closure of $\rightarrow$. An element $x \in S$ is *irreducible* if there is no $y \in S$ such that $x \rightarrow y$. For $x, y \in S$, if $x \xrightarrow{*} y$ and y is irreducible, then y is called a *$\rightarrow$-normal form* of x.

2. Let $T_1 = (V, E, c)$ be a tree which includes adjacent edges $e_1 = \{v_1, v_2\}$ and $e_2 = \{v_2, v_3\}$ with $c(e_1) = c(e_2)$ (see Fig. 8 (a)). Let T_2 be the tree obtained from T_1 by identifying v_3 with v_1 together with the adjacent edges e_1 and e_2 (see Fig. 8 (b)). Then we say that T_2 is an *edge-folding of* T_1. The binary relation $\rightarrow_F$ on the set of trees is defined to be the set of pairs (T_1, T_2) such that T_2 is an edge-folding of T_1.

Lemma 7. (1) *A tree T realizes a walk for a string x if and only if a linear chain l with label x is an F-expansion of T, i.e., $l \xrightarrow{*}_F T$.*

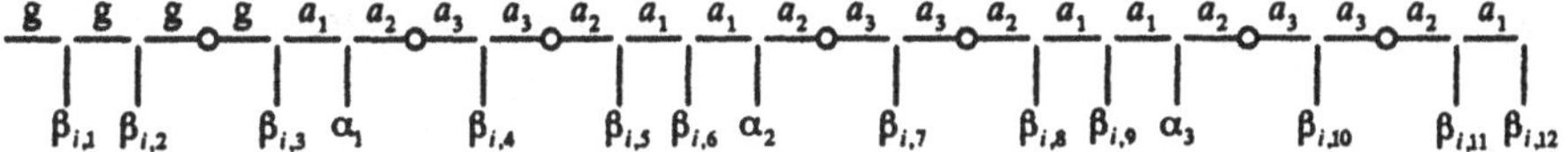

Fig. 9. The role of this (1,1)-caterpillar in the proof of Theorem 8 is almost the same as that of T_{X_i} in the proof of Theorem 1.

(2) *The binary relation* $\rightarrow_F$ *on the set of trees is confluent, namely, for any trees* x, y_0, y_1, $x \xrightarrow{*}_F y_0$ *and* $x \xrightarrow{*}_F y_1$ *imply that there is a tree* z *such that* $y_0 \xrightarrow{*}_F z$ *and* $y_1 \xrightarrow{*}_F z$.

(3) *Let* x *be a string and* l *be a linear chain with label* x. *Then, a* $\rightarrow_F$*-normal form of* l *is unique and it is the smallest tree that realizes a walk for* x.

(4) *Suppose that* t *is an arbitrary tree realizing a walk for a string* x *and* t' *is the smallest tree realizing a walk for* x. *We denote those walks by* w *and* w', *respectively. Then, for any integers* $0 \leq i < j \leq |x| - 1$, *if* $\{w'[i], w'[i+1]\} \neq \{w'[j], w'[j+1]\}$, *then* $\{w[i], w[i+1]\} \neq \{w[j], w[j+1]\}$.

4 Inferring a (1,1)-caterpillar from a walk

A *caterpillar* is a tree which is created by a linear chain, called the *backbone*, and various other appendage linear chains attached to the nodes of the backbone, called *hairs* [6]. A caterpillar is called a (1,1)-caterpillar if the number of hairs of each node in the backbone is at most 1 and the length of a hair is 1. We can say that (1,1)-caterpillars are the simplest trees of bounded degree 3 since at most one edge is attached to each node of a linear chain. The class of (1,1)-caterpillars is denoted by (1,1)-Caterpillar. We next consider GIW((1,1)-Caterpillar), the graph inference from a walk for (1,1)-caterpillars. Recall that the problem for linear chains is solvable in polynomial time [3, 10]. However, if each node of a linear chain is allowed to append at most one edge to itself, the graph inference problem turns to be NP-complete. The following can be shown by a reduction from the vertex cover problem in a way similar to that in the proof of Theorem 1 (See Fig. 9).

Theorem 8. *For any integers* $k, l \geq 1$, *the graph inference from a walk for* (k,l)*-caterpillars is NP-complete.*

5 Approximability

In this section, we describe some results of approximability of the problems we have dealt with so far. An optimization problem consists of a set I of possible instances, a map S which maps each $x \in I$ to a set of feasible solutions, and a measure $m : S(I) \rightarrow Q^+$. For a solution s, we call $m(s)$ the cost of s. An algorithm $\mathcal{A}$ for an optimization problem is called an ϵ-approximation algorithm if $cost(\mathcal{A}(x))/opt(x) \leq \epsilon$, where $cost(\mathcal{A}(x))$ is the cost of the solution of x produced by $\mathcal{A}$ and $opt(x)$ is the cost of an optimal solution of x.

Theorem 9. *Let $1 \leq \epsilon < 2$. If there is a polynomial-time ϵ-approximation algorithm for the graph inference from a walk for trees of bounded degree k for some $k \geq 3$, then $P = NP$.*

The following fact is a key to the proof of Theorem 9:

Claim 10. *Let G and K be an instance of the vertex cover problem and T be a tree of bounded degree 3 which realizes a walk for the string produced by applying the reduction in the proof of Theorem 1 to G and K.*

1. *Assume that G has a vertex cover U with $|U| \leq K$. If T is the smallest tree, there are exactly $3\mu - 1$ edges in T. Otherwise, there are at least 4μ edges in T.*
2. *If G does not have any vertex cover U with $|U| \leq K$, there are at least 4μ edges in T.*

We next show that GIW(k-Deg-Tree) is MAXSNP-hard for any $k \geq 3$. By the result due to Arora et al. [2], this implies that there is no polynomial time approximation scheme for GIW(k-Deg-Tree) unless P = NP.

Let Π_1 and Π_2 be two optimization (maximization or minimization) problems. We say that Π_1 *L-reduces* to Π_2 if there are polynomial-time algorithms f and g and constants α and $\beta > 0$ such that:

1. Given an instance I_1 of Π_1, the algorithm f produces an instance I_2 of Π_2 that satisfies $opt(I_2) \leq \alpha \cdot opt(I_1)$, and
2. Given any feasible solution s_2 of I_2, the algorithm g produces a solution s_1 of I_1 such that $|cost(s_1) - opt(I_1)| \leq \beta \cdot |cost(s_2) - opt(I_2)|$.

Some basic facts about L-reductions are as follows: First, the composition of two L-reductions is also an L-reduction. Second, if problem Π_1 L-reduces to problem Π_2 and Π_2 can be approximated in polynomial time with relative error δ, i.e., there is an algorithm $\mathcal{A}$ for Π_2 with $\delta \geq |opt(x) - cost(\mathcal{A}(x))|/opt(x)$, then Π_1 can be approximated with relative error $\alpha\beta\delta$. In particular, if Π_2 has a polynomial time approximation scheme, then so does Π_1.

The class MAXSNP$_0$ is the class of maximization problems defined syntactically in Papadimitriou and Yannakakis [8, 9]. It is known that every problem in this class can be approximated within *some* constant factor. MAXSNP is defined as the class of all optimization problems that are L-reducible to a problem in MAXSNP$_0$. A problem is MAXSNP-hard if every problem in MAXSNP can be L-reduced to it.

The following can be shown by slightly modifying the proof of Theorem 1.

Theorem 11. *The graph inference from a walk for trees of bounded degree 3 is MAXSNP-hard.*

We can also see the following:

Theorem 12. *Let $1 \leq \epsilon < 2$. If there is a polynomial-time ϵ-approximation algorithm for the graph inference from a walk for (k,l)-caterpillars for some integers $k, l \geq 1$, then $P = NP$.*

Theorem 13. *For any integers $k, l \geq 1$, the graph inference from a walk for (k,l)-caterpillars is MAXSNP-hard.*

Concluding Remarks

We have shown that the graph inference from a walk for trees of bounded degree k is NP-complete for any $k \geq 3$ even if the alphabet size is restricted to $k+1$. We also have shown that the graph inference from a walk for (k,l)-caterpillars is NP-complete for $k,l \geq 1$. In addition we have seen that these problems are MAXSNP-hard and the approximation rate cannot be less than 2 unless P=NP. The following problems remain open:

(1) Is there any polynomial-time ϵ-approximation algorithm for GIW(3-Deg-Tree), for some $\epsilon \geq 2$?
(2) Let $k,l \geq 1$. Does GIW((k,l)-Caterpillar) remain NP-complete even if the alphabet size is restricted to a constant?
(3) Let $\epsilon \geq 2$. Is there any polynomial-time ϵ-approximation algorithm for GIW((k,l)-Caterpillar) for $k,l \geq 1$.
(4) Is GIW((k,l)-Caterpillar) solvable in polynomial time if either k or l is unbounded, or both are unbounded?

References

1. D. Angluin. On the complexity of minimum inference of regular sets. *Inform. Control*, 39:337–350, 1978.
2. S. Arora, C. Lund, R. Motwani, M. Sudan, and M. Szegedy. Proof verification and hardness of approximation problems. In *Proc. 33rd IEEE Symp. Foundations of Computer Science*, pages 14–23, 1992.
3. J. A. Aslam and R. L. Rivest. Inferring graphs from walks. In *Proc. 3rd Workshop on Computational Learning Theory*, pages 359–370, 1990.
4. M.R. Garey and D.S. Johnson. *Computers and Intractability: A Guide to the Theory of NP-Completeness*. W.H. Freeman and Company, 1979.
5. E. M. Gold. Complexity of automaton identification from given data. *Inform. Control*, 37:302–320, 1978.
6. J. Haralambides, F. Makedon, and B. Monien. Bandwidth minimization: An approximation algorithm for caterpillars. *Math. Systems Theory*, 24:169–177, 1991.
7. O. Maruyama and S. Miyano. Inferring a tree from walks. In *Proc. 17th Mathematical Foundations of Computer Science, Lecture Notes in Computer Science*, volume **629**, pages 383–391, 1992; To appear in Theoretical Computer Science.
8. C. Papadimitriou and M. Yannakakis. Optimization, approximation and complexity classes. *J. Comput. System Sci.*, 43(3):425–440, 1991.
9. C. H. Papadimitriou. *Computational Complexity*. Addison-Wesley Publishing Company, 1994.
10. V. Raghavan. Bounded degree graph inference from walks. *J. Comput. System Sci.*, 49:108–132, 1994.
11. S. Rudich. Inferring the structure of a Markov chain from its output. In *Proc. 26th IEEE Symp. Foundations of Computer Science*, pages 321–326, 1985.

Honeycomb networks

Ivan Stojmenović
Computer Science Department
University of Ottawa
Ottawa, Ontario K1N 9B4, Canada

Abstract

The honeycomb mesh, based on hexagonal plane tessellation, is considered as a multiprocessor interconnection network. A honeycomb mesh network with n nodes has degree 3 and diameter $\approx 1.63\sqrt{n}$ -1, which is 25% smaller degree and 18.5% smaller diameter then the mesh connected computer with approximately the same number of nodes. A convenient addressing scheme for nodes is introduced which provides simple computation of shortest paths and the diameter. Simple and optimal (in the number of required communication steps) routing algorithm is developed. Vertex and edge symmetric honeycomb torus network is obtained by adding wrap around edges to the honeycomb mesh. The network cost, defined as the product of degree and diameter, is better for honeycomb networks than for the two other families based on square (mesh connected computers and tori) and triangular (hexagonal meshes and tori) tessellations. The average distance in honeycomb torus with n nodes is proved to be approximately $0.54\sqrt{n}$.

1. Introduction

Various research and development results on how to interconnect multiprocessor components have been reported in literature. Several surveys of parallel computing architectures exist [A, D, KGGK, Q, TW]. One of most popular architectures is the mesh connected computer (see Fig. 1), in which processors are placed in a square or rectangular grid with each processor being connected by a communication link to its neighbors in up to four directions. Tori [M] are meshes with wrap-around connections to achieve vertex and edge symmetry. Meshes and tori are among the most frequent multiprocessor networks available today on the market.

It is well known that there are three possible tessellations of a plane with regular polygons of the same kind: square (Fig. 1), triagonal (Fig. 2) and hexagonal (Fig. 3), corresponding to dividing a plane into regular squares, triangles and hexagons, respectively. The square tessellation is basis for mesh connected computers, which are widely studied in literature. The triangular tessellation is used in [SRD, CSK] to define hexagonal mesh (Fig. 2) multiprocessor (we will preserve the original network name from literature). There are only about half a dozen papers that study the network. The hexagonal mesh was used in the HARTS project at the University of Michigan [S]. Addressing, routing and broadcasting in hexagonal meshes was studied in [CSK]. The time and space optimization problems involved in the mapping of parallel algorithms onto a hexagonal mesh architecture has been explored in [RS] (note that in [RS] the hexagonal mesh architecture is called "honeycomb" one). Embeddings of tree in hexagonal arrays were studied in [GKS] while performance was analyzed in [DRS].

Hexagonal tessellations were used in literature for various applications. Examples are cellular phone station placement [G], the representation of benzenoid hydrocarbons in chemistry [L, TMSBCC], computer graphics [LS] and image processing [Y,B,BHM]. To the best of our knowledge, they were not previously used as a basis for an interconnection network. Here we propose to study the honeycomb mesh interconnection network (Fig. 3), based on the hexagonal tessellation. The name "honeycomb" was selected because it is often used in association with hexagonal grids (their yet another application in the honey production). By adding wrap-around edges, we define the corresponding honeycomb torus network. We will study the basic topological properties and communication algorithms for honeycomb meshes and tori.

A topology is evaluated in terms of a number of parameters. The main ones are: degree, diameter, and symmetry. The degree of a network is the maximal number of neighbors of a processor. The distance between two processors is the smallest number of communication links that a message has to traverse in order to be routed between the two processors. It corresponds to the number of edges in the shortest path between two processors. The diameter of a network is the farthest distance between any two processors. A graph is vertex (edge) symmetric if the graph looks the same from each of its vertices (edges, respectively). The existence of vertex or edge symmetries in networks simplifies the design of algorithms. Asymmetry in networks causes premature saturation of certain links and large message queues at certain nodes under heavy message traffic, resulting in an increase in message delays.

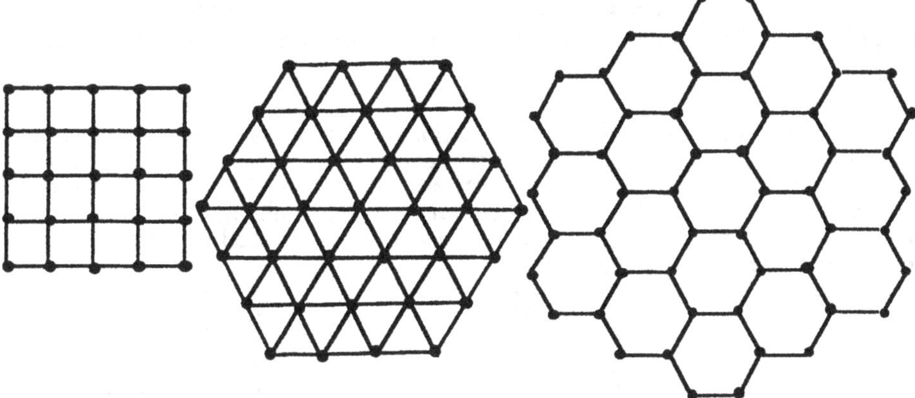

Figure 1. Square mesh Figure 2. Hexagonal mesh Figure 3. Honeycomb mesh

Further important measures of "goodness" of a network are bisection width (the minimum number of links that, when cut, separate the network into two parts with equal number of processors), wire length (or layout aspects), existence of optimal data communication techniques such as routing, broadcasting, gossiping, sorting, permutation, prefix scan etc., node disjoint paths (or fault tolerance), embeddability and recursive decomposition (or scalability). In this paper, we are interested in the symmetry, diameter, degree, bisection width and routing. The remaining aspects of honeycomb meshes and tori are currently open research problems. Although all characteristics are important, it seems that the network cost, defined as the product of the degree and diameter (measured with respect to the number of nodes) is the most important parameter of a network.

Section 2 of this paper describes topological properties of honeycomb meshes and introduces a convenient addressing scheme for nodes. In section 3 optimal routing algorithm for honeycomb meshes is presented. Honeycomb torus network is defined in section 4; its topological properties are easily derived as extensions of the corresponding results for honeycomb meshes. Section 5 lists further results and some open problems on the honeycomb networks. The full version of this paper in a technical report [St].

2. Topological properties of honeycomb meshes

Hexagonal and honeycomb meshes are dual graphs (one can obtain the honeycomb mesh by joining the centers of each triangle in a hexagonal mesh with centers of neighboring triangles, and vice versa).

To maximize symmetry, honeycomb meshes are built as follows: one hexagon is a honeycomb mesh of size 1, denoted HM_1. The honeycomb mesh HM_2 of size 2 is obtained by adding six hexagons to the boundary edges of HM_1. Inductively, honeycomb mesh HM_t of size t is obtained from HM_{t-1} by adding a layer of hexagons around the boundary of HM_{t-1}. For instance, Fig. 2 is honeycomb mesh of size 3, i.e. HM_3. Alternatively, the size t of HM_t is determined as the number of hexagons between the center and boundary of HM_t (inclusive).

Lemma 1. The number of nodes of the honeycomb mesh of size t is $6t^2$.

Proof. It is easy to observe that the boundary of HM_t has 12 more nodes than the boundary of HM_{t-1}. Thus, it is possible to prove (by induction on t) that the boundary of HM_t has 12t-6 nodes. These are the only new nodes to be added to the nodes of HM_{t-1}. The number of nodes of HM_t follows by induction on t. ♦

Lemma 2. The number of links in HM_t is $9t^2$-3t.

Proof. It is straightforward to show that the boundary of HM_t has 6t nodes of degree 2, while all other nodes of HM_t have degree 3. Therefore, the total number of links is $(3(6t^2-6t)+2(6t))/2=9t^2-3t$. ♦

We shall introduce a convenient coordinate system for nodes and edges of honeycomb meshes. Let x-, y- and z-axes start at the center of the honeycomb mesh and be parallel to three edge directions, respectively. Edges parallel to x-axis have vector coordinates (1,0,0) or (-1,0,0), depending on their direction. Similarly, edges parallel to y-direction have coordinates (0,1,0) and (0,-1,0) while edges parallel to z direction have vector coordinates (0,0,1) and (0,0,-1).

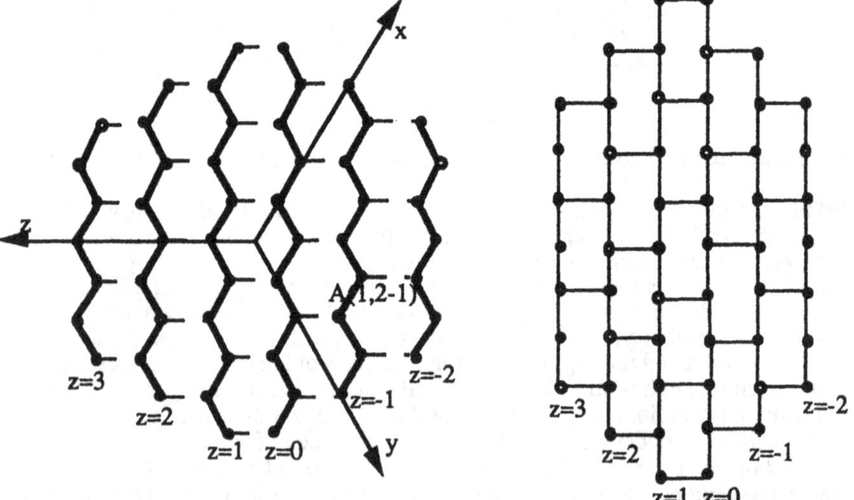

Figure 4. z-coordinates of nodes

Figure 5. Brick drawing of HM_3

Once edge vectors are defined, consider what are coordinates of nodes. The z-coordinate of all nodes reachable from a given node A by travelling along edges (±1, 0, 0) or (0, ±1, 0) (i.e. parallel to x- or y-axis) is the same as the z-coordinate of A. All nodes with a fixed (say) z-coordinate belong to a zigzag chain. The z-coordinate will change only by following an edge parallel to z-axis, i.e. edge (0, 0, 1) or (0, 0, -1). If two central chains are given z-coordinates 1 and 0, the 6 zigzag chains with respect to z-axis are z=-2, z=-1, z=0, z=1, z=2 and z=3; they are drawn in bold in Fig. 4. Similar zigzag chains can be defined for x- and y-coordinates. For instance, the coordinates of node A in Fig. 4 are (1, 2, -1). If each zigzag chain with a fixed z-coordinate is drawn as a vertical line, the honeycomb mesh receives the shape of bricks in a wall network (Fig. 5). The network drawn in this way clearly shows that the number of edges parallel to z-axis in a shortest path between two nodes is greater or equal to the difference in their z coordinate. It easily follows that the coordinates of all nodes are integers (x,y,z) such that $-t+1 \le x,y,z \le t$. Moreover, we can prove the following lemma.

Lemma 3. Nodes of a honeycomb network of size t can be coded by integer triples (u,v,w) such that $-t+1 \le u,v,w \le t$ and $1 \le u+v+w \le 2$. Two nodes (u',v',w') and (u",v",w") are connected by an edge iff $|u'-u''|+|v'-v''|+|w'-w''|=1$.

Proof. The honeycomb mesh is a bipartite graph. All nodes can be subdivided into two groups, which will be called black and white nodes, such that any edge joins a black and a white node. Fig. 4 indicates black and white nodes in HM_3. Edges going from a black node to a white node have vector coordinates (1,0,0), (0,1,0) or (0,0,1), while edges going out of white vertices toward black ones have vector coordinates (-1,0,0), (0,-1,0) or (0,0,-1). Therefore edges going from a black node to a white node join (u,v,w) to either (u+1,v,w), (u,v+1,w) or (u,v,w+1) and thus the sum u+v+w increases by 1. Analogously, edges joining from a white node to a black one join (u,v,w) to one of (u-1,v,w), (u,v-1,w) or (u,v,w-1), thus decreasing the sum u+v+w by 1. Since u+v+w alternatively increases and decreases by 1, it obviously follows that u+v+w=1 for each black node and u+v+w=2 for each white node. Two nodes are connected by an edge iff they differ in exactly one coordinate. ♦

Consider two zigzag chains x=u and y=v. If they intersect, the intersection consists of one or two points. Because u+v+w=1 or 2, the intersection node(s) has the z-coordinate either w=1-u-v or w=2-u-v, provided it is in the interval [-t+1,t].

Lemma 4. The distance between nodes (u',v',w') and (u",v",w") of a hexagonal mesh is $|u'-u''| + |v'-v''| + |w'-w''|$.

Proof. Since every edge connects two nodes whose two coordinates are equal and the third one differs by 1, it is not possible to connect two nodes without traversing at least $|u'-u''|$ edges parallel to x-coordinate, $|v'-v''|$ edges parallel to y-axis and $|w'-w''|$ edges parallel to z-axis. This proves that the distance cannot be smaller than $|u'-u''| + |v'-v''| + |w'-w''|$. We will show now that there exist a path between the two nodes with exactly that length. The proof is by mathematical induction on distance d between the two nodes. If d=1 then two coordinates of nodes must be equal (say u'=u", v'=v") while the third coordinate differs by 1 (i.e. w"=w'+1 or w"=w'-1). If w"=w'+1 then u'+v'+w'=1, u"+v"+w"=2, (u',v',w') is a black node, (u",v",w") is a white node and the edge (1,0,0) joins (u',v',w') to (u",v",w"). The case w"=w'-1 is analogous.

Suppose now that every two nodes (p',q',r') and (p",q",r") such that $|p'-p''|+|q'-q''|+|r'-r''|=d'<d$ can be connected by a path of length d'. We shall prove that any two nodes (u',v',w') and (u",v",w") such that $|u'-u''| + |v'-v''| + |w'-w''|=d$ can also be connected by a path of length d.

If (u',v',w') is a black node then consider three cases:

- If u'<u" then nodes (u',v',v') and (u'+1,v',w') are connected by an edge (with direction vector (1,0,0)) and $|u'+1-u''|+|v'-v''|+|w'-w''|=d-1$. By inductive assumption, there exist a path of length d-1 between nodes (u'+1,v',w') and (u",v",w"). A path of length d between (u',v',w') and (u",v",w") is obtained by adding the edge joining nodes (u',v',w') and (u'+1,v',w') to the path of length d-1 between nodes (u'+1,v',w') and (u",v",w").

- If u'≥u" but v'<v" then nodes (u',v', w') and (u',v'+1,w') are connected by an edge and the conclusion follows similarly as in the previous case.

- If u'≥u" and v'≥v" then from $u'+v'+w'=1 \le u''+v''+w''$ it follows that w'<w" (the two nodes are distinct), and an edge between (u',v',w') and (u',v',w'+1) exists. Conclusion follows similarly as in the previous two cases.

If (u',v',w') is a white node then, analogously to the previous cases, we can show that at least one of the three neighboring nodes of node (u',v',w') is at distance d-1 to node (u",v",w"). The neighbor is (u'-1,v',w') if u'>u", (u',v'-1,w') if v'>v" and (u',v',w'-1) if w'>w", and at least one of the three conditions is satisfied. ♦

Lemma 5. The diameter of honeycomb mesh of size t is 4t-1.

Proof. The distance between nodes (t,-t+1,0) and (-t+1,t,1) is $|2t-1|+|2t-1|+1=4t-1$. We will prove by induction that the distance between any two nodes of HM_t is $\le 4t-1$. Clearly, any two nodes of HM_1 are at distance ≤ 3. Suppose that any two nodes of HM_{t-1} are at distance $\le 4(t-1)-1$. Each node on the boundary of HM_t is at distance 1 or 2 from a node of HM_{t-1} (recall that HM_t is constructed from HM_{t-1} by adding a layer of hexagons around the boundary of HM_{t-1}). A node of HM_{t-1} is at distance 0 from a node of HM_{t-1}, e.g. itself. Consider two nodes A and B of HM_t. Let $|AB|$ denote the distance between nodes A and B. There exist two nodes A' and B' from HM_{t-1} such that $|AA'|\le 2$ and $|BB'|\le 2$. Then $|AB| \le |AA'| + |A'B'| + |B'B| \le 2 + 4(t-1)-1 + 2 = 4t-1$. ♦

Theorem 1. Honeycomb mesh network with n nodes has degree 3 and diameter $4\sqrt{\frac{n}{6}}-1 \approx 1.63\sqrt{n}-1$.

Proof. Follows from Lemmas 1 and 5. ♦

Therefore honeycomb meshes have 25% smaller degree and 18.5% smaller diameter then the mesh connected computer with the same number of nodes. This is an important advantage of honeycomb meshes over square ones. The advantage can be explained as follows. It is clear from Fig. 5, which also shows that honeycomb mesh can be embedded onto the square grid, that the distance between two nodes remains virtually same if a quarter of edges is eliminated from the grid. Further, by making a hexagonal rather than square boundary, the boundary is closer to a circular shape thus reducing its diameter.

Let us compare the network costs of the networks based on regular plane tessellations.

Theorem 2. The network costs of a mesh connected computer, hexagonal and honeycomb meshes with n nodes are $\approx 8\sqrt{n}$, $6.93\sqrt{n}$, and $4.90\sqrt{n}$, respectively.

Proof. The network cost for a honeycomb network with n nodes is $12\sqrt{\frac{n}{6}}-3= 2\sqrt{6}\sqrt{n}-3 \approx 4.90\sqrt{n}$. The number of nodes of a hexagonal mesh of size t is $n=3t^2-3t+1$ [CSK] while its diameter is 2t-2. The degree of nodes is 6. Therefore $n \approx 3t^2$ and $t \approx \frac{\sqrt{3}}{3}\sqrt{n}$. The network cost is therefore $\approx 6(2\frac{\sqrt{3}}{3}\sqrt{n}) = 4\sqrt{3}\sqrt{n} \approx 6.93\sqrt{n}$. The diameter of a square mesh connected computer with n nodes is $2\sqrt{n}-2$ and its degree is 4. Thus the cost of a mesh connected computer is $\approx 8\sqrt{n}$. ♦

Therefore hexagonal mesh has approximately 13% smaller cost than a mesh connected computer with the same number of nodes. Honeycomb mesh, however, has smaller cost than either of these two networks that are used in practice for designing multiprocessors. The cost of a honeycomb network is approximately 29% smaller than the cost of a hexagonal mesh and about 39% smaller than the cost of a mesh connected computer. The later is a significant reduction in the cost compared to (arguably) the most popular network on the market.

3. Routing in honeycomb meshes

The problem of finding a path from a source to destination and forwarding a message along the path is known as the routing problem. In this section we will describe routing algorithm for the honeycomb mesh networks.

Suppose that the source node (in a routing problem) is node source=(u',v',w') while the destination node is node dest=(u",v",w"). Let Δx=u"-u', Δy=v"-v' and Δz=w"-w'. The vector (Δx, Δy, Δz) is the "translation" vector for the message. The shortest path between the two nodes consists of $|\Delta x|$ edges parallel to x-axis, $|\Delta y|$ edges parallel to y-axis and $|\Delta z|$ edges parallel to z-axis. A routing algorithm can be designed following the proof of Lemma 4. In short, the routing algorithm checks at each current node which of the edge directions x, y, or z (in this order) would reduce the distance to the destination, and will send the message on that edge. Proof of lemma 4 guarantees that at least one edge would lead to a node closer to the destination.

Let the sign of a node T be s(T)=+1 for a black node and sign(T)=-1 for a white one. Clearly sign((u,v,w))=1 if u+v+w=1 and sign((u,v,w))=-1 otherwise. The current node (node currently holding the message) is denoted current-node=(u,v,w). The routing algorithm is as follows.

```
Route_Honeymesh(source,dest);
  current-node ← source; (* u ← u'; v ← v'; w ← w'; *)
  Δx ← u"-u'; Δy ← v"-v'; Δz ← w"-w';
  while current-node ≠ dest do
        if Δx*sign(current-node) > 0 then
              {send message on edge parallel to x-axis;
              Δx ← Δx-sign(current-node);
              u ← u+sign(current-node) }
                         else if Δy*sign(current-node) > 0    then
              {send message on edge parallel to y-axis;
              Δy ← Δy-sign(current-node);
              v ← v+sign(current-node) }
                                                              else
              {send message on edge parallel to z-axis;
              Δz ← Δz-sign(current-node);
              w ← w+sign(current-node)};
```

The algorithm is clearly optimal in the number of communication steps, and asymptotically optimal in the number of computation steps (i.e. has constant number of instructions between any two communication steps).

Lemma 6. The shortest path between source and destination nodes can be explicitly described (with constant number of parameters) on the basis of their addresses and consists of two zigzag chains.

Proof. Suppose that the source is a black node (the case of white node source is symmetric and will be studied later). Consider few possible cases:

1) $\Delta x>0$, $\Delta y\le 0$, $\Delta z\le 0$. The path is $(xy)^{|\Delta y|}(xz)^{|\Delta z|}x^c$, where a^b denotes aa...a (b times), x, y and z denote the message being sent on an edge parallel to x, y and z-axis, respectively, c=1 if destination is a white node and c=0 otherwise. In other words, the path consists of two zigzag chains, z=w' and y=v".

2) $\Delta x>0$, $\Delta y<0$ and $\Delta z>0$. The path is $(xy)^{|\Delta x|}(zy)^{|\Delta z|-1}zy^c$ (i.e. chain z=w' followed by chain x=u"); c=1 for black node destination and c=0 otherwise.

3) $\Delta x>0$, $\Delta y>0$, $\Delta z<0$. The path is $(xz)^{|\Delta x|}(yz)^{|\Delta y|-1}yz^c$ (chains y=v' and x=u"); c determined as in case 2).

4) $\Delta x\leq 0$, $\Delta y\leq 0$, $\Delta z>0$. The path is $(zx)^{|\Delta x|}(zy)^{|\Delta y|}z^c$ (chains y=v' and x=u"); c determined as in case 1).

5) $\Delta x<0$, $\Delta y>0$, $\Delta z>0$. The path is $(yx)^{|\Delta y|}(zx)^{|\Delta z|-1}zx^c$ (chains z=w' and y=v"); c determined as in case 2).

6) $\Delta x\leq 0$, $\Delta y>0$, $\Delta z\leq 0$. The path is $(yx)^{|\Delta x|}(yz)^{|\Delta z|}y^c$ (chains z=w' and x=u"); c determined as in case 1).

The shortest path therefore has the form $(pq)^a(rs)^b$ for a black node destination. If the destination is a white node then the path is corrected by either deleting the last edge s from the path (if $\Delta x\Delta y\Delta z<0$) or adding edge r to the path (otherwise). Edges p, q, r, s (each of them is either x, y or z) and their repetitions a and b (each of them being either $|\Delta x|$, $|\Delta y|$, or $|\Delta z|$) are determined according to one of six above cases.♦

4. Honeycomb torus network

Honeycomb torus network can be obtained by joining pairs of nodes of degree 2 (i.e. their unused ports) of the honeycomb mesh. In order to achieve edge and vertex symmetry, the best choice for wrapping around seems to be the pairs of nodes that are mirror symmetric with respect to three lines, passing through the center of hexagonal mesh, and normal to each of three edge orientations.

Figure 6 shows how to wrap around honeycomb mesh of size 3 (HM_3) to obtain HT_3, the honeycomb torus of dimension 3. The three lines of mirror symmetry for wrap around edges are shown in dashed lines. The same edge is given the same number. For example, edges 4ed5gf in Fig. 6 make a hexagon, and edges 7a1b6c also make a hexagon. Thus by wrapping around as indicated, we receive new hexagons. In general, the nodes that are joined by an edge are the following pairs:

(-t+1, t+1-p, p) and (t, -p+1, p-t) for $1\leq p\leq t$,

(p, -t+1,t +1-p) and (p-t, t, -p+1) for $1\leq p\leq t$,

(t+1-p, p, -t+1) and (-p+1, p-t, t) for $1\leq p\leq t$.

Note that vertices that are joined are on the boundary and the difference between them is either (2t-1,-t,-t), (-t,2t-1,-t) or (-t,-t,2t-1), depending on the direction of their missing edge.

One can observe that it is possible to move from chain z=0 to chain z=t, using edge 1 (see Fig. 4 and 5 for t=3), without making any step in the z direction. The chains z=0 and z=t can therefore be considered as one chain. In fact, pair of chains z=p and z=p-t for each p, $1\leq p\leq t$, may similarly be considered as one chain. Analogous observations can be made for chains in x and y directions. Moreover, each pair of chains contains exactly 6t nodes, i.e. the same number of nodes. Although it is possible to introduce a new notation due to merging chains, we shall keep our node notation because of its convenience.

Fig. 7 illustrates the edge and vertex symmetry of honeycomb tori. Honeycomb torus HT_3 centered at hexagon T is shown with bold edges on the "boundary" (it is only the boundary of the corresponding honeycomb mesh while the honeycomb torus includes outside hexagons adjacent to the border in wrap around fashion). The same network is redrawn so that it is centered at hexagon T' which is adjacent to T (the new "boundary" is indicated in dashed lines in Fig. 7). The same letters correspond to the same hexagons while the same numbers point to the same edges. It is clear that both tori, one centered at T and one centered at T' consist of the same edges and hexagons. For instance, both tori consists of hexagons A, B, C, D, E, F, G, H, I, J, K, P and some others (hexagons that are clearly joint to both tori are not labeled in Fig. 7). Therefore any hexagon can be considered as the center of the honeycomb torus.

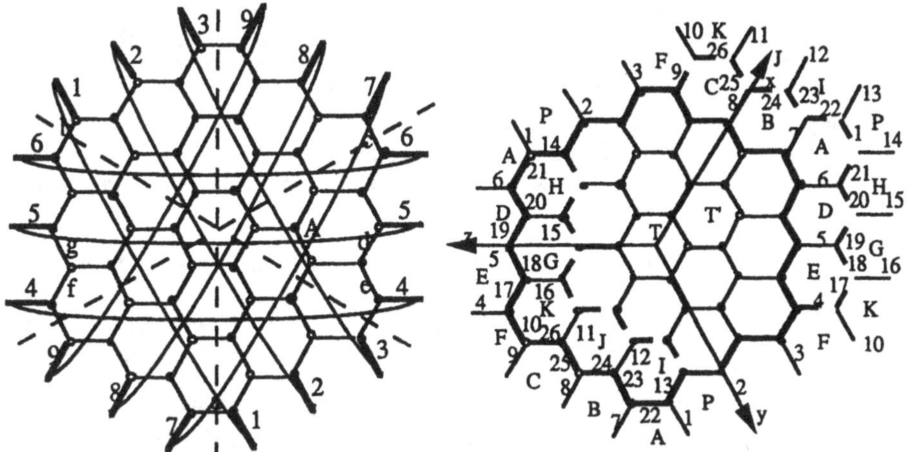

Figure 6. Honeycomb torus of size 3   Figure 7. Translation of center of HT_3

Lemma 7. The diameter of honeycomb torus HT_t is 2t.

Proof. The proof is by induction. The claim is trivially correct for t=1. Suppose that it is correct for honeycomb tori of size <t. Let a and b be two nodes at the diameter distance. Because of symmetry (Fig. 7), we can "translate" one of the hexagons containing node a to the position of the central hexagon; let the new coordinates of node a be, for example, at a=(0,1,0) (the other five positions are symmetric for the analysis). If node b is, after that translation, inside HT_{t-1} then the distance to a is ≤2(t-1). If node b is on the boundary of HT_t then in at most two steps the node can reach a node of HT_{t-1}, and that node is at distance ≤2(t-1) from node a. Therefore in both cases the distance is ≤2+2(t-1)= 2t. On the other hand, the distance between nodes (0,1,0) and (t,-t+1,0) is 2t. A path of length 2t between them is $(xy)^t$, i.e. t times edges (1,0,0) and (0,-1,0). This is also the shortest path between the two nodes if only hexagonal mesh edges are used. Note that paths $(yz)^t$ and $(zx)^t$ also connect (0,1,0) to (t, -t+1, 0). Node (0,1,0) is in the center of HT_t while node (t,-t+1,0) is on the boundary of HT_t. The distance from node (0,1,0) to the nearest boundary node with a wrap around edge is 2t-2, and (t,-t+1,0) is not at that distance. Since the two nodes have the same color, two more edges are needed to connect one of reached boundary node to the destination (t, -t+1, 0).♦

Therefore the diameter of honeycomb tori is approximately twice smaller than the diameter of the corresponding honeycomb meshes. This is the same ratio as in the case of tori that expand mesh connected computers and hexagonal meshes. Therefore, the cost of all three tori is twice smaller than the cost of the corresponding meshes (Theorem 2), and the comparison of costs remains the same as given earlier for meshes.

Let us compare now the bisection widths of the six networks under consideration.

Lemma 8. The bisection widths of mesh connected computer, torus, hexagonal mesh, hexagonal torus, honeycomb mesh, and honeycomb torus with n nodes are approximately $\sqrt{n}$, $2\sqrt{n}$, $2.31\sqrt{n}$, $4.61\sqrt{n}$, $0.82\sqrt{n}$ and $2.04\sqrt{n}$, respectively.

Proof. The bisection width of mesh connected computers and tori are well known. Hexagonal meshes and tori of size t have bisection widths approximately 4t and 8t, i.e. $\approx 2.31\sqrt{n}$ and $\approx 4.61\sqrt{n}$, respectively. Honeycomb meshes and tori of size t have bisection widths approximately 2t and 5t, i.e. $\approx 0.82\sqrt{n}$ and $\approx 2.04\sqrt{n}$, respectively.♦

We can observe that the bisection width of honeycomb torus is higher that the bisection width of (square) torus with the same number of nodes (in spite of 25% reduction in the number of edges). On the other hand, hexagonal meshes and tori have better bisection widths than honeycomb ones. Let us also consider bisection widths with respect to node degrees; the ratios bisection width/degree for considered six networks are $0.25\sqrt{n}$, $0.5\sqrt{n}$, $0.39\sqrt{n}$, $0.77\sqrt{n}$, $0.27\sqrt{n}$ and $0.68\sqrt{n}$, respectively.

We shall now consider the problem of finding the distance, shortest paths and routing a message between two nodes.

Lemma 9. The distance between two nodes (u',v',w') and (u",v",w") of honeycomb torus of size t is

min (|u"-u'| + |v"-v'| + |w"-w'|, |u"-u'+2t| + |v"-v'-t| + |w"-w'-t|, |u"-u'-2t| + |v"-v'+t| + |w"-w'+t|, |u"-u'-t| + |v"-v'+2t| + |w"-w'-t |, |u"-u'+t| + |v"-v'-2t| + |w"-w'+t|, |u"-u'-t| + |v"-v'-t| + |w"-w'+2t|, |u"-u'+t| + |v"-v'+t| + |w"-w'-2t|).

Proof. Suppose that HT_t is drawn on a (larger) hexagonal grid such that there are multiple copies of the same node. Given a source Σ and destination Ω, the shortest path between Σ and Ω on honeycomb torus can be obtained by choosing the shortest among paths from Σ to all copies of Ω on the hexagonal grid. It is not necessary to consider the unlimited number of copies of the same destination, since only its original and 6 copies obtained by translating it by one of vectors (2t,-t,-t), (-t,2t,-t), (-t,-t,2t), (-2t,t,t), (t,-2t,t) or (t,t,-2t) have chance to be the closest to the source (a composition of any two out of six translation vectors, i.e. their sum, either leads to another vector from the same group, a null vector or a vector that has ±3t as two of its coordinates; the distance from source to any later address is clearly ≥ 2d). The distances and paths on the hexagonal grid can be found by using the lemmas and algorithm developed for the hexagonal meshes in the previous section.♦

Theorem 3. The average distance between any two nodes in HT_t is

$$\frac{4}{3}t - \frac{1}{6t} \approx \frac{2}{9}\sqrt{6}\sqrt{n} \approx 0.54\sqrt{n}.$$

Proof. Because of symmetry, it suffices to determine the average distance from a source Σ to all other nodes. There are 3 nodes at distance 1 from Σ, 6 nodes at distance 2, 9 nodes at distance 3, ..., 3(2t-1) nodes at distance 2t-1 and 3(t-1)+2=3t-1 nodes at distance 2t. The sum of all distances from Σ to other nodes is $0\cdot 1 + 1\cdot 3 + 2\cdot 6 + 3\cdot 9 + \ldots + (2t-1)\cdot 3(2t-1) + 2t\cdot(3t-1) = 3(1^2 + 2^2 + 3^2 + \ldots + (2t-1)^2) + 6t^2 - 2t = 3\frac{1}{6}(2t-1)(2t)(4t-1) + 6t^2 - 2t = 8t^3 - t$. The average distance is $\frac{8t^3-t}{6t^2} = \frac{4}{3}t - \frac{1}{6t}$.♦

5. Further results and open problems

The broadcasting algorithms for honeycomb meshes and tori, and a routing algorithm for honeycomb tori are given in the full version of this paper [St]. Honeycomb meshes with square, rectangle, and rhombus boundaries are studied in [St]. In fault tolerant applications it is important to construct the maximal possible number of edge disjoint paths between any two nodes. In case of honeycomb networks, the node degree 3 limits the number of such paths to 3. It is not difficult to observe that three disjoint paths between any two nodes (of degree 3) always exist. The length of the longest of these paths should be minimized, which is less trivial. There always exist three disjoint paths between two nodes of the same (different) color such that the longest of them has length d+6 (d+4, respectively), where d is the distance between them, and these bounds are optimal.

There are a number of problems on honeycomb meshes and tori that remain for further investigation. The embeddings of rings (i.e. the construction of Hamiltonian paths), trees, hypercubes, star and other networks into honeycomb meshes and tori (and vice versa) shall be studied (few straightforward results in this direction are known). Fig. 5 suggests the study of possible simulation of algorithms devised for mesh connected computer to run on honeycomb meshes. The existence of a deadlock free routing procedures shall be searched. The basic data communication techniques (parallel prefix, sorting, merging, personalized communication etc.) need to be developed. The network scalability seems to be a problem, especially for honeycomb tori (it faces similar scalability problems at the popular torus network).

The properties of the direct products of honeycomb meshes with itself or other types of meshes may be investigated, to find new attractive networks. Finally, the generalization(s) of honeycomb meshes to three and more dimensions shall be defined and studied.

References

[A] Akl S.G., The Design and Analysis of Parallel Algorithms, Prentice Hall, 1989.

[B] Borgefors G., Distance transformations on hexagonal grids, Pattern recognition Letters, 9, 1989,97-105.

[BHM] Bell S.B.M., Holroyd F.C., and Mason D.C., A digital geometry for hexagonal pixels, Image and Vision Computing, 7, 1989, 194-204.

[CSK] Chen M.S., Shin K.G., and Kandlur D.D., Addressing, routing, and broadcasting in hexagonal mesh multiprocessors, IEEE Trans. on Comp., 39, 1, 1990, 10-18.

[D] Duncan R., A survey of parallel computer architectures, IEEE Survey & Tutorial Series, 30-31, 1990.

[DRS] J. W. Dolter J.W., Ramanathan P. and Shin K. G. , Performance Analysis of Virtual Cut-Through Switching in HARTS: A Hexagonal Mesh Multicomputer, IEEE Transactions on Computers, 40, 6, 669--680,1991.

[G] Gamst A., Homogeneous distribution of frequencies in a regular hexagonal cell system, IEEE Transactions on Vehicular Technology, 31, 3, 1982, 132-144.

[GKS] D. Gordon D., I. Koren I., and Silberman G. M., Embedding Tree Structures in VLSI Hexagonal Arrays, IEEE Transactions on Computers, 33, 104-107, 1984.

[KGGK] Kumar V., Grama A., Gupta A., and Karypis G., Introduction to Parallel Computing, Design and Analysis of Algorithms, Benjamin/Cummings Company, Inc. 1994.

[L] Lunnon W.F., Counting hexagonal and triangular polyominoes, in: Graph Theory and Computing (R.C. Read, ed.), Academic Press, 1972.

[LS] Lester L.N. and Sandor J., Computer graphics on a hexagonal grid, Computers and Graphics, 8, 1984, 401-409.

[M] Martin A.J., The torus: an exercize in constructing a processing surface, Proc 2nd Caltech Conf. VLSI, 1981, 527-537.

[Q] Quinn M.J., Parallel Computing, Theory and Practice, McGraw and Hill, 1994.

[RS] Robic B. and Silc J., High-performance computing on a honeycomb architecture, Proc. 2nd Int. ACPC Parallel Computation Conf., LNCS, Austria, 1993.

[S] Shin K.G., HARTS: A distributed real-time architecture, Computer, May 1991, 25-35.

[St] Stojmenovic I., Honeycomb networks: Topological properties and communication algorithms, TR-95-01, Computer Science Department, University of Ottawa, January 1995.

[SRD] Stevens K.S., Robinson S.V., and Davis A.L., The post office - communication support for distributed ensemble architectures, Proc. 6th Int. Conf. Distrib. Comput. Sys., 1986, 160-166.

[TMSBCC] Tosic R., Masulovic D., Stojmenovic I., Brunvoll J., Cyvin B.N. and Cyvin S.J., Enumeration of polyhex hydrocarbons to h=17, Journal of Chemical Information and Computer Sciences, 35, 1995, 181-187.

[TW] Trew A. and Wilson G. (ed.), Past, Present, Parallel, a Survey of Available Parallel Computing Systems, Springer-Verlag, 1991.

[Y] Yong-Kui L., The generation of circular arcs and straight lines on hexagonal grids, Computer Graphics Forum, 12, 1993, 21-32.

Witness-Isomorphic Reductions and the Local Search Problem (Extended Abstract*)

Sophie Fischer,[1] Lane Hemaspaandra,[2] and Leen Torenvliet[1]

[1] University of Amsterdam, Department of Computer Science, Plantage Muidergracht 24, 1018 TV Amsterdam. Supported (in part) by grants NWO/SION 612316801 and HC&M grant ERB4050PL93-0516.
[2] Department Computer Science, University of Rochester, Rochester, NY 14627. Supported in part by grants NSF-CCR-8957604, NSF-INT-9116781/ JSPS-ENGR-207, and NSF-CCR-9322513. Work done in part while visiting the Tokyo Institute of Technology, the UEC–Tokyo, and the Univ. of Amsterdam.

Abstract. We study witness-isomorphic reductions, a type of structure-preserving reduction between *NP*-decision problems. We show that witness-isomorphic reductions can be used in a uniform approach to the local search problem

1 Introduction

The "natural" *NP*-complete decision problems are very much alike. They not only are of the same complexity, but also are in the same polynomial-time isomorphism degree [BH77], and the reductions/isomorphisms between many of these problems are parsimonious [Sim75]. One would expect that such a tight connection between *NP*-complete problems "of interest" would lead to an integrated approach when dealing with the closely related optimization problems. This however is not common practice in operations research. Indeed, typically, for each individual *NP*-optimization problem new techniques and heuristics are invented. It seems that though existing reductions show a tight connection between solutions to the problem, the connection is not strong enough still to allow translation of search techniques from one problem to another.

A first step towards tightening the relation between problems further than parsimonious reductions can, was taken by Lynch and Lipton [LL78] who defined "structure-preserving reductions." This notion was later applied to optimization problems by Ausiello, D'Atri and Protasi [ADP80]. A structure-preserving reduction f is accompanied by a polynomial-time computable function g that computes from each witness for a given x a witness for $f(x)$. More recently, Agrawal and Biswas [AB92] studied the complementary approach. They stated a problem A to have a "universal relation" if for any problem B reduced to A a witness for $x \in B$ can be computed from a witness for $f(x) \in A$.

In this paper we further study the existence of reductions that preserve the properties of the witness spaces. Instead of just asking that the reduction pre-

* Full vers.: http://www.cs.rochester.edu/trs/theory-trs.html, as 94.tr.522.

serves the *number* of solutions, we demand an *isomorphism* between the witnesses. We will see that even this extremely restrictive reducibility notion can indeed often link the relations (witness schemes) that define *NP*-complete problems. Yet, surprisingly, there exist very natural witness schemes for problems in the isomorphism degree of *Sat* for which it is unlikely that such a tight connection between these problems and *Sat* exists.

Such witness-isomorphic reductions (for short, wi-reductions) can be used to obtain insight into the structural properties of local search problems. Local search is a technique for optimization problems introduced by Johnson, et al. [JPY88]. Instead of searching for a globally optimal solution, local search techniques try to improve a given initial solution until a local optimum is reached. Fischer [Fis95] defines a class of decision problems related to local search and shows these problems *NP*-complete. In this paper we show that witness-isomorphic reductions exists between standardized witnessing relations for some of these problems, and we infer from this that a local search strategy for one problem can be polynomially translated into a local search strategy for the other.

Many different witnessing schemes can define an *NP*-decision problem and the witness-isomorphic reductions in this paper are defined in terms of these relations rather than in terms of the problem. Our classification of problems through the tool of witness-isomorphic reductions might be more satisfying if we could frame witness-isomorphic reductions as a property of problems rather than a property of the relations. One way of achieving such a goal would be to "quantify out" the relation. For problems A and B one might be able to show that witness-isomorphic reductions exist regardless of which witness schemes are chosen to define A and/or B. In Section 5 we study possible approaches along this line, and determine their computational power. We conclude that some are trivial and that amongst the remaining ones there is no compelling reason to prefer one over the other. This section also provides some new observations on the question of $\#P$ completeness of *NP* counting problems. In particular, $\#P$ is often thought of as the counting version of *NP*. However Valiant [Val79a] has shown that not only *NP*-complete problems have $\#P$ hard counting versions. We look at the flip question: Do all *NP*-complete problems have (only) $\#P$-complete counting versions? We give a structural condition sufficient to ensure that the answer to this question is "no."

2 Definitions and Notation

Sets are denoted by capital letters and are subsets of Γ^*, where $\Gamma = \{0,1\}$. The cardinality of a set A is denoted as $\|A\|$. Strings are denoted as small letters $x, y, u, v, \ldots$ and are elements of Γ^*. *NP* is the class of all sets that can be recognized by nondeterministic Turing machines running in polynomial time. We will use the following standard equivalent definition of *NP*. A set A is in *NP* if and only if there exists a polynomial-time relation R_A and a polynomial p_A such that $x \in A \Longleftrightarrow (\exists y)[|y| \leq p_A(|x|) \wedge R_A(x,y)]$. The relation R_A is called a *witness scheme* for A, and a string y for which $R_A(x,y)$ is called a *witness* for

$x \in A$. Via padding, each set in *NP* has a countable infinitely number of witness schemes. We will often assume that the polynomial p_A is given and not mention it separately.

2.1 Witness-Isomorphic Reductions

Definition 1. Let A and B be languages in *NP* and let R_A be a witness scheme for A and let R_B be a witness scheme for B. We will say that (A, R_A) reduces (polynomial-time) *witness-isomorphically* to (B, R_B) ($(A, R_A) \leq_{wi} (B, R_B)$) if and only if there exist polynomial-time computable and polynomial-time invertible functions f and g such that:

1. $(\forall x)[x \in A \iff f(x) \in B]$. That is, $A \leq_m^P B$ via f.
2. $\forall x, y$: if $R_A(x, y)$ then $(\exists z)[g(\langle x, y\rangle) = \langle f(x), z\rangle \wedge R_B(f(x), z)]$.
3. $\forall x, y_1 \neq y_2$: if $R_A(x, y_1)$ and $R_A(x, y_2)$ then $g(\langle x, y_1\rangle) \neq g(\langle x, y_2\rangle)$.
4. $\forall w, z$: if $(\exists x)[f(x) = w \wedge R_B(w, z)]$ then $(\exists x, y)[R_A(x, y) \wedge g(\langle x, y\rangle) = \langle w, z\rangle]$.

We say, in the above situation, that $(A, R_A) \leq_{wi} (B, R_B)$ via f and g.

Based on wi-reductions, a notion of witness-isomorphic isomorphism can be defined. Just as in the case of many-one reductions and p-isomorphism, we can find sufficient conditions for two pairs of sets with associated witness schemes to be wi-isomorphic. A function is *length increasing* if the length of its output is greater than the length of its input. A function is called *1-invertible* if it is 1-1, and its inverse can be computed in polynomial time.

Definition 2. Let A and B be two sets in *NP* and let R_A be a witness scheme for A and let R_B be a witness scheme for B. The pair (A, R_A) is *wi-isomorphic* to (B, R_B), notated $(A, R_A) \equiv_{wi}^{iso} (B, R_B)$, if and only if there are functions f and g such that $(A, R_A) \leq_{wi} (B, R_B)$ via f and g and $(B, R_B) \leq_{wi} (A, R_A)$ via f^{-1} and g^{-1}.

Theorem 3. *Let A and B be two sets in NP and let R_A be a witness scheme for A and let R_B be a witness scheme for B. Suppose that $(A, R_A) \leq_{wi} (B, R_B)$ via f_1 and g_1 and $(B, R_B) \leq_{wi} (A, R_A)$ via f_2 and g_2. Suppose that both f_1 and f_2 are length increasing and 1-invertible. Then $(A, R_A) \equiv_{wi}^{iso} (B, R_B)$.*

Using a polynomial-time version of the Schröder-Bernstein theorem, Berman and Hartmanis [BH77] showed that all paddable *NP*-complete problems are polynomial-time isomorphic. Since all currently known natural *NP*-complete sets are paddable, this implies that these sets belong to a single p-isomorphism degree of *NP*, namely that of *Sat*. In this paper we will show for three well-known natural *NP*-complete problems that they are wi-isomorphic to each other, and that there exist natural *NP*-complete problems that are highly unlikely to be wi-isomorphic to these problems. Thus, using wi-isomorphism, we are able to nontrivially refine the p-isomorphism degree of *Sat*.

We finish this subsection by giving a necessary condition for the existence of a witness-isomorphic reduction. We also note a set of sufficient conditions.

Theorem 4. *Let R_1 and R_2 be relations (implicitly representing two problems). For each $b \in \{1, 2\}$ and each $i \in \{0, 1, \cdots\}$, define $Y_{b,i} = \{x \mid [R_b$ provides exactly i witnesses for $x]\}$. Define two conditions as follows:*

(D1) $P = P^{\#P}$.
(D2) *There exists a polynomial q such that, for each $z \in \Sigma^*$ and each i, it holds that: if $z \in Y_{1,i}$ then $(\exists y \in Y_{2,i})\,[q(|z|) \geq |y|$ and $q(|y|) \geq |z|]$.*

Then the following two claims hold: (1) If (D1) and (D2) hold, then R_1 witness-isomorphically reduces to R_2, and (2) If (D2) fails to hold, then R_1 does not witness-isomorphically reduce to R_2.

2.2 Local Search

Definition 5. [JPY88] A *Polynomial Local Search(PLS)* problem A is a five tuple $\langle I_A, \mathcal{FS}_A, f_A, opt_A, N_A\rangle$, where I_A is the set of instances of A, for each $I \in I_A$ the set $\mathcal{FS}_A(I)$ is the set of feasible solutions of I, f_A assigns to every feasible solution an integer value, opt_A is either *min* or *max* depending on the optimization nature of the problem, and for each $I \in I_A, s \in \mathcal{FS}_A(I)$, $N_A(I, s)$ is the set of neighbors of s. Furthermore, $I_A \in P$, for each $I \in I_A$ an initial solution in $\mathcal{FS}_A(I)$ can be computed in polynomial time, and for given $s \in \mathcal{FS}_A(I)$ we can either decide in polynomial time whether s is locally optimal or compute an $s' \in N_A(I, s)$ with a better cost.

The set of feasible solutions of a local search problem, together with a neighborhood structure, can be interpreted as a directed graph. The nodes of this graph are feasible solutions and edges point from feasible solutions to other feasible solutions with better cost. A path in this graph, such that each solution on this path has a cost better than the previous one, is called an augmenting path. A local search algorithm can be viewed as walking along an augmenting path in the graph from an arbitrary node (initial solution) to a sink (local optimum).

For a problem $A \in PLS$, one can define a decision variant A^* as follows.

Definition 6. [Fis95] Let $A \in PLS$. Define decision problem A^* as

Given $I \in I_A$, $s \in \mathcal{FS}_A(I)$, 0^d.
Question Is there a path p and a locally optimal solution s', such that p is an augmenting path between s and s' and p has length at most d?

Solution s is called the ***initial solution*** and value d is called the ***distance***. The problem A^* is called the ***starred version*** of problem A.

For $A \in PLS$, the set A^* belongs to NP, and so it is characterized by polynomial-time computable relations. We consider in this paper one such relation, the relation R_A. Relation $R_A(\langle I, s, 0^d\rangle, lsp)$ evaluates to true if and only if lsp is an augmenting path of length at most d from s to a locally optimal solution. Such an augmenting path is called a ***short*** augmenting path. Relation R_A is called the ***natural witness scheme*** of A^*.

We will consider the following three *PLS* problems.

1: The instance set of the problem *MaxSat* consists of Boolean formulas in CNF, where each clause has a weight. The set of feasible solutions of such a formula ϕ is formed by all assignments τ to the variables of ϕ. The cost of τ equals the sum of the weights of the clauses satisfied by τ. An assignment τ' is a neighbor of τ if we can obtain τ' from τ by flipping the value of one variable in τ. This neighborhood is called the *flip* neighborhood.

2: The instance set of the problem *MinPartition* consists of multisets A of integers. The set of feasible solutions of A is formed by all partitions of the multiset A into two disjoint multisets. The cost of a partition is the absolute value of the difference of the sums of the values of the two sets. We wish to minimize this cost. A partition (A', B') is a neighbor of partition of (A, B), if we can obtain (A', B') from (A, B) by either moving an element from A to B or moving an element from B to A. This neighborhood is called the *swap* neighborhood.

3: The instance set of the problem $MinVC$ consists of graphs G. The set of feasible solutions of G is formed by all vertex covers of G. The cost of a vertex cover of G equals the number of vertices in the vertex cover. A vertex cover VC' is a neighbor of a vertex cover VC if we can obtain VC' from VC by deleting one vertex from VC. This neighborhood is called the *remove* neighborhood.

3 Witness-Isomorphic Reductions

For problems whose globally optimal solutions are beyond the reach of feasible computation, one may turn to the local search approach in hope of finding a locally optimal solution in reasonable time. Note that a witness-isomorphic reduction between two (starred versions) of local search problems establishes a tight connection between search paths that translates these search paths back and forth. Thus, such a reduction makes a strategy concocted for one problem usable for the other. We give two examples of witness-isomorphic reductions from standard *NP*-problems to the starred versions of local search problems. From this we conclude that there is a "wi-connection" between the two starred versions. Let *Sat* be the set of satisfiable Boolean formulas. Let R_{Sat} be the witness scheme for *Sat* that on input ϕ and τ decides whether τ is a satisfying assignment for ϕ. Let *Partition* be the set of multi-sets containing positive integers. Let R_{Part} be the witness scheme for *Partition* that on input A and (A_0, B_0) decides whether (A_0, B_0) is a partition of the elements of A, i.e., whether the elements in A_0 sum up to the same value as the elements of B_0.

Theorem 7. *There exists a witness-isomorphic reduction from (Sat,R_{Sat}) to (MaxSat*,R_{MS}).*

Proof. (sketch) For input formula F on n variables, we construct a formula F' such that on an augmenting path starting from the all zero initial solution variables can be flipped to true only in increasing order of their index and can never be flipped to false. Furthermore, the assignment to F' obtained after all such augmenting flips for all n variables is locally optimal if and only if the assignment thus created satisfies F. Hence for each truth assignment there exists a *single* augmenting path of length n ending in a local optimum. □

Theorem 8. *There exists a witness-isomorphic reduction from (Partition,R_{Part}) to (MinPartition*,R_{MP}).*

Proof. (idea) From a given instance of partition $A = \{a_1, a_2, \ldots, a_n\}$, we construct an instance of *MinPartition**, $\langle A', (A'_0, B'_0), 0^{2n}\rangle$, in which each integer a_i is represented by the elements α_i^1, α_i^2, β_i^1 and β_i^2. These elements ensure that a path from (A'_0, B'_0) to a local optimum (which is a partition of the original problem) is indeed unique. Let (A'_s, B'_s) be a partition of A' reachable after at most $2n$ swaps. By inserting enough elements of weight 1, we ensure that (A_s, B_s) is locally optimal if and only if $A_s = B_s$. □

In the full paper the reductions of both theorems and a wi-reduction from (Sat,R_{Sat}) to (Partition,R_{Part}) can be found. We conclude by Theorem 3 and the forthcoming Theorem 17 that (MaxSat*,R_{MS})$\equiv_{wi}^{iso}$ (MinPartition*,R_{MP}).

4 A Non Wi-Isomorphism

In the previous section we gave witness-isomorphic reductions from (Sat,R_{Sat}) to starred versions of local search problems (always with the "short path witness scheme"). By Theorem 17 we can use these reductions to obtain tight relations between the (starred versions of) these local search problems. It would be very nice if such reductions could be found between *all* (starred versions of) local search problems with their short path witness schemes. This could motivate the search for a *uniform* search strategy, applicable via translation, to *any problem* in *PLS*. We note however that witness-isomorphic reductions are *not* always possible.

A very simple example shows this. Define for instance a variant of $MaxSat$, the problem VMS, that has the same instance as $MaxSat$. Suppose that the set of solutions belonging to a Boolean formula ϕ contains tuples $\langle\tau, l\rangle$, where τ is an assignment to the variables in ϕ and $l \in \{0,1\}$. Two tuples $\langle\tau, l\rangle$ and $\langle\tau', l'\rangle$ are neighbors if τ' is a neighbor of τ according to the flip neighborhood. Like $MaxSat$, the problem VMS belongs to *PLS*. Define for VMS its starred version VMS^* as we did before, and let R_{VMS} be its natural witness scheme. Since there are Boolean formulas that have exactly one satisfying assignment, (Sat,R_{Sat})$\not\leq_{wi}$(VMS*,R_{VMS}).

Note that we have broken condition ($D2$) of Theorem 4 in a particularly simple way: by ensuring that there are no instances of $VMaxSat^*$ having an odd number of witnesses. In fact, the counterexample just given is exactly the type of mismatch that was of interest to Edwards and Welsh [EW].

We now turn our attention to an optimization problem with a well-known neighborhood structure. Consider the $MinVC$ problem with the remove neighborhood. We will show now that if $R \neq NP$ then there is a structural difference between $MaxSat$ and $MinVC$ in terms of their short local search paths. Furthermore, separation of these two problems seems to resist simple combinatorial arguments as used above.

Theorem 9. *$MinVC^*$ is NP-complete.*

Lemma 10. *Let G be an instance of MinVC, let VC_0 be any feasible solution in $\mathcal{FS}_{MinVC}$. Let VC be a locally optimal solution reachable from VC_0 after k local search steps. Then there are $k!$ augmenting paths from VC_0 to VC.*

Theorem 11. *If there exists a wi-reduction from (Sat, R_{Sat}) to $(MinVC^*, R_{MVC})$ then $R = NP$.*

Proof. (Sketch) Suppose that such a reduction exists. On an input formula, F, we use the Valiant-Vazirani [VV85] construction to obtain a new formula (different coin flips may yield different formulas). The Valiant-Vazirani construction has the following properties. If F is not satisfiable, then for all coin flips the new formula obtained is not satisfiable. There is a polynomial h (independent of F) such that if F is satisfiable, then with probability at least $1/h(|F|)$ the formula obtained has exactly one satisfying assignment. Apply the assumed wi-reduction on the new formula obtained as above. We obtain a graph with an initial vertex cover and (with probability $1/h(|F|)$ if F is satisfiable but with probability zero if f is not satisfiable) a unique optimal vertex cover at distance 1. We search the distance-1 neighborhood of the initial solution to retrieve this vertex cover, and accept (on the current probabilistic computation path) if we find it. If F is satisfiable (respectively, is not satisfiable), this algorithm accepts with probability $1/h(|F|)$ (respectively, 0), thus $R = NP$. □

5 Models of Witness-Isomorphic Reduction

5.1 Witness-Isomorphic Reduction Definitions

We will define several variants of the wi-reduction. These variations arise from different possible quantifications in the definition. There are six possible combinations of existential and universal quantification, and Definition 12 presents each of them. We will consider all these types of reductions. Our results completely order the strengths of these six notions of witness-isomorphic reduction. We will also address the incidental, but interesting, issue of whether all counting versions of NP-complete sets are $\#P$-complete.

Definition 12. For each $A, B \in NP$,

1. $A \leq^P_{wi\exists\exists} B$ if and only if there exists a witness scheme R_A for A and a witness scheme R_B for B such that $(A, R_A) \leq_{wi} (B, R_B)$.
2. $A \leq^P_{wi\forall\forall} B$ if and only if for each witness scheme R_A for A and for each witness scheme R_B for B, $(A, R_A) \leq_{wi} (B, R_B)$.
3. $A \leq^P_{wi\forall_r\exists_\ell} B$ if and only if for each witness scheme R_B for B there exists a witness scheme R_A for A such that $(A, R_A) \leq_{wi} (B, R_B)$.

4. $A \leq^P_{wi\forall_\ell\exists_r} B$ if and only if for each witness scheme R_A for A there exists a witness scheme R_B for B such that $(A, R_A) \leq_{wi} (B, R_B)$.
5. $A \leq^P_{wi\exists_r\forall_\ell} B$ if and only if there exists a witness scheme R_B for B such that for each witness scheme R_A for A, $(A, R_A) \leq_{wi} (B, R_B)$.
6. $A \leq^P_{wi\exists_\ell\forall_r} B$ if and only if there exists a witness scheme R_A for A such that for each witness scheme R_B for B, $(A, R_A) \leq_{wi} (B, R_B)$.

The mnemonic is that the "wi" subscript gives the order of the quantifiers and which set ("ℓ" for left or "r" for right) the quantifier belongs to in cases where this is ambiguous. Some of the relations between these reductions are immediate from the definitions. The remaining ones (viewing the reductions as shorthands for the subset of $NP \times NP$ for which they hold), are stated in the following theorem.

Theorem 13. *The relations of the various reductions of Definition 12 on NP is* $\leq^P_{wi\exists_\ell\forall_r} = \leq^P_{wi\forall\forall} \subsetneq \leq^P_{wi\exists_r\forall_\ell} \subsetneq \leq^P_{wi\forall_\ell\exists_r} \subsetneq \leq^P_{wi\forall_r\exists_\ell} = \leq^P_{wi\exists\exists} = \leq^P_m$.

We prove this theorem by considering the properties of these reductions.

Since *Sat* is a lodestar in the study of *NP*, we note, in contrast to some of the other reduction types soon to be discussed, that we trivially have here broad equivalence to *Sat*. (We adopt the standard notational shorthand $E^P_r(B) = \{A \mid [A \leq^P_r B \text{ and } B \leq^P_r A]\}$.)

Corollary 14. $E^P_{wi\exists\exists}(Sat) = E^P_{wi\forall_r\exists_\ell}(Sat) = NP\text{-} \leq^P_m$ *-complete.*

5.2 The Reductions $\leq^P_{wi\exists\exists}$, $\leq^P_{wi\forall_r\exists_\ell}$, $\leq^P_{wi\forall\forall}$ and $\leq^P_{wi\exists_\ell\forall_r}$

In the next theorem we see that $\leq^P_{wi\exists\exists}$ and $\leq^P_{wi\forall_r\exists_\ell}$ are, on *NP*, just new names for $\leq^P_m$. The proof is based on the fact that we can use as a witness scheme for set A (the set reduced from) any witness scheme of set B (the set reduced to). We essentially steal for A the witness scheme of B.

Theorem 15. *1.* $(\forall A, B \in NP)[A \leq^P_{wi\exists\exists} B$ *if and only if* $A \leq^P_m B]$.
2. $(\forall A, B \in NP)[A \leq^P_{wi\forall_r\exists_\ell} B$ *if and only if* $A \leq^P_m B]$.

The reductions $\leq^P_{wi\forall\forall}$ and $\leq^P_{wi\exists_\ell\forall_r}$ are pathological. They relate only the empty set to itself.

Theorem 16. *For any sets* $A, B \in NP : A \leq^P_{wi\forall\forall} B \iff A \leq^P_{wi\exists_\ell\forall_r} B \iff A = B = \emptyset$.

The above observation is inspired by a paper of Edwards and Welsh [EW] that used a similar observation to "disprove," in a certain nonstandard sense, the Berman-Hartmanis Isomorphism Conjecture.

5.3 The $\leq^P_{wi\exists_r\forall_\ell}$-reduction

Note how strong the claim $A\leq^P_{wi\exists_r\forall_\ell}B$ is. It says that there is some relationship for B so flexible that *any* relation for A yields a witness-isomorphic reduction to B with respect to the flexible relation. Nonetheless, such tremendous flexibility can and does exist. In fact, any sufficiently careful proof of the Cook's Theorem yields the following claim.

Theorem 17. $(\forall A \in NP)[A\leq^P_{wi\exists_r\forall_\ell}Sat]$. *Furthermore, not only is the existentially quantified relation for Sat the same for all $R_{A'}$ for a particular set A', it in fact is the same for any witness relation of any NP set.*

The good behavior of $\leq^P_{wi\exists_r\forall_\ell}$ is further certified by its transitivity. However, it is not in general reflexive.

Proposition 18.

1. $(\forall A, B, C \in NP)$ $[(A\leq^P_{wi\exists_r\forall_\ell}B$ *and* $B\leq^P_{wi\exists_r\forall_\ell}C) \Longrightarrow A\leq^P_{wi\exists_r\forall_\ell}C]$.
2. *For each finite set A,* $A\not\leq^P_{wi\exists_r\forall_\ell}A$. *If* $P \neq NP$, *then there is a set A in* $NP-P$ *such that* $A\not\leq^P_{wi\exists_r\forall_\ell}A$.

It is instructive to compare our $\leq^P_{wi\exists_r\forall_\ell}$ reductions to the "universal relation" notion proposed by Agrawal and Biswas [AB92]. Our notion is more demanding than theirs in that it requires witness isomorphism, rather than allowing mere equivalence as filtered through their elaborate "masking" mechanism. On the other hand, our notion is less demanding than theirs in that our definition applies to arbitrary *NP* sets, rather than forcing *NP*-completeness and applying with all *NP* sets as the potential left-hand side of the reduction.

5.4 $\leq^P_{wi\forall_\ell\exists_r}$-Reducibility

Note that $\leq^P_{wi\forall_\ell\exists_r}$ is a rather unusual reduction, as it requires that structure be projected "forward." As already noted, it is a more general reduction than $\leq^P_{wi\exists_r\forall_\ell}$, and a less general reduction than $\leq^P_m$. First note that the first inclusion is strict. Consider for instance reducing a set with one element to another set with one element. We will first give necessary conditions for $\leq^P_{wi\forall_\ell\exists_r}$-reducibility. Then we show that the second inclusion is strict. Finally, we show that on a subclass of *NP* that $\leq^P_{wi\forall_\ell\exists_r}$-reducibility equals many-one reducibility.

Definition 19. Let C and D be two disjoint sets. Set C is *NP*-separable from D if and only if there exists a set $E \in NP$, such that $C \subseteq E$ and E and D are disjoint.

Theorem 20. *Let* $A, B \in NP$. *Suppose that* $A \leq^P_{1-1,honest} B$ *via a reduction f such that* $\overline{f(A)} \cap B$ *is NP-separable from* $f(A)$. *Then* $A\leq^P_{wi\forall_\ell\exists_r}B$.

What is the relationship between $\leq^P_{wi\forall_\ell\exists_r}$ and $\leq^P_m$? Clearly, for any finite sets S and T such that $|S| > |T|$, we have $S \leq^P_m T$ yet $S \not\leq^P_{wi\forall_\ell\exists_r} T$. This pigeon-hole trick can be easily also used on infinite sets (e.g., on $S = \{0^{2^{2^k}} | k \geq 1\} \cup \{1^{2^{2^k}} | k \geq 1\}$ and $T = \{0^{2^{2^k}} | k \geq 1\}$). This is indeed just a trick based on the lack of enough strings to which to map. That is, it does not hold that

$$(**) \qquad (\exists \text{ polynomial } f)\,(\forall n)\,[||S^{\leq n}|| \leq ||T^{\leq f(n)}||].$$

However, there are relativized worlds where there are sets A and B such that $A \leq^P_m B$ and there are enough strings to map to, yet A does not $\leq^P_{wi\forall_\ell\exists_r}$ reduce to B. There are also relativized worlds (e.g., via collapsing classes dramatically) such that all *NP* sets related by a many-one reduction and satisfying $(**)$ in fact are related by the $\leq^P_{wi\forall_r\exists_\ell}$ reduction.

So, we have given necessary conditions for $\leq^P_{wi\forall_\ell\exists_r}$-reducibility. Furthermore we have shown that the $\leq^P_{wi\forall_\ell\exists_r}$ reduction does not equal the many-one reduction. However, there is a subclass of *NP* on which these two kinds of reductions coincide.

Theorem 21. *Let A and B be two NP-complete sets. Suppose that A and B are both 1-invertibly paddable. Then $A \leq^P_m B$ if and only if $A \leq^P_{wi\forall_\ell\exists_r} B$.*

5.5 #*P*-completeness

In the penumbra of these notions lies an interesting question about #*P*-completeness. Many people, quite informally, think of #*P* as the counting version of *NP*. However, Valiant [Val79a] has noted that some *P* problems have #*P*-complete counting versions. We investigate a flip side of the issue: Are all *NP*-complete sets #*P*-complete in their counting versions? In particular, are there *NP*-complete sets that with respect to some witness scheme are not #*P*-complete?

We use #*P*-completeness in its most natural form, namely, with respect to 1-T reductions (see [Zan91], and also [Val79a], for some discussion of the issues involved in completeness types for #*P*). That is, f is #*P*-complete if and only if $f \in \#P$ and for each $g \in \#P$, it holds that $g \in FP^f_{1\text{-}T}$.

We first prove the following theorem concerning sets in *NP* having a witness scheme such that the counting version of the set is not #*P*-complete with respect to this witness scheme.

Theorem 22. *1. If there is a NP-complete set L that with respect to some witnessing relation R_L is not #P-complete, then $P \neq P^{\#P}$.*
2. If $P \neq P^{\#P}$ and NP = FewP, then each NP-complete set has some witnessing scheme with respect to which it fails to be #P-complete.

Now we turn to the question whether every set in *NP* has a witness scheme such that the set is #*P*-complete with respect to this witness scheme. Let *NP*-$\leq_r$-complete be the set of decision problems that are complete for *NP* with respect to the $\leq_r$-reduction.

Theorem 23. *If NP-$\leq_m$-complete = NP-$\leq^P_{1\text{-}1,\ onto,\ honest}$-complete, then every NP-complete set L has a witness scheme R_L, such that the counting version of L is #P-complete with respect to R_L.*

One might hope to sidestep Theorem 22 by asking whether every *NP*-complete set has some witness scheme with respect to which it *is* #*P*-complete. For #*P*-$\leq^P_{1\text{-}T}$-completeness this is an interesting open question. However, there are nontrivial relativized worlds (i.e., worlds in which P and NP differ) in which there are *NP*-complete sets that are not (in the natural sense) #*P*-$\leq^P_m$-complete sets with respect to any legal witness relation. For example, the pathological *NP*-complete sets constructed in [HH91] are not even $\leq^P_m$-hard for the P function $f(n) = n$.

Acknowledgment: We thank M. Ogihara for helpful discussions, and H. Buhrman for suggesting the proof of Theorem 11.

References

[AB92] M. Agrawal and S. Biswas. Universal relations. In *Proceedings of the 7th Structure in Complexity Theory Conference*, pages 207–220, Boston, Mass., June 1992. IEEE Computer Society Press.

[ADP80] G. Ausiello, A. D'Atri, and M. Protasi. Structure preserving reductions among convex optimization problems. *J. Computer and System Sciences*, 21:136–153, 1980.

[BH77] L. Berman and H. Hartmanis. On isomorphisms and density of NP and other complete sets. *SIAM J. Comput.*, 6:305–322, 1977.

[EW] K. Edwards and D. Welsh. On the complexity of uniqueness problems. Manuscript, early 1980s.

[Fis95] S. Fischer. On the complexity of local search problems. *Information Processing Letters*, 53:69–75, 1995.

[HH91] J. Hartmanis and L. Hemachandra. One-way functions and the non-isomorphism of NP-complete sets. *Theoretical Computer Science*, 81(1):155–163, 1991.

[JPY88] D. Johnson, C. Papadimitriou, and M. Yannakakis. How easy is local search? *J. Comput. System Sci.*, 37:79–100, 1988.

[LL78] N. Lynch and R. Lipton. On structure preserving reductions. *SIAM J. Comp.*, 7(2):119–125, 1978.

[Sim75] J. Simon. On some central problems in computational complexity. Technical report, Cornell University, Ithaca NY, 1975. TR 75-224.

[Val79a] L. Valiant. The complexity of computing the permanent. *Theoretical Computer Science*, 8:189–201, 1979.

[Val79b] L. Valiant. The complexity of enumeration and reliability problems. *SIAM Journal on Computing*, 8(3):410–421, 1979.

[VV85] L. Valiant and V. Vazirani. NP is as easy as detecting unique solutions. In *Proc. 17th ACM Symp. Theory of Computing*, pages 458–463, 1985.

[Zan91] V. Zankó. #P-completeness via many-one reductions. *International Journal of Foundations of Computer Science*, 2(1):76–82, 1991.

Multiple Product Modulo Arbitrary Numbers

Claudia Bertram-Kretzberg and Thomas Hofmeister

Lehrstuhl Informatik II, Universität Dortmund, D-44221 Dortmund, Germany
bertram,hofmeist@Ls2.informatik.uni-dortmund.de

Abstract. Let n binary numbers of length n be given. The Boolean function "Multiple Product" MP_n asks for (some binary representation of) the value of their product. It has been shown in [SR],[SBKH] that this function can be computed in polynomial-size threshold circuits of depth 4. For a lot of other arithmetic functions, circuits of depth 3 are known. They are mostly based on the fact that the value of the considered function modulo some prime numbers p can be computed easily in threshold circuits.
In this paper, we show that the difficulty in constructing smaller depth circuits for MP_n stems from the fact that for all numbers m which are divisible by a prime larger than 3, computing MP_n modulo m already cannot be computed in depth 2 and polynomial size. This result still holds if we allow m to grow exponentially in n ($m < 2^{cn}$, for some constant c). This improves upon recent results in [K1].
We also investigate moduli of the form $2^i 3^j$. In particular, we show that there are depth-2 polynomial-size threshold circuits for computing MP_n modulo m if $m \in \{2,4,8\}$, and that no such circuits exist if m is divisible by 9 or 16.

1 Introduction

In the last few years, threshold circuits of constant depth have been intensively studied. Although a threshold gate is a rather simple device which can only decide whether the number of 1s in its input is above some threshold, it turned out that it seems rather difficult to prove any superpolynomial lower bound even for circuits with depth bounded by 3. The first exponential lower bound for threshold circuits of depth 2 is by [HMPST] for the "Inner Product modulo 2", defined by $IP_n : \{0,1\}^{2n} \to \{0,1\}$, $IP_n(x_1, y_1, \ldots, x_n, y_n) := x_1 y_1 \oplus \cdots \oplus x_n y_n$. Further techniques for depth 2 were developed, but could not be extended to depth 3. The lack of negative results was then complemented by a series of results which proved threshold circuits to be surprisingly powerful. If we abbreviate by TC_k^0 all Boolean functions which can be computed in threshold circuits of polynomial size and depth k, then the following complex Boolean functions are now known to be contained in TC_3^0: Sorting of n binary numbers which have length n each; multiplication of two binary numbers of length n; computing the $n-$th power of an input number; computing an approximation of the division of two binary numbers of length n. If we want to add n numbers of length n, we even get away with TC_2^0 ([GK, GHR]). For a survey or for lower bounds, see e.g. [H, R, W].

One of the few exceptions of arithmetic functions where we know of a small-depth (actually, depth 4, see [SR]) threshold circuit, but of no TC_3^0 circuit, is the "multiple product".
The technique which was used when realizing complex functions like division consisted of computing the result modulo small prime numbers and then reconstructing the result via Chinese Remaindering. A notion which also turned out to be rather useful is that of 1-approximability. For a formal definition, we refer the reader to, e.g., [H]. Informally, a 1-approximable function can be computed in TC_2^0-circuits which have some special property. Namely, on any input, the number of ones which are fed into the output gate is restricted to some small range. This means that the output gate has a weak task and can be omitted if there are other gates underneath. The set of 1-approximable functions is a proper subclass of TC_2^0.
Though it may seem a random decision to consider "multiple product", it should be seen that this function is close to the boundary of what we know. It seems natural to investigate why the decomposition via Chinese Remaindering fails when applied to the multiple product.
First results obtained in this direction were given by Krause [K1] who has shown that for all $O(\log n)$-bit numbers m which have a prime factor larger than 3, the problem of computing the multiple product modulo m is not 1-approximable. The proof of this was based on communication complexity arguments. This indicates already why Chinese Remaindering cannot be successful.
In this paper, we improve upon this result in two respects. First, we show that the above negative statement can be strengthened to TC_2^0 instead of 1-approximability. Second, we are able to extend the statement to numbers m which consist of $c \cdot n$ bits (for some constant c). Our proof is also rather simple. We then extend our investigations to numbers which have not been tackled in [K1]. In particular, we are able to classify exactly for which numbers of the form $m := 2^i$ the multiple product modulo m can be computed in TC_2^0.
It should be noted that considering powers of 2 is perhaps the most natural case since it corresponds to computing the actual bits in the output of the multiple product. In this respect, we are able to design TC_2^0-circuits which compute the 3 least significant bits of the multiple product. The way the circuits are designed also reveals that those 3 bits are actually 1-approximable. We are then able to show that higher order bits are not computable in TC_2^0. Finally, the negative results are extended to all moduli m which are divisible by 16 or 9.

2 Definitions and basic properties

Let us recall some basic number theoretic notions. For a natural number m, let Z_m be the residue class modulo m, and Z_m^* denote the multiplicative group modulo m. For an $a \in Z_m^*$, we denote – slightly abusing notation – by $\frac{1}{a}$ the multiplicative inverse of a. The modulus will be clear from the context.
Let $\mathrm{ord}_m(a)$ denote the order of a, i.e. the smallest $i \geq 1$ such that $a^i \equiv 1 \bmod m$. An element $a \in Z_m^*$ is called a "primitive root" modulo m if $\mathrm{ord}_m(a) = |Z_m^*|$.

Throughout this paper, we will assume that $z_1, \ldots, z_n$ are binary input numbers of length n each. If the number of factors is not equal to their length, then we implicitly pad with dummy inputs. We identify the z_i with the natural numbers they represent and denote by $MP_n^{(m)}(z_1, \ldots, z_n)$ the binary representation of the value $z_1 \cdots z_n \bmod m$. A *projection reduction* from a Boolean function $f(x_1, \ldots, x_n)$ to a function $g(y_1, \ldots, y_t)$ is a mapping $p : \{1, \ldots, t\} \rightarrow \{0, 1, x_1, \ldots, x_n, \overline{x_1}, \ldots, \overline{x_n}\}$ such that $f(x_1, \ldots, x_n) = g(p(1), \ldots, p(t))$. A projection reduction is called *polynomial* if t is bounded by a polynomial in n. As an example, consider the projection reduction sketched in Fig. 1. Multiplying, modulo 16, the three given binary numbers (corresponding to the rows) means computing the 4 least significant bits of $(4y+1)(10x+1)(12y+2x+1)$. It turns out that in the result, bit 3 is equal to the AND of x and y. I.e., Fig. 1 describes a projection reduction from the AND-function to the Multiple Product modulo 16.

0	y	0	1
x	0	x	1
y	y	x	1

Fig. 1

Projection reductions are "depth-preserving", i.e., if there is a polynomial projection reduction from f to g, and f needs exponential size in threshold circuits of depth 2, then so does g. In this paper, we provide polynomial projection reductions from IP_n to $MP^{(m)}$ showing that computing Multiple Product modulo m is difficult in depth-2 threshold circuits.
As in Fig. 1, projection reductions to the Multiple Product can be described as the product of some linear terms. This motivates the following definition where we consider linear terms which contain at most two variables.

Definition 1. Let $m \geq 2$ be an integer. Call a polynomial of the form $ax+by+c$, where $a, b, c \in Z_m$, a "linear combination". A polynomial $f(x, y)$ which is the product of linear combinations is called a PLC.

In the sequel, we will construct PLCs which have certain properties. We want to use them to construct projection reductions, so we have to transform them into rows. Unfortunately, for even moduli m, this is not always possible. For example, the linear combination $2x + 2y + 1$ cannot be turned into a row modulo 16, since the values of all bit positions larger than 3 are equivalent to 0 modulo 16, so we have the bit with value 2 only once at our disposal. Nevertheless, we need it twice to represent $2x$ and $2y$. (Using negations of variables also won't help.)
This motivates the following definition:

Definition 2. A linear combination $ax + by + c$ can be "represented modulo m" if a, b, and c possess binary representations modulo m, $a = \sum_{i=0}^{N} a_i 2^i$, $b = \sum_{i=0}^{N} b_i 2^i$, $c = \sum_{i=0}^{N} c_i 2^i$, such that for all i the bits a_i, b_i, c_i "do not collide", i.e., for all i, at most one of the bits a_i, b_i, c_i is 1. The number N is called the representation size. A PLC "can be represented modulo m" if all of its linear combinations can be represented.

If the bits do not collide, then we can transform a PLC $ax + by + c$ into a row by putting an x into all positions where $a_i = 1$, y into all positions where $b_i = 1$ etc. The only moduli causing trouble are even, as the following lemma shows. It also reveals small representations of the linear combinations.

Lemma 3. *If m is odd, then any linear combination $ax+by+c$ can be represented modulo m, using $O(\log m)$ bits.*

Proof. Let $j := \lceil \log m \rceil$. Since m is odd, the inverses of powers of 2 exist. We binary encode the numbers a, $b/(2^j)$, and $c/(2^{2j})$ with j bits each. We then plug the encoding of these numbers into the bit positions $0, \ldots, j-1$, $j, \ldots, 2j-1$, $2j, \ldots, 3j-1$, respectively. The representation size is $O(\log m)$. □

We now show how we can deal with the cases where the modulus m is even, assuming that we can handle the powers of 2:

Lemma 4. *If the linear combination $ax + by + c$ can be represented modulo 2^k, then it can be represented modulo $m := 2^k \cdot r$, for all odd r, with $O(\log m)$ bits.*

Proof. (Sketch:) By the Chinese Remainder Theorem, it suffices to find a representation which simultaneously works modulo r and 2^k. We take the representation of $ax + by + c$ modulo 2^k which occupies the least significant k bits only. Modulo r, this represents also a linear combination, call it G. Higher order bits contribute nothing modulo 2^k, hence, by the method from Lemma 3, we can use the bits at positions larger than $k - 1$ to represent the linear combination $ax+by+c-G$ modulo r. The representation size is $k+O(\log r) = O(\log m)$. □

We want to use the PLCs to simulate the behaviour of the inner product function. If we feed the variable pairs one by one into the inner product function, then it changes its output each time a pair has the value $(1, 1)$. We want to achieve a similar behaviour with PLCs, hence the following definition is motivated:

Definition 5. We call a PLC f a "2-PLC modulo m" if it has the following property: $f(0,0) \equiv f(0,1) \equiv f(1,0) \equiv 1 \bmod m$, and $\text{ord}_m(f(1,1)) = 2$.
Analogously, a PLC f is called a "3-PLC" if $f(1,1)$ has order 3 instead of 2. (Note that 3-PLCs will be useful when dealing with the Inner Product modulo 3 instead of the Inner Product modulo 2.)

For example, $f(x,y) := (3x + 3y + 1)^2$ is a 2-PLC modulo 5 since $f(0,0) = 1$, $f(0,1) = f(1,0) = 16$ are equivalent to 1 modulo 5 and $f(1,1) = 49$ is equivalent to -1 modulo 5 which is an element of order 2.
We have reduced the problem of finding a projection reduction to the problem of finding a 2-PLC f modulo m which is representable. The reason is the following: For every pair of variables (x_i, y_i), we take the PLC $f(x_i, y_i)$ and consider the linear terms as rows of the multiple product.
The rows which correspond to a variable pair $(x_i, y_i) \neq (1,1)$ only contribute a factor of 1 modulo m. Let t be the number of variable pairs $(x_i, y_i) = (1,1)$. The output of $MP^{(m)}$ is $f(1,1)^t$. Since the order of $f(1,1)$ is 2, this is equal to $f(1,1)$ if t is odd and 1 if t is even. As a consequence, there is one bit in the output of $MP^{(m)}$ which is 1 iff t is odd. Hence, this bit is identical to $IP(x_1, y_1, \ldots, x_n, y_n)$.
The 2-PLCs we construct consist of 3 linear combinations which are representable with at most $c' \log m$ bits. This has the following consequence: Given n rows

consisting of n bits each, we can store the PLCs of $n/3$ variables in those rows if $c' \log m \leq n$, hence for all $m \leq 2^{cn}$, the PLCs can be used to give a polynomial projection reduction from $IP_{n/3}$ to $MP_n^{(m)}$. This then yields that $MP_n^{(m)}$ needs exponential size in threshold circuits of depth 2.
We can now concentrate our attention on finding appropriate 2-PLCs.

3 Numbers containing a prime factor larger than 3

In this section, we give 2-PLCs for every number m which contains a prime larger than 3 in its prime factorization.

Lemma 6. *The following PLC f is a 2-PLC modulo m, for every $m \geq 5$ which is neither divisible by 2 nor 3:* $(-2x+1-\frac{y}{3}) \cdot (-2x+3y+1) \cdot (1-\frac{5}{8}y)$.

Proof. Since m is not divisible by 2 or 3, the existence of $\frac{1}{8}$ and $\frac{1}{3}$ is guaranteed. We have $f(x,0) = (-2x+1)^2 = 1$ for $x \in \{0,1\}$. Furthermore, $f(0,1) = (1-\frac{1}{3}) \cdot 4 \cdot (\frac{3}{8}) \equiv 1 \bmod m$, and $f(1,1) = (-1-\frac{1}{3}) \cdot 2 \cdot (\frac{3}{8}) \equiv -1 \bmod m$. Since $\mathrm{ord}_m(-1) = 2$, we have shown that f is a 2-PLC modulo m. □

Lemma 6 leaves open the question what we can show for numbers which are divisible by 2 or 3. The next lemma provides us with a method to obtain 2-PLCs for numbers m which contain at least one other prime besides 2 and 3 in their factorization.

Lemma 7. *Let $m_1, m_2 \geq 2$ be relatively prime. Assume that f is a 2-PLC modulo m_1. Let $f = f_1 \cdots f_k$ be the factorization of f into its linear combinations. There are two numbers r_1 and r_2 which only depend on m_1 and m_2 such that $f' := \prod_{i=1}^{k}(r_1 \cdot f_i + r_2)$ is a 2-PLC modulo $m_1 \cdot m_2$.*

Proof. By the Chinese Remainder Theorem, we can choose two numbers r_1 and r_2 such that $r_1 \equiv 1 \bmod m_1$, $r_1 \equiv 0 \bmod m_2$, and $r_2 \equiv 0 \bmod m_1$, $r_2 \equiv 1 \bmod m_2$. This yields that $f'(x,y) \equiv f(x,y) \bmod m_1$ and $f'(x,y) \equiv 1 \bmod m_2$. We apply $\mathrm{ord}_{m_1 \cdot m_2}(a) = \mathrm{lcm}(\mathrm{ord}_{m_1}(a), \mathrm{ord}_{m_2}(a))$ to $a := f'(x,y)$ and find that since $\mathrm{ord}_{m_2}(a) = 1$, $f'(x,y)$ has the same order modulo $m_1 m_2$ as $f(x,y)$ has modulo m_1. Hence, f' is a 2-PLC modulo $m_1 m_2$. □

It should be noted that we need not know a 2-PLC modulo m_2 in the above lemma, hence it can also be applied if e.g. $m_2 = 3$. Note further that the lemma can also be applied if we are searching for 3-PLCs instead of 2-PLCs.
We are allowed to apply Lemma 7 to construct 2-PLCs in the case when one of m_1, m_2 is even. But, in order to get a projection reduction from these 2-PLCs, we also have to ensure that the PLCs can be represented. We now show that 2-PLCs constructed according to Lemma 7 have this property if we apply it carefully.
Assume therefore that we apply Lemma 7 with $m_1 = 2^i$, m_2 odd, and a PLC f modulo m_1 which is representable modulo m_1. A linear combination $ax + by + c$

within this PLC is turned by the technique of Lemma 7 into a linear combination which is equivalent to $ax + by + c$ modulo m_1. Lemma 4 shows that all linear combinations in the PLC f' can be represented modulo $m_1 m_2$.
The other case is when we apply Lemma 7 with m_1 odd and $m_2 = 2^i$. In that case, every linear combination within f' is equivalent to 1 modulo m_2 which is surely representable modulo m_2. Applying Lemma 4 again yields that f' is representable modulo $m_1 m_2$. Altogether, we have proved the following theorem:

Theorem 8. *For every $m \geq 5$ which contains a prime factor larger than 3, one can construct a 2-PLC modulo m which is also representable modulo m with only $O(\log m)$ many bits. As a consequence, there is a constant c such that if $m \leq 2^{cn}$ has a prime factor larger than 3, then $MP_n^{(m)}$ needs exponential size when computed in threshold circuits of depth 2.*

Proof. We apply Lemma 6 to the largest number which divides m and which is not divisible by 2 or 3, and then use Lemma 7 in case m is divisible by 2 or 3. The fact that the second statement in the theorem is a consequence of the first was already discussed in Section 2. □

Example 1. Let $m_1 = 5^2$ and $m_2 = 2^2$. Modulo m_1, we have $1/3 = 17, \quad 1/8 = 22$. Lemma 6 yields the 2-PLC $f := (-2x+1-17y)\,(-2x+3y+1)\,(1-10y)$ modulo 25. Applying Lemma 7 (with $r_1 = 76$, $r_2 = 25$), we find $(48x + 8y + 1)(48x + 28y + 1)(40y + 1)$ which is the desired (representable) 2-PLC modulo 100.

The only moduli m which remain to be investigated are of the form $2^i 3^j$. The next two sections are devoted to numbers of this form.

4 Powers of 2

Computing $MP_n^{(2^i)}$ corresponds to splitting off the bits $0, \ldots, i-1$ of MP_n. This means that $MP_n^{(2^{i+1})}$ contains $MP_n^{(2^i)}$ as a subproblem. Thus, from a statement like "$MP_n^{(2^i)}$ cannot be computed in TC_2^0", it would follow immediately that $MP_n^{(2^{i+1})}$ cannot be computed in TC_2^0. Nevertheless, this would not tell us anything about whether we could compute bit i in TC_2^0 or not.
Hence, to make our statements as strong as possible, we consider in this section the functions $h_n^{(2^i)}$ which are 1 iff bit number $i-1$ in MP_n is 1.
First, we exhibit 2-PLCs which show that for $i \geq 4$, $h_n^{(2^i)}$ cannot be computed in TC_2^0. We then show that for $i < 4$, $h_n^{(2^i)}$ can in fact be computed in TC_2^0.

Lemma 9. *Let $i \geq 4$ and $a := 2^{i-2}$. Then the following PLC f is a 2-PLC modulo 2^i which is also representable modulo 2^i: $(ay+1) \cdot (3ay+(a-2)x+1) \cdot ((3a-2)x+1)$. f also has the property that $f(1,1) \equiv (2^{i-1}+1) \mod 2^i$.*

Proof. For $i \geq 4$, it holds that $a^2 = 2^{2i-4} \equiv 0 \mod 2^i$. We conclude $f(0,y) = (ay+1) \cdot (3ay+1) = 3a^2y^2 + 4ay + 1 \equiv 1 \mod 2^i$ and $f(1,0) = (a-1) \cdot (3a-$

$1) = 3a^2 - 4a + 1 \equiv 1 \bmod 2^i$. And, $f(1,1) = (a+1) \cdot (4a-1) \cdot (3a-1) \equiv -(3a^2 + 2a - 1) \equiv 1 - 2a \equiv 2^i + 1 - 2^{i-1} \equiv 2^{i-1} + 1 \equiv 2a + 1 \bmod 2^i$. Since $(2a+1)^2 = 4a^2 + 4a + 1 \equiv 1 \bmod 2^i$, we have that $f(1,1)$ is an element of order 2. Hence, f is a 2-PLC modulo 2^i.

Every linear combination within f is representable modulo 2^i: For the first and third linear combination, this is obvious since a and $3a-2$ are even numbers, for the second linear combination it suffices to see that $3a = 2a + a = 2^{i-1} + 2^{i-2}$, and $a - 2 = 2^{i-3} + \cdots + 2^1$. □

Figure 1 in Section 2 shows the projection reduction which corresponds to the 2-PLC modulo 16 constructed according to Lemma 9. Looking at the way we construct projection reductions from PLCs, we find that because of $f(1,1) \equiv (2^{i-1} + 1) \bmod 2^i$, it is bit number $i-1$ which in the projection reduction is identical to the Inner Product modulo 2. Hence, $h_n^{(2^i)}$ is not in TC_2^0 for $i \geq 4$. The representation size of the PLC from Lemma 9 is $i-1$, hence if i is allowed to grow with n, we this time get: As long as $4 \leq i \leq n$, there is a projection reduction from $IP_{n/3}$ to $h_n^{(2^i)}$ which proves that the bits in positions 3 to $n-1$ are not computable in TC_2^0. The following should be noted: There is a reduction in [HMPST] which shows that the multiplication of two numbers cannot be computed in TC_2^0. That reduction can be used if i is growing in some way with n. The strength of our reduction is that it already works for very small i.

For $i \leq 3$, the situation is different. For those i, $h_n^{(2^i)}$ can be computed in TC_2^0. We first prove that $h_n^{(2)}$, $h_n^{(4)}$ and $h_n^{(8)}$ can be computed in circuits of the following form, with polynomially many gates. The output OR-gate gets some AND-gates as inputs. The AND-gates either only get literals as inputs or literals plus exactly one parity-gate which also only gets literals as inputs. (A literal is a variable or the negation of a variable.)

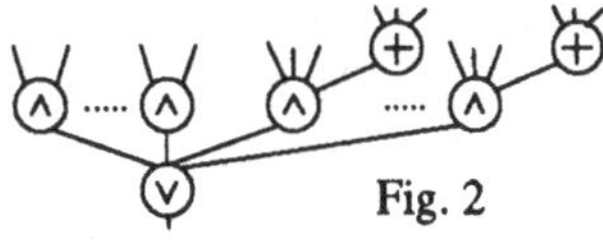

Fig. 2

The following property will be quite useful: *If the number x is even, then* $x \bmod 2^k = 2(\frac{x}{2} \bmod 2^{k-1})$. This property can be exploited as follows: Assume that we want to compute $h^{(2^k)}(z_1, \ldots, z_n)$. If one of the input numbers, say z_i, is even, then the value of $h^{(2^k)}$ on this input is identical to the value of $h^{(2^{k-1})}$ on input $z_1, \ldots, z_{i-1}, z_i/2, z_{i+1}, \ldots, z_n$. To realize our idea, we define the following test functions $t_1, \ldots, t_{n+1}$ which check whether some input numbers z_i are even: $t_i := z_{1,0} \wedge \cdots \wedge z_{i-1,0} \wedge \overline{z_{i,0}}$ for $i \leq n$ and $t_{n+1} := z_{1,0} \wedge \cdots \wedge z_{n,0}$. Especially, (for $1 \leq i \leq n$), $t_i = 1 \Leftrightarrow z_i$ is the first even number. t_{n+1} is 1 if all z_i are odd. It should be noted that by definition, exactly one function t_i computes 1, the others compute 0.

$h_n^{(2)}$ is 1 iff all input numbers are odd, hence it is identical to t_{n+1} and can be computed in a circuit of the above form (using some dummy gates).

We now compute $h^{(4)}$ using $h^{(2)}$. Since $h^{(4)}$ only depends on the 2 least significant bits of the z_i, we can assume that all input numbers are smaller than 4.

Define the functions $G_i := h^{(2)}(z_1, \ldots, z_{i-1}, z_i', z_{i+1}, \ldots, z_n)$, for $1 \leq i \leq n$, where z_i' is obtained from z_i by shifting the bits one position to the right and ignoring the least significant bit.

If z_i is even, then by the above remarks, G_i is identical to $h^{(4)}(z_1, \ldots, z_n)$.
Suppose that every z_i is odd. Consequently, all input numbers are either 1 or 3. The product of these numbers is either 1 or 3 modulo 4. Since $3^2 = 1 \bmod 4$, we find that $h^{(4)}$ is 1 iff there is an odd number of 3's in the input. This can easily be tested by $G_{n+1} := z_{1,1} \oplus \cdots \oplus z_{n,1}$.
Altogether, we get the following formula: $h^{(4)} = \bigvee_{i=1}^{n+1} (t_i \wedge G_i)$.
For each G_i $(1 \leq i \leq n)$, we have already designed circuits of the form described in Figure 2. The expression $(t_i \wedge G_i)$ can be realized by putting the literals which occur in t_i into the AND-gates of the circuit for G_i. The OR-gate can be melted together with the OR-gate of the G_i's. $G_{n+1} \wedge t_{n+1}$ contributes an AND-gate with a parity as input.
We proceed in a similar fashion with $h^{(8)}$. Again, we can assume that all input numbers are smaller than 8. We will use the following proposition in which $a_i := \#\{j | z_j = i\}$ counts how many inputs have the value i. Its proof is immediate from the graphical representation of the multiplication table modulo 8 given below.

Proposition 10. *If* $z_1, \ldots, z_n \bmod 8 \in \{1,3,5,7\}$, *then* $z_1 \cdots z_n \bmod 8$ *is in* $\{5,7\}$ *if and only if* $a_5 + a_7$ *is odd.*

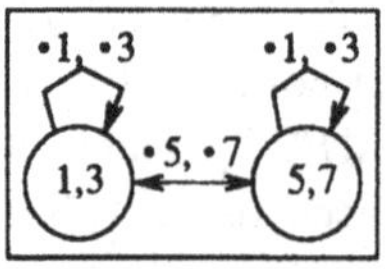

To construct a circuit for $h^{(8)}$, we proceed as follows. If one of the input numbers is even, we can compute, as we did for $h^{(4)}$, the function $t_i \wedge G'_i$, where G'_i is obtained from G_i by replacing $h^{(2)}$ by $h^{(4)}$. We now have to consider the case where all input numbers are odd, i.e., from $\{1,3,5,7\}$. By Proposition 10, we only have to count how many input numbers are 5 or 7. As all numbers are odd, we can identify the 5's and 7's by bit number 2, namely: $z_i \in \{5,7\} \Leftrightarrow z_{i,2} = 1$. Consequently, $a_5 + a_7$ is odd if and only if $G_{n+1} := z_{1,2} \oplus \cdots \oplus z_{n,2} = 1$. We get a term $t_{n+1} \wedge G_{n+1}$. Analogously to $h^{(4)}$, we can now compute $h^{(8)}$ in a circuit of the form described in Figure 2.
We now sketch how such a circuit can be transformed into a TC_2^0-circuit. Consider an AND-gate which has a parity function and literals as input. Using a known trick called "wire-encoding" (see e.g. [H]), it can be computed by a "symmetric" gate. Let us sketch this shortly: Let the literals entering the parity gate be $v_1, \ldots, v_t$ and the other literals be $w_1, \ldots, w_T$. Then the output of the AND-gate only depends on the value of $(T+1)\sum_{i=1}^{t} v_i + \sum_{i=1}^{T} w_i$. Such "symmetric" functions are easy to realize in depth-2 threshold circuits; furthermore, they are 1-approximable.
This means that the output OR-gate can be seen as a gate which gets 1-approximable functions as input and hence the whole circuit can be simulated in polynomial-size, depth-2 threshold circuits.
(As a remark, it should be noted that due to the choice of our test functions, the above circuit also shows that $h^{(2)}, h^{(4)}$, and $h^{(8)}$ are 1-approximable. Namely, at most one input of the OR-gate is 1. Therefore, the output can be regarded as exactly representable by 1-approximable functions. As a consequence, the function computed by the whole circuit is also 1-approximable.)

5 Powers of 3

We start by showing that the situation for computing the multiple product modulo 3 is different. Namely, we show that there is no projection reduction from the Inner Product modulo 2 to $MP_n^{(3)}$. This means that the reduction technique which is behind Theorem 8 has to fail when applied to $MP^{(3)}$.

Theorem 11. *For all n, there is no projection reduction from IP_5 to $MP_n^{(3)}$.*

Proof. In order to get a contradiction, let us assume that we can find a projection reduction. Again, we visualize the factors as rows where in the bit positions we have variables or constants. (Negations of variables can easily be simulated since $-1 = 2 \bmod 3$.) Let $V := \{x_1, y_1, \ldots, x_5, y_5\}$ be the set of binary variables. We recall that a row corresponds to an expression of the form $a_1x_1 + b_1y_1 + \cdots + a_5x_5 + b_5y_5 + c$, where all a_i, b_i and c are taken from the set $\{0, 1, 2\}$.
We consider first in which situations we can force the value of a row to 0 (modulo 3) by some variable assignment. Let the row be given by the above expression. If $c = 0$, we can set all variables to 0 and force the value of the row to 0. If $c = 1$, and there is one variable v where the coefficient of v is 2, then we set $v := 1$, and all other variables to 0. If $c = 1$, and there are at least two variables v_1, and v_2 which have the coefficient 1, then we set $v_1 := v_2 := 1$, and all other variables to 0. The case $c = 2$ can be treated analogously. Thus, the only rows which cannot be forced to 0 are of the form $1, 2, (v+1)$, or $2(v+1)$ for some variable v.
We now return to the projection reduction. Assume that no row in this projection reduction can be forced to 0 by some variable assignment. By the above arguments, the projection reduction then corresponds to a PLC f in which every linear combination is of the form $1, 2, (v+1)$ or $2(v+1)$ for some variable v.
f has to depend essentially on all variables since IP_5 depends essentially on all variables. Furthermore, we have $(v+1)^2 \equiv 1 \bmod 3$ for $v \in \{0,1\}$. This means that for some $i \in \{0,1\}$, f is equivalent to $2^i(x_1+1)(y_1+1)\cdots(x_n+1)(y_n+1)$. Then we have $f(0,0,0,\ldots,0) = f(1,1,0,\ldots,0) \bmod 3$, but the Inner Product modulo 2 yields 0 on the first, and 1 on the second input. Thus, f cannot correspond to a projection reduction which yields a contradiction. This contradiction was caused by the assumption that there is no row in the projection reduction which can be forced to 0.
We now investigate a row which can be forced to 0 and the corresponding variable assignment more closely. Let the value of IP_5 on this assignment be s. The value of the multiple product modulo 3 on this assignment is of course 0.
For every pair (x_i, y_i) it holds that changing it either to $(0,0)$ or to $(1,1)$ will change the output of IP_5. Hence, the value of the row under consideration also needs to change since otherwise the multiple product would remain 0.
For all pairs (x_i, y_i) we mark by which amount the value of the row will change. Let us call this value d_i. We have just seen that $d_i \in \{1, 2\}$.
We have 5 variable pairs, hence, by the pigeonhole principle, there are at least three d_i which are equal, let us assume w.l.o.g. that $d_1 = d_2 = d_3$.

By changing the assignments of these pairs, the output of IP_5 will change 3 times, hence it is then equal to $s \oplus 1$. On the other hand, the value of the row will be changed by an amount of $3d_1 \equiv 0 \bmod 3$, hence the multiple product is still zero. This is a contradiction. □

By a finer analysis, one could improve upon the constant 5 in Theorem 11. Three further things should be noted: First, the proof of Theorem 11 shows more than that there are no 2-PLCs modulo 3 since in general there might be projection reductions which work in a different manner. This is why we have to deal with zero rows in the above proof. Second, it can easily be seen that computing whether the multiple product is divisible by 3 is in TC_2^0. Nevertheless, this does not tell us anything about how the bits in the representation can be computed. Third, it is easy to see that 2-PLCs modulo 3^i are also 2-PLCs modulo 3, hence there are none. This indicates that we have to treat powers of 3 differently.
One way out is to consider the "inner product modulo 3", IP^*, defined by $IP^* = x_1y_1 + \cdots + x_ny_n \bmod 3$. In order to turn IP^* into a Boolean function $f^{(IP3)}$, we have to find some appropriate encoding. We choose $f^{(IP3)} = 1 \Leftrightarrow IP^* = 0$.
It has been shown in [KW] that if we have a threshold circuit of depth 2 which gets binary coded values from $\{0, 1, 2\}$ as input and which has to compute some binary encoding of IP^* (over Z_3), then this circuit needs exponential size. This result can be used to show that the Boolean function $f^{(IP3)}$ cannot be computed in TC_2^0 ([K2]).
This suggests that one should try to find 3-PLCs modulo 3^i. We omit the details why the existence of a 3-PLC modulo 3^i guarantees that there is a projection reduction from $f^{(IP3)}$ to $MP^{(3^i)}$ and report instead the 3-PLCs that we have found. We need the following number theoretic proposition: (see e.g. [S], p.61)

Proposition 12. *Let $i \geq 2$. If p is an odd prime, then the set of primitive roots modulo p^i consists of all elements x which are primitive roots modulo p and which fulfill $x^{p-1} \not\equiv 1 \bmod p^2$. In particular, 2 is a primitive root modulo 3^i.*

Lemma 13. *For $i \geq 2$, let $w = 2^{2 \cdot 3^{i-2}}$, $b = \frac{w+1}{2} - 1$, $a = \frac{2}{w+1} - 1$. Then the PLC $f := (-2x + 1) \cdot (-2x + ay + 1) \cdot (by + 1)$ is a 3-PLC modulo 3^i.*

Proof. We first have to ensure that the inverses modulo 3^i used in the definition of the parameters do exist. For $1/2$, this is clear. w is a power of 4, hence $w \equiv 1 \bmod 3$, and $w + 1 \equiv 2 \bmod 3$ has an inverse. Now we evaluate f: $f(x, 0) = (-2x+1)^2 = 1$, $f(0, 1) = (a+1)(b+1) \equiv 1 \bmod 3^i$ and $f(1, 1) = (1-a)(b+1) \equiv w \bmod 3^i$. The order of $f(1, 1)$ is 3, by the following argument: 2 is a primitive root modulo 3^i, hence it has order $2 \cdot 3^{i-1}$. Thus, w has order 3. □

For example, $(-2x + 1) \cdot (-2x + 3y + 1) \cdot (6y + 1)$ is a 3-PLC modulo 9.
Lemma 13 shows that there is a bit in the binary representation of $MP^{(3^i)}, i \geq 2$ fixed, which cannot be computed in TC_2^0.
We have noted earlier that the technique from Lemma 7 can also be used to obtain 3-PLCs for numbers m which are of the form $3^i \cdot r$, $i \geq 2$.

This yields that the only moduli that we were not able to classify are of the form $3 \cdot 2^i$, with $i \leq 3$ since to all other numbers of the form $2^i 3^j$, one of the PLC construction methods can be applied.

6 Final remarks

We were able to classify for all fixed numbers $m \notin \{3, 6, 12, 24\}$, whether the multiple product modulo m can be computed in polynomial-size threshold circuits of depth 2. For $m = 24$, we have the strange situation that we are able to provide 2-PLCs modulo 24, nevertheless, we have not found a 2-PLC which is also representable. One example of such a PLC is $(-2x+12y+1)(-2x+18y+1)(6y+1)$.

Acknowledgments Our thanks go to Petr Savický for suggesting to us an improvement in Theorem 11, to Hanno Lefmann for pointing us to Proposition 12, and to Matthias Krause for stimulating discussions, in particular for suggesting the investigation of 3-PLCs instead of 2-PLCs for computing modulo 9.

References

[HMPST] A. Hajnal, W. Maass, P. Pudlák, M. Szegedy, G. Turán, *Threshold circuits of bounded depth,* Proceedings of 28th FOCS, 1987, 99-110.

[GHR] M. Goldmann, J. Håstad, A. Razborov, *Majority gates vs. general weighted threshold gates,* Proc. 7th Structures (1992), pp. 2-13.

[GK] M. Goldmann, M. Karpinski, *Simulating threshold circuits by majority circuits,* Proc. 25th STOC, 1993, p. 551-560.

[H] T. Hofmeister, *Depth-efficient threshold circuits for arithmetic functions,* Chap. 2 in: Theoretical Advances in Neural Computation and Learning, V. Roychowdhury, K-Y. Siu, and A. Orlitsky (eds.), Kluwer Academic Publ.

[K1] M. Krause, *On realizing iterated multiplication by small depth threshold circuits,* Proc. of 12th STACS (1995), 83-94.

[K2] M. Krause, pers. comm.

[KW] M. Krause, S. Waack, *Variation ranks of communication matrices and lower bounds for depth two circuits having symmetric gates with unbounded fan-in,* Proc. of 32nd FOCS, 1991, 777-782.

[R] A. Razborov, *On small depth threshold circuits,* In Proc. 3rd Scandinavian Workshop on Algorithm Theory, 42-52, LNCS 621, 1992.

[S] A. Scholz, B. Schoeneberg, *Einführung in die Zahlentheorie,* Sammlung Göschen, Band 5131, Walter de Gruyter, 1973

[SBKH] K.-Y. Siu, J. Bruck, T. Kailath, T. Hofmeister, *Depth efficient neural networks for division and related problems,* IEEE Transactions on Information Theory, May 1993, p. 946-956.

[SR] K.-Y. Siu, V. Roychowdhury, *On optimal depth threshold circuits for multiplication and related problems,* SIAM Journal on Discrete Mathematics 7 (1994), p. 285-292.

[W] I. Wegener, *Optimal lower bounds on the depth of polynomial-size threshold circuits for some arithmetic functions,* Inf. Proc. Letters 46 (1993), p. 85-87.

Lower Bounds for the Majority Communication Complexity of Various Graph Accessibility Problems

Christoph Meinel[1] and Stephan Waack[2]

[1] Theoretische Informatik, Fachbereich IV, Universität Trier, D–54286 Trier
[2] Inst. für Num. und Angew. Mathematik, Univ. Göttingen, Lotzestr. 16–18, D–37083 Göttingen

Introduction

The *graph accessibility problem* GAP $= (\mathrm{GAP}_n)_{n\in\mathbf{N}}$ consists in the decision whether there is a path in a given directed, acyclic n-node graph $G = (V, E)$, $V = \{1, \ldots, n\}$ and $E \subseteq V \times V$, that leads from vertex 1 to vertex n. As usual, let G be given by its adjacency matrix $G = (a_{ij})_{1\le i,j\le n, i\ne j}$ with

$$a_{ij} = a(i,j) = \begin{cases} 1 & \text{if } (i,j) \in E\,; \\ 0 & \text{otherwise.} \end{cases}$$

$\mathrm{GAP}_n : \{0,1\}^{n^2} \longrightarrow \{0,1\}$, is defined by

$$(a_{ij}) \longrightarrow \begin{cases} 1 & \text{if there is a path in the graph described by } (a_{ij}) \text{ from 1 to } n; \\ 0 & \text{otherwise.} \end{cases}$$

The major property of GAP is the following one.

Theorem 1. GAP *is complete for the complexity class* NL *of languages acceptable by nondeterministic logarithmic space-bounded Turing machines via logspace reductions (see [15]), via projection translations (see [6]), and via p-projection reductions for nonuniform* NL *(see [8]).* □

Soon it was realized (see, e.g.,[9]) that certain modified GAPs, denoted by MOD_k-GAP, $k \geq 2$, have similar properties for the complexity classes MOD_k–L, defined by logarithmic space–bounded Turing machines equipped with the counting acceptation mode MOD_k. Here, an input is accepted, if and only if the number of accepting computations is *not* congruent 0 modulo k.

$\mathrm{MOD}_k\text{-GAP}_n : \{0,1\}^{n^2} \longrightarrow \{0,1\}$, is defined by

$$(a_{ij}) \longrightarrow \begin{cases} 1 & \text{the number of paths in } (a_{ij}) \text{ from 1 to } n \text{ is not divisible by } k; \\ 0 & \text{otherwise.} \end{cases}$$

A generalization of Theorem 1 yields the following theorem which is true for the various reduction notions. (For a proof, e.g. of the p-projection completeness, we refer to [10].)

Theorem 2. MOD_k-GAP *is complete for* MOD_k-L, $k \geq 2$. □

From Theorems 1 and 2 it becomes clear why it is an important goal in complexity theory to characterize the complexity of graph accessibility problems. In [17], Yao started the study of the communication complexity of graph problems. In [5], the deterministic communciation complexity of *connectivity* and *s-t-connectivity* (for undirected graphs) was investigated. There the problem of proving lower bounds on the *probabilistic communication complexity* of graph problems was raised. In the following we contribute to the solution of this problem by investigating the *majority communication complexity* of the graph accessibility problems GAP and MOD_k-GAP, $k \geq 2$.

Let a graph $G = (V, E)$ be given, in arbitarily distributed form, to two processors P_1 and P_2 with unbounded computational power. In order to solve GAP or MOD_k-GAP, both processors have to communicate via a common communication tape. The computation of the whole structure, which is called a *communication protocol* or simply a *protocol*, is going on in *rounds*. Starting with P_1, the processors write alternatingly bits on the communication tape. These bits depend on the input available to the processor which is to move and on the bits already written on the communication tape before. We assume without loss of generality that in each round exactly one bit is written on the communication tape and that all (nondeterministic) computations of a protocol are of equal length, say L. If the last bit written on the communication tape is "1" or "0", the particular computation is called *accepting* or *rejecting*, respectively. (Since we shall assume the processors to be nondeterministic, this last bit need not to coincide with the output of the protocol.) So co-operative computations can be thought of as to be Boolean strings. The length L of the string is the *communication complexity* of the computation. (For more reading on communciation complexity we refer, e.g., to [1], [2], [3], [4], [7]). Since our processors are nondeterministic we have to define the *output of* of a protocol by means of a certain *acception mode*. In this paper we consider the probabilistic *majority acception mode* in which a protocol *accepts* an input, if the number of accepting computations is greater than the number of rejecting ones.

We prove that all graph accessibility problems, defined before, have majority communication complexity $\Omega(n)$, where n is the number of nodes of the graph under consideration.

Simular bounds could be proved recently for the modular communication complexity of GAP and MOD_m-GAP [11]. For the nondeterministic communication complexity Raz and Spieker derived the lower bound $\Omega(n \log\log n)$ [14]. However, the optimal lower bound $\theta(n \log n)$ could be proved up to now merely for the deterministic communication complexity [5].

1 The Computational Model

In order to be able to receive our results we need a precise formal definition of the considered computational model which was described informally already in the introduction. Let $f : S_1 \times S_2 \to \{0,1\}$ be given in distributed form. (Throughout this paper, S_1 and S_2 are either $\{0,1\}^n$ or $\mathbb{Z}/m\mathbb{Z}$.) A *protocol of length* L consisting of two processors P_1 and P_2 which access inputs of S_1 and S_2, respectively, can be described by two functions

$$\Phi_i : S_i \times \{0,1\}^{\leq L} \to \{0,1\},$$

$i = 1,2$. The interpretation is as follows. Let $\gamma = \gamma_1 \dots \gamma_j$, $\gamma_k \in \{0,1\}$. If $\Phi_i(s_i, \gamma) = 1$, and if $|\gamma| - i$ is even, then the corresponding processor P_i is able to write γ_j on the communication tape provided that it has read $\gamma_1 \dots \gamma_{j-1}$ on the communication tape and that it has s_i as input. If, however, $\Phi_i(s_i, \gamma) = 0$, then P_i is not able to write γ_j.

The work of a protocol P of length L can be described in terms of two $\#S_1 \times \#S_2$–matrices Acc^P and Rej^P. For $(s_1, s_2) \in S_1 \times S_2$, $Acc^P_{s_1,s_2}$ gives the number of accepting computations of the protocol P on the input (s_1, s_2), and $Rej^P_{s_1,s_2}$ gives the number of rejecting computations.

In order to make this approach unique, we agree that $\Phi_i(s_i, \gamma) = 1$, if $|\gamma| - i$ is odd, for $i = 1,2$.

$$Acc^P_{s_1,s_2} \stackrel{def}{=} \sum_{\gamma_1 \cdots \gamma_L \in \{0,1\}^L, \gamma_L = 1} \prod_{j=1}^{L} \Phi_{(1+(j+1) \bmod 2)}(s_{(1+(j+1) \bmod 2)}, \gamma_1 \dots \gamma_j) \quad (1)$$

$$Rej^P_{s_1,s_2} \stackrel{def}{=} \sum_{\gamma_1 \cdots \gamma_L \in \{0,1\}^L,\ \gamma_L = 0} \prod_{j=1}^{L} \Phi_{1+((j+1) \bmod 2)}(s_{1+((j+1) \bmod 2)}, \gamma_1 \dots \gamma_j) \quad (2)$$

Increasing the length of P by at most two, it can be achieved that $Acc^P_{s_1,s_2} \neq Rej^P_{s_1,s_2}$ for all inputs (s_1, s_2). In the following, we assume that all protocols will have this property.

A *counting accepting mode* μ for a protocol P is a function $\mu : \mathbf{N}^2 \to \{0,1\}$ such that P accepts a distributed input (s_1, s_2) if and only if $\mu(Acc^P_{s_1,s_2}, Rej^P_{s_1,s_2}) = 1$. Otherwise P rejects the input. In the following we consider the probabilistic *majority accepting mode* $\text{MAJ}(n_1, n_2) = 1 \stackrel{def}{\iff} n_1 > n_2$. which leads to an acception of a given input if the number of accepting computations exeeds that of rejecting computations.

Definition 3. *A protocol P equipped with the accepting mode* MAJ *is called a* majority-protocol. *The* majority communication complexity MAJ-Comm(f) *of a function $f : S_1 \times S_2 \to \{0,1\}$ is defined by*
MAJ-Comm(f) $\stackrel{def}{=}$ $\min\{$ *length*$(P) \mid f_P = f$ $\}$, *where f_P denotes the function computed by the majority-protocol P.*

Investigating communication complexity, the appropriate type of reduction is that of rectangular reductions which are defined as follows: Let $F = (F_{2n} : \Sigma^n \times \Sigma^n \to \{0,1\})_{n \in \mathbf{N}}$ and $G = (G_{2n} : \Gamma^n \times \Gamma^n \to \{0,1\})_{n \in \mathbf{N}}$ be two decision problems. F is *rectangularly reducible* to G with respect to q (denoted by $F \leq^q_{rec} G$), where $q : \mathbf{N} \to \mathbf{N}$ is a nondecreasing function, if, for each n, there are two transformations $l_n, r_n : \Sigma^n \to \Gamma^{q(n)}$ such that for all $\mathbf{x}, \mathbf{y} \in \Sigma^n$ $F_{2n}(\mathbf{x}, \mathbf{y}) = G_{2q(n)}(l_n(\mathbf{x}), r_n(\mathbf{y}))$.

Rectangular reductions can be used for proving lower bounds on the majority communication complexity in the following way: Let $q : \mathbb{N} \to \mathbb{N}$ be an unbounded nondecreasing function. Then we define $q^{(-1)}$ by $q^{(-1)}(i) = \max\{j | \; q(j) \leq i\}$. Standard arguments yield

Lemma 4. *Assume there are given two sequences of functions* $F = (F_{2n} : \Sigma^n \times \Sigma^n \to \{0,1\})_{n\in\mathbb{N}}$ *and* $G = (G_{2n} : \Gamma^n \times \Gamma^n \to \{0,1\})_{n\in\mathbb{N}}$. *If* $c(n) \leq$ MAJ-Comm(F) *and* $F \leq^q_{rec} G$, *then* $c \circ q^{(-1)}(n) \leq$ MAJ-Comm(G). □

One efficient way to get rectangular reductions is to work with projection reductions [16] which are defined as follows.

Definition 5. Let $F = (F_n : \Sigma^n \to \{0,1\})_{n\in\mathbb{N}}$ and $G = (G_n : \Gamma^n \to \{0,1\})_{n\in\mathbb{N}}$. The mapping $\pi_n : \{y_1, \ldots, y_m\} \to \{x_1, \ldots, x_n, \neg x_1, \ldots, \neg x_n\} \cup \Gamma$ is called a *projection reduction* from F_n to G_m if $F_n(x_1, \ldots, x_n) = G_m(\pi(y_1), \ldots, \pi(y_m))$. If F_n and G_m are given in distributed form,

$$F_{2n} : \Sigma^n \times \Sigma^n \to \{0,1\} \text{ and } G_{2m} : \Gamma^m \times \Gamma^m \to \{0,1\}$$

then a projection reduction π_n is said to *respect the distribution* of the variables if

$$\pi_n^{-1}\{x_1, \ldots, x_n, \neg x_1, \ldots, \neg x_n\} \subseteq \{y_1, \ldots, y_m\}$$

and

$$\pi_n^{-1}\{x_{n+1}, \ldots, x_{2n}, \neg x_{n+1}, \ldots, \neg x_{2n}\} \subseteq \{y_{m+1}, \ldots, y_{2m}\}.$$

A sequence $\pi = (\pi_n)_n \in \mathbb{N}$ of reduction projections π_n is called a *$p(n)$–projection reduction* and we write $F \leq^p_\pi G$ if $p(n)$ is a nondecreasing function with $m \leq p(n)$.

From Lemma 4 we immediately get

Lemma 6. *Assume that we are given two sequences of functions* $F = (F_{2n} : \Sigma^n \times \Sigma^n \to \{0,1\})_{n\in\mathbb{N}}$ *and* $G = (G_{2m} : \Gamma^m \times \Gamma^m \to \{0,1\})_{m\in\mathbb{N}}$ *with* $F \leq^p_\pi G$, *where p is increasing and* $\pi = (\pi_n)_{n\in\mathbb{N}}$ *is a sequence of projection reductions that respects the distribution of the variables. If* $c(n) \leq$ MAJ-Comm(F), *then* $c \circ q^{(-1)}(n) \leq$ MAJ-Comm(G). □

2 Rank Arguments for Lower Bounds

Following an approach of Mehlhorn and Schmidt, rank arguments can be used for proving lower bounds on the length of communication protocols. Throughout this section, f denotes a function $f : S_1 \times S_2 \to \{0,1\}$ with $N = \#S_1 = \#S_2$. M^f denotes the *communication matrix* of f, which is defined by $M^f_{s_1,s_2} = f(s_1, s_2)$.

Lemma 7. **[12]** *Let R be any semiring. Let P be a protocol of the length L on the input set $S_1 \times S_2$, $\#S_1 = \#S_2 = N$, and let Acc^P and Rej^P be the $N \times N$–matrices defined in equations 1, and 2. Then*

$$\mathrm{rank}_R(Acc^P) \leq 2^{L-1}, \tag{3}$$

$$\mathrm{rank}_R(Rej^P) \leq 2^{L-1}. \ \square \tag{4}$$

In order to derive lower bounds on the length of protocols equipped with the *majority* acceptance mode, we adopt the concept of variation ranks of communication matrices first developed in [7].

Definition 8. *Two real $N \times N$–matrices A and B with nonzero coefficients are called* order–equivalent *if, for all indices i and j, $a_{ij} \cdot b_{ij} \geq 0$. Let θ be a positive natural number, and let A be a real matrix with non-zero coefficients. The* variation rank var-rank$_{\leq,\theta}(A)$ *is the minimum over all numbers* $\mathrm{rank}_{\mathbf{R}} B$*, where B is a $N \times N$–matrix with $b_{ij} \in \{0, \pm 1, \pm 2, \ldots, \pm\theta\}$ that is order–equivalent to A.*

If J denotes the $N \times N$–matrix whose coefficients are equal to 1, then Lemma 7 implies the following corollary.

Corollary 9. $\log_2\left(\text{var-rank}_{\leq,2^L}(2M^f - J)\right) \leq L$, *where L is the length of any* MAJ*-protocol computing f.* $\square$

In order to estimate the variation rank of the matrix $(2M^f - J)$, some linear algebraic considerations and computations are nessecary. Recall that if $\mathbf{R}^N$ is the N–dimensional real vector space of column vectors and if $\mathbf{x}^T\mathbf{y}$ denotes the standard scalar product, then $||\mathbf{x}|| = \sqrt{\mathbf{x}^T\mathbf{x}}$ is the norm induced by this scalar product. Let $A = (a_{ij})$ be a real $N \times N$–matrix. Then $||A|| := \sup\{||A\mathbf{x}|| \mid ||\mathbf{x}|| = 1\}$ is the *spectral norm*, and $||A||_2 := \sqrt{\sum_{i,j} |a_{ij}|^2}$ is the l_2*–norm* of the matrix A. The matrix A is called *orthogonal* if and only if $A^{-1} = A^T$. The following theorem, which is well–known in linear algebra, relates these notions to each other.

Theorem 10. *1.* $\frac{1}{\sqrt{N}}||A||_2 \leq ||A|| \leq ||A||_2$.

2. $\frac{1}{\sqrt{N}}||A||_2 = ||A||$ *if and only if $A = d \cdot U$, where $0 \leq d \in \mathbf{R}$ and U is an orthogonal matrix.* $\square$

Due to the next lemma, the variation rank of a matrix M with coefficients from $\{-1, 1\}$ can be estimated in terms of the norms of certain matrices A which are order–equivalent to M.

Lemma 11. [7] *Let M be an $N \times N$–matrix with $m_{i,j} \in \{-1, 1\}$ If $A = (a_{ij})$ is any $N \times N$–matrix over* $\mathbf{R}$ *that is order–equivalent to M with $1 \leq |a_{ij}| \leq \theta$ for all $1 \leq i, j \leq N$, then* $\frac{||A||_2^2}{\theta^2 \cdot ||A||^2} \leq$ var-rank$_{\leq,\theta}(M)$. $\square$

A straightforward computation using Lemma 11 together with Corollary 9 yields

Lemma 12. *Let A be a real matrix which is order equivalent to $2M^f - J$, where $1 \leq |a_{ij}| \leq \theta$, for all $1 \leq i, j \leq N$. Let $\tilde{A}$ be a square submatrix of A. Then*

$$\frac{2}{3} \log_2 \left(\frac{\|\tilde{A}\|_2}{\|\tilde{A}\|} \right) - 2 \log_2 \theta \;\leq\; \text{MAJ-Comm}(f) \;. \quad \Box$$

Due to Theorem 10, a matrix $\tilde{A}$ is optimal in Lemma 12 if $\tilde{A} = d \cdot \tilde{U}$, where $\tilde{U}$ is orthogonal.

Corollary 13. *If, moreover, $\tilde{A}$ is assumed to be an $\tilde{N} \times \tilde{N}$-submatrix of the matrix A, and if there are a real number $d > 0$ and an orthogonal matrix $\tilde{U}$ such that $\tilde{A} = d \cdot \tilde{U}$, then $\frac{1}{3} \log_2 \tilde{N} - 2 \log_2 \theta \;\leq\; \text{MAJ-Comm}(f)$.* $\Box$

Using Corollary 13, we start to prove lower bounds on the length of majority protocols for some concrete functions. We consider the *MOD_m-orthogonality-test-function* $\text{ORT}^{[m]} = (\text{ORT}_{2n}^{[m]})_{n \in \mathbf{N}}$, $m \geq 2$, which is defined by

$$\text{ORT}_{2n}^{[m]} : (\mathbf{Z}/m\mathbf{Z})^n \times (\mathbf{Z}/m\mathbf{Z})^n \to \{0,1\}_{n \in \mathbf{N}},$$

$$(x_1, \ldots, x_n, y_1, \ldots, y_n) \mapsto \begin{cases} 1 \text{ if } \sum x_i y_i = 0 \text{ in } \mathbf{Z}/m\mathbf{Z}; \\ 0 \text{ otherwise.} \end{cases}$$

The problem is to find a quadratic submatrix M' of $M^{\text{ORT}^{[m]}}$ with large degree, and to find an optimal comparison matrix $\tilde{A}$ of M' in the sense of Corollary 13.

First we look for an appropriate submatrix M' of M. We describe M' by giving its set $\mathcal{R}$ of column indices, $\mathcal{R} \subset (\mathbf{Z}/m\mathbf{Z})^n \cong \left(\mathbf{Z}/p_1^{l_1}\mathbf{Z}\right)^n \times \cdots \times \left(\mathbf{Z}/p_r^{l_r}\mathbf{Z}\right)^n$. Let us assume that the elements of $(\mathbf{Z}/m\mathbf{Z})^n$ and $\left(\mathbf{Z}/p^l\mathbf{Z}\right)^n$ are column vectors. We adopt the usual definition of $\mathbf{Z}/p^l\mathbf{Z}$–linear independence. The following lemma can be proved by the help of arguments from linear algebra.

Lemma 14. *Let $A = (a_{ij})$ be an integer $n \times k$–matrix. Then the vectors $((a_{1j} \bmod p^l), \ldots, (a_{nj} \bmod p^l))^T$, for $j = 1, \ldots k$, are linearly independent over $\mathbf{Z}/p^l\mathbf{Z}$ if and only if the vectors $((a_{1j} \bmod p), \ldots, (a_{nj} \bmod p))^T$, for $j = 1, \ldots k$, are linearly independent over $\mathbf{Z}/p\mathbf{Z}$.* $\Box$

Now we define on the set $\{\mathbf{x} | \mathbf{x} \in \left(\mathbf{Z}/p^l\mathbf{Z}\right)^n, \mathbf{x} \text{ linearly independent}\}$ the equivalence relation

$$\mathbf{x} \sim \mathbf{y} \overset{def}{\iff} \mathbf{x} \text{ and } \mathbf{y} \text{ are linearly dependent over } \mathbf{Z}/p^l\mathbf{Z}.$$

Let, for $p_i = p$, $\mathcal{R}_i$ denote an arbitrary but fixed system of representatives, and let $\mathcal{R} \overset{def}{=} \mathcal{R}_1 \times \cdots \times \mathcal{R}_r$. Then we get

Corollary 15. $\#\mathcal{R} = \frac{p_1^n - 1}{p_1 - 1} \cdot \ldots \cdot \frac{p_r^n - 1}{p_r - 1}$. $\Box$

After having found via $\mathcal{R}$ an appropriate quadratic submatrix M' of $M^{\mathrm{ORT}^{[m]}}$ that is of large degree, we have to construct an optimal comparison matrix $\tilde{A}$ in the sense of Corollary 13. In order to do this, we use the following fact.

Lemma 16. *Let* $\mathbf{x}, \mathbf{y} \in \mathcal{R}$, $\mathbf{x} \neq \mathbf{y}$.

1. $\omega_1^{(n)} \stackrel{def}{=} \#\{\mathbf{z} \mid (\mathbf{z}^T\mathbf{x} = 0) \wedge (\mathbf{z}^T\mathbf{y} = 0)\}/\#\mathcal{R} = \prod_{i=1}^r \frac{p_i^{n-2}-1}{p_i^n-1}$,
2. $\omega_2^{(n)} \stackrel{def}{=} \#\{\mathbf{z} \mid (\mathbf{z}^T\mathbf{x} \neq 0) \wedge (\mathbf{z}^T\mathbf{y} \neq 0)\}/\#\mathcal{R} =$
$= 1 - 2 \cdot \prod_{i=1}^r \frac{p_i^{n-1}-1}{p_i^n-1} + \prod_{i=1}^r \frac{p_i^{n-2}-1}{p_i^n-1}$. □

Proposition 17. *If* $m = p_1^{l_1} \cdot \ldots \cdot p_r^{l_r}$, *where the* p_i *are pairwise different prime numbers, then, for sufficiently large* n,

$$\text{MAJ-Comm}(\mathrm{ORT}_{2n}^{[m]}) \geq \frac{n-7}{3} \log_2(p_1 \cdot \ldots \cdot p_r).$$

Proof. We consider first the following quadratic equation and one of its solutions $t^{(n)}$.

$$0 = T^2 - \frac{1-(\omega_1^{(n)} + \omega_2^{(n)})}{\omega_1^{(n)}} T + \frac{\omega_2^{(n)}}{\omega_1^{(n)}}$$

$$t^{(n)} = \frac{1-(\omega_1^{(n)} + \omega_2^{(n)})}{2\omega_1^{(n)}} + \sqrt{D^{(n)}}$$

The numbers $\omega_i^{(n)}$ were defined in Lemma 16.

Now we define the following matrix $\tilde{A}$ indexed by $\mathcal{R} \times \mathcal{R}$.

$$\tilde{a}_{\mathbf{xy}} \stackrel{def}{=} \begin{cases} t^{(n)} \cdot p_1 \cdot \ldots \cdot p_r & \mathbf{x}^T\mathbf{y} = 0; \\ -p_1 \cdot \ldots \cdot p_r & \text{otherwise}, \end{cases}$$

which is order–equivalent to the corresponding submatrix of $2M^{\mathrm{ORT}^{[m]}} - J$. It can be show that $\tilde{A}^T A = d \cdot I$, for sufficiently large n. The claim follows from Corollary 13 now. □

3 Graph Accessibility Problems

In order to make graph accessibility problems tractable for the model of distributed computation, we assume that the set of input variables is partitioned in an arbitrary way into two sets of equal size. If we speak about projection reductions to GAPs in the sequel, we always mean ones which respect the pre-assigned partition. We visualize the graph, which is the transpose[3] $\pi_n^t(\sigma)$ of a vector $\sigma \in \Sigma^n$, in such a way that the edges which are not constant are drawn as thin lines and are labelled by the corresponding predicates (see Figure 2). All other edges are drawn as thick lines.

[3] The *transpose* $\pi_n^t : \{0,1\}^n \to \{0,1\}^m$ of the projection reduction π is defined by $\pi_n^t(\mathbf{u}) = (\pi_n(y_1)(\mathbf{u}), \ldots, \pi_n(y_m)(\mathbf{u}))$, where $\mathbf{u} = (x_1(\mathbf{u}), \ldots, x_n(\mathbf{u})) \in \{0,1\}^n$.

Lemma 18. *[10] Let $E_1 \cup E_2$ be any partition of the set of all edges $\{1,\dots,n\} \times \{1,\dots,n\}$ into two sets of equal size $\frac{n(n-1)}{2}$. Then there are subsets $E_1' \subseteq E_1$ and $E_2' \subseteq E_2$ such that*

- $\#E_i' \geq \lfloor n/8 - 1 \rfloor$
- *the edges from $E_1' \cup E_2'$ are pairwise vertex-disjoint*
- *neither vertex 1 nor vertex n is incident with any edge from $E_1' \cup E_2'$.* □

The proof of Proposition 19 is easy and that's why omitted.

Proposition 19. *Assume that the input variable set of* GAP *is partitioned in an arbitrary way into two subsets of equal size. Then $\neg\mathrm{ORT}^{[2]} = (\neg\mathrm{ORT}_N)_{N\in\mathbb{N}}$ is reducible to* GAP *via a $(O(n^4))$-projection reduction which respects that partition.* □

Proposition 20. *Let $m \in \mathbb{N}$. Assume that the input variables of* MOD$_m$-GAP *are partitioned in an arbitrary way into two subsets of equal size. Then $\neg\mathrm{ORT}^{[m]} = (\neg\mathrm{ORT}_N^{[m]})_{N\in\mathbb{N}}$ is reducible to* MOD$_m$-GAP *via a $\left((4\binom{m}{2}+1)^2 \cdot n^4\right)$-projection reduction which respects that partition.*

Proof. Let $Y \cup Z$ be the preassigned partition of the set of variables of MOD$_m$-GAP$_{n(n-1)}$ and let

$$Y \supseteq Y' \stackrel{def}{=} \left\{ x_{i_{\kappa,\nu} j_{\kappa,\nu}} \mid \kappa = 1,\dots,r/\binom{m}{2},\ \nu = 1,\dots,\binom{m}{2} \right\}$$

$$Z \supseteq Z' \stackrel{def}{=} \left\{ x_{k_{\kappa,\nu} l_{\kappa,\nu}} \mid \kappa = 1,\dots,r/\binom{m}{2},\ \nu = 1,\dots,\binom{m}{2} \right\}$$

be the two subsets whose existence is insured by Lemma 18. Then we have $r = \lfloor n/8 - 1 \rfloor$ and we assume w.l.o.g. that r is divisible by $\binom{m}{2}$, since m is a universal constant. The projection reduction

$$\pi_{2r/\binom{m}{2}} : \{x_{i,j}\} \to \left\{ 0, 1, (t_\nu = a), (u_\nu = a) \mid \nu = 1,\dots,r/\binom{m}{2}, a \in \mathbb{Z}/m\mathbb{Z} - \{0\} \right\}$$

is defined by means of Figure 2 and Figure 1, in which the transpose $\pi^t_{2r/\binom{m}{2}}$ is shown.

If $(\mathbf{t},\mathbf{u}) \in \{0,1\}^{2r/\binom{m}{2}}$, then an easy calculation reveals that for the number $\left[1 \stackrel{\pi^t(\mathbf{t},\mathbf{u})}{\longrightarrow} n\right]$ of directed paths from vertex 1 to vertex n in the graph $\pi^t(\mathbf{t},\mathbf{u})$ holds

$$\left[1 \stackrel{\pi^t(\mathbf{t},\mathbf{u})}{\longrightarrow} n\right] \equiv \mathbf{t}^T\mathbf{u} \pmod{m},$$

where $\mathbf{t}^T\mathbf{u}$ denotes the standard inner product. □

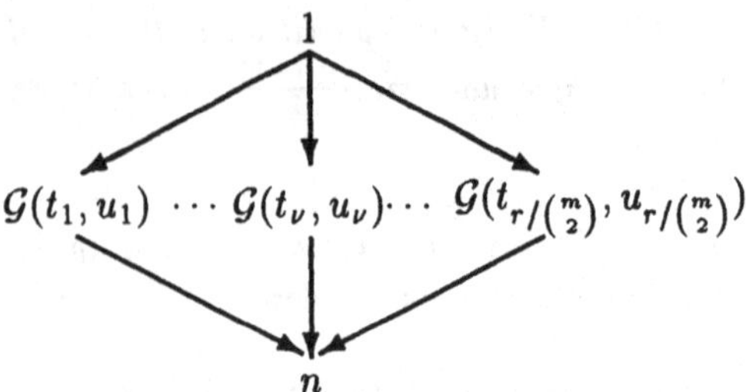

Figure 1. The graph transposed to the instance $(\mathbf{t}, \mathbf{u})$ of $\neg\mathrm{ORT}^{[m]}$

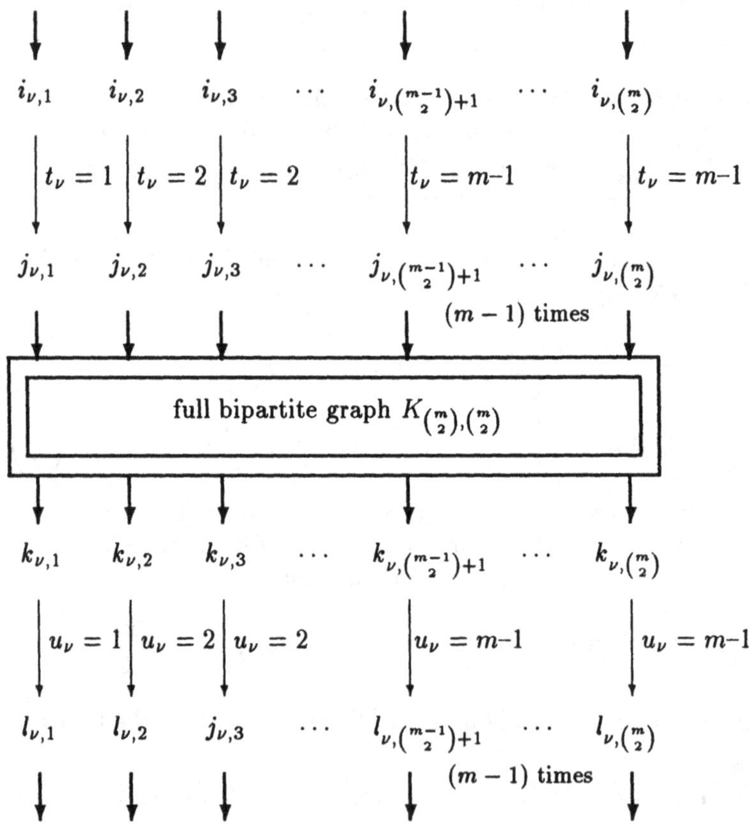

Figure 2. *The subgraph $\mathcal{G}(t_\nu, u_\nu)$ of Figure 1.*

Putting altogether one obtain the announced main theorem of this paper.

Theorem 21.

1. *It holds* MAJ-Comm(GAP_n) = $\Omega(n)$.
2. *Let m be an arbitrary number. Then* MAJ-Comm(MOD_m-GAP_n) = $\Omega(n)$. □

References

1. A. V. Aho, J. D. Ullman, M. Yannakakis, *On notions of information transfer in VLSI circuits*, in: Proc. 15th ACM STOC 1983, pp. 133–183.
2. L. Babai, P. Frankl, J. Simon, *Complexity classes in communication complexity theory*, in: Proc. 27th IEEE FOCS, pp. 337–347, 1986.
3. B. Halstenberg, R. Reischuk, *Relations between Communication Complexity Classes*, in: Proc. 3rd IEEE Structure in Complexity Theory Conference, pp. 19–28, 1988.
4. C. Damm, M. Krause, Ch. Meinel, St. Waack, *Separating counting communication complexity classes*, in: Proc. 9th STACS, Lecture Notes in Computer Science **577**, Springer Verlag 1992, pp. 281–293.
5. A. Hajnal, W. Maass, G. Turan, *On the communication complexity of graph problems*, in: Proc. 20th ACM STOC 1988, pp. 186–191.
6. N. Immerman, *Languages that capture complexity classes*, SIAM J. Comput., **16**(4)(1978), pp. 760–778.
7. M. Krause, St. Waack, *Variation ranks of communication matrices and lower bounds for depth two circuits having symmetric gates with unbounded fan–in*, in: Proc. 32nd IEEE FOCS 1991, pp. 777–782.
8. Ch. Meinel, *p-Projection reducibility and the complexity classes L(nonuniform) and NL(nonuniform)*, in: Proc. 12th MFCS, 1986, LNCS 233, 527–535.
9. Ch. Meinel, *Modified branching programs and their computational power*, LNCS 370, Springer-Verlag, 1989.
10. Ch. Meinel, St. Waack, *Upper and lower bounds for certain graph-accessibility problems on bounded alternating ω-branching programs*, in: Complexity Theory - current research, Eds. K. Ambos-Spies, S. Homer, U. Schöning, Cambridge University Press 1993, 273–290.
11. Ch. Meinel, St. Waack, *Lower Bounds on the Modular Communication Complexity of various graph-accessibility problems*, in: Proc. LATIN'95, LNCS 911, 427–435.
12. K. Mehlhorn, E. M. Schmidt, *Las Vegas is better than determinism in VLSI and distributed computing*, in: Proc. 14th ACM STOC 1982, pp. 330–337.
13. R. Paturi, J. Simon, *Probabilistic communication complexity*, Journ. of Computer and System Science **33**(1986), pp. 106–124.
14. R. Raz, B. Spieker, *On the "log rank"–conjecture in communication complexity*, in: Proc. 34th IEEE FOCS 1993, pp. 168–176.
15. W. Savitch, *Relationship between nondeterministic and deterministic tape complexities*, J. Comput. System Sci. **4**(1970), pp. 244–253.
16. Skyum, L. V. Valiant, *A complexity theory based on Boolean algebra*, Proc. 22nd IEEE FOCS, pp. 244-253.
17. A. Yao, *The entropic limitations of VLSI computations*, Proc. 13th ACM STOC 1981, pp. 308–311.

Strong Optimal Lower Bounds for Turing Machines that Accept Nonregular Languages*

Alberto Bertoni, Carlo Mereghetti, and Giovanni Pighizzini

Dipartimento di Scienze dell'Informazione
Università degli Studi di Milano
via Comelico, 39 - 20135 Milano - Italy

Abstract. In this paper, simultaneous lower bounds on space and input head reversals for deterministic, nondeterministic and alternating Turing machines accepting *nonregular* languages are studied.
Three notions of space complexity, namely strong, middle, and weak, are considered; moreover, another notion called accept, is introduced. For all cases we obtain tight lower bounds. In particular, we prove that while in the deterministic and nondeterministic case these bounds are "strongly" optimal—in the sense that we exhibit a nonregular language over a *unary* alphabet exactly fitting them—in the alternating case optimal lower bounds for tally languages turn out to be higher than those for arbitrary languages.

1 Introduction

Gap results for space complexity of nonregular languages are well known. In the pioneering work by Stearns, Hartmanis, and Lewis [SHL65] deterministic Turing machines accepting nonregular languages by halting on any input of length n within $s(n)$ work space are studied proving that, for one-way machines, $s(n) \geq d \cdot \log n$ must hold for a suitable constant $d > 0$ and infinitely many n ($s(n) = \Omega_\infty(\log n)$ for short) while, for two-way devices, $s(n) = \Omega_\infty(\log\log n)$. Hopcroft and Ullman [HU69] generalize such lower bounds to nondeterministic machines further dropping the halting property. Optimality of these bounds is then guaranteed by several languages.

Here, a key point which is worth noting is that the $s(n)$ space bound holds for *all* the computations on inputs of length n (strong space). Different notions of space complexity have been introduced: closer to the idea of nondeterminism, Alberts evaluates $s(n)$ on the basis of the existence of a $s(n)$ space bounded accepting computation on any accepted input of length n (weak space, [Alb85]) while Szepietowski proposes an intermediate notion by computing $s(n)$ on all the computations on accepted inputs of length n (middle space, [Sze88]).

We remark that all these space notions are easily seen to be equivalent when dealing with fully space constructible bounds. Since Geffert [Gef91] shows that

* This work was supported in part by the ESPRIT Basic Research Action No. 6317: "Algebraic and Syntactic Methods in Computer Science (ASMICS 2)" and by the Ministero dell'Università e della Ricerca Scientifica e Tecnologica (MURST).

there are no monotone increasing sublogarithmic fully space constructible functions, this leads us to search possible differences among above notions of space complexity by considering sublogarithmic bounds. In this sense, our paper continues the line of investigations on the complexity world below logspace (see, for instance, [Gef93, BMP94a, DH94, LR94, Sze94]) where a convenient setting to work into is certainly represented by the analysis of minimal resource requirements for nonregular languages acceptance.

We introduce a new notion of space complexity, called accept, where space bound $s(n)$ is computed on *all the accepting computations* on inputs of length n. Accept space concept turns out to be very useful especially when related to the other computational resource we will be concerned with, namely the number $i(n)$ of input head reversals.

We prove that:

1. one–way nondeterministic Turing machines accepting nonregular languages in accept $s(n)$ space must satisfy $s(n) = \Omega_\infty(\log n)$;
2. $s(n) \cdot i(n) = \Omega_\infty(\log n)$ for deterministic Turing machines using any of the four notions of space, and for nondeterministic machines as well except for weak case where $s(n) \cdot i(n) = \Omega_\infty(\log \log n)$.

We design a new algorithm that accepts the complement of Alt–Mehlhorn's language $\mathcal{L}$ [AM75] in weak nondeterministic $O(\log \log n)$ space by one input scan. This allows to prove that all the considered lower bounds are optimal with respect to either general or tally languages.

For alternating Turing machines, we obtain slightly different results. In particular, we get a $\log \log n$ lower bound for the accept case. Moreover, we show that $s(n) \cdot i(n) = \Omega_\infty(\log \log n)$ with the only exception of the strong case where $s(n) \cdot i(n) = \Omega_\infty(\log n)$.

Lower bounds for the alternating case are optimal with respect to general languages, but the study of their optimality for tally languages permits us to single out important differences from deterministic and nondeterministic cases. First of all, we show how to recognize $\mathcal{L}$ within accept $O(\log \log n)$ space on a one–way alternating machine by using the power of universal states. This proves the optimality of the corresponding lower bound, and witnesses that one–way alternation in accept $O(\log \log n)$ space is strictly more powerful than nondeterminism under the same restrictions. Subsequently, we consider middle space and show that, unlike other presented cases, the optimal space lower bound for nonregular tally languages accepted by one–way devices is *strictly higher* than that with respect to general languages. More precisely, we prove that

> one–way alternating Turing machines accepting nonregular tally languages within middle $s(n)$ space must satisfy $s(n) = \Omega_\infty(\log n)$.

For the sake of brevity, all the proofs in this version of the paper are just outlined.

2 Preliminaries

We briefly recall some basic notions. For more details, the reader is referred to any of the standard introductory texts on formal languages and complexity theory (e.g., [HU79, BDG87]).

Let Σ^* be the set of all the strings on the alphabet Σ. The length of a string $x \in \Sigma^*$ is denoted by $|x|$, and the complement of a language $L \subseteq \Sigma^*$ by L^c. L is said to be *tally* (or *unary*) if and only if Σ contains only one symbol.

Throughout the paper, we consider *Turing machines* equipped with a read–only input tape containing input strings surrounded by two endmarkers, and a read/write work tape. Space complexity is measured on the only work tape hence allowing sublinear bounds. W.l.o.g. we assume that Turing machines never print the *blank* symbol onto their work tape. An *internal configuration* is a triple specifying work tape content, position of the head on the work tape, and state of the control. We recall that a *computation* of a deterministic or nondeterministic Turing machine is represented by a sequence of internal configurations while, on *alternating Turing machines*, it may be depicted by a *computation tree* [CKS81].

Let M be a deterministic, nondeterministic, or alternating Turing machine:

- M works in strong $s(n)$ space if and only if each computation on any input of length n uses at most $s(n)$ work tape cells;
- M works in middle $s(n)$ space if and only if each computation on any accepted input of length n uses at most $s(n)$ work tape cells;
- M works in accept $s(n)$ space if and only if each accepting computation on any input of length n uses at most $s(n)$ work tape cells;
- M works in weak $s(n)$ space if and only if on each accepted input of length n there exists an accepting computation using at most $s(n)$ work tape cells.

As recalled in the Introduction, all these notions are equivalent when considering overlogarithmic space complexities. Moreover, in the deterministic case, middle, accept, and weak notions coincide even for sublogarithmic bounds.

A Turing machine M is said to be *one–way* whenever its input head can never move toward left, otherwise M is *two–way*. We can formalize intermediate situations by imposing a bound $i(n)$ on the *number of input head reversals* (also *inversions*). We always compute $i(n)$ by considering those computations by which space is defined. So, for instance, we say that an alternating Turing machine M *simultaneously* works within weak $s(n)$ space and $i(n)$ input head reversals if and only if on any accepted input of length n there exists an accepting computation tree using at most $s(n)$ work tape cells and where input head direction is reversed at most $i(n)$ times on each path from the root. For technical reasons, we stipulate $i(n) = 1$ for one–way devices.

We recall that, for any two functions $f, g : \mathbf{N} \to \mathbf{N}$, $f(n) = \Omega_\infty(g(n))$ if and only if $f(n) \geq d \cdot g(n)$ for a constant $d > 0$ and infinitely many n.

3 Deterministic and Nondeterministic Turing Machines Accepting Nonregular Languages

In this section, we first study minimal space requirements for one–way and for two–way, deterministic and nondeterministic Turing machines accepting nonregular languages under the four different space notions previously introduced. In particular, we concentrate on accept space bounded models of computation. Thereafter, we extend the lower bounds on the product $s(n) \cdot i(n)$ given in [BMP94b] for the strong case to middle, accept and weak machines. Finally, we focus our attention on proving that the lower bounds presented are tight even with respect to tally languages. To this aim, we start by briefly presenting some properties of a simple nonregular tally language and of its complement.

3.1 The Languages $\mathcal{L}$ and $\mathcal{L}^c$

For any positive integer n, let $q(n)$ be the smallest positive integer not dividing n. Thus, let $\mathcal{L}$ be the language defined as

$$\mathcal{L} = \{1^n : q(n) \text{ is a power of } 2\}.$$

The language $\mathcal{L}$ was first considered by Alt and Mehlhorn in [AM75] where they proved that it is a nonregular language acceptable in strong deterministic $O(\log \log n)$ space. Such a space bound is a direct consequence of the fact that $q(n) = O(\log n)$ for any n.

Recently, this result was strengthened in [BMP94b] by showing:

Theorem 1. *The language $\mathcal{L}$ can be recognized in* strong *$O(\log \log n)$ space by a deterministic Turing machine with $O(\frac{\log n}{\log \log n})$ input head reversals.*

Let us turn to the complement of $\mathcal{L}$. A well known result in [Sip80] states that strong deterministic space complexity classes are closed under complement. However, the proof of such a result makes use of a simulation technique which is not input head reversals preserving. On the other hand, a trivial modification of the algorithm exhibited in [BMP94b] for proving Theorem 1 shows that even $\mathcal{L}^c$ can be accepted in strong deterministic $O(\log \log n)$ space and $O(\frac{\log n}{\log \log n})$ input head reversals. We now prove that we can do better on input head reversals by using weak space.

Theorem 2. *The language $\mathcal{L}^c$ can be recognized in* weak *$O(\log \log n)$ space by a one–way nondeterministic Turing machine.*

Proof. (outline) It can be shown that, for any n, $q(n)$ is not a power of 2 if and only if there exist two positive integers s, t with $2^s < t < 2^{s+1}$, $t = O(\log n)$, and such that $n \equiv 0 \pmod{2^s}$ and $n \not\equiv 0 \pmod{t}$.

Hence, we can construct a nondeterministic Turing machine M accepting $\mathcal{L}^c$ that implements the following procedure:

input(1^n)
guess an integer s, $s > 1$
guess an integer t, $2^s < t < 2^{s+1}$
if $n \equiv 0 \pmod{2^s}$ *and* $n \not\equiv 0 \pmod{t}$ **then** *accept*
else *reject*

It can be immediately seen that M works in weak $O(\log\log n)$ space. Moreover, condition $n \equiv 0 \pmod{2^s}$ *and* $n \not\equiv 0 \pmod{t}$ is easily checkable by scanning the input once while counting its length modulo 2^s and t. □

3.2 Tight Lower Bounds

We briefly recall that space lower bounds for one–way and for two–way, deterministic and nondeterministic Turing machines accepting nonregular languages are proved for the strong case in [SHL65, HU69]. Such lower bounds remain the same even when considering middle space [Sze88]. Different lower bounds for weak space are obtained in [Alb85] (see Table 1, next page).

Let us now focus on accept space. By above results and trivial relationships among space notions, it is easy to see that $s(n) = \Omega_\infty(\log n)$ and $s(n) = \Omega_\infty(\log\log n)$ for one–way deterministic and for two–way deterministic or nondeterministic machines, respectively. The only case which deserves our attention is then examined in the following:

Theorem 3. *Let M be a one–way nondeterministic Turing machine recognizing a nonregular language L in* accept *$s(n)$ space. Then $s(n) = \Omega_\infty(\log n)$.*

Proof. (outline) $L \subseteq \Sigma^*$ being nonregular, for any positive integer k we can assume $x = a_1 a_2 \ldots a_n$, with $a_i \in \Sigma$, to be one of the shortest strings accepted by M in *at least* k space. So, there exist $n+1$ internal configurations $c_0, c_1, \ldots, c_n$ of M such that c_0 is the initial internal configuration, for each $1 \le i \le n$, c_i can be reached from c_{i-1} by consuming the ith input symbol, and c_n is an accepting internal configuration using at least k space. Note that if $c_i = c_j$ for some $0 \le i < j \le n$, then even $x' = a_1 \ldots a_i a_{j+1} \ldots a_n$ is accepted by using at least k space. But $|x'| < |x|$ which clearly contradicts our assumption on x. Hence, we must require the existence of at least $n+1$ different internal configurations of M on inputs of length n, thus obtaining $2^{O(s(n))} \ge n+1$. □

Table 1 resumes space lower bounds so far considered and obtained. Their optimality is witnessed by several languages in literature. Such languages are mainly defined over alphabets with two or more symbols. Here, we want to stress an even *stronger* optimality condition, namely that with respect to *tally* languages. To this aim, we consider the languages $\mathcal{L}$ and $\mathcal{L}^c$ studied in Section 3.1. As a consequence of Theorem 1, we can provide algorithms for accepting $\mathcal{L}$ whose space complexity exactly fits all the lower bounds for two–way machines. Furthermore, it is not difficult to construct a one–way logarithmic space bounded deterministic machine that accepts $\mathcal{L}$ by first storing in binary notation input length on its work tape. Thus, $\mathcal{L}$ is also able to fulfill all the lower bounds for one–way

	Strong	Middle	Accept	Weak
One–way Deterministic	$\log n$	$\log n$	$\log n$	$\log n$
One–way Nondeterministic	$\log n$	$\log n$	$\log n$	$\log\log n$
Two–way Deterministic	$\log\log n$	$\log\log n$	$\log\log n$	$\log\log n$
Two–way Nondeterministic	$\log\log n$	$\log\log n$	$\log\log n$	$\log\log n$

Table 1. Space lower bounds: strong [SHL65, HU69], middle [Sze88], weak [Alb85], accept Theorem 3

devices except for the nondeterministic weak space case[2]. It seems difficult to design nondeterministic algorithms that accept $\mathcal{L}$ in weak $O(\log\log n)$ space by one input scan. However, in Section 3.1, we have provided a one–way nondeterministic machine accepting $\mathcal{L}^c$ within weak $O(\log\log n)$ space. As a matter of fact, one could make use of $\mathcal{L}^c$ for proving the optimality of all the proposed lower bounds.

Theorem 4. *All the lower bounds given in Table 1 are optimal even with respect to tally languages.*

Let us now investigate how input head reversals can explicitly concur in defining lower bounds for deterministic and nondeterministic machines recognizing nonregular languages. We show how to suitably adapt the proof given in [BMP94b] for strong bounded machines to the other space notions.

The following simulation result in part motivates the introduction of the accept space complexity notion:

Lemma 5. *Let M be a deterministic or nondeterministic Turing machine working within either* strong *or* middle *or* accept *(*weak*) $s(n)$ space, and $i(n)$ input head reversals. Then, there exists an equivalent one–way nondeterministic machine M' using* accept *(*weak*) $O(s(n) \cdot i(n))$ space.*

Proof. (outline) Any accepting computation of M on inputs of length n can be suitably represented by a sequence of $n+1$ *crossing sequences* [Hen65] of at most $i(n)+1$ internal configurations of M. Thus, M' simulates M by guessing, step by step, a crossing sequence and locally testing "compatibility" with the previous one on the currently scanned input symbol. The space needed to store each guessed crossing sequence of an accepting computation of M is clearly $O(s(n) \cdot i(n))$ whenever M is either strong or middle or accept space bounded. Hence, in these three cases, M' turns out to be a one–way nondeterministic machine using accept $O(s(n) \cdot i(n))$ space. On the other hand, was M weak space bounded, then it is easy to notice that so would do M'. □

[2] We recall that the optimality of the weak $\log\log n$ space lower bound for one–way nondeterministic machines accepting general nonregular languages was first proved in [Fre79] by means of the language $\{0^n 1 0^k : n \neq k\}$.

Theorem 6. *Let* $r \in$ {Deterministic, Nondeterministic}, c $\in$ {Strong, Middle, Accept, Weak}, *and* $l(n)$ *be the* (r, c)*th entry of Table 2. For any* r *Turing machine* M *accepting a nonregular language in* c *space* $s(n)$ *with* $i(n)$ *input head reversals,* $s(n) \cdot i(n) = \Omega_\infty(l(n))$. *This lower bound is optimal even with respect to tally languages.*

	Strong	Middle	Accept	Weak
Deterministic	$\log n$	$\log n$	$\log n$	$\log n$
Nondeterministic	$\log n$	$\log n$	$\log n$	$\log \log n$

Table 2. Simultaneous lower bounds on the product $s(n) \cdot i(n)$: strong [BMP94b], and middle, accept, weak Theorem 6

Proof. (outline) By Lemma 5, we can construct from M an equivalent one–way nondeterministic machine M' working in accept or weak $O(s(n) \cdot i(n))$ space. Thus, by applying to M' the lower bounds in Table 1, the desired result follows.

For what is concerned with optimality, arguments in Section 3.1 can be used to show that the tally language $\mathcal{L}^c$ fits all the lower bounds in Table 2. □

4 Alternating Turing Machines Accepting Nonregular Languages

Let us now analyze minimal resource requirements for alternating Turing machines accepting nonregular languages. Lower bounds for strong space are proved in [Sud80], for middle space in [Sze88], and for weak space in [Iwa93]. Accept space lower bounds can be easily obtained by considering the relationship with middle and weak machines (Table 3).

	Strong	Middle	Accept	Weak
One–way Alternating	$\log n$	$\log \log n$	$\log \log n$	$\log \log n$
Two–way Alternating	$\log \log n$	$\log \log n$	$\log \log n$	$\log \log n$

Table 3. Space lower bounds: strong [Sud80], middle [Sze88], weak [Iwa93]

By also taking into account input head reversals, we get the lower bounds summarized in Table 4, and proved in the following:

Theorem 7. *Let* M *be an alternating Turing machine accepting a nonregular language in* strong *(*middle *or* accept *or* weak*) space* $s(n)$ *with* $i(n)$ *input head reversals. Then,* $s(n) \cdot i(n) = \Omega_\infty(\log n)$ $(s(n) \cdot i(n) = \Omega_\infty(\log \log n))$.

	Strong	Middle	Accept	Weak
Alternating	$\log n$	$\log\log n$	$\log\log n$	$\log\log n$

Table 4. Simultaneous lower bounds on the product $s(n) \cdot i(n)$: Theorem 7

Proof. (outline) For the strong case, we can "forget" the fact that M is an alternating machine, since computational resources are measured without distinguishing between accepting and nonaccepting computations. Thus, we can apply the technique used in [BMP94b] for the corresponding nondeterministic case. The other results follow by observing that the lower bounds for the corresponding one–way and two–way devices coincide. □

Let us now investigate the optimality of the bounds in Tables 3 and 4. We begin by observing that the lower bounds for strong and weak cases coincide with the corresponding ones for nondeterministic machines, whence their optimality (even for tally languages) comes immediately out. The same argument works for two–way machines using middle and accept space. So, to complete the optimality analysis of Table 3, it remains to consider middle and accept space lower bounds for one–way alternating machines.

For the accept case, from Table 1 we first notice that no one–way nondeterministic machine recognizing a nonregular language in accept $O(\log\log n)$ space can exist. So, in order to show the optimality of the $\log\log n$ lower bound, we actually have to use the power of universal branching as in the following:

Theorem 8. *The language $\mathcal{L}$ can be recognized in* accept $O(\log\log n)$ *space by a one–way alternating Turing machine.*

Proof. (outline) We can construct an alternating Turing machine M accepting $\mathcal{L}$ that implements the following procedure:

input(1^n)
existentially guess an integer r, $r > 2$
universally generate all the integers s, $2 \leq s \leq r$
if $s < r$ **then**
  if $n \equiv 0 \pmod{s}$ **then** *accept*
      else *reject*
else
  if $n \not\equiv 0 \pmod{s}$ *and* s is a power of 2 **then** *accept*
      else *reject*

The universal branching checks whether a guessed integer r is the smallest not dividing n and whether r is a power of 2. M accepts whenever both these conditions are satisfied. Accept $O(\log\log n)$ space bound can be obtained by observing that the only guess leading to acceptance is the one corresponding to $q(n)$, and recalling that $q(n) = O(\log n)$. Further, computing the length of the input modulo a given integer can be accomplished in one input scan. □

Let us now turn to the middle model. The optimality of the $\log\log n$ space lower bound for one–way alternating machines was first proved in [Sze88] by means of the nonregular language

$$\mathcal{A} = \{a^k b^m : m \text{ is a common multiple of all } r \leq k\}.$$

The language $\mathcal{A}$ is defined over a two letter alphabet, and this is fundamental for efficiently computing membership since the algorithm proposed in [Sze88] is crucially based on the internal structure of the strings in $\mathcal{A}$. Up to now, the existence of a unary—and hence structureless—language matching the considered lower bound has been an open question.

Here, we solve this problem by giving a negative answer. In fact, we obtain an higher optimal lower bound for tally languages.

Theorem 9. *Let M be a one–way alternating Turing machine accepting a nonregular tally language L in* middle *$s(n)$ space. Then, $s(n) = \Omega_\infty(\log n)$. Moreover, this bound is tight.*

Proof. (outline) By contradiction, assume $s(n) = o(\log n)$. So, we can find an integer n' such that $2^{s(n')} < n'$ (*) and the string $1^{n'}$ belongs to L. Let c be an internal configuration reachable by M in $m \geq n'$ moves. Then, there exists a sequence $c_0, c_1, \ldots, c_{n'}, \ldots, c_m$ where c_0 is the initial internal configuration, $c_m = c$, and c_{i+1} is an immediate successor of c_i for each $0 \leq i \leq m-1$. L being unary, internal configurations $c_0, c_1, \ldots, c_{n'}$ can be reached on input $1^{n'}$, and hence, by the middle space bound, use at most $s(n')$ space. From the inequality (*), there must exist $0 \leq i < j \leq n'$ such that $c_i = c_j$ thus implying that c is even reachable in less than m moves. By iterating this argument, we get that any configuration reachable by M can be reached within less then n' moves. This implies that L is regular whence a contradiction follows.

For the optimality, it is enough to consider the language $\mathcal{L}$. □

Theorem 9 completes optimality analysis of the bounds in Table 3 by remarking the only difference, so far obtained, on minimal resource requirements between tally and general nonregular languages acceptance.

Further, the optimality of the bounds in Table 4 can be immediately drawn from the corresponding one–way case except for middle machines accepting nonregular tally languages. We conjecture that the difference pointed out in Theorem 9 holds even in this case, and we leave, as an open problem, to prove or disprove that $\log\log n$ is an optimal lower bound on the product middle space$\times$input head reversals for alternating Turing machines accepting nonregular tally languages.

Acknowledgment. The authors wish to thank anonymous referees for useful comments and remarks. In particular, observations made by a referee helped in simplifying the proof of Theorem 2.

References

[Alb85] M. Alberts. Space complexity of alternating Turing machines. In *Fundamentals of Computation Theory, Proceedings*, Lecture Notes in Computer Science 199, pages 1–7. Springer Verlag, 1985.

[AM75] H. Alt and K. Mehlhorn. A language over a one symbol alphabet requiring only $O(\log\log n)$ space. *SIGACT news*, 7:31–33, 1975.

[BDG87] J. Balcázar, J. Díaz, and J. Gabarró. *Structural Complexity I.* EATCS Monographs on Theoretical Computer Science 11. Springer Verlag, 1987.

[BMP94a] A. Bertoni, C. Mereghetti, and G. Pighizzini. On languages accepted with simultaneous complexity bounds and their ranking problem. In *Mathematical Foundations of Computer Science 1994, Proceedings*, Lecture Notes in Computer Science 841, pages 245–255. Springer Verlag, 1994.

[BMP94b] A. Bertoni, C. Mereghetti, and G. Pighizzini. An optimal lower bound for nonregular languages. *Information Processing Letters*, 50:289–292, 1994. Corrigendum. *ibid.*, 52:339, 1994.

[CKS81] A. Chandra, D. Kozen, and L. Stockmeyer. Alternation. *Journal of the ACM*, 28:114–133, 1981.

[DH94] C. Damm and M. Holzer. Inductive counting below LOGSPACE. In *Mathematical Foundations of Computer Science 1994, Proceedings*, Lecture Notes in Computer Science 841, pages 276–285. Springer Verlag, 1994.

[Fre79] R. Freivalds. On time complexity of deterministic and nondeterministic Turing machines. *Latvijskij Matematiceskij Eshegodnik*, 23:158–165, 1979. (In Russian).

[Gef91] V. Geffert. Nondeterministic computations in sublogarithmic space and space constructibility. *SIAM J. Computing*, 20:484–498, 1991.

[Gef93] V. Geffert. Tally version of the Savitch and Immerman–Szelepcsényi theorems for sublogarithmic space. *SIAM J. Computing*, 22:102–113, 1993.

[Hen65] F. Hennie. One–tape, off–line Turing machine computations. *Information and Control*, 8:553–578, 1965.

[HU69] J. Hopcroft and J. Ullman. Some results on tape–bounded Turing machines. *Journal of the ACM*, 16:168–177, 1969.

[HU79] J. Hopcroft and J. Ullman. *Introduction to automata theory, languages, and computations.* Addison–Wesley, Reading, MA, 1979.

[Iwa93] K. Iwama. ASPACE($o(\log\log n)$) is regular. *SIAM J. Computing*, 22:136–146, 1993.

[LR94] M. Liśkiewicz and R. Reischuk. The complexity world below logarithmic space. In *Structure in Complexity Theory, Proceedings*, pages 64–78, 1994.

[SHL65] R. Stearns, J. Hartmanis, and P. Lewis. Hierarchies of memory limited computations. In *IEEE Conf. Record on Switching Circuit Theory and Logical Design*, pages 179–190, 1965.

[Sip80] M. Sipser. Halting space–bounded computations. *Theoretical Computer Science*, 10:335–338, 1980.

[Sud80] I. Sudborough. Efficient algorithms for path system problems and applications to alternating and time–space complexity classes. In *Proc. 21st IEEE Symposium on Foundations of Computer Science*, pages 62–73, 1980.

[Sze88] A. Szepietowski. Remarks on languages acceptable in $\log\log n$ space. *Information Processing Letters*, 27:201–203, 1988.

[Sze94] A. Szepietowski. *Turing Machines with Sublogarithmic Space.* Lecture Notes in Computer Science 843. Springer Verlag, 1994.

A superpolynomial lower bound for $(1, +k(n))$-branching programs

Stanislav Žák

Institute of Computer Science
Academy of Sciences of the Czech Republic
Pod vodárenskou věží 2
182 00 Prague 8
Czech Republic
stan@uivt.cas.cz

Abstract. By $(1, +k(n))$-branching programs (b. p.s) we mean those b. p.s which during each of their computations are allowed to test at most $k(n)$ input bits repeatedly. For a Boolean function J computable within polynomial time a trade-off has been proven between the number of repeatedly tested bits and the size of each b. p. P which computes J. If at most $\lfloor \sqrt{n}/48(log(c(n)))^2 \rfloor - 1$ repeated tests are allowed then the size of P is at least $c(n)$. This yields superpolynomial lower bounds for e. g. $(1, +\sqrt{n}/48(log(n)loglog(n))^2)$-b. p.'s and for $(1, +\sqrt{n}/48(log(n))^4)$-b. p.'s.

The presented result is a step towards a superpolynomial lower bound for 2-b. p.'s which is an open problem since 1984 when the first superpolynomial lower bounds for 1-b. p.s were proven [6], [7].

1 Introduction

The main goal of the theory of branching programs (b. p.s) is to prove a superpolynomial lower bound for a Boolean function computable within polynomial time. This would solve the $P =?LOG$ problem.

In 1984 the first superpolynomial lower bounds for 1-b. p.s which are allowed to test each input bit at most once during each computation were proven [6], [7]. Since that time a more general open problem stands to prove a superpolynomial lower bounds for k-b. p.s, especially for 2-b. p.s.

The first steps towards the case of 2-b. p.s were made with real-time b. p.s,which perform at most n steps during each computation on any input of length n. The results were a quadratic lower bound [3], a subexponential lower bound [8] and an exponential lower bound [4].

Another attempt was to prove lower bounds for nondeterministic syntactic k-b. p.s where the restriction that at most k tests of each input bit are allowed is applied not only upon the computations but upon all paths in the b. p. in question. For nondeterministic syntactic k-b. p.s exponential lower bounds have been proven [1], [2]. For syntactic $(1, +k(n))$-b. p.s tight hierarchies (in $k(n)$) are proven in [5].

However the problem for 2-b. p.s remains open. Another idea is to prove lower bounds for b. p.s for which some k input bits may be tested repeatedly ($(1,+k)$-b. p.s) with the hope that it will be possible to reach the lower bound for 2-b. p.s by extending k to n. We prove superpolynomial lower bounds for a large $k(n)$, $k(n) \leq \sqrt{n}/48(log(n)loglog(n))^2$. This follows from a trade off between the number of allowed tests and the size of b. p.s - as mentioned in the Abstract. The proof is achieved through simple means.

2 Preliminaries

We shall now introduce a usual definition of branching programs and of other concepts we shall use in the next sections.

Definition 1. Let n be a natural number, $n > 0$, and $I = \{1, ..., n\}$ be the set of bits. By a branching program P (over I) we understand a directed acyclic (finite) graph with one source. The out-degree of each vertex is not greater than 2. The branching vertices (out-degree = 2) are labeled by bits from I, one out-going edge is labeled by 0, the other one by 1. The sinks (out-degree = 0) are labeled by 0 and 1.

Definition 2. Let u be an input word for a branching program P, $u \in \{0,1\}^n$. By the computation of the program P on the word u - *comp*(u) - we mean the sequence $\{v_i\}_{i=1}^k$ of vertices of P such that
a) v_1 is the source of P
b) v_k is a sink of P
c) If the out-degree of v_i = 1 then v_{i+1} is the vertex pointed to by the edge out-going from v_i.
d) If the out-degree of $v_i = 2$ and the label of $v_i = j \in I$ then v_{i+1} is the vertex pointed to by the edge out-going from v_i which is labeled by u_j ($u = (u_1, ...u_n) \in \{0,1\}^n$).

We know that each input word determines a path in P from the source to a sink. - Sometimes we can say that an input word u or a computation *comp*(u) goes through a vertex v.

Definition 3. Let P be a branching program.

a) If u is an input word then say that *comp*(u) tests a bit i iff there is a vertex $v \in comp(u)$ with out-degree = 2 which is labeled by i (*comp*(u) tests i in v; it is an inquiry of i; i is tested during *comp*(u)).

b) We say that P is a k-branching program iff for each bit i and each input word u the computation *comp*(u) tests bit i in at most k vertices of P.

c) We say that P is $(1,+k)$-branching program iff for each input word u at most k bits are tested more than once during *comp*(u).

d) By the size $|P|$ we mean the number of its vertices.

e) By the Boolean function f_P of n variables computed by P we understand the function which is given as follows: for $u \in \{0,1\}^n$, $f_P(u)$ is equal to the label of the last vertex of *comp*(u) (this vertex is a sink).

Definition 4. Let f_n be a Boolean function of n variables. By the complexity of f_n we mean the size of a minimal branching program which computes f_n. Let $\{f_n\}$ be a sequence of Boolean functions. By its complexity we mean a function s such that $s(n)$ is the complexity of f_n .

A language $L \subseteq \{0,1\}^+$ determines a sequence of Boolean functions; thus, we speak about the complexity of L.

We know that we can also define the complexity of a sequence of Boolean functions using branching programs which are restricted in some sense (e. g. k-branching programs). Naturally, the derived complexity grows with the severity of the restriction.

Let us recall a usual operation relevant to branching programs. It is possible to reduce the sets of vertices and edges to those which are used by computations on a subset of input words. The resulting structure is a b. p. too.

3 The definition of the Boolean function J

For the purposes of our definition we shall organize the n $(=(2m)^2)$ input bits in a binary matrix with $2\sqrt{n}$ rows and $\sqrt{n}/2$ columns. On this matrix we shall define a move which will be given by iterations of the function *Jump* from the following definition.

Definition 5. Let A be a $2\sqrt{n} \times \sqrt{n}/2$ binary matrix $(n = (2m)^2)$. We define a function $Jump : \{0,1\}^{2\sqrt{n}} \times \{1, ..., \sqrt{n}/2\} \rightarrow \{0,1\}^{2\sqrt{n}} \times \{-\sqrt{n}, ..., \sqrt{n} + \sqrt{n}/2\}$ as follows: Let $M \in \{0,1\}^{2\sqrt{n}}$ and $k \in \{1, ..., \sqrt{n}/2\}$. $Jump(M,k) = (M', k')$ where $M' = M \oplus C_k$ ($\oplus$ is the componentwise sum modulo 2 and C_k is the k-th column of A) and $k' = k + (||M'||_1 - ||M'||_0)/2$ where $||M'||_1$ is the number of one's in M', $||M'||_0$ the number of zeroes. (M is called the input memory, M' the output memory.)

We see that if $k' \in \{1, ..., \sqrt{n}/2\}$ it is possible to iterate the function *Jump* on arguments M', k' $(Jump(M', k'))$.

Definition 6. Let A be a $2\sqrt{n} \times \sqrt{n}/2$ binary input matrix. The value $J(A)$ is given as follows: We start the iterations of *Jump* with the values $M = \{0\}^{2\sqrt{n}}$ and $k = 1$. We iterate *Jump* until $k' \notin \{1, ..., \sqrt{n}/2\}$ or $\sqrt{n}/2$ iterations are performed. We define $J(A) = 1$ iff k' of the last iterations of *Jump* equals $\sqrt{n}/2 + 1$. In the other cases $J(A) = 0$.

It is clear that J is computable within polynomial time, J is in P. On the other hand J seems to be hard for Turing machines with logarithmic tape and for branching programs of polynomial sizes.

4 The lower bounds

Before the proof of the following theorem we introduce a technical definition.

Definition 7. Let $I = \{1, ..., n\}$ be the set of bits. Let $A \subseteq I, A \neq \emptyset$. By an assignment α of A we mean a mapping $\alpha : A \to \{0,1\}$. If $B \subseteq I, B \neq \emptyset, B \cap A = \emptyset$ and β is an assignment of B then by $[\alpha, \beta]$ we mean the assignment of $A \cup B$ where $[\alpha, \beta](i) = \alpha(i)$ if $i \in A$ and $[\alpha, \beta](i) = \beta(i)$ otherwise. If a is a word, $a \in \{0,1\}^n$, then we can understand a as an assignment of I. For $A \subseteq I, a\lceil A$ is an assignment of A.

Theorem 8. *Let c be a function, $c : N \to N, n \leq c(n) \leq 2^{\sqrt[4]{n}/4\sqrt{3}}$. On $(1, +\lfloor\sqrt{n}/48(log(c(n)))^2\rfloor - 1)$-b. p.'s, the complexity of J is at least c.*

Proof. By contradiction. We suppose that there is a number $n, n \in N$, and $(1, +\lfloor\sqrt{n}/48(log(c(n)))^2\rfloor - 1)$-b. p. P which computes J on inputs of length n and the size of P is less than $c(n)$. We shall construct an input word a which will require (on P) to test at least $x = \lfloor\sqrt{n}/48log(c(n))^2\rfloor$ bits two times. This will be a contradiction.

We shall construct a and a sequence of input words $b_1, ..., b_x$. For each $i, 1 \leq i \leq x$, the inputs a and b_i will differ only on a set A_i of bits, $|A_i| < 2log(c(n))$; for different i, j it will hold $A_i \cap A_j = \emptyset$. We shall prove that for each i *comp*(a) and *comp*(b_i) must branch at least two times. This fact, with regard to the construction of a and b_i, will require that at least one bit from A_i must be tested at least two times during *comp*(a). This will be our contradiction.

We follow the computations of P until $log(c(n))$ tests of bits are performed during each of them. Since $|P| < c(n)$ there are two computations on inputs c_1, c_2 which branch and then they are sticked in a vertex. Let C_1 be the set of bits tested by *comp*(c_1) and C_2 be the set of bits tested by *comp*(c_2). Let $A_1 = C_1 \cup C_2$. We see that $|A_1| < 2log(c(n))$. Now we define parts of inputs a and b_1. a equals c_1 on C_1 and a equals c_2 on $C_2 - C_1$. b_1 equals c_2 on C_2 and b_1 equals c_1 on $C_1 - C_2$. We see that *comp*(a) follows *comp*(c_1) and *comp*(b_1) follows *comp*(c_2) until *comp*(a) and *comp*(b_1) join in a vertex. It is clear that there is a bit in A_1 on which a and b_1 differ. Such bits will be called important bits of the set A_1. On bits outside of A_1, b_1 will equal a (as follows).

If A_i, b_i are constructed we continue in the following way: We take only those inputs which equal a on $\bigcup_{j=1}^{i} A_j$. These inputs define a subprogram P_i of P. Since $|\bigcup_{j=1}^{i} A_j| \leq 2log(c(n))x \leq \sqrt{n}/2$ each computation of P_i is longer than $log(c(n))$. (If not, then during a computation of P at most $\sqrt{n}/2 + log(c(n)) \leq \sqrt{n}/2 + \sqrt[4]{n}$ bits are tested. This is unsufficient for giving the correct answer - accept or reject.) We follow the computations of P_i to the depth $log(c(n))$ and we define a, b_{i+1}, A_{i+1} as a, b_1, A_1 above. We see that $A_{i+1} \cap \bigcup_{j=1}^{i} A_j = \emptyset$.

At this moment we have defined the inputs $a, b_1, ...b_x$ on the set $A = \bigcup_{i=1}^{x} A_i$ (and the important bits for each A_i). Outside of A, $a, b_1, ..., b_x$ will be the same. The content of bits outside of A will be such that it will hold $J(a) = 1$ and

$J(b_1) = J(b_2) = ...J(b_x) = 0$. It is clear that for each i $comp(a)$ and $comp(b_i)$ branch, then they are sticked in a vertex, and after that they will branch for the second times. According to the construction of a, b_i, A_i there will be a bit in A_i which will be tested during $comp(a)$ the second time. Hence during $comp(a)$, x bits will be tested repeatedly.

Since $|A| \leq \sqrt{n}/2$ there are $3\sqrt{n}/2$ rows (in each of the input matrices $a, b_1, ..., b_x$) without any bits of A. Without loss of generality we assume that they are the last $3\sqrt{n}/2$ rows.

Now it is necessary to define a and $b_1, ..., b_x$ outside of A. We shall do it in steps. In each step the contents of some bits will be defined in such a way that for some i's it will be clear that $J(b_i) = 0$.

Before the first step we say that a column C of the input matrix is free if $C \cap A = \emptyset$. The other columns are called non-free. The number of the non-free columns is at most $|A| \leq x2log(c(n)) \leq \sqrt{n}/24log(c(n))$. During the construction the number of non-free columns will increase.

Let us describe the first step of our construction. We are in the situation when the first column of the input matrix is pointed to (to be an argument for the first iteration of $Jump$) and the input memory is $0^{2\sqrt{n}}$. If the first column does not contain any important bit (of any A_i) we define the contents of bits which do not belong to A in such a way that $Jump$ points to a column C_1 which contains some important bits (with a memory $M \in \{0,1\}^{2\sqrt{n}}$). After this action the first column of the input matrix is non-free.

Let $i_1, ..., i_k$ be all indices such that some important bits of $A_{i_1}, ..., A_{i_k}$ belong to C_1. Our task is to define an assignment α of bits from $C_1 - A$ in such a way that $Jump(M, .)$ points to free columns if the arguments $[\alpha, a\lceil(C_1 \cap A)]$, $[\alpha, b_{i_1}\lceil(C_1 \cap A)]$, ... , $[\alpha, b_{i_k}\lceil(C_1 \cap A)]$ are used. Since a and b_i differ at most on A_i and $|A_i| < 2log(c(n))$, the maximal distance between columns which will be pointed to is at most $4log(c(n)) - 1$. There are many free columns (as it is demonstrated at the end of the proof), therefore, it is possible to find $4log(c(n)) - 1$ adjacent free columns. Further it is possible to choose α such that all columns which are pointed to belong to these $4log(c(n)) - 1$ adjacent free columns. The contents of the (free) columns which are pointed to but which are not pointed to by $Jump(M, [\alpha, a\lceil(C_1 \cap A)])$ we choose in such a way that the next iteration(s) of $Jump$ points to outside of the input matrix - for example to the left. For those inputs b_i $J(b_i) = 0$. The mentioned columns become non-free.

Now let us investigate the free column C_2 pointed to by $Jump(M, [\alpha, a\lceil(C_1 \cap A)])$. In the case that for some i C_2 is pointed to by $Jump(M, [\alpha, b_i\lceil(C_1 \cap A)])$ too, we continue as follows.

We know that the iterations of $Jump$ on a and the iterations on b_i reach C_2 with the input memories which a/ differ on the first $\sqrt{n}/2$ bits, b/ are the same on the remaining $3\sqrt{n}/2$ bits, and c/ differ on the rows on which important bits of A_i lie. Therefore in the first $\sqrt{n}/2$ bits of C_2 we give only one 1 on one row on which one important bit of A_i lies. On the other $\sqrt{n}/2 - 1$ bits we give zeroes. The content of the remaining $3\sqrt{n}/2$ bits will be such that the columns pointed to by the next iterations will be free. It is possible to manage it as above. C_2 becomes non-free.

From the construction of the content of the first $\sqrt{n}/2$ bits of C_2 it follows that the free columns pointed to by the next iteration of $Jump$ on a and by the next iteration of $Jump$ on b_i are different. The number of b_is such that iterations of $Jump$ on them follow the iterations of $Jump$ on a is decreased.

The contents of the columns which are pointed to by the iterations of $Jump$ on b_i's but not pointed to by the iteration of $Jump$ on a are defined in such a way that the next iterations of $Jump$ on them points to the left outside of the input matrix. ($J(b_i) = 0$.)

If there are b_i's such that iterations of $Jump$ on them follow the iteration on a then we repeat the last operation of decreasing of the number of such b_i's. In the other case there are two possibilities: a/ there is another column with important bits - we start the next step of our construction with this column; b/ if there is not such a column we define the content of the column pointed to by the last iteration of $Jump$ on a in such a way that the next iteration of $Jump$ on a points to the right immediately after the last column of the input matrix ($J(a) = 1$).

It remains to prove that in each step of our construction it is possible to find $4log(c(n)) - 1$ adjacent free columns. Since the first column is non-free there are at most NF groups of adjacent free columns where NF stands for the number of non-free columns after the last step of our construction. It suffices to prove $(\sqrt{n}/2 - NF)/NF \geq 4log(c(n)) - 1$. It is clear that $NF \leq |A| + 3x + 1$ since in our construction for each input $b_1, ..., b_x$ we need at most 3 free columns for the proof that $J(b_i) = 0$. We see that
$NF \leq x(2log(c(n)) - 1) + 3x + 1 \leq 6xlog(c(n))$. It suffices to prove that $(\sqrt{n}/2)/6xlog(c(n)) \geq 4log(c(n))$. It follows from the choice of x. Q.E.D.

Corollary. a/ On $(1, +\lfloor\sqrt{n}/48(log(n)loglog(n))^2\rfloor - 1)$-branching programs, the complexity of J is at least $(log(n))^{log(n)}$;
b/ On $(1, +\lfloor\sqrt{n}/48(log(n))^4\rfloor - 1)$-branching programs, the complexity of J is at least $n^{log(n)}$.

Comment. The bounds are superpolynomial.

References

[1] A. Borodin, A.Razborov, R. Smolensky - On Lower Bounds for Read-k-times Branching Programs - Computational Complexity 3, 1 - 18.

[2] S. Jukna - A Note on Read-k-times Branching Programs - Universität Dortmund - Forschungsbericht Nr. 448, 1992

[3] M. Ftáčnik, J. Hromkovič - Nonlinear Lower Bound for Real-Time Branching Programs.

[4] K. Kriegel, S. Waack - Exponential Lower Bounds for Real-time Branching Programs - Proc. FCT'87, LNCS 278, 263 - 267.

[5] D. Sieling - New Lower Bounds and Hierarchy Results for Restricted Branching Programs

[6] I. Wegener - On the Complexity of Branching Programs and Decision Trees for Clique Functions - JACM 35, 1988, 461 - 471.

[7] S. Žák - An Exponential Lower Bound for One-time-only Branching Programs - MFCS'84, LNCS 176, 562 - 566.

[8] S. Žák - An Exponential Lower Bound for Real-time Branching Programs - Information and Control, Vol. 71, No 1/2, 87 - 94.

Deterministic Parsing for Augmented Context-free Grammars*

Luca Breveglieri[†] Alessandra Cherubini[‡] Stefano Crespi Reghizzi[†]

[†]Dipartimento di Elettronica e Informazione
[‡]Dipartimento di Matematica
Politecnico di Milano
Piazza Leonardo Da Vinci n. 32
I-20133 Milano, Italy

Abstract. *In contrast to the usual depth-first derivations of context-free (CF) grammars, breadth-first derivations (also in combination with depth-first ones) yield a class of augmented context-free grammars (ACF) (also termed multi-breadth-depth grammars) endowed with greater generative capacity, yet manageable. The inadequacy of CF grammars to treat distant dependencies is overcome by the new model. ACF grammars can be classified with respect to their disposition, a concept related to the data structure needed to parse their strings. For such augmented CF grammars we consider the $LL(k)$ condition, that ensures top-down deterministic parsing. We restate the condition as an adjacency problem and we prove that it is decidable for any disposition. The deterministic linear-time parser differs from a recursive descent parser by using instead of a LIFO stack a more general data structure, involving FIFO queues and LIFO stacks in accordance with the disposition. ACF grammars can be also viewed as a formalized version of ATN (Augmented Transition Networks).*

1 Introduction

Context-free (CF) grammars cannot define some important aspects of programming languages, such as long distance dependencies and agreements, but context-sensitive grammars are too complex to be used in practice. Recently a new attempt to extend the generative capacity of CF grammars, still retaining their essential properties, has been made. Such augmented CF (ACF) grammars (also called multi-breadth-depth or MBD) have the same structure as CF productions (one symbol on the lefthand side) but use a more general operation than concatenation for combining the constituents occurring in the right part of the production. The combination depends on the disposition of the grammar, which can be depth-first (D) (coinciding with usual CF rewriting), breadth-first (B)

* Work partially supported by MURST 60% (Italy), ESPRIT-BRA ASMICS 2 n. 6317 (E.U.) and CNR-CSISEI (Italy)

[1, 5] or any combination of D and B. In terms of generation, an ACF grammar generates a tree as the underlying CF grammar, which is visited in an order depending on the disposition, e.g. it is breadth-first for disposition B. Such languages are recognized by automata with an array of LIFO and FIFO segments, depending on the rewriting disposition. An interesting subfamily are the D^+ grammars, which correspond to automata with an array of PD segments, and can be parsed in polynomial time [6].

For practical use in compilers, any grammar family must dispose of a systematic technique for building fast, linear time parsers. For CF grammars we recall the $LL(k)$ top-down parsers [11], implementing deterministic PD automata, which recognize by empty PD stack and are essentially stateless.

We show that the notion of $LL(k)$ grammar can be extended to ACF grammars. Using a recent result (the generalised Chomsky-Schützenberger theorem for ACF grammars [4]) we prove that the $LL(k)$ test is effective for any disposition, and we show how to systematically build generalised top-down deterministic parsers for $LL(1)$ ACF grammars. The result is similar to the "ad hoc" parsers obtained by the well-known ATN approach [15]: a deterministic automaton with a tape made of an array of LIFO or FIFO segments.

This research provides a new approach for defining the syntax of artificial languages with greater precision than possible with CF grammars, without compromising the efficiency of recognition. Practical experimentation will be needed to evaluate the convenience of ACF grammars.

In comparison to other extensions to CF grammars, one has to note that ACF phrases are permutations of CF phrases, hence ACF languages are semilinear (in Parikh's sense) in contrast to most past extensions, e.g. matrix grammars, which loose this property.

Some relation is to be found between ACF grammars and other models proposed for computational linguistics: tree adjoining grammars [10] and equivalent models [14], and coupled context-free grammars [8].

The $LL(k)$ coupled CF grammars have been studied by Pitsch [12], while we examined the $LL(k)$ condition for ACF grammars with the special disposition Depth-Breadth in [3], but the "ad hoc" methods used in both studies are hardly extensible to the general case of grammars with dispositions including queues and PD stacks.

2 Preliminaries

ACF grammars are best introduced by referring to a Greibach CF normal form, where each production $A \to bBC$ is an instruction for a PDA saying that, when A is on top of the PD stack and b is on the input tape, the input tape pointer has to be advanced, A has to be popped and the string BC has to be pushed. ACF productions act as instructions for an automaton having a memory organised as an array of segments, each segment being either a PD stack (LIFO) or a queue (FIFO). The arrangement of the segments is called the ***disposition*** of the grammar, and is denoted as a function $r : [1, n] \to \{B, D\}$, where $n \geq 1$ is the number of segments. The value $r(i) = D$ (with $1 \leq i \leq n$) means that the ith segment of the array is a PD stack, $r(i) = B$ that it is a FIFO queue.

Definition 1. An ACF grammar G, with disposition $r : [1,n] \to \{B, D\}$ ($n \geq 1$), is a 5-tuple $G = (V_N, V_T, S, P, r)$, where V_N and V_T are the non-terminal and terminal alphabet, respectively, $S \in V_N$ is the axiom and P is the set of the productions, of the form $A \to v(\alpha_1)_{r(1)} \ldots (\alpha_n)_{r(n)}$, where $v \in V_T^*$ and $\alpha_i \in V_N^*$, for any $1 \leq i \leq n$; the α's are the segments of the production. □

Productions $A \to w(\varepsilon)_{r(1)} \ldots (\varepsilon)_{r(n)}$ and $A \to (\varepsilon)_{r(1)} \ldots (\varepsilon)_{r(n)}$ can be shortened as $A \to w$ and $A \to \varepsilon$, respectively.

Definition 2. Given an ACF grammar $G = (V_N, V_T, S, P, r)$, with disposition $r : [1,n] \to \{B, D\}$ ($n \geq 1$), let:

$$S_1 = u(\beta_1)_{r(1)} \ldots (\beta_{i-1})_{r(i-1)}(A\beta_i)_{r(i)}(\beta_{i+1})_{r(i+1)} \ldots (\beta_n)_{r(n)}$$

be a sentential form of G, where $A \in V_N$, $u \in V_T^*$, $\beta_i \in V_N^*$, for any $1 \leq i \leq n$, and $\beta_j = \varepsilon$, for any $1 \leq j < i$. The β's and $A\beta_i$ are the segments of S_1. Let also:

$$p : A \to v(\alpha_1)_{r(1)} \ldots (\alpha_n)_{r(n)}$$

be a (labeled) production of G, where $A \in V_N$, $v \in V_T^*$ and $\alpha_i \in V_N^*$, for any $1 \leq i \leq n$. The sentential form S_2 *derives* from S_1 by means of the production p, as follows:

$$S_1 \overset{p}{\Rightarrow}_G uv(\alpha_1)_{r(1)} \ldots (\alpha_{i-1})_{r(i-1)}(\gamma_i)_{r(i)}(\gamma_{i+1})_{r(i+1)} \ldots (\gamma_n)_{r(n)} = S_2$$

where if $r(j) = D$ then $\gamma_j = \alpha_j\beta_j$ and if $r(j) = B$ then $\gamma_j = \beta_j\alpha_j$, for any $i \leq j \leq n$. □

Note that derivations are leftmost and the non-terminal A occurring on the left in the ith segment can be rewritten iff all preceding segments are void. The language generated by an ACF grammar G is:

Definition 3. $L(G) = \{w | \quad w \in V_T^* \wedge (S)_{r(1)}(\varepsilon)_{r(2)} \ldots (\varepsilon)_{r(n)} \overset{*}{\Rightarrow}_G w\}$ □

Definition 4. The ACF grammars with disposition r constitute a family denoted $\mathcal{G}_r$ and the corresponding family of languages is denoted $\mathcal{L}_r$. □

Since $\mathcal{G}_D$ includes CF grammars in Greibach normal form[2], $\mathcal{L}_D$ is the family of CF languages. ACF grammars retain the fundamental properties of CF grammars: thus each ACF language is the hom. image of the intersection of a regular language and a generalised Dyck language (generalised Chomsky-Schützenberger theorem [4]). For the disposition B the generalised Dyck language is the AntiDyck or FIFO language [2, 7]. Consider arrivals (a_k) and departures (a_k'') of $1 \leq k \leq n$ customers at a job shop with FIFO service. The sequence of events corresponding to the service of the incoming request is the AntiDyck language, defined by the ACF grammar with disposition $r(1) = B$:

[2] Productions of type $A \to w(\alpha)_D$, with $w = \varepsilon$, are allowed.

Example 1 FIFO or AntiDyck.

$$S \rightarrow (SS)_B \mid a_k(SA''_k)_B \mid \varepsilon \quad 1 \le k \le n \qquad A''_k \rightarrow a''_k(S)_B \qquad 1 \le k \le n$$

$$\begin{aligned}
&(S)_B \Rightarrow (\mathbf{SS})_B \Rightarrow \mathbf{a_1}(S\mathbf{SA''_1})_B \Rightarrow a_1\mathbf{a_2}(SA''_1\mathbf{SA''_2})_B \Rightarrow a_1a_2(A''_1SA''_2)_B \Rightarrow \\
&\Rightarrow a_1a_2\mathbf{a''_1}(SA''_2S)_B \Rightarrow a_1a_2a''_1\mathbf{a_3}(A''_2S\mathbf{SA''_3})_B \Rightarrow a_1a_2a''_1a_3\mathbf{a''_2}(SSA''_3\mathbf{S})_B \Rightarrow \\
&\Rightarrow a_1a_2a''_1a_3a''_2(SA''_3S)_B \Rightarrow a_1a_2a''_1a_3a''_2(A''_3S)_B \Rightarrow a_1a_2a''_1a_3a''_2\mathbf{a''_3}(S\mathbf{S})_B \Rightarrow \\
&\Rightarrow a_1a_2a''_1a_3a''_2a''_3(S)_B \Rightarrow a_1a_2a''_1a_3a''_2a''_3(\varepsilon)_B = a_1a_2a''_1a_3a''_2a''_3
\end{aligned}$$

A richer example, the Dyck-AntiDyck language corresponding to the disposition $r(1) = D$ and $r(2) = B$, is shown in section 5.

Consider procedure declarations, with the procedure identifier repeated after the procedure end; the disposition of the grammar is $r(1) = D$ and $r(2) = B$:

Example 2 Procedure Declarations.

$$\begin{aligned}
&S \rightarrow (\langle PDECL\rangle)_D(\langle PLIST\rangle)_B \mid (\langle PDECL\rangle)_D(\varepsilon)_B \\
&\langle PDECL\rangle \rightarrow proc(\langle PID\rangle\langle BLOCK\rangle\langle END\rangle)_D(\varepsilon)_B \\
&\langle PID\rangle \rightarrow a(\langle PID\rangle)_D(A)_B \mid b(\langle PID\rangle)_D(B)_B \mid \ldots \mid \varepsilon \\
&\langle PLIST\rangle \rightarrow (\varepsilon)_D(S)_B \\
&\langle A\rangle \rightarrow a \qquad\qquad \langle B\rangle \rightarrow b \quad \ldots \\
&\langle BLOCK\rangle \rightarrow (\langle STAT\rangle\langle BLOCK\rangle)_D(\varepsilon)_B \mid (\langle STAT\rangle)_D(\varepsilon)_B \\
&\langle STAT\rangle \rightarrow begin(\langle BLOCK\rangle\langle END\rangle)_D(\varepsilon)_B \mid simplestat \\
&\langle END\rangle \rightarrow end
\end{aligned}$$

Figure 1 shows a derivation tree for this grammar; note that the subtree corresponding to the B segment must be visited breadth-first. The D segment

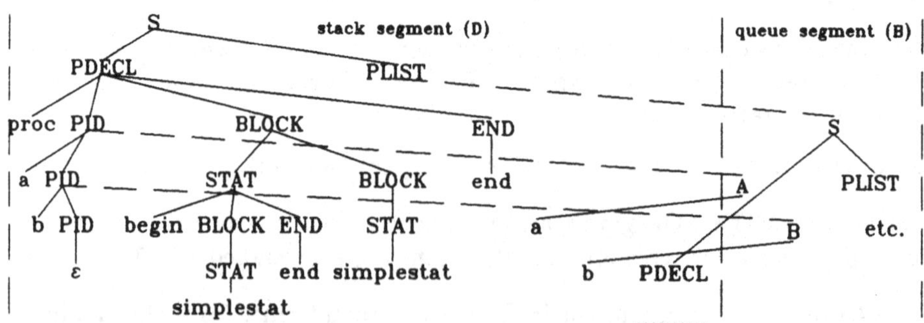

Fig. 1. *Partial syntactic tree for procedure declarations.*

accounts for block nesting in the procedure body, whereas the B segment stores the procedure identifier for later reuse. Procedures cannot be nested, but this feature can be implemented by using the disposition $r(1) = r(2) = D$ instead of $r(1) = D$ and $r(2) = B$ [6].

3 $LL(1)$ ACF grammars

The next definition subsumes the classical one for CF grammars:

Definition 5. The ACF grammar G is $LL(1)$ iff there do not exist two derivations:

$$S \stackrel{*}{\Rightarrow} u(\varepsilon)_{r(1)} \cdots (\varepsilon)_{r(i-1)}(A\beta_i)_{r(i)}(\beta_{i+1})_{r(i+1)} \cdots (\beta_n)_{r(n)} \stackrel{p_h P^*}{\Longrightarrow} uax\,\chi$$
$$S \stackrel{*}{\Rightarrow} v(\varepsilon)_{r(1)} \cdots (\varepsilon)_{r(j-1)}(A\gamma_j)_{r(j)}(\gamma_{j+1})_{r(j+1)} \cdots (\gamma_n)_{r(n)} \stackrel{p_k P^*}{\Longrightarrow} uby\,\xi$$

where $a \neq b$, with $a, b \in V_T$, and $\chi = (\chi_1)_{r(1)} \cdots (\chi_n)_{r(n)}, \xi = (\xi_1)_{r(1)} \cdots (\xi_n)_{r(n)}$

The two productions $p_h, p_k \in P$ are alternatives with the same left member; $\beta_r, \gamma_s, \chi_t, \xi_t \in V_N^*$, for any $i, j \leq r, s \leq n$ and $1 \leq t \leq n$, are contents of segments; and $u, v, x, y \in V_T^*$ are terminal strings. □

Intuitively G is $LL(1)$ iff there do not exist two distinct derivations, starting from the same non-terminal A, such that the next generated terminal character is the same.

It is immediate to give the definition of look-ahead set of a production:

Definition 6. Given the ACF grammar G, the look-ahead set $LA(p) \subseteq V_T \cup \{\dashv\}$ ($\dashv$ is the end-marker) of the production p is defined as the largest set satisfying the two following relationships:

$$a \in LA(p) \Leftrightarrow S \stackrel{*}{\Rightarrow} u(\varepsilon)_{r(1)} \cdots (\varepsilon)_{r(i-1)}(A\beta_i)_{r(i)}(\beta_{i+1})_{r(i+1)} \cdots (\beta_n)_{r(n)} \stackrel{pP^*}{\Rightarrow} uax\chi$$
$$\dashv \in LA(p) \Leftrightarrow S \stackrel{*}{\Rightarrow} u(\varepsilon)_{r(1)} \cdots (\varepsilon)_{r(j-1)}(A\beta_j)_{r(j)}(\beta_{j+1})_{r(j+1)} \cdots (\beta_n)_{r(n)} \stackrel{pP^*}{\Rightarrow} u$$

where the symbols have the same meaning as in definition 5. □

Proposition 7. *An ACF grammar G is $LL(1)$ iff, for any two alternative productions p_h, p_k, with $h \neq k$, it holds $LA(p_h) \cap LA(p_k) = \emptyset$.* □

Lemma 8. *For any ACF grammar G and any production p, the look-ahead set $LA(p)$ is computable.* □

The proof is deferred to section 4.

Theorem 9. *It is decidable whether an ACF grammar G is $LL(1)$.* □

Proof. By proposition 7 and lemma 8, the disjoint intersection emptiness test of the look-ahead sets allows to decide effectively the $LL(1)$ property.

4 Computation of look-ahead sets

The computation of look-ahead sets is based on an algebraic theory of adjacencies in ACF grammars [4].

4.1 Recall of Adjacency Theory for ACF Grammars

The separator character $\perp$ prevents two characters from becoming adjacent. Consider a string over the alphabet $V \cup \{\perp\}$, where the special character $\perp$ acts as a *separator*. It makes no sense to write two adjacent separators; i.e. one has the relationship $\perp^2 = \perp$.

These concepts can be compactly embedded into the definition of a new monoid M:

Definition 10. Given any alphabet V, let $\cong_\perp$ be the congruence, over the free monoid $(V \cup \{\perp\})^*$, generated by the relationship $\perp^2 = \perp$. Define the quotient monoid $M = (V \cup \{\perp\})^* / \cong_\perp$. □

By definition of quotient monoid the elements of the monoid M can be identified with the strings over the extended alphabet $V \cup \{\perp\}$ wherein no two adjacent separators $\perp$ occur. The free monoid V^* is clearly a submonoid of M.

We write AB **in** α, where $A, B \in V$, to mean that the string $\alpha \in M$ can be factorised as $\alpha_1 AB \alpha_2$, i.e. it contains at least one instance of the adjacent letter pair AB.

The following transformation compresses strings preserving adjacencies:

Definition 11. Given some alphabet V, let $\tau : M \to 2^M$ be a function defined:

$$\tau(\alpha) = \{\beta | \quad \beta \in M \ \wedge \ (\beta \text{ is } \textbf{fixpoint} \text{ of } \alpha = \alpha_1 ABC \alpha_2 \mapsto \alpha_1 A \perp C \alpha_2)\}$$

where if none of A, B is $\perp$ then AB **in** $\alpha_1 A$ and if none of B, C is $\perp$ then BC **in** $\alpha_1 A$. The symbols are $\alpha, \alpha_1, \alpha_2, \beta \in M$ and $A, B, C \in V \cup \{\perp\}$. □

The transformation τ enjoys the following properties, proven in [4]:

1. **Existence/Uniqueness**: for any string $\alpha \in M$ there exists $\beta \in M$ such that $\beta \in \tau(\alpha)$ and for any other $\gamma \in M$ such that $\gamma \in \tau(\alpha)$ it holds $\beta = \gamma$, i.e. any string α admits one and only one τ-image.
2. **Finiteness**: there exists a positive integer K, depending only on the alphabet V, such that for any string $\alpha \in M$ and $\beta \in \tau(\alpha)$, it holds $|\beta| \leq K$, i.e. any string α has τ-images of bounded length.
3. **Absorption**: for any strings $\alpha, \beta \in M$ it holds $\tau(\alpha\beta) = \tau(\tau(\alpha)\tau(\beta))$.

Thanks to point (1) τ can be assumed to be a total function on M to M.

For any two strings $\alpha, \beta \in M$, define: $\alpha \odot \beta = \tau(\alpha\beta)$; $\odot$ is associative and admits a neutral element (the string ε, because $\tau(\varepsilon) = \varepsilon$), hence is a concatenation operator, called τ-concatenation. Here is an example of τ-concatenation: $ABCDE \odot ABCDE = \tau(ABCDEABCDE) = ABCDEA{\perp}{\perp}{\perp}E \cong_\perp ABCDE$ $A{\perp}E$ (this also gives an example of computation of the function τ).

Proposition 12. *The function $\tau : M \to T$ is a surjective monoid hom. on the monoid $M = \langle M, \cdot, \varepsilon \rangle$, under concatenation, onto the finite monoid $T = \langle \tau(M), \odot, \varepsilon \rangle$, under τ-concatenation. It holds $T = M / \cong_\tau$, where $\cong_\tau$ is the natural equivalence on M induced by the function τ.* □

The proof is given by points (2) and (3) above.

We can extend ACF grammars to the monoid T, by replacing concatenation with τ-concatenation; such grammars will be named τ-ACF. A segment of a τ-ACF sentential form is a string belonging to the finite monoid T, and since the disposition is finite, a τ-ACF grammar is equivalent to a finite state device.

The next step is to convert an ACF grammar into a τ-ACF one, featuring the same adjacencies. A production $p \in P$ of an ACF grammar $G = (V_N, V_T, S, P, r)$ is mapped onto a production $\tau(p)$ of a τ-ACF grammar $G_\tau = (V_N, V_T \cup \{\perp\}, S, P_\tau, r)$ as follows:

$$p : A \rightarrow v(\alpha_1)_{r(1)}, \ldots, (\alpha_n)_{r(n)} \mapsto \tau(p) : A \rightarrow \tau(v)(\tau(\alpha_1))_{r_\tau(1)}, \ldots, (\tau(\alpha_n))_{r_\tau(n)}$$

A similar rule allows to map sentential forms; note that the segments of $\tau(p)$ retain their D (LIFO) or B (FIFO) nature, but under τ-concatenation.

Proposition 13. *Given any ACF grammar G and its τ-ACF image G_τ, for any derivation step $S_1 \overset{p}{\Rightarrow}_G S_2$ of G there exists a hom. image of G_τ, obtained by means of the function τ, namely $\tau(S_1) \overset{\tau(p)}{\Rightarrow}_{G_\tau} \tau(S_2)$.* □

Note that two symbols A and B, placed in different segments as in $(\ldots A)_{r(i)}$ $(\varepsilon)_{r(i+1)} \cdots (\varepsilon)_{r(i+j-1)}$ $(B \ldots)_{r(i+j)}$ are considered adjacent. The round brackets () are only separators, not involved in adjacencies.

Remark. Although in G_τ there may exist derivations that are not hom. images, through τ, of derivations in G, it is however possible to decide whether a derivation of G_τ is a hom. image of at least one derivation of G: it suffices to attempt to reproduce it in G [4]. It is also decidable whether an *infinite* but *regular* set of derivations of G_τ contains at least one derivation that is a hom. image of a derivation of G [4].

In [4] proposition 13 is used to solve the adjacency problem: decide whether an ACF grammar G admits a derivation $S \overset{*}{\Rightarrow} S_i$ such that the symbols $A, B \in V_T \cup V_N$ are adjacent in the sentential form S_i, i.e. whether AB **in** S_i. In fact, the function τ has the property to preserve adjacencies; hence the adjacency problem of G is equivalent to that of G_τ (see remark 4.1), where it can be solved by extensive check, because G_τ is in turn equivalent to a finite state device and the function τ is computable [4].

4.2 Look-ahead Sets of ACF Grammars

The function τ will next be used to compute the look-ahead sets. The production set P can be partitioned into the set P_T of the productions that contain terminal characters and the set P_N of those that do not. Denote $FS(p) = \{a|$ terminal a occurs in production $p\} \subseteq V_T$ to be the set of terminal characters contained in the production $p \in P$, if any (FS stands for first-set).

Given an ACF grammar $G \in \mathcal{G}_r$, the (leftmost) Szilard language of G is the set $S(G) \subseteq P^*$ of the label traces of the derivations of G. Since derivations are leftmost, the Szilard language of any ACF grammar is in $\mathcal{L}_r$. The look-ahead set can be reformulated as follows:

Definition 14. The look-ahead set of production p is:

$$LA(p) = \begin{cases} \text{if } p \in P_T & FS(p) \\ \text{if } p \in P_N & \{a | \, p_i \in P_T \,\wedge\, a \in FS(p_i) \,\wedge\, (P^* p P_N^* p_i P^* \cap S(G) \neq \emptyset)\} \end{cases}$$

and $\dashv \in LA(p)$ if $p \in P_N \wedge (P^* p P_N^* \cap S(G) \neq \emptyset)$. □

This is equivalent to definition 6, for if $p \in P_T$ then $FS(p)$ immediately gives the look-ahead set of p, otherwise we must check whether there exists a derivation that, after using the production p at some step, uses the production p_i that generates a, possibly after using some productions that do not generate immediately any terminal character. The end-marker $\dashv$ must be added to the look- ahead set of p whenever after using p no more terminal characters are generated.

Combining proposition 13 and reformulation 14, the look-ahead set can be computed. Here follows the proof of lemma 8:

Lemma 8. Given any ACF grammar G, there exists an algorithm to compute the look-ahead sets of its productions. □

Proof. The proof is essentially a recollection of previous lemmas and propositions. Let $G \in \mathcal{G}_r$ be an ACF grammar. By definition 14, in order to compute $LA(p_o)$ for $p_o \in P$ we need look for strings of types $P^* p_o P_N^* p_i P^*$ and $P^* p_o P_N^*$ in the Szilard language of G. The language $S(G)$ is generated by a grammar $G^S = (V_N, P, S, P, r) \in \mathcal{G}_r$; G^S uses the labels of the productions of G as its terminal characters. Let $G_\tau^S = (V_N, P \cup \{\perp\}, S, P_\tau, r_\tau)$ be the hom. τ-image of G^S, through the function τ. By proposition 13 and remark 4.1 any derivation step of G^S admits a computable homomorphic τ-image of G_τ^S. The derivation relation of G_τ^S is finite, since the set of all sentential forms of G_τ^S is finite; hence it can be computed extensively. Suppose the arcs of the finite directed graph of the derivation relation of G_τ^S are labeled with the productions in P_τ. Deciding the existence of paths of the types $P_\tau^* p_{o,\tau} P_{N,\tau}^* p_{i,\tau} P_\tau^*$ and $P_\tau^* p_{o,\tau} P_{N,\tau}^*$ amounts to checking the intersection emptiness of two regular languages. Let $path(p_o) = graph(G) \cap P_\tau^* p_{o,\tau} P_{N,\tau}^* p_{i,\tau} P_\tau^*$ or $path(p_o) = graph(G) \cap P_\tau^* p_{o,\tau} P_{N,\tau}^*$, then $path(p_o)$ is a regular set. Since, by remark 4.1, it is possible to decide whether at least one path in $path(p_o)$ admits a counterimage path in the derivation relation of G^S, we can decide whether, for any production $p_i \in P$, it holds $FS(p_i) \subseteq LA(p_o)$ or $\dashv \in LA(p_o)$. The computation of the set $FS(p_i)$ is immediate.

Lemma 8 implies the decidability of the $LL(1)$ property of ACF grammars (see theorem 9).

5 Construction of the deterministic parser

For a $LL(1)$ ACF grammar it is straightforward to construct a deterministic recogniser. It suffices to show an example.

Example 3 Recursive Descent ACF Parser. The construction extends the classical one adding a FIFO structure to the recursive descent stack. We illustrate the procedure by implementing a $LL(1)$ parser for the Dyck-AntiDyck language [4] with two letters a, b, defined by the ACF grammar G, with disposition $r(1) = D$ and $r(2) = B$:

$$V_T = \{a, a', a'', b, b', b''\} \qquad V_N = \{S, E, A', A'', B', B''\}$$
$$S \rightarrow \varepsilon \qquad E \rightarrow \varepsilon$$
$$S \rightarrow a(EA')_D(A'')_B \mid b(EB')_D(B'')_B \qquad E \rightarrow a(EA')_D(A'')_B \mid b(EB')_D(B'')_B$$
$$A' \rightarrow a'(E)_D(\varepsilon)_B \qquad A'' \rightarrow a''(E)_D(\varepsilon)_B$$
$$B' \rightarrow b'(E)_D(\varepsilon)_B \qquad B'' \rightarrow b''(E)_D(\varepsilon)_B$$

Some strings of this language are: ε, $aa'a''$, $abb'a'a''b''$, $aa'bb'a''b''$, $aa'a''bb'b''$, $abb'a'a''aa'b''a''$, ... The lookahead sets of grammar G are:

$$LA(A'' \rightarrow a''(E)_D(\varepsilon)_B) = \{a''\} \qquad LA(B'' \rightarrow b''(E)_D(\varepsilon)_B) = \{b''\}$$
$$LA(A' \rightarrow a'(E)_D(\varepsilon)_B) = \{a'\} \qquad LA(B' \rightarrow b'(E)_D(\varepsilon)_B) = \{b'\}$$
$$LA(E \rightarrow a(EA')_D(A'')_B) = \{a\} \qquad LA(E \rightarrow b(EB')_D(B'')_B) = \{b\}$$
$$LA(E \rightarrow \varepsilon) = \{\dashv, a', a'', b', b''\} \qquad LA(S \rightarrow a(EA')_D(A'')_B) = \{a\}$$
$$LA(S \rightarrow b(EB')_D(B'')_B) = \{b\} \qquad LA(S \rightarrow \varepsilon) = \{\dashv\}$$

A syntactic procedure is provided for each non-terminal; the main program is shown at the end. The first segment nature is $r(1) = D$, which requires a PD stack, implemented by the stack of activation records of the syntactic procedures. On the contrary the second segment, $r(2) = B$, is implemented by a separate FIFO structure, the queue. Other implementations would of course be possible, including the use of the system queues provided by operating systems for managing remote procedure calls or entry calls in Ada.

```
procedure A'';                procedure A';
begin                         begin
    if char = a'' then            if char = a' then
        read(char);                   read(char);
        call E                        call E
    else error                    else error
end A'';                      end A';
```

The procedures for the non-terminals B' and B'' are formally identical to procedures A' and A'' and are omitted.

```
procedure E;
const
    FIN = {⊣, a', a'', b', b''}
begin
    case char of
    a: read(char);
        call enqueue(A'');
        call E;
        call A'
    b: read(char);
        call enqueue(B'');
        call E;
        call B'
    else if char ∉ FIN then error
    end case
end E;
```

```
program PARSER;
var
    queue: array of procname;
    size : integer;
    char: character
begin
    size := 0;
    read(char);
    case char of
    a: read(char);
        call enqueue(A'');
        call E;
        call A'
    b: read(char);
        call enqueue(B'');
        call E;
        call B'
    else if char ≠⊣ then error
    end case
    while size > 0 do call head
end PARSER.
```

The data structure *queue* is a sequence of procedure names; the $LL(1)$ parser uses two auxiliary procedures (not shown) for queue handling: *enqueue*, that appends with a FIFO policy the name of the procedure to the *queue* of procedure names; *head*, that returns the address of the procedure, the name of which is on top of the *queue* of procedure names, and deletes the top of the *queue* of procedure names.

The example can be easily generalised to any disposition. Given a $LL(1)$ ACF grammar G, its parser will always have a linear-time complexity. In fact, the parser is deterministic, as a consequence of the $LL(1)$ property of G, hence in any derivation of G two productions p_k and p_h, containing terminals, are separated by a bounded number of productions of P_N, which do not contain terminals. Were not so, the derivation would be an everlooping one. But the bound depends only on G, hence the length of the derivation is a linear function of the length of the generated string.

6 Conclusion

The structure of the parser motivates the name "augmented" CF of these languages, because they can be viewed as a formal model of the augmented transition networks ATN (Woods [15]), a well-known semi-formal approach for writing parsers. The ATN's use certain registers to store information during parsing and allow transitions to be enabled by the presence of specified data in the registers. In our model a similar behaviour can be obtained by using a suitable disposition of memory segments. Notice however that the generative capacity of ACF grammars is more restricted than ATN's, which accept any recursively enumerable set, because they allow unrestricted use of their registers.

References

1. E. Allevi, A. Cherubini, S. Crespi Reghizzi, "Breadth-first Phrase-Structure Grammars and Queue Automata", in *LNCS* 324, 1988, pp. 162-170
2. F. Brandenburg, "On the Intersections of Stacks and Queues", in *Theoretical Computer Science* 226, 1981, pp. 61-68
3. L. Breveglieri, C. Citrini, S. Crespi Reghizzi, "Deterministic Dequeue Automata and $LL(1)$ Parsing of Breadth-Depth Grammars", in *LNCS* 529, 1991, pp. 146-156
4. L. Breveglieri, A. Cherubini, S. Crespi Reghizzi, "A Chomsky-Schützenberger Property for generalised (augmented) Context-free Languages", Internal Report n. 93-062, Dipartimento di Elettrnonica e Informazione, Politecnico di Milano, 1994
5. A. Cherubini, C. Citrini, S. Crespi Reghizzi, D. Mandrioli, "QRT FIFO Automata, Breadth-first Grammars and their Relations", in *Theoretical Computer Science* 85, 1991, pp. 171-203
6. A. Cherubini, P. San Pietro, "Polynomial Time Parsing Algorithm for k-Depth Languages", to appear in *Journal of Computer and Systems Science*, 1995
7. B. Franchi Zannettacci, B. Vauquelin, "Automates à File" (in French) (Queue Automata), in *Theoretical Computer Science* 11, 1980, pp. 221-225
8. Y. Guan, G. Hotz, A. Reichert, "Tree Grammars with multilinear Interpretation", Technical Report, University of Saarbrücken, 1992
9. G. Hotz, G. Pitsch, "On Parsing Coupled Context-free Languages", submitted for publication, 1994
10. A. K. Joshi, L. S. Levi, M. Takahashi, "Tree adjunct Grammars", in *Journal on Computer Systems Science* 10, 1975, pp. 136-173
11. P. M. II Lewis, R. E. Stearns, "Syntax-directed Transduction", in *Journal of ACM* 15, 1968, pp. 464-488
12. G. Pitsch, "LL(k) Coupled Context-free Grammars", in *Journal on Information and Processing Cybernetics*, EIK 29, 6, 1993, pp. 389-413
13. G. Satta, "Tree-adjoining Grammar Parsing and Matrix Multiplication", in *Computational Linguistics*, 20, 2, 1994, pp. 173-191
14. K. Vijay Shanker, D. J. Weir, "The Equivalence of four Extensions of Context-free Grammars", in *Mathematical Systems Theory* 27, 1994, pp. 511-546
15. W. A. Woods, "Transition Network Grammars for natural Language Analysis", in *Communications of ACM*, 13, 10, 1970, pp. 591-606

A Periodicity Theorem on Words and Applications*

Filippo Mignosi, Antonio Restivo and Sergio Salemi

Dipartimento di Matematica ed Applicazioni, Università di Palermo
via Archirafi 34 - 90123 Palermo - ITALY

Abstract. We prove a periodicity theorem on words that has strong analogies with the Critical Factorization theorem and we show three applications of it.

1 Introduction

The study of periodicity is a central topic in combinatorics on words and presents some important applications in algebra, in formal language theory and in string searching algorithms. The main results concerning periodicity on words are the theorem of Fine and Wilf and the Critical Factorization theorem. In the Critical Factorization theorem one considers a word $a_1a_2\cdots a_n$ and, for any integer i ($1 \leq i \leq n-1$), one looks at the shortest repetition (a *square*) *centered* in this position, i.e. one looks at the shortest (virtual) suffix of $a_1a_2\cdots a_i$ which is also a (virtual) prefix of $a_{i+1}a_{i+2}\cdots a_n$ (cf. [6], [8] and [11]). The local period at position i is defined as the length of this shortest suffix. The Critical Factorization theorem states, roughly speaking, that the global period of $a_1a_2\cdots a_n$ is the maximum of the local periods.

The main result of this paper states a new periodicity theorem on words that presents some analogies with the Critical Factorization theorem.

Two main points make the difference. Firstly, we define a local period by considering, for any position in the word, instead of a shortest repetition *centered* in that position, a shortest φ^2-repetition *ending* in that position.

The second differencen is that by a φ^2-repetition we here mean (instead of a *square*, i.e. a word having period P and length $2P$), a word having period P and length greater than or equal to $\varphi^2 P$, where φ is the golden number.

By taking into account this new notion of local period, our main result states a relationship between the period of a word to its local periods. We further prove that the number $\varphi^2 = 2.618\cdots$ is tight for this result, in the sense that for any real number smaller than φ^2 (for instance 2) this result cannot be achieved.

Remark that this theorem also improves some combinatorial lemmas obtained in [10] and [1] and motivated by string matching problems.

We then derive three applications of this result. In the first application we show, answering a question of J. Shallit [14], that an infinite word $w = a_1a_2a_3\cdots$ is ultimately periodic if and only if there exists a positive integer k such that for any

* Work partially supported by the ESPRIT II Basic Research Actions Program of the EC under Project ASMICS 2 (contract No. 6317)

$n \geq k$ the finite word $a_1 a_2 \cdots a_n$ has a suffix that is a φ^2-repetition. By using the Fibonacci word we show that the number φ^2 is tight for this result.

The second application concernes the perfectness of some families of infinite words and it is related to some problems posed by J. D. Currie [2]. We show that the family of α-power free infinite words over an alphabet of cardinality greater than or equal to 2, with $\alpha \geq \varphi^2 + 1$, is a perfect set. This improves some results obtained by J. D. Currie [3].

As a third application we improve the upper bound on the number of comparisons in the text processing of the Galil-Seiferas's string matching algorithm [10].

2 A Periodicity Theorem

In this section we prove the main result of this paper. Before stating it we give four lemmas; the first three are elementary and we state them without proofs.

For any notations not explicitely defined in this paper we refer to [11]

We start with the classical definition of periodicity in words.

Definition 1. Let $w = a_1 \cdots a_k$. We say that w has period P if for any integers r, s such that $1 \leq r \leq s \leq k$

$$r \equiv s \pmod{P} \Longrightarrow a_r = a_s.$$

Lemma 2. *Let $w = vu$ be a word having two periods, P and Q, with $Q < P$ and $|u| = Q$. Then v has period $P - Q$.*

Lemma 3. *Let u, v, w be words such that uv and vw have period P and $|v| \geq P$ Then the word uvw has period P.*

The *golden number*, here denoted by φ, plays an important role in this paper. Let us recall that φ is the real positive root of the equation $x^2 - x - 1 = 0$. Since by definition $\varphi^2 = \varphi + 1$, in the proofs of this paper we shall sometimes interchange φ^2 and $\varphi + 1$ without mentioning it explicitely.

Lemma 4. *Let φ be the golden number and let P, Q be two positive integers with $Q < P$. The following two inequalities are equivalent.*

i) $(\varphi/(\varphi+1))P \leq Q$
ii) $(\varphi P - Q)/(P - Q) \geq \varphi^2$.

In order to state the mail result of this paper we need the following definitions and notations

Let v be a word having period P and let α be a real positive number. The word v is here called an *α-repetition* if $|v|/P \geq \alpha$. For instance a square is a 2-repetition. If a α-repetition v is a suffix (rep. prefix) of a word w we say that w has a *α-suffix with period P* (resp. a *α-prefix with period P*).

Lemma 5. *Let $w = a_1 a_2 \cdots a_j$ be a word which has periods P, Q with $Q < P$, and let us suppose that $|w| \geq \varphi P$. If $Q < (\varphi/(\varphi+1))P$ then w has a φ^2-suffix with period Q; if $Q \geq (\varphi/(\varphi+1))P$ then w has a φ^2-suffix with period $P - Q$.*

Proof: We can suppose that the length of w is $\lceil \varphi P \rceil$ (otherwise we consider the suffix of w having this length).

If $Q < (\varphi/(\varphi+1))P$ then $(\varphi P)/Q > \varphi + 1 = \varphi^2$ then the statement of the proposition is true, because w has an $\lceil \varphi P \rceil / Q$-suffix with period Q (w itself).

Let us suppose that $Q \geq (\varphi/(\varphi+1))P$, i.e. $(\varphi+1)Q \geq \varphi P$ (see next figure).

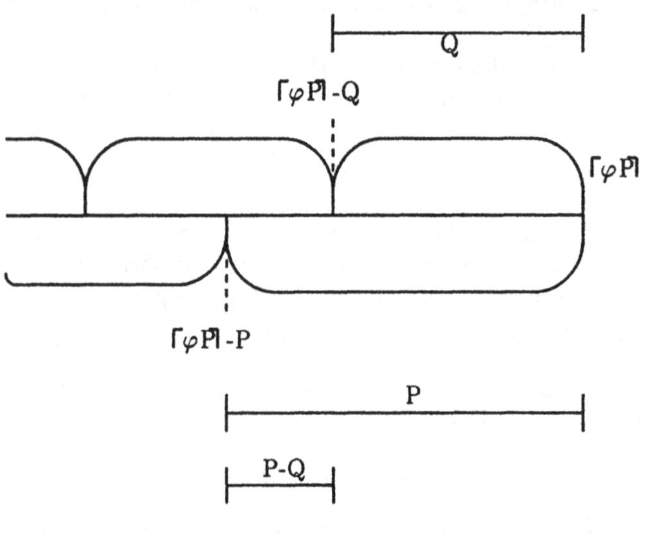

Fig. 1

By Lemma 2 it follows that the word

$$v = a_1 a_2 \cdots a_{j-Q}$$

has period $P - Q$. One has that

$$|v|/(P-Q) = (\lceil \varphi P \rceil - Q)/(P-Q) \geq (\varphi P - Q)/(P-Q).$$

By Lemma 4, $|v|/(P-Q) \geq \varphi^2$ and, so, by definition v is a φ^2-repetition with period $P-Q$. Since w has period Q, its prefix v of length $|w| - Q$, is also a suffix of w. Therefore w has a φ^2-suffix with period $P-Q$. □

In the following theorem we consider two positive integers k, t and a word $x = a_1 \cdots a_k \cdots a_t$ such that for any n, $k \leq n \leq t$, the word $a_1 \cdots a_n$ has a φ^2-suffix, where φ is the golden number.

We define the *φ-local period* $p(n)$ as follows

$$p(n) = min\{d \,|\, a_1 \cdots a_n \text{ has a } \varphi^2\text{-suffix with period } d\}.$$

We also define

$$P = max\{p(n) \,|\, k \leq n \leq t\}.$$

$$Z = min\{n \,|\, k \leq n \leq t \text{ and } p(n) = P\}.$$

$$S = max\{n \,|\, k \leq n \leq t \text{ and } p(n) = P\}.$$

Theorem 6. *The word $a_{Z-\lceil\varphi^2 P\rceil+1}\cdots a_S$ has period P. Moreover $Z < k+P$.*

Proof: The proof is by induction on the number m of indices n such that $p(n) = P$.

We first prove the statement for $m = 1$ (the base of the induction).

If $m = 1$ there exists only one natural n such that $p(n) = P$. In this case $Z = S$ and, by definition, $a_{Z-\lceil\varphi^2 P\rceil+1}\cdots a_Z$ has period P.

It remains to show that $Z < k+P$. The proof is by contradiction. Suppose that $Z - P \geq k$, then the word $a_1\cdots a_{Z-P}$ has, by definition, a φ^2-suffix with period $p(Z-P) = Q$. Notice that, since $m = 1$, $Q < P$.

Two cases are possible: either $Q > (\varphi/(\varphi+1))P$, or $Q \leq (\varphi/(\varphi+1))P$.

If $Q > (\varphi/(\varphi+1))P$, then $(\varphi+1)Q = \varphi^2 Q > \varphi P$. Since by hypothesis $a_1\cdots a_{Z-P}$ has a φ^2-suffix of period Q then the length of this suffix is $\geq \varphi^2 Q > \varphi P$. It follows that the word w of length $\lceil\varphi P\rceil$

$$w = a_{Z-P-\lceil\varphi P\rceil+1}\cdots a_{Z-P}$$

has period Q.

Since $a_1\cdots a_Z$ has a $\varphi^2 = (\varphi+1)$-suffix with period P, then $a_1\cdots a_{Z-P}$ has a φ-suffix with same period P. It follows that the word w has also period P. By Lemma 5 w (and consequently $a_1\cdots a_{Z-P}$) has a φ^2-suffix of period $P-Q$.

We note that $P - Q < Q$, because $Q \geq (\varphi/(\varphi+1))P$, and, so, $Q > P/2$. This contradicts the fact that $p(Z-P) = Q$.

In the case $Q \leq (\varphi/(\varphi+1))P$ we also derive a contradiction. Indeed, since the word $a_1\cdots a_Z$ and the word $a_1\cdots a_{Z-P}$ have the same suffix of length $\lceil\varphi P\rceil$, and since the φ^2-suffix of $a_1\cdots a_{Z-P}$ has in this case length $\leq \varphi P$, then $p(Z) \leq Q \leq (\varphi/(\varphi+1))P < P$, against the hypothesis that $p(Z) = P$.

We have now to prove the inductive step. Let $m > 1$. Denote by $\hat{n}$, the greatest among the numbers $n < S$ such that $p(n) = P$.

By inductive hypothesis, the word $a_{Z-\lceil(1+\varphi)P\rceil+1}\cdots a_{\hat{n}}$ has period P. Moreover $Z < k+P$.

Set $\hat{k} = \hat{n}+1$. The word $x = a_1\cdots a_{k+t} = a_1\cdots a_{\hat{k}}\cdots a_{k+t}$ satisfies the hypothesis of the theorem by changing k with $\hat{k}$, and we are in same situation than the previous case $m = 1$. Therefore the word $a_{S-\lceil(1+\varphi)P\rceil+1}\cdots a_S$ has period P. Moreover $S < \hat{k}+P$.

Set $u = a_{Z-\lceil(1+\varphi)P\rceil+1}\cdots a_{S-\lceil(1+\varphi)P\rceil}$, $v = a_{S-\lceil(1+\varphi)P\rceil+1}\cdots a_{\hat{n}}$, and $w = a_{\hat{k}}\cdots a_S$. We know that uv and vw have period P. We now show that $|v| \geq P$. One has

$$|v| = \hat{n} - (S - \lceil(1+\varphi)P\rceil) = \hat{n} - S + P - \lceil\varphi P\rceil.$$

Since $S < \hat{k} + P \leq \hat{k} + P - 1 = \hat{n} + P$,

$$|v| \geq \hat{n} - \hat{n} - \lceil\varphi P\rceil = \lceil\varphi P\rceil > P.$$

By Lemma 3 the statement of the theorem follows. □

The hypothesis in the previous theorem that for any n, $k \leq n \leq t$, the word $a_1\cdots a_n$ has a φ^2-suffix, is quite strong. In order to skip this hypothesis (analogously as done in the Critical Factorization Theorem by J. P. Duval, cf. [6], [8] and [11]), we extend the notion of φ-local period to the notion of *virtual* φ-local period.

In the following Proposition we consider a word $x = a_1 \cdots a_t$.

For any n, $1 \leq n \leq t$, we define the *φ-virtual local period* $\hat{p}(n)$ as follows

$$\hat{p}(n) = min\{d \,|\, a_1 \cdots a_n \text{ has a } \varphi^2\text{-suffix with period } d \text{ or } a_1 \cdots a_n \text{ has period } d\}.$$

We define

$$\hat{P} = max\{\hat{p}(n) \,|\, 1 \leq n \leq t\}.$$

$$\hat{Z} = min\{n \,|\, 1 \leq n \leq t \text{ and } \hat{p}(n) = \hat{P}\}.$$

$$\hat{S} = max\{n \,|\, 1 \leq n \leq t \text{ and } \hat{p}(n) = \hat{P}\}.$$

Proposition 7. *The word $a_1 \cdots a_{\hat{S}}$ has period $\hat{P}$. Moreover $\hat{Z} < \varphi^2 \hat{P}$.*

Proof. It is easy to verify that if $p(n)$ is defined (i.e. $a_1 \cdots a_{n_2}$ has a φ^2-suffix), then $p(n) = \hat{p}(n)$. Moreover, if $p(n)$ is not defined (i.e. $a_1 \cdots a_{n_2}$ has no φ^2-suffixes), then for any m, $1 \leq m \leq n$, $\hat{p}(m) \leq \hat{p}(n)$.

Consider now the set $\mathbf{X} = \{n \,|\, 1 \leq n \leq t \text{ and } \hat{p}(n) = \hat{P}\}$.

It is easy to prove that, supposing $n_1 < n_2$ with $n_1, n_2 \in \mathbf{X}$, if $p(n_2)$ is not defined then $p(n_1)$ is not defined. Analogously, if $p(n_1)$ is defined then $p(n_2)$ is defined.

If for any $n \in \mathbf{X}$, $p(n)$ is not defined, then $a_1 \cdots a_{\hat{S}}$, by definition of $\hat{p}(\hat{S})$, has period $\hat{P}$ and $|a_1 \cdots a_{\hat{S}}| = \hat{S} < \varphi^2 \hat{P}$, and, so, the proposition holds.

Hence we can suppose that there exists a smallest number $n_1 \in \mathbf{X}$ such that $p(n_1)$ is defined. The number n_1 cannot be the smallest element of $\mathbf{X}$ (i.e. $n_1 = \hat{Z}$) otherwise, by Lemma 5, $\hat{p}(n_1 - \hat{P}) = \hat{P}$, i.e. $n_1 - \hat{P} \in \mathbf{X}$, a contradiction. Set $k = n' + 1$ where n' is the greatest element of $\mathbf{X}$ smaller than n_1.

We claim that for any n, $k \leq n \leq t$, the word $a_1 \cdots a_n$ has a φ^2-suffix. If not then there exists a number n, $k \leq n \leq t$, such that $a_1 \cdots a_n$ has no φ^2-suffixes (i.e. $p(n)$ is not defined) and such that $\hat{p}(n) < \hat{P}$. Previous conditions imply that for any m, $1 \leq m \leq n$, $\hat{p}(m) \leq \hat{p}(n) < \hat{P}$, against the hypothesis that $\hat{p}(n') = \hat{P}$. Thus the claim is proved and it is now possible to apply Theorem 6 to the word x with the previously defined number k. By Theorem 6 $a_{n_1 - \lceil \varphi^2 \hat{P} \rceil + 1} \cdots a_{\hat{S}}$ has period $\hat{P}$ and $n_1 < n' + 1 - \hat{P}$, i. e. $n_1 \leq n' - \hat{P}$.

Since $p(n')$ is not defined and $\hat{p}(n') = \hat{P}$ then $a_1 \cdots a_{n'}$ has period $\hat{P}$. By Proposition 3, setting $u = a_1 \cdots a_{n_1 - \lceil \varphi^2 \hat{P} \rceil}$, $v = a_{n_1 - \lceil \varphi^2 \hat{P} \rceil + 1} \cdots a_{n'}$ and $w = a_{n'+1} \cdots a_{\hat{S}}$, since $|v| = n' - n_1 + \lceil \varphi^2 \hat{P} \rceil \geq n' - n' - \hat{P} + \lceil \varphi^2 \hat{P} \rceil = \lceil \varphi \hat{P} \rceil \geq \hat{P}$, $a_1 \cdots a_{\hat{S}}$ has period $\hat{P}$.

It remains to prove that $\hat{Z} < \varphi^2 \hat{P}$. We know that $\hat{Z} \leq n'$ and, consequently, $p(\hat{Z})$ is not defined, i.e. $a_1 \cdots a_{\hat{Z}}$ has no φ^2-suffixes; this fact and the fact that $\hat{p}(\hat{Z}) = \hat{P}$ implies that $|a_1 \cdots a_{\hat{Z}}| = \hat{Z} < \varphi^2 \hat{P}$, q.e.d. □

3 Ultimately Periodic Words

We state now the first application of our theorem that is a characterization of infinite words that are ultimately periodic. This result, which answer a question asked by J.

Shallit [14], is of independent interest and has also some interesting consequences. Indeed we will use it in the next section.

Let us recall that an infinite word $\mathbf{w} = a_1a_2\cdots$ is *ultimately periodic* if there exist natural numbers $M > 0$, $h > 0$, such that the infinite word $a_Ma_{M+1}\cdots$ is periodic with period h.

Theorem 8. *An infinite word* $\mathbf{w} = a_1a_2a_3\cdots$ *is ultimately periodic if and only if there exists a number* k *such that for any* $n \geq k$ *the finite word* $a_1a_2\cdots a_n$ *has a* φ^2*-suffix.*

Proof: If $\mathbf{w} = a_1a_2a_3\cdots$ is ultimately periodic then there exist natural numbers $M > 0$, $h > 0$, such that the infinite word $a_Ma_{M+1}\cdots$ is periodic with period h. Since $\varphi^2 < 3$, for any $n \geq M + 3h$ the finite word $a_1a_2\cdots a_n$ has an φ^2-suffix.

Let us suppose now that there exists a number k such that for any $n \geq k$ the finite word $a_1a_2\cdots a_n$ has an φ^2-suffix; we will show that $\mathbf{w} = a_1a_2a_3\cdots$ is ultimately periodic.

We firstly claim that $Sup\{p(n) \mid n \geq k\} < k$; we recall that we have defined $p(n)$ as $p(n) = min\{d \,|a_1\cdots a_n$ has a φ^2-suffix with period $d\}$. Let us suppose by contradiction that there exists an n such that $p(n) = P \geq k$. Let Z be the smallest n satisfiing this condition. This means that $a_1a_2\cdots a_Z$ has an φ^2-suffix with period P. Hence the length Z of $a_1a_2\cdots a_Z$ must be greater than $\varphi^2P = (1+\varphi)P = P + \varphi P \geq k + \varphi P > k + P$. By Theorem 6, applied to the word $a_1a_2\cdots a_Z$, one has that $Z < k + P$, a contradiction and the claim is proved.

Let us now denote by $P = Sup\{p(n) \mid n \geq k\} < k$

The proof of the proposition is by induction on P.

If $P = 1$, for any $n \geq k$ the word $a_1a_2\cdots a_n$ ends with a cube of period 1, i.e. it ends with a^3 where a is a letter. Trivially the infinite word $\mathbf{w}$ is ultimately periodic.

Let us suppose now that the statement is true for any P', $1 \leq P' \leq P$.

Two cases are possible.

First case: there are infinitely many number n such that $p(n) = P$. We want to prove that the infinite word $a_ka_{k+1}\cdots$ is periodic with period P. Let $i, j \geq k$, $i < j$, with $i = j \pmod{P}$; we want to prove that $a_i = a_j$. Take S such that $S \geq j$ and $p(S) = P$. By Theorem 6 applied to the word $a_1a_2\cdots a_S$ the word $a_k\cdots a_S$ is P-periodic and, consequently, $a_i = a_j$.

Second case: there are finitely many number n such that $p(n) = P$; let S be the greatest of such numbers. Set $k' = S + 1$. Since $Sup\{p(n) \mid n \geq k'\} = P' < P$ then $\mathbf{w}$ satisfies the inductive hypothesis (considering k' instead of k) and, consequently, it is ultimately periodic. □

We remark that the smallest number M such that the infinite word $a_Ma_{M+1}\cdots$ is periodic cannot be bounded by a function of k. We only know (by the previous proof) that the period of the word $a_Ma_{M+1}\cdots$ is smaller than k. An example is given by the word $(baaa)^n aaaaa\cdots$, $n \geq 3$; here the number k can be chosen equal to 12 and $M = 4n - 3$.

The following proposition shows that the number φ^2 is tight for both Theorem 6 and for Theorem 8; its proof makes use of properties of the Fibonacci words (cf. [12]).

Proposition 9. *For any real number $\epsilon > 0$ there exists a natural number $k > 0$ such that for any $n \geq k$ the prefix of length n of the infinite Fibonacci word has a $(\varphi^2 - \epsilon)$-suffix.*

By using results from [6] and [8] we can prove, in a non trivial way, the following Theorem, that is analogous to Theorem 8.

Theorem 10. *An infinite word $\mathbf{w} = a_1a_2a_3\cdots$ is ultimately periodic if and only if there exists a number k such that for any $n \geq k$ the finite word $a_1a_2\cdots a_n$ has a suffix that is equal to a prefix of the infinite word $a_na_{n+1}\cdots$.*

We remark that in this theorem we have a situation which is complementary to the one of Theorem 8: the smallest period P of the word $a_Ma_{M+1}\cdots$ cannot be bounded by a function of k, where M is the smallest number such that the infinite word $a_Ma_{M+1}\cdots$ is periodic. However we have that $M \leq k$. An example is given by the word $ba^nba^nba^nba^n\cdots$, $n \geq 2$; here the number k can be chosen equal to 2 and $P = n+1$.

4 Perfect Sets of Infinite Words

An infinite word $\mathbf{x}$ is α-power free for a real number $\alpha > 1$ if no factor of $\mathbf{x}$ is an α-repetition. The words that are 2-power free and 3-power free are usually called square-free and cube-free respectively. Given an alphabet A, we denote by $X(\alpha, A)$ as the set of infinite words over A that are α-power free.

Several authors have studied the topological properties of the set $X(\alpha, A)$ for different *integer* values of the number α and for different alphabets (cf [2]). In particular Shelton and Sony in [15] proved that $X(2, A)$ is a perfect set for *Card(A)*$= 3$.

The most recent results have been obtained by J. D. Currie [3] who has shown that $X(\alpha, A)$ is a perfect set for any *integer* α greater than or equal to two and such that $\alpha+$*Card(A)*≥ 5, except possibly in the case $\alpha = 3$ and *Card(A)*$= 2$. This last case is posed as an open problem in [2] and recently solved, as announced in [4]. In [5] it is shown that $X(\alpha, A)$ is a perfect set for any *real* number α, $1 < \alpha < 2$ and large enough alphabet A.

In this section we prove that $X(\alpha, A)$ is a perfect set for any *real* number $\alpha \geq \varphi^2 + 1$ and *Card(A)*≥ 2.

Definition 11. An infinite word $\mathbf{x} = a_1a_2a_3\cdots$ has the α-extention property over the alphabet A if for any $h > 0$ the prefix $a_1a_2a_3\cdots a_h$ of $\mathbf{x}$ is also a prefix of another infinite word $\mathbf{y}$ over the alphabet A which is α-power free and $\mathbf{x} \neq \mathbf{y}$.

There is a strong connection between the previous definition and the topological notion of *perfect set*. Indeed, if we consider the usual topology of infinite words (cf [11]), then $X(\alpha, A)$ is a perfect set if and only if any word $\mathbf{x}$ in $X(\alpha, A)$ has the α-extention property over A.

In next propositions we shall use the infinite Thue-Morse word $\mathbf{t} = v_1v_2v_3\cdots$ (cf. [11]). Let us denote by $\mathbf{t}_h$ the h-th suffix of the Thue-Morse word which is the infinite word: $\mathbf{t}_h = v_hv_{h+1}v_{h+2}\cdots$.

Recall that an infinite word is *overlap-free* if it is $(\alpha+\epsilon)$-power free for any $\epsilon > 0$. It is well known (cf. [11]) that the Thue-Morse word $\mathbf{t}$ is overlap-free. The perfectness of the set of overlap free infinite words is well known (cf. [9] and [13]) and is used in the proof of the following lemma.

In the sequel, by the alphabet of a word w we mean the set of letters that appear in the word w.

Lemma 12. *Let k, h be positive integres and let $\mathbf{t}_h$ be the h-th suffix of the Thue Morse word. If the word $\mathbf{x} = a_1a_2\cdots a_k\mathbf{t}_h$ is α-power free with $\alpha > 3$, then $\mathbf{x}$ has the α-extention property over the same alphabet of $\mathbf{x}$.*

Proof: Let $\mathbf{t}_h = v_hv_{h+1}\cdots$. It is known (cf [13]) that for any $i \geq 0$, $v_h\cdots v_{h+i}$ is prefix of another infinite word $\hat{\mathbf{t}}_h$, $\hat{\mathbf{t}}_h \neq \mathbf{t}_h$, which is also overlap-free. Choose $i > \alpha k$ and the corresponding $\hat{\mathbf{t}}_h$. We prove that the infinite word $\mathbf{y} = a_1a_2\cdots a_k\hat{\mathbf{t}}_h$ is α-power free. Let us suppose, by contradiction, that $\mathbf{y}$ contains an α-power. Set

$$\begin{aligned}
&u = a_1a_2\cdots a_k && |u| = k\\
&v = v_hv_{h+1}\cdots v_{h+i} && |v| > \alpha k\\
&\hat{\mathbf{t}}_h = v\mathbf{s}\\
&\mathbf{s} = v'_{h+i+1}v'_{h+i+2}\cdots.
\end{aligned}$$

Then we can write: $\mathbf{y} = uv\mathbf{s}$.

If $\mathbf{y}$ contains an α-power, with $\alpha \geq 3$, then there exists a prefix of $\mathbf{y}$ of the form $wz'z^n$, with z' suffix of z, $|z'z^n|/|z| > \alpha$. We have $n = \lfloor\alpha\rfloor \geq 3$.

The word $wz'z$ is prefix of u, otherwise there exists a suffix z'' of z such that $z''z^{n-1}$ is prefix of $\hat{\mathbf{t}}_h$, contraddicting the hypothesis that $\hat{\mathbf{t}}_h$ is overlap-free. Thus $|z| < k$. On the other hand uv is a proper prefix of $wz'z^n$, otherwise $\mathbf{x}$ contains an α-power. It follows that z^{n-2} is not a factor of v and then $(n-2)|z| > |v| > \alpha k$. From this we derive $|z| > \frac{\alpha}{(n-2)}k$ and, since $n = \lfloor\alpha\rfloor$, one has $|z| > \frac{\alpha}{(n-2)}k > k$, which is a contradiction. This concludes the proof. □

Lemma 13. *Let $\alpha > 3$. If $a_1a_2\cdots a_k$ is α-power free and has no $(\alpha-1)$ suffixes, then there exists a number i such that $a_1a_2\cdots a_k\mathbf{t}_i$ is α-power free, where $\mathbf{t}_i$ is the i-th suffix of the word of Thue-Morse.*

Proof: Let us consider the infinite word $a_1a_2\cdots a_k\mathbf{t}_1$; if it is not α-power free, then it contains a word u that is a power with exponent $\geq \alpha$ and period P. We can write

$$a_1a_2\cdots a_k\mathbf{t}_1 = vu\mathbf{x}$$

where v is a finite word prefix of $a_1a_2\cdots a_k\mathbf{t}_1$ and $\mathbf{x}$ is an infinite word, suffix of $a_1a_2\cdots a_k\mathbf{t}_1$. Since $\mathbf{t}_1$ is overlap free then $|v| < k$ and since $a_1a_2\cdots a_k$ has no $(\alpha-1)$ suffixes then $|vu| > k$.

Hence we can decompose $u = u'u''$ such that $a_1a_2\cdots a_k = vu'$ and $\mathbf{t}_1 = u''\mathbf{x}$.

Since $\mathbf{t}_1$ is overlap free then $|u'|/P \geq \alpha - 2$ and since $a_1a_2\cdots a_k$ has no $(\alpha-1)$ suffixes then $|u''|/P > 1$, i.e.

1) $k \geq |u'| \geq (\alpha-2)P > P$,
2) $|u''| > P$.

By 1) and 2), since u is P periodic, $a_{k-P+1}a_{k-P+2}\cdots a_k\mathbf{t}_{P+1} = \mathbf{t}_1$.

Let us now consider the word $a_1a_2\cdots a_k\mathbf{t}_{P+1}$; if it is not α-power free, then it contains a word u_2 that is a power with exponent $\geq \alpha$ and period P_2. We can write

$$a_1a_2\cdots a_k\mathbf{t}_{P+1} = v_2u_2\mathbf{x}_2$$

where v_2 is a finite word prefix of $a_1a_2\cdots a_k\mathbf{t}_{P+1}$ and $\mathbf{x}_2$ is an infinite word, suffix of $a_1a_2\cdots a_k\mathbf{t}_{P+1}$.

With same argument developed above we can decompose $u_2 = u_2'u_2''$ such that $a_1a_2\cdots a_k = vu_2'$ and $\mathbf{t}_1 = u_2''\mathbf{x}_2$ and such that

3) $k \geq |u_2'| \geq (\alpha-2)P_2 > P_2$
4) $|u_2''| > P_2$.

By 3) and 4), since u_2 is P_2 periodic, $a_{k-P_2+1}a_{k-P_2+2}\cdots a_k\mathbf{t}_{P+P_2+1} = \mathbf{t}_{P+1}$.

We claim that $P_2 > P$; indeed by 3) and 4), since u_2 is P_2 periodic the word $a_{k-P_2+1}a_{k-P_2+2}\cdots a_k\mathbf{t}_{P+1}$ has a $2+(1/P)$-prefix with period P; if $P_2 \leq P$ then $a_{k-P_2+1}a_{k-P_2+2}\cdots a_k\mathbf{t}_{P+1}$ is contained in $a_{k-P+1}a_{k-P+2}\cdots a_k\mathbf{t}_{P+1} = \mathbf{t}_1$, that is impossible because $\mathbf{t}_1$ is overlap-free.

We can iterate this construction and obtain a sequence of integers $P = P_1 < P_2 < \cdots$ such that for any j, $P_j \leq k$. Hence this sequence must be a finite sequence $P = P_1 < P_2 < \cdots P_q$, and this means that there exists number $i = P_1 + P_2 + \cdots P_q$ such that $a_1a_2\cdots a_k\mathbf{t}_i$ is α-power free. □

Theorem 14. *$X(\alpha, A)$ is a perfect set for any* real *number $\alpha \geq \varphi^2+1$ and* Card(A)$\geq$ 2.

Proof: It is sufficient to prove that if $\mathbf{x} = a_1a_2a_3\cdots$ is α-power free, with $\alpha \geq \varphi^2+1$ then $\mathbf{x}$ has the α-extention property over the alphabet of $\mathbf{x}$.

If there exists a natural number $h > 0$ such that for any $n \geq h$, $a_1a_2\cdots a_n$ has an $(\alpha-1)$-suffix, then by Theorem 8 the word $\mathbf{x}$ would be ultimately periodic and, consequently, not α-power free (contracdiction). Hence for any $h > 0$ there exists a $k \geq h$ such that $a_1a_2a_3\cdots a_k$ has no $(\alpha-1)$ suffixes. By Lemma 13 there exists a number i such that $\mathbf{y} = a_1a_2\cdots a_k\mathbf{t}_i$ is α-power free, where $\mathbf{t}_i$ is the i-th suffix of the word of Thue-Morse. If $\mathbf{y} \neq \mathbf{x}$ then the thesis of the theorem holds. If $\mathbf{y} = \mathbf{x}$ then by Lemma 12 the thesis of the theorem holds too. □

We can generalize the notion of overlap free word in the following way: we say that a word is *weakly* α-power free if it is $(\alpha+\epsilon)$-power free for any $\epsilon > 0$. For instance the set of the overlap-free words coincides with the set of the weakly 2-power free words. We denote by $W(\alpha, A)$ the set of infinite words over A that are weakly α-power free.

One has that $X(\alpha, A) \subset W(\alpha, A)$; it is also easy to see that if α is not a rational number $X(\alpha, A) = W(\alpha, A)$. Moreover, in general, $X(\alpha, A) \neq W(\alpha, A)$; indeed if we consider a binary alphabet A the set $X(2, A)$ is empty while the set of overlap free words over a binary alphabet $W(2, A)$ it is well known to be non empty.

We can state the following two questions:

Question 15. If α is rational and $X(\alpha, A) \neq \emptyset$ is it true that $X(\alpha, A) \neq W(\alpha, A)$?

Question 16. If α is rational and $W(\alpha, A) \neq \emptyset$ is it true that $X(\alpha, A) \neq W(\alpha, A)$?

Even if the two questions are very similar, the second seems much deeper because it is probably linked to a famous conjecture of Dejan (cf. [11]).

We can prove in an analogous way as Theorem 14 that $W(\alpha, A)$ is a perfect set for any *real* number $\alpha \geq \varphi^2 + 1$ and *Card(A)*≥ 2.

Motivated by this result, by the results and questions in [2] and [3], and by the fact that the set $W(2, A)$ is perfect over a binary alphabet (cf. [13]) we state the following question:

Question 17. Is it true that for any real number α and for any alphabet A, the set $X(\alpha, A)$ ($W(\alpha, A)$ respectively) is either empty or perfect?

5 String Matching

In [10] Galil and Seiferas give a time-space-optimal string matching algorithm. A main tool in [10] is a combinatorial theorem on words that the authors call "Decomposition Theorem". This result has been improved by Crochemore and Rytter in [1].

We here further improve the Decomposition Theorem as an application of our main theorem. As a consequence one can give a better upper bound on the number of comparisons in the text processing in the algorithms of [10] and [1].

Recall that a word w having period P is called an *α-repetition*, where α is a real positive number, if $|w|/P \geq \alpha$. Suppose that P is the shortest period of w; the suffix of length P of w is here called the *base* of w. A base is always a primitive word.

The following lemma is a direct consequence of Proposition 7 and is an improvement of [10, Lemma 3].

Lemma 18. *For each primitive word v of length P there is a parse $v = v_1 v_2$ such that, for any word v' having a φ-suffix of base v, $v'v_1$ has no φ^2-suffix of period shorter than P.*

Proof: Consider the $(1+\varphi) = \varphi^2$-suffix $x = a_1 \cdots a_t$ of base $|v|$ of the word $v'v$. By Proposition 7, $a_1 \cdots a_{\hat{S}}$ has period $\hat{P}$.

Since x has period $|v|$, $\hat{S} > t - |v| + 1$. By Lemma 5, since $|a_1 \cdots a_{\hat{S}}| > \varphi|v|$, $\hat{P} = |v|$. Hence, if we write $x = a_1 \cdots a_{\hat{S}} v_2$ then $|v_2| < |v|$ and , consequently we can write $v = v_1 v_2$; it is easy to chek that this is the required parse. □

Remark that previous proof is does not give directly a fast algorithm for finding the parse; however, analogously as in [10] it is possible to develop a "constructive" proof making use of Lemma 5 that gives rice to a linear algorithm.

The proof of the next theorem follows the lines of that of the Decomposition Theorem in [10] making use our Lemma 18 instead of [10, Lemma 3]. In the proof we use also our Lemma 5.

Theorem 19. *Each word w has a parse $w = uu'$ such that u does not contain two φ^2-suffixes having different bases and $|u'| < C \cdot P(u)$, where $P(u)$ is the shortest period of u and $C = \frac{4\varphi+3}{2\varphi+2}$.*

Proof: We obtain the word u by deleting appropriate suffixes from w until the remainder does not contain two φ^2-suffixes having different bases.

Suppose that w has two φ^2-suffixes having different bases (if not then set $u = w$ and v the empty string); let v be the *second* shorter base. Then $w = v'v$ where v' has a φ-suffix. By Lemma 18 find the parse $v = v_1 v_2$ and set $w_1 = v'v_1$. Repeat same arguments and get a finite sequence $w = w_0, w_1, \cdots, w_h$, where w_h does not contain two φ^2-suffixes having different bases and for any $i < h$, w_i has two φ^2-suffixes having different bases.

Set $u = w_h$; since u is a prefix of w we can write $w = uu'$. We claim that this is the requred parse of w. It remains only to prove that $|u'| \leq C \cdot P(u)$, where $P(u)$ is the shortest period of u.

Since u is a prefix of w_{h-1}, we can write $w_{h-1} = uu_{h-1}$ where $|u_{h-1}|$ is smaller than the length of the base v_{h-1} of a φ^2 suffix of w_{h-1}. We claim that the shortest period of u is greater than or equal to the length of v_{h-1}. Indeed, u has a φ-suffix of length $|v_{h-1}|$; if it has period Q with $Q < |v_{h-1}|$ then, by Lemma 5, it would have a φ^2-suffix of length smaller than $|v_{h-1}|$, a contradiction because u, by construction, has by Lemma 18 no φ^2-suffix of length smaller than $|v_{h-1}|$.

Since w_{i+1} is a prefix of w_i, $0 \leq i \leq h-1$, we can write $w_i = w_{i+1}u_i$.

We claim that $u_i \leq \beta^{h-1-i}|v_{h-1}|$ with $\beta = 1/(2 + \frac{1}{\varphi^3})$; in this case, by previous claim, since $|u'| = \Sigma_{j=o}^{h-1}|u_j|$ and $C = \Sigma_{j=0}^{\infty}\beta^j$, the proof of the theorem would be concluded.

In order to prove the claim, it is sufficient to show that for any i, $0 \leq i \leq h-2$, $|v_i| \geq \frac{1}{\beta}|v_{i-1}|$, where v_i is the *second* shorter base of a φ^2-suffix of w_i; this because, by Lemma 18, $|u_i| < |v_i|$.

First of all, by construction and Lemma 18, the *first* shorter base z of a φ^2-suffix of w_i has lenght $L > |v_{i-1}|$.

In order to prove the claim we want to prove that $|v_i| \geq \frac{1}{\beta}L$.

By the Theorem of Fine and Wilf, $|v_i| \geq (\varphi^2 - 1)L = \varphi L$.

Suppose that $\varphi L < |v_i| < 2L = 2|z|$. Let y be the φ^2-repetition that is the suffix of w_i having z as base and length $|y| = \lceil \varphi^2 L \rceil$. Since $v_i v_i$ is a suffix of w_i, we can write $y = y'zz = y''v_i$ where y' is suffix of z (and, so, of v_i) and y'' is a suffix of v_i with $|y''| > |y'|$. Hence y' is a suffix and also a prefix of y''; this implies that y'' has period $|y''| - |y'|$ and exponent $\frac{|y''|}{|y''|-|y'|} = 1/(1 - \frac{|y'|}{|y''|}) \geq 1/(1 - \frac{(\varphi^2-2)L}{L}) \geq \varphi^2$. Therefore y'' is a φ^2-suffix of v_i and it has a base of length $|y''| - |y'| < L$, a contradiction.

If $|v_i| = 2L = 2|z|$ then v_i would not be a base of a φ^2-suffix of w_i, because, by definition, a base is a primitive word.

Hence $|v_i| > 2L$; suppose that $|v_i| < \frac{1}{\beta}L$. We derive a contradiction, analogously as done just above. Let y be the φ^2-repetition that is the suffix of w_i having z as base and length $|y| = \lceil \varphi^2 L \rceil$. Since $v_i v_i$ is a suffix of w_i, we can write $y = y'zz = y''v_i$ where y' is suffix of z (and, so, of v_i) and y'' is a suffix of v_i with $|y'| > |y''|$.

Hence y'' is a suffix and also a prefix of y'; this implies that y' has period $|y'| - |y''|$ and exponent $\frac{|y'|}{|y'|-|y''|} \geq \frac{|y'|}{\frac{1}{\varphi^3}L} \geq \varphi^2$. Therefore y' is a φ^2-suffix of v_i and it has a base of length $|y'| - |y''| < L$, a contradiction.

This proves the claim and, consequently, concludes the proof of the theorem. □

In next proposition we show that the constant φ^2 in previous theorem is tight (cf. [1, Proposition 9]). The proof make use of Proposition 9.

Proposition 20. *For any constant $C > 0$ and for any $\epsilon > 0$ there exists a word w with the following property: if $w = uu'$ is a parse such that u does not contain two $\varphi^2 - \epsilon$-suffixes having different bases, then $\frac{|u'|}{P(u)} \geq C$.*

As in [10] and in [1] one can use Theorem 19 to design a string matching algorithm. If we consider the parse of the pattern as in Theorem 19, the algorithm TEXT-SEARCH in [1] and [10], which computes the positions of occurrences of the pattern inside the text t, makes at most $(\varphi^2 + C)|t|$ symbol comparisons, where C is defined in Theorem 19.

Acknowledgements

We wish to thank J. P. Allouche and D. Breslauer for discussions and suggestions.

References

1. Crochemore M. and Rytter W., "Squares, Cubes and Time-Space Efficient String-Searching", Tech. Rep. LITP **91.47** (july 1991).
2. Currie J. D., "Open Problems in Pattern Avoidance" Amer. Math. Montly, **100**, pp. 790-793, october 1993.
3. Currie J. D., "On the Structure and Extendibility of k-Power Free Words", Preprint, 1995.
4. Currie J. D., Shelton R., Private Communication 1995.
5. Currie J. D., Shelton R., "Cantor Sets and Dejean's Conjecture", Preprint 1995.
6. Cesari Y. and Vincent M. "Une Caractérisation des Mots Périodiques" C. R. Acad. Sc. Paris, **t. 286** (19 juin 1978) Série A pp. 1175-1177.
7. de Luca A., "A Combinatorial Property of the Fibonacci Words", Inform. Process. Lett., **12** *n°*4 (1981), pp. 195-195.
8. Duval J. P., "Périodes et Répetitions des Mots du Monoide Libre" Theor. Comp. Science **9** (1979) pp. 17-26.
9. Fife E.D., "Binary Sequence which contains no BBb" Trans. Amer. Math. Society **261** (1) (1980), 115-136.
10. Galil Z. and Seiferas J., "Time-Space Optimal String Matching" J. of Computer and Sys. Sciences **26** (1983), pp. 280-294.
11. Lothaire M., "Combinatorics on Words", Addison Wesley, vol. 17 Enciclopedia of Matematics and its Applications (1983).
12. Mignosi F. Pirillo G., "Repetitions in the Fibonacci Infinite Word" RAIRO Theor. Informatics and Applications, vol **26**, n^O 3, (1992), pp. 199-204.
13. Restivo A. and Salemi S., "Overlap Free Words on Two Symbols" Lecture Notes in Comp. Science Vol **192** (1984) pp. 198-206.
14. Shallit J., Private Communication, 1994.
15. Shelton R. and Sony R., " Aperiodic Words on the Three Symbols 1, 2, 3", J. Reine Angew. Math. **321** (1982), pp. 195-209, in Combinatorics on Words, Cumming L. ed. (Academic Press, New York), pp. 101-118 (1993), J. Reine Angew. Math. **330** (1984), pp. 44-52.

A New Approach to Analyse Coupled-Context-Free Languages

Günter Hotz Gisela Pitsch

FB 14 – Informatik, Universität des Saarlandes
D-66123 Saarbrücken, Germany, Email hotz|pitsch@cs.uni-sb.de

Abstract. Coupled-Context-Free Grammars are a natural generalization of context-free ones obtained by combining nonterminals to corresponding parentheses which can only be substituted simultaneously. Refering to their generative capacity we obtain an infinite hierarchy of languages that comprises the context-free ones as the first and all those generated by Tree Adjoining Grammars (TAGs) as the second element. Here, we present a completely new approach to analyse this language hierarchy. It solves the word problem for the class of languages generated by TAGs in time $O(n^6)$, n length of the input, by reducing it to the analysis of sequences of parentheses.

1 Introduction

The syntax of natural languages cannot be modelled by context-free grammars (cf. [16]) while the appropriate context-sensitive grammars are known to be PSPACE-complete. To solve this dilemma, people are looking for classes in between context-free and context-sensitive languages that are powerful enough to model the syntax of natural languages but showing a polynomial time complexity as to the analysis. Coupled-Context-Free Grammars represent such a formalism. Their suitability to model syntactical phenomena follows from the fact that they include the languages generated by the Tree Adjoining Grammars (TAGs) of [10] as one subclass. The linguistic significance of TAGs is well explored (cf. [1, 11], e.g.). In particular, both formalisms are able to model the linguistic phenomenon of cross-serial dependencies, which is not context-free but frequently appears in natural languages (cf. [2, 16]).

Coupled-Context-Free Grammars have been introduced in [5,6], and further studied in [8, 9, 13]. It belongs to the family of regulated string rewriting systems investigated in [4]. Many regulated string rewriting systems obtain a generalization of context-free grammars by allowing simultaneous rewriting of arbitrary finite combinations of elements. In [4], it is shown that this results in languages which are not semilinear. But semilinearity is important since it formalizes the "constant-growth property" of natural languages. In contrast to these formalisms, all languages defined by Coupled-Context-Free Grammars are semilinear because of restrictions on the rewriting steps: They consider elements rewritten simultaneously as components of a parenthesis which can only be substituted in parallel, if they form themselves a parenthesis produced by the same rewriting step, and only by sequences of parentheses which are correctly nested. When characterizing Coupled-Context-Free Grammars by the maximal number of elements rewritten simultaneously – their *rank* – we get an infinite hierarchy, whose smallest element – the one of rank 1 – is represented by the context-free grammars. The next element, namely Coupled-Context-Free Grammars of rank 2, generates the same class of languages as TAGs do. This growth of the generative capacity permits to extend the context-free languages by continuously growing semilinear language classes.

Since Coupled-Context-Free Grammars are a natural generalization of context-free ones, all efficient context-free parsing algorithms represent possibilities to develop such an algorithm for them. Thus, the well-known algorithms of Earley resp. Younger were used to develop algorithms to analyse TAGs (cf. [17] resp. [18]) and Coupled-Context-Free Grammars of rank 2 (cf. [6] resp. [8]). But all of them are essentially based on the context-free counterpart, not on the special features of the formalisms. Therefore, to get a lower time complexity of the analysis, we should try to exploit these special features. Coupled-Context-Free Grammars are defined via expressions over sets of parentheses. Therefore, a natural way to solve their word problem seems to be the reduction of the problem to the investigation of sequences of parentheses. This is possible, if we are able to translate any combination of input word/Coupled-Context-Free Grammar into a set of parentheses expressions which uniquely represents this instance of the general word problem. Here, we present a realisation for his approach for the first time.

In the context-free case, the representation theorem of Shamir (cf. [15]) can be used to construct a directed graph for any combination of input word/grammar in Greibach normalform. Its edges are marked such that the input word is an element of the language analysed iff there exists a path from the distinguished begin node to the distinguished end node of the graph which is marked by a sequence of parentheses correctly nested. Based on this, we construct such a graph for Coupled-Context-Free Grammars of rank 2. But here, its marking on the edges consists of two components. The first one stores the information about context-free derivability as before, the second one stores the information about the coupling between two components of a parenthesis. Now, we aim to find a path through the graph whose marking represents a correct sequence of parentheses in the first as well as in the second component. The direct translation of the context-free algorithm onto our situation leads to the solution of an NP-complete problem (cf. [12]). Therefore, we have to develop an alternative strategy. It looks at first on the correctness of the coupling, i.e. on the second component of the marking. Only then, the context-free derivability is tested relative to this coupling, i.e. the first component is investigated.

The complexity of the algorithm resulting for Coupled-Context-Free Grammars of rank 2 amounts to $O(n^6)$, where n is the length of the input. This equals the time bound as it is achieved by [17] or [8]. But since it mainly relies on the special features of the formalism, it represents the best starting point for future research. Besides, the algorithm provides new insights on the general structure of these grammars which already led to a representation theorem for them in [9].

2 Coupled-Context-Free Grammars

Here, we introduce the formalism of Coupled-Context-Free Grammars. An extensive characterization can be found in [5, 6]. Coupled-Context-Free Grammars are defined over extended semi-Dyck sets, a generalization of semi-Dyck sets. Their elements can be regarded as sequences of parentheses that are correctly nested. Semi-Dyck sets play an important role in the theory of formal languages. [3] show that they are a generator of context-free languages. To extend the family of context-free languages we consider parentheses of arbitrary finite order and extended semi-Dyck sets over them defined as follows:

Definition 1 Parentheses Set.

A finite set $\mathcal{K} := \{(k_{i,1}, \ldots, k_{i,m_i}) \mid i, m_i \in \mathrm{N}\}$ is a *Parentheses Set* iff it satisfies $k_{i,j} \neq k_{l,m}$ for $i \neq l$ or $j \neq m$. The elements of $\mathcal{K}$ are called *Parentheses*. All parentheses of a fixed length $r \geq 1$ are summarized as $\mathcal{K}[r] := \{(k_{i,1}, \ldots, k_{i,m_i}) \in \mathcal{K} \mid m_i = r\}$ where $\mathcal{K}[0] := \{\varepsilon\}$ (the empty word). The set of all components of parentheses in $\mathcal{K}$ is denoted by $comp(\mathcal{K}) := \{k_i \mid (k_1, \ldots, k_i, \ldots, k_r) \in \mathcal{K}\}$.

Notation *When dealing with parentheses of length at most 2 (the used situation), we denote pairs of parentheses by* $(X, \overline{X})$, $(Y, \overline{Y})$, ... *instead of* (X_1, X_2), (Y_1, Y_2), ... *This simplifies the formulas since we can use* X_1, X_2, ... *for other purposes.*

Definition 2 Extended Semi-Dyck Set.

Let $\mathcal{K}$ be a parentheses set, T an arbitrary finite set where $T \cap \mathcal{K} = T \cap comp(\mathcal{K}) = \emptyset$. $ED(\mathcal{K}, T)$, the *Extended Semi-Dyck Set over* $\mathcal{K}$ *and* T, is inductively defined by

$(E1)$ $T^* \subseteq ED(\mathcal{K}, T)$.
$(E2)$ $\mathcal{K}[1] \subseteq ED(\mathcal{K}, T)$.
$(E3)$ $u_1, \ldots, u_r \in ED(\mathcal{K}, T), (k_1, \ldots, k_{r+1}) \in \mathcal{K}[r+1] \implies k_1 u_1 \cdots k_r u_r k_{r+1} \in ED(\mathcal{K}, T)$.
$(E4)$ $u, v \in ED(\mathcal{K}, T) \implies u \cdot v \in ED(\mathcal{K}, T)$.
$(E5)$ $ED(\mathcal{K}, T)$ is the smallest set fulfilling conditions $(E1) - (E4)$.

Definition 3 Coupled-Context-Free Grammar.

A *Coupled-Context-Free Grammar over* $ED(\mathcal{K}, T)$ is an ordered 4-tuple $G = (\mathcal{K}, T, P, S)$ where $S \in \mathcal{K}[1]$ and P is a finite, nonempty set of productions of the form $\{(k_1, \ldots, k_r) \rightarrow (\alpha_1, \ldots, \alpha_r) \mid (k_1, \ldots, k_r) \in \mathcal{K}, \alpha_1 \cdot \ldots \cdot \alpha_r \in ED(\mathcal{K}, T)\}$. The set of all these grammars is denoted by $CCFG$.

The term "coupled" expresses that here, a certain number of context-free rewritings is executed in parallel and controlled by $\mathcal{K}$. Therefore, $\mathcal{K}$ can be regarded as a set of coupled nonterminals.

To be short, we denote the left resp. right side of $p := (k_1, \ldots, k_r) \rightarrow (\alpha_1, \ldots, \alpha_r) \in P$ by

- $\mathcal{S}(p) := (k_1, \ldots, k_r)$, the *source* of p, resp.
- $\mathcal{D}(p) := (\alpha_1, \ldots, \alpha_r)$, the *drain* of p.

The same abbreviation is used for any edge $e = (v_1, v_2) \in E$ in a directed graph $G = (V, E)$ to denote the source $(\mathcal{S}(e) = v_1)$ resp. the drain $(\mathcal{D}(e) = v_2)$ of e.

At last, we give the definition of derivation for $CCFG$. Let $G = (\mathcal{K}, T, P, S) \in CCFG$ and $V := comp(\mathcal{K}) \cup T$. We define the relation $\Rightarrow_G$ as a subset of $V^* \times V^*$ consisting of all *derivation steps of rank* r for G with $r \geq 1$. $\phi \Rightarrow_G \psi$ holds for $\phi, \psi \in V^*$ if and only if there exist $u_1, u_{r+1} \in V^*$, $u_2, \ldots, u_r \in ED(\mathcal{K}, T)$ and $(k_1, \ldots, k_r) \rightarrow (\alpha_1, \ldots, \alpha_r) \in P$ such that

$$\phi = u_1 k_1 u_2 k_2 \cdots u_r k_r u_{r+1} \quad \text{and} \quad \psi = u_1 \alpha_1 u_2 \alpha_2 \cdots u_r \alpha_r u_{r+1} .$$

$\stackrel{*}{\Rightarrow}_G$ denotes the reflexive, transitive closure of $\Rightarrow_G$. Obviously, for the above ϕ and ψ, $u_1 \cdot u_{r+1} \in ED(\mathcal{K}, T)$ follows from $S \stackrel{*}{\Rightarrow}_G \phi$ since the result of the substitution is a sequence of parentheses correctly nested iff the original word was. $L(G) := \{w \in T^* \mid S \stackrel{*}{\Rightarrow}_G w\}$ is the language generated by G.

To describe exactly the generative capacity of our grammars showing different ranks, we need

Definition 4 Rank, $CCFG(l)$.
For any $G = (\mathcal{K}, T, P, S) \in CCFG$, let the *rank* of G be defined as $rank(G) := \max\{r \mid (k_1, \ldots, k_r) \in \mathcal{K}\}$. Then, we define for all $l \geq 1$ that $CCFG(l) := \{G \in CCFG \mid rank(G) \leq l\}$.

[6] proves that $CCFG$ builds up an infinite hierarchy of languages and, at the same time, represents a proper extension of context-free grammars not exceeding the power of context-sensitive ones.

Sometimes, it is useful to "neglect" the relations between the components of a parenthesis. Then, we investigate instead of $G = (\mathcal{K}, T, P, S) \in CCFG$ the grammar $G' := (comp(\mathcal{K}), T, P', S)$ for

$$P' := \bigcup_{(k_1,\ldots,k_r)\to(\alpha_1,\ldots,\alpha_r)\in P} \{k_i \to \alpha_i \mid 1 \leq i \leq r\}.$$

Since G' is certainly a context-free grammar, we denote G' (resp. P') by $CF(G)$ (resp. $CF(P)$) in the sequel. Obviously, G' satisfies $L(G) \subseteq L(G')$.

Note: Throughout this paper, we assume w.l.o.g. that $\varepsilon \notin L(G)$ for any $G \in CFG$ or $G \in CCFG$. This simplifies the presentation while everything presented could also be done if $\varepsilon \in L(G)$ holds.

3 The Context-Free Case

We first introduce the understanding of production sets as systems of formal equations. In [7], this and the Greibach normalform for context-free grammars are used to prove elegantly a variant of the representation theorem of Shamir. Here, we present the idea of this constructive proof since it allows to translate the word problem for context-free languages into the search for a path in a directed graph. Its edges are marked such that the input word is in the language analysed iff this path is marked by a sequence of parentheses correctly nested. We define this graph before closing by the algorithm itself.

3.1 The Theorem of Shamir

Let $G = (N, T, P, S)$ a context-free grammar in Greibach normalform, i.e. $P \subseteq N \times TN^*$. Instead of considering each $p \in P$ as a substitution rule, we can take it as a formal equation. Here, the elements of N represent variables while terminal symbols are treated as constants. Thus, $X \to YbCD \in P$, e.g., results in $X = YbCD$. We can manipulate these equations as usual in the algebra, whereby the multiplication of variables is associative, but not commutative. As done in [3], we can assign to each P an equation system for formal power series. This system is solvable by algebraic series. In general, we can use this understanding to prove results in the theory of context-free languages by elegant algebraic means. The well-known representation theorems of Chomsky–Schützenberger in [3] and of Shamir in [15] are developed on this background. In addition, this algebraic view can be used to construct the Greibach normalform causing only a cubic growth of the context-free grammar's size (cf. [14]).

Let $G = (N, T, P, S)$ in Greibach normalform. Then, all equations resulting from P are of the form

$$X = tX_1X_2\ldots X_k, \quad X, X_1, \ldots, X_k \in N, \; t \in T.$$

Therefrom, we can uniquely define the mapping $\varphi_G(t) := \{X^{-1}u^R \mid X \to tu \in P\}$ for each $t \in T$, where u^R is defined as $(w_1w_2\ldots w_k)^R := w_k \ldots w_2w_1$, while X_i^{-1} is the formal inverse of the variable $X_i \in N$. Intuitively, X^{-1} means "*replace* X", while X says "*generate* X". Therefore, each element of $\varphi_G(t)$ represents one possibility how to generate $t \in T$ during a derivation process relative to G. For any context-free grammar G, φ_G just defined can be extended to a monoid homomorphism $\varphi_G : T^* \longrightarrow \wp((N \cup N^{-1})^*)$ where the concatenation is the only monoid operation. $\wp((N \cup N^{-1})^*)$ denotes the set of all finite subsets of $(N \cup N^{-1})^*$. In [7], φ_G is used to prove the following variant of the representation theorem of Shamir in [15] in an elegant and constructive way:

Theorem 5. *For any context-free language $L \subseteq T^+$, there exists an alphabet N, an $S \in N$, and a monoid homomorphism $\varphi_G : T^* \longrightarrow \wp((N \cup N^{-1})^*)$, such that with $D(N) := ED(\{(X, X^{-1}) \mid X \in N\}, \emptyset)$, it holds: $w \in L \iff \varphi_G(w) \cap S^{-1} \cdot D(N) \neq \emptyset$. Besides, it holds $\varphi_G(t) \subset N^{-1}N^* \; \forall t \in T$.*

This theorem and φ_G could be used to solve the word problem for $w \in T^+$ relative to G as follows:

1. For each $t \in T$, regard $\varphi_G(t)$ as a formal sum instead of a set of products.
2. Replace each $w_i \in T$, $1 \leq i \leq n$, in $w = w_1 \ldots w_n$ by the formal sum $\varphi_G(w_i)$.
3. Multiply the resulting product of sums out. During this process, substitute subsequences $X_iX_i^{-1}$, $X_i \in N$, by ε. I.e., reduce relative to the congruence relation $\rho_G := \{(X_iX_i^{-1}, \varepsilon) \mid X_i \in N\}$.
4. From Theorem 5, it follows that the result contains $S^{-1} \iff w \in L(G)$ holds.

The representation as product of sums is very compact. This compactness is destroyed when multiplying out. In the worst case, we get $O(|P|^n)$ partial sums which have to be tested modulo ρ_G. Thus, we would get an exponential runtime. Consequently, we have to work on the original representation to get an efficient procedure. Here, we do that by translating the product of sums to a graph where we work on. This answers the word problem without enumerating all possible derivations.

3.2 The Greibach Graph

The main idea is to construct a *column* of a graph for each w_i in $w = w_1 \dots w_n$. The sequence of these columns equals the sequence of the symbols in w.

At first, the graph gets a start node representing column 0 (it also represents the only row in column 0). $|\varphi_G(w_1)|$ edges directed to column 1 start there.

Each of the columns 1 up to n consists of $|\varphi_G(w_i)|$ rows if we construct the column for w_i. Each *row* represents an element of $\varphi_G(w_i)$ and contains as many nodes as the element it represents contains nonterminals. Let this length be denoted by $|r_j^{w_i}|$. From column 1 to n, there are two kinds of edges: inside a row and from column to column. *Inside* a row j, there are only edges from node v to $v+1$, $1 \leq v < |r_j^{w_i}|$. The l-th edge in this sequence is marked by the $(l+1)$-th symbol of the element of $\varphi_G(w_i)$ represented by row j. *Between columns*, there are only edges from column i to column $i+1$, $0 \leq i < n$. For each row in column i, there are $|\varphi_G(w_i)|$ edges starting at the last node in the row. They are directed to all the different starting nodes of the rows in column $(i+1)$. All of these edges leading to the same row in column $(i+1)$ are marked by the same symbol, namely the first symbol of the element of $\varphi_G(w_{i+1})$ represented by this row. Fig. 1. shows an example of such a row.

Additionally, the graph gets a final node $\mathcal{F}$ representing column $n+1$. It is the endpoint of $|\varphi_G(w_n)|$ edges marked by ε which start at the different end nodes of the rows in column n.

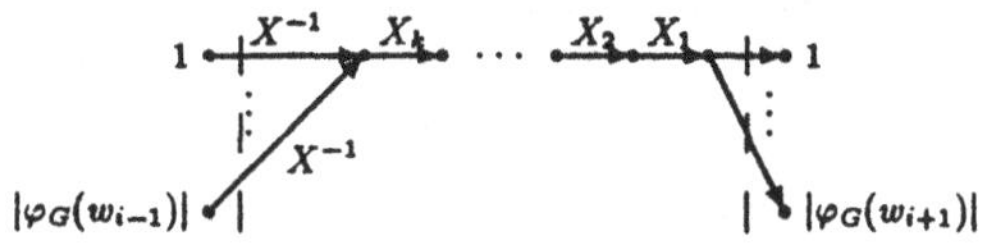

Fig. 1. A row in column i of the Greibach graph resulting from $X^{-1}X_k \dots X_1 \in \varphi_G(w_i)$

The connection to the multiplication is that obviously, each term in the result of the formal multiplication corresponds to the marking of a path from the start to the end node in the graph. Thus, we can say that $w \in L(G)$ holds iff there is a path whose marking modulo ρ_G equals S^{-1}. The procedure presented in Section 5 solves this decision problem.

To get an elegant description, we add a begin node $\mathcal{B}$ to the graph (column -1), which is the start of one edge leading to the only node in column 0 and marked by S. Thus, our problem is reduced to a search for a path from $\mathcal{B}$ to $\mathcal{F}$, whose marking modulo ρ_G is ε. All this can be formalized as

Definition 6 Greibach Graph.

Let $G = (N, T, P, S)$ a context-free grammar in Greibach normalform, and $w \in T^+$, $n := |w| > 0$. We define for all $t \in T$ the set $P(t) := \{X \to X_1 \dots X_k \mid X \to tX_1 \dots X_k \in P\}$. The elements of $P(t)$ are enumerated as p_j^t, $1 \leq j \leq |P(t)|$. *GNF-Graph*$_G(w)$, the *Greibach Graph of* w *relative to* G, is defined by the node set V_{GNF} and the edge set E_{GNF} defined as

$$V_{GNF} := \{\mathcal{B}\} \cup \{(0,1,0)\} \cup \bigcup_{i=1}^{n} \bigcup_{j=1}^{|P(w_i)|} \bigcup_{l=0}^{|\mathcal{D}(p_j^{w_i})|} \{(i,j,l)\} \cup \{\mathcal{F}\},$$

$$\begin{aligned} E_{GNF} := {} & \{(\mathcal{B},(0,1,0))\} \cup \{(0,1,0)\} \times \bigcup_{j=1}^{|P(w_1)|} \{(1,j,0)\} \cup \\ & \bigcup_{i=2}^{n} \Big(\bigcup_{j=1}^{|P(w_{i-1})|} \{(i-1,j,|\mathcal{D}(p_j^{w_{i-1}})|)\} \times \bigcup_{j=1}^{|P(w_i)|} \{(i,j,0)\}\Big) \\ & \cup \bigcup_{i=1}^{n} \bigcup_{j=1}^{|P(w_i)|} \bigcup_{l=0}^{|\mathcal{D}(p_j^{w_i})|-1} \{((i,j,l),(i,j,l+1))\} \cup \bigcup_{j=1}^{|P(w_n)|} \{(n,j,|\mathcal{D}(p_j^{w_n})|)\} \times \{\mathcal{F}\}. \end{aligned}$$

The mapping $\gamma : E_{GNF} \longrightarrow N \cup N^{-1} \cup \{\varepsilon\}$, the marking on the edges, is defined as

$$\gamma(e) := \begin{cases} \mathcal{S}(p_j^t)^{-1} & \text{if } t = w_i,\ \mathcal{D}(e) = (i,j,s),\ s = 0. \\ (\mathcal{D}(p_j^t))_s & \text{if } t = w_i,\ \mathcal{D}(e) = (i,j,s),\ s > 0. \\ S & \text{if } \mathcal{S}(e) = \mathcal{B}. \\ \varepsilon & \text{if } \mathcal{D}(e) = \mathcal{F}. \end{cases}$$

γ can be extended to a monoid homomorphism $\gamma : E^*_{GNF} \longrightarrow (N \cup N^{-1})^*$ on the paths in the graph.

Definition 7. Given $G = (N, T, P, S) \in CFG$, we define the parentheses congruence relation for G by $\rho_G := \{(X_i X_i^{-1}, \varepsilon) \mid X_i \in N\}$.

Now, we get from Theorem 5 (cf. [12] for details)

Lemma 8. *Let* $G = (N, T, P, S)$ *a context-free grammar in Greibach normalform and* $w \in T^+$. *It holds:*

$$w \in L(G) \iff \text{In } \textit{GNF-Graph}_G(w), \text{ there exists a path } u \in E^*_{GNF} \text{ fulfilling } \mathcal{S}(u) = \mathcal{B},\ \mathcal{D}(u) = \mathcal{F}, \text{ and } \gamma(u) \equiv_{\rho_G} \varepsilon.$$

3.3 The Analysis

Now, we present the algorithm solving the word problem by searching a path. This is done efficiently by representing partial expressions which are congruent to ε modulo ρ_G by a single edge marked by ε.

The idea is to search locally for short cuts on all paths from $\mathcal{B}$ to $\mathcal{F}$. These short cuts are represented by a new edge s^* leading from the start to the endpoint of the short cut and marked by ε. The only thing we do now is trying to prolong these short cuts.
At the beginning, a short cut corresponds to sequences of two edges with inverse marks. Later on, short cuts are either sequences of two new edges marked by ε (condition ($E4$) of Definition 2) or sequences of an old edge, a new edge, and finally an old edge where the marks of the two old edges are inverse (condition ($E3$)). Thus, we use the definition of Dyck-sets to develop an efficient procedure. Obviously, our investigation can work locally and treat each new edge only once for the two possibilities. Each new edge represents compactly a reducible partial expression in the product. No edge is generated twice.

We denote by *GNF-Graph*$^*_G(w)$ the graph (V_*, E_*) determined by the procedure *GNF-analysis*(*GNF-Graph*$_G(w)$) given on the right which results from these considerations. Its correctness follows from:

procedure *GNF-analysis*(*GNF-Graph*$_G(w)$)
$V_* := V_{GNF}$; $E_* := E_{GNF}$; $\mathcal{E} := \emptyset$;
(1) **for all** $s, s' \in E_{GNF}$ **where**
$\mathcal{D}(s) = \mathcal{S}(s')$ **and** $\gamma(s), \gamma(s') \neq \varepsilon$
do
if $\gamma(s) \cdot \gamma(s') \equiv_\rho \varepsilon$
then
$s^* := (\mathcal{S}(s), \mathcal{D}(s'))$; $\gamma(s^*) := \varepsilon$;
$E_* := E_* \cup \{s^*\}$; $\mathcal{E} := \mathcal{E} \cup \{s^*\}$;

while $\mathcal{E} \neq \emptyset$
do /* let $s \in \mathcal{E}$ fixed */
(2) **for all** $s' \in E_*$ **where** $\gamma(s') = \varepsilon$ **and**
$(\mathcal{D}(s') = \mathcal{S}(s)$ or $\mathcal{S}(s') = \mathcal{D}(s))$
do
if $\mathcal{D}(s') = \mathcal{S}(s)$
then $s^* := (\mathcal{S}(s'), \mathcal{D}(s))$
else $s^* := (\mathcal{S}(s), \mathcal{D}(s'))$;
$\gamma(s^*) := \varepsilon$;
if $s^* \notin E_*$
then $E_* := E_* \cup \{s^*\}$; $\mathcal{E} := \mathcal{E} \cup \{s^*\}$;
(3) **for all** $s', s'' \in E_*$ **where** $\gamma(s'), \gamma(s'') \neq \varepsilon$
and $\mathcal{D}(s') = \mathcal{S}(s)$, $\mathcal{S}(s'') = \mathcal{D}(s)$
do
if $\gamma(s') \cdot \gamma(s'') \equiv_{\rho_G} \varepsilon$
then
$s^* := (\mathcal{S}(s'), \mathcal{D}(s''))$; $\gamma(s^*) := \varepsilon$;
if $s^* \notin E_*$
then $E_* := E_* \cup \{s^*\}$; $\mathcal{E} := \mathcal{E} \cup \{s^*\}$;
$\mathcal{E} := \mathcal{E} \setminus \{s\}$;

Lemma 9. *Let $G = (N, T, P, S)$ a context-free grammar in Greibach normalform and $w \in T^+$. It holds:*

In GNF-Graph$_G(w)$, there exists a path $u \in E^*_{GNF}$ where $\mathcal{S}(u) = \mathcal{B}$, $\mathcal{D}(u) = \mathcal{F}$, and $\gamma(u) \equiv_\rho \varepsilon$.
$\iff$ *In GNF-Graph$^*_G(w)$, there exists an edge $s^* = (\mathcal{B}, \mathcal{F})$ where $\gamma(s^*) = \varepsilon$.*

Proof. obvious (by induction on the length of partial paths). For details see [12].

Theorem 10. *Let $G = (N, T, P, S)$ a context-free grammar in Greibach normalform. The procedure GNF-analysis solves the word problem for any $w \in T^+$, $n := |w|$, relative to G in time $O(n^3)$.*

Proof. (1) is executed only once at the start. Because of the graph structure, two edges with inverse marking can only follow each other when connecting one column to the next one. Thus, (1) costs $O(n)$.

The next steps are executed once for each element of $\mathcal{E}$. Since no edge in $\mathcal{E}$ is produced twice and since each edge in $\mathcal{E}$ connects two different columns, $\mathcal{E}$ gets at most $O(n^2)$ elements.

(2) can only generate a new ε-edge for a fixed $s \in \mathcal{E}$ if there is another ε-edge s' which shares an endpoint with s. Because of the construction of *GNF-Graph*$_G(w)$, there are at most $O(n)$ such edges.

In contrast to this, for any fixed $s \in \mathcal{E}$, (3) demands the existence of two edges s', s'' fulfilling $\gamma(s')$, $\gamma(s'') \neq \varepsilon$ to produce a new ε-edge. In addition, s' and s'' have to share an endpoint with s. In *GNF-Graph*$_G(w)$, there are at most $|P|^2$ such edges.

Remark: Given an acyclic graph with one begin and one final node as well as a marking γ from $\Sigma \cup \Sigma^{-1}$, Σ finite alphabet, and a congruence relation ρ, our algorithm answers the question whether there exists a path u from $\mathcal{B}$ to $\mathcal{F}$ fulfilling $\gamma(u) \equiv_\rho \varepsilon$, too. There, it needs for $O(n)$ nodes $O(n^4)$ operations.

4 The Idea

In the context-free case, it was successful to reduce the wordproblem to the analysis of sequences of parentheses. Therefore, we want to use the same approach for $CCFG(2)$. Consequently, we have to construct a graph where we search for a path, whose marking expresses derivability/non-derivability of the input word relative to the underlying grammar. Here, context-free derivability does not suffice, but we additionally have to test the correctness of the coupling relative to the two components of nonterminal parentheses inside any derivation. Thus, we need a marking on the edges consisting in two different components, one for each of the two different tests to be performed. Now, the idea is to define a Greibach normalform for all $G \in CCFG(2)$ such that the graph and the first component of the marking (modelling context-free derivability) can be constructed as before using $CF(G)$ instead of G.

To get the second component of the marking, each $(X, \overline{X}) \rightarrow (\alpha, \overline{\alpha}) \in P$ is uniquely named by $(p, \overline{p})$, $p \in \Sigma$, Σ arbitrary alphabet. $(p, \overline{p})$ is understood as a parenthesis, i.e. we define the parentheses set $\pi_\Sigma := \{(p, \overline{p}) \mid p \in \Sigma, \nu^{-1}(p) \in P\}$. Thus, we can define a new congruence relation as $\sigma_G := \{(p\overline{p}, \varepsilon) \mid (p, \overline{p}) \in \pi_\Sigma\}$. It remains to use p resp. $\overline{p}$ as second marking such that it holds:

$$w \in L(G) \Longleftrightarrow \exists u \in E^*_{GNF} : \mathcal{S}(u) = \mathcal{B}, \mathcal{D}(u) = \mathcal{F}, \gamma_1(u) \equiv_{\rho_G} \varepsilon, \gamma_2(u) \equiv_{\sigma_G} \varepsilon.$$

We do that by taking p resp. $\overline{p}$ as second component for edges marked in the first component by X^{-1} resp. $\overline{X}^{-1}$, where X^{-1} resp. $\overline{X}^{-1}$ resulted from those terms in φ_G coming from $X \rightarrow \alpha$ resp. $\overline{X} \rightarrow \overline{\alpha}$ (i.e. the left-hand side of the productions). All other second components of the marking are set to ε.

4.1 The Normalform

Let $G \in CCFG(2)$. To generalize our algorithm, we first have to generalize the Greibach normalform. Therefore, it seems to be the best to demand Greibach normalform for $CF(G)$. Obviously, this generalization could easily be extended for $CCFG(l)$, $l > 2$. But in [12], it is shown that such a generalization is not suitable for our purpose. Thus, we need a more sophisticated normalform to perform the context-free as well as the coupled part of the analysis by reducing relative to a congruence relation.

When constructing φ_G, each $X \rightarrow tX_1 \dots X_k$ is transformed into $t = X^{-1}X_k \dots X_1$. Inside the graph, $X_1^{-1}, \dots, X_k^{-1}$ appear on the right of this sequence. In addition, the nonterminal components coupled to $X_1, \dots, X_k$ have to appear still farther on the right. To produce such a correct sequence of parentheses, $\overline{X}^{-1}$ has to be situated on the right of these coupled components. This can be achieved, if the second component of coupled productions is of a symmetric form as the first one is.

Definition 11 Generalized GNF.
$G = (\mathcal{K}, T, P, S) \in CCFG(2)$ is in *Generalized Greibach Normalform* (*GNF*), iff it satisfies:

(1) $P|_{\mathcal{K}[1]} \subseteq \mathcal{K}[1] \times T \cdot (comp(\mathcal{K}))^*$.
(2) $P|_{\mathcal{K}[2]} \subseteq \mathcal{K}[2] \times \left(T \cdot (comp(\mathcal{K}))^* \times (comp(\mathcal{K}))^* \cdot T\right)$.

__Remark:__ Up to now, it is still open how to construct a $G' \in CCFG(2)$ in generalized Greibach normalform fulfilling $L(G) = L(G')$ for each $G \in CCFG(2)$.

Let $G = (\mathcal{K}, T, P, S) \in CCFG(2)$ in generalized GNF. Using $CF(P)$, we can define φ_G uniquely in analogy to the context-free case. The symmetric form of second components of productions leads to

$$\varphi_G(t) := \{X^{-1}u^R \mid X \rightarrow tu \in CF(P)\} \cup \left\{u^R\overline{X}^{-1} \mid \overline{X} \rightarrow ut \in CF(P)\right\}.$$

This can also be extended to a monoid homomorphism $\varphi_G : T^* \longrightarrow \wp((comp(\mathcal{K}) \cup comp(\mathcal{K})^{-1})^*)$. This homomorphism defines the first component of the marking of the edges for our graph as usual.

Notation *To simplify the presentation, we talk about* red *and* black *edges in the sequel. Thereby, edges marked by X^{-1} or $\overline{X}^{-1}$ (the former $\mathcal{S}(p)$ for some $p \in CF(P)$) are said to be red, all the others black. In the figures, red edges are represented by thick lines while black edges are represented dotted.*

4.2 The Modified Graph

Let $G = (\mathcal{K}, T, P, S) \in CCFG(2)$ in generalized GNF. For any $w \in T^*$, the edges in $GNF\text{-}Graph_{CF(G)}(w)$ are constructed as before. The differences consist in the marking of the edges:

1. Each edge $s \in E_{GNF}$ is marked by $\gamma(s) := (\gamma_1(s), \gamma_2(s))$. Here, γ_1 results from $\varphi_G(t)$ as in the context-free case. For $\gamma_2(s)$, the following holds:
   __$\gamma_2(s) = \varepsilon$,__ if s is a black edge, i.e. $\gamma_1(s) \in comp(\mathcal{K})$, or if $\gamma_1(s) = X^{-1} \in \mathcal{K}[1]^{-1}$.
   __$\gamma_2(s) := \nu(p)$,__ if s is a red edge and $\gamma_1(s) = X^{-1}$ resulted from $X \rightarrow tX_1 \dots X_k \in CF(P)$, the first component of $p := (X, \overline{X}) \rightarrow (tX_1 \dots X_k, \alpha) \in P$.
   __$\gamma_2(k) := \overline{\nu(q)}$,__ if s is a red edge and $\gamma_1(s) = \overline{X}^{-1}$ resulted from $X \rightarrow X_1 \dots X_k t \in CF(P)$, the second component of $q := (Y, X) \rightarrow (\alpha, X_1 \dots X_k t) \in P$.

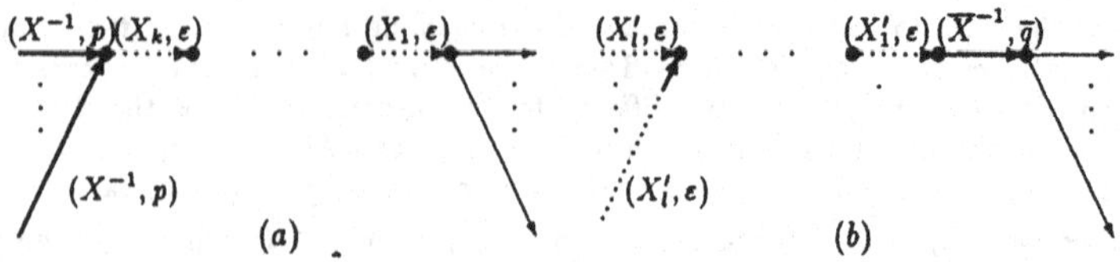

Fig. 2. $\gamma := (\gamma_1, \gamma_2)$, the marking of the edges

2. Now, the elements of $\varphi_G(t)$ are of the form $X^{-1}X_k \dots X_1 \in \varphi_G(t)$ (a) for first components of productions ($X \to tX_1 \dots X_k \in CF(P)$ holds), while for second components ($\overline{X} \to X'_1 \dots X'_l t' \in CF(P)$) they are as $X'_l \dots X'_1 \overline{X}^{-1} \in \varphi_G(t')$. (b) For $p := \nu((X,\overline{X}) \to (tX_1 \dots X_k, \alpha))$, $q := \nu((X,\overline{X}) \to (\beta, X'_1 \dots X'_l t'))$, the difference is shown in Fig. 2. We see that red edges appear on the left of their respective black edges except from the situation if their (red) marking resulted from the second component of a coupled production.
3. The additional edge $(\mathcal{B}, (0,1,0))$ necessary to have a uniform context-free analysis is not needed here. Thus, we remove it and identify $\mathcal{B}$ and $(0,1,0)$.
4. The graph resulting from $G \in CCFG(2)$ via $CF(G)$ in this way is denoted by *NF-Graph*$_G(w)$.

We finish the graph construction by an example, which is also used to explain the algorithm.

Example 1. Let $G \in CCFG(2)$ for $\mathcal{K} = \{S, (X,\overline{X}), (Y,\overline{Y})\}$, $T = \{\$, a, b, c, d\}$, $P = \{S \to \$X\overline{X},\ (Y,\overline{Y}) \overset{(h,\overline{h})}{\to} (b,c),\ (X,\overline{X}) \overset{(f,\overline{f})}{\to} (aXY, \overline{Y}\,\overline{X}d),\ (X,\overline{X}) \overset{(g,\overline{g})}{\to} (aY, \overline{Y}d)\}$. It holds $L(G) = \{\$a^n b^n c^n d^n \mid n \geq 1\}$. P defines the mapping φ_G for all $t \in T$ as

$$\varphi(\$) = S^{-1}\overline{X}X,\ \ \varphi(a) = X^{-1}YX + X^{-1}Y,$$
$$\varphi(b) = Y^{-1},\ \ \varphi(c) = \overline{Y}^{-1},\ \ \varphi(d) = \overline{X}\,\overline{Y}\,\overline{X}^{-1} + \overline{Y}\,\overline{X}^{-1}.$$

For $w := \$aabbccdd$, *NF-Graph*$_G(w)$ is shown in Fig. 4. while its derivation tree is shown in Fig. 3. To simplify Fig. 4., we omit all ε-markings. For all the others, γ_1 and γ_2 are written on different sides of the edge.

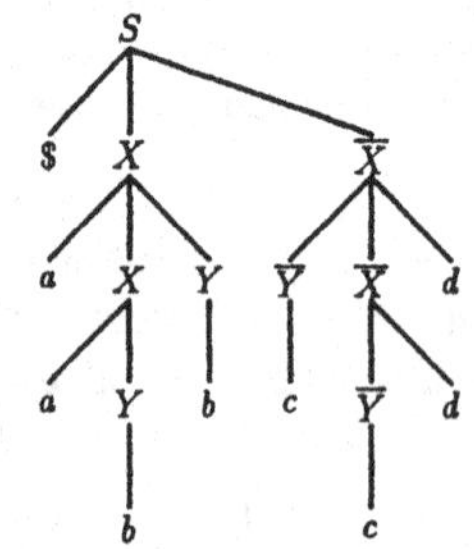

Fig. 3. Derivation tree for $w = \$aabbccdd$

4.3 The Principle of the Analysis

Let $G = (\mathcal{K}, T, P, S) \in CCFG(2)$ in generalized GNF. As we already scetched, the idea is to search a path u in *NF-Graph*$_G(w)$, which shows a sequence of parentheses correctly nested in the first as well as in the second component of its marking. We still have to show how this path can be found efficiently.

The first idea is to use the context-free algorithm on γ_1. Each time a new ε-edge is created γ_2 could be collected from the edges used for this construction. This means that we could not forget the partial paths leading to the construction of the ε-edge as it was possible in the context-free case. Since the context-free and the coupled information are distributed very differently on the graph and, in general, cannot be reduced together, the consequence would be that each ε-edge could show an exponential amount of second-component markings. This is too expensive for an efficient procedure. Besides, since this procedure would not take special properties of the graph into account, an efficient solution would mean the efficient solution of an NP-complete problem as shown in [12].

Thus, we decide to trace the derivation process for X and $\overline{X}$ in $(X,\overline{X}) \in \mathcal{K}[2]$ in parallel. This means to search at first for couplings in the graph. Therefore, it suffices to examine red edges and the second component of their marking. Relative to the couplings found we test context-free derivability. In fact, this means to investigate the context-free derivability of the black edges belonging to these red edges, i.e. to investigate the first component of their marking. Both operations are performed in turn.

We start with the most simplest cases, which are investigated in a preprocessing performed only once. These cases stand for $N \to w_i \in P$, $N \in \mathcal{K}[1]$, and $(X,\overline{X}) \to (w_j, w_{j+1}) \in P$, $(X,\overline{X}) \in \mathcal{K}[2]$. They are easy to find since they are represented by one ore two continuous red edges only. They model the smallest correct sequences of parentheses (ε or $p\overline{p}$) we can find in the whole graph.

In the sequel, the procedure incrementally constructs continuously growing paths in *NF-Graph*$_G(w)$. The first condition each path u has to fulfill is $\gamma_2(u) \equiv_{\rho_G} \varepsilon$. Therefore, we only test red edges. Following the definition of $ED(\mathcal{K}, T)$, there are 3 cases to distinguish:

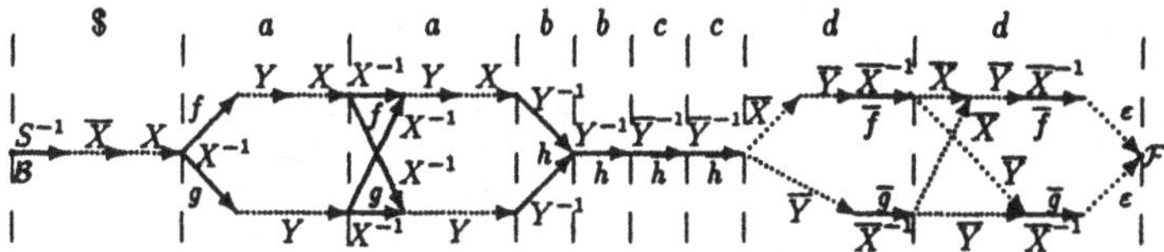

Fig. 4. $NF\text{-}Graph_G(w)$ for $w = \$aabbccdd$

1. $u, v \in ED(\pi_\Sigma, \emptyset) \implies u \cdot v \in ED(\pi_\Sigma, \emptyset)$
2. $N \in \mathcal{K}[1],\ v \in ED(\pi_\Sigma, \emptyset) \implies \varepsilon_N \cdot v \in ED(\pi_\Sigma, \emptyset)$
3. $(p, \overline{p}) \in \pi_\Sigma,\ v \in ED(\pi_\Sigma, \emptyset) \implies pv\overline{p} \in ED(\pi_\Sigma, \emptyset)$

Hereby, 2. is a special case of 3. and models the situation of red edges s fulfilling $\gamma_2(s) = \varepsilon$, i.e. $(\gamma_1(s))^{-1} \in \mathcal{K}[1]$. The algorithm realizes each condition as separate steps which are iterated successively.

The second condition each path u has to fulfill is, if u leads from column i to column j and if $\gamma_1(u) \equiv_{\rho_G} W$, $W^{-1} \overset{*}{\Rightarrow}_G w_i \dots w_j$ has to hold. This condition is tested separately inside each step.

Example 2. (Example 1 continued)

Relative to the derivation tree in Fig. 3., the algorithm works bottom-up and from the inside to the outside of the tree. Thus, it finds at first the coupling $(Y, \overline{Y}) \to (b, c)$ (columns 5/6 of the graph) in the preprocessing, again $(Y, \overline{Y}) \to (b, c)$ (col. 4/7) then $(X, \overline{X}) \to (aY, \overline{Y}d)$ (col. 3/8) thereby reducing with the relation σ_G, $(X, \overline{X}) \to (aXY, \overline{YX}d)$ (col. 3/8) - all by Step 3 - and finally $S \to \$X\overline{X}$ by Step 2.

5 The Algorithm

Notation *Let $G \in CCFG(2)$ in generalized GNF and $w \in T^+$.*

- *The set of all red edges in $NF\text{-}Graph_G(w)$ is denoted by $RED_G(w)$.*
- *As formal calculation rule, we define $(X^{-1})^{-1} := X$ for $X \in comp(\mathcal{K})$; for $X_1, \dots, X_j \in comp(\mathcal{K})$, we define: $v := X_1^{-1} \cdot \dots \cdot X_j^{-1} \implies v^{-1} = X_1 \cdot \dots \cdot X_j$.*

Now, let $s \in RED_G(w)$. We define:

- *$Col(s) := i \iff \mathcal{D}(s) = (i, j, k)$.*
- *$Prod(s) := \gamma_1(u) = v \in (comp(\mathcal{K}))^+ \iff \Big(\gamma_1(s)^{-1} \to w_{Col(s)}v^R \in CF(P)$ and $\mathcal{D}(s) = \mathcal{S}(u)\Big)$ or $\Big(\gamma_1(s)^{-1} \to v^R w_{Col(s)} \in CF(P)$ and $\mathcal{D}(u) = \mathcal{S}(s)\Big)$.*

The algorithm marks the couplings it finds by green edges (the new "ε-edges"). All these are collected in $GREEN_G(w)$. Green edges generated by Step 1 or 3 have to store everything inside this coupling. This is done by markings which store sequences of green edges which themselves store red edges as follows:

Definition 12 single, composed.

Let $G = (\mathcal{K}, T, P, S) \in CCFG(2)$ in generalized GNF, $w \in T^+$. $k \in GREEN_G(w)$ is called ***single***, if there is no mark on k. Otherwise, k is called ***composed***. The marks of a composed k are denoted by <u>*marks*</u>(k). It consists of the lists <u>*linear*</u>(k) determined by Step 1 and <u>*nested*</u>(k) constructed by Step 3.

Definition 13 Forrest, Yield.

Let $G = (\mathcal{K}, T, P, S) \in CCFG(2)$ in generalized GNF, $w \in T^+$. For all $k := (s, s') \in GREEN_G(w)$, the directed graph $Forrest(k) := (V(k), E(k))$ and the mapping $Yield(k)$ are defined as:

<u>1. Let $k = (s, s')$ single.</u> If $(\gamma_1(s))^{-1} \in \mathcal{K}[1]$, we have $Forrest(k) := (\{s, k\}, \{(k, s)\})$, $Yield(k) := \gamma_1(s)$. If $\left((\gamma_1(s))^{-1}, (\gamma_1(s'))^{-1}\right) \in \mathcal{K}[2]$, it is $Forrest(k) := (\{s, s', k\}, \{(k, s), (k, s')\})$, $Yield(k) := \gamma_1(s) \cdot \gamma_1(s')$.

<u>2. Let $k = (s, s')$ nested</u> and marked by $linear(k)$ consisting of $m_{lin} \geq 0$ marks to green edge pairs (k_1^j, k_2^j), $0 \leq j \leq m_{lin}$, as well as by $nested(k)$ consisting of $m_{nes} \geq 0$ marks to single green edges k^j, $0 \leq j \leq m_{nes}$. It holds $m_{lin} + m_{nes} > 0$. We have

$$Forrest(k) := \bigcup_{j=1}^{m_{lin}} Forrest_{lin}(k, j) \cup \bigcup_{j=1}^{m_{nes}} Forrest_{nes}(k, j),$$

```
PREPROCESSING

GREEN_G(w) := ∅;
for all s ∈ RED_G(w) where
        ( Col(s) = i and (γ1(s))^-1 → w_i ∈ P )
do
   GREEN_G(w) := GREEN_G(w) ∪ {(s,s)};
   single((s,s)) := true;
od;
for all s, s' ∈ RED_G(w) where
        (D(s) = S(s'))
do
   if ((γ1(s))^-1, (γ1(s'))^-1) ∈ K[2]
     and (γ2(s), γ2(s')) ∈ π_Σ
   then
     GREEN_G(w) := GREEN_G(w) ∪ {(s,s')};
     single((s,s')) := true;
od;

ITERATION

for d := 1 to (n+2)
do
   for all s, s' ∈ RED_G(w) where
        Col(s') − Col(s) = d
   do
(1)    for all k, k' ∈ GREEN_G(w) where
             (S(k) = s, D(k') = s'
              and D(D(k)) = S(S(k')) )
       do
          k* := (s, s');
          if k* ∉ GREEN_G(w)
          then
               GREEN_G(w) :=
                          GREEN_G(w) ∪ {k*};
               single(k*) := false;
          linear(k*) := linear(k*) ∪ {(k, k')};
       od;
(2)  if (γ1(s))^-1 ∈ K[1]
     then
       if ∃k ∈ GREEN_G(w) where
          ( ( Col(S(k)) = Col(s) + 1 ) and
           (D(k) = s') and ∃v ∈ Yield(k)
           where (Prod(s) · v ≡_ρG ε) )
       then
         k* := (s, s');
         if k* ∉ GREEN_G(w)
         then
              GREEN_G(w) := GREEN_G(w) ∪ {k*};
         single(k*) := true;
(3) if ((γ1(s))^-1, (γ1(s'))^-1) ∈ K[2]
       and (γ2(s), γ2(s')) ∈ π_Σ
    then
      for all k ∈ GREEN_G(w) where
           ( Col(S(k)) = Col(s) + 1
             and Col(D(k)) = Col(s') − 1 )
      do
        k* := (s, s');
        for all v1 v2 v3 ∈ Yield(k) where
              (a) Prod(s) · v1 ≡_ρG ε
              (b) (v3 · Prod(s'))^R ≡_ρG ε
        do
          if k* ∉ GREEN_G(w)
          then
            GREEN_G(w) := GREEN_G(w) ∪ {k*};
            single(k*) := false;
          if v2 = ε
          then single(k*) := true;
          else
            Let k' ∈ V(k) where Yield(k') = v2
               in Forrest(k) = (V(k), E(k))
            nested(k*) := nested(k*) ∪ {k'};
            /* (γ1(S(k*))^-1, γ1(D(k*))^-1) ∈ K[2] */
        od;
```

Fig. 5. The Procedure

$$Yield(k) := \bigcup_{j=1}^{m_{lin}} Yield_{lin}(k,j) \cup \bigcup_{j=1}^{m_{nes}} Yield_{nes}(k,j).$$

For all $(k_1^j, k_2^j) \in linear(k)$, it holds

$Forrest_{lin}(k,j) := (V(k_1^j) \cup V(k_2^j) \cup \{k\}, E(k_1^j) \cup E(k_2^j) \cup \{(k,k_1^j),(k,k_2^j)\}),$
$Yield_{lin}(k,j) := \{u \cdot v \mid u \in Yield(k_1^j), v \in Yield(k_2^j)\}.$

For all $k^j \in nested(k)$, we have

$Forrest_{nes}(k,j) := (V(k^j) \cup \{k,s,s'\}, E(k^j) \cup \{(k,s),(k,k^j),(k,s')\})$,
$Yield_{nes}(k,j) := \{\gamma_1(s) \cdot u \cdot \gamma_1(s') \mid u \in Yield(k^j)\}.$

Let $G = (\mathcal{K}, T, P, S) \in CCFG(2)$ in generalized GNF, $w \in T^+$, $n := |w|$, $\rho_G := \{(XX^{-1}, \varepsilon) \mid X \in comp(\mathcal{K})\}$, $\pi_\Sigma := \{(p, \overline{p}) \mid p \in \Sigma\}$, and $NF\text{-}Graph_G(w)$ constructed. The algorithm can be formalized as shown in Fig. 5. It fulfills the following two lemmata as invariants. They are formally proved in [12] by induction on the distance of the columns any $k \in GREEN_G(w)$ connects.

Lemma 14. *Let $G \in CCFG(2)$ in generalized GNF, $w \in T^+$, $n := |w|$. For all $k \in GREEN_G(w)$ where $Col(S(k)) = i$ and $Col(\mathcal{D}(k)) = j$, it holds: $v \in Yield(k) \implies v^{-1} \overset{*}{\Rightarrow}_G w_i \dots w_j$*

Lemma 15. *Let $G \in CCFG(2)$ in generalized GNF, $w \in T^+$, $n := |w|$. For all $W \in ED(\mathcal{K}, \emptyset)$, it holds:*

$$W \overset{*}{\Rightarrow}_G w_i \dots w_j \implies \exists k \in GREEN_G(w) : Col(S(k)) = i, Col(\mathcal{D}(k)) = j, W^{-1} \in Yield(k)$$

From these lemmata, the correctness of our procedure follows, since then, we have:

$w \in L(G) \iff \exists k \in GREEN_G(w)$: $Col((S(k)) = 1$, $Col(\mathcal{D}(k)) = n$, and $Yield(k) = S^{-1}$

6 The Complexity

Each edge in $GREEN_G(w)$ is created only once. Different paths leading to the same edge are modelled by *marks*. For each $k \in GREEN_G(w)$, $|linear(k)| \leq O(|CF(P)|^2 \cdot n)$ and $|nested(k)| \leq O(|CF(P)|^2 \cdot n^2)$ hold because of their construction by the algorithm.

The preprocessing costs $O(|CF(P)|^2 \cdot n)$ operations. No more situations have to be examined, since only n transitions from one column to the next one exist.
The iteration investigates red edges s, s', where $d := Col(s') - Col(s)$ grows from 1 to $(n+2)$. Thus, each step is iterated at most $O(|CF(P)|^2 \cdot n^2)$ times. Now, let s, s' be arbitrary, but fixed.
Step (1) applies to at most $|CF(P)|^2 \cdot n$ situations, where each costs only $O(1)$ operations.
Step (2) applies to at most $|CF(P)|$ situations, where each costs $O(n^4)$ to search a $v \in Yield(k)$ fulfilling $(Prod(s) \cdot v \equiv_{\rho_G} \varepsilon)$, if $marks(k)$ is realized as a matrix. (For each sign in the *Yield*, we have to investigate n^2 situations where each can cost $O(n^2)$ because of the length of *marks*.) Everything else costs $O(1)$.
Step (3) applies to at most $|CF(P)|^2$ situations, but the most time-consuming operation is, as for Step (2), the search for a suitable element inside a yield.

Theorem 16. *Let $G \in CCFG(2)$ in generalized GNF, $w \in T^+$, and $n := |w|$. Our procedure solves the wordproblem for w relative to G in time $O(n^6)$.*

References

[1] A. Abbeillé: *Parsing French with Tree Adjoining Grammars: Some Linguistic Accounts.* In Proc. of the 12th Conf. on Comput. Linguistics 1988, pp. 7-12

[2] J. Bresnan, R. Kaplan, P. Peters, A. Zaenen: *Cross-serial Dependencies in Dutch.* Linguistic Inquiry 13 (1982), pp. 613-635

[3] N. Chomsky, N. Schützenberger: *The Algebraic Theory of Context-Free Languages.* In "Computer Programming and Formal Systems" Amsterdam, North Holland 1963

[4] J. Dassow, G. Păun: *Regulated Rewriting in Formal Language Theory.* Springer 1989

[5] Y. Guan, G. Hotz, A. Reichert: *Tree Grammars with multilinear Interpretation.* Technical Report, Univ. of Saarbrücken 1992

[6] Y. Guan: *Klammergrammatiken, Netzgrammatiken und Interpretationen von Netzen.* PhD thesis, Univ. of Saarbrücken 1992

[7] G. Hotz, T. Kretschmer: *The Power of the Greibach Normal Form.* EIK 25 (1989), pp. 507-512

[8] G. Hotz, G. Pitsch: *Fast Uniform Analysis of Coupled-Context-Free Grammars.* In Proc. of ICALP 1994, pp. 412-423

[9] G. Hotz, G. Pitsch: *A Representation Theorem for Coupled-Context-Free Grammars.* In Proc. of Conf. on Semigroups, Automata, and Languages, Porto 1994, pp. 88-91

[10] A.K. Joshi, L.S. Levy, M. Takahashi: *Tree Adjunct Grammars.* J. Comput. Syst. Sci. 10 (1975), pp. 136-163

[11] T. Kroch, A.K. Joshi. *The Linguistic Relevance of Tree Adjoining Grammars.* Technical Report MS-CIS-85-16, Univ. of Pennsylvania, Philadelphia 1985

[12] G. Pitsch: *Analyse von Klammergrammatiken.* PhD thesis, Univ. of Saarbrücken 1993. also Technical Report 10/1994, Univ. of Saarbrücken, 1994.

[13] G. Pitsch: *LL(k)-Parsing of Coupled-Context-Free Grammars.* Comput. Intelligence 10, pp. 563-578

[14] D.J. Rosenkrantz. *Matrix Equations and Normal Forms for Context-Free Grammars.* J. ACM 14 (1967), pp. 501-507

[15] E. Shamir. *A Representation Theorem for Algebraic and Context-Free Power Series in Noncommuting Variables.* Information and Control 11 (1967), pp. 239-254

[16] S. Shieber: *Evidence against Context-Freeness of Natural Language.* Linguistics and Philosophy 8 (1986), pp. 333-343

[17] Y. Schabes, A.K. Joshi. *An Early-Type Parsing Algorithm for Tree Adjoining Grammars.* In Proc. of the 26th Meeting of the Assoc. for Comput. Linguistics 1988

[18] K. Vijay-Shanker, A.K. Joshi. *Some Computational Properties of Tree Adjoining Grammars.* In Proc. of the 23th Meeting of the Assoc. for Comput. Linguistics 1985, pp. 82-93

Computational Complexity of Simultaneous Elementary Matching Problems

(Extended Abstract)

Miki Hermann[1,*] Phokion G. Kolaitis[2,†]

[1] CRIN (CNRS) and INRIA-Lorraine, BP 239, 54506 Vandœuvre-lès-Nancy, France. (hermann@loria.fr)

[2] Computer and Information Sciences, University of California, Santa Cruz, CA 95064, U.S.A. (kolaitis@cse.ucsc.edu)

Abstract. The simultaneous elementary E-matching problem for an equational theory E is to decide whether there is an E-matcher for a given system of equations in which the only function symbols occurring in the terms to be matched are the ones constrained by the equational axioms of E. We study the computational complexity of simultaneous elementary matching problems for the equational theories A of semigroups, AC of commutative semigroups, and ACU of commutative monoids. In each case, we delineate the boundary between NP-completeness and solvability in polynomial time by considering two parameters, the number of equations in the systems and the number of constant symbols in the signature. Moreover, we analyze further the intractable cases of simultaneous elementary AC-matching and ACU-matching by taking also into account the maximum number of occurrences of each variable. Using graph-theoretic techniques, we show that if each variable is restricted to having at most two occurrences, then several cases of simultaneous elementary AC-matching and ACU-matching can be solved in polynomial time.

1 Introduction and Summary of Results

The design of matching and unification algorithms is one of the principal challenges faced by researchers in automated deduction. This challenge can become particularly intriguing when the terms to be matched or unified contain function symbols satisfying the axioms of an equational theory E, in which case we speak of E-matching and E-unification algorithms. Among the various equational theories that have been investigated with respect to matching and unification during the past twenty years, the equational theory AC of commutative semigroups occupies a prominent place, because of its important rôle in term rewriting and its conspicuous presence in applications (cf. [BHK*88, JK91, BS93]). In addition to AC, there has been also an extensive study of unification in the equational theories A of semigroups and ACU of commutative monoids. Indeed, A-unification algorithms solve the classical Markov's problem for word equations, while ACU-unification algorithms are used widely as building blocks for AC-unification algorithms.

Benanav, Kapur, and Narendran [BKN87] analyzed the computational complexity of decision problems for matching in various equational theories and established that A-matching, AC-matching, and ACU-matching are all NP-complete problems. Benanav et

*Partially supported by a NATO grant. Research was carried out while this author was visiting the University of California, Santa Cruz.

†Partially supported by a Guggenheim Fellowhsip and NSF Grant CCR-9307758.

al. [BKN87] discovered also that AC1-matching, the restriction of AC-matching to terms in which each variable occurs only once, is solvable in polynomial-time. This tractable case of AC-matching turned out to be the rather isolated, since Verma and Ramakrishnan [VR92] showed that AC-matching is NP-complete even if each variable is allowed to have only two occurrences in the terms being matched. Aiming to develop a different perspective on the complexity of matching, Kolaitis and Hermann [HK94] introduced and studied a class of counting problems that arise naturally in this context. More specifically, if E is an equational theory, then #E-matching is the following problem: given a term s and a ground term t, find the cardinality of a minimal complete set of E-matchers of s and t. The motivation for considering these counting problems comes from the fact that matching and unification algorithms should not only decide whether two given terms can be E-matched (E-unified), but should also return a minimal complete set of E-matchers (E-unifiers). In particular, such algorithms can solve at the same time the corresponding #E-matching problem. Thus, by identifying the computational complexity of #E-matching, we gain a deeper insight into the expected behavior of matching and unification algorithms than the insight obtained from the analysis of the corresponding decision problem. In the paper [HK94], it was shown that #A-matching, #AC-matching, and #ACU-matching are all #P-complete problems. The concept of #P-completeness was introduced by Valiant [Val79] as a means of quantifying the computational difficulty of counting problems. In many respects, a #P-completeness result for a counting problem indicates a higher level of intractability than a NP-completeness result for the corresponding desision problem. Valiant [Val79] showed also that there exist polynomial-time decision problems whose counting version is #P-complete. As it turns out, this phenomenon occurs also in matching, because in [HK94] it was shown that that #AC1-matching is a #P-complete problem.

If one takes a closer look at the above NP-hardness and #P-hardness results for matching, then one realizes that their proofs make use of terms containing *free* function symbols, i.e., function symbols that are not constrained by the axioms of the underlying equational theory. To put it differently, in these hardness results the signature over which the terms are built is allowed to vary and is given as part of the input of the decision and counting problem under consideration. In turn, this raises the question: does the complexity of the matching problems change, if the signature contains no free function symbols? There are several other situations where it has been established that the presence of free function symbols affects the properties of matching and unification. As Baader and Siekman [BS93] write, "It is important to note that the signature over which the terms of the unification problems may be built has considerable influence on the unification type and on the existence of unification algorithms". For this reason, in studying an equational theory E one distinguishes between the case of *elementary* E-matching (E-unification), where the signature contains no free function symbols, and the case of *general* E-matching (E-unification), where the signature contains free function symbols of arbitrary arity. In both cases the signature may contain one or more free constant symbols. Elementary E-matching (E-unification) extends naturally to *simultaneous elementary* E-matching (E-unification), where, instead of just a single equation $s \stackrel{?}{=}_{\mathrm{E}} t$, one is given a *system* of equations $s_1 \stackrel{?}{=}_{\mathrm{E}} t_1, \ldots, s_k \stackrel{?}{=}_{\mathrm{E}} t_k$ for which an E-matcher (E-unifier) is sought. Note that in the case of general E-matching (E-unification) such systems reduce to a single equation $f(s_1, \ldots, s_k) \stackrel{?}{=}_{\mathrm{E}} f(t_1, \ldots, t_k)$, where f is a free function symbol.

In this paper, we carry out a systematic investigation of the computational complexity of simultaneous elementary E-matching decision and counting problems, where E is one of the equational theories A, AC or ACU. Our goal is to identify the rôle of the signature on the complexity of matching and to delineate the boundary between intractability and tractability for elementary matching in these theories. We classify simultaneous elementary matching problems according to the number of equations in the system and the number of free constant symbols in the signature. Eker [Eke93] proved that elementary AC-matching is NP-complete for single equations over signatures with an unbounded number of free constant symbols. At the other end of the scale, Baader and Siekmann [BS93] pointed out that simultaneous elementary AC-matching is NP-complete for systems of unbounded length over signatures with two free constant symbols. In fact, a slight modification of that reduction shows that a single free constant symbol suffices for establishing NP-hardness. We complement the above results in two ways. First, we point out that in these cases the corresponding counting problem is #P-complete. After this, we establish that if the systems are of fixed length and the signature contains a fixed number of free constant symbols, then both the decision problem and the counting problem for simultaneous elementary AC-matching can be solved in polynomial time using dynamic programming. Thus, intractability occurs in AC-matching only when the length of the systems or the number of free constant symbols grow beyond any bounds.

We use the same classification to study and identify the complexity of decision and counting problems in simultaneous elementary A-matching and ACU-matching. It turns out that A-matching is tractable in fewer cases than AC-matching, whereas ACU-matching is tractable in more cases. We show that simultaneous elementary A-matching is solvable in polynomial time only when the systems are of fixed length and the signature has a single free constant symbol. In all other cases, the decision problem is NP-complete and the counting problem is #P-complete. In contrast, simultaneous elementary ACU-matching is solvable in polynomial time as long as the systems are of fixed length, even if the signature has an unbounded number of free constant symbols.

Finally, we take a closer look at the intractable cases of simultaneous elementary AC-matching and ACU-matching by considering a third parameter as a resource, namely the maximum number of variable occurrences in the systems. While for general AC-matching one occurrence suffices for establishing #P-hardenss and two occurrences suffice for establishing NP-hardness, we show that here the dividing line between tractability and intractability is one level higher at two occurrences and three occurrences, respectively. In particular, we show that the decision problem for simultaneous elementary AC-matching with each variable occurring twice is solvable in polynomial time over signatures with one free constant symbol, even if the systems are of unbounded length. Moreover, the decision problem for simultaneous elementary ACU-matching with each variable occurring twice is solvable in polynomial time, even if the signature contains an unbounded number of free constant symbols and the systems are of unbounded length. We derive polynomial-time algorithms for these problems by reducing them to a class of graph-theoretic problems, known as *b-matching*, that ask whether a given graph contains a subgraph whose nodes satisfy certain degree constraints. Although *b*-matching problems have been studied extensively in the context of graph theory to our knowledge this is the first time that a connection has been made between these graph-theoretic problems and matching problems in equational theories. This connection opens the road for incorporating efficient *b*-matching algorithms into AC-matching and ACU-matching algorithms.

2 Preliminaries

This section contains the definitions of the main concepts and a minimum amount of the necessary background material from equational matching and computational complexity. Additional material on these topics can be found in [JK91, BS93] and [Pap94].

Matching Problems in Equational Theories and their Complexity

A *signature* $\mathcal{F}$ is a countable set of function and constant symbols. If $\mathcal{X}$ is a countable set of variables, then $\mathcal{T}(\mathcal{F},\mathcal{X})$ denotes the set of all terms over the signature $\mathcal{F}$ and the variables in $\mathcal{X}$. Capital letters $X, Y, Z, \ldots$, as well as capital letters with subscripts $X_i, Y_i, Z_i, \ldots$ will be used to denote variables in $\mathcal{X}$.

An *identity* over $\mathcal{F}$ is a first-order sentence of the form $(\forall X_1)\ldots(\forall X_n)(l = r)$, where l and r are terms in $\mathcal{T}(\mathcal{F},\mathcal{X})$ with variables among $X_1,\ldots,X_n$. Every set E of identities can be viewed as the set of *equational axioms* of an *equational theory* Th(E) consisting of all identities over $\mathcal{F}$ that are logically implied by E. By an abuse of terminology, we will often say the "equational theory E", instead of "the equational theory Th(E)". The notation $s =_{\mathrm{E}} t$ denotes that the identity $(\forall X_1)\ldots(\forall X_n)(s = t)$ is a member of Th(E).

Our main focus will be on the equational theory AC of commutative semigroups and on the equational theory ACU of commutative monoids. For both these theories, the signature $\mathcal{F}$ contains a binary function symbol $+$ that is assumed to be associative and commutative. Thus, the equational axioms of AC are

$$\text{A: } (\forall X)(\forall Y)(\forall Z)(X + (Y + Z) = (X + Y) + Z) \qquad \text{C: } (\forall X)(\forall Y)(X + Y = Y + X)$$

For ACU, the signature $\mathcal{F}$ contains also a constant symbol 0, which is the *unit* element for $+$. Thus, ACU satisfies also the identity U: $(\forall X)(X + 0 = X)$. We also consider the equational theory A of semigroups, whose only equational axiom is associativity.

A *substitution* is a mapping $\rho: \mathcal{X} \rightarrow \mathcal{T}(\mathcal{F},\mathcal{X})$ such that $X\rho = X$ for all but finitely many variables X. We say that a term s *E-matches* a ground term t if there is a substitution ρ such that $s\rho =_{\mathrm{E}} t$. In this case, we call ρ an *E-matcher* of s and t. It can be shown that a term s E-matches a ground term t if and only if the equation $s \stackrel{?}{=}_{\mathrm{E}} t$ can be solved in the quotient algebra $\mathcal{T}(\mathcal{F},\mathcal{X})/{=_{\mathrm{E}}}$.

E-matching is the following decision problem: given a term s and a ground term t over a signature $\mathcal{F}$, decide whether s E-matches t. Benanav, Kapur, and Narendran [BKN87] investigated the computational complexity of E-matching and showed that A-matching, AC-matching, and ACU-matching are all NP-complete problems.

Beside the decision problem, there is an another important (and often more challenging) algorithmic problem arising in matching, namely the problem of designing algorithms which not only decide whether a given term s E-matches a ground term t, but also return as value a *minimal complete* set $\mu\mathrm{CSM}_{\mathrm{E}}(s,t)$ of E-matchers of s and t, provided that s E-matches t. An insight into this problem can be gained by studying a related *counting* problem in equational matching, that asks for the number of E-matchers in a minimal complete set. Before describing this approach in more detail, we state the basic relevant facts from computational complexity.

#P is the class of all counting problems that are computable in polynomial-time using *counting* Turing machines, i.e., non-deterministic Turing machines equipped with an additional output tape on which it prints in binary the number of its accepting computations. The class #P was introduced by Valiant [Val79], who established the existence of #P-*complete* problems, i.e., counting problems in #P such that every problem in #P can be reduced to them via restricted polynomial-time reductions that preserve the number of solutions (*parsimonious* reductions) or at least make it possible to compute the number of solutions of one problem from the other (*counting* reductions). The prototypical #P-complete problem is #SAT, which asks for the number of satisfying assignments of a given Boolean formula. Valiant [Val79] discovered also that there are polynomial-time decision problems, such as perfect matching in bipartite graphs, whose corresponding counting problem is #P-complete. The prevalent view in complexity theory is that a #P-completeness result indicates a higher level of intractability than a NP-completeness result does. No #P-complete problem is known to be (nor is believed to be) a member of the class FPH, the functional analog of the polynomial hierarchy PH (cf. [Pap94]).

In [HK94], we introduced a class of *counting* problems in equational matching and studied their computational complexity using tools from the theory of #P-completeness. More precisely, #E-*matching* is the following counting problem: given a term s and a ground term t, find the cardinality of $\mu CSM_E(s,t)$. This problem is well-defined for every *finitary* equational theory E. Observe that, on the face of it, #E-matching is a problem of intermediate difficulty between the decision problem for E-matching and the problem of designing matching algorithms that return minimal complete sets of E-matchers. Thus, a #P-completeness result about the #E-matching problem of some equational theory E suggests that computing minimal complete sets of E-matchers is a truly intractable problem. In [HK94] we showed that #A-matching, #AC-matching, and #ACU-matching are all #P-complete problems. Moreover, we established there that even #AC1-matching is #P-complete, where AC1 is the restriction of AC to *linear terms* (terms in which each variable occurs only once). In contrast, [BKN87] showed that the decision problem for AC1-matching is solvable in polynomial time.

Simultaneous Elementary Matching

Let $\mathcal{F}$ be a signature, $\mathcal{X}$ a set of variables, and E an equational theory whose axioms are identities over $\mathcal{F}$. The signature $\mathcal{F}$ may contain function or constant symbols that do not occur in the equational axioms of E. Such symbols are called *free*, since they are not constrained in any way by E. As mentioned earlier, the existence of free function or constant symbols in the signature may affect the structural properties of an equational theory E and have an impact on unification or matching algorithms for E (cf. [BS93]). Closer to our interests here, it should be noted that the proof in [BKN87] that AC-matching is NP-hard makes an essential use of free function symbols in the signature. More recently, Eker [Eke93] showed that AC-matching remains NP-hard over signatures with no free function symbols; in the proof of this result, however, the signature at hand contains an unbounded number of free constant symbols. The #P-hardness proofs for #AC-matching and #AC1-matching in [HK94] depend on free function symbols and free constant symbols in the signature. Thus, it is natural to ask whether and how the computational complexity of E-matching and #E-matching changes, if the instances of these problems are restricted to terms over signatures having no free function symbols and possibly only a bounded number of free constant symbols.

The *elementary* E-*matching problem* is the restriction of E-matching to signatures with no free function symbols. Thus, given a pair (s,t), where s is a term and t is a ground term with function symbols among those in the equational axioms of E, the question is to decide whether there is a substitution ρ such that $s\rho =_{\mathrm{E}} t$. The *elementary #E-matching problem* is the analogous restriction of #E-matching. In the sequel, we will also be interested in extensions of elementary matching problems where each instance can be a finite set of pairs of terms, instead of just a single pair of terms.

The *simultaneous elementary* E-*matching problem* is the following decision problem: given a finite set $\{(s_1,t_1),\ldots,(s_k,t_k)\}$, where each s_i is a term and each t_i is a ground term with function symbols among those in the equational axioms of E, decide whether there is a substitution ρ such that $s_i\rho =_{\mathrm{E}} t_i$ for every $i \leq k$. Such a substitution is called an E-*matcher of the set* $\{(s_1,t_1),\ldots,(s_k,t_k)\}$. Similarly, the *simultaneous elementary #E-matching problem* is the following counting problem: given a finite set of pairs of terms as above, find the cardinality of a minimal complete set of E-matchers of that set. From now on, the notation $s_1 \stackrel{?}{=}_{\mathrm{E}} t_1,\ldots,s_k \stackrel{?}{=}_{\mathrm{E}} t_k$ will be used to represent an instance of the simultaneous elementary E-matching (or #E-matching) problem.

In effect, the simultaneous elementary E-matching problem asks for the solution of a *system* of equations $s_1 \stackrel{?}{=}_{\mathrm{E}} t_1,\ldots,s_k \stackrel{?}{=}_{\mathrm{E}} t_k$ in the quotient algebra $\mathcal{T}(\mathcal{F},\mathcal{X})/=_{\mathrm{E}}$, where the function symbols of $\mathcal{F}$ are exactly the function symbols occurring in the equational axioms of E. Of course, one can consider simultaneous E-matching problems over arbitrary signatures. However, the simultaneous E-matching problem over arbitrary signatures is reducible to the E-matching problem, because one can use free function symbols to encode a system of equations into a single equation. We will classify simultaneous elementary matching problems using two parameters, namely the *number of equations* in a given system, called the *length* of the system, and the *number of free constants* in the signature. Note that the number of free constant symbols is unimportant for matching problems over signatures with free function symbols, since a set $\{C_1, C_2,\ldots,C_m\}$ of free constant symbols can be represented by the set $\{g(C), g(g(C)),\ldots,g^m(C)\}$, where C is a free constant symbol and g is a free unary function symbol.

If k and m are two positive integers, then the $\epsilon\mathrm{E}(k,m)$-*matching* problem consists of all instances of simultaneous elementary E-matching with at most k equations and at most m free constants. We also put

$$\epsilon\mathrm{E}(k,\omega) = \bigcup_{m=1}^{\infty} \epsilon\mathrm{E}(k,m) \quad \text{and} \quad \epsilon\mathrm{E}(\omega,m) = \bigcup_{k=1}^{\infty} \epsilon\mathrm{E}(k,m)$$

Thus, in $\epsilon\mathrm{E}(k,\omega)$-matching the signature has an unbounded number of free constant symbols, while in $\epsilon\mathrm{E}(\omega,m)$-matching the systems of equations have unbounded length. We define similarly #$\epsilon\mathrm{E}(k,m)$-matching, #$\epsilon\mathrm{E}(k,\omega)$-matching, and #$\epsilon\mathrm{E}(\omega,m)$-matching.

3 Simultaneous Elementary AC-Matching

If $+$ is an associative and commutative binary function symbol, then every term built using $+$, variables from $\mathcal{X}$, and free constants can be brought into an equivalent *flattened* form. This means that all parentheses have been removed and all occurrences of identical variables and free constants have been grouped together using multiplicity coefficients, so that if t is a variable or a free constant, then every term of the form $t+\cdots+t$ with α summands equal to t is replaced by the expression αt. Thus, an instance of the elementary

AC-matching problem is an equation of the form

$$\alpha_1 X_1 + \cdots + \alpha_n X_n \stackrel{?}{=}_{\mathrm{AC}} \gamma_1 C_1 + \cdots + \gamma_m C_m,$$

where each X_i is a variable from $\mathcal{X}$, each C_j is a free constant, and each α_i and each γ_j is a positive integer. The *size* of such an instance of elementary AC-matching is equal to $n \max\{\alpha_1, \ldots, \alpha_n\} + m \max\{\gamma_1, \ldots, \gamma_m\}$, i.e., all integers occurring in this instance are viewed as written in *unary notation*. In other words, the size of an instance $s \stackrel{?}{=}_{\mathrm{AC}} t$ of elementary AC-matching is essentially the sum of all occurrences of variables and free constants occurring in s and t, before s and t are flattened. By the same token, the *size* of an instance $s_1 \stackrel{?}{=}_{\mathrm{AC}} t_1, \ldots, s_k \stackrel{?}{=}_{\mathrm{AC}} t_k$ of the simultaneous AC-matching problem is equal to the sum of the sizes of each instance $s_i \stackrel{?}{=}_{\mathrm{AC}} t_i$, $1 \leq i \leq k$.

It is well known that there is a close relationship between the elementary AC-matching problem and the problem of solving systems of linear Diophantine equations subject to certain additional constraints. Let $\alpha_1 X_1 + \cdots + \alpha_n X_n \stackrel{?}{=}_{\mathrm{AC}} \gamma_1 C_1 + \cdots + \gamma_m C_m$ be an instance of elementary AC-matching and assume that ρ is an AC-matcher for it. The substitution ρ assigns to each variable X_i, $1 \leq i \leq n$, a certain number (possibly zero) of copies of each constant symbol C_j, $1 \leq j \leq m$. This can be expressed formally by $X_i \mapsto x_{i1} C_1 + \cdots + x_{im} C_m$, $1 \leq i \leq n$, where each x_{ij} is an *arithmetic* variable ranging over non-negative integers and expressing how many copies of the constant symbol C_j will be assigned to the variable X_i. Let us consider now how the copies of each constant symbol C_j are distributed among the variables X_i: out of a total of γ_j copies of C_j, we have that x_{1j} copies are assigned to X_1, x_{2j} copies are assigned to X_2, and so on until x_{nj} copies are assigned to X_n. We arrive at the following system of linear Diophantine equations

$$\begin{array}{rcl} \alpha_1 x_{11} + \cdots + \alpha_n x_{n1} & = & \gamma_1 \\ \vdots \qquad\qquad \vdots & & \vdots \\ \alpha_1 x_{1m} + \cdots + \alpha_n x_{nm} & = & \gamma_m \end{array} \tag{1}$$

Note that an integer solution of the above system does not necessarily give rise to an AC-matcher of the instance $\alpha_1 X_1 + \cdots + \alpha_n X_n \stackrel{?}{=}_{\mathrm{AC}} \gamma_1 C_1 + \cdots + \gamma_m C_m$, unless it satisfies certain constraints arising from the assignments $X_i \mapsto x_{i1} C_1 + \cdots + x_{im} C_m$, $1 \leq i \leq n$. More specifically, each x_{ij} must be a non-negative integer and each variable must be assigned *at least one* copy of *at least one* of the constants symbols. Thus, there is a one-to-one and onto correspondence between AC-matchers of $\alpha_1 X_1 + \cdots + \alpha_n X_n \stackrel{?}{=}_{\mathrm{AC}} \gamma_1 C_1 + \cdots + \gamma_m C_m$ and integer solutions of the system (1) that satisfy the constraints

$$x_{ij} \geq 0, \quad 1 \leq i \leq n,\ 1 \leq j \leq m \tag{2}$$

$$\sum_{j=1}^{m} x_{ij} \geq 1, \quad 1 \leq i \leq n. \tag{3}$$

In elementary ACU-matching, constraints (3) are not necessary, because we can always assign the constant 0 of the unit axiom U to a variable. As a result, ACU-matchers correspond to solutions of the system (1) that satisfy just the non-negativity constraints (2).

Eker [Eke93] established that ϵAC$(1, \omega)$-matching is a NP-complete problem by reducing the following 3-PARTITION problem to the elementary AC-matching problem over signatures with an unbounded number of free constants symbols.

3-PARTITION: Given a finite set $S = \{a_1, \ldots, a_{3m}\}$ with $3m$ elements, a positive integer γ, and a positive integer weight $s(a_i)$ for every $a_i \in S$ such that $\gamma/4 < s(a_i) < \gamma/2$ and $\sum_{i=1}^{3m} s(a_i) = m\gamma$, decide whether S can be partitioned into m disjoint sets $S_1, \ldots, S_m$ such that $\sum_{a \in S_j} s(a) = \gamma$ for every $j \leq m$.

Using systems of linear Diophantine equations with constraints of the form (2) and (3) as an intermediary, an instance of 3-PARTITION can be reduced to an instance $s(a_1)X_1 + \cdots + s(a_{3m})X_{3m} \stackrel{?}{=}_{AC} \gamma C_1 + \cdots + \gamma C_m$ of the elementary AC-matching problem, where $C_1, \ldots, C_{3m}$ are free constant symbols. It is known that 3-PARTITION is a *strongly* NP-complete problem, which means that it remains NP-complete even when all integers occurring in it are given in unary (cf. [GJ79]). This property of 3-PARTITION is indispensable here, since the preceding reduction is in polynomial-time only when the weights $s(a_i)$, $1 \leq i \leq 3m$, and the integer γ are in unary[3]. Moreover, this reduction of 3-PARTITION to ϵAC$(1,\omega)$-matching is parsimonious, which in turn implies that the counting problem #ϵAC$(1,\omega)$-matching is #P-hard. The preceding findings establish the following result.

Theorem 3.1 *ϵAC$(1,\omega)$-matching is* NP-*complete and* #ϵAC$(1,\omega)$-*matching is* #P-*complete.*

The above result identifies the computational complexity of simultaneous elementary AC-matching for the case in which the system consists of a single equation and the signature contains an unbounded number of free constant symbols. At the other end of the classification of elementary matching problems according to the length of the system and the number of free constants, we have the case in which the systems of equations are of unbounded length and the signature contains a single free constant symbol.

Theorem 3.2 *ϵAC$(\omega,1)$-matching is* NP-*complete and* #ϵAC$(\omega,1)$-*matching is* #P-*complete.*

Proof: (*Hint*) Refinement of the reduction of 1-IN-3 SAT to ϵAC$(\omega,2)$-matching, which was given in [BS93]. □

The main result of this section shows that if both the length of the system and the number of free constants are kept bounded, then the elementary AC-matching decision and counting problems are tractable. In what follows, P stands for the class of decision problems solvable in deterministic polynomial time, while FP denotes the class of functions computable in deterministic polynomial time.

Theorem 3.3 *ϵAC(k,m)-matching is in* P *and* #ϵAC(k,m)-*matching is in* FP, *for all* $k \geq 1$ *and all* $m \geq 1$.

Proof: (*Hint*) Dynamic programming algorithm for counting the solutions of systems of linear Diophantine equations (given in unary) subject to certain constraints. □

The preceding Theorems 3.1, 3.2, and 3.3 give a complete picture of the computational complexity of simultaneous elementary AC-matching problems. In the full paper, we study the complexity of ACU-matching and unveil a different picture, since simultaneous elementary ACU-matching turns out to be tractable for systems of bounded length, even if the signature contains an unbounded number of free constants.

[3]Benanav et al. [BKN87] state that Chandra and Kanellakis (unpublished) showed that elementary AC-matching is NP-hard by reducing the BIN PACKING problem to it. BIN PACKING is a strongly NP-complete problem that contains 3-PARTITION as a special case (cf. [GJ79]).

Table 1: Complexity Results for Simultaneous Elementary Matching

Simultaneous Elementary A-Matching

number of equations	number of constants		
	1	$m \geq 2$	ω
$k \geq 1$	P / FP	NP-complete / #P-complete	NP-complete / #P-complete
ω	NP-complete / #P-complete	NP-complete / #P-complete	NP-complete / #P-complete

Simultaneous Elementary AC-Matching

number of equations	number of constants		
	1	$m \geq 2$	ω
$k \geq 1$	P / FP	P / FP	NP-complete / #P-complete
ω	NP-complete / #P-complete	NP-complete / #P-complete	NP-complete / #P-complete

Simultaneous Elementary ACU-Matching

number of equations	number of constants		
	1	$m \geq 2$	ω
$k \geq 1$	P / FP	P / FP	P / FP
ω	NP-complete / #P-complete	NP-complete / #P-complete	NP-complete / #P-complete

Theorem 3.4 *ϵACU$(\omega, 1)$-matching is* NP*-complete and* #ϵACU$(\omega, 1)$*-matching is* #P*-complete. On the other hand,* ϵACU(k, ω)*-matching is in* P *and* #ϵACU(k, ω)*-matching is in* FP*, for all* $k \geq 1$.

We analyze also the complexity of elementary matching for the equational theory A of semigroups. Our findings are summarized in the following result, which shows that simultaneous elementary A-matching becomes intractable as soon as the signature $\mathcal{F}$ contains two free constant symbols, even if the system consists of a single equation.

Theorem 3.5 *ϵA$(1, m)$-matching is* NP*-complete and* #ϵA$(1, m)$*-matching is* #P*-complete, for all* $m \geq 2$. *ϵA$(\omega, 1)$-matching is* NP*-complete and* #ϵA$(\omega, 1)$*-matching is* #P*-complete. On the other hand,* ϵA$(k, 1)$*-matching is in* P *and* #ϵA$(k, 1)$*-matching is in* FP*, for all* $k \geq 1$.

The results of this section are illustrated in Table 1.

4 Elementary Matching with Bounded Occurrences of Variables

Up to this point, we classified and studied simultaneous elementary matching problems by utilizing two parameters, the number of equations in a given system and the number of free constants in the signature. There is, however, a third natural parameter that often comes into play in equational matching, namely the maximum number of occurrences of variables in the instances of the matching problem under consideration. The rôle of this parameter is completely understood for the case of AC-matching over signatures containing free function symbols. Indeed, let AC*i*-matching be the restriction of AC-matching to instances in which each variable has at most i occurrences, where i is a positive integer. As mentioned earlier, Benanav et al. [BKN87] showed that the decision problem for AC1-matching is solvable in polynomial time, whereas Hermann and Kolaitis [HK94] proved that the counting problem #AC1-matching is #P-complete (and, hence, for every $i \geq 2$, #AC*i*-matching is #P-complete as well). Benanav et al. [BKN87] also pointed out that the decision problem for AC3-matching is NP-complete, but left the complexity of AC2-matching as an open question. This was settled by Verma and Ramakrishnan [VR92], who established that the decision problem for AC2-matching is NP-complete. By exploiting the existence of free function symbols in a clever way, Verma and Ramakrishnan [VR92] showed that SAT restricted to instances in which each Boolean variable has at most three occurrences can be reduced to AC2-matching[4]. Free function symbols are also used in a crucial way when proving that #AC1-matching is #P-hard [HK94].

Next, we investigate the computational complexity of simultaneous elementary AC-matching problems in which variables have a bounded number of occurrences. This is done by carrying out a finer analysis of ϵAC(k,ω)-matching and ϵAC(ω, m)-matching, which in the previous section were shown to be the intractable cases of simultaneous elementary AC-matching. If i, k, and m are positive integers, then ϵACi(k,ω)-matching is the restriction of ϵAC(k,ω)-matching to instances in which each variable has at most i occurrences in a given system of k equations. Similarly, we define the classes ϵACi(ω, m)-matching, ϵACi(ω,ω)-matching, and the corresponding classes of counting problems.

All cases of simultaneous elementary AC1-matching turn out to be tractable. Thus, free function symbols are indispensable for showing that #AC1-matching is #P-hard.

Theorem 4.6 *ϵAC1(ω,ω)-matching is in* P *and #ϵAC1(ω,ω)-matching is in* FP.

Proof: (*Hint*) For each equation, we find the number of elementary ACU-matchers using Theorem 3.4 and subtract the number of ACU-matchers violating the constraints (3). If each variable occurs once, the latter computation can be done in polynomial time. □

Recall that ϵAC($1,\omega$)-matching is proved NP-hard and that #ϵAC($1,\omega$)-matching is proved #P-hard using a parsimonious reduction from 3-PARTITION (cf. Theorem 3.1). This reduction generates instances of AC-matching in which variables have an unbounded number of occurrences. The following result reveals that if we bound the number of occurrences of variables, then we cross the dividing line between intractability and tractability.

Theorem 4.7 *ϵACi(k,ω) is in* P *and #ϵACi(k,ω) is in* FP, *for all $i \geq 1$ and all $k \geq 1$.*

Proof: (*Hint*) Dynamic programming algorithm for systems of linear Diophantine equations (in unary) of bounded length and with bounded coefficients. □

To complete the analysis, we consider ϵAC(ω, m)-matching with bounds on the number of occurrences of variables. It turns out that here three occurrences suffice to establish NP-hardness and #P-hardness, even over signatures with only one free constant symbol.

Theorem 4.8 *ϵAC3(ω, 1)-matching is* NP-*complete and #ϵAC3(ω, 1)-matching is #P-complete.*

Proof: (*Hint*) Parsimonius reduction from POSITIVE 1-IN-3 SAT. □

It remains to examine simultaneous elementary AC-matching problems in which the systems are of unbounded length, but each variable has at most two occurrences. In order to analyze this case, we bring into the picture concepts and techniques from graph theory. Recall that if $G = (V, E)$ is a graph, then a *matching* is a subset M of the set E of edges such that no two edges in M have a common node, while a *complete matching*

[4] This restriction of SAT is NP-complete (cf. [GJ79]). In contrast, SAT restricted to instances in which each variable has at most two occurrences can be decided in polynomial time using resolution.

is a matching M such that every node of G is incident upon an edge in M. The following generalizations of these concepts turn out to be extremely useful here.

If $G = (V, E)$ is a graph (not necessarily a bipartite one) and $b = (b_i : i \in V)$ is a sequence of positive integers, then a *b-matching* is a subset M of E such that every node i of G is incident upon at most b_i edges in M. A *complete b-matching* is a b-matching such that every node i of G is incident upon exactly b_i edges in M. The *b-matching problem* asks: given a graph $G = (V, E)$ and a sequence $b = (b_i : i \in V)$ of positive integers, is there a complete b-matching of G? This problem has been studied extensively in the literature and efficient algorithmic solutions have been found. In particular, Edmonds and Johnson [EJ69] established that b-matching is solvable in polynomial time. Moreover, Berge [Ber73] considered the b-matching problem for *multigraphs* and showed that it has a polynomial-time reduction to the b-matching problem for graphs. We now have all the necessary tools to obtain the following result.

Theorem 4.9 *ϵAC2$(\omega, 1)$-matching is in* P, *but #ϵAC2$(\omega, 1)$-matching is #P-complete.*

Proof: (*Hint*) Every instance of ϵAC2$(\omega, 1)$-matching can be transformed into a system of linear Diophantine equations such that the elements of the matrix are either 0 or 1, and each column has exactly two non-zero entries. Such a matrix can be viewed as the node-edge incidence matrix of a multigraph. As a result, every instance of the original ϵAC2$(\omega, 1)$-matching problem can be reduced in polynomial time to an instance of a b-matching problem on a multigraph. For the counting problem, use a parsimonious reduction of #PERFECT MATCHINGS [Val79] to #ϵAC2$(\omega, 1)$-matching. □

It is an open problem to identify the exact complexity of ϵAC2(ω, m)-matching for $m \geq 2$. In this case the decision problem appears to become more difficult, because it reduces to a b-matching problem with additional *coloring* constraints. The state of affairs is clear, however, for the counting problem, since the preceding Theorem 4.9 implies that #ϵAC2(ω, m)-matching is #P-complete for every $m \geq 2$.

In the full paper, we study also the complexity of simultaneous elementary ACU-matching problems with bounds on the number of occurrences of variables. The following result summarizes our findings.

Theorem 4.10 *ϵACU2(ω, ω)-matching is in* P, *whereas ϵACU3$(\omega, 1)$-matching is* NP-*complete. Moreover, #ϵACU2$(\omega, 1)$-matching is #P-complete.*

The results of this section are illustrated in Table 2.

We conclude by pointing out that some of our results in this section provide a partial explanation as to why all known combination algorithms for equational unification have superpolynomial worst-case behavior. Indeed, by Theorem 4.10, simultaneous elementary ACU2-matching is solvable in polynomial time, while general ACU2-matching is NP-complete [VR92]. Thus, unless P = NP, the decision problem for general ACU2-matching can not be solved via a polynomial-time algorithm that combines a decision procedure for simultaneous elementary ACU2-matching with a syntactic matching algorithm for terms in which each variable occurs at most twice. Moreover, by Theorem 4.6, simultaneous elementary #AC1-matching is in FP, while general #AC1-matching is #P-complete [HK94]. Thus, unless FP = #P, no general AC1-matching algorithm can be designed using a polynomial-time combination algorithm that combines an elementary AC1-matching algorithm with a syntactic matching algorithm for linear terms.

Table 2: Simultaneous Elementary Matching with Bounded Variable Occurrence

Simultaneous Elementary AC1-Matching & ACU1-Matching

number of equations	number of constants		
	1	$m \geq 2$	ω
$k \geq 1$	P / FP		
ω			

Simultaneous Elementary AC2-Matching

number of equations	number of constants		
	1	$m \geq 2$	ω
$k \geq 1$	P / FP		
ω	P / #P-c	? / #P-complete	

Simultaneous Elementary ACU2-Matching

number of equations	number of constants		
	1	$m \geq 2$	ω
$k \geq 1$	P / FP		
ω	P / #P-complete		

Simultaneous Elementary ACi-Matching & ACUi-Matching, $i \geq 3$

number of equations	number of constants		
	1	$m \geq 2$	ω
$k \geq 1$	P / FP		
ω	NP-complete / #P-complete		

References

[Ber73] C. Berge. *Graphs and hypergraphs.* North-Holland, Amsterdam, 2nd edition, 1973.

[BHK*88] H-J. Bürckert, A. Herold, D. Kapur, J.H. Siekmann, M.E. Stickel, M. Tepp, and H. Zhang. Opening the AC-unification race. *Journal of Automated Reasoning*, 4(4):465–474, 1988.

[BKN87] D. Benanav, D. Kapur, and P. Narendran. Complexity of matching problems. *Journal of Symbolic Computation*, 3:203–216, 1987.

[BS93] F. Baader and J.H. Siekmann. Unification theory. In D.M. Gabbay, C.J. Hogger, and J.A. Robinson, editors, *Handbook of Logic in Artificial Intelligence and Logic Programming*, Oxford University Press, Oxford (UK), 1993.

[EJ69] J. Edmonds and E.L. Johnson. Matching: a well-solved class of integer linear programs. In *Combinatorial Structures and Their Applications, Calgary (Canada)*, pages 89–92, Gordon and Breach, 1969.

[Eke93] S.M. Eker. *Improving the efficiency of AC matching and unification.* Research report 2104, Institut de Recherche en Informatique et en Automatique, November 1993.

[GJ79] M.R. Garey and D.S. Johnson. *Computers and intractability: A guide to the theory of NP-completeness.* W.H. Freeman and Co, 1979.

[HK94] M. Hermann and P.G. Kolaitis. The complexity of counting problems in equational matching. In A. Bundy, editor, *Proceedings 12th International Conference on Automated Deduction, Nancy (France)*, pages 560–574, Springer-Verlag, June 1994.

[JK91] J.-P. Jouannaud and C. Kirchner. Solving equations in abstract algebras: a rule-based survey of unification. In J.-L. Lassez and G. Plotkin, editors, *Computational Logic. Essays in honor of Alan Robinson*, chapter 8, pages 257–321, MIT Press, Cambridge (MA, USA), 1991.

[Pap94] C.H. Papadimitriou. *Computational complexity.* Addison-Wesley, 1994.

[Val79] L.G. Valiant. The complexity of computing the permanent. *Theoretical Computer Science*, 8:189–201, 1979.

[VR92] R.M. Verma and I.V. Ramakrishnan. Tight complexity bounds for term matching problems. *Information and Computation*, 101:33–69, 1992.

Graph Reducibility of Term Rewriting Systems

M. R. K. Krishna Rao

Computer Science Group
Tata Institute of Fundamental Research
Colaba, BOMBAY 400 005, INDIA
e-mail: **krishna@tifrvax.bitnet**

Abstract. Term rewriting is generally implemented using graph rewriting for efficiency reasons. Graph rewriting allows sharing of common structures thereby saving both time and space. This implementation is sound in the sense that computation of a normal form of a graph yields a normal form of the corresponding term. However, certain properties of term rewriting systems are not reflected in their graph rewriting implementations. Weak normalization is one such property. An undesirable side effect of this is that it may be impossible to compute a normal form of a normalizable term. In this paper, we present some sufficient conditions for preservation of weak normalization and discuss the implication of the results to modularity.

1 Introduction

In the last few decades, term rewriting systems (TRS, for short) have played a fundamental role in the analysis and implementation of abstract data type specifications, decidability of word problems, theorem proving, computability theory, design of functional programming languages, integration of functional programming and logic programming paradigms, etc.

Term rewriting is often implemented using graph rewriting to cut down the evaluation costs. Graph (directed acyclic) representation of terms facilitate sharing of structures - unlike the tree representation - and hence saves both space and time. This implementation is both sound and complete in the following sense. If a graph G reduces to G' then the term corresponding to G rewrites to the term corresponding to G' (soundness) and two graphs are convertible if and only if the corresponding terms are convertible (completeness). One of the nice fallouts of this is that the computation of a normal form of a given graph yields a normal form of the corresponding term.

A graph rewriting step using a non-right-linear rewrite rule does not make multiple copies of the subgraphs corresponding to non-linear variables, but enforces sharing of these subgraphs - however it does not enforce identification of two equal subterms (subgraphs) of the right-hand side term of the rule. Due to this enforced sharing, certain properties of the given TRS are not reflected in the graph rewriting implementation. For example, the graph rewriting relation corresponding to a given confluent TRS need not be confluent. The same holds for the weak normalization property. One of the undesirable side-effects of this is that one may not be able to compute a normal form of a graph corresponding to a normalizable term (i.e., term which has a normal form w.r.t. term rewriting).

In this paper, we study the theoretical question of when can one ensure weak normalization of the graph rewriting corresponding to a given weakly normalizing TRS. A TRS is said to be 'graph reducible' if all the graphs representing a normalizable term are normalizable. The graph reducibility of TRSs has been studied earlier by Plump in [6], where he identified some classes of graph reducible systems using a kind of parallel rewriting derivations. In these derivations, all occurrences of a redex in a given term are reduced at once using the same rewrite rule. Such a parallel rewriting step can be easily simulated by one or more graph rewriting steps. It may take more than one graph rewriting steps to simulate a parallel rewrite step as graph rewriting does not enforce complete sharing of structures. Clearly, parallelly normalizing systems (systems under which, any normalizable term can be reduced to normal form through parallel rewriting) are graph reducible. Plump [6] identified two classes of parallelly normalizing systems, namely, parallelly terminating and orthogonal systems.

Since, parallel rewriting reduces all the occurrences of a redex in a term at once, parallel normalization does not capture graph reducibility completely, i.e., there are graph reducible systems which are not parallelly normalizing. In a sense, parallel normalization assumes complete sharing of subgraphs. In this paper, we identify some classes of graph reducible systems without assuming complete sharing. Our main result is that every weakly innermost normalizing system is graph reducible. We compare our results with Plump's results by establishing various relationships between parallel normalization and innermost normalization properties.

The rest of the paper is organized as follows. The next section gives preliminary definitions of graph rewriting. In section 3, we study graph reducibility; review the existing results based on parallel rewriting and present new results based on innermost rewriting. The relationship between the various parallel rewriting properties and innermost rewriting properties is studied in section 4. Section 5 discusses the preservation of confluence and graph reducibility based on other properties. Section 6 concludes with a summary.

2 Preliminaries

We assume that the reader is familiar with the basic terminology of term rewriting systems and give definitions only when they are required. The notations not defined in the paper can be found in Dershowitz and Jouannaud [3], Klop [4], Plump [8] or Courcelle [2].

In the following, $\mathcal{T}(\Sigma, X)$ denotes the set of terms constructed from set of function symbols Σ and set of variables X. We recall the following definitions from Plump [7, 8].

Definition 1 (hypergraph) A *hypergraph* G over Σ is a system $\langle V, E, s, t, l\rangle$, where V, E are finite sets of nodes and hyperedges, $s : E \to V$, $t : E \to V^*$ are mappings that assign a source node and a string of target nodes to each hyperedge, and $l : E \to \Sigma \cup X$ is a mapping that labels each hyperedge e such that $arity(l(e))$ is the length of $t(e)$.

The components of a hypergraph G are refered to as V_G, E_G, s_G, t_G and l_G. A node v is a *predecessor* of a node v' if there is an edge e such that v' occurs in $t_G(e)$. The relations $>_G$ and $\geq_G$ are the transitive and reflexive-transitive closures of the predecessor relation. For each node v, G/v is the subhypergraph of G consisting of all the nodes v' with $v \geq_G v'$ and all the edges outgoing from these nodes.

Definition 2 (collapsed tree) A hypergraph C over Σ is a *collapsed tree* if

1. there is a node $root_C$ such that $root_C \geq v$ for each node v,
2. the predecessor relation of C is acyclic and
3. each node has a unique outgoing edge, i.e., s_C is bijective.

Definition 3 Let C be a collapsed tree. Then the mapping $term_C : V_C \to T(\Sigma, X)$ is defined as

$$\begin{aligned} term_C(v) &= l_C(e) && \text{if } t_C(e) \text{ is an empty string } \lambda,\\ term_C(v) &= l_C(e)(term_C(v_1), \ldots, term_C(v_n)) && \text{if } t_C(e) = v_1 \ldots v_n, \end{aligned}$$

where e is the unique edge with source v. In the following $term_C$ stands for $term_C(root_C)$.

Definition 4 Let G, H be hypergraphs. A *hypergraph morphism* $g : G \to H$ is a pair of mappings $\langle g_v : V_G \to V_H, g_e : E_G \to E_H\rangle$ that preserve sources, targets and labels, i.e., $s_H \circ g_e = g_v \circ s_G$, $t_H \circ g_e = g_v^* \circ t_G$ and $l_H \circ g_e = l_G$.[1]

Definition 5 A collapsed tree C is a *tree with shared variables* if (1) for each node v, $indegree_C(v) > 1$ implies $term_C(v) \in X$ and (2) for all nodes v, v', $term_C(v) = term_C(v') \in X$ implies $v = v'$.

In the following, $\Diamond t$ denotes a tree with shared variables such that $term_C(\Diamond t) = t$ and $\underline{C}$ denotes the hypergraph obtained from C by removing all the edges labelled with variables.

Now, we define the graph rewriting relation induced by a TRS $\mathcal{R}$.

Definition 6 (evaluation step) Let C, D be collapsed trees. Then there is an *evaluation step* from C to D, denoted by $C \Rrightarrow_{\mathcal{E}} D$, if there is a rule $l \to r \in \mathcal{R}$ and hypergraph morphism $g : \underline{\Diamond l} \to C$ such that D is isomorphic to the collapsed tree constructed as follows:

[1] Given a mapping $f : A \to B$, $f^* : A^* \to B^*$ sends λ to λ and $a_1 \ldots a_n$ to $f(a_1) \ldots f(a_n)$.

1. Remove hyperedge outgoing from $g_v(root_{\Diamond l})$, yielding a hypergraph C'.
2. Build the disjoint union $C' + \underline{\Diamond r}$ and
   - identify $g_v(root_{\Diamond l})$ with $root_{\Diamond r}$,
   - for each pair $\langle u, u' \rangle \in V_{\Diamond l} \times V_{\Diamond r}$ with $term_{\Diamond l}(u) = term_{\Diamond r}(u') \in X$, identify $g_v(u)$ with u'.

   Let C'' be the resulting hypergraph.
3. Remove garbage, resulting a collapsed tree $C''/root_C$.

For evaluations with non-left-linear rules, we need to 'fold' collapsed trees.

Definition 7 (folding step) Let C, D be collapsed trees. Then there is a *folding step* $C \Rrightarrow_{\mathcal{F}} D$ if there are distinct edges $e, e' \in E_C$ with $l_C(e) = l_C(e')$ and $t_C(e) = t_C(e')$, and D is isomorphic to the collapsed tree obtained from C by identifying e with e' and $s_C(e)$ with $s_C(e')$.

We denote the relation $\Rrightarrow_{\mathcal{E}} \cup \Rrightarrow_{\mathcal{F}}$ by $\Rrightarrow_{\mathcal{R}}$ and omit the subscript if it does not lead to any confusion.

Example 1 This figure shows an evaluation step on a collapsed tree C representing term $(((0 + x) \times (0 + x)) + x)$ with rewrite rule $x \times (y + z) \to (x \times y) + (x \times z)$. Here, *the hyperedges are represented by boxes and the nodes are represented by circles.* The morphism locating the left-hand side $\underline{\Diamond(x \times (y + z))}$ identifies the nodes representing x and $(y + z)$ with the node representing $(0 + x)$ in C.
In the examples below, we simplify the pictures of collapsed trees by deleting the nodes and replacing every hyperedge having n target nodes by n arcs, without introducing any confusion.

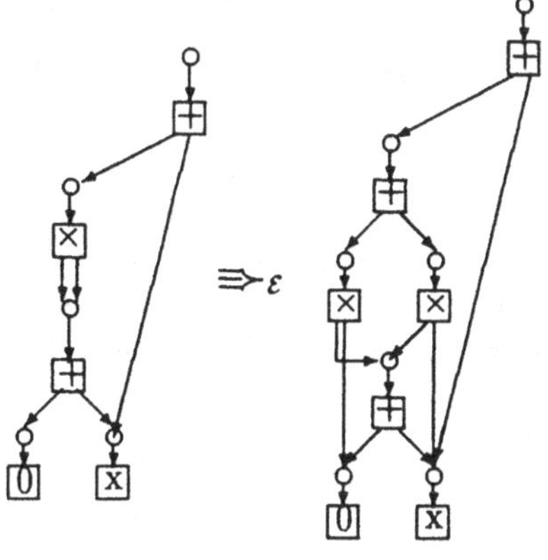

3 Graph Reducibility

In this section, we define the notion of graph reducibility (introduced in [1] and [6]) of term rewriting systems and present some sufficient conditions for it.

Definition 8 (graph reducibility) A term rewriting system $\mathcal{R}$ is called *graph reducible* if every collapsed tree represting a term t has a normal form w.r.t. $\Rrightarrow_{\mathcal{R}}$ whenever t has a normal form w.r.t. $\mathcal{R}$.

If a term rewriting system is graph reducible, every normalizable term can be normalized through graph rewriting. Before presenting our results, we first show that a weakly normalizing system need not be graph reducible and then briefly review the existing results on graph reducibility.

Example 2 The system $\{f(x) \to g(x,x);\ a \to b;\ g(a,b) \to c;\ g(b,b) \to f(a)\}$ (from [6]) is weakly normalizing, but not graph reducible as the two possible $\Rrightarrow$-derivations from $f(a)$ loop.

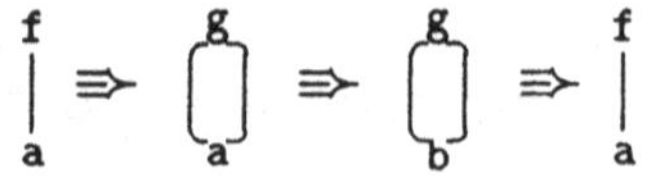

$$f(a) \Rrightarrow g(a,a) \Rrightarrow g(b,b) \Rrightarrow f(a) \quad \text{and} \quad f(a) \Rrightarrow f(b) \Rrightarrow g(b,b) \Rrightarrow f(a)$$

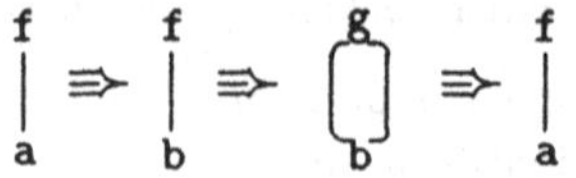

3.1 Earlier results

Plump [6] introduced the notion of parallel normalization to study graph reducibility.

Definition 9 Given a term t and a redex position π in t, $t \dashv\!\!|\!|_\pi\ u$ denotes a parallel rewrite step in which all the occurrences of the subterm $t_{|\pi}$ in t are reduced using the same rewrite rule.

Definition 10 (parallel normalization) A term rewriting system $\mathcal{R}$ is called *parallelly normalizing* if for every term t having a normal form, there is a parallel rewrite sequence $t \dashv\!\!|\!|^* u$ reducing t to a normal form u.

The following result is proved in [6].

Theorem 1 *Every parallelly normalizing system is graph reducible.*

Plump [6] identified two classes of parallelly normalizing systems, namely, parallelly terminating systems and orthogonal systems. Since parallel outermost reduction strategy is normalizing for orthogonal systems, one can easily get a parallelly normalizing reduction from every normalizable term, i.e., orthogonal systems are parallelly normalizing.

Definition 11 (parallel termination) A term rewriting system $\mathcal{R}$ is called *parallelly terminating* if all its parallel rewrite sequences are of finite length.

Theorem 2 (from [6]) *A system is parallelly normalizing (and hence graph reducible) if it is parallelly terminating or orthogonal.*

Remark: The above remarks about orthogonal systems are valid for the class of weakly orthogonal systems and they too are parallelly normalizing.

3.2 New Results: based on innermost normalization

Every parallel reduction step can be easily simulated using $\Rrightarrow$. However, every $\Rrightarrow$-step cannot be simulated using parallel reduction. In the parallel reduction, complete sharing (folding) is assumed, whereas $\Rrightarrow$ does not enforce complete sharing. In the following, we establish some results on graph reducibility based on innermost reductions which do not require complete sharing. Our main result is:

Theorem 3 *Every weakly innermost normalizing (WIN) system is graph reducible.*

We need the following lemmas in proving this theorem. We say a subgraph at node v in a hypergraph is shared if there is a node $v' \geq v$ with $indegree(v') > 1$.

Lemma 1 If $C \Rrightarrow_{\mathcal{R}} C'$ is an innermost reduction and C is a collapsed tree such that no redex in it is shared, then no redex in C' is shared.

Proof: There are two cases: (i) $C \Rrightarrow_{\mathcal{F}} C'$ and (ii) $C \Rrightarrow_{\mathcal{E}} C'$. In case (i), if e and e' are identified, then $term_C(s_C(e)) = term_C(s_C(e'))$ is irreducible and the lemma holds.

Case (ii): Let $l \rightarrow r$ be the rewrite rule and $g : \underline{\Diamond l} \rightarrow C$ be the morphism used in the reduction. The sharing introduced in the reduction is only over the nodes $\{g_v(u) \mid term_{\Diamond l}(u) \in var(l)\}$. Since $C \Rrightarrow_{\mathcal{R}} C'$ is an innermost reduction, each $term_{\Diamond l}(v)$ is irreducible. Hence, no redex in C' is shared. □

The following lemma explains when can a term rewrite step be imitated (by $\Rrightarrow$) on the collapsed trees. A rewrite step $t \Rightarrow t'$ at position π can be imitated by $\Rrightarrow$ if the redex is not shared in the corresponding graph.

Lemma 2 If $t \Rightarrow_\pi t'$ and C is any collapsed tree such that (i) $term(C) = t$ and (ii) $t_{|\pi}$ is not shared, then there exists a collapsed tree C' such that $C \Rrightarrow^* C'$ and $term(C') = t'$.

Proof: If the applied rewrite rule is left-linear, it can be applied on C resulting in C'. It is easy to see that $term(C') = t'$ since the redex is not shared in C. If the applied rewrite rule is non-left-linear, it can be applied after suitably collapsing C. □

The following example illustrates the need for condition (ii) above.

Example 3 Consider the system in Example 2 and the rewrite step $\mathtt{g(a,a)} \Rightarrow \mathtt{g(a,b)}$ and the collapsed tree C shown here. This collapsed tree cannot be reduced to any C' such that $term(C') = \mathtt{g(a,b)}$ as the redex a is shared in C.

Now, we are in a position to prove Theorem 3.

Proof of Theorem 3:
Let t be a minimal term (w.r.t. the subterm relation) such that a collapsed tree C is not normalizable and $term(C) = t$. That's, every proper subtree of C is normalizable. Now, normalize every 'shared' subtree of C to obtain a collapsed tree C_1 so that no redex in C_1 is shared. Let t_1 be the term $term(C_1)$ and $t_1 \Rightarrow t_2 \Rightarrow \cdots \Rightarrow t_n$ be an innermost derivation reducing t_1 to a normal form t_n. From the above two lemmas, it follows that there exists a sequence $C_1 \Rrightarrow^* C_2 \Rrightarrow^* \cdots \Rrightarrow^* C_n$ such that $term(C_i) = t_i$. Since t_n is a normal form, only folding steps are possible on C_n and one can normalize C_n using the folding steps, yielding a normal form of C, contradicting the assumption that C is not normalizable. □

Example 4 The system $\{\mathtt{f(x,x)} \to \mathtt{f(c,c)};\ \mathtt{c} \to \mathtt{a};\ \mathtt{c} \to \mathtt{b}\}$ is weakly innermost normalizing and hence graph reducible by the above theorem.

None of the earlier results prove the graph reducibility of this system as it is not parallelly normalizing - $\mathtt{f(c,c)}$ cannot be normalized using parallel rewriting. □

The above theorem assumes normalization of every term, i.e., weak normalization property of the TRS. We can weaken this requirement and generalize the theorem as follows.

Theorem 4 *A* TRS $\mathcal{R}$ *is graph reducible if* t' *is weakly innermost normalizing whenever* $t \Rightarrow_{\mathcal{R}} t'$ *and* t *is weakly innermost normalizing.*

Proof: The proof of the above theorem holds in this case as (i) weak innermost normalization of t implies weak innermost normalization of every subterm of t and (ii) $term(C_1)$ is weakly innermost normalizing by the above property. □

The following example illustrates this theorem.

Example 5 The following system (from [6])
$\{\mathtt{add(0,y)} \to \mathtt{y};\ \mathtt{add(s(x),y)} \to \mathtt{s(add(x,y))};\ \mathtt{add(x,y)} \to \mathtt{add(y,x)}\}$
is weakly innermost normalizing on any term t with at most one variable. Hence the above requirement holds and this system is graph reducible by the above theorem. Note that this system is not weakly innermost normalizing (on every term), so Theorem 3 cannot be used. □

The above theorem requires that the set of weakly innermost normalizing terms are closed under rewriting. The following example shows that this requirement cannot be relaxed. In particular, a weakly innermost normalizing term need not be graph reducible.

Example 6 The term $\mathtt{f(c,c)}$ (with normal form $\mathtt{f(a,b)}$) is weakly innermost normalizing w.r.t. the system $\{\mathtt{f(x,x)} \to \mathtt{f(x,x)};\ \mathtt{c} \to \mathtt{a};\ \mathtt{c} \to \mathtt{b}\}$, but a collapsed tree representing this term (with c shared) is not reducible to a normal form, i.e., this term is not graph reducible. □

4 Relationship between parallel normalization and innermost normalization properties

In this section, we study relationships between various parallel normalization and innermost normalization properties. Example 4 shows that the class of weakly innermost normalizing is not a subclass of the class of parallelly normalizing systems. The following example shows that the converse is not true either.

Example 7 The system $\{\mathtt{a} \to \mathtt{f(a)};\ \mathtt{f(x)} \to \mathtt{b}\}$ is orthogonal and hence parallelly normalizing. But it is not weakly innermost normalizing as the term a is not normalizable through innermost reduction (the only innermost derivation from a is $\mathtt{a} \Rightarrow \mathtt{f(a)} \Rightarrow \mathtt{f(f(a))} \cdots$). □

Theorem 5 *(i) Parallel normalization* $\not\Rightarrow$ *weak innermost normalization.*
(ii) Weak innermost normalization $\not\Rightarrow$ *parallel normalization.*

However, strong innermost normalization (SIN) implies parallel normalization.

Theorem 6 *Every strongly innermost normalization system is parallelly normalizing.*

Proof: One can easily get a normalizing parallel rewriting derivation from any given term by reducing innermost redeces every time. □

Parallel termination is a sufficient condition for parallel normalization. Now, we study the relationship between parallel termination and (both weak and strong) innermost normalization.

Theorem 7 *Every parallelly terminating system is weakly innermost normalizing.*

Proof: Parallel termination implies that every parallel derivation starting from any term is of finite length. In particular, a parallel derivation in which only innermost redeces are rewritten is of finite length. From such a derivation, one can easily obtain a terminating innermost derivation implying the weak innermost normalization property. □

Example 4 shows that the converse of this theorem does not hold. The following two examples show that parallel termination neither implies nor is implied by strong innermost normalization.

Example 8 The system $\{\mathtt{f(a,b)} \rightarrow \mathtt{f(c,c)};\ \mathtt{c} \rightarrow \mathtt{a};\ \mathtt{c} \rightarrow \mathtt{b}\}$ is parallelly terminating. But it is not strongly innermost normalizing as we have a looping derivation $\mathtt{f(a,b)} \Rightarrow_{\mathtt{in}} \mathtt{f(c,c)} \Rightarrow_{\mathtt{in}} \mathtt{f(a,c)} \Rightarrow_{\mathtt{in}} \mathtt{f(a,b)} \Rightarrow_{\mathtt{in}} \cdots$. □

Example 9 The system $\{\mathtt{f(a,a)} \rightarrow \mathtt{f(a,a)};\ \mathtt{a} \rightarrow \mathtt{b}\}$ is strongly innermost normalizing. But it is not parallelly terminating as we have a looping derivation (applying the first rule) $\mathtt{f(a,a)} \twoheadrightarrow\!\! \parallel \mathtt{f(a,a)} \twoheadrightarrow\!\! \parallel \cdots$. □

Theorem 8 *(i) Parallel termination* $\not\Rightarrow$ *strong innermost normalization.*
(ii) Strong innermost normalization $\not\Rightarrow$ *parallel termination.*

The following diagram presents the different classes of graph reducible systems.

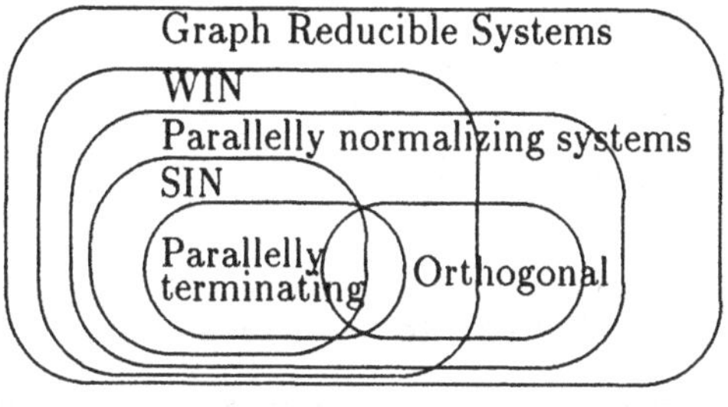

5 Discussion

Like weak normalization, confluence is not preserved in the implementation of term rewriting by graph rewriting, i.e., $\mathcal{R}$ can be confluent while $\Rrightarrow_{\mathcal{R}}$ is not confluent.

Example 10 The system $\{a \to f(a);\ g(x,x) \to g(x,x);\ g(x,f(x)) \to b\}$ is confluent. But $\Rrightarrow_{\mathcal{R}}$ is not confluent as we have the following reductions and the collapsed trees representing $g(a,a)$ (with a shared) and b are not joinable by $\Rrightarrow_{\mathcal{R}}$.

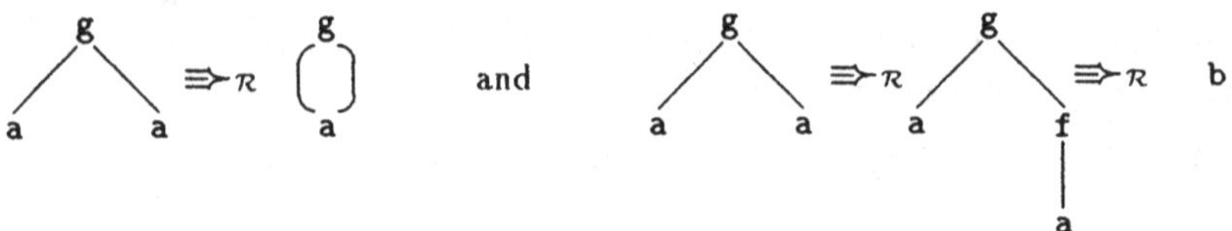

Plump [7, 8] proved that $\Rrightarrow_{\mathcal{R}}$ is confluent if and only if $\mathcal{R}$ is confluent, when $\Rrightarrow_{\mathcal{R}}$ is weakly normalizing. Since, we proved that $\Rrightarrow_{\mathcal{R}}$ is weakly normalizing if $\mathcal{R}$ is weakly innermost normalizing, we have the following result.

Theorem 9 Let $\mathcal{R}$ be a (i) weakly innermost normalizing system or (ii) parallelly normalizing system. *Then $\mathcal{R}$ is confluent if and only if $\Rrightarrow_{\mathcal{R}}$ is confluent.*

Confluence is not modular for graph rewriting, unlike term rewriting. That's, confluence of relations $\Rrightarrow_{\mathcal{R}_0}$ and $\Rrightarrow_{\mathcal{R}_1}$ does not imply confluence of $\Rrightarrow_{\mathcal{R}_0 \cup \mathcal{R}_1}$, even if the signatures of $\mathcal{R}_0$ and $\mathcal{R}_1$ are disjoint. Plump [7] and Kurihara and Ohuchi [5] assume termination of the two relations to ensure the modularity of confluence, i.e., they prove that completeness (confluence + termination) is modular for graph rewriting. Since it is well known that weak innermost normalization is modular, we can establish that semi-completeness (confluence + weak normalization) is modular for this class of systems.

Theorem 10 (modularity of semi-completeness) Let $\mathcal{R}_0$ and $\mathcal{R}_1$ be two weakly innermost normalizing systems with disjoint signatures. Then, the following statements are equivalent.

1. $\Rrightarrow_{\mathcal{R}_0 \cup \mathcal{R}_1}$ is confluent,
2. $\Rrightarrow_{\mathcal{R}_0 \cup \mathcal{R}_1}$ is semi-complete,
3. $\Rrightarrow_{\mathcal{R}_0}$ and $\Rrightarrow_{\mathcal{R}_1}$ are confluent,
4. $\Rrightarrow_{\mathcal{R}_0}$ and $\Rrightarrow_{\mathcal{R}_1}$ are semi-complete,
5. $\mathcal{R}_0$ and $\mathcal{R}_1$ are confluent,
6. $\mathcal{R}_0$ and $\mathcal{R}_1$ are semi-complete.

Remark: The disjointness requirement of this theorem can be relaxed as in [7, 5]. For lack of space, we do not go into the details.

It is interesting to see whether non-overlapping systems are graph reducible. Since there is precisely one choice for the rewrite rule to apply at any redex, one may expect that the sharing of a redex is immaterial in this context. However, the following example shows that a non-overlapping system need not be graph reducible.

Example 11 The rewrite system in the above example is non-overlapping but not graph reducible as the following collapsed tree (representing term g(a, a) with normal form b) is not normalizable.

Another interesting investigation is to see whether we can get graph reducibility results using outermost reductions instead of innermost reductions. The following example shows that the answer for this question is negative as well.

Example 12 The system { f(x) → h(x, g(x)); h(a, g(b)) → c; h(b, g(a)) → c; h(b, g(b)) → f(a); a → b } is strongly outermost normalizing. But it is not graph reducible as the collapsed tree (representing f(a) with normal form c) is not normalizable. The two possible derivations loop.

f(a) ⇛ h(·, g(a)) sharing a ⇛ h(·, g(b)) sharing b ⇛ f(a) and f(a) ⇛ f(b) ⇛ h(·, g(b)) sharing b ⇛ f(a)

One might conjecture that *right linear* TRSs are graph reducible as graph reduction involving right linear rewrite rule does not introduce extra sharing in the graph. The following example refutes this conjecture.

Example 13 The right linear system {d → a; d → b; g(a, b) → c; g(x, y) → g(x, y)} is not graph reducible as the three possible ⇛-derivations from the collapsed tree (representing term g(d, d) with normal form c) sharing d loop.

(1) g(d, d) shared ⇛ g(d, d) shared (2) g(d, d) shared ⇛ g(a, a) shared ⇛ g(a, a) shared (3) g(d, d) shared ⇛ g(b, b) shared ⇛ g(b, b) shared

In the above example, the starting graph is sharing the node representing d and the evaluation step identifies the nodes representing x and y in $\Diamond\underline{g(x,y)}$ with this node and the sharing propagates throughout the derivation. However, if the initial term has no sharing, right linear rewrite rules do not introduce any sharing.

Definition 12 (weak graph reducibility) A term rewriting system $\mathcal{R}$ is called *weakly graph reducible* if there exists a normalizable (w.r.t. $\Rrightarrow_{\mathcal{R}}$) collapsed tree represting t whenever t has a normal form w.r.t. $\mathcal{R}$.

Theorem 11 *Every right linear* TRS *is weakly graph reducible.*

6 Conclusion

In this paper, we presented some sufficient conditions for graph reducibility of term rewriting systems and compared our results with the existing results. The implications of the results to the preservation and modularity of confluence in the graph implementation of term rewriting are discussed. We presented some solutions to the three open questions posed by Plump [6].

1. A sufficient condition for graph reducibility is provided in terms of a term rewriting notion, *weak innermost normalization*.
2. A sufficient *syntactic* condition, which goes beyond orthogonality, for (weak) graph reducibility is provided, *right-linearity*.
3. Two classes of TRSs (other than the orthogonal systems) are identified, under which all the normal forms of a term can be computed through graph rewriting, i.e., (i) *right-linear systems* and (ii) *strongly innermost normalizing overlay*[2] *systems*. All the normal forms of a given term t can be computed by graph reducing a collapsed tree with shared variables C representing t.

References

1. H.P. Barendregt, M.C.J.D. van Eekelen, J.R.W. Gauert, J.R. Kennaway, M.J. Plasmeijer and M.R. Sleep (1987), *Term graph rewriting*, Proc. PARLE'87, Lecture Notes in Computer Science **259**, pp. 141-158, Springer-Verlag.
2. B. Courcelle (1990), *Graph rewriting: an algebraic and logic approach*, In J. van Leeuwen (ed.), *Handbook of Theoretical Computer Science*, Vol. **B**, pp. 193-242, North-Holland.
3. N. Dershowitz and J.-P. Jouannaud (1990), *Rewrite Systems*, In J. van Leeuwen (ed.), *Handbook of Theoretical Computer Science*, Vol. **B**, pp. 243-320, North-Holland.
4. J.W. Klop (1992), *Term Rewriting Systems*, tech rep. CS-R9073, CWI, Amsterdam. Also appears as a chapter in S. Abramsky, D. Gabbay and T. Maibaum (ed.), *Handbook of Logic in Computer Science*, Vol. **2**, Oxford Press, 1992.
5. M. Kurihara and A. Ohuchi (1995), *Modularity in noncopying term rewriting*, to appear in Theoretical Computer Science.
6. D. Plump (1990), *Graph-reducible term rewriting systems*, Proc. 4th workshop on graph grammars and their applications to Computer Science, Lecture Notes in Computer Science **532**, pp. 622-636, Springer-Verlag.
7. D. Plump (1992), *Collapsed tree rewriting: completeness, confluence and modularity*, Proc. CTRS'92, Lecture Notes in Computer Science **656**, pp. 97-112, Springer-Verlag.
8. D. Plump (1993), *Evaluation of functional expressions by hypergraph rewriting*, Ph.D. Thesis, University of Bremen.

[2] Overlay systems allow overlapping of the left-hand sides only at the top level, i.e., the left-hand side term l_i does not unify with any non-variable proper subterm of any left-hand side term l_j.

Positive Recursive Type Assignment*

Paweł Urzyczyn
Institute of Informatics, Warsaw University,
ul. Banacha 2, 02-097 Warsaw, Poland.
(urzy@mimuw.edu.pl)

Abstract. We consider several different definitions of type assignment with positive recursive types, from the point of view of their typing ability. We discuss the relationships between these systems. In particular, we show that the class of typable pure lambda terms remains the same for different type disciplines involving positive type fixpoints, and that type reconstruction is decidable.

1 Introduction

This paper subject is to study "Curry style" type assignment with recursive types. By "Curry style", as opposed to fully typed "Church style", we mean the approach where types are assigned, as predicates, to pure lambda terms. A type assignment system proves judgements of the form $E \vdash M : \tau$, where M is a term of untyped lambda calculus, τ is a type, and E is a set of type assumptions about free variables (a type environment).

By recursive types we mean "type fixpoints" represented by expressions of the form $\mu\alpha\tau$, where τ is a type and α is a type variable. Such a fixpoint type is identified with its unfolding $\tau[\mu\alpha\tau/\alpha]$. For instance, if τ is $(\alpha \to \beta) \to \beta$ then $\mu\alpha\tau$ is equivalent to $((\mu\alpha\tau) \to \beta) \to \beta$, and this equivalence allows to derive e.g., $E \vdash z(xy)(yx) : \beta$, where the environment E consists of the type assumptions: $(x : \mu\alpha\tau)$, $(y : (\mu\alpha\tau) \to \beta)$ and $(z : \beta \to \beta \to \beta)$.

A type containing occurrences of the constructor μ is often represented as an infinite regular tree obtained by unwinding all its fixpoints. But the notion of equivalence between types induced by such presentation is stronger than the above "syntactic" equivalence: different types may unwind to the same tree (see [4]).

Type assignment with arbitrary fixpoints was studied for instance in the papers [2], [3], [4]. See also [1], for a survey of major properties. However, arbitrary recursive types are in a sense too strong. Let σ be $\mu\alpha(\alpha \to \alpha)$. One can easily show that all terms can be assigned the type σ. This means that all terms are typable.

In order to keep the class of typable terms within the bounds of strong normalization property, one imposes the positivity condition: $\mu\alpha\tau$ is a legal type only if α does not occur in τ to the left of an odd number of arrows. Mendler ([7])

* Partly supported by NSF Grant CCR-9113196, KBN Grant 2 P301 031 06 and by ESPRIT BRA7232 "Gentzen".

proves (essentially) that the positivity condition is sufficient for strong normalization, and that it is the weakest possible: adding an arbitrary negative fixpoint always allows to type a non-normalizable term.

In the present paper we concentrate on the positive recursive types. The goal is to compare the existing approaches to positive recursive type assignment, with respect to their typing ability. We first consider the approach based on the fixpoint constructor μ as described above. But there are two ways of understanding the equivalence between a fixpoint and its unfolding. One possibility is to provide rules to replace a typing $M : \mu\alpha\tau$ with $M : \tau[\mu\alpha\tau/\alpha]$, and conversely (folding and unfolding at the top level). The other way is to identify these types entirely, which generates a congruence on the set of all types, and then to replace freely all congruent types with each other.

An entirely different approach is to use "type constraints", i.e., to introduce type constants, and postulate equations of the form e.g. "$c = (c \to \beta) \to \beta$". Such c then behaves in a similar way to $\mu\alpha((\alpha \to \beta) \to \beta)$. This is the approach of [2] and [7].

As we mentioned before, recursive types are conveniently presented by regular trees. We would like to do the same with positive recursive types, but as noted in [3] and [4], the tree model is not adequate here. The difficulty is that a positive fixpoint may unwind to the same tree as a negative one, which means introducing "bad behaviour" in an implicit way. To avoid this we propose in Section 3 to use labelled trees to preserve the polarity information.

Our main result is that all the four type assignment systems are of equal typing power, in the following sense: a pure lambda term is typable in one of these systems iff it is typable in any other (but not necessarily into the same type). We also show how to use our tree representation to prove that self-application is not typable (Example 3.3), and that typability is decidable (Corollary 4.4).

Section 2 introduces the type assignment systems based on the constructor μ and Section 3 introduces our trees. The last Section 4 deals with type constraints and contains our main result, Theorem 4.3. Due to space limitations, most details are omitted.

2 The basic type assignment systems

The positive recursive types are defined by mutual induction, together with the notion of positive and negative free variables. For a type τ, we use the notation $FV_+(\tau)$ and $FV_-(\tau)$ to denote the sets of variables occurring positively (resp. negatively) in τ.

- Type variables are types, and we have $FV_+(\alpha) = \{\alpha\}$ and $FV_-(\alpha) = \emptyset$;
- If σ and τ are types then $(\sigma \to \tau)$ is a type, satisfying $FV_+(\sigma \to \tau) = FV_+(\tau) \cup FV_-(\sigma)$ and $FV_-(\sigma \to \tau) = FV_-(\tau) \cup FV_+(\sigma)$;
- If σ is a type and α is a type variable, such that $\alpha \notin FV_-(\sigma)$, then $(\mu\alpha\sigma)$ is a type, and we define $FV_+(\mu\alpha\sigma) = FV_+(\sigma) - \{\alpha\}$, and $FV_-(\mu\alpha\sigma) = FV_-(\sigma)$

The notational conventions are as follows: the operator μ is of higher priority than arrow, and arrows associate to the right. Unnecessary parentheses are omitted. That is, e.g., the notation "$\mu\alpha\sigma \to \tau \to \rho$" is equivalent to "$((\mu\alpha\sigma) \to (\tau \to \rho))$". Since μ binds variables, we allow for alpha conversion, i.e., we identify types that are the same except for a renaming of their bound variables. Also the notion of substitution, denoted $\tau[\sigma/\alpha]$, is as usual, with a possible alpha conversion of τ. A *type environment* is a set E of pairs of the form $(x : \sigma)$, where x is an object variable and σ is a type, such that if $(x : \sigma), (x : \sigma') \in E$ then $\sigma = \sigma'$. Thus, an environment is a finite partial function from variables into types. If E is an environment then $E(x : \sigma)$ is an environment such that

$$E(x:\sigma)(y) = \begin{cases} \sigma, & \text{if } x \equiv y; \\ E(y), & \text{if } x \not\equiv y. \end{cases}$$

The terms of the pure λ-calculus are defined as usual by the grammar

$$M ::= \ x \mid (M\,M) \mid (\lambda x\,M)$$

A *judgement* is an expression of the form $E \vdash M : \tau$ where E is a type environment. We consider two basic systems to derive judgements involving positive recursive types. Both these systems contain the ordinary simple type assignment rules:

(Var) $\quad E \vdash x : \sigma \quad$ if $(x : \sigma)$ is in E

(App) $$\frac{E \vdash M : \tau \to \sigma,\ E \vdash N : \tau}{E \vdash (MN) : \sigma}$$

(Abs) $$\frac{E(x:\tau) \vdash M : \sigma}{E \vdash (\lambda x.M) : \tau \to \sigma}$$

The simplest way to introduce positive recursive types is to extend this core system by the following two rules:

(Fold) $$\frac{E \vdash M : \sigma[(\mu\alpha\tau)/\alpha]}{E \vdash M : \mu\alpha\tau}$$

(Unfold) $$\frac{E \vdash M : \mu\alpha\tau}{E \vdash M : \tau[(\mu\alpha\tau)/\alpha]}$$

We use the notation $\vdash_{FU}$ to denote derivability in the above system. Our second system, which will be referred to by the notation $\vdash_{\sim}$, has only one new rule in addition to (Var), (App) and (Abs):

$$(\sim) \qquad \frac{E \vdash M : \sigma, \quad \sigma \sim \tau}{E \vdash M : \tau}$$

Here, the relation $\sim$ is the smallest congruence on types satisfying

$$\mu\alpha\tau \sim \tau[(\mu\alpha\tau)/\alpha].$$

Clearly, rules (Fold) and (Unfold) are then seen as special cases of rule ($\sim$), and we have the obvious implication:

$$\text{If } E \vdash_{FU} M : \tau \text{ then } E \vdash_{\sim} M : \tau.$$

The converse implication does not hold, for the simple reason that

$$(x : \mu\alpha(\beta \to \alpha) \to \beta) \not\vdash_{FU} x : (\beta \to \mu\alpha(\beta \to \alpha)) \to \beta,$$

while the two types are obviously $\sim$-related. Note that the above example shows also that typing under $\vdash_{FU}$ is not closed under eta reduction. Indeed, a correct $\vdash_{FU}$-judgement is obtained from the above if x is replaced by $\lambda y.xy$ at the right hand side. On the other hand, it is not difficult to prove that $E \vdash_{\sim} M : \tau$ implies $E \vdash_{\sim} M' : \tau$, for all M' such that $M \twoheadrightarrow_{\eta} M'$.

However, there is more between $\vdash_{\sim}$ and $\vdash_{FU}$ than just eta reduction. For instance, we can derive

$$(x : \mu\alpha(\mu\beta(\alpha \to \beta) \to \alpha)) \vdash_{\sim} x : \mu\alpha((\alpha \to \mu\beta(\alpha \to \beta)) \to \alpha),$$

while, for all eta expansions X of x,

$$(x : \mu\alpha(\mu\beta(\alpha \to \beta) \to \alpha)) \not\vdash_{FU} X : \mu\alpha((\alpha \to \mu\beta(\alpha \to \beta)) \to \alpha).$$

Two important properties of the positive recursive type assignment are as follows:

Theorem 2.1. *Let $E \vdash M : \tau$, where $\vdash$ is either $\vdash_{\sim}$ or $\vdash_{FU}$. Then:*

1. *The term M is strongly normalizable;*
2. *If $M \twoheadrightarrow_{\beta} N$ then also $E \vdash N : \tau$.*

Proof. Part (1) follows from Mendler's paper [7], because of the equivalence between type constraints and recursive type assignment (see Theorem 4.3). For part (2), we need to prove the following claim:

$$\text{If } E(x : \tau) \vdash M : \sigma \text{ and } E \vdash N : \tau \text{ then } E \vdash M[N/x] : \sigma.$$

This goes by an easy induction on M. Details are left to the reader. ∎

We conclude this section with a remark on the power of recursive types. Let $\tau = \mu\alpha(\beta \to \alpha)$. We have $\tau \sim (\beta \to \tau)$ and one can easily derive that $(x : \tau) \vdash \lambda y.\, x : \tau$. This means that the combinator $\mathbf{K} \equiv \lambda xy.\, x$ has type $\tau \to \tau$. If $\mathbf{2} \equiv \lambda fx.\, f(fx)$ then of course we have $\mathbf{2} : (\tau \to \tau) \to \tau \to \tau$ and we conclude that $\mathbf{22K} : \tau$. On the other hand we have:

Lemma 2.2. *The term* **22K** *is untypable in the second order polymorphic lambda calculus (System* **F***).*

It follows that recursive types cannot be replaced by polymorphic types as long as typability is concerned: the class of terms typable with positive type fixpoints is not a subset of polymorphically typable terms. In Section 3 we show that the converse inclusion is also not true.

3 Labelled trees

Arbitrary recursive types are often represented as their unfoldings to infinite regular trees, see e.g. [3] and [4]. This representation can be useful, although it is not fully adequate, as two different types can sometimes be unfolded to the same tree. However, when one restricts attention to positive fixpoints only, the ordinary tree model becomes just inconsistent. Consider the type $\tau = \mu\alpha((\alpha \to \beta) \to \beta)$. There is nothing really wrong if it is represented by the same tree as $\mu\alpha((((\alpha \to \beta) \to \beta) \to \beta) \to \beta)$, but the serious problem is different. Let $\sigma = (\tau \to \beta)$. Then we have $\tau \sim (\sigma \to \beta)$ and both τ and σ unfold to exactly the same tree. Now, τ is a "negative" subtype of σ and equating these two types results in a calculus which is no longer strongly normalizable (see [7]).

A tree-like representation of positive recursive types is useful because it allows sometimes for graph-theoretical reasoning about type inference (especially when one wants to prove non-typability). Since the polarity information is lost after unfolding, we must keep it visible by adding extra decoration to our trees. That's why we propose to use labelled trees instead. In what follows a *tree* is defined as a function $T : \mathrm{Dom}(T) \to \mathrm{TVar} \cup \mathcal{L}$, such that

- TVar denotes the set of all type variables;
- the symbol $\mathcal{L}$ stands for a set of *labels*;
- $\mathrm{Dom}(T)$ is a nonempty downward closed subset of $\{L, R\}^*$, i.e., $wv \in \mathrm{Dom}(T)$ implies $w \in \mathrm{Dom}(T)$;
- for each $w \in \mathrm{Dom}(T)$, either $T(w) \in \mathcal{L}$ and $wR, wL \in \mathrm{Dom}(T)$, or $T(w)$ is a variable and w is a leaf.

By $T|_w$ we denote the *subtree* of T *rooted at* w, i.e., a tree with domain $\{v : wv \in \mathrm{Dom}(T)\}$, defined by $T|_w(v) = T(wv)$. A tree is called *regular* iff it has only a finite number of different subtrees. (In particular there is only a finite number of labels.)

Let T and T' be regular trees such that $\mathrm{Dom}(T) = \mathrm{Dom}(T')$. We identify T with T' if the equality $T(w) = T'(w)$ holds *for almost every* $w \in \mathrm{Dom}(T)$, including necessarily all the leaves. That is, from now on, we write $T = T'$ even if there is a finite number of differences in the labelling of T and T', but only at the internal nodes. In particular, this means that internal labelling of finite trees can be ignored altogether, so our finite trees are equivalent to ordinary finite types.

A node w is *positive* iff it has an even number of L's, otherwise it is called *negative*. Now we would like to define a positive tree as one that satisfies $T(w) \neq T(wv)$, for each w and each negative v. This would lead to difficulties because of our convention to identify trees with labels equal almost everywhere, so we must relax this condition as follows: a tree T is called *positive* iff $T(w) \neq T(wv)$ holds for almost every pair (w, v), with negative v (provided both sides are defined).

If T_1 and T_2 are trees then $T_1 \rightarrow T_2$ denotes the only tree T satisfying $T|_L = T_1$ and $T|_R = T_2$. Note that, due to our convention, the label $T(\varepsilon)$ does not matter.

For our *tree assignment system*, we define a *tree environment*, as a finite partial function from variables to positive regular trees, and we use the notation $\mathcal{E}(x : T)$ as for ordinary environments. The rules are as follows:

(Var) $\qquad \mathcal{E} \vdash x : S \qquad$ if $(x : S)$ is in $\mathcal{E}$

(App) $\qquad \dfrac{\mathcal{E} \vdash M : T \rightarrow S,\ \mathcal{E} \vdash N : T}{\mathcal{E} \vdash (MN) : S}$

(Abs) $\qquad \dfrac{\mathcal{E}(x : T) \vdash M : S}{\mathcal{E} \vdash (\lambda x.M) : T \rightarrow S}$

We use the symbol $\vdash_t$ to denote derivability in the tree assignment systems. Clearly, if $\mathcal{E} \vdash_t M : T$ then T must be positive and regular. The above system behaves very much like the ordinary simple assignment system; in particular it is easy to show that $\mathcal{E} \vdash_t M : T$ implies $\mathcal{E} \vdash_t M : T'$, for all T' such that $T \twoheadrightarrow_{\beta\eta} T'$.

In order to find a translation from recursive type assignment to tree assignment, we need the following definition. Let τ be a type and w be a path. We write $\tau[w]$ for the subtype of τ rooted at w, and we define a type $\tau(w)$ as follows:

$$\begin{aligned}
\tau(\varepsilon) &= \tau; \\
(\tau \rightarrow \sigma)(Lw) &= \tau(w); \\
(\tau \rightarrow \sigma)(Rw) &= \sigma(w); \\
(\mu\alpha\tau)(w) &= \tau(w)[\mu\alpha\tau/\alpha], \text{ if } \tau(w) \text{ is defined;} \\
(\mu\alpha\tau)(wv) &= (\mu\alpha\tau)(v), \text{ if } \tau[w] = \alpha.
\end{aligned}$$

The only case where the two conditions of the above definition can overlap is when $\tau[w] = \alpha$ and we want to define $\mu\alpha\tau$. Thus, to see that the above definition is correct, it suffices to prove by induction w.r.t. τ that:

$$\text{if } \tau[w] = \alpha \text{ and } \alpha \text{ is free in } \tau \text{ then also } \tau(w) = \alpha,$$

(with no ambiguity possible). Then we obtain $(\mu\alpha\tau)(w) = \mu\alpha\tau$, either way.

Now for an arbitrary type τ, we define its tree representation T_τ, by $T_\tau(w) = [\tau(w)]_\sim$. If we identify the equivalence class of a variable with the variable itself, then we can say that this definition is correct:

Lemma 3.1.

1. *T_τ is a positive regular tree, for each type τ. (The set $\mathcal{L}$ of labels is the set of equivalence classes of non-variable types.) In particular, for each τ and w, we have $\tau(w) \not\sim \tau$.*
2. *If $\tau \sim \sigma$ then $T_\tau = T_\sigma$, and conversely.*

Proof. Omitted.

Note that the equality of trees $T_\tau = T_\sigma$ is quite different than the relation $\approx$ of [4] (identical tree unfoldings), because the latter identifies more types than $\sim$.

If E is a type environment then by $\mathcal{T}_E$ we denote the corresponding tree environment, given by $\mathcal{T}_E(x) = T_{E(x)}$, for all x. The main result of this section is:

Proposition 3.2. *If $E \vdash_\sim M : \tau$ then $\mathcal{T}_E \vdash_t M : T_\tau$.*

An application of the tree assignment is demonstrated by the following example:

Example 3.3 *There is no type τ such that $\vdash_\sim \lambda x.\, xx : \tau$.*

Proof. Suppose the contrary. By Proposition 3.2, there is a positive regular tree T, such that our tree assignment derives $\vdash \lambda x.\, xx : T$. Let S be the left subtree of T. One can easily see that we must have $S = S \to S'$, for some S', and thus all labels on the leftmost path in S are the same. This contradicts the positivity condition. ∎

Together with Lemma 2.2, the above proves that recursive types and quantificational polymorphism are orthogonal with respect to their typing power. Indeed, $\lambda x.\, xx$ is easily typable in System **F**.

4 Type constraints

In this section we consider positive type constraints, in the spirit of [7]. If TConst is a fixed set of *type constants* then we define *simple types with constants* with help of the grammar:

$$\tau ::= \alpha \mid c \mid \tau \to \tau,$$

where the metavariables α and c range over type variables and type constants, respectively. The subtype notation $\tau[w]$ is used also for types with constants and has the obvious meaning. A *type constraint* is an equation of the form "$c = \tau$", where $c \in$ TConst and τ is a simple type with constants. A *system of constraints* is a finite set of constraints such that all the left-hand sides are different constants.

A system of constraints $\mathcal{C}$ determines an equivalence relation $\sim_{\mathcal{C}}$ as the smallest congruence satisfying $c \sim_{\mathcal{C}} \tau$, whenever "$c = \tau$" is in $\mathcal{C}$. Such a system $\mathcal{C}$ is *positive* iff, for all constants c, the equivalence $c \sim_{\mathcal{C}} \tau$ implies that $\tau[w] = c$ may only hold for positive w (Mendler's condition **P**).

Type inference for simple types with constants is defined relative to a given positive set of constraints $\mathcal{C}$. The rules are the ordinary (Var), (App), (Abs) and in addition:

$$(\sim_{\mathcal{C}}) \qquad \frac{E \vdash M : \sigma, \quad \sigma \sim_{\mathcal{C}} \tau}{E \vdash M : \tau}$$

We use the symbol $\vdash_{\mathcal{C}}$ to denote type assignment with help of the system of constraints $\mathcal{C}$. It was shown by Mendler that typable terms have strong normalization property iff $\mathcal{C}$ is positive. An analogous result can be obtained (as shown by Marz, [6]) for generalized constraints, i.e., arbitrary equations of the form "$\tau = \sigma$", with an appropriate generalized notion of positivity. We conjecture that the set of typable terms also remains unchanged in this case.

We are particularly interested in derivations of a specific simple shape. We write $E \vdash^{\bullet}_{\mathcal{C}} M : \tau$ if $E \vdash_{\mathcal{C}} M : \tau$ can be derived so that rule $(\sim_{\mathcal{C}})$ is used only at the "top level", i.e., in one of the two restricted forms:

$$\frac{E \vdash M : c}{E \vdash M : \tau} \qquad\qquad \frac{E \vdash M : \tau}{E \vdash M : c}$$

where "$c = \tau$" is a constraint in $\mathcal{C}$.

Our aim is now to translate the tree assignment system of Section 3 into type inference with constraints. More precisely, we show the following result.

Proposition 4.1. *If $\mathcal{E} \vdash_t M : T$ then there exists a system $\mathcal{C}$ of constraints such that $E \vdash^{\bullet}_{\mathcal{C}} M : \tau$, for some E and τ.*

Proof. For each positive regular tree T, let c_T be a new constant. Our system $\mathcal{C}$ of constraints consists of all equations of the form:

$$\begin{aligned} c_{T \to S} &= c_T \to c_S; \\ c_T &= \alpha, \quad \text{if } T(\varepsilon) = \alpha. \end{aligned}$$

Details are omitted. ∎

Our last step is from constraints back to recursive types. For this it is convenient to extend our language so that both constants and fixpoints may occur in types. Thus, we allow for all types constructed according to the folowing grammar:

$$\tau ::= \alpha \mid c \mid \tau \to \tau \mid \mu\alpha\tau,$$

with only positive μ-bindings. We generalize appropriately the notion of a constraint and for a given system of constraints $\mathcal{C}$, we redefine the relation $\sim_{\mathcal{C}}$ as the smallest congruence satisfying both conditions:

$$\mu\alpha\tau \sim_C \tau[(\mu\alpha\tau)/\alpha];$$
$$c \sim_C \tau, \qquad \text{for "} c = \tau \text{" in } \mathcal{C}.$$

Of course, $\mathcal{C}$ is always assumed to be positive. The meaning of "$E \vdash_C M : \tau$" for the extended language should now be clear. We also use the notation $E \vdash^{\bullet}_{\mathcal{C}} M : \tau$ if the judgement $E \vdash M : \tau$ is derivable with help of rules (Var), (App), (Abs), (Fold), (Unfold), and the two restricted forms of ($\sim_C$), as above. Note that $\vdash_{\emptyset}$ is just $\vdash_{\sim}$, and that $\vdash^{\bullet}_{\emptyset}$ is equivalent to $\vdash_{FU}$. We are going to eliminate one constant at a time. The main technical lemma is as follows:

Lemma 4.2. *Let $\mathcal{C}$ be a positive system of n constraints ($n > 0$), and assume that $E \vdash_C M : \sigma$. There exists a positive system $\mathcal{D}$ of $n-1$ constraints, such that $E' \vdash_{\mathcal{D}} M : \sigma'$, for some E' and σ'. In addition, if $E \vdash^{\bullet}_{\mathcal{C}} M : \sigma$ then $E' \vdash^{\bullet}_{\mathcal{D}} M : \sigma'$.*

The above lemma applied repeatedly allows one to get rid of all constants and constraints at the cost of introducing μ's. Let us note here that the result of this process is not unique and depends on the order in which the constants are eliminated.

We have concluded the loop connecting our systems, and we can now state our main result: each of them is of the same power w.r.t. typability of pure lambda terms.

Theorem 4.3. *For every pure lambda term M, the following conditions are equivalent:*

1. *$E \vdash_{FU} M : \tau$, for some E and τ;*
2. *$E \vdash_{\sim} M : \tau$, for some E and τ;*
3. *$\mathcal{E} \vdash_t : T$, for some $\mathcal{E}$ and T;*
4. *$E \vdash_C : \tau$, for some positive system $\mathcal{C}$, and some E and τ.*

Proof. That (1) implies (2) is an obvious inclusion. The implication from (2) to (3) follows from Proposition 3.2, and the implication from (3) to (4) is given by Proposition 4.1. Condition (4) implies (2) because by Lemma 4.2, we can eliminate step by step all occurrences of constants, resulting in a derivation of the form $E' \vdash_{\emptyset} M : \tau'$. Finally, (3) implies (1) because Proposition 4.1 guarantees a derivation in the special form $E \vdash^{\bullet}_{\mathcal{C}} M : \tau$, and the elimination process of Lemma 4.2 will result in $E' \vdash^{\bullet}_{\emptyset} M : \tau'$. ∎

Corollary 4.4. *It is decidable whether a given term M is typable with respect to $\vdash_{\sim}$.*

Proof. Due to the equivalence of conditions (1) and (3) of Theorem 4.3, we ask whether M is typable in the tree assignment system. First we follow essentially a standard algorithm for ordinary finite types. We assign an unknown t_P to each subterm P of M (with different occurrences of non-variable subterm counted as different subterms). Then we set equations of the form: $t_P = t_Q \to t_{PQ}$ and $t_{\lambda x.P} = t_x \to t_P$. It remains to solve these equations over positive regular trees. It is not difficult to show that a solution exists iff our equations form a positive system of constraints, and this is decidable in polynomial time. ∎

5 Conclusion

We have shown the equivalence of typability under different type disciplines involving the combination of simple types (arrow types) and recursion. We have also constructed an equivalent tree model of positive recursive types. We would like to extend these results to systems involving quantificational polymorphism. However, the generalization will not be immediate. The difficulty is the substitution. It seems that one needs a notion of substitution on trees, satisfying $T_{\tau[\sigma/\alpha]} = T_\tau\,[T_\sigma/\alpha]$ and the naive solution does not satisfy this property, because of the different labelling.

References

1. Barendregt., H.P., Lambda Calculi with Types, Chapter 1 in: *Handbook of Logic in Computer Science*, vol **2**, (S. Abramsky, Dov.M. Gabbay, and T.S.E. Maibaum, Eds.) Clarendon Press, 1992, pp. 118–310.
2. Breazu-Tannen, V., Meyer, A.R., Lambda calculus with constrained types, in: *Logics of Programs* (R. Parikh, Ed.), LNCS 193, Springer, Berlin, 1985.
3. Cardone, F., Coppo, M., Two extensions of Curry's type inference system, in: *Logic and Computer Science* (P. Oddifreddi, Ed.), Academic Press, 1990, pp. 19–75.
4. Cardone, F., Coppo, M., Type inference with recursive types: syntax and semantics, *Information and Computation*, **92** (1991), 48–80.
5. Klop, J.W., *Combinatory Reduction Systems*, Mathematisch Centrum, Amsterdam, 1980.
6. Marz, M., Private communication, 1994.
7. Mendler, N.P., Inductive types and type constraints in the second-order lambda calculus, *Annals of Pure and Applied Logic*, **51** (1991), 159–172.

String Recognition on Anonymous Rings

Evangelos Kranakis[12] Danny Krizanc[12] Flaminia L. Luccio[12]

[1] Carleton University, School of Computer Science, Ottawa, ON, Canada. K1S 5B6
[2] Research supported in part by National Sciences Engineering Research Council of Canada grant.

Abstract. We consider the problem of recognizing whether a given binary string of length n is equal (up to rotation) to the input of an anonymous oriented ring of n processors. Previous algorithms for this problem have been "global" and do not take into account "local" patterns occurring in the string. Such patterns may be repetitive or discriminating, and can be used to provide efficient algorithms for recognizing strings. In this paper we give new upper and lower bounds on the bit complexity of string recognition. For the case of periodic strings, near optimal bounds are given which depend on the period of the string. For the case of a randomly chosen string, an optimal algorithm for the problem is given. In particular, we show that almost all strings can be recognized by communicating $\Theta(n \log n)$ bits. It is interesting to note that Kolmogorov complexity theory is used in the proof of our *upper* bound, rather than its traditional application to the proof of lower bounds.

1 Introduction

There have been several studies in the literature concerning the construction of communication efficient algorithms for computing functions on anonymous rings [2, 4, 5, 6, 1, 10], as well as on more general anonymous networks, like tori [3], hypercubes [7], Cayley networks [8], etc. In general, studies of the bit complexity of computing boolean functions of the inputs mainly resort to input collection before determining the output of the boolean function.

In particular, Attiya, Snir and Warmuth [2] showed that all the functions that are computable on an anonymous asynchronous ring of processors, can be computed using $O(n^2)$ messages (one bit message if the functions are boolean) using input collection. They also proved that every algorithm that computes the minimum of all inputs (the OR function in the boolean case), requires $\Omega(n^2)$ messages, i.e., the bounds in this case are tight. Furthermore, they show that almost all boolean functions on n variables require $\Omega(n^2)$ bits to compute. On the other hand, Moran and Warmuth [10] gave an $\Omega(n \log n)$ lower bound for computing any non-constant function and presented functions (derived from a recursive application of de Bruijn sequences) with a $O(n \log n)$ bit complexity.

In this paper we further investigate the bit complexity of computing boolean functions on an anonymous ring by concentrating on an interesting class of functions related to the problem of recognizing an input as being equivalent up to rotation to a fixed string. These functions are shown to exhibit behavior opposite to what was described above, i.e., almost all such functions can be computed using $O(n \log n)$ bits and functions requiring $\Omega(n^2)$ bits are the exception, not the rule. The bit complexity of string recognition is shown to be closely related to the underlying symmetry of the string.

1.1 Results of the paper

Let $x = x_1 x_2 \cdots x_n, y = y_1 y_2 \cdots y_n \in \{0,1\}^n$ be binary strings of length n and suppose that for each $i = 1, \ldots, n$ the i-th processor of an anonymous ring knows the i-th bit y_i of y as well as the entire string x. Give an efficient algorithm such that all n processors recognize whether or not the input string y is identical (up to rotation) to the string x is known as the **string recognition problem.**

We can reformulate our problem in terms of boolean functions. For any string $x \in \{0,1\}^n$ define the boolean function $f_x : \{0,1\}^n \rightarrow \{0,1\}$ as follows:

$$f_x(y) = \begin{cases} 1 \text{ if } y \text{ is a cyclic shift of } x \\ 0 \text{ otherwise.} \end{cases}$$

Clearly, being invariant under rotations, the function f_x is computable in the oriented anonymous ring [2]. We are interested in determining the bit complexity of computing $f_x(y)$.

The input collection algorithm of Attiya, Snir and Warmuth [2] implies that for every x, $f_x(y)$ can be computed using $O(n^2)$ bits. Such an algorithm is "global", in the sense that the same algorithm is executed regardless of x or the input to the network. In the sequel, we show how taking into account repetitive or discriminating patterns within a string might provide more efficient algorithms for our problem. For the case of symmetric or repetitive strings we specify upper bounds (section 2.1) and lower bounds (section 3) which depend on the period k of a string x of length n, where $x = w^t v$, $t \geq 0$, v a prefix of w, and $k = |w|$. If $v = \emptyset$ then we give an $O(nk + \frac{n^2}{k})$ upper bound and $\Omega(n \log n + \frac{n^2}{k})$ lower bound. If $v \neq \emptyset$ then we give an $O(nk + n \log n)$ upper bound and $\Omega(n \log n)$ lower bound.

In section 2.2, we show that almost all strings can be recognized using $\Theta(n \log n)$ bits. Our upper bound is an interesting application of Kolmogorov complexity theory which has traditionally been used to show lower bounds. From an intuitive point of view, Kolmogorov complexity theory deals with the amount of information that a string contains [9, 12]. This quantity can be calculated in terms of the size of the shortest program that computes the string. For a random string x of length n, the length of its shortest program is very close to n, with high probability. A string with this property is called incompressible. We use this fact to derive an upper bound of $O(n \log n)$ bits for almost all strings, by showing that if no efficient algorithm exists to recognize a string then a short program exists to compute the string, contradicting its incompressibility.

1.2 Preliminaries

As our model of computation we consider the standard anonymous, asynchronous, ring of n processors [2]. The size n of the ring is known to the processors, and initially the processors are given a single bit as well as a string x of length n. By anonymity, the processors execute the same algorithm given the same data. At the end, it is desired that all the processors determine correctly whether or not the given string is a rotation of the input.

In the proofs below we further assume that the ring is oriented, i.e., the processors can distinguish in a "globally consistent" manner their left from their right neighbor. Nevertheless, all our results are valid for unoriented rings with only minor modifications in the definitions and the statements of the results.

Let n be the number of processors and let $0 \leq i < n$ denote the i-th processor. If b_p is the input to processor p then $\langle b_p : p < n \rangle$ denotes the network input. The right (respectively, left) neighbourhood of processor p of length k is the sequence of bits $\langle b_{p+i} : 0 \leq i < k \rangle$ (respectively, $\langle b_{p-i} : 0 \leq i < k \rangle$), where the operations $+, -$ are done modulo n.

Before we proceed with the description of our algorithms we give some necessary definitions.

Definition 1. Call u (respectively, v) a *prefix* (respectively, *suffix*) of the string x, if $x = uv$ for some string v (respectively, u); the prefix (respectively, suffix) is called *proper* if it is not equal to x. For any string x of length n let the *period* of x be the smallest integer $k \leq n$ such that for some strings w, v we have that: w has length k, v is a prefix of w, and $x = w^{\lfloor n/k \rfloor} v$. For any string u, let $|u|$ denote its length. Given a string $x = x_1 x_2 \dots x_n$ of length n, let $x \uparrow s = x_1 x_2 \dots x_s$ denote the first s bits of x, and $x^r = x_{r+1} x_{r+2} \dots x_n x_1 x_2 \dots x_r$ the r-th rotation of x. S_x^t is the set of all the different substrings of x, and of all its rotations, that are of length $t \leq n$, i.e., $S_x^t = \{x^i \uparrow t \mid i = 1, \dots, n\}$.

Definition 2. Given a string x of length n, a program p of length $|p|$, a programming language S, let $K_S(x)$ denote the length of the minimum program that outputs x using S, i.e., $K_S(x) = \min\{|p| : S(p) = x\}$.

From now on we will use the notation $K(x)$ to refer to the Kolmogorov complexity of x with respect to an optimal method of specification S, i.e., a method whose complexity differs by at most a constant from other methods that compute x. If $K(x) \geq |x| - O(\log |x|)$ we say that the string x is *Kolmogorov random.* It is easy to derive the fact that almost every string of a given length is Kolmogorov random. To simplify our presentation we assume from now on that the string x is Kolmogorov random if $K(x) \geq |x| - \log |x|$. In particular, this implies that a string of length n is Kolmogorov random with probability at least $1 - 1/n$.

2 Upper Bounds

2.1 Periodic strings

We now give an efficient algorithm for the string recognition problem. We can prove the following theorem.

Theorem 3. *Let $x = w^{\lfloor n/k \rfloor}v$ be a string of period k such that $|x| = n$, $|w| = k$ and v is a proper prefix of w. There is an algorithm for recognizing the string x on an n processor anonymous oriented ring with bit complexity $O(nk + \frac{n^2}{k})$ if $v = \emptyset$, and $O(nk + n \log n)$ if $v \neq \emptyset$.*

PROOF The main proof of the theorem consists of an efficient input collection algorithm satisfying the requirements above. Let a string x be known to all the processors and let b_p be the input to processor p. In the output of the algorithm it is determined whether or not x is a rotation of the input. Each processor executes the following algorithm which is described in several phases.

Phase 1 The processor computes the period k of the given string x as well as strings w, v such that v is a proper substring of w and in addition $x = w^t v$, for some integer $t \geq 0$. This is a local step executed initially by all the processors and does not contribute in any way to the overall bit complexity of the final algorithm.

Phase 2 Let k be the period of the string x as computed in Phase 1. The processors now compute their left neighborhood of length k as well as their right neighborhood of length $2k + 1$ by executing the following algorithm.

/* computing the right neighborhood */ send b_p to the left;
for $i = 1$ to $2k$ **do** send bit received from the right to the left **od**
/* computing the left neighborhood */ send b_p to the right;
for $i = 1$ to $k - 1$ **do** send bit received from the left to the right **od**

The idea of this phase is to compute a *small* length neighborhood of the input string and use this to decide whether or not the input string is a rotation of x. It will become apparent in the case $v \neq \emptyset$ (discussed in the sequel) why we need to compute a neighborhood of length $2k + 1$ to the right and a neighborhood of length k to the left (for the time being we will only have use for the left neighborhood of length k). Clearly, the bit complexity of Phase 2 is $O(nk)$.

Phase 3 In this phase the processors will execute the main part of the algorithm that will determine whether or not the given string is a rotation of the input. The rest of the algorithm depends on whether or not $v = \emptyset$.

CASE $v = \emptyset$: Let u_p be the first k bits of the right neighborhood computed by processor p in Phase 2 above. Now p executes the following algorithm.

if u_p is not a rotation of w
  then broadcast "no" x is not a rotation of the input;
  else /* u_p is a rotation of w */
  if u_p is the lexicographically maximal rotation of w
    then send a "yes" around the ring;
    every processor that receives a "yes" forwards it around the ring;
    every processor that receives a "no" forwards it around the ring and halts;
  if u_p is the lexicographically maximal rotation of w and processor p receives
    $\lfloor \frac{n}{k} \rfloor$ "yes" messages **then** broadcast x is a rotation of the input;
    else /* it receives a "no"*/ broadcast x is not a rotation of the input; **fi**
  fi

At the confirmation stage at most $\lfloor \frac{n}{k} \rfloor$ processors participate (i.e., the ones that have a lexicographically maximal rotation of w); each processor sends a "yes" or a "no" message around the ring (confirming that it has a lexicographically maximal rotation of w) and waits for $\lfloor \frac{n}{k} \rfloor$ "yes" messages or a "no" message. At most $\lfloor \frac{n}{k} \rfloor$ "yes" messages are sent and travel n steps. Finally, if any processor either has a neighborhood of length k which is not a rotation of w or receives a "no" message, it sends it to its neighbor and does not transmit again. Thus the overall bit complexity of this phase is $O(\frac{n^2}{k})$. (The "yes" or "no" messages require only $O(1)$ bits.)

At the end of this phase all processors will know whether or not all processors have seen a rotation of w. If indeed, all processors have seen a rotation of w then the string x is accepted else the string is rejected. The correctness of this last assertion is proved in the sequel. In the following argument we assume that the strings x, w, v are as in the statement of Theorem 3.

If there exists a processor $p \in \{i = 1, \dots, n\}$ that does not see a rotation of the input, this obviously implies $x \neq w^t$, and p will broadcast a message to stop the other processors.

If all the processors have seen a rotation of the input, then $x = w^t$ must hold. Let us assume on the contrary that there exist a processor p whose left neighborhood $w^{(t-1)} = w_t \dots w_k w_1 \dots w_{t-1}, t = 1, \dots, k$ is a rotation of the input, but its neighbor $p+1$ sees another rotation $w^{(s-1)} = w_s \dots w_k w_1 \dots w_{s-1}, s = 1, \dots, n$, which is not adjacent. Since p and $p+1$ are adjacent, their left neighborhood must have $k-2$ bits that are the same, i.e., $w_{(t+1)\text{mod}k} \dots w_k w_1 \dots w_{t-1} = w_s \dots w_k w_1 \dots w_{s-2}$. Moreover, if the two rotations cannot be adjacent, we have $w_t \neq w_{s-1}$, and since we are working with binary strings, we have $w_t = \overline{w_{s-1}}$. We now need the following:

Lemma 4. *Every rotation $w^{(t-1)} = w_t \dots w_k w_1 \dots w_{t-1}$, $t = 1, \dots, k$, of the binary string $w^{(0)} = w_1 \dots w_k$ of length k has the same number of ones.*

PROOF Proof omitted. ■

We have assumed that there can be two rotations with a different number of ones since $w_t \neq w_{s-1}$, but the above lemma shows that this is not possible, i.e., we have a contradiction. If each processor sees a rotation of the input, then the string can only be $x = w^t$.

CASE $v \neq \emptyset$: We assume that $x = w^t v$, where $v = v_1 \dots v_l$ is a proper prefix of w of length l, i.e., $v = w_1 \dots w_l$. Using the fact that w is the period of the string x, and assuming $x = x_1 \dots x_n$, we can easily prove the following lemma.

Lemma 5. *There exists a substring $z = z_1 \dots z_k$ of length k of x that has weight (i.e., number of bits equal to 1) different from the weight of w.*

PROOF Omitted. ■

Let v_p be the neighborhood of length $3k$ computed by processor p in Phase 2. It consists of the left neighborhood of length $2k+1$ and the right neighborhood of length k. In view of the representation of x in the form $w^t v$ it is an immediate consequence of Lemma 5 that there is a *unique* position in the string x whose

k-neighborhood is not a rotation of w, but such that the k-neighborhoods of all k positions to its left are indeed rotations of w and the k positions to its right have the *correct* values.

However, the converse of this is also true, in the sense that if the input string has a unique position satisfying the above conditions, as well as the k positions to its right have the correct k-neighborhoods, and in addition all other positions have a k neighborhood which is a rotation of w then in fact the input string itself must be a rotation of x. In the proof of the following lemma we assume that $x = w^{\lfloor \frac{n}{k} \rfloor} v$, $\lfloor \frac{n}{k} \rfloor \geq 2$. The case $x = wv$ can be solved using input collection with $O(n^2)$ bit complexity.

Lemma 6. *If after Phase 2 of the algorithm there exists at least one processor whose 3k-bit string obtained in Phase 2 is different from 3k bits of the string* $w^3 v w^3$, *then* $x \neq w^{\lfloor \frac{n}{k} \rfloor} v$. *If on the other hand all the processors see a correct 3k-neighborhood, then* $x = w^{\lfloor \frac{n}{k} \rfloor} v$, *or* $x = w^{s_1} v w^{s_2} v \ldots w^{s_i} v$, *for* $s_j \geq 2$, $j = 1, \ldots i$, $i \geq 2$.

PROOF Proof omitted. ■

It is now easy to convert this characterization into an $O(nk + n \log n)$ algorithm for determining whether or not the input is a rotation of x. The algorithm for processor p is as follows.

if a proper rotation is not seen **or** a halt is received
  then broadcast x is not a rotation of the input and halt
  else if in the "unique" position
      then send a message around the ring with a counter a **fi**;
    counter a is incremented by every processor;
    if in the "unique" position, and a counter $a < n$ is received,
    then broadcasts x is not a rotation of the input and halt
    else if $a = n$, **then** broadcast x is a rotation of the input; **fi**
    fi
fi

The observations made above prove the correctness of the algorithm. Only one processor can be in the unique position. If there is more then one, this situation is detected by another processor in a unique position, by receiving $a < n$. Note that it is not possible that every processor has w^3 as a neighborhood ($|x| = n$ cannot be divided by $|w|$, since $|v| < |w|$). The bit complexity of the algorithm is straightforward. In the worst case in this step, a message of at most $\log n$ bits travels for n steps. The total bit complexity of the algorithm, in the case $v \neq 0$ is then $O(nk + n \log n)$. This completes the proof of Theorem 3. ■

2.2 Kolmogorov random strings

We now present an algorithm that optimally recognizes a Kolmogorov random string (i.e., almost every string) using $\Theta(n \log n)$ bits. (The lower bound follows from [10].)

Theorem 7. *Let x be a Kolmogorov random string of length n. There is an algorithm for recognizing the string x on an n processor anonymous oriented ring with bit complexity $O(n \log n)$.*

PROOF Let x be a Kolmogorov random string of length n, given as an input to all the processors, and let b_p be the single bit of input at processor p. In the output of the algorithm it is determined whether or not the input bit configuration is a rotation of x. In the algorithm we use a constant a that will be more precisely calculated below. We will refer to Lemma 8 and 9 to justify the fact that, if the $c\lceil \log n \rceil$ neighborhood of a processor coincides with one of the strings contained in $S_x^t = \{x^i \uparrow t \mid i = 1, \ldots, n\}$ (see Definition 1), then, for n large enough, the input string must be x or one of its rotations.

Let $c = \max\{c', c''\}$, where c' and c'' are constants given in Lemma 8 and 9 below. A generic processor p executes the following phases.

Phase 1 Compute and store S_x^t, for $t = c \log n$. This is a local step and it does not contribute to the overall bit complexity of the final algorithm.

Phase 2 Compute the right neighborhood of length t as Phase 2 of algorithm above.

/*computing the right neighborhood*/ send b_p to the left;
for $i = 1$ to t **do** send bit received from the right to the left; **od**
Check whether the t-neighborhood coincides with one of the strings contained in S_x^t. The cost of this phase, in terms of bits transmitted, is $O(n \log n)$.

Phase 3 In this phase p will determine if the input string is a rotation of x. Since x is a Kolmogorov random string, if after $t-1$ steps all the processors have seen strings of S_x^t, then the input string must be x (see Lemma 9), otherwise, if at least one finds a different substring, it is not x. Let u_p be the t-neighborhood of processor p. Now p executes the following:

if $u_p \notin S_x^t$, **then** broadcast x is not a rotation of the input and halt;
  else if u_p is the maximal string **then** send a counter a around the ring;
    /* counter a is only incremented by processors who have seen an acceptable string */
    if a counter value $a = n$ is received
     then broadcast x is a rotation of the input and halt;
     else /* $a < n$, or another processor has seen an unacceptable string and has sent a halt */ broadcast x is not a rotation of the input and halt **fi**
    else /* u_p is not a maximal string */
    if an unacceptable string is seen
     then broadcast x is not a rotation of the input and halt
     else if a counter a is received **then** broadcast $a := a + 1$
      else /*a halt is received*/ store the information "x is (is not) a rotation of the input", broadcast it and halt **fi**
    fi
    fi
  fi

We can now precisely define a method to find the right value of c and we can justify Phase 2 and 3 of the algorithm.

We have the following lemmas:

Lemma 8. *Given a string $x = x_1 x_2 \dots x_n$ of length n, and an integer $t \leq n$, there exist a constant $c' \in \mathcal{N}$, such that, if n is large enough, for each $t \geq c' \log n$, if $|S_x^t| < n$, then x is not Kolmogorov random.*

PROOF The proof follows from results reported in [11]. ∎

Lemma 9. *There exist a constant $c'' \in \mathcal{N}$, such that, for n sufficiently large and for all $t \geq c'' \log n$, for any two strings $x = x_1 x_2 \dots x_n$ and $y = y_1 y_2 \dots y_n$ of length n, if x is Kolmogorov random, and $S_y^t \subseteq S_x^t$, then $x = y$ up to rotation.*

PROOF Proof omitted. ∎

If the input string is x then from Lemma 8 there exists a unique leader since only one processor sees a maximal substring. Therefore the bit complexity in this case is $O(\sum_{i=0}^{\log n} 2^i (i+1)) + O(n) = O(n \log n)$. If the input string is not x, then there are at most $\frac{n}{c \log n}$ processors that see the maximal string and that send a counter. In this case the bit complexity is still $O(n \log n) + O(n) = O(n \log n)$ since each counter will stop after reaching the next of these processors, i.e., $c \log n$ bit messages will travel for at most n steps. The correctness of the algorithm is straightforward. If the input string is x, then there is a unique leader that acknowledges the fact that each processor has seen an acceptable neighborhood, and Lemma 9 states that this condition is sufficient. On the other hand, if there is more then one leader, or at least one processor finds an unacceptable neighborhood (and from Lemma 9, if x is not the input string then this must happen), then a halt is sent and eventually all the processors will end their computation.

The overall bit complexity of these phases is $O(n \log n)$. This completes the proof of Theorem 7. ∎

3 Lower Bounds

In this section we prove lower bounds for the string recognition problem. In the case of Kolmogorov random string we need only the lower bound of $\Omega(n \log n)$ of [10] and the equivalent boolean function formulation of the string recognition problem stated in the introduction. This lower bound implies the optimality of the algorithm given above. For the case of $x = w^t v$ we have the following;

Theorem 10. *Let $x = w^{\lfloor \frac{n}{k} \rfloor} v$ be a string of period k such that $|x| = n$, $|w| = k$ and v is a proper prefix of w. The lower bound for recognizing any n-ary string on an n processors anonymous oriented ring is $\Omega(n \log n + \frac{n^2}{k})$ if $v = \emptyset$, $\Omega(n \log n)$ if $v \neq \emptyset$.*

PROOF Let x be a string as in the statement of the theorem. The $\Omega(n \log n)$ bound follows from [10]. Hence we only need to prove the $\Omega(\frac{n^2}{k})$ lower bound for the case $v = \emptyset$.

By Theorem 5.1 in [2] we know that a lower bound on the bit complexity of computing a function can be derived as follows. Given two input configurations y and z of length n, every algorithm that computes the function on input y requires at least $\sum_{i=0}^{\alpha} SI(y,i)$ messages in the worst case. Here α is a constant, such that there exist two processors p and q in the ring, for which p has the same α-neighborhood in y as q in z, but their output (at the end of the algorithm) is different. $SI(y,i)$ is the symmetry index function of the string y, i.e., the minimum number of elements in a equivalent i-neighborhood for processors in the configuration y.

Consider the string recognition problem with an input string $x = w^{\lfloor \frac{n}{k} \rfloor}$, $v = \emptyset$ and run the algorithm with input configurations $z = w^{\lfloor \frac{n}{k} \rfloor - 1} w_0 \ldots w_{k-1} \overline{w_k}$, and $y = x$. There exist two processors p in y and q in z, that have the same $\lfloor \frac{n}{4} \rfloor - 1$-neighborhood, but their output for the problem is different since $y = x$, and $z \neq x$. On input y there are at least $\frac{\lfloor \frac{n}{k} \rfloor}{2}$ processors who see the same $\lfloor \frac{n}{4} \rfloor - 1$-neighborhood, we have then:

$$\sum_{i=0}^{\alpha} SI(y,i) = \sum_{i=0}^{\lfloor \frac{n}{4} \rfloor - 1} \frac{\lfloor \frac{n}{k} \rfloor}{2} = \lfloor \frac{n}{4} \rfloor \frac{\lfloor \frac{n}{k} \rfloor}{2}, \tag{1}$$

i.e., the lower bound is $\Omega(\frac{n^2}{k})$. ∎

4 Conclusions and open problems

In this paper we have studied the string recognition problem on anonymous, asynchronous, n-processor rings.

We have shown a $\Theta(n \log n)$ bit complexity bound for Kolmogorov random strings, which in turns implies this same bit complexity for almost all strings. For strings of the form $x = w^t v$, $t \geq 0$, $|w| = k$, we have shown an $O(nk + n \log n)$ bit upper bound when $v \neq \emptyset$ and an $O(nk + \frac{n^2}{k})$ bit upper bound when $v = \emptyset$. When $v = \emptyset$ we have also shown an $\Omega(n \log n + \frac{n^2}{k})$ bit lower bound which shows that the upper bound is tight, for $k = O(\sqrt{n})$. When $v \neq \emptyset$ the upper bound $O(nk + n \log n)$ is tight for $k = O(\log n)$. An interesting open problem would be tighten these bounds in all cases.

As a final remark, we observe that the proof given for the string recognition problem when x is a Kolmogorov random string can be modified and extended to other networks like tori, meshes, etc.

Acknowledgments

The authors would like to thank Paul Vitányi for pointing out the usefulness of reference [11] in proving lemma 9. Thanks also to Nicola Santoro for the idea on how to tighten the bounds in the case of periodic strings with $v = \emptyset$.

References

1. H. Attiya and Y. Mansour, "Language Complexity on the Synchronous Anonymous Ring", *Theoretical Computer Science*, **53** 169-185, (1987).
2. H. Attiya, M. Snir and M. Warmuth, "Computing on an Anonymous Ring", *Journal of the ACM*, **35 (4)**, 845-875, (1988).
3. P.W. Beame and H.L. Bodlaender, "Distributed Computing on Transitive Networks: The Torus", *6th Annual Symposium on Theoretical Aspects of Computer Science, STACS*, Springer Verlag LNCS,**349**, 294-303, (1989).
4. H.L. Bodlaender, S. Moran, M.K. Warmuth, "The Distributed Bit Complexity of the Ring: from the Anonymous to the Non-Anonymous Case", *Information and Computation*, **108 (1)**, 34-50, (1994).
5. P. Ferragina, A. Monti and A. Roncato, "Trade-off between Computation Power and Common Knowledge in Anonymous Rings", *Pre-Proceedings of Colloquium on Structural Information and Communication Complexity*, Ottawa, Canada, May 16-18 (1994).
6. O. Goldreich, L. Shrara, "On the Complexity of Global Computation in the Presence of Link Failures: the Case of Ring Configuration", *Distributed Computing*, **5**, **(3)**, 121-131, (1991).
7. E. Kranakis and D. Krizanc, "Distributed Computing on Anonymous Hypercube Networks", *Proceedings of the 3rd IEEE Symposium on Parallel and Distributed Processing*, Dallas, Dec. 2-5, 722-729, (1991).
8. E. Kranakis and D. Krizanc, "Computing Boolean Functions on Cayley Networks", *Proceedings of the 4th IEEE Symposium on Parallel and Distributed Processing*, Arlington, Texas, Dec. 1-4, 222-229, (1992).
9. M. Li, P.M.B. Vitanyi, "Kolmogorov Complexity and its Applications", Handbook of Theoretical Computer Science, Algorithms and Complexity. The MIT Press, Cambridge, Massachusetts, (1990).
10. S. Moran and M. K. Warmuth, "Gap Theorems for Distributed Computation", *Proceedings of the 5th ACM Symposium on Principles of Distributed Computing*, 131-140, (1986).
11. J. Seiferas, "A Simplified Lower Bound for Context-free Language Recognition," Information and Control, **69**, 255-260, (1986).
12. A.K. Zvonkin, L.A. Levin, "The Complexity of Finite Objects and the Development of the Concepts of Information and Randomness by means of the Theory of Algorithms", *Russian Math. Surveys*, **25**, 83-124, (1970).

The Firing Squad Synchronization Problem on Cayley Graphs *

Zsuzsanna Róka

Laboratoire de l'Informatique du Parallélisme
Ecole Normale Supérieure de Lyon
46, Allée d'Italie, 69364 Lyon Cedex 07, France
e-mail: zroka@lip.ens-lyon.fr.

Abstract. The Firing Squad Synchronization Problem (FSSP for short) has been intensively studied in the one-dimensional space. The problem consists in the synchronization of a segment of automata. We generalize this problem on Cayley graphs. We give minimal time solutions for (*a*) synchronizing all cells in all minimal paths between any pair of cells of a Cayley graph; (*b*) synchronizing all cells in all minimal paths starting at a given cell G (the "general") and leading to all cells at a given distance from G in a Cayley graph. In solutions for (b), in some cases, all cells of a ball in a Cayley graph will be synchronized, in other cases this is not possible because of the existence of "culs-de-sac".

1 Introduction

Some recent papers study cellular automata on Cayley graphs. This notion is a generalization of the classical one, where cellular automata are defined in the n-dimensional space $\mathbb{Z}^n$. As Cayley graphs are more various but regular enough to be considered as possible underlying graphs for cellular automata, it is possible to model many more phenomena (such as parallel machines or crystal growing) on Cayley graphs than in $\mathbb{Z}^n$. That is why it is interesting to study this notion. A natural question arises: what are properties of cellular automata in $\mathbb{Z}^n$ true also on Cayley graphs? The problem "what are the Cayley graphs such that, for finite configurations, the injectivity of a cellular automaton is equal to its surjectivity?" was studied by Machí *et al.* in [3]. It was also shown in [6] that if the Cayley graph is a context-free graph, then there exists an algorithm which decides, when given a state set and a local transition function, whether or not the global transition function is surjective (or injective).

In this paper, we study whether the solutions for the FSSP in the one-dimensional space can be generalized for Cayley graphs. Recall that, the classical FSSP can be stated as follows. Consider a segment of automata on the line, with the "general" at the left-most end of the segment: the only automaton being in a non-quiescent state. Let us define the automata in such a way that, at a certain time T, all of them, synchronously and for the first time, enter in a special state, called a "firing" state.

* This work was partially supported by the Esprit Basic Research Action "Algebraic and Syntactical Methods In Computer Science" and by a Grant of the French Government.

This problem has been intensively studied, solutions have been given in [1, 2, 4]. Some generalizations were also found: among them, synchronization in optimal time of a segment ([5]) and of a rectangle ([10]) with the general placed anywhere, and synchronization of non-oriented graphs with bounded vertex-degree in time linear in the number of vertices of the graph ([7]). Here, we give time-optimal solutions to synchronize all cells in all minimal paths between any pair of cells of a Cayley graph and to synchronize all cells in all minimal paths starting at a given cell G (the "general") and leading to all cells at a given distance from G in a Cayley graph. We shall show that there exists a property of graphs that can lead to some difficulties in these algorithms: the existence of "culs-de-sac" (a cul-de-sac is a dead-end road). The decidability of the existence of "culs-de-sac" in a graph, as far as we know, is an open problem.

2 Cellular automata on Cayley graphs

Let us first recall the definitions of Cayley graphs and of cellular automata on Cayley graphs.

Definition 1. For every group presentation $G = \langle \mathcal{G} \mid \mathcal{R} \rangle$ (where $\mathcal{G}$ is the generating set and $\mathcal{R}$ is the relating set) there is an associated *Cayley graph* $\Gamma = (V, A)$: the vertices (V) correspond to the elements of the group, and the arcs (A) are colored with generators in the following way. There exists a directed edge colored with generator g from a vertex x to a vertex y, if and only if $y = xg$ in G.

Definition 2. Let x and y be two vertices in a Cayley graph Γ. The *distance* between x and y is the length of a minimal path from x to y and is denoted by $\mathrm{d}(x, y)$.

As Cayley graphs are graphical representations of groups, they are regular, hence their underlying graph can be considered as a communication graph of cellular automata. We put copies of the same finite automaton in the vertices of a Cayley graph Γ that we call *cells*. In order to compute its new state, each cell can communicate with some other, called *neighbor* cells. Without loss of generality (see [8]), we can suppose that these neighbors are some of the automata connected to the cell by an arc in Γ. A formal definition of cellular automata on Cayley graphs can be given as follows.

Definition 3. A *cellular automaton on a Cayley graph* $\Gamma = (V, A)$ is a 4-tuple $\mathcal{A} = (S, \Gamma, N, \delta)$ where

- S is a finite set, called the *set of states*,
- Γ is the *Cayley graph* of a finitely presented group
  $$G = \langle \mathcal{G} \mid \mathcal{R} \rangle = \langle g_1, g_2, \ldots, g_n \mid R_1, R_2, \ldots, R_k \rangle,$$
  We denote by $\mathcal{G}^{-1}$ the set of the inverse elements of $\mathcal{G}$.
- The *neighborhood* is $N = (w_1, w_2, \ldots, w_m)$ where $\forall i, w_i$ is in $\mathcal{G} \cup \mathcal{G}^{-1} \cup \{1\}$,
- $\delta : S^m \to S$ is the *local transition rule*.

The new state of each cell is computed via δ in parallel and synchronously. Thus we obtain the global behavior of the cellular automaton. We call a *configuration* an application c from G to S. The set C of all configurations is S^G. Thus, a cellular automaton transforms a configuration into another one:

$$\forall c \in C,\ \forall i \in G,\ \mathcal{A}(c)(i) = \delta(c(iw_1), c(iw_2) \ldots, c(iw_m)).$$

In the following, we only study cellular automata with full neighborhood (note that the neighborhood must be symmetrical, because synchronization requires two-way communications between cells), that is, the neighborhood contains all generators, all their inverses and the neutral element: $N = (g_1, g_2, \ldots, g_n, g_1^{-1}, g_2^{-1}, \ldots, g_n^{-1}, 1)$.

Definition 4. A state q is said to be *quiescent*, if $\delta(q, q, \ldots, q) = q$.

3 The FSSP on Cayley graphs

First of all, let us explain in more details the FSSP for a segment of automata. The goal is to give a cellular automaton with four distinguished states: G ("general"), F ("fire"), B ("border") and s_q (a quiescent state) which evolves as follows. At time 0, one cell is in state G, the cell at distance $n-1$ at his right is in state B and all other cells are in state s_q. At the end of the synchronization, all cells between the general and the border will enter in state F. All other cells stay in state s_q all along the evolution of the cellular automaton.

Let us consider now the Cayley graph Γ_1 of the group $\langle a \mid \emptyset \rangle$. This graph corresponds to the line $\mathbb{Z}$. Let $\mathcal{A}$ be a cellular automaton which is a minimal-time solution for the problem described above. It is clear that a cellular automaton $\mathcal{A}_1 = (S, \Gamma_1, N, \delta)$, where S is the set of states of $\mathcal{A}$, δ is the transition function of $\mathcal{A}$, and $N = (a, a^{-1}, 1)$, is a minimal-time solution for the same problem stated in terms of cellular automata on the Cayley graph Γ_1.

Let us remark that, in the solutions, the general "knows", from the beginning, that the cells to be synchronized are at his right-hand-side (resp. in the direction of the neighbor defined by the generator a) and that the cellular automaton does not depend on n.

Here, we shall give solutions for the following problems:

Problem 1 Synchronize all cells located on a minimal length path leading from a cell X to another cell Y in a Cayley graph.

Problem 2 Synchronize all cells located on a minimal length path leading from a cell X to all cells Y at a given distance from X in a Cayley graph.

3.1 Synchronization of all minimal paths between two cells

For most Cayley graphs, saying that Y is at the right-hand-side of X does not make sense. Hence, we shall suppose that, in the solutions for Problem 1, the general "does not know" in which direction to synchronize. He will try to do it in every possible directions in the neighborhood, hence we allow that cells not to be synchronized do not stay in the quiescent state during the evolution of the cellular automaton; we do not care about their states. Hence, the FSSP for Problem 1 can be formulated as follows.

Definition 5 (FSSP1). Let Γ be the Cayley graph of a group $G = \langle \mathcal{G} \mid \mathcal{R} \rangle$ and let u and v be two vertices of Γ. Let the distance between u and v be $n-1$. Let $\mathcal{P} = \{w \in \Gamma \mid w \text{ is on a minimal length path starting at } u \text{ ending at } v\}$. The *FSSP1* is to define a cellular automaton $\mathcal{A} = (S, \Gamma, N, \delta)$ with four distinguished states: s_q (a quiescent state), G (the "general"), B (the "border") and F (the "fire") such that, for all integers n, starting from the initial configuration c_0 defined by

$$c_0(u) = G,\ c_0(v) = B;\ \forall x \in \Gamma \setminus \{v, u\},\ c_0(x) = s_q$$

there exists a time t_F (the firing time) such that

$$\forall w \in \mathcal{P},\ c_{t_F}(w) = F;\ \forall v \in \Gamma,\ \forall 0 \leq t < t_F,\ c_t(v) \neq F.$$

First solution. Let us first remark that the solution that we present here is not a general solution to Problem 1. It works only for graphs that do not contain so-called "culs-de-sac" (we explain this phenomenon in section 1).

Before giving the formal algorithm of this solution, we explain the main idea. Let the distance between the general X and the border cell Y be $n-1$. From X, we build all minimal paths to Y, and then, we synchronize all cells of these paths simultaneously, as if they were segments of automata on the line: we shall consider that the general is at the leftmost end of all such paths; each of its neighbors (cells at distance 1) is in a minimal path (leading somewhere, not necessarily to Y), hence each of them will act as if it was the right-neighbor of the general in a segment of automata. We shall say that they are "right"-neighbors of the general. Conversely, the general will act as if it was the left-neighbor of all these cells at distance 1 in a segment of automata. Respectively, we shall say that the general is their "left"-neighbor. Then, at time 1, the general chooses its "right"-neighbors and all of its neighbors choose it as their "left"-neighbor. Notice that, at time 1 of the synchronization, only states of the general and its "right"-neighbors can be changed and that, in order to compute the new states of these neighbors, only the state of the general is needed. At time 2, cells at distance 2 can choose all their "left"-neighbors among cells being at distance 1, and conversely, cells at distance 1 can choose all their "right"-neighbors among cells being at distance 2. In order to compute the state of cells at distance 2 at time 2 of the synchronization, only the state of their "left"-neighbors is needed. In the minimal paths, these cells know their "left"-neighbors, and cells being nearer to the general already know both their "right"- and "left"-neighbors. Thus, the construction of minimal paths (that is, the choice of "right"- and "left"-neighbors) can be done in parallel with the synchronization.

The algorithm has two main parts shown in Figure 1a. The first part is executed in the part A of the synchronization (see Figure 1a). As we have described before, in parallel with the synchronization, we build all minimal paths of length $n-1$: cells choose their "left"- and "right"-neighbors. As there is not a unique cell at distance $n-1$, among these paths, there can be paths which lead to another vertex than Y. At the moment of this choice cells cannot know which are neighbors leading to Y: each cell has to choose all possible "right"-neighbors. The second main part is executed in part B of the synchronization: Y is reached at time $n-1$, so at this time, its "left"-neighbors know that they are in "good" paths. This information (by signal 2) flows back through all "left"-neighbors of cells to the general and reaches all cells being in a minimal path to Y: these are the cells which will be synchronized.

Let us describe in more details the algorithm presented above. We use a cellular automaton $\mathcal{A}_1$ which is a minimal-time solution for Γ_1. Let Γ' be a Cayley graph, we construct a cellular automaton $\mathcal{B} = (S', \Gamma', N', \delta')$ which synchronizes with the help of $\mathcal{A}_1$, all cells in all minimal paths between cell X (being in state G') and another cell Y (being in state B'). We define the set of states S' by

$$S' = \{active_0, active_1, active_2, active_3\} \times S \times M$$

where S is the set of states of $\mathcal{A}_1$ and M is a new finite set which will be used as a memory to keep in "right"- and "left"-neighbors. We consider that $G' = (active_1, G, \emptyset)$, $\tilde{q}' = (active_0, \tilde{q}, \emptyset)$ and $B' = (active_3, B, \emptyset)$. We do not define completely δ', we only give the way to construct transitions. We do not care about the states used for the synchronization on the line, we only study how to construct minimal paths from X to Y. The facts that

> (1) $\mathcal{A}_1$ solves the problem on the line (2) each cell can participate in the synchronization of minimal paths on which it can be found (3) if a cell occurs on two minimal paths then it occurs at the same position in them and (4) the S components of the states of cells on minimal paths being at the *same* distance from the general are the *same*

allow to say that $\mathcal{B}$ solves our synchronization problem on Γ'. In the following, we define only the evolution of the first and the third components of the states $(active_i,.,m)$.

The third component is used to keep in mind which cells among the neighbors of a cell must be considered as its "left"- and "right"-neighbors. As only a finite number of combinations are possible, M is a finite memory. We denote by $Right_u$ and $Left_u$ the set of "right"- and "left"-neighbors of a cell u, and the component M, at a given time, represents these two sets. Until they are not defined, their values are $\emptyset$. At the beginning, a cell X is in state G', and another one Y is in state B'; all other cells are in state $\tilde{q}'$.

ALGORITHM 1 (Choosing neighbors – first version): Each cell u, executes at each time unit the following process:

Case 1: u is in the $active_0$ state and there exists a set of cells V being in $active_1$ state in its neighborhood: $Left_u := V$; u enters the $active_1$ state.
Case 2: u is in the $active_1$ state and there exists a set of cells V being in $active_0$ state in its neighborhood: $Right_u := V$; u enters the $active_2$ state.
Case 3: u is in the $active_1$ state and there exists a set of cells V being in $active_3$ state in its neighborhood: $Right_u := V$; u enters the $active_2$ state.
Case 4: u is in the $active_3$ state and there exists a set of cells V being in the $active_1$ state in its neighborhood: $Left_u := V$.
Case 5: u is in the $active_2$ state and some of his "right"-neighbors are in the $active_3$ state; the others (forming a set denoted by V, possibly empty) are in the $active_2$ state:
u use the second component of the state of the $active_3$ cells for computing its transition in the synchronization process, u enters the $active_3$ state; $Right_u := Right_u \setminus V$.

Case 6: If u is not in any previous cases, then, if it is in a quiescent ($\tilde{q}'$) state or is the border and it does not change, otherwise it has well defined "right"- and "left"-neighbors and it continues the synchronization process on the second component of its state.

Cases 1-4 occur in the first part (A) of the algorithm, and cases 5-6 in the second part (B). Notice that a cell becomes $active_1$ at the same time when it is reached by signal 1, and becomes $active_3$ when it is reached by signal 2 (see Figure 1b).

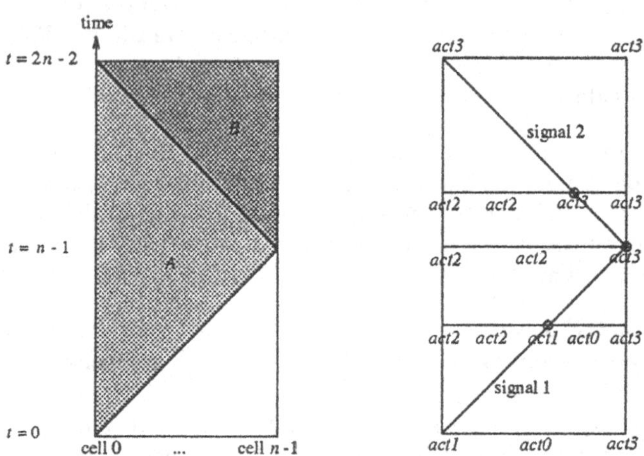

Fig. 1. Zones of the synchronization and first state-components.

Clearly, at the end of the synchronization, all $active_3$ cells will be synchronized: they are exactly the cells being in minimal paths from X to Y. Any classical algorithm can be applied at the same time, so the synchronization needs $2n-2$ time steps ($2n-2$ is also the time, when the general can become $active_3$ for the first time). This time is optimal, otherwise we could synchronize a segment of automata in less than the optimal time.

Unfortunately, this algorithm does not consider the case when there exist cells such that after becoming $active_1$, in their neighborhoods there are no cells being in a quiescent state. It is a problem, because if it is the case, then it is possible that a cell has two right-neighbors in different states: which one should be chosen for computing its new state? This algorithm works correctly only if all cells to be synchronized that are at the same distance from the general are in the same state. Before solving this problem, let us study this phenomenon.

"Culs-de-sac". First of all, let us see the following example.

Example 1 (*No "right"-neighbors*):

Let $G = \langle a, b, c \mid b = a^3, c = a^4 \rangle$. Let $X = 1$ and $Y = a^9$. We want to synchronize all cells being in minimal paths from X to Y. See Figure 2.

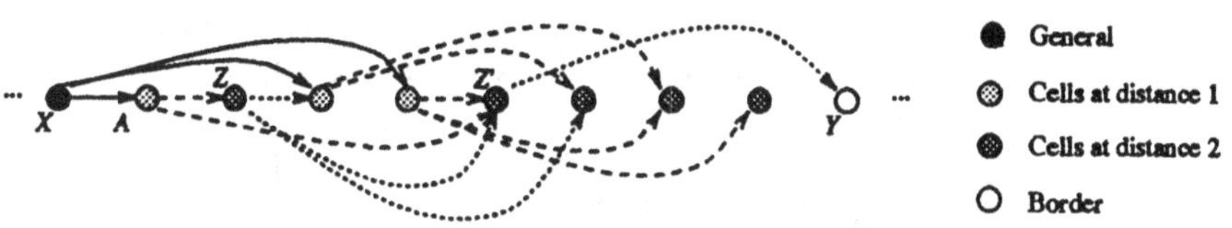

Fig. 2. Right-neighbors.

Arrows go from a cell to its "right"-neighbors defined by generators. We do not illustrate the arrows going to the "right"-neighbors defined by the inverse of the generators. In the first step, the general has all cells at distance 1 as "right"-neighbors. In the second step, we illustrate by dotted arrows the "right"-neighbors of all cells being at distance 1: these are cells at distance 2. Then, we see that for cell Z, there is no possible "right"-neighbor. It causes a problem: Z is the "right"-neighbor of cell A, but A has also a second right-neighbor Z', which, not as Z, has a "right"-neighbor (Y). It means, that in the rest of the computation, the two "right"-neighbors of A can be in different states: which one A should choose? We shall say that Z is a "cul-de-sac" of order 1 (it is at some distance n from the origin and has no neighbors at distance $n+1$).

Definition 6. A cell at distance n from the origin is a *cul-de-sac of order k* if the ball of radius k centered on this cell is included in the ball of radius $n+k-1$ centered on the origin.

The existence of "culs-de-sac" is a property of graphs and is independent of colorings. We do not know which graphs have such "culs-de-sac", but we know that they can occur even in planar graphs. See [9] for some examples.

Second – modified – solution. In order to give a solution for Problem 1 which is correct even if there exist "culs-de-sac" in the graph, we modify the set of states of $\mathcal{B}$ by adding a new state † representing the "death" of a cell:

$$S' = \{active_0, active_1, active_2, active_3, \dagger\} \times S \times M.$$

Then, each cell u, executes at each time unit the following process:

ALGORITHM 2 (Choosing neighbors – second version):

Case 1: u is in the $active_0$ state and there exists a set of cells V being in the $active_1$ state in its neighborhood: $Left_u := V$; u enters the $active_1$ state.

Case 2: u is in the $active_1$ state and there exists a set of cells V being in the $active_0$ state in its neighborhood: $Right_u := V$; u enters the $active_2$ state.

Case 3: u is in the $active_1$ state and it has no neighbors in the $active_0$ state: u enters the † state.

Case 4: u is in the $active_2$ or the $active_3$ state, but if it is $active_2$, then it has not any $active_3$ neighbors. Let V the set of its dead "right"-neighbors:
u uses the second component of the state of its non-dead "right"-neighbors in order to compute its transition in the synchronization process; $Right_u = Right_u \setminus V$.

Case 5: u has only dead "right"-neighbors; u dies and enters in † state.

Case 6: u is in the *active*$_1$ state and there exists a set of cells V being in the *active*$_3$ state in its neighborhood: $Right_u := V$; u enters the *active*$_2$ state.

Case 7: u is in the *active*$_3$ state and there exists a set of cells V being in the *active*$_1$ state in its neighborhood: $Left_u := V$.

Case 8: u is in the *active*$_2$ state, and it has *active*$_3$ "right"–neighbors. Some of its "right"-neighbors (set V) are in the *active*$_2$ state, and some others (but not all) are died (set W):
u uses the second component of the state of its non-dead *active*$_3$ "right"–neighbors in order to compute its transition in the synchronization process; $Right_u = Right_u \setminus (V \cup W)$.

Case 9: If u is not in any previous cases, then, if it is in a quiescent ($\tilde{q}'$) state or is the border and it does not change, otherwise it has well defined "right"- and "left"-neighbors and it continues the synchronization process on the second component of its state.

With this modification, all "right"-("left"-)neighbors of a cell have the same states which are always well computed. See the different steps of the algorithm for the CA of Example 1 in Figure 3.

At time $t = 2$, every cell at distance 1 can choose a "right"-neighbor and the states of all cells are well computed. Hence, at time $t = 3$, the states of all cells are well computed except Z who becomes *dead* and B who is not in any minimal path from X to Y. All cells at distance 2 becomes *active*$_3$ except Z (*dead*) and B (stays *active*$_2$). At time $t = 4$, for computing the new states of cells, the states of Z and B are ignored and they are not "right"-neighbors of any cell anymore. At time $t = 5$, all other cells are synchronized.

Remark, that the state of a cell becoming *dead* at time T is well computed until time $T-1$, hence the states of all of its neighbors are well computed until time T. This is also true for cells never becoming *active*$_3$: until all cells at the same distance are *active*$_2$, their states are the same, if some of them become *active*$_3$ at time T, the states are the same until time $T-1$, and the states of all of their neighbors are well computed until time T. From time $T+1$ on, only the well-computed states are considered.

4 Synchronization of balls in Cayley graphs

Let us now study Problem 2. In this case, the general must synchronize in every possible directions in its neighborhood. Hence, we can require that in a solution, all cells not to be synchronized stay in a quiescent state all along the evolution of the cellular automaton. Formally, the FSSP for Problem 2 can be stated as follows.

Definition 7 (FSSP2). Let Γ be the Cayley graph of a group $G = \langle \mathcal{G} \mid \mathcal{R} \rangle$, let u be a vertex of Γ and n an integer. Let $\mathcal{B} = \{b \in \Gamma \mid \mathrm{d}(u,b) = n-1\}$ and $\mathcal{P} = \{w \in \Gamma \mid w$ is on a minimal length path starting at u and ending at a cell b in $\mathcal{B}\}$. The *FSSP2* is to define a cellular automaton $\mathcal{A} = (S, \Gamma, N, \delta)$ with four distinguished states: s_q (a quiescent state), G (the "general"), B (the "border") and F (the "fire") such that, for all integer n, starting from the initial configuration c_0 defined by

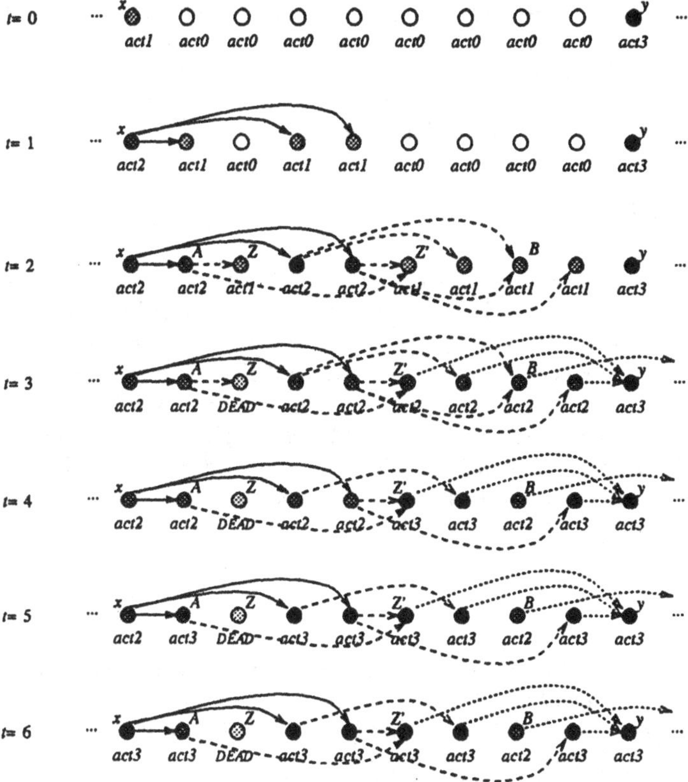

Fig. 3. Different steps of Algorithm 2.

$$c_0(u) = G;\ \forall v \in \mathcal{B},\ c_0(v) = B;\ \forall x \in \Gamma \setminus (\mathcal{B} \cup \{u\}),\ c_0(x) = s_q$$

there exists a time t_F (the firing time) such that

$$\forall w \in \mathcal{P},\ c_{t_F}(w) = F;\ \forall w \notin \mathcal{P},\ c_{t_F}(w) = s_q;\ \forall v \in \Gamma,\ \forall 0 \le t < t_F,\ c_t(v) \neq F.$$

If there is no "culs-de-sac" in the graph, then such a cellular automaton synchronizes all cells of the ball of radius $n-1$ centered in u.

In order to solve this problem, Algorithm 2 can be used with more border cells. The synchronization needs $2n-2$ time units in all cases. However, the set of states can be big. Sometimes, for Problem 2, we do not need to keep in mind all "right"- and "left"-neighbors of a cell. Let us see now for what kind of graphs this is the case.

Condition 1: Let Γ be a Cayley graph and u a vertex of Γ. Let $\mathrm{d}(1,u) = k$. Then, there exists a vertex v among the neighbor vertices of u such that $\mathrm{d}(1,v) = k+1$ (Γ has no "cul-de-sac").

In other words, this condition says that, during the synchronization, every cell can choose at least one "right"-neighbor.

Theorem 8. *Let Γ be a Cayley graph. In order to solve Problem 2 on Γ, it is sufficient to choose exactly one "right"- and one "left"-neighbor for each cell, if and only if Condition 1 holds.*

The proof of this theorem can be found in [9].

5 Conclusion

In this paper, we have given a generalization of the FSSP on the line for Cayley graphs. A natural question is whether one can give algorithms for synchronizing all cells of a ball in a Cayley graph, even if there are some "culs-de-sac" in the graph. If their order is bounded, then we can modify the original solutions for the line such that the answer is positive. But there also exist Cayley graphs where this order is not bounded, see for example the Cayley graph of the group $G = \langle a, b, c \mid ab = ba, cac^{-1} = ab, cbc^{-1} = ab^2 \rangle$ (Poincaré's group). Another question to answer is to characterize graphs having "culs-de-sac". As far as we know, it is an open problem.

References

1. R. Balzer. A 8 state minimal time solution to the Firing Squad Synchronization Problem. *Information and Control*, 10:22–42, 1967.
2. C. Culik. Variation of the Firing Squad Synchronization Problem. *Information Processing Letter*, pages 152–157, 1989.
3. A. Machí and F. Mignosi. Garden of Eden configurations for cellular automata on Cayley graphs of groups. *SIAM Journal on Discrete Mathematics*, 6(1):44–56, 1993.
4. J. Mazoyer. A six states minimal time solution to the Firing Squad Synchronization Problem. *Theoretical Computer Science*, 50:183–238, 1987.
5. F.R. Moore and G.G. Langdon. A generalized firing squad problem. *Information and Control*, (12):212–220, 1968.
6. D.E. Muller and P.E. Schupp. Pushdown automata, ends, second-order logic and reachability problems. In *13th Annual ACM Symp. on the Theory of Computing*, Milwaukee, 1981.
7. A. Holliger P. Rosenstiehl, J.R. Fiksel. *Graph Theory and Computing*, chapter Intelligent graphs: Networks of finite automata capable of solving graph problems. Lectures in Computer Science. R. C. Read, academic press edition, 1972.
8. Zs. Róka. *Cellular automata on Cayley graphs.* PhD thesis, Ecole Normale Supérieure de Lyon, France, July 1994.
9. Zs. Róka. The Firing Squad Synchronization Problem on Cayley graphs. *preprint*, 1995.
10. H. Szwerinsky. Time optimal solution for the Firing Squad Synchronization Problem for n-dimensional rectangles with the general at any position. *Theoretical Computer Science*, 19:305–320, 1982.

Solving Cheap Graph Problems on Meshes

Jop F. Sibeyn[1] and Michael Kaufmann[2]

[1] Max-Planck-Institut für Informatik, Im Stadtwald, 66123 Saarbrücken, Germany. E-mail: jopsi@mpi-sb.mpg.de.
[2] Fakultät Informatik, Universität Tübingen, Sand 13, 72076 Tübingen, Germany. E-mail: mk@informatik.uni-tuebingen.de

Abstract. Efficient mesh algorithms exist for 'expensive' graph problems like transitive closure and computing *all* shortest paths, taking $\mathcal{O}(n)$ time on an $n \times n$ mesh for a graph with n vertices. This is work-optimal. On the other hand, there are so far no efficient algorithms for 'cheap' graph problems like finding the connected components, constructing a minimum spanning tree, or finding a path between a pair of vertices. These problems are cheap in the sense that sequentially they can be solved in time (almost) linear in n and m, where m is the number of edges.
In this paper we show that the mentioned cheap problems can be solved on an $\sqrt{N} \times \sqrt{N}$ mesh in $\mathcal{O}((n \cdot m/N)^{1/2} + \log n \cdot (\sqrt{N} + m/N))$ time. We derive a lower bound of $\Omega((n \cdot m/N)^{1/2} + \sqrt{N} + m/N)$. Hence, the algorithms have optimal time order for most n, m and N. The algorithms are work-optimal to within a factor $\log n$ for $N \leq m/n$.

1 Introduction

Fundamental Graph Problems. One of the central graph problems is the determination of their connected components. In our case, the graph $G = (V, E)$ is undirected, has $n = |V|$ vertices, and $m = |E| \geq n/2$ edges. The connected components of G are the maximal subsets of V such that any two vertices in a subset are connected by a path in G. Other important problems are the construction of a minimal spanning tree of G or finding paths between pairs of vertices. The ratio m/n is called the **density** of the graph. If the density is around 1 (close to n), the graph is said to be **sparse** (**dense**).

Sequentially these problems can easily be solved in $\mathcal{O}(n + m)$ or $\mathcal{O}(n + m \cdot \log n)$ time using (variants of) breadth-first search. However, in parallel they are much harder. A connected-components algorithm can also be used to construct a minimum spanning tree or to find a path between a pair of vertices.

Meshes. Various models for parallel computers have been considered. Because of their regularity, scalability, and programmability, meshes of various dimensions are among the most studied machines with a fixed interconnection network. In a d-dimensional **mesh** consisting of N PUs, the processing units, **PUs**, are laid out in a d-dimensional $N^{1/d} \times \cdots \times N^{1/d}$ grid, in which a PU is connected to its (at most) $2 \cdot d$ immediate neighbors.

Every PU has its own local memory, which is assumed to be of limited size. In our case, for a graph with n vertices and m edges, every PU can store $\mathcal{O}((n+m)/N)$ entries of the graph.

The PUs communicate by the exchange of **packets**. In our case, a packet consists of the information concerning one vertex or edge, plus some information for directing it. The PUs can communicate with all their neighbors at the same time: in a single step they can send and receive at most $2 \cdot d$ packets. If on a real mesh this assumption does not hold, then one step of our mesh can trivially be split into several more elementary steps.

The performance of an algorithm is measured in the first place by the maximal number of communication steps T_{comm} required, and by the queue size Q that may occur during its execution. Other quality parameters are the maximal number T_{comp} of computation steps a PU may make, and the work $W = T \cdot N$. Here $T = T_{\text{comm}} + T_{\text{comp}}$. An algorithm is work-optimal if $W = \mathcal{O}(T_{\text{seq}})$, where T_{seq} is the sequential time consumption.

Previous Work. Many researchers investigated parallel algorithms for the connected-components problem. Most attention has gone to algorithms for the PRAM. A fundamental algorithm, which serves as a basis for most investigations, including ours, was given by Hirschberg et al. [8]. Subsequently, better and specialized algorithms were developed for the various PRAM models and for the special case of sparse graphs [3, 18]. For more references and an overview of the merits of each paper we refer to [9, pp. 259–262]. Here we only mention the algorithm by Han and Wagner [7], which has running time $\mathcal{O}((m + n \cdot \log n)/N + \log^2 n)$.

For the mesh there are several algorithms, the first by Nassimi and Sahni [12]. They essentially give an implementation of the algorithm of [8] on the mesh. On an $n \times n$ mesh $T = \mathcal{O}(D \cdot n \cdot \log n)$, where D equals the maximal degree of G. Atallah and Kosaraju [2] extend and improve the results of this paper. Among other things, they prove that the connected components of a graph with n vertices can be computed on an $n \times n$ mesh with $T = \mathcal{O}(n)$. The problem has also been considered by Hambrusch [6]. The results of this paper ($T = n^{3/2}$, with n PUs and $\mathcal{O}(n)$ total area) are hard to compare, as the data are processed here in a systolic fashion. As far as we could check, there are no more recent papers on the connected-components problem on meshes. A more recent algorithm for the hypercube is given by Ryu and JáJá [13]. It is based on the PRAM algorithm of Shiloach and Vishkin [18], and achieves the optimal time order for $N \leq n^{1-\epsilon}$ for any $\epsilon > 0$.

Greiner [5] analyzes the performance of several algorithms in practice. He also provides references to other papers describing implementations, most of which are for two- and three-dimensional meshes. However, these papers do not provide substantial theoretical contributions.

The connected components can be determined by first computing the transitive closure of a graph using the Warshall algorithm (see [2]). On an $n \times n$ mesh this gives $T = \mathcal{O}(n)$ and $W = \mathcal{O}(n^3)$. As sequentially the problem takes $\mathcal{O}(n + m)$ time, this is a very poor performance, particularly for sparse graphs. Once a spanning tree is known, the algorithm of Atallah and Hambrusch [1] can be applied, taking $\mathcal{O}(\sqrt{n})$ time on an $\sqrt{n} \times \sqrt{n}$ mesh, but how is a spanning tree computed?

This Paper. We provide a thorough analysis of the connected-components problems on meshes. We incorporate the many new ideas that have evolved in the past few years, and add numerous ideas specific to the problem.

For a two-dimensional mesh with N PUs, we prove a lower bound of $\Omega((n \cdot m/N)^{1/2} + \sqrt{N} + m/N)$. We present an algorithm with: $T_{\text{comm}} = \mathcal{O}((n \cdot m/N)^{1/2} + \log n \cdot \sqrt{N})$ and $T_{\text{comp}} = \mathcal{O}(\log^2 n \cdot m/N)$. The hidden constants are moderate, and the algorithm might be practical. The algorithm has optimal time order for all $m/n \cdot \log^4 n \leq N \leq \sqrt{n \cdot m}/\log n$. For $N \leq m/n$, the computation time is only $\mathcal{O}(\log n \cdot m/N)$: the algorithm is work-optimal to within a factor $\log n$ for these N. The same bounds hold for computing a spanning tree and for finding a path between a pair of vertices. Similar results are derived for higher dimensional meshes.

Comparing with earlier results we see that for the first time the performance depends on n, m and N. This overcomes the unrealistic assumption that the graph and the network are the same size. In practical applications the parallel systems are small in comparision with the problem solved on them. Some key results are summarized in Table 1. To see how good the achieved bounds really are, consider

	N	T	W
[2]	n^2	n	n^3
[6]	n	$n^{3/2}$	$n^{5/2}$
now	$\sqrt{n \cdot m}/\log n$	$(n \cdot m)^{1/4} \cdot \sqrt{\log n}$	$(n \cdot m)^{3/4}/\sqrt{\log n}$
now	m/n	n	m

Table 1. Time consumptions for the connected components problem. Constants are omitted.

the basic problem of routing $m \geq N$ keys on an $\sqrt{N} \times \sqrt{N}$ mesh. This requires $\Theta(m/\sqrt{N})$ steps. For all $m = \omega(n)$, this is of a larger order than the time required by our algorithm to solve the connected-components problem for a graph with n vertices and m edges.

Method. Like most of the earlier algorithms, our algorithm goes back to the scheme of Hirschberg [8]. Initially each vertex constitutes a component by itself. Components are identified with the index of their smallest vertex. Then the following steps are repeated $\log n$ times:

1. Hook a component i_2 onto component i_1 if $i_2 > i_1$, and there is an edge from a vertex in component i_2 to a vertex in component i_1.
2. Contract the thus constructed (pseudo) tree of connected components.

We implement Step 1 by a 'multiple-minimum computation'. In most cases this step determines the running time of the algorithm. Its cost is relatively high because of the small bisection width of a mesh. For Step 2, there are two possibilities: (1) Pointer jumping (see Section 5.1), a technique commonly known from the development of PRAM algorithms, is suited for practical implementation because of its simplicity. However, if G is sparse, the running time is $\Omega(\log n)$ times larger than optimal. (2) We prefer a more elaborate method, involving the Euler-tour technique (see Section 5.2). The Euler-tour technique requires the application of several subroutines, one of which is list ranking.

Contents. The remainder of the paper is organized as follows: after preliminaries we analyze some basic problems. Then we show how pointer-jumping and the Euler-tour technique can be performed efficiently on the mesh. In Section 6 we discuss the connected-components problem. Finally, we extend our ideas to higher dimensional meshes, to the computation of spanning trees and to the problem of finding a path between two vertices. Due to space requirements we omit most of the proofs, especially for lower bounds and multi-dimensional meshes. They can be found in [16].

2 Preliminaries

A **pseudotree** is a rooted tree with a self-loop at its root. A set of pseudotrees is called **pseudoforest**.

Indexings. In a two-dimensional mesh, the PU at position (i,j), $0 \leq i,j < \sqrt{N}$, is denoted $P_{i,j}$. Here position $(0,0)$ lies in the upper-left corner. There are several natural index functions I, giving the PUs an index in $\{0,1,\ldots,N-1\}$. In the row-major indexing $I(P_{i,j}) = i\cdot\sqrt{N}+j$. In the column-major indexing $I(P_{i,j}) = i+j\cdot\sqrt{N}$. In the snake-like row-major indexing, the indices in the odd rows run from right to left. For a given indexing, P_i, denotes the PU with index i.

Data Organization. Lower and upper bounds for the connected components problem essentially depend on the organization of the data. For PRAM algorithms, it is commonly assumed that the graph is given either in the form of an adjacency list or as an adjacency matrix. This is quite restrictive, and may limit the applicability of an algorithm as a subroutine. For our algorithms, the input may be completely arbitrary; we only assume that the data are evenly distributed:

Assumption 1 *Initially each PU holds the information related to m/N edges.*

Work Allocation. The work specifically related to a vertex i is performed by $P_{i \bmod N}$. The work related to an edge is performed by the PU in which this edge is stored. The necessary data are stored accordingly.

Routing and Sorting. There are numerous results in packet routing and sorting on meshes. We cite only those which will be used in the sequel, namely for k-k routing and sorting [11, 10, 15], and for the more general k-l routing [17]. In k-l routing, each PU sends up to k packets and receives at most l packets. In a sorting problem all packets are provided with a key from a totally ordered set. They must be rearranged such that eventually they will appear in sorted order with respect to the indexing of the mesh. The following asymptotically optimal results have been achieved:

Lemma 1 [11, 10, 15] *k-k routing and sorting on d-dimensional meshes can be performed deterministically in $(1+o(1))\cdot\max\{2\cdot d\cdot N^{1/d}, k\cdot N^{1/d}/2\}$ steps.*

Lemma 2 [17] *Routing k-l distributions on two-dimensional meshes takes $(1+o(1))\cdot(k\cdot l\cdot N)^{1/2}/2+\mathcal{O}(\min\{k,l\}\cdot N^{1/2})$.*

List Ranking. We need some results of list ranking on meshes.

A linked list, hereafter just **list**, consists of a set of nodes together with a successor function s. For a node i, $s(i)$ either gives the index of another node or has value 0. For every value j there is at most one i with $s(i)=j$. In the **list-ranking problem**, we have a set of lists, consisting of n nodes in total. The task is to determine the **rank** of every node: the distance to the last node on the list. Actually, we only need to identify the last node on the list. We call this **list rooting**. If there is more than one list, then list rooting is as hard as list ranking.

There are several different approaches for the list-ranking problem on meshes, e.g. [1], [4], [14]. On a $\sqrt{n}\times\sqrt{n}$ mesh they require $\mathcal{O}(\sqrt{n})$ steps, which is the optimal time *order*. The most practical algorithm [14] requires about $120\cdot\sqrt{n}$ steps, the others even more. If n/N is large, then the performance is better:

Lemma 3 [14] *List ranking and rooting on d-dimensional $N^{1/d}\times\cdots\times N^{1/d}$ meshes can be performed in $11\cdot n/N^{1-1/d}+\mathcal{O}(d\cdot N^{1/d})$ steps for lists of total length n.*

3 Multiple Minimum

We consider a central subtask. Let m numbers be evenly distributed over the N PUs of a network. Suppose that each number is colored with a color from $\{0, 1, \ldots, C-1\}$, and that we want to determine the minima of the numbers with the same colors. This problem we call the **multiple-minimum problem**, *mmp*(C, m, N).

Lower Bound By a bisection-bound-like argument we get a lower bound on the number of routing steps required by *mmp*(C, m, N):

Lemma 4 *On a two-dimensional mesh mmp*(C, m, N) *takes at least* $3/8 \cdot (C \cdot m/N)^{1/2}$ *steps. On d-dimensional meshes it takes* $(1 - 1/2^d) \cdot m \cdot (C \cdot N/m)^{1/d}/(d \cdot N)$ *steps.*

Algorithm. Our algorithm for the *mmp* consists of two phases. During Phase 1 the algorithm operates in non-overlapping submeshes that hold precisely C packets. All submeshes are indexed by the same (e.g. row-major) indexing. In the second phase, the obtained partial results are combined.

The following steps are performed in each $(C \cdot N/m)^{1/2} \times (C \cdot N/m)^{1/2}$ submesh:

Algorithm MULTIPLE-MINIMUM

1. Sort the packets lexicographically, first by color and then by value, in snake-like row-major order.

2. Eliminate all packets that are not the smallest of their color.

3. Route the surviving ones: the packet with color c to the PU with index $c \bmod (N \cdot C/m)$ in the submesh.

Lemma 5 *Phase 1 takes* $(1+o(1)) \cdot (C \cdot m/N)^{1/2}$ *steps. Hereafter the PU with index i within its submesh,* $0 \leq i < N \cdot C/m$ *holds the minima of the packets with color* $i + j \cdot N \cdot C/m$*, for all* $0 \leq j < m/N$.

In Phase 2 the results of the submeshes are repeatedly 'merged': the following step is repeated for $x = 2 \cdot (N \cdot C/m)^{1/2}, 4 \cdot (N \cdot C/m)^{1/2}, \ldots, \sqrt{N}$:

4. Perform within each $x \times x$ submesh routing and elimination operations such that afterwards the PU with index i within its submesh, $0 \leq i < x^2$, holds the minima of the packets with color $i + j \cdot x^2$, for all $0 \leq j < C/x^2$.

The routing operations can easily be solved optimally, while the elimination of the non-minima are trivial operations. No edge contention occur and we achieve

Lemma 6 *Phase 2 takes fewer than* $3/4 \cdot (C \cdot m/N)^{1/2} + 2 \cdot \sqrt{N}$ *steps. Hereafter* P_i, $0 \leq i < N$ *holds the minima of the packets with colors* $i + j \cdot N$*, for all* $0 \leq j < m/N$.

Theorem 1 MULTIPLE-MINIMUM *solves mmp*(C, m, N) *on a two-dimensional mesh in fewer than* $(1\frac{3}{4} + o(1)) \cdot (C \cdot m/N)^{1/2} + 2 \cdot \sqrt{N}$ *steps. The maximal occurring queue size can be bounded to* $m/N + \mathcal{O}(1)$.

MULTIPLE-MINIMUM can easily be extended to meshes of arbitrary dimension:

Theorem 2 MULTIPLE-MINIMUM *solves mmp*(C, m, N) *on a d-dimensional mesh in fewer than* $(1 + \frac{2^d - 1}{d \cdot (2^d - 2)} + o(1)) \cdot (C \cdot N/m)^{1/d} \cdot m/N + d \cdot N^{1/d}$ *steps.*

Performance Ratio. Comparing the results of Lemma 4 and Theorem 1 we get

Lemma 7 *For two-dimensional meshes, the performance ratio of* MULTIPLE-MINIMUM *is* $17/3$*, and for d-dimensional meshes, the performance ratio is* $d + o(d)$.

4 Concurrent Read

Concurrent read and write are important operations when simulating a PRAM step on a network. In the **concurrent read problem**, $crp(n, s, N)$, s data items are stored in a network with N PUs, and n items have to be read. Every PU requests at most $\lceil n/N \rceil$ and stores at most $\lceil s/N \rceil$ items. Here we give an algorithm for the *crp*. It is similar to the above algorithms. Concurrent write can be solved analogously.

Lemma 8 *$crp(n, s, N)$ requires $\Omega((n \cdot s/N)^{1/2} + \sqrt{N})$ steps.*

We show that the lower bound can be matched up to a constant factor.

Algorithm CONCURRENT-READ

1. Sort the requests on the indices of the requested items in snake-like order.
2. Determine for every request for a data item e whether it is the one residing in the PU with the lowest index among the requests for e. These are the superrequests.
3. Route the superrequests to the PUs where the requested items reside, and then route the requested items back to the superrequests.
4. Spread the requested items from the superrequests over the other requests for the same items.
5. Route the requested items to the PUs that requested them.

Theorem 3 CONCURRENT-READ *solves $crp(n, s, N)$ on a two-dimensional mesh, in $(1 + o(1)) \cdot (n \cdot s/N)^{1/2} + \mathcal{O}(n/\sqrt{N} + \sqrt{N})$ steps.*

Proof: Step 1 and 6 are n/N-n/N sorting operations and essentially take $n/(2 \cdot \sqrt{N})$ steps each. Step 2 takes 1 step. Step 3 consists of n/N-s/N and s/N-n/N routings, and essentially takes $(n \cdot s/N)^{1/2}/2$ steps. Step 5 takes $2 \cdot \sqrt{N}$. □

For the special cases $n = s$ and $s \leq n$, we can derive even easier methods and get:

Theorem 4 *$crp(n, n, N)$ can be solved in $(2 + o(1)) \cdot n/N^{1/2} + \mathcal{O}(\sqrt{N})$ steps. For $s \leq n$, $crp(n, s, N)$ can be solved in $(2\frac{3}{4} + o(1)) \cdot (n \cdot s/N)^{1/2} + \mathcal{O}(\sqrt{N})$ steps.*

5 Tree Rooting

We need one more basic subroutine for the connected-components algorithm. Suppose that we have a pseudoforest consisting of n vertices, and let the parent of a vertex i be given by $s(i)$. In the **tree-rooting problem**, $trp(n, N)$, using N PUs for each vertex the root of the pseudotree has to be determined in which it lies (we do not require that $s(i)$ is *set* to the root). Distance and bisection bound arguments give:

Lemma 9 *If on a two-dimensional mesh, vertex i and the value of $s(i)$ are stored in $P_{i \bmod N}$, then $trp(n, N)$ takes at least $\max\{n/(4 \cdot \sqrt{N}), 2 \cdot \sqrt{N}\}$ steps.*

5.1 Pointer Jumping

With CONCURRENT-READ as a subroutine we can implement tree rooting on a mesh by the well-known technique of pointer-jumping [9]. Because $s = n$, and we may assume that $s(i)$ is stored in $P_{i \bmod N}$, this gives a $crp(n, n, N)$. Hence,

Theorem 5 *On a mesh $trp(n, N)$ can be solved with* POINTER-JUMPING *in $\log n \cdot ((3/2 + o(1)) \cdot n/\sqrt{N} + \mathcal{O}(\sqrt{N}))$ steps.*

By the small constant in the leading term of Theorem 5, and because for all practical purposes $\log n < 30$, the simple pointer-jumping technique performs reasonably, although far from optimally. To achieve the optimal time order $\mathcal{O}(n/\sqrt{N})$, we were not able to use pointer jumping, but the Euler-tour technique [19] [9, Sec. 3.2]. Here we summarize its main ideas, and then describe an implementation on the mesh.

5.2 Euler-Tour Technique

Tour Construction. The idea is to replace every edge (i, j), by two directed edges: (i, j) and (j, i). For every vertex i, the incident edges (i, j) are cyclically ordered, defining a successor function *suc* for every edge: if, according to the order of the edges starting in i, edge (i, j') follows after (i, j) (cyclically), then $suc(j, i) = (i, j')$. Following the edges in the '*suc*' - order gives one Euler tour for every tree. These tours are turned into paths by cutting them open. Determining the ranks of the edges leads to efficient PRAM algorithms for many important graph problems.

Mesh Algorithm. We describe how this transformation can be performed on meshes. The lists start with edges leaving from a root and end with edges pointing to a root. For every edge, identity and memory position of its successor are determined.

Algorithm EULER-PATHS

1. For every undirected edge (i, j), $i \neq j$, create two directed edges (i, j) and (j, i).
2. Sort copies of all directed edges (i, j), in snake-like row-major order, lexicographically on the i and j values. Mark where they come from.
3. As a result of the sorting, the edges leaving from any vertex i are stored in consecutive memory positions. This defines an *order* on these edges. Send a packet from the last edge leaving from i to the first.
4. For all (i, j), $i \neq j$, let j' be such that $order(i, j') = order(i, j) - 1$. Send a packet containing (i, j) and its memory position to the PU holding (j', i).
5. For all (i, j), $i \neq j$, if (i, j) receives a packet (j, i'), then $suc(i, j) := (j, i')$, else if no packet is received, then $suc(i, j) = 0$: (i, j) is a final node.

Lemma 10 *Given a pseudoforest with n vertices,* EULER-PATHS *creates a set of linear lists with $2 \cdot n$ nodes in total. On a two-dimensional mesh with N PUs this takes $(2 + o(1)) \cdot n/\sqrt{N} + \mathcal{O}(\sqrt{N})$ steps.*

Proof: Step 2 and 4 are sorting problems in which every PU holds $2 \cdot n/N$ packets. They take $(1 + o(1)) \cdot n/\sqrt{N} + \mathcal{O}(\sqrt{N})$ steps each. We implement Step 3 as follows: From every last edge (i, j), one packet is sent along the row towards the PUs with smaller indices. Another packet is sent along the column until it comes to a PU without any further edges leaving from i. In every row it reaches, a packet is sent, in the manner of the first packet. The horizontal and vertical moves take at most $\sqrt{N} - 1$ steps each. □

By the Euler-tour technique, tree rooting is transformed to list rooting. Lemma 10 shows that setting up these lists on meshes is only four times as expensive as an $n/\sqrt{N}$-$n/\sqrt{N}$ routing. Combining with Lemma 3,

Theorem 6 *$trp(n, N)$ can be solved by applying* EULER-PATHS *and list rooting in $13 \cdot n/\sqrt{N} + \mathcal{O}(\sqrt{N})$ steps.*

The full range of applications of the Euler-tour technique can be obtained with a comparable time consumption.

6 Connected Components

Let $ccp(n, m, N)$ denote the problem of computing the connected components of a graph with n vertices and m edges, using N PUs.

6.1 Lower Bounds

The idea for lower bound of the multiple-minimum problem also applies here:

Lemma 11 *We consider $ccp(n, m, N)$ on a two-dimensional mesh. If the data are stored arbitrarily only satisfying Assumption 1, then the number of steps is at least*

$$\max\{\left(\frac{(n - 1/2 - \sqrt{2 \cdot m}) \cdot m}{48 \cdot N}\right)^{1/2}, 2 \cdot \sqrt{N}\}.$$

Corollary 1 *For $m \leq n^2/4$, $ccp(n, m, N)$ requires at least $(n \cdot m/N)^{1/2}/13$ steps.*

6.2 PRAM Algorithm

First we give an approach based on the PRAM algorithm from [8]. There are n vertices.

We use a function $c : \{0, \ldots, n-1\} \to \{0, \ldots, n-1\}$. Initially $c(i) = i$, for all $0 \leq i < n$. A **supervertex** is a vertex i, with $c(i) = i$. Eventually, every vertex i in a component of the graph will have $c(i)$ equal to the index of the smallest vertex in its component. The following procedure is iterated until no more changes occur:

Algorithm SHRINK

1. For all supervertices i, $0 \leq i < n$, $c'(i) := \min\{c(k) | (j, k)$ is an edge, $c(j) = i$ and $c(k) \neq i\}$.
2. For all supervertices i, $0 \leq i < n$, $c'(i) := \min\{c'(i), c'(c'(i))\}$.
3. For all supervertices i, $0 \leq i < n$, $c''(i) :=$ index of the root of the pseudotree in which i lies.
4. For all vertices i, $0 \leq i < n$, $c(i) := c''(c(i))$.

On a PRAM, we should set $c'(i) := i$ in Step 1, if the set over which the minimum is taken is empty. After Step 1, the function c' defines a set of trees with possible cycles of length two at their roots [8]. In Step 2, these cycles are contracted. Thus, we obtain a pseudoforest. In Step 3, the roots of these trees are determined. In Step 4, the c values are updated.

A supervertex i is said to be **active** in iteration t of SHRINK, if there is an edge (j, k), with $c(j) = i$ and $c(k) \neq i$. Otherwise it is called **passive**. The performance analysis is based on the following two lemmas:

Lemma 12 *A supervertex i is passive iff every node j in the component of i has $c(j) = i$. Hence, a passive supervertex remains passive.*

Lemma 13 *In iteration t, $t = 1, 2, \ldots$, of SHRINK, there are at most $n/2^{t-1}$ active supervertices. Hence, SHRINK is applied at most $\lfloor \log n \rfloor$ times.*

Knowing this, it can be shown that the algorithm runs on a PRAM with $n + m$ PUs in $\mathcal{O}(\log^2 n)$ time [8]. More refined algorithms perform better on the PRAM, but they appear unnecessarily complicated for the mesh.

6.3 Implementation on Mesh

The presentation of SHRINK was given with implementation on the mesh in mind. By Assumption 1, the edges are evenly spread over the PUs. We will make sure that the following invariants hold. Initially they are satisfied:

Invariant 1 *At the beginning of each iteration, every PU knows the current c values for all endpoints of its edges.*

Invariant 2 *If n' is the current number of active supervertices, then these are numbered from 0 through $n'-1$.*

Lemma 14 *On a two-dimensional mesh, Step 1 takes $(1\frac{3}{4}\cdot\sqrt{2}+o(1))\cdot(n'\cdot m/N)^{1/2}+\mathcal{O}(\sqrt{N})$ steps. Hereafter, for an* active *supervertex i, $c'(i)$ stands in $P_{i \bmod N}$.*

Proof: For each edge (i,j) with $c(i)\neq c(j)$ two packets are created: one with color $c(i)$ and value $c(j)$, and one with color $c(j)$ and value $c(i)$. With Invariant 1 this is easy. The required minima can be computed as an instance of $mmp(n', 2\cdot m, N)$. □

Now we should restore Invariant 2: only after renumbering we can profit from the fact that n' has become smaller. The following procedure renumbers the previously active supervertices. Note that a supervertex i is allocated to $P_{i \bmod N}$.

Algorithm RENUMBER

1. Each supervertex $i<n'$ creates a packet (x,i). Here $x=0$ if i is active, else $x=1$. Sort the packets lexicographically on first and second field. If (j,i) ends up in memory position i^*, then i is renumbered i^*.
2. Determine the new number n'' of active supervertices by finding the highest-indexed memory position storing a packet $(0,i)$, and broadcast it to all PUs.
3. Each supervertex $i^*<n''$ sends a packet containing i^* to $P_{i \bmod N}$.
4. Each supervertex $i<n'$ with $i*<n''$ reads the value of $c'(i)^*$ in $P_{c'(i) \bmod N}$.
5. Each supervertex $i<n'$ with $i*<n''$ sends $c'(i)^*$ to $P_{i^* \bmod N}$.

n' and n'' further denote the number of active supervertices in the previous and current iteration of SHRINK, respectively. In the first iteration, $n''=n'=n$, and RENUMBER is omitted. Restoring Invariant 1 is postponed until Step 4. RENUMBER is implemented by simple routing and sorting operations and solving a $crp(n',n',N)$ in Step 4.

Lemma 15 *On a two-dimensional mesh,* RENUMBER *takes $3\frac{1}{2}\cdot n'/N+\mathcal{O}(\sqrt{N})$ steps.*

Step 2 and Step 3 are instances of $crp(n'',n'',N)$ and $trp(n'',N)$, respectively.

Lemma 16 *On a two-dimensional mesh, Step 2 and Step 3 takes $(2+o(1))\cdot n''/\sqrt{N}+\mathcal{O}(\sqrt{N})$ and $13\cdot n''/\sqrt{N}+\mathcal{O}(\sqrt{N})$ steps respectively.*

Step 4 restores Invariant 1. For every endpoint i of an edge with $i<n'$, we want to know the new value of $c(i)$. Because of the renumbering $c(i)$ is known in $P_{i \bmod N}$, but not $c(i)^*$. So, we cannot simply read $c''(c(i)^*)$. Therefore we add the following step before Step 4:

Each supervertex $i^*<n''$ sends a packet containing $c''(i^*)$ to $P_{i \bmod N}$.

This sending takes $(1/2 + o(1)) \cdot n'/\sqrt{N}$ steps. Hereafter $c''(c(i)^*)$ is available in $P_{c(i) \bmod N}$.

Lemma 17 *On a two-dimensional mesh, Step 4 takes* $(2\frac{3}{4} \cdot \sqrt{2} + o(1)) \cdot (n' \cdot m/N)^{1/2} + \mathcal{O}(\sqrt{N})$ *steps.*

Proof: Every PU sends at most $2 \cdot m/N$ requests, and holds at most n'/N data. This is an instance of $crp(2 \cdot m, n', N)$. □

Summing over all steps in all iterations gives our main result:

Theorem 7 *Iterating* SHRINK *solves* $ccp(n, m, N)$ *on a two-dimensional mesh, in* $29 \cdot (n \cdot m/N)^{1/2} + \mathcal{O}(\log n \cdot \sqrt{N} + n/\sqrt{N})$ *communication steps.*

7 Further Results

7.1 Higher Dimensional Meshes

Observation 1 *The five steps of an implementation of* SHRINK *on a network can be categorized in two ways: those with the complexity of* $mmp(n', m, N)$*, and those with the complexity of* $trp(n', N)$*.*

Theorem 8 *Iterating* SHRINK *solves* $ccp(n, m, N)$ *on a* d*-dimensional mesh, in* $\mathcal{O}(N^{1/d} \cdot (n/N + d \cdot \log n + d \cdot m/N \cdot (n/m)^{1/d}))$ *communication steps.*

7.2 Spanning Trees and Paths

The parallel implementation of Sollin's algorithm for computing minimum spanning trees follows the strategy of the connected components algorithm [9, pp. 223–227]:

Theorem 9 *Variants of the connected components algorithm solve the minimum spanning tree problem and determine a path between a pair of vertices. On a two-dimensional mesh with* N *PUs and for graphs with* n *vertices and* m *edges, this takes* $\mathcal{O}((n \cdot m/N)^{1/2} + \log n \cdot \sqrt{N})$ *communication steps.*

7.3 Computation Time

So far, we have only considered the number of *communication* steps, T_{comm}. Generally the communication time largely dominates the computation time. But for very large m/N, this may be different. Here we briefly consider the number of *computation* steps, T_{comp}.

We use Observation 1. Consider a step with the complexity of $mmp(n', m, N)$. For small m/N, its computation time is dominated by communication-related terms; for large m/N, by the sorting inside the PUs, which is performed in Step 1 of SHRINK. It takes $\mathcal{O}(m/N \cdot \log(m/N)) = \mathcal{O}(m/N \cdot \log n)$ steps. In $trp(n', N)$ there are only $n'/N \lesssim m/N$ packets in every PU.

Theorem 10 *The number of non-communication related computation steps is bounded by* $\mathcal{O}(m/N \cdot \log^2 n)$*.*

Now consider the case $N \leq m/n$. Then every PU holds $m/N \geq n$ packets. This means that the submeshes in an application of $mmp(n', m, N)$ consist of a single PU. The operations within a PU can be performed in $\mathcal{O}(m)$ time by using a bucket for each 'color'. This gives

Theorem 11 *If* $N \leq m/n$*, then the number of non-communication related computation steps can be bounded to* $\mathcal{O}(m/N \cdot \log n)$*.*

8 Conclusion

Developing several subroutines, we constructed an implementation of Hirschberg's connected-components algorithm, running in $\mathcal{O}((n \cdot m/N)^{1/2} + \log n \cdot (\sqrt{N} + m/N))$ on two-dimensional meshes. For all but very sparse graphs this is optimal. Considering that even a single rearrangement of the data takes $\Omega(m/\sqrt{N})$, these are surprising results. If the number of processors is moderate the algorithm even becomes work-optimal up to a factor $\mathcal{O}(\log n)$. Further research should settle the question whether work-optimality can be achieved. Possibly we could incorporate ideas from [7].

Acknowledgement

This paper has profited from the extremely helpful comments by two of the referees.

References

1. Atallah, M.J., S.E. Hambrusch, 'Solving Tree Problems on a Mesh-Connected Processor Array,' *Information and Control*, 69, pp. 168-187, 1986.
2. Atallah M.J., S.R. Kosaraju, 'Graph Problems on a Mesh-Connected Processor Array,' *Journal of the ACM*, 31(3), pp. 649–667, 1984.
3. Chin, F.Y., J. Lam, I. Chen, 'Efficient Parallel Algorithms for some Graph Problems,' *Communications of the ACM*, 25(9), pp. 659-665, 1982.
4. Gibbons, A.M., Y. N. Srikant, 'A Class of Problems Efficiently Solvable on Mesh-Connected Computers Including Dynamic Expression Evaluation,' *International Processing Letters*, 32, pp. 305-311, 1989.
5. Greiner, J., 'A Comparison of Parallel Algorithms for Connected Components,' *Proc 6th Symp. on Par. Algs and Architectures*, pp. 16–25, ACM, 1994.
6. Hambrusch, S.E., 'VLSI Algorithms for the Connected Components Problem,' SIAM Journal on Computing, 12, pp. 354–365, 1983.
7. Han, Y., R.A. Wagner, 'An Efficient and Fast Parallel-Connected Component Algorithm,' *Journal of the ACM*, Vol. 37, No. 3, pp. 626–642, 1990.
8. Hirschberg, D.S., A.K. Chandra, D.V. Sarwate, 'Computing Connected Components on Parallel Computers,' *Communications of the ACM*, 22(8), pp. 461–464, 1979.
9. JáJá, J., *An Introduction to Parallel Algorithms*, Addison-Wesley, 1992.
10. Kaufmann, M., J.F. Sibeyn, T. Suel, 'Derandomizing Algorithms for Routing and Sorting on Meshes,' *Proc. Symp. on Discrete Algorithms*, pp. 669–679, ACM-SIAM, 1994.
11. Kunde, M., 'Block Gossiping on Grids and Tori: Deterministic Sorting and Routing Match the Bisection Bound,' *Proc. European Symp. on Algorithms*, LNCS 726, pp. 272–283, Springer-Verlag, 1993.
12. Nassimi, D., S. Sahni, 'Finding Connected Components and Connected Ones On a Mesh-Connected Parallel Computer,' *SIAM Journal of Computing*, Vol. 9, No. 4, 1980.
13. Ryu, K.W., J. JáJá, 'Efficient Algorithms for List Ranking and for Solving Graph Problems on the Hypercube,' *IEEE Trans. Par. and Dist. Systems*, pp. 83-90, 1990.
14. Sibeyn, J.F., 'Independent Sets and List Ranking on Meshes,' *Proc. Computing Science in the Netherlands*, pp. 271–280, SION, Amsterdam, 1994.
15. Sibeyn, J.F., 'Desnakification of Mesh Sorting Algorithms,' *Proc. 2nd European Symp. on Algorithms*, LNCS 855, pp. 377–390, Springer-Verlag, 1994.
16. Sibeyn, J.F., M. Kaufmann, 'Solving Cheap Graph Problems on Meshes,' *Technical Report WSI-95-9*, Wilhelm-Schickard-Institut für Informatik, Tübingen, 1995.
17. Sibeyn, J.F., M. Kaufmann, 'Deterministic 1-k Routing on Meshes,' *Proc. 11th Symp. on Theoretical Aspects of Computer Science*, LNCS 775, pp. 237–248, Springer, 1994.
18. Shiloach, Y., U. Vishkin, 'An $\mathcal{O}(\log n)$ Parallel Connectivity Algorithm,' *Journal of Algorithms*, 3(1), pp. 57–67, 1982.
19. Tarjan, R.E., U. Vishkin, 'Finding Biconnected Components and Computing Tree Functions in Logarithmic Parallel Time,' *SIAM Journal of Computing*, 13, pp. 862–874, 1985.

An Elementary Bisimulation Decision Procedure for Arbitrary Context-Free Processes

Olaf Burkart[1], Didier Caucal[2], Bernhard Steffen[3]

[1] Lehrstuhl für Informatik II, RWTH Aachen, Ahornstraße 55, 52074 Aachen, Germany,

[2] IRISA, Campus de Beaulieu, 35042 Rennes, France

[3] Fakultät für Mathematik und Informatik, Universität Passau, Innstraße 33, 94032 Passau, Germany

Abstract. We present an elementary algorithm for deciding bisimulation between arbitrary context-free processes. This improves on the state of the art algorithm of Christensen, Hüttel and Stirling consisting of two semi-decision procedures running in parallel, which prohibits any complexity estimation. The point of our algorithm is the effective construction of a finite relation characterizing all bisimulation equivalence classes, whose mere existence was exploited for the above mentioned decidability result.

1 Introduction

Algebraic descriptions of concurrent systems are usually formulated using a process calculus such as CSP [Hoa85], CCS [Mil89], or ACP [BW90], and their semantics in terms of labelled transition graphs together with a notion of behavioural equivalence which reflects some notion of observation. A number of such behavioural equivalences have been considered depending on the suggested observational power (cf. [Gla90]): their main rationale has been to capture aspects like nondeterministic, parallel or nonterminating behaviours, which are not taken into account in classical language theory. Besides their observational power, decidability is of practical interest. For example, from classical language theory it is known that language equivalence is decidable for regular systems. However, if one moves further to context-free languages the problem becomes undecidable. In the 'finer' process algebraic setting the situation is different, as *bisimilarity* is decidable for *strongly normed* context-free processes (BPA processes)[BBK87], which are defined by reduced context-free grammars, and can terminate in finitely many steps at any point of the execution. This exceptional property of the bisimulation equivalence led to an intense investigation (cf. [Cau90, Gro91, HS91, HT94, HM94]), which resulted in a polynomial time decision procedure for normed processes [HJM94]. The treatment of general context-free processes requires completely new techniques, as the decomposition properties for the normed case fail to hold. Nevertheless, considering *bisimulation bases B* characterizing the bisimulation equivalence as the least congruence w.r.t. sequential composition containing B, it is possible to prove that bisimulation is decidable also in this case [CHS92]. The existence of such a finite relation

B can be exploited for a decision algorithm based on two semi-decision procedures: one for searching a bisimulation base, and one for the enumeration of all non-bisimilar pairs of processes.

In this paper we show how to effectively compute a bisimulation base B, and exploit it for the construction of an elementary bisimulation decision procedure for arbitrary context-free processes. The key idea behind the construction of B is the determination of a new bound for the number of transitions needed to separate two normed non-bisimilar processes along the lines of [Cau89]. This bound allows the construction of an 'initial' base, which subsequently must be refined by means of a fixpoint iteration similar to the one used in [HJM94] to obtain B. The decision algorithm is then completed by a straightforward branching algorithm. - Detailed proofs are given in [BCS94].

Section 2 introduces the kind of processes and the behavioural equivalence we are interested in, while Sect. 3 presents the new bound for the number of transitions needed to separate two non-bisimilar normed context-free processes. Finally, in Sect. 4 we develop our new bisimulation base construction algorithm to obtain the proposed decision procedure.

2 Context-Free Processes and Bisimulation

We first review some basic definitions and facts concerning the class of processes and the behavioural equivalence we want to consider. A *labelled transition system* is a triple $(\mathcal{P}, Act, \rightarrow)$ consisting of a set of *states* or *processes* $\mathcal{P}$, a set of *actions* Act and a *transition relation* $\rightarrow \subseteq \mathcal{P} \times Act \times \mathcal{P}$, written $p \xrightarrow{a} p'$ for $(p, a, p') \in \rightarrow$. As usual, we extend the transition relation by reflexivity and transitivity to allow $p \xrightarrow{w} p'$ for $w \in Act^*$, and we call a process p *terminating* if no transition evolves from p, also written as $p \not\rightarrow$. A labelled transition system is called *finitely branching* if for each process p the set $\{ p \xrightarrow{a} p' \mid a \in Act, p' \in \mathcal{P} \}$ is finite. We will concentrate on the class of processes defined by guarded recursive BPA (Basic Process Algebra) systems [BBK87].

Definition 1. A *BPA expression* is defined by the following abstract syntax

$$E ::= \epsilon \mid a \mid X \mid E + E \mid E \cdot E$$

where a ranges over Act and X over a family of variables. Here ϵ represents the empty process, while the operator $+$ is interpreted as nondeterministic choice and $\cdot$ denotes sequential composition – henceforth we usually omit the $\cdot$.

A *BPA system* $\mathcal{C}$ is a quadruple (V, Act, Δ, X_1) consisting of a finite set of *variables* or *nonterminals* $V = \{ X_1, \ldots, X_n \}$, a finite set of *actions* or *terminals* Act, a finite set of recursive process equations $\Delta = \{ X_i = E_i \mid 1 \leq i \leq n \}$, where each E_i is a BPA expression with free variables in V which does not contain ϵ, and a variable $X_1 \in V$, called the *root*.

Definition 2. We call an occurrence of a variable X in a BPA term t *guarded* if t has a subterm $a.t'$ such that a is an atomic action and t' contains the occurrence of X. A BPA term t is guarded if every variable occurrence is guarded and a BPA system is guarded if each E_i is guarded for $1 \leq i \leq n$.

In the remainder of this paper we use $X, Y, \ldots$ to range over variables in V and Greek letters $\alpha, \beta, \ldots$ to range over elements in V^*. For technical convenience, we identify the empty process ϵ with the empty variable sequence and use the convention $\epsilon\alpha = \alpha\epsilon = \alpha$. The function $|.|$ gives the length of a sequence.

Definition 3. Any guarded BPA system $\mathcal{C} = (V, Act, \Delta, X_1)$ defines a labelled transition system $\mathcal{T}_\mathcal{C}$ where the transition relations are given as the least relations satisfying the following rules:

$$a \xrightarrow{a} \epsilon; \quad \frac{E \xrightarrow{a} E'}{X \xrightarrow{a} E'}, X = E \in \Delta; \quad \frac{E \xrightarrow{a} E'}{EF \xrightarrow{a} E'F}; \quad \frac{E \xrightarrow{a} E'}{E + F \xrightarrow{a} E'}; \quad \frac{F \xrightarrow{a} F'}{E + F \xrightarrow{a} F'}$$

The states of $\mathcal{T}_\mathcal{C}$ are also called *BPA processes*. Since all processes reachable from the root are variable sequences we will restrict our attention to the labelled transition subsystem of $\mathcal{T}_\mathcal{C}$ with state set V^*.

Bisimulation equivalence, which we are going to decide for arbitrary context-free processes in this paper, is defined as follows [Par81, Mil89]:

Definition 4. A binary relation R between processes is a *bisimulation* if whenever $(p, q) \in R$ then for each $a \in Act$:

1. $p \xrightarrow{a} p'$ implies $\exists\, q'.\, q \xrightarrow{a} q' \ \wedge\ (p', q') \in R$, and
2. $q \xrightarrow{a} q'$ implies $\exists\, p'.\, p \xrightarrow{a} p' \ \wedge\ (p', q') \in R$.

Two processes p and q are said to be *bisimulation equivalent* or *bisimilar*, written $p \sim q$, if $(p, q) \in R$ for some bisimulation R. In the remainder of the paper we write $[p]_\sim$ for the bisimulation equivalence class of p. Now a basic result of [BBK87] states that any guarded BPA system can effectively be transformed into *K-Greibach Normal Form* (K-GNF), while preserving bisimulation equivalence. A BPA system is said to be in K-GNF, when each equation is of the form $X_i =_{df} \sum_{j=1}^{m_i} a_{ij}\alpha_{ij}$ with the additional restriction that each variable sequence α_{ij} has length of at most K. Another useful notion is the one of *self-bisimulation* [Cau90]. It is defined by means of the least congruence w.r.t. sequential composition of a relation R on V^*, denoted by $\leftrightarrow^*_R$.

Definition 5. Given a binary relation R between processes of V^* we define $p \cong_R q$ if for each $a \in Act$:

1. $p \xrightarrow{a} p'$ implies $\exists\, q'.\, q \xrightarrow{a} q' \ \wedge\ p' \leftrightarrow^*_R q'$, and
2. $q \xrightarrow{a} q'$ implies $\exists\, p'.\, p \xrightarrow{a} p' \ \wedge\ p' \leftrightarrow^*_R q'$.

A binary relation R between processes is a *self-bisimulation* iff $R \subseteq \cong_R$. Thus a self-bisimulation is simply a bisimulation up to congruence w.r.t. sequential composition. Self-bisimulations are important because $\leftrightarrow^*_R \subseteq \sim$, whenever R is a self-bisimulation [Cau90].

2.1 Normedness and Cancellations

The *norm* of a process p, written as $||p||$, is the length of the shortest transition sequence from p to a terminating state. A process is said to be *normed* if its norm is finite. Moreover, a transition $p \xrightarrow{a} p'$ of a normed process p is called a *norm-reducing* transition if $||p'|| = ||p|| - 1$. Finally, a BPA system is called normed if all defined variables are normed. In the remainder of this section we state some properties of normed BPA processes. In particular, normedness allows us to take advantage of some important cancellation rules.

First recall that the norm is additive wrt. sequential composition, i.e. $||\alpha\beta|| = ||\alpha|| + ||\beta||$, that bisimulation preserves the norm, i.e. $\alpha \sim \beta$ implies $||\alpha|| = ||\beta||$, and that bisimulation is a congruence wrt. sequential composition, i.e. if $\alpha \sim \alpha'$ and $\beta \sim \beta'$ then $\alpha\beta \sim \alpha'\beta'$.

Lemma 6. *Let $C = (V, Act, \Delta, X_1)$ be a normed BPA system in K-GNF with maximal variable norm $\mathcal{N}$. Whenever $\alpha \xrightarrow{w} \alpha'$ with $\alpha, \alpha' \in V^*$ and $|w| = l$ then we have*

$$||\alpha'|| \leq (l(K-1) + |\alpha|)\mathcal{N}.$$

Lemma 7 (Cancellation rules for normed BPA processes). *Let α, β and γ be normed. Then 1. $\gamma\alpha \sim \gamma\beta$ implies $\alpha \sim \beta$ and 2. $\alpha\gamma \sim \beta\gamma$ implies $\alpha \sim \beta$.*

Note however that both implications of the cancellation lemma fail to hold when dealing with unnormed processes:

1. Let $X = a + aX + aY$ and $Y = bY$ then we have $XY \sim XXY$ but $Y \not\sim XY$.
2. Let $X = a$ and $Y = aY$ then we have $XY \sim XXY$ but $X \not\sim XX$.

A crucial property of normed processes is stated in the following splitting lemma [Cau90].

Lemma 8 (Splitting rule for normed BPA processes). *Let $X\alpha, Y\beta \in V^+$ be normed such that $||X|| \leq ||Y||$. Then*

$$X\alpha \sim Y\beta \quad \textit{iff} \quad X\gamma \sim Y \textit{ and } \alpha \sim \gamma\beta \textit{ for some } \gamma.$$

In contrast, in the presence of unnormed processes we only have the trivial right-cancellation rule $\alpha X \beta \sim \alpha X$, for any unnormed variable X.

3 A Separability Bound for Normed BPA

The development of this section is based on a fixed-point construction, which Milner [Mil89] proposed to characterize bisimulation of finitely branching transition systems in terms of sequences of approximations. *Separability* is defined in terms of the complements of these approximations. It characterizes the number of transitions needed to separate two non-bisimilar processes.

Definition 9. Let R be a binary relation between processes. Then $(p,q) \in \mathcal{F}(R)$ iff for each $a \in Act$:

1. $p \xrightarrow{a} p'$ implies $\exists\, q'.\ q \xrightarrow{a} q' \ \wedge\ (p',q') \in R$, and
2. $q \xrightarrow{a} q'$ implies $\exists\, p'.\ p \xrightarrow{a} p' \ \wedge\ (p',q') \in R$.

It is well-known that $\sim\ = \ \bigcap \{\mathcal{F}^i(\mathcal{P} \times \mathcal{P}) \mid i \geq 0\}$, whenever the labelled transition graph $(\mathcal{P}, Act, \rightarrow)$ is finitely branching. Based on this iterative characterization of bisimulation we define when two processes are said to be m-bisimilar, which leads to the notion of separability.

Definition 10. Let $p, q \in \mathcal{P}$ be two processes. p and q are said to be *m-bisimilar*, written $p \sim_m q$, if $(p,q) \in \mathcal{F}^{\,m}(\mathcal{P} \times \mathcal{P})$. Moreover, we define the *separability* of p and q as $\mathrm{Sep}(p,q) =_{\mathrm{df}} \max\{\, m \mid p \sim_m q\,\} + 1$. If the separability of p and q is finite[4], say m, then p and q are also called *m-separable.*

The adequate notion when considering transitions to separate non-bisimilar processes is a *separating transition.*

Lemma 11. *If two processes $p, q \in \mathcal{P}$ are m-separable, then one of the following conditions hold.*

1. *$p \xrightarrow{a} p'$ for some a, p' and $\forall\, q'.\ q \xrightarrow{a} q' \Rightarrow p' \not\sim_{m-1} q'$; or*
2. *$q \xrightarrow{a} q'$ for some a, q' and $\forall\, p'.\ p \xrightarrow{a} p' \Rightarrow p' \not\sim_{m-1} q'$.*

In the first case we call $p \xrightarrow{a} p'$ a separating transition *for p and q, and in the later case $q \xrightarrow{a} q'$, respectively.*

In contrast to bisimilarity, separability has got little attention in the past. Our algorithm is based on a new bound for the separability of strongly normed context-free processes. Such a bound was first developed in [Cau89] for *simple grammars* which can be interpreted as normed *deterministic* BPA systems. It is surprising that these results can be extended to the nondeterministic case.
Let $\mathcal{C} = (V, Act, \Delta, X_1)$ be a normed BPA system. Abbreviating $\min\{\, \|\alpha\|, \|\beta\|\,\}$ by $\|\alpha, \beta\|$ and $\max\{\, \|E\| \mid X =_{\mathrm{df}} E \in \Delta\,\} - 1$ by $\mathcal{E}$, we have, for $\alpha, \beta \in V^*$:

Theorem 12. *If α is not bisimilar to β, then $Sep(\alpha,\beta) \leq \mathcal{B}_{\alpha,\beta}$, where*

$$\mathcal{B}_{\alpha,\beta} = \begin{cases} \|\alpha,\beta\| + 1 & \text{if } \|\alpha\| \neq \|\beta\|, \text{ and} \\ (n-1)\mathcal{E} + 1 + \|\alpha,\beta\| & \text{if } \|\alpha\| = \|\beta\|. \end{cases}$$

In the next section we will apply this theorem to a slightly larger class of processes, namely BPA_δ. The constant symbol δ represents *deadlock*, i.e. a process which cannot proceed. Its behaviour is captured by the axioms $E+\delta = E$ and $\delta E = \delta$. A BPA_δ system is *normed*, if each variable X is either normed in the usual sense or deadlocks immediately after each possible transition. It is easy to show that the bound given above is still valid for normed BPA_δ systems. This technical but straightforward variant is important for the proof of Proposition 20.

[4] Note that $p \sim q$ implies $\mathrm{Sep}(p,q) = \infty$.

4 The Algorithm

In this section we present our three step algorithm for deciding bisimilarity of context-free processes. The first two steps are required for the construction of a *bisimulation base* B. Bisimulation bases characterize bisimulation equivalence as the least congruence w.r.t. sequential composition containing B. This can be exploited for a branching algorithm, which completes the decision procedure in a third step. We will concentrate on the first step here, as the second step can be obtained by combining results from (cf. [CHS92, HJM94]), and the third step is rather straightforward. Thus we start by sketching the second step, which also serves as a good motivation for the subsequently presented first step of our algorithm. Finally, we summarize the results to obtain the complete decision procedure.

Henceforth assume that we have a guarded BPA system $\mathcal{C} = (V, Act, \Delta, X_1)$ in K-GNF, where the variables $V = \{X_1, \ldots, X_n\}$ are ordered by nondecreasing norm. Moreover, we divide the set of variables into disjoint subsets $V_N = \{X \in V \mid X \text{ is normed}\}$ and $V_U = V \setminus V_N$. Due to the right-cancellation rule for unnormed processes we restrict our attention to variable sequences $\alpha \in \mathcal{P}(V^*) =_{\text{df}} V_N^* \cup V_N^* V_U$. Additionally, we write $\mathcal{P}(V^+)$ for $\mathcal{P}(V^*) \setminus \{\epsilon\}$, and we denote the maximal finite norm of all given variables by $\mathcal{N}$. Finally, we assume that the given BPA system is *normalized*, i.e. if α is an unnormed right-hand side summand of some normed variable X, then α must be of the form $a.Y$. This additional assumption does not impose any restriction, since every guarded BPA system in K-GNF can be normalized by means of the following transformation:

> If $a.\beta$ with $\beta \notin V$ is an unnormed right-hand side summand of some normed variable X, replace β by some fresh variable Y and add the equation $Y =_{\text{df}} \beta$ to Δ. Then transform the resulting BPA system again into K-GNF.

The transformation will eventually terminate since every newly created variable is unnormed.

4.1 Bisimulation Bases

An important difference between the theory of normed and unnormed BPA processes is the existence of two kinds of bisimilar pairs, *decomposable* and *elementary* pairs (cf. [CHS92]).

Definition 13. Let $X_i\alpha \sim X_j\beta$ with $i \leq j$ and $X_i, X_j \in V_N$. We say that the pair $(X_i\alpha, X_j\beta)$ is *decomposable* if there exists some γ such that $\alpha \sim \gamma\beta$ and $X_i\gamma \sim X_j$. If the pair is not decomposable it is said to be *elementary*.

An immediate consequence of this definition is that if $(X_i\alpha, X_j\beta)$ is elementary, then α and β must be unnormed. Thus in the normed case only decomposable pairs can occur.

In order to prove termination, we extend the notion of norm to a *seminorm* on arbitrary context-free processes as follows: we define the *seminorm* of a variable sequence $\alpha \in \mathcal{P}(V^*)$ as $||\alpha X||_s = ||\alpha X||$ if $X \in V_N$ and $||\alpha X||_s = ||\alpha||$ otherwise. The seminorm is used to define a well-founded ordering on $\mathcal{P}(V^*) \times \mathcal{P}(V^*)$ by $(\alpha_1, \alpha_2) \sqsubseteq (\beta_1, \beta_2)$ iff $\max\{\, ||\alpha_1||_s, ||\alpha_2||_s \,\} \leq \max\{\, ||\beta_1||_s, ||\beta_2||_s \,\}$.

Definition 14.

- A *base* is a binary relation consisting of pairs $(X_i\alpha, X_j\beta) \in \mathcal{P}(V^+) \times \mathcal{P}(V^+)$ with $i \leq j$.
- A base B is called *bisimulation-complete* iff whenever $X_i\alpha \sim X_j\beta$ with $i \leq j$ then one of the following conditions hold:
  1. $(X_i\alpha, X_j\beta)$ is decomposable, i.e. we have in particular $X_i\gamma \sim X_j$ for some γ, and $(X_i\gamma', X_j) \in B$ for some $\gamma' \sim \gamma$.
  2. $(X_i\alpha, X_j\beta)$ is elementary and $(X_i\alpha', X_j\beta') \in B$ for some $\alpha' \sim \alpha$ and $\beta' \sim \beta$ such that $(\alpha', \beta') \sqsubseteq (\alpha, \beta)$.
- The relation $\equiv_B$ is defined recursively by:
  1. $\epsilon \equiv_B \epsilon$ and
  2. $X_i\alpha \equiv_B X_j\beta$ iff (a) $(X_i\gamma, X_j) \in B$ and $\alpha \equiv_B \gamma\beta$ or
     (b) $(X_i\alpha', X_j\beta') \in B$, $\alpha \equiv_B \alpha'$ and $\beta \equiv_B \beta'$.

The importance of the relation $\equiv_B$ is revealed by the following lemma.

Lemma 15.
1. $\equiv_B \subseteq \leftrightarrow^*_B$ *2. If B is bisimulation-complete then* $\sim \subseteq \equiv_B$.

The key structure for our decidability result are *bisimulation bases*, which are relations B satisfying $\sim = \leftrightarrow^*_B$. They are important as they characterize bisimulation equivalence as the least congruence w.r.t. sequential composition containing B. As a consequence of Lemma 15, one of the inclusions, $\sim \subseteq \leftrightarrow^*_B$, is guaranteed for bisimulation-complete relations B. A sufficient condition for the inverse inclusion, which can be proved for our construction, is 'self-bisimulation'.

Definition 16. Given a base B, define the subbase $\mathcal{R}(B)$ by: $(\alpha, \beta) \in \mathcal{R}(B)$ iff $(\alpha, \beta) \in B$ and 1. $\alpha \xrightarrow{a} \alpha'$ implies $\exists\, \beta'.\ \beta \xrightarrow{a} \beta' \ \wedge\ \alpha' \equiv_B \beta'$, and 2. $\beta \xrightarrow{a} \beta'$ implies $\exists\, \alpha'.\ \alpha \xrightarrow{a} \alpha' \ \wedge\ \alpha' \equiv_B \beta'$.

That $\mathcal{R}$ is a good candidate for successively reducing a bisimulation-complete relation to a bisimulation base is a consequence of the following lemma.

Lemma 17. *Let B be a bisimulation-complete base. Then the following holds:*
1. If $(\alpha, \beta) \in B$ and $\alpha \sim \beta$ then $(\alpha, \beta) \in \mathcal{R}(B)$. 2. $\mathcal{R}(B)$ is bisimulation-complete.

Along the lines of [HJM94], this can be exploited to verify that the successive $\mathcal{R}$-refinement of a bisimulation-complete relation yields indeed a bisimulation base: the (additional) fixpoint property of $B_\sim$ is sufficient to establish that $B_\sim$ is a self-bisimulation.

Theorem 18. *If B_0 is a bisimulation-complete base then $B_\sim =_{df} \bigcap \{\mathcal{R}^i(B_0) \mid i \geq 0\}$ is a bisimulation base, i.e. we have $\sim = \leftrightarrow^*_{B_\sim}$.*

4.2 The Computation of an Initial Base

Recall that we consider a normalized unnormed BPA system $\mathcal{C} = (V, Act, \Delta, X_1)$. We say a variable $Y \in V_U$ is *crossing*, if Y occurs on the right-hand side of some $X \in V_N$, and we denote the set of all crossing variables by V_C. Intuitively, starting with a normed process we can only reach an unnormed one by "crossing" a variable of V_C. If $\sim_{\mathcal{C}}$ denotes the bisimilarity wrt. $\mathcal{C}$, we construct a normed BPA$_\delta$ system $\mathcal{C}' = (V', Act', \Delta', X_1)$ from $\mathcal{C}$ as follows.

- $V' = V_N \cup V_C$,
- $Act' = Act \cup \{ a_{[Y]_{\sim_\mathcal{C}}} \mid Y \in V_C \}$, where each $a_{[Y]_{\sim_\mathcal{C}}}$ is an action not occurring in Act,
- $\Delta' = \{ X =_{\text{df}} E \in \Delta \mid X \in V_N \} \cup \{ Y =_{\text{df}} a_{[Y]_{\sim_\mathcal{C}}} \delta \mid Y \in V_C \}$.

The constructed BPA$_\delta$ $\mathcal{C}'$ system is obviously normed. It represents the behaviour of the normed part of $\mathcal{C}$ as stated in the following proposition.

Proposition 19. *For all $\alpha, \beta \in V_N^* \cup V_C$ we have: $\alpha \sim_\mathcal{C} \beta$ iff $\alpha \sim_{\mathcal{C}'} \beta$.*

The proposition is easily proved by showing that the equality $\sim_{\mathcal{C}'} = \sim_{\mathcal{C}} \restriction_{V_N^* \cup V_C} \cup \{ (\delta, \delta) \}$ holds. The key point to observe is that the behaviour of crossing variables is encoded in the transitions leading to a deadlock since we have, for any $Y, Z \in V_C$, $a_{[Y]_{\sim_\mathcal{C}}} = a_{[Z]_{\sim_\mathcal{C}}}$ iff $Y \sim_\mathcal{C} Z$. By means of this proposition we are now able to apply the separability bound $\mathcal{B}_{\alpha,\beta}$ obtained in the previous section.

Proposition 20. *Consider the BPA system $\mathcal{C}$ and let ζ be normed with $\zeta \not\sim \eta$, $||\zeta|| \leq ||\eta||$ and $\zeta\beta \sim \eta\beta$. Then $\beta \sim X$ where $X =_{\text{df}} \gamma X$ for some $\gamma \neq \epsilon$ such that the following conditions hold.*

- *If $||\zeta|| < ||\eta||$ then $\eta \stackrel{w}{\rightarrow} \gamma$ for some fixed w where $\zeta \stackrel{w}{\rightarrow} \epsilon$ is a norm-reducing transition sequence.*
- *If $||\zeta|| = ||\eta||$ then without loss of generality $\zeta \stackrel{w}{\rightarrow} \epsilon$ and $\eta \stackrel{w}{\rightarrow} \gamma$ in $|w| \leq \mathcal{B}(\zeta, \eta)$ steps where $\mathcal{B}(\zeta, \eta) =_{\text{df}} \mathcal{B}_{\zeta,\eta} + (\mathcal{B}_{\zeta,\eta}(K-1) + |\zeta|)\mathcal{N}$.*

Proof. First assume $||\zeta|| < ||\eta||$. Let $\zeta \stackrel{w}{\rightarrow} \epsilon$ be a norm-reducing transition sequence. Then $\zeta\beta \stackrel{w}{\rightarrow} \beta, \eta\beta \stackrel{w}{\rightarrow} \gamma\beta$ and $\beta \sim \gamma\beta$ for some γ such that $\eta \stackrel{w}{\rightarrow} \gamma$ in $|w| = ||\zeta||$ steps. Since any system of guarded equations has a unique solution up to bisimulation, we conclude that $\beta \sim X$ where $X =_{\text{df}} \gamma X$, which completes the first part.

Now suppose $||\zeta|| = ||\eta||$. By Proposition 19, $\text{Sep}_{\mathcal{C}'}(\zeta, \eta) = m$ for some $m \geq 1$. Thus we have the following situation: $\zeta = \zeta_m \not\sim_{m,\mathcal{C}'} \eta_m = \eta$. Let $\zeta_m \stackrel{a}{\rightarrow} \zeta_{m-1}$ wlog. be a separating transition. Since $\zeta_m\beta \stackrel{a}{\rightarrow} \zeta_{m-1}\beta$ we also have $\eta_m\beta \stackrel{a}{\rightarrow} \eta_{m-1}\beta$ for some η_{m-1} such that $\zeta_{m-1}\beta \sim_\mathcal{C} \eta_{m-1}\beta$ and $\zeta_{m-1} \not\sim_{m-1,\mathcal{C}'} \eta_{m-1}$ due to the separating property of the transition. This construction can repeatedly be applied to obtain sequences $\zeta_m, \ldots, \zeta_1$ and $\eta_m, \ldots, \eta_1$ such that $\zeta_i \not\sim_{i,\mathcal{C}'} \eta_i$ and $\zeta_i\beta \sim_\mathcal{C} \eta_i\beta$ for all $1 \leq i \leq m$. An illustration is given in Fig. 1. As the situation is symmetric in this case we may assume $||\zeta_1|| \leq ||\eta_1||$. In order to complete the proof we consider two cases:

Case 1: $||\eta_1|| < \infty$. This implies $||\zeta_1|| < \infty$, and since $\mathcal{C}$ and $\mathcal{C}'$ coincide on $V_N^* \times V_N^*$, we have also $\zeta_1 \not\sim_{1,\mathcal{C}} \eta_1$. As $\zeta_1\beta \sim_\mathcal{C} \eta_1\beta$, we obtain $\zeta_1 = \epsilon$. Hence $\gamma = \eta_1$ will work and we have $|w| = m - 1 = \mathrm{Sep}_{\mathcal{C}'}(\zeta, \eta) - 1 \leq \mathcal{B}_{\zeta,\eta} - 1$.

Case 2: $||\eta_1|| = \infty$. From $\zeta_1 \not\sim_{\mathcal{C}'} \eta_1$ we conclude by Proposition 19 that $\zeta_1 \not\sim_\mathcal{C} \eta_1$. Since $\zeta_1\beta \sim_\mathcal{C} \eta_1\beta$, we have $||\zeta_1|| < \infty$. Hence with $|w| = m-1+||\zeta_i|| \leq \mathcal{B}_{\zeta,\eta}+(\mathcal{B}_{\zeta,\eta}(K-1)+|\zeta|)\mathcal{N}$ there exists again some γ such that $\eta = \eta_m \xrightarrow{w} \eta_1 = \gamma$ in $m-1 = |w| \leq \mathcal{B}_{\zeta,\eta}+(\mathcal{B}_{\zeta,\eta}(K-1)+|\zeta|)\mathcal{N}$ steps and $\beta \sim X$ where $X =_{\mathrm{df}} \eta_1 X$.

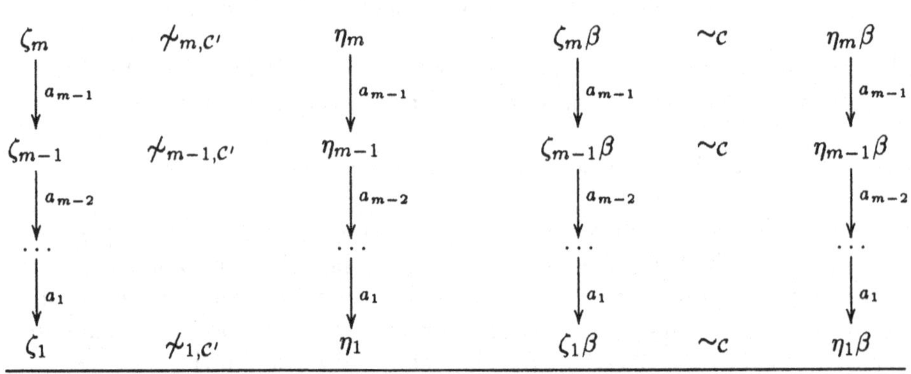

Fig. 1. The construction of a separating transition track.

The first step of the initial base construction consists of a *completion* procedure for the given BPA system.

Algorithm 21. *The* elementary completion Δ^ω *of a set of equations* Δ *is defined as follows:*

- *Every equation of* Δ *is contained in* Δ^ω.
- *For each* i *and* j *in the range* $1 \leq i \leq j \leq n$ *such that* $X_i, X_j \in V_N$ *fix some norm-reducing transition sequence* $X_i \xrightarrow{u} \epsilon$. *Then for each pair* $(X_i\gamma, X_j)$ *such that* $X_j \xrightarrow{u} \gamma$ *for some* γ *we do the following:*
  1. *If* $||X_i\gamma|| < ||X_j||$ *then fix some norm-reducing transition sequence* $X_i\gamma \xrightarrow{w} \epsilon$ *and add for each* ζ *such that* $X_j \xrightarrow{w} \zeta$ *the equations* $Y =_{\mathrm{df}} \zeta Y$ *and* $Y' =_{\mathrm{df}} \gamma Y$ *to* Δ^ω *where* Y, Y' *are fresh variables.*
  2. *If* $||X_i\gamma|| > ||X_j||$ *then fix some norm-reducing transition sequence* $X_j \xrightarrow{w} \epsilon$ *and add for each* ζ *such that* $X_i\gamma \xrightarrow{w} \zeta$ *the equations* $Y =_{\mathrm{df}} \zeta Y$ *and* $Y' =_{\mathrm{df}} \gamma Y$ *to* Δ^ω *where* Y, Y' *are fresh variables.*
  3. *If* $||X_i\gamma|| = ||X_j||$ *then add for each* ζ *such that* $X_i\gamma \xrightarrow{w} \epsilon \wedge X_j \xrightarrow{w} \zeta$, *or* $X_j \xrightarrow{w} \epsilon \wedge X_i\gamma \xrightarrow{w} \zeta$ *in* $|w| \leq \mathcal{B}(X_i\gamma, X_j)$ *steps the equations* $Y =_{\mathrm{df}} \zeta Y$ *and* $Y' =_{\mathrm{df}} \gamma Y$ *to* Δ^ω *where* Y, Y' *are fresh variables.*

The equations generated from a pair $(X_i\gamma, X_j)$ are also called the elementary completion *of* $(X_i\gamma, X_j)$.

During this completion we will add new equations to Δ in order to be able to explicitly denote some needed bisimulation classes. Note, however, that each equation added to Δ defines an unnormed variable which is bisimilar to $\gamma\zeta^\omega$ for some γ, ζ, and that no new variable is reachable from any of the original variables. Thus the bisimulation classes generated by finite sequences over V are unchanged after completion.

Algorithm 22 (Initial base B_0 construction).
Let Δ^ω be the elementary completion of Δ with variables V_N and $V_U^\omega = V_U \cup V_U^{new}$.

Step 1: *For each i and j in the range $1 \leq i \leq j \leq n$ such that $X_i, X_j \in V_N$ fix some $[X_j]_{||X_i||}$ such that $X_j \stackrel{w}{\to} [X_j]_{||X_i||}$ in $|w| = ||X_i||$ norm-reducing steps. Then $(X_i[X_j]_{||X_i||}, X_j) \in B_0$.*

Step 2: *For each i and j in the range $1 \leq i \leq j \leq n$ such that $X_i, X_j \in V_N$ let u be the path labelling chosen during the elementary completion. Then for each γ such that $X_j \stackrel{u}{\to} \gamma$ let $(X_iY', X_jY) \in B_0$, if $Y =_{df} \zeta Y$ and $Y' =_{df} \gamma Y$ are contained in the elementary completion of $(X_i\gamma, X_j)$.*

Step 3: *For each i and j in the range $1 \leq i \leq j \leq n$ such that $X_i, X_j \in V_U^\omega$ let $(X_i, X_j) \in B_0$.*

Step 4: *For each $X_i \in V_N$ and $X_j \in V_U^\omega$ let $\{ (X_i[X_j]_{||X_i||}, X_j) \mid X_j \stackrel{w}{\to} [X_j]_{||X_i||}$ in $|w| = ||X_i||$ steps$\} \subseteq B_0$. Moreover, let Ω be the maximal seminorm of all $[X_j]_{||X_i||}$ obtained. Then add also $\{ (X_i\alpha, X_j) \mid ||\alpha||_s < \Omega \}$ to B_0.*

Bisimulation completeness follows by construction:

Theorem 23. *The initial base B_0 is bisimulation-complete.*

4.3 Summary of the Decision Procedure

The overall algorithm proceeds in three steps:

1. Computation of an initial base B_0 by means of the algorithm presented in the previous subsection. This algorithm terminates with a base of elementary size.
2. Refinement of B_0 by iterative application of $\mathcal{R}$ until a bisimulation base is reached, which is the case after at most $|B_0|$ iterations. As B_0 is of elementary size and each iteration itself is elementary also this step is elementary.
3. Decision of $\alpha \sim \beta$ by means of a straightforward (obviously elementary) branching algorithm exploiting the bisimulation completeness of the constructed bisimulation base.

Summarizing we can conclude:

Theorem 24 Main Theorem.
Our three step bisimulation decision algorithm is elementary.

Remark: Our complexity analysis is quite rough. A more careful analysis would reveal quite a small 'exponentiality'. Indeed we conjecture that some straightforward optimizations will yield a doubly exponential algorithm.

References

[BBK87] J.C.M. Baeten, J.A. Bergstra, and J.W. Klop. Decidability of Bisimulation Equivalence for Processes Generating Context-Free Languages. In *PARLE '87, LNCS 259*, pages 94–113. Springer, 1987. Full version appeared as: Technical Report CS-R8632, CWI, Sep. 1987.

[BCS94] O. Burkart, D. Caucal, and S. Steffen. An Elementary Bisimulation Decision Procedure for Arbitrary Context-Free Processes. Technical Report AIB-94-28, RWTH Aachen, 1994.

[BW90] J.C.M. Baeten and W.P. Weijland. *Process Algebra*, volume 18 of *Cambridge Tracts in TCS*. Cambridge University Press, 1990.

[Cau89] D. Caucal. A Fast Algorithm to Decide on Simple Grammars Equivalence. In *Int. Symposium on Optimal Algorithms, LNCS 401*, pages 66–85. Springer, 1989.

[Cau90] D. Caucal. Graphes Canoniques de Graphes Algébriques. *RAIRO*, 24(4):339–352, 1990. A preliminary version appeared as: Rapport de Recherche 872, INRIA, July 1988.

[CHS92] S. Christensen, H. Hüttel, and C. Stirling. Bisimulation Equivalence is Decidable for all Context-Free Processes. In *CONCUR '92, LNCS 630*, pages 138–147. Springer, 1992.

[Gla90] R.J. van Glabbeek. The Linear Time - Branching Time Spectrum. In *CONCUR 90, LNCS 458*, pages 278–297. Springer, 1990.

[Gro91] J.F. Groote. A Short Proof of the Decidability of Bisimulation for Normed BPA-Processes. Technical Report CS-R9151, CWI, Dec 1991.

[HJM94] Y. Hirshfeld, M. Jerrum, and F. Moller. A Polynomial Algorithm for Deciding Bisimilarity of Normed Context-Free Processes. Technical Report ECS-LFCS-94-286, LFCS, Edinburgh, March 1994. To be presented at FOCS '94.

[HM94] Y. Hirshfeld and F. Moller. A Fast Algorithm for Deciding Bisimilarity of Normed Context-Free Processes. In *CONCUR '94, LNCS 836*, pages 48–63, 1994.

[Hoa85] C.A.R. Hoare. *Communicating Sequential Processes*. Prentice–Hall, 1985.

[HS91] H. Hüttel and C. Stirling. Actions Speak Louder than Words: Proving Bisimilarity for Context-Free Processes. In *LICS '91*, pages 376–386. IEEE Computer Society Press, 1991.

[HT94] D.T. Huynh and L. Tian. Deciding Bisimilarity of Normed Context-Free Processes is in Σ_2^p. *Theoretical Computer Science*, 123:183–197, 1994.

[Mil89] R. Milner. *Communication and Concurrency*. Prentice–Hall, 1989.

[Par81] D. Park. Concurrency and Automata on Infinite Sequences. In *5th GI Conference, LNCS 104*, pages 167–183. Springer, 1981.

On Congruences and Partial Orders*

Serge Bauget and Paul Gastin

Institut Blaise Pascal, LITP
4, place Jussieu, F-75252 Paris Cedex 05
{Serge.Bauget,Paul.Gastin}@litp.ibp.fr

Abstract. Mazurkiewicz trace theory is not powerful enough to describe concurrency paradigms as, for instance, the "Producer / Consumer". We propose in this paper a generalization of Mazurkiewicz trace monoids which allows to model such problems. We consider quotients of the free monoids by congruences which preserve the commutative images of words. An equivalence class in the quotient monoid consists of all the sequential observations of a distributed computation. In order to characterize congruences which do model concurrency, we study the relationship of this approach and the classical representation of distributed computations with partial orders. We show that the only congruences for which the classes can be represented by partial orders and the concatenation transfers modularly to partial orders are congruences generated by commutations, that is trace congruences. We prove necessary conditions and sufficient conditions on congruences so that their classes can be represented by partial orders. In particular, an important sufficient condition covers both trace congruences and the "Producer / Consumer" congruence.

1 Introduction

In computer science, Mazurkiewicz introduced trace monoids in order to describe behaviors of distributed systems [Maz77]. In such systems, actions executed by different components may be completely independent. Thus, considering a distributed computation, different external observers may perceive independent actions in different orders. Therefore a distributed computation can be modelized by the collection of all its sequential observations, called a trace, which is precisely an equivalence class in some free monoid. If A is the alphabet which represents the possible actions and $I \subseteq A \times A$ is the symmetric and irreflexive relation which contains the independent letters, the trace monoid over (A, I) is the quotient of the free monoid A^* by the congruence generated by $\{(ab, ba) \mid (a, b) \in I\}$. For detailed presentations of traces, the reader is referred to surveys [Maz87, AR88, Per89], to the monograph [Die90] or to the Book of Traces [DR95].

* This research has been supported by the ESPRIT Basic Research Actions No. 6317 ASMICS II.

However, trace theory is not powerful enough to describe the behaviors of all concurrency problems. For instance, the classical "Producer / Consumer" example cannot be described within this model. But on the other hand, the "Producer / Consumer" paradigm can all the same be described by the quotient of the free monoid $\{P, C\}^\star$ by the congruence generated by the pair (PPC, PCP), where P and C stand for *produce* and *consume*. This congruence is different from a trace congruence because a commutation of P and C depends on a left context. In this paper, we will study congruences which allow us to describe distributed systems which cannot be represented in trace theory. In this way, an equivalence class will represent the sequential observations of a parallel computation. These observations are of course composed with the same actions but the order of actions may change. So we require that the congruences preserve the number of occurrences of each letter of a word. Recently, other works has adopted the same framework [Lac92, BR94].

The theory of semi-commutations [CL87, CLR95] provides another generalization of Mazurkiewicz traces in which, for instance, the "Producer / Consumer" example can be represented. However, the point of view of semi-commutation is fully different since it consists of a rewriting system which may be non symmetric. Yet another generalization of traces linked with Petri nets and which covers in particular the "Producer / Consumer" paradigm can be found in [HKT92].

Other well-known models of distributed systems are based on partial orders, see for instance [Win88, NW95]. In such approaches, the description does not insist on the possible observations of a behavior, but on the occurrences of its actions and on their causal relations described by the partial order. In trace theory, the two approaches are equivalent. The sequential observations of a distributed computation are precisely the linear extensions of its associated partial order. Conversely, the partial order associated with a distributed computation is the intersection of (the total orders defined by) its sequential observations. In our generalized theory, we require that a congruence preserves the number of occurrences of each letter of a word. Hence, we may still associate a partial order with a distributed computation: the intersection of the total orders of its sequential observations. However, in general, the set of linear extensions of the partial order may strictly contain the set of sequential observations. When modeling distributed systems, this situation is clearly undesirable. We say that a congruence is represented by partial orders if each equivalence class is equal to the set of linear extensions of the associated partial order. The aim of this paper is to characterize congruences which are represented by partial orders. In other words, we want to find the congruences which do model concurrency.

When a congruence $\equiv$ is represented by partial orders, one may transfer the structure of the quotient monoid $A^\star/\equiv$ to the set of partial orders which represent classes. In Section 3 we characterize congruences for which the concatenation of partial orders is modular, that is, the concatenation of two partial orders may only add edges from the first one to the second one. Surprisingly, we prove that a congruence is represented by partial orders with a modular concatenation if and only if it is a trace congruence.

In the following, we are looking for characterizations of congruences which are represented by partial orders. In Section 4 we give some necessary conditions. In particular, we show that a right cancellative congruence which is represented by partial orders is necessarily generated by commutations under left contexts.

In the last section, we focus on congruences which are generated by commutations under left contexts. We show that, in general, they neither are represented by partial orders, nor are right cancellative. We give sufficient conditions for such congruences to ensure that they are represented by partial orders and are right cancellative. One such condition is that the width of each partial order is at most two. This is the case for instance for the "Producer / Consumer" example. This condition may seem restrictive but is the key point for a much more general one. We say that two letters are independent if they commute under some context. We show that a congruence is represented by partial orders (and is right cancellative) if whenever there exist three pairwise independent letters, these letters commute without any context. This sufficient condition covers in particular trace congruences and the "Producer / Consumer" congruence.

For lack of space, proofs have to be omitted. They are contained in a full version of this paper which is available as a technical report and may be published elsewhere.

2 Preliminaries

In this section, we recall basic definitions of trace theory. We consider a finite alphabet A and $A^\star$ denotes the free monoid over A, which is the set of the finite words over A with the usual concatenation. For u in $A^\star$, $alph(u)$ denotes the set of letters of u, $|u|$ the length of u and $|u|_a$ the number of occurrences of the letter a in the word u. In the trace model, the letters of A are considered as actions or events in a distributed system. And, intuitively, two events a and b are said to be independent when they can be executed concurrently or in an irrelevant order. More precisely, let $I \subseteq A \times A$ be a symmetric and irreflexive relation over the alphabet A, called the independence relation. The trace monoid over (A, I), denoted by $\mathbb{M}(A, I)$, is the quotient of the free monoid $A^\star$ by the congruence generated by $\{(ab, ba) \mid (a, b) \in I\}$. However, the trace theory is not powerful enough to describe the behaviors of all concurrency problems. The classical "Producer / Consumer" example cannot be described within this model. On the other hand, the "Producer / Consumer" paradigm can be described by the quotient of the free monoid $\{P, C\}^\star$ by the congruence generated by the pair (PPC, PCP), where P and C stand for *produce* and *consume*.

We are looking in the following to generalize these situations. The aim is still to represent a behavior of a distributed systems by its set of sequential observations. We will retain the structure of a quotient monoid of $A^\star$ through a congruence. Since the different observations of a distributed computation are all composed with the same actions (in an order which may change), we will simply require that the congruence preserves the number of the occurrences of any letter and therefore the length of any word. We will say that a congruence

$\equiv$ on $A^\star$ *preserves the commutative image* if $u \equiv v$ implies $|u|_a = |v|_a$ for all $a \in A^\star$. If $\mathcal{R}$ is a relation on $A^\star \times A^\star$, we denote by $\equiv_{\mathcal{R}}$ (or simply $\equiv$ if it is not ambiguous) the congruence generated by $\mathcal{R}$, that is the transitive and reflexive closure of the relation $\{(w'uw'', w'vw'') \mid w', w'' \in A^\star, (u,v) \in \mathcal{R}\}$. For any word u in $A^\star$, we denote by $[u]_{\mathcal{R}}$ (or simply by $[u]$) the class of u in $A^\star/\equiv_{\mathcal{R}}$. We associate with a word u its occurrence total order $To(u) = (E_u, \leq_u)$ defined by: $E_u = \{(a,i) \mid a \in A, 1 \leq i \leq |u|_a\}$ and $(a,i) \leq_u (b,j)$ if and only if the i-th occurrence of a precedes the j-th occurrence of b in u.

From now on, we will assume that the congruence $\equiv$ preserves the commutative image. Note that if $u \equiv v$ then $E_u = E_v$. This allows us to associate with the class of u its occurrence partial order, denoted by $Po(u)$, which is obtained as the intersection of the occurrence (total) orders of its representatives, that is to say:

$$Po(u) = \bigcap_{v \in [u]} To(v) = (E_u, \leq_{[u]}).$$

The relation $\leq_{[u]}$ is thus defined for all occurrences $x, y \in E_u$ by: $x \leq_{[u]} y \iff \forall v \in [u], x \leq_v y$.

To illustrate this definition, let us consider the "Producer / Consumer" example. Let $A = \{P, C\}$ and the congruence be generated by the relation $\mathcal{R} = \{(PPC, PCP)\}$. Let $u = PPCCP$. We have

$$[u] = \{PPPCC, PPCPC, PPCCP, PCPPC, PCPCP\}$$

and $Po(u)$ is defined by $E_u = \{(P,1), (P,2), (P,3), (C,1), (C,2)\}$ and

$$\leq_u = \{((P,1),(P,2)), ((P,1),(P,3)), ((P,2),(P,3)), \\ ((C,1),(C,2)), ((P,1),(C,1)), ((P,1),(C,2)), ((P,2),(C,2))\}.$$

Note that, in order to lighten the pictures, we only draw the transitive reductions (the Hasse diagrams) of partial orders. Moreover, we will not precise the occurrence numbers. Hence, the previous partial order will be simply depicted as

$$Po(u) = \left\{ \begin{array}{ccccc} P & \longrightarrow & P & \longrightarrow & P \\ & \searrow & & \searrow & \\ & & C & \longrightarrow & C \end{array} \right. .$$

Clearly we have, for all words u and v: $u \equiv v \Longrightarrow Po(u) = Po(v)$. However, the converse property: $Po(u) = Po(v) \Longrightarrow u \equiv v$ is not generally true. We can verify this with the following example: Let $A = \{a, b, c\}$ and $\equiv$ be generated by the relation $\mathcal{R} = \{(acb, cab), (bac, bca), (acb, bac), (abc, cba)\}$. Let $u = acb$. We have $[u] = \{acb, cab, bac, bca\}$ and

$$Po(u) = \left\{ \begin{array}{c} a \\ b \\ c \end{array} \right. .$$

Now let $v = abc$. We have $[v] = \{abc, cba\}$ and $Po(v) = Po(u)$ but $u \not\equiv v$.

However, this converse property holds in trace monoids : If $\equiv$ is a trace congruence then $u \equiv v \Longleftrightarrow Po(u) = Po(v)$ for all words u and v. The mapping Po from $\mathbb{M}(A, I)$ into the set $\mathcal{PO}$ of finite partial orders is thus injective and we can identify $\mathbb{M}(A, I)$ with its image through Po. In other words, we can identify a trace and its partial order. In order to clarify the relevance in associating the equivalence class and the partial order, let us take a look at three examples, after having given the following definition. If $P = (E_P, \leq_P)$ is a partial order, a word u is called *a linear extension of* P if $E_u = E_P$ and $\leq_P \subseteq \leq_u$, that is, $x \leq_P y \Longrightarrow x \leq_u y$ for all $x, y \in E_u$. We denote by $LE(P)$ the set of linear extensions of a partial order P.

1) The trace monoid: $A = \{a, b, c\}$ and $I = c \text{---} a \text{---} b$ is the independence relation. The congruence $\equiv$ is thus generated by: $\mathcal{R} = \{(ab, ba), (ac, ca)\}$. Let $u = acbac$. We have

$$[u] = \{acbac, cabac, acabc, acbca, caabc, cabca, aacbc, cbaac, cbaca, cbcaa\}$$

and

$$Po(u) = \begin{cases} a \longrightarrow a \\ c \longrightarrow b \longrightarrow c \end{cases}.$$

We can clearly see that, in this example, we have $LE(Po(u)) = [u]$.

2) Consider again the "Producer / Consumer" example presented above with $u = PPCCP$. We also have $LE(Po(u)) = [u]$.

3) Let $A = \{a, b\}$ and $\equiv$ be generated by $\mathcal{R} = \{(aab, baa)\}$. Let $u = baa$. We have $[u] = \{baa, aab\}$ and

$$Po(u) = \begin{cases} a \longrightarrow a \\ b \end{cases}$$

In this case, we have $LE(Po(u)) \neq [u]$. For instance, $aba \in LE(Po(u)) \setminus [u]$. The following definition will allow us to distinguish the previous situations.

Definition 1. We will say that a congruence $\equiv$ is represented by partial orders when it preserves the commutative image and when for each word $u \in A^\star$, $[u] = LE(Po(u))$.

When the congruence $\equiv$ preserves the commutative image, the mapping Po from $A^\star/\equiv$ into $\mathcal{PO}$ allows us to associate with each equivalence class a partial order. However in the case of a congruence represented by partial orders, we can be more precise:

Lemma 2. *If a congruence $\equiv$ is represented by partial orders, then the mapping Po from $A^\star/\equiv$ into $\mathcal{PO}$ is injective.*

Almost all the work which follows aims at characterizing the congruences represented by partial orders. The study of traces has already provided us with an example. We will also show that the case of the "Producer / Consumer" is a similar example.

3 Modular Concatenation

We start here with the study of the behavior of the concatenation with respect to partial orders. We will prove that the congruences for which the concatenation transposes itself naturally over partial orders are trace congruences only. Within this section, $\equiv$ denotes a congruence represented by partial orders. Lemma 2 is of great importance. First of all, it allows us to identify an equivalence class and its partial order. However it also allows us to define a concatenation over the set of the partial orders associated with words from $A^\star$. Indeed, the mapping Po from $A^\star/\equiv$ into $\mathcal{PO}$ is injective and $A^\star/\equiv$ is a monoid, thus we can define a structure of monoid on $Po(A^\star/\equiv)$ by setting down: $Po(u) \cdot Po(v) = Po(uv)$, for all $u, v \in A^\star$.

The concatenation on partial orders which are associated with equivalence classes does not have the same properties in the case of traces as in that of the "Producer / Consumer". To illustrate this difference, let us take another look at the previous examples.

1) The trace monoid: Let $A = \{a, b, c, d\}$ and $I = c \longrightarrow a \longrightarrow b \qquad d$ be the independence relation. Let $u = acbac$ and $v = dab$. The concatenation $Po(u) \cdot Po(v)$ of their partial orders is

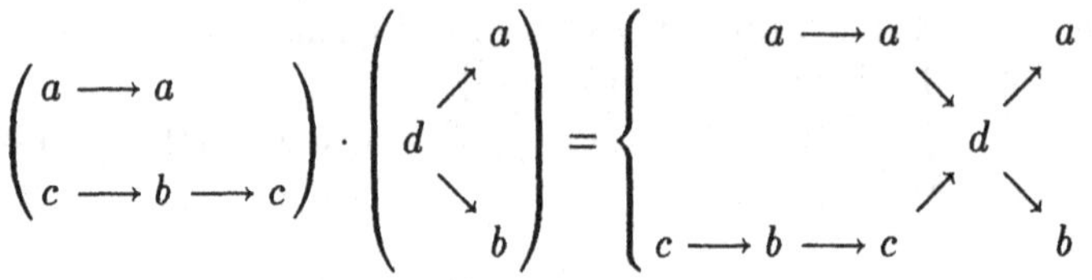

$$\begin{pmatrix} a \longrightarrow a \\ \\ c \longrightarrow b \longrightarrow c \end{pmatrix} \cdot \begin{pmatrix} & a \\ \nearrow & \\ d & \\ \searrow & \\ & b \end{pmatrix} = \left\{ \begin{array}{ccccc} a \longrightarrow a & & & & a \\ & \searrow & & \nearrow & \\ & & d & & \\ & \nearrow & & \searrow & \\ c \longrightarrow b \longrightarrow c & & & & b \end{array} \right.$$

In this example, the concatenation is simply obtained by taking the disjoint union of the partial orders and adding edges from the first one to the second one.

2) The "Producer / Consumer" example: Let $u = P$ et $v = CP$. We have

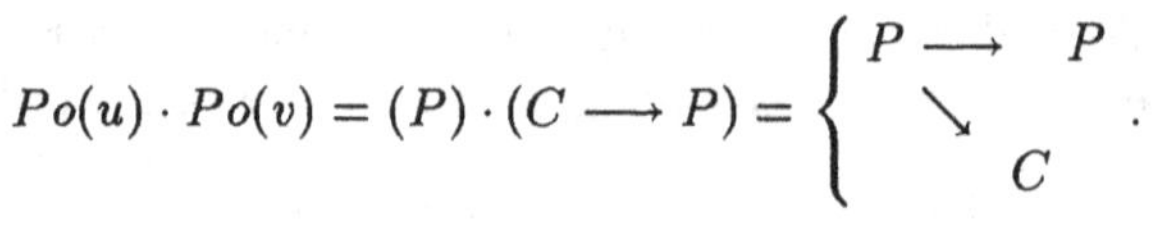

$$Po(u) \cdot Po(v) = (P) \cdot (C \longrightarrow P) = \left\{ \begin{array}{ccc} P & \longrightarrow & P \\ & \searrow & \\ & & C \end{array} \right. .$$

In this case, the link $C \longrightarrow P$ of the second partial order has been destroyed by the concatenation.

The different behaviors which are observed in the previous two examples lead us to set out the following definition. To formalize this definition, we introduce the translation $t_u : A \times \mathbb{N} \longrightarrow A \times \mathbb{N}$ defined by $t_u(a, i) = (a, i + |u|_a)$. Note that, for $u, v \in A^\star$, we have $E_{uv} = E_u \cup t_u(E_v)$.

Definition 3. We say that a congruence is modularly represented by partial orders if it is represented by partial orders and if the concatenation of two partial orders is obtained by taking their disjoint union and by possibly adding edges from the first one to the second one, that is, if for all words u and v of $A^\star$, it holds:

1. $\leq_{[uv]} \cap E_u \times E_u = \leq_{[u]}$
2. $\leq_{[uv]} \cap t_u(E_v) \times t_u(E_v) = t_u(\leq_{[v]})$
3. $\leq_{[uv]} \cap t_u(E_v) \times E_u = \emptyset$

If a congruence is modularly represented by partial orders, we will show that it can be generated by a relation in which the rules are all commutations of two letters. And thus, we prove that the congruences which are modularly represented by partial orders are exactly the trace congruences.

Theorem 4. *Let $\equiv_{\mathcal{R}}$ be a congruence generated by a relation $\mathcal{R}$. Let $\equiv_{\mathcal{C}}$ be the congruence generated by $\mathcal{C} = \{(u,v) \in \mathcal{R} \mid |u| = |v| = 2\}$. If $\equiv_{\mathcal{R}}$ is modularly represented by partial orders, then $\equiv_{\mathcal{R}} = \equiv_{\mathcal{C}}$.*

4 Necessary Conditions

In this section, we study some necessary conditions for congruences to be represented by partial orders.

Proposition 5. *Let $\equiv$ be a congruence represented by partial orders. If $ua \equiv vb$ with $a \neq b$ then $ua \equiv wba \equiv wab \equiv vb$ for some $w \in A^\star$.*

This proposition can easily be generalized to:

Proposition 6. *Let $\equiv$ be a congruence represented by partial orders.*
If $uav \equiv u'bv$ with $a \neq b$ then $uav \equiv wbav \equiv wabv \equiv u'bv$ for some $w \in A^\star$.
If $uav \equiv ubv'$ with $a \neq b$ then $uav \equiv uabw \equiv ubaw \equiv ubv'$ for some $w \in A^\star$.

We will now study right cancellative congruences. Recall that a congruence is right cancellative if $uw \equiv vw$ implies $u \equiv v$ for all $u, v, w \in A^\star$. We will show that a congruence represented by partial orders and which is right cancellative is necessarily a congruence which can be generated by a relation in which all the rules are commutations under a left context. First, note that if there exists a rule of the form $ua \equiv va$ in the relation $\mathcal{R}$ which defines $\equiv$, we then know that $u \equiv v$. The equivalence $ua \equiv va$ is thus a consequence of the equivalence of u and v. Hence the pair (ua, va) can be removed from the relation $\mathcal{R}$ without changing the generated congruence. Therefore, without loss of generality, we may assume that the rules which define $\equiv$ are formed by words which end with distinct letters. Next, remark that Proposition 5 becomes now:

Proposition 7. *Let $\equiv$ be a right cancellative congruence represented by partial orders. If $ua \equiv vb$ with $a \neq b$ then $u \equiv wb$ and $v \equiv wa$ for some $w \in A^\star$.*

We can now obtain the following main result. Indeed, this theorem admits a symmetric version when one consider left cancellative congruences.

Theorem 8. *Let $\equiv$ be a congruence represented by partial orders and which is right cancellative, then $\equiv$ can be generated by a relation in which the rules are all commutations under a left context, that is to say rules of the form: $uab \equiv uba$.*

We have just established that a congruence represented by partial orders and which is right cancellative can be generated by a relation in which the rules are all commutations under left contexts (Theorem 8). There are of course two questions which must be addressed. Let $\equiv$ be a congruence which is defined by commutations under left contexts. Is $\equiv$ right cancellative? Can $\equiv$ be represented by partial orders? The answer to these questions is no, not necessarily. To realize this, let us consider the congruence defined by the relation $\mathcal{R} = \{(cab, cba), (bac, bca), (abc, acb)\}$. $\equiv$ is not right cancellative: it is easy to show that $abcbca \equiv acbcba$ and $abcbc \not\equiv acbcb$. Moreover, $\equiv$ is not represented by partial orders. Let $u = abca$. We have $[u] = \{abca, acba, acab, abac\}$ and

$$Po(u) = \left\{ \begin{array}{ccc} & & a \\ & \nearrow & \\ a & \rightarrow & b \\ & \searrow & \\ & & c \end{array} \right. .$$

There are six linear extensions of $Po(u)$ and only four elements in $[u]$.

In fact, this example is very characteristic. The letters which commute (under a certain context) are a and b, a and c, and b and c. And if we define the independence relation I by $I = \{(a,b) \in A \times A \mid a \neq b \text{ and } wab \equiv wba \text{ for some } w \in A^\star\}$, then the graph of I is a triangle. We will come back to this situation latter.

5 Commutations under Left Contexts

The purpose of this section is to determine a family of congruences defined by commutations under left contexts and which can in addition be represented by partial orders. The following results depend on the "width" of the partial orders associated with the words. If $P = (E_P, \leq_P)$ is a partial order, recall that *an antichain* of P is a set of vertices pairwise incomparable for $\leq_P$ and *the width of* P is the maximal length of antichains of P. The first essential result which we will prove is the following:

Theorem 9. *Let $\equiv$ be a congruence generated by (a relation in which the rules are) commutations under left contexts. If for each word $u \in A^\star$, the partial order $Po(u)$ is of width at most two, then the congruence $\equiv$ is represented by partial orders and it is right cancellative.*

This theorem is a direct consequence of the following three lemmas.

Lemma 10. *Let $\equiv$ be a congruence which preserves the commutative image. Let u be a word of $A^\star$ such that the partial order $Po(u)$ has at most two maximal elements. If an occurrence of the letter a is maximal in $Po(u)$, then there exists a word v such that $u \equiv va$.*

For instance, let $\equiv$ be the congruence generated by $\mathcal{R} = \{(cca, cac), (cab, cba)\}$. Let $u = cacab$, we have $[u] = \{cacab, ccaab, cacba, ccaba, ccbaa\}$. The letter a has a maximal occurrence in $Po(u)$ and we do have $u \equiv va$ if we take for example $v = ccab$. Let us now compare $Po(u)$ and $Po(v)$. We have $[v] = \{ccab, cacb, ccba\}$ and we can see that $Po(v)$ is obtained by canceling in $Po(u)$ the last occurrence of a. The next lemma state that this is a general fact.

$$Po(u) = \left\{ \begin{array}{ccccc} & & a & \longrightarrow & a \\ & \nearrow & & & \\ c & & & \nearrow & \\ & \searrow & & & \\ & & c & \longrightarrow & b \end{array} \right. \qquad Po(v) = \left\{ \begin{array}{ccccc} & & a & & \\ & \nearrow & & & \\ c & & & & \\ & \searrow & & & \\ & & c & \longrightarrow & b \end{array} \right.$$

Let $P = (E_P, \leq_P)$ be a partial order and let $x \in E_P$ be a maximal vertex of P, we denote by $P \setminus \{x\}$ the partial order $(E \setminus \{x\}, \leq_P \bigcap (E \setminus \{x\} \times E \setminus \{x\})$.

Lemma 11. *Let $\equiv$ be a congruence generated by commutations under left contexts. Let u be a word of $A^\star$ such that the partial order $Po(u)$ is of width at most two. If α is an occurrence of the letter a maximal in $Po(u)$ and v is a word such that $u \equiv va$, then $Po(u) \setminus \{\alpha\} = Po(v)$.*

Lemma 12. *Let $\equiv$ be a congruence generated by commutations under left contexts. $\equiv$ is represented by partial orders and is right cancellative if and only if*

(i) for any word u of $A^\star$, if the letter a has a maximal occurrence in $Po(u)$, then there exits a word v such that $u \equiv va$

(ii) for all words u and v such that $u \equiv va$, if we denote by α the last occurrence of a in u, then $Po(u) \setminus \{\alpha\} = Po(v)$.

Corollary 13. *When A is an alphabet of two letters, every congruence generated by commutations under left contexts is represented by a partial order and is right cancellative. It is of course the case of the "Producer / Consumer" paradigm.*

The following results provide other families of congruences defined by commutations under left contexts which are represented by partial orders and which are right cancellative. If $\equiv$ is generated by a relation $\mathcal{R}$ in which the rules are commutations under left contexts, the independence relation associated with $\equiv$ is $I = \{(a, b) \in A \times A \mid a \neq b \text{ and } (uab, uba) \in \mathcal{R} \text{ for some } u \in A^\star\}$. We say that I contains a *triangle* if it contains a clique of three elements, that is to say when $I \supseteq \{(a, b), (b, c), (c, a), (a, c), (c, b), (b, a)\}$ for some $a, b, c \in A$.

Proposition 14. *Let $\equiv$ be a congruence generated by commutations under left contexts. If the independence relation associated with $\equiv$ does not contain a triangle, then, for every word $u \in A^\star$, the partial order $Po(u)$ has a width at most two (and thus $\equiv$ is represented by partial orders and is right cancellative).*

Theorem 15. *Let* $\equiv$ *be a congruence generated by commutations under left contexts. If, for each triangle* $\{(a,b),(b,c),(c,a),(a,c),(c,b),(b,a)\}$ *contained in the independence relation* I *associated with* $\equiv$*, the rules which commute* a *and* b*,* b *and* c *and* a *and* c *are simply commutations without context, then* $\equiv$ *is represented by partial orders and is right cancellative.*

References

[AR88] I.J. Aalbersberg and G. Rozenberg. Theory of traces. *Theoretical Computer Science*, 60:1–82, 1988.

[BR94] I. Biermann and B. Rozoy. Context traces and transition systems. In S. Kuru, M.U. Caglayan, E. Gelembe, H.L. Akin, and C. Ersoy, editors, *Proceedings of the 9th International Symposium on Computer and Information Science ISCIS IX*, pages 301–309. Bogazici University Printhouse, Turkey, 1994.

[CL87] M. Clerbout and M. Latteux. Semi-Commutations. *Information and Computation*, 73:59–74, 1987.

[CLR95] M. Clerbout, M. Latteux, and Y. Roos. Semi-commutations. In G. Rozenberg and V. Diekert, editors, *The Book of Traces*, pages 487–552. World Scientific, Singapore, 1995.

[Die90] V. Diekert. *Combinatorics on Traces*. Number 454 in Lecture Notes in Computer Science. Springer Verlag, 1990.

[DR95] V. Diekert and G. Rozenberg, editors. *Book of Traces*. World Scientific, Singapore, 1995. to appear.

[HKT92] P.W. Hoogers, H.C.M. Kleijn, and P.S. Thiagarajan. A trace semantics for petri nets. In W. Kuich, editor, *Proceedings of the 19th International Colloquium on Automata Languages and Programming (ICALP'92)*, number 623 in Lecture Notes in Computer Science, pages 595–604. Springer Verlag, 1992.

[Lac92] J. Lacaze. Parties reconnaissables de monoïdes définis par générateurs et relations. *R.A.I.R.O. — Informatique Théorique et Applications*, 26:541–552, 1992.

[Maz77] A. Mazurkiewicz. Concurrent program schemes and their interpretations. Tech. rep. DAIMI PB 78, Aarhus University, 1977.

[Maz87] A. Mazurkiewicz. Trace theory. In W. Brauer et al., editors, *Advances in Petri Nets'86*, number 255 in Lecture Notes in Computer Science, pages 279–324. Springer Verlag, 1987.

[NW95] M. Nielsen and G. Winskel. Trace structures and other models for concurrency. In G. Rozenberg and V. Diekert, editors, *The Book of Traces*, pages 271–306. World Scientific, Singapore, 1995.

[Per89] D. Perrin. Partial commutations. In G. Ausiello et al., editors, *Proceedings of the 16th International Colloquium on Automata, Languages and Programming (ICALP'89)*, number 372 in Lecture Notes in Computer Science, pages 637–651. Springer Verlag, 1989.

[Win88] G. Winskel. An introduction to event structures. In J.W. de Bakker, W.-P. de Roever, and G. Rozenberg, editors, *Linear Time, Branching Time and Partial Order in Logics and Models for Concurrency*, number 354 in Lecture Notes in Computer Science, pages 123–172. Springer Verlag, 1988.

Performance Preorder: Ordering Processes with Respect to Speed*

Flavio Corradini[1] and Roberto Gorrieri[2] and Marco Roccetti[2]

[1] Dipartimento di Scienze dell'Informazione, Università "La Sapienza"
Via Salaria 113, I-00189 Roma, Italy
e-mail: corradini@dsi.uniroma1.it

[2] Dipartimento di Scienze dell'Informazione, Università di Bologna
Piazza di Porta S. Donato 5, I-40127 Bologna, Italy
e-mail: {gorrieri,roccetti}@cs.unibo.it

Abstract. The theory of processes with durational actions proposed in [8] is equipped here with a preorder based on execution speed, called performance preorder. Two processes P and Q are related if they are strong bisimilar (i.e., functional equivalent) and the first one is at least as fast as the second one. Hence, this preorder supports the stepwise refinement "from specification to implementation" by increasing efficiency while retaining the same functionality. We show that the problem of finding faster implementations for a specification is connected to the problem of finding more distributed implementations of the same specification. This is an immediate consequence of the proof that the location preorder, which is based on a measure of distribution, implies the performance preorder.

1 Introduction

Recently, in the field of semantics for process description languages, a great deal of interest has been stirred up by equivalence notions which incorporate some measure of efficiency (see, e.g., [12, 3, 8]). Some of them [2, 7, 8] rely on the basic idea that processes are discriminated not only according to their *functionality* (what actions the processes can do), but also considering their *performance* (a measure of the time consumed for their execution).

Any action a is assumed to have a duration $f(a)$ which represents the time needed for its execution. Every sequential subprocess is equipped with a clock, whose elapsing is set by the execution of actions. Whenever an action a is executed by a sequential subcomponent F, the value n of the clock of F is incremented to $n + f(a)$, whilst the local clocks of those sequential components not involved in the execution of a are unaffected. Hence, if F is idle during a transition, its local clock value cannot increase. In other words, each sequential subprocess is always *eager* to perform an executable action (or dually actions are *urgent*): the time value is incremented locally only when the executable action is performed. A simple example may be helpful. Consider the term $E = a.c|b$. Since

* Research partially supported by MURST, CNR and Esprit BRA n. 8130 LOMAPS.

the clock is set to 0 before starting the execution of E, $s = (0 \Rightarrow a.c) \,|\, (0 \Rightarrow b)$ is the initial state of the transition system, where the auxiliary operator $n \Rightarrow F$ means that the execution of F starts exactly after n time units of the global clock. One of the two transitions out of s is labelled $< a, f(a) >$ and reaches $(f(a) \Rightarrow c)|(0 \Rightarrow b)$. By executing b, it reaches the state $(f(a) \Rightarrow c)|(f(b) \Rightarrow nil)$; finally the execution of c produces a transition labelled $< c, f(a) + f(c) >$ with target state $(f(a) + f(c) \Rightarrow nil) \,|\, (f(b) \Rightarrow nil)$. It is immediate observing that the time needed for the complete execution of E is $max\{f(a)+f(c), f(b)\}$. Standard bisimulation on this labelled transition system defines a new semantics for process algebras, called *performance equivalence* in [8], which equates systems whenever they perform the *same* actions in the *same* amount of time.

This paper is in the line of [8], but here we focus on the problem of *ordering processes with respect to speed*, allowing to consider degrees of efficiency among processes, for example by forcing implementations to be faster than (although functionally equivalent to) specifications. The tool used to this aim is a preorder, called *performance preorder* and denoted by $\sqsubseteq_p$, which is based on the classical notion of bisimulation. Intuitively, $E_1 \sqsubseteq_p E_2$ if and only if E_1 and E_2 are strong bisimilar but E_1 is at least as fast as E_2. The kernel of this preorder gives rise to a new equivalence, called *competitive equivalence* and denoted $\simeq_c$, which relates processes by considering only the optimal (or fastest) and worst (or slowest) executions. This equivalence is more discriminating than interleaving bisimulation [10]. Indeed, the equation $a \,|\, b \simeq_c a.b + b.a$ does not hold in our setting because $a|b \sqsubseteq_p a.b+b.a$ but $a.b+b.a \not\sqsubseteq_p a|b$. To see this consider the possible transitions which $a.b + b.a$ and $a \,|\, b$ can perform:

$$0 \Rightarrow a.b + b.a \overset{<a,f(a)>}{\longrightarrow} f(a) \Rightarrow b \overset{<b,f(a)+f(b)>}{\longrightarrow} f(a) + f(b) \Rightarrow nil$$

$$0 \Rightarrow a \,|\, 0 \Rightarrow b \overset{<a,f(a)>}{\longrightarrow} f(a) \Rightarrow nil \,|\, 0 \Rightarrow b \overset{<b,f(b)>}{\longrightarrow} f(a) \Rightarrow nil \,|\, f(b) \Rightarrow nil$$

Thus, we can see that all the actions of the former state can be performed in a less or equal time of the corresponding "matching" transitions of the latter state. Competitive equivalence is weaker than performance equivalence: $E_1 = a.a.a + a|a|a$ and $E_2 = a.a.a + a|a|a + a.a|a$ provide the needed example. We claim that competitive equivalence is more appropriate when one is interested in extimating the time intervals for the optimal and worst cases only.

The paper is organized as follows. In Section 2 we introduce a simple process algebra (with recursion, but without communication), together with its operational semantics. In Section 3 we recall performance equivalence from [8] and describe performance preorder and competitive equivalence. In Section 4 we compare competitive equivalence with the best known untimed non-interleaving semantics proposed in the literature. This includes a comparison of performance preorder with the *causal preorder* [1] and with the *location preorder* [4]. The latter comparison is particularly interesting as it proves the (quite expected) result that the more distributed a process is, the more efficient it is. Finally, Section 5 is devoted to comparison with related work and further research.

2 Language and Operational Semantics

Let *Act* be the set of *actions*, ranged over by a, b, c, ... and X be the set of variables, ranged over by x, y, z, ... The process terms are freely generated by the following syntax:

$$F \quad ::= \quad nil \quad \Big| \quad a.F \quad \Big| \quad F+F \quad \Big| \quad F \mid F \quad \Big| \quad x \quad \Big| \quad \mathrm{rec}\ x.\,F$$

This is the subset of *CCS* [10], where the parallel operator | does not allow communication. In the following, we will focus on the set P of the closed terms (called *agents* or *processes*), ranged over by E. The set of *finite processes* (i.e., without recursion) will be denoted by P_{fin}.

The final goal of any program is to be executed, and the measure of the time it consumes strictly depends on the chosen machine. Our assumptions on abstract machines are the following:

1) *maximal parallelism:* whenever a new subprocess is activated, there is always a processor free, ready to execute it.
2) *eagerness:* there is no time-passing in between the execution of actions from the same subprocess; equivalently actions happen as soon as possible.
3) *static duration:* the amount of time needed for the execution of an action is fixed on the basis of the features of the abstract machine.

As the duration of actions can be different for different machines, we should take this parameter into account. One possibility is to introduce *duration functions* (ranged over by f, g) which associate to each action the number of time units needed for its execution. In the following, we choose any duration function $f\,:\,Act \rightarrow N^+$, simply to fix this parameter. Our language is equipped with an SOS semantics in terms of labelled transition systems.

Definition 1. A *labelled transition system* is a triple $< S, M, T >$ where S is a set of *states*, M is a set of *labels* and $T = \{\stackrel{\mu}{\longrightarrow} \subseteq S \times S \mid \mu \in M\}$ is the *transition relation*. We will write $s \stackrel{\mu}{\longrightarrow} s'$ instead of $< s, s' > \in \stackrel{\mu}{\longrightarrow}$.

In our case, the states are terms of a syntax extending the one for agents with a local *clock prefixing* operator, $n \Rightarrow \_$, which records the evolution of different parts of a distributed state.

Definition 2. The states are terms generated by the following syntax:

$$s \quad ::= \quad n \Rightarrow nil \quad \Big| \quad n \Rightarrow a.E \quad \Big| \quad s+s \quad \Big| \quad s \mid s \quad \Big| \quad n \Rightarrow \mathrm{rec}\ x.\,F$$

where E and $\mathrm{rec}\ x.\,F$ denote agents. The set of states is denoted by S.

The equations in Table 1, called *clock distribution equations*, show that the operator $n \Rightarrow \_$ may be applied to any agent E, which can be canonically reduced to a state, when interpreting these equations as rewrite rules from left to right.

$n \Rightarrow (E \mid E') = (n \Rightarrow E) \mid (n \Rightarrow E')$
$n \Rightarrow (E + E') = (n \Rightarrow E) + (n \Rightarrow E')$

Table 1. Clock Distribution Equations.

Each transition is labelled by a pair of the form $< a, n >$ meaning that action a has been completed exactly n time units after the computation began. Hence, the set of labels for the transition system is $\Pi = Act \times N^+$. The transition relation is given through a set of inference rules (Table 2) defined in a structural inductive manner. It is worthwhile observing that these rules are parametric w.r.t. the chosen duration function f. Hence, to be precise, we should write $\longrightarrow_f$.

$$Act \quad \frac{}{n \Rightarrow a.E \xrightarrow{<a,k>} k \Rightarrow E} \quad k = n + f(a)$$

$$Alt_1 \quad \frac{s_1 \xrightarrow{<a,n>} s_1'}{s_1 + s_2 \xrightarrow{<a,n>} s_1'} \qquad Alt_2 \quad \frac{s_2 \xrightarrow{<a,n>} s_2'}{s_1 + s_2 \xrightarrow{<a,n>} s_2'}$$

$$Par_1 \quad \frac{s_1 \xrightarrow{<a,n>} s_1'}{s_1 \mid s_2 \xrightarrow{<a,n>} s_1' \mid s_2} \qquad Par_2 \quad \frac{s_2 \xrightarrow{<a,n>} s_2'}{s_1 \mid s_2 \xrightarrow{<a,n>} s_1 \mid s_2'}$$

$$Rec \quad \frac{n \Rightarrow E[\text{rec } x.\, E/x] \xrightarrow{<a,n>} s'}{n \Rightarrow \text{rec } x.\, E \xrightarrow{<a,n>} s'}$$

Table 2. The Structural Rules for the Operational Semantics.

A few comments are now in order. Rule *Act* states that an action a, executable at time n, is completed at time $k = n + f(a)$; the number k denotes the time which passed for all the sequential subprocesses of E. Note that $k \Rightarrow E$ may be not a state; in such a case, applications of the clock distribution equations will eventually transform $k \Rightarrow E$ into a state. Rules Alt_1, Alt_2, Par_1 and Par_2 are as usual. Finally, note that $n \Rightarrow E[\text{rec } x.\, E/x]$ in the premise of rule *Rec* may need applications of the clock distribution equations to become a state.

3 Behavioural Semantics

In this section we first recall the definition of performance equivalence from [8] and prove that it is a congruence. Then, we study performance preorder and the induced competitive equivalence.

3.1 Performance Equivalence

The observational semantics we are interested in is based on the branching-time semantics of bisimulation; as a matter of fact, performance bisimulation is nothing but (ordinary) strong bisimulation on the transition system labelled by pairs of the form $< a, n >$.

Definition 3. (*Performance Equivalence*)

1) Let Rel denote the set of binary relations over S. The functional $R : Rel \longrightarrow Rel$ is defined, for each $\Re \in Rel$, as follows: $(s_1, s_2) \in R(\Re)$ if, for each $a \in A$,
   i) $s_1 \stackrel{<a,n>}{\longrightarrow} s'_1$ implies $s_2 \stackrel{<a,n>}{\longrightarrow} s'_2$ such that $(s'_1, s'_2) \in \Re$;
   ii) $s_2 \stackrel{<a,n>}{\longrightarrow} s'_2$ implies $s_1 \stackrel{<a,n>}{\longrightarrow} s'_1$ such that $(s'_1, s'_2) \in \Re$.
2) A relation $\Re \in Rel$ will be called a $R-$ ***bisimulation*** if $\Re \subseteq R(\Re)$.
3) We say that two states s_1 and s_2 are *f-performance equivalent*, denoted $s_1 \sim^f s_2$, if and only if there exists a $R-$ ***bisimulation*** $\Re$ such that $(s_1, s_2) \in \Re$.
4) We say that two agents E_1, E_2 are *f-performance equivalent*, denoted $E_1 \sim_p^f E_2$, if and only if $0 \Rightarrow E_1 \sim^f 0 \Rightarrow E_2$.

Again, when f is clear from the context, we can omit the superscript f, as in $s_1 \sim s_2$ and $E_1 \sim_p E_2$. This observational semantics equates systems whenever they perform the same actions at the same time thus introducing a simple form of performance evaluation in process algebra.

Proposition 4. Performance equivalence is a congruence on P.

3.2 The Performance Preorder

In order to relate processes with respect to speed, we propose a preorder $\sqsubseteq_p^f$ over P: $E_1 \sqsubseteq_p^f E_2$ if and only if E_1 and E_2 have the same functional behavior but E_1 is at least as fast as E_2 according to duration function f.

Definition 5. (*Performance Preorder*)

1) Let Rel denote the set of binary relations over S. The functional $G : Rel \longrightarrow Rel$ is defined, for each $\Re \in Rel$, as follows: $(s_1, s_2) \in G(\Re)$, if for each $a \in A$,
   i) $s_1 \stackrel{<a,n>}{\longrightarrow} s'_1$ implies $s_2 \stackrel{<a,m>}{\longrightarrow} s'_2$ such that $n \leq m$ and $(s'_1, s'_2) \in \Re$;
   ii) $s_2 \stackrel{<a,n>}{\longrightarrow} s'_2$ implies $s_1 \stackrel{<a,m>}{\longrightarrow} s'_1$ such that $n \geq m$ and $(s'_1, s'_2) \in \Re$.
2) A relation $\Re \in Rel$ will be called a $G-$ ***bisimulation*** if $\Re \subseteq G(\Re)$.
3) We say that two states s_1 and s_2 are in the relation of *f-performance preorder* (denoted $s_1 \sqsubseteq^f s_2$) if and only if there exists a $G-$***bisimulation*** $\Re$ such that $(s_1, s_2) \in \Re$.
4) We say that $E_1 \sqsubseteq_p^f E_2$ if and only if $0 \Rightarrow E_1 \sqsubseteq^f 0 \Rightarrow E_2$.

Whenever clear from the context we will omit the superscript duration function. Hence, we will often write $s_1 \sqsubseteq s_2$ or $E_1 \sqsubseteq_p E_2$.

Example 1. A few examples are now in order.

$$a \mid b \sqsubseteq_p a.b + b.a, \qquad a.b + b.a \not\sqsubseteq_p a \mid b$$
$$a \mid b + a.b + b.a \sqsubseteq_p a.b + b.a, \qquad a.b + b.a \not\sqsubseteq_p a \mid b + a.b + b.a$$
$$a \mid b \sqsubseteq_p a \mid b + a.b + b.a, \quad a \mid b + a.b + b.a \not\sqsubseteq_p a \mid b$$

Relation $\sqsubseteq_p$ is reflexive and transitive but not symmetric as the examples above show. When relating processes with respect to speed by means of $\sqsubseteq_p$, of each set of functionally-equivalent computations we focus only on the fastest one and on the slowest one, which provide a lower and upper bound to the time needed for executions. For instance, in $a \mid b + a.b + b.a$ there are two different computations for the sequence ab, with different temporal behaviour. We have that $E_1 = a \mid b + a.b + b.a \sqsubseteq_p E_2 = a.b + b.a$ because the fastest computation for ab in E_1 is faster than the fastest (actually unique) ab computation from E_2, as well as the slowest computation for ab is faster than the slowest ab computation from E_2. All the "performance-intermediate" functionally-equivalent computations are irrelevant, as the following example shows.

Example 2. Consider the following two processes $E_1 = a.a.a + a|a|a$ and $E_2 = a.a.a + a|a|a + a.a|a$. We have that $E_1 \sqsubseteq_p E_2$ and $E_2 \sqsubseteq_p E_1$. This shows that the "intermediate" aaa computations due to subagent $a.a|a$ have no influence on the preorder.

Proposition 6. Performance preorder is a precongruence over P.

Relation $\sqsubseteq_p^f$ depends on the choice of the duration function f, as the following example shows.

Example 3. Consider $E_1 = a.a \mid c$ and $E_2 = a.a \mid c + c.(a \mid a)$. We can show that $E_1 \sqsubseteq_p^f E_2$ if and only if $f(a) \leq f(c)$. In fact, every transition of $0 \Rightarrow E_1$ can be matched (in the same time) by a transition of $0 \Rightarrow E_2$. Similarly, transitions performed by the summand $0 \Rightarrow a.a \mid c$ of E_2 can be matched by transitions of $0 \Rightarrow E_1$. Consider now the transitions from $0 \Rightarrow c.(a \mid a)$. This term can perform $0 \Rightarrow c.(a \mid a) \xrightarrow{<c,f(c)>} f(c) \Rightarrow a \mid f(c) \Rightarrow a$ and, in order to match this transition, $0 \Rightarrow E_1$ can only perform $0 \Rightarrow E_1 \xrightarrow{<c,f(c)>} 0 \Rightarrow a.a \mid f(c) \Rightarrow nil$. Now, $0 \Rightarrow a.a \mid f(c) \Rightarrow nil \sqsubseteq^f f(c) \Rightarrow a \mid f(c) \Rightarrow a$ if and only if $f(a) \leq f(c)$ because the second a of the left state will be completed after $2 \times f(a)$ units of time, while the second a of the right one after $f(c) + f(a)$.

3.3 Competitive Equivalence

In a natural way, the kernel of the preorder gives rise to a notion of equivalence, called *competitive equivalence*.

Definition 7. Two agents E_1 and E_2 are *competitive* equivalent (denoted $E_1 \simeq_p E_2$) if $E_1 \sqsubseteq_p E_2$ and $E_2 \sqsubseteq_p E_1$. In other words, $\simeq_p = \sqsubseteq_p \cap \sqsupseteq_p$.

Analogously to performance preorder, competitive equivalence discriminates agents only by considering the fastest computation and the slowest one for any set of functionally-equivalent computations. Two agents are equivalent if these upper and lower bounds coincide. Also in this case, all the "performance-intermediate" functionally-equivalent computations are irrelevant, as Example 2 shows: $E_1 \simeq_p E_2$ even if E_2 has additional "intermediate" aaa computations.

Relation $\simeq_p$ enjoys the same properties of congruence enjoyed by the preorder. In particular it is preserved by every syntactic construct of the language, including recursion. Moreover, similarly to the preorder, competitive equivalence does depend on the duration assigned to every action.

Proposition 8. Let E_1 and E_2 be two agents and f be a duration function. Then $E_1 \simeq_p^f E_2$ does not imply $E_1 \simeq_p^g E_2$ for any action duration function g.

Proof. Consider processes $E_1 = a.a|c + c.a.a$ and $E_2 = a.a|c + c.a.a + c.(a|a)$. We can show that $E_1 \simeq_p^f E_2$ if and only if $f(a) \leq f(c)$. To prove $E_1 \simeq_p^f E_2$ we have to show both $E_1 \sqsubseteq_p^f E_2$ and $E_2 \sqsubseteq_p^f E_1$. The latter immediately follows whatever is the time assigned to actions a and c. The former follows if and only if $f(a) \leq f(c)$ by similar arguments of Example 3.

The same does not happen for the specific case of constant durational functions, as stated in the following proposition.

Proposition 9. Let E_1 and E_2 be two agents and f, g be any two constant duration functions. Then $E_1 \simeq_p^f E_2$ implies $E_1 \simeq_p^g E_2$.

We now compare performance and competitive equivalences. Because $=$ implies $\leq$ and $=$ implies $\geq$ in N^+, $\sim_p$ is indeed a $G-$ ***bisimulation***.

Proposition 10. For E_1, $E_2 \in P$ and any f, we have that $E_1 \sim_p^f E_2$ implies $E_1 \simeq_p^f E_2$.

The converse implication does not hold, i.e. $\simeq_p^f$ is strictly weaker than $\sim_p^f$. To this, consider the two agents in Example 2, which are $\simeq_p^f$-equivalent but not $\sim_p^f$-equivalent.

4 Comparative Performance Semantics

In this section we first show how our preorder relates with *strong bisimulation equivalence*. Then we compare our preorder with *causal preorder* [1] and *location preorder* [4]. Finally, we establish how competitive equivalence relates with the best known untimed non-interleaving semantics proposed in the literature, namely *location* [4], *causal* [6], *ST* [9] and *step* [13] equivalences.

4.1 Relationships with Strong Bisimulation Equivalence

Performance preorder is related to bisimulation equivalence $\sim$ as illustrated in the following theorem (where P_{seq} is the set of processes built without parallel composition).

Theorem 11. Let $E_1 \in P_{seq}$, E_2, $E_3 \in P$ and f is any duration function. Then:

1) $E_1 \sim E_2$ iff $E_2 \sqsubseteq_p^f E_1$.
2) $E_2 \sqsubseteq_p^f E_3$ implies $E_2 \sim E_3$,

4.2 Relationships with Non-interleaving Preorders

We first consider the case of the causal preorder [1]. In this semantic theory, transitions are of the form $E_1 \xrightarrow{u} E_2$ where E_1 and E_2 are P terms, while u is a pomset of actions in Act, called computation. A preorder $\leq_C$ over computations/pomsets is defined: $u \leq_C v$ if u and v correspond to the execution of the same actions, but performed in a less caused fashion in the computation v. The syntax preorder $\leq_C$ is used to induce a preorder, called causal preorder and denoted $\sqsubseteq_c$, over the set of processes P. This preorder preorder does not reduce concurrency to sequentiality and nondeterminism. Its definition is very similar to that of performance preorder but instead of relating natural numbers, it relates pomsets with respect to $\leq_C$. The following proposition shows that $\sqsubseteq_c$ is incomparable with our performance preorder.

Proposition 12. Let E_1 and E_2 be two P terms. Then:

i) $E_1 \sqsubseteq_c E_2$ does not imply $E_1 \sqsubseteq_p^f E_2$
ii) $E_1 \sqsubseteq_c E_2$ does not imply $E_1 \sqsupseteq_p^f E_2$
iii) $E_1 \sqsubseteq_p^f E_2$ does not imply $E_1 \sqsubseteq_c E_2$
iv) $E_1 \sqsubseteq_p^f E_2$ does not imply $E_1 \sqsupseteq_c E_2$

Proof. We provide a pair of processes related by $\sqsubseteq_c$ but not by $\sqsubseteq_p^f$ or $\sqsupseteq_p^f$ and vice versa. i) $a.b+b.a \sqsubseteq_c a \mid b$ but $a.b+b.a \not\sqsubseteq_p^f a \mid b$ for any duration function f. ii) $a.(b+c)+a|b \sqsubseteq_c a.(b+c)+a|b+a.b$ but $a.(b+c)+a|b \not\sqsupseteq_p^f a.(b+c)+a|b+a.b$ for any duration function f. iii) $a \mid b \sqsubseteq_p^f a.b+b.a$ for any f but $a \mid b \not\sqsubseteq_c a.b+b.a$. vi) $a.a|a.a \sqsubseteq_p^f a.a.(a|a)$ for any f, but $a.a.(a|a) \not\sqsubseteq_c a.a|a.a$. It is clear that $a.a|a.a \sqsubseteq_p^f a.a.(a|a)$. To show that $a.a.(a|a) \not\sqsubseteq_c a.a|a.a$ consider the transitions $a.a|a.a \xrightarrow{a.a} nil|a.a \xrightarrow{a.a} nil|nil$ which cannot be successfully matched by $a.a.(a|a)$.

For similar reasons the kernel of the causal preorder, $\simeq_c$, does not coincide with our competitive equivalence. Processes $E_1 = a.(b+c) + a|b + a.b$ and $E_2 = a.(b+c)+a|b$ are $\simeq_c$-equivalent but not competitive equivalent (note that $E_1 \not\sqsubseteq_p^f E_2$). To prove that $\simeq_p^f$ does not imply $\simeq_c$, consider the pair of processes in Proposition 8 which are $\simeq_p^f$-equivalent (for $f(a) \leq f(c)$) but not $\simeq_c$-equivalent. It follows that $\simeq_p^f$ and $\simeq_c$ are incomparable.

Let us now consider location preorder from [4]. The intuition behind this preorder is that two processes are related if the first is "more distributed" over the space than the other one. Technically, location names (taken from an infinite set Loc of names) are dynamically assigned to performed actions. This is achieved by means of a transition relation of the form $\xrightarrow{a,u}$, where a is an action, $u = l_1 ... l_n l$ is a word over Loc. For $u, v \in Loc^*$, $u \leq v$ holds if u is a subword of v. This preorder on location names induces a preorder $\sqsubseteq_l$ on processes. Its definition is very similar to that of performance preorder but instead of relating natural numbers, it relates locations with respect to $\leq$. We state that location preorder strictly implies performance preorder so that if E_1 is "more distributed than" E_2, then E_1 is "faster than" E_2, but the vice versa is not always true.

Proposition 13. Let E_1 and E_2 be in P.Then, $E_1 \sqsubseteq_l E_2$ implies $E_1 \sqsubseteq_p E_2$.

For the counter-example, let us consider the pair of processes in Example 3. They are $\sqsubseteq_p^f$-related if $f(a) \leq f(c)$, but they are not $\sqsubseteq_l$-related.

The same holds when considering the kernel of location preorder (defined as usual by $\simeq_l = \sqsubseteq_l \cap \sqsupseteq_l$) and competitive equivalence.

Proposition 14. Let E_1 and E_2 be in P. Then, $E_1 \simeq_l E_2$ implies $E_1 \simeq_p E_2$.

4.3 Relationships with Non-interleaving Equivalences

Proposition 15. For processes in P, location equivalence as well as causal equivalence and ST equivalence strictly imply competitive equivalence.

It is worth noting that competitive equivalence is incomparable with *step equivalence*, the coarsest non-interleaving semantics proposed so far. Intuitively the transitions of the step semantics are labelled by multisets of actions which are concurrently executable. Thus for example $a|b \sim_{Step} a|b + a.b$. Clearly $a|b \not\simeq_p^f a|b + a.b$ for any f because $a|b + a.b \not\sqsubseteq_p^f a|b$. To see that $\simeq_p^f$ does not imply $\sim_{Step}$ consider the pair of processes E_1 and E_2 in Proposition 8 which are $\simeq_p^f$-equivalent (for $f(a) \leq f(c)$) but not $E_1 \sim_{Step} E_2$. In fact process $E_2 \xrightarrow{c} a|a$ while E_1 can perform c but the resulting two a actions can be performed sequentially only.

5 Conclusions

In this paper we presented a semantic theory for a process description language which is based on a preorder $\sqsubseteq_p$ relating two processes E_1 and E_2 if they have the same functional behaviour and E_1 is at least as fast as E_2. We have proved the intutive and expected fact that the more distributed a process is, the more efficient it is. In [5] a complete and sound axiomatization of performance preorder and competitive equivalence is provided, together with an example of stepwise refinement of a specification to its optimal implementation.

5.1 Related Work

Two preorders relating processes with respect to speed have been proposed in the process algebra literature. Both have in common with us only the goal because they conceive "time passing" in a completely different way. In [3] a notion of efficiency is based on the number of communications that have taken place. Hence, E_1 is "faster" than E_2 if E_1 never need to perform more internal (τ-) actions than E_2. This notion has an intuitive justification in the fact that communications are often the most expensive operations to be performed. However, no performance measure is available for a language without communication. In [12] a "faster than" relation has been studied in the so-called abstract time approach: actions are atomic and time passes "in between" them. We claim that this approach to timed agents, even if appropriate for specific applications, is less natural than ours as only in our approach one can formally prove the basically intutive statement that "the more distributed a process is, the more efficient it is".

5.2 Open Problems and Future Research

Extending our theory to communicating processes seems not trivial. In the setting of durational actions, two different synchronization rules have been proposed [2, 8]. However, in both cases performance preorder is not a precongruence for parallel composition with synchronization. Further work will be devoted to solve this problem. Another, quite interesting line of research is the study of "optimal implementations": given a specification E_1, find the fastest E_2 which is functionally equivalent to E_1. This means that we would like to study algorithms for finding the minimal elements in the performance preorder. Due to the comparison with the location preorder, it seems clear that this problem is tightly related to the problem of finding *parallel decompositions* of processes, where the notion of decomposition we have in mind has some connection with the one in [11].

Acknowledgements

The first author thanks Rocco De Nicola for his encouragement to explore this area of research.

References

1. L.Aceto, *On Relating Concurrency and Nondeterminism*, Technical Report SI/RR–89/06, University of Sussex, 1989.
2. L.Aceto, D.Murphy, *Timing and Causality in Process Algebra*, Technical Report 9/93, University of Sussex, 1993, to appear in Acta Informatica.
3. S.Arun-Kumar and M.Hennessy, *An Efficiency Preorder for Processes*, Acta Informatica **29**, pp.737-760, 1992.
4. G.Boudol, I.Castellani, M.Hennessy, A.Kiehn, *A Theory of Processes with Localities*, Formal Aspects of Computing **6**, pp. 165-200, 1993.
5. F.Corradini, R.Gorrieri and M.Roccetti, *Performance Preorder and Competitive equivalence*, Tech.Rep. LFCS-95-1, University of Bologna, January 1995.
6. Ph.Darondeau, P.Degano, *Causal trees*, In Automata, Languages and Programming, Springer, LNCS **372**, 1989.
7. G-L.Ferrari and U.Montanari, *Observing Time-Complexity of Concurrent Programs*, Technical Report, Dipartimento di Informatica, Università di Pisa, 1993.
8. R.Gorrieri, M.Roccetti and E. Stancampiano, *A Theory of Processes with Durational Actions*, Theoretical Computer Science **140** (1), pp. 73-94, March 1995.
9. R.J. van Glabbeek, F.Vaandrager, *Petri Net Models for Algebraic Theories of Concurrency*, In Proc. of PARLE II, Springer, LNCS **259**, pp. 224-242, 1987.
10. R.Milner, *Communication and concurrency*, International Series on Computer Science, Prentice Hall International, 1989.
11. R.Milner, F.Moller, *Unique Decomposition of Processes.* Theoretical Computer Science **107**, pp. 357-363, 1993.
12. F.Moller, C.Tofts, *Relating Processes with Respect to Speed.* In CONCUR'91, LNCS **527**, Springer-Verlag, pp. 424-438, 1991.
13. M.Nielsen, P.S.Thiagarajan, *Degrees of Nondeterminism and Concurrency*, In Proc. 4th Conf. on FST & TCS, Springer, LNCS **181**, pp. 89-117, 1984.

Towards a Semantic Theory of CML
Extended Abstract

W. Ferreira
M. Hennessy

University of Sussex

Abstract. A simple untyped language based on *CML*, Concurrent ML, is defined and analysed. The language contains a *spawn* operator for initiating new independent threads of computation and constructs for the exchange of data between these threads. A denotational model for the language is presented where denotations correspond to computations of values rather than simply values. It is shown to be fully abstract with respect to a behavioural preorder based on contextual testing.

1 Introduction

The language Concurrent ML (*CML*), [16], is one of a number of recent languages which seeks to combine aspects of functional and concurrent programming. Standard ML, [19], is augmented with the ability to spawn off new independent threads of computation. Further constructs are added to enable these threads to synchronise and exchange data on communication channels. Although it has been implemented there has been very little work on its semantic foundations.

As a first step in this direction we consider a relatively simple language which nevertheless contains some of the key features of *CML*. It is a language for the evaluation of simple untyped expressions which contains a *spawn* operator for introducing new threads of computation. To this is added a range of constructs, based on those of *CCS*, for receiving and sending values. The resulting language combines the production of values, the spawning of concurrent threads and the exchange of data among these threads in a computationally non-trivial manner.

In Section 2 we give the syntax of our language and an operational semantics. This is more general than the corresponding reduction relations of [16, 3], as it also determines the communication potentials of expressions and their ability to produce values; the operational semantics is given in terms of an extended *labelled transition system*. This would enable us to define a notion of observational equivalence for expressions but instead in this paper we consider a Morris style behavioural preorder [13] $\sqsubset\!\!\!\sim$, based on the ability to guarantee the production of values,

The remainder of the paper is devoted to building a fully-abstract denotational model for this preorder. The starting point is the value passing version of Acceptance Trees, [7], considered in [8] which is extended to a new model **D** to take into account the ability of expressions to produce values. However the key point is the recognition that elements of the model correspond not to values but to *computations* of values. Thus a monadic interpretation, [12], of the model is required and this leads to the interpretation of the language in a *retract* of **D**, called **E**, which is shown to be fully-abstract with respect to $\sqsubset\!\!\!\sim$. We end with a brief comparison with other work.

In this extended abstract all proofs are omitted; instead emphasis is placed explaining the operational semantics of the languages and giving an overview of the construction of the model.

2 The Language and its Operational Semantics

We start with a simple sequential language for evaluating expressions over some datatype such as the Natural Numbers. Parallelism may be introduced into such a sequential language by adding an operator called *spawn* which can initiate a new computational thread. An abstract syntax for such a language could be given by the following:

$$\begin{aligned} e &::= d \mid op(\underline{d}) \mid let\ x = e\ in\ e \mid b \mapsto e, e \mid spawn(e) \\ d &::= v \mid x \end{aligned}$$

Here v ranges over a set of basic values *Val* which we assume contains a distinguished value *null*, x over a set of variables *Var* and *op* over a set of function or operator symbols *Op*. We also assume the existence of a set of boolean expressions *BExp* ranged over by b.

The intended meaning of these constructs should be apparent but note that for convenience we only allow expressions of the form $op(\underline{e})$ when each e_i has one of the simple forms x or v. The effect of $op(\underline{e})$ for more general e_i can be obtained using the expression $let\ x_1 = e_1\ in\ let\ x_2 = e_2\ in\ \ldots op(x_1, \ldots, x_k)$. Thus the *let* construct is used in the language to make more explicit the order in which sub-expressions are evaluated.

The language as it stands is very limited. Although multiple evaluation threads can be activated, in expressions such as $let\ x = spawn(e_1)\ in\ e_2$, independent threads can not co-operate or share information. So we add to the language untyped versions of the communication primitives of *CML*,

- $n?\lambda x.e$, input a value along the communication channel n and apply the function $\lambda x.e$ to it
- $n!v.e_2$, output the value v along the channel n and then evaluate e_2,

and an untyped choice operator $e_1 + e_2$, meaning carry out the evaluation associated with the expression e_1 or that associated with e_2.

In addition to these operators which have their direct counterparts in *CML* we add a parallel operator $e_1 \parallel e_2$, meaning carry out the evaluation of e_1 and e_2 concurrently. Such an operator does not appear in the syntax of *CML* but it enables us to express directly in the syntax of the language the states which are generated as the evaluation of an expression proceeds.

The complete abstract syntax of our language is given by the following:

$$\begin{aligned} e &::= d \mid op(\underline{d}) \mid let\ x = e\ in\ e \mid b \mapsto e, e \mid spawn(e) \\ &\quad \mid n?\lambda x.e \mid n!d.e \mid e + e \mid e \parallel e \\ &\quad \mid local\ n\ in\ e\ end \mid \delta \mid e \oplus e \mid let\ rec\ P\ in\ e \mid P \\ d &:= v \mid x \end{aligned}$$

Note again that we restrict the output expressions to the form $n!d.e$ where d can only be a value or a constant. But once more the more general form $n!e_1.e_2$ can be taken to be an abbreviation for the expression $let\ x = e_1\ in\ n!x.e_2$ where x is a fresh variable. The constructs not explained are

- $local\ n\ in\ e\ end$ – meaning that n is a local channel name for the evaluation of e,
- δ – an evaluation which can no longer proceed,
- $e_1 \oplus e_2$ – an internal or spontaneous choice between the evaluation of e_1 and e_2

$$(VT)\ v \xrightarrow{\surd v} \delta \qquad (PT)\ \frac{e_2 \xrightarrow{\surd v} e_2'}{e_1 \parallel e_2 \xrightarrow{\surd v} e_1 \parallel e_2'}$$

$$(BT)\ \frac{e_1 \xrightarrow{\surd v} e_1',\ [\![b]\!] = true}{b \mapsto e_1, e_2 \xrightarrow{\surd v} e_1'} \qquad (LT)\ \frac{e \xrightarrow{\surd v} e'}{local\ n\ in\ e\ end \xrightarrow{\surd v} local\ n\ in\ e'\ end}$$

Fig. 1. Operational semantics: value production rules

- $let\ rec\ P\ in\ e$ – recursive definitions using a set of predefined expression names $P \in PN$.

We now consider an operational semantics for closed expressions in the language, *PExp*. For the sake of simplicity we ignore the evaluation of boolean expressions. That is we assume that for each closed boolean expression b there is a corresponding truth value $[\![b]\!]$ and more generally for any boolean expression b and mapping ρ from variables to values there is a boolean value $[\![b]\!]\rho$. The operational semantics for *CML*, in papers such as [6, 16, 3], are given in terms of a reduction relation between multi-sets of closed expressions, but because we have introduced the parallel operator $\parallel$ our reduction relation is expressed simply as a binary relation $\xrightarrow{\tau}$ over closed expressions; $e \xrightarrow{\tau} e'$ means that in one step the closed expression e can be reduced to e'. Also these papers use a two-level approach to the operational semantics, the lower-level expressing reductions of individual expressions and the upper-level using these lower-level relations to define reductions between multi-sets of expressions. Instead, as is common for process algebras, we use auxiliary relations $\xrightarrow{n?v}$ and $\xrightarrow{n!v}$ to define our reduction relation $\xrightarrow{\tau}$.

There is one further ingredient. A sequence of reductions should eventually lead to the production of a value which in normal sequential languages also means that the computation has terminated. We use a special relation $\xrightarrow{\surd}$ to indicate the final production of a value. Thus the rule $v \xrightarrow{\surd} v$ may be used to capture the idea that the simple expression v terminates in the production of the value v while the two rules

$$e_1 \xrightarrow{\tau} e_1' \text{ implies } let\ x = e_1\ in\ e_2 \xrightarrow{\tau} let\ x = e_1'\ in\ e_2$$
$$e_1 \xrightarrow{\surd} v \text{ implies } let\ x = e_1\ in\ e_2 \xrightarrow{\tau} e_2[v/x]$$

could adequately describe the semantics of local declarations of variables.

However the correct handling of the *spawn* construct requires some care. This is best discussed in terms of a degenerate form of local declarations; let $e_1; e_2$ be a shorthand notation for *let* $x = e_1$ *in* e_2 where x does not occur free in e_2. We could therefore derive from above the natural rules:

$$e_1 \xrightarrow{\tau} e_1' \text{ implies } e_1; e_2 \xrightarrow{\tau} e_1'; e_2$$
$$e_1 \xrightarrow{\surd} v \text{ implies } e_1; e_2 \xrightarrow{\tau} e_2.$$

Intuitively $spawn(e_1); e_2$ should proceed by creating a new processor to handle the evaluation of e_1 which could proceed at the same time as the evaluation of e_2. However this requires a reinterpretation of the sequential composition operator ; as in [1]; $e_1; e_2$ no longer means when the evaluation of e_1 is finished start with the evaluation of e_2. Instead we interpret $e_1; e_2$ as "start the evaluation of e_2 as soon as an initialisation signal has been received from e_1". This initialisation signal is of course a $\surd$-move and the above judgement can be inferred if we allow the inferences

$$spawn(e) \xrightarrow{\surd} e$$
$$e_1 \xrightarrow{\surd} e_1' \text{ implies } e_1; e_2 \xrightarrow{\tau} e_1' \parallel e_2$$

(*LtI*) $$\frac{e_1 \xrightarrow{\surd v} e_1'}{let\ x = e_1\ in\ e_2 \xrightarrow{\tau} e_1' \parallel e_2[v/x]}$$

(*SI*) $$spawn(e) \xrightarrow{\tau} e \parallel null$$

(*ECI*) $$\frac{e_1 \xrightarrow{\surd v} e_1'}{e_1 + e_2 \xrightarrow{\tau} e_1' \parallel v} \qquad \frac{e_2 \xrightarrow{\surd v} e_2'}{e_1 + e_2 \xrightarrow{\tau} e_2' \parallel v}$$

(*Com*) $$\frac{e_1 \xrightarrow{n?v} e_1',\ e_2 \xrightarrow{n!v} e_2'}{e_1 \parallel e_2 \xrightarrow{\tau} e_1' \parallel e_2'} \qquad \frac{e_1 \xrightarrow{n!v} e_1',\ e_2 \xrightarrow{n?v} e_2'}{e_1 \parallel e_2 \xrightarrow{\tau} e_1' \parallel e_2'}$$

(*IC*) $$e_1 \oplus e_2 \xrightarrow{\tau} e_1 \qquad e_1 \oplus e_2 \xrightarrow{\tau} e_2$$

(*Rec*) $$let\ rec\ P\ in\ e \xrightarrow{\tau} e[let\ rec\ P\ in\ e/x]$$

(*ECA*1) $$\frac{e_1 \xrightarrow{\tau} e_1'}{e_1 + e_2 \xrightarrow{\tau} e_1' + e_2} \qquad \frac{e_2 \xrightarrow{\tau} e_2'}{e_1 + e_2 \xrightarrow{\tau} e_1 + e_2'}$$

Fig. 2. Operational semantics: main reduction rules

In the second rule e_2 is initiated and its evaluation runs in parallel with that of the continuation, e_1', of e_1.

This discussion indicates a potential conflict between the two uses of the predicate $\surd$, one to produce values and the other to produce continuations. However this conflict can be resolved if we revise $\surd$ so that it has the type

$$\xrightarrow{\surd} \subseteq CPExp \times (Val \times CPExp).$$

When applied to a term it produces both a value and a continuation, for which we use the notation $e \xrightarrow{\surd v} e'$. The revised rule for simple values now becomes: $v \xrightarrow{\surd v} \delta$ where δ is the "deadlocked evaluation " and we use the rule

$$spawn(e) \xrightarrow{\tau} e \parallel null,$$

where *null* is a special distinguished value, rather than

$$spawn(e) \xrightarrow{\surd null} e.$$

Local declarations are now interpreted as follows:

$$e_1 \xrightarrow{\tau} e_1' \text{ implies } let\ x = e_1\ in\ e_2 \xrightarrow{\tau} let\ x = e_1'\ in\ e_2$$
$$e_1 \xrightarrow{\surd v} e_1' \text{ implies } let\ x = e_1\ in\ e_2 \xrightarrow{\tau} e_1' \parallel e_2[v/x].$$

Using these rules one can check that the evaluation of $spawn(e_1); e_2$ can proceed by initiating a thread for the evaluation of e_1 and then at any time launch a new thread which evaluates e_2.

The defining rules for the operational semantics are given in Figures 1,2,3. The first contains the rules for the relations $\xrightarrow{\surd v}$ while the second contains the most important rules for the reduction relation $\xrightarrow{\tau}$. The final Figure contains the rules for the external actions $\xrightarrow{n?v}$, $\xrightarrow{n!v}$ and routine rules for the reduction relation $\xrightarrow{\tau}$. Here

---

$$(ECA2)\ \frac{e_1 \xrightarrow{a} e_1'}{e_1 + e_2 \xrightarrow{a} e_1'} \qquad \frac{e_2 \xrightarrow{a} e_2'}{e_1 + e_2 \xrightarrow{a} e_2'}$$

$$(PA)\ \frac{e_1 \xrightarrow{\mu} e_1'}{e_1 \parallel e_2 \xrightarrow{\mu} e_1' \parallel e_2} \qquad \frac{e_2 \xrightarrow{\mu} e_2'}{e_1 \parallel e_2 \xrightarrow{\mu} e_1 \parallel e_2'}$$

$$(BoolA)\ \frac{e \xrightarrow{\mu} e', [\![b]\!] = true}{b \mapsto e \xrightarrow{\mu} e'} \qquad (SA)\ \frac{e \xrightarrow{\mu} e'}{spawn(e) \xrightarrow{\mu} spawn(e')}$$

$$(LcA)\ \frac{e \xrightarrow{\mu} e', chan(\mu) \neq n}{local\ n\ in\ e\ end \xrightarrow{\mu} local\ n\ in\ e'\ end} \qquad (In)\ n?x.e \xrightarrow{n?v} e[v/x] \quad \text{for every value } v$$

$$(LtA)\ \frac{e_1 \xrightarrow{\mu} e_1'}{let\ x = e_1\ in\ e_2 \xrightarrow{\mu} let\ x = e_1'\ in\ e_2} \qquad (Out)\ n!v.e \xrightarrow{n!v} e$$

Fig. 3. Operational semantics: Auxiliary rules

μ ranges over the set of actions Act_τ which denotes $Act \cup \{\tau\}$, where Act denotes the set of external actions $\{n?v \mid n \in N,\ v \in Val\} \cup \{n!v \mid n \in N,\ v \in Val\}$. Most of these rules have either already been explained or are readily understood. However it is worth pointing out the asymmetry in the termination rule for parallel, (PT). In the expression $e \parallel e'$ only e' can produce a value using a $\surd$ action. Of course e can evaluate independently and indirectly contribute to this production by communicating with e' using the rule (Com). Also the rule for external choice (ECI) might be unexpected. It implies, for example, that if e_1 can produce a value v with a continuation e_1' then the external choice $e_1 + e_2$ can evolve to a state where the value v is available to the environment while the evaluation of continuation e_1' proceeds. Both these rules are designed to reflect the evaluation of *CML* programs as explained in [16].

3 Value Production Systems

The operational semantics of *PExp* determines a labelled transition system with a number of special properties. These are encapsulated in the following definition:

Definition 1. A value production system, vps, is a collection system

$$\langle E, \delta, Val, Act_\tau, \longrightarrow, \xrightarrow{\surd} \rangle \text{ where}$$

1. E is a set of *(closed) expressions*
2. Val is a set of values such that $Val \subseteq E$
3. $\longrightarrow \subseteq E \times Act_\tau \times E$
4. $\xrightarrow{\surd} \subseteq E \times Val \times E$
5. δ is a deadlocked expression, i.e. $\delta \not\xrightarrow{\mu}$ for every $\mu \in Act_\tau$ and $\delta \not\xrightarrow{\surd}$
6. the only move from the expression v is $v \xrightarrow{\surd} \delta$, i.e. $v \xrightarrow{\surd v} \delta$, $v \not\xrightarrow{\mu}$ for every $\mu \in Act_\tau$ and $v \xrightarrow{\surd w} e$ implies $e = \delta$ and $v = w$
7. *single-valuedness:* if $e \xrightarrow{\surd v} e'$ then $e' \xrightarrow{\surd w}$ for no value w
8. *value-determinacy:* $e \xrightarrow{\surd v} e'$ and $e \xrightarrow{\surd w} e''$ implies e' is e'' and $v = w$.
9. *forward commutativity:* If $e \xrightarrow{\mu} e_1$ and $e \xrightarrow{\surd v} e_2$ then there exists an e_3 such that

$$\begin{array}{ccc} e & \xrightarrow{\mu} & e_1 \\ {\scriptstyle \surd v}\downarrow & & \downarrow{\scriptstyle \surd v} \\ e_2 & \xrightarrow{\mu} & e_3 \end{array}$$

10. *backward commutavity:* If $e \xrightarrow{\surd v} e_1$ and $e_1 \xrightarrow{\mu} e_2$ then there exists e_3 such that

$$\begin{array}{ccc} e & \xrightarrow{\sqrt{v}} & e_1 \\ \mu\downarrow & & \downarrow\mu \\ e_3 & \xrightarrow{\sqrt{v}} & e_2 \end{array}$$

Theorem 2. *The operational semantics of the previous section determines a vps with PExp as the set of expressions.*

We can now investigate properties of the operational semantics of *PExp* by deriving properties of an arbitrary vps. In this extended abstract we omit the definitions of strong and weak bisimulation equivalence, $\sim$ and $\approx$, for any arbitrary vps; one only needs to add to the standard requirements that processes should have the same ability to produce values. We also omit the details of how operators such as $\|$ and $let\ x = e\ in\ f$ for any function f from *Val* to E can be defined over an arbitrary vps.

Theorem 3. *In any vps if* $e \xrightarrow{\sqrt{v}} e'$ *then* $e \sim e' \parallel v$.

This theorem demonstrates that values can only be produced by expressions in *PExp* in a very restricted manner. Essentially values can only be offered to the environment and subsequent behaviour can not depend on the value being absorbed by the environment.

Theorem 4. *In any vps*

1. $let\ x = e\ in\ \lambda x.x \approx e$
2. $let\ x = v\ in\ f \approx f(v)$ *for every value* v
3. $let\ x_2 = (let\ x_1 = e\ in\ f)\ in\ g \sim let\ x_1 = e\ in\ \lambda v.(let\ x_2 = f(v)\ in\ g)$.

If we translate these results for the particular vps for *PExp* it means that any behavioural equivalence containing $\approx$ satisfies the following axioms:

$$let\ x = e\ in\ x = e$$
$$let\ x = v\ in\ e = e[v/x]$$
$$let\ x_2 = (let\ x_1 = e_1\ in\ e_2)\ in\ e_3 = let\ x_1 = e_1\ in\ (let\ x_2 = e_2\ in\ e_3)$$
$$\text{provided } x_1 \notin fv(e_3).$$

Note that Theorem 3 is crucial for the first law to hold and in the operational semantics this is ensured by the rules (ECI) and (SI). If in place of the former we had

$$\frac{e_1 \xrightarrow{\sqrt{v}} e_1'}{e_1 + e_2 \xrightarrow{\sqrt{v}} e_1'}$$

and its symmetric counterpart then the two expressions $v + n!v.\delta$ and $let\ x = v + n!v.\delta\ in\ x$ would not be *weakly bisimilar*.

We end this section with the definition of a behavioural preorder over expressions. It is based loosely on the contextual preorder originally defined in [13] for the λ-calculus. However since our language is nondeterministic there are two reasonable adaptations, refered to as *may* and *must* testing in [7]. Here we concentrate on the latter.

The basic test applied to an expression is whether or not it can produce a value. We formalise this as follows. A computation of a closed expression e is any maximal sequence (i.e. it is infinite, or finite and cannot be extended) of τ derivations from e. Let $Comp(e)$ denote the set of computations of e and for any $c \in Comp(e)$ let c_i denote the ith component of c.

For any $v \in Val$ let e *must* v if for all $c \in Comp(e)$ there exists some i such that $c_i \xrightarrow{\surd v}$.

Definition 5. For any pair of expressions expressions e_1, e_2 let $e_1 \sqsubseteq e_2$ if for any value v not appearing in e_1, e_2 and for every closing context $C[\ ]$, $C[e_1]$ *must* v implies $C[e_2]$ *must* v.

Thus expressions are compared by their ability to provoke surrounding contexts into guaranteeing values. In the remaining sections we outline how to build a denotational model which is fully abstract with respect to this behavioural preorder.

4 Natural Interpretations

PExp is a language for defining recursive terms over a set of operators together with a *let construct* and a set of prefix operators. In this section we outline the general requirements on a model in order to interpret the language.

For convenience let Σ denote the set of standard operator symbols of the language:

- the constant δ
- a unary symbol $n!v$, for each $n \in N$ and each $v \in Val$
- a unary symbol *local* n *in* $-$ *end*, for each $n \in N$
- a unary operator *spawn*
- the binary symbols $+$, $\oplus$, $\|$.

To interpret recursive terms over this alphabet we use a Σ-domain which consists of a domain D, i.e. an algebraic cpo, together with a continuous function f_D over D for each operator symbol f. To interpret input prefixing we require, for each channel $n \in N$ a continuous function of type $[[Val \longrightarrow D] \longrightarrow D]$.

Thus far the requirements are very similar to those used in [8] but we also need to interpret the *let* construct. Expressions in *PExp* produce, or evaluate to, values from *Val* but because of their concurrent nature many significantly different evaluations can lead to the same value. Thus it is appropriate to think of elements of the domain D as *computations* of values from *Val* and the *let* construct as a mechanism for manipulating computations rather than values. A general denotational theory of programming languages based on the idea that programs denote computations rather than values has been developed in [12] using monads and we follow this approach. Two functions are required:

1. a function η_D which associates with each value v a trivial computation $\eta(v)$ for producing this value
2. a continuous functional $\ ^{*^D}$ which extends a function f from values to computations to a function f^{*^D} from computations to computations.

Definition 6. An Interpretation for the language *PExp* consists of a 4-tuple

$\langle D, in_D, \eta_D, \ {}^{*^D} \rangle$ where

1. D is a Σ-domain
2. $in_D\colon Chan \longrightarrow [[Val \longrightarrow D] \longrightarrow D]$
3. $\eta_D\colon Val \longrightarrow D$
4. ${}^{*^D}\colon [(Val \longrightarrow D) \longrightarrow [D \longrightarrow D]]$

Given such an interpretation a denotational semantics for the language can be given as a function

$$D[\![\ ]\!] : PExp \longrightarrow [Env_{Val} \longrightarrow [Env_D \longrightarrow D]],$$

where Env_{Val} denotes the set of *Val* environments, i.e. mappings from the set of variables *Var* to the set of values *Val* and Env_D is the set of D environments, mappings from the set of process names *PN* to the domain D. We also assume that each operator *op* has an interpretation op_v as a function over values. The semantics is then defined by structural induction on expressions in the standard manner. The only non-trivial clause is

$$D[\![let\ x = e_1\ in\ e_2]\!]\rho = (\lambda v.D[\![e_2]\!]\rho[v/x])^{*^D} D[\![e_1]\!]\rho$$

However there are some reasonable requirements on the interpretation of the *let* construct which are best expressed as properties of the functions η and ${}^{*^D}$; these are derived directly from the monad laws given in [12].

Definition 7. An Interpretation is *Natural* if

1. $(\eta_D)^{*^D} = id_D$
2. $f^{*^D} \circ \eta_D = f$ for every $f\colon Val \longrightarrow D$
3. $f^{*^D} \circ g^{*^D} = (f^{*^D} \circ g)^{*^D}$ for every $f,\ g\colon Val \longrightarrow D$.

These properties ensure that the interpretation of the *let* construct has some expected properties:

Proposition 8. *If D is a Natural Interpretation then*

1. $D[\![let\ x = e\ in\ x]\!] = D[\![e]\!]$
2. $D[\![let\ x = v\ in\ e]\!] = D[\![e[v/x]]\!]$
3. $D[\![let\ x_2 = (let\ x_1 = e_1\ in\ e_2)\ in\ e_3]\!] = D[\![let\ x_1 = e_1\ in\ (let\ x_2 = e_2\ in\ e_3)]\!]$ *provided* $x_1 \notin fv(e_3)$.

In the next section we outline a a Natural Interpretation which is fully-abstract with respect to the behavioural preorder $\sqsubseteq$.

5 Acceptance Trees

We first review the version of Acceptance Trees, [7], used in [8] to model a value-passing process language. We then discuss how it might be modified so as to interpret *PExp*.

Acceptance trees are models of processes where the branches are labelled by the actions a process can perform and each node represents the set of possible states a process can reach after the sequence of actions labelling the path from the root of the tree to the node. The nondeterministic behaviour of processes is represented by ***acceptance sets*** attached to the nodes. These are finite collections of nonempty sets of communication potentials closed with respect to set union and convex closed with respect to subset inclusion. In order to accommodate value-passing these trees are modified so that the branches from a node do not lead directly to another node but rather to a function from values to trees which represent the functional behaviour of the process on reception or transmission of a value along a channel. In addition to the input and output of values expressions from *PExp* can produce values, i.e. perform $\surd$ actions. These can be accommodated by adding $\surd$ as a possible component to the acceptance sets.

We now define a recursive domain equation whose solution, in the category of domains with embeddings [15], is a formal representation of these trees. If N is the set of communication channels let cN represent the set $\{ n?, n! \mid n \in N \}$; nodes in the trees will be represented by acceptance sets over cN. Let I be a domain representing the ***sequel*** of a process after performing an input, O a corresponding domain for output and T a corresponding domain for $\surd$. Then $H_D(N, I, O, T)$ denotes the set of pairs $\langle \mathcal{A}, f \rangle$ which satisfy:

- $\mathcal{A}$ is an acceptance set over cN, i.e. a finite collection of finite non-empty subsets of cN,
- f is a function from cN to the disjoint union of I and O, i.e $f : cN \rightharpoonup_f I + O + T$, such that $domain(f) = |\mathcal{A}|$, i.e. the union of all the sets in $\mathcal{A}$.
- $f(\alpha) \in I$ whenever $\alpha = n?$ for some channel n
- $f(\alpha) \in O$ whenever $\alpha = n!$ for some channel n
- $f(\surd) \in T$ whenever it is defined.

Elements of $H_P(N, I, O)$ can be ordered by:

> $\langle \mathcal{A}, f \rangle \leq \langle \mathcal{B}, g \rangle$ if $\mathcal{B} \subseteq \mathcal{A}$ and $f \leq g$, i.e. $f(\alpha) \leq g(\alpha)$ for every α in the domain of g.

If I, O and T are predomains, i.e. are domains except they may possibly lack a least element, then one can check that so is $H_D(N, I, O, T)$. Moreover H_P can be used to induce a functor in the category of predomains with continuous functions as morphisms. So we can solve the domain equation

$$
\begin{aligned}
\mathbf{P} &= H_P(N, \mathbf{I}, \mathbf{O})_\perp \\
\mathbf{I} &= Val \longrightarrow \mathbf{P} \\
\mathbf{O} &= Val \rightharpoonup_f \mathbf{P} \\
\mathbf{T} &= Val \rightharpoonup_f \mathbf{P}.
\end{aligned}
$$

in the category of domains with embeddings as morphism, [15]. The domain representing the input sequels is the set of functions from values to processes. Operationally processes can only output a finite number of different values on any given channel and therefore the set of finite non-empty functions from values to processes, $Val \longrightarrow_f \mathbf{P}$ is used for both output and termination sequels. Note that $\mathbf{O}$ and $\mathbf{P}$ are predomains rather than domains.

Many of the operators in *PExp* have been interpreted over a domain $\mathbf{P}$ in [8] and these definitions are easily modified to to $\mathbf{D}$. Moreover the extra operators such as *spawn* can also be interpreted and following operational intuitions we can also give reasonable definitions of $\eta_{\mathbf{D}}$ and $*^{\mathbf{D}}$ which can be used to interpret the *let* construct. Because of space limitations these are omitted. However this means that we have an Interpretation of *PExp*.

Unfortunately it is not a Natural Interpretation as the requirement

$$\eta_{\mathbf{D}}^{*^{\mathbf{D}}} = id_{\mathbf{D}}$$

is not satisfied. The problem occurs because there are many compact elements in the domain $\mathbf{D}$ which are not denotable under this interpretation by expressions in *PExp*. A typical example is any d element of the form $\langle\{n!, \surd\}, f\rangle_\perp$ where $f(\surd) = \delta_{\mathbf{D}}$. It turns out that $\eta_{\mathbf{D}}^{*^{\mathbf{D}}} d$ has the form $fold\ \langle \mathcal{A}, g\rangle_\perp$ where $\{\surd\} \in \mathcal{A}$ and therefore this must be different from d. However we can use a domain retract to cut down the model $\mathbf{D}$ so as to get a Natural Interpretation.

We have seen in Section 3 that the operational behaviour of expressions is constrained in that the properties of Value Production Systems are satisfied. To define a Natural Interpretation we need to isolate a sub-domain of $\mathbf{D}$ which satisfies the semantic counterparts to these properties. To do so we use the function $\eta_{\mathbf{D}}^{*^{\mathbf{D}}}$ which can be shown to be a domain retract. Let $\mathbf{E}$ denote its range. This can be viewed as an Interpretation by using the functions already defined over $\mathbf{D}$. Specifically

1. for each symbol $f \in \Sigma$ let $f_{\mathbf{E}}$ be defined as $\eta_{\mathbf{D}}^{*^{\mathbf{D}}} \circ (f_{\mathbf{D}} \lceil \mathbf{E})$,
2. the input function is defined as before, $in_{\mathbf{E}}\ n\ f = fold\ \langle\{\{n?\}\}, n? \mapsto f\rangle_\perp$
3. $\eta_{\mathbf{E}} = \eta_{\mathbf{D}} \lceil \mathbf{E}$
4. for $f \in [\,Val \longrightarrow \mathbf{E}]$ let $f^{*^{\mathbf{E}}} = (f^{*^{\mathbf{D}}}) \lceil \mathbf{E}$.

With these definitions we have:

Proposition 9. $\mathbf{E}$ *is a Natural Interpretation.*

The main result of the paper is:

Theorem 10. *The Natural Interpretation based on* $\mathbf{E}$ *is* fully-abstract, *i.e.* $\mathbf{E}[\![e]\!] \leq \mathbf{E}[\![e']\!]$ *if and only if* $e \sqsubseteq e'$.

The proof of this theorem is long and complicated. First it involves an alternative characterisation of the behavioural preorder $\sqsubseteq$ using convergence predicates and operational acceptance sets. An *internal full abstraction* result is then obtained for the model, using similar concepts but this time defined model theoretically. Finally these characteristics of expressions e are related to the corresponding characteristics of their denotations $\mathbf{E}[\![e]\!]$. This in turn involves finding a notion of *head normal form* for expressions and a set of rewrite rules which can be used to transform all convergent terms into head normal forms. The details may be found in the technical report [17] which is the full version of this extended abstract.

6 Related Work

There has already been a number of attempts at giving an operational semantics for *CML* , or rather core subsets of *CML* but as far as we are aware very few of these have been used to develop a semantic theory or denotational model for the language. For example in [16, 3] the core language λ_{cv} is given a two-level operational semantics which results in a reduction relation between multi-sets of language expressions. Although this gives a formal semantics which may be referenced by implementors it is insufficient as the basis of a behavioural theory. A similar approach is taken in [6] where a hierarchy of languages is defined and each is given a bisimulation semantics. Starting with a *CCS* like language in which the parallel operator has been replaced with a *fork* operator for process creation, restriction, guarded choice and finally private channel names are added. This last refinement produces a language which is more reminiscent of the $\pi - calculus$ and in particular it does not include any notion of the production of values.

More recently in [2] an operational semantics is given to a language called *FPI* which has many of the programming constructs of *CML*. However it lacks any *spawn* or *fork* construct and indeed later in the same thesis the author notes[1] that in order to accommodate such an operator his operational semantics would have to be modified considerably. Furthermore the operational semantics of value production within the context of the parallel operator in not consistent with that of CML in [16]. In the same thesis a denotational semantics, based on Acceptance Trees, is given for a language very similar to λ_{cv}. However this is not in the style of a semantic function

$$\mathcal{D}: \lambda_{cv} \longrightarrow \mathbf{D}$$

where **D** is a semantic domain; instead there is an extra parameter which is defined in terms of a notion of "dynamic types". There is also no result corresponding to our Theorem 10, the *full-abstraction* result, as there is no behavioural semantics given for λ_{cv}.

There has also been some related work on *higher-order processes languages* such as *CHOCS*, [18] and *FACILE*, [4]. Again here the main theoretical emphasis has been on the development of operational semantics in terms of labelled transition systems and to a certain extent the investigation of appropriate versions of bisimulation equivalence for these languages. Another strand of research has been on the development of *type systems* for these kinds of languages, [14], and we will certainly need to build on such work if we are to extend our results to languages which include more of the features of *CML*.

Acknowledgements: The authors would like to thank Alan Jeffrey for many valuable discussions and suggestions. This work has been supported by the ESPRIT/BRA CONCUR2 project and a EPSRC grant GR/H16537. The first author would like to acknowledge the generous support of a British Telecom (BT) CASE Award.

1 on page 163

References

1. J.C.M. Baeten and F.W. Vaandrager. An algebra for process creation. *Acta Informatica*, 29(4):303–334, 1992.
2. Mourad Debabi. Integration des Paradigmes de Programmation Parallele, Fonctionnelle et Imperative: Fondement Semantiques. PhD thesis, Universite Paris-Sud, U.F.R Scientifique d'Orsay, July 1994.
3. R. Milner D. Berry and D. Turner. A Semantics for ML Concurrency Primitives. In *Proceedings of the 19th ACM Symposium on Principles of Programmings Languages*, 1992.
4. A. Giacalone, P. Mishra and S. Prasad. Facile: A symetric integration of concurrent and functional programming. In *Proceedings of TAPSOFT 89* pp.184-209, *Lecture Notes in Computer Science 352, Springer-Verlag, 1989.*
5. Carl A. Gunter. *Semantics of Programming Languages.* MIT Press, Cambridge Massachusetts, 1992.
6. K. Havelund. *The Fork Calculus: Towards a Logic for Concurrent ML.* PhD thesis, Ecole Normale Superieur, Paris, 1994.
7. M. Hennessy. *Algebraic Theory of Processes.* MIT Press, Cambridge, Massachusetts, 1988.
8. M. Hennessy and A. Ingolfsdottir. A Theory of Communicating Processes with Value-Passing. Report 7/91, School of Cognitive and Computing Sciences, Sussex University, 1991.
9. C.A.R. Hoare. *Communicating Sequential Processes.* Prentice-Hall International, Englewood Cliffs, 1985.
10. A. Ingolfsdottir. *Semantic Models for Communicating Processes with Value Passing.* PhD thesis, University of Sussex, 1994.
11. R. Milner. *Communication and Concurrency.* Prentice-Hall International, Englewood Cliffs, 1989.
12. E. Moggi. Computational Lambda Calculus and Monads. Report ECS-LFCS-88-66, Edinburgh LFCS, 1988.
13. James Morris. *Lambda-Calculus Models of Programming Languages.* PhD thesis, MIT, June 1968.
14. F. Nielson and H.R. Nielson. From CML to Process Algebras Technical Report DAIMI PB-433 Computer Science Department, Aarhus University, March 1993.
15. G.D. Plotkin. Lecture notes in domain theory, 1981. University of Edinburgh.
16. John Reppy. *Higher-Order Concurrency.* PhD thesis, Cornell University, June 1992. Technical Report TR 92-1285.
17. W. Ferreira and M. Hennessy Towards a Semantic Theory of CML. Sussex University Technical Report CS-02-95, Department of Computer Science, 1995.
18. Bent Thomsen. *A calculus of higher order communicating systems.* PhD thesis, Imperial College of Science, Technology and Medicine, Department of Computing, September 1990.
19. M.Tofte, R.Milner and R.Harper. *The Definition of Standard ML.* MIT Press, 1990.

Modular constructions of distributing automata

Sébastien Huguet, Antoine Petit

LIFAC
Ecole Normale Supérieure de Cachan
61, Avenue du président Wilson
94235 Cachan Cedex, France
E-Mail: {huguet,petit}@lifac.ens-cachan.fr

Topics: Automata and formal languages, Models of computation, Parallel and distributed computing

1 Introduction

The notion of traces has been introduced in 1977 by A. Mazurkiewicz in order to modelize the finite behaviors of some subclasses of Petri nets [Maz77]. Since this original work, trace theory has been considerably studied in particular as one of the most interesting and powerful formal model for concurrent systems. The book edited recently by V. Diekert and G. Rozenberg [DR95] summarizes the principal works done in trace theory in the past 18 years.

It can be seen in this book that the subfamily of recognizable trace languages, i.e. the languages describing the behaviors of finite state concurrent processes, has been in particular intensively studied. From an algebraic point of view, this family has been characterized by E. Ochmański [Och85]. Extending the famous Kleene's theorem, he proves that the family of recognizable trace languages coincides with the family of trace languages constructed from the finite languages by closure under union, trace concatenation and trace iteration.

From automata point of view, a great deal of attention has been given to the definition of suitable deterministic finite state parallel machines able to describe exactly the recognizable trace languages. The easiest notion of such machines is the one of I-diamond automata in which, for any independent actions a and b, the state reached after the sequence ab is the same than the state reached after the sequence ba. Even if these automata characterize exactly recognizable trace languages, they have the main drawback that in such automata, the parallelism reduces to logical parallelism ($a \parallel b = ab + ba$). In other words, there is no true parallelism in I-diamond automata. On the contrary, in an asynchronous (cellular) automata, as defined by W. Zielonka, two independent actions are performed by disjoint sets of processors and can thus be executed "simultaneously". The deep and difficult result of Zielonka [Zie87, CMZ93] states that a trace language is recognizable if and only if it is recognized by some deterministic asynchronous (cellular) automaton. The well known drawbacks of these automata are the fact that they are difficult to construct in practical cases and moreover they have often huge state spaces even for "small" languages (see e.g. [Per89]). The notion of distributing automata (under the name of $\mathbb{N}$–distributed automata) has been proposed as an alternative to asynchronous cellular automata [Pet93]. In such an automaton, two independent actions are performed "simultaneously" by independent processors. But contrary to the asynchronous cellular automata, the synchronizations between the processors are explicitly performed by a centralized processor: the synchronizer. From the parallelism point of view, this synchronizer can, of course, be seen as a drawback. Nevertheless a distributing automaton can be constructed from any I-diamond automata in a much simpler way than an asynchronous cellular automaton as proved by the implementation work proposed in [Cér92].

From a practical point of view, a very important point on these finite state parallel machines relies on the possibility, or not, to construct them in a modular way. Namely, any real (concurrent) program is built in a structured way step by step. Therefore, for any suitable based model, it has to be possible to construct these automata also step by step from "small" ones to "big" ones using the operations of union, trace concatenation and trace iteration. The modularity results for I-diamond automata and asynchonous cellular automata can be summarized as follows.

- Modular constructions exist for I-diamond automata. In fact, such constructions have even been proposed in order to prove the closure of recognizable trace languages by trace concatenation [CP85] and trace iteration [Mét86]. The constructed automata are non deterministic but it is immediate to see that the classical procedure to determinize finite automata preserves the I-diamondness.
- Concerning asynchronous cellular automata, modular constructions can be obtained through the results of G. Pighizzini on asynchronous automata [Pig93]. Once again the obtained automata are non deterministic. But unfortunately it turns out that the determinization of asynchronous cellular automata is a difficult problem. The only known solutions [KMS94, Mus94] do not allow easy constructions of deterministic asynchronous cellular automata from non deterministic ones. On the contrary, it seems that it is not much simpler to construct a deterministic asynchronous cellular automata from a non deterministic one than from an I-diamond automaton.

In the case of distributing automata, there does not exist yet any modular constructions. The aim of this paper is precisely to fill this gap. Note that, as in the case of modular constructions of asynchronous automata [Pig93], the proposed constructions are suitable generalizations of those existing for I-diamond automata.

The next section is devoted to some preliminaries on traces, recognizable trace languages and modular constructions. Distributing automata are defined in Section 3. The proposed definition is a non-deterministic generalization of the original one [Pet93]. Then an easy determinization procedure is given. Modular constructions of distributing automata are presented in Section 4.

For lack of space, this paper does not contain any proof. A complete presentation can be found in the technical report [HP95].

2 Preliminaries

We assume that the reader is familiar with the basic notions of formal languages theory: alphabet, words, language, concatenation... (see e.g. [HU79]).

2.1 Basic definitions

A concurrent alphabet is a pair (A, I) where A is a finite alphabet and $I \subseteq A \times A$, a symmetric and irreflexive relation called independence relation. The dependence relation D is the complement of I: $D = A \times A \backslash I$.

The equivalence $\sim_I$ is defined as the reflexive and transitive closure of the relation $\{(\alpha ab\beta, \alpha ba\beta)/\alpha, \beta \in A^* \textit{ and } (a,b) \in I\}$. For $v, w \in A^*, v \sim_I w$ means that w can be obtained from v by a sequence of permutations of independent letters. It's easy to see that $\sim_I$ is a congruence: for $u, u', v, v' \in A^*$, if $u \sim_I u'$ and $v \sim_I v'$ then $uu' \sim_I vv'$.

The trace monoid generated by (A, I) — also called the free partially commutative monoid (fpcm) [CF69] — is the quotient monoid, $A^*/\sim_I$ [Maz77] denoted in the sequel by $\mathbb{M}(A, I)$. The neutral element of $\mathbb{M}(A, I)$ is denoted by ε. A trace is an element of $\mathbb{M}(A, I)$ and a trace language is a subset of this monoid. The canonical surjection from A^* to $\mathbb{M}(A, I)$ is denoted by φ. A word language $L \subseteq A^*$ is I–closed if $L = \varphi^{-1}(\varphi(L))$ i.e. $\forall u \in L, \forall v \in A^*, v \sim_I u$ implies $v \in L$. A trace t can be identified with the set $\varphi^{-1}(t)$ of pairwise $\sim_I$–equivalent words. Then a trace language T can be identified with the I–closed word language $\varphi^{-1}(T)$.

In this paper, we are mainly interested by recognizable trace languages i.e. trace languages which describe the finite state systems. Formally, these languages can be define as follows.

2.2 Recognizable languages

Recall that in any monoid M (see e.g. [Ber79]), a deterministic M–automaton $\mathcal{A}$ is a 4–tuple (Q, δ, q_0, F) where Q is a finite set of states, $q_0 \in Q$ is the initial state, $F \subseteq Q$ is the set of final states and $\delta : Q \times M \to Q$ is the transition function verifying:

- $\delta(q, \varepsilon) = q$ where ε is the neutral element of M.
- $\forall q \in Q, \forall m, n \in M, \delta(\delta(q, m), n) = \delta(q, mn)$.

The language recognized by $\mathcal{A}$ is then $L(\mathcal{A}) = \{m \in M / \ \delta(q_0, m) \in F\}$. A language, $L \subseteq M$, is recognizable if there exists some M–automaton $\mathcal{A}$ such that $L(\mathcal{A}) = L$.

In the case where M is the free monoid A^*, the definition above reduces obviously to the classical notion of finite automaton and recognizable word language. When M is a trace monoid $\mathbb{M}(A, I)$, the definition above leads to the notion of recognizable trace language. In fact, we will use mainly in this paper the well–known following characterization (see e.g. [CP85]).

Proposition 1. A trace language $T \subseteq \mathbb{M}(A, I)$ is recognizable if and only if the word language $\varphi^{-1}(T) \subseteq A^*$ is recognizable.

This proposition allows to identify recognizable trace languages with recognizable I–closed word languages. This identification will now be done throughout this paper.

A natural and interesting question arises then: what kind of suitable "deterministic parallel finite state machines" can be used to define these recognizable I–closed word languages? More precisely, we are looking for a family *Aut* of "deterministic parallel finite state machines" such that an I–closed word language is recognizable if and only if there exists some element of *Aut* recognizing it. Such machines of *Aut* should of course take into account the independence of actions.

As we explained in details in the introduction, the first and easiest notion of such machines is the one of I–diamond automata. Then, W. Zielonka introduced the famous notion of asynchronous (cellular) automata. Finally, the notion of distributing automata has been proposed in [Pet93].

For such families of "deterministic parallel finite state machines", the possibility (or not) to construct these machines in a modular way is a very important aspect. Namely, "big" machines can thus be obtained step by step from "smaller" ones in order to get models of real programs built themselves in a modular way. We give now a formal definition of modular constructions.

2.3 Modular constructions

In the sequential case, the famous Kleene's theorem states that the family of word languages recognized by finite automata coincides with the family of word languages constructed in a modular way starting from some basic languages ($\emptyset, \{\varepsilon\}, \{a\}$ for $a \in A$) and using a finite number of operations of union, concatenation and iteration. This theorem has been extended to recognizable trace languages by E. Ochmański [Och85] in the following way. Since the equivalence relation is a congruence, the surjection φ induces a concatenation and an iteration between trace languages. Through the identification of trace languages and I–closed word language, these trace concatenation and trace iteration correspond to the following operations between I–closed word languages. Let L, L' be two I–closed word languages, then we define

$$L \cdot_I L' = \varphi^{-1}(\varphi(L \cdot L'))$$
$$L^{*_I} = \varphi^{-1}(\varphi(L^*))$$

Example 1 : *Let $A = \{a, b, c, d\}$ and I be the independence relation represented by the following graph:*

$$a — c — b \quad d$$

Let $u = ca$ and $v = abd$. As explained above, the trace languages $T = \{\varphi(u)\}$ and $T' = \{\varphi(v)\}$ are identified with the I-closed word languages $L = \varphi^{-1}(T) = \{ac, ca\}$ and $L' = \varphi^{-1}(T') = \{abd\}$. Moreover,

- $L \cdot_I L' = \varphi^{-1}(\varphi(\{ac, ca\} \cdot \{abd\})) = \varphi^{-1}(\varphi(\{acabd, caabd\})) = \{caabd, acabd, aacbd, aabcd\}$
- $L^{*_I} = \varphi^{-1}(\varphi(\{ac, ca\}^*)) = \{u \in \{a, c\}^* / |u|_a = |u|_c\}$

Note that whereas L is of course recognizable, L^{*_I} is no more a recognizable word language. In order to obtain recognizable languages under the operation ^{*_I}, the notion of connected word or trace is useful. The alphabet of a trace t is the common alphabet of the words of $\varphi^{-1}(t)$. The alphabet of a trace (resp. a word) t is denoted by $alph(t)$. A trace (resp. a word) t is connected if the graph of the relation $D \cap (alph(t) \times alph(t))$ is a connected one. For instance, in the example above, the word $u = ac$ is not connected whereas the words $v = abd$ and acd are connected. A trace language (resp. a word language) is connected if all its elements are connected.

Ochmański's theorem [Och85] can thus be stated as follows. The family of recognizable trace languages coincides with the smallest family of trace languages containing $\emptyset, \{\varepsilon\}, \{a\}$ for $a \in A$ and closed under union, trace concatenation and trace iteration restricted to connected languages. As explained in [Bau92], using a decomposition result of G. Pighizzini [Pig93], it is even possible to restrict the iteration to languages where all the traces have the same connected alphabet. Using the identification between recognizable trace languages and recognizable I–closed word languages, these results can be reformulated as follows. The family of recognizable I–closed word languages is the smallest family of word languages $\mathcal{F}$ such that:

1. $\emptyset \in \mathcal{F}, \{\varepsilon\} \in \mathcal{F}, \{a\} \in \mathcal{F}$ for $a \in A$
2. If $L \in \mathcal{F}$ and $L' \in \mathcal{F}$ then $L \cup L' \in \mathcal{F}$
3. If $L \in \mathcal{F}$ and $L' \in \mathcal{F}$ then $L \cdot_I L' \in \mathcal{F}$
4. If $L \in \mathcal{F}$ and all the elements of L have the same connected alphabet then $L^{*_I} \in \mathcal{F}$.

Therefore a family $\mathcal{A}ut$ of "parallel finite state machines" is compatible with the modularity of recognizable I–closed languages if for any elements $\mathcal{A}$, $\mathcal{B}$ of $\mathcal{A}ut$, it is possible to construct elements of $\mathcal{A}ut$ recognizing the languages $L(\mathcal{A}) \cup L(\mathcal{B})$, $L(\mathcal{A}) \cdot_I L(\mathcal{B})$ and $L(\mathcal{A})^{*_I}$ when $L(\mathcal{A})$ verifies the conditions above.

As explained in the introduction, the aim of this paper is to propose modular constructions for distributing automata that we will now define.

3 Distributing automata

We define formally in this section the notion of distributing automaton. This definition is a non deterministic generalization of the one proposed in [Pet93]. For a detailed discussion on (non–deterministic) distributing automata see [Hug95].

A subset $C \subseteq A$ is a clique of the graph (A, I) if and only if for any $a, b \in C, (a, b) \in I$. The set of all cliques of (A, I) is denoted in the sequel by Cl. For any $X \subseteq A$, we note $D(X) = \{y \in A / \exists x \in X, (x, y) \in D\}$ and $I(X) = A \backslash D(X) = \{y \in A / \forall x \in X, (x, y) \in I\}$.

A distributing automaton $\mathcal{A}$ on an independent alphabet (A, I) is a 5–tuple:

$$\mathcal{A} = (S, s_0, F, (Q_x, \delta_x, B_x)_{x \in A}, Syn)$$

where:

- S is the finite set of synchronization states
- $s_0 \in S$ is the initial synchronization state
- $F \subseteq S$ is the set of final synchronization states
- For any $x \in A, (Q_x, \delta_x, B_x)$ is the local automaton for x defined by:
  - the finite set of local states Q_x
  - the local (non deterministic) transition function $\delta_x : Q_x \to \mathcal{P}(Q_x)$
  - the set of initial local states $B_x \subseteq Q_x$
- Syn is the partial synchronization function from the set of global states $\mathcal{G}(\mathcal{A}) = \{(s, (q_c)_{c \in C}) / s \in S, C \in Cl, q_c \in Q_c$ for any $c \in C\}$ into S. This function verifies

$Syn(s) = s$ for any $s \in S$ and for any independent actions x and y and any global state $(s, (q_c)_{c \in C})$:

$$Syn(Syn(s, (q_c)_{c \in C \cap D(x)}), (q_c)_{c \in C \cap I(x) \cap D(y)}) = Syn(s, (q_c)_{c \in C \cap (D(x) \cup D(y))})$$

To understand easily the behavior of a distributing automaton, it is convenient to see such an automaton as a global one (note that such a global approach is also mostly used in the presentation of asynchronous cellular automata, see e.g. [Zie87, CMZ93]).

The global transition function $\Delta : \mathcal{G}(\mathcal{A}) \times A \to \mathcal{P}(\mathcal{G}(\mathcal{A}))$ associated with the distributing automaton given above is defined as follows. For any global state $g = (s, (q_c)_{c \in C})$ and any action $x \in A$, we distinguish two cases:

- $x \in C$: $\Delta(g, x) = \{(s, (q_c)_{c \in C \setminus \{x\}}, q'_x) / q'_x \in \delta_x(q_x)\}$
- $x \notin C$: $\Delta(g, x) = \{(Syn(s, (q_c)_{c \in C \cap D(x)}), (q_c)_{c \in C \cap I(x)}, q'_x) / q'_x \in \delta_x(B_x)\}$

For any $G \in \mathcal{P}(\mathcal{G}(\mathcal{A}))$ and $x \in A, \Delta(G, x) = \{g' / g' \in \Delta(g, x), g \in G\}$ and $Syn(G) = \{Syn(g) / g \in G\}$. Then, the language recognized by the distributing automaton is

$$L(\mathcal{A}) = \{u \in A^* / Syn(\Delta(s_0, u)) \cap F \neq \emptyset\}$$

Note that it is immediate to verify that the global automaton associated with a distributing automaton is I–diamond.

As explained in [Cér92], distributing automata can be implemented with true concurrency. Roughly, this true parallelism can be explained as follows. Any global state $g = (s, (q_c)_{c \in C})$ corresponds in fact to $|C| + 1$ processors: the synchronizer and one for each action of C. Since the letters of C are pairwise independent, these processors in charge of executing the actions can perform their tasks simultaneously. The synchronizer takes place, for a partial or global synchronization, only to manage the execution of dependent actions.

Example 2 *: Let $A = \{a, b, c, d\}$ and $I = a - c - b \quad d$. We define the distributing automaton*

$$\mathcal{A} = (\{1, 2, 3, 4\}, \{1\}, \{2\}, (Q_x, \delta_x, B_x)_{x \in A}, Syn)$$

where

- $Q_a = \{0_a, 1_a\}$, $B_a = \{0_a\}$, $\delta_a(0_a) = 1_a$
- $Q_b = \{0_b, 1_b\}$, $B_a = \{0_b\}$, $\delta_b(0_b) = \delta_b(1_b) = 1_b$
- $Q_c = \{0_c, 1_c, 2_c\}$, $B_a = \{0_c\}$, $\delta_c(0_c) = 1_c, \delta(1_c) = 2_c, \delta(2_c) = 1_c$
- $Q_d = \{0_d, 1_d\}$, $B_a = \{0_d\}$, $\delta_d(0_d) = 1_d$

and the synchronization function is given by

- $Syn(1, 1_a) = 2$
- $Syn(2, 1_b, 2_c) = 3$
- $Syn(2, 1_b, 1_c) = 4$
- $Syn(3, 1_d) = 1$
- $Syn(4, 1_d) = 2$
- $Syn(s) = s$ *for any* $s \in \{1, 2, 3, 4\}$.

The global automaton associated with this distributing automaton is represented in the figure below. As usual, the non productive states has not been represented.

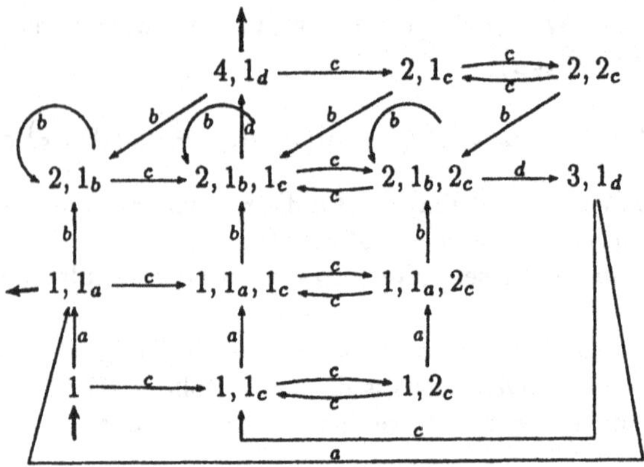

The "real" behaviour of the distributing automaton can be deduced from the global automaton. For instance, in the part

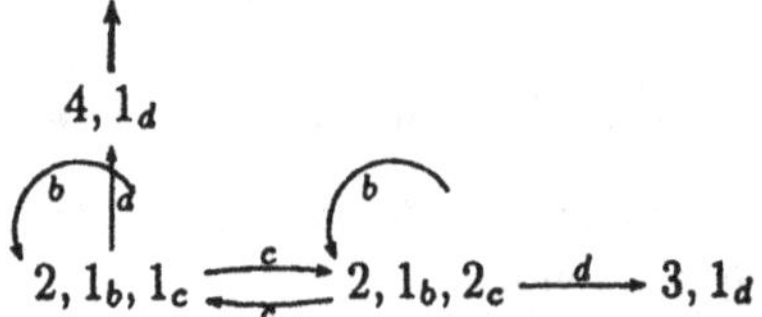

the independent actions b and c are executed simultaneously by distinct processors until an action d generates a synchronization of the two processors by the synchronizer. In the part

$2, 1_b, 1_c$ $2, 1_b, 2_c$

$1, 1_a, 1_c$ $1, 1_a, 2_c$

$1, 1_c$ $1, 2_c$

actions c are executed simultaneously with the action a and then actions b. The synchronization between the "a" and the "b"'s is a partial one which do not affect the action c which is independent of both a and b.

When, for any $x \in A$, the local automaton (Q_x, δ_x, B_x) is deterministic i.e. $|B_x| = 1$ and for any $q_x \in Q_x, |\delta_x(q_x)| \leq 1$, the distributing automaton is said deterministic. Obviously, the associated global automaton is in this case also deterministic. This notion of deterministic distributing automaton is equivalent to the definition of $\mathbb{N}$-distributed automaton [Pet93]. As stated by the following result, these automata are suitable for recognizable I-closed word languages.

Theorem 2 [Pet93]. *An I-closed word language is recognizable if and only if it is recognized by some deterministic distributing automaton.*

It is not difficult to prove that any distributing automaton is equivalent, i.e. recognizes the same language, than a deterministic one. The construction of the determinized of a distributing automaton is very closed than the classical subset construction for finite automata. Note nevertheless that even if the non determinism has been defined only at the level of the local automata, the determinization involves a subset construction on both local states and synchronization states. More precisely, let $\mathcal{A} = (S, s_0, F, (Q_x, \delta_x, B_x)_{x\in A}, Syn)$ be a non deterministic distributing automaton. We define the determinized $det(\mathcal{A})$ of $\mathcal{A}$ as the 5-tuple

$$(\mathcal{P}(S), \{s_0\}, F', (\mathcal{P}(Q_x), \delta'_x, \{B_x\})_{x\in A}, Syn')$$

where:

- $F' = \{S' \in \mathcal{P}(S) / S' \cap F \neq \emptyset\}$.
- $\delta'_x : \mathcal{P}(Q_x) \to \mathcal{P}(Q_x)$ is defined for any $Q \subseteq Q_x$ by

$$\delta'_x(Q) = \{q' \in Q_x / q' \in \delta_x(q) \text{ for some } q \in Q\}$$

- Syn' is the partial function from $\{(S', (Q'_c)_{c\in C}) / S' \in \mathcal{P}(S), C \in Cl, Q'_c \in \mathcal{P}(Q_c)$ for any $c \in C\}$ into $\mathcal{P}(S)$ defined by:

$$Syn'(S', (Q'_c)_{c\in C}) = \{Syn(s', (q'_c)_{c\in C}) / s' \in S', q'_c \in Q'_c \text{ for any } c \in C\}$$

Using the definition of the global automaton associated with a distributing automaton and the idea of the proof of the classical subset construction for finite automata, it can be proved:

Proposition 3. *Let $\mathcal{A}$ be a non deterministic distributing automaton. Then $det(\mathcal{A})$ is a deterministic distributing automaton which recognizes the same language than $\mathcal{A}$.*

Note that this proposition contains two results. First, the object $det(\mathcal{A})$ is a distributing automaton and second, it recognizes the same language than $\mathcal{A}$.

A similar remark has of course to be done for the three propositions of the next section.

4 Modular constructions of distributing automata

We propose in this section modular constructions of distributing automata for the operations of union, trace concatenation ($\cdot_I$) and (restricted) trace iteration (^{*_I}) defined in Section 2. Note that, as in the case of modular constructions of asynchronous automata [Pig93], these constructions are suitable generalizations of those existing for I–diamond automata.

4.1 Union

As for classical finite automata, the construction reduces to a cartesian product. On distributing automata, the cartesian product is done at both levels of synchronizer states and local states. As usual we may assume without generality that automata are complete.

Let $\mathcal{A}'$ and $\mathcal{A}''$ be two complete distributing automata:
$\mathcal{A}' = (S', s'_0, F', (Q'_x, \delta'_x, B'_x)_{x\in A}, Syn')$; $\mathcal{A}'' = (S'', s''_0, F'', (Q''_x, \delta''_x, B''_x)_{x\in A}, Syn'')$.
The union of $\mathcal{A}'$ and $\mathcal{A}''$ is defined by $union(\mathcal{A}', \mathcal{A}'') =$

$$(S' \times S'', (s'_0, s''_0), (F' \times S'') \cup (S' \times F''), (Q'_x \times Q''_x, \delta_x, (B'_x, B''_x))_{x\in A}, Syn)$$

where:

- δ_x is defined for any $x \in A$ and $q = (q', q'') \in Q'_x \times Q''_x$ by
$$\delta_x(q) = \{(q'_x, q''_x)/q'_x \in \delta'_x(q'), q''_x \in \delta''_x(q'')\}$$
- Syn is defined for $g = ((s', s''), (q'_c, q''_c)_{c\in C})$ by
$$Syn(g) = (Syn'(s', (q'_c)_{c\in C}), Syn''(s'', (q''_c)_{c\in C}))$$

Proposition 4. *Let $\mathcal{A}'$ and $\mathcal{A}''$ be two distributing automata. Then $union(\mathcal{A}', \mathcal{A}'')$ is a distributing automaton which recognizes the union $L(\mathcal{A}') \cup L(\mathcal{A}'')$.*

Note that if $\mathcal{A}'$ and $\mathcal{A}''$ are deterministic then so is $union(\mathcal{A}, \mathcal{A}'')$.

4.2 Trace concatenation

Recall that the operation of trace concatenation $\cdot_I$ can easily be characterized as follows. Let L' and L'' be two I–closed languages, then

$$L' \cdot_I L'' = \{u_0v_0u_1v_1 \cdots u_kv_k / \forall i, u_i, v_i \in A^*,$$
$$u_0u_1 \cdots u_k \in L', v_0v_1 \cdots v_k \in L'', (v_j, u_i) \in I \text{ for any } j < i\}$$

The concatenation of two distributing automata is based on this characterization. The idea is to add binary flags to the local automata. Initially both flags have the value 0. When an action is performed, the flag is set to 1. These flags are used to ensure that any letter performed by a local automaton of the first distributing automaton is independent of all the letters already executed by the local automata of the second distributing automaton.

Let $\mathcal{A}' = (S', s'_0, F', (Q'_x, \delta'_x, B'_x)_{x\in A}, Syn')$ and $\mathcal{A}'' = (S'', s''_0, F'', (Q''_x, \delta''_x, B''_x)_{x\in A}, Syn'')$ be two distributing automata. The concatenation $concat(\mathcal{A}', \mathcal{A}'')$ is the 5–tuple

$$(S' \times S'' \times \mathcal{P}(A), (s'_0, s''_0, \emptyset), F' \times F'' \times \mathcal{P}(A),$$
$$(Q'_x \times \{0,1\} \times Q''_x \times \{0,1\}, \delta_x, B'_x \times \{0\} \times B''_x \times \{0\})_{x\in A}, Syn)$$

where

- for any $q_x = (q', \alpha, q'', \beta) \in Q'_x \times \{0,1\} \times Q''_x \times \{0,1\}$,
$$\delta_x(q_x) = \begin{cases} \{(\overline{q}', 1, q'', \beta)/\overline{q}' \in \delta'_x(q')\} \cup \{(q', \alpha, \overline{q}'', 1)/\overline{q}'' \in \delta''_x(q'')\} & \text{if } \beta = 0 \\ \{(q', \alpha, \overline{q}'', 1)/\overline{q}'' \in \delta''_x(q'')\} & \text{if } \beta = 1 \end{cases}$$
- Syn is the partial function from $\mathcal{G}(\mathcal{A})$ into $S' \times S'' \times \mathcal{P}(A)$ defined for any $g = ((s', s'', E), (q'_c, \alpha_c, q''_c, \beta_c)_{c\in C})$, if $\{c \in C/\alpha_c = 1\} \subseteq I(E)$, by
$$Syn(g) = (Syn'(s', (q'_c)_{c\in C \& \alpha_c = 1}), Syn''(s'', (q''_c)_{c\in C \& \beta_c = 1}),$$
$$E \cup \{c \in C/\beta_c = 1\})$$
with $\mathcal{G}(\mathcal{A}) = \{(s, (q_c)_{c\in C})/s \in S' \times S'' \times \mathcal{P}(A), C \in Cl, q_c \in Q'_c \times \{0,1\} \times Q''_c \times \{0,1\}$ for any $c \in C\}$

Proposition 5. *Let $\mathcal{A}'$ and $\mathcal{A}''$ be two distributing automata. Then $concat(\mathcal{A}', \mathcal{A}'')$ is a distributing automaton which recognizes the trace concatenation $L(\mathcal{A}') \cdot_I L(\mathcal{A}'')$.*

4.3 (Restricted) trace iteration

Let $\mathcal{A}$ be a distributing automaton recognizing a recognizable I–closed word language L whose elements have all the same connected alphabet. In order to construct a distributing automaton recognizing L^{*_I}, we will use the following characterization given in [Bau92] from the results of [Mét86] and [Pig93].

Let $u, v \in A^*$. Then $uv \in L^{*_I}$ if and only if
$\exists 0 \leq n \leq |A|,\ y, z \in L^{*_I},\ u_i, v_i \in A^*, (1 \leq i \leq n)$ such that:

1. $u \sim_I y u_1 u_2 \cdots u_n$,
2. $v \sim_I v_1 v_2 \cdots v_n z$,
3. $u_i \neq \varepsilon, v_i \neq \varepsilon$,
4. $u_i v_i \in L$,
5. $(v_i, u_{i+1} u_{i+2} \cdots u_n) \in I, 1 \leq i \leq n$.

The idea of the construction of the trace iteration of a distributing automaton $\mathcal{A}$ relies on a principle similar to the one used for the concatenation. We will consider several copies of $\mathcal{A}$ and we will perform non determiniscally the actions in these copies. Of course, an action can be executed in copy i only if it is independent of all the actions already performed in copies $i+1, \cdots$. This condition will be checked with flags, as in the concatenation case. The main consequence of the above characterization of L^{*_I} is that the number of copies can be bounded.

Let $\mathcal{A} = (S, s_0, F, (Q_x, \delta_x, B_x)_{x \in A}, Syn)$ be a distributing automaton recognizing an I–closed language, L, in which all the words have the same connected alphabet, A. The iteration, $iter(\mathcal{A})$, is defined as the 5–tuple

$$((S \times \mathcal{P}(A))^m, (s_0, \emptyset)^m, \{(s_0, \emptyset)^m\} \cup (\{(s, A)/s \in F\} \times (s_0, \emptyset)^{m-1}),$$
$$((Q_x \times \{0,1\})^m, \delta_x^*, (B_x \times \{0\})^m)_{x \in A}, Syn^*)$$

where:

- $m = |A| + 2$,
- δ_x^* is defined for any $x \in A$ and for $q = (q_i, \alpha_i)_{1 \leq i \leq m} \in (Q_x \times \{0,1\})^m$ by
$$\delta_x^*(q) = \{(q_i^*, \alpha_i^*)_{1 \leq i \leq m} \in (Q_x \times \{0,1\})^m / \exists j \in [1, m], \forall i \in [j+1, m],$$
$$\alpha_i = 0, q_j^* \in \delta_x(q_j), \alpha_j^* = 1, \forall k \neq j, q_k^* = q_k, \alpha_k^* = \alpha_k\}$$
- let $g = ((s_i, E_i)_{1 \leq i \leq m}, (q_{c,i}, \alpha_{c,i})_{c \in C, 1 \leq i \leq m}) \in \mathcal{G}(iter(\mathcal{A}))$, $Syn^*(g)$ is defined only if
$$\forall 1 \leq i \leq m, \{x \in C / \alpha_{x,i} \neq 0\} \subseteq I(\cup_{i < j \leq m} E_j)$$
This condition means that the actions executed by the local processors of the copy i are independent of all the actions already performed in copies $i+1, \cdots, m$. Under this condition, we compute first
$$(s_i', E_i')_{1 \leq i \leq m} = (Syn(s_i, (q_{c,i})_{c \in C}), E_i \cup \{c \in C / \alpha_{c,i} \neq 0\})_{1 \leq i \leq m}$$
If some E_k' is equal to A then no action can be further executed in the copies $1, \cdots, k-1$. These copies are closed and we have to check that the corresponding states are final. Formally, let $k = max(\{1\} \cup \{i/1 \leq i \leq m, E_i' = A\})$, $Syn^*(g)$ is defined only if
$$k = 1 \text{ or } \forall i, 1 \leq i \leq k-1, s_i' = Syn(s_i, (q_{c,i})_{c \in C}) \in F)$$

If all these necessary conditions are fulfilled, we define

$$Syn^*(g) = ((s'_{k+i}, E'_{k+i})_{0 \leq i \leq m-k}, (s_0, \emptyset)^{k-1})$$

Proposition 6. *Let $\mathcal{A}$ be a distributing automaton recognizing L, a connected I-closed language in which all the words have the same connected alphabet. Then $iter(\mathcal{A})$ is a distributing automaton which recognizes the trace iteration L^{*_I}.*

5 Conclusion

We proposed in this paper modular constructions of distributing automata. These constructions give non deterministic automata which can be determinized through the determinization procedure given in section 3. These constructions will be implemented in the distributing automata manipulation package initialized in [Cér92]. As we recall in the introduction, such modular constructions are essential in order to modelize real concurrent programs.

References

[Bau92] S. Bauget. Reconnaissabilité de l'itération d'un langage connexe dans le monoïde des traces. Technical report, Institut Blaise Pascal, Université Paris VI, 1992.

[Ber79] J. Berstel. Transductions and context free langages. *Teubner Studienbucher Informatik*, 1979.

[Cér92] C. Cérin. *Applications de la théorie des traces à la mesure et l'implantation d'algorithmes de distribution*. PhD thesis, Université Paris–Sud, France, 1992.

[CF69] P. Cartier and D. Foata. Problèmes combinatoires de commutation et réarrangements. *Lecture Notes in Mathematics*, 85, Springer 1969.

[CMZ93] R. Cori, Y. Métivier, and W. Zielonka. Asynchronous mappings and asynchronous cellular automata. *Information and computation*, 2(106):159–202, 1993.

[CP85] R. Cori and D. Perrin. Automates et commutations partielles. *RAIRO Theor. Inf. Appl.*, 19:21–32, 1985.

[DR95] V. Diekert and G. Rozenberg. Book of traces. *World scientific, Singapore*, 1995.

[HP95] S. Huguet and A. Petit. Modular constructions of distributing automata. Technical report, LIFAC, ENS–Cachan, France, 1995.

[HU79] J.E. Hopcroft and J.D. Ullman. Introduction to automata theory, languages and computation. *Addison Wesley, Reading, MA*, 1979.

[Hug95] S. Huguet. Le non-déterminisme dans les automates distribuants. Technical report, LIFAC, ENS–Cachan, France, 1995.

[KMS94] N. Klarlund, M. Mukund, and M. Sohoni. Determinized asynchronous automata. *Proceedings of ICALP'94, LNCS 820*, pages 130–141, 1994.

[Maz77] A. Mazurkiewicz. Concurrent program schemes and their interpretations. Technical report, DAIMI, Aarhus University, 1977. Rep. PB-78.

[Mét86] Y. Métivier. Une condition suffisante de reconnaissabilité dans un monoïde partiellement commutatif. *RAIRO Theor. Inf. Appl.*, 20(2):121–127, 1986.

[Mus94] A. Muscholl. On the complementation of büchi asynchronous cellular automata. *Proceedings of ICALP'94, LNCS 820*, pages 142–153, 1994.

[Och85] E. Ochmański. Regular behaviour of concurrent systems. *EATCS Bulletin*, 27:56–67, 1985.

[Per89] D. Perrin. Partial commutation. *Proceedings of ICALP'89, LNCS 372*, pages 637–651, 1989.

[Pet93] A. Petit. Recognizable trace langages, distributed automata and the distribution problem. *Acta Informatica*, 30:89–101, 1993.

[Pig93] G. Pighizzini. Synthesis of nondeterministic asynchronous automata. In *Semantic of Programming Languages and Model Theory*, pages 109–126. Algebra, Logic and Applications, vol 5, Gordon and Breach Science, 1993.

[Zie87] W. Zielonka. Notes on finite asynchronous automata and trace langages. *RAIRO Theor. Inf. Appl.*, 21:99–135, 1987.

On the Proof Method for Bisimulation (extended abstract)

Davide Sangiorgi

INRIA- Sophia Antipolis, France. Email: davide@cma.cma.fr.

1 Introduction

In concurrency theory, *bisimilarity* is widely accepted as the finest (extensional) behavioural equivalence one would want to impose. Intense research conducted has evidenced the robustness and elegance of its mathematical theory.

On a labelled transition system, bisimilarity, abbreviated $\sim$, is defined as the largest symmetric relation $\mathcal{R}$ on processes s.t. $(P, Q) \in \mathcal{R}$ implies:

$$\text{if } P \xrightarrow{\mu} P', \text{ then there is } Q' \text{ s.t. } Q \xrightarrow{\mu} Q' \text{ and } (P', Q') \in \mathcal{R} . \qquad (*)$$

A relation $\mathcal{R}$ which satisfies clause $(*)$, without necessarily being the largest such relation, is called a *bisimulation relation.* By definition of $\sim$, a bisimulation relation is contained in $\sim$, and hence it consists of only pairs of bisimilar processes. This immediately suggests a proof method for $\sim$ — by far the most popular one: To demonstrate that $(P, Q) \in \sim$ holds, find a bisimulation relation containing the pair (P, Q).

Note that in clause $(*)$, the same relation $\mathcal{R}$ is mentioned in the hypothesis and in the thesis. In other words, when we check the bisimilarity clause on a pair (P, Q), all needed pairs of derivatives, like (P', Q'), must be present in $\mathcal{R}$. We cannot discard any such pair of derivatives from $\mathcal{R}$, even "manipulate" its process components. In this way, a bisimulation relation often contains many pairs strongly related with each other, in the sense that, at least, the bisimilarity between the processes in some of these pairs implies that between the processes in other pairs. (For instance, in a process algebra a bisimulation relation might contain pairs of processes obtainable from other pairs through application of algebraic laws for $\sim$, or obtainable as combinations of other pairs and of the operators of the language.) These redundancies can make both the definition and the verification of a bisimulation relation annoyingly heavy and tedious: It is difficult at the beginning to guess all pairs which are needed; and clause $(*)$ must be checked on all pairs introduced.

As an example, let P be a non-deadlocked process from a CCS-like language, and $!P$ the process defined thus: $!P \stackrel{\text{def}}{=} P \mid !P$. Process $!P$ represents the *replication* of P, i.e., a countable number of copies of P in parallel. A property that we naturally expect to hold is that duplication of replication has no behavioural effect, i.e, $!P \mid !P \sim !P$. To prove this, we would like to use the *singleton* relation

$$\mathcal{R} \stackrel{\text{def}}{=} \{(!P \mid !P \,,\, !P)\} .$$

But $\mathcal{R}$ is easily seen not to be a bisimulation relation. If we add pairs of processes to $\mathcal{R}$ so to make it into a bisimulation relation, then we might find that the simplest solution is to take the *infinite* relation

$$\mathcal{R}' \stackrel{\text{def}}{=} \{(Q_1, Q_2) \ : \ \text{for some } R, \, Q_1 \sim R \mid !P \mid !P \ \text{ and } \ Q_2 \sim R \mid !P\}.$$

The size augmentation in passing from $\mathcal{R}$ to $\mathcal{R}'$ is rather discouraging. But it does seems somehow unnecessary, for the bisimilarity between the two processes in $\mathcal{R}$ already implies that between the processes of all pairs of $\mathcal{R}'$.

The study reported in this paper aims at relieving the work involved with the bisimulation proof method. We anticipate that on the previous example our proof techniques allow us to prove the property $!P \mid !P \sim !P$ simply using the singleton $\mathcal{R}$.

We generalise the bisimulation proof method by relaxing the bare recursion in $(*)$. First, we introduce the notion of *progression*: A relation $\mathcal{R}$ progresses to a relation $\mathcal{S}$ if matching actions of processes in $\mathcal{R}$ yield derivatives which are in $\mathcal{S}$. We allow a relation $\mathcal{R}$ to progress to a different relation $\mathcal{F}(\mathcal{R})$, where $\mathcal{F}$ is a function on relations. Functions which can be safely used in this way (i.e., such that if $\mathcal{R}$ progresses to $\mathcal{F}(\mathcal{R})$, then $\mathcal{R}$ only includes pairs of bisimilar processes) are *sound*. We give a simple condition, called *respectfulness*, which ensures soundness. We show that the class of respectful functions contains non-trivial functions and we prove closure properties of the class w.r.t. various important function constructors, like composition, union and iteration. These properties allow us to construct sophisticated sound functions — and hence sophisticated proof techniques for bisimilarity — from simpler ones.

As examples of application of our techniques, we derive simpler proofs of some standard results of CCS. Further applications can be found in [BS94, San95], where these techniques play a crucial role in the proof of the main results.

In this short version of the paper, most of the proofs are omitted. Full details can be found in [San94].

2 Progressions and respectful functions

The results in this section hold for any transition system $(\mathcal{P}r, Act, \longrightarrow)$ with domain $\mathcal{P}r$, set of *actions* (or *labels*) Act and transition relation $\longrightarrow \subseteq \mathcal{P}r \times Act \times \mathcal{P}r$. We use P, Q and R to range over $\mathcal{P}r$ and call them *processes*; μ and λ range over Act. We write $P \xrightarrow{\mu} Q$ when $(P, \mu, Q) \in \longrightarrow$.

We let $\mathcal{R}$ and $\mathcal{S}$ range over binary relations on processes. The union of relations $\mathcal{R}$ and $\mathcal{S}$ is $\mathcal{R} \cup \mathcal{S}$, and their composition is $\mathcal{R}\mathcal{S}$. We often use the infix notation for relations. We use letters I and J for countable indexing sets in unions and sums.

Definition 1 (progression). Given two relations $\mathcal{R}$ and $\mathcal{S}$, we say that $\mathcal{R}$ *progresses to* $\mathcal{S}$, written $\mathcal{R} \rightarrowtail \mathcal{S}$, if $P \,\mathcal{R}\, Q$ implies:

1. whenever $P \xrightarrow{\mu} P'$, there is Q' s.t. $Q \xrightarrow{\mu} Q'$ and $P' \,\mathcal{S}\, Q'$;

2. the converse, i.e., whenever $Q \xrightarrow{\mu} Q'$, there is P' s.t. $P \xrightarrow{\mu} P'$ and $P' \mathcal{S} Q'$.

When $\mathcal{R}$ and $\mathcal{S}$ coincide, the above clauses are the ordinary ones of the definition of a bisimulation relation. Two processes P and Q are said *bisimilar*, written $P \sim Q$, if $P \mathcal{R} Q$ holds, for some bisimulation relation $\mathcal{R}$. This is the basis of the standard method for proving the bisimilarity between two processes: Find a relation $\mathcal{R}$ which progresses to itself and which includes the pair of given processes.

However, self-progressions $\mathcal{R} \rightarrowtail \mathcal{R}$ are special cases of progressions, but not the only ones by which process bisimilarities can be inferred. In the paper, we look for general conditions on progressions which guarantee this property.

We shall consider progressions of the form $\mathcal{R} \rightarrowtail \mathcal{F}(\mathcal{R})$ where $\mathcal{F}$ is a function from relations to relations. We call these *first-order functions*, briefly *functions*. Below, $\mathcal{F}$ and $\mathcal{G}$ range over such functions.

Definition 2 (soundness). A function $\mathcal{F}$ is *sound* if, for any $\mathcal{R}$, $\mathcal{R} \rightarrowtail \mathcal{F}(\mathcal{R})$ implies $\mathcal{R} \subseteq \sim$.

Not all functions are sound. An example is the function which maps every relation to the universal relation $\mathcal{P}r \times \mathcal{P}r$. We wish to determine a class of sound functions for which membership is easy to check, which includes interesting functions and satisfies interesting properties. We propose the class of *respectful* functions.

Definition 3 (respectfulness). A function $\mathcal{F}$ is *respectful* if whenever $\mathcal{R} \subseteq \mathcal{S}$ and $\mathcal{R} \rightarrowtail \mathcal{S}$ holds, then $\mathcal{F}(\mathcal{R}) \subseteq \mathcal{F}(\mathcal{S})$ and $\mathcal{F}(\mathcal{R}) \rightarrowtail \mathcal{F}(\mathcal{S})$ also holds.

Remark. If we replaced the respectfulness requirement by two separate ones, namely

(a) $\mathcal{R} \subseteq \mathcal{S}$ implies $\mathcal{F}(\mathcal{R}) \subseteq \mathcal{F}(\mathcal{S})$, and
(b) $\mathcal{R} \rightarrowtail \mathcal{S}$ implies $\mathcal{F}(\mathcal{R}) \rightarrowtail \mathcal{F}(\mathcal{S})$,

then we would get a stronger definition (i.e, a stronger condition on $\mathcal{F}$) which would not capture important sound functions, like the function $\mathcal{C}$ for the closure under contexts (Section 3).

Theorem 4 (soundness of respectful functions). *If $\mathcal{F}$ is respectful, then $\mathcal{F}$ is sound.*

Theorem 4 shows that a respectful first-order function yields a sound proof technique for bisimilarity. We can push further and look for ways of combining respectful functions in which respectfulness is preserved.

We call a function which takes first-order functions as arguments and yields back another first-order function as a result, a *second-order function* or, briefly, a *constructor*. A constructor is *respectful* if whenever its first-order function arguments are respectful, then also the first-order function result is respectful. This hierarchy of functions could be continued, by defining respectful third-order functions, respectful fourth-order functions and so on... . We stop at second order because it will be enough for our purposes.

We present a few primitive respectful functions and constructors. They are rather simple, but give rise to interesting compounds. Two simple primitive respectful functions are the following:

$$\mathcal{I}(\mathcal{R}) \stackrel{\text{def}}{=} \mathcal{R} \qquad\qquad \mathcal{U}(\mathcal{R}) \stackrel{\text{def}}{=} \sim$$

$\mathcal{I}$ is the identity function. $\mathcal{U}$ is the constant-to-$\sim$ function, mapping every relation onto the bisimilarity relation. Later we shall introduce a further primitive respectful function, roughly, a function which returns the closure of a relation under contexts.

The primitive respectful constructors we consider are *composition* ($\circ$), *union* ($\cup$) and chaining ($\frown$), so defined:

$$(\mathcal{G} \circ \mathcal{F})(\mathcal{R}) \stackrel{\text{def}}{=} \mathcal{G}(\mathcal{F}(\mathcal{R}))$$
$$(\bigcup_{i \in I} \mathcal{F}_i)(\mathcal{R}) \stackrel{\text{def}}{=} \bigcup_{i \in I}(\mathcal{F}_i(\mathcal{R}))$$
$$(\mathcal{G} \frown \mathcal{F})(\mathcal{R}) \stackrel{\text{def}}{=} \mathcal{G}(\mathcal{R})\ \mathcal{F}(\mathcal{R})$$

Here are some examples of functions and constructors that we can derive from the primitive ones. Derived functions are:

$$\text{for } n > 0, \mathcal{D}_n \stackrel{\text{def}}{=} \mathcal{I} \frown \ldots \frown \mathcal{I}, \quad n \text{ times}$$
$$\mathcal{B} \stackrel{\text{def}}{=} \mathcal{U} \frown \mathcal{I} \frown \mathcal{U} \qquad\qquad \mathcal{T} \stackrel{\text{def}}{=} \bigcup_{n>0} \mathcal{D}_n$$

Function $\mathcal{B}$ represents the classical *bisimulation up-to* $\sim$, as in Milner's book [Mil89] Function $\mathcal{T}$ returns the transitive closure of a relation. Examples of derived constructors are exponentiation and iteration, defined using composition and union as follows:

$$\mathcal{F}^n(\mathcal{R}) \stackrel{\text{def}}{=} \mathcal{F}((\ldots(\mathcal{F}(\mathcal{R}))\ldots)), \quad n \text{ times}$$
$$\mathcal{F}^*(\mathcal{R}) \stackrel{\text{def}}{=} \bigcup_n \mathcal{F}^n(\mathcal{R})$$

As a consequence of the respectfulness of the basic functions and constructors, these derived functions and constructors are respectful too.

3 Closure of a relation under contexts

We now consider the case — standard in process algebras — in which the class of processes is defined as the term algebra generated by some signature. We call $\mathcal{P}r_\Sigma$ the process language determined by a signature Σ; then a process is an element of $\mathcal{P}r_\Sigma$. A *functional operator* is a symbol in Σ whose arity is greater than 0. A *Σ-context* is a context for the language $\mathcal{P}r_\Sigma$ with at most one occurrence of the hole $[\cdot]$ in it. We use C to range over Σ-contexts. If C is a Σ-context and $P \in \mathcal{P}r_\Sigma$, then $C[P] \in \mathcal{P}r_\Sigma$ is the process obtained from C by filling the hole $[\cdot]$ with P. We utilise contexts to define a function $\mathcal{C}_\Sigma$ on process relations which makes the closure of a relation $\mathcal{R}$ under a certain class of contexts.

$$\mathcal{C}_\Sigma(\mathcal{R}) \stackrel{\text{def}}{=} \bigcup_{C \text{ faithful}} \{(C[P], C[Q]) : (P, Q) \in \mathcal{R}\}. \tag{1}$$

Before saying what a faithful context is, note that in the definition of $\mathcal{C}_\Sigma$ the contexts used may have at most one occurrence of a unique hole $[\cdot]$. More sophisticated closures, involving contexts which may contain different holes can be recovered as a combination of function $\mathcal{C}_\Sigma$ and other respectful functions of the previous section (see Lemma 9).

Definition 5. The class of *faithful contexts* is the largest set Cont of Σ-contexts s.t., for all $C \in$ Cont and $P \in \mathcal{P}r_\Sigma$, whenever $C[P] \xrightarrow{\mu} R$, there exist $C' \in$ Cont s.t. either

(a) $R = C'[P]$ and, for all Q, we have $C[Q] \xrightarrow{\mu} C'[Q]$, or
(b) there are $P' \in \mathcal{P}r_\Sigma$ and $\lambda \in Act$ s.t. $P \xrightarrow{\lambda} P'$ and $R = C'[P']$ and, moreover, for all $Q, Q' \in \mathcal{P}r_\Sigma$ s.t. $Q \xrightarrow{\lambda} Q'$, we have $C[Q] \xrightarrow{\mu} C'[Q']$.

In familiar process algebras, such as ACP and CCS, all contexts are faithful. Indeed, faithful contexts correspond to Larsen and Liu's *1-to-1 contexts* [LL91].

The transition relation for the processes of the language generated by a signature Σ can be defined structurally , assigning a set of *transition rules* to each symbol in Σ. In some cases, it suffices to look at the format of such transition rules to know that contexts of the language are faithful. We show that this is indeed the case for the *unary De Simone format over* Σ. This is a simplified version of the format introduced by De Simone [DS85] (the main restriction is that only one action at a time is observable). In rule (2) below, X_r, $1 \le r \le n$, and Y_j, $j \in J$, are metavariables which are instantiated with processes when the rule is applied.

Definition 6 (unary De Simone format). A transition rule

$$\frac{X_j \xrightarrow{\lambda_j} Y_j \; (j \in J)}{f(X_1, \ldots, X_n) \xrightarrow{\mu} t} \tag{2}$$

is in *unary De Simone format over* Σ if: n is the arity of f in Σ; $J \subseteq \{1, \ldots, n\}$; $X_r, 1 \le r \le n$, and $Y_j, j \in J$, are distinct variables; t is a term in $\mathcal{P}r_\Sigma(X'_1, \ldots, X'_n)$, where for all $1 \le r \le n$, each X'_r occurs at most once in t, and $X'_r = Y_r$ if $r \in J$, $X'_r = X_r$ otherwise.

Theorem 7. *Consider the process language over a signature Σ in which the meaning of all functional symbols in Σ is given using a set of rules in unary De Simone format over Σ. Then all Σ-contexts are faithful.*

In the remainder of the paper, to simplify the notation we omit the indication of the signature. Thus, we shall call a Σ-context simply a context, and we shall abbreviate function $\mathcal{C}_\Sigma$ in (1) as $\mathcal{C}$.

Lemma 8 (closure under contexts). The function $\mathcal{C}$ is respectful. □

In the sequel, we often abbreviate $\mathcal{C}(\mathcal{R})$ as $\mathcal{R}^\mathcal{C}$ and $\mathcal{T}(\mathcal{R})$ as $\mathcal{R}^\mathcal{T}$ (that is, $\mathcal{R}^\mathcal{C}$ is the closure of $\mathcal{R}$ under faithful contexts and $\mathcal{R}^\mathcal{T}$ is the transitive closure of $\mathcal{R}$).

4 Examples of applications

We assume some familiarity with CCS. Its syntax is as in [Mil89]; so for instance, the process language includes a set of constants, each of which has a unique defining equation. To apply to CCS the whole theory of proof techniques for bisimilarity developed in Section 2, we only have to understand which contexts are faithful; these are needed in the definition of function $\mathcal{C}$. An easy inspection on the transitional rules of the functional operators of the CCS signature shows that they all fit the De Simone format. By Theorem 7, we get that all CCS contexts are faithful.

4.1 Uniqueness of solutions of equations

An interesting example of application of our proof techniques to CCS is the proof of uniqueness of solutions of equations, as from Milner's book [Mil89].

We use a tilde to denote a finite (and possibly empty) tuple. All notations we introduce are generalised to tuples componentwise. For notational convenience, in this section we work with polyadic contexts, i.e., contexts which may contain an arbitrary number of different holes $[\cdot]_1, \ldots, [\cdot]_n$, and, moreover, each of these holes may appear more than once. We can recover the closure of a relation under polyadic contexts as the transitive closure of the closure under the monadic ones.

Lemma 9. If $(P_i, Q_i) \in \mathcal{R}$, $i \le i \le n$, and C is an n-ary context, then $(C[P_1, \ldots, P_n], C[Q_1, \ldots, Q_n]) \in (\mathcal{R}^\mathcal{C})^\mathcal{T}$. □

We say that a context C is *weakly guarded* if each occurrence of each hole of C is within some subexpression of the form $\alpha. C'$, where α is a prefix. The two lemmas below are easily proved by an inductive argument.

Lemma 10 (Lemma 4.13 in [Mil89]). If C is weakly guarded and $C[\widetilde{P}] \xrightarrow{\mu} P'$, then P' is of the form $C'[\widetilde{P}]$, and moreover, for any $\widetilde{Q}$, $C[\widetilde{Q}] \xrightarrow{\mu} C'[\widetilde{Q}]$. □

Lemma 11 (Proposition 4.14(1) in [Mil89]). If $A \stackrel{def}{=} P$, then $A \sim P$. □

Proposition 12. (**unique solution of equations, Proposition 4.14(2) in [Mil89]**) *Suppose $\widetilde{C}$ are weakly guarded contexts, with $\widetilde{P} \sim \widetilde{C}[\widetilde{P}]$ and $\widetilde{Q} \sim \widetilde{C}[\widetilde{Q}]$. Then $\widetilde{P} \sim \widetilde{Q}$.*

Proof. Let $\mathcal{R} \stackrel{\text{def}}{=} \{(P_i, Q_i) : 1 \le i \le n\}$, where n is the length of vectors $\widetilde{C}$, $\widetilde{P}$ and $\widetilde{Q}$. Suppose $P_i \xrightarrow{\mu} P_i'$. From Lemmas 10 and 11 we deduce that there are C_i' and Q_i' s.t. the following two diagrams commute:

$$\begin{array}{ccc} P_i & \sim & C_i[\widetilde{P}] \\ \mu\downarrow & & \mu\downarrow \\ P_i' & \sim & C_i'[\widetilde{P}] \end{array} \qquad\qquad \begin{array}{ccc} C_i[\widetilde{Q}] & \sim & Q_i \\ \mu\downarrow & & \mu\downarrow \\ C_i'[\widetilde{Q}] & \sim & Q_i' \end{array}$$

By Lemma 9, this shows that $\mathcal{R} \rightarrowtail \sim (\mathcal{R}^{\mathcal{C}})^{\mathcal{T}} \sim$ holds. Since function $\sim (-^{\mathcal{C}})^{\mathcal{T}} \sim$ is sound, we infer $\mathcal{R} \subseteq \sim$, which proves the proposition. □

In the proof of Proposition 12, the cardinality of the relation $\mathcal{R}$ is the same as the cardinality of the vector of given contexts $\widetilde{C}$. In particular, if we are dealing with only one context (i.e., only one equation), then $\mathcal{R}$ consists of *one* only pair. For the proof of Proposition 12, Milner [Mil89] shows that

$$\mathcal{R}' \stackrel{\text{def}}{=} \bigcup_{C} \{(C[\widetilde{P}], C[\widetilde{Q}])\}$$

is a bisimulation up-to $\sim$ (i.e., $\mathcal{R}' \rightarrowtail \sim \mathcal{R}' \sim$ holds), proceeding on induction on the structure of C. Note that in $\mathcal{R}'$ the contexts in the union are *all* contexts — including the unguarded ones.

4.2 Some properties of replication

Given a process P, its *replication* $!\,P$ is defined by the equation $!\,P \stackrel{\text{def}}{=} P \,|\, !\,P$, and stands for a countable infinite number of copies of P in parallel. In certain process algebras like the π-calculus, replication is the only form of recursion allowed. This because replication gives enough expressive power and enjoys interesting algebraic properties. For instance, for any pair of processes P and Q we have:

$$(1)\ \ !\,P \,|\, !\,P \sim !\,P; \qquad (2)\ \ !\,(P \,|\, Q) \sim !\,P \,|\, !\,Q;$$
$$(3)\ !\,(P+Q) \sim !\,(P \,|\, Q).$$

With our proof techniques based on sound functions, we can prove these assertions by exhibiting progressions of the form $\mathcal{R} \rightarrowtail \sim \mathcal{R}^{\mathcal{C}} \sim$. For (1) (2) and (3), the relations to use are, respectively,

$$\mathcal{R}_1 \stackrel{\text{def}}{=} \{(!\,P \,|\, !\,P, !\,P)\}, \qquad \mathcal{R}_2 \stackrel{\text{def}}{=} \{(!\,(P \,|\, Q), !\,P \,|\, !\,Q)\},$$
$$\mathcal{R}_3 \stackrel{\text{def}}{=} \{(!\,(P+Q), !\,(P \,|\, Q))\}.$$

The possibility of cutting contexts off, achieved through the closure under contexts, reduces the size of the relations to exhibit sensibly. Relations $\mathcal{R}_i$ only contain *one* pair of processes. Without the closure under contexts, each $\mathcal{R}_i$ would contain an infinity of pairs. For instance, $\mathcal{R}_3$ would become

$$\mathcal{R}_3' \stackrel{\text{def}}{=} \bigcup_{R} \{(R \,|\, !\,(P+Q), R \,|\, !\,(P \,|\, Q))\}$$

($\mathcal{R}_3'$ progresses to $\sim \mathcal{R}_3' \sim$). Having $\mathcal{R}_3'$ in place of $\mathcal{R}_3$ does not make the proof conceptually more difficult, but it does make it more tedious.

5 Related work

Some of the proof techniques described in the paper, or special cases of them, have already appeared in the literature. But we should stress that there has never been a systematic study of the topic. For instance, we feel that we lacked the capability of combining simpler proof techniques into more powerful ones, which is made possible by the theory developed in this paper.

We mentioned Milner's *bisimulation up-to* $\sim$ technique [Mil89], in which the closure of a bisimulation relation is achieved up to bisimilarity itself. Two special cases of the up-to-context technique had been previously put forward: In [Cau90], Caucal defines a notion of *self-bisimulation* and uses it to establish a decidability result for the class of BPA processes, which can be viewed as the processes generated by a context-free grammar. Self-bisimulation is used to eliminate common prefixes and suffixes in the derivatives of two processes. Another form of up-to-context technique is Milner, Parrow and Walker' *bisimulation up-to restriction* [MPW92], with which common outermost restrictions in the derivatives of two processes can be discarded.

6 Further developments

One of our most useful primitive proof techniques is an "up-to context" technique which allows us to cancel a common context in the derivatives of two processes. We have shown that if the transition rules for the operators of the language are in unary De Simone format, then this technique is sound. The proof of this result uses the fact that the operators specifiable with transition rules in unary De Simone format preserve bisimilarity. There are other formats of transition rules which go beyond the De Simone format and which enjoy this property. For instance, Groote and Vaandrager' *tyft* format [GV92], and Bloom, Istrail and Meyer' *GSOS* format [BIM88]. It would be interesting to examine whether a soundness result for the up-to-context technique also holds for the *tyft* and the *GSOS* formats. We think that some constraints would have to be imposed on them: For instance one might have to disallow lookaheads greater than one in the *tyft* format (such lookaheads allow the definition of operators which, in order to release some action, require the release of a *sequence* of actions — as opposed to *one* — from some of their arguments).

In the full paper, we examine the application of our proof techniques to the π-*calculus* [MPW92] in detail. The π-calculus is a development of CCS which allows name communications. Our interest for the π-calculus is motivated, besides by its relevance as a process algebra, by certain peculiarities of its transition system, which deviates from a standard system, like the one for CCS, in some important aspects: Firstly, the π-calculus is a (special case of) a value-passing calculus. Secondly, π-calculus transition rules utilise alpha conversion and substitution on names. These features have to be taken into account in the definition of bisimilarity and affect, in an important way, the definition of the function $\mathcal{C}$ (closure under contexts). The peculiarities of π-calculus transition system also suggest other primitive respectful functions. One is a function which allows us to apply injective substitutions on names to the derivatives of two processes. This function yields a form of "up-to injective substitution" technique which is very handy when dealing with universally-quantified substitutions on names — which are common in the π-calculus.

In this paper, we confined ourselves to strong bisimilarities, where all actions are treated equally. A natural development of our work is to look at *weak bisimilarities*, where a special action, called *silent action*, is distinguished from the others and partially ignored in the bisimilarity clause. This issue is non-trivial, though: See the concluding section of [San94] for a discussion.

We believe that our proof techniques could be very advantageous in *higher-order calculi* , i.e calculi in which terms can be exchanged in a communication. For instance, a few rather involved proofs in [San92], dealing with the Higher-Order π-calculus, should become simpler using some form of "bisimulation up-to context" (see Remark 6.6.18 in [San92]). Our proof techniques should also be useful in higher-order functional languages, for instance to reason about *applicative bisimilarity* of programs [Abr89].

The bisimulation proof method stems from the theory of fixed-points and the co-induction principle [Mil89, MT91]. On a complete lattice (i.e., a partial order with all joins) the co-induction principle says:

> *Let $(D, <)$ be a complete lattice, and $\mathcal{G} : D \to D$ a monotone function with greatest fixed-point $\mu_{\mathcal{G}}$. To prove that $x < \mu_{\mathcal{G}}$ it suffices to prove that x is a post-fixed point of $\mathcal{G}$, i.e, $x < \mathcal{G}(x)$.*

When the bisimilarity relation $\sim$ is interpreted as the greatest fixed-point of a certain continuous function on relations [Mil89, Section 4.6], this translate into saying that to prove $\mathcal{R} \subseteq\sim$ it suffices to prove that $\mathcal{R}$ is a bisimulation relation. We would like to see whether our study of the bisimulation proof method leads to interesting generalisation of the co-induction principle. A possible generalisation, suggested by the definition of respectful functions and the proof of Theorem 4, uses an auxiliary function $\mathcal{F}$ as follows:

Theorem 13. *Let $(D, <)$ be a complete lattice, and $\mathcal{G} : D \to D$ a monotone function with greatest fixed-point $\mu_{\mathcal{G}}$. Suppose $\mathcal{F} : D \to D$ and that, for all $z, y \in D$, $z < y$ and $z < \mathcal{G}(y)$ implies $\mathcal{F}(z) < \mathcal{F}(y)$ and $\mathcal{F}(z) < \mathcal{G}(\mathcal{F}(y))$. Then to prove $x < \mu_{\mathcal{G}}$ it suffices to prove $x < \mathcal{G}(\mathcal{F}(x))$.* □

Theorem 4 is an instance of this theorem, and the proof is essentially the same. A more elegant but weaker formulation of Theorem 13 could require that $\mathcal{F}$ is monotone and that $\mathcal{F} \circ \mathcal{G} < \mathcal{G} \circ \mathcal{F}$ (i.e., for all z, $(\mathcal{F} \circ \mathcal{G})(z) < (\mathcal{G} \circ \mathcal{F})(z)$). It is worth pointing out that if $\mathcal{F}$ is monotone, then the condition $\mathcal{F} \circ \mathcal{G} < \mathcal{G} \circ \mathcal{F}$ is the same as the condition "for all $z, y \in D$, $z < \mathcal{G}(y)$ implies $\mathcal{F}(z) < \mathcal{F}(\mathcal{G}(y))$". In terms of respectful functions for bisimilarity, this formulation would amount to having the same conditions as in the remark after Definition 3.

Acknowledgements

I would also like to thank Glenn Bruns, Martin Hofmann, Marcelo Fiore, Robin Milner, Andrew Pitts, Jan Rutten, Daniele Turi, David N. Turner, David Walker, and an anonymous referee whose comments helped me to improve the technical presentation. Also, thanks to an anonymous referee for his suggestions on TeX. This research has been supported by the ESPRIT BRA project 6454 "CONFER".

References

[Abr89] S. Abramsky. The lazy lambda calculus. In D. Turner, editor, *Research Topics in Functional Programming*. Addison-Wesley, 1989.

[BIM88] B. Bloom, S. Istrail, and A.R. Meyer. Bisimulation can't' be traced: preliminary report. In *15th POPL*, 1988.

[BS94] M. Boreale and D. Sangiorgi. A fully abstract semantics for causality in the π-calculus. Technical Report ECS–LFCS–94–297, Edinburgh Univ., 1994. An extract in proc. *STACS'95*, LNCS 900.

[Cau90] D. Caucal. Graphes canoniques de graphes algébriques. *Informatique Théorique et Applications (RAIRO)*, 24(4):339–352, 1990.

[DS85] R. De Simone. Higher level synchronising devices in MEIJE-SCCS. *Theoretical Computer Science*, 37:245–267, 1985.

[Gro90] J.F. Groote. Transition system specifications with negative premises. In *Proc. CONCUR '90*, LNCS 458, 1990.

[GV92] J.F. Groote and F.W. Vaandrager. Structured operational semantics and bisimulation as a congruence. *Information and Computation*, 100:202–260, 1992.

[LL91] K.G. Larsen and X. Liu.. Compositionality through an operational semantics of contexts. *J. Logic Computat.*, 1(6):761–795, 1991.

[Mil89] R. Milner. *Communication and Concurrency*. Prentice Hall, 1989.

[MPW92] R. Milner, J. Parrow, and D. Walker. A calculus of mobile processes, (Parts I and II). *Information and Computation*, 100:1–77, 1992.

[MT91] R. Milner and M. Tofte. Co-induction in relational semantics. *Theoretical Computer Science*, 87:209–220, 1991.

[San92] D. Sangiorgi. *Expressing Mobility in Process Algebras: First-Order and Higher-Order Paradigms*. PhD thesis CST–99–93, University of Edinburgh, 1992.

[San94] D. Sangiorgi. On the bisimulation proof method. Technical Report ECS–LFCS–94–299, LFCS, Dept. of Comp. Sci., Edinburgh Univ., 1994. Revised version available via anonymous ftp from `cma.cma.fr` as `pub/papers/davide/bis-proof.ps.Z`.

[San95] D. Sangiorgi. Lazy functions and mobile processes. Technical Report RR-2515, INRIA-Sophia Antipolis, 1995. available via anonymous ftp from `cma.cma.fr` as `pub/papers/davide/RR-2515.ps.Z`.

Towards a Calculus of Predicate Transformers

Clare Martin

University of Buckingham, Buckingham MK18 1EG, UK.

Abstract. The main purpose of this paper is to investigate whether the relationship between the categories of total functions, relations and predicate transformers described in [7] can be used to develop a calculus of predicate transformers for program derivation in the style of [13] directly from the well-established calculus of functions [2]. The results are mixed in the sense that although many laws of the functional calculus can be generalised to predicate transformers, they must be weakened in order to do so.

1 Introduction

In [7], it is shown that there is a single categorical construction which, when applied to the category of total functions yields the category of relations, and when applied to the category of relations yields the category of monotonic predicate transformers. Associated with this construction are extensions of functors, natural transformations, and initial algebras which offer the potential to extend the laws of the well-established functional calculus to both relations and predicate transformers in a uniform way. The main advantage of a calculus of relations over a functional calculus lies in its treatment of non-deterministic programs. The main advantage of a calculus of predicate transformers over a relational calculus is that it provides a semantic category for the refinement calculus [13], in which one can reason about non-deterministic programs in a way which is impossible in a purely relational setting. For example, there exist refinements of non-deterministic programs which cannot be proved correct in a purely relational calculus [14].

In recent years there has been a considerable amount of work on the development of a relational calculus [1, 5, 6, 11], but very little on a corresponding calculus of predicate transformers. One reason for this is that many equational laws of the functional calculus generalise to relations in a straightforward way, but must be weakened to inequations when extended to predicate transformers. Nevertheless, it is arguable that such inequational laws could still prove useful since the refinement calculus is mainly concerned with program *refinement*, unlike the functional calculus which is used for program *transformation*.

This paper represents a first step towards the development of a calculus of predicate transformers. As such, we will restrict our attention to a small subset of four laws of the functional calculus. By discussing how such laws might be extended to predicate transformers we will develop some general techniques which could be applied to a wider set of laws. We will begin with some notation.

1.1 Notation

We will use the following notation for functional programming operators: the function τ maps its argument a to the singleton list $[a]$; $f*$ denotes the 'map f' function, which applies the function f to each member of a list; $+\!\!+$ denotes the concatenate operator which takes two lists as argument and appends the right hand one to the left; and the reduce operator / takes an associative binary operator $\oplus$ as its left-hand argument and a list $[x_1, x_2, ...x_n]$ as its right-hand argument where

$$\oplus/[a_1, a_2, ..., a_n] = a_1 \oplus a_2 \oplus ... \oplus a_n$$

The number 1 denotes the singleton type consisting of one distinguished element, which we will denote by 0, and the identity function on a type A is written as I_A. Functional application is denoted by juxtaposition and binds most tightly in expressions. It associates to the right, so fgx means f applied to $g(x)$.

The letter $\mathcal{S}$ denotes the category of total functions, $\mathcal{R}$ denotes the category of relations and $\mathcal{T}$ denotes the category of predicate transformers, where a predicate transformer is a total function between powersets which is monotonic with respect to the subset inclusion ordering. Composition in each category is denoted by semicolon; so if $f : A \to B$ and $g : B \to C$, $f;g : A \to C$. The converse of any relation $R : A \to B$ in $\mathcal{R}$ is denoted by $R^\circ : B \to A$. The product and coproduct functors in $\mathcal{S}$ are represented by the standard symbols $\times$ and $+$ respectively. The standard notation is also used for the product arrow $< f, g >: A \to B \times C$, and the coproduct arrow $[f, g] : A + B \to C$, where f and g are of appropriate type in each case. Although the notation used for the coproduct arrow is the same as that used for lists, there should be no confusion since both are standard and are used in different contexts.

The set $\mathbb{P}A$ is the powerset of A, and the *existential image* functor $\mathcal{E} : \mathcal{R} \to \mathcal{T}$ maps each relation $R : A \to B$ to the function $\mathcal{E}R : \mathbb{P}A \to \mathbb{P}B$ defined by

$$(\mathcal{E}R)X = \{b|(\exists a \in X : aRb)\}$$

Its restriction to $\mathcal{S}$, considered as a functor from $\mathcal{S}$ to itself is the covariant power functor, denoted by $\mathbb{P} : \mathcal{S} \to \mathcal{S}$. The *universal image* functor $\mathcal{A} : \mathcal{R} \to \mathcal{T}$ maps each relation $R : A \to B$ to the function $\mathcal{A}R : \mathbb{P}B \to \mathbb{P}A$ defined by

$$(\mathcal{A}R)Y = \cup\{X|((\mathcal{E}R)X \subseteq Y)\}$$

Each of the three categories considered here has a partial order on its homsets: the pointwise ordering in $\mathcal{T}$, inclusion in $\mathcal{R}$ and the trivial equality ordering in $\mathcal{S}$. An arrow $f : A \to B$ in a category with such an ordering $\sqsubseteq$ on its homsets for which there exists $g : B \to A$ such that

$$I_A \sqsubseteq f;g \quad \text{and} \quad g;f \sqsubseteq I_B$$

is called a *map*, and g is its *comap*. For any relation R, $\mathcal{E}R$ is a map in $\mathcal{T}$ and $\mathcal{A}R$ is its comap.

1.2 Promotion Rules

The subset of laws of the functional calculus which will be discussed here is known as the set of *promotion* rules [2], and is given below:

one-point rules

$$[\,];f* = f;[\,] \tag{1}$$
$$[\,];\oplus/ = I \tag{2}$$

join rules

$$+\!\!+/;f* = f**;+\!\!+/ \tag{3}$$
$$+\!\!+/;\oplus/ = (\oplus/*);\oplus/ \tag{4}$$

The first step towards the generalisation of such laws to predicate transformers is the extension of functors, which is described in section 2. The second step is the extension of initial algebras, which is described in section 3. The extension of the promotion theorems themselves is given in Section 4, before the concluding remarks in Section 5.

2 Functors

We will restrict attention to functors which are monotonic with respect to the ordering on homsets of the categories considered here. Not all such functors have an extension to predicate transformers; those that do are called *relators* [5] and can be characterised by the property that they preserve factorisation of relations into functions: a functor F is a relator if for all total functions f, g, h and k,

$$f;g^\circ = h^\circ;k \Rightarrow Ff;(Fg)^\circ = (Fh)^\circ;Fk$$

Every endofunctor F which is a relator in $\mathcal{S}$ has a unique extension to an endofunctor in $\mathcal{R}$ [11]. The same is true of any functor whose source and target has been constructed from $\mathcal{S}$ using some combination of product or coproduct functors. For example, the product functor $\times : \mathcal{S} \times \mathcal{S} \to \mathcal{S}$ extends to $\otimes : \mathcal{R} \times \mathcal{R} \to \mathcal{R}$ where $\otimes$ agrees with $\times$ on objects, and for all relations R, S in $\mathcal{R}$,

$$(a,b)R \otimes S(c,d) \Leftrightarrow aRc \text{ and } bSd$$

Each such functor on relations can be extended once again to an *upfunctor* $\hat{F}$ on predicate transformers [7], which is to say that:

$$\hat{F}I_A = I_{\hat{F}A}$$
$$\hat{F}(p;q) \sqsubseteq \hat{F}p;\hat{F}q$$

The dual concept to an upfunctor, given by reversing the inequality will be called a *downfunctor*. Although $\hat{F}$ is not necessarily a functor, it does have the property that if p is a map and r is a comap in $\mathcal{T}$, then for all q in $\mathcal{T}$ of appropriate type,

$$\hat{F}(p;q;r) = \hat{F}p;\hat{F}q;\hat{F}r \tag{5}$$

This fact will prove essential to the extension of promotion theorems in Section 4.

Some examples of extended functors on predicate transformers are given below. More examples, including the exponential functor can be found in [10]. Unfortunately, the extension of the product functor, which is fundamental to many data types, is not a functor.

Examples

1. The **product** functor extends to $p\hat{\times}q : \mathbb{P}(A \times C) \to \mathbb{P}(B \times D)$, where
$$(p\hat{\times}q)Y = \cup\{pS \times qT | S \times T \subseteq Y\}$$
2. The extension of the **coproduct** functor is isomorphic to the cartesian product functor:
$$\mathbb{P}(A + B) \cong \mathbb{P}A \times \mathbb{P}B \text{ and } p\hat{+}q \cong p \times q$$
3. The extension of the **map** functor on lists is similar to the product functor: let $A_1 \times A_2 \times .... \times A_n$ denote the set of all lists of length n in which the ith element is drawn from the set A_i, then $p\hat{*} : \mathbb{P}A* \to \mathbb{P}B*$ is given by
$$p\hat{*}Y = \cup\{pX_1 \times pX_2 \times ....pX_n | X_1 \times X_2 \times .... \times X_n \subseteq Y\}$$

If definitions such as these are to be used in program refinements in the style of the refinement calculus, they must be translated into that language. Any monotonic predicate transformer has a representation as a specification statement in the refinement calculus, and conversely, the meaning of every statement is given by a unique predicate transformer. Suppose that the predicate transformer p represents the specification statement:

$$|[con\ X : E \bullet [pre(X), post(X)]]|$$

Any program satisfying this specification will, when activated in an initial state satisfying $pre(X)$ establish a final state satisfying $post(X)$. The specification statement corresponding to $p\hat{*}$ is:

$$|[con\ [X_1, X_2, ...X_n] : E* \bullet [\forall i \bullet pre(X_i), \forall i \bullet post(X_i)]]|$$

Although this definition is not very surprising, the advantage of developing it algebraically is that its properties are revealed more clearly. For example, it is easy to show that every extended functor $\hat{F}$ preserves all conjunctivity and disjunctivity properties of predicate transformers.[10]

3 Initial Algebras

Let F be an upfunctor from some category $\mathcal{D}$ to itself. An *initial F-algebra* is an arrow $\alpha : FA \to A$ such that for each arrow ϕ of type $FB \to B$ for some B, there exists an arrow $(\!|\phi|\!) : A \to B$ such that

$$(\alpha; \psi = F\psi; \phi) \Leftrightarrow \psi = (\!|\phi|\!) \tag{6}$$

Arrows of the form $(\!|\phi|\!)$ are called *catamorphisms*. Every initial algebra α is characterised up to isomorphism by its defining equation (6). This definition can be dualised: an initial F^{op}–algebra in $\mathcal{C}^{op}$ is called a *final F-coalgebra* in $\mathcal{C}$. If $(\!|\phi|\!)$ is a catamorphism in $\mathcal{C}^{op}$, we say it is an *anamorphism* in $\mathcal{C}$, which is written as $[\!(\phi)\!]$.

It is well-known that initial algebras in $\mathcal{S}$ are preserved under the extension of functors to relations [8]. Moreover, the following theorem [12] shows that such initial algebras are also transformed to final coalgebras in $\mathcal{T}$. This result gives a natural way to extend functional programming operators such as fold-left operator and the reduce operator (/) to predicate transformers.

Theorem 1. *Let $F : \mathcal{S} \to \mathcal{S}$ be a relator with initial algebra α. Then $A\alpha$ is a final coalgebra of $\hat{F} : \mathcal{T} \to \mathcal{T}$.*

This theorem can be applied to a variety of data types [9]. Initially, we will concentrate on the type of *snoc-lists*, and give some examples of catamorphisms on this data type, in order to illustrate how fold-left behaves on predicate transformers. Then we will look at some algebraic properties of the type of *join*-lists, in order to meet our original goal of attempting to generalise promotion laws (1)-(4) to predicate transformers.

The type of snoc-lists consists of the type of all finite sequences, as constructed from the empty list function $\eta : 1 \to A*$ which returns the empty list [ ], together with the snoc operator $+\!\!\!+\!\!<: A * \times A \to A*$ which takes a list and an element of A and appends the element to the list:

$$[a_1, a_2, ..., a_{n-1}] +\!\!\!+\!\!< a_n = [a_1, a_2, ..., a_n]$$

This data type can also be characterised as an initial algebra: consider the functor $F : \mathcal{S} \to \mathcal{S}$, defined for all $f : X \to Y$ by

$$FX = 1 + (X \times A)$$
$$Ff = I_1 + (f \times I_A)$$

The initial algebra of F is the coproduct arrow $[\eta, +\!\!\!+\!\!<]$. So standard functional programming operators that are usually defined using recursion equations can be given an alternative definition as a single catamorphism. In particular, the recursive definition of the fold-left operator, denoted by $\oplus\!\not\rightarrow_e$, for all $\oplus : B \times A \to B$ and $e : 1 \to B$:

$$\eta; \oplus\!\not\rightarrow_e = e \tag{7}$$
$$+\!\!\!+\!\!<; \oplus\!\not\rightarrow_e = (\oplus\!\not\rightarrow_e \times I); \oplus \tag{8}$$

is equivalent to the following statement:

$$\oplus\!\not\rightarrow_e = (\!| e, \oplus |\!)$$

where $(\!| e, \oplus |\!)$ is an abbreviation for $(\!| [e, \oplus] |\!)$. Since initial algebras are preserved under the embedding of $\mathcal{S}$ into $\mathcal{R}$, this definition can be generalised immediately to relations [3] simply by replacing the product $\times$ by its extension $\otimes$. The resulting notion of a relational fold is illustrated by the example below.

Example

Let $\oplus : \mathbb{N} \times \mathbb{N} \to \mathbb{N}$ and $e : 1 \to \mathbb{N}$ be defined by $\oplus = \max; \leq$ and $e = \{(0,0)\}$. Then $\oplus\!\not\rightarrow_e$ is characterised by the following recusion equations:

$$[\,] \oplus\!\not\rightarrow_e 0$$
$$[a_1, a_2, ..., a_n] \oplus\!\not\rightarrow_e b \Leftrightarrow \forall i \bullet a_i \leq b$$

Although this definition is unsurprising, its mathematical derivation ensures that it is the canonical extension of the fold-left operator to relations. Furthermore, its characterisation as a catamorphism is suitable for manipulation in program transformations, as illustrated in [3].

We will now use Theorem 1 to extend the definition of fold-left to predicate transformers. Since $\mathcal{A}[\eta, +\!\!+\!\!<]$ is a final coalgebra of $\hat{F}$ in $\mathcal{T}$, we have that for all $\oplus : \mathbb{P}B \to \mathbb{P}(A \times B)$ and $e : \mathbb{P}A \to \mathbb{P}1$,

$$\oplus \not\to_e ; \mathcal{A}\eta = e$$
$$\oplus \not\to_e ; \mathcal{A} +\!\!+\!\!< \; = \oplus ; (\oplus \not\to_e \hat{\times} I).$$

Expanding these equations using the definition of $\hat{\times}$ gives

$$[\,] \in \oplus \not\to_e X\} \Leftrightarrow eX = \{0\} \tag{9}$$
$$\{(as, a) | as +\!\!+\!\!< a \in \oplus \not\to_e X\} = \bigcup \{\oplus \not\to_e A \times B | A \times B \subseteq \oplus X\} \tag{10}$$

In its present form, this definition is rather more difficult to apply than the previous one. The problem is that any meaningful example must first be expressed in the refinement calculus, then converted into a predicate transformer, and then translated back into the refinement calculus once its fold has been calculated. This is illustrated by the example below.

Example

Let P be a specification which considers the values of two variables x and y, which are allowed to range over the natural numbers, and if y is greater than or equal to x, assigns the value of y to a third variable z. In the refinement calculus this is expressed as follows:

$$P = x \leq y \to |[con\ Y : \mathbb{N} \bullet [y = Y, z = Y]]|$$

Let Q be a specification which establishes an initial value to variable x of zero:

$$Q = [\text{true}, x = 0]$$

If we let the meaning of specifications P and Q be given by predicate transformers $\oplus$ and e respectively, then we can use the laws of the refinement calculus to calculate that for all $X \in \mathbb{P}\mathbb{N}$,

$$\oplus X = (\mathbb{N} \times X) \cup \{(n, m) : \mathbb{N} \times \mathbb{N} | n > m\}$$
$$eX = \begin{cases} \{0\} & \text{if } 0 \in X \\ \emptyset & \text{otherwise} \end{cases}$$

Equations(9) and (10) can now be used to calculate that $\oplus \not\to_e X$ is given by

$$\{as +\!\!+\!\!< a | (as, a) \in \mathbb{N} * \times X\} \cup \{[a_1, a_2, ..., a_n] : \mathbb{N} * | \exists k \bullet a_k > a_{k+1}\} \cup \chi$$

where $\chi = \{[\,]\}$ if $0 \in X$, otherwise $\emptyset$. When converted back into the refinement calculus, this predicate transformer, perhaps unsurprisingly, yields the specification which examines a list as, and if as is increasing, it assigns the value of the last element of as to a variable z. If as is the empty list, then z is assigned the value of zero:

$$(\mathsf{inc}\ as \rightarrow |[con\ Y : \mathbb{N} \bullet [\mathsf{last}(as) = Y, z = Y]]|) \ddagger [as = [\,], z = 0]$$

where a list as satisfies predicate inc if each member of as is greater than or equal to the preceding member, and last(as) denotes the last member of as. The ‡ operator denotes program conjunction: the conjunction of a family of programs is the worst program that is better than each member of that family [14].

This example shows that the extension of the fold-left operator to predicate transformers behaves exactly as we would expect. The advantage of the predicate transformer formulation of this definition over its relational counterpart is that it can be used to express a wider variety of programs. For example, consider the following specification

$$\begin{aligned} x \leq y \rightarrow (&|[con\ Y : \mathbb{N} \bullet [y = Y, z = Y \sqcup z = Y + 1]]| \ddagger \\ &|[con\ Y : \mathbb{N} \bullet [y = Y, z = Y + 1 \sqcup z = Y + 2]]|) \end{aligned}$$

This specification represents a program which considers the values of two variables x and y to see whether y is greater than or equal to x. If so, then the program is the worst which is better than the program which non-deterministically assigns variable z the value of y or $y+1$ and that which non-deterministically assigns it the value of $y+1$ or $y+2$. The meaning of this specification is given by the predicate transformer $\oplus$, where

$$\oplus X = \{(n,m) | (\{n, n+1\} \subseteq X \text{ or } \{n+1, n+2\} \subseteq X) \ \&\ m \in \mathbb{N}\} \cup \{(n,m) | n > m\}$$

This predicate transformer is particularly badly behaved: it is neither conjunctive nor disjunctive. Therefore the meaning of this specification could not be given by a single relation, yet the meaning of its fold over lists can be calculated in the same way as the example above, to give a corresponding result. This technique of translating each specification into a predicate transformer in order to calculate the meaning of its fold over lists is clearly very inefficient. What is really needed is a new refinement rule, but that is left as a topic of future research.

4 Promotion Theorems

The promotion rules given in Section 1.2 are all special cases of a more general promotion theorem given in [1, 4]. In order to apply this theorem to predicate transformers, it must be dualised from catamorphisms to anamorphisms, and then weakened slightly. The reason for the weakening is that relators in $\mathcal{S}$ do not necessarily extend to functors in $\mathcal{T}$. We will begin with the following lemma, the proof of which is omitted.

Lemma 2. *If p is a map or a comap in $\mathcal{T}$, then $[\![p]\!]$ is also a map or a comap, respectively.*

The following analog of the promotion theorem relies on the fact that whenever a unique solution of the equation $X = FX$ exists, it is also the least solution of $X \sqsupseteq FX$ and the greatest solution of $X \sqsubseteq FX$.

Theorem 3 (Promotion). *Let $p : A \to B$, $q : B \to FB$ and $r : A \to FA$ in some category $\mathcal{C}$ with an ordering $\sqsubseteq$ on its homsets. Then*

$$p; q = r; Fp \Rightarrow p; [\![q]\!] = [\![r]\!] \text{ if } F \text{ is a functor} \tag{11}$$
$$p; q \sqsubseteq r; Fp \Rightarrow p; [\![q]\!] \sqsubseteq [\![r]\!] \text{ if } F \text{ is a downfunctor} \tag{12}$$
$$p; q \sqsupseteq r; Fp \Rightarrow p; [\![q]\!] \sqsupseteq [\![r]\!] \text{ if } F \text{ is an upfunctor} \tag{13}$$

The proof of this theorem is omitted, since it is only slightly different from that given for relations in [1], where F is required to be a functor. The following Corollary is a fairly immediate consequence of the theorem, together with Lemma 2 and equation (5), and will be useful in the examples that follow.

Corollary 4. *If p is a comap or q is a map, then equation (11) of Theorem 3 holds for any extended relator $\hat{F} : \mathcal{T} \to \mathcal{T}$, even if it is not a functor.*

The significance of Theorem 3 is not obvious until it is applied to an actual data type. In order to apply it to the promotion rules of Section 1.2, we must examine its consequences on the type of join-lists rather than snoc-lists. This is the type defined in $\mathcal{S}$ by the initial algebra $[\eta, \tau, +\!\!+] : GA* \to A*$ where the functor $G : \mathcal{S} \to \mathcal{S}$ is defined for all $f : X \to Y$ in $\mathcal{S}$ by

$$GX = 1 + A + X \times X$$
$$Gf = I_1 + I_A + f \times f$$

For brevity, we will denote the final coalgebra of $\hat{G}$ in $\mathcal{T}$ by $\langle \tilde{\eta}, \tilde{\tau}, \tilde{+\!\!+} \rangle : \mathbb{P}A* \to \mathbb{P}1 \times \mathbb{P}A \times \mathbb{P}(A * \times A*)$ where $\tilde{\eta} = A\eta$, $\tilde{\tau} = A\tau$ and $\tilde{+\!\!+} = A +\!\!+$. We obtain the following evaluation rules for join-list anamorphisms:

$$[\![1_\oplus, p, \oplus]\!]; \tilde{\eta} = 1_\oplus \tag{14}$$
$$[\![1_\oplus, p, \oplus]\!]; \tilde{\tau} = p \tag{15}$$
$$[\![1_\oplus, p, \oplus]\!]; \tilde{+\!\!+} = \oplus; [\![1_\oplus, p, \oplus]\!] \hat{\times} [\![1_\oplus, p, \oplus]\!] \tag{16}$$

Part (13) of the promotion theorem, together with Corollary 4 gives the following theorem for join-lists:

Theorem 5.

$$p; \oplus \sqsupseteq \ominus; p \hat{\times} p \Rightarrow p; [\![1_\oplus, q, \oplus]\!] \sqsupseteq [\![p; 1_\oplus, p; q, \ominus]\!]$$

where the $\sqsupseteq$ sign can be replaced by equality if $\oplus$, q and $1_\oplus$ are maps, or if p is a comap.

In order to see how this is used, we need the definitions of map and reduce for predicate transformers. These are direct translations of the definitions for $\mathcal{S}$ given in [9].

Definition 6 (Map).

$$p\hat{*} \triangleq [\![\tilde{\eta}, (\tilde{\tau}; p), \tilde{+\!\!+}]\!] : \mathbb{P}(A*) \to \mathbb{P}(B*) \tag{17}$$

The definition of $p\hat{*}$ given in Section 2 can be shown to satisfy the equations corresponding to (14), (15) and (16) for this anamorphism. Therefore the two definitions are equivalent. The definition of reduce for predicate transformers is also a straight analog of that for total functions:

Definition 7 (Reduce). Suppose $\oplus : \mathbb{P}A \to \mathbb{P}(A \times A)$ is associative and has unit $1_\oplus$, then $\oplus/$ is defined by

$$\oplus/ \triangleq [\![1_\oplus, I, \oplus]\!] : \mathbb{P}(A) \to \mathbb{P}(B*) \tag{18}$$

It follows from Lemma 2 that if both $\oplus$ and $1_\oplus$ are maps, then $\oplus/$ is a map.

In the functional calculus, these definitions can be used to show that each join-list catamorphism can be expressed as the composition of a reduction and a map. The same is not true of predicate transformers, but we can show that each anamorphism is refined by the composition of a reduction and a map.

Theorem 8 (Factorisation Theorem).

$$[\![1_\oplus, p, \oplus]\!] \sqsubseteq \oplus/; p\hat{*}$$

where this becomes an equality if p is a map or $\oplus$ and $1_\oplus$ are comaps.

Proof The justification for the use of Theorem 5 in the calculation below comes from definitions (18) and (16), which together imply that $\oplus/; \tilde{+\!\!+} = \oplus; \oplus/ \hat{\times} \oplus /$.

$$\begin{array}{rcll} \oplus/; p\hat{*} & = & \oplus/; [\![\tilde{\eta}, \tilde{\tau}; p, \tilde{+\!\!+}]\!] & \text{(definition (17))} \\ & \sqsupseteq & [\![\oplus/; \tilde{\eta}, \oplus/; \tilde{\tau}; p, \oplus]\!] & \text{(Theorem 5)} \\ & = & [\![1_\oplus, p, \oplus]\!] & \text{(definitions (14),(15),(18))} \end{array}$$

It follows from Corollary 4 that this result can be strengthened to an equality if p is a map or $\oplus$ and $1_\oplus$ are comaps.

This theorem can be used to achieve our original goal, which was to extend the promotion rules of Section 1.2 to predicate transformers. The one-point rules are immediate from definitions (15), (17) and (18), but the join-rules are not so trivial. The extension of law (4) is given below.

Theorem 9.

$$\oplus/; \tilde{+\!\!+}/ \sqsubseteq \oplus/; \oplus/\hat{*}$$

Proof The crucial step in the proof below is the application of the promotion theorem, which is justified since $\oplus/$ is an anamorphism:

$$\begin{array}{rcll} \oplus/; \tilde{+\!\!+}/ & = & \oplus/; [\![\tilde{\eta}, I, \tilde{+\!\!+}]\!] & \text{(definition (18), since } I_{\tilde{+\!\!+}} = \tilde{\eta}) \\ & = & [\![\oplus/; \tilde{\eta}, \oplus/, \oplus]\!] & \text{(Theorem 5, since } \tilde{\eta} \text{ and } \tilde{+\!\!+} \text{ are maps)} \\ & = & [\![\tilde{\eta}, \oplus/, \oplus]\!] & \text{(definitions (14),(18))} \\ & \sqsubseteq & \oplus/; \oplus/\hat{*} & \text{(Theorem 8)} \end{array}$$

A similar proof can be used to derive the following analog of promotion law 3:

$$p\hat{*}; \tilde{+\!\!+}/ = \tilde{+\!\!+}/; p\hat{*}\hat{*}$$

The main difference from the above proof is that the equational version of Theorem 4 could be used, since $\tilde{+\!\!+}$ is a comap.

5 Conclusions and Future Work

In this paper some algebaic properties of predicate transformers have been used to extend a selection of functional programming operators and their associated laws to predicate transformers. The techniques developed to do so could now be applied to a much wider set of laws. They could also be generalised further: for example, Theorem 8 could be expressed in terms of an arbitrary data type. However, in order for such laws to be meaningful, those developed so far must first be translated back from the semantic domain of predicate transformers into a real specification language such as the refinement calculus. This would allow the development of some more realistic examples than those of Section 3. Future research could then be guided by the use of such examples in genuine program derivations.

References

1. R. Backhouse, P.J. de Bruin, G. Malcolm, E. Voermans, J. avn der Woude *A Relational Theory of Datatypes.* in Proceedings of Workshop on Constructive Algorithmics: The Role of Relations in Program Development (1990)
2. R.S. Bird *Lectures on Constructive Functional Programming.* Technical Monograph PRG-69.
3. R.S. Bird and O. de Moor *Solving Optimisation Problems with Catamorphisms.* Springer-Verlag Lecture Notes in Computer Science 669 (1992) 45-66.
4. R.S. Bird and O. de Moor *Relational Program Derivation and Context-free Language Recognition* In: A Classical Mind. Essays in Honour of C.A.R. Hoare. Prentice-Hall (1994) 17-36.
5. A. Carboni, M. Kelly and R. Wood *A 2-Categorical Approach to Geometric Morphisms I.* Sydney Pure Mathematics Research Reports 89-19 (1989), Department of Pure Mathematics, University of Sydney, NSW 2006, Australia.
6. P.J. Freyd and A. Scedrov *Categories, Allegories.* North Holland Mathematical Library (1989).
7. P. Gardiner, C.E. Martin and O. de Moor *An Algebraic Construction of Predicate Transformers.* Science of Computer Programming 22: 21-44 (1994)
8. S. Eilenberg and J.B. Wright *Automata in General Algebras.* Information and Control, 11(4):452-470, 1967.
9. G. Malcolm *Data Structures and Program Tansformation.* Science of Computer Programming, 14 (1990) 255-279
10. C. E. Martin *Preordered Categories and Predicate Transformers* D.Phil thesis, Computing Laboratory, Oxford (1991).
11. O. de Moor *Categories, Relations and Dynamic Programming* D.Phil thesis. Technical Monograph PRG-98, Computing Laboratory, Oxford (1992).
12. O. de Moor *Inductive Data Types* IPL? (to be added) (1994)
13. C.C. Morgan *Programming From Specifications (Second Edition)* Prentice-Hall, Englewood Cliffs, NJ. (1994)
14. C.C. Morgan, K. Robinson and P.H.B. Gardiner *On the Refinement Calculus* PRG Technical Monograph PRG-70, Programming Research Group, Oxford (1988)

An Abstract Account of Composition

Martín Abadi[1] and Stephan Merz[2]

[1] Digital Equipment Corporation, Systems Research Center, 130 Lytton Avenue, Palo Alto, CA 94301, U.S.A.
[2] Institut für Informatik, Technische Universität München, Arcisstr. 21, 80290 München, Germany

Abstract. We present a logic of specifications of reactive systems. The logic is independent of particular computational models, but it captures common patterns of reasoning with assumption-commitment specifications. We use the logic for deriving proof rules for TLA and CTL* specifications.

1 Assumption-commitment specifications

Modularity is a central concern in the design of specification methods. In general terms, modularity is the ability to reduce reasoning about a complete system to reasoning about its components. These components are not expected to operate in fully arbitrary environments. In the context of the complete system, each component can assume that its environment is to some extent well behaved, for instance that it adheres to certain communication protocols. Therefore, it is common to specify each component by describing both the function required of the component and the properties assumed of its environment. In the realm of sequential programs, for example, the requirements are postconditions and the assumptions are preconditions. In the broader realm of reactive systems, which we consider in this paper, there are several forms of assumption-commitment specifications [17, 11, 18, 1, 2, 19, 6, 22, 7, 12].

An assumption-commitment specification for a component of a reactive system consists of a formula A, which expresses assumptions about the environment, and a formula C, which expresses the requirements that an implementation of the component has to meet. Clearly, the meaning of such a specification depends somehow on A and C. In the simplest approach, the meaning is that if A holds then C holds, and if A does not hold then the implementation is completely unconstrained. One may therefore write the specification in the form $A \Rightarrow C$, where $\Rightarrow$ is the classical implication connective. This formulation seems intuitive; as we will see, however, stronger forms of assumption-commitment specifications are preferable for reasoning.

Suppose that we have two components specified by $A_1 \Rightarrow C_1$ and $A_2 \Rightarrow C_2$, and that we would like to prove that their composition satisfies the property P. Representing composition by conjunction and implementation by implication, we would have to prove that the formula $(A_1 \Rightarrow C_1) \wedge (A_2 \Rightarrow C_2) \Rightarrow P$ is valid. In the composite system, each component is part of the other's environment;

therefore, the assumption of each component may reflect the commitment of the other. So we would like to be able to use the commitment of each component to discharge the other's assumption. This argument suggests the following proof rule:

$$\frac{C_1 \Rightarrow A_2 \quad C_2 \Rightarrow A_1 \qquad C_1 \wedge C_2 \Rightarrow P}{(A_1 \Rightarrow C_1) \wedge (A_2 \Rightarrow C_2) \Rightarrow P}$$

Unfortunately, this rule is unsound—it is an instance of circular reasoning.

One remedy is to strengthen the hypotheses in order to break the circularity, for example by demanding that $A_1 \vee A_2$ be valid; with this, the rule becomes classically sound but weak. Another remedy, which is more useful and common, is to strengthen assumption-commitment specifications. For each specification $A \Rightarrow C$, one can add tnat C holds for longer than A in case A does not hold forever. The motivation for the stronger form of specification comes from the observation that no reasonable implementation of $A \Rightarrow C$ will produce an execution that violates first C and later A. To do this, an implementation would have to predict the future behavior of the environment. In some formalisms, such prophetic implementations are excluded altogether, for example by continuity requirements.

The literature contains a number of sound variants of the unsound rule. Typically, the sound variants are justified using induction along computations. In one of the simplest cases, the reasoning may go: C_1 is not falsified before A_1, which is implied by C_2, so C_1 is not falsified before C_2; analogously, C_2 is not falsified before C_1; hence neither C_1 nor C_2 is ever falsified; therefore, P must hold, since $C_1 \wedge C_2$ implies P. There are many more delicate and more powerful arguments.

Despite the breadth of the literature, we believe that a few general logical ideas account for an interesting part of the work on composition. The purpose of this paper is to present an abstract logic of specifications; the logic is independent of particular computational models, but it captures much of the reasoning common in formalisms with assumption-commitment specifications. Using the abstract logic, we derive proof rules for concrete specification methods. However, we do not attempt to capture every aspect of these specification methods; we focus on simple, basic results with broad applicability.

Our logic borrows from that of Abadi and Plotkin [5]. In particular, we take the idea of using intuitionistic reasoning for assumption-commitment specifications. However, for the sake of simplicity and generality, we do not adopt some non-standard constructs of that logic (for example, "constrains at most").

Cau, Collette, and Xu have given another interesting, unifying perspective on rules for composition [22, 7]. Their work treats abstract rules semantically; concurrent processes, with either shared variables or message passing, are then embedded in a common semantic structure based on labelled sequences. This structure could provide a model for our logic (much like the model of section 3). In comparison, our abstract treatment of composition is primarily syntactic. We resort to semantic reasoning about computations only in applications to particular formalisms. This approach enables us to consider non-linear well-founded structures, for example in the context of branching-time logics.

The next section introduces our abstract logic. Sections 3 and 4 apply the logic to justify rules for TLA [16] and for CTL* [8]. Section 5, in conclusion, discusses the results.

2 A logic of specifications

Our logic of specifications is a propositional intuitionistic logic. We use the standard connectives $\wedge$ and $\rightarrow$. In addition, we introduce a new connective, $\stackrel{+}{\rightarrow}$; this connective will be useful in treating assumption-commitment specifications. In the models of interest to us, $P \stackrel{+}{\rightarrow} Q$ is equivalent to $(Q \rightarrow P) \rightarrow Q$. Next we discuss the models in some detail.

Assume given a nonempty set Σ and a pre-order $\sqsubseteq$ on Σ. We define $\sigma \sqsubset \tau$ as $\sigma \sqsubseteq \tau$ and $\tau \not\sqsubseteq \sigma$. A set $S \subseteq \Sigma$ is downward closed if $\tau \in S$ and $\sigma \sqsubseteq \tau$ imply that $\sigma \in S$. We take Σ as the set of worlds of a Kripke frame [20, p.77], whose accessibility relation is the inverse of $\sqsubseteq$ (that is, τ is accessible from σ iff $\tau \sqsubseteq \sigma$). Since this accessibility relation is reflexive and transitive, we obtain a Kripke model of propositional intuitionistic logic. The interpretation of atomic proposition, $\wedge$, and $\rightarrow$ is the standard one; we give an interpretation for $\stackrel{+}{\rightarrow}$:

- Each atomic proposition has a truth value at each element of Σ. It is required that atomic propositions are true on downward-closed subsets of Σ: if p_i is an atomic proposition, $\sigma \models p_i$, and $\sigma' \sqsubseteq \sigma$, then $\sigma' \models p_i$.
- For the connectives, we have:
  $\sigma \models P \wedge Q$ iff $\sigma \models P$ and $\sigma \models Q$
  $\sigma \models P \rightarrow Q$ iff for all $\tau \sqsubseteq \sigma$: if $\tau \models P$ then $\tau \models Q$
  $\sigma \models P \stackrel{+}{\rightarrow} Q$ iff for all $\tau \sqsubseteq \sigma$: if $\rho \models P$ for all $\rho \sqsubset \tau$ then $\tau \models Q$

It follows from these definitions that all formulas are true on downward-closed subsets of Σ. Below, we sometimes identify propositions and downward-closed subsets of Σ.

Somewhat surprisingly, $\stackrel{+}{\rightarrow}$ can be defined from $\rightarrow$ if $\sqsubset$ is a well-founded relation:

Proposition 1. *Assume that $(\Sigma, \sqsubseteq)$ is a pre-order and that $\sqsubset$ is a well-founded relation on Σ. For all $\sigma \in \Sigma$ and all formulas P and Q,*

$$\sigma \models P \stackrel{+}{\rightarrow} Q \quad \textit{iff} \quad \sigma \models (Q \rightarrow P) \rightarrow Q$$

Proof. "only if": The proof proceeds by well-founded induction on $\sqsubset$, exploiting the hypothesis that $\sqsubset$ is well-founded. Assume that $\sigma \models P \stackrel{+}{\rightarrow} Q$, that $\tau \sqsubseteq \sigma$, and that $\tau \models Q \rightarrow P$, to prove that $\tau \models Q$. Since $\sigma \models P \stackrel{+}{\rightarrow} Q$, if $\rho \models P$ for all $\rho \sqsubset \tau$ then $\tau \models Q$. Therefore, we let $\rho \sqsubset \tau$ and prove that $\rho \models P$. Since $\sigma \models P \stackrel{+}{\rightarrow} Q$, downward closure yields $\tau \models P \stackrel{+}{\rightarrow} Q$ and $\rho \models P \stackrel{+}{\rightarrow} Q$. By induction hypothesis,

$\rho \models (Q \to P) \to Q$. Since $\tau \models Q \to P$, downward closure yields $\rho \models Q \to P$. Finally, $\rho \models Q$ and $\rho \models P$ follow by intuitionistic logic.

"if": Assume that $\sigma \models (Q \to P) \to Q$, that $\tau \sqsubseteq \sigma$, and that $\rho \models P$ for all $\rho \sqsubset \tau$; we have to show that $\tau \models Q$. Assume, to the contrary, that $\tau \not\models Q$. First, we show that $\tau \models Q \to P$. Assume that $\rho \models Q$ for some $\rho \sqsubseteq \tau$. Either $\tau \sqsubseteq \rho$ or $\rho \sqsubset \tau$. If $\tau \sqsubseteq \rho$ then $\tau \models Q$ by downward closure, in contradiction with our assumptions. Hence, $\rho \sqsubset \tau$, so $\rho \models P$; it follows that $\tau \models Q \to P$. Since $\sigma \models (Q \to P) \to Q$, downward closure yields $\tau \models (Q \to P) \to Q$. Finally, $\tau \models Q$ follows by intuitionistic logic. $\diamond$

From now on, we assume that $\sqsubset$ is well-founded, and treat $P \xrightarrow{+} Q$ as if it were a shorthand for $(Q \to P) \to Q$. The original semantic definition of $P \xrightarrow{+} Q$ is still important, as it gives the meaning of $(Q \to P) \to Q$ directly and clearly.

We can reason syntactically about $\to$ and $\xrightarrow{+}$, using any of the standard axiomatizations of propositional intuitionistic logic. We adopt sequent notation; the sequent $P_1, \ldots, P_n \vdash P$ means that the conjunction of $P_1, \ldots, P_n$ implies P.

Proposition 2. *The following sequents are derivable:*

$$P \xrightarrow{+} Q, P \xrightarrow{+} (Q \to R) \vdash P \xrightarrow{+} R \tag{1}$$

$$\bigwedge_{i \in I} (P_i \xrightarrow{+} Q_i) \vdash (\bigwedge_{i \in I} P_i) \xrightarrow{+} (\bigwedge_{i \in I} Q_i) \tag{2}$$

$$P \xrightarrow{+} Q \vdash P \to Q \tag{3}$$

$$P \xrightarrow{+} P \vdash P \tag{4}$$

Sequents (1) and (2) state implication-like properties of $\xrightarrow{+}$. Sequent (3) says that $\xrightarrow{+}$ is stronger than $\to$. Sequent (4) can be understood as an abstract formulation of computational induction.

Beyond these elementary results, we are interested in sequents that represent rules for refining specifications, as we explain below. Adopting the convention that $\wedge$ binds tighter than $\to$ and $\xrightarrow{+}$, we obtain the following results:

Theorem 3. *The following sequents are derivable:*

$$P \to (Q \to P') \vdash (P' \xrightarrow{+} Q) \to (P \xrightarrow{+} Q) \tag{5}$$

$$P \to (P' \wedge Q \xrightarrow{+} P') \vdash (P' \to Q) \to (P \to Q) \tag{6}$$

We present two concrete interpretations of the logic in the remainder of the paper. Very roughly, Σ represents a set of computations, and $\sigma \sqsubseteq \tau$ holds if computation σ may evolve to computation τ. A proposition represents a specification; $\sigma \models P$ means that σ is allowed by P. From this perspective, $\sigma \models P \to Q$ means that Q holds for at least as long as P along σ; similarly, $\sigma \models P \xrightarrow{+} Q$ means that Q holds for strictly longer than P (or forever) along σ. We can write assumption-commitment specifications in either of the forms $P \to Q$ and $P \xrightarrow{+} Q$.

We also view $P \rightarrow Q$ as asserting that P refines Q, because $P \rightarrow Q$ is valid iff every computation allowed by P is also allowed by Q. Correspondingly, refinement rules for assumption-commitment specifications establish formulas of the forms $(P' \rightarrow Q') \rightarrow (P \rightarrow Q)$ or $(P' \stackrel{+}{\rightarrow} Q') \rightarrow (P \stackrel{+}{\rightarrow} Q)$. Theorem 3 deals with special cases of such formulas. That theorem allows us to use the commitment Q to establish the assumption P'. In this respect, it contains the essence of rules for composing mutually dependent assumption-commitment specifications. Despite its circular flavor, it is sound because of the distinction between $\rightarrow$ and $\stackrel{+}{\rightarrow}$.

3 Composition in TLA

In our first application of the general logic, we consider specifications written in linear-time temporal logics. For concreteness we emphasize a particular linear-time temporal logic, TLA [16]. Using the tools of section 2, we reproduce part of the previous work on assumption-commitment specifications in TLA [2].

Formulas of linear-time temporal logics are normally interpreted over infinite sequences $\sigma = \langle s_0, s_1, \ldots \rangle$ of states. A formula is valid if it is holds of all sequences of states. For the formulation of assumption-commitment specifications, it is convenient to interpret formulas also over finite sequences, as follows: a formula F holds of a finite sequence ρ if ρ is empty or if there exists some infinite sequence σ that extends ρ such that F holds of σ. A formula F is a safety property if F holds of an infinite sequence whenever it holds of all its finite prefixes.

The connective $\wedge$ and $\Rightarrow$ are the usual, classical ones; several interesting, additional connectives are definable in TLA [3]:

- $\mathcal{C}(F)$ holds of a sequence σ iff F holds of all finite prefixes of σ.
- $F \rightarrow\!\!\triangleright G$ holds of σ iff, for all (finite or infinite) prefixes ρ of σ, if F holds of ρ then so does G. Although $\rightarrow\!\!\triangleright$ is strictly stronger than $\Rightarrow$, $F \Rightarrow G$ and $F \rightarrow\!\!\triangleright G$ are equivalid.
- $F \stackrel{+}{\rightarrow\!\!\triangleright} G$ holds of $\sigma = \langle s_0, s_1, \ldots \rangle$ iff both:
  1. for all $n \geq 0$, if F holds of $\langle s_0, \ldots, s_{n-1} \rangle$, then G holds of $\langle s_0, \ldots, s_n \rangle$;
  2. if F holds of σ then G holds of σ.

It follows that $\mathcal{C}(F)$ denotes the strongest safety property implied by F; and F is equivalent to $\mathcal{C}(F)$ iff F is a safety property. If F and G are safety properties then $F \rightarrow\!\!\triangleright G$ and $F \stackrel{+}{\rightarrow\!\!\triangleright} G$ are safety properties too. For all F and G, we have:

$$F \rightarrow\!\!\triangleright G \equiv (\mathcal{C}(F) \rightarrow\!\!\triangleright \mathcal{C}(G)) \wedge (F \Rightarrow G) \tag{7}$$

$$F \stackrel{+}{\rightarrow\!\!\triangleright} G \equiv (\mathcal{C}(F) \stackrel{+}{\rightarrow\!\!\triangleright} \mathcal{C}(G)) \wedge (F \Rightarrow G) \tag{8}$$

Finite sequences yield a model of the abstract logic of section 2. Specifically, let Σ be the set of finite sequences of states, and $\sqsubseteq$ be the prefix order on Σ. Clearly, $\sqsubset$ is well-founded on Σ. To each formula F corresponds the set $\mathcal{M}(F)$ of finite sequences of which F holds; this is a downward-closed subset of Σ, and we may treat it as a proposition of the abstract logic. We have

$$\mathcal{M}(F \rightarrow\!\!\triangleright G) = \mathcal{M}(F) \rightarrow \mathcal{M}(G) \tag{9}$$

$$\mathcal{M}(F \stackrel{+}{\rightarrow\!\!\triangleright} G) = \mathcal{M}(F) \stackrel{+}{\rightarrow} \mathcal{M}(G) \tag{10}$$

Furthermore, if F_i is a safety property for every $i \in I$, then:

$$\mathcal{M}(\bigwedge_{i \in I} F_i) = \bigwedge_{i \in I} \mathcal{M}(F_i) \tag{11}$$

The correspondence between the abstract logic and this model is close enough for our purposes, but not complete. In particular, there are downward-closed subsets of Σ that are not denoted by any TLA formula, for example the empty set. In addition, this model validates some formulas that are not intuitionistically valid, for example:

$$((P_1 \rightarrow P_2) \rightarrow Q) \land ((P_2 \rightarrow P_1) \rightarrow Q) \rightarrow Q$$

This formula is a disjunction-free version of the traditional formula $(P_1 \rightarrow P_2) \lor (P_2 \rightarrow P_1)$, which expresses a kind of linearity [10].

In the previous work on TLA, the composition of specifications is their conjunction, and refinement is implication. The assumption-commitment specification with assumption A and commitment C is either $A \mathrel{-\!\!\triangleright} C$ or $A \overset{+}{\mathrel{-\!\!\triangleright}} C$. When $A \mathrel{-\!\!\triangleright} C$ is chosen [1, 5], semantic conditions guarantee the equivalence of $A \mathrel{-\!\!\triangleright} C$ and $A \overset{+}{\mathrel{-\!\!\triangleright}} C$; therefore, we consider only $A \overset{+}{\mathrel{-\!\!\triangleright}} C$. In [2] there is a rule for proving that a conjunction of specifications, each of the form $A_i \overset{+}{\mathrel{-\!\!\triangleright}} C_i$, implies another specification $A \overset{+}{\mathrel{-\!\!\triangleright}} C$. The following result is a variation of that rule, restricted to safety properties:

Theorem 4. *If the TLA formulas A, C, A_i, C_i are safety properties (for $i \in I$), then the following formula is valid:*

$$(A \land \bigwedge_{i \in I} C_i \mathrel{-\!\!\triangleright} \bigwedge_{i \in I} A_i) \land (A \overset{+}{\mathrel{-\!\!\triangleright}} (\bigwedge_{i \in I} C_i \mathrel{-\!\!\triangleright} C)) \mathrel{-\!\!\triangleright} (\bigwedge_{i \in I}(A_i \overset{+}{\mathrel{-\!\!\triangleright}} C_i) \mathrel{-\!\!\triangleright} (A \overset{+}{\mathrel{-\!\!\triangleright}} C))$$

Proof. Since the formula is a safety property, it suffices to show that it is valid on finite sequences. Using (9), (10), and (11), we prove the validity of the sequent:

$$(A \land \bigwedge_{i \in I} C_i \rightarrow \bigwedge_{i \in I} A_i), (A \overset{+}{\rightarrow} (\bigwedge_{i \in I} C_i \rightarrow C)) \vdash \bigwedge_{i \in I}(A_i \overset{+}{\rightarrow} C_i) \rightarrow (A \overset{+}{\rightarrow} C)$$

1. Assume $(A \land \bigwedge_{i \in I} C_i \rightarrow \bigwedge_{i \in I} A_i)$ and $(A \overset{+}{\rightarrow} (\bigwedge_{i \in I} C_i \rightarrow C))$ and $\bigwedge_{i \in I}(A_i \overset{+}{\rightarrow} C_i)$.
2. $(\bigwedge_{i \in I} A_i \overset{+}{\rightarrow} \bigwedge_{i \in I} C_i) \rightarrow (A \overset{+}{\rightarrow} \bigwedge_{i \in I} C_i)$
   From step 1, which implies $A \rightarrow (\bigwedge_{i \in I} C_i \rightarrow \bigwedge_{i \in I} A_i)$, by Theorem 3(5).
3. $\bigwedge_{i \in I} A_i \overset{+}{\rightarrow} \bigwedge_{i \in I} C_i$
   From step 1 by Proposition 2(2).
4. $A \overset{+}{\rightarrow} \bigwedge_{i \in I} C_i$
   From steps 2 and 3.
5. $A \overset{+}{\rightarrow} C$
   From steps 1 (which says $A \overset{+}{\rightarrow} (\bigwedge_{i \in I} C_i \rightarrow C)$) and 4, by Proposition 2(1).

◊

This proof shows that the abstract logic of section 2 accounts for the rule for composing specifications in the case of safety properties. Starting from Theorem 4, classical reasoning justifies a rule for arbitrary properties; the extra argument requires only the validity of $F \Rightarrow \mathcal{C}(F)$ and of the equivalences (7) and (8):

Theorem 5. *For any TLA formulas A, C, A_i, C_i (for $i \in I$), the following formula is valid:*

$$\begin{pmatrix} \mathcal{C}(A) \wedge \bigwedge_{i \in I} \mathcal{C}(C_i) \twoheadrightarrow \bigwedge_{i \in I} A_i \\ \wedge \\ A \wedge \bigwedge_{i \in I} C_i \twoheadrightarrow C \\ \wedge \\ \mathcal{C}(A) \overset{+}{\twoheadrightarrow} (\bigwedge_{i \in I} \mathcal{C}(C_i) \twoheadrightarrow \mathcal{C}(C)) \end{pmatrix} \Rightarrow (\bigwedge_{i \in I} (A_i \overset{+}{\twoheadrightarrow} C_i) \Rightarrow (A \overset{+}{\twoheadrightarrow} C))$$

Theorem 5 yields a rule for composing specifications quite similar to that of Abadi and Lamport [2]. That work also develops techniques for establishing the hypotheses of the rule, for example techniques for proving formulas of the form $\mathcal{C}(A) \overset{+}{\twoheadrightarrow} (\bigwedge_{i \in I} \mathcal{C}(C_i) \twoheadrightarrow \mathcal{C}(C))$. Those techniques rely on TLA-specific ideas, outside the scope of our abstract logic. With this caveat, we believe that Theorems 4 and 5 reproduce the previous work faithfully and clarify its logical contents.

The same line of reasoning can be used to justify rules for other linear-time temporal logics, provided $\mathcal{C}$, $\twoheadrightarrow$, and $\overset{+}{\twoheadrightarrow}$ are definable. We treat branching-time logics in the next section.

4 Composition in CTL*

We apply the logic of section 2 to assumption-commitment specifications in the branching-time temporal logic CTL* [8]. This application is somewhat more tentative than that of section 3, in part because of the expressiveness of CTL*, which allows many different styles of assumption-commitment specifications. We restrict attention to the fragment of CTL* where formulas are invariant under finite stuttering [15]—specifically, we do not allow the next-time operator.

Formulas of branching-time temporal logics are normally interpreted over infinite trees. They include state formulas, which are evaluated at a state in a tree, and path formulas, which are evaluated on a path in a tree. We write $M, s \models F$ if the state formula F is true at state s in tree M.

We extend the semantics of state formulas to finite trees. We say that M is a subtree of N, and write $M \sqsubseteq N$, if M has the same root as N and M's accessibility relation is included in N's. For a finite tree M and a state s, we write $M, s \models F$ if s is not a node of M or if there exists some infinite tree N such that $M \sqsubseteq N$ and $N, s \models F$.

When s is the root of M, we may simply say that F is true of M, and write $M \models F$. A specification is given by a state formula F; it describes the set of trees N such that $N \models F$. A state formula F is a safety property if $N \models F$ whenever $M \models F$ for all finite subtrees $M \sqsubseteq N$.

As in the linear-time case, we have the connectives $\mathcal{C}$, $\twoheadrightarrow$, and $\overset{+}{\twoheadrightarrow}$:

- If F is a state formula, then $\mathcal{C}(F)$ is a state formula, with $N, s \models \mathcal{C}(F)$ iff $M, s \models F$ holds for all finite subtrees $M \sqsubseteq N$.
- If F and G are state formulas, then $F \mathrel{-\!\!\triangleright} G$ is a state formula, with $N, s \models F \mathrel{-\!\!\triangleright} G$ iff for all (finite and infinite) subtrees M of N, if $M, s \models F$ then $M, s \models G$.
- If F and G are state formulas, then $F \overset{+}{-\!\!\triangleright} G$ is a state formula, with $N, s \models F \overset{+}{-\!\!\triangleright} G$ iff both:
  1. for all finite subtrees $M \sqsubseteq N$, if $T, s \models F$ for all $T \sqsubset M$ then $M, s \models G$
  2. $N, s \models F \mathrel{-\!\!\triangleright} G$.

Again, $\mathcal{C}(F)$ denotes the strongest safety property implied by F; and F is equivalent to $\mathcal{C}(F)$ iff F is a safety property. If F and G are safety properties then $F \mathrel{-\!\!\triangleright} G$ and $F \overset{+}{-\!\!\triangleright} G$ are safety properties too. For all F and G, we have:

$$(F \mathrel{-\!\!\triangleright} G) \;\Rightarrow\; (\mathcal{C}(F) \mathrel{-\!\!\triangleright} \mathcal{C}(G)) \wedge (F \Rightarrow G) \tag{12}$$

$$F \overset{+}{-\!\!\triangleright} G \;\equiv\; (\mathcal{C}(F) \overset{+}{-\!\!\triangleright} \mathcal{C}(G)) \wedge (F \mathrel{-\!\!\triangleright} G) \tag{13}$$

Note the differences with the corresponding definitions and results for TLA. The differences arise because an infinite tree may have infinite proper subtrees, while the proper subsequences of an infinite sequence are all finite.

Finite trees yield another model of the abstract logic of section 2. Specifically, let Σ be the set of finite trees ordered by $\sqsubseteq$. Clearly, $\sqsubset$ is well-founded on Σ. To each state formula F corresponds the set $\mathcal{T}(F)$ of finite trees of which F is true; this is a downward-closed subset of Σ. For finite trees, we get the analogues of (9) and (10), with $\mathcal{M}$ replaced by $\mathcal{T}$. For safety properties F_i, the analogue of (11) holds as well; this would not be true if we had allowed the next-time operator.

We represent the assumption-commitment specification with assumption A and commitment C by the formula $A \overset{+}{-\!\!\triangleright} C$. We obtain the following theorem for specifications of the form $A \overset{+}{-\!\!\triangleright} C$:

Theorem 6. *If the CTL* formulas A, C, A_i, C_i are safety properties and do not contain the next-time operator (for $i \in I$), then the following formula is valid:*

$$(A \wedge \bigwedge_{i \in I} C_i \mathrel{-\!\!\triangleright} \bigwedge_{i \in I} A_i) \wedge (A \overset{+}{-\!\!\triangleright} (\bigwedge_{i \in I} C_i \mathrel{-\!\!\triangleright} C)) \mathrel{-\!\!\triangleright} (\bigwedge_{i \in I} (A_i \overset{+}{-\!\!\triangleright} C_i) \mathrel{-\!\!\triangleright} (A \overset{+}{-\!\!\triangleright} C))$$

The proof uses exactly the same reasoning as the corresponding proof for TLA. Going beyond safety properties, we can obtain a CTL* analogue for Theorem 5; the proof is basically the same as that of Theorem 5, and relies on the validity of $F \Rightarrow \mathcal{C}(F)$, the implication-like properties of $\mathrel{-\!\!\triangleright}$, and (12) and (13).

In branching-time temporal logics, the composition of modules does not in general implement the conjunction of the specifications of the modules. The application of our theorems as composition rules will therefore require additional arguments. This complication is not unique to our work; several authors [13, 9] have advocated restricting commitments to the fragment ∀CTL* in order to ensure that specifications are preserved by composition.

Josko [13, 14] has suggested representing an assumption-commitment specification as a pair (A, C) where A is a linear-time formula and C is a branching-time formula; Vardi [21] has studied the complexity of model-checking for specifications of this form. With Josko's definitions, a tree M satisfies a specification (A, C) with assumption A and commitment C iff $M' \models C$ where M' is the subtree of M that consists of those paths that satisfy A. Instead of Josko's (A, C), we can write $(\forall A) \stackrel{+}{\triangleright} C$, which is similar but logically stronger. The similarity between (A, C) and $(\forall A) \stackrel{+}{\triangleright} C$ is even closer under the substantial hypotheses of Josko's rules for dealing with mutual dependencies [14].

5 Conclusion

We have studied specifications in a general logical framework. We then inferred concrete proof rules for composing specifications from general logical facts. We believe that this approach explains some of the principles that underly the rules and helps in comparing rules.

Both of the applications described in detail in this paper are for temporal logics. However, our approach is not intrinsically limited to temporal logics: we have also used it on specifications of stream-processing functions [6, 19]. An assumption-commitment specification for a stream-processing function gives a property of the result of the function under assumptions about the inputs of the functions. Inductive reasoning arises when the function is defined as a fixpoint. We can represent that reasoning in our abstract logic, and thus prove variants of the proof rules of Stølen et al. [19]. We omit the details, which are long and perhaps not so natural.

Our exposition has been confined to the propositional level; we did not address the interplay of quantification and composition. In particular, existential quantification corresponds to hiding, which we have largely ignored. However, a general logical treatment of hiding may well be possible, and quite desirable. (Such a treatment was once started but not completed [4].)

References

1. Martín Abadi and Leslie Lamport. Composing specifications. *ACM Transactions on Programming Languages and Systems*, 15(1):73–132, January 1993.
2. Martín Abadi and Leslie Lamport. Conjoining specifications. Research Report 118, Digital Equipment Corporation, Systems Research Center, 1993. To appear in *ACM Transactions on Programming Languages and Systems.*
3. Martín Abadi and Stephan Merz. On TLA as a logic. In Manfred Broy, editor, *Deductive Program Design*, NATO ASI Series. Springer-Verlag, Berlin, 1995. To appear.
4. Martín Abadi and Gordon Plotkin. A logical view of composition and refinement. In *Proceedings of the Eighteenth Annual ACM Symposium on Principles of Programming Languages*, pages 323–332. ACM, January 1991.
5. Martín Abadi and Gordon Plotkin. A logical view of composition. *Theoretical Computer Science*, 114(1):3–30, June 1993.

6. Manfred Broy. A functional rephrasing of the assumption/commitment specification style. SFB-Bericht 342/10/94, TUM-I9417, Techn. Univ. München, Munich, April 1994.
7. Antonio Cau and Pierre Collette. Parallel composition of assumption-commitment specifications: a unifying approach for shared variable and distributed message passing concurrency. *Acta Informatica*, 1995. To appear.
8. E. Allen Emerson. Temporal and modal logic. In Jan van Leeuwen, editor, *Handbook of theoretical computer science*, pages 997–1071. Elsevier Science Publishers B.V., 1990.
9. Orna Grumberg and David E. Long. Model checking and modular verification. *ACM Transactions on Programming Languages and Systems*, 16(3):843–871, May 1994.
10. Alfred Horn. Logic with truth values in a linearly ordered Heyting algebra. *Journal of Symbolic Logic*, 34(3):395–408, September 1969.
11. Cliff B. Jones. Tentative steps toward a development method for interfering programs. *ACM Transactions on Programming Languages and Systems*, 5(4):596–619, October 1983.
12. Bengt Jonsson and Yih-Kuen Tsay. Assumption/guarantee specifications in linear-time temporal logic. In *Proceedings of TAPSOFT '95*, Lecture Notes in Computer Science, Berlin, May 1995. Springer-Verlag.
13. Bernhard Josko. Verifying the correctness of AADL modules using model checking. In J. W. de Bakker, W.-P. de Roever, and G. Rozenberg, editors, *Stepwise Refinement of Distributed Systems: Models, Formalisms, Correctness*, volume 430 of *Lecture Notes in Computer Science*, pages 386–400. Springer-Verlag, Berlin, 1989.
14. Bernhard Josko. Modular specification and verification of reactive systems. Habilitationsschrift, Univ. Oldenburg, Fachbereich Informatik, April 1993.
15. Leslie Lamport. What good is temporal logic? In R. E. A. Mason, editor, *Information Processing 83: Proceedings of the IFIP 9th World Congress*, pages 657–668, Paris, September 1983. IFIP, North-Holland.
16. Leslie Lamport. The temporal logic of actions. *ACM Transactions on Programming Languages and Systems*, 16(3):872–923, May 1994.
17. Jayadev Misra and K. Mani Chandy. Proofs of networks of processes. *IEEE Trans. Software Engineering*, 7(4):417–426, July 1981.
18. Amir Pnueli. In transition from global to modular temporal reasoning about programs. In Krzysztof R. Apt, editor, *Logics and Models of Concurrent Systems*, NATO ASI Series, pages 123–144. Springer-Verlag, October 1984.
19. Ketil Stølen, Frank Dederichs, and Rainer Weber. Assumption/commitment rules for networks of asynchronously communicating agents. SFB-Bericht 342/2/93, TUM-I9303, Techn. Univ. München, Munich, February 1993.
20. A. S. Troelstra and D. van Dalen. *Constructivism in Mathematics: An Introduction*, volume 1. North Holland, Amsterdam, 1988.
21. Moshe Vardi. On the complexity of modular model checking. In *Proceedings of the Tenth Symposium on Logic in Computer Science*. IEEE, June 1995.
22. Qiwen Xu, Antonio Cau, and Pierre Collette. On unifying assumption-commitment style proof rules for concurrency. In Bengt Jonsson and Joachim Parrow, editors, *Proceedings of the Fifth International Conference on Concurrency Theory (CONCUR '94)*, volume 836 of *Lecture Notes in Computer Science*, pages 267–282, Berlin, 1994. Springer-Verlag.

Syntax and Semantics of Procol

Roel van der Goot and Arie de Bruin

Erasmus University Rotterdam, The Netherlands

Abstract. A metric semantics of the parallel object-based programming language Procol is introduced. It is divided into three layers [2], a global layer, an object layer, and a statement layer. At the global level, the sequence in the interactions between the objects (represented in the object layer) is described. The object level expresses the abstract behavior of one object, i.e., only those aspects that are relevant for the outside world. It specifies the interactions an object is willing to perform, and also in what sequence it is able to do so. The statement layer is the most concrete one. It gives a direct representation of a Procol program. In this layer all constituent statements of a program are still recognizable. It forms the basis for the two higher layers, containing all possible sequences of communication statements needed at the object and global layer. Two transformation functions between these three levels can be defined, one from the statement layer to the object layer, and one from the object layer to the global layer. In this paper only the latter transformation will be introduced. New in our approach are a new denotation of the global layer, and a more intuitive transformation to this layer.

1 Introduction

Procol [3, 5] is an object-based language in which objects are executed in parallel. Objects themselves are strictly sequential, although the choice of a communication partner is nondeterministic. An object performs actions. Per object only one action is in execution at any moment. So the parallelism resides at the object level, not at the action level. Objects can communicate with each other by synchronous message passing. Procol is an extension to any imperative language. In this paper we will use ANSI C as the host language.

Pierre America and Jan Rutten have used metric denotational semantics to define the object-oriented language Pool [1, 2]. Their work has laid the foundation for this paper. However, significant additions to this basis are needed to model the more advanced features of Procol. The use of sender, receiver, and creator keywords is new. The possibility to delegate to other objects, as well as the idea that objects can delete each other, are new. The use of an init and a cleanup action at creation and deletion of the object are related to this last feature. But by far the strongest effect on the semantics is caused by the introduction of protocols, the major idea of Procol. The use of protocols causes a lot more nondeterminism at the statement layer leading to more intricate domain equations. Most of the changes these innovations caused, are described in this paper. Besides the features of Procol another novel idea is introduced at the global layer. The denotations of a program describe only interactions that really take place. Attempts at communication that are not honored are no longer visible at this level. This result has been obtained by introducing a new and more intuitive abstraction from the object layer to the global layer.

2 Syntax and Informal Semantics

In this section we will provide the syntax of the language. Based on this syntax we will try to make the reader familiar with all concepts of the language Procol. The syntax of Procol is defined in a C like fashion, because we choose C as the host language in this paper. We first introduce the whole syntax before we give an informal semantics of it. The sans serif font denotes the non-terminals, while the American typewriter font denotes the terminals in the grammar. The non-terminals CName and AName, denote classes of identifiers representing names of classes and actions, respectively. The non-terminal OName denotes the class of object-valued variables. The domains Variables, Formal-Parameters, Actual-Parameters, and Result-Parameters denote sequences of variable declarations, formal parameter declarations, expressions and variables, respectively. The first three of these four sequences may be empty.

```
Program            ::= Classes
Classes            ::= Class | Class Classes
Class              ::= obj CName ( Formal-Parameters )
                          { Variables Actions Protocol }
Actions            ::= Action | Action Actions
Action             ::= action AName ( Formal-Parameters )
                          { Variables Command }
Protocol           ::= protocol { Compound-Protocol }
Compound-Protocol ::= Selection-Protocol || Compound-Protocol
                     | Selection-Protocol
Selection-Protocol  ::= Protocol-Sequence + Selection-Protocol
                     | Protocol-Sequence
Protocol-Sequence   ::= Repetition-Protocol ; Protocol-Sequence
                     | Repetition-Protocol
Repetition-Protocol ::= Guarded-Protocol * | Guarded-Protocol
Guarded-Protocol    ::= Expression : Protocol-Item | Protocol-Item
Protocol-Item       ::= ( Compound-Protocol )
                     | FName -> AName ( Formal-Parameters )
Command             ::= ... | del ( OName ) | reply ( Actual-Parameters )
                     | FName . AName ( Actual-Parameters )
                     | @ FName . AName ( Actual-Parameters )
                     | FName . AName ( Actual-Parameters ) ->
                          ( Result-Parameters )
Expression          ::= ... | sender | receiver | creator | self
                     | OName | new ( CName ( Actual-Parameters ))
FName ::= CName | OName
```

A Procol program contains one or more class definitions. One of these definitions must be the definition of class *main*. At the beginning of the program execution only one object is active, which will be an object of this class.

A class definition consists of its name, its formal parameters (used for initialization), its data, its actions, and its protocol. Its syntax is not very surprising, except that all variables have to be defined before any code can be written (different from ANSI C). There are two special actions namely *init* and *cleanup*, which, if defined in a class, are executed at creation (new) and termination (del) of an object of this class, respectively.

In a Procol program objects run in parallel. If they are ready with an action, they are willing to accept messages from other objects. As a reaction to the acceptance of a message a new action will be executed. Protocols specify the sequence of messages an object is willing to receive. A protocol tells what objects are allowed to initiate what actions, and in what order. They are built out of Protocol-Items also known as interaction terms by applying the operators compound (||), select (+), sequence (;), repeat (*), and guard(:). The interaction terms are of the form *FN* -> *AN* (*FPs*), and state that the object is willing to accept a message from an object in family *FN* involving action *AN* with arguments *FPs*. The compound operator merges two possible action sequences. The select operator allows a nondeterministic choice between two possible action sequences. The guard operator initiates its subprotocol only if the guard expression evaluates to TRUE. Please note that the expression in a guarded protocol may contain side-effects thanks to the host language C. However it is good programming practice not to use these side-effects, moreover it violates the spirit of Procol. Our semantics is flexible enough to model such side-effects however.

A Procol command can be one of the following statements.

- ...: A C statement, which will not be further explained in this semantics.
- *FN* . *AN* (*APs*): A send statement telling to initiate action *AN* with arguments *APs* in one of the objects in family *FN*. After execution of this statement the predefined variable `receiver` (see our discussion of expressions below) is updated with the identity of the object that accepted the send.
- *FN* . *AN* (*APs*) -> (*RPs*): This is a request statement doing almost the same as the send statement. The only difference is that after sending the message, the object performing this statement will wait for an answer. The answer is stored in the parameters *RPs*.
- @ *FN* . *AN* (*APs*): A delegate statement telling to initiate action *AN* with arguments *APs* in any object of the family *FN*. The object that accepts this delegation message sends its answer directly to the object that initiated the action in which this statement occurs. This is a dynamic alternative to inheritance where almost the same happens by defining a derived class.
- `reply` (*APs*): A reply statement sending arguments *APs* back to the requesting object, i.e., the object that initiated the action.
- `del` (*ON*): A delete statement telling to delete object *ON*. Deletes can only have effect on an object when it has arrived at its protocol.

A Procol expression can be one of the following terms.

- ...: A C expression, not treated in this paper.
- *ON*: An object name expression resulting in the identity of that object.
- `sender`, `receiver`, `creator` or `self`: Predefined variables containing, respectively, the identity of the object that initiated the present action, the identity of the object that received the latest send or delegate message, the identity of the creator of the object, the own identity of the object.
- `new` (*CN* (*APs*)): A new expression telling to create a new object of class *CN* with initial arguments *APs*. The identity of the created object is returned. In the newly created object the predefined variable `creator` is initialized with the identity of the creator.

3 Example

Now it is time to make this informal semantics a bit more understandable by an example. In this example a referee (main) activates a game between two players. One of the players gets the ball in order to serve. It serves the ball to his opponent, the opponent hits it back, etcetera. Every time a player plays the ball to the opponent it has chance 0.1 to mishit the ball, in which case the opponent will get a point and the next serve (rally-point system in volley-ball). The player who first reaches the score of 15 points is declared the winner.

```
obj player()
{
   player opponent;

   action meet_opponent(player op) { opponent = op; }

   action hit_ball() { if (random() < 0.9) opponent.hit_ball();
      else creator.update_score(); }

   protocol { creator -> meet_opponent(player op) ;
      (opponent -> hit_ball() + creator -> hit_ball()) * }
}

obj main()
{
   player player1, player2; int score1, score2; bool active;

   action init() { score1 = score2 = 0; active = true;
      player1 = new(player()); player2 = new(player());
      player1.meet_opponent(player2);
      player2.meet_opponent(player1); player1.hit_ball(); }
   action cleanup() { del(player1); del(player2); }
```

```
   action update_score() {
      switch(sender) {
      case player1: if (++score2 < 15) player2.hit_ball();
         else { printf("player 2 won!\n"); active = false; }
         break;
      case player2: if (++score1 < 15) player1.hit_ball();
         else { printf("player 1 won!\n"); active = false; }
         break;
      default: printf("Error: Should not reach this point"); } }

   protocol { (active: player -> update_score()) * }
}
```

4 Global and Object Process Domains

At the highest level of abstraction the running program with all its active objects is found. These objects are communicating with each other, creating new objects, and deleting others. The general domain GProc (global process) consists of all possible sequences of such events.

$$
\begin{aligned}
\mathsf{GProc} &= \textit{deadlock} + \textit{steps}\ \mathcal{P}_{co}(\mathsf{GStep}) \\
\mathsf{GStep} &= \textit{termination}\ \mathsf{Obj} \times \mathsf{GProc} + \textit{divergence}\ \mathsf{Obj} \times \mathsf{GProc} + \\
&\quad\ \textit{creation}\ \mathsf{Obj} \times \mathsf{Obj} \times \mathsf{CName} \times \mathsf{GProc} + \\
&\quad\ \textit{deletion}\ \mathsf{Obj} \times \mathsf{Obj} \times \mathsf{GProc} + \\
&\quad\ \textit{communication}\ \mathsf{Obj} \times \mathsf{Obj} \times \mathsf{Obj} \times \mathsf{Comm} \times \mathsf{Arg}^* \times \mathsf{GProc} \\
\mathsf{Comm} &= \textit{action}\ \mathsf{AName} + \textit{reply} \\
\mathsf{Arg} &= \ldots + \textit{object}\ \mathsf{Obj} \\
\mathsf{Obj} &= \ldots
\end{aligned}
$$

The domain Arg denotes all possible argument values in the underlying language together with all object values from domain Obj. Domain Obj is a denumerable infinite set of object identities. The domains GProc and GStep are defined by a recursive set of equations, describing in essence a tree structure, where the branches are labeled by elements from Obj, Obj × Obj × CName, Obj × Obj, or Obj × Obj × Obj × Comm × Arg*. The operator $\mathcal{P}_{co}$ applied to a metric space A yields the class of all compact subsets of A.

The domain GProc can distinguish between a deadlocked program and a running program. A program deadlocks when all active objects are waiting for an interaction to occur but no matches can be made. This should be contrasted with a terminated program, in which there are no more interacting objects. This will be modeled by the empty set. The running program is represented by an abstract tree, the paths of which specify all possible sequences of events generated by the program. Each element in the domain GStep describes one such event and the future of the computation after this event (again a tree structure, denoted by general process gp in the list below). The following events are distinguished.

- *termination* (o_c, gp): Object o_c has terminated.
- *divergence* (o_c, gp): Object o_c will continue to execute forever without engaging in an interaction with the other objects.
- *creation* (o_c, o_s, cn, gp): Object o_c has created a server object o_s of class cn.
- *deletion* (o_c, o_s, gp): Client object o_c has deleted server object o_s.
- *communication* $(o_c, o_s, o_o, \textit{action } an, \vec{a}_{cs}, gp)$: Client o_c has sent or delegated (depending on whether objects o_c and o_o are equal or not) action an with arguments $\vec{a}_{cs}$ to server o_s.
- *communication* $(o_s, o_o, o_s, \textit{reply}, \vec{a}_{so}, gp)$: Server o_s has replied to the originator o_o by sending the result argument list $\vec{a}_{so}$.

At a lower level of abstraction objects with all their event intentions are defined. The lifetime of an object is denoted by an element of OProc. Every object is willing to communicate with, create, and delete other objects according to its internal state. The events an object is willing to participate in, partly depend on its state. However, this internal state is not present in the object process's domain OProc. It can only be found at the lowest level of abstraction, i.e., the statement level. An OProc defines the sequence of communication intentions with other objects for one object only.

$$\begin{aligned}
\mathsf{OProc} = {} & \textit{terminated} + \textit{diverged} + \\
& \textit{new}\ \mathsf{CName} \times \mathsf{Arg}^* \times (\mathsf{Obj} \rightarrow \mathsf{OProc}) + \textit{delete}\ \mathsf{Obj} \times \mathsf{OProc} + \\
& \textit{send}\ \mathsf{Fam} \times \mathsf{AName} \times \mathsf{Arg}^* \times (\mathsf{Obj} \rightarrow \mathsf{OProc}) + \\
& \textit{receive}\ \mathsf{Arg}^* \rightarrow \mathsf{OProc} + \textit{reply}\ \mathsf{Obj} \times \mathsf{Arg}^* \times \mathsf{OProc} + \\
& \textit{delegate}\ \mathsf{Fam} \times \mathsf{Obj} \times \mathsf{AName} \times \mathsf{Arg}^* \times (\mathsf{Obj} \rightarrow \mathsf{OProc}) + \\
& \textit{protocol}\ \mathcal{P}_{co}(\mathsf{OPStep}) \times \mathsf{OProc} \\
\mathsf{OPStep} = {} & \mathsf{Fam} \times \mathsf{AName} \times (\mathsf{Obj} \rightarrow \mathsf{Obj} \rightarrow \mathsf{Arg}^* \rightarrow \mathsf{OProc}) \\
\mathsf{Fam} = {} & \textit{object}\ \mathsf{Obj} + \textit{class}\ \mathsf{CName}
\end{aligned}$$

An object distinguishes the following intentions to participate in an event.

- *terminated*: The object is terminated.
- *diverged*: The object has diverged due to an infinite loop or an infinite recursion. The object will make no attempt to participate in an event anymore.
- *new* $(cn, \vec{a}_{cs}, o2op)$: The object wants to create a new object of class cn initialized with the arguments $\vec{a}_{cs}$. The original object will proceed after receiving the identity o_s of the created object as defined in object process $o2op(o_s)$.
- *delete* (o, op): The object wants to delete object o, and to proceed as object process op.
- *send* $(f_s, an, \vec{a}_{cs}, o2op)$: The object wants to send action an with arguments $\vec{a}_{cs}$ to an object of family f_s. If this send action succeeds the object will receive the identity o_s of the receiver and proceed as object process $o2op(o_s)$.

- *receive* $\vec{a}2op$: The object wants to receive a reply in the form of a list $\vec{a}_{sc}$. The receiving object will continue as defined in object process $\vec{a}2op(\vec{a}_{sc})$. A request statement is modeled by two events of which a receive is the second one, in which the result parameters are sent back. The first part of a request statement is modeled as an ordinary send event.
- *reply* $(o_c, \vec{a}_{sc}, op)$: The object wants to reply to a request of object o_c by sending arguments $\vec{a}_{sc}$, it will proceed as defined in object process op.
- *delegate* $(f_s, o_o, an, \vec{a}_{cs}, o2op)$: The object wants to delegate action an with arguments $\vec{a}_{cs}$ to an object in family f_s, the reply has to be sent to object o_o. The delegating object continues as defined in object process $o2op(o_s)$, where o_s is the identity of the receiving object.
- *protocol* (p, op): For every element $(f_c, an, o2o2\vec{a}2op)$ of p, the object is willing to accept a message containing action an from any object in family f_c. The continuation depends on the object o_c that sent this message. Because it is possible that this object has delegated the message, another object o_o is relevant too, i.e., the object that initiated the chain of messages. Notice that o_o can be equal to o_c. The continuation is also dependent on the arguments $\vec{a}_{cs}$ object o_c sends with the action name. So the protocol object proceeds with object process $o2o2\vec{a}2op(o_c)(o_o)(\vec{a}_{cs})$. At this stage it is also possible that a delete request for the object is honored. In that case the object proceeds as described in object process op (which models the cleanup action of the object).

5 From Object to Global Semantics

In an object process we specify what one process does. At the global level we want to know what a program does, and thus how multiple objects interact with each other. To this end we define a function Ψ combining a set of object processes into a global process.

Object processes interact with each other using object identities, values from Obj. The combinator Ψ has therefore to be provided with the identity of every object process, i.e., it has to be a function defined on a (finite) set of ordered pairs in Obj $\times$ OProc. However, we want to make sure that every object has a unique identity. Therefore we will model the set of ordered pairs by a function Obj $\rightarrow$ OProc, only defined on a finite subset of Obj. We will call such an ordered pair a maplet, and its notation will be $o \mapsto op$ instead of (o, op).

$$\mathsf{Pool} = \mathsf{Obj} \overset{fi}{\rightarrow} \mathsf{OProc}.$$

More information is needed though. On creation of an object a new object process is started, defined by the class of the new object. Therefore an environment is needed, associating each class name with a function. This function yields an OProc, depending on the arguments passed by the creating object, the object identity and the identity of its creator.

$$\mathsf{Environ} = \mathsf{CName} \rightarrow (\mathit{bound}\ \mathsf{Arg}^* \rightarrow \mathsf{Obj} \rightarrow \mathsf{Obj} \rightarrow \mathsf{OProc} + \mathit{unbound})$$

One function is defined on this environment, namely $find(env, cn)$ yielding the function that is associated with class name cn in environment env.

For the definition of Ψ also dynamic information, coded as a store is needed. This has to do with the concept of family. For instance an object can specify the receiver of a send action by a family, in essence a class name. This means that "at run-time" the class names of every existing object must be available.

$$\mathsf{Store} = \mathsf{Obj} \rightarrow (\mathit{stored}\ \mathsf{CName} + \mathit{unused} + \mathit{undefined})$$

Four definitions are defined on this store[1]. Function $allocate(sto)$ yields a tuple (sto', obj) where store sto' is store sto after the allocation of a new object identifier obj. Function $deallocate(sto, obj)$ yields a store that changes store sto by freeing the location of object identifier obj. Function $update(sto, obj, cn)$ yields a new store where class name cn is stored in location obj. Function $fetch(sto, obj)$ yields the class name that is associated with object obj in store sto.

All this leads to the following functionality of Ψ.

$$\Psi : \mathsf{Pool} \rightarrow \mathsf{Environ} \rightarrow \mathsf{Store} \rightarrow \mathsf{GProc}$$

Think of this transformation as follows. There is a pool of objects. Each object raises signs upon which currently possible (object) events are written, one per sign. A person at the side of the pool collects these signs. Another person collects pairs of signs. The first person takes from the objects in the pool signs with specific events on them. The second person takes specific combinations of two signs from different objects. Accepting a sign, or a combination of two signs corresponds with an event, an element from **GStep**. After a sign of an object is taken, having generated such a general event, the object can proceed, and in general it will raise other signs later on in its lifetime. The order in which the signs are taken is maintained. This order forms one of many possible general processes.

The work of the two persons is modeled by two functions called *one* and *two*, depicting the number of signs the person takes out of the pool at a time. The definition of the transformation function Ψ is built upon these two functions.

$$
\begin{aligned}
&\Psi(p)(env)(sto) = \\
&\quad \mathbf{if}\ p = \emptyset\ \mathbf{then}\ steps\ \emptyset \\
&\quad \mathbf{else} \\
&\qquad \mathbf{let}\ gp = \bigcup\{one(o \mapsto op)(p - \{o \mapsto op\})(env)(sto) : o \mapsto op \in p\} \cup \\
&\qquad\quad \bigcup\{two(o_1 \mapsto op_1)(o_2 \mapsto op_2)(p - \{o_1 \mapsto op_1, o_2 \mapsto op_2\})(env)(sto) : \\
&\qquad\qquad o_1 \mapsto op_1 \in p, o_2 \mapsto op_2 \in p\}\ \mathbf{in} \\
&\qquad \mathbf{if}\ gp = \emptyset\ \mathbf{then}\ deadlock \\
&\qquad \mathbf{else}\ steps\ gp
\end{aligned}
$$

$$one : (\mathsf{Obj} \times \mathsf{OProc}) \rightarrow \mathsf{Pool} \rightarrow \mathsf{Environ} \rightarrow \mathsf{Store} \rightarrow \mathcal{P}_{co}(\mathsf{GStep})$$

[1] The concepts environment and store originate from David Watt's book [6].

$$one(o_c \mapsto terminated)(p)(env)(sto) =$$
$$\{termination\ (o_c, \Psi(p)(env)(deallocate(sto, o_c)))\}$$
$$one(o_c \mapsto diverged)(p)(env)(sto) = \{divergence\ (o_c, \Psi(p)(env)(sto))\}$$

The information that an object has terminated or diverged, is passed on to the general process. The general process (unlike the object process) must be able to proceed after these events, because other objects may still be alive.

$$one(o_c \mapsto new(cn, \vec{a}_{cs}, o2op))(p)(env)(sto) =$$
$$\textbf{let } (sto_1, o_s) = allocate\ sto \textbf{ in}$$
$$\textbf{let } sto_2 = update(sto_1, o_s, cn) \textbf{ in}$$
$$\textbf{let } obj = find(env, cn) \textbf{ in}$$
$$\{creation\ (o_c, o_s, cn,$$
$$\Psi(p \cup \{o_c \mapsto o2op(o_s), o_s \mapsto obj\ \vec{a}_{cs}\ o_s\ o_c\})(env)(sto_2))\}$$

Object o_c wants to create a new object of class *cn*, initialized with arguments $\vec{a}_{cs}$. Some work has to be done for this new object. The object has to have a unique identity, the store needs to be updated, the object process has to be found, and this object has to be added to the pool.

Application of *one* to any other object event results in the empty set.

$$two : (\mathsf{Obj} \times \mathsf{OProc}) \to (\mathsf{Obj} \times \mathsf{OProc}) \to$$
$$\mathsf{Pool} \to \mathsf{Environ} \to \mathsf{Store} \to \mathcal{P}_{co}(\mathsf{GStep})$$

$$two(o_c \mapsto delete\ (o_s, op_1))(o_s \mapsto protocol\ (p_1, op_2))(p_2)(env)(sto) =$$
$$\{deletion\ (o_c, o_s, \Psi(p_2 \cup \{o_c \mapsto op_1, o_s \mapsto op_2\})(env)(sto))\}$$

Object o_c wants to delete object o_s. This is only allowed when object o_s is in its protocol. The deletion is registered in the global process, object o_c continues, and object o_s starts its cleanup section *op*.

$$two(o_c \mapsto send\ (f_s, an, \vec{a}_{cs}, o2op))(o_s \mapsto protocol\ (p_1, op))(p_2)(env)(sto) =$$
$$\{communication\ (o_c, o_s, o_c, action\ an, \vec{a}_{cs},$$
$$\Psi(p_2 \cup \{o_c \mapsto o2op(o_s), o_s \mapsto o2o2\vec{a}2op(o_c)(o_c)(\vec{a}_{cs})\})(env)(sto)) :$$
$$(f_c, an, o2o2\vec{a}2op) \in p_1, member(o_c, f_c, sto), member(o_s, f_s, sto)\}$$

Object o_c wants to send a message containing action *an* and arguments $\vec{a}_{cs}$ to an object in family f_s. At the same time object o_s wants to receive that kind of message from an object of family f_c. If object o_s is a member (the function *member* is defined below) of family f_s, and object o_c is a member of family f_c, then a communication can take place. Both objects proceed like specified in their continuations.

$$two(o_c \mapsto delegate\ (f_s, o_o, an, \vec{a}_{cs}, o2op))(o_s \mapsto protocol\ (p_1, op))$$
$$(p_2)(env)(sto) = \{communication\ (o_c, o_s, o_o, action\ an, \vec{a}_{cs},$$
$$\Psi(p_2 \cup \{o_c \mapsto o2op(o_s), o_s \mapsto o2o2\vec{a}2op(o_c)(o_o)(\vec{a}_{cs})\})(env)(sto)) :$$
$$(f_c, an, o2o2\vec{a}2op) \in p_1, member(o_c, f_c, sto), member(o_s, f_s, sto)\}$$

Same story for delegation, only this time the originator o_o is different from the sender o_c.

$$two(o_s \mapsto reply\ (o_o, \vec{a}_{so}, op))(o_o \mapsto receive\ \vec{a}2op)(p)(env)(sto) =$$
$$\{communication\ (o_s, o_o, o_s, reply, \vec{a}_{so},$$
$$\Psi(p \cup \{o_s \mapsto op, o_o \mapsto \vec{a}2op(\vec{a}_{so})\})(env)(sto))\}$$

Object o_s wants to reply the requested arguments $\vec{a}_{so}$ to the originator o_o of the action now in execution. Object o_o is waiting for these arguments.

Application of *two* on other pairs of events results in the empty set. In the definition of *two* we introduced a function *member* which checks whether an object is a member of a specific family.

$$member : \mathsf{Obj} \times \mathsf{Fam} \times \mathsf{Store} \rightarrow \{\text{TRUE}, \text{FALSE}\}$$

$$member(o, object\ o, sto) = \text{TRUE}$$
$$member(o, class\ cn, sto) = (fetch(sto, o) = cn)$$

A full description of both syntax and semantics is available as a technical report [4].

References

1. P.H. America and J.J.M. Rutten, *A parallel object-oriented language: Design and semantic foundations*, Ph.D. thesis, Centre for Mathematics and Computer Science (CWI), 1989.
2. P.H. America and J.J.M. Rutten, *A layered semantics for a parallel object-oriented language*, Formal Aspects of Computing **4** (1992), 376–408.
3. J. van den Bos and J.C. Laffra, *Procol – a concurrent object-oriented language with protocols delegation and constraints*, Acta Informatica **28** (1991), 511–538.
4. A. de Bruin and R.A. van der Goot, *Syntax and semantics of Procol*, Tech. Report EUR-CS-94-07, Erasmus University Rotterdam, 1994, ftp://ftp.cs.few.eur.nl/pub /doc/techreports/1994.
5. J.C. Laffra, *Procol – a concurrent object language with protocols, delegation, persistence and constraints*, Ph.D. thesis, Erasmus University Rotterdam, 1992.
6. D.A. Watt, *Programming language syntax and semantics*, Prentice Hall, 1991.

Synthesizing Distinguishing Formulae for Real Time Systems –Extended Abstract *

Jens Chr. Godskesen[1] and Kim G. Larsen[2]

[1] Tele Danmark Research, Lyngsø Allé 2, DK-2970 Hørsholm, Denmark.
[2] BRICS, Aalborg Univ., Fr. Bajers Vej 7, DK-9220 Aalborg, Denmark.

1 Introduction

Research in the area of process algebras has created interest in *behavioural relations* as a tool for verifying correctness of processes [14, 12, 2]. In this approach, specifications as well as implementations are formalized as process algebraic expressions, and verification consists of establishing a suitable behavioural relationship between an implementation and its specification. A number of equivalences has been proposed and several tools support verification for finite-state systems based on such equivalences (e.g. [13, 6, 9]). However, for a tool to be of real assistance it is crucial that *diagnostic* information is offered in case of erroneous design. For a variety of *bisimulation equivalences* [14] the theoretical basis for generation of such diagnostic information is given in terms of a *logical* characterization of the equivalence: two systems are equivalent exactly when they satisfy the same formulae in a particular modal logic [11]. Thus when two systems are found to be inequivalent, one may explain why by a formula satisfied by one but not the other. Algorithms for generating distinguishing formulae for finite-state systems has been described in [5, 3] and implemented in at least two tools [9, 6]. During the last few years a number of real-time process algebras has been introduced [7, 16, 1]. Due to the use of the non-negative reals as time domain, even the simplest processes describe infinite state systems. Thus, decidability of bisimilarity cannot be achieved using the standard techniques for finite-state systems. However, decidability of bisimulation equivalence between networks of timed regular processes has recently been established [15]. The underlying algorithmic techniques has later been implemented in the verification tool EPSILON [4]. Our goal in this paper is to describe the method used in EPSILON for generating diagnostic information for the bisimulation equivalence. The method may be seen as an extension of the algorithm in [15] to which information of time-quantities has been added sufficient for generating distinguishing formulae. The full version of this paper can be found in [8].

2 Timed Processes

Our language for timed processes is based on the real–time calculus TCCS [16]. In order to explain our algorithmic ideas most clearly we have made certain

* This work has been supported by the Danish Basic Research Foundation project BRICS and the ESPRIT Basic Research Action 7166, CONCUR2.

simplifications in comparison to TCCS. However, the algorithmic ideas extend to the full calculus of TCCS and moreover it generalizes easily to the *modal* extension of TCCS, TMS, defined in [4] in which a variety of equivalences and preorders is considered [10].

2.1 Syntax and Semantics Let $\mathcal{A}$ be a fixed set of actions ranged over by $a, b, c, \ldots$. We denote by $\mathcal{R}_{>0}$ the set of positive reals ranged over by d. Similarly, $\mathcal{R}_{\geq 0}$ denotes the set of non–negative reals ranged over by e. NAT denotes the set of natural numbers (including 0), and finally, $\mathcal{D}$ denotes the set $\{\epsilon(d) \mid d \in \mathcal{R}_{>0}\}$. We use σ to range over elements of the set $\mathcal{A} \cup \mathcal{D}$. Assume a *finite* set of process variables $\mathcal{V}$ and for each process variable X a defining equation of the following (normal) form:

$$X \stackrel{def}{=} \sum_{i=1}^{n} \epsilon(e_i).a_i.X_i \tag{1}$$

where $e_i \in$ NAT and $X_i \in \mathcal{V}$. We denote by Δ the set of recursive definitions.[3]

Intuitively, the definition of X in (1) describes a behaviour which after a delay of d will "offer" to its environment all actions a_i for which $e_i \leq d$; if the environment "accepts" the offered action, X may evolve to the behaviour determined by X_i. Formally, the behaviour of a regular process described by Δ is given in terms of a transition system with transitions labelled by actions ($\mathcal{A}$) or delays ($\mathcal{D}$). First, let for $d \in \mathcal{R}_{>0}$, X^d denote the term $\sum_{i=1}^{n} \epsilon(e_i \dot{-} d).a_i.X_i$ assuming that X is defined as in (1).[4] Also, we let $X^0 = X$. Then the labelled transition system $\langle \mathbf{X}, \mathcal{A} \cup \mathcal{D}, \longrightarrow \rangle$ is induced where $\mathbf{X} = \{X^e \mid X \in \mathcal{V}, e \in \mathcal{R}_{\geq 0}\}$ and $\longrightarrow \subseteq \mathbf{X} \times (\mathcal{A} \cup \mathcal{D}) \times \mathbf{X}$ is defined by the two axioms below assuming (1) is the defining equation for X. We shall use $P, Q, \ldots$ to range over $\mathbf{X}$.

$$X^e \xrightarrow{a_i} X_i \text{ when } e_i \leq e \qquad\qquad X^e \xrightarrow{\epsilon(d)} X^{e+d}$$

Example 1. Consider [5] $Z \stackrel{def}{=} \epsilon(1).a.Z_b + \epsilon(1).b.Z_a + b.X$, $Z_a \stackrel{def}{=} a$, $Z_b \stackrel{def}{=} b$, and $X \stackrel{def}{=} \epsilon(1).a$. The semantics yields:

$$Z \xrightarrow{\epsilon(\frac{1}{2})} \epsilon(\tfrac{1}{2}).a.Z_b + \epsilon(\tfrac{1}{2}).b.Z_a + b.X \xrightarrow{b} X \xrightarrow{\epsilon(\frac{1}{2})} \epsilon(\tfrac{1}{2}).a$$

A *network* (over Δ and $\mathcal{V}$) is a term of the form $(X_1 \mid \ldots \mid X_n)$ where $X_i \in \mathcal{V}$. The set of n–ary networks induces a labelled transition system $\mathcal{N}_n = \langle \mathbf{Net}_n, \mathcal{A} \cup \mathcal{D}, \longrightarrow \rangle$, where $\mathbf{Net}_n = \{(X_1^{e_1} \mid \ldots \mid X_n^{e_n}) \mid X_i \in \mathcal{V}, e_i \in \mathcal{R}_{\geq 0}\}$ and $\longrightarrow \subseteq \mathbf{Net}_n \times (\mathcal{A} \cup \mathcal{D}) \times \mathbf{Net}_n$ is defined by the following axiom and inference rule:

$$(X_1^{e_1} \mid \ldots \mid X_n^{e_n}) \xrightarrow{\epsilon(d)} (X_1^{e_1+d} \mid \ldots \mid X_n^{e_n+d})$$

$$\frac{X_i^{e_i} \xrightarrow{a} X_i'}{(X_1^{e_1} \mid \ldots \mid X_i^{e_i} \mid \ldots \mid X_n^{e_n}) \xrightarrow{a} (X_1^{e_1} \mid \ldots \mid X_i' \mid \ldots \mid X_n^{e_n})}$$

Thus, in a network, the regular components synchronize on delay transitions and interleave on action transitions. We shall use $\overline{P}, \overline{Q}, \ldots$ to range over $\mathbf{Net}_n$.

[3] In (1) we restrict to integer delays. However, the semantic time domain is that of the positive reals, thus derivatives of processes will not in general contain integral delay.

[4] $\dot{-}$ denotes *monus* on $\mathcal{R}_{\geq 0}$. That is for $e, f \in \mathcal{R}_{\geq 0}$, $e \dot{-} f = \max\{e - f, 0\}$.

[5] *nil* is the the empty sum. We use $a.P$ for $\epsilon(0).a.P$, and a for $a.nil$.

Example 2. Consider $X \stackrel{def}{=} \epsilon(1).a$ and $Y \stackrel{def}{=} b$. Applying the operational semantics yields:

$$X \mid Y \xrightarrow{\epsilon(\frac{1}{2})} (\epsilon(\tfrac{1}{2}).a \mid b) \xrightarrow{b} (\epsilon(\tfrac{1}{2}).a \mid nil) \xrightarrow{\epsilon(\frac{1}{2})} (a \mid nil) \xrightarrow{a} (nil \mid nil)$$

2.2 Distinguishing Formulae As networks semantically constitute labelled transition systems we may compare them with respect to a number of behavioural relations such as bisimilarity [14].

Definition 1. *Let $\mathcal{T} = \langle S, A, \longrightarrow \rangle$ be a labelled transition system. A simulation $\mathcal{S}$ is a binary relation on S such that whenever $p\mathcal{S}q$ and $a \in A$ then if $p \xrightarrow{a} p'$ also $q \xrightarrow{a} q'$ for some q' with $p'\mathcal{S}q'$. A binary relation $\mathcal{B}$ is a bisimulation if $\mathcal{B}$ and $\mathcal{B}^{-1}$ are simulations.*[6] *We say that p and q are bisimilar and write $p \sim q$ if $p\mathcal{B}q$ for some bisimulation $\mathcal{B}$.*

Example 3. Consider the union of the equation systems from Examples 1 and 2. Then the executions demonstrated in the two examples clearly prove that $X \mid Y \not\sim Z$.

The above example illustrates two non-bisimilar networks. Ideally, an automatic verification tool should not only report this fact but also provide *explanations* as to why there is a lack of bisimilarity. The well known Hennessy–Milner Logic [11] provides the key to such explanations. The formulas of Hennessy–Milner Logic, $\mathcal{M}$, are given by the following abstract syntax:

$$F ::= \mathrm{tt} \mid F \wedge G \mid \neg F \mid \langle \sigma \rangle F$$

We interpret Hennessy–Milner Logic relative to the labelled transition system $\mathcal{N}_n$. I.e. we define a *satisfaction* relation $\models$ between networks ($\mathbf{Net}_n$) and formulae ($\mathcal{M}$). For propositional constructs the definition is straightforward, and for the modality, we define:

$$\overline{P} \models \langle \sigma \rangle F \;\Leftrightarrow\; \exists \overline{P}'.\overline{P} \xrightarrow{\sigma} \overline{P}' \wedge \overline{P}' \models F$$

Now let $\mathcal{M}(\overline{P})$ be the set of properties satisfied by $\overline{P}$. Then the following characterization result [11] shows that Hennessy–Milner Logic can be applied for explanations:

Theorem 2. $\overline{P} \sim \overline{Q}$ *if and only if* $\mathcal{M}(\overline{P}) = \mathcal{M}(\overline{Q})$.

Example 4. Consider $X \mid Y$ and Z from Example 3. That $X \mid Y \not\sim Z$ is "explained" by the formula $\langle \epsilon(\frac{1}{2}) \rangle \langle b \rangle \langle \epsilon(\frac{1}{2}) \rangle \langle a \rangle \mathrm{tt}$, which is satisfied by $X \mid Y$ but not by Z.

[6] $\mathcal{B}^{-1} = \{(q,p) \mid (p,q) \in \mathcal{B}\}$.

3 Symbolic Processes

It is obvious that the standard semantics of networks is infinitary; thus decidability of bisimilarity between networks is beyond the standard techniques for finite state systems. However, in [15] an algorithm for deciding bisimilarity for networks was presented. In the following we shall give a simplified presentation of the algorithm. Then in the next section we show how to extend the algorithm in order that distinguishing formulae may be generated.

3.1 Symbolic States Given two networks $(X_1 \mid \ldots \mid X_m)$ and $(Y_1 \mid \ldots \mid Y_n)$ their bisimilarity will be reduced to deciding a suitable property of an induced joint *finite-state symbolic* transition system, in which states represent *sets* of pairs of networks.

A *symbolic state* (of arity (m,n)) is a finite list $\phi = [(M_1,N_1),\ldots,(M_k,N_k)]$ where M_i and N_i are multisets of $\{X^l \mid X \in \mathcal{V},\, l \in \textrm{NAT}\}$ with $|\biguplus_i M_i| = m$ and $|\biguplus_i N_i| = n$, and with $M_i \uplus N_i \neq \emptyset$ for $i > 1$. ϕ is said to be *interior* in case $M_1 \uplus N_1 = \emptyset$ and *boundary* otherwise. ϕ *represents* a whole family of pairs of networks. More precisely, all pairs of the form:

$$((M_1^{v_1} \mid \ldots \mid M_k^{v_k})\ ,\ (N_1^{v_1} \mid \ldots \mid N_k^{v_k})) \tag{2}$$

where $0 = v_1 < v_2 < \cdots < v_k < 1$, and for a multiset $M = \{X_1, \ldots X_j\}$, $M^e = (X_1^e \mid \ldots \mid X_j^e)$. Now, call $\overline{v} = (v_1,\ldots,v_k) \in \mathcal{R}^k_{\geq 0}$ *well-ordered and fractional* (W) if $0 = v_1 < v_2 < \cdots < v_k < 1$. Then for $\phi = [(M_1,N_1),\ldots,(M_k,N_k)]$ a symbolic state and $\overline{v} = (v_1,\ldots,v_k) \in W$, $\phi(\overline{v}) = (\phi_1(\overline{v}), \phi_2(\overline{v}))$ denotes the pair in (2). Thus, the set of pairs represented by ϕ is $\|\phi\| = \{\phi(\overline{v}) \mid \overline{v} \in W\}$.

Example 5. Consider once more the union of the equation systems from Examples 1 and 2. The symbolic state $[(\{X,Y\},\{Z\})]$ represents the single pair $(X|Y,\ Z)$. The symbolic state $[(\emptyset,\emptyset),\ (\{X,Y\},\{Z\})]$ represents all pairs of the form $(\epsilon(1-d).a|b,\ \epsilon(1-d).a.Z_b + \epsilon(1-d).b.Z_a + b.X)$, where $0 < d < 1$.

We let $\textrm{SS}_{m,n}$ denote the set of symbolic states (of arity (m,n)). It may be concluded that the set of symbolic states $\textrm{SS}_{m,n}$ is finite.

3.2 Symbolic Semantics In order to determine which symbolic states represent bisimilar pairs we provide a symbolic semantics for $\textrm{SS}_{m,n}$. Thus, let $\phi = [(M_1,N_1),\ldots,(M_k,N_k)]$ be a symbolic state (of arity (m,n)), then the symbolic action transitions $\longmapsto_1$, $\longmapsto_2$ and the symbolic delay transition $\overset{w}{\longmapsto}$ are defined by the rules in Table 1 where $\langle\!\langle \ldots \rangle\!\rangle$ denotes the list resulting from removing all pairs $(\emptyset,\emptyset)$ from the original list; we denote by $\overset{a}{\hookrightarrow}_1$ and $\overset{a}{\hookrightarrow}_2$ the two transition relations which are defined using the rules for $\overset{a}{\longmapsto}_1$ and $\overset{a}{\longmapsto}_2$ except that pairs of empty sets are *not* removed in the resulting "symbolic" state; finally, for M a multiset and $d \in \mathcal{R}_{>0}$, $M^{-d} = \{X^{n+d} \mid X^n \in M\}$.

Example 6. Recall Examples 1 and 2. Figure 1 illustrates (part of) the symbolic transition system for the initial symbolic state induced by the pair $(X \mid Y, Z)$. Symbolic states are indicated by boxes with symbolic state tuples occurring just below their associated box. For additional information we have indicated inside the boxes the families of network pairs represented by the symbolic state.

$$\frac{X \xrightarrow{a} X'}{\phi \xmapsto{a}_1 \langle\!\langle(\{X'\} \uplus M_1', N_1), \ldots, (M_k', N_k)\rangle\!\rangle} \quad \begin{array}{l} M_i = M_i' \uplus \{X\} \\ M_j = M_j' \ (i \neq j) \end{array}$$

$$\frac{Y \xrightarrow{a} Y'}{\phi \xmapsto{a}_2 \langle\!\langle(M_1, \{Y'\} \uplus N_1'), \ldots, (M_k, N_k')\rangle\!\rangle} \quad \begin{array}{l} N_i = N_i' \uplus \{Y\} \\ N_j = N_j' \ (i \neq j) \end{array}$$

$$\phi \xmapsto{w} [(\emptyset, \emptyset), (M_1, N_1), \ldots, (M_k, N_k)] \quad \phi \text{ is boundary}$$

$$\phi \xmapsto{w} \langle\!\langle(M_k^{-1}, N_k^{-1}), (M_1, N_1), \ldots, (M_{k-1}, N_{k-1})\rangle\!\rangle \quad \phi \text{ is interior}$$

Table 1. Rules for symbolic transitions.

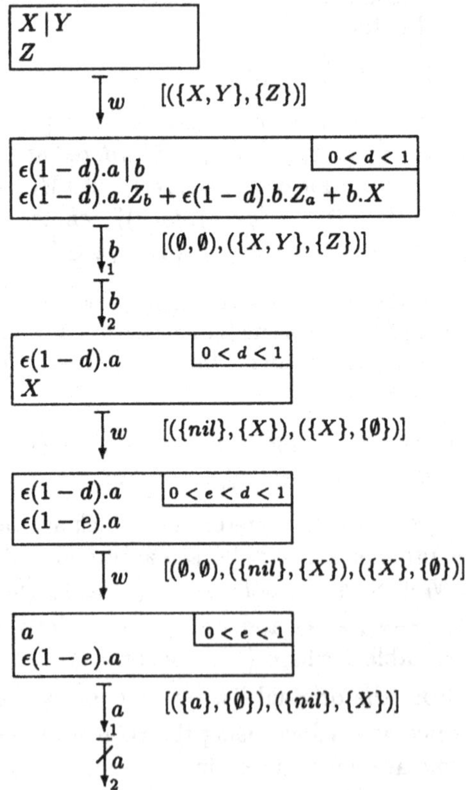

Fig. 1. Part of the symbolic transition system induced by $X \,|\, Y$ and Z.

The close relationship between the semantics of a symbolic state and the (standard) semantics of the (pairs of) networks it represents are as below. Obviously, Lemma 3 *1* and *2* may be dualised with $\longmapsto_2$ replacing $\longmapsto_1$.

Lemma 3 (Correspondence).

1. $\phi \overset{a}{\longmapsto}_1 \phi'$ and $(\overline{P},\overline{Q}) \in \|\phi\|$ implies $\exists \overline{P}'.\ \overline{P} \overset{a}{\longrightarrow} \overline{P}'$ such that $(\overline{P}',\overline{Q}) \in \|\phi'\|$;
2. $(\overline{P},\overline{Q}) \in \|\phi\|$ and $\overline{P} \overset{a}{\longrightarrow} \overline{P}'$ implies $\exists \phi'.\ \phi \overset{a}{\longmapsto}_1 \phi'$ with $(\overline{P}',\overline{Q}) \in \|\phi'\|$;
3. $\phi \overset{w}{\longmapsto} \phi'$ and $(\overline{P},\overline{Q}) \in \|\phi\|$ implies $\exists d \in \mathcal{R}_{>0}.\ (\overline{P}^d,\overline{Q}^d) \in \|\phi'\|$;[7]
4. $(\overline{P},\overline{Q}) \in \|\phi\|$ implies $\forall d\ \exists \phi'.\ \phi(\overset{w}{\longmapsto})^*\phi'$ with $(\overline{P}^d,\overline{Q}^d) \in \|\phi'\|$;

3.3 Symbolic Bisimulation

Definition 4. *$\mathcal{B} \subseteq SS_{m,n}$ is a symbolic bisimulation if whenever $\phi \in \mathcal{B}$ and $a \in \mathcal{A}$ the following holds:*

1. Whenever $\phi \overset{a}{\longmapsto}_1 \phi'$ then $\phi' \overset{a}{\longmapsto}_2 \phi''$ for some ϕ'' with $\phi'' \in \mathcal{B}$,
2. Whenever $\phi \overset{a}{\longmapsto}_2 \phi'$ then $\phi' \overset{a}{\longmapsto}_1 \phi''$ for some ϕ'' with $\phi'' \in \mathcal{B}$
3. Whenever $\phi \overset{w}{\longmapsto} \phi'$ then $\phi' \in \mathcal{B}$

We write $\phi \in \sim_s$ whenever ϕ is contained in some symbolic bisimulation.

As $\mathrm{SS}_{m,n}$ is finite-state and $\sim_s$ is a maximal fixedpoint of a simple monotonic function on sets of symbolic states it follows from standard techniques that questions of the form $\phi \in \sim_s$ are decidable. Moreover, using Lemma 3 the following close relationships between (ordinary) bisimulation and the symbolic counterparts may be easily established:

Theorem 5. *Let $(\overline{P},\overline{Q}) \in \|\phi\|$. Then $\overline{P} \sim \overline{Q}$ if and only if $\phi \in \sim_s$.*

It follows that in order to decide whether two networks $(X_1 \mid \ldots \mid X_m)$ and $(Y_1 \mid \ldots \mid Y_n)$ are bisimilar we may alternatively decide whether the initial symbolic state $[(\{X_1,\ldots,X_m\},\{Y_1,\ldots,Y_n\})]$ is a member of the symbolic bisimulation. For instance, using the definition of symbolic bisimilarity it follows clearly from Figure 1 and Theorem 5 that $X \mid Y \not\sim Z$.

4 Pointed Symbolic Processes

Section 3 provides a finite symbolic semantics based on which bisimilarity between networks can be decided. However, the semantics has abstracted away from time-quantities, and it is not possible to synthesize distinguishing formulae based on this semantics. Therefore, we provide in this section a more informative yet still (sufficiently) finitary *pointed* symbolic semantics with explicit time information. We show that this semantics provides the basis for an algorithm constructing distinguishing formulae.

4.1 Pointed Semantics A *pointed symbolic state* is a pair $\langle\phi,\overline{v}\rangle$, where ϕ is a symbolic state and $\overline{v}$ is a (corresponding) well-ordered fractional. We

[7] Here $\overline{P}^d$ denotes the unique network such that $\overline{P} \overset{\epsilon(d)}{\longrightarrow} \overline{P}^d$.

denote by $\mathrm{PSS}_{m,n}$ the set of all pointed symbolic states (of arity (m,n)). Observe that $\mathrm{PSS}_{m,n}$ in contrast to $\mathrm{SS}_{m,n}$ is infinite. A pointed symbolic state $\langle\phi,\overline{v}\rangle$ *represents* both the family of network pairs represented by ϕ, i.e. $\|\phi\|$, as well as the particular network pair pointed out by $\overline{v}$, i.e. $\phi(\overline{v})$.

The symbolic semantics of $\mathrm{PSS}_{m,n}$ refines that of $\mathrm{SS}_{m,n}$ in that symbolic wait transitions are parameterized with time-quantities in order to capture the corresponding delay transition between the represented networks. Before giving the symbolic semantics of $\mathrm{PSS}_{m,n}$ we need some notation: for $\overline{v}=(v_1,\ldots,v_k)\in W$ we define $\overline{v}^*=(1-v_k)$, $\mathrm{next}_B(\overline{v})=(0,v_1+(\frac{\overline{v}^*}{2}),\ldots,v_k+(\frac{\overline{v}^*}{2}))$ and $\mathrm{next}_I(\overline{v})=(0,v_1+\overline{v}^*,\ldots,v_{k-1}+\overline{v}^*)$. Now let $\langle\phi,\overline{v}\rangle\in\mathrm{PSS}_{m,n}$. Then the $\Longrightarrow_1$, $\Longrightarrow_2$ and $\overset{w(d)}{\Longrightarrow}$ transition relations are defined by the rules below:

$$\frac{\phi\overset{a}{\hookrightarrow}_1\phi'}{\langle\phi,\overline{v}\rangle\overset{a}{\Longrightarrow}_1\langle\!\langle\phi',\overline{v}\rangle\!\rangle}\qquad\frac{\phi\overset{w}{\longmapsto}\phi'}{\langle\phi,\overline{v}\rangle\overset{w(\overline{v}^*/2)}{\Longrightarrow}\langle\phi',\mathrm{next}_B(\overline{v})\rangle}\ \phi\text{ is boundary}$$

$$\frac{\phi\overset{a}{\hookrightarrow}_2\phi'}{\langle\phi,\overline{v}\rangle\overset{a}{\Longrightarrow}_2\langle\!\langle\phi',\overline{v}\rangle\!\rangle}\qquad\frac{\phi\overset{w}{\longmapsto}\phi'}{\langle\phi,\overline{v}\rangle\overset{w(\overline{v}^*)}{\Longrightarrow}\langle\phi',\mathrm{next}_I(\overline{v})\rangle}\ \phi\text{ is interior}$$

where $\langle\!\langle\phi,\overline{v}\rangle\!\rangle$ denotes the pointed symbolic state resulting from removing all pairs $(\emptyset,\emptyset)$ from ϕ and at the same time removing the corresponding component v_i from $\overline{v}$.

Example 7. Figure 2 is the pointed version of Figure 1.

Though $\mathrm{PSS}_{m,n}$ is an infinite set the above symbolic semantics is finitary in the following important sense: the total set of immediate $\Longrightarrow$-derivatives of any pointed symbolic state $\langle\phi,\overline{v}\rangle$ is finite! [8]

The following Correspondence Lemma shows that the pointed symbolic semantics indeed is an extension of the symbolic semantics from the previous section. Obviously, clause *1* and *2* have analogous counterparts for $\Longrightarrow_2$.

Lemma 6 (Correspondence).

1. $(\overline{P},\overline{Q})=\phi(\overline{v})$ and $\overline{P}\overset{a}{\longrightarrow}\overline{P}'$ implies $\langle\phi,\overline{v}\rangle\overset{a}{\Longrightarrow}_1\langle\phi',\overline{v}'\rangle$ and $(\overline{P}',\overline{Q})=\phi'(\overline{v}')$ for some ϕ' and $\overline{v}'$.
2. $\langle\phi,\overline{v}\rangle\overset{a}{\Longrightarrow}_1\langle\phi',\overline{v}'\rangle$ implies $\phi_1(\overline{v})\overset{a}{\longrightarrow}\phi_1'(\overline{v}')$ and $\phi_2(\overline{v})=\phi_2'(\overline{v}')$.
3. $\phi\overset{w}{\longmapsto}\phi'$ implies for all $\overline{v}$, $\langle\phi,\overline{v}\rangle\overset{w(d)}{\Longrightarrow}\langle\phi',\overline{v}'\rangle$ for some $\overline{v}'$ and d.
4. $\langle\phi,\overline{v}\rangle\overset{w(d)}{\Longrightarrow}\langle\phi',\overline{v}'\rangle$ implies $\phi_1(\overline{v})\overset{\epsilon(d)}{\longrightarrow}\phi_1'(\overline{v}')$, $\phi_2(\overline{v})\overset{\epsilon(d)}{\longrightarrow}\phi_2'(\overline{v}')$ and $\phi\overset{w}{\longmapsto}\phi'$.

4.2 Pointed Symbolic Bisimulation

Definition 7. *$\mathcal{B}\subseteq PSS_{m,n}$ is a pointed symbolic bisimulation if whenever $\langle\phi,\overline{v}\rangle\in\mathcal{B}$, $a\in\mathcal{A}$ and $d\in\mathcal{R}_{>0}$ the following holds:*

1. $\langle\phi,\overline{v}\rangle\overset{a}{\Longrightarrow}_1\langle\phi',\overline{v}'\rangle$ implies $\exists\phi'',\overline{v}''.\ \langle\phi',\overline{v}'\rangle\overset{a}{\Longrightarrow}_2\langle\phi'',\overline{v}''\rangle$ with $\langle\phi'',\overline{v}''\rangle\in\mathcal{B}$,

[8] The set of derivatives of $\langle\phi,\overline{v}\rangle$ is the union of the sets $\{\langle\phi',\overline{v}'\rangle\mid\exists a.\exists i.\langle\phi,\overline{v}\rangle\overset{a}{\Longrightarrow}_i\langle\phi',\overline{v}'\rangle\}$ and $\{\langle\phi',\overline{v}'\rangle\mid\exists d\in\mathcal{R}_{>0}.\langle\phi,\overline{v}\rangle\overset{w(d)}{\Longrightarrow}\langle\phi',\overline{v}'\rangle\}$.

$X \mid Y$
Z

$\Downarrow w(\frac{1}{2})$ $[(\{X,Y\},\{Z\})]$ (0)

$\epsilon(1-d).a \mid b$ $d = \frac{1}{2}$
$\epsilon(1-d).a.Z_b + \epsilon(1-d).b.Z_a + b.X$

$\Downarrow b_1$ $[(\emptyset,\emptyset),\ (\{X,Y\},\{Z\})]$ $(0,\frac{1}{2})$

$\Downarrow b_2$

$\epsilon(1-d).a$ $d = \frac{1}{2}$
X

$\Downarrow w(\frac{1}{4})$ $[(\{nil\},\{X\}),\ (\{X\},\{\emptyset\})]$ $(0,\frac{1}{2})$

$\epsilon(1-d).a$ $e = \frac{1}{4} d = \frac{3}{4}$
$\epsilon(1-e).a$

$\Downarrow w(\frac{1}{4})$ $[(\emptyset,\emptyset),\ (\{nil\},\{X\}),\ (\{X\},\{\emptyset\})]$ $(0,\frac{1}{4},\frac{3}{4})$

a $e = \frac{1}{2}$
$\epsilon(1-e).a$

$\Downarrow a_1$ $[(\{a\},\{\emptyset\}),\ (\{nil\},\{X\})]$ $(0,\frac{1}{2})$

$\not\Downarrow a_2$

Fig. 2. Part of the *pointed* symbolic transition system induced by $X \mid Y$ and Z.

2. $\langle \phi, \overline{v} \rangle \overset{a}{\Longrightarrow}_2 \langle \phi', \overline{v}' \rangle$ implies $\exists \phi'', \overline{v}''.\ \langle \phi', \overline{v}' \rangle \overset{a}{\Longrightarrow}_1 \langle \phi'', \overline{v}'' \rangle$ with $\langle \phi'', \overline{v}'' \rangle \in \mathcal{B}$
3. $\langle \phi, \overline{v} \rangle \overset{w(d)}{\Longrightarrow} \langle \phi', \overline{v}' \rangle$ implies $\langle \phi', \overline{v}' \rangle \in \mathcal{B}$

We write $\langle \phi, \overline{v} \rangle \in \sim_{ps}$ *if* $\langle \phi, \overline{v} \rangle$ *is contained in a pointed symbolic bisimulation.*

For $\mathcal{B} \subseteq \mathrm{SS}_{m,n}$, let $\mathcal{B}^{\uparrow} = \{\langle \phi, \overline{v} \rangle \mid \phi \in \mathcal{B}\}$. Dually, for $\mathcal{B} \subseteq \mathrm{PSS}_{m,n}$ let $\mathcal{B}^{\downarrow} = \{\phi \mid \langle \phi, \overline{v} \rangle \in \mathcal{B}\}$.

Lemma 8. *If $\mathcal{B}$ is a symbolic bisimulation then $\mathcal{B}^{\uparrow}$ is a pointed symbolic bisimulation. If $\mathcal{B}$ is a pointed symbolic bisimulation then $\mathcal{B}^{\downarrow}$ is a symbolic bisimulation.*

This leads directly to the following using the existing result of Theorem 5:

Theorem 9. $\langle \phi, \overline{v} \rangle \in \sim_{ps}$ *if and only if* $\phi_1(\overline{v}) \sim \phi_2(\overline{v})$.

Thus, two networks $(X_1 \mid \ldots \mid X_m)$ and $(Y_1 \mid \ldots \mid Y_n)$ are bisimilar just in case the initial pointed symbolic state $\langle [(\{X_1, \ldots, X_m\}, \{Y_1, \ldots, Y_n\})], (0) \rangle$ is a member of the pointed symbolic bisimulation. However, due to the infinite nature of

$PSS_{m,n}$ this does not directly lead to an alternative algorithm for bisimilarity, a problem we will deal with in the following subsection.

4.3 Computing Distinguishing Formulae In standard fashion we may define for n a natural number the n'th approximations of the various symbolic relations $\sim_s$ and $\sim_{ps}$. The 0'th approximate is simply the entire set of (pointed) symbolic states, and the $(n+1)$'th approximate is defined using the definition schemas of Definitions 4 and 7 with the n'th approximate substituting $\mathcal{B}$ in the (relevant) defining clauses. For $\equiv$ one of the above relations the corresponding n'th approximate will be denoted $\equiv^n$. It is easy to see that in both cases $\equiv^n$ will be decreasing in n. Also, in both cases $\equiv^n$ approximates $\equiv$ in the sense that $\equiv$ equals the intersection of all its approximations (i.e. $\equiv = \bigcap_{n\in\omega} \equiv^n$).

As the set of symbolic states is finite, there exists a K (being simply the number of symbolic states of the given arity) such that $\sim_s^n$ will be constant when n exceeds K. This fact leads directly to an iterative algorithm for deciding $\sim_s$ and hence – due to Theorem 5 – for deciding $\sim$. In contrast, the set of pointed symbolic states is infinite and there is therefore no a priori guarantee that the decreasing sequence $\langle\sim_{ps}^n\rangle_n$ will converge at any finite stage. However, finite convergence is ensured by the following Lemma relating symbolic and pointed symbolic approximates:

Lemma 10. *For all n, $(\sim_{ps}^n)^\downarrow = \sim_s^n$ and $(\sim_s^n)^\uparrow = \sim_{ps}^n$.*

Thus the pointed symbolic approximates converges at the same iteration as the symbolic counterparts. Furthermore, as any pointed symbolic state has only a finite (and computable) set of immediate derivatives, it follows that $\sim_{ps}^n$ is decidable for any n. Hence bisimilarity between networks may alternatively be computed by deciding $\sim_{ps}^K$-membership problems for a sufficiently large K.

In addition, the use of *pointed* symbolic bisimulation enables the generation of distinguishing formulae in cases of non-bisimilarity as stated by the following theorem. The proof given is constructive and constitutes the generation algorithm.

Theorem 11. *Whenever $\langle\phi,\overline{v}\rangle \notin \sim_{ps}$ then $\exists F.\ \phi_1(\overline{v}) \models F$ and $\phi_2(\overline{v}) \not\models F$.*

Proof: The proof is by induction in n, where $\langle\phi,\overline{v}\rangle \notin \sim_{ps}^n$. We only show the induction step. Assume $\langle\phi,\overline{v}\rangle \notin \sim_{ps}^{n+1}$. There are three cases to consider depending on which of the conditions for membership of $\sim_{ps}^{n+1}$ that fails. We only show two of the cases. Assume $\langle\phi,\overline{v}\rangle \stackrel{a}{\Longrightarrow}_1 \langle\phi',\overline{v}'\rangle$ but whenever $\langle\phi',\overline{v}'\rangle \stackrel{a}{\Longrightarrow}_2 \langle\phi^j,\overline{v}^j\rangle$ $(j = 1\ldots m)$ then $\langle\phi^j,\overline{v}^j\rangle \notin \sim_{ps}^n$. Now, using the Induction Hypothesis we may conclude that there exists some formula F_j such that ${\phi^j}_1(\overline{v}^j) \models F_j$ but ${\phi^j}_2(\overline{v}^j) \not\models F_j$. Now, let $F = \langle a\rangle(F_1 \wedge \ldots \wedge F_m)$ then it follows easily using Lemma 6 that $\phi_1(\overline{v}) \models F$ whereas $\phi_2(\overline{v}) \not\models F$. Assume $\langle\phi,\overline{v}\rangle \stackrel{w(d)}{\Longrightarrow} \langle\phi',\overline{v}'\rangle$ but $\langle\phi',\overline{v}'\rangle \notin \sim_{ps}^n$. Now, using the Induction Hypothesis we may conclude that there exists a formula F' such that $\phi_1'(\overline{v}') \models F'$ but $\phi_2'(\overline{v}') \not\models F'$. Now let $F = \langle\epsilon(d)\rangle F'$, then it follows from the Lemma 6 that $\phi_1(\overline{v}) \models F$ whereas $\phi_2(\overline{v}) \not\models F$. □

Applying the construction of the above Theorem 11 to the pointed symbolic transition system induced by $X \mid Y$ and Z (partially shown in Figure 2) we may generate the formula $\langle\epsilon(\frac{1}{2})\rangle\langle b\rangle\langle\epsilon(\frac{1}{4})\rangle\langle\epsilon(\frac{1}{4})\rangle\langle a\rangle \mathrm{tt}$ distinguishing $X \mid Y$ and Z.

References

1. J.C.M. Baeten and J.A. Bergstra. Real time process algebra. Technical Report P8916, University of Amsterdam, 1989.
2. J. A. Bergstra, J. Heering, and P. Klint. Algebra of communicating processes. In *CWI symposium on Mathematics and Computer Science*. North–Holland, 1986.
3. U. Celikkan and R. Cleaveland. Diagnostic information for behavioral preorders. In *Proceedings of CAV'92*, volume 663 of *Lecture Notes In Computer Science, Springer Verlag*. Springer-Verlag, 1992.
4. K. Čerāns, J.C. Godskesen, and K.G. Larsen. Timed modal specifications — theory and tools. In *Proceedings of CAV'93*, volume 697 of *Lecture Notes In Computer Science*, pages 253–267. Springer-Verlag, 1993.
5. R. Cleaveland. On automatically distinguishing inequivalent processes. In *Proceedings of CAV'90*, volume 531 of *Lecture Notes In Computer Science*. Springer-Verlag, 1990.
6. R. Cleaveland, J. Parrow, and B. Steffen. The concurrency workbench. Technical Report ECS-LFCS-89-83, LFCS, University of Edinburgh, Scotland, 1989.
7. J. Davis and S. Schneider. An introduction to timed CSP. Technical Report PRG–75, Oxford University Computing Laboratory, 1989.
8. J.C. Godskensen and K.G. Larsen. Synthesizing Distiniguishing Formulae for Real Time Systems. BRICS Report Series RS-94-48, BRICS, Aalborg University, December 1994. Accessible via WWW: http://www.brics.aau.dk/BRICS.
9. J.C. Godskesen, K.G. Larsen, and M. Zeeberg. TAV – users manual. Technical Report R 89-19, University of Aalborg, Denmark, 1989.
10. J.C. Godskesen. *Timed Modal Specifications -A Theory for Verification of Real-Time Concurrent Systems*. Phd. thesis, Aalborg University, Denmark, 1994.
11. M. Hennessy and R. Milner. Algebraic laws for nondeterminism and concurrency. *Journal of the Association for Computing Machinery*, pages 137–161, 1985.
12. C.A.R. Hoare. Communicating sequential processes. *Communications of the ACM*, 21(8):666–677, 1978.
13. V. Lecompte, E. Madelaine, and D. Vergamini. Auto: A verification system for parallel and communicating processes. INRIA, Sophia–Antipolis, 1988.
14. R. Milner. *Calculus of Communicating Systems*, volume 92 of *Lecture Notes In Computer Science, Springer Verlag*. Springer Verlag, 1980.
15. K. Čerāns. Decidability of bisimulation equivalences for processes with parallel timers. In *Proceedings of CAV'92*, volume 663 of *Lecture Notes In Computer Science, Springer Verlag*. Springer-Verlag, 1992.
16. Y. Wang. Real–time behaviour of asynchronous agents. In *Proceedings of CONCUR'90*, volume 458 of *Lecture Notes In Computer Science, Springer Verlag*. Springer-Verlag, 1990.

From Timed Automata to Logic — and Back *

François Laroussinie[1], Kim G. Larsen[1], Carsten Weise[2]

[1] **BRICS*****, Aalborg Univ., Denmark
[2] Aachen Univ., Germany

Abstract. In this paper, we define a timed logic L_ν which is sufficiently expressive that we for any timed automaton may construct a single *characteristic* L_ν formula uniquely characterizing the automaton up to timed bisimilarity.
Also, we prove decidability of the *satisfiability* problem for L_ν with respect to given bounds on the number of clocks and constants of the timed automata to be constructed.

1 Introduction

One of the most successful techniques for *automatic verification* is that of *model-checking*; i.e. a property is given as a formula of a propositional temporal logic and automatically compared with an automaton representing the actual behaviour of the system. Extremely efficient model–checking algorithms have been obtained for *finite* automata with respect to the branching–time temporal logics CTL [7, 22, 8] and the modal μ–calculus [17, 4, 10, 9, 3, 24]. In the last few years, model–checking has been extended to real–time systems, with time considered to be a dense linear order. A timed extension of finite automata through addition of a finite set of real–valued clocks has been put forward [2], and the corresponding model–checking problem has been proven decidable for a number of timed logics including timed extensions of CTL (TCTL) [1] and a timed μ–calculus (T_μ) [13].

In this paper we continue this transfer of existing techniques from the setting of finite (untimed) automata to that of timed automata. In particular a timed logic L_ν is put forward, which is sufficiently expressive that we for any timed automaton may (effectively) construct a single *characteristic* L_ν formula uniquely characterizing the automaton up to timed bisimilarity. The construction is a timed extension of those in [5, 12, 16], and reduces timed bisimilarity between automata to a model–checking problem, which — when combined with the model–checking algorithm for L_ν — yields an alternative algorithm for timed bisimulation compared with [6]. In addition, characteristic formula constructions may be given for other behavioural preorders [19, 11], immediately yielding decision procedures for these relationships as well. Secondly, we prove decidability of

* This work has been supported by the European Communities under CONCUR2, BRA 7166

*** Basic Research in Computer Science, Centre of the Danish National Research Foundation.

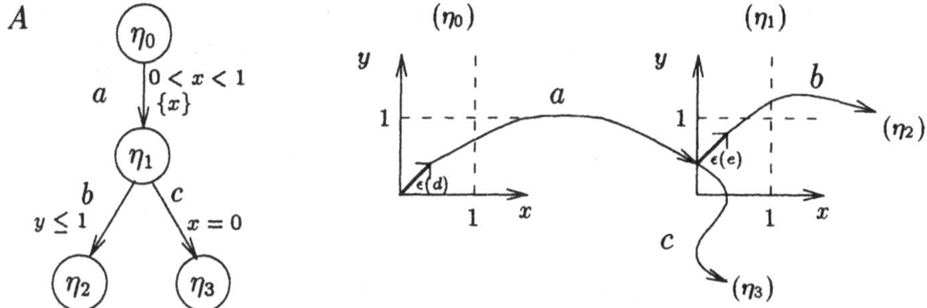

Fig. 1. An automaton and its behaviour

bounded satisfiable for L_ν. That is, we present a model–construction algorithm, which given a formula of L_ν and bounds k and M will synthesize a timed automaton with no more than k clocks and no clock being compared with constants greater than M (provided any such exits).

Combining the characteristic formula construction with the bounded model-construction algorithm enables us to decide whether an automaton can be simplified in terms of number of clocks and constants used for comparison.

A full version can be found in [18].

2 Timed Automata

Let $\mathcal{A}$ be a fixed set of actions ranged over by $a, b, c, \ldots$. We denote by $\mathbf{N}$ the set of natural numbers and by $\mathbf{R}$ the set of non–negative real numbers. $\mathcal{D}$ denotes the set of delay actions $\{\epsilon(d) \mid d \in \mathbf{R}\}$, and $\mathcal{L}$ denotes the union $\mathcal{A} \cup \mathcal{D}$. If C is a set of clocks, $\mathcal{B}(C)$ denotes the set of formulas built using boolean connectives over atomic formulas of the form $x \leq m$, $m \leq x$, $x \leq y + m$ and $y + m \leq x$ with $x, y \in C$ and $m \in \mathbf{N}$. Moreover $\mathcal{B}_M(C)$ denotes the subset of $\mathcal{B}(C)$ with no constant greater than M.

Definition 1. A timed automaton A is a tuple $\langle \mathcal{A}, N, \eta_0, C, E \rangle$ where $\mathcal{A}$ is a finite set of actions, N is a finite set of nodes, η_0 is the initial node, C is a finite set of clocks, and $E \subseteq N \times N \times \mathcal{A} \times 2^C \times \mathcal{B}(C)$ corresponds to the set of edges. $e = \langle \eta, \eta', a, r, b \rangle \in E$ represents an edge from the node η to the node η' with action a, r denoting the set of clocks to be reset and b is the enabling condition over the clocks of A.

Informally, the system starts at node η_0 with all its clocks initialized to 0. The values of the clocks increase synchronously with time. At any time, the automaton whose current node is η can change node by following an edge $\langle \eta, \eta', a, r, b \rangle \in E$ provided the current values of the clocks satisfy b. With this transition the clocks in r get reset to 0.

A *time assignment* v for C is a function from C to $\mathbf{R}$. We denote by $\mathbf{R}^C$ the set of time assignments for C. For $v \in \mathbf{R}^C$, $x \in C$ and $d \in \mathbf{R}$, $v + d$ denotes the time assignment which maps each clock x in C to the value $v(x)+d$. For $C' \subseteq C$, $[C' \mapsto 0]v$ denotes the assignment for C which maps each clock in C' to the value 0 and agrees with v over $C \setminus C'$. Given a condition $b \in \mathcal{B}(C)$ and a time assignment $v \in \mathbf{R}^C$, $b(v)$ is a boolean value describing whether b is satisfied by v or not. Finally a k-clock automaton is a timed automaton $\langle \mathcal{A}, S, \eta_0, C, E \rangle$ such that $|C| = k$.

A *state* of an automaton A is a pair $\langle \eta, v \rangle_A$ where η is a node of A and v a time assignment for C. The initial state of A is $\langle \eta_0, v_0 \rangle_A$ where v_0 is the time assignment mapping all clocks in C to 0. The semantics of A is given by a labelled transition system $\mathcal{M}_A = \langle \Sigma_A, \mathcal{L}, \sigma_0, \longrightarrow_A \rangle$, where Σ_A is the set of states of A, σ_0 is the initial state $\langle \eta_0, v_0 \rangle_A$, and $\longrightarrow_A$ is the transition relation defined as follows: $\langle \eta, v \rangle \xrightarrow{a}_A \langle \eta', v' \rangle$ iff $\exists r, b.$ s.t. $\langle \eta, \eta', a, r, b \rangle \in E \wedge b(v) \wedge v' = [r \rightarrow 0]v$ and $\langle \eta, v \rangle \xrightarrow{\epsilon(d)}_A \langle \eta', v' \rangle$ iff $\eta = \eta'$ and $v' = v + d$

We may now apply the standard notion of bisimulation [20, 21] to the labelled transition systems determined by two automata A and B. Letting s_A and s_B range over states of respectively A and B, *strong timed bisimulation* $\sim$ is defined as the largest symmetric relation over $\Sigma_A \times \Sigma_B$ such that whenever $s_A \sim s_B$, $\ell \in \mathcal{A} \cup \mathcal{D}$ and $s_A \xrightarrow{\ell}_A s'_A$ then there exists s'_B such that $s_B \xrightarrow{\ell}_B s'_B$ and $s'_A \sim s'_B$. We say that A and B are *strong timed bisimular* if their initial states are strong bisimilar.

Example 1. Consider the automaton A of Figure 1. The two coordinate systems in the right part of the Figure indicate (some of) the states of A. Each point of the coordinate systems represents a unique time assignment, with the left (resp. right) coordinate system representing states involving the node η_0 (resp. η_1). In the Figure we have indicated some transition sequences (with $d < 1$ and $e + d \leq 1$).

3 Timed Modal Logic L_ν

We consider a dense-time logic L_ν with clocks and recursion. This logic may be seen as a certain fragment of the μ-calculus T_μ presented in [13].

Definition 2. Let K a finite set of clocks, Id a set of identifiers and k an integer. The set L_ν of formulae over K, Id and k is generated by the abstract syntax with φ and ψ ranging over L_ν:

$$\varphi ::= \mathtt{tt} \mid \mathtt{ff} \mid \varphi \wedge \psi \mid \varphi \vee \psi \mid \exists \varphi \mid \forall \varphi \mid \langle a \rangle \varphi \mid [a] \varphi$$
$$\mid x \,\mathsf{in}\, \varphi \mid x + n \bowtie y + m \mid x \bowtie m \mid Z$$

where $a \in \mathcal{A}$; $x, y \in K$; $n, m \in \{0, 1, \ldots, k\}$; $\bowtie \in \{=, <, \leq, >, \geq\}$ and $Z \in \mathsf{Id}$.

The meaning of the identifiers is specified by a declaration $\mathcal{D}$ assigning a formula of L_ν to each identifier. When $\mathcal{D}$ is understood we write $Z \stackrel{\mathrm{def}}{=} \varphi$ for $\mathcal{D}(Z) = \varphi$. The K clocks are called *formula clocks* and a formula φ is said to be *closed* if every formula clock x occurring in φ is in the scope of an "x in ..." operator.

Given a timed automaton $A = \langle \mathcal{A}, N, \eta_0, C, E \rangle$, we interpret the L_ν formulas over an *extended state* $\langle \eta, vu \rangle_{A^+}$ where $\langle \eta, v \rangle_A$ is a state of A and u a time assignment for K. Transitions between extended states are defined by: $\langle \eta, vu \rangle_{A^+} \xrightarrow{\epsilon(d)} \langle \eta', v+d\, u+d \rangle_{A^+}$ and $\langle \eta, vu \rangle_{A^+} \xrightarrow{a} \langle \eta', v'u' \rangle_{A^+}$ iff $\langle \eta, v \rangle_A \xrightarrow{a} \langle \eta', v' \rangle_A$ and $u = u'$. Formally, the satisfaction relation between extended states and formulas is defined as follows:

Definition 3. Let A be a timed automaton and $\mathcal{D}$ a declaration. The satisfaction relation $\models_\mathcal{D}$ is the largest relation satisfying the following implications :

$$
\begin{array}{rcl}
\langle \eta, v\, u \rangle_{A^+} \models_\mathcal{D} \mathtt{tt} & \Rightarrow & \text{true} \\
\langle \eta, v\, u \rangle_{A^+} \models_\mathcal{D} \mathtt{ff} & \Rightarrow & \text{false} \\
\langle \eta, v\, u \rangle_{A^+} \models_\mathcal{D} \varphi \land \psi & \Rightarrow & \langle \eta, v\, u \rangle_{A^+} \models_\mathcal{D} \varphi \text{ and } \langle \eta, v\, u \rangle_{A^+} \models_\mathcal{D} \psi \\
\langle \eta, v\, u \rangle_{A^+} \models_\mathcal{D} \exists\, \varphi & \Rightarrow & \exists d \in \mathbf{R}.\ \ \langle \eta, v{+}d\ u{+}d \rangle_{A^+} \models_\mathcal{D} \varphi \\
\langle \eta, v\, u \rangle_{A^+} \models_\mathcal{D} \langle a \rangle\, \varphi & \Rightarrow & \exists\, \langle \eta', v' \rangle_A.\ \ \langle \eta, v \rangle_A \xrightarrow{a} \langle \eta', v' \rangle_A \text{ and } \langle \eta', v'\, u \rangle_{A^+} \models_\mathcal{D} \varphi \\
\langle \eta, v\, u \rangle_{A^+} \models_\mathcal{D} x{+}m \bowtie y{+}n & \Rightarrow & u(x) + m \bowtie u(y) + n \\
\langle \eta, v\, u \rangle_{A^+} \models_\mathcal{D} x \,\mathsf{in}\, \varphi & \Rightarrow & \langle \eta, v\, u' \rangle_{A^+} \models_\mathcal{D} \varphi \text{ where } u' = [\{x\} \to 0]u \\
\langle \eta, v\, u \rangle_{A^+} \models_\mathcal{D} Z & \Rightarrow & \langle \eta, v\, u \rangle_{A^+} \models_\mathcal{D} \mathcal{D}(Z)
\end{array}
$$

Any relation satisfying the above implications is called a *satisfiability* relation. It follows from standard fixpoint theory [23] that $\models_\mathcal{D}$ is the union of all satisfiability relations and that the above implications in fact are biimplications for $\models_\mathcal{D}$. We say that A satisfies a closed L_ν formula φ and write $A \models \varphi$ when $\langle \eta_0, v_0\, u \rangle_{A^+} \models_\mathcal{D} \varphi$ for any u. Note that if φ is closed, then $\langle \eta, vu \rangle_{A^+} \models_\mathcal{D} \varphi$ iff $\langle \eta, vu' \rangle_{A^+} \models_\mathcal{D} \varphi$ for any $u, u' \in \mathbf{R}^K$.

The real–time interval modality $\exists]m;n[$ (resp. $\forall]m;n[$) introduced in [14] which denotes existential (resp. universal) quantification over delay between m and n, can be defined in L_ν [4]. A formula is called a *q-clocks formula* if it contains no more than q formula clocks.

Example 2. The initial state $\langle \eta_0, v_0\, u_0 \rangle$ of the automaton from Figure 1 satisfies the following L_ν formula φ:

$$
\varphi = \exists\,]0;1[\, \langle a \rangle \left[\left(\langle c \rangle\, \mathtt{tt} \right) \land \left(\forall\,]0;1[\, [c]\, \mathtt{ff} \right) \land \left(\exists\,]0;1[\, \langle b \rangle\, \mathtt{tt} \right) \land \left(\exists\,]0;1[\, [b]\, \mathtt{ff} \right) \right] \qquad (1)
$$

4 Model Checking

The model-checking problem for L_ν consists in deciding if a given timed automaton A satisfies a given specification φ in L_ν. This problem is decidable using the region technique of Alur and Dill [2, 1] which provides an abstract semantics of timed automata in the form of finite labelled transition systems with the truth value of L_ν formulas being maintained. The basic idea is that, given a timed automaton A, two states $\langle \eta, v_1 \rangle_A$ and $\langle \eta, v_2 \rangle_A$ which are close enough with respect to their clocks values (we will say that v_1 and v_2 are in the same *region*) can perform the same actions, and two extended states $\langle \eta, v_1\, u_1 \rangle_{A^+}$ and $\langle \eta, v_2\, u_2 \rangle_{A^+}$

[4] $\exists]m;n[\varphi \stackrel{\text{def}}{=} x \,\mathsf{in}\big(\exists(x > m \land x < n \land \varphi)\big)$ and $\forall]m;n[\varphi \stackrel{\text{def}}{=} x \,\mathsf{in}\big(\forall(x \le m \lor x \ge n \lor \varphi)\big)$

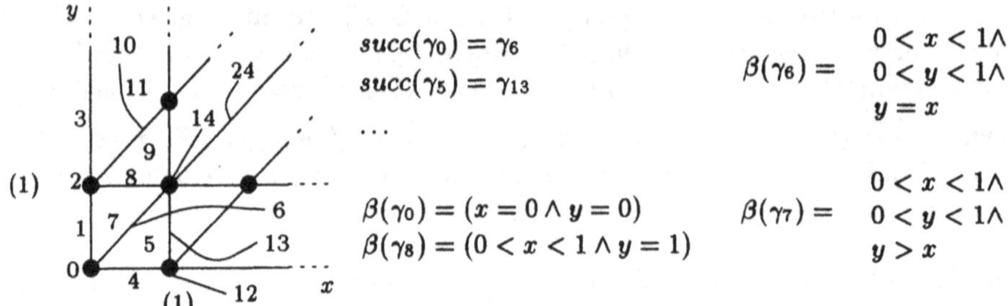

Fig. 2. $\mathcal{R}_k^C$ with $C = \{x, y\}$ and $k = 1$

where $v_1\, u_1$ and $v_2\, u_2$ are in the same region, satisfy the same L_ν formulas. In fact the regions are defined as equivalence classes of a relation $\doteq$ over time assignments [13]. Formally, given C a set of clocks and k an integer, we say $u \doteq v$ if and only if u and v satisfy the same conditions of $\mathcal{B}_k(C)$. $[u]$ denotes the region which contains the time assignment u. $\mathcal{R}_k^C$ denotes the set of all regions for a set C of clocks and the maximal constant k. From a decision point of view it is important to note that $\mathcal{R}_k^C$ is finite.

For a region $\gamma \in \mathcal{R}_k^C$, we can define $b(\gamma)$ as the truth value of $b(u)$ for any u in γ. Conversely given a region γ, we can easily build a formula of $\mathcal{B}(C)$, called $\beta(\gamma)$, such that $\beta(\gamma)(u) = \mathtt{tt}$ iff $u \in \gamma$. Thus, given a region γ', $\beta(\gamma)(\gamma')$ is mapped to the value $\mathtt{tt}$ precisely when $\gamma = \gamma'$. Finally, note that $\beta(\gamma)$ itself can be viewed as a L_ν formula.

Given a region $[u]$ in $\mathcal{R}_k^C$ and $C' \subseteq C$ we define the following reset operator: $[C' \to 0][u] = [[C' \to 0]u]$. Moreover given a region γ, we can define the successor region of γ (denoted by $succ(\gamma)$): Informally the change from γ to $succ(\gamma)$ correspond to the minimal elapse of time which can modify the enabled actions of the current state(a formal definition is given in [18]).

We denote by γ^l the lth successor region of γ (i.e. $\gamma^l = succ^l(\gamma)$). From each region γ, it is possible to reach a region γ' s.t. $succ(\gamma') = \gamma'$, and we denote by l_γ the required number of step s.t. $\gamma^{l_\gamma} = succ(\gamma^{l_\gamma})$.

Example 3. The Figure 2 gives an overview of the set of regions defined by two clocks x and y, and the maximal constant 1. In this case there are 32 different regions. In general successor regions are determined by following 45° lines upwards to the right.

Given a timed automata $A = \langle \mathcal{A}, N, \eta_0, C, E \rangle$, let k_A be the maximal constant occurring in the enabling condition of the edges E. Then for any $k \geq k_A$ we can define a symbolic semantics of A over symbolic states $[\eta, \gamma]_A$ where $\eta \in N$ and $\gamma \in \mathcal{R}_k^C$ as follows: for any $[\eta, \gamma]$ we have $[\eta, \gamma]_A \xrightarrow{a} [\eta', \gamma']_A$ iff $\exists\, u \in \gamma,\ \langle \eta, u \rangle_A \xrightarrow{a} \langle \eta', u' \rangle_A$ and $u' \in \gamma'$.

Consider now L_ν with respect to formula clock set K and maximal constant k_L. Also consider a given timed automaton $A = \langle \mathcal{A}, N, \eta_0, C, E \rangle$ (s.t. K and C are disjoint). Then an *extended symbolic state* is a pair $[\eta, \gamma]_{A^+}$ where $\eta \in N$ and $\gamma \in \mathcal{R}_k^{C^+}$ with $C^+ = C \cup K$ and $k = max(k_A, k_L)$. We can define the

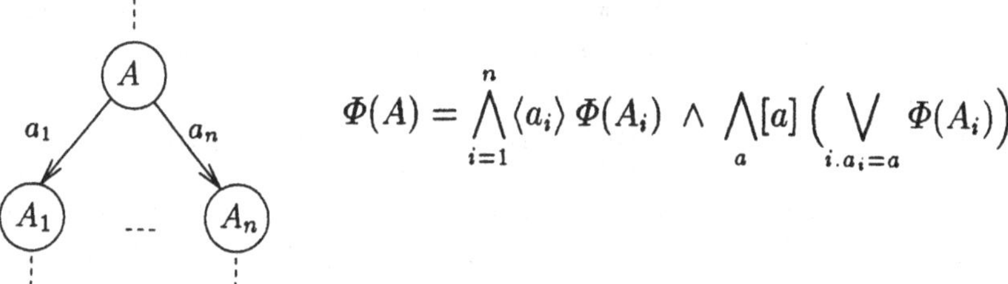

Fig. 3. Characteristic formula for finite automata.

symbolic semantics for L_ν, i.e. the truth value of L_ν formulas over the extended symbolic state. Due to space limitation we only give the two main implications defining the *symbolic satisfiability relation* $\vdash_{\mathcal{D}}$ [5]:

$$[\eta,\gamma]_{A^+} \vdash_{\mathcal{D}} \exists\, \varphi \;\Rightarrow\; \exists l \in \mathbf{N}.\;\; [\eta, succ^l(\gamma)]_{A^+} \vdash_{\mathcal{D}} \varphi$$
$$[\eta,\gamma]_{A^+} \vdash_{\mathcal{D}} \langle a\rangle\, \varphi \;\Rightarrow\; \exists\, [\eta, \gamma_{|C}]_A \xrightarrow{a} [\eta', \gamma'_{|C}]_A \text{ s.t. } \gamma'_{|K} = \gamma_{|K} \wedge [\eta', \gamma']_{A^+} \vdash_{\mathcal{D}} \varphi$$

We have the following important result: Let φ be a formula of L_ν, and let $\langle \eta, v\, u\rangle_{A^+}$ be an extended state over some timed automaton A, then we have [6]:

$$\langle \eta, v\, u\rangle_{A^+} \models_{\mathcal{D}} \varphi \quad \text{if and only if} \quad [\eta, [v \cdot u]]_{A^+} \vdash_{\mathcal{D}} \varphi$$

It follows that the model checking problem for L_ν is decidable since, given $\varphi \in L_\nu$, it suffices to check the truth value of any given L_ν formula φ with respect to a finite transition system corresponding to the extended symbolic semantics of A.

5 Characteristic Properties

First let us recall the characteristic formula construction for finite automata [16, 12, 5] (see Figure 3). The construction defines the characteristic formula $\Phi(A)$ of a node A in terms of similar characteristic formulas of the derivates $A_1 \ldots A_n$ of A: whenever A has an a_i–transition to A_i this is reflected in $\Phi(A)$ by addition of a conjunct $\langle a_i\rangle\Phi(A_i)$. To characterize A up to strong bisimilarity $\Phi(A)$ contains in addition a conjunct $[a]\Psi_a$ for each action a, where Ψ_a is a disjunction over all a–transitions out of A. In general the definitions of characteristic formulas $\Phi(A)$ constitutes a simultaneous recursive definition (as the automaton may have cycles), and to obtain the desired characterization the solution sought is the maximum one. For timed automata the characteristic formula construction must necessarily take account of the time assignment in addition to the actual node. Thus, for a timed automaton $A = \langle \mathcal{A}, N, \eta_0, C, E\rangle$, we shall define characteristic formulas of the form $\Phi(\eta, \gamma)$, where η is a node of A

[5] $\gamma_{|C}$ (resp. $\gamma_{|K}$) denotes the set of time-assignments in γ restricted to the automata (resp. formula) clocks.

[6] where $v \cdot u$ is the time assignment over $C \cup K$ such that $(v \cdot u)(x) = v(x)$ if $x \in C$ and $(v \cdot u)(x) = u(x)$ if $x \in K$.

and γ is a region over the clocks of A. The construction of $\Phi(\eta,\gamma)$ follows closely the pattern from the finite automa case. However, we first need to be able to determine the (a–) edges out of η which are enabled in the region γ. Given an edge $e = \langle \eta, \eta', a, r, b\rangle$ in E, η_e (resp. η'_e, a_e, r_e, b_e) denotes η (resp. η', a, r, b). Given $\eta \in N$ and $\gamma \in \mathcal{R}^C_{k_A}$, we define $E(\eta,\gamma) = \{e \mid \eta_e = \eta \text{ and } b_e(\gamma) = \mathtt{tt}\}$ and $E(\eta,\gamma,a) = \{e \in E(\eta,\gamma) \mid a_e = a\}$. Thus, $E(\eta,\gamma)$ (resp. $E(\eta,\gamma,a)$) is the set of all enabled transitions (resp. a-transitions) from $[\eta,\gamma]_A$. We may now present the characteristic formula construction for timed automata:

Definition 4. Let A be a timed automaton $\langle \mathcal{A}, N, \eta_0, C, E\rangle$. For any region γ in $\mathcal{R}^C_{k_A}$, and node η in N, we introduce an identifier $\Phi(\eta,\gamma)$ (the characteristic formula) associated with the symbolic state $[\eta,\gamma]_A$. The definition (declaration) for $\Phi(\eta,\gamma)$ is:

$$\Phi(\eta,\gamma) \stackrel{\text{def}}{=} \left(\begin{array}{c} \bigwedge_{e\in E(\eta,\gamma)} \langle a_e\rangle \left(r_e \,\mathsf{in}\, \Phi(\eta'_e, r_e(\gamma))\right) \wedge \bigwedge_a [a] \left(\bigvee_{e\in E(\eta,\gamma,a)} \left(r_e \,\mathsf{in}\, \Phi(\eta'_e, r_e(\gamma))\right)\right) \\ \wedge\, \mathbf{\forall}\Big(\bigwedge_{l=0..l_\gamma} \beta(\gamma^l) \Rightarrow \Phi(\eta,\gamma^l)\Big) \end{array}\right)$$

We denote by Id_A the set of identifiers $\Phi(\eta,\gamma)$ and by $\mathcal{D}_A$ the corresponding declaration.

Note that the declaration for $\Phi(\eta,\gamma)$ is not quite a L_ν formula due to the presence of implication. However, it is easy to transform it into an equivalent L_ν formula because the negation of $\beta(\gamma)$ can be expressed in L_ν. Moreover ($r \,\mathsf{in}\, \varphi$) is an abbreviation for $(c_1 \,\mathsf{in}\, (c_2 \,\mathsf{in} \ldots (c_n \,\mathsf{in}\, \varphi)))$ whenever r is $\{c_1,\ldots,c_n\}$. Finally $r(\gamma)$ denotes $[r \to 0]\gamma$. Note that $\mathcal{D}_A$ uses no more than $|C|$ formula clocks.

The declaration for $\Phi(\eta,\gamma)$ contains three groups of conjunctions the two first of which are closely related to the characteristic formula construction for finite automata. The first group contains a $\langle a_e\rangle$–formula for any edge e, which is enabled at η in the region γ. Following this edge clearly takes the automaton to the extended state $[\eta'_e, r_e(\gamma)]$. The second group of conjuncts contains for each action a a formula of the type $[a]\Psi_a$, where Ψ is a disjunction over all a–labelled edges being enabled at η in the region γ. Whereas the two first groups exhaustively characterizes the action behaviour of the extended state $[\eta,\gamma]$, the third conjunct is a $\mathbf{\forall}$–formula dealing with all delay transitions by requiring that any delay leading to a particular successor region γ^l should satisfy the corresponding characteristic formula.

Example 4. Reconsider the timed automaton A described in Example 1 and the corresponding regions from Example 3. Below we give the declaration of some of the characteristic formulas. We define $\varphi_{nil} \stackrel{\text{def}}{=} \bigwedge_a [a]\,\mathtt{ff}$ and we denote $\beta(\gamma_i)$ by β_i. We have:

$$\begin{aligned}\Phi(\eta_0,\gamma_0) &\stackrel{\text{def}}{=} \varphi_{nil} \wedge \mathbf{\forall}\Big[(\beta_0 \Rightarrow \Phi(\eta_0,\gamma_0)) \wedge (\beta_6 \Rightarrow \Phi(\eta_0,\gamma_6)) \wedge (\beta_{14} \Rightarrow \Phi(\eta_0,\gamma_{14})) \\ &\qquad \wedge (\beta_{24} \Rightarrow \Phi(\eta_0,\gamma_{24}))\Big] \\ \Phi(\eta_0,\gamma_6) &\stackrel{\text{def}}{=} \langle a\rangle\, x \,\mathsf{in}\, \Phi(\eta_1,\gamma_1) \wedge [a]\, x \,\mathsf{in}\, \Phi(\eta_1,\gamma_1) \wedge [b]\,\mathtt{ff} \wedge [c]\,\mathtt{ff} \\ &\qquad \wedge \mathbf{\forall}\Big[(\beta_6 \Rightarrow \Phi(\eta_0,\gamma_6)) \wedge (\beta_{14} \Rightarrow \Phi(\eta_0,\gamma_{14})) \wedge (\beta_{24} \Rightarrow \Phi(\eta_0,\gamma_{24}))\Big]\end{aligned}$$

We have the following Main Theorem the proof of which is given in [18].

Theorem 5. *Let* $A = \langle \mathcal{A}, N, \eta_0, C, E\rangle$ *and* $B = \langle \mathcal{A}, M, \rho_0, K, F\rangle$ *be two timed automata. Then for any* $\rho \in M$, $\eta \in N$, $v \in \boldsymbol{R}^K$ *and* $u \in \boldsymbol{R}^C$: $\langle \rho, v\rangle_B \sim \langle \eta, u\rangle_A$ *iff* $\langle \rho, v\ u\rangle_{B^+} \models_{\mathcal{D}_A} \Phi(\eta, [u])$ *where* $\mathcal{D}_A$ *corresponds to the previous definition of* $\Phi(\eta, \gamma)$ *for each* $\eta \in N$ *and* $\gamma \in \mathcal{R}^C_{k_A}$.

As model–checking of L_ν is decidable we may use the above characteristic formula construction to decide timed bisimilarity between timed automata: to decide if two timed automata are timed bisimilar simply compare one automaton to the characteristic formula of the other.

6 Model Construction

In this section we address the *satisfiability* problem for L_ν. That is we want to decide whether there exists a timed automaton A satisfying a given L_ν–formula φ. The hardness of this problem is illustrated by the following 1-clock formula:

$$\Psi_l \stackrel{\text{def}}{=} \Big(\underbrace{\exists]0;\infty[\,\langle a\rangle \cdots \exists]0;\infty[\,\langle a\rangle}_{l}\Big)\Big[\bigwedge_{i=1..l} \exists]0;1[\,\Big(\langle a_i\rangle\,\mathtt{tt} \wedge \bigwedge_{j\neq i}[a_j]\,\mathtt{ff}\Big)\Big]$$

where $l \in \mathbf{N}$. Indeed Ψ_l is satisfiable by some p-clock automata if and only if $l \leq 2p+1$. As a consequence of this remark (see [18]) we cannot deduce the number of clocks in the automaton from the number of clocks in φ. In fact, similar to the results for TCTL and T_μ, we conjecture that the satisfiability problem for L_ν is undecidable.

Instead, we address the following more restricted *bounded satisfiability* problem in which bounds have been placed on both the number of automaton clocks as well as the size of the constants these clocks are compared to: given a formula φ (over a declaration $\mathcal{D}$), a set of clocks C and an integer M, we want to decide (and synthesize) whether there exists a (C, M)–automaton s.t. $A \models_{\mathcal{D}} \varphi$. We have the following main result:

Theorem 6. *The bounded satisfiability problem for* L_ν *is decidable.*

The remainder of this section is devoted to the proof of this theorem and to an example of bounded satisfiability checking. The decision procedure is closely related to the canonical model construction for modal logic [15].
Let φ be a given L_ν formula with k_φ as maximal constant. Let K be the set of formula clocks occurring in φ. Given C a set of clocks (with $C \cap K = \emptyset$) and M an integer, we want to decide if there exists a (C, M)–automaton satisfying φ. Let $C^+ = C \cup K$. Let L^φ_ν be the set of all subformulae of φ. Obviously L^φ_ν is finite.

A *problem* Π is a subset of $\mathcal{R}^{C^+}_k \times L^\varphi_\nu$ where $k = max(M, k_\varphi)$. A problem Π is said to be *satisfiable* if there exists a (C, M)-automaton A and a node η of A such that for any $(\gamma, \psi) \in \Pi$ we have $[\eta, \gamma]_{A^+} \models_{\mathcal{D}} \psi$. We call A a solution to Π. A problem Π is said to be *maximal* if it satisfies the classical closure conditions for the boolean operators and the following ones: $(\gamma, \exists\psi) \in \Pi \Rightarrow \exists l.\ (\gamma^l, \psi) \in \Pi$; $(\gamma, \forall\psi) \in \Pi \Rightarrow \forall l.\ (\gamma^l, \psi) \in \Pi$; $(\gamma, x \text{ in } \psi) \in \Pi \Rightarrow ([\{x\} \to 0]\gamma, \psi) \in \Pi$;

We have the two following remarks, the proofs of which are trivial: (1) If $\Pi \subseteq \Pi'$ and Π' is satisfiable then also Π is satisfiable, and (2) If Π is satisfiable then there exists a maximal problem Π' containing Π and being satisfiable.

Thus it suffices to consider satisfiability of maximal problems. Given a problem Π, a region γ and an action a we define the problem $\Pi_a^{\gamma,r}$ as the set $\{(r(\gamma), \psi) \mid (\gamma, [a]\,\psi) \in \Pi\}$. Now we introduce a new notion about problems. Let $\mathcal{C}$ be a set of maximal problems. Then $\mathcal{C}$ is a *consistency relation* if whenever $\Pi \in \mathcal{C}$ then:

1– $(\gamma, x + m \bowtie y + n) \in \Pi \Rightarrow \gamma(x) + m \bowtie \gamma(y) + n$
2– $\forall\gamma,\ (\gamma, \mathrm{ff}) \notin \Pi$
3– $(\gamma, \langle a\rangle\,\psi) \in \Pi \Rightarrow \exists\, r \subseteq C, b \in \mathcal{B}_M(C)$ and $\Pi' \in \mathcal{C}$ **s.t.** : $b(\gamma) = \mathrm{tt}\ \wedge$
$\quad (\ (r(\gamma), \psi) \cup \Pi_a^{\gamma,r} \subseteq \Pi'\ ) \wedge (\forall\gamma',\ b(\gamma') = \mathrm{tt} \Rightarrow \Pi_a^{\gamma',r} \subseteq \Pi')$

We say that a maximal problem is consistent if it belongs to some consistency relation. We have the following key lemma:

Lemma 7. *Let Π be a maximal problem. Then Π is consistent if and only if Π is satisfiable.*

Proof. $\Rightarrow$ Let $\mathcal{C}$ be a consistency relation (containing Π). Now construct the canonical automaton $A_{\mathcal{C}} = \langle \mathcal{A}, N, \eta_0, C, E\rangle$ s.t. : $N = \{\eta_\Pi \mid \Pi \in \mathcal{C}\}$, η_0 is some $\eta_\Pi \in N$, and $\langle \eta_\Pi, \eta_{\Pi'}, a, r, b\rangle \in E$ iff whenever $(\gamma, [a]\,\psi) \in \Pi$ and $b(\gamma) = \mathrm{tt}$ then $(r(\gamma), \psi) \in \Pi'$.

Now it can be shown that $A_{\mathcal{C}}$ solves all problems of $\mathcal{C}$. In particular whenever $(\gamma, \psi) \in \Pi$ for some $\Pi \in \mathcal{C}$, then $[\eta_\Pi, \gamma]_{A_C^+} \models_{\mathcal{D}} \psi$. Finally we have:

Lemma 8. *It is decidable whether a maximal problem is consistent.*

Proof. Let S_{Π_m} be the set of maximal problems over $\mathcal{R}_k^{C^+} \times L_\nu^\varphi$. Clearly S_{Π_m} is finite (since L_ν^φ and $\mathcal{R}_k^{C^+}$ are too). Thus the set of relations $\mathcal{C}$ over maximal problems is finite. Now given a relation $\mathcal{C}$ it is easy to check whether $\mathcal{C}$ is consistent since the choices for possible reset set r over C and the set $\mathcal{B}_M(C)$ are both finite.

Thus given a formula φ and bounds C and M, we can consider the (finitely many) maximal problems Π over C and M containing (γ_0, φ). It follows that φ is (C, M)–satisfiable precisely if one of these maximal problems is consistent, which is decidable due to Lemma 8. Note that the proof of Lemma 7 is constructive: given a consistency relation it gives a (C, M)-timed automata satisfying φ.

Example 5. Consider the formula φ in Example 2: We can use the model construction algorithm presented above to show that no $(1,1)$-automaton satisfies φ.

Thus the formula in the above example is satisfiable by a 2–clock automaton but by no $(1,1)$–automata. Using the easily established fact that timed bisimilar automata satisfy the same L_ν–formulas it follows that the automaton of Example 2 is inequivalent to all $(1,1)$–automata with respect to timed bisimilarity. Now combining the above bounded model–construction algorithm with the characteristic property construction of the previous section we obtain an algorithm for deciding whether a timed automaton can be simplified in either its number clocks or the size of the constants these clocks are compared to: given a timed automaton A, a clock set C and a natural number M, it is decidable whether there exists a (C, M)–automaton being timed bisimilar to A.

Conclusion

This paper has presented two main results relating timed automata and the real–timed logic L_ν: a *characteristic formula* construction, and, a *bounded model construction* algorithm. The results presented may be pursued and improved in a number of directions: The notion of a characteristic formula construction may be applied to other behavioural preorders. In related work, we have already shown that characteristic formula constructs also exists for the "faster–than"–relation in [11] and the time–abstracted equivalence in [19]; The results of this paper only settles decidability of a *bounded* satisfiability problem for L_ν. However, it follows from this result that the unconstrained satisfiability problem is at least r.e. Decidability of the satisfiability problem with only bounds on the number of clocks remains an open problem. Finally, future work includes study of the decidability of the satisfiability problems for extensions of L_ν.

References

1. R. Alur, C. Courcoubetis, and D. Dill. Model–checking for Real–Time Systems. In *Proceedings of Logic in Computer Science*, pages 414–425. IEEE Computer Society Press, 1990.
2. R. Alur and D. Dill. Automata for Modelling Real–Time Systems. *Theoretical Computer Science*, 126(2):183–236, April 1994.
3. H.R. Andersen. Model checking and boolean graphs. In *Proceedings of ESOP'92*, volume 582 of *Lecture Notes in Computer Science, Springer Verlag*, Berlin, 1992. Springer.
4. A. Arnold and P. Crubille. A linear algorithm to solve fixed–point equations on transition systems. *Information Processing Letters*, 29, 1988.
5. M. C. Browne, E. M. Clarke, and O. Grümberg. Characterizing finite Kripke structures in propositional temporal logic. *Theoretical Computer Science*, 59:115–131, 1988.
6. Karlis Cerans. Decidability of bisimulation equivalences for parallel timer processes. In *Proc. of CAV'92*, volume 663 of *Lecture Notes in Computer Science, Springer Verlag*, Berlin, 1992. Springer Verlag.
7. E. M. Clarke and E. A. Emerson. Design and synthesis of synchronization skeletons using Branching Time Temporal Logic. In *Proc. Workshop on Logics of*

Programs, volume 131 of *Lecture Notes in Computer Science*, pages 52–71, Berlin, 1981. Springer Verlag.

8. E. M. Clarke, E. A. Emerson, and A. P. Sistla. Automatic verification of finite state concurrent system using temporal logic. *ACM Trans. on Programming Languages and Systems*, 8(2):244–263, 1986.
9. R. Cleaveland and B. Steffen. Computing behavioural relations, logically. In *Proceedings of 18th International Colloquium on Automata, Languages and Programming*, volume 510 of *Lecture Notes in Computer Science, Springer Verlag*, Berlin, 1991. Springer.
10. E.A. Emerson and C.L Lei. Efficient model checking in fragments of the propositional mu–calculus. In *Proceedings of Logic in Computer Science*, pages 267–278. IEEE Computer Society Press, 1986.
11. F.Moller and C. Tofts. Relating Processes with Respect to Speed. Technical Report ECS–LFCS–91–143, Department of Computer Science, University of Edinburgh, 1991.
12. S. Graf and J. Sifakis. A Modal Characterization of Observational Congruence on Finite Terms of CCS. *Information and Control*, 68:125–145, 1986.
13. T. A. Henzinger, Z. Nicollin, J. Sifakis, and S. Yovine. Symbolic model checking for real-time systems. In *Logic in Computer Science*, 1992.
14. U. Holmer, K.G. Larsen, and W. Yi. Decidability of bisimulation equivalence between regular timed processes. In *Proceedings of CAV'91*, volume 575 of *Lecture Notes in Computer Science, Springer Verlag*, Berlin, 1992.
15. G.E. Hughes and M.J. Cresswell. *An Introduction to Modal Logic*. Methuen and Co., 1968.
16. A. Ingolfsdottir and B. Steffen. Characteristic formulae. *Information and Computation*, 110(1), 1994. To appear.
17. D. Kozen. Results on the propositional mu–calculus. In *Proc. of International Colloquium on Algorithms, Languages and Programming 1982*, volume 140 of *Lecture Notes in Computer Science, Springer Verlag*, Berlin, 1982.
18. F. Laroussinie, K. G. Larsen, and C. Weise. From Timed Automata to Logic — and Back. Technical Report RS–95–2, BRICS, 1995. Accessible through WWW: http://www.brics.aau.dk/BRICS.
19. K.G. Larsen and Y. Wang. Time Abstracted Bisimulation: Implicit Specifications and Decidability. *In Proceedings of MFPS'93*, 1993.
20. R. Milner. *Communication and Concurrency*. prentice, Englewood Cliffs, 1989.
21. D. Park. Concurrency and automata on infinite sequences. In *Proceedings of 5th GI Conference*, volume 104 of *Lecture Notes in Computer Science, Springer Verlag*, Berlin, 1981. Springer.
22. J. P. Queille and J. Sifakis. Specification and verification of concurrent programs in CESAR. In *Proc. 5th Internat. Symp. on Programming*, volume 137 of *Lecture Notes in Computer Science*, pages 195–220, Berlin, 1982. Springer Verlag.
23. A. Tarski. A lattice–theoretical fixpoint theorem and its applications. *Pacific Journal of Math.*, 5, 1955.
24. Liu Xinxin. *Specification and Decomposition in Concurrency*. PhD thesis, Aalborg University, 1992. R 92–2005.

Incremental Model Checking for Decomposable Structures (Extended Abstract)

J.A. MAKOWSKY* and E.V. RAVVE **

Department of Computer Science
Technion - Israel Institute of Technology
Haifa, Israel
e-mail: {cselena,janos}@cs.technion.ac.il

Abstract. Assume we are given a transition system which is composed from several well identified components. We propose a method which allows us to reduce the model checking of Monadic Second Order formulas in the complex system to model checking of derived formulas in Monadic Second Order Logic in the components.

1 Introduction

In hardware verification (but not only) we find the following situation: We are given a mathematical model of a finite state device in form of a finite relational structure $\mathcal{A}$ (transition system) and a formalized property ϕ. Usually ϕ is given in advance and $\mathcal{A}$ is being built with the aim to satisfy ϕ. Checking whether ϕ holds in $\mathcal{A}$ is to be automatized. This process is called model checking. The literature is rich in papers addressing this problem, [Eme90].

Very often $\mathcal{A}$ is built from components $\mathcal{A}_i$ where $i \in I$ is some index set or structure. In the process of building $\mathcal{A}$ several candidate structures $\mathcal{A}^j$ have to be checked for ϕ, where j denotes the jth attempt of designing $\mathcal{A}$. Often $\mathcal{A}^j$ differs from $\mathcal{A}^{j+1}$ in one component $\mathcal{A}_i^{j+1}$.

The problem we address here, is: How can we exploit this modularity to make the model checking process more efficient. To make this question meaningful, we have to make various aspects more precise.

Choice of the logic. We shall argue in section 2, that Monadic Second Order Logic ($MSOL$) is a good choice to deal with this problem for three reasons: It allows for a workable definition of modularity of structures to be checked, and hence also of the incrementality of model checking. A theorem due to Courcelle and Walukiewicz [Cou93, CW95] allows us to apply our method,

* Partially supported by a grant of the French-Israeli Binational Foundation, by a grant of the German–Israeli Foundation, and by the Fund for Promotion of Research of the Technion–Israeli Institute of Technology

** This paper contains parts of the M.Sc.thesis of the second author, written under the supervision of the first author

at a certain cost, to all other specification languages used in the literature. In [MR95b] we show that similar theorems with less cost involved are valid for Transitive Closure and Fixed Point Logics.

Precise definition of modularity. We propose a notion of modularity based on a generalization of disjoint unions of structures *with additional links between the components*, which depend only on the index structure and specified nodes in the components as described by some table. The table will be represented syntactically by a translation scheme Φ, defined in section 4. Such generalized disjoint unions have a long history in mathematical logic, [Mak85], but were, so far, not exploited for model checking purposes. We shall call them Φ–sums. A motivating example is discussed in great detail in section 3. In section 6 we shall discuss realistic examples which falls under this definition, and exhibit others which provably do not.

Complexity measures. To measure the advantage of this method we shall differ from the usual approach, which looks at the cost of checking *once*, whether $\mathcal{A}$ satisfies ϕ, and uses either the size of $\mathcal{A}$, the size of ϕ or the sum of the two as the relevant input size. We shall ask, what our method can gain by repeating this process many times, with small changes at a time. For this purpose we also look at the size of the changed component and the number of iterations. A detailed discussion of these cost evaluations is given in section 7.

Our main result shows how the truth of ϕ in $\mathcal{A}$ depends on the components $\mathcal{A}_i$ of $\mathcal{A}$ and the index structure $\mathcal{I}$. The exact formulation of this is rather involved and is explained in detail in section 5. It is an extension of the Feferman–Vaught Theorem, [FV59] for First Order Logic to $MSOL$, which seems to be new. Special cases have been considered in the literature ad hoc in [She75, Gur79, She92]. For First Order Logic the Feferman–Vaught theorem covers a very wide class of generalized products and sums of structures (here representing transition systems or processes) and is extremely powerful. Our extension of this theorem for Monadic Second Order Logic works only for a more restricted class of *sum-like* structures. As a negative result we show in section 6 that our theorem does not apply to certain synchronized product construction used in building parallel synchronized transition systems.

From the theorem we derive a method for checking ϕ in $\mathcal{A}$ which proceeds as follows:

Preprocessing. Given ϕ and Φ, but no $\mathcal{A}$, we construct a sequence of formulas $\psi_{i,j}$ and a boolean function $F_{\Phi,\phi}$. This construction is polynomial in the size of ϕ and Φ.

Initialization. Assume our first structure $\mathcal{A}^0$ has to be checked. In a first run we compute the boolean values $b_{i,j}$ defined by

$$b_{i,j} = 1 \text{ iff } \mathcal{A}_i \models \psi_{i,j}.$$

Checking ϕ. The theorem now states that $\mathcal{A}^0 \models \phi$ iff $F_{\Phi,\phi}(\bar{b}) = 1$.

Iteration. If a new $\mathcal{A}^1$ has to be checked differing from $\mathcal{A}^0$ only in, say, $\mathcal{A}_1^1$, we only have to recompute the values $a_{1,j}$ and $F_{\Phi,\phi}$.

A close analysis in section 7 of this process reveals that, even if the model checking procedure is already polynomial, considerable gains in efficiency are possible under our scenario of incremental, i.e. stepwise building and verification of the design.

2 Why Monadic Second Order Logic

2.1 Basics

Our choice of hardware specification language is Monadic Second Order Logic (MSOL). Recall that Second Order Logic (SOL) is like first order logic, but allows also variables and quantification over relation variables of various but fixed arities. Monadic Second Order Logic is the sublogic of SOL where relation variables are restricted to be unary. The meaning function of formulas is explained for arbitrary τ–structures where τ is the vocabulary, i.e. a finite set of relation and constant symbols. We do not consider here the case of adding function symbols. We denote by $\mathcal{A}, \mathcal{B}$ structures and their underlying sets by A, B.

The relation variables will range also over infinite sets, when the structures considered are infinite.

The quantifier rank of formulas is defined as usual taking the maximum for $\vee, \wedge$ and $\neg$, and augmenting by 1 in case of quantification.

Two structures $\mathcal{A}$ and $\mathcal{B}$ are n-equivalent with respect to some logic $\mathcal{L}$, which we denote it by $\mathcal{A} \equiv_n \mathcal{B}(\mathcal{L})$, if all the formulas of logic $\mathcal{L}$ with quantifier depth n have the same truth value in these structures. Similarly, We denote by $Th^n_{\mathcal{L}}(\mathcal{A})$ a set of all formulas with n quantifier of some logic $\mathcal{L}$, which hold in $\mathcal{A}$, and by $Th_{\mathcal{L}}(\mathcal{A})$ a set of all formulas of $\mathcal{L}$, which are true in $\mathcal{A}$. If the context makes it clear we shall omit $\mathcal{L}$.

2.2 Expressive Power of Monadic Second Order Logic

Monadic Second Order Logic has considerable expressive power. Most of the logics used in hardware verification are sublogics of it. Very often in hardware specification one models the device by a finite relational structure $\mathcal{A}$ and associates with it an infinite structure $bhv(\mathcal{A})$ the behaviour of $\mathcal{A}$. By abuse of notation, one speaks of formulas true in $\mathcal{A}$, but they are really explained on $bhv(\mathcal{A})$. However, using powerful tools based on ideas related to Rabin's theorem on the decidability of $MSOL$ on infinite trees, [Rab69], Courcelle [Cou93], and Courcelle and Walukiewicz [CW95] proved:

Theorem 1 (Courcelle and Walukiewicz). *Every $MSOL$ expressible property of the behavior of a transition system is equivalent to some $MSOL$ expressible property of the transition system.*

This theorem justifies our restriction to MSOL over finite structures (transition systems). However, the translation of formulas over the behaviour to formulas over the transition system comes at a considerable cost and is at best feasible for small formulas.

3 Motivating Examples

In this section we show how several well known $MSOL$-properties over some graph composition can be reduced to components.

Assume we are given two undirected finite graphs $\mathcal{A}_1 = \langle V_{A_1}, E_{A_1}, P_{A_1} \rangle$ and $\mathcal{A}_2 = \langle V_{A_2}, E_{A_2}, Q_{A_2} \rangle$, where V_{A_i} denotes a set of vertices, E_{A_i} denotes a set of edges and P_{A_1}, Q_{A_2} are one place relations (vertex colorings) respectively. Let $\mathcal{A}$ be the disjoint union of $\mathcal{A}_1$ and $\mathcal{A}_2$ with additional edges forming a complete bipartite graph on the colored vertices. We define this composition of two colored graphs formally as follows: $\mathcal{A} = \mathcal{A}_1 \heartsuit \mathcal{A}_2 = \langle V_A = V_{A_1} \dot{\cup} V_{A_2}, E \rangle$, where $V_{A_1} \dot{\cup} V_{A_2}$ denotes disjoint union of sets of vertices, and a pair of vertices (x, y) of ${V_A}^2$ belongs to E iff

$$\Phi : (x, y) \in E_{A_1} \vee (x, y) \in E_{A_2} \vee (x \in P_{A_1} \wedge y \in Q_{A_2}) \vee (x \in Q_{A_2} \wedge y \in P_{A_1})$$

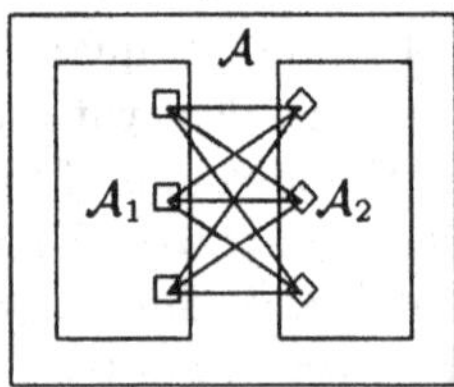

Fig. 1. Composition of Two Graphs: $\mathcal{A}_1$ and $\mathcal{A}_2$.

We want to check whether $\mathcal{A}$ is connected, has cycles or is 3–colourable.

3.1 Connectivity

It is easily seen that

(*) $\mathcal{A}$ is connected iff both in $\mathcal{A}_1$ and $\mathcal{A}_2$ it is true that every connected component has at least one colored vertex.

We observe the following:

- Connectivity can be expressed by a formula of Monadic Second Order Logic ϕ_{conn}.

- The property that every connected component has at least one colored vertex can be expressed by formulas of Monadic Second Order Logic ψ_1 and ψ_2 respectively.
- Φ can be expressed by a formula of Monadic Second Order over the disjoint union of $\mathcal{A}_1$ and $\mathcal{A}_2$. Actually, in this example, $\Phi(x, y)$ is a quantifierfree First Order formula.
- To check whether $\mathcal{A}$ is connected ($\mathcal{A} \models \phi_{conn}$) it suffices to check, using (*), that $\mathcal{A}_1 \models \psi_1$ and $\mathcal{A}_2 \models \psi_2$.
- Moreover, by defining boolean values $b_i = 1$ iff $\mathcal{A}_i \models \psi_i$ there is a boolean function F such that $\mathcal{A} \models \phi_{conn}$ iff $F(b_1, b_2) = 1$.
- To check whether $\mathcal{A}$ is not connected ($\mathcal{A} \models \neg\phi_{conn}$) it suffices to evaluate F again and to check that $F(b_1, b_2) = 0$.
- The formulas ψ_i and the boolean function F depend only on the syntactic structure of Φ and ϕ_{conn}, but not on the structures $\mathcal{A}_i$.
- If we have checked the connectivity of $\mathcal{A}$ and now wish to check the connectivity of $\mathcal{A}' = \mathcal{A}'_1 \heartsuit \mathcal{A}_2$ for a different $\mathcal{A}'_1$ we just have to recompute $\mathcal{A}'_1 \models \psi_1$, and $F(b'_1, b_2)$ for $b'_1 = 1$ iff $\mathcal{A}'_1 \models \psi_1$, but we do not have to recompute b_2.

3.2 Cycles and 3–Colorability

To check whether $\mathcal{A}$ has cycles we observe that

> (**) $\mathcal{A}$ has a cycle iff $\mathcal{A}_1$ has a cycle, or $\mathcal{A}_2$ has a cycle, or there are at least two connected colored vertices in $\mathcal{A}_1$ and at least one colored vertex in $\mathcal{A}_2$, or the same with 1 and 2 inverted.

and proceed similarly as follows.

- We first write the property as a formula ϕ in Monadic Second Order Logic.
- Then, using (**), which depends only on ϕ and Φ, we look for formulas $\psi_{1,1}, \ldots, \psi_{1,n_1}$ and $\psi_{2,1}, \ldots, \psi_{2,n_2}$ in Monadic Second Order Logic, which will give us the properties to be checked in $\mathcal{A}_1$ and $\mathcal{A}_2$ respectively.
- Then, again using (**), we look for a boolean function F in n_1+n_2 arguments $b_{1,1}, \ldots, b_{2,n_2}$.
- Now we put $b_{i,j} = 1$ iff $\mathcal{A}_i \models \psi_{i,j}$ and hope to conclude that $\mathcal{A} \models \phi$ iff $F(b_{1,1}, \ldots, b_{2,n_2}) = 1$.

Surprisingly, our main theorem 11 implies that this method can be mechanized, even if (**) is not given in advance. The reader should convince himself of this by computing the case 3-Colorability directly. We note here also, that the finiteness of the structures is not needed in the proof.

3.3 Generalizations

We have explained our main result by using a very simple example of a disjoint union of two colored graphs with some edges added, defined by Φ. The general theorem generalizes to combination of more than two structures and more complicated additional relations.

To make this more transparent we proceed in two stages:

- We first look at the disjoint union of structures $\mathcal{A}_i$ where I is a larger index set, and more generally, an index structure $\mathcal{I}$ equipped with its own relations such as successor, order, or, in the most general case, any finite number of relations. For the exact formulation of the most general situation we have to assume that $\mathcal{I}$ has a definable partition into finitely many sets. The general method for such disjoint unions is described in theorem 9.
- Disjoint unions are not very interesting as such. To get the method applicable to real life situations we take advantage of translation schemes, described in section 4. Combined in this way with translation schemes disjoint unions capture the most general situation in which the method works. The Φ used in the above example is a simple instance of such a translation scheme.

More complicated examples are given in section 6.

4 Translation Schemes

In this section we introduce the general framework for syntactically defined translation schemes. We introduce also the notion of abstract translation schemes which goes back to Rabin [Rab65], but see also [Imm87, Dah82] and [Cou94].

Definition 2. Translation Schemes Φ.
Let τ and σ be two vocabularies and $\mathcal{L}$ be a logic, such as FOL or $MSOL$. Let $\sigma = \{R_1, \ldots, R_m\}$ and let $\rho(R_i)$ be the arity of R_i. Let $\Phi = \langle \phi, \psi_1, \ldots, \psi_m \rangle$ be formulas of $\mathcal{L}(\tau)$. Φ is *k-feasible for σ over τ* if ϕ has exactly k distinct free first order variables and each ψ_i has $k\rho(R_i)$ distinct free first order variables. Such a $\Phi = \langle \phi, \psi_1, \ldots, \psi_m \rangle$ is also called a *k-τ-σ-translation scheme* or, shortly, a *translation scheme*, if the parameters are clear in the context.
k is a vectorization parameter. We call translation schemes *scalar (non-vectorized)* if $k = 1$.

With a translation scheme Φ we can naturally associate (partial) functions

Φ^* from τ-structures to σ-structures and
$\Phi^\#$ from $\mathcal{L}(\sigma)$-formulas to $\mathcal{L}(\tau)$-formulas.

For details, cf. [Cou94, EFT94, MR95a].

Observation 3. *(i) $\Phi^\#(\theta) \in FOL$ (SOL) provided $\theta \in FOL$ (SOL), even for vectorized Φ $(k \geq 2)$.*
(ii) $\Phi^\#(\theta) \in MSOL$ provided $\theta \in MSOL$, but only for non-vectorized Φ $(k = 1)$.

In the sequel, we assume that Φ^* is not vectorized, unless stated otherwise.
The following facts hold (for proof see [EFT94]).

Proposition 4.
Let $\Phi = \langle \phi, \psi_1, \ldots, \psi_m \rangle$ be a k-τ-σ-translation scheme, $\mathcal{A}$ a τ-structure and θ a $\mathcal{L}(\sigma)$-formula. Then $\mathcal{A} \models \Phi^\#(\theta)$ iff $\Phi^*(\mathcal{A}) \models \theta$.

Proposition 5.
Let $\Phi = \langle \phi, \psi_1, \ldots, \psi_m \rangle$ be a k-τ-σ-translation scheme, $\mathcal{A}$ a τ-structure. In this case if $Th(\mathcal{A})$ is decidable then $Th(\Phi^*(\mathcal{A}))$ is decidable too.

5 Piecing Structures Together

In this section we discuss various ways of obtaining transition systems from smaller components.

5.1 Disjoint Union

The *Disjoint Union* of a family of structures is the simplest example of juxtaposing structures where none of the components are linked to each other.

Definition 6 (Disjoint Union).
Let $\tau_\imath = \langle R_1^\imath, \ldots, R_{j^\imath}^\imath, c_1^\imath, \ldots, c_{\ell^\imath}^\imath \rangle$ be a vocabulary of $\mathcal{A}_\imath$. In the general case the resulting structure is $\mathcal{A} = \bigsqcup_{\imath \in I} \mathcal{A}_\imath = \langle I \cup \dot{\bigcup}_{\imath \in I} A_\imath, P(\imath, x), I(x), R_j^I(1 \leq j \leq \jmath^I), R_{j^\imath}^\imath(\imath \in I, 1 \leq j^\imath \leq \jmath^\imath), c_{l^\imath}^\imath(\imath \in I, 1 \leq l^\imath \leq l^\imath) \rangle$ for all $\imath \in I$, where $P(\imath, x)$ is true iff x came from $\mathcal{A}_\imath$ and $I(x)$ is true iff x came from $\mathcal{I}$.

Definition 7 (Partitioned Index Structure). Let $\mathcal{I}$ be an index structure. $\mathcal{I}$ is called *finitely partitioned* into ℓ parts if there are unary predicates I_α, $\alpha < \ell$, in the vocabulary of $\mathcal{I}$ such that their interpretation forms a partition of the universe of $\mathcal{I}$.

Using *Ehrenfeucht-Fraïssé* games for $MSOL$, [Ehr61], it is easy to see that

Theorem 8. *Let $\mathcal{I}, \mathcal{J}$ be two (not necessary finitely) partitioned index structures over the same vocabulary such that for $i, j \in I_\ell$ and $i', j' \in J_\ell$ $\mathcal{A}_i$ and $\mathcal{A}_j$ ($\mathcal{B}_{i'}$ and $\mathcal{B}_{j'}$) are isomorphic.*

(i) If $\mathcal{I} \equiv_{MSOL}^n \mathcal{J}$, and $\mathcal{A}_i \equiv_{MSOL}^n \mathcal{B}_i$ then $\dot{\bigcup}_{i \in I} \mathcal{A}_i \equiv_{MSOL}^n \dot{\bigcup}_{j \in J} \mathcal{B}_j$.
(ii) If $\mathcal{I} \equiv_{MSOL}^n \mathcal{J}$, and $\mathcal{A}_i \equiv_{FOL}^n \mathcal{B}_i$ then $\dot{\bigcup}_{i \in I} \mathcal{A}_i \equiv_{FOL}^n \dot{\bigcup}_{j \in J} \mathcal{B}_j$.

. If, as in our applications, there are only finitely many different components, we can prove a stronger statement, dealing with formulas rather than theories.

Theorem 9. *Let $\mathcal{I}$ be a finitely partitioned index structure.*
Let $\mathcal{A} = \bigsqcup_{i \in I} \mathcal{A}_i$ be a τ-structure, where each $\mathcal{A}_i$ is isomorphic to some $\mathcal{B}_1, \ldots, \mathcal{B}_\ell$ over the vocabularies $\tau_1, \ldots, \tau_\ell$, in accordance to the partition (ℓ is the number of the classes).
For every $\phi \in MSOL(\tau)$ there are:

- *a boolean function $F_\phi(b_{1,1}, \ldots, b_{1,j_1}, \ldots, b_{\ell,1}, \ldots, b_{\ell,j_\ell}, b_{I,1}, \ldots, b_{I,j_I})$*
- *$MSOL$-formulas $\psi_{1,1}, \ldots, \psi_{1,j_1}, \ldots, \psi_{\ell,1}, \ldots, \psi_{\ell,j_\ell}$*
- *$MSOL$-formulas $\psi_{I,1}, \ldots, \psi_{I,j_I}$*

such that for every $\mathcal{A}$, $\mathcal{I}$ and $\mathcal{B}_\imath$ as above with $\mathcal{B}_\imath \models \psi_{\imath,\jmath}$ iff $b_{\imath,\jmath} = 1$ and $\mathcal{B}_I \models \psi_{I,\jmath}$ iff $b_{I,\jmath} = 1$ we have

$$\mathcal{A} \models \phi$$

iff

$$F_\phi(b_{1,1}, \ldots, b_{1,j_1}, \ldots, b_{\ell,1}, \ldots, b_{\ell,j_\ell}, b_{I,1}, \ldots, b_{I,j_I}) = 1$$

Moreover, F_ϕ and the $\psi_{\imath,\jmath}$ are computable from ϕ, ℓ and vocabularies alone, but are exponential in the quantifier depth of ϕ.

Proof: By analyzing the proof of theorem 8 and tedious book keeping. □

5.2 Sum–like Structures

The disjoint union as such is not very interesting. However, combining it with translation schemes gives as a rich repertoire of patching techniques.

Definition 10 Sum–like Structures. Let $\mathcal{I}$ be a finitely partitioned index structure.
Let $\mathcal{A} = \dot{\bigsqcup}_{i\in I}\mathcal{A}_i$ be a τ–structure, where each $\mathcal{A}_i$ is isomorphic to some $\mathcal{B}_1,\ldots,\mathcal{B}_\ell$ over the vocabularies $\tau_1,\ldots,\tau_\ell$, in accordance with the partition.
Furthermore let Φ be a scalar (i.e. non–vectorized) τ–σ $MSOL$–translation scheme.
The Φ–sum of $\mathcal{B}_1,\ldots,\mathcal{B}_\ell$ over $\mathcal{I}$ is the structure $\Phi^*(\mathcal{A})$, or rather any structure isomorphic to it.

Theorem 11. *Let $\mathcal{I}$ be a finitely partitioned index structure and let $\mathcal{A}$ be the Φ–sum of $\mathcal{B}_1,\ldots,\mathcal{B}_\ell$ over $\mathcal{I}$, as above.*
For every $\phi \in MSOL(\tau)$ there are:

- *a boolean function $F_{\Phi,\phi}(b_{1,1},\ldots,b_{1,j_1},\ldots,b_{\ell,1},\ldots,b_{\ell,j_\ell},b_{I,1},\ldots,b_{I,j_I})$*
- *$MSOL$–formulas $\psi_{1,1},\ldots,\psi_{1,j_1},\ldots,\psi_{\ell,1},\ldots,\psi_{\ell,j_\ell}$*
- *$MSOL$–formulas $\psi_{I,1},\ldots,\psi_{I,j_I}$*

such that for every $\mathcal{A}$, $\mathcal{I}$ and $\mathcal{B}_\imath$ as above with $\mathcal{B}_\imath \models \psi_{\imath,\jmath}$ iff $b_{\imath,\jmath} = 1$ and $\mathcal{B}_I \models \psi_{I,\jmath}$ iff $b_{I,\jmath} = 1$ we have

$$\mathcal{A} \models \phi$$

iff

$$F_{\Phi,\phi}(b_{1,1},\ldots,b_{1,j_1},\ldots,b_{\ell,1},\ldots,b_{\ell,j_\ell},b_{I,1},\ldots,b_{I,j_I}) = 1$$

Moreover, $F_{\Phi,\phi}$ and the $\psi_{\imath,\jmath}$ are computable from $\Phi^{\#}$ and ϕ , but are exponential in the quantifier depth of ϕ.

Proof: By analyzing the proof of theorem 9 and using theorem 4. □

6 Examples

Now we will consider several examples. The first is asynchronous parallel composition of processes, including the pipeline design. However, it is much more general and is better described as *uniform graph substitution.* The next is synchronized parallel composition of processes.

6.1 Uniform Graph Substitution (Pipelines)

Let us consider the following composition of two input graphs $\mathcal{H}$ and $\mathcal{G}$. $\mathcal{G}$ can be viewed as a display graph, where on each node we want to have a copy of $\mathcal{H}$, such that certain additional edges are added. In practice this is a model on how a pipeline works. The nodes marked with L^j are the latches.

Let $\mathcal{G} = \langle G, R\rangle$ and $\mathcal{H} = \langle H, S, L^j(j \in J)\rangle$ be two relational structures (J is finite), then their composition $\mathcal{C} = \langle C, L^1_C, ..., L^{|J|}_C, S_C, R^j_C(j \in J)\rangle$ is defined as following (according to notations of definition 6):

- $C = \dot{\bigcup}_{g \in G} H^g$;
- $L^j_C(w)$ is true if w belongs to L^j;
- $S_C = \{(w, v) : w \in H^g, v \in H^g, S(w, v)\}$;
- $R^j_C = \{(w, v) : L^j(w), L^j(v), P(i, w), P(i', v), R(i, i')\}$.

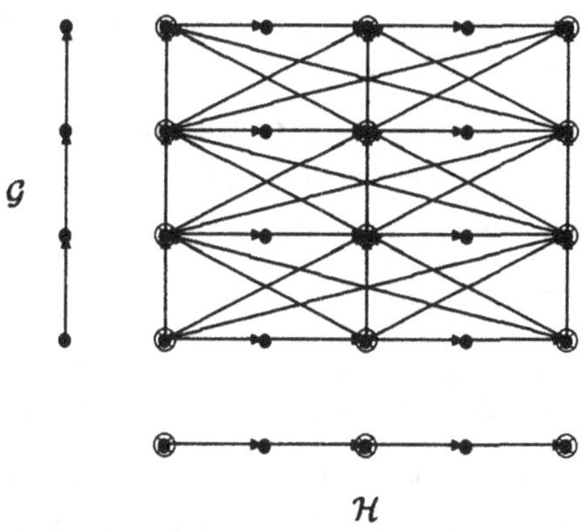

Fig. 2. Uniform Graph Substitution.

In Fig. 2 we give an example of such a substitution, where $\mathcal{H}$ has only one predicate L, labeled by $\otimes$. It is easy to see that this construction can be obtained from the Cartesian product $\mathcal{G} \times \mathcal{H}$ by a FOL translation scheme without vectorization. However, the Cartesian product cannot be obtained from $\dot{\bigsqcup}_{g \in G} \mathcal{H}$ without vectorization. However, $\mathcal{C}$ can also be obtained from the disjoint union $\dot{\bigsqcup}_{g \in G} \mathcal{H}$ by a FOL translation scheme without vectorization. The following proposition makes precise.

Proposition 12.
$\mathcal{C}$ is isomorphic to $\Phi^*(\dot{\bigsqcup}_{g \in G} \mathcal{H})$ with $\Phi = \langle \phi, \psi_{L^1_C}, \ldots, \psi_{L^J_C}, \psi_S, \psi_{R^1_C}, \ldots, \psi_{R^J_C} \rangle$ and $\phi = \exists i(P(i, x) \wedge I(i)), \psi_{L^j_C} = \exists i((P(i, x) \wedge I(i)) \wedge L^j(x)), \psi_S = \exists i((I(i) \wedge (P(i, w) \wedge P(i, v))) \wedge S(w, v)), \psi_{R^j_C} = \exists i \exists i'((((I(i) \wedge I(i')) \wedge R(i, i')) \wedge (L^j(w) \wedge L^j(v))) \wedge (P(i, w) \wedge P(i', v)))$.

In this example, depending on the choice of the interpretation of the L^j's, more sophisticated parallel computations can be modelled, but not all.

6.2 Synchronous Parallel Composition

Our next example is a synchronized parallel transition system, which is not sum–like. We consider the parallel composition of transition systems as studied in [GL94]. The transition systems here are given as follows.

Definition 13. Given a structure $\mathcal{S} = \langle S; S_0, R, X_\wp(\wp \in \Re)\rangle$, where.

(i) S is a finite set of states.
(ii) S_0 is a relation for set of initial states.
(iii) $R \subseteq S \times S$ is a transition relation.
(iv) $X_\wp = \{s \in S : s \models \wp\}$ where $\Re$ is a finite set of atomic propositions.

Now the synchronous product is defined as follows ($\Im(s)$ denotes a set of all atomic propositions, which are true in s):

Definition 14. Let $\mathcal{S}$ and $\mathcal{S}'$ be two structures as above. The composition of $\mathcal{S}$ and $\mathcal{S}'$, denoted $\mathcal{S} \parallel \mathcal{S}'$, is the structure $\mathcal{S}''$ defined by

Atomic Propositions $\Re'' = \Re \cup \Re'$.
States $S'' = \{(s, s') \in S \times S' \mid \Im(s) \cap \Re' = \Im(s') \cap \Re\}$.
Initial States $S_0'' = (S_0 \times S_0') \cap S''$.
Unary Predicates $(s, s') \in X_\wp''$ iff $s \in X_\wp$ or $s' \in X_\wp'$.
Transition Relation $R''((s, s'), (t, t'))$ iff $R(s, t)$ and $R'(s', t')$.

Theorem 15. *There are no unary Φ, $\mathcal{I}$ and $\mathcal{S}_\imath$, such that $\mathcal{S}'' = \mathcal{S} \| \mathcal{S}'$ is isomorphic to $\Phi(\dot{\bigsqcup}_{\imath \in I} \mathcal{S}_\imath)$. In other words, the synchronized parallel composition of two transition systems is not, in general, sum–like.*

Proof:
The simplest case of this composition is the Cartesian Product of components. Now, by Büchi's theorem, the $MSOL$–theory of one successor is decidable, whereas, the $MSOL$–theory of the Cartesian product of two copies of one successor relation is not. □

7 Complexity Consideration

In this section we discuss under what conditions theorem 9 improves the complexity of model checking, when measured in the size of the composed structure only. Our scenarios are as follows: A formula (set of formulas) ϕ is given in advance. A structure (transition system) is now submitted to the model checker and we want to know, how long it takes to check whether ϕ is true. The first scenario (Scenario A) consists of checking one structure. More realistically, in Scenario B, we check several structures, which differ from each other only in small components.

Model checking for $MSOL$ is likely to be non–polynomial, as it sits fully in the polynomial hierarchy PH.

Most Hardware Verification Languages are stronger than FOL but weaker than $MSOL$, and their model checking complexity is polynomial. In [MR95b] we discuss our method for such languages. From theorem 9 we conclude that:

Observation 16. *(i) Function $F_{\Phi,\phi}$ gives a Model Checker of $\mathcal{A}$ with the help of Model Checkers of $\mathcal{A}_i$ and index structure $\mathcal{I}$.*
(ii) Theorem 9 is useless if the $\mathcal{A}_i$ and index structure $\mathcal{I}$ are not "easily" obtained from $\mathcal{A}$.

Assume that $\mathcal{A}$ is sum-like. Its components are $\mathcal{A}_i$ with index structure $\mathcal{I}$, and we want to check whether ϕ is true in $\mathcal{A}$. Assume that:

- $\mathcal{T}(N)$ denotes time to solve the problem by the usual way (N denotes the size of structure $\mathcal{A}$);
- $\mathcal{E}_I$ denotes time to extract index structure $\mathcal{I}$ from $\mathcal{A}$;
- $\mathcal{E}_i$ denotes time to extract each $\mathcal{A}_i$ from $\mathcal{A}$;
- $\mathcal{C}_I(n_I)$ denotes time to compute all values of $b_{I,j}$, where n_I is the size of I;
- $\mathcal{C}_i(n_i)$ denotes time to compute all values of $b_{i,j}$, where n_i is the size of A_i;
- $\mathcal{T}_{F_{\Phi,\phi}}$ denotes time to build $F_{\Phi,\phi}$;
- $\mathcal{T}_{search} = \mathcal{T}_S$ denotes time to search one result in the table of $F_{\Phi,\phi}$.

According to these symbols new checking time is:

$$\mathcal{T}_{new} = \mathcal{E}_I + \Sigma_{i\in I}\mathcal{E}_i + \mathcal{C}_I + \Sigma_{i\in I}\mathcal{C}_i + \mathcal{T}_{F_{\Phi,\phi}} + \mathcal{T}_S$$

and the question to answer is: Under what conditions is it true that $\mathcal{T} > \mathcal{T}_{new}$.

In the case of Scenario A, time gain is only obtained when the property to be checked is not polynomially checkable. However, in Scenario B time is saved already after a small number of iteration. A detailed analysis is given in the full paper [MR95a].

8 Conclusion

We have shown how to use the Feferman–Vaught Theorem and its generalization to Monadic Second Order Logic in the context of model checking of transition systems. In [MR95b] we have analyzed the same method also for Transitive Closure and Fixed Point Logic.

In the case of Φ-sums the method yields considerable complexity reductions for model checking of $MSOL$-formulas in the case of incremental model checking.

We concentrated here on model checking of properties of transition systems. But the method is much more general and in future work we shall analyze other applications as well.

Acknowledgements

We are would like to thank S.Shelah, who gave us his manuscript [She92]. The first author had stimulating discussions with Y. Hirshfeld and E. Clarke in the early stages of this research. In later stages, B. Courcelle, A. Arnold, D.Niwiński and O. Grumberg helped us in finding more examples to which we could apply our method. We would also like to thank the referees of MFCS'95 for their constructive comments.

References

[Cou93] B. Courcelle. The monadic second-order logic of graphs IX: Machines and their behaviours. Preprint, 1993.

[Cou94] B. Courcelle. Monadic second order graph transductions: A survey. *Theoretical Computer Science*, 126:53–75, 1994.

[CW95] B. Courcelle and I. Walukiewicz. Monadic second order logic, graphs and unfoldings of transition systems. Paper in preparation, 1995.

[Dah82] E. Dahlhaus. *Combinatorial and Logical Properties of Reductions to some Complete Problems in NP and NL.* PhD thesis, Technische Universität Berlin, Germany, 1982.

[EFT94] H.D. Ebbinghaus, J. Flum, and W. Thomas. *Mathematical Logic, 3rd edition.* Undergraduate Texts in Mathematics. Springer-Verlag, 1994.

[Ehr61] A. Ehrenfeucht. An application of games to the completeness problem for formalized theories. *Fundamenta Mathematicae*, 49:129–141, 1961.

[Eme90] E.A. Emerson. Temporal and modal logic. In J. van Leeuwen, editor, *Handbook of Theoretical Computer Science*, volume 2, chapter 16. Elsevier Science Publishers, 1990.

[FV59] S. Feferman and R. Vaught. The first order properties of products of algebraic systems. *Fundamenta Mathematicae*, 47:57–103, 1959.

[GL94] O. Grumberg and D.E. Long. Model checking and modular verification. *ACM Trans. on Programming Languages and Systems*, 16(3):843–871, 1994.

[Gur79] Y. Gurevich. Modest theory of short chains, I. *Journal of Symbolic Logic*, 44:481–490, 1979.

[Imm87] N. Immerman. Languages that capture complexity classes. *SIAM Journal on Computing*, 16(4):760–778, Aug 1987.

[Mak85] J.A. Makowsky. Compactness, embeddings and definability. In *Model-Theoretic Logics*, Perspectives in Mathematical Logic, chapter 18. Springer Verlag, 1985.

[MR95a] J.A. Makowsky and E. Ravve. Incremental model checking for decomposable structures. Technical Report TR848, revised version, April 1995, Department of Computer Science, Technion–Israel Institute of Technology, Haifa, Israel, 1995.

[MR95b] J.A. Makowsky and E. Ravve. Incremental model checking for fixed point properties of decomposable structures. Technical Report TR844, revised version, April 1995, Department of Computer Science, Technion–Israel Institute of Technology, Haifa, Israel, 1995.

[Rab65] M.A. Rabin. A simple method for undecidability proofs and some applications. In Y. Bar Hillel, editor, *Logic, Methodology and Philosophy of Science II*, Studies in Logic, pages 58–68. North Holland, 1965.

[Rab69] M. Rabin. Decidability of second order theories and automata on infinite trees. *Transactions of American Mathematical Society*, 141:1–35, 1969.

[She75] S. Shelah. The monadic theory of order. *Annals of Mathematics*, 102:379–419, 1975.

[She92] S. Shelah. On the very weak 0–1 law for random graphs with orders. Preprint, 1992.

Automata for the modal μ-calculus and related results

David Janin
LaBRI[1]
U.E.R. de Mathématiques et d'Informatique
Université de Bordeaux I
351, Cours de la Libération,
FR-33405 Talence Cedex, France
e-mail: janin@labri.u-bordeaux.fr

Igor Walukiewicz
BRICS[2,3]
Department of Computer Science
University of Aarhus
Ny Munkegade
DK-8000 Aarhus C, Denmark
e-mail: igw@daimi.aau.dk

Abstract. The propositional μ-calculus as introduced by Kozen in [4] is considered. The notion of disjunctive formula is defined and it is shown that every formula is semantically equivalent to a disjunctive formula. For these formulas many difficulties encountered in the general case may be avoided. For instance, satisfiability checking is linear for disjunctive formulas. This kind of formula gives rise to a new notion of finite automaton which characterizes the expressive power of the μ-calculus over all transition systems.

1 Introduction

We consider the propositional μ-calculus as introduced by Kozen [4]. Subsequent research showed that the μ-calculus is an interesting logic when specification and verification is concerned. It is an expressive logic; on binary trees it is as expressive as the monadic second order logic of two successors [8, 3]. On the other hand, if computational complexity is concerned, the propositional μ-calculus is not much more difficult than classical propositional logic as its decidability problem is EXPTIME complete. Because of these and other features the logic is considered to be one of the most interesting logics of programs.

The two main results we present here are:

- Definition of the class of *disjunctive formulas* and the proof that every formula is equivalent to a disjunctive formula.
- Characterization of the μ-calculus by means of a new kind of automata on transition systems.

The methods developed here allow us also to obtain other know results as corollaries. In particular we show that our results subsume the results of Niwinski and Emerson and Jutla [8, 3]. We obtain yet another proof of Rabin's complementation lemma.

It was already discovered by Kozen in [4] that the interplay of all the connectives of the μ-calculus raises some challenging difficulties. Here we try to analyze these difficulties. Our first step is to give alternative "operational" semantics of the μ-calculus formulas. We look at a formula as an automaton-like device checking a property of the unwinding of a model from a given state.

If we are to check that $\langle a \rangle \alpha$ holds, we choose an edge from this state labeled by a leading to a state where α holds. If we are to check that $\alpha \vee \beta$ holds, we choose (nondeterministically) one of the disjuncts. If we are to check $\sigma X.\alpha(X)$, when σ is μ or ν, we try the equivalent formula $\alpha(\sigma X.\alpha(X))$. The distinction between least (μ) or greatest (ν) fixed points is achieved using suitable infinitary acceptance conditions. When we check $\alpha \wedge \beta$ we must check that this state satisfies both α and β.

While disjunctions act like nondeterministic choices, conjunctions act rather like universal branching of alternating automata. Such an alternating behavior of conjunctions is the source of many difficulties.

From automata theory we know that alternating automata are equivalent to nondeterministic ones [7]. This suggests that every formula should be equivalent to a formula which does not have universal branching behaviors represented by conjunctions. Of course we cannot discard conjunctions completely from positive formulas as shown by the formula $(\langle a \rangle p) \wedge [a](p \vee q)$. Note that the conjunction in this formula does not act as a universal branching. It is rather like an implicit conjunction from (usual, not alternating) automata on trees where transition relation forces the right son to be labeled by one state and the left son by another one. Such a kind of implicit conjunction is the only form of conjunction that appears in the fixpoint notation for sets of trees defined by Niwiński [8]. It was proved that this fixpoint language has the same expressive power as the monadic second order logic of n successors. Hence adding explicit conjunction to this language will not increase its expressive power.

These considerations lead to the notion of *disjunctive formulas* which are formulas where the role of conjunction is restricted so that it never acts as an universal branching. We show that every formula is equivalent to a disjunctive formula. It turns out that the satisfiability problem is linear for disjunctive formulas. There is also a straightforward method of model construction for such formulas. In comparison, the satisfiability problem for arbitrary formulas is EXPTIME-complete and the only known method of model construction involves nontrivial reduction to Rabin automata on infinite trees.

Disjunctive formulas also hint the possibility of giving automata-like characterization of the μ-calculus. In [8, 3] it was shown that over binary trees the μ-calculus is as expressive as the monadic second order logic (MS-logic for short). Nevertheless it is not true that over arbitrary transition systems the μ-calculus is as expressive as MS-logic. It is not even true when we restrict the class of models to trees with nodes of finite but unbounded degrees. In both cases μ-calculus is strictly weaker than MS-logic.

Notice that these general trees can be encoded into binary trees. For a given μ-calculus formula we can construct, say, a Rabin automaton which recognizes codings of the models of the formula. But this is only a one way mapping. It is not true that for every Rabin automaton there is a μ-calculus formula having as models exactly the transition systems of which codings are accepted by the automaton.

We propose a notion of automaton of which expressive power is exactly the same as the μ-calculus. Restricted to binary trees these automata are just alternating automata with so-called parity conditions [6, 3]. They are more general because they admit runs over arbitrary transition systems. We show that there are direct translations between disjunctive formulas and this kind of automata. This proves that the set of recognizable languages induced by our notion of automata is closed under all boolean operators hence also complementation. If we consider μ-calculus restricted to binary trees then our constructions give us ordinary (non alternating) parity automata on trees. This way we obtain a proof of Rabin's complementation lemma and the results from [8, 3].

The paper is organized as follows. We start by giving basic definitions including a new formula constructor and the notion of binding functions. In the second section we describe operational semantics of formulas. In the third we present the notion of disjunctive formulas and prove properties of such formulas. Next section is devoted to the new kind of automata which we call μ-automata.

2 Preliminary definitions

Let $Prop = \{p, q, \ldots\} \cup \{\bot, \top\}$ be a set of propositional letters, $Var = \{X, Y, \ldots\}$ a set of variables and $Act = \{a, b, \ldots\}$ a set of actions. Formulas of the μ-calculus over these sets can be defined by the following grammar:

$$F := Prop \mid \neg Prop \mid Var \mid F \vee F \mid F \wedge F \mid \langle Act \rangle F \mid [Act]F \mid \mu Var.F \mid \nu Var.F$$

Note that we allow negations only before propositional constants. As we will be interested mostly in closed formulas this is not a restriction. All the results presented here extend to the general case when negation before variables is also allowed, restricting as usual to positive occurrences of bound variables.

In the following, $\alpha, \beta, \gamma, \ldots$ will denote formulas, and $A, B, C \ldots$ will denote finite sets of formulas. We shall use σ to denote either μ or ν. Variables, propositional constants and their negations will be called *literals*.

Formulas are interpreted in *transition systems* of the form $\mathcal{M} = \langle S, R, \rho \rangle$, where:

- S is a nonempty set of states,
- $R : Act \to \mathcal{P}(S \times S)$ is a function assigning a binary relation on S to each action in Act.
- $\rho : Prop \to \mathcal{P}(S)$ is a function assigning a set of states to every propositional constant.

For a given model $\mathcal{M}$ and an assignment $Val : Var \to \mathcal{P}(S)$, the set of states in which a formula α is true, denoted $\|\alpha\|^{\mathcal{M}}_{Val}$, is defined inductively as follows (we will omit superscript $\mathcal{M}$ when it causes no ambiguity):

$$\|p\|_{Val} = \rho(p) \quad \|\bot\|_{Val} = \emptyset \quad \|\top\|_{Val} = S$$
$$\|\neg p\|_{Val} = S - \rho(p)$$
$$\|X\|_{Val} = Val(X)$$
$$\|\alpha \vee \beta\|_{Val} = \|\alpha\|_{Val} \cup \|\beta\|_{Val}$$
$$\|\alpha \wedge \beta\|_{Val} = \|\alpha\|_{Val} \cap \|\beta\|_{Val}$$
$$\|\langle a\rangle\alpha\|_{Val} = \{s : \exists s'.(s,s') \in R(a) \wedge s' \in \|\alpha\|_{Val}\}$$
$$\|[a]\alpha\|_{Val} = \{s : \forall s'.(s,s') \in R(a) \Rightarrow s' \in \|\alpha\|_{Val}\}$$
$$\|\mu X.\alpha(X)\|_{Val} = \bigcap\{S' \subseteq S : \|\alpha\|_{Val[S'/X]} \subseteq S'\}$$
$$\|\nu X.\alpha(X)\|_{Val} = \bigcup\{S' \subseteq S : S' \subseteq \|\alpha\|_{Val[S'/X]}\}$$

here $Val[S'/X]$ is the valuation such that, $Val[S'/X](X) = S'$ and $Val[S'/X](Y) = Val(Y)$ for $Y \neq X$. We shall write $\mathcal{M}, s, Val \models \alpha$ when $s \in \|\alpha\|^{\mathcal{M}}_{Val}$.

2.1. Definition (Binding). We call a formula *well named* iff every variable is bound at most once in the formula and free variables are distinct from bound variables. For a variable X bound in a well named formula α there exists a unique subterm of α of the form $\sigma X.\beta(X)$, from now on called the *binding definition of X in α* and denoted $\mathcal{D}_\alpha(X)$. We will omit subscript α when it causes no ambiguity. We call X a *μ-variable* when $\sigma = \mu$, otherwise we call X a *ν-variable.*

The function $\mathcal{D}_\alpha$ assigning to every bound variable its *binding definition* in α will be called the *binding function* associated with α.

2.2. Definition (Dependency order). Given a formula α we define the *dependency order* over the bound variables of α, denoted $\leq_\alpha$, as the least partial order relation such that if X occurs free in $\mathcal{D}_\alpha(Y)$ then $X \leq_\alpha Y$. We will say that a bound variable Y depends on a bound variable X in α when $X \leq_\alpha Y$.

2.3. Definition. Variable X in $\mu X.\alpha(X)$ is *guarded* iff every occurrence of X in $\alpha(X)$ is in the scope of some modality operator $\langle\,\rangle$ or $[\,]$. We say that a formula is guarded iff every bound variable in the formula is guarded.

2.4. Proposition (Kozen). *Every formula is equivalent to some guarded formula.*

This proposition allows us to restrict ourselves to guarded, well-named formulas. From now on, we shall only consider formulas of this kind. This restriction is not essential to what follows but simplifies definitions substantially.

In construction of our tableaux we shall distinguish some occurrences of conjunction which should not be reduced by ordinary (*and*) rule.

2.5. Definition. We extend the syntax of the μ-calculus by allowing new construction of the form $a \to A$, where a is an action and A is a finite set of formulas. Such a formula will be semantically equivalent to $\bigwedge\{\langle a\rangle\alpha | \alpha \in A\} \wedge [a] \bigvee A$. Namely state q satisfies formula $a \to A$ when any formula of A is satisfied by at least one a-successor of state q, and any a-successor of state q satisfies at least one formula of A. We adopt the convention that the conjunction of the empty set of formulas is the formula $\top$ and disjunction of the empty set is $\bot$.

2.6. Remark. A formula $\langle a\rangle\alpha$ is equivalent to $a \rightarrow \{\alpha, \top\}$ and a formula $[a]\alpha$ is equivalent to $a \rightarrow \{\alpha\} \vee a \rightarrow \emptyset$. It follows that any formula can be written with this new construction in place of modalities. All the notions defined in this section like bound variable definitions, guardedness, etc. extend to formulas with this new construction.

3 "Operational semantics"

Here we will describe alternative "operational" semantics for the formulas of the μ-calculus. We will show that a formula is satisfied in a state s of a structure $\mathcal{M}$ with a valuation *Val* iff there is a consistent marking of a tableau for the formula. This characterization gives us a tool for proving equivalence of formulas.

Let γ be a well-named, guarded formula where construction $a \rightarrow A$ is used instead of $\langle a\rangle\alpha$ and $[a]\alpha$ constructions.

3.1. Definition. We define the system of tableau rules $\mathcal{S}^{\gamma}$ parameterized by a formula γ, or rather its binding function:

$$(and)\ \frac{\{\alpha,\beta,C\}}{\{\alpha\wedge\beta,C\}} \qquad (or)\ \frac{\{\alpha,C\}\quad\{\beta,C\}}{\{\alpha\vee\beta,C\}}$$

$$(\mu)\ \frac{\{\alpha(X),C\}}{\{\mu X.\alpha(X),C\}} \qquad (\nu)\ \frac{\{\alpha(X),C\}}{\{\nu X.\alpha(X),C\}}$$

$$(reg)\qquad \frac{\{\alpha(X),C\}}{\{X,C\}} \qquad \text{whenever } X \text{ is a bound variable of } \gamma \text{ and } \mathcal{D}_{\gamma}(X)=\sigma X.\alpha(X)$$

$$(mod)\quad \frac{\{\alpha\}\cup\{\bigvee B : a\rightarrow B\in\{C\}, B\neq A\} \quad \text{for every } a\rightarrow A\in\{C\}, \alpha\in A}{\{C\}}$$

with $\bigvee\emptyset$ interpreted as $\bot$.

3.2. Remark. The rule (*mod*) has as many premises as there are formulas in the sets A such that $a \rightarrow A \in C$. For instance

$$\frac{\{\alpha_1,\alpha_3\}\quad\{\alpha_2,\alpha_3\}\quad\{\alpha_1\vee\alpha_2,\alpha_3\}\quad\{\beta_1\}\quad\{\beta_2\}}{\{a\rightarrow\{\alpha_1,\alpha_2\}, a\rightarrow\{\alpha_3\}, b\rightarrow\{\beta_1,\beta_2\}\}}$$

is an instance of the rule.

3.3. Remark. We see applications of the rules as a process of reduction. Given a finite set of formulas C we want to derive, we look for the rule the conclusion of which matches our set. Then we apply the rule and obtain the assumptions of the instance of the rule whose conclusion is C.

3.4. Definition. A *tableau* for γ is a pair $\langle T, L\rangle$, where T is a tree and L is a labeling function such that:

1. the root of T is labeled by $\{\gamma\}$,

2. the sons of any node n are created and labeled according to the rules of system $\mathcal{S}^\gamma$, with *rule (mod) applied only when no other rule is applicable.*

Leaves and nodes where (*mod*) rule was applied will be called *modal nodes*. The root of $\mathcal{T}$ and sons of modal nodes will be called *choice nodes*. We will say that m is *near* n iff there is a path from n to m in the tableau without an application of modal rule.

3.5. Remark. Returning to our example of an instance of the rule (*mod*) from Remark 3.2. If a node n is labeled by the conclusion of this instance then it has five sons labeled by corresponding assumptions. We will call a son obtained by *reducing* an action a an *a-son*. In our example n has three a-sons and two b-sons. Node n is a modal node, its sons are choice nodes.

3.6. Definition (Marking). For a tableau $\mathcal{T} = \langle T, L\rangle$ we define its *marking* with respect to a structure $\mathcal{M} = \langle S, R, \rho\rangle$ and state s_0 to be a relation $M \subseteq S \times T$ satisfying the following conditions:

1. $(s_0, r) \in M$, where r is a root of T.
2. If some pair (s, m) belongs to M and a rule other than (*mod*) was applied in m, then for some son n of m, $(s, n) \in M$.
3. If $(s, m) \in M$ and rule (*mod*) was applied in a node m then for every action a for which exists a formula of the form $a \dot{\rightarrow} A$ in $L(n)$:
   (a) for every a-son n of m there exists a state t such that $(s, t) \in R(a)$ and $(t, n) \in M$.
   (b) for every state t such that $(s, t) \in R(a)$ there exists an a-son n of m such that $(t, n) \in M$.

3.7. Definition (Trace). Given a path $\mathcal{P}$ of a tableau $\mathcal{T} = \langle T, L\rangle$, a *trace* on $\mathcal{P}$ will be a function F assigning a formula to every node in some initial segment of $\mathcal{P}$ (possibly to the whole $\mathcal{P}$), satisfying the following conditions:

- If $F(n)$ is defined then $F(n) \in L(n)$.
- Let m be a node with $F(m)$ defined and let $n \in \mathcal{P}$ be a son of m. If a rule applied in m does not reduce the formula $F(m)$ then $F(n) = F(m)$. If $F(m)$ is reduced in m then $F(n)$ is one of the results of the reduction. This should be clear for all the rules except (*mod*). In case m is a modal node and n is labeled by $\{\delta\} \cup \{\bigvee B : a \rightarrow B \in C, B \neq A\}$ for some $a \rightarrow A \in L(m)$ and $\delta \in A$, then $F(n) = \delta$ if $F(m) = a \rightarrow A$ and $F(n) = \bigvee B$ if $F(m) = a \rightarrow B$ for some $a \rightarrow B \in C$, $B \neq A$. Traces from other formulas end in node m.

3.8. Definition (μ-trace). We say that there is a *regeneration* of a variable X on a trace F on some path iff for some node m and its son n on the path $F(m) = X$ and $F(n) = \alpha(X)$ with $\mathcal{D}_\gamma(X) = \sigma X.a(X)$, i.e. rule (*reg*) was applied to variable X.

We call a trace *μ-trace* iff it is an infinite trace (defined for the whole path) on which the smallest variable, with respect to $\leq_\alpha$ ordering, regenerated i.o. is a μ-variable. Similarly a trace will be called a *ν-trace* iff it is an infinite trace where the the smallest variable, with respect to $\leq_\alpha$ ordering, regenerated i.o. is a ν-variable.

3.9. Remark. Every infinite trace is either a μ-trace or a ν-trace because all the rules except regenerations decrease the size of formulas and formulas are guarded hence every formula is eventually reduced. Observe that even though $\leq_\alpha$ is a partial ordering there is always the least variable required in the above definition.

3.10. Definition (Consistent marking). Using notation from the Definition 3.6, a marking M of $\mathcal{T}$ with respect to $\mathcal{M}$ and s is *consistent* with respect to $\mathcal{M}, s$, *Val* iff it satisfies the following conditions:

local consistency for every modal node m and state t, if $(t, m) \in M$ then $\mathcal{M}, t, Val \models A'$, where A' is the set of all the literals occurring in $L(m)$,
global consistency for every path $\mathcal{P} = n_0, n_1, \ldots$ of T such that for every $i = 0, 1, \ldots$ there exist s_i with $(s_i, n_i) \in M$ there is no μ-trace on $\mathcal{P}$.

The following theorem gives a characterization of satisfiability by means of consistent markings.

3.11. Theorem. *A positive guarded formula γ is satisfied in a structure $\mathcal{M}$, state s and valuation Val iff there exists a marking M of a tableau for γ consistent with $\mathcal{M}, s$, Val.*

Proof. The proof uses transfinite approximations of fixed point expressions and signatures in the style of those defined in [9].

4 A disjunctive normal form theorem

In this section we define a notion of *disjunctive formula* and show that every formula is equivalent to a disjunctive formula.

4.1. Definition. The set of *disjunctive formulas*, $\mathcal{F}_d$ is the smallest set defined by the following clauses:

1. every variable is a disjunctive formula,
2. if $\alpha, \beta \in \mathcal{F}_d$ then $\alpha \vee \beta \in \mathcal{F}_d$; if moreover X occurs only positively in α and not in the context $X \wedge \gamma$ for some γ, then $\mu X.\alpha, \nu X.\alpha \in \mathcal{F}_d$,
3. formula $\alpha_1 \wedge \ldots \wedge \alpha_n$ is a disjunctive formula provided that every α_i is either a literal or a formula of a form $a \to A$ with $A \subseteq \mathcal{F}_d$. Moreover we require that for any action a there can be at most one conjunct of the form $a \to A$ among $\alpha_1, \ldots, \alpha_n$.

4.2. Remark. Many properties can be "naturally" expressed by disjunctive formulas. For example the properties q holds almost always and q holds infinitely often can be written as the following disjunctive formulas:

$$\mu X.((a \to \{X\}) \vee \nu Y.(q \wedge a \to \{Y\})) \qquad \nu X.\mu Y.((q \wedge a \to \{X\}) \vee a \to \{Y\})$$

4.3. Remark. Modulo the order of application of (*and*) rules, disjunctive formulas have unique tableaux. Moreover on any infinite path there is one and only one infinite trace.

4.4. Theorem. *For every formula there exists an equivalent disjunctive formula.*

Proof. Let $\mathcal{T}$ be a regular tableau for a formula γ. A graph obtained from a tree by adding edges from some leaves to their ancestors will be called a *tree with back edges*. Added edges will be called *back edges*. First one needs to prove:

4.5. Lemma. *It is possible to construct a finite tree with back edges $\mathcal{T}_l = \langle T_l, L_l \rangle$, satisfying the following conditions:*

1. *$\mathcal{T}_l$ unwinds to $\mathcal{T}$.*
2. *Every node to which a back edge points can be assigned color magenta or navy in such a way that for any infinite path from the unwinding of $\mathcal{T}_l$ we have: there is a μ-trace on the path iff the highest node of $\mathcal{T}_l$ through which the path goes i.o. is colored magenta.*

To prove the lemma one takes a deterministic parity automaton $\mathcal{A}$ [6, 3] which recognizes paths of $\mathcal{T}$ having μ-trace on them. Then one can run $\mathcal{A}$ on every path of $\mathcal{T}$. This gives an assignment of states of $\mathcal{A}$ to nodes of $\mathcal{T}$. Obtained tree is still regular and we can use parity condition to present it in the desired form.

Next one constructs from $\mathcal{T}_l$ a disjunctive formula $\widehat{\gamma}$ which has a tableau equivalent to $\mathcal{T}$. The construction starts in the leaves of the tree and proceeds to the root. All back edges leading to a node n are assigned the same variable X_n and the color of the node is used to decide which fixpoint operator should be used to close this variable when we reach n in our construction.

In [9] the general technique of model construction for the μ-calculus formulas was described. Till now it remains essentially the only known technique for model construction (see [5] for different approach). It turns out that in case of disjunctive formulas model construction is much easier. This is described in the following theorem.

4.6. Theorem. *A closed disjunctive formula α is satisfiable iff the formula β obtained from α by replacing all occurrences of μ-variables by $\bot$ and all ν-variables by $\top$ is satisfiable.*

Proof. Let $\mathcal{T}_\alpha$ and $\mathcal{T}_\beta$ be tableaux for α and β respectively. There exists a function h which for any node of $\mathcal{T}_\alpha$ gives us the corresponding node of $\mathcal{T}_\beta$, mapping variables to corresponding constants. This situation is schematically represented in Figure 1. It is quite easy to show that if α is satisfiable then β is satisfiable. This can be done by induction on the structure of α.

Conversely, assume β is satisfiable and let M be a minimal (w.r.t. inclusion) marking of $\mathcal{T}_\beta$ consistent w.r.t. some arbitrary model $\mathcal{M}$ for β. It is quite easy, using h^{-1} and the modal nodes occurring in M, to build a regular model of β together with a marking M' of $\mathcal{T}_\alpha$ consistent with that model such that no μ-variable is ever regenerated on any path of that marking.

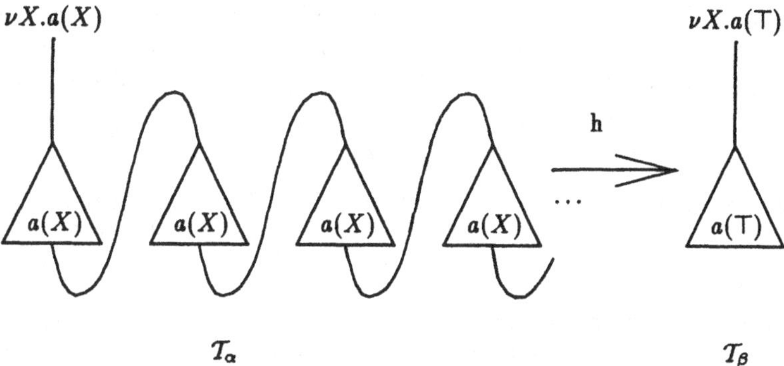

Fig. 1. Relation between $\mathcal{T}_\alpha$ and $\mathcal{T}_\beta$

Because β in the above theorem is a disjunctive formula without fixpoint operators we have:

4.7. Corollary. *Satisfiability checking for disjunctive formulas can be done in linear time.*

5 Automata for the μ-calculus

The question we ask here is what concept of automaton characterizes the expressive power of the μ-calculus over transition systems.

The idea of constructing automata able to deal with arbitrary branching was already considered in [1] but the construction proposed there would give us to big expressive power.

5.1. Definition. A *μ-automaton* is a tuple $\mathcal{A} = \langle Q, \Sigma_p, \Sigma_a, q_0, \delta, \Omega \rangle$ where: Q is a finite set of states, Σ_p, Σ_a are finite alphabets called *proposition* and *action* alphabets respectively, $q_0 \in Q$ is the initial state, $\delta : Q \to \mathcal{P}(\Sigma_p \times (\Sigma_a \dot{\to} \mathcal{P}(Q)))$ is a transition function and $\Omega : Q \to \mathcal{N}$ is a indexing function defining acceptance conditions. Here, $\Sigma_a \dot{\to} \mathcal{P}(Q)$ denotes the set of partial functions from Σ_a to $\mathcal{P}(Q)$.

5.2. Definition. A *labeled transition system restricted* to Σ_a and Σ_p is a tuple

$$\mathcal{T} = \langle S, s_0 \in S, R : \Sigma_a \to \mathcal{P}(S \times S), \rho : S \to \Sigma_p \rangle$$

where s_0 is the *initial state*, ρ defines labeling of states and R defines edges between states together with their labeling.

5.3. Remark. From given finite sets of actions Σ_a and literals L_p and given transition system with some valuation it is straightforward to construct a labeled transition system restricted to Σ_a and $\Sigma_p = \mathcal{P}(L_p)$. There is also an obvious translation in the opposite direction assuming, say, that all variables not in Σ_p are always false and that there are no other edges.

5.4. Definition. For a restricted transition system $\mathcal{T}$ and an automaton $\mathcal{A}$ as the above we define a *run* of $\mathcal{A}$ on $\mathcal{T}$ to be an infinite labeled tree T satisfying the following conditions:

- The root is labeled by (q_0, s_0).
- For any node of the tree labeled (q, s) there is a pair $(p, f) \in \delta(q)$ such that $p = \rho(s)$ and for every action a in the domain of f (assumed partial):
  - ⋆ for every $q_a \in f(a)$ there is a son labeled (q_a, t) for some t with $(s, t) \in R(a)$,
  - ⋆ for every t with $(s, t) \in R(a)$ there is $q_a \in f(a)$ and a son labeled (q_a, t)

The run is accepting iff for any path $\mathcal{P}$, $\min\{\Omega(q) : q$ appears i.o. on $\mathcal{P}\}$ is even.

We would like to prove that automata of this kind have exactly the same expressive power as the μ-calculus.

5.5. Theorem. *For any disjunctive formula γ there is an equivalent μ-automaton.*

Proof. Let $\mathcal{T}$ be a tree with back edges unwinding into a tableau for γ. We build an automaton recognizing exactly the models of γ. Its set of states is $Q = (CN \times BV)$ where CN is the set of choice nodes (see Definition 3.4). Transitions are build from a state (n, X) to a state (m, Y) whenever m is near n, with Y the smallest variables regenerated on the path from n to m or $*$ if there is no such.

5.6. Theorem. *For any μ-automaton $\mathcal{A}$ we can construct an equivalent disjunctive formula.*

Proof. Construct a tree with back edges from the automaton in the style of Lemma 4.5. Then construct a formula from this tree.

5.7. Corollary. *μ-automata are closed under all the connectives of the μ-calculus. In particular they are closed under negation.*

5.8. Remark. A transition system is called *labeled binary tree* iff every state has exactly two transitions: one labeled "l" and one labeled "r". Exactly the same argument as in Theorem 4.4 shows that over labeled binary trees every formula of the μ-calculus is equivalent to a disjunctive formula where each special conjunction is of the form $l \to \{\alpha_l\} \wedge r \to \{\alpha_r\} \wedge \Gamma$ with Γ containing only literals. It follows that μ-automata built from such formulas correspond exactly to usual (non alternating) automata with so called *parity condition*[6, 3]. This shows that μ-calculus is equivalent to Rabin automata and that μ-automata are closed under boolean connectives. In particular this gives a proof of Rabin's complementation lemma.

References

1. O. Bernholtz and O. Grumberg. Branching time temporal logic and amorphous tree automata. In *Proc. 4th Conference on Concurrency Theory*, volume 715 of *Lecture Notes in Computer Science*, pages 262–277. Springer-Verlag, 1993.
2. E.A. Emerson and C.S. Jutla. The complexity of tree automata and logics of programs. In *29th IEEE Symp. on Foundations of Computer Science*, 1988.
3. E.A. Emerson and C.S. Jutla. Tree automata, mu calculus and determinacy. In *Proc. FOCS 91*, 1991.
4. D. Kozen. Results on the propositional mu-calculus. *Theoretical Computer Science*, 27:333–354, 1983.
5. D. Kozen. A finite model theorem for the propositional μ-calculus. *Studa Logica*, 47(3):234–241, 1988.
6. A.W. Mostowski. Regular expressions for infinite trees and a standard form of automta. In A. Skowron, editor, *Fith Symposium on Computation Theory*, volume 208 of *LNCS*, pages 157–168, 1984.
7. D.E. Muller and P.E. Schupp. Alternating automata on infinite trees. *Theoretical Computer Science*, 54:267–276, 1987.
8. D. Niwiński. Fixed points vs. infinite generation. In *Proc. 3rd. IEEE LICS*, pages 402–409, 1988.
9. R.S. Street and E.A. Emerson. An automata theoretic procedure for the propositional mu-calculus. *Information and Computation*, 81:249–264, 1989.

[1] Laboratoire Bordelais de Recherche en Informatique

[2] Basic Research in Computer Science,
Centre of the Danish National Research Foundation.

[3] On leave from: Institute of Informatics, Warsaw University, Banacha 2, 02-097 Warsaw, POLAND

A ν-Calculus with Local Views for Systems of Sequential Agents

Peter Niebert

Institut für Informatik, Universität Hildesheim
niebert@informatik.uni-hildesheim.de

Abstract. We present $\nu TrTL$, a (partial order) logic based on "local" next operators and fixpoint definitions. It extends Thiagarajan's trace based generalization of propositional temporal logic (TrPTL). Both logics are interpreted over systems consisting of a fixed number of sequential processes (locations) running concurrently and occasionally synchronizing via joint actions.
We give a reduction of $\nu TrTL$ formulas to Büchi asynchronous automata, which also yields decision procedures for both satisfiability and model checking.

1 Introduction

Temporal logics are a widely accepted specification and verification formalism in several areas of computer science, in particular in the field of *reactive systems*. The most widely used approach assumes a discrete and totally ordered time structure (natural numbers as time instances), as the logic LTL (linear time temporal logic), which is based on the temporal operators "next" and "until". In such a framework the connection to the behaviour of concurrent systems is given by an *interleaving semantics*, which assumes events observed in a total order.

On the other hand *partial order semantics* for concurrent systems, where the ordering of events represents *causal dependency*, are sometimes more appropriate than interleaving models, because they are more abstract, yet contain all meaningful information about the concurrent behaviour: this explains the successful application of partial order models in model checking.

A recent and promising approach to logics for partial order semantics has been taken by Thiagarajan with his *trace based extension of temporal logic* $TrPTL$ [Thi94]. Thiagarajan's framework uses a semantic model related to Mazurkiewicz traces, presented by a fixed number of processes at a set of locations *Loc*, which communicate by synchronizing events. A global state of such a system is the product of the local states of the locations. The key idea is to interpret temporal operators such as 'until' and in particular "next" only relatively to the "view" of one location (local time), and it assumes that atomic properties are local to some location.

Moreover Thiagarajan has demonstrated how to extend the automata theoretic approach [VW86] to the satisfiability and model checking problems of $TrPTL$. For this purpose, *Büchi Asynchronous automata*, a special class of Büchi automata running on traces, are used. At the same time this gives an upper bound for the expressiveness of $TrPTL$.

In this paper we present a fixpoint extension of Thiagarajan's trace based temporal logic. For temporal logics in the world of interleaving semantics it is well known that the usual temporal operators such as "until" can be expressed using next-step modalities and fixpoint definitions [Koz83], see also [Sti92]. Usually such logics (based on some kind of next and fixpoints) are of greater expressiveness, but they also have the conceptual advantage of separating problems related to relatively simple "next" operators on the one hand and the problems related to fixpoints or iteration/recursion on the other hand. This general observation is also reflected in the construction of this paper.

The logic in [Thi94] already contains local next-operators (similar to modalities in the propositional μ-calculus). Based on these "simple" modalities and *local* fixpoints we develop the logic $\nu TrTL$, which subsumes trace based temporal logic.

We show how to extend the automata theoretic construction for $TrPTL$ to our logic (by combining the methods of [ES89] with those in [Thi94] and [MS93]). The difficult part was to map the Streett-Emerson framework to asynchronous automata, for which a positive (complement free) formulation of acceptance conditions was necessary. Moreover we have simplified the construction of [Thi94] in several respects by defining an adapted automaton model. As a result we obtain decision procedures for both satisfiability and model checking.

The results of this work are not surprising, and we consider them as one of several intermediate steps in the development of location or causality based partial order temporal logics. There still remain many unanswered expressiveness questions, for example, whether $\nu TrTL$ is expressively equivalent or (as we expect) weaker than the automaton model.

In section 2 we introduce the underlying semantic model. In section 3 the logic is defined and we indicate how to define $TrPTL$ operators with fixpoints. In section 4 we define asynchronous automata with local Büchi conditions. In section 5 we analyse technical properties to prepare the translation of formulas to equivalent automata, which is given in section 6. In section 7 we summarize the decidability results achieved by the construction.

2 Semantic Models

The location based approach to Mazurkiewicz traces considers parallel system of sequential processes, which communicate via joint actions [Thi94].

More precisely we assume a set of locations $Loc = \{1, ..., K\}$, a *distributed alphabet* $\widetilde{\Sigma} = (\Sigma_1, ..., \Sigma_K)$, and a set $\widetilde{\mathcal{P}} = (\mathcal{P}_1, ..., \mathcal{P}_K)$ of local propositions, where $\mathcal{P}_i$ denotes the set of propositions affiliated with location i. The sets Σ_i may overlap and we define $\Sigma = \bigcup_{i=1}^{K} \Sigma_i$ as the set of all actions. Likewise the sets $\mathcal{P}_i$ may overlap, i.e. a proposition may be affiliated with several locations, and we define $\mathcal{P} = \bigcup_{i=1}^{K} \mathcal{P}_i$. A frequently used notion is the set of locations participating in an action a, hence the notation $Loc(a) = \{i \in Loc;\ a \in \Sigma_i\}$, and similarly $Loc(P) = \{i;\ P \in \mathcal{P}_i\}$.

For a partial order $(E, \leq)$ and $M \subseteq E$, let $\downarrow M = \{e \in E; \exists e' \in M. e \leq e'\}$, the *downward closure* of M. We write $\downarrow e$ for $\downarrow \{e\}$.

Now we define partially ordered runs over such systems: a *frame* over $\widetilde{\Sigma}$ is a labelled poset $F = (E, \leq, \lambda)$, where E is a countable set of *events*, with $\leq$ a partial order on E, and $\lambda : E \longrightarrow \Sigma$ a labelling. Further let $E_i = \{e \in E;\ \lambda(e) \in \Sigma_i\}$, the set of i-events. For each i the restriction $\leq|_{E^i \times E^i}$ is total, (i.e. the events of one agent are causally ordered), and the global order $\leq$ is the least partial order containing the local (total) orders.

A *configuration* c of a frame F is a finite, downward closed set of events (i.e. $\downarrow c = c$). Let C_F denote the set of all configurations of the frame F. We define a *localization* of configurations, the *i-view*: $\downarrow^i c := \downarrow (c \cap E_i)$, i.e. the least configuration, that coincides with c on i-events. On configurations we define a *successor relation*, such that $c \xrightarrow{a} d$ iff $d = c \cup \{e\}$ for an $e \in E$ with $\lambda(e) = a$.

An *interpretation of a frame* is a mapping $I : \widetilde{\mathcal{P}} \longrightarrow 2^{C_F}$ such that $\downarrow^i c = \downarrow^i c'$ implies that $c \in I(P)$ iff $c' \in I(P)$ for all $P \in \mathcal{P}_i$, i.e. the interpretation of propositions affiliated with location i depends only on i-events. Moreover this implies that a proposition affiliated with several locations may only be changed by joint actions of these locations.

3 The logic

Now we define the logic $\nu TrTL$. For the moment we will do so in a rather general fashion. Later it turns out, that further restrictions on the syntax of allowed formulas are necessary.

Let $\widetilde{\mathcal{P}}$ and $\widetilde{\Sigma}$ be as above. Let $\mathcal{V}$ be a set of propositional variables. Elements of $\mathcal{V}$ are denoted by $X, Y, Z, \ldots$.

Definition 1 (Syntax). The logic $\nu TrTL$ is inductively defined as follows: $P, \neg P \in \nu TrTL$ for $P \in \mathcal{P}$; similarly $X, \neg X \in \nu TrTL$ for $X \in \mathcal{V}$; for $\phi, \psi \in \nu TrTL$, $\phi \wedge \psi, \phi \vee \psi \in \nu TrTL$, for $a \in \Sigma, i \in Loc(a)$, $\phi \in \nu TrTL$, $(\phi)_i$, $\langle a \rangle_i \phi$, $[a]_i \phi \in \nu TrTL$, for $\phi \in \nu TrTL$, $X \in \mathcal{V}$, such that no free occurrence of X in ϕ is negated, also $\mu X.\phi, \nu X.\phi \in \nu TrTL$.
The operators μ and ν bind the variables. By $\phi[X/\psi]$ we denote the formula obtained by substituting all free occurrences of X in ϕ by ψ. A formula that does not contain any free variables is *closed*.

For convenience we only allow negation of atomic propositions (formally the negation of variables is also allowed, but only in the case of free variables!). However the logic is closed under negation, because every operator has its *dual*, and negations can be drawn inside down to the atomic propositions. Let $not(\phi)$ denote the negation of ϕ.

$\nu TrTL$ is evaluated over interpreted frames (F, I). Since formulas may also contain free variables, we additionally need valuations $v : \mathcal{V} \longrightarrow C_F$, which assign sets of configurations to variables. While I is required to respect locality, v may be arbitrary.

Definition 2 (Semantics). The semantics of a formula ϕ w.r.t. (F, I) and a valuation v is a set of configurations, denoted by $[\phi]_v^{(F,I)}$, where we omit (F, I) and v if clear from the context. It is inductively defined, except for the modalities in the obvious way:
$[P]_v^{(F,I)} = I(P)$ for $P \in \mathcal{P}$, $[X]_v^{(F,I)} = v(X)$ for $X \in \mathcal{V}$;
$[\neg\phi)] = C_F \backslash [\phi]$, $[\phi \wedge \psi] = [\phi] \cap [\psi]$, $[\phi \vee \psi] = [\phi] \cup [\psi]$;
$[\mu X.\phi]_v^{(F,I)} = \bigcap\{A;\ [\phi]_{v[X/A]}^{(F,I)} \subseteq A\}$, $[\nu X.\phi]_v^{(F,I)} = \bigcup\{A;\ A \subseteq [\phi]_{v[X/A]}^{(F,I)}\}$.
Here $v[X/A](X) = A$ and for $Y \neq X$ we have $v[X/A](Y) = v(Y)$.
The semantic rules for the modalities:

- $[(\phi)_i]_v^{(F,I)} = \{c;\ \downarrow^i c \in [\phi]_v^{(F,I)}\}$,
- $[\langle a\rangle_i\phi]_v^{(F,I)} = \{c;\ \exists d, c'.\ \downarrow^i c = \downarrow^i c' \text{ and } c' \xrightarrow{a} d \text{ and } \downarrow^i d \in [\phi]_v^{(F,I)}\}$,
- $[[a]_i\phi]_v^{(F,I)} = \{c;\ \forall d, c'.\ (\downarrow^i c = \downarrow^i c' \text{ and } c' \xrightarrow{a} d) \Rightarrow \downarrow^i d \in [\phi]_v^{(F,I)}\}$,

We say ϕ is satisfied in a configuration $c \in C_F$ iff $c \in [\phi]_v^{(F,I)}$, and we also write $(F, I), c \models \phi$ for this. We use $(F, I) \models \phi$ to denote $(F, I), \emptyset \models \phi$: a model has some property iff its initial configuration has it.

Note that even with a linear framework we need two kinds of next operators ($\langle a\rangle_i$ and $[a]_i$). Similar to the case of LTL with past, which requires two previous operators, the reason is that local components are allowed to stop.

TrPTL as subset of *νTrTL*

Without going into the details, we argue that Thiagarajan's $TrPTL$ is a subset of $\nu TrTL$. $TrPTL$ (see [Thi94] for a complete definition) has a local until operator as main connective, which can be expressed in $\nu TrTL$ by defining:
$\phi\ U_i\ \psi := \mu X.(\psi')_i \vee ((\phi')_i \wedge \bigvee_{a\in\Sigma_i}\langle a\rangle_i X)$.

4 Automata

In this section we introduce a class of automata capable of specifying languages of interpreted frames – or equivalently of Mazurkiewicz traces. Zielonka [Zie89] introduced *asynchronous automata* which specify languages of finite traces. These were generalized by Gastin and Petit [GP92] for languages of infinite (real) traces using Büchi acceptance conditions.

There are several variants around now. In the following we introduce a version, which is tailored towards the application for program logics in that the translation of formulas from TrPTL of $\nu TrTL$ can be done *in a natural way*. Although this version is expressively equivalent with all the other models (e.g. those in [GP92]), translations from one variant to another can be very expensive.

Definition 3. A *Local Büchi Asynchronous Automaton with Valuation* over *Loc*, $\widetilde{\Sigma}$ and $\widetilde{\mathcal{P}}$, is a structure $\mathcal{A} = (\widetilde{S}, \longrightarrow, S_{in}, \widetilde{F}, \widetilde{R}, v)$ where $\widetilde{S} = (S_1, ..., S_K)$ with each S_i is a nonempty finite set of states of location i; $S_G = S_1 \times \cdots \times S_K$ is the set of global states; $S_{in} \subseteq S_G$ is a set of global initial states. $\widetilde{F} = (F_1, ..., F_K)$, $\widetilde{R} = (R_1, ..., R_K)$, and for each i the sets $F_i, R_i \subseteq S_i$ are the local (final and recurring) acceptance sets.

$\longrightarrow \subseteq S_G \times \Sigma \times S_G$ is a set of (global) transitions such that:

1. If $s \stackrel{a}{\longrightarrow} s'$, then for all i with $a \notin \Sigma_i$ we have $s[i] = s'[i]$.
2. If $s \stackrel{a}{\longrightarrow} s'$ then also $t \stackrel{a}{\longrightarrow} t'$ for all t, t' such that $s[i] = t[i]$ and $s'[i] = t'[i]$ for all $i \in Loc(a)$, and $t[j] = t'[j]$ for all $j \notin Loc(a)$.

This means that transitions are local to the locations participating in the action they are labelled with.

The valuation v is a mapping $v : S_G \longrightarrow 2^{\mathcal{P}}$ such that

1. if $s[i] = t[i]$ for all $i \in Loc(P)$, then $P \in v(s)$ iff $P \in v(t)$;
2. if $Loc(P) \not\subseteq Loc(a)$ (i.e. if not all locations that are required to change P participate in a), then $P \in v(s)$ iff $P \in v(t)$ for $s \stackrel{a}{\longrightarrow} t$.

In the following we refer to local Büchi asynchronous automata with valuations as LBAV or simply as automata, because we mostly consider this class. We also consider automata without valuations and call these LBA. To the automata defined in [GP92] we refer as BA (as they have global Büchi conditions and no valuations). Now we define the acceptance of LBAVs:

Definition 4. Let (F, I) be an interpreted frame. A run ρ of (F, I) over the LBAV $\mathcal{A}$ is a map $\rho : C_F \longrightarrow S_G$ with $\rho(\emptyset) \in S_{in}$, $p \stackrel{a}{\longrightarrow} q$ in (F, I) implies $\rho(p) \stackrel{a}{\longrightarrow} \rho(q)$, and for all $P \in \mathcal{P}$ we have $p \in I(P)$ iff $P \in v(\rho(p))$ (for LBA without valuations the last condition is simply omitted).

For a run ρ of (F, I) over $\mathcal{A}$ we define for each i the set $\inf_i(\rho)$ of infinitely often visited local states: $\inf_i(\rho) = \{s_i;\ s_i = \rho(\downarrow e)[i]$ for infinitely many $e \in E_i\}$.

A run ρ is accepting iff for each i either E_i is finite and $\rho(\downarrow E_i)[i] \in F_i$ (an accepted final state) or E_i is infinite and $\inf_i(\rho) \cap R_i \neq \emptyset$. An interpreted frame (F, I) is accepted by an automaton $\mathcal{A}$ iff there exists an accepting run for it over $\mathcal{A}$. The set (language) of interpreted frames accepted by $\mathcal{A}$ is called $\mathcal{L}(\mathcal{A})$.

5 Analysis of the logic

In this section we introduce some useful notions for the automaton construction.

Definition 5. A formula ϕ *is of simple type* i iff $\phi = P$ or $\phi = \neg P$ with $P \in \mathcal{P}_i$, $\phi = (\psi)_i$, $\phi = [a]_i\psi$ or $\phi = \langle a \rangle_i \psi$. Inductively we define that a formula ϕ *is of (general) type* i iff ϕ is of simple type i; $\phi = \psi_1 \vee \psi_2$ or $\phi = \psi_1 \wedge \psi_2$, and ψ_1, ψ_2 are of type i; $\phi = \mu X.\psi$ or $\phi = \nu X.\psi$ and ψ is of type i.

The use of this notion lies in the following simple but important observation:

Lemma 6. *If a formula ϕ is of type i, then for any c: $c \in [\phi]$ iff $\downarrow^i c \in [\phi]$.*

Definition 7. A formula is *guarded*, iff every free occurrence of the fixpoint variable in the body of a fixpoint sub-formula lies within the range of a modality. A formula has *local fixpoints* if for every sub-formula $\mu X.\phi$ or $\nu X.\phi$ there exists an i so that all sub-formulas of ϕ with free occurrences of X are of type i.

Every formula can be translated to an equivalent guarded formula, so we can use this special form for a simpler framework . The restriction to local fixpoints is necessary for expressing certain fixpoint properties with Büchi conditions. Henceforth only guarded, positive formulas with local fixpoints are considered.

Definition 8. Let M be a set of $\nu TrTL$ formulas. M is called *Fischer-Ladner-closed* (FL-closed) iff the following conditions hold: If $\phi \in M$, then also $not(\phi)$. If $\langle a\rangle_i\psi$ or $[a]_i\psi \in M$ or $\psi(i) \in M$ then $\psi \in M$. If $\psi_1 \vee \psi_2 \in M$ or $\psi_1 \wedge \psi_2 \in M$ then $\psi_1, \psi_2 \in M$. If $\mu X.\psi \in M$, then $\psi[X/\mu X.\psi] \in M$, and if $\nu X.\psi \in M$, then $\psi[X/\nu X.\psi] \in M$.

$FL(\phi)$ is the least FL-closed set containing ϕ, the *Fischer-Ladner-Closure*.

$FL(\phi)$ is always finite and in fact has at most as many members as ϕ has symbols (see e.g. [Sti92]). Intuitively only the formulas in the FL-Closure need to be evaluated in order to evaluate ϕ. This is reflected by the definitions of atoms (9) and local atoms (10), which represent evaluations at global and local states. The following lemma (11) shows how global states (atoms) can be represented by tuples of local atoms, which is used in the automaton construction.

Definition 9 (Atoms). Let A be a subset of $FL(\phi)$, then A is called an *atom generated by* ϕ, iff the following conditions hold: for $\psi \in FL(\phi)$ *either* $\psi \in A$ *or* $not(\psi) \in A$; if $\psi_1 \wedge \psi_2 \in FL(\phi)$, then $\psi_1 \wedge \psi_2 \in A$ iff $\psi_1 \in A$ and $\psi_2 \in A$; $\mu X.\psi \in A$ iff $\psi[X/\mu X.\psi] \in A$; $\langle a\rangle_i\psi_1, \langle b\rangle_i\psi_2 \in A$ implies $a = b$.

AT denotes the set of atoms generated by ϕ.

Definition 10 (Type i Atoms). By AT_i we denote *atoms of type i generated by* ϕ, more precisely the set of all sets A_i of formulas of type i in $FL(\phi)$, such that the following conditions hold: for all $\psi \in FL(\phi)$ with ψ of type i either $\psi \in A_i$ or $not(\psi) \in A_i$, but not both; if $\psi_1 \wedge \psi_2 \in FL(\phi)$ of type i, then $\psi_1 \wedge \psi_2 \in A_i$ iff $\psi_1 \in A_i$ and $\psi_2 \in A_i$; $\mu X.\psi \in A_i$ iff $\psi[X/\mu X.\psi] \in A_i$; $\langle a\rangle_i\psi_1, \langle b\rangle_i\psi_2 \in A_i$ implies $a = b$. For shorthand we write $[AT]$ for $AT_1 \times \cdots \times AT_K$.

Let $rep : AT \rightarrow [AT]$ such that $rep(A) = (A_1, \ldots, A_K)$, where $A_i = A \cap \{\psi;\ \psi \text{ is of type } i\}$. Let conversely *expand* be a mapping from $[AT]$ to partitions of $FL(\phi)$, such that $A = expand(A_1, \ldots, A_K)$, where A is inductively defined as follows: if $T \in FL(\phi)$, then $T \in A$; if ψ is of type i, then $\psi \in A$ iff $\psi \in A_i$; $\psi_1 \wedge \psi_2 \in A$ iff $\psi_1, \psi_2 \in A$; $\psi_1 \vee \psi_2 \in A$ iff $\psi_1 \in A$ or $\psi_2 \in A$.

Lemma 11. *$Im(expand) = AT$, i.e. the expansion always yields correct atoms. rep and expand are inverse function and thus bijections between AT and $[AT]$.*

For representation purposes we define how to restrict the semantics of models to finite sets of formulas:

Definition 12. Given a FL-closed set of formulas L and an interpreted frame (F, I), a *partial evaluation* of (F, I) w.r.t. L is a mapping $e : C_F \longrightarrow 2^L$ such that: $\forall \phi \in L, d \in C_F : \phi \in e(d) \Leftrightarrow d \in [\phi]^M$.

The Streett-Emerson approach

The automata construction in the next section has the purpose of ensuring the existence of certain partial evaluations for interpreted frames as input.

The key idea of the technically involved Streett-Emerson approach to this problem, which we cannot present formally due to lack of space (see [ES89]), is to split the concept of partial evaluations in two parts: into *preevaluations* (called premodel in [ES89]) and *choice functions*. Preevaluations are the same as partial evaluations except that the fixpoint formulas are interpreted as arbitrary fixpoints rather than least or greatest; the advantage of preevaluations is, that their conditions can be checked locally.

Partial evaluations are preevaluations. To make preevaluations partial evaluations, Streett-Emerson use notions of *derivation* and *reproduction relations* (for the least fixpoint formulas), which are linked to the inductive definition of the semantics of formulas. Derivation relations (and then reproduction relations) are determined by *choice functions*, which choose for all disjunctions in a premodel, which disjunct should be satisfied.

If there exists a choice function such that the induced reproduction relation of least fixpoints is well-founded, then the preevaluation is called well-founded and is in fact a partial evaluation. Hence the task to ensure that a preevaluation is a partial evaluation is to look for a witness choice function. While this framework was conceived for sequential program logics, the results carry over to $\nu TrTL$ and many similar settings without substantial changes in the proofs.

6 Translation to automata

In this section we give the translation of $\nu TrTL$-formulas to Büchi asynchronous automata. We loosely follow the construction given in [Thi94] and adapt it to our requirements. The idea is essentially to use atoms as states of the automaton. In the final stage of the construction it is intended that the formulas belonging to such a state should be true for a certain configuration, which is evaluated to this state in some successful run. In particular, the state of component i is supposed to represent the partial evaluation of the i-view of a configuration.

Notation. Let $s = (s_1, \ldots, s_K)$ and $t = (t_1, \ldots, t_K)$ be K-tuples. Then $s[i] = s_i$ denotes the ith component of s. We write $s \otimes t$ for $((s_1, t_1), \ldots, (s_K, t_K))$. This notation is extended to sets of K-tuples by $S \otimes T := \{s \otimes t;\ s \in S,\ t \in T\}$.

We start by defining the first component of the local automaton, which for an interpreted frame "guesses" a preevaluation. Opposed to constructions for the sequential case we cannot use AT or $[AT]$ to represent the global state; rather we will use these sets to represent the local views of the global state:

Let $\mathcal{A}_0 = (\widetilde{S^0}, \longrightarrow_0 S^0_{in}, \widetilde{F^0}, \widetilde{R^0}, v^0)$ with the following properties:

Each local state set S^0_i is the subset of $[AT]$, such that for all $A \in S^0_i$ and for all $(\psi)_i \in FL(\phi)$ we have: $(\psi)_i \in expand(A)$ iff $\psi \in expand(A)$.

$S^0_{in} = \{(A^1, \ldots, A^K);\ \forall i,j \in Loc : A^i = A^j \wedge \phi \in expand(A^i)\}$; $\widetilde{R^0} = \widetilde{S^0}$; $F^0_i := S^0_i \setminus \{A;\ \langle a\rangle_i\psi \in expand(A)$ for some $a \in \Sigma_i, \psi \in FL(\phi)\}$.

$v^0(A^1, \ldots, A^K) = \bigcup_{i=1}^{K}(expand(A^i) \cap \mathcal{P}_i)$, i.e. v extracts the propositions of type i from the ith component).

Finally and most important the transition relation satisfies:
$(A^1, \ldots, A^K) \xrightarrow{a}_0 (B^1, \ldots, B^K)$ iff

- $\forall i \notin Loc(a) : A^i = B^i$ and $\forall i,j \in Loc(a) : B^i = B^j$.
- If $a \in \Sigma_i$ and $\langle a\rangle_i\psi \in FL(\phi)$ then $\langle a\rangle_i\psi \in A^i[i]$ iff $\psi \in expand(B^i)$.
- If $a \in \Sigma_i$ and $[a]_i\psi \in FL(\phi)$ then $[a]_i\psi \in A^i[i]$ iff $\psi \in expand(B^i)$.
- If $\langle b\rangle_i \in A^i[i]$ and $a \in \Sigma_i$ then $a = b$.

Obviously $\mathcal{A}_0$ is an LBAV. The acceptance condition (in combination with the transition relation) enforces that properties of the kind $\langle a\rangle_i\psi$ must be fulfilled, because the component i may not stop with such a formula.

Next we have to ensure the invariant that the local states represent the local views. This is achieved by combining our automaton with a *gossip automaton* that keeps track of the information, which of the locations has the relatively newest information about the other locations. More precisely given a set of locations X and some frame F, it provides a function $Latest_{F,X}$, which will name for each configuration c and each location i, a specific location $j \in X$ with the latest information concerning i, and for uniqueness it chooses the location j with the smallest index:
$Latest_{F,X}(c,i) = \hat{i} \in X$ such that $\forall j \in X.\ \downarrow^i (\downarrow^j (c)) \subseteq \downarrow^i (\downarrow^{\hat{i}} c)$, and if $j \in X$ and $\downarrow^i (\downarrow^j c) = \downarrow^i (\downarrow^{\hat{i}} c)$ then $\hat{i} \leq j$ (as ordered by the integer ordering of Loc).

Lemma 13 [MS93]. *For each fixed $\widetilde{\Sigma}$, there exists a deterministic (L)BA $\mathcal{A}_\Gamma = (\widetilde{S^\Gamma}, \longrightarrow_\Gamma, S^\Gamma_{in}, \widetilde{F^\Gamma}, \widetilde{R^\Gamma})$ such that $\widetilde{F^\Gamma} = \widetilde{R^\Gamma} = \widetilde{S^\Gamma}$ and $\mathcal{A}_\Gamma$ accepts any frame, and for each $\emptyset \neq X \subseteq Loc$ there exists an (effectively computable) function $g_X : S^\Gamma_1 \times \cdots \times S^\Gamma_K \times Loc \to X$ such that for every configuration c of a frame F and for every $i \in Loc$, $Latest_{F,X}(c,i) = g_X(\rho_F(c), i)$, where ρ_F is the unique accepting run for F.*

As in [Thi94] the safety automaton $\mathcal{A}_1$ is defined as follows. We construct a "product" automaton of $\mathcal{A}_0$ and $\mathcal{A}_\Gamma$, where we add constraints on the transitions, which we obtain from the gossip information:

$\mathcal{A}_1 = (\widetilde{S^1}, \longrightarrow_1, S^1_{in}, \widetilde{F^1}, \widetilde{R^1}, v^1)$ where

- $\widetilde{S^1} = \widetilde{S^0} \otimes \widetilde{S^\Gamma}$; $S^1_{in} = S^0_{in} \otimes S^\Gamma_{in}$; $\widetilde{F^1} = \widetilde{F^0} \otimes \widetilde{F^\Gamma}$; $\widetilde{R^1} = \widetilde{R^0} \otimes \widetilde{R^\Gamma}$;
- $v^1(s \otimes g) = v^0(s)$;

- Let $t,\ t' \in S_G^1,\ g,\ g' \in S_G^\Gamma$.
  $t \otimes g \xrightarrow{a}_1 t' \otimes g'$ iff $t \xrightarrow{a}_0 t'$, $g \xrightarrow{a}_\Gamma g'$, and $\forall j \in Loc(a), \forall i \notin Loc(a).(t'_j[i] = t_{\hat{j}}[i]$ where $g_{Loc(a)}(g_{l_1}, \ldots, g_{l_n}, i) = \hat{j}$ and $Loc(a) = \{l_1, \ldots, l_n\}$, i.e. after communicating all participants "know" of all non-participants, what the best informed participant believed before the communication.

Again it is clear, that $\mathcal{A}_1$ is a LBAV. It is intended that this automaton recognizes preevaluations. More precisely each successful run decorates the configurations with atoms, which represent a preevaluation. To complete the construction we need to extend $\mathcal{A}_1$ to check for the existence of a well-founded choice function (as indicated in the last section). The construction in [ES89] involves a negative formulation plus a complementation, which we want to avoid with asynchronous automata. Therefore we give a positive reformulation with some detail.

First of all we let the automaton guess a choice function, which is represented by marking each disjunction with "left" or "right". Thus a derivation relation and a reproduction relation is fixed, which has to be checked for wellfoundedness, i.e. that every least fixpoint finally stops reproducing. To keep track of several fixpoints at once, we maintain four pools: one with those fixpoints that have not yet come up (*sleep*); one with fixpoints that will not reproduce (*dead*); one with reproducing fixpoints which we currently observe (*observed*); and one with other reproducing fixpoints which have to be observed later (*pending*). Whenever the observed pool gets empty, we note a *checkpoint* and shift the pending pool over to the observed pool. Then checking that every fixpoint finally stops reproducing is equivalent to checking for infinitely many checkpoints, a Büchi condition.

Definition 14. A *marking of a formula* ϕ is a mapping $m : \{\mu X.\psi;\ \mu X.\psi$ sub-formula of $\phi\} \longrightarrow \{sleep, dead, observed, pending\}$.

Let m be a marking of ϕ and m' a marking of ψ. We say m *may derive* m' iff for all $\mu X.\xi$, which are sub-formulas of both ϕ and ψ, the pair $(m(\mu X.\xi), m'(\mu X.\xi))$ obeys the following restrictions: if $m = dead$, then $m' = dead$; if $m = observed$, then $m' \in \{observed, dead\}$; if $m = pending$, then $m' \in \{pending, observed, dead\}$.

A marking of type i of an atom $(A_1, \ldots, A_K) = rep(A)$, is a pair (m, ch) where m is a family of markings $\{m_\phi;\ \phi \in A_i\}$ and ch is a mapping $ch : \{\phi \vee \psi; \phi \vee \psi \in A\} \longrightarrow \{l, r\}$ such that

- If $\phi_l \vee \phi_r \in A$, then $\phi_{ch(\phi_l \vee \phi_r)} \in A$.
- Let $\rightsquigarrow_{ch}$ be the least reflexive and transitive relation on A such that
  - $\phi_l \vee \phi_r \rightsquigarrow_{ch} \phi_{ch(\phi_l \vee \phi_r)}$; $\phi_l \wedge \phi_r \rightsquigarrow_{ch} \phi_l$; $\phi_l \wedge \phi_r \rightsquigarrow_{ch} \phi_l$;
  - $(\phi)_i \rightsquigarrow_{ch} \phi$ (for this i only!);
  - $\mu X.\psi \rightsquigarrow_{ch} \psi[X/\mu X.\psi]$; $\nu X.\psi \rightsquigarrow_{ch} \psi[X/\nu X.\psi]$;
- If $\phi, \psi \in A_i$ and $\phi \rightsquigarrow_{ch} \psi$, then m_ϕ may derive m_ψ (for this i only);
- If $\mu X.\psi \in A_i$ then: $m_{\mu X.\psi}(\mu X.\psi) \in \{observed, pending\}$;

A marking (m, ch) is a *checkpoint*, if for all sub-formulas $\mu X.\psi$ occurring in any formula $\phi \in A_i$ *of simple type* i the following holds: $m_\phi(\mu X.\psi) \neq observed$.

With these concepts we can define $\mathcal{A}_2$, which extends the automaton $\mathcal{A}_1$ to track down the reproduction of least fixpoints (the state components named t originate from $\mathcal{A}_0$, those named g from $\mathcal{A}_\Gamma$):

$\mathcal{A}_2 = (\widetilde{S^2}, \longrightarrow_2, S^2_{in}, \widetilde{F^2}, \widetilde{R^2}, v^2)$ is defined by $S^2_i = \{(t_i, g_i, r_i);\ (t_i, g_i) \in S^1_i, r_i = (m_i, ch_i)$ marking of type i for $t_i[i]\}$, and:

$t \otimes g \otimes r \xrightarrow{a}_2 t' \otimes g' \otimes r'$ iff

- $t \otimes g \xrightarrow{a}_1 t' \otimes g'$;
- for each $i \notin Loc(a)$ the marking does not change: $r_i = r'_i$;
- for each $i \in Loc(a)$: Let $A_i = t_i[i]$, $A'_i = t'_i[i]$ (the type i atom of the ith component), $r_i = (m, ch)$, $r'_i = (m', ch')$ be the corresponding markings. Then the following has to hold:
  - if (m, ch) is not a checkpoint, then for $\langle a\rangle_i\phi \in A_i$ and for each $\phi \leadsto_{ch'} \psi \in A'_i$ the marking $m_{\langle a\rangle_i\phi}$ may derive m'_ψ (and similarly for $[a]_i\phi \in A_i$).
  - if (m, ch) is a checkpoint, then the same holds, but no fixpoint may be marked *pending* in m'.

$F^2_i = \{(t_i, g_i, r_i) \in S^2_i;\ t_i \in F^0_i\}$. $R^2_i = \{(t_i, g_i, r_i);\ r_i$ is a checkpoint$\}$.

$S^2_{in} = \{t \otimes g \otimes r \in S^2_G;\ t \otimes g \in S^1_{in}\}$.

$v^2(t \otimes g \otimes r) = v^0(t)$.

$\mathcal{A}_\phi := \mathcal{A}_2$ is again a LBAV, and it accepts the language of all those models, which satisfy the original formula ϕ, as is explained in the next section.

7 Decidability

Theorem 15. *For every formula ϕ we can effectively construct an LBAV $\mathcal{A}_\phi$ such that for all (F, I) holds: $(F, I) \models \phi$ iff $(F, I) \in \mathcal{L}(\mathcal{A}_\phi)$.*

The construction is exactly that of the last section. A detailed proof of its correctness can be found in [Nie95].

Corollary 16. *The satisfiability problem for $\nu TrTL$ is decidable.*

Proof. A formula ϕ is satisfiable iff $L(\mathcal{A}_\phi) \neq \emptyset$. The emptiness problem for BAs was shown to be decidable (c.f. [Thi94]) and the result carries over to LBAVs.

LBAVs can also be used as system descriptions. The linear time behaviour of a system is its accepted language. A system satisfies a property, if all its runs do.

Definition 17. Let $\mathcal{A}$ be a LBAV, ϕ a formula. We say that $\mathcal{A}$ satisfies ϕ (or symbolic: $\mathcal{A} \models \phi$) iff $(F, I) \models \phi$ for all $(F, I) \in \mathcal{L}(\mathcal{A})$.

The *model checking problem* for $\nu TrTL$ is the set $\{(\mathcal{A}, \phi);\ \mathcal{A} \models \phi\}$

Corollary 18. *The model checking problem for $\nu TrTL$ is decidable.*

Proof. We use the standard construction: $\mathcal{A} \models \phi$ iff $\mathcal{L}(\mathcal{A}) \cap \mathcal{L}(\mathcal{A}_{\neg\phi}) = \emptyset$. Without proof we state that there exists a "product construction" on LBAVs such that for every pair $\mathcal{A}$ and $\mathcal{B}$ of LBAVs we effectively obtain an automaton $\mathcal{A} \otimes \mathcal{B}$ with $\mathcal{L}(\mathcal{A} \otimes \mathcal{B}) = \mathcal{L}(\mathcal{A}) \cap \mathcal{L}(\mathcal{B})$. We obtain the reduction to the emptiness problem: $\mathcal{A} \models \phi$ iff $\mathcal{L}(\mathcal{A} \otimes \mathcal{A}_{\neg\phi}) = \emptyset$.

We have not investigated the complexity of the construction and related algorithms in detail. A careful estimation yields the same upper bounds given for *TrPTL* in [Thi94], i.e. an upper bound of $2^{O(|\phi|^3 \log(|\phi|))}$ for the global state space and transition relation of $\mathcal{A}_\phi$, and thus for the time complexity of the satisfiability (emptiness) problem. An upper bound for the model checking complexity is $O(|\mathcal{A}|)2^{O(|\phi|^3 \log(|\phi|))}$.

Acknowledgements

I am grateful to Ursula Goltz, Michaela Huhn, Wojciech Penczek, P.S. Thiagarajan, and Heike Wehrheim for their interest, valuable suggestions, encouragement, and patience, while this work was carried out. Part of this work was supported by the Esprit Working Group No. 6067 CALIBAN (Causal Calculi Based on Nets).

References

[ES89] E. Allen Emerson and Robert S. Streett. An automata theoretic decision procedure for the propositional mu-calculus. *Information and Computation*, 81:249–264, 1989.

[GP92] Paul Gastin and Antoine Petit. Asynchronous cellular automata for infinite traces. In *ICALP* '92, LNCS 623, pages 583–594, 1992.

[Koz83] Dexter Kozen. Results on the propositional μ-calculus. *Theoretical Computer Science*, 27:333–354, 1983.

[MS93] Madhavan Mukund and Milind Sohoni. Keeping track of the latest gossip: Bounded time-stamps suffice. internal report tcs-93-3, School of Mathematics, SPIC Science Foundation, Madras, India, 1993.

[Nie95] Peter Niebert. A μ-calculus with local views for systems of sequential agents. Technical report, Univ. Hildesheim.

[Sti92] Colin Stirling. Modal and temporal logics. In S. Abramsky, D. Gabbay, and T. Maibaum, editors, *Handbook of Logic in Computer Science*. Oxford University Press, 1992

[Thi94] P.S. Thiagarajan. A trace based extension of Linear Time Temporal Logic. In *Proceedings of the 9th annual IEEE symposium on Logic in Computer Science (LICS)*, 1994.

[VW86] Moshe Y. Vardi and Pierre Wolper. An automata-theoretic approach to automatic program verification. In *Proceedings of the 1st annual IEEE Symposium on Logic in Computer Science (LICS)*, pages 332–344, 1986.

[Zie89] Wieslaw Zielonka. Safe executions of recognizable trace languages by asynchronous automata. In *Logic at Botik*, LNCS 363, pages 278–289, 1989.

An Operator Calculus Approach to the Evolution of Dynamic Data Structures

P. Feinsilver, [1] and R. Schott [2]

Abstract. In this paper, we present an original method based on operator calculus for the analysis of dynamic data structures applicable for Knuth's model as well as the Markovian model. Our approach uses techniques developed by the authors for the study of algebraic structures related to Lie groups. By this approach, we recover readily the average complexity of dynamic algorithms previously proved through analytical tools. Here, we indicate how to analyse the case of multiple files. Our operator calculus approach is suitable for investigating a variety of related problems in complexity analysis.

I. Introduction

The analysis of dynamic data structures was developed in the work of Flajolet, Françon, Vuillemin, see, e.g., [4] [5] [7] [8] following the interest generated by Jonassen & Knuth [11] and continued in [9], all of these works using analytical tools. A probabilistic approach was developed by Louchard, Maier et al., see [14] [15] [16]. A new approach has been given in [1] using operator calculus. A feature of this method is that any questions concerning the asymptotic distribution, such as higher moments, are readily answered. The present paper is a continuation of those developments.

First, we give the basics of the operator calculus methods we use. Then we present the formulation of the Markovian model and Knuth's model for the evolution of dynamic data structures for multiple files. The theory as developed in [1] for a single file is thus extended to the case of multiple files.

II. Background on the operator calculus method

The techniques here are based on connecting recurrence formulas with shift operators and transition operators. This involves two steps:

1) Formulation of a recurrence in *time:* writing a dynamical system in terms of a transition operator "multiplication by X". This is the basic idea of 'duality theory.'

2) Formulation of a three-term recurrence in terms of shift operators acting on a basis of a vector space. This is the connection with representations of Lie algebras.

Remark. Generally, n and k will denote multi-indices, $n = (n_1, \ldots, n_d)$, $k = (k_1, \ldots, k_d)$, with i and j single indices. For a multi-index, we have, e.g., $|n| = \sum_i n_i$, $n! = n_1! \cdots n_d!$, $n = \sum_i n_i e_i$, with e_i the standard basis in $\mathbf{N}^d$, $e_1 = (1, 0, \ldots, 0)$, and so on. Inequalities are componentwise, e.g., $n \geq 0$ means $n_i \geq 0$, $1 \leq i \leq d$. For a variable $x = (x_1, \ldots, x_d)$, $x^n = x_1^{n_1} x_2^{n_2} \cdots x_d^{n_d}$, etc.

2.1 ELEMENTS OF DUALITY THEORY

Here we indicate the general approach to duality.

Consider a discrete dynamical system of the form

$$\mathrm{C}_{n+1} = A\mathrm{C}_n$$

[1] Department of Mathematics, Southern Illinois University, Carbondale, Illinois 62901 USA

[2] CRIN, INRIA-Lorraine, Université de Nancy I, B.P. 239, 54506 Vandoeuvre-lès-Nancy, France

with $\mathbf{C}_n$ a vector of components $\mathbf{C}_n(k)$. This gives a matrix $\{ c_{nk} \}$, with $c_{nk} = \mathbf{C}_n(k)$. Determine the operator X by the relation

$$X^n \phi_0 = \sum_k c_{nk} \phi_k = \mathbf{C}_n \cdot \Phi$$

where Φ is a column of the basis vectors ϕ_j. Thus

$$X^n \phi_0 = \mathbf{C}_n \cdot \Phi = A^n \mathbf{C}_0 \cdot \Phi = \mathbf{C}_0 \cdot (A^*)^n \Phi$$

So the action of X on Φ is dual to that of A on $\mathbf{C}$: $X\Phi = A^*\Phi$. We have the correspondence between the recurrence ($d = 1$)

$$c_{n+1,k} = \sum_l A_{kl} c_{nl}$$

and the action of X

$$X \phi_k = \sum_l A_{lk} \phi_l$$

For example, the Stirling numbers of the second kind, defined by $x^n = \sum_k s_{n,k} x^{(k)}$, with $x^{(n)} = x(x-1)\cdots(x-n+1)$, satisfy $s_{n+1,k} = s_{n,k-1} + k\, s_{n,k}$. This is dual to the action of X, $X\phi_k = \phi_{k+1} + k\,\phi_k$, with $\phi_k = x^{(k)}$.

For a multi-component system, we have $A = (A_1, \cdots, A_d)$, $X = (X_1, \cdots, X_d)$. We assume that $A_i A_j = A_j A_i$, $X_i X_j = X_j X_i$, $\forall i, j$, and we have, with n, k multi-indices,

$$X_j X^n \phi_0 = X^{n+e_j} \phi_0 = \mathbf{C}_{n+e_j} \cdot \Phi$$

dual to $\mathbf{C}_{n+e_j} = A_j \mathbf{C}_n$.

2.2 OPERATOR CALCULUS

Consider a vector space with basis $\{ \psi_n \}_{n \geq 0}$, $n = (n_1, \ldots, n_d)$. The *raising* and *velocity* (so-called because of the analogy to differentiation) operators are defined by the action on the basis

$$R_i \psi_n = \psi_{n+e_i}, \qquad V_i \psi_n = n_i \psi_{n-e_i}$$

They satisfy the commutation relations $[V_j, R_i] = \delta_{ij} I$, I denoting the identity operator, with the Lie bracket denoting the commutator $[V_j, R_i] = V_j R_i - R_i V_j$. This is the basic link to Lie algebras. The operators $\{ R_i, V_i \}$ are called *boson operators* and they generate the (associative) Heisenberg-Weyl algebra. The most familiar realization of these operators is given by $\psi_n = x^n$, the usual basis for polynomials in the variables $(x_1, \ldots, x_d)$, with R_i acting by multiplication by x_i and V_i acting by partial differentiation $\partial/\partial x_i$.

Observe that $R_i V_i \psi_n = n_i \psi_n$ and thus the operator $\nu = \sum_i R_i V_i$ acts as

$$\nu \psi_n = |n| \psi_n$$

and is called the *number operator*.

These operators are used to express the action of operators such as X in a useful form. For example, the action

$$X \psi_n = \psi_{n+1} + n\psi_n + 3n\psi_{n-1}$$

can be expressed by the equation $X = R + RV + 3V$. In terms of files, the operator R indicates insertion of an item, while V indicates the deletion of any of the n items present in a file of size n. The operator RV ($d = 1$) is useful for computing costs depending on the current file size. Similarly, when considering multiple files, R_i indicates insertion into the ith file, while the number operator is used to indicate costs, e.g., that depend on the total number of items in the files combined. For a single file, Chapter 2 of [1] shows how this calculus may be used to analyze dynamic data structures. Now we will see how the approach applies to the case of multiple files.

III. Dynamic data structures

We review the approach based on path counting, used in the study of random walks. Using the method of duality indicated above, this leads to orthogonal polynomials and an associated operator calculus. The operator calculus is then employed for the analysis of data structures.

Here we review the basics of dynamic data structures. The motivation is to compare the efficiency of the various data structures. Two basic ideas are *time costs* and *space costs*, involving respectively the complexity due to the number of operations involved and the complexity due to storage — memory — requirements. Here we study time costs.

3.1 HISTORIES

We present a useful formalism. Let $\mathcal{O}$ denote the *alphabet of operations*, in our case we have $\mathcal{O} \subset \{I, D, Q^+, Q^-\}$, where I, D, Q^+, Q^- stand respectively for insertion, deletion, positive query and negative query. Thus, a word means a sequence of elements belonging to $\mathcal{O}$. We denote the set of words over the alphabet $\mathcal{O}$ by $\mathcal{O}^*$. We want to count the number of operations involved when the operations are performed on files under constraints imposed according to the various data structures. First, we make a general definition, corresponding to the necessary condition that a file cannot be of negative size.

3.1.1 Definition. For $w \in \mathcal{O}^*$ and $O \in \mathcal{O}$, denote by $|w|_O$ the number of times O appears in w.

3.1.2 Definition. For $w \in \mathcal{O}^*$, the *height* of w, $h(w)$, is defined by

$$h(w) = |w|_I - |w|_D$$

Note that the difference between the number of insertions and deletions is just the size of the file. Now we have

3.1.3 Definition. A *schema* is a word $w = O_1 O_2 \ldots O_n \in \mathcal{O}^*$ such that the sequence of subwords $w_i = O_1 O_2 \ldots O_i$ satisfies $h(w_i) \geq 0$, for all i, $1 \leq i \leq n$.

When counting file operations involving keys, we consider only their relative order. The method of counting the number of ways an operation can be applied to a given file in a given situation is determined by a sequence of nonnegative integers, ranks, corresponding to (the relative ordering of) keys.

3.1.4 Definition. Let $r_1, \ldots, r_n$ be a sequence of nonnegative integers, *ranks*. A *history* is a sequence of ordered pairs $\{(O_1, r_1), \ldots, (O_n, r_n)\}$ such that $O_1 O_2 \ldots O_n$ is a schema and $r_1, \ldots, r_n$ are admissible ranks (for a given model).

The ranks allowed determine the particular models. Below, we discuss two models that have been studied: the *markovian model* and *Knuth's model*. So a model is determined by the alphabet $\mathcal{O}$ and, for each data structure, the specification of allowed histories.

Here we continue with a sketch of the general approach, assuming a model has been given.

3.1.5 Definition. For an operation O, the *number of possibilities* $\mathrm{Npos}(O, k)$ is the number of ranks r for which O is defined on a file of size k.

If an operation is not allowed at a given time, we set $\mathrm{Npos}(O, k) = 0$. This determines the count of the number of operations of a given type that are permitted to be performed on a file.

3.2 TIME COSTS

First some notation.

3.2.1 Definition. For a given class of histories:

1) $\mathcal{H}_{k,l,n}$ denotes the set of histories of length n with initial height k and final height l. Denote the cardinality $|\mathcal{H}_{k,l,n}|$ by $H_{k,l,n}$.
2) $\mathcal{H}_n$ denotes the set of histories starting and ending with an empty file, i.e., $\mathcal{H}_n = \mathcal{H}_{0,0,n}$. Denote the cardinality $|\mathcal{H}_n|$ by H_n.

Suppose we are given a cost functional on the set of histories: cost(h), some measure of the complexity of the histories. Then we have

3.2.2 Definition. The *integrated cost* over $\mathcal{H}_n$ is

$$K_n = \frac{1}{H_n} \sum_{h \in \mathcal{H}_n} \text{cost}(h)$$

In order to analyze time costs, it is convenient that the data structure satisfy a condition of *stationarity*. Many implementations commonly used in computer science have the required property. Here is one way of stating what is needed. Denote by E_k the set of all states of a structure of size k. This depends on the particular implementation. For example, for a sorted list, there is only one state for each k, while there are $k!$ possible states of size k for an unsorted list. As another example, there are $k!$ pagodas of size k. One defines

3.2.3 Definition. The *standard probability distribution* on E_k is determined by giving equal weight to all states of size k corresponding to the schema I^k. We denote by $p_s(e)$ the corresponding probability of a state $e \in E_k$.

3.2.4 Definition. A data structure is *stationary* if for all k, probabilities induced on E_k by histories corresponding to schema $I^{k+1}D$, I^kQ^-, and I^kQ^+ (respectively) coincide with the standard probability distribution p_s.

The structures we will consider are known to be stationary. This property permits the calculation of costs in a particularly effective manner. Namely, we can use the notion of individual costs.

3.2.5 Definition. The *individual cost* of operation O on a file of size k is given by

$$CO_k = \sum_{e \in E_k} p_s(e) \, \text{cost}(O, e)$$

where cost(O, e) is the cost of performing operation O on the state e.

Here costs are determined by the average number of comparisons of keys required for the operation. The following table gives the average costs of operations for various implementations.

(In this table we use the notation $h_k = 1 + \frac{1}{2} + \cdots + \frac{1}{k}$.)

Data type	Implementation	CI_k	CD_k	CQ^+_k	CQ^-_k
Linear list	Sorted list	$\frac{k+2}{2}$	$\frac{k+1}{2}$		
	Unsorted list	0	$\frac{k+1}{2}$		
Priority queue	Sorted list	$\frac{k+2}{2}$	0		
	Unsorted list	0	$k-1$		
	Binary tournament	$h_{k+1} - \frac{1}{2}$	$2\left(h_k + \frac{1-2k}{k}\right)$		
	Pagodas	$2\frac{k}{k+1}$	$2\left(h_k + \frac{1-2k}{k}\right)$		
Dictionary	Sorted list	$\frac{k+2}{2}$	$\frac{k+1}{2}$	$\frac{k+1}{2}$	$\frac{k+2}{2}$
	Unsorted list	0	$\frac{k+1}{2}$	$\frac{k+1}{2}$	k
Symbol table	Sorted list	$\frac{k+2}{2}$	$k-1$	$\frac{k+1}{2}$	
	Unsorted list	0	0	$\frac{k+1}{2}$	

From this table we can see that the relative efficiencies are not evident. For example, look at dictionaries. The table shows that, implemented as a list, the average cost of an insertion in a dictionary of size k is $(k+2)/2$ if the list is sorted, 0 if unsorted. The average cost for deletions and positive queries is independent of whether the list is sorted, while the average cost of a negative query is $(k+2)/2$ for sorted lists, k for unsorted. Comparing these costs, it is unclear how to determine which list structure is more efficient. This is where the idea (of Françon, Knuth, et al.) to consider the dynamic behavior of these structures comes from.

To compute the average (integrated) cost we use the individual costs CO_k. First we have

3.2.6 Definition. The *level crossing number* $NO_{k,n}$ is the number of operations of type O performed on a file of size k in the course of the histories $\mathcal{H}_n$.

We can thus write

$$NO_{k,n} = \text{Npos}\,(O_k) \cdot \sum_{i=0}^{n-1} H_{0,k,i}\, H_{0,k',n-i-1} \tag{3.2.1}$$

where

$$k' = \begin{cases} k, & \text{for } O = Q^+ \text{ or } Q^- \\ k+1, & \text{for } O = I \\ k-1, & \text{for } O = D \end{cases}$$

From the definitions, we see that

3.2.7 Proposition. *For stationary structures, the integrated cost is given by*

$$K_n = \frac{1}{H_n} \sum_{O \in \mathcal{O}} \sum_k CO_k \cdot NO_{k,n}$$

3.3 POSSIBILITY FUNCTIONS: MARKOVIAN MODEL, KNUTH'S MODEL

The models presented here differ principally in the way one counts insertions (and negative queries). In [13], Knuth discusses two types of insertions in a data structure. Take the interval $[0,1]$ as the set of keys. Consider inserting the next key into a file of k keys:

I_0 means insertion of a random number by order in the sense that the new number is equally likely to fall in any of the $k+1$ intervals determined by the keys in the file

I means the insertion of a random number uniformly distributed on the interval $[0,1]$, independent of previously inserted numbers.

G.D. Knott[12] showed that I_0 differs from I. Considering insertions of type I_0 gives the *markovian model* (studied in [5], [7], [14], [16]).

3.3.1 Markovian model

For this model the specification of histories is as follows (recall that $h(w)$ is the height of the word w, i.e., it is the size of the corresponding file):

1. For linear lists, the alphabet of operations $\mathcal{O} = \{I, D\}$ with admissible ranks satisfying:

$$\begin{aligned} 0 \le r_j &< h(O_1 \dots O_{j-1}) \qquad & O_j = D \\ 0 \le r_j &\le h(O_1 \dots O_{j-1}) \qquad & O_j = I \end{aligned}$$

2. For priority queues, $\mathcal{O} = \{I, D\}$ with admissible ranks satisfying:

$$\begin{aligned} r_j &= 0 \qquad & O_j = D \\ 0 \le r_j &\le h(O_1 \dots O_{j-1}) \qquad & O_j = I \end{aligned}$$

3. For dictionaries, $\mathcal{O} = \{ I, D, Q^+, Q^- \}$ with admissible ranks satisfying:

$$\begin{array}{ll} 0 \le r_j < h(O_1 \ldots O_{j-1}) & O_j = D \text{ or } Q^+ \\ 0 \le r_j \le h(O_1 \ldots O_{j-1}) & O_j = I \text{ or } Q^- \end{array}$$

4. For symbol tables, $\mathcal{O} = \{ I, D, Q^+ \}$ with admissible ranks satisfying:

$$\begin{array}{ll} r_j = 0 & O_j = D \\ 0 \le r_j < h(O_1 \ldots O_{j-1}) & O_j = Q^+ \\ 0 \le r_j \le h(O_1 \ldots O_{j-1}) & O_j = I \end{array}$$

Thus, the possibility functions for this model are:

Data type	Npos (I,k)	Npos (D,k)	Npos (Q^+,k)	Npos (Q^-,k)
Linear list	$k+1$	k		
Priority queue	$k+1$	1		
Dictionary	$k+1$	k	k	$k+1$
Symbol table	$k+1$	1	k	

3.3.2 Knuth's model

Considering insertions of type I gives *Knuth's model.* Here is an example of how this works for a linear list. Consider the sequence of operations $IIIDI$, starting from an empty file. Let $x < y < z$ be the first three keys inserted. We have x, y and z equally likely to be deleted. Let w be the fourth key inserted. Whichever key has been deleted, considering all four keys, the four possibilities: $w < x < y < z$, $x < w < y < z$, $x < y < w < z$, $x < y < z < w$ — are equally likely. Thus, we count 4 possibilities for the fourth insertion, even though the file consists of only two items. In general, consider a sequence of operations $O_1 \ldots O_n$ on an initially empty file. Let O_n be the i-th I of the sequence. Let $x_1 < \cdots < x_{i-1}$ be the keys inserted during the first $n-1$ operations. Let w be the i-th key inserted. All of the possibilities $w < x_1 < \cdots < x_{i-1}, \ldots, x_1 < \cdots < x_{i-1} < w$ are equally likely, whatever the keys deleted. In combinatorial terms: after n operations, consisting of i I's and $n-i$ D's, the data structure thus being of size $k = 2i - n$, the keys are considered as a subset of a set of size i where any of the $\binom{i}{k}$ subsets of size k are equally likely. Thus, the number of possibilities for the i-th I equals i — regardless of the size of the structure at that point — while in the markovian model, the number of possibilities for an insertion is $k+1$ for a data structure of size k. For dictionaries, a similar argument applies to negative queries as for insertions.

For Knuth's model the specification of histories is as follows:

1. For linear lists, $\mathcal{O} = \{ I, D \}$ with admissible ranks satisfying:

$$\begin{array}{ll} 0 \le r_j < h(O_1 \ldots O_{j-1}) & O_j = D \\ 0 \le r_j \le |O_1 \ldots O_{j-1}|_I & O_j = I \end{array}$$

2. For priority queues, $\mathcal{O} = \{ I, D \}$ with admissible ranks satisfying:

$$\begin{array}{ll} r_j = 0 & O_j = D \\ 0 \le r_j \le |O_1 \ldots O_{j-1}|_I & O_j = I \end{array}$$

3. For dictionaries, $\mathcal{O} = \{ I, D, Q^+, Q^- \}$ with admissible ranks satisfying:

$$\begin{array}{ll} 0 \le r_j < h(O_1 \ldots O_{j-1}) & O_j = D \text{ or } Q^+ \\ 0 \le r_j \le |O_1 \ldots O_{j-1}|_I + |O_1 \ldots O_{j-1}|_{Q^-} & O_j = I \text{ or } Q^- \end{array}$$

4. For symbol tables, $\mathcal{O} = \{I, D, Q^+\}$ with admissible ranks satisfying:

$$\begin{array}{ll} r_j = 0 & O_j = D \\ 0 \le r_j < h(O_1 \ldots O_{j-1}) & O_j = Q^+ \\ 0 \le r_j \le |O_1 \ldots O_{j-1}|_I & O_j = I \end{array}$$

Thus, the possibility functions are given by:

Data type	Npos (i^{th} I or Q^-)	Npos (D,k)	Npos (Q^+,k)
Linear list	i	k	
Priority queue	i	1	
Dictionary	i	k	k
Symbol table	i	1	k

First, we indicate how to enumerate histories. Then we obtain expressions for the integrated costs using level crossing numbers and the individual costs. Thus, one is able to compare the relative efficiency of different implementations.

3.4 ENUMERATION OF HISTORIES

We have a multiple-file system of d files. Here we are working with the Markovian model. We consider insertions, deletions and queries on any individual file. A new feature is that we allow transferring of items between files. Thus, at a given (time-)step, we have possibilities as indicated

$$i_k^{(j)} = \text{Npos}(I,k,j), \quad q_k^{(j)} = \text{Npos}(Q,k,j), \quad d_k^{(j)} = \text{Npos}(D,k,j)$$

where Npos is the number of possibilities for that operation to be carried out on file j when the system is of size $k = (k_1, \ldots, k_d)$. The query operation here has the extended meaning that for subscript k it refers indeed to a query, while for a subscript of the form $k + e_a - e_b$ it indicates the transfer of an item from file a to file b. The 'time' noted by the index n is now a multi-index, referring to the number of times operations have been performed on (referred to) given files. Then we have, considering a one-step transition from n to $n + e_j$,

3.4.1 Proposition. *Let c_{nk} denote the number of ways starting from level 0 to reach level k in n steps. The c_{nk} satisfy the recurrence*

$$c_{n+e_j\,k} = i_{k-e_j}^{(j)}\, c_{n\,k-e_j} + \sum_{a,b} q_{k+e_a-e_b}^{(j)}\, c_{n\,k+e_a-e_b} + d_{k+e_j}^{(j)}\, c_{n\,k+e_j}$$

with $c_{0\,0} = 1$, $c_{0\,k} = 0$, $k \ne 0$.

For $d = 1$, we can identify this recurrence with the *transition matrix*

$$\begin{pmatrix} q_0 & i_0 & 0 & 0 & \cdots \\ d_1 & q_1 & i_1 & 0 & \cdots \\ 0 & d_2 & q_2 & i_2 & \cdots \\ 0 & 0 & d_3 & q_3 & \ddots \\ 0 & 0 & 0 & d_4 & \ddots \\ 0 & 0 & 0 & 0 & \ddots \\ \cdots & \cdots & \cdots & \cdots & \cdots \end{pmatrix} \tag{3.4.1}$$

where the kl entry indicates the number of ways of going from level k to level l in one step, $k, l \ge 0$. The nth power of this matrix thus gives the number of ways of going from one level to another in n steps.

Now look at the dual recurrence. Introduce the transition operator(s) $X = (X_1, \ldots, X_d)$. The operator X is the one-step transition operator. As in the discussion of duality, we find a recurrence for the action of the X_j on a basis $\{\phi_k\}$. The basis will be thus expressed as orthogonal polynomials in the variables X. We denote integration with respect to the corresponding distribution, expected value, by $\langle \cdot \rangle$.

3.4.2 Proposition. *The action of X_j on the basis $\{\phi_k\}$ satisfies*

$$X_j\phi_k = i_k^{(j)}\phi_{k+e_j} + \sum_{a,b} q_k^{(j)}\phi_{k-e_a+e_b} + d_k^{(j)}\phi_{k-e_j}$$

Proof: Apply X_j to the relation

$$X^n\phi_0 = \sum_k c_{nk}\phi_k$$

and use the relation in the above Proposition for the c_{nk} to find the corresponding action of X_j on the ϕ_k. ■

At this point, it is best to give an example. A generalization of the Meixner class (see [1]), where i, d, and q depend at most linearly on k is given according to the recurrence ([3], [2])

$$X_j\phi_k = \gamma_j(\tau + |k|)\,\phi_{k+e_j} + \sum_{a,b} \alpha_{aj}^b k_a\phi_{k+e_b-e_a} + k_j\phi_{k-e_j} \tag{3.4.2}$$

Here we can write the recurrence for the monic polynomials

$$\psi_k = \gamma^k(\tau)_{|k|}\,\phi_k$$

with $\|\psi_k\|^2 = k!\gamma^k\Gamma(\tau + |k|)/\Gamma(\tau) = k!\gamma^k(\tau)_{|k|}$, $\psi_0 = \phi_0 = 1$,

$$X_j\psi_k = \psi_{k+e_j} + \sum_{a,b} \alpha_{aj}^b k_a\psi_{k+e_b-e_a} + \gamma_j(\tau + |k| - 1)k_j\psi_{k-e_j}$$

And $\varepsilon_k = \|\phi_k\|^2 = \dfrac{k!}{\gamma^k(\tau)_{|k|}}$. These are a family of orthogonal polynomials in several variables. They may be expressed in terms of Lauricella polynomials.

Generally, when we have ϕ_k a system of orthogonal polynomials, with squared norms $\varepsilon_k = \|\phi_k\|^2$, we have as in the case $d = 1$, here with multi-indices,

3.4.3 Theorem. *The number of histories $H_{k,l,n}$, going from level l to level k in n steps is given by the expected value*

$$H_{k,l,n} = \langle X^n\phi_k\phi_l\rangle/\varepsilon_l$$

In particular,

$$H_{0,k,n} = \langle X^n\phi_k\rangle/\varepsilon_k, \qquad H_{k,0,n} = \langle X^n\phi_k\rangle$$

with

$$H_{0,0,n} = \langle X^n\rangle = \mu_n$$

the moments.

3.5 KNUTH'S MODEL

For Knuth's model, insertions are treated differently than in the Markovian model. As above, insertions into file j occur only when operating on that file. Denote by c_{nk}^s, the number of paths starting from 0 that are of height k after n steps, with s the number of insertions (also one can include negative queries which we will ignore here). Here, $s = (s_1, \ldots, s_d)$ indicates insertions made into the various files. The recurrence in Proposition 3.4.1 takes the form

$$c_{n+e_j\,k}^s = s_j\,c_{n\,k-e_j}^{s-e_j} + \sum_{a,b} q_{k+e_a-e_b}^{(j)}\,c_{n\,k+e_a-e_b}^s + d_{k+e_j}^{(j)}\,c_{n\,k+e_j}^s$$

Introduce the generating function in the variables $(t_1,\dots,t_d)$

$$C_{nk}(t)=\sum_{s\geq 0}\frac{t^s}{s!}c^s_{nk}$$

Thus, the s is summed out, leading to a situation similar to the markovian model. We see immediately that

3.5.1 Proposition. *The $C_{nk}(t)$ satisfy the recurrence*

$$C_{n+e_j\,k}=t_j\,C_{n\,k-e_j}+\sum_{a,b}q^{(j)}_{k+e_a-e_b}\,C_{n\,k+e_a-e_b}+d^{(j)}_{k+e_j}\,C_{n\,k+e_j}$$

Here we have operators X_t acting on a basis $\{\,\phi_k(x,t)\,\}$ such that

$$(X_t)^n\,\phi_0=\sum_k C_{nk}(t)\,\phi_k$$

Dual to Prop. 3.5.1 is

3.5.2 Proposition. *The polynomials $\{\,\phi_k(x,t)\,\}$ satisfy the recurrence*

$$X_j\phi_k=t_j\phi_{k+e_j}+\sum_{a,b}q^{(j)}_k\phi_{k-e_a+e_b}+d^{(j)}_k\phi_{k-e_j}$$

Note that the t_j correspond to the factors γ_j in equation (3.4.2). With $H^s_{k,l,n}$ the number of histories from level k to level l in n steps with s insertions, we consider the generating function

$$H_{k,l,n}(t)=\sum_{s\geq 0}\frac{t^s}{s!}H^s_{k,l,n}$$

To get back to the number of histories from $H^s_{k,l,n}(t)$ we integrate out the t variables as follows.

3.5.3 Proposition. *The number of histories $H_{k,l,n}$ is given by the integral*

$$H_{k,l,n}=\int_0^\infty\cdots\int_0^\infty e^{-(t_1-t_2-\dots-t_d)}\,H_{k,l,n}(t)\,dt_1dt_2\cdots dt_d$$

which takes into account all possible insertions.

We can as well consider insertions from the point of view of the system. I.e., we consider the total number of insertions at a given point when counting an insertion. Then we have only one t with the generating function

$$C_{nk}(t)=\sum_{s\geq 0}\frac{t^{|s|}}{|s|!}\binom{|s|}{s_1,\dots,s_d}c^s_{nk}$$

Similarly, to recover the histories, we have to integrate out only t.

3.6 OPERATOR CALCULUS AND DATA STRUCTURES: KNUTH'S MODEL

Now we apply this to the analysis of data structures. Given a model for the data structures, define operators $\xi_{\mathcal{O}}$ incorporating the action, such as insertion or deletion (cf. R and V) and the corresponding number of possibilities for the operation $\mathcal{O}$. Thus we have the operators $\xi_I(j)$, for insertions, $\xi_Q(j)$, for queries, and $\xi_D(j)$, for deletions. For Knuth's model, $i_k(j)$ becomes t_j. For $d_k(j)=k_j$, e.g. for linear lists and dictionaries, we have effectively $\xi_D(j)=V_j$.

At this point, we recall the main results for $d=1$. Using multi-indices and the formulation in the preceding, these results extend directly to the case $d>1$.

3.6.1 Lemma. *In Knuth's model, the level crossing numbers satisfy*

$$NO_{kn}(t)=\sum_i\langle X_t^{n-i-1}\xi_{\mathcal{O}}\phi_k\rangle\langle X_t^i\phi_k\rangle/\varepsilon_k$$

Proof: In the formula

$$NO_{kn}(t)=\text{Npos}\,(O,k)\sum_i H_{0,k,i}(t)H_{k',0,n-i-1}(t)$$

substitute the formulas giving the path numbers in terms of matrix elements. Expanding in t, the superscripts denoting the number of insertions:

$$\sum_{s=0}^{\infty} \frac{t^s}{s!} NO^s_{kn} = \text{Npos}(O,k) \sum_i \sum_{a,b=0}^{\infty} \frac{t^a t^b}{a!\,b!} H^a_{0,k,i} H^b_{k',0,n-i-1}$$

Combining like powers of t on the right-hand side yields

$$NO^s_{kn} = \text{Npos}(O,k) \sum_i \sum_a \binom{s}{a} H^a_{0,k,i} H^{s-a}_{k',0,n-i-1}$$

This shows the counting of insertions along the path, equally distributed along the initial and final segments, with the break at the kth step. ■

Now we express the cost CO_k of the operation O on a file of size k in terms of a *cost operator*, $C_{\mathcal{O}}(RV)$ such that $C_{\mathcal{O}}(RV)\phi_k = CO_k\,\phi_k$.

3.6.2 Theorem. *Main formula for integrated cost (case d = 1)*

For an operation $\mathcal{O}$ and corresponding operator $\xi_{\mathcal{O}}$

$$KO_n(t)H_n = \sum_i \langle X_t^{n-i-1} \xi_{\mathcal{O}} C_{\mathcal{O}}(RV)\, X_t^i \rangle$$

Proof: Applying the cost operator to the level crossing formula given by the lemma

$$\begin{aligned}
\sum_k CO_k NO_{kn}(t) &= \sum_k \sum_i \langle X_t^{n-i-1} \xi_{\mathcal{O}} C_{\mathcal{O}}(RV)\phi_k\rangle \langle X_t^i \phi_k\rangle / \varepsilon_k \\
&= \sum_k \sum_i \langle C^*_{\mathcal{O}}(RV) \xi^*_{\mathcal{O}} X_t^{n-i-1} \phi_k\rangle \langle X_t^i \phi_k\rangle / \varepsilon_k \\
&= \sum_i \langle C^*_{\mathcal{O}}(RV) \xi^*_{\mathcal{O}} X_t^{n-i-1} X_t^i \rangle \\
&= \sum_i \langle X_t^{n-i-1} \xi_{\mathcal{O}} C_{\mathcal{O}}(RV) X_t^i \rangle
\end{aligned}$$

where Parseval's formula is used to go from the second to the third line. ■

3.6.3 Corollary. *The total cost satisfies:*

$$K_n(t)H_n = \sum_i \langle X_t^{n-i-1} \sum_{\mathcal{O}} \xi_{\mathcal{O}} C_{\mathcal{O}}(RV)\, X_t^i \rangle$$

For dictionaries in Knuth's model, e.g., one readily finds the results of [5] [15] by the method indicated here, as shown in [1]. Below, we will look at a two-file model as an example.

The general results extend to the case $d > 1$ as follows. The formula for the level crossing numbers has the form

$$NO_{kn}(t) = \sum_j \sum_l H_{0,k,l}(t) H_{k',0,n-l-e_j}(t)$$

thus the previous Lemma reads

$$NO_{kn}(t) = \sum_j \sum_l \langle X_t^{n-l-e_j} \xi^{(j)}_{\mathcal{O}} \phi_k\rangle \langle X_t^l \phi_k\rangle / \varepsilon_k$$

And we have the theorem

3.6.4 Theorem. *Main formula for integrated cost (case d > 1)*

For an operation $\mathcal{O}$ and corresponding operator $\xi_{\mathcal{O}}$

$$KO_n(t)H_n = \sum_j \sum_l \langle X_t^{n-l-e_j} \xi^{(j)}_{\mathcal{O}} C_{\mathcal{O}}(RV)^{(j)}\, X_t^l \rangle$$

Example: Consider the system according to the recurrences:

$$x_1\phi_k = t\phi_{k+e_1} + q|k|\,\phi_k + k_1\phi_{k-e_1}$$
$$x_2\phi_k = t\phi_{k+e_2} + q\,(k_1\phi_{k-e_1+e_2} + k_2\phi_{k-e_2+e_1}) + Qk_2\phi_k + k_2\phi_{k-e_2}$$

where q and Q are constants. Changing over to the monic polynomials, $\psi_k = t^{|k|}\phi_k$, we have

$$x_1\psi_k = \psi_{k+e_1} + q|k|\,\psi_k + tk_1\psi_{k-e_1}$$
$$x_2\psi_k = \psi_{k+e_2} + q\,(k_1\psi_{k-e_1+e_2} + k_2\psi_{k-e_2+e_1}) + Qk_2\psi_k + tk_2\psi_{k-e_2}$$

In operator terms, we have

$$\begin{aligned} X_1 &= R_1 + q(R_1V_1 + R_2V_2) + tV_1 \\ X_2 &= R_2 + q(R_1V_2 + R_2V_1) + QR_2V_2 + tV_2 \end{aligned} \tag{3.6.1}$$

The main formula for determining the structure involved is

$$e^{-VR}Xe^{VR}\Omega = (t\dot{H} + \dot{V}R)\Omega$$

(the dot referring to differentiation with respect to a parameter) which comes from the general theory of *Appell systems*, where the distribution of X is given according to $\langle e^{sX}\rangle = e^{tH(s)}$, so that knowing $H(s)$ one can find the moments $\mu_n(t)$ and hence the number of histories, H_n by integration, cf. Prop. 3.5.3. In the multivariate case, $X = z_1X_1 + z_2X_2$ and H and V become functions of (z_1, z_2) upon setting $s = 1$. Here we get the system for H

$$\frac{\partial H}{\partial z_1} = V_1, \qquad \frac{\partial H}{\partial z_2} = V_2$$

and for the V's we have the Jacobian matrix

$$\begin{pmatrix} \frac{\partial V_1}{\partial z_1} & \frac{\partial V_1}{\partial z_2} \\ \frac{\partial V_2}{\partial z_1} & \frac{\partial V_2}{\partial z_2} \end{pmatrix} = \begin{pmatrix} 1 + qV_1 & qV_2 \\ qV_2 & 1 + qV_1 + QV_2 \end{pmatrix} \tag{3.6.2}$$

The system for the V's can be solved explicitly. Letting r and s denote the roots of the quadratic equation $x^2 - Qx - q^2 = 0$, we have

$$V_1 = \frac{1}{q}\left[e^{qz_1}\,\frac{re^{sz_2} - se^{rz_2}}{r - s} - 1\right]$$
$$V_2 = \frac{e^{qz_1}}{r - s}\left[\frac{r}{s - Q}\,e^{sz_2} - \frac{s}{r - Q}e^{rz_2}\right]$$

From equations (3.6.2), we see that near the origin V_i behave like z_i, which act on functions of (x_1, x_2) like the partial derivatives $\partial/\partial x_i$. This is like the case of dictionaries or linear lists in the single-file case.

To illustrate how the computation of the integrated cost goes, we take the example of the Hermite polynomials, Gaussian distribution, with

$$V = D, \qquad R = x - D$$

where D denotes $\dfrac{d}{dx}$. From equation (3.6.1), we see that the operators corresponding to deletions are tV_i (not just V_i) so for deletions at cost l we have the operator $tVRV$, the RV giving the factor l for the cost and the tV corresponding to deletions. We give the computation for $d = 1$, for linear lists, as the dictionary case is similar, but requires analysis of the poles of $1 - H$ to get the correct constants. The general behavior in terms of n, the file size, however, is found similarly as for the case $d = 1$. First, we recall that the moments of a Gaussian distribution with variance t are given by $\mu_{2n}(t) = t^n(2n)!/(2^n n!)$. Thus,

$$H_{2n} = \int_0^\infty \mu_n(t)\,dt = \frac{(2n)!}{2^n}$$

We want the asymptotic behavior of

$$\sum_l \langle X^{n-l-1} tVRV X^l \rangle = t \sum_l \left[l(l-1)\langle X^{n-2}\rangle - l(l-1)(l-2)\langle X^{n-4}\rangle \right]$$

The first term is of the order of $t\mu_{n-2}(t)\, n^3/3$, the second term is seen to be of a lower order of growth. Setting $n = 2p$, we have, then, using the formula for the moments,

$$(8p^3/3)\, t^p \frac{(2p-2)!}{2^{p-1}(p-1)!}$$

which yields, upon integrating out t times e^{-t} from 0 to ∞,

$$K_n H_n \sim (8p^4/3) \frac{(2p-2)!}{2^{p-1}}$$

with $H_{2p} = (2p)!\, 2^{-p}$, dividing by H_n gives the result

$$K_n \sim 4p^2/3 = n^2/3$$

IV. Conclusion

With these results adapted to various models, the analysis of the corresponding dynamic data structures can be carried through. This approach is completely general and permits computation of all moments of the asymptotic distributions. The formulation given here permits analysis of problems involving three-term recurrences, thus connected to orthogonal polynomials and special functions, e.g., Bessel functions.

Acknowledgments. The first author thanks the CRIN-INPL for kind hospitality and support. This work has been done with the help of NATO Grant 931395.

REFERENCES

1. P. Feinsilver & R. Schott, *Special Functions and Computer Science*, Kluwer Academic Publishers, 1994.
2. P.Feinsilver & R. Schott, *Krawtchouk polynomials and finite probability theory*, Probability Measures on Groups X, Plenum, (1991) 129–135.
3. P. Feinsilver, *Orthogonal polynomials and coherent states*, Symmetries in Science V, Plenum Press, (1991) 159–172.
4. Ph. Flajolet, *Analyse d'algorithmes de manipulation d'arbres et de fichiers*, Cahiers du B.U.R.O., **34–35** (1981) 1-209.
5. Ph. Flajolet, J.Françon and J. Vuillemin, *Sequence of operations analysis for dynamic data structures*, J. of Algorithms, **1** (1981) 111–141.
6. Ph. Flajolet and J.S. Vitter, *Average-case analysis of algorithms and data structures*, Handbook of Theoretical Computer Science, 1990 chapter 9, Elsevier Sc. Pub. B. V..
7. J. Françon, *Combinatoire des structures de données*, Thèse de doctorat d'Etat, Université de Strasbourg, 1979.
8. J. Françon, *Histoires de fichiers*, RAIRO Inf. Th., **12** (1978) 49–62.
9. J. Françon, B. Randrianarimanana and R. Schott, *Analysis of dynamic algorithms in D.E. Knuth's model*, T.C.S., **72**, (1990) 147–167.
10. J. Françon, G. Viennot, and J. Vuillemin, *Description and analysis of an efficient priority queue representation*, Proceedings of the 19th Annual Symp. on Foundations of Computer Science, 1978, 1–7.
11. A. Jonassen and D.E. Knuth, *A trivial algorithm whose analysis isn't*, J. Comput. System Sci., **16** (1978) 301–332.

12. G.D. Knott, *Deletion in binary storage trees*, Report Stan–CS 75-491, 1975.

13. D.E. Knuth, *Deletions that preserve randomness*, IEEE Trans. Software Eng., **SE-3**, 5 (1977) 351–359.

14. G. Louchard, *Random walks, Gaussian processes and list structures*, T.C.S., **53**, (1987) 99–124.

15. G. Louchard, B. Randrianarimanana and R. Schott, *Probabilistic analysis of dynamic algorithms in D.E. Knuth's model*, T.C.S., **93**, (1992) 201–225.

16. R.S. Maier, *A path integral approach to data structures evolution*, Journal of Complexity, **7**, 3, (1991) 232-260.

Authors Index

Springer-Verlag and the Environment

We at Springer-Verlag firmly believe that an international science publisher has a special obligation to the environment, and our corporate policies consistently reflect this conviction.

We also expect our business partners – paper mills, printers, packaging manufacturers, etc. – to commit themselves to using environmentally friendly materials and production processes.

The paper in this book is made from low- or no-chlorine pulp and is acid free, in conformance with international standards for paper permanency.

Lecture Notes in Computer Science

For information about Vols. 1–899

please contact your bookseller or Springer-Verlag

Vol. 900: E. W. Mayr, C. Puech (Eds.), STACS 95. Proceedings, 1995. XIII, 654 pages. 1995.

Vol. 901: R. Kumar, T. Kropf (Eds.), Theorem Provers in Circuit Design. Proceedings, 1994. VIII, 303 pages. 1995.

Vol. 902: M. Dezani-Ciancaglini, G. Plotkin (Eds.), Typed Lambda Calculi and Applications. Proceedings, 1995. VIII, 443 pages. 1995.

Vol. 903: E. W. Mayr, G. Schmidt, G. Tinhofer (Eds.), Graph-Theoretic Concepts in Computer Science. Proceedings, 1994. IX, 414 pages. 1995.

Vol. 904: P. Vitányi (Ed.), Computational Learning Theory. EuroCOLT'95. Proceedings, 1995. XVII, 415 pages. 1995. (Subseries LNAI).

Vol. 905: N. Ayache (Ed.), Computer Vision, Virtual Reality and Robotics in Medicine. Proceedings, 1995. XIV,

Vol. 906: E. Astesiano, G. Reggio, A. Tarlecki (Eds.), Recent Trends in Data Type Specification. Proceedings, 1995. VIII, 523 pages. 1995.

Vol. 907: T. Ito, A. Yonezawa (Eds.), Theory and Practice of Parallel Programming. Proceedings, 1995. VIII, 485 pages. 1995.

Vol. 908: J. R. Rao Extensions of the UNITY Methodology: Compositionality, Fairness and Probability in Parallelism. XI, 178 pages. 1995.

Vol. 909: H. Comon, J.-P. Jouannaud (Eds.), Term Rewriting. Proceedings, 1993. VIII, 221 pages. 1995.

Vol. 910: A. Podelski (Ed.), Constraint Programming: Basics and Trends. Proceedings, 1995. XI, 315 pages. 1995.

Vol. 911: R. Baeza-Yates, E. Goles, P. V. Poblete (Eds.), LATIN '95: Theoretical Informatics. Proceedings, 1995. IX, 525 pages. 1995.

Vol. 912: N. Lavrac, S. Wrobel (Eds.), Machine Learning: ECML – 95. Proceedings, 1995. XI, 370 pages. 1995. (Subseries LNAI).

Vol. 913: W. Schäfer (Ed.), Software Process Technology. Proceedings, 1995. IX, 261 pages. 1995.

Vol. 914: J. Hsiang (Ed.), Rewriting Techniques and Applications. Proceedings, 1995. XII, 473 pages. 1995.

Vol. 915: P. D. Mosses, M. Nielsen, M. I. Schwartzbach (Eds.), TAPSOFT '95: Theory and Practice of Software Development. Proceedings, 1995. XV, 810 pages. 1995.

Vol. 916: N. R. Adam, B. K. Bhargava, Y. Yesha (Eds.), Digital Libraries. Proceedings, 1994. XIII, 321 pages. 1995.

Vol. 917: J. Pieprzyk, R. Safavi-Naini (Eds.), Advances in Cryptology - ASIACRYPT '94. Proceedings, 1994. XII, 431 pages. 1995.

Vol. 918: P. Baumgartner, R. Hähnle, J. Posegga (Eds.), Theorem Proving with Analytic Tableaux and Related Methods. Proceedings, 1995. X, 352 pages. 1995. (Subseries LNAI).

Vol. 919: B. Hertzberger, G. Serazzi (Eds.), High-Performance Computing and Networking. Proceedings, 1995. XXIV, 957 pages. 1995.

Vol. 920: E. Balas, J. Clausen (Eds.), Integer Programming and Combinatorial Optimization. Proceedings, 1995. IX, 436 pages. 1995.

Vol. 921: L. C. Guillou, J.-J. Quisquater (Eds.), Advances in Cryptology – EUROCRYPT '95. Proceedings, 1995. XIV, 417 pages. 1995.

Vol. 922: H. Dörr, Efficient Graph Rewriting and Its Implementation. IX, 266 pages. 1995.

Vol. 923: M. Meyer (Ed.), Constraint Processing. IV, 289 pages. 1995.

Vol. 924: P. Ciancarini, O. Nierstrasz, A. Yonezawa (Eds.), Object-Based Models and Languages for Concurrent Systems. Proceedings, 1994. VII, 193 pages. 1995.

Vol. 925: J. Jeuring, E. Meijer (Eds.), Advanced Functional Programming. Proceedings, 1995. VII, 331 pages. 1995.

Vol. 926: P. Nesi (Ed.), Objective Software Quality. Proceedings, 1995. VIII, 249 pages. 1995.

Vol. 927: J. Dix, L. Moniz Pereira, T. C. Przymusinski (Eds.), Non-Monotonic Extensions of Logic Programming. Proceedings, 1994. IX, 229 pages. 1995. (Subseries LNAI).

Vol. 928: V.W. Marek, A. Nerode, M. Truszczynski (Eds.), Logic Programming and Nonmonotonic Reasoning. Proceedings, 1995. VIII, 417 pages. 1995. (Subseries LNAI).

Vol. 929: F. Morán, A. Moreno, J.J. Merelo, P. Chacón (Eds.), Advances in Artificial Life. Proceedings, 1995. XIII, 960 pages. 1995 (Subseries LNAI).

Vol. 930: J. Mira, F. Sandoval (Eds.), From Natural to Artificial Neural Computation. Proceedings, 1995. XVIII, 1150 pages. 1995.

Vol. 931: P.J. Braspenning, F. Thuijsman, A.J.M.M. Weijters (Eds.), Artificial Neural Networks. IX, 295 pages. 1995.

Vol. 932: J. Iivari, K. Lyytinen, M. Rossi (Eds.), Advanced Information Systems Engineering. Proceedings, 1995. XI, 388 pages. 1995.

Vol. 933: L. Pacholski, J. Tiuryn (Eds.), Computer Science Logic. Proceedings, 1994. IX, 543 pages. 1995.

Vol. 934: P. Barahona, M. Stefanelli, J. Wyatt (Eds.), Artificial Intelligence in Medicine. Proceedings, 1995. XI, 449 pages. 1995. (Subseries LNAI).

Vol. 935: G. De Michelis, M. Diaz (Eds.), Application and Theory of Petri Nets 1995. Proceedings, 1995. VIII, 511 pages. 1995.

Vol. 936: V.S. Alagar, M. Nivat (Eds.), Algebraic Methodology and Software Technology. Proceedings, 1995. XIV, 591 pages. 1995.

Vol. 937: Z. Galil, E. Ukkonen (Eds.), Combinatorial Pattern Matching. Proceedings, 1995. VIII, 409 pages. 1995.

Vol. 938: K.P. Birman, F. Mattern, A. Schiper (Eds.), Theory and Practice in Distributed Systems. Proceedings,1994. X, 263 pages. 1995.

Vol. 939: P. Wolper (Ed.), Computer Aided Verification. Proceedings, 1995. X, 451 pages. 1995.

Vol. 940: C. Goble, J. Keane (Eds.), Advances in Databases. Proceedings, 1995. X, 277 pages. 1995.

Vol. 941: M. Cadoli, Tractable Reasoning in Artificial Intelligence. XVII, 247 pages. 1995. (Subseries LNAI).

Vol. 942: G. Böckle, Exploitation of Fine-Grain Parallelism. IX, 188 pages. 1995.

Vol. 943: W. Klas, M. Schrefl, Metaclasses and Their Application. IX, 201 pages. 1995.

Vol. 944: Z. Fülöp, F. Gécseg (Eds.), Automata, Languages and Programming. Proceedings, 1995. XIII, 686 pages. 1995.

Vol. 945: B. Bouchon-Meunier, R.R. Yager, L.A. Zadeh (Eds.), Advances in Intelligent Computing - IPMU '94. Proceedings, 1994. XII, 628 pages.1995.

Vol. 946: C. Froidevaux, J. Kohlas (Eds.), Symbolic and Quantitative Approaches to Reasoning and Uncertainty. Proceedings, 1995. X, 420 pages. 1995. (Subseries LNAI).

Vol. 947: B. Möller (Ed.), Mathematics of Program Construction. Proceedings, 1995. VIII, 472 pages. 1995.

Vol. 948: G. Cohen, M. Giusti, T. Mora (Eds.), Applied Algebra, Algebraic Algorithms and Error-Correcting Codes. Proceedings, 1995. XI, 485 pages. 1995.

Vol. 949: D.G. Feitelson, L. Rudolph (Eds.), Job Scheduling Strategies for Parallel Processing. Proceedings, 1995. VIII, 361 pages. 1995.

Vol. 950: A. De Santis (Ed.), Advances in Cryptology - EUROCRYPT '94. Proceedings, 1994. XIII, 473 pages. 1995.

Vol. 951: M.J. Egenhofer, J.R. Herring (Eds.), Advances in Spatial Databases. Proceedings, 1995. XI, 405 pages. 1995.

Vol. 952: W. Olthoff (Ed.), ECOOP '95 - Object-Oriented Programming. Proceedings, 1995. XI, 471 pages. 1995.

Vol. 953: D. Pitt, D.E. Rydeheard, P. Johnstone (Eds.), Category Theory and Computer Science. Proceedings, 1995. VII, 252 pages. 1995.

Vol. 954: G. Ellis, R. Levinson, W. Rich. J.F. Sowa (Eds.), Conceptual Structures: Applications, Implementation and Theory. Proceedings, 1995. IX, 353 pages. 1995. (Subseries LNAI).

VOL. 955: S.G. Akl, F. Dehne, J.-R. Sack, N. Santoro (Eds.), Algorithms and Data Structures. Proceedings, 1995. IX, 519 pages. 1995.

Vol. 956: X. Yao (Ed.), Progress in Evolutionary Computation. Proceedings, 1993, 1994. VIII, 314 pages. 1995. (Subseries LNAI).

Vol. 957: C. Castelfranchi, J.-P. Müller (Eds.), From Reaction to Cognition. Proceedings, 1993. VI, 252 pages. 1995. (Subseries LNAI).

Vol. 958: J. Calmet, J.A. Campbell (Eds.), Integrating Symbolic Mathematical Computation and Artificial Intelligence. Proceedings, 1994. X, 275 pages. 1995.

Vol. 959: D.-Z. Du, M. Li (Eds.), Computing and Combinatorics. Proceedings, 1995. XIII, 654 pages. 1995.

Vol. 960: D. Leivant (Ed.), Logic and Computational Complexity. Proceedings, 1994. VIII, 514 pages. 1995.

Vol. 961: K.P. Jantke, S. Lange (Eds.), Algorithmic Learning for Knowledge-Based Systems. X, 511 pages. 1995. (Subseries LNAI).

Vol. 962: I. Lee, S.A. Smolka (Eds.), CONCUR '95: Concurrency Theory. Proceedings, 1995. X, 547 pages. 1995.

Vol. 963: D. Coppersmith (Ed.), Advances in Cryptology -CRYPTO '95. Proceedings, 1995. XII, 467 pages. 1995.

Vol. 964: V. Malyshkin (Ed.), Parallel Computing Technologies. Proceedings, 1995. XII, 497 pages. 1995.

Vol. 965: H. Reichel (Ed.), Fundamentals of Computation Theory. Proceedings, 1995. IX, 433 pages. 1995.

Vol. 966: S. Haridi, K. Ali, P. Magnusson (Eds.), EURO-PAR '95: Parallel Processing. Proceedings, 1995. XV, 734 pages. 1995.

Vol. 967: J.P. Bowen, M.G. Hinchey (Eds.), ZUM '95: The Z Formal Specification Notation. Proceedings, 1995. XI, 571 pages. 1995.

Vol. 969: J. Wiedermann, P. Hájek (Eds.), Mathematical Foundations of Computer Science 1995. Proceedings, 1995. XIII, 588 pages. 1995.

Vol. 970: V. Hlaváč, R. Šára (Eds.), Computer Analysis of Images and Patterns. Proceedings, 1995. XVIII, 960 pages. 1995.

Vol. 971: T.E. Schubert, P.J. Windley, J. Alves-Foss (Eds.), Higher Order Logic Theorem Proving and Its Applications. Proceedings, 1995. VIII, 400 pages. 1995.

Vol. 972: J.-M. Hélary, M. Raynal (Eds.), Distributed Algorithms. Proceedings, 1995. XI, 333 pages. 1995.

Vol. 973: H.H. Adelsberger, J. Lažanský, V. Mařík (Eds.), Information Management in Computer Integrated Manufacturing. IX, 665 pages. 1995.

Vol. 974: C. Braccini, L. DeFloriani, G. Vernazza (Eds.), Image Analysis and Processing. Proceedings, 1995. XIX, 757 pages. 1995.

Vol. 975: W. Moore, W. Luk (Eds.), Field-Programming Logic and Applications. Proceedings, 1995. XI, 448 pages. 1995.

Vol. 978: N. Revell, A M. Tjoa (Eds.), Database and Expert Systems Applications. Proceedings, 1995. XV, 654 pages. 1995.